RACE, CLASS, AND GENDER IN THE UNITED STATES

RACE, CLASS, AND GENDER IN THE UNITED STATES

AN INTEGRATED STUDY

Eleventh Edition

Paula S. Rothenberg

with

Christina Hsu Accomando
Humboldt State University

worth publishers
Macmillan Learning
New York

Senior Vice President, Content Strategy: Charles Linsmeier
Program Director, Social Sciences: Shani Fisher
Executive Program Manager: Chris Cardone
Program Editor: Sarah Berger
Development Editor: Len Neufeld
Editorial Assistant: Nick Rizzuti
Executive Marketing Manager: Kate Nurre
Marketing Assistant: Chelsea Simens
Director of Media Editorial and Assessment, Social Sciences: Noel Hohnstine
Media Editor: Stephanie Matamoros
Director, Content Management Enhancement: Tracey Kuehn
Senior Managing Editor: Lisa Kinne
Senior Workflow Project Manager: Jennifer Wetzel
Senior Content Project Manager: Kerry O'Shaughnessy
Project Manager: Murugesh Namasivayam, Lumina Datamatics, Inc.
Executive Permissions Editor: Robin Fadool
Text Permissions Editor: Michael McCarty
Director of Design, Content Management: Diana Blume
Design Services Manager: Natasha Wolfe
Cover Designer: John Callahan
Art Manager: Matthew McAdams
Production Supervisor: Brianna Lester
Media Project Manager: Joe Tomasso
Composition: Lumina Datamatics, Inc.
Printing and Binding: King Printing Co., Inc.
Cover Photo: Xan Padrón, *Time Lapse. West Palm Beach,* courtesy of Saatchi Art

Library of Congress Control Number: 2019946842

ISBN-13: 978-1-319-14365-7
ISBN-10: 1-319-14365-2

4 5 6   25 24 23 22

Worth Publishers
One New York Plaza
Suite 4600
New York, NY 10004-1562
www.macmillanlearning.com

CONTENTS

PREFACE

Owning the past can only enhance the future. Failing to acknowledge the past leaves the present confused and confusing. Naming injustice for the sole purpose of assigning blame will divide us; identifying injustice in order to address it has the potential to move us toward a society that values both diversity and community.

—PAULA S. ROTHENBERG

In 1988, Paula S. Rothenberg published the first edition of this anthology, under the title *Racism and Sexism: An Integrated Study*. Her collection was a groundbreaking contribution to teaching a wide range of courses—women's studies, ethnic studies, sociology, history, politics, philosophy, composition, and more—with an integrated and intersectional approach. With the new title *Race, Class, and Gender in the United States*, the anthology has seen ten editions since then and has been used by more than half a million students in a rich array of undergraduate and graduate courses.

After more than five decades of publishing, teaching, and organizing, Paula S. Rothenberg died on June 7, 2018. She taught philosophy and women's studies at William Paterson University in New Jersey for thirty-seven years, and she also served as director of The New Jersey Project on Inclusive Scholarship, Curriculum, and Teaching, a statewide curriculum transformation project. Rothenberg sparked controversy in 1990 when her anthology was adopted as a required textbook at the University of Texas–Austin and subsequently attacked by syndicated columnist George Will and other high-profile conservatives, including Lynne Cheney. The anthology's reach has only expanded since then, and Rothenberg went on to author numerous other influential textbooks as well as her autobiographical work, *Invisible Privilege: A Memoir About Race, Class, and Gender*. A chapter of the memoir is dedicated to the genesis of the anthology and the firestorm it created in the early years of the "culture wars." The collection grew out of a team-taught course on racism and sexism, and Rothenberg recounts her efforts to get the course approved through her university's curriculum committee: a conservative historian on the committee voted against the course proposal "on the grounds that it began with the assumption that racism and sexism existed in the United States instead of allowing students to make up their own minds." The same professor wanted her to "add a section discussing the benefits of slavery."[1] Needless to say, she did not bend to these criticisms.

At my small state university in rural northern California, I began teaching from the anthology in the fall of 2000. Our new chair of women's studies—who was dedicated to curricular transformation and to teaching about oppression and resistance in an

---

[1] Paula S. Rothenberg, *Invisible Privilege: A Memoir about Race, Class, and Gender* (University Press of Kansas, 2000), p. 165.

intersectional way—created a new cross-listed women's studies / ethnic studies course, "Power/Privilege: Race, Class, Gender, and Sexuality." We knew we wanted a textbook that focused on social constructions of identities, and we did not want an "additive" approach (e.g., a women's studies textbook that merely *added* race and class, or an ethnic studies textbook that *added* gender and sexuality). It was clear that Paula S. Rothenberg's anthology was the perfect vehicle for this new interdisciplinary and intersectional course. The two of us alternated teaching the class, and we organized the syllabus around Rothenberg's notions of the social construction of difference, institutionalized hierarchies, grappling with history, and envisioning change. Each semester, around week 10, one of us would call the other to say, "This course is impossible—what were we thinking?" By week 15, however, when students were presenting their creative final projects (ranging from poetry 'zines on resistance and collages challenging stereotypes to a 12-step brochure "for recovering homophobes" that one young athlete presented to his football team), we would call each other again, this time to say, "This class is transformational!" For some students, the class provided a language to articulate their lived experience; for others, it tore down the blinders of privilege as they began to question entitlement, prejudice, and deeply held beliefs of meritocracy. For many students the course did both, as they learned to grapple with the complexities of social location and the interlocking relations of power and privilege. Rothenberg's lively anthology, with selections ranging from social theory, court cases, and statistics to personal narratives and the occasional poem, gave us a rigorous grounding and made this transformational work possible.

After two decades of teaching Rothenberg's text to hundreds of students, it was an honor to be invited to work on the eleventh edition of *Race, Class, and Gender in the United States*. I never met Paula Rothenberg, but we started an email exchange when she was working on the seventh edition, and it was abundantly clear that she cared passionately about the integrity and relevance of this anthology and about the issues themselves, which, to her (and to me), were never just academic or theoretical.

In Rothenberg's 2015 preface to the tenth edition (reproduced below), she noted the significance of Barack Obama's election as the first African American president and of Hillary Clinton leading the polls in the presidential race (at that time). While these were significant milestones, clearly neither achievement signaled the end of racism or sexism in our nation, and the work to be done by this anthology remains as relevant as ever. In fact, our country's political climate at the time of this writing underscores the vital necessity of this text and the courses that embrace it. My hope is that the next generation of students engage with this text with a sense of urgency, eager to learn about the structures and discourses that have revived long-standing patterns of oppression and spread them in new forms.

New to *Race, Class, and Gender*, Eleventh Edition

The eleventh edition of *Race, Class, and Gender*, like previous editions, views the problems facing our country and our communities as structural and seeks to contribute to conversations about fairness and justice. We examine racism, sexism, heterosexism, and class privilege, and we explore the interlocking nature of these systems of oppression as they work in combination and impact every aspect of life in U.S. society today. New to this edition, Kimberlé Crenshaw's essay "Why Intersectionality Can't Wait" explains how she coined the term *intersectionality* in 1989 and why there is a continued need for an accessible metaphor that captures the complexity of multiple, simultaneous, and interlocking forms of oppression. This intersectional framework is one that we rely on throughout the book to illustrate the complex dimensions of race, gender, sexuality, and class. This edition features recent pieces about contemporary social movements written by the founders of those movements, as well as some earlier foundational works of intersectional analysis that are new to this volume.

Part I introduces the social construction of difference by examining the ways that race, gender, sexuality, and class have been socially and hierarchically constructed to the benefit of some and to the disadvantage of others. Aurora Levins Morales's piece, new to this edition, uses global and personal history to explore the paradox of race as a social construction with real consequences. She makes connections between knowing our history and changing our future: "If we can teach the history of racism in the United States as a history of the shifting needs of empire, as a history of both impositions and choices, alliances and betrayals, a history with roots far outside and long before the first colonial encounters, if we can hold the tension between disbelief in race and belief in what racism does to us, we will enable more and more young people to remake old and seemingly immutable decisions about where their interests lie and with whom." The updated title of Pem Davidson Buck's selection ("Derailing Rebellion: Inventing White Privilege") emphasizes how the elite intentionally deploys constructions of race to set working people against one another and derail impulses toward protest and rebellion, a point also illustrated by Morales. In another new piece, poet and hip hop artist Tim'm T. West reveals the intersections of gender, sexuality, and race, as a gay black man "interested in 'flipping the script'—in challenging the ways that black men internalize identities that we ourselves took no part in creating."

Part II opens with Crenshaw's essay on intersectionality as "an analytic sensibility, a way of thinking about identity and its relationship to power." She emphasizes how the term makes visible not only the complexity of identity but also "institutions that use identity to exclude and privilege." Her essay is followed by an updated version of Beverly Tatum's critical piece on defining racism as a "system of advantage based on race." Ian Hancy López's selection on strategic racism, from his influential book on dog-whistle politics, joins the selections by Tatum and other writers in Part II who offer nuanced understandings of racism as something that goes beyond personal prejudice. Gregory Mantsios's "Class in America" has been updated with current statistics, showing that the class myths and realities he identified are still operating and that, in many cases, economic disparities are even greater today. Three pivotal selections from elsewhere in the tenth edition— essays by Ta-Nehisi Coates, Evelyn Alsultany, and Joan L. Griscom—have been moved to Part II to emphasize their contributions to understanding institutionalized hierarchies and interlocking modes of oppression.

Part III, which has been retitled "Citizenship and Immigration: Constructing Nationality, Borders, and Belonging," features six new pieces—including two poems—that explore the social and legal notions of nationality that have been central to constructions of difference in the United States since its founding. Ian Haney López and Angelica Quintero trace legal restrictions on citizenship and immigration based on race and other categories. Aviva Chomsky, in a selection from her book *Undocumented: How Immigration Became Illegal*, reveals how illegality is itself a construction. Jaclyn Granick and Britt Tevis, in the wake of a mass shooting at a Pittsburgh synagogue in 2018, analyze the links between nativism and antisemitism, both historically and in the present. Poets Bao Phi and Javier Zamora tell personal stories of the trauma involved in fleeing their homelands. They came to this country as children in different ways—Phi as a refugee from the U.S. war in Vietnam, Zamora as an unaccompanied minor crossing the U.S.–Mexico border by foot—and they both struggle with questions of belonging in their adopted home.

Part IV features nine new pieces on everyday discrimination, addressing voter suppression, "living while black," sexual assault, immigration, queer identities, and environmental racism. "Standing Rock, Flint, and the Color of Water" makes connections across different struggles for environmental protection and self-determination. The authors argue: "Linking the politics surrounding the Dakota Access Pipeline project to Flint, Michigan's lead-poisoning crisis is critical for understanding how race and class inform presumed social risk, vulnerability to premature death, and access to democratic decision-making." Several other pieces foreground intersections of identity, including Mohammad's "Queer and Undocumented" and Raven E. Heavy Runner's "First Nations, Queer and Education."

Three of the new pieces offer intersectional analysis of sexualized violence and simultaneously acknowledge and complicate the impact of the #MeToo movement. "They Treat Me Like a Criminal, but They Are the Criminals" tells the story of Aura Hernández, who came to this country fleeing domestic violence, only to be sexually assaulted by a border patrol agent. Hernández now faces deportation to Guatemala, and the article points out that "largely missing from the #MeToo movement are the stories of women who have been sexually abused by members of the largest law-enforcement agency in the United States: Customs and Border Protection." Yolonda Wilson addresses our nation's racialized history of sexualized violence—in contexts ranging from slavery to gynecology to the law—to explain why black women have a different relationship to #MeToo than do white women. Chris Linder and Jessica Harris identify specific strategies for addressing campus sexual violence with an awareness of unequal power relations. Discussing issues of sexual violence in the classroom poses numerous challenges, including the risk of triggering survivors to experience flashbacks or to suffer other symptoms associated with PTSD. We encourage instructors to contextualize the readings beforehand to give survivors and other students the opportunity to prepare themselves for such content.[2] Instructors also might

---

[2] While critics charge that trigger warnings coddle students and exclude challenging material from the classroom, the opposite is true. Instructors provide such warnings precisely because they *do* include such material and because they want students to engage with the material as fully as possible. History professor Onni Gust considers trigger warnings the opposite of infantilization: "They implicitly demand that students assess their own needs and take responsibility for them." He also values their impact on the instructor: "Having 'triggers' in mind forces me to think about the potential diversity of experiences in my classroom, not to make assumptions about my students' lives and to think carefully about the language I use and the framing of the topic" ("I use trigger warnings—but I'm not mollycoddling my students," *The Guardian*,

consider providing students with a list of campus as well as national resources for survivors.[3] At the same time, articles on sexual violence can provide a powerful opportunity to discuss this vital issue in complex, nuanced, and survivor-centered ways. Students are confronting sexualized violence in their lives and on our campuses, whether or not our colleges and curricula provide a space to identify the power dynamics involved as well as strategies aimed at preventing such violence.

Part V includes four new pieces, including a classic essay by Dorothy Allison, "A Question of Class," which offers a personal, structural, and intersectional analysis of class issues from the perspective of a queer white Southern woman who grew up categorized and otherized as "white trash" in America. The other new pieces provide current statistics and policy analysis to help us understand the lasting impact of the subprime crisis (Jillian Olinger), the debt trap faced by poor people and communities of color (Alexandra Bastien), and the inequities of public school funding (an NPR publication).

Part VI has been retitled "Living Knowledge and Testimony" to reflect its focus on personal testimony and what Cherríe Moraga calls *theory in the flesh*—knowledge that emanates from and is applicable to lived experience. Moraga's "La Güera" is a foundational piece of intersectional analysis and Chicana feminism. The three-part caution she articulates in this autobiographical essay resonates throughout Part VI: "The danger lies in ranking the oppressions. *The danger lies in failing to acknowledge the specificity of the oppression.* The danger lies in attempting to deal with oppression purely from a theoretical base." Deborah Miranda addresses the history of the California missions through an analysis of curriculum and of her own experiences as a "proud, mixed-blood California Indian woman." Dhaha Nur tells a personal story of being separated from his mother, initially as a result of civil war in his native Somalia, and now as a result of the 2017 "Muslim ban." In his essay "Male-on-Male Rape," another challenging but vital selection addressing sexualized violence, Michael Scarce recounts his experience with campus sexual assault in order to break the silence around male rape, analyze the complexity of causes, and offer concrete strategies for change.

June 14, 2016). Literature professor Colleen Clemens argues that having a trigger warning in her syllabus prompts an important conversation on the first day of class that sets the stage for the thoughtful but difficult discussions to follow: "Having that conversation about trigger warnings may help a veteran, sexual assault survivor or another person with post-traumatic stress disorder see that my classroom honors their challenges and resilience" ("Why I Support Trigger Warnings," *Teaching Tolerance*, June 6, 2016). Graduate student and instructor Lynne Alexander offers concrete strategies for supporting survivors in the classroom, including these: know that survivors can be anyone; set clear guidelines for class discussion; prepare students for difficult topics; consider the pedagogical value of graphic material; be prepared for disclosures (including knowing your role as a mandated reporter); and believe your students ("Not Just Trigger Warnings: Supporting Survivors of Sexual & Domestic Violence in the Classroom," https://gcci.uconn.edu/2018/11/21/not-just-trigger-warnings-supporting-survivors-of-sexual-domestic-violence-in-the-classroom/#).

[3] Many campuses have a Title IX coordinator or campus advocate, a counseling center, a women's center, or other resources that can assist survivors of all genders. Some campuses coordinate with community hotlines or shelters. Examples of national resources include the Rape, Abuse & Incest National Network (RAINN), which has a website (www.rainn.org), a 24-hour National Sexual Assault Hotline (800.656.HOPE), and an online hotline (online.rainn.org). The Me Too movement also has a website (metoomvmt.org) with valuable resources for healing and advocacy.

Part VII, now titled "How It Happens: Legal Constructions of Power and Privilege," has six new selections and several new or updated introductions. The 1773 "Petition of the Africans, Living in Boston" is a protest document demonstrating black resistance to enslavement in the colonial period. An excerpt from the South Carolina Black Codes, passed immediately after ratification of the Thirteenth Amendment in 1865, is an important primary document revealing the postwar refusal to accept the emancipation of enslaved Americans. South Carolina was the first, but such codes swept the south after the Civil War. *Bradwell* v. *Illinois* is an 1873 Supreme Court ruling that allowed states to prohibit women from practicing law, based on both "Divine law" and assertions of women's "natural and proper timidity and delicacy." *McCleskey* v. *Kemp* is a 1987 Supreme Court ruling that upheld a death sentence despite compelling statistical evidence that Georgia's application of capital punishment was infused with systemic racial bias. The justices did not disagree with the robust statistical evidence but rejected McCleskey's ability to make a claim of discrimination in the absence of proof of intentional bias in his specific case. The importance of this ruling lies in its essentially closing the courthouse doors to claims of racial bias based on *systemic* racism, as opposed to explicit articulations of racist intent. *Shelby County* v. *Holder* is the 2013 case that gutted a key provision of the Voting Rights Act of 1965 and that thereby opened the floodgates to a wide range of voter suppression laws and practices. The selection on *Obergefell* v. *Hodges*, the 2015 ruling that struck down bans on same-sex marriage, now includes excerpts from Justice Anthony Kennedy's majority opinion.

Part VIII includes a timely excerpt from Jason Stanley's book *How Fascism Works*, providing an overview of fascist political tactics and an in-depth look at "unreality" — what happens when truth is replaced by power. Another recent piece, "Understanding Antisemitism" (from Jews for Racial and Economic Justice) examines both history and recent events to explain the complex and at times seemingly contradictory workings of antisemitic rhetoric, policies, and practices. This excerpt addresses the notion that antisemitism is simply something from the past or encountered only outside the United States. Michael Yellow Bird's essay uses the trope of "cowboys and Indians" as a way to explore the history and legacies of settler colonialism and the genocide of Indigenous peoples.

Part IX expands upon the theme of "making a difference" with nine new essays. Classic feminist essays by Audre Lorde and bell hooks are followed by Amit Taneja's personal essay about his own feminist journey "from oppressor to activist" as a gay immigrant man of color. Andrea Ayvazian's piece on the power of allied behavior is now followed by a piece that identifies some of the pitfalls of allyship, when it becomes mere performance. This essay (which I coauthored with Kristin J. Anderson) proposes coalition building as a more fruitful way than ally performance to conceptualize and practice working across differences in pursuit of social justice and meaningful social transformations. We have also added a new piece by Alicia Garza, emphasizing the intersectionality at the core of the Black Lives Matter movement, which she cofounded, and critiquing those who would appropriate the movement without honoring its roots. Tarana Burke comments on the misinterpretations of the movement she founded as "me too" more than a decade ago and speaks to its vibrant future as a tool for individual healing and collective change. Loretta Ross and Rickie Solinger speak to another vital movement in the twenty-first century, a movement conceptualized as "reproductive justice," that was created by black women and goes dramatically beyond abortion rights to encompass the right to *have* a child, the right *not* to have a child, and the right to parent children in a safe environment. The next two selections take different abolitionist approaches to social change. Angela Davis argues for a new constellation of transformative options to replace an obsolete prison system. Morgan Bassichis, Alex Lee, and Dean Spade propose radical and transformative solutions to current problems (solutions that go beyond the "official" solutions offered by mainstream organizations) as they work to build an abolitionist trans and queer movement. In "What the Dreamers Can Teach the Parkland Kids," a young immigration rights activist, Gaby Pacheco, speaks to the even younger organizers of a new movement to end gun violence after yet another mass shooting at a school. Finally, Chief Arvol Looking Horse reframes what happened at Standing Rock, seeing it not as a defeat but as the beginning and continuation of a broad new transnational movement to protect our water and our Earth.

New Pedagogy in the Eleventh Edition

The eleventh edition includes several new, student-centered pedagogical features to support instructors as they assign readings, facilitate class discussions, and assess student learning. The Introduction to the book and the essays introducing each of the nine parts have all been revised and updated, with new opening epigraphs that capture key themes and help frame the topics.

The introduction to each part now concludes with a list of accessible guiding questions that point students toward key terms, central concepts, and critical lenses in particular readings, as well as salient themes across multiple selections. These questions connect theory to praxis and motivate students to apply their critical thinking skills to the readings. Unlike single-author textbooks, *Race, Class, and Gender in the United States* offers a multitude of diverse voices from different eras and different disciplines. The guiding questions highlight points of connection and contrast among the readings within each part and among the different sections of the book—for example, questions that ask students to apply a key insight from one reading to other readings or otherwise place the authors in dialogue.

Throughout the anthology, guiding questions also return to fundamental concepts, such as intersectional analysis, social constructions of difference, and the relationship between history and the present. Many of the questions ask readers to identify moments of resistance or positive strategies for change, which are not always immediately evident in readings that highlight stories of oppression. Some of the prompts encourage students to identify key concepts in the essays and make connections to their own lives and communities. Overall, the guiding questions help students become agents in their own learning, showing how key terms and concepts can function as lenses, empowering students to look differently at other readings and at the world around them. Finally, it should be noted that the guiding questions are in no way exhaustive—they should encourage readers to think of and answer their own questions as well.

Most of the selections are now accompanied by another new framing element, brief author biographies that help students engage more fully with the material by foregrounding relevant information about the writer's background, field of expertise, and publications.

In addition, many of the editor's notes introducing individual selections—particularly the legal documents in Part VII—are either new or significantly updated. These notes provide context for readers with limited background in the issues addressed in the selections (such as students in lower-division general education courses), as well as for more advanced students who might want guidance for engaging in additional research.

Finally, each part concludes with an updated list of suggestions for further reading, selected for their usefulness for students with research or presentation assignments as well as for readers embarking on their own explorations.

Acknowledgments

Instructors across the country have contributed insightful feedback on the eleventh edition. Reviewers include Ash R. Allee, Johnson County Community College; Becky Anthony, Salisbury University; R. Dianne Bartlow, California State University, Northridge; Debra Berry, College of Southern Nevada; Jon Cabiria, Delaware County Community College; Elizabeth Cramer, Virginia Commonwealth University; Patricia Cullinan, Truckee Meadows Community College; Bosah Ebo, Rider University; Michelle Emerson-Lewis, Michigan State University; Elaine Gunnison, Seattle University; Alicia Gutierrez-Romine, La Sierra University; Denise Isom, California Polytechnic State University–San Luis Obispo; Navita James, University of South Florida; Joachim Kibirige, Missouri Western State University; Jeff Knapp, University of Nebraska at Omaha; Rebecca Lasher, Western Carolina University; Jodie M. Lawston, California State University–San Marcos; Enid Logan, University of Minnesota; David Lucander, Rockland Community College; Shari Lyman, College of Southern Nevada; Gail Markle, Kennesaw State University; Rain L. Marshall, Humboldt State University; Miranda Miller, Gillette College; Kathryn L. Norsworthy, Rollins College; Sonja Peterson-Lewis, Tempe University; Lindsay A. Phillips, Albright College; Peter D. Schwartz, Ramapo College of New Jersey; Tara Schwitzman, New Jersey City University; Glennie Fitzgerald Sewell, Norwich University; Joan Tropnas, St. John's University; and Ken Weidner, Saint Joseph's University.

I deeply appreciate Sarah Berger for her commitment to the project, her intellectual engagement, her openness to new approaches, and her trusting me with this work. I want to thank Len Neufeld for his meticulous editing and for vibrant debates in the margins of track changes and across time zones.

I am indebted to my brilliant and generous colleagues and collaborators who provided recommendations, close readings, and extensive feedback at multiple stages of this project, including Judith E. Coker, María Eugenia Corral Rocha, Janet Winston, Rain Archambeau Marshall, Anne Shea, Kristin J. Anderson, Maral Attallah, Ramona Bell, Scott Bentley, Kim Berry, Loren Cannon, Barbara Brinson Curiel, Jennifer Ryan Hsu, Louis Hsu, Kerry Marsden, Raven Marshall, Eli Pence, Nancy Pérez, Tessa Pitré, Karla Rivas, Nancy Roman, Mary Sue Savage, Corrina Wells, and Jess Whatcott. I also owe profound gratitude to hundreds of students over the past two decades who have helped me see new things in this book every semester.

Finally, I must thank my best teachers—Claire Hsu Accomando, Allan Accomando, Nicolette Laloy Hsu, and Fuyun Hsu—for instilling in me their love of books, passion for teaching, and commitment to justice.

In honor of this anthology's author–editor for its first ten editions and to bring forward her profound perspectives on the supremely important issues at the heart of this book, we reproduce here Paula S. Rothenberg's reflections on and acknowledgments for the tenth edition.

Reflections from the First to the Tenth Edition of *Race, Class, and Gender*—Paula S. Rothenberg, 2015

When the first edition of *Race, Class, and Gender in the United States* was published in 1988 under the title *Racism and Sexism: An Integrated Study*, there was no World Wide Web. There were no smart phones. Smoking was still allowed on airplanes. China was one of the poorest nations in the world, the Soviet Union still existed, and apartheid was alive—if not well—in South Africa. In fact, the next president of South Africa and famed civil rights leader Nelson Mandela was still in prison in 1988, serving the 25th year of his sentence.

In the United States, the Reagan Administration was defending the secret sale of U.S. arms to Iran, while the Supreme Court was asked to decide whether one of the largest associations of "businessmen"—the Rotary Club—had a constitutional right to refuse to admit women as members. Scholars were arguing over the relationship between race and intelligence—a debate that was about to get even more heated in the decade that followed. Three quarters of the American population thought homosexual relations between two consenting adults was *always* wrong and the state had the right to outlaw such conduct.* As for the issue of economic inequality, it was nowhere to be found in the public discourse.

Much has happened in the intervening years. With a surge in voter turnout in 2008, a black man was elected president, and as of this writing, a woman is leading the polls for—and, by the time you are reading this, may even have won—the presidency of the United States. Given the setbacks for the feminist, black, and Latino/a movements of the 1960s and 1970s, most Americans in the 1980s did not expect to witness this type of cultural and political change in their lifetime. Even more inconceivable, given the cultural landscape, was that a growing LGBT (lesbian, gay, bisexual, and transgender) movement would help make gay marriage legal, and gender reassignment would enter the popular culture. An Occupy Wall Street movement helped put the issue of economic inequality squarely on the national and international agenda, seemingly overnight. And while many had hoped for a growing environmental movement, few anticipated the emergence of a global approach to climate change.

On the other hand, nearly three decades after the first edition of this book was published, so much has stayed the same or worsened. In 1988, the richest 20% of Americans

---

* Tom W. Smith, "Public Attitudes toward Homosexuality." NORC/University of Chicago: September, 2011. The right of states to outlaw acts of homosexuality by consenting adults was based on the 1986 Supreme Court decision *Bowers v. Hardwick*.

held 83% of total household wealth: today, that 20% holds 93% of the nation's wealth. Women have made significant strides politically, socially, and economically, yet they still make only 77 cents for every dollar a man makes—and the gap is even greater for women of color (64 cents for African American women). While racial profiling has finally caught the attention of the media, its persistence—and its expansion to Muslim and Sikh communities—continues to destroy lives and families. Policies, like affirmative action, that were designed to remedy inequities have been deeply weakened. So too, have organizations, like unions, that had for so long been such an important check on inequality and injustice. Twenty-two percent of the children in the United States live in poverty, a proportion nearly identical to what it was 30 years ago. How ironic that so much change can co-exist with so much stagnation.

How do we make sense of all of this? In the introduction to the first edition of the book, I put it simply: "An integrated approach to the study of racism and sexism within the context of class provides us with a more comprehensive, more accurate, more useful analysis of the world in which we live out our lives." This is as true now as it was nearly three decades ago.

Paula S. Rothenberg's Acknowledgments for the Tenth Edition

Many people contributed to *Race, Class, and Gender*—and its evolution over the course of nearly three decades. First, I owe a profound debt to the old 12th Street study group, with whom I first studied black history and first came to understand the centrality of the issue of race. I am also indebted to the group's members, who provided me with a lasting example of what it means to commit one's life to the struggle for equality and justice for all people.

Next, I owe an equally profound debt to my friends and colleagues in the New Jersey Project on Inclusive Scholarship, Curriculum, and Teaching, and to friends, colleagues, and students at William Paterson University who have been involved in the various race and gender projects we have carried out over the years. I have learned a great deal from all of them. I would also like to thank the faculty and students, too many to name, at the many colleges and universities where I have lectured over the years.

This edition would not have been possible without the work of three collaborators to whom I am deeply indebted: Soniya Munshi for her research, writing, and revisions to this edition; Sarah Berger, my hands-on editor, for her insights, sensitivity, perseverance, and deep commitment to the project; and Greg Mantsios for his invaluable assistance and good judgment about all things related to this and all previous editions.

Finally, I want to thank Greg for being such a remarkable partner as well as collaborator; our children, Alexi Mantsios and Andrea Mantsios; and their partners, Caroline Donohue and Luis Armando Ocaranza Ordaz, for their insights, observations, and most of all, their extraordinary support through thick and thin.

ABOUT THE AUTHORS

Paula S. Rothenberg was a professor of philosophy and women's studies at William Paterson University of New Jersey. Her areas of expertise included multicultural curriculum transformation, inequality and equity, globalizing the curriculum, and white privilege. From 1989 to 2006, she served as director of the New Jersey Project on Inclusive Scholarship, Curriculum, and Teaching, a statewide initiative to develop a more inclusive and multicultural curriculum. In the late 1970s, she coedited with Alison Jaggar one of the first women's studies texts, *Feminist Frameworks: Alternative Theoretical Accounts of Relations Between Women and Men*. Rothenberg published several other influential anthologies, including *White Privilege: Readings on the Other Side of Racism*; *Beyond Borders: Thinking Critically About Global Issues*; *What's the Problem? A Brief Guide to Critical Thinking*; and *Creating an Inclusive College Curriculum: A Teaching Sourcebook*. She also published *Invisible Privilege: A Memoir about Race, Class, and Gender*. Her essays appear in journals and anthologies across the disciplines, and have been widely reprinted. She passed away in June 2018.

Christina Hsu Accomando is a professor of English and Critical Race, Gender, and Sexuality Studies at Humboldt State University in Arcata, California. She teaches multiethnic U.S. literature, ethnic studies, women's studies, and multicultural queer studies. Drawing upon critical race studies and women of color feminism, her scholarship focuses on the law and literature of U.S. slavery and resistance, particularly the work of Harriet Jacobs and Sojourner Truth, as well as contemporary issues of race, gender, and U.S. law. She is the author of *"The Regulations of Robbers": Legal Fictions of Slavery and Resistance*, and her essays have appeared in *Still Seeking an Attitude: Critical Reflections on the Work of June Jordan* and the Norton Critical Edition of Harriet Jacobs' *Incidents in the Life of a Slave Girl*. She blogs with Kristin J. Anderson for *Psychology Today*, and her work has also been published in *MELUS*, *African American Review*, *Feminism & Psychology*, and *The Antioch Review*. In addition, Accomando coedited and wrote the introduction for the expanded second edition of Tim'm West's *RED DIRT REVIVAL: a poetic memoir in 6 breaths*.

INTRODUCTION

Race—racism—is a device. . . . It is simply a means. An invention to justify the rule of some men over others. . . . [A] device is a device, but . . . it also has consequences: Once invented it takes on a life, a reality of its own. So, in one century, men invoke the device of religion to cloak their conquests. In another, race. Now, in both cases you and I may recognize the fraudulence of the device, but the fact remains that a man . . . who is shot . . . because he is black—is suffering the utter reality of the device. And it is pointless to pretend that it doesn't exist—merely because it is a lie!

—LORRAINE HANSBERRY

The election of Barack Obama in 2008 heralded for many Americans a turning point in U.S. politics—if an African American man can become president, surely we have moved past those old racial hierarchies and have entered a new era of equality and democracy. In the years since, much indeed has changed, but not necessarily in the direction of a more robust democracy.

Challenges we continue to face include mass shootings at schools and places of worship; sharp increases in hate crimes; increased numbers of murdered and missing Indigenous women; rising rates of maternal mortality (particularly for African American and Indigenous women); high rates of immigrant detention and deportation, migrant family separation, and asylum seekers refused entry; mass incarceration (with stark racial disparities and with women as the fastest-growing prison population); police shootings of unarmed African Americans; a proliferation of anti-transgender policies and a rollback of existing LGBT protections; restrictions on the right to vote; rising income inequality; obstacles to labor organizing and unionization; environmental racism, including the prioritizing of profits over safe water supplies in marginalized communities; devastating hurricanes and other consequences of climate change; and a rise of authoritarianism across the globe. Clearly, hierarchies remain and we face deeply entrenched obstacles to genuine democracy and a truly inclusive society.

At the same time, powerful movements for social justice have emerged and gained strength. Me Too—founded in 2006 by Tarana Burke as a grassroots effort to support survivors of sexualized violence—rose to national and global prominence in 2017 and has grown into a widespread movement to empower individual healing and systemic change. Black Lives Matter—created in 2013 by Alicia Garza, Patrisse Cullors, and Opal Tometi—has expanded into a global network with a broad and intersectional agenda. Indigenous coalitions formed during the Standing Rock water protection protests sparked an international movement to protect water and land resources. Students from Parkland, Florida, to Chicago, Illinois, have forged a national movement to end gun violence. Even as migrants and asylum seekers have been detained, deported, and banned, activists have come together across differences to mount legal challenges, create sanctuary cities, and demand a more just immigration policy. Massive women's marches across the globe have prompted grassroots organizing as well as difficult conversations about how to create a truly intersectional feminist movement for meaningful and lasting change. Teachers are forming powerful coalitions for change, spurred in part by successful 2018 strikes in Oklahoma, Kentucky, and West Virginia. Voters in a range of states decided in 2018 to raise the minimum wage, expand Medicaid, restore voting rights, and elect the most diverse Congress in U.S. history. In 2019, schoolchildren in the United States and across the globe organized massive protests to demand action on climate change.

How should we understand the complicated dynamics at work in our world today? It is impossible to make sense out of either the past or the present without using race, class, gender, and sexuality as central categories of description and analysis. Yet many of us are the products of an educational system that has taught us to ignore these socially constructed categories and thus not to see the differences in power and privilege based on them. A basic premise of this book is that much of what passes for a neutral perspective across the disciplines and in cultural life smuggles in elements of class, race, and gender bias and distortion. Learning to identify these and other fundamental categories and to analyze the associated biases and distortions is essential if we wish to understand our own lives and the lives of others.

The Challenges of Studying Race, Class, Gender, and Sexuality

As we begin our study together, some differences from other academic enterprises are immediately apparent. Whereas participants in an introductory chemistry class rarely begin the semester with deeply felt and firmly held attitudes toward the subject, almost every student in a course that deals with issues of race, class, gender, and sexuality enters the room on the first day with strong feelings, and every faculty member does so as well. Under the best conditions, if we acknowledge our feelings head-on, those feelings can provide the basis for a passionate study of the topics and can give this course real meaning, with long-term consequences. It is also important to acknowledge that we all come to this material with both knowledge and ignorance, and we must be prepared to have some of our paradigms shifted.

Racism, sexism, heterosexism, and class exploitation are all systems of oppression with their own particular history. Therefore, it is important to explore each of these systems on its own terms; at the same time, these systems operate in conjunction with one another to form an enormously complex set of interlocking and self-perpetuating relations of domination and subordination. It is essential that we understand the ways in which these systems overlap, intersect, and play off one another. A central principle of this anthology is *intersectionality*, a term coined by legal scholar Kimberlé Crenshaw (see Selection 1 in Part II). This analytical framework uses multiple lenses to explore intersections of identity and intertwined systems of oppression and privilege. Intersectional analysis has powerfully transformed critical scholarship as well as social movements.

The Structure of This Book

Lorraine Hansberry, in her play *Les Blancs,* succinctly describes the fundamental paradox of race as a social construction with real consequences: "it is pointless to pretend that it doesn't *exist*—merely because it is a *lie.*" This book begins with an examination of the ways in which race, class, gender, and sexuality have been socially constructed in the United States as "differences" used to form hierarchies. Once invented, these categories have profound material and ideological consequences. What exactly does it mean to claim that someone or some group of people is "different"? How is the construction of "difference" used to justify inequality, exclusion, exploitation, and even extermination? The readings in the first half of this volume are intended to initiate a dialogue about the ways in which U.S. society constructs difference, and the personal, social, and political consequences that flow from that construction.

Part I shows how ideas of human difference are socially constructed. Each author demonstrates how differences that may appear "natural" are actually socially produced and how the meanings and values associated with those differences create a hierarchy of power and privilege. Some of the readings scrutinize one particular category of difference, while others illuminate intersections among multiple categories. Taken as a whole, the readings in Part I reveal a complex web of social, political, and cultural constructions.

Part II examines racism, sexism, homophobia, and class exploitation as intersecting systems of privilege and oppression that ensure advantages for some and diminished opportunities for others. Bias is often understood as a purely interpersonal dynamic, but the authors in this section reveal the subtle, structural, and institutionalized ways in which discrimination operates.

Part III addresses legal and cultural constructions of nationality, borders, and belonging. The diverse scholars, journalists, and poets in this section interrogate the complexities and mythologies of American identity. Designations like "citizen" or "undocumented" might seem clear-cut, but they are not; they are complex social and legal constructions with profound consequences.

Part IV provides concrete examples of how interlocking systems of oppression operate in contemporary U.S. society. The stories of everyday discrimination include voter suppression, mass incarceration, gender policing, homophobia, Islamophobia, sexualized violence, racialized violence, and environmental racism. Several of the readings also address strategies for individual resistance and collective activism.

Part V focuses on the impact of economic structures on people's lives. The readings in this part build upon the analyses in previous parts and illuminate the ways in which race and gender intersect with the economic inequalities that define class.

Socially constructed differences result in real differences in opportunity, expectations, and treatment. These differences are brought to life in the testimonies in Part VI, which articulate the connections between individual experiences and structural oppression. The authors in this part address the flesh-and-blood impact of such forces as colonialism, internment, immigration policies, sexualized and racialized violence, transphobia, microaggressions, gentrification, and internalized oppression. In some cases, these stories will resonate with our own lives, while in other cases, they will represent new and shocking information. When we study in a systematic way the devastating personal and social costs of racism, sexism, heterosexism, and class exploitation, it is easy to become overwhelmed or immobilized. How can we reconcile the dominant American narrative of "liberty and justice for all" with the reality presented in these pages? At this point we turn to history.

Part VII examines fundamental contradictions in U.S. history by focusing on primary documents that address race and gender issues in American law, beginning in the years before the American Revolution. When these documents are read in the context of the earlier material describing social constructions of race, class, gender, and sexuality in contemporary society, they give us a way of using the past to make sense of the present.

Why do these divisions continue to exist in our society, and how are they reproduced? Part VIII offers some insights. Systems of oppression and privilege structure our society *and* structure our ways of thinking. The selections in Part VIII focus on how our conceptions of others—and, equally important, our conceptions of ourselves—can help perpetuate racism, sexism, heterosexism, and class exploitation. Stereotypes and ideology are key to maintaining social hierarchies. They make it difficult to identify both the origins of an unjust distribution of resources and the forces that maintain the injustice. Systems of unequal power and privilege have been institutionalized, rationalized, and normalized. We grow up being taught that the prevailing hierarchy in society is natural and inevitable, which hinders our ability to imagine and work toward social transformation.

The authors in Part IX challenge this prevailing hierarchy at its core and offer conceptual and concrete strategies for positive change. These scholars and activists articulate ways we can build coalitions across differences—rather than allowing differences to divide us or pretending they do not exist—in order to create a more socially just community and a planet that can sustain us. Several selections articulate a vision for intersectional feminism as a way to redefine difference and transform our society. Many of the authors describe powerful movements they have helped to create—movements for human rights, restorative justice, a life-sustaining planet, and an end to interpersonal and state violence. They describe not only abolishing oppressive institutions but also creating, in Angela Davis's words, "a constellation of alternative strategies and institutions." These readings invite all of us to imagine new constellations and new ways of thinking. In the words of poet Martín Espada, "we have to envision a more just world before the world can become more just."

The Social Construction of Difference: Race, Class, Gender, and Sexuality

It's in that space of critical curiosity and historical context, in the tension held between layers of truth, that insight emerges.

—Aurora Levins Morales

Every society grapples with the question of how to distribute its wealth, power, resources, and opportunities. In some cases, the distribution is relatively egalitarian; in others, it is dramatically unequal. Those societies that tend toward an unequal distribution have adopted various criteria to use in apportioning privilege; some have used age, others have used ancestry. In the United States, as in many other places, society uses race, class, and gender. To this end, gender and race differences have often been represented as unbridgeable and immutable.

Men and women have historically been portrayed as polar opposites with innately different abilities and capacities. The very traits that are considered positive in a man are often seen as signs of dysfunction in a woman, and the qualities that are praised in women are often ridiculed in men. We need only look at the representation of women in U.S. politics where, despite making up a majority of the population, women hold less than a quarter of congressional seats,[1] or at the small number of male nurses (9 percent of all nurses[2]) to see that ideas about gender differences shape our view of what women and men can and cannot do.

So-called "race" difference also has been portrayed in a binary fashion. "Whites" (i.e., relatively light-skinned people of European origin) have historically viewed themselves as innately superior in intelligence and ability to people with darker skin. As both the South Carolina "Act for the Better Ordering and Governing of Negroes and Slaves" of 1712 and the *Dred Scott* ruling of 1857 make clear (excerpts from both appear in Part VII of this volume), African Americans were constructed as members of a different and lesser race. Their enslavement, like the genocide carried out against Native Americans, was justified on the basis of constructed biological differences. In the Southwest, Anglo landowners claimed that Asians and Mexicans were naturally suited to perform certain kinds of brutal farm labor to which whites were "physically unable to adapt."[3]

Class status, too, has been correlated with supposed differences in innate ability and moral worth. Property qualifications for voting have been used not only to prevent African Americans from exercising the right to vote, but also to exclude poor whites. From the beginnings of U.S. society, owning property was considered an indication of superior intelligence and character.

We begin this book with an entirely different premise. All the readings in this first part argue that far from reflecting natural and innate differences among people, the categories of gender, race, and class are socially constructed. Rather than being "given" in nature, they reflect culturally constructed differences that maintain the prevailing distribution of power and privilege in a society, and they change in relation to changes in social, political, and economic life.

Social scientists often distinguish between "sex" as a category that is assigned at birth and "gender" as the particular set of socially constructed meanings that are associated with each sex. Although "sex" is often assumed to be natural or biological, even sex is socially constructed. As Susan Stryker shows in Selection 9, sex collapses complex and diverse physiological, genetic, and other biological differences into only two available options: male and female.

Classification as a man or as a woman carries connotative differences in meaning from culture to culture and within each society, as well as over different periods of time. What is understood as "naturally" masculine or feminine behavior in one culture or society may be the exact opposite of what is considered "natural" for women or men in another culture or society. Furthermore, while it is true that most societies have sex-role stereotypes that identify certain jobs or activities as appropriate for women and others for men, there is little consistency across societies in the kinds of tasks that have been so categorized. In some societies it is women who are responsible for agricultural labor, and in others it is men. Even within cultures that construct women as unsuited for heavy manual labor, some women (in the United States, usually women of color and poor white working women) have always been expected and required to perform backbreaking physical work—on plantations, in factories, on farms, in commercial laundries, and in their homes.

Anthropologist Gayle Rubin argues that "far from being an expression of natural differences, exclusive gender identity is the suppression of natural similarities."[4] From birth, children are under enormous pressure to conform to sex-role stereotypes that divide basic human attributes between two sexes. In Selection 5, Judith Lorber argues that assumed differences between women and men are never merely differences but are constructed hierarchically so that women are always portrayed as different in the sense of being deviant and deficient. Central to this construction of difference is the social construction of sexuality, a process Jonathan Ned Katz and Michael Kimmel analyze in Selections 6 and 7. In Selection 8, Tim'm West argues that understanding scripts of gender cannot be separated from an analysis of race and sexuality. In Selection 9, Susan Stryker asks us to evaluate our assumptions about the relationships among sex, gender, and sexuality, and posits that transgender feminism reveals the limits of theorizing about gender on the basis of sexed bodies.

The idea of race also has been socially constructed. The claim that race is a social construction challenges the assumption that people are born into different races that have biologically based differences in intellect, temperament, and character. The idea of ethnicity, in contrast to race, focuses on the shared social/cultural experiences and heritages of various groups. The important difference here is that the notion of race implies biological (including genetic) similarities and differences, whereas ethnicity emphasizes commonalities that are understood as social, not biological, in origin.

Historian and ethnic studies scholar Ronald Takaki suggests that in the United States, "[r]ace. . . has been a social construction that has historically set apart racial minorities from European immigrant groups."[5] As Aurora Levins Morales argues in Selection 1, the "seemingly real, obvious, and biological foundations of racial categories are completely fabricated, constantly shifting, and . . . used to justify gross economic and social inequities." Michael Omi and Howard Winant, the authors of Selection 2, would agree. They maintain that categorization by race is politically motivated rather than based on biological or other scientific criteria. They point to the relatively arbitrary way in which the category of race has been constructed and suggest that changes in the meaning and use of racial distinctions can be correlated with economic and political changes in U.S. society. Dark-skinned men and women from Spain were once classified as "white" along with light-skinned immigrants from England and Ireland, whereas early Greek immigrants were often classified as "Orientals" and subjected to the same discrimination that Chinese and Japanese immigrants experienced under the laws of California and other Western states. In South Africa, Japanese immigrants were categorized as "white," not "black" or "colored," presumably because the South African economy depended on trade with Japan. In contemporary U.S. society, dark-skinned Latinas and Latinos are often categorized as "black" by those who continue to equate something called "race" with skin color. In Selection 3, Pem Davidson Buck argues that whiteness and white privilege were constructed historically along with race difference in order to divide working people and set them against each other and in this way protect the wealth and power of a small, privileged elite. In "How Jews Became White Folks" (Selection 4), Karen Brodkin provides a detailed account of the specific ways in which the status and classifications of one group, Jewish immigrants to the United States, changed over time as a result of and in relation to economic, political, and social changes in our society.

The claim that race is a social construction is not meant to deny that people differ in skin color and other physical characteristics. Rather, it sees these differences as occurring along a continuum of diversity and not reflecting any categorical biological distinctions among peoples or any innate differences in intelligence, abilities, or moral nature. Scientists have long argued that all human beings are descended from a common lineage and that genetic differences among individuals *within* so-called racial groups are actually greater than the differences *between* groups.

Algerian-born French philosopher Albert Memmi argues that racism (or, by analogy, sexism) consists of stressing real or imagined differences between individuals or populations and interpreting those differences in ways that lead to subordination. That is, racism means assigning a value to a particular difference in a way that discredits an individual or group to the advantage of another and that transforms mere difference into deficiency.[6] In the United States, both race and gender differences have been carefully constructed as hierarchy and used to rationalize racism and sexism.

Hierarchical systems like these are intertwined in complex ways. "The shifting ground of race serves the shifting interests of class," notes Aurora Levins Morales in Selection 1. Michael Kimmel argues in Selection 7 that homophobia is "intimately interwoven with both sexism and racism." According to Kimmel, the ideal of masculinity that prevails in U.S. society today is one that reflects the needs and interests of capitalism. It effectively defines "women, nonwhite men, nonnative-born men, homosexual men" as "other" and deficient, and in this way renders members of all these groups, as well as large numbers of white working-class and middle-class men, powerless in contemporary society. In Selection 8, Tim'm West explores the ways that the scripts of black masculinity have been shaped by both racism and homophobia. As "a gay brotha who is largely inspired by . . . studies of feminism," he calls for ways to think "creatively and critically about manhood."

Our understanding of the ways in which race and gender differences have been constructed is further enriched by Douglas Baynton's analysis in Selection 11. Baynton argues that the idea of disability has functioned historically to justify unequal treatment for women and minority groups as well as to justify inequality for disabled people themselves. Focusing on women's suffrage, civil rights, and immigration, he explores the ways in which the *concept* of disability has been used at different moments in history to disenfranchise various groups in U.S. society and to legitimize discrimination against them.

The social construction of class is analogous, but not identical, to that of race and gender. Differences between rich and poor, which result from particular ways of structuring the economy, are socially constructed as innate differences among people. These differences are then used to rationalize or justify the unequal distribution of wealth and power that results from economic decisions made to perpetuate privilege. In addition, straightforward numerical differences in earnings are rarely the basis for conferring class status. For example, schoolteachers and college professors are usually considered to have a higher status than plumbers and electricians, even though the earnings of plumbers and electricians are often significantly higher. Where people are presumed to fit into the class hierarchy has less to do with clear-cut numerical categories than it does with the socially constructed superiority of those who are seen as performing mental labor (i.e., work with their heads) over those who are seen as performing manual labor (i.e., work with their hands). In addition, the status of various occupations and the class position the occupations imply often change depending on whether the occupation is predominantly female or male and on its racial composition.

Equally significant, differences in wealth and family income have been overladen with value judgments and stereotypes to the extent that identifying someone as middle class, working class, or poor carries implications about his or her moral character and ability. In the nineteenth century, proponents of Calvinism and social Darwinism maintained that being poor in itself indicated that an individual was morally flawed and thus deserved his or her poverty—relieving society of any responsibility for social ills. More recently, as Susan Greenbaum discusses in Selection 10, the idea that poverty can be blamed on family structure and cultural values was brought to the fore again in the 1965 government-issued Moynihan Report, which claimed that African American family values were producing a "tangle of pathology." This approach to blaming the poor for being poor refuses to see poverty as a social and economic problem that we can collectively address.

Finally, class differences can be viewed as socially constructed in a way that parallels the social construction of differences in race and gender. In this respect, the organization of U.S. society makes class hierarchy (or class itself) appear natural and inevitable. We grade and rank children from their earliest ages and claim to be sorting them according to something called "natural ability." The tracking that permeates our system of education both reflects and creates the expectation that there are A people, B people, C people, and so forth, and simultaneously rationalizes and hides the correlations between class and success. Well before high school, children come to define themselves and others in this hierarchical way and to accept this kind of classification as natural. Consequently, quite apart from accepting the particular mythology or ideology of class difference prevalent at any given moment (i.e., "the poor are lazy and worthless" versus "the poor are meek and humble and will inherit the earth"), we come to think it natural and inevitable that there should be class differences in the first place, just as race and gender differences are thought of as natural and inevitable. In the final essay in Part I, Jean Baker Miller asks and answers this question: "What do people do to people who are different from them and why?"

NOTES

1. Drew DeSilver, "A record number of women will be serving in the new Congress," *Pew Research Center Fact Tank*. Dec. 18, 2018. (http://www.pewresearch.org/fact-tank/2018/12/18/record-number-women-in-congress/).

2. Women continue to comprise more than 90% of the nursing workforce, yet male nurses earn more than women in comparable positions. See Megan Knowles, "Male nurses make 7% more than female peers, survey finds," *Becker's Hospital Review*. October 10, 2018. (https://www.beckershospitalreview.com/compensation-issues/male-nurses-make-7-more-than-female-peers-survey-finds.html).

3. Ronald Takaki, *A Different Mirror: Multicultural American History* (Little, Brown, 1993), p. 321.

4. Gayle Rubin, "The Traffic in Women," in *Toward an Anthropology of Women*, Rayna R. Reiter, ed. (Monthly Review Press, 1975), p. 180.

5. Takaki, *A Different Mirror*.

6. Albert Memmi, *Dominated Man* (Beacon Press, 1968).

GUIDING QUESTIONS FOR PART I

1. Morales describes the "tightrope walk" of exposing biological race as a fabrication while also exposing the "devastating injuries brought about by racism." How does each of the readings in Part I reveal the apparent paradox between viewing race and other categories of identity as social constructions and recognizing their real consequences?

2. How are various social constructions of difference "used to justify gross economic and social inequities" (Morales)? What happens when people come together across different identities? Why do some forces in U.S. society find such alliances dangerous?

3. According to Buck and other authors in Part I, what are some of the tactics used by the ruling elite to "divide and rule their labor force"? In what ways is an exploitable labor force useful for the ruling elite?

4. Omi and Winant argue that race is a "pre-eminently *sociohistorical* concept." What are some institutions and social practices that have played a role in constructing race historically in the United States? How have culture, politics, science, and religion affected the meanings we ascribe to race?

5. Brodkin argues that "Jews became white" in the United States in the aftermath of World War II, and Morales states that she and her brother "became *spics* overnight" when they moved from Puerto Rico to Chicago. What does it mean that social categories like race can be so contextual and variable?

6. Lorber argues that "everyone 'does gender'" without thinking about it." Why does she think it's important to get people to think about it?

7. What are some of the different ways the authors in Part I address homophobia (e.g., West and Kimmel)? Why is it useful to see homophobia from multiple viewpoints? How does homophobia intersect with other forms of oppression?

8. "The shifting ground of race serves the shifting interests of class," argues Morales. Identify moments when different categories of identity (including race, class, gender, sexuality, and ability) intersect with each other. Why is it important to examine the construction and operation of these identities in conjunction with each other?

9. "So what causes poverty?" asks Greenbaum. Why do the non-poor blame the poor for causing their own poverty? How do the readings in Part I offer a complex understanding of poverty and class oppression?

10. "Disability is everywhere in history," argues Baynton, "once you begin looking for it." After reading Baynton's analysis, what happens if you look at citizenship, inequality, and American history through a lens that makes constructions of disability visible? Do the other articles in Part I begin to look different?

11. Most of the articles in Part I detail patterns of oppression and discrimination in the United States. What are some examples of resistance, rebellion, or activism in the readings?

1   What Race Isn't: Teaching about Racism

Aurora Levins Morales

The biggest challenge in teaching about racism is to have double vision: on the one hand, to continually point out that the seemingly real, obvious, and biological foundations of racial categories are completely fabricated, constantly shifting, and in spite of their widespread acceptance, not obvious at all; on the other, to explicitly map, over and over again, the devastating injuries brought about by racism and expose the ways that ideas of race are used to justify gross economic and social inequities.

It's a tightrope walk, requiring dexterity in handling contradiction. To expose the notion of biological race as fraudulent, to look at the actual genetics of human diversity and see that there is no such thing as race, no human subspecies, without allowing any quarter to the liberal pretensions of colorblindness, to the literal whitewashing of real differences in culture, experience, power, resources. To demolish the idea of fundamental biological difference and refuse to let anyone get away with "We're all human beings" meaning "We're all like me" or use the true statement that all lives are important to undermine and dismiss the specific power of saying, in the face of systematic and deadly racist violence, that Black Lives Matter.

To bear witness to all of the bloody history of racism, to expose the manipulations and brutalities, the wicked roots of the ideologies and their ruthless implementation, and to make ample space for righteous rage, without allowing a speck of essentialism to creep into the anger of students of color, conceding no space at all to ideas of "blood" determining our moral and political stances.

It is extremely useful to teach students about the flexibility of racist ideology, how adaptable it is to the needs of the elite, to see how it serves those who wield it. What does it mean that in the early twentieth century an attorney in the Minnesota Iron Range tried to classify Finns as "Mongolian" to exclude radical miners, many of them Finnish, from citizenship, but failed, because the broader elite powers didn't want to raise questions about the whiteness of any Europeans? Or that in 1923 the United States Supreme Court ruled, in spite of the expert "race science" testimony of anthropologists, that a high-caste Hindu man might be Aryan but was not white because the "common understanding" of white excluded him? What does it mean that in mid-nineteenth-century debates in California Mexicans were considered white and Chinese people weren't, not because of their features but because

Aurora Levins Morales is a writer, artist, and historian. Her books include *Medicine Stories: Essays for Radicals*; *Kindling: Writings on the Body*; and *Remedios: Stories of Earth and Iron from the History of Puertorriqueñas*.

of their relative positions in the economy of the time and place? And see how 150 years has reversed that classification: Mexican Americans are most definitely no longer seen as white, while Asian Americans, economically exploited as the working-class immigrant population continues to be, are considered the people of color closest to "almost white." This has everything to do with the economic rise of Japan and China and the industrialization of parts of the Pacific Rim, not any increased tolerance or enlightenment among European Americans. The shifting ground of race serves the shifting interests of class.

It's in that space of critical curiosity and historical context, in the tension held between layers of truth, that insight emerges. Those moments of insight in my own life came from being abruptly shifted across categories in the eyes of others. In 1967 my family moved from rural Puerto Rico to Chicago. On the island my light brown hair was called *rubia*, or blonde, and although I was a Caribbean girl with indigenous and African ancestors and a colonial subject, my middle-class access in a community of farm laborers, my U.S. Jewish father, and my light skin color made me a blanquita.

In Chicago, in the private university high school my father's faculty status entitled us to, my brother and I became *spics* overnight. My skin color got lighter in the long sunless winters, and my English was accent-free, something that people still marvel over in congratulatory voices. But as a Puerto Rican girl in a big U.S. city, I acquired social color. Some of us are dark enough and Spanish-speaking enough to bear the brunt of immediate and constant recognition and unambiguous classification as a target. Others, like me, become the tokens, exotic but conditionally acceptable. We are the ones who are told we don't look Puerto Rican, don't sound Puerto Rican, the ones who are always being invited to collude in despising our own kinfolk, the ones people confide their racism to as between friends. Nevertheless I was racially recategorized by getting on a plane.

Redefined by migration as a young woman of color, and fortunate enough to find communities of activism where I could give voice to the complexity of my social identities, the loosely knit web of U.S. feminist women of color became my home and the root place of my political coming of age. But "woman of color" is essentially a political term, not a racial one. It is a name that is not claimed by every female with dark skin and ancestors from outside of Europe. It's a name defined by collective opposition to racism, a unity created by a politicized shared experience. It brings together peoples who have been at war with one another for centuries. It brings together people whose features, colors, languages, customs have very little in common but who, confronted with U.S. racism, were subjected to similar abuses.

Just as "white" was invented to cover all those invited to partake of the colonial pie, some sooner, some later, and defined always against someone else's not-whiteness. In 1744, when sailors pressed into the service of England joined with indentured servants, slaves, relocated indigenous people, and others to riot against the elites of New York City and burn their mansions, English sailors spoke of going out to attack white people as if it were obvious that this category did not include them. Many Europeans had already become white in relationship to imperialism. Others came to this country as racialized minorities in Europe, Irish, Eastern European Jewish, Roma, Slavs, and Sicilians, despised by the English, French, and Germans whose elites were the dominant imperialist powers. They became white in relation to specific groups of people who were not.

One of the challenges I offer European American students is to figure out in relation to whom their family took on this identity. For Scandinavians in Minnesota, it was most likely the Ojibwe; for the Irish and the Ashkenazi Jews of eastern cities it was African Americans; for settlers in the Southwest it was indigenous and mestizx peoples from both sides of the new border who credentialed their whiteness; in California most likely a mixture of Mexican, Chinese, Japanese, Filipinx, and Native American. For all their weight in our lives, the racial categories that define how injustice will be measured out are extremely circumstantial.

If we can teach the history of racism in the United States as a history of the shifting needs of empire, as a history of both impositions and choices, alliances and betrayals, a history with roots far outside and long before the first colonial encounters, if we can hold the tension between disbelief in race and belief in what racism does to us, we will enable more and more young people to remake old and seemingly immutable decisions about where their interests lie and with whom.

2 Racial Formation
Michael Omi and Howard Winant

In 1982–83, Susie Guillory Phipps unsuccessfully sued the Louisiana Bureau of Vital Records to change her racial classification from black to white. The descendant of an eighteenth-century white planter and a black slave, Phipps was designated "black" in her birth certificate in accordance with a 1970 state law which declared anyone with at least one-thirty-second "Negro blood" to be black. The legal battle raised intriguing questions about the concept of race, its meaning in contemporary society, and its use (and abuse) in public policy. Assistant Attorney General Ron Davis defended the law by pointing out that some type of racial classification was necessary to comply with federal record-keeping requirements and to facilitate programs for the prevention of genetic diseases. Phipps's attorney, Brian Begue, argued that the assignment of racial categories on birth certificates was unconstitutional and that the one-thirty-second designation was inaccurate. He called on a retired Tulane University professor who cited research indicating that most whites have one-twentieth "Negro" ancestry. In the end, Phipps lost. The court upheld a state law which quantified racial identity, and in so doing affirmed the legality of assigning individuals to specific racial groupings.[1]

The Phipps case illustrates the continuing dilemma of defining race and establishing its meaning in institutional life. Today, to assert that variations in human physiognomy are racially based is to enter a constant and intense debate. *Scientific* interpretations of race have not been alone in sparking heated controversy; *religious* perspectives have done so as well.[2] Most centrally, of course, race has been a matter of *political* contention. This has been particularly true in the United States, where the concept of race has varied enormously over time without ever leaving the center stage of U.S. history.

What Is Race?

Race consciousness, and its articulation in theories of race, is largely a modern phenomenon. When European explorers in the New World "discovered" people who looked different than themselves, these "natives" challenged then existing conceptions of the origins of

Michael Omi is a professor of ethnic studies, sociology, and gender and women's studies at the University of California, Berkeley. He has served as associate director of the Haas Institute for a Fair and Inclusive Society.

Howard Winant is a professor of sociology at the University of California, Santa Barbara, and the founder of the University of California Center for New Racial Studies.

the human species, and raised disturbing questions as to whether *all* could be considered in the same "family of man."[3] Religious debates flared over the attempt to reconcile the Bible with the existence of "racially distinct" people. Arguments took place over creation itself, as theories of polygenesis questioned whether God had made only one species of humanity ("monogenesis"). Europeans wondered if the natives of the New World were indeed human beings with redeemable souls. At stake were not only the prospects for conversion, but the types of treatment to be accorded them. The expropriation of property, the denial of political rights, the introduction of slavery and other forms of coercive labor, as well as outright extermination, all presupposed a worldview which distinguished Europeans— children of God, human beings, etc.—from "others." Such a worldview was needed to explain why some should be "free" and others enslaved, why some had rights to land and property while others did not. Race, and the interpretation of racial differences, was a central factor in that worldview.

In the colonial epoch science was no less a field of controversy than religion in attempts to comprehend the concept of race and its meaning. Spurred on by the classificatory scheme of living organisms devised by Linnaeus in *Systema Naturae,* many scholars in the eighteenth and nineteenth centuries dedicated themselves to the identification and ranking of variations in humankind. Race was thought of as a *biological* concept, yet its precise definition was the subject of debates which, as we have noted, continue to rage today. Despite efforts ranging from Dr. Samuel Morton's studies of cranial capacity[4] to contemporary attempts to base racial classification on shared gene pools,[5] the concept of race has defied biological definition. . . .

Attempts to discern the *scientific meaning* of race continue to the present day. Although most physical anthropologists and biologists have abandoned the quest for a scientific basis to determine racial categories, controversies have recently flared in the area of genetics and educational psychology. For instance, an essay by Arthur Jensen which argued that hereditary factors shape intelligence not only revived the "nature or nurture" controversy, but raised highly volatile questions about racial equality itself.[6] Clearly the attempt to establish a *biological* basis of race has not been swept into the dustbin of history, but is being resurrected in various scientific arenas. All such attempts seek to remove the concept of race from fundamental social, political, or economic determination. They suggest instead that the truth of race lies in the terrain of innate characteristics, of which skin color and other physical attributes provide only the most obvious, and in some respects most superficial, indicators.

Race as a Social Concept

The social sciences have come to reject biologistic notions of race in favor of an approach which regards race as a *social* concept. Beginning in the eighteenth century, this trend has been slow and uneven, but its direction clear. In the nineteenth century Max Weber discounted biological explanations for racial conflict and instead highlighted the social and political factors which engendered such conflict.[7] The work of pioneering cultural anthropologist Franz Boas was crucial in refuting the scientific racism of the early twentieth century by rejecting the connection between race and culture, and the assumption of a continuum of "higher" and "lower" cultural groups. Within the contemporary social science literature, race is assumed to be a variable which is shaped by broader societal forces.

Race is indeed a pre-eminently *sociohistorical* concept. Racial categories and the meaning of race are given concrete expression by the specific social relations and historical context in which they are embedded. Racial meanings have varied tremendously over time and between different societies.

In the United States, the black/white color line has historically been rigidly defined and enforced. White is seen as a "pure" category. Any racial intermixture makes one "nonwhite." In the movie *Raintree County*, Elizabeth Taylor describes the worst of fates to befall whites as "havin' a little Negra blood in ya'—just one little teeny drop and a person's all Negra."[8] This thinking flows from what Marvin Harris has characterized as the principle of *hypo-descent*:

> By what ingenious computation is the genetic tracery of a million years of evolution unraveled and each man [*sic*] assigned his proper social box? In the United States, the mechanism employed is the rule of hypo-descent. This descent rule requires Americans to believe that anyone who is known to have had a Negro ancestor is a Negro. We admit nothing in between. . . . "Hypo-descent" means affiliation with the subordinate rather than the superordinate group in order to avoid the ambiguity of intermediate identity. . . . The rule of hypo-descent is, therefore, an invention, which we in the United States have made in order to keep biological facts from intruding into our collective racist fantasies.[9]

The Susie Guillory Phipps case merely represents the contemporary expression of this racial logic.

By contrast, a striking feature of race relations in the lowland areas of Latin America since the abolition of slavery has been the relative absence of sharply defined racial groupings. No such rigid descent rule characterizes racial identity in many Latin American societies. Brazil, for example, has historically had less rigid conceptions of race, and thus a variety of "intermediate" racial categories exists. Indeed, as Harris notes, "One of the most striking consequences of the Brazilian system of racial identification is that parents and children and even brothers and sisters are frequently accepted as representatives of quite opposite racial types."[10] Such a possibility is incomprehensible within the logic of racial categories in the United States.

To suggest another example: The notion of "passing" takes on new meaning if we compare various American cultures' means of assigning racial identity. In the United States, individuals who are actually "black" by the logic of hypo-descent have attempted to skirt the discriminatory barriers imposed by law and custom by attempting to "pass" for white.[11] Ironically, these same individuals would not be able to pass for "black" in many Latin American societies.

Consideration of the term "black" illustrates the diversity of racial meanings which can be found among different societies and historically within a given society. In contemporary British politics the term "black" is used to refer to all nonwhites. Interestingly, this designation has not arisen through the racist discourse of groups such as the National Front. Rather, in political and cultural movements, Asian as well as Afro-Caribbean youth are adopting the term as an expression of self-identity.[12] The wide-ranging meanings of "black" illustrate the manner in which racial categories are shaped politically.[13]

The meaning of race is defined and contested throughout society, in both collective action and personal practice. In the process, racial categories themselves are formed, transformed, destroyed, and re-formed. We use the term *racial formation* to refer to the process by which social, economic and political forces determine the content and importance of racial categories, and by which they are in turn shaped by racial meanings. Crucial to this formulation is the treatment of race as a *central axis* of social relations which cannot be subsumed under or reduced to some broader category or conception.

Racial Ideology and Racial Identity

The seemingly obvious, "natural" and "common sense" qualities which the existing racial order exhibits themselves testify to the effectiveness of the racial formation process in constructing racial meanings and racial identities.

One of the first things we notice about people when we meet them (along with their sex) is their race. We utilize race to provide clues about *who* a person is. This fact is made painfully obvious when we encounter someone whom we cannot conveniently racially categorize—someone who is, for example, racially "mixed" or of an ethnic/racial group with which we are not familiar. Such an encounter becomes a source of discomfort and momentarily a crisis of racial meaning. Without a racial identity, one is in danger of having no identity.

Our compass for navigating race relations depends on preconceived notions of what each specific racial group looks like. Comments such as, "Funny, you don't look black," betray an underlying image of what black should be. We also become disoriented when people do not act "black," "Latino," or indeed "white." The content of such stereotypes reveals a series of unsubstantiated beliefs about who these groups are and what "they" are like.[14]

In U.S. society, then, a kind of "racial etiquette" exists, a set of interpretative codes and racial meanings which operate in the interactions of daily life. Rules shaped by our perception of race in a comprehensively racial society determine the "presentation of self,"[15] distinctions of status, and appropriate modes of conduct. "Etiquette" is not mere universal adherence to the dominant group's rules, but a more dynamic combination of these rules with the values and beliefs of subordinated groupings. This racial "subjection" is quintessentially ideological. Everybody learns some combination, some version, of the rules of racial classification, and of their own racial identity, often without obvious teaching or conscious inculcation. Race becomes "common sense"—a way of comprehending, explaining and acting in the world.

Racial beliefs operate as an "amateur biology," a way of explaining the variations in "human nature."[16] Differences in skin color and other obvious physical characteristics supposedly provide visible clues to differences lurking underneath. Temperament, sexuality, intelligence, athletic ability, aesthetic preferences, and so on are presumed to be fixed and discernible from the palpable mark of race. Such diverse questions as our confidence and trust in others (for example, clerks or salespeople, media figures, neighbors), our sexual preferences and romantic images, our tastes in music, films, dance, or sports, and our very ways of talking, walking, eating, and dreaming are ineluctably shaped by notions of race. Skin color "differences" are thought to explain perceived differences in intellectual, physical, and artistic temperaments, and to justify distinct treatment of racially identified individuals and groups.

The continuing persistence of racial ideology suggests that these racial myths and stereotypes cannot be exposed as such in the popular imagination. They are, we think, too essential, too integral, to the maintenance of the U.S. social order. Of course, particular meanings, stereotypes, and myths can change, but the presence of a *system* of racial meanings and stereotypes, of racial ideology, seems to be a permanent feature of U.S. culture.

Film and television, for example, have been notorious in disseminating images of racial minorities which establish for audiences what people from these groups look like, how they behave, and "who they are."[17] The power of the media lies not only in their ability to reflect the dominant racial ideology, but in their capacity to shape that ideology in the first place. D. W. Griffith's epic *Birth of a Nation*, a sympathetic treatment of the rise of the Ku Klux Klan during Reconstruction, helped to generate, consolidate, and "nationalize" images of blacks which had been more disparate (more regionally specific, for example) prior to the film's appearance.[18] In U.S. television, the necessity to define characters in the briefest and most condensed manner has led to the perpetuation of racial caricatures, as racial stereotypes serve as shorthand for scriptwriters, directors, and actors, in commercials, etc. Television's tendency to address the "lowest common denominator" in order to render programs "familiar" to an enormous and diverse audience leads it regularly to assign and reassign racial characteristics to particular groups, both minority and majority.

These and innumerable other examples show that we tend to view race as something fixed and immutable—something rooted in "nature." Thus we mask the historical construction of racial categories, the shifting meaning of race, and the crucial role of politics and ideology in shaping race relations. Races do not emerge full-blown. They are the results of diverse historical practices and are continually subject to challenge over their definition and meaning.

Racialization: The Historical Development of Race

In the United States, the racial category of "black" evolved with the consolidation of racial slavery. By the end of the seventeenth century, Africans whose specific identity was Ibo, Yoruba, Fulani, etc. were rendered "black" by an ideology of exploitation based on racial logic—the establishment and maintenance of a "color line." This of course did not occur overnight. A period of indentured servitude which was not rooted in racial logic preceded the consolidation of racial slavery. With slavery, however, a racially based understanding of society was set in motion which resulted in the shaping of a specific *racial* identity not only for the slaves but for the European settlers as well. Winthrop Jordan has observed: "From the initially common term *Christian*, at mid-century there was a marked shift toward the terms *English* and *free*. After about 1680, taking the colonies as a whole, a new term of self-identification appeared—*white*."[19]

We employ the term *racialization* to signify the extension of racial meaning to a previously racially unclassified relationship, social practice, or group. Racialization is an ideological process, an historically specific one. Racial ideology is constructed from pre-existing conceptual (or, if one prefers, "discursive") elements and emerges from the struggles of competing political projects and ideas seeking to articulate similar elements differently. An account of racialization processes that avoids the pitfalls of U.S. ethnic history[20] remains to be written.

Particularly during the nineteenth century, the category of "white" was subject to challenges brought about by the influx of diverse groups who were not of the same Anglo-Saxon stock as the founding immigrants. In the nineteenth century, political and ideological struggles emerged over the classification of Southern Europeans, the Irish, and Jews, among other "non-white" categories.[21] Nativism was only effectively curbed by the institutionalization of a racial order that drew the color line *around*, rather than *within*, Europe.

By stopping short of racializing immigrants from Europe after the Civil War, and by subsequently allowing their assimilation, the American racial order was reconsolidated in the wake of the tremendous challenge placed before it by the abolition of racial slavery.[22] With the end of Reconstruction in 1877, an effective program for limiting the emergent class struggles of the later nineteenth century was forged: the definition of the working class *in racial terms*—as "white." This was not accomplished by any legislative decree or capitalist maneuvering to divide the working class, but rather by white workers themselves. Many of them were recent immigrants, who organized on racial lines as much as on traditionally defined class lines.[23] The Irish on the West Coast, for example, engaged in vicious anti-Chinese race-baiting and committed many pogrom-type assaults on Chinese in the course of consolidating the trade union movement in California.

Thus the very political organization of the working class was in important ways a racial project. The legacy of racial conflicts and arrangements shaped the definition of interests and in turn led to the consolidation of institutional patterns (e.g., segregated unions, dual labor markets, exclusionary legislation) which perpetuated the color line *within* the working class. Selig Perlman, whose study of the development of the labor movement is fairly sympathetic to this process, notes that:

> The political issue after 1877 was racial, not financial, and the weapon was not merely the ballot, but also "direct action"—violence. The anti-Chinese agitation in California, culminating as it did in the Exclusion Law passed by Congress in 1882*, was doubtless the most important single factor in the history of American labor, for without it the entire country might have been overrun by Mongolian [sic] labor and *the labor movement might have become a conflict of races instead of one of classes.*[24]

More recent economic transformations in the United States have also altered interpretations of racial identities and meanings. The automation of southern agriculture and the augmented labor demand of the postwar boom transformed blacks from a largely rural, impoverished labor force to a largely urban, working-class group by 1970.[25] When boom became bust and liberal welfare statism moved rightwards, the majority of blacks came to be seen, increasingly, as part of the "underclass," as state "dependents." Thus the

---

*See "The Chinese Exclusion Act," in Part VII of this volume.

particularly deleterious effects on blacks of global and national economic shifts (generally rising unemployment rates, changes in the employment structure away from reliance on labor intensive work, etc.) were explained once again in the late 1970s and 1980s (as they had been in the 1940s and mid-1960s) as the result of defective black cultural norms, of familial disorganization, etc.[26] In this way new racial attributions, new racial myths, are affixed to "blacks."[27] Similar changes in racial identity are presently affecting Asians and Latinos, as such economic forces as increasing Third World impoverishment and indebtedness fuel immigration and high interest rates, Japanese competition spurs resentments, and U.S. jobs seem to fly away to Korea and Singapore.[28] . . .

Once we understand that race overflows the boundaries of skin color, superexploitation, social stratification, discrimination and prejudice, cultural domination and cultural resistance, state policy (or of any other particular social relationship we list), once we recognize the racial dimension present to some degree in *every* identity, institution, and social practice in the United States—once we have done this, it becomes possible to speak of *racial formation*. This recognition is hard-won; there is a continuous temptation to think of race as an *essence*, as something fixed, concrete, and objective, as (for example) one of the categories just enumerated. And there is also an opposite temptation: to see it as a mere illusion, which an ideal social order would eliminate.

In our view it is crucial to break with these habits of thought. The effort must be made to understand race as *an unstable and "decentered" complex of social meanings constantly being transformed by political struggle*. . . .

NOTES

1. *San Francisco Chronicle*, 14 September 1982, 19 May 1983. Ironically, the 1970 Louisiana law was enacted to supersede an old Jim Crow statute which relied on the idea of "common report" in determining an infant's race. Following Phipps's unsuccessful attempt to change her classification and have the law declared unconstitutional, a legislative effort arose which culminated in the repeal of the law. See *San Francisco Chronicle*, 23 June 1983.
2. The Mormon church, for example, has been heavily criticized for its doctrine of black inferiority.
3. Thomas F. Gossett notes:

   Race theory . . . had up until fairly modern times no firm hold on European thought. On the other hand, race theory and race prejudice were by no means unknown at the time when the English colonists came to North America. Undoubtedly, the age of exploration led many to speculate on race differences at a period when neither Europeans nor Englishmen were prepared to make allowances for vast cultural diversities. Even though race theories had not then secured wide acceptance or even sophisticated formulation, the first contacts of the Spanish with the Indians in the Americas can now be recognized as the beginning of a struggle between conceptions of the nature of primitive peoples which has not yet been wholly settled. (Thomas F. Gossett, *Race: The History of an Idea in America* [Schocken Books, 1965], p. 16).

   Winthrop Jordan provides a detailed account of early European colonialists' attitudes about color and race in *White Over Black: American Attitudes Toward the Negro, 1550–1812* (Norton, 1977 [1968]), pp. 3–43.

4. Pro-slavery physician Samuel George Morton (1799–1851) compiled a collection of 800 crania from all parts of the world which formed the sample for his studies of race. Assuming that the larger the size of the cranium translated into greater intelligence, Morton established a relationship between race and skull capacity. Gossett reports that:

> In 1849, one of his studies included the following results: The English skulls in his collection proved to be the largest, with an average cranial capacity of 96 cubic inches. The Americans and Germans were rather poor seconds, both with cranial capacities of 90 cubic inches. At the bottom of the list were the Negroes with 83 cubic inches, the Chinese with 82, and the Indians with 79. (Ibid., p. 74).

On Morton's methods, see Stephen J. Gould, "The Finagle Factor," *Human Nature* (July 1978).

5. Definitions of race founded upon a common pool of genes have not held up when confronted by scientific research which suggests that the differences *within* a given human population are greater than those *between* populations. See L. L. Cavalli-Sforza, "The Genetics of Human Populations," *Scientific American* (September 1974), pp. 81–9.

6. Arthur Jensen, "How Much Can We Boost IQ and Scholastic Achievement?" *Harvard Educational Review*, vol. 39 (1969), pp. 1–123.

7. Ernst Moritz Manasse, "Max Weber on Race," *Social Research*, vol. 14 (1947), pp. 191–221.

8. Quoted in Edward D. C. Campbell, Jr., *The Celluloid South: Hollywood and the Southern Myth* (Knoxville: University of Tennessee Press, 1981), pp. 168–70.

9. Marvin Harris, *Patterns of Race in the Americas* (Norton, 1964), p. 56.

10. Ibid., p. 57.

11. After James Meredith had been admitted as the first black student at the University of Mississippi, Harry S. Murphy announced that he, and not Meredith, was the first black student to attend "Ole Miss." Murphy described himself as black but was able to pass for white and spent nine months at the institution without attracting any notice (ibid., p. 56).

12. A. Sivanandan, "From Resistance to Rebellion: Asian and Afro-Caribbean Struggles in Britain," *Race and Class*, vol. 23, nos. 2–3 (Autumn–Winter 1981).

13. Consider the contradictions in racial status which abound in the country with the most rigidly defined racial categories—South Africa. There a race classification agency is employed to adjudicate claims for upgrading of official racial identity. This is particularly necessary for the "coloured" category. The apartheid system considers Chinese as "Asians" while the Japanese are accorded the status of "honorary whites." This logic nearly detaches race from any grounding in skin color and other physical attributes and nakedly exposes race as a juridical category subject to economic, social and political influences. (We are indebted to Steve Talbot for clarification of some of these points.) [*Editor's note:* South Africa's system of racial apartheid officially ended in 1994.]

14. Gordon W. Allport, *The Nature of Prejudice* (Doubleday, 1958), pp. 184–200.

15. We wish to use this phrase loosely, without committing ourselves to a particular position on such social psychological approaches as symbolic interactionism, which are outside the scope of this study. An interesting study on this subject is S. M. Lyman and W. A. Douglass, "Ethnicity: Strategies of Individual and Collective Impression Management," *Social Research*, vol. 40, no. 2 (1973).

16. Michael Billig, "Patterns of Racism: Interviews with National Front Members," *Race and Class*, vol. 20, no. 2 (Autumn 1978), pp. 161–79.

17. "Miss San Antonio USA Lisa Fernandez and other Hispanics auditioning for a role in a television soap opera did not fit the Hollywood image of real Mexicans and had to darken their faces before filming." Model Aurora Garza said that their faces were bronzed with powder because they looked too white. "'I'm a real Mexican [Garza said] and very dark anyway. I'm even darker right now because I have a tan. But they kept wanting me to make my face darker and darker'" (*San Francisco Chronicle*, 21 September 1984). A similar dilemma faces Asian American actors who feel that Asian character lead roles inevitably go to white actors who make themselves up to be Asian. Scores of Charlie Chan films, for example, have been made with white leads (the last one was the 1981 *Charlie Chan and the Curse of the Dragon Queen*). Roland Winters, who played in six Chan features, was asked by playwright Frank Chin to explain the logic of casting a white man in the role of Charlie Chan: "'The only thing I can think of is, if you want to cast a homosexual in a show, and you get a homosexual, it'll be awful. It won't be funny . . . and maybe there's something there . . .'" (Frank Chin, "Confessions of the Chinatown Cowboy," *Bulletin of Concerned Asian Scholars*, vol. 4, no. 3 [Fall 1972]).

18. Melanie Martindale-Sikes, "Nationalizing 'Nigger' Imagery Through 'Birth of a Nation,'" paper prepared for the 73rd Annual Meeting of the American Sociological Association, 4–8 September 1978, in San Francisco.

19. Winthrop D. Jordan, op. cit., p. 95; emphasis added.

20. Historical focus has been placed either on particular racially defined groups or on immigration and the "incorporation" of ethnic groups. In the former case the characteristic ethnicity theory pitfalls and apologetics such as functionalism and cultural pluralism may be avoided, but only by sacrificing much of the focus on race. In the latter case, race is considered a manifestation of ethnicity.

21. The degree of antipathy for these groups should not be minimized. A northern commentator observed in the 1850s: "An Irish Catholic seldom attempts to rise to a higher condition than that in which he is placed, while the Negro often makes the attempt with success." Quoted in Gossett, op. cit., p. 288.

22. This analysis, as will perhaps be obvious, is essentially DuBoisian. Its main source will be found in the monumental (and still largely unappreciated) *Black Reconstruction in the United States, 1860–1880* (New York: Atheneum, 1977 [1935]).

23. Alexander Saxton argues that:

North Americans of European background have experienced three great racial confrontations: with the Indian, with the African, and with the Oriental. Central to each transaction has been a totally one-sided preponderance of power, exerted for the exploitation of nonwhites by the dominant white society. In each case (but especially in the two that began with systems of enforced labor), white workingmen have played a crucial, yet ambivalent, role. They have been both exploited and exploiters. On the one hand, thrown into competition with nonwhites as enslaved or "cheap" labor, they suffered economically; on the other hand, being white, they benefited by that very exploitation which was compelling the nonwhites to work for low wages or for nothing. Ideologically they were drawn in opposite directions. *Racial identification cut at right angles to class consciousness.* (Alexander Saxton, *The Indispensable Enemy: Labor and the Anti-Chinese Movement in California* (Berkeley and Los Angeles: University of California Press, 1971), p. 1; emphasis added.)

24. Selig Perlman, *The History of Trade Unionism in the United States* (Augustus Kelley, 1950), p. 52; emphasis added.

25. Whether southern blacks were "peasants" or rural workers is unimportant in this context. Sometime during the 1960s blacks attained a higher degree of urbanization than whites. Before World War II most blacks had been rural dwellers and nearly 80 percent lived in the South.

26. See George Gilder, *Wealth and Poverty* (New York: Basic Books, 1981); Charles Murray, *Losing Ground* (New York: Basic Books, 1984).

27. A brilliant study of the racialization process in Britain, focused on the rise of "mugging" as a popular fear in the 1970s, [appears] in Stuart Hall *et al.*, *Policing the Crisis* (London: Macmillan, 1978).

28. The case of Vincent Chin, a Chinese American man beaten to death in 1982 by a laid-off Detroit auto worker and his stepson who mistook him for Japanese and blamed him for the loss of their jobs, has been widely publicized in Asian American communities. On immigration conflicts and pressures, see Michael Omi, "New Wave Dread: Immigration and Intra–Third World Conflict," *Socialist Review*, no. 60 (November–December 1981).

3 Derailing Rebellion: Inventing White Privilege

Pem Davidson Buck

Constructing Race

Improbable as it now seems, since Americans live in a society where racial characterization and self-definition appear to be parts of nature, in the early days of colonization before slavery was solidified and clearly distinguished from other forms of forced labor, Europeans and Africans seem not to have seen their physical differences in that way.[1] It took until the end of the 1700s for ideas about race to develop until they resembled those we live with today. Before Bacon's Rebellion, African and European indentured servants made love with each other, married each other, ran away with each other, lived as neighbors, liked or disliked each other according to individual personality. Sometimes they died or were punished together for resisting or revolting. And masters had to free both Europeans and Africans if they survived to the end of their indentures. Likewise, Europeans initially did not place all Native Americans in a single racial category. They saw cultural, not biological, differences among Native Americans as distinguishing one tribe from another and from themselves.

Given the tendency of slaves, servants, and landless free Europeans and Africans to cooperate in rebellion, the elite had to "teach Whites the value of whiteness" in order to divide and rule their labor force.[2] After Bacon's Rebellion they utilized their domination of colonial legislatures that made laws and of courts that administered them, gradually building a racial strategy based on the earlier tightening and lengthening of African indenture. Part of this process was tighter control of voting. Free property owning blacks, mulattos, and Native Americans, all identified as *not* of European ancestry, were denied the vote in 1723.[3]

To keep the racial categories separate, a 1691 law increased the punishment of European women who married African or Indian men; toward the end of the 1600s a white woman could be whipped or enslaved for marrying a black. Eventually enslavement for white women was abolished because it transgressed the definition of slavery as black. The problem of what to do with white women's "black" children was eventually partially solved by the control of white women's reproduction to prevent the existence of such children. The potentially "white" children of black women were defined out of existence; they were "black" and shifted from serving a thirty-year indenture to being slaves. To facilitate these reproductive distinctions and to discourage the intimacy that can lead to solidarity and revolts, laws were passed requiring separate quarters for black and white laborers.

Pem Davidson Buck is a professor of anthropology at Elizabethtown Community and Technical College in Kentucky. Her work focuses on whiteness, discourses of inequality, incarceration, and the relationship between state formation and punishment.

Kathleen Brown points out that the control of women's bodies thus became critical to the maintenance of whiteness and to the production of slaves.[4] At the same time black men were denied the rights of colonial masculinity as property ownership, guns, and access to white women were forbidden. Children were made to inherit their mother's status, freeing European fathers from any vestiges of responsibility for their offspring born to indentured or enslaved African mothers. This legal shift has had a profound effect on the distribution of wealth in the United States ever since; slaveholding fathers were some of the richest men in the country, and their wealth, distributed among *all* their children, would have created a significant wealthy black segment of the population.

At the same time a changing panoply of specific laws molded European behavior into patterns that made slave revolt and cross-race unity more and more difficult.[5] These laws limited, for instance, the European right to teach slaves to read. Europeans couldn't use slaves in skilled jobs, which were reserved for Europeans. Europeans had to administer prescribed punishment for slave "misbehavior" and were expected to participate in patrolling at night. They did not have the legal right to befriend blacks. A white servant who ran away with a black was subject to additional punishment beyond that for simply running away. European rights to free their slaves were also curtailed.

Built into all this, rarely mentioned but nevertheless basic to the elite's ability to create and maintain whiteness, slavery, and exploitation, was the use of force against both blacks and whites. Fear kept many whites from challenging, or even questioning, the system. It is worth quoting Lerone Bennett's analysis of how the differentiation between black and white was accomplished:

> The whole system of separation and subordination rested on official state terror. The exigencies of the situation required men to kill some white people to keep them white and to kill many blacks to keep them black. In the North and South, men and women were maimed, tortured, and murdered in a comprehensive campaign of mass conditioning. The severed heads of black and white rebels were impaled on poles along the road as warnings to black people and white people, and opponents of the status quo were starved to death in chains and roasted slowly over open fires. Some rebels were branded; others were castrated. This exemplary cruelty, which was carried out as a deliberate process of mass education, was an inherent part of the new system.[6]

Creating White Privilege

White privileges were established. The "daily exercise of white personal power over black individuals had become a cherished aspect of Southern culture," a critically important part of getting whites to "settle for being white."[7] Privilege encouraged whites to identify with the big slaveholding planters as members of the same "race." They were led to act on the belief that all whites had an equal interest in the maintenance of whiteness and white privilege, and that it was the elite—those controlling the economic system, the political system, and the judicial system—who ultimately protected the benefits of being white.[8]

More pain could be inflicted on blacks than on whites.[9] Whites alone could bear arms; whites alone had the right of self-defense. White servants could own livestock; Africans couldn't. It became illegal to whip naked whites. Whites but not Africans had to be given their freedom dues at the end of their indenture. Whites were given the right to beat any blacks, even those they didn't own, for failing to show proper respect. Only whites could be hired to force black labor as overseers. White servants and laborers were given lighter tasks and a monopoly, for a time, on skilled jobs. White men were given the right to control "their" women without elite interference; blacks as slaves were denied the right to family at all, since family would mean that slave husbands, not owners, controlled slave wives. In 1668, all free African women were defined as labor, for whom husbands or employers had to pay a tithe, while white women were defined as keepers of men's homes, not as labor; their husbands paid no tax on them. White women were indirectly given control of black slaves and the right to substitute slave labor for their own labor in the fields.

Despite these privileges, landless whites, some of them living in "miserable huts," might have rejected white privilege if they saw that in fact it made little *positive* difference in their lives, and instead merely protected them from the worst *negative* effects of elite punishment and interference, such as were inflicted on those of African descent.[10] After all, the right to whip someone doesn't cure your own hunger or landlessness. By the end of the Revolutionary War unrest was in the air. Direct control by the elite was no longer politically or militarily feasible. Rebellions and attempted rebellions had been fairly frequent in the hundred years following Bacon's Rebellion.[11] They indicated the continuing depth of landless European discontent. Baptist ferment against the belief in the inherent superiority of the upper classes simply underscored the danger.[12]

So landless Europeans had to be given some *material* reason to reject those aspects of their lives that made them similar to landless Africans and Native Americans, and to focus instead on their similarity to the landed Europeans—to accept whiteness as their defining characteristic. Landless Europeans' only real similarity to the elite was their European ancestry itself, so that ancestry had to be given real significance: European ancestry was identified with upward mobility and the right to use the labor of the non-eligible in their upward climb. So, since land at that time was the source of upward mobility, land had to be made available, if only to a few.

Meanwhile, Thomas Jefferson advocated the establishment of a solid white Anglo-Saxon yeoman class of small farmers, who, as property owners, would acquire a vested interest in law and order and reject class conflict with the elite. These small farmers would, by upholding "law and order," support and sometimes administer the legal mechanisms—jails, workhouses and poorhouses, and vagrancy laws—that would control other whites who would remain a landless labor force. They would support the legal and illegal mechanisms controlling Native Americans, Africans, and poor whites, becoming a buffer class between the elite and those they most exploited, disguising the elite's continuing grip on power and wealth. . . .

The Psychological Wage

The initial construction of whiteness had been based on a material benefit for whites: land, or the apparently realistic hope of land. By the 1830s and 1840s, most families identified by their European descent had had several generations of believing their whiteness was real. But its material benefit had faded. Many whites were poor, selling their labor either as farm renters or as industrial workers, and they feared wage slavery, no longer certain they were much freer than slaves.[13] But this time, to control unrest, the elite had no material benefits they were willing to part with. Nor were employers willing to raise wages. Instead, politicians and elites emphasized whiteness as a benefit in itself.

The work of particular white intellectuals, who underscored the already existing belief in white superiority and the worries about white slavery, was funded by elites and published in elite-owned printing houses.[14] These intellectuals provided fodder for newspaper discussions, speeches, scientific analysis, novels, sermons, songs, and blackface minstrel shows in which white superiority was phrased as if whiteness in and of itself was naturally a benefit, despite its lack of material advantage. This sense of superiority allowed struggling northern whites to look down their noses at free blacks and at recent immigrants, particularly the Irish. This version of whiteness was supposed to make up for their otherwise difficult situation, providing them with a "psychological wage" instead of cash—a bit like being employee of the month and given a special parking place instead of a raise.

Many whites bought into the psychological wage, expressing their superiority over non-whites and defining them, rather than the capitalists, as the enemy. They focused, often with trade union help, on excluding blacks and immigrants from skilled trades and better-paying jobs. Employers cooperated in confining blacks and immigrants to manual labor and domestic work, making a clear definition of the work suitable for white men.[15] Native white men began shifting away from defining themselves by their landowning freedom and independence. Instead they accepted their dependence on capitalists and the control employers exercised over their lives, and began to define themselves by their class position as skilled "mechanics" working for better wages under better working conditions than other people. They became proud of their productivity, which grew with the growing efficiency of industrial technology, and began using it to define whiteness—and manhood. The ethic of individual hard work gained far wider currency. Successful competition in the labor marketplace gradually became a mark of manhood, and "white man's work" became the defining characteristic of whiteness.[16] Freedom was equated with the right to own and sell your own labor, as opposed to slavery, which allowed neither right. Independence was now defined not only by property ownership but also by possession of skill and tools that allowed wage-earning men to acquire status as a head of household controlling dependents.[17]

This redefinition of whiteness was built as much on changing gender as on changing class relationships.[18] Many native white men and women, including workers, journalists, scientists, and politicians, began discouraging married women from working for wages, claiming that true women served only their own families. Despite this claim—the cult of domesticity, or of true womanhood—many wives of working class men actually did work outside the home. They were less likely to do so in those cases where native men were able, through strikes and the exclusion of women, immigrants, and free blacks, to create an artificial labor shortage. Such shortages gave native working class men the leverage to force employers to pay them enough to afford a non-earning wife. Women in the families of such men frequently did "stay home" and frequently helped to promote the idea that people who couldn't do the same were genetically or racially or culturally inferior.

But native whites whose wages actually weren't sufficient struggled on in poverty. If a native woman worked for wages, particularly in a factory, the family lost status. Many female factory workers were now immigrants rather than native whites. Many had no husband or had husbands whose wages, when they could get work, came nowhere near supporting a family.[19] It is no wonder immigrant women weren't particularly "domestic." Such families didn't meet the cultural requirements for white privilege — male "productivity" in "white man's work" and dependent female "domesticity." These supposed white virtues became a bludgeon with which to defend white privilege and to deny it to not-quite-whites and not-whites, helping to construct a new working class hierarchy. This new hierarchy reserved managerial and skilled jobs for "productive" native whites. So, for the price of reserving better jobs for some native whites, the capitalist class gained native white consent to their own loss of independence and to keeping most of the working class on abysmally low wages.

In the South, where there was less industry, the psychological wage slowly developed an additional role. It was used not only to gain consent to oppressive industrial relations, but also to convince poor farming whites to support Southern elites in their conflict with Northern elites. Du Bois points out that by the Civil War

> . . . it became the fashion to pat the disenfranchised poor white man on the back and tell him after all he was white and that he and the planters had a common object in keeping the white man superior. This virus increased bitterness and relentless hatred, and after the war it became a chief ingredient in the division of the working class in the Southern States.[20]

NOTES

1. My discussion of the construction of race and racial slavery is deeply indebted to Lerone Bennett, *The Shaping of Black America* (New York: Penguin Books, 1993 [1975]), 1–109. See also Theodore Allen, *Invention of the White Race*, vol. II, *The Origin of Racial Oppression in Anglo-America* (New York: Verso, 1997), 75–109; Audrey Smedley, *Race in North America: Origin and Evolution of a Worldview* (Boulder: Westview Press, 1993), 100–1, 109, 142–3, 198; Kathleen Brown, *Good Wives, Nasty Wenches, and Anxious Patriarchs: Gender, Race, and Power in Colonial Virginia* (Chapel Hill: University of North Carolina Press, 1996), 107–244; bell hooks, *Ain't I a Woman: Black Women and Feminism* (South End Press, 1981), 15–51.
2. Bennett, *Shaping of Black America*, 74–5.
3. Allen, *Invention*, vol. II, 241.
4. Brown, *Good Wives*, pays particular attention to control of women's bodies and status in producing slavery and race (see especially 181, 129–33, 116); also see Allen, *Invention*, vol. II, 128–35, 146–7, 177–88; Bennett, *Shaping of Black America*, 75.
5. For this section, see Bennett, *Shaping of Black America*, 72; Edmund Morgan, *American Slavery, American Freedom: The Ordeal of Colonial Virginia* (New York: W. W. Norton and Co, 1975), 311–3; Allen, *Invention*, vol. II, 249–53.
6. Bennett, *Shaping of Black America*, 73–4.
7. The first quote is from Smedley, *Race in North America*, 224; the second is from David Roediger, *The Wages of Whiteness: Race and the Making of the American Working Class* (New York: Verso, 1991), 6.

8. Allen, *Invention*, vol. II, 162, 248–53, emphasizes that elites invented white supremacy to protect their own interests, although working-class whites did much of the "dirty work" of oppression.

9. Morgan, *American Slavery*, 312–3. On white privileges, see Ronald Takaki, *A Different Mirror: A History of Multicultural America* (Boston: Little, Brown, 1993), 67–8; Allen, *Invention*, vol. II, 250–3; Brown, *Good Wives*, 180–3.

10. The quote is from Allen, *Invention*, vol. II, 256, citing a contemporary traveler.

11. Howard Zinn, *A People's History of the United States* (HarperCollins, 1995, 2nd ed.), 58.

12. Smedley, *Race in North America*, 174–5.

13. See David Roediger, *The Wages of Whiteness: Race and the Making of the American Working Class* (New York: Verso, 1991), 13–4, 65–87, for a discussion of white attitudes toward "wage slavery" and "white slavery."

14. For discussion of elite manipulation of attitudes, see particularly Alexander Saxton, *The Rise and Fall of the White Republic: Class Politics and Mass Culture in Nineteenth-Century America* (New York: Verso,1990); Smedley, *Race in North America*; Allen, *Invention of the White Race*, vol. I, 163–5.

15. Allen, *Invention*, vol. I, 192–9, Critiques the common assumption that the focus on "job competition" was natural as opposed to manipulated by elites.

16. Noel Ignatiev, *How the Irish Became White* (New York: Routledge, 1995), 112, 115; Allen, *Invention*, vol. I, 195. On "Marketplace Man," see Michael Kimmel, "Masculinity as Homophobia: Fear, Shame, and Silence in the Construction of Gender Identity," in Harry Brod and Michael Kaufman, eds., Theorizing Masculinities (Thousand Oaks: Sage Publications, 1994), 123; Jonathan Edmonds, "'Meat vs Rice': Euro-American Labor and Feminization of the Chinese American Working Class" (term paper, Seminar on Chinese American Labor, Oberlin College, 1997).

17. On independence and labor as a free man's own property, see Lacy Ford, "Frontier Democracy: The Turner Thesis Revisited," *Journal of the Early Republic*, vol.13 (1993), 158–9; McCurry, "The Politics of the Yeoman Households in South Carolina"; Smedley, *Race in North America*, 47–8; Hahn, "The Yeomanry of the Nonplantation South," 33.

18. For issues raised in this section, see Karen Brodkin, *How Jews Became White Folks and What That Says about Race in America* (New Brunswick: Rutgers University Press, 1998), 77–102; Julie Matthaei, *An Economic History of Women in America: Women's Work, the Sexual Division of Labor, and the Development of Capitalism* (New York: Schocken Books, 1982), 124–40; Alice Abel Kemp, *Women's Work: Degraded and Devalued* (Englewood Cliffs: Prentice Hall, 1994), 149–59.

19. Leith Mullings, "Uneven Development: Class, Race, and Gender in the United States before 1900," in Eleanor Leacock and Helen Safa, eds., *Women's Work: Development and the Division of Labor by Gender* (South Hadley, MA: Bergin and Garvey, 1986), 50–1.

20. Du Bois, *Black Reconstruction*, 80.

4 How Jews Became White Folks, and What That Says About Race in America

Karen Brodkin

The American nation was founded and developed by the Nordic race, but if a few more million members of the Alpine, Mediterranean and Semitic races are poured among us, the result must inevitably be a hybrid race of people as worthless and futile as the good-for-nothing mongrels of Central America and Southeastern Europe.

—KENNETH ROBERTS, "WHY EUROPE LEAVES HOME"

It is clear that Kenneth Roberts did not think of my ancestors as white, like him. The late nineteenth century and early decades of the twentieth saw a steady stream of warnings by scientists, policymakers, and the popular press that "mongrelization" of the Nordic or Anglo-Saxon race—the real Americans—by inferior European races (as well as by inferior non-European ones) was destroying the fabric of the nation.

I continue to be surprised when I read books that indicate that America once regarded its immigrant European workers as something other than white, as biologically different. My parents are not surprised; they expect antisemitism to be part of the fabric of daily life, much as I expect racism to be part of it. They came of age in the Jewish world of the 1920s and 1930s, at the peak of antisemitism in America.[1] They are rightly proud of their upward mobility and think of themselves as pulling themselves up by their own bootstraps. I grew up during the 1950s in the Euro-ethnic New York suburb of Valley Stream, where Jews were simply one kind of white folks and where ethnicity meant little more to my generation than food and family heritage. Part of my ethnic heritage was the belief that Jews were smart and that our success was due to our own efforts and abilities, reinforced by a culture that valued sticking together, hard work, education, and deferred gratification.

I am willing to affirm all those abilities and ideals and their contribution to Jews' upward mobility, but I also argue that they were still far from sufficient to account for Jewish success. . . . Instead I want to suggest that Jewish success is a product not only of ability but also of the removal of powerful social barriers to its realization.

It is certainly true that the United States has a history of antisemitism and of beliefs that Jews are members of an inferior race. But Jews were hardly alone. American anti-semitism was part of a broader pattern of late-nineteenth-century racism against all southern

---

Karen Brodkin is a professor emerita of anthropology at the University of California, Los Angeles. Her books include *Power Politics* and *Making Democracy Matter: Identity and Activism in Los Angeles.*

and eastern European immigrants, as well as against Asian immigrants, not to mention African Americans, Native Americans, and Mexicans. These views justified all sorts of discriminatory treatment, including closing the doors, between 1882 and 1927, to immigration from Europe and Asia. This picture changed radically after World War II. Suddenly, the same folks who had promoted nativism and xenophobia were eager to believe that the Euro-origin people whom they had deported, reviled as members of inferior races, and prevented from immigrating only a few years earlier, were now model middle-class white suburban citizens.[2]

It was not an educational epiphany that made those in power change their hearts, their minds, and our race. Instead, it was the biggest and best affirmative action program in the history of our nation, and it was for Euromales. That is not how it was billed, but it is the way it worked out in practice. I tell this story to show the institutional nature of racism and the centrality of state policies to creating and changing races. Here, those policies reconfigured the category of whiteness to include European immigrants. There are similarities and differences in the ways each of the European immigrant groups became "whitened." I tell the story in a way that links antisemitism to other varieties of anti-European racism because this highlights what Jews shared with other Euro-immigrants.

Euroraces

The United States' "discovery" that Europe was divided into inferior and superior races began with the racialization of the Irish in the mid-nineteenth century and flowered in response to the great waves of immigration from southern and eastern Europe that began in the late nineteenth century. Before that time, European immigrants — including Jews — had been largely assimilated into the white population. However, the 23 million European immigrants who came to work in U.S. cities in the waves of migration after 1880 were too many and too concentrated to absorb. Since immigrants and their children made up more than 70 percent of the population of most of the country's largest cities, by the 1890s urban America had taken on a distinctly southern and eastern European immigrant flavor. Like the Irish in Boston and New York, their urban concentrations in dilapidated neighborhoods put them cheek by jowl next to the rising elites and the middle class with whom they shared public space and to whom their working-class ethnic communities were particularly visible.

The Red Scare of 1919 clearly linked anti-immigrant with anti-working-class sentiment — to the extent that the Seattle general strike by largely native-born workers was blamed on foreign agitators. The Red Scare was fueled by an economic depression, a massive postwar wave of strikes, the Russian Revolution, and another influx of postwar immigration. . . .

Not surprisingly, the belief in European races took root most deeply among the wealthy, United States-born Protestant elite, who feared a hostile and seemingly inassimilable working class. By the end of the nineteenth century, Senator Henry Cabot Lodge pressed Congress to cut off immigration to the United States; Theodore Roosevelt raised the alarm of "race suicide" and took Anglo-Saxon women to task for allowing "native" stock to be outbred by inferior immigrants. In the early twentieth century, these fears gained a great deal of social legitimacy thanks to the efforts of an influential network of aristocrats and scientists who developed theories of eugenics — breeding for a "better" humanity — and scientific racism. . . .

By the 1920s, scientific racism sanctified the notion that real Americans were white and that real whites came from northwest Europe. Racism by white workers in the West fueled laws excluding and expelling the Chinese in 1882. Widespread racism led to closing the immigration door to virtually all Asians and most Europeans between 1924 and 1927, and to deportation of Mexicans during the Great Depression.

Racism in general, and antisemitism in particular, flourished in higher education. Jews were the first of the Euro-immigrant groups to enter college in significant numbers, so it was not surprising that they faced the brunt of discrimination there. The Protestant elite complained that Jews were unwashed, uncouth, unrefined, loud, and pushy. Harvard University President A. Lawrence Lowell, who was also a vice president of the Immigration Restriction League, was open about his opposition to Jews at Harvard. The Seven Sisters schools had a reputation for "flagrant discrimination.". . .

Columbia's quota against Jews was well known in my parents' community. My father is very proud of having beaten it and been admitted to Columbia Dental School on the basis of his skill at carving a soap ball. Although he became a teacher instead because the tuition was too high, he took me to the dentist every week of my childhood and prolonged the agony by discussing the finer points of tooth-filling and dental care. . . .

My parents believe that Jewish success, like their own, was due to hard work and a high value placed on education. They attended Brooklyn College during the Depression. My mother worked days and went to school at night; my father went during the day. Both their families encouraged them. More accurately, their families expected it. Everyone they knew was in the same boat, and their world was made up of Jews who were advancing just as they were. . . .

How we interpret Jewish social mobility in this milieu depends on whom we compare them to. Compared with other immigrants, Jews were upwardly mobile. But compared with nonimmigrant whites, that mobility was very limited and circumscribed. The existence of anti-immigrant, racist, and antisemitic barriers kept the Jewish middle class confined to a small number of occupations. Jews were excluded from mainstream corporate management and corporately employed professions, except in the garment and movie industries, in which they were pioneers. Jews were almost totally excluded from university faculties (the few who made it had powerful patrons). Eastern European Jews were concentrated in small businesses, and in professions where they served a largely Jewish clientele. . . .

My parents' generation believed that Jews overcame antisemitic barriers because Jews are special. My answer is that the Jews who were upwardly mobile were special among Jews (and were also well placed to write the story). My generation might well respond to our parents' story of pulling themselves up by their own bootstraps with "But think what you might have been without the racism and with some affirmative action!" And that is precisely what the post-World War II boom, the decline of systematic, public, anti-Euro racism and antisemitism, and governmental affirmative action extended to white males let us see.

Whitening Euro-ethnics

By the time I was an adolescent, Jews were just as white as the next white person. Until I was eight, I was a Jew in a world of Jews. Everyone on Avenue Z in Sheepshead Bay was Jewish. I spent my days playing and going to school on three blocks of Avenue Z, and visiting my grandparents in the nearby Jewish neighborhoods of Brighton Beach and Coney Island. There were plenty of Italians in my neighborhood, but they lived around the corner. They were a kind of Jew, but on the margins of my social horizons. Portuguese were even more distant, at the end of the bus ride, at Sheepshead Bay. The *shul*, or temple, was on Avenue Z, and I begged my father to take me like all the other fathers took their kids, but religion wasn't part of my family's Judaism. Just how Jewish my neighborhood was hit me in first grade, when I was one of two kids to go to school on Rosh Hashanah. My teacher was shocked—she was Jewish too—and I was embarrassed to tears when she sent me home. I was never again sent to school on Jewish holidays. We left that world in 1949 when we moved to Valley Stream, Long Island, which was Protestant and Republican and even had farms until Irish, Italian, and Jewish ex-urbanities like us gave it a more suburban and Democratic flavor.

Neither religion nor ethnicity separated us at school or in the neighborhood. Except temporarily. During my elementary school years, I remember a fair number of dirt-bomb (a good suburban weapon) wars on the block. Periodically, one of the Catholic boys would accuse me or my brother of killing his god, to which we'd reply, "Did not," and start lobbing dirt bombs. Sometimes he'd get his friends from Catholic school and I'd get mine from public school kids on the block, some of whom were Catholic. Hostilities didn't last for more than a couple of hours and punctuated an otherwise friendly relationship. They ended by our junior high years, when other things became more important. Jews, Catholics, and Protestants, Italians, Irish, Poles, "English" (I don't remember hearing WASP as a kid), were mixed up on the block and in school. We thought of ourselves as middle class and very enlightened because our ethnic backgrounds seemed so irrelevant to high school culture. We didn't see race (we thought), and racism was not part of our peer consciousness. Nor were the immigrant or working-class histories of our families.

As with most chicken-and-egg problems, it is hard to know which came first. Did Jews and other Euro-ethnics become white because they became middle-class? That is, did money whiten? Or did being incorporated into an expanded version of whiteness open up the economic doors to middle-class status? Clearly, both tendencies were at work.

Some of the changes set in motion during the war against fascism led to a more inclusive version of whiteness. Antisemitism and anti-European racism lost respectability. The 1940 census no longer distinguished native whites of native parentage from those, like my parents, of immigrant parentage, so Euro-immigrants and their children were more securely white by submersion in an expanded notion of whiteness.[3]

Theories of nurture and culture replaced theories of nature and biology. Instead of dirty and dangerous races that would destroy American democracy, immigrants became ethnic groups whose children had successfully assimilated into the mainstream and risen to the middle class. In this new myth, Euro-ethnic suburbs like mine became the measure of American democracy's victory over racism. Jewish mobility became a new Horatio Alger story. In time and with hard work, every ethnic group would get a piece of the pie, and the United States would be a nation with equal opportunity for all its people to become part of a prosperous middle-class majority. And it seemed that Euro-ethnic immigrants and their children were delighted to join middle America.

This is not to say that antisemitism disappeared after World War II, only that it fell from fashion and was driven underground. . . .

Although changing views on who was white made it easier for Euro-ethnics to become middle class, economic prosperity also played a very powerful role in the whitening process. . . .

. . . The postwar period was a historic moment for real class mobility and for the affluence we have erroneously come to believe was the American norm. It was a time when the old white and the newly white masses became middle class.[4]

The GI Bill of Rights, as the 1944 Serviceman's Readjustment Act was known, is arguably the most massive affirmative action program in American history. It was created to develop needed labor force skills and to provide those who had them with a lifestyle that reflected their value to the economy. The GI benefits that were ultimately extended to 16 million GIs (of the Korean War as well) included priority in jobs—that is, preferential hiring, but no one objected to it then—financial support during the job search, small loans for starting up businesses, and most important, low-interest home loans and educational benefits, which included tuition and living expenses. This legislation was rightly regarded as one of the most revolutionary postwar programs. I call it affirmative action because it was aimed at and disproportionately helped male, Euro-origin GIs.[5] . . .

Education and Occupation

It is important to remember that, prior to the war, a college degree was still very much a "mark of the upper class," that colleges were largely finishing schools for Protestant elites. Before the postwar boom, schools could not begin to accommodate the American masses. Even in New York City before the 1930s, neither the public schools nor City College had room for more than a tiny fraction of potential immigrant students.[6]

Not so after the war. The almost 8 million GIs who took advantage of their educational benefits under the GI Bill caused "the greatest wave of college building in American history." White male GIs were able to take advantage of their educational benefits for college and technical training, so they were particularly well positioned to seize the opportunities provided by the new demands for professional, managerial, and technical labor. . . .

The reason I refer to educational and occupational GI benefits as affirmative action programs for white males is because they were decidedly not extended to African Americans or to women of any race. Theoretically they were available to all veterans; in practice women and black veterans did not get anywhere near their share. Women's Army and Air Force units were initially organized as auxiliaries, hence not part of the military. When that status was changed, in July 1943, only those who reenlisted in the armed forces were eligible for veterans' benefits. Many women thought they were simply being demobilized and returned home. The majority remained and were ultimately eligible for veterans' benefits. But there was little counseling, and a social climate that discouraged women's careers and independence cut down on women's knowledge and sense of entitlement. The Veterans Administration kept no statistics on the number of women who used their GI benefits.[7]

The barriers that almost completely shut African American GIs out of their benefits were even more formidable. In Neil Wynn's portrait, black GIs anticipated starting new lives, just like their white counterparts. Over 43 percent hoped to return to school, and most expected to relocate, to find better jobs in new lines of work. The exodus from the South toward the North and West was particularly large. So it was not a question of any lack of ambition on the part of African American GIs. White male privilege was shaped against the backdrop of wartime racism and postwar sexism. . . .

The military, the Veterans Administration, the United States Employment Services (USES), and the Federal Housing Administration effectively denied African American GIs access to their benefits and to new educational, occupational, and residential opportunities. Black GIs who served in the thoroughly segregated armed forces during World War II served under white officers. African American soldiers were given a disproportionate share of dishonorable discharges, which denied them veterans' rights under the GI Bill. Between August and November 1946, for example, 21 percent of white soldiers and 39 percent of black soldiers were dishonorably discharged. Those who did get an honorable discharge then faced the Veterans Administration and the USES. The latter, which was responsible for job placements, employed very few African Americans, especially in the South. This meant that black veterans did not receive much employment information and that the offers they did receive were for low-paid and menial jobs. "In one survey of 50 cities, the movement of blacks into peacetime employment was found to be lagging far behind that of white veterans: in Arkansas ninety-five percent of the placements made by the USES for Afro-Americans were in service or unskilled jobs."[8] African Americans were also less likely than whites, regardless of GI status, to gain new jobs commensurate with their wartime jobs. For example, in San Francisco, by 1948, black Americans "had dropped back halfway to their prewar employment status."[9]

Black GIs faced discrimination in the educational system as well. Despite the end of restrictions on Jews and other Euro-ethnics, African Americans were not welcome in white colleges. Black colleges were overcrowded, but the combination of segregation and prejudice made for few alternatives. About 20,000 black veterans attended college by 1947, most in black colleges, but almost as many, 15,000, could not gain entry. Predictably, the disproportionately few African Americans who did gain access to their educational benefits were able, like their white counterparts, to become doctors and engineers, and to enter the black middle class.[10]

Suburbanization

In 1949, ensconced in Valley Stream, I watched potato farms turn into Levittown and Idlewild (later Kennedy) airport. This was the major spectator sport in our first years on Long Island. A typical weekend would bring various aunts, uncles, and cousins out from the city. After a huge meal, we'd pile into the car—itself a novelty—to look at the bull-dozed acres and comment on the matchbox construction. During the week, my mother and I would look at the houses going up within walking distance. . . .

At the beginning of World War II, about one-third of all American families owned their houses. That percentage doubled in twenty years. . . .

The Federal Housing Administration (FHA) was key to buyers and builders alike. Thanks to the FHA, suburbia was open to more than GIs. People like us would never have been in the market for houses without FHA and Veterans Administration (VA) low-down-payment, low-interest, long-term loans to young buyers. . . .

The FHA believed in racial segregation. Throughout its history, it publicly and actively promoted restrictive covenants. Before the war, these forbade sales to Jews and Catholics as well as to African Americans. The deed to my house in Detroit had such a covenant, which theoretically prevented it from being sold to Jews or African Americans. Even after the Supreme Court outlawed restrictive covenants in 1948, the FHA continued to encourage builders to write them in against African Americans. FHA underwriting manuals openly insisted on racially homogeneous neighborhoods, and their loans were made only in white neighborhoods. . . .

The result of these policies was that African Americans were totally shut out of the suburban boom. An article in *Harper's* described the housing available to black GIs.

> On his way to the base each morning, Sergeant Smith passes an attractive air-conditioned, FHA-financed housing project. It was built for service families. Its rents are little more than the Smiths pay for their shack. And there are half-a-dozen vacancies, but none for Negroes.[11]

. . . Urban renewal was the other side of the process by which Jewish and other working-class Euro-immigrants became middle class. It was the push to suburbia's seductive pull. The fortunate white survivors of urban renewal headed disproportionately for suburbia, where they could partake of prosperity and the good life. . . .

If the federal stick of urban renewal joined the FHA carrot of cheap mortgages to send masses of Euro-Americans to the suburbs, the FHA had a different kind of one-two punch for African Americans. Segregation kept them out of the suburbs, and redlining made sure they could not buy or repair their homes in the neighborhoods in which they were allowed to live. The FHA practiced systematic redlining. This was a practice developed by its predecessor, the Home Owners Loan Corporation (HOLC), which in the 1930s developed an elaborate neighborhood rating system that placed the highest (green) value on all-white, middle-class neighborhoods, and the lowest (red) on racially nonwhite or mixed and working-class neighborhoods. High ratings meant high property values. The idea was that low property values in redlined neighborhoods made them bad investments. The FHA was, after all, created by and for banks and the housing industry. Redlining warned banks not to lend there, and the FHA would not insure mortgages in such neighborhoods. Redlining created a self-fulfilling prophecy. . . . The FHA's and VA's refusal to guarantee loans in redlined neighborhoods made it virtually impossible for African Americans to borrow money for home improvement or purchase. Because these maps and surveys were quite secret, it took the civil rights movement to make these practices and their devastating consequences public. As a result, those who fought urban renewal, or who sought to make a home in the urban ruins, found themselves locked out of the middle class. They also faced an ideological assault that labeled their neighborhoods slums and called them slumdwellers.[12]

Conclusion

The record is very clear. Instead of seizing the opportunity to end institutionalized racism, the federal government did its level best to shut and double-seal the postwar window of opportunity in African Americans' faces. It consistently refused to combat segregation in the social institutions that were key to upward mobility in education, housing, and employment. Moreover, federal programs that were themselves designed to assist demobilized GIs and young families systematically discriminated against African Americans. Such programs reinforced white/nonwhite racial distinctions even as intrawhite racialization was falling out of fashion. This other side of the coin, that white men of northwestern European ancestry and white men of southeastern European ancestry were treated equally in theory and in practice with regard to the benefits they received, was part of the larger postwar whitening of Jews and other eastern and southern Europeans.

The myth that Jews pulled themselves up by their own bootstraps ignores the fact that it took federal programs to create the conditions whereby the abilities of Jews and other European immigrants could be recognized and rewarded rather than denigrated and denied. The GI Bill and FHA and VA mortgages, even though they were advertised as open to all, functioned as a set of racial privileges. They were privileges because they were extended to white GIs but not to black GIs. Such privileges were forms of affirmative action that allowed Jews and other Euro-American men to become suburban homeowners and to get the training that allowed them—but much less so women vets or war workers—to become professionals, technicians, salesmen, and managers in a growing economy. Jews and other white ethnics' upward mobility was due to programs that allowed us to float on a rising economic tide. To African Americans, the government offered the cement boots of segregation, redlining, urban renewal, and discrimination.

Those racially skewed gains have been passed across the generations, so that racial inequality seems to maintain itself "naturally," even after legal segregation ended. Today, I own a house in Venice, California, like the one in which I grew up in Valley Stream, and my brother until recently owned a house in Palo Alto much like an Eichler house. Both of us are where we are thanks largely to the postwar benefits our parents received and passed on to us, and to the educational benefits we received in the 1960s as a result of affluence and the social agitation that developed from the black Freedom Movement. I have white, African American, and Asian American colleagues whose parents received fewer or none of America's postwar benefits and who expect never to own a house despite their considerable academic achievements. Some of these colleagues who are a few years younger than I also carry staggering debts for their education, which they expect to have to repay for the rest of their lives.

Conventional wisdom has it that the United States has always been an affluent land of opportunity. But the truth is that affluence has been the exception and that real upward mobility has required massive affirmative action programs. . . .

NOTES

1. Gerber 1986; Dinnerstein 1987, 1994.
2. Not all Jews are white or unambiguously white. It has been suggested, for example, that Hasidim lack the privileges of whiteness. Rodriguez (1997, 12, 15) has begun to unpack the claims of white Jewish "amenity migrants" and the different racial meanings of Chicano claims to a crypto-Jewish identity in New Mexico. See also Thomas 1996 on African American Jews.
3. This census also explicitly changed the Mexican race to white (United States Bureau of the Census 1940, 2:4).
4. Nash et al. 1986, 885–886.
5. On planning for veterans, see F. J. Brown 1946; Hurd 1946; Mosch 1975; "Postwar Jobs for Veterans" 1945; Willenz 1983.
6. Willenz 1983, 165.
7. Willenz 1983, 20–28, 94–97. I thank Nancy G. Cattell for calling my attention to the fact that women GIs were ultimately eligible for benefits.
8. Nalty and MacGregor 1981, 218, 60–61.
9. Wynn 1976, 114, 116.
10. On African Americans in the U.S. military, see Foner 1974; Dalfiume 1969; Johnson 1967; Binkin and Eitelberg 1982; Nalty and MacGregor 1981. On schooling, see Walker 1970, 4–9.
11. Quoted in Foner 1974, 195.
12. See Gans 1962.

REFERENCES

Binkin, Martin, and Mark J. Eitelberg. 1982. *Blacks and the Military.* Washington, D.C.: Brookings Institution.

Brown, Francis J. 1946. *Educational Opportunities for Veterans.* Washington, D.C.: Public Affairs Press American Council on Public Affairs.

Dalfiume, Richard M. 1969. *Desegregation of the U.S. Armed Forces: Fighting on Two Fronts, 1939–1953.* Columbia: University of Missouri Press.

Dinnerstein, Leonard, 1987. *Uneasy at Home: Anti-Semitism and the American Jewish Experience.* New York: Columbia University Press.

_____. 1994. *Anti-Semitism in America.* New York: Oxford University Press.

Foner, Jack. 1974. *Blacks and the Military in American History: A New Perspective.* New York: Praeger Publishers.

Gans, Herbert. 1962. *The Urban Villagers.* New York: Free Press of Glencoe.

Gerber, David, ed. 1986. *Anti-Semitism in American History.* Urbana: University of Illinois Press.

Hurd, Charles. 1946. *The Veterans' Program: A Complete Guide to Its Benefits, Rights and Options.* New York: McGraw-Hill Book Company.

Johnson, Jesse J. 1967. *Ebony Brass: An Autobiography of Negro Frustration Amid Aspiration.* New York: The William Frederick Press.

Mosch, Theodore R. 1975. *The GI Bill: A Breakthrough in Educational and Social Policy in the United States.* Hicksville, N.Y.: Exposition Press.

Nalty, Bernard C., and Morris J. MacGregor, eds. 1981. *Blacks in the Military: Essential Documents.* Wilmington, Del.: Scholarly Resources, Inc.

Nash, Gary B., Julie Roy Jeffrey, John R. Howe, Allen F. Davis, Peter J. Frederick, and Allen M. Winkler. 1986. *The American People: Creating a Nation and a Society.* New York: Harper and Row.

"Postwar Jobs for Veterans."1945. *The Annals of the American Academy of Political and Social Science* 238 (March).

Rodriguez, Sylvia. 1997. "Tourism, Whiteness, and the Vanishing Anglo." Paper presented at the conference "Seeing and Being Seen: Tourism in the American West." Center for the American West, Boulder, Colorado, 2 May.

Thomas, Laurence Mordekhai. 1996. "The Soul of Identity: Jews and Blacks." In *People of the Book*, ed. S. F. Fishkin and J. Rubin-Dorsky. Madison: University of Wisconsin Press, 169–186.

United States Bureau of the Census. 1940. *Sixteenth Census of the United States*, V. 2. Washington, D.C.: United States Government Printing Office.

Walker, Olive. 1970. "The Windsor Hills School Story." *Integrated Education: Race and Schools* 8, 3:4–9.

Willenz, June A. 1983. *Women Veterans: America's Forgotten Heroines*. New York: Continuum.

Wynn, Neil A. 1976. *The Afro-American and the Second World War*. London: Paul Elek.

5 "Night to His Day": The Social Construction of Gender

Judith Lorber

Talking about gender for most people is the equivalent of fish talking about water. Gender is so much the routine ground of everyday activities that questioning its taken-for-granted assumptions and presuppositions is like thinking about whether the sun will come up.[1] Gender is so pervasive that in our society we assume it is bred into our genes. Most people find it hard to believe that gender is constantly created and re-created out of human interaction, out of social life, and is the texture and order of that social life. Yet gender, like culture, is a human production that depends on everyone constantly "doing gender" (West and Zimmerman 1987).

And everyone "does gender" without thinking about it. Today, on the subway, I saw a well-dressed man with a year-old child in a stroller. Yesterday, on a bus, I saw a man with a tiny baby in a carrier on his chest. Seeing men taking care of small children in public is increasingly common—at least in New York City. But both men were quite obviously stared at—and smiled at, approvingly. Everyone was doing gender—the men who were changing the role of fathers and the other passengers, who were applauding them silently. But there was more gendering going on that probably fewer people noticed. The baby was wearing a white crocheted cap and white clothes. You couldn't tell if it was a boy or a girl. The child in the stroller was wearing a dark blue T-shirt and dark print pants. As they started to leave the train, the father put a Yankee baseball cap on the child's head. Ah, a boy, I thought. Then I noticed the gleam of tiny earrings in the child's ears, and as they got off, I saw the little flowered sneakers and lace-trimmed socks. Not a boy after all. Gender done.

Gender is such a familiar part of daily life that it usually takes a deliberate disruption of our expectations of how women and men are supposed to act to pay attention to how it is produced. Gender signs and signals are so ubiquitous that we usually fail to note them— unless they are missing or ambiguous. Then we are uncomfortable until we have successfully placed the other person in a gender status; otherwise, we feel socially dislocated. . . .

For the individual, gender construction starts with assignment to a sex category on the basis of what the genitalia look like at birth.[2] Then babies are dressed or adorned in a way that displays the category because parents don't want to be constantly asked whether their baby is a girl or a boy. A sex category becomes a gender status through naming, dress, and the use of other gender markers. Once a child's gender is evident, others treat those in

Judith Lorber is a professor emerita of sociology and women's studies at the CUNY Graduate Center and Brooklyn College of the City University of New York. Her books include *Gender Inequality: Feminist Theories and Politics* and *Gendered Bodies: Feminist Perspectives*.

From *Paradoxes of Gender*, pp. 13–18, 22, 23–27, 29, 30, 32–35, and notes on pp. 304–305. Copyright © 1994 by Yale University. All Rights Reserved. Reprinted by permission of Yale University Press as publisher.

one gender differently from those in the other, and the children respond to the different treatment by feeling different and behaving differently. As soon as they can talk, they start to refer to themselves as members of their gender. Sex doesn't come into play again until puberty, but by that time, sexual feelings and desires and practices have been shaped by gendered norms and expectations. Adolescent boys and girls approach and avoid each other in an elaborately scripted and gendered mating dance. Parenting is gendered, with different expectations for mothers and for fathers, and people of different genders work at different kinds of jobs. The work adults do as mothers and fathers, and as low-level workers and high-level bosses, shapes women's and men's life experiences, and these experiences produce different feelings, consciousness, relationships, skills—ways of being that we call feminine or masculine.[3] All of these processes constitute the social construction of gender.

Gendered roles change—today fathers are taking care of little children, girls and boys are wearing unisex clothing and getting the same education, women and men are working at the same jobs. Although many traditional social groups are quite strict about maintaining gender differences, in other social groups they seem to be blurring. Then why the one-year-old's earrings? Why is it still so important to mark a child as a girl or a boy, to make sure she is not taken for a boy or he for a girl? What would happen if they were? They would, quite literally, have changed places in their social world.

To explain why gendering is done from birth, constantly and by everyone, we have to look not only at the way individuals experience gender but at gender as a social institution. As a social institution, gender is one of the major ways that human beings organize their lives. Human society depends on a predictable division of labor, a designated allocation of scarce goods, assigned responsibility for children and others who cannot care for themselves, common values and their systematic transmission to new members, legitimate leadership, music, art, stories, games, and other symbolic productions. One way of choosing people for the different tasks of society is on the basis of their talents, motivations, and competence—their demonstrated achievements. The other way is on the basis of gender, race, ethnicity—ascribed membership in a category of people. Although societies vary in the extent to which they use one or the other of these ways of allocating people to work and to carry out other responsibilities, every society uses gender and age grades. Every society classifies people as "girl and boy children," "girls and boys ready to be married," and "fully adult women and men," constructs similarities among them and differences between them, and assigns them to different roles and responsibilities. Personality characteristics, feelings, motivations, and ambitions flow from these different life experiences so that the members of these different groups become different kinds of people. The process of gendering and its outcome are legitimated by religion, law, science, and the society's entire set of values. . . .

Western society's values legitimate gendering by claiming that it all comes from physiology—female and male procreative differences. But gender and sex are not equivalent, and gender as a social construction does not flow automatically from genitalia and reproductive organs, the main physiological differences of females and males. In the construction of ascribed social statuses, physiological differences such as sex, stage of development, color of skin, and size are crude markers. They are not the source of the social statuses of gender, age grade, and race. Social statuses are carefully constructed through prescribed processes of teaching, learning, emulation, and enforcement. Whatever genes, hormones, and biological evolution contribute to human social institutions is materially as well as qualitatively transformed by social practices. Every social institution has a material base, but culture and social practices transform that base into something with qualitatively different patterns and constraints. The economy is much more than producing food and goods and distributing them to eaters and users; family and kinship are not the equivalent of having sex and procreating; morals and religions cannot be equated with the fears and ecstasies of the brain; language goes far beyond the sounds produced by tongue and larynx. No one eats "money" or "credit"; the concepts of "god" and "angels" are the subjects of theological disquisitions; not only words but objects, such as their flag, "speak" to the citizens of a country.

Similarly, gender cannot be equated with biological and physiological differences between human females and males. The building blocks of gender are *socially constructed statuses*. . . .

Genders, therefore, are not attached to a biological substratum. Gender boundaries are breachable, and individual and socially organized shifts from one gender to another call attention to "cultural, social, or aesthetic dissonances" (Garber 1992, 16). . . .

For Individuals, Gender Means Sameness

Although the possible combinations of genitalia, body shapes, clothing, mannerisms, sexuality, and roles could produce infinite varieties in human beings, the social institution of gender depends on the production and maintenance of a limited number of gender statuses and of making the members of these statuses similar to each other. Individuals are born sexed but not gendered, and they have to be taught to be masculine or feminine.[4] As Simone de Beauvoir said: "One is not born, but rather becomes, a woman . . . ; it is civilization as a whole that produces this creature . . . which is described as feminine" (1953, 267).

Children learn to walk, talk, and gesture the way their social group says girls and boys should. Ray Birdwhistell, in his analysis of body motion as human communication, calls these learned gender displays *tertiary* sex characteristics and argues that they are needed to distinguish genders because humans are a weakly dimorphic species—their only sex markers are genitalia (1970, 39–46). Clothing, paradoxically, often hides the sex but displays the gender.

In early childhood, humans develop gendered personality structures and sexual orientations through their interactions with parents of the same and opposite gender. As adolescents, they conduct their sexual behavior according to gendered scripts. Schools, parents, peers, and the mass media guide young people into gendered work and family roles. As adults, they take on a gendered social status in their society's stratification system. Gender is thus both ascribed and achieved (West and Zimmerman 1987). . . .

Gender norms are inscribed in the way people move, gesture, and even eat. In one African society, men were supposed to eat with their "whole mouth, wholeheartedly, and not, like women, just with the lips, that is halfheartedly, with reservation and restraint"

(Bourdieu [1980] 1990, 70). Men and women in this society learned to walk in ways that proclaimed their different positions in the society:

> The manly man . . . stands up straight into the face of the person he approaches, or wishes to welcome. Ever on the alert, because ever threatened, he misses nothing of what happens around him. . . . Conversely, a well brought-up woman . . . is expected to walk with a slight stoop, avoiding every misplaced movement of her body, her head or her arms, looking down, keeping her eyes on the spot where she will next put her foot, especially if she happens to have to walk past the men's assembly. (70)

. . . For human beings there is no essential femaleness or maleness, femininity or masculinity, womanhood or manhood, but once gender is ascribed, the social order constructs and holds individuals to strongly gendered norms and expectations. Individuals may vary on many of the components of gender and may shift genders temporarily or permanently, but they must fit into the limited number of gender statuses their society recognizes. In the process, they re-create their society's version of women and men: "If we do gender appropriately, we simultaneously sustain, reproduce, and render legitimate the institutional arrangements. . . . If we fail to do gender appropriately, we as individuals—not the institutional arrangements—may be called to account (for our character, motives, and predispositions)" (West and Zimmerman 1987, 146).

The gendered practices of everyday life reproduce a society's view of how women and men should act (Bourdieu [1980] 1990). Gendered social arrangements are justified by religion and cultural productions and backed by law, but the most powerful means of sustaining the moral hegemony of the dominant gender ideology is that the process is made invisible; any possible alternatives are virtually unthinkable (Foucault 1972; Gramsci 1971).[5]

For Society, Gender Means Difference

The pervasiveness of gender as a way of structuring social life demands that gender statuses be clearly differentiated. Varied talents, sexual preferences, identities, personalities, interests, and ways of interacting fragment the individual's bodily and social experiences. . . . In the social construction of gender, it does not matter what men and women actually do; it does not even matter if they do exactly the same thing. The social institution of gender insists only that what they do is *perceived* as different. . . .

If men and women are doing the same tasks, they are usually spatially segregated to maintain gender separation, and often the tasks are given different job titles as well, such as executive secretary and administrative assistant (Reskin 1988). If the differences between women and men begin to blur, society's "sameness taboo" goes into action (Rubin 1975, 178). At a rock and roll dance at West Point in 1976, the year women were admitted to the prestigious military academy for the first time, the school's administrators "were reportedly perturbed by the sight of mirror-image couples dancing in short hair and dress gray trousers," and a rule was established that women cadets could dance at these events only if they wore skirts (Barkalow and Raab 1990, 53).[6] Women recruits in the United States Marine Corps are required to wear makeup – at a minimum, lipstick and eye shadow – and they have to take classes in makeup, hair care, poise, and etiquette. This feminization is part of a deliberate policy of making them clearly distinguishable from men Marines. Christine Williams quotes a twenty-five-year-old woman drill instructor as saying, "A lot of the recruits who come here don't wear makeup; they're tomboyish or athletic. A lot of them have the preconceived idea that going into the military means they can still be a tomboy. They don't realize that you are a Woman Marine" (1989, 76–77)[7]. . . .

Since gender differences are socially constructed, all men and all women can enact the behavior of the other, because they know the other's social script: "'Man' and 'woman' are at once empty and overflowing categories. Empty because they have no ultimate, transcendental meaning. Overflowing because even when they appear to be fixed, they still contain within them alternative, denied, or suppressed definitions" (Scott 1988, 49). . . .

For one transsexual man-to-woman, the experience of living as a woman changed his/her whole personality. As James, Morris had been a soldier, foreign correspondent, and mountain climber; as Jan, Morris is a successful travel writer. But socially, James was superior to Jan, and so Jan developed the "learned helplessness" that is supposed to characterize women in Western society:

> We are told that the social gap between the sexes is narrowing, but I can only report that having, in the second half of the twentieth century, experienced life in both roles, there seems to me no aspect of existence, no moment of the day, no contact, no arrangement, no response, which is not different for men and for women. The very tone of voice in which I was now addressed, the very posture of the person next in the queue, the very feel in the air when I entered a room or sat at a restaurant table, constantly emphasized my change of status.
>
> And if other's responses shifted, so did my own. The more I was treated as woman, the more woman I became. I adapted willy-nilly. If I was assumed to be incompetent at reversing cars, or opening bottles, oddly incompetent I found myself becoming. If a case was thought too heavy for me, inexplicably I found it so myself. . . . Women treated me with a frankness which, while it was one of the happiest discoveries of my metamorphosis, did imply membership of a camp, a faction, or at least a school of thought; so I found myself gravitating always towards the female, whether in sharing a railway compartment or supporting a political cause. Men treated me more and more as junior, . . . and so, addressed every day of my life as an inferior, involuntarily, month by month I accepted the condition. I discovered that even now men prefer women to be less informed, less able, less talkative, and certainly less self-centered than they are themselves; so I generally obliged them. (1975, 165–66)[8]

Gender as Process, Stratification, and Structure

As a social institution, gender is a process of creating distinguishable social statuses for the assignment of rights and responsibilities. As part of a stratification system that ranks these statuses unequally, gender is a major building block in the social structures built on these unequal statuses.

As a *process*, gender creates the social differences that define "woman" and "man." In social interaction throughout their lives, individuals learn what is expected, see what is expected, act and react in expected ways, and thus simultaneously construct and maintain the gender order: "The very injunction to be a given gender takes place through discursive routes: to be a good mother, to be a heterosexually desirable object, to be a fit worker, in sum, to signify a multiplicity of guarantees in response to a variety of different demands all at once" (Butler 1990, 145). Members of a social group neither make up gender as they go along nor exactly replicate in rote fashion what was done before. In almost every encounter, human beings produce gender, behaving in the ways they learned were appropriate for their status, or resisting or rebelling against these norms. Resistance and rebellion have altered gender norms, but so far they have rarely eroded the statuses.

Gendered patterns of interaction acquire additional layers of gendered sexuality, parenting, and work behaviors in childhood, adolescence, and adulthood. Gendered norms and expectations are enforced through informal sanctions of gender-inappropriate behavior by peers and by formal punishment or threat of punishment by those in authority should behavior deviate too far from socially imposed standards for women and men. . . .

As part of a *stratification* system, gender ranks men above women of the same race and class. . . .

The further dichotomization by race and class constructs the gradations of a heterogeneous society's stratification scheme. . . . The dominant categories are the hegemonic ideals, taken so for granted as the way things should be that white is not ordinarily thought of as a race, middle class as a class, or men as a gender. The characteristics of these categories define the Other as that which lacks the valuable qualities the dominants exhibit.

In a gender-stratified society, what men do is usually valued more highly than what women do because men do it, even when their activities are very similar or the same. In different regions of southern India, for example, harvesting rice is men's work, shared work, or women's work: "Wherever a task is done by women it is considered easy, and where it is done by [men] it is considered difficult" (Mencher 1988, 104). A gathering and hunting society's survival usually depends on the nuts, grubs, and small animals brought in by the women's foraging trips, but when the men's hunt is successful, it is the occasion for a celebration. Conversely, because they are the superior group, white men do not have to do the "dirty work," such as housework; the most inferior group does it, usually poor women of color (Palmer 1989). . . .

Societies vary in the extent of the inequality in social status of their women and men members, but where there is inequality, the status "woman" (and its attendant behavior and role allocations) is usually held in lesser esteem than the status "man." Since gender is also intertwined with a society's other constructed statuses of differential evaluation—race, religion, occupation, class, country of origin, and so on—men and women members of the favored groups command more power, more prestige, and more property than the members of the disfavored groups. Within many social groups, however, men are advantaged over women. . . .

As a *structure*, gender divides work in the home and in economic production, legitimates those in authority, and organizes sexuality and emotional life (Connell 1987, 91–142). . . .

When gender is a major component of structured inequality, the devalued genders have less power, prestige, and economic rewards than the valued genders. In countries that discourage gender discrimination, many major roles are still gendered; women still do most of the domestic labor and child rearing, even while doing full-time paid work; women and men are segregated on the job and each does work considered "appropriate"; women's work is usually paid less than men's work. Men dominate the positions of authority and leadership in government, the military, and the law; cultural productions, religions, and sports reflect men's interests. . . .

Gender inequality—the devaluation of "women" and the social domination of "men"—has social functions and a social history. It is not the result of sex, procreation, physiology, anatomy, hormones, or genetic predispositions. It is produced and maintained by identifiable social processes and built into the general social structure and individual identities deliberately and purposefully. The social order as we know it in Western societies is organized around racial ethnic, class, and gender inequality. I contend, therefore, that the continuing purpose of gender as a modern social institution is to construct women as a group to be the subordinates of men as a group. The life of everyone placed in the status "woman" is "night to his day—that has forever been the fantasy. Black to his white. Shut out of his system's space, she is the repressed that ensures the system's functioning" (Cixous and Clément [1975] 1986, 67).

NOTES

1. Gender is, in Erving Goffman's words, an aspect of *Felicity's Condition:* "any arrangement which leads us to judge an individual's . . . acts not to be a manifestation of strangeness. Behind Felicity's Condition is our sense of what it is to be sane" (1983, 27). Also see Bem 1993; Frye 1983, 17–40; Goffman 1977.
2. In cases of ambiguity in countries with modern medicine, surgery is usually performed to make the genitalia more clearly male or female.
3. See Butler 1990 for an analysis of how doing gender *is* gender identity.
4. For an account of how a potential man-to-woman transsexual learned to be feminine, see Garfinkel 1967, 116–85, 285–88. For a gloss on this account that points out how, throughout his encounters with Agnes, Garfinkel failed to see how he himself was constructing his own masculinity, see Rogers 1992.
5. The concepts of moral hegemony, the effects of everyday activities (praxis) on thought and personality, and the necessity of consciousness of these processes before political change can occur are all based on Marx's analysis of class relations.
6. Carol Barkalow's book has a photograph of eleven first-year West Pointers in a math class, who are dressed in regulation pants, shirts, and sweaters, with short haircuts. The caption challenges the reader to locate the only woman in the room.
7. The taboo on males and females looking alike reflects the United States' military's homophobia (Bérubé 1989). If you can't tell those with a penis from those with a vagina, how are you going to determine whether their sexual interest is heterosexual or homosexual unless you watch them having sexual relations?
8. See Bolin 1988, 149–50, for transsexual men-to-women's discovery of the dangers of rape and sexual harassment. Devor's "gender blenders" went in the opposite direction. Because they found that it was an advantage to be taken for men, they did not deliberately cross-dress, but they did not feminize themselves either (1989, 126–40).

REFERENCES

Barkalow, Carol, with Andrea Raab. 1990. *In the men's house*. New York: Poseidon Press.

Bem, Sandra Lipsitz. 1993. *The lenses of gender: Transforming the debate on sexual inequality*. New Haven: Yale University Press.

Bérubé, Allan. 1989. Marching to a different drummer: Gay and lesbian GIs in World War II. In Duberman, Vicinus, and Chauncey.

Birdwhistell, Ray L. 1970. *Kinesics and context: Essays on body motion communication*. Philadelphia: University of Pennsylvania Press.

Bolin, Anne. 1988. *In search of Eve: Transsexual rites of passage*. South Hadley, Mass.: Bergin & Garvey.

Bourdieu, Pierre. [1980] 1990. *The logic of practice*. Stanford, Calif.: Stanford University Press.

Butler, Judith. 1990. *Gender trouble: Feminism and the subversion of identity*. New York and London: Routledge.

Cixous, Hélène, and Catherine Clément. [1975] 1986. *The newly born woman*, translated by Betsy Wing. Minneapolis: University of Minnesota Press.

Connell, R.[Robert] W. 1987. *Gender and power: Society, the person, and sexual politics*. Stanford, Calif.: Stanford University Press.

de Beauvoir, Simone. 1953. *The second sex*, translated by H. M. Parshley. New York: Knopf.

Devor, Holly. 1989. *Gender blending: Confronting the limits of duality*. Bloomington: Indiana University Press.

Duberman, Martin Bauml, Martha Vicinus, and George Chauncey, Jr. (eds.). 1989. *Hidden from history: Reclaiming the gay and lesbian past*. New York: New American Library.

Dwyer, Daisy, and Judith Bruce (eds.). 1988. *A home divided: Women and income in the Third World*. Palo Alto, Calif.: Stanford University Press.

Foucault, Michel. 1972. *The archeology of knowledge and the discourse on language*, translated by A. M. Sheridan Smith. New York: Pantheon.

Frye, Marilyn. 1983. *The politics of reality: Essays in feminist theory*. Trumansburg, N.Y.: Crossing Press.

Garber, Marjorie. 1992. *Vested interests: Cross-dressing and cultural anxiety*. New York and London: Routledge.

Garfinkel, Harold. 1967. *Studies in ethnomethodology*. Englewood Cliffs, N.J.: Prentice-Hall.

Goffman, Erving. 1977. The arrangement between the sexes. *Theory and Society* 4:301–33.

———. 1983. Felicity's condition. *American Journal of Sociology* 89:1–53.

Gramsci, Antonio. 1971. *Selections from the prison notebooks*, translated and edited by Quintin Hoare and Geoffrey Nowell Smith. New York: International Publishers.

Mencher, Joan. 1988. Women's work and poverty: Women's contribution to household maintenance in South India. In Dwyer and Bruce.

Morris, Jan. 1975. *Conundrum*. New York: Signet.

Palmer, Phyllis. 1989. *Domesticity and dirt: Housewives and domestic servants in the United States, 1920–1945*. Philadelphia: Temple University Press.

Reskin, Barbara F. 1988. Bringing the men back in: Sex differentiation and the devaluation of women's work. *Gender & Society* 2:58–81.

Rogers, Mary F. 1992. They were all passing: Agnes, Garfinkel, and company. *Gender & Society* 6:169–91.

Rubin, Gayle. 1975. The traffic in women: Notes on the political economy of sex. In *Toward an anthropology of women*, edited by Rayna R[app] Reiter. New York: Monthly Review Press.

Scott, Joan Wallach. 1988. *Gender and the politics of history*. New York: Columbia University Press.

West, Candace, and Don Zimmerman. 1987. Doing gender. *Gender & Society* 1:125–51.

Williams, Christine L. 1989. *Gender differences at work: Women and men in nontraditional occupations*. Berkeley: University of California Press.

6 The Invention of Heterosexuality
Jonathan Ned Katz

Heterosexuality is old as procreation, ancient as the lust of Eve and Adam. That first lady and gentleman, we assume, perceived themselves, behaved, and felt just like today's heterosexuals. We suppose that heterosexuality is unchanging, universal, essential: ahistorical.

Contrary to that common-sense conjecture, the concept of heterosexuality is only one particular historical way of perceiving, categorizing, and imagining the social relations of the sexes. Not ancient at all, the idea of heterosexuality is a modern invention, dating to the late nineteenth century. The heterosexual belief, with its metaphysical claim to eternity, has a particular, pivotal place in the social universe of the late nineteenth and twentieth centuries that it did not inhabit earlier. This essay traces the historical process by which the heterosexual idea was created as ahistorical and taken-for-granted. . . .

By not studying the heterosexual idea in history, analysts of sex, gay and straight, have continued to privilege the "normal" and "natural" at the expense of the "abnormal" and "unnatural." Such privileging of the norm accedes to its domination, protecting it from questions. By making the normal the object of a thoroughgoing historical study we simultaneously pursue a pure truth and a sex-radical and subversive goal: We upset basic preconceptions. We discover that the heterosexual, the normal, and the natural have a history of changing definitions. Studying the history of the term challenges its power.

Contrary to our usual assumption, past Americans and other peoples named, perceived, and socially organized the bodies, lusts, and intercourse of the sexes in ways radically different from the way we do. If we care to understand this vast past sexual diversity, we need to stop promiscuously projecting our own hetero and homo arrangement. Though lip service is often paid to the distorting, ethnocentric effect of such conceptual imperialism, the category heterosexuality continues to be applied uncritically as a universal analytical tool. Recognizing the time-bound and culturally-specific character of the heterosexual category can help us begin to work toward a thoroughly historical view of sex. . . .

Before Heterosexuality: Early Victorian True Love, 1820–1860

In the early nineteenth-century United States, from about 1820 to 1860, the heterosexual did not exist. Middle-class white Americans idealized a True Womanhood, True Manhood, and True Love, all characterized by "purity"—the freedom from sensuality.[1]

Jonathan Ned Katz is an independent scholar and investigative historian who focuses on lesbian, gay, bisexual, transgender, and heterosexual American history; he is also a visual artist.

Presented mainly in literary and religious texts, this True Love was a fine romance with no lascivious kisses. This ideal contrasts strikingly with late nineteenth- and twentieth-century American incitements to a hetero sex.*

Early Victorian True Love was only realized within the mode of proper procreation, marriage, the legal organization for producing a new set of correctly gendered women and men. Proper womanhood, manhood, and progeny—not a normal male-female eros—was the main product of this mode of engendering and of human reproduction.

The actors in this sexual economy were identified as manly men and womanly women and as procreators, not specifically as erotic beings or heterosexuals. Eros did not constitute the core of a heterosexual identity that inhered, democratically, in both men and women. True Women were defined by their distance from lust. True Men, though thought to live closer to carnality, and in less control of it, aspired to the same freedom from concupiscence.

Legitimate natural desire was for procreation and a proper manhood or womanhood; no heteroerotic desire was thought to be directed exclusively and naturally toward the other sex; lust in men was roving. The human body was thought of as a means towards procreation and production; penis and vagina were instruments of reproduction, not of pleasure. Human energy, thought of as a closed and severely limited system, was to be used in producing children and in work, not wasted in libidinous pleasures.

The location of all this engendering and procreative labor was the sacred sanctum of early Victorian True Love, the home of the True Woman and True Man—a temple of purity threatened from within by the monster masturbator, an archetypal early Victorian cult figure of illicit lust. The home of True Love was a castle far removed from the erotic exotic ghetto inhabited most notoriously then by the prostitute, another archetypal Victorian erotic monster. . . .

Late Victorian Sex-Love: 1860–1892

"Heterosexuality" and "homosexuality" did not appear out of the blue in the 1890s. These two eroticisms were in the making from the 1860s on. In late Victorian America and in Germany, from about 1860 to 1892, our modern idea of an eroticized universe began to develop, and the experience of a heterolust began to be widely documented and named. . . .

In the late nineteenth-century United States, several social factors converged to cause the eroticizing of consciousness, behavior, emotion, and identity that became typical of the twentieth-century Western middle class. The transformation of the family from producer to consumer unit resulted in a change in family members' relation to

---

*Some historians have recently told us to revise our idea of sexless Victorians: Their experience and even their ideology, it is said, were more erotic than we previously thought. Despite the revisionists, I argue that "purity" was indeed the dominant, early Victorian, white middle-class standard. For the debate on Victorian sexuality see John D'Emilio and Estelle Freedman, *Intimate Matters: A History of Sexuality in America* (New York: Harper & Row, 1988), p. xii.

their own bodies; from being an instrument primarily of work, the human body was integrated into a new economy, and began more commonly to be perceived as a means of consumption and pleasure. Historical work has recently begun on how the biological human body is differently integrated into changing modes of production, procreation, engendering, and pleasure so as to alter radically the identity, activity, and experience of that body.[2]

The growth of a consumer economy also fostered a new pleasure ethic. This imperative challenged the early Victorian work ethic, finally helping to usher in a major transformation of values. While the early Victorian work ethic had touted the value of economic production, that era's procreation ethic had extolled the virtues of human reproduction. In contrast, the late Victorian economic ethic hawked the pleasures of consuming, while its sex ethic praised an erotic pleasure principle for men and even for women.

In the late nineteenth century, the erotic became the raw material for a new consumer culture. Newspapers, books, plays, and films touching on sex, "normal" and "abnormal," became available for a price. Restaurants, bars, and baths opened, catering to sexual consumers with cash. Late Victorian entrepreneurs of desire incited the proliferation of a new eroticism, a commoditized culture of pleasure.

In these same years, the rise in power and prestige of medical doctors allowed these upwardly mobile professionals to prescribe a healthy new sexuality. Medical men, in the name of science, defined a new ideal of male-female relationships that included, in women as well as men, an essential, necessary, normal eroticism. Doctors, who had earlier named and judged the sex-enjoying woman a "nymphomaniac," now began to label women's *lack* of sexual pleasure a mental disturbance, speaking critically, for example, of female "frigidity" and "anesthesia."*

By the 1880s, the rise of doctors as a professional group fostered the rise of a new medical model of Normal Love, replete with sexuality. The new Normal Woman and Man were endowed with a healthy libido. The new theory of Normal Love was the modern medical alternative to the old Cult of True Love. The doctors prescribed a new sexual ethic as if it were a morally neutral, medical description of health. The creation of the new Normal Sexual had its counterpart in the invention of the late Victorian Sexual Pervert. The attention paid the sexual abnormal created a need to name the sexual normal, the better to distinguish the average him and her from the deviant it.

Heterosexuality: The First Years, 1892–1900

In the periodization of heterosexual American history suggested here, the years 1892 to 1900 represent "The First Years" of the heterosexual epoch, eight key years in which the idea of the heterosexual and homosexual were initially and tentatively formulated by

---

*This reference to females reminds us that the invention of heterosexuality had vastly different impacts on the histories of women and men. It also differed in its impact on lesbians and heterosexual women, homosexual and heterosexual men, the middle class and working class, and on different religious, racial, national, and geographic groups.

U.S. doctors. The earliest-known American use of the word "heterosexual" occurs in a medical journal article by Dr. James G. Kiernan of Chicago, read before the city's medical society on March 7, 1892, and published that May—portentous dates in sexual history.[3] But Dr. Kiernan's heterosexuals were definitely not exemplars of normality. Heterosexuals, said Kiernan, were defined by a mental condition, "psychical hermaphroditism." Its symptoms were "inclinations to both sexes." These heterodox sexuals also betrayed inclinations "to abnormal methods of gratification," that is, techniques to insure pleasure without procreation. Dr. Kiernan's heterogeneous sexuals did demonstrate "traces of the normal sexual appetite" (a touch of procreative desire). Kiernan's normal sexuals were implicitly defined by a monolithic other-sex inclination and procreative aim. Significantly, they still lacked a name.

Dr. Kiernan's article of 1892 also included one of the earliest-known uses of the word "homosexual" in American English. Kiernan defined "Pure homosexuals" as persons whose "general mental state is that of the opposite sex." Kiernan thus defined homosexuals by their deviance from a gender norm. His heterosexuals displayed a double deviance from both gender and procreative norms.

Though Kiernan used the new words heterosexual and homosexual, an old procreative standard and a new gender norm coexisted uneasily in his thought. His word heterosexual defined a mixed person and compound urge, abnormal because they wantonly included procreative and non-procreative objectives, as well as same-sex and different-sex attractions.

That same year, 1892, Dr. Krafft-Ebing's influential *Psychopathia Sexualis* was first translated and published in the United States.[4] But Kiernan and Krafft-Ebing by no means agreed on the definition of the heterosexual. In Krafft-Ebing's book, "hetero-sexual" was used unambiguously in the modern sense to refer to an erotic feeling for a different sex. "Homo-sexual" referred unambiguously to an erotic feeling for a "same sex." In Krafft-Ebing's volume, unlike Kiernan's article, heterosexual and homosexual were clearly distinguished from a third category, a "psycho-sexual hermaphroditism," defined by impulses toward both sexes.

Krafft-Ebing hypothesized an inborn "sexual instinct" for relations with the "opposite sex," the inherent "purpose" of which was to foster procreation. Krafft-Ebing's erotic drive was still a reproductive instinct. But the doctor's clear focus on a different-sex versus same-sex sexuality constituted a historic, epochal move from an absolute procreative standard of normality toward a new norm. His definition of heterosexuality as other-sex attraction provided the basis for a revolutionary, modern break with a centuries-old procreative standard.

It is difficult to overstress the importance of that new way of categorizing. The German's mode of labeling was radical in referring to the biological sex, masculinity or femininity, and the pleasure of actors (along with the procreant purpose of acts). Krafft-Ebing's heterosexual offered the modern world a new norm that came to dominate our idea of the sexual universe, helping to change it from a mode of human reproduction and engendering to a mode of pleasure. The heterosexual category provided the basis for a move from a production-oriented, procreative imperative to a consumerist pleasure principle—an institutionalized pursuit of happiness. . . .

Only gradually did doctors agree that heterosexual referred to a normal, "other-sex" eros. This new standard-model heterosex provided the pivotal term for the modern regularization of eros that paralleled similar attempts to standardize masculinity and femininity, intelligence, and manufacturing.[5] The idea of heterosexuality as the master sex from which all others deviated was (like the idea of the master race) deeply authoritarian. The doctors' normalization of a sex that was hetero proclaimed a new heterosexual separatism — an erotic apartheid that forcefully segregated the sex normals from the sex perverts. The new, strict boundaries made the emerging erotic world less polymorphous — safer for sex normals. However, the idea of such creatures as heterosexuals and homosexuals emerged from the narrow world of medicine to become a commonly accepted notion only in the early twentieth century. In 1901, in the comprehensive *Oxford English Dictionary*, "heterosexual" and "homosexual" had not yet made it.

The Distribution of the Heterosexual Mystique: 1900–1930

In the early years of this heterosexual century the tentative hetero hypothesis was stabilized, fixed, and widely distributed as the ruling sexual orthodoxy: The Heterosexual Mystique. Starting among pleasure-affirming urban working-class youths, southern blacks, and Greenwich Village bohemians as defensive subculture, heterosex soon triumphed as dominant culture.[6]

In its earliest version, the twentieth-century heterosexual imperative usually continued to associate heterosexuality with a supposed human "need," "drive," or "instinct" for propagation, a procreant urge linked inexorably with carnal lust as it had not been earlier. In the early twentieth century, the falling birth rate, rising divorce rate, and "war of the sexes" of the middle class were matters of increasing public concern. Giving vent to heteroerotic emotions was thus praised as enhancing baby-making capacity, marital intimacy, and family stability (Only many years later, in the mid-1960s, would heteroeroticism be distinguished completely, in practice and theory, from procreativity and male-female pleasure sex justified in its own name.)

The first part of the new sex norm — hetero — referred to a basic gender divergence. The "oppositeness" of the sexes was alleged to be the basis for a universal, normal, erotic attraction between males and females. The stress on the sexes' "oppositeness," which harked back to the early nineteenth century, by no means simply registered biological differences of females and males. The early twentieth-century focus on physiological and gender dimorphism reflected the deep anxieties of men about the shifting work, social roles, and power of men over women, and about the ideals of womanhood and manhood. That gender anxiety is documented, for example, in 1897, in *The New York Times'* publication of the Reverend Charles Parkhurst's diatribe against female "andromaniacs," the preacher's derogatory, scientific-sounding name for women who tried to "minimize distinctions by which manhood and womanhood are differentiated."[7] The stress on gender difference was a conservative response to the changing social-sexual division of activity and feeling which gave rise to the independent "New Woman" of the 1880s and eroticized "Flapper" of the 1920s.

The second part of the new hetero norm referred positively to sexuality. That novel upbeat focus on the hedonistic possibilities of male-female conjunctions also reflected a social transformation—a revaluing of pleasure and procreation, consumption and work in commercial, capitalist society. The democratic attribution of a normal lust to human females (as well as males) served to authorize women's enjoyment of their own bodies and began to undermine the early Victorian idea of the pure True Woman—a sex-affirmative action still part of women's struggle. The twentieth-century Erotic Woman also undercut nineteenth-century feminist assertion of women's moral superiority, cast suspicions of lust on women's passionate romantic friendships with women, and asserted the presence of a menacing female monster, "the lesbian."[8] . . .

In the perspective of heterosexual history, this early twentieth-century struggle for the more explicit depiction of an "opposite-sex" eros appears in a curious new light. Ironically, we find sex-conservatives, the social purity advocates of censorship and repression, fighting against the depiction not just of sexual perversity but also of the new normal heterosexuality. That a more open depiction of normal sex had to be defended against forces of propriety confirms the claim that heterosexuality's predecessor, Victorian True Love, had included no legitimate eros. . . .

The Heterosexual Steps Out: 1930–1945

In 1930, in *The New York Times*, heterosexuality first became a love that dared to speak its name. On April 30th of that year, the word "heterosexual" is first known to have appeared in *The New York Times Book Review*. There, a critic described the subject of André Gide's *The Immoralist* proceeding "from a heterosexual liaison to a homosexual one." The ability to slip between sexual categories was referred to casually as a rather unremarkable aspect of human possibility. This is also the first known reference by *The Times* to the new hetero/homo duo.[9]

The following month the second reference to the hetero/homo dyad appeared in *The New York Times Book Review*, in a comment on Floyd Dell's *Love in the Machine Age*. This work revealed a prominent antipuritan of the 1930s using the dire threat of homosexuality as his rationale for greater heterosexual freedom. *The Times* quoted Dell's warning that current abnormal social conditions kept the young dependent on their parents, causing "infantilism, prostitution and homosexuality." Also quoted was Dell's attack on the "inculcation of purity" that "breeds distrust of the opposite sex." Young people, Dell said, should be "permitted to develop normally to heterosexual adulthood." "But," *The Times* reviewer emphasized, "such a state already exists, here and now." And so it did. Heterosexuality, a new gender-sex category, had been distributed from the narrow, rarified realm of a few doctors to become a nationally, even internationally, cited aspect of middle-class life.[10] . . .

Heterosexual Hegemony: 1945–1965

The "cult of domesticity" following World War II—the reassociation of women with the home, motherhood, and child care; men with fatherhood and wage work outside the home—was a period in which the predominance of the hetero norm went almost unchallenged, an era of heterosexual hegemony. This was an age in which conservative mental-health professionals reasserted the old link between heterosexuality and procreation. In contrast, sex liberals of the day strove, ultimately with success, to expand the heterosexual ideal to include within the boundaries of normality a wider-than-ever range of nonprocreative, premarital, and extramarital behaviors. But sex-liberal reform actually helped to extend and secure the dominance of the heterosexual idea, as we shall see when we get to Kinsey.

The postwar sex-conservative tendency was illustrated in 1947, in Ferdinand Lundberg and Dr. Marnia Farnham's book, *Modern Woman: The Lost Sex.* Improper masculinity and femininity were exemplified, the authors decreed, by "engagement in heterosexual relations . . . with the complete intent to see to it that they do not eventuate in reproduction."[11] Their procreatively defined heterosex was one expression of a postwar ideology of fecundity that, internalized and enacted dutifully by a large part of the population, gave rise to the postwar baby boom.

The idea of the feminine female and masculine male as prolific breeders was also reflected in the stress, specific to the late 1940s, on the homosexual as sad symbol of "sterility"—that particular loaded term appears incessantly in comments on homosex dating to the fecund forties.

In 1948, in *The New York Times Book Review,* sex liberalism was in ascendancy. Dr. Howard A. Rusk declared that Alfred Kinsey's just published report on *Sexual Behavior in the Human Male* had found "wide variations in sex concepts and behavior." This raised the question: "What is 'normal' and 'abnormal'?" In particular, the report had found that "homosexual experience is much more common than previously thought," and "there is often a mixture of both homo and hetero experience."[12]

Kinsey's counting of orgasms indeed stressed the wide range of behaviors and feelings that fell within the boundaries of a quantitative, statistically accounted heterosexuality. Kinsey's liberal reform of the hetero/homo dualism widened the narrow, old hetero category to accord better with the varieties of social experience. He thereby contradicted the older idea of a monolithic, qualitatively defined, natural procreative act, experience, and person.[13]

Though Kinsey explicitly questioned "whether the terms 'normal' and 'abnormal' belong in a scientific vocabulary," his counting of climaxes was generally understood to define normal sex as majority sex. This quantified norm constituted a final, society-wide break with the old qualitatively defined reproductive standard. Though conceived of as purely scientific, the statistical definition of the normal as the-sex-most-people-are-having substituted a new, quantitative moral standard for the old, qualitative sex ethic—another triumph for the spirit of capitalism.

Kinsey also explicitly contested the idea of an absolute, either/or antithesis between hetero and homo persons. He denied that human beings "represent two discrete populations, heterosexual and homosexual." The world, he ordered, "is not to be divided into sheep and goats." The hetero/homo division was not nature's doing: "Only the human mind invents categories and tries to force facts into separated pigeon-holes. The living world is a continuum."[14]

With a wave of the taxonomist's hand, Kinsey dismissed the social and historical division of people into heteros and homos. His denial of heterosexual and homosexual personhood rejected the social reality and profound subjective force of a historically constructed tradition which, since 1892 in the United States, had cut the sexual population in two and helped to establish the social reality of a heterosexual and homosexual identity.

On the one hand, the social construction of homosexual persons has led to the development of a powerful gay liberation identity politics based on an ethnic group model. This has freed generations of women and men from a deep, painful, socially induced sense of shame, and helped to bring about a society-wide liberalization of attitudes and responses to homosexuals.[15] On the other hand, contesting the notion of homosexual and heterosexual persons was one early, partial resistance to the limits of the hetero/homo construction. Gore Vidal, rebel son of Kinsey, has for years been joyfully proclaiming:

> there is no such thing as a homosexual or a heterosexual person. There are only homo- or heterosexual acts. Most people are a mixture of impulses if not practices, and what anyone does with a willing partner is of no social or cosmic significance.
>
> So why all the fuss? In order for a ruling class to rule, there must be arbitrary prohibitions. Of all prohibitions, sexual taboo is the most useful because sex involves everyone. . . . we have allowed our governors to divide the population into two teams. One team is good, godly, straight; the other is evil, sick, vicious.[16]

Heterosexuality Questioned: 1965–1982

By the late 1960s, anti-establishment counterculturalists, fledgling feminists, and homosexual-rights activists had begun to produce an unprecedented critique of sexual repression in general, of women's sexual repression in particular, of marriage and the family—and of some forms of heterosexuality. This critique even found its way into *The New York Times*.

In March 1968, in the theater section of that paper, freelancer Rosalyn Regelson cited a scene from a satirical review brought to New York by a San Francisco troupe:

> a heterosexual man wanders inadvertently into a homosexual bar. Before he realizes his mistake, he becomes involved with an aggressive queen who orders a drink for him. Being a broadminded liberal and trying to play it cool until he can back out of the situation gracefully, he asks, "How do you like being a ah homosexual?" To which the queen drawls drily, "How do you like being ah whatever it is you are?"

Regelson continued:

> The Two Cultures in confrontation. The middle-class liberal, challenged today on many fronts, finds his last remaining fixed value, his heterosexuality, called into question. The theater . . . recalls the strategies he uses in dealing with this ultimate threat to his world view.[17]

Heterosexual History: Out of the Shadows

Our brief survey of the heterosexual idea suggests a new hypothesis. Rather than naming a conjunction old as Eve and Adam, heterosexual designates a word and concept, a norm and role, an individual and group identity, a behavior and feeling, and a peculiar sexual-political institution particular to the late nineteenth and twentieth centuries.

Because much stress has been placed here on heterosexuality as word and concept, it seems important to affirm that heterosexuality (and homosexuality) came into existence before it was named and thought about. The formulation of the heterosexual idea did not create a heterosexual experience or behavior; to suggest otherwise would be to ascribe determining power to labels and concepts. But the titling and envisioning of heterosexuality did play an important role in consolidating the construction of the heterosexual's social existence. Before the wide use of the word "heterosexual," I suggest, women and men did not mutually lust with the same profound, sure sense of normalcy that followed the distribution of "heterosexual" as universal sanctifier.

According to this proposal, women and men make their own sexual histories. But they do not produce their sex lives just as they please. They make their sexualities within a particular mode of organization given by the past and altered by their changing desire, their present power and activity, and their vision of a better world. That hypothesis suggests a number of good reasons for the immediate inauguration of research on a historically specific heterosexuality.

The study of the history of the heterosexual experience will forward a great intellectual struggle still in its early stages. This is the fight to pull heterosexuality, homosexuality, and all the sexualities out of the realm of nature and biology [and] into the realm of the social and historical. Feminists have explained to us that anatomy does not determine our gender destinies (our masculinities and femininities). But we've only recently begun to consider that *biology does not settle our erotic fates.* The common notion that biology determines the object of sexual desire, or that physiology and society together cause sexual orientation, are determinisms that deny the break existing between our bodies and situations and our desiring. Just as the biology of our hearing organs will never tell us why we take pleasure in Bach or delight in Dixieland, our female or male anatomies, hormones, and genes will never tell us why we yearn for women, men, both, other, or none. That is because desiring is a self-generated project of individuals within particular historical cultures. Heterosexual history can help us see the place of values and judgments in the construction of our own and others' pleasures, and to see how our erotic tastes—our aesthetics of the flesh—are socially institutionalized through the struggle of individuals and classes.

The study of heterosexuality in time will also help us to recognize the *vast historical diversity of sexual emotions and behaviors*—a variety that challenges the monolithic heterosexual hypothesis. John D'Emilio and Estelle Freedman's *Intimate Matters: A History of Sexuality in America* refers in passing to numerous substantial changes in sexual activity and feeling: for example, the widespread use of contraceptives in the nineteenth century, the twentieth-century incitement of the female orgasm, and the recent sexual conduct changes by gay men in response to the AIDS epidemic. It's now a commonplace of family history that people in particular classes feel and behave in substantially different ways under different historical conditions.[18] Only when we stop assuming an invariable essence of heterosexuality will we begin the research to reveal the full variety of sexual emotions and behaviors.

The historical study of the heterosexual experience can help us *understand the erotic relationships of women and men in terms of their changing modes of social organization.* Such modal analysis actually characterizes a sex history well under way.[19] This suggests that the eros-gender-procreation system (the social ordering of lust, femininity and masculinity, and baby-making) has been linked closely to a society's particular organization of power and production. To understand the subtle history of heterosexuality we need to look carefully at correlations between (1) society's organization of eros and pleasure; (2) its mode of engendering persons as feminine or masculine (its making of women and men); (3) its ordering of human reproduction; and (4) its dominant political economy. This General Theory of Sexual Relativity proposes that substantial historical changes in the social organization of eros, gender, and procreation have basically altered the activity and experience of human beings within those modes.[20]

A historical view locates heterosexuality and homosexuality in time, helping us distance ourselves from them. This distancing can help us formulate new questions that clarify our long-range sexual-political goals: What has been and is the social function of sexual categorizing? Whose interests have been served by the division of the world into heterosexual and homosexual? Do we dare not draw a line between those two erotic species? Is some sexual naming socially necessary? Would human freedom be enhanced if the sex-biology of our partners in lust was of no particular concern, and had no name? In what kind of society could we all more freely explore our desire and our flesh?

As we move [into the year 2000], a new sense of the historical making of the heterosexual and homosexual suggests that these are ways of feeling, acting, and being with each other that we can together unmake and radically remake according to our present desire, power, and our vision of a future political-economy of pleasure.

NOTES

1. Barbara Welter, "The Cult of True Womanhood: 1820–1860," *American Quarterly*, vol. 18 (Summer 1966); Welter's analysis is extended here to include True Men and True Love.

2. See, for example, Catherine Gallagher and Thomas Laqueur, eds., "The Making of the Modern Body: Sexuality and Society in the Nineteenth Century," *Representations*, no. 14 (Spring 1986) (republished, Berkeley: University of California Press, 1987).

3. Dr. James G. Kiernan, "Responsibility in Sexual Perversion," *Chicago Medical Recorder*, vol. 3 (May 1892), pp. 185–210.

4. R. von Krafft-Ebing, *Psychopathia Sexualis, with Especial Reference to Contrary Sexual Instinct: A Medico-Legal Study*, trans. Charles Gilbert Chaddock (Philadelphia: F. A. Davis, 1892), from the 7th and revised German ed. Preface, November 1892.

5. For the standardization of gender, see Lewis Terman and C. C. Miles, *Sex and Personality, Studies in Femininity and Masculinity* (New York: McGraw Hill, 1936). For the standardization of intelligence, see Lewis Terman, *Stanford-Binet Intelligence Scale* (Boston: Houghton Mifflin, 1916). For the standardization of work, see "scientific management" and "Taylorism" in Harry Braverman, *Labor and Monopoly Capital: The Degradation of Work in the Twentieth Century* (New York: Monthly Review Press, 1974).

6. See D'Emilio and Freedman, *Intimate Matters*, pp. 194–201, 231, 241, 295–96; Ellen Kay Trimberger, "Feminism, Men, and Modern Love: Greenwich Village, 1900–1925," in *Powers of Desire: The Politics of Sexuality*, ed. Ann Snitow, Christine Stansell, Sharon Thompson (New York: Monthly Review Press, 1983), pp. 131–52; Kathy Peiss, "'Charity Girls' and City Pleasures: Historical Notes on Working Class Sexuality, 1880–1920," in *Powers of Desire*, pp. 74–87; and Mary P. Ryan, "The Sexy Saleslady: Psychology, Heterosexuality, and Consumption in the Twentieth Century," in her *Womanhood in America*, 2nd ed. (New York: Franklin Watts, 1979), pp. 151–82.

7. [Rev. Charles Parkhurst], "Woman. Calls Them Andromaniacs. Dr. Parkhurst So Characterizes Certain Women Who Passionately Ape Everything That Is Mannish. Woman Divinely Preferred. Her Supremacy Lies in Her Womanliness, and She Should Make the Most of It— Her Sphere of Best Usefulness the Home," *The New York Times*, May 23, 1897, p. 16:1.

8. See Lisa Duggan, "The Social Enforcement of Heterosexuality and Lesbian Resistance in the 1920s," in *Class, Race, and Sex: The Dynamics of Control*, ed. Amy Swerdlow and Hanah Lessinger (Boston: G. K. Hall, 1983), pp. 75–92; Rayna Rapp and Ellen Ross, "The Twenties Backlash: Compulsory Heterosexuality, the Consumer Family, and the Waning of Feminism," in *Class, Race, and Sex*; Christina Simmons, "Companionate Marriage and the Lesbian Threat," *Frontiers*, vol. 4, no. 3 (Fall 1979), pp. 54–59; and Lillian Faderman, *Surpassing the Love of Men* (New York: William Morrow, 1981).

9. Louis Kronenberger, review of André Gide, *The Immoralist*, New York Times Book Review, April 20, 1930, p. 9.

10. Henry James Forman, review of Floyd Dell, *Love in the Machine Age* (New York: Farrar & Rinehart), *New York Times Book Review*, September 14, 1930, p. 9.

11. Ferdinand Lundberg and Dr. Marnia F. Farnham, *Modern Woman: The Lost Sex* (New York: Harper, 1947).

12. Dr. Howard A. Rusk, *New York Times Book Review*, January 4, 1948, p. 3.

13. Alfred Kinsey, Wardell B. Pomeroy, Clyde E. Martin, *Sexual Behavior in the Human Male* (Philadelphia: W. B. Saunders, 1948), pp. 199–200.

14. Kinsey, *Sexual Behavior*, pp. 637, 639.

15. See Steven Epstein, "Gay Politics, Ethnic Identity: The Limits of Social Constructionism," *Socialist Review* 93/93 (1987), pp. 9–54.

16. Gore Vidal, "Someone to Laugh at the Squares With" [Tennessee Williams], *New York Review of Books*, June 13, 1985; reprinted in his *At Home: Essays, 1982–1988* (New York: Random House, 1988), p. 48.

17. Rosalyn Regelson, "Up the Camp Staircase," *The New York Times*, March 3, 1968, Section II, p. 1:5.

18. D'Emilio and Freedman, *Intimate Matters*, pp. 57–63, 268, 356.

19. Ryan, *Womanhood*; John D'Emilio, "Capitalism and Gay Identity," in *Powers of Desire*, pp. 100–13; Jeffrey Weeks, *Coming Out: Homosexual Politics in Britain from the Nineteenth Century to the Present* (London: Quartet Books, 1977); D'Emilio and Freedman, *Intimate Matters*; Katz, "Early Colonial Exploration, Agriculture, and Commerce: The Age of Sodomitical Sin, 1607–1740," *Gay/Lesbian Almanac*, pp. 23–65.

20. This tripartite system is intended as a revision of Gayle Rubin's pioneering work on the social-historical organization of eros and gender. See "The Traffic in Women: Notes on the Political-Economy of Sex," in *Toward an Anthropology of Women*, ed. Rayna R. Reiter (New York: Monthly Review Press, 1975), pp. 157–210, and "Thinking Sex: Notes for a Radical Theory of the Politics of Sexuality," in *Pleasure and Danger: Exploring Female Sexuality*, ed. Carole S. Vance (Boston: Routledge & Kegan Paul, 1984), pp. 267–329.

7 | Masculinity as Homophobia: Fear, Shame, and Silence in the Construction of Gender Identity

Michael S. Kimmel

We think of manhood as eternal, a timeless essence that resides deep in the heart of every man. We think of manhood as a thing, a quality that one either has or doesn't have. We think of manhood as innate, residing in the particular biological composition of the human male, the result of androgens or the possession of a penis. We think of manhood as a transcendent tangible property that each man must manifest in the world, the reward presented with great ceremony to a young novice by his elders for having successfully completed an arduous initiation ritual. . . .

In this chapter, I view masculinity as a constantly changing collection of meanings that we construct through our relationships with ourselves, with each other, and with our world. Manhood is neither static nor timeless; it is historical. Manhood is not the manifestation of an inner essence; it is socially constructed. Manhood does not bubble up to consciousness from our biological makeup; it is created in culture. Manhood means different things at different times to different people. We come to know what it means to be a man in our culture by setting our definitions in opposition to a set of "others"—racial minorities, sexual minorities, and, above all, women. . . .

Classical Social Theory as a Hidden Meditation of Manhood

Begin this inquiry by looking at four passages from that set of texts commonly called classical social and political theory. You will, no doubt, recognize them, but I invite you to recall the way they were discussed in your undergraduate or graduate courses in theory:

> The bourgeoisie cannot exist without constantly revolutionizing the instruments of production, and thereby the relations of production, and with them the whole relations of society. Conservation of the old modes of production in unaltered form, was, on the contrary, the first condition of existence for all earlier industrial classes. Constant revolutionizing of production, uninterrupted disturbance of all social conditions, everlasting uncertainty and agitation distinguish the bourgeois epoch from all earlier ones. All fixed, fast-frozen relations, with their train of ancient and venerable prejudices and opinions are swept away, all newformed ones become antiquated before they can ossify. All that is solid melts into air, all that

Michael S. Kimmel is a professor of sociology and gender studies at Stony Brook University, where he founded the Center for the Study of Men and Masculinities

is holy is profaned, and man is at last compelled to face with sober senses, his real conditions of life, and his relation with his kind. (Marx & Engels, 1848/1964)

An American will build a house in which to pass his old age and sell it before the roof is on; he will plant a garden and rent it just as the trees are coming into bearing; he will clear a field and leave others to reap the harvest; he will take up a profession and leave it, settle in one place and soon go off elsewhere with his changing desires. . . . At first sight there is something astonishing in this spectacle of so many lucky men restless in the midst of abundance. But it is a spectacle as old as the world; all that is new is to see a whole people performing in it. (Tocqueville, 1835/1967)

Where the fulfillment of the calling cannot directly be related to the highest spiritual and cultural values, or when, on the other hand, it need not be felt simply as economic compulsion, the individual generally abandons the attempt to justify it at all. In the field of its highest development, in the United States, the pursuit of wealth, stripped of its religious and ethical meaning, tends to become associated with purely mundane passions, which often actually give it the character of sport. (Weber, 1905/1966)

We are warned by a proverb against serving two masters at the same time. The poor ego has things even worse: it serves three severe masters and does what it can to bring their claims and demands into harmony with one another. These claims are always divergent and often seem incompatible. No wonder that the ego so often fails in its task. Its three tyrannical masters are the external world, the super ego and the id. . . . It feels hemmed in on three sides, threatened by three kinds of danger, to which, if it is hard pressed, it reacts by generating anxiety. . . . Thus the ego, driven by the id, confined by the super ego, repulsed by reality, struggles to master its economic task of bringing about harmony among the forces and influences working in and upon it; and we can understand how it is that so often we cannot suppress a cry: "Life is not easy!" (Freud, "The Dissection of the Psychical Personality," 1933/1966)

If your social science training was anything like mine, these were offered as descriptions of the bourgeoisie under capitalism, of individuals in democratic societies, of the fate of the Protestant work ethic under the ever rationalizing spirit of capitalism, or of the arduous task of the autonomous ego in psychological development. Did anyone ever mention that in all four cases the theorists were describing men? Not just "man" as in generic mankind, but a particular type of masculinity, a definition of manhood that derives its identity from participation in the marketplace, from interaction with other men in that marketplace— in short, a model of masculinity for whom identity is based on homosocial competition? Three years before Tocqueville found Americans "restless in the midst of abundance," Senator Henry Clay had called the United States "a nation of self-made men."

What does it mean to be "self-made"? What are the consequences of self-making for the individual man, for other men, for women? It is this notion of manhood—rooted in the sphere of production, the public arena, a masculinity grounded not in land ownership or in artisanal republican virtue but in successful participation in marketplace competition—this has been the defining notion of American manhood. Masculinity must be proved, and no sooner is it proved than it is again questioned and must be proved again— constant, relentless, unachievable, and ultimately the quest for proof becomes so meaningless that it takes on the characteristic, as Weber said, of a sport. He who has the most toys when he dies wins. . . .

Masculinity as History and the History of Masculinity

The idea of masculinity expressed in the previous extracts is the product of historical shifts in the grounds on which men rooted their sense of themselves as men. To argue that cultural definitions of gender identity are historically specific goes only so far; we have to specify exactly what those models were. In my historical inquiry into the development of these models of manhood[1] I chart the fate of two models for manhood at the turn of the nineteenth century and the emergence of a third in the first few decades of that century.

In the late eighteenth and early nineteenth centuries, two models of manhood prevailed. The *Genteel Patriarch* derived his identity from landownership. Supervising his estate, he was refined, elegant, and given to casual sensuousness. He was a doting and devoted father, who spent much of his time supervising the estate and with his family. Think of George Washington or Thomas Jefferson as examples. By contrast, the *Heroic Artisan* embodied the physical strength and republican virtue that Jefferson observed in the yeoman farmer, independent urban craftsman, or shopkeeper. Also a devoted father, the Heroic Artisan taught his son his craft, bringing him through ritual apprenticeship to status as master craftsman. Economically autonomous, the Heroic Artisan also cherished his democratic community, delighting in the participatory democracy of the town meeting. Think of Paul Revere at his pewter shop, shirtsleeves rolled up, a leather apron—a man who took pride in his work.

Heroic Artisans and Genteel Patriarchs lived in casual accord, in part because their gender ideals were complementary (both supported participatory democracy and individual autonomy, although patriarchs tended to support more powerful state machineries and also supported slavery) and because they rarely saw one another: Artisans were decidedly urban and the Genteel Patriarchs ruled their rural estates. By the 1830s, though, this casual symbiosis was shattered by the emergence of a new vision of masculinity, *Marketplace Manhood.*

Marketplace Man derived his identity entirely from his success in the capitalist marketplace as he accumulated wealth, power, status. He was the urban entrepreneur, the businessman. Restless, agitated, and anxious, Marketplace Man was an absentee landlord at home and an absent father with his children, devoting himself to his work in an increasingly homosocial environment—a male-only world in which he pits himself against other men. His efforts at self-making transform the political and economic spheres, casting aside the Genteel Patriarch as an anachronistic feminized dandy—sweet, but ineffective and outmoded, and transforming the Heroic Artisan into a dispossessed proletarian, a wage slave.

As Tocqueville would have seen it, the coexistence of the Genteel Patriarch and the Heroic Artisan embodied the fusion of liberty and equality. Genteel Patriarchy was the manhood of the traditional aristocracy, the class that embodied the virtue of liberty. The Heroic Artisan embodied democratic community, the solidarity of the urban shopkeeper or craftsman. Liberty and democracy, the patriarch and the artisan, could, and did, coexist. But Marketplace Man is capitalist man, and he makes both freedom and equality problematic, eliminating the freedom of the aristocracy and proletarianizing the equality of the artisan. In one sense, American history has been an effort to restore, retrieve, or reconstitute the virtues of Genteel Patriarchy and Heroic Artisanate as they were being transformed in the capitalist marketplace.

Marketplace Manhood was a manhood that required proof, and that required the acquisition of tangible goods as evidence of success. It reconstituted itself by the exclusion of "others"—women, nonwhite men, nonnative-born men, homosexual men—and by terrified flight into a pristine mythic homosocial Eden where men could, at last, be real men among other men. The story of the ways in which Marketplace Man becomes American Everyman is a tragic tale, a tale of striving to live up to impossible ideals of success leading to chronic terrors of emasculation, emotional emptiness, and a gendered rage that leave[s] a wide swath of destruction in its wake.

Masculinities as Power Relations

Marketplace Masculinity describes the normative definition of American masculinity. It describes his characteristics—aggression, competition, anxiety—and the arena in which those characteristics are deployed—the public sphere, the marketplace. If the marketplace is the arena in which manhood is tested and proved, it is a gendered arena, in which tensions between women and men and tensions among different groups of men are weighted with meaning. These tensions suggest that cultural definitions of gender are played out in a contested terrain and are themselves power relations.

All masculinities are not created equal; or rather, we are all *created* equal, but any hypothetical equality evaporates quickly because our definitions of masculinity are not equally valued in our society. One definition of manhood continues to remain the standard against which other forms of manhood are measured and evaluated. Within the dominant culture, the masculinity that defines white, middle class, early middle-aged, heterosexual men is the masculinity that sets the standards for other men, against which other men are measured and, more often than not, found wanting. Sociologist Erving Goffman (1963) wrote that in America, there is only "one complete, unblushing male":

> a young, married, white, urban, northern heterosexual, Protestant father of college education, fully employed, of good complexion, weight and height, and a recent record in sports. Every American male tends to look out upon the world from this perspective. . . . Any male who fails to qualify in any one of these ways is likely to view himself . . . as unworthy, incomplete, and inferior. (p. 128)

This is the definition that we will call "hegemonic" masculinity, the image of masculinity of those men who hold power, which has become the standard in psychological evaluations, sociological research, and self-help and advice literature for teaching young men to become "real men" (Connell, 1987). The hegemonic definition of manhood is a man *in* power, a man *with* power, and a man *of* power. We equate manhood with being strong, successful, capable, reliable, in control. The very definitions of manhood we have developed in our culture maintain the power that some men have over other men and that men have over women.

Our culture's definition of masculinity is thus several stories at once. It is about the individual man's quest to accumulate those cultural symbols that denote manhood, signs that he has in fact achieved it. It is about those standards being used against women to prevent their inclusion in public life and [to consign them] to a devalued private sphere. It is about the differential access that different types of men have to those cultural resources that confer manhood and about how each of these groups then develops their own modifications to preserve and claim their manhood. It is about the power of these definitions themselves to serve to maintain the real-life power that men have over women and that some men have over other men.

This definition of manhood has been summarized cleverly by psychologist Robert Brannon (1976) into four succinct phrases:

1. "No Sissy Stuff!" One may never do anything that even remotely suggests femininity. Masculinity is the relentless repudiation of the feminine.
2. "Be a Big Wheel." Masculinity is measured by power, success, wealth, and status. As the current saying goes, "He who has the most toys when he dies wins."
3. "Be a Sturdy Oak." Masculinity depends on remaining calm and reliable in a crisis, holding emotions in check. In fact, proving you're a man depends on never showing your emotions at all. Boys don't cry.
4. "Give 'em Hell." Exude an aura of manly daring and aggression. Go for it. Take risks.

These rules contain the elements of the definition against which virtually all American men are measured. Failure to embody these rules, to affirm the power of the rules and one's achievement of them, is a source of men's confusion and pain. Such a model is, of course, unrealizable for any man. But we keep trying, valiantly and vainly, to measure up. American masculinity is a relentless test.[2] The chief test is contained in the first rule. Whatever the variations by race, class, age, ethnicity, or sexual orientation, being a man means "not being like women." This notion of antifemininity lies at the heart of contemporary and historical conceptions of manhood, so that masculinity is defined more by what one is not rather than who one is.

Masculinity as the Flight from the Feminine

Historically and developmentally, masculinity has been defined as the flight from women, the repudiation of femininity. . . .

The drive to repudiate the mother as the indication of the acquisition of masculine gender identity has three consequences for the young boy. First, he pushes away his real mother, and with her the traits of nurturance, compassion, and tenderness she may have embodied. Second, he suppresses those traits in himself, because they will reveal his incomplete separation from mother. His life becomes a lifelong project to demonstrate that he possesses none of his mother's traits. Masculine identity is born in the renunciation of the feminine, not in the direct affirmation of the masculine, which leaves masculine gender identity tenuous and fragile.

Third, as if to demonstrate the accomplishment of these first two tasks, the boy also learns to devalue all women in his society as the living embodiments of those traits in himself he has learned to despise. Whether or not he was aware of it, Freud also described the origins of sexism—the systematic devaluation of women—in the desperate efforts of the boy to separate from mother. We may *want* "a girl just like the girl that married dear old Dad," as the popular song had it, but we certainly don't want to *be like* her.

This chronic uncertainty about gender identity helps us understand several obsessive behaviors. Take, for example, the continuing problem of the school-yard bully. Parents remind us that the bully is the *least* secure about his manhood, and so he is constantly trying to prove it. But he "proves" it by choosing opponents he is absolutely certain he can defeat; thus the standard taunt to a bully is to "pick on someone your own size." He can't, though, and after defeating a smaller and weaker opponent, which he was sure would prove his manhood, he is left with the empty gnawing feeling that he has not proved it after all, and he must find another opponent, again one smaller and weaker, that he can again defeat to prove it to himself.[3] . . .

When does it end? Never. To admit weakness, to admit frailty or fragility, is to be seen as a wimp, a sissy, not a real man. But seen by whom?

Masculinity as a Homosocial Enactment

Other men: We are under the constant careful scrutiny of other men. Other men watch us, rank us, grant our acceptance into the realm of manhood. Manhood is demonstrated for other men's approval. It is other men who evaluate the performance. Literary critic David Leverenz (1991) argues that "ideologies of manhood have functioned primarily in relation to the gaze of male peers and male authority" (p. 769). Think of how men boast to one another of their accomplishments—from their latest sexual conquest to the size of the fish they caught—and how we constantly parade the markers of manhood—wealth, power, status, sexy women—in front of other men, desperate for their approval.

That men prove their manhood in the eyes of other men is both a consequence of sexism and one of its chief props. "Women have, in men's minds, such a low place on the social ladder of this country that it's useless to define yourself in terms of a woman," noted playwright David Mamet. "What men need is men's approval." Women become a kind of currency that men use to improve their ranking on the masculine social scale. (Even those moments of heroic conquest of women carry, I believe, a current of homosocial evaluation.) Masculinity is a *homosocial* enactment. We test ourselves, perform heroic feats, take enormous risks, all because we want other men to grant us our manhood. . . .

Masculinity as Homophobia

. . . That nightmare from which we never seem to awaken is that those other men will see that sense of inadequacy, they will see that in our own eyes we are not who we are pretending to be. What we call masculinity is often a hedge against being revealed as a fraud, an exaggerated set of activities that keep others from seeing through us, and a frenzied effort to keep at bay those fears within ourselves. Our real fear "is not fear of women but of being ashamed or humiliated in front of other men, or being dominated by stronger men" (Leverenz, 1986, p. 451).

This, then, is the great secret of American manhood: *We are afraid of other men.* Homophobia is a central organizing principle of our cultural definition of manhood. Homophobia is more than the irrational fear of gay men, more than the fear that we might be perceived as gay. "The word 'faggot' has nothing to do with homosexual experience or even with fears of homosexuals," writes David Leverenz (1986). "It comes out of the depths of manhood: a label of ultimate contempt for anyone who seems sissy, untough, uncool" (p. 455). Homophobia is the fear that other men will unmask us, emasculate us, reveal to us and the world that we do not measure up, that we are not real men. We are afraid to let other men see that fear. Fear makes us ashamed, because the recognition of fear in ourselves is proof to ourselves that we are not as manly as we pretend, that we are, like the young man in a poem by Yeats, "one that ruffles in a manly pose for all his timid heart." Our fear is the fear of humiliation. We are ashamed to be afraid.

Shame leads to silence—the silences that keep other people believing that we actually approve of the things that are done to women, to minorities, to gays and lesbians in our culture. The frightened silence as we scurry past a woman being hassled by men on the street. That furtive silence when men make sexist or racist jokes in a bar. That clammy-handed silence when guys in the office make gay-bashing jokes. Our fears are the sources of our silences, and men's silence is what keeps the system running. This might help to explain why women often complain that their male friends or partners are often so understanding when they are alone and yet laugh at sexist jokes or even make those jokes themselves when they are out with a group.

The fear of being seen as a sissy dominates the cultural definitions of manhood. It starts so early. "Boys among boys are ashamed to be unmanly," wrote one educator in 1871 (cited in Rotundo, 1993, p. 264). I have a standing bet with a friend that I can walk onto any playground in America where 6-year-old boys are happily playing and by asking one question, I can provoke a fight. That question is simple: "Who's a sissy around here?" Once posed, the challenge is made. One of two things is likely to happen. One boy will accuse another of being a sissy, to which that boy will respond that he is not a sissy, that the first boy is. They may have to fight it out to see who's lying. Or a whole group of boys will surround one boy and all shout "He is! He is!" That boy will either burst into tears and run home crying, disgraced, or he will have to take on several boys at once, to prove that he's not a sissy. (And what will his father or older brothers tell him if he chooses to run home crying?) It will be some time before he regains any sense of self-respect.

Violence is often the single most evident marker of manhood. Rather it is the willingness to fight, the desire to fight. The origin of our expression that one has a chip on one's shoulder lies in the practice of an adolescent boy in the country or small town at the turn of the century, who would literally walk around with a chip of wood balanced on his shoulder—a signal of his readiness to fight with anyone who would take the initiative of knocking the chip off (see Gorer, 1964, p. 38; Mead, 1965).

As adolescents, we learn that our peers are a kind of gender police, constantly threatening to unmask us as feminine, as sissies. One of the favorite tricks when I was an adolescent was to ask a boy to look at his fingernails. If he held his palm toward his face and curled his fingers back to see them, he passed the test. He'd look at his nails "like a man." But if he held the back of his hand away from his face, and looked at his fingernails with arm outstretched, he was immediately ridiculed as sissy.

As young men we are constantly riding those gender boundaries, checking the fences we have constructed on the perimeter, making sure that nothing even remotely feminine might show through. The possibilities of being unmasked are everywhere. Even the most seemingly insignificant thing can pose a threat or activate that haunting terror. On the day the students in my course "Sociology of Men and Masculinities" were scheduled to discuss homophobia and male-male friendships, one student provided a touching illustration. Noting that it was a beautiful day, the first day of spring after a brutal northeast winter, he decided to wear shorts to class. "I had this really nice pair of new Madras shorts," he commented. "But then I thought to myself, these shorts have lavender and pink in them. Today's class topic is homophobia. Maybe today is not the best day to wear these shorts."

Our efforts to maintain a manly front cover everything we do. What we wear. How we talk. How we walk. What we eat. Every mannerism, every movement contains a coded gender language. Think, for example, of how you would answer the question: How do you "know" if a man is homosexual? When I ask this question in classes or workshops, respondents invariably provide a pretty standard list of stereotypically effeminate behaviors. He walks a certain way, talks a certain way, acts a certain way. He's very emotional; he shows his feelings. One woman commented that she "knows" a man is gay if he really cares about her; another said she knows he's gay if he shows no interest in her, if he leaves her alone.

Now alter the question and imagine what heterosexual men do to make sure no one could possibly get the "wrong idea" about them. Responses typically refer to the original stereotypes, this time as a set of negative rules about behavior. Never dress that way. Never talk or walk that way. Never show your feelings or get emotional. Always be prepared to demonstrate sexual interest in women that you meet, so it is impossible for any woman to get the wrong idea about you. In this sense, homophobia, the fear of being perceived as gay, as not a real man, keeps men exaggerating all the traditional rules of masculinity, including sexual predation with women. Homophobia and sexism go hand in hand. . . .

Homophobia as a Cause of Sexism, Heterosexism, and Racism

Homophobia is intimately interwoven with both sexism and racism. The fear—sometimes conscious, sometimes not—that others might perceive us as homosexual propels men to enact all manner of exaggerated masculine behaviors and attitudes to make sure that no one could possibly get the wrong idea about us. One of the centerpieces of that exaggerated masculinity is putting women down, both by excluding them from the public sphere and by the quotidian put-downs in speech and behaviors that organize the daily life of the American man. Women and gay men become the "other" against which heterosexual men project their identities, against whom they stack the decks so as to compete in a situation in which they will always win, so that by suppressing them, men can stake a claim for their own manhood. Women threaten emasculation by representing the home, workplace, and familial responsibility, the negation of fun. Gay men have historically played the role of the consummate sissy in the American popular mind because homosexuality is seen as an inversion of normal gender development. There have been other "others." Through American history, various groups have represented the sissy, the non-men against whom American men played out their definitions of manhood, often with vicious results. In fact, these changing groups provide an interesting lesson in American historical development.

At the turn of the nineteenth century, it was Europeans and children who provided the contrast for American men. The "true American was vigorous, manly, and direct, not effete and corrupt like the supposed Europeans," writes Rupert Wilkinson (1986). "He was plain rather than ornamented, rugged rather than luxury seeking, a liberty loving common man or natural gentleman rather than an aristocratic oppressor or servile minion" (p. 96). The "real man" of the early nineteenth century was neither noble nor serf. By the middle of the century, black slaves had replaced the effete nobleman. Slaves were seen as dependent, helpless men, incapable of defending their women and children, and therefore less than manly. Native Americans were cast as foolish and naive children, so they could be infantilized as the "Red Children of the Great White Father" and therefore excluded from full manhood.

By the end of the century, new European immigrants were also added to the list of the unreal men, especially the Irish and Italians, who were seen as too passionate and emotionally volatile to remain controlled sturdy oaks, and Jews, who were seen as too bookishly effete and too physically puny to truly measure up. In the mid-twentieth century, it was also Asians—first the Japanese during the Second World War, and more recently, the Vietnamese during the Vietnam War—who have served as unmanly templates against which American men have hurled their gendered rage. Asian men were seen as small, soft, and effeminate—hardly men at all.

Such a list of "hyphenated" Americans—Italian-, Jewish-, Irish-, African-, Native-, Asian-, gay—composes the majority of American men. So manhood is only possible for a distinct minority, and the definition has been constructed to prevent the others from achieving it. Interestingly, this emasculation of one's enemies has a flip side—and one that is equally gendered. These very groups that have historically been cast as less than manly were also, often simultaneously, cast as hypermasculine, as sexually aggressive, violent rapacious beasts, against whom "civilized" men must take a decisive stand and thereby rescue civilization. Thus black men were depicted as rampaging sexual beasts, women as carnivorously carnal, gay men as sexually insatiable, southern European men as sexually predatory and voracious, and Asian men as vicious and cruel torturers who were immorally disinterested in life itself, willing to sacrifice their entire people for their whims. But whether one saw these groups as effeminate sissies or as brutal savages, the terms with which they were perceived were gendered. These groups become the "others," the screens against which traditional conceptions of manhood were developed. . . .

Power and Powerlessness in the Lives of Men

I have argued that homophobia, men's fear of other men, is the animating condition of the dominant definition of masculinity in America, that the reigning definition of masculinity is a defensive effort to prevent being emasculated. In our efforts to suppress or overcome those fears, the dominant culture exacts a tremendous price from those deemed less than fully manly: women, gay men, nonnative-born men, men of color. This perspective may help clarify a paradox in men's lives, a paradox in which men have virtually all the power and yet do not feel powerful (see Kaufman, 1993).

Manhood is equated with power—over women, over other men. Everywhere we look, we see the institutional expression of that power—in state and national legislatures, on the boards of directors of every major United States corporation or law firm, and in every school and hospital administration. . . .

When confronted with the analysis that men have all the power, many men react incredulously. "What do you mean, men have all the power?" they ask. "What are you talking about? My wife bosses me around. My kids boss me around. My boss bosses me around. I have no power at all! I'm completely powerless!"

Men's feelings are not the feelings of the powerful, but of those who see themselves as powerless. These are the feelings that come inevitably from the discontinuity between the social and the psychological, between the aggregate analysis that reveals how men are in power as a group and the psychological fact that they do not feel powerful as individuals. They are the feelings of men who were raised to believe themselves entitled to feel that power, but do not feel it. No wonder many men are frustrated and angry. . . .

Why, then, do American men feel so powerless? Part of the answer is because we've constructed the rules of manhood so that only the tiniest fraction of men come to believe that they are the biggest of wheels, the sturdiest of oaks, the most virulent repudiators of femininity, the most daring and aggressive. We've managed to disempower the overwhelming majority of American men by other means—such as discriminating on the basis of race, class, ethnicity, age, or sexual preference. . .

Others still rehearse the politics of exclusion, as if by clearing away the playing field of secure gender identity of any that we deem less than manly—women, gay men, nonnative-born men, men of color—middle-class, straight, white men can reground their sense of themselves without those haunting fears and that deep shame that they are unmanly and will be exposed by other men. This is the manhood of racism, of sexism, of homophobia. It is the manhood that is so chronically insecure that it trembles at the idea of lifting the ban on gays in the military, that is so threatened by women in the workplace that women become the targets of sexual harassment, that is so deeply frightened of equality that it must ensure that the playing field of male competition remains stacked against all newcomers to the game.

Exclusion and escape have been the dominant methods American men have used to keep their fears of humiliation at bay. The fear of emasculation by other men, of being humiliated, of being seen as a sissy, is the leitmotif in my reading of the history of American manhood. Masculinity has become a relentless test by which we prove to other men, to women, and ultimately to ourselves, that we have successfully mastered the part. The restlessness that men feel today is nothing new in American history; we have been anxious and restless for almost two centuries. Neither exclusion nor escape has ever brought us the relief we've sought, and there is no reason to think that either will solve our problems now. Peace of mind, relief from gender struggle, will come only from a politics of inclusion, not exclusion, from standing up for equality and justice, and not by running away.

NOTES

1. Much of this work is elaborated in *Manhood: The American Quest* (in press). [This was published in 1996 as *Manhood in America: A Cultural History.*]
2. Although I am here discussing only American masculinity, I am aware that others have located this chronic instability and efforts to prove manhood in the particular cultural and economic arrangements of Western society. Calvin, after all, inveighed against the disgrace "for men to become effeminate," and countless other theorists have described the mechanics of manly proof (see, for example, Seidler, 1994).
3. Such observations also led journalist Heywood Broun to argue that most of the attacks against feminism came from men who were shorter than 5 ft. 7 in. "The man who, whatever his physical size, feels secure in his own masculinity and in his own relation to life is rarely resentful of the opposite sex" (cited in Symes, 1930, p. 139).

REFERENCES

Brannon, R. (1976). The male sex role—and what it's done for us lately. In R. Brannon & D. David (Eds.), *The forty-nine percent majority* (pp. 1–40). Reading, MA: Addison-Wesley.

Connell, R. W. (1987). *Gender and power.* Stanford, CA: Stanford University Press.

Freud, S. (1933/1966). *New introductory lectures on psychoanalysis* (L. Strachey, ed.). New York: Norton.

Goffman, E. (1963). *Stigma.* Englewood Cliffs, NJ: Prentice Hall.

Gorer, G. (1964). *The American people: A study in national character.* New York: Norton.

Kaufman, M. (1993). *Cracking the armour: Power and pain in the lives of men.* Toronto: Viking Canada.

Leverenz, D. (1986). Manhood, humiliation and public life: Some stories. *Southwest Review, 71,* Fall.

Leverenz, D. (1991). The last real man in America: From Natty Bumppo to Batman. *American Literary Review, 3.*

Marx, K., & F. Engels. (1848/1964). The communist manifesto. In R. Tucker (ed.), *The Marx-Engels reader.* New York: Norton.

Mead, M. (1965). *And keep your powder dry.* New York: William Morrow.

Rotundo, E. A. (1993). *American manhood: Transformations in masculinity from the revolution to the modern era.* New York: Basic Books.

Seidler, V. J. (1994). *Unreasonable men: Masculinity and social theory.* New York: Routledge.

Symes, L. (1930). The new masculinism. *Harper's Monthly, 161,* January.

Tocqueville, A. de. (1835/1967). *Democracy in America.* New York: Anchor.

Weber, M. (1905/1966). *The Protestant ethic and the spirit of capitalism.* New York: Charles Scribner's.

Wilkinson, R. (1986). *American tough: The tough-guy tradition and American character.* New York: Harper & Row.

8 Flipping the Script: Black Manhood and the Proactive Process of Becoming

Tim'm T. West

Black Men Loving Black Men Is The Revolutionary Act.

—Marlon Riggs, *Tongues Untied*

It is necessary to grow a new skin, to develop new thoughts, to set afoot a new man.

—Frantz Fanon

Diamonds are coals under pressure.

—Nina Simone

As a young male growing up in several U.S. ghettos (both urban and rural), I was aware of the multiple implications of being black. I came to know that being a black male meant being subjected to a whole host of incompatible representations. As if it was not enough to be subjugated by white racism, there were the judgments made by other blacks or the reproach of my own self-reflexive gaze. Ambitious, project-boy . . . not like the others, not hardly a delinquent (not yet), promising, but a little hostile . . . yeah. There were, in addition, prescriptions for what kind of black man I should become: a tough, intelligent, well assimilated, and still-down-with-my-people, streetsmart man. Unsurprisingly, I struggled with how to uncover a sense of self from all the expectations. The images of black men made available through the media and television were either hypermasculine superheroes in Blaxploitation flicks or frustrated "boyz in the hood" whose rage with societal racism frequently got played out in multiple, self-destructive reactions. I tried to counter these images with a paradoxical performance of ghettoman savvy: black enough and man enough to substantiate that I was "down" with the brothas, yet articulate and poised enough to maneuver my way through the complex maze of white sociality and privilege.

There were moments when I thought that I would lose myself in whiteness; but I believed strongly that acting like a good *boy* would save me from the racist presuppositions that seemed most inescapable. I figured that I could charm "The Man"—a near-omnipotent whiteness that was too disparate and subtle to locate but that was always working to subjugate. I naively believed that self-alignment could be a sure way out of the realities of race and believed that if my performance was shrewd enough, I might be

Tim'm T. West is a poet, scholar, educator, and hip-hop artist. He directs the LGBTQ Community Initiative at Teach For America, and his books include *Pre|dispositions*, *Red Dirt Revival*, and *Flirting*.

granted some room to breathe—perhaps even a space to create. This mediating space was, no doubt, a difficult place to be. I was embittered about this tense place in the middle that demanded constant negotiation: between Africa and America, home and the academy, between a self that I thought I knew and the one I was trying to find. I was searching for a social space void of contradictions and did not yet realize that no such place existed.

In college, my resistance took the form of a shaky appropriation of Afro-centric episte-mology and a nostalgic appreciation for Black Power. I was trying to undo all the accultur-ation and find a (my)self that did not even exist. . . . The search for self makes an enticing but deceptive promise; and I would later realize that searching for me was a much less productive process than becoming me.

[M]y current intellectual projects scrutinize systems of domination that would have black men believe that the only identities available are the ones "The Man" prescribes. . . . I am interested in "flipping the script"—in challenging the ways that black men inter-nalize identities that we ourselves took no part in creating. I am specifically concerned about the ways that socially constituted antagonisms between black men hinder politically effective coalitions and want to interrogate this outgrowth of internalized oppression and its consequences. I am most troubled when I see the ways that the black male scripts we perform are complicit with our own domination.

For many black men, the Million Man March* provided one such opportunity to rein-vigorate a political struggle that would address American racism and its multiple effects. Black men gathered to acknowledge the ways in which our conduct is often in accord with the distressing predicaments and negative indicators within our community. Impera-tive political transformations would not occur without black men undertaking a personal introspective process directed towards self-evaluation and personal development. For some of us, the March was about launching personal interventions, teasing out complexities, owning our fabrications and performances, and reconstructing black male experience in order to transform ourselves and the communities in which we live. I found some hopeful-ness in the possibility that black men were interested in engaging in a self-fashioning that reminded me of the ethical experience Michel Foucault celebrates in the latter volumes of *History of Sexuality*. I especially thought about his belief that the "work of the self on the self" can become indispensable to understanding (and engaging in) political struggle. Directing political acts that are grounded in ethical reflection seems a more productive strategy than either hoping for some divine rescue or organizing antihero militias with no real objectives beyond destroying "The Man." . . .

October 16, 1995, was a day that, for me, marked the possibility for collectively recon-ceptualizing black male experience. Because it was principally a day about possibilities, I was ambivalent about precisely what kind of re-conceptualization would take place. I feared that any national conversation about black manhood could potentially promote some icon of black manhood that negates much of what I am: black and male certainly, but a good deal more as well. As a gay brotha who is largely inspired by my studies of

---

*On October 16, 1995, hundreds of thousands of African American men gathered at the National Mall in Washington, D.C., in a historic march organized by Nation of Islam leader Louis Farrakhan, the National African American Leadership Summit, and numerous other civil rights organizations.

feminism, I feared that mobilizing American black men would lead to essentializing, one-dimensional conceptions of manhood that reinforce and mirror the white heteronormative standards I have struggled against since childhood. White patriarchy in blackface can hardly characterize political subversion; it can only reinforce the current order.

My reservations about attending the Million Man March were connected with the race-essentializing, patriarchal and heterosexist ideology so subtly central to much of its inception. Like many others, I would cling to the more general call for personal introspection: the kind of self-evaluation that I believe is so central to building self-confidence, promoting self-determination, and actualizing political transformation. An optimist, I hoped that this mobilization would be the impetus for the creation of strong coalitions upon which political struggles can depend. Black men would collectively raise thoughtful challenges to institutional racism as well as social and economic injustice. Men markedly different than me would recognize that despite our differences, we share common concerns. The March would be a forum where black men could address our (often) antagonistic relationships to each other and to the women and children in our lives. We might recognize the extent to which patriarchal models necessitate the very domination and subjugation we struggle against. It would be a day filled with both idealism and anxiety, the kind of apprehensive excitability common to all great moments in history.

. . .

. . . I would reconcile my differences with the March organizers by recognizing that my participation was itself a struggle that would provide its own meaningful lesson: the realization that there is no singular model for black men and that our collective strength lies in our diversity.

A few years after the March and having developed a strong desire to grapple intellectually with the complex nature of black male experience, I have located academia as a place where I can think productively about systems of subjectification, the relation between power and the subject, ethical self-formation, and political agency. From this vantage point, there seemed to be a lack of clarity about what March leaders' call for atonement was asking of us. In one sense, atoning involves self-critique. Black men *should* think about what within us is lacking, about dreams deferred, about talents we have not ourselves recognized amid all the preoccupation with scrutiny from the whites, from black women, from each other.

. . . While atonement as the recognition of a problem can be productive in the sense that it calls for self-evaluation and redescription, it fails as long as it is more concerned with undoing and atoning than creating and becoming. Our subjugation and psychological scars are not things we can undo; neither are our mistakes and failures. As with the Deleuzean[1] fold, there is something fundamentally unproductive about the attempts to unfold. Once the crease is made, it makes little sense to keep pressing eternally in order to undo the (undoable) fold. Even a reversal of the fold is no more than a new fold—a return (or folding back) to the initial injury rather than an undoing of it. I believe that instead of struggling and pressing to erase our subjugation, black men should concern ourselves with (and focus our energies towards) the creative process of seizing the agency to make new folds. I am not advocating the kinds of stylistic folds that open up a space for creative expression (such as some forms of Hip-Hop music*) but which devalue black life through promoting material excess and violence within our communities. Rather, I am proposing that black men produce folds that are always self-critical and that attempt to anticipate and eschew the forms of domination responsible for our subjugation. . . .

A year following the March I was in Bedstuy,[2] daily reciprocating screwface gestures at brothas on the corner. Screwface is a gaze that scrutinizes the authenticity of another's manhood. It is a ritualistic practice that is so internalized and ingrained that the stroll around the corner store triggers an impulsive performance. I begin to contradict all those politically subversive stands that I relentlessly advocate in consciousness. The change in my pace marks the confrontation, the rhythm in my stride anticipates judgment, and I remove any visible signs of happiness (the last thing I want to do is to appear "gay"). So it is a habitual response to perform the mean-mug or screwface. Gnawing the teeth, perfectly reciprocating the daunting stares, a slight nod of the head and other small gestures constitute the complex game of reading the gaze:

> *Is this brotha tryin' to test me or size me up? Might it be all right to speak? If I look one second too long at this brotha I might incite an unwanted confrontation. Damn he looks good! What was that look about? Oh shit, I forgot to hide my Foucault books. Look kinda silly frontin' like there is such a thing as a hard-core academician (an image that the brothas on this corner aren't likely to accept anytime soon).*

What is most problematic about this *round-the-way* ritual is not its performative nature. It is no more dramatic or exaggerated than the intellectual performance at the academic conference. In either situation I am capable of performing the gestures and jargon acceptably. I know what is expected of me and am familiar with the respective codes of conduct. So I am not writing about black men, masculine anxiety, and subjugation because I am interested in problematizing (inescapable) performances, but rather because I have serious concerns about misrecognizing the ways certain of our performances are complicit with our own subjugation. That I can act—that I can consciously employ a subversive performance—opens up possibilities for understanding how performance can be exercised for survival and resistance. . . . [T]his idea of performative strategies of resistance is central to my examinations of black masculinity.

Resistance. What would it mean, for example, for me to deny the screwface performance on my Bedstuy streetcorner? What might he do if I extended my hand or initiated a brotherly embrace? Put a knife to my throat? Ask me out on a date? The possibilities are many; but the fear of antagonism is often enough to squelch attempts at bravery. Fear continues to operate as a mutual and reiterative function between black men. Too often, we are afraid to express love for each other. Let us show each other how afraid we are: (Screwface and head-nod: "*What up dawg?*" he says. "*Nothin, yo,*" I reply.) End scene.

---

*For more on West's examination of hip-hop, see his essays "Keepin' It Real: Disidentification and Its Discontents," in *Black Cultural Traffic: Crossroads in Global Performance and Popular Culture*, edited by Kennell Jackson and Harry Elam (University of Michigan Press, 2005), and "It's All One: A Conversation between Juba Kalamka and Tim'm West," in *Total Chaos: The Art and Aesthetics of Hip-Hop*, edited by Jeff Chang (Civitas Books, 2006).

. . .

I invoke the late Marlon Riggs' sentiment that "Black Men Loving Black Men Is *The* Revolutionary Act" because black men fighting and killing each other is the "business as usual" that I feared we would revert to upon return from the Million Man March. Riggs recognized the danger that is connected with black men having to assume roles that lead to self-loathing. He wanted to call in question the lack of respect for brothas who are thinking creatively and critically about manhood. The very systems of power that work to subordinate black men are often the same systems that applaud our antagonism towards each other. . . . Black men have been conditioned to recognize the worthlessness we some-times feel for ourselves in our mirror images—in each other. We repeatedly project our own self-loathing on those who most resemble us. Precisely who is the "bitch ass nigga" customarily referenced in so much of contemporary hip-hop? How do sexism and hetero-sexism inform this kind of scrutiny? Is this what the screwface signifies? . . .

While I disagree that there is revolutionary potential that is particular to love between black men (romantic or otherwise) or that revolution should be reduced to the "act,"[3] I believe that it is precisely fear of love between brothas manifesting itself romantically (homophobia), that has long prevented love between black men which is not apologetic, defensive, or anxiety-ridden. Homophobia functions to rebuke what appears to be an extreme manifestation of love between men. Often, the capacity for one brotha to love another must be perpetually negated each time desire is felt. Getting beyond this fear, which I argue involves getting beyond black male homophobia, is a courageous process that is indeed revolutionary.

Both W.E.B. DuBois and James Baldwin referred to a double-edgedness, a special sense, that comes from having to endure the process of subjugation. Can the injury per-formed by the violating other be reorganized in order to provide a strategic advantage—a counter-performance that transforms injury into insurgency? Might the physical and psy-chological scars dealt to black men give rise to what feminist Gloria Anzaldúa calls *la facultad*[4]—that special sensibility that those who are daily beaten down rely on for sur-vival? My belief is that if black men can begin to disavow unhappy attachments to our subjection, then we can begin the proactive process of becoming. Becoming expresses an optimistic and creative process that is not preoccupied with fighting off a subjection that we can never fully escape, but rather is about discovering ways to transform our subjection into a self-determined and politically viable existence.

. . . I continue to rise despite the obstacles of race, gender, and sexuality because they are the very sites of struggle from which I discover my strengths. . . . The experience of engaging the questions that I pose here demonstrates one way that ethical experience can take the shape of an intellectual project. With each new discovery I make and with each question I encounter, I change my surroundings and my relationship to it. As I perform insurgent scholarship and as I accept the errors in judgment that reflect my naiveté, I am living. With each word that I write (and unwrite), I am consoled by the certainty that I can become. I am becoming!

NOTES

1. As I understand Gilles Deleuze's essay "How Do You Make Yourself a Body Without Organs?" the Body Without Organs describes a plane of consistency that resists organization (shaping) into a subjected organism. The fold signifies a moment of violence against the individual which cannot be undone. However, the BwO after subjectification is not rendered helpless: "We are continually stratified . . . . The BwO is that glacial reality where the alluvions, sedimentations, coagulations, foldings, and recoilings that compose an organism—and also signification and subject—occur" (pg. 159). The "wrongfully folded" BwO might conceive of this folding as an opportunity for subversive agency. . . .

2. Bedstuy (Bedford-Stuyvesant), Brooklyn, is one of the largest black communities in the United States. It was my neighborhood through the duration of my research at The Graduate Faculty at The New School for Social Research.

3. Though Riggs' film *Tongues Untied* focuses on the self-determination of the black gay subject and celebrating romantic love and desire between black men, it does not follow that the "act" that he refers to when he suggests that "Black men loving black men is the revolutionary act" is necessarily a sexual one. I would caution against reducing revolution to any singular act, in the way that some counter-effective militant actions get labeled "revolutionary" based on the mere radical nature of the act.

4. In *Borderlands/La Frontera*, Gloria Anzaldúa defines *La facultad* as: "the capacity to see in surface phenomena the meaning of deeper realities, to see the deep structure below the surface. It is an instant 'sensing,' a quick perception arrived at without conscious reasoning. . . . Those who do not feel psychologically safe or physically safe in the world are more apt to develop this sense. Those who are pounced on the most have it the strongest—the females, the homosexuals of all races, the darkskinned, the outcast, the persecuted, the marginalized, the foreign" (aunt lute books, San Francisco, 1987, page 38).

9 Transgender Feminism: Queering the Woman Question

Susan Stryker

Many years ago, I paid a visit to my son's kindergarten room for parent-teacher night. Among the treats in store for us parents that evening was a chance to look at the *My Favorite Things* book that each child had prepared over the first few weeks of classes. Each page was blank except for a preprinted line that said "My favorite color is (blank)" or "My favorite food is (blank)," or "My favorite story is (blank)"; students were supposed to fill in the blanks with their favorite things and draw an accompanying picture. My son had filled the blanks and empty spaces of his book with many such things as "green," "pizza" and "*Goodnight Moon*," but I was unprepared for his response to "My favorite animal is (blank)". His favorite animal was "yeast." I looked up at the teacher, who had been watching me in anticipation of this moment. "Yeast?" I said, and she, barely suppressing her glee, said, "Yeah. And when I asked why yeast was his favorite animal, he said, 'It just makes the category animal seem more interesting.'"

At the risk of suggesting that the category "woman" is somehow not interesting *enough* without a transgender supplement, which is certainly not my intent, I have to confess that there is a sense in which "woman," as a category of human personhood, is indeed, for me, *more* interesting when we include transgender phenomena within its rubric. The work required to encompass transgender within the bounds of womanhood takes women's studies, and queer feminist theorizing, in important and necessary directions. It takes us directly into the basic questions of the sex/gender distinction, and of the concept of a sex/gender system, that lie at the heart of Anglophone feminism. Once there, transgender phenomena ask us to follow basic feminist insights to their logical conclusion (biology is not destiny, and one is not born a woman, right?). And yet, transgender phenomena simultaneously threaten to refigure the basic conceptual and representational framework within which the category "woman" has been conventionally understood, deployed, embraced, and resisted.

Perhaps "gender," transgender tells us, is not related to "sex" in quite the same way that an apple is related to the reflection of a red fruit in the mirror; it is not a mimetic relationship. Perhaps "sex" is a category that, like citizenship, can be attained by the non-native residents of a particular location by following certain procedures. Perhaps gender has a more complex genealogy, at the level of individual psychobiography as well as collective socio-historical process, than can be grasped or accounted for by the currently dominant

Susan Stryker is a professor of gender and women's studies at the University of Arizona and the founder of the Transgender Studies Initiative. Her award-winning works include *The Transgender Studies Reader* and the documentary *Screaming Queens: The Riot at Compton's Cafeteria*.

From *Third Wave Feminism*, edited by Stacy Gillis, Gillian Howie and Rebecca Munford, published 2004. Reproduced with permission of SNCSC.

binary sex/gender model of Eurocentric modernity. And perhaps what is to be learned by grappling with transgender concerns is relevant to a great many people, including non-transgendered women and men. Perhaps transgender discourses help us think in terms of embodied specificities, as *women's* studies has traditionally tried to do, while also giving us a way to think about gender as a system with multiple nodes and positions, as *gender* studies increasingly requires us to do. Perhaps transgender studies, which emerged in the academy at the intersection of feminism and queer theory over the course of the last decade or so, can be thought of as one productive way to "queer the woman question."[1] If we define "transgender phenomena" broadly as anything that disrupts or denaturalizes normative gender, and which calls our attention to the processes through which normativity is produced and atypicality achieves visibility, "transgender" becomes an incredibly useful analytical concept. What might "transgender feminism"—a feminism that focuses on marginalized gender expressions as well as normative ones—look like?

As an historian of the United States, my training encourages me to approach currently salient questions by looking at the past through new eyes. Questions that matter now, historians are taught to think, are always framed by enabling conditions that precede them. Thus, when I want to know what transgender feminism might be, I try to learn what it has already been. When I learned, for example, that the first publication of the post-WWII transgender movement, a short-lived early 1950s magazine called *Transvestia*, was produced by a group calling itself The Society for Equality in Dress (Meyerowitz 2002, 179), I not only saw that a group of male transvestites in Southern California had embraced the rhetoric of first-wave feminism and applied the concept of gender equality to the marginalized topic of cross-dressing; I also came to think differently about Amelia Bloomer and the antebellum clothing reform movement. To the extent that breaking out of the conventional constructions of womanhood is both a feminist and transgender practice, what we might conceivably call transgender feminism arguably has been around since the first half of the nineteenth century.

Looking back, it is increasingly obvious that transgender phenomena are not limited to individuals who have "transgendered" personal identities. Rather, they are signposts that point to many different kinds of bodies and subjects, and they can help us see how gender can function as part of a more extensive apparatus of social domination and control. Gender as a form of social control is not limited to the control of bodies defined as "women's bodies," or the control of female reproductive capacities. Because genders are categories through which we recognize the personhood of others (as well as ourselves), because they are categories without which we have great difficulty in recognising personhood at all, gender also functions as a mechanism of control when some loss of gender status is threatened, or when claims of membership in a gender are denied. Why is it considered a heterosexist put-down to call some lesbians mannish? Why, if a working-class woman does certain kinds of physically demanding labor, or if a middle-class woman surpasses a certain level of professional accomplishment, is their feminine respectability called into question? Stripping away gender, and misattributing gender, are practices of social domination, regulation, and control that threaten social abjection; they operate by attaching transgender stigma to various unruly bodies and subject positions, not just to "transgendered" ones.[2] . . .

Transgender issues also engage many of the foundational questions in the social sciences and life sciences as they pertain to feminist inquiry. The biological body, which is typically assumed to be a single organically unified natural object characterized by one and only one of two available sex statuses, is demonstrably no such thing. The so-called "sex of the body" is an interpretive fiction that narrates a complex amalgamation of gland secretions and reproductive organs, chromosomes and genes, morphological characteristics and physiognomic features. There are far more than two viable aggregations of sexed bodily being. At what cost, for what purposes, and through what means do we collapse this diversity of embodiment into the social categories "woman" and "man"? How does the psychical subject who forms in this material context become aware of itself, of its embodied situation, of its position in language, family or society? How does it learn to answer to one or the other of the two personal pronouns "he" or "she," and to recognize "it" as a disavowed option that forecloses personhood? How do these processes vary from individual to individual, from place to place, and from time to time? These are questions of importance to feminism, usually relegated to the domains of biology and psychology, that transgender phenomena can help us think through. Transgender feminism gives us another axis, along with critical race studies or disability studies, to learn more about the ways in which bodily difference becomes the basis for socially constructed hierarchies, and helps us see in new ways how we are all inextricably situated, through the inescapable necessity of our own bodies, in terms of race, sex, gender or ability.

For all the reasons I have suggested, transgender phenomena are *interesting* for feminism, women's studies, gender studies, sexuality studies, and so forth. But *interesting*, by itself, is not enough, when hard decisions about budgets and staffing have to be made in academic departments, priorities and commitments actualized through classroom allocations and affirmative action hiring. *Interesting* also has to be *important*, and transgender is rarely considered important. All too often transgender is thought to name only a largely irrelevant class of phenomena that occupy the marginal fringe of the hegemonic gender categories man and woman, or else it is seen as one of the later, minor accretions to the gay and lesbian movement, along with bisexual and intersexed. At best, transgender is considered a portent of a future that seems to await us, for good or ill. But it remains a canary in the cultural coal mine, not an analytical workhorse for pulling down the patriarchy and other associated social ills. As long as transgender is conceived as the fraction of a fraction of a fraction of a movement, as long as it is thought to represent only some inconsequential outliers in a bigger and more important set of data, there is very little reason to support transgender concerns at the institutional level. Transgender will always lose by the numbers. The transgender community is tiny. In (so-called) liberal democracies that measure political strength by the number of votes or the number of dollars, transgender does not count for much, or add up to a lot. But there is another way to think about the importance of transgender concerns at this moment in our history.

One measure of an issue's potential is not how many people directly identify with it but, rather, how many other issues it can be linked with in a productive fashion. How, in other words, can an issue be *articulated*, in the double sense of "articulation," meaning both "to bring into language," and "the act of flexibly conjoining."[3] Articulating a transgender politics is part of the specialized work that I do as an activist transgender intellectual. How many issues can I link together through my experience of the category transgender?

To the extent that I am perceived as a woman (which is most of the time), I experience the same misogyny as other women, and to the extent that I am perceived as a man (which happens every now and then), I experience the homophobia directed toward gay men—both forms of oppression, in my experience, being rooted in a cultural devaluation of the feminine. My transgender status, to the extent that it is apparent to others, manifests itself through the appearance of my bodily surface and my shape, in much the same way that race is constructed, in part, through visuality and skin, and in much the same way that the beauty system operates by privileging certain modes of appearance. My transsexual body is different from most other bodies, and while this difference does not impair me, it has been medicalized, and I am sometimes disabled by the social oppression that takes aim at the specific form of my difference. Because I am formally classified as a person with a psychopathology known as Gender Identity Disorder, I am subject to the social stigma attached to mental illness, and I am more vulnerable to unwanted medical-psychiatric interventions. Because changing personal identification documents is an expensive and drawn-out affair, I have spent part of my life as an undocumented worker. Because identification documents such as drivers, licenses and passports are coded with multiple levels of information, including previous names and "AKAs," my privacy, and perhaps my personal safety, is at risk every time I drive too fast or cross a border. When I travel I always have to ask myself whether some aspect of my appearance, some bit of data buried in the magnetic strip on some piece of plastic with my picture on it, will create suspicion and result in my detention? In this era of terror and security, we are all surveyed, we are all profiled, but some of us have more to fear from the state than others. Staying home, however, does not make me safer. If I risk arrest by engaging in non-violent demonstrations, or violent political protest, the incarceration complex would not readily accommodate my needs; even though I am a post-operative male-to-female transsexual, I could wind up in a men's prison where I would be at extreme risk of rape and sexual assault. Because I am transgendered, I am more likely to experience discrimination in housing, employment and access to health care, and more likely to experience violence. These are not abstract issues: I have lost jobs, and not been offered jobs, because I am transgendered. I have had doctors walk out of exam rooms in disgust; I have had more trouble finding and retaining housing because I am transgendered; I have had my home burglarized and my property vandalized, and I have been assaulted, because I am transgendered.

Let me recapitulate what I can personally articulate through transgender: misogyny, homophobia, racism, looksism, disability, medical colonization, coercive psychiatrization, undocumented labor, border control, state surveillance, population profiling, the prison-industrial complex, employment discrimination, housing discrimination, lack of health care, denial of access to social services, and violent hate crimes. These issues are my issues, not because I think it is chic to be politically progressive. These issues are my issues, not because I feel guilty about being white, highly educated, or a citizen of the United States. These issues are my issues, not because my bodily being lives the space where these issues intersect. I articulate these issues when my mouth speaks the words that my mind puts together from what my body knows. It is by winning the struggles over these issues that my body as it is lived for me survives—or by losing them, that it will die. If these issues are your issues as well, then transgender needs to be part of your intellectual and political agenda. It is one of your issues.

I conclude now with some thoughts on yet another aspect of transgender articulation, the one mentioned in my title, which is how transgender issues articulate, or join together, feminist and queer projects. "Trans-" is troublesome for both LGBT communities and feminism, but the kind of knowledge that emerges from this linkage is precisely the kind of knowledge that we desperately need in the larger social arena.

Trans is not a "sexual identity," and therefore fits awkwardly in the LGBT rubric. That is, "transgender" does not describe a sexual orientation (like homosexual, bisexual, heterosexual or asexual), nor are transgender people typically attracted to other transgender people in the same way that lesbians are attracted to other lesbians, or gay men to other gay men. Transgender status is more like race or class, in that it cuts across the categories of sexual identity.[4] Neither is transgender (at least currently, in Eurocentric modernity) an identity term like "woman" or "man" that names a gender category within a social system. It is a way of being a man or a woman, or a way of marking resistance to those terms. Transgender analyses of gender oppression and hierarchy, unlike more normative feminist analyses, are not primarily concerned with the differential operations of power upon particular identity categories that create inequalities within gender systems, but rather with how the system itself produces a multitude of possible positions that it then works to centre or to marginalize.

Transgender practices and identities are a form of gender trouble, in that they call attention to contradictions in how we tend to think about gender, sex and sexuality. But the transgender knowledges that emerge from these troubling contradictions, I want to argue, can yoke together queer and feminist projects in a way that helps break the impasse of identity politics that has so crippled progressive movements in the United States. Since the early 1970s, progressive politics have fragmented along identity lines practically to the point of absurdity. While it undoubtedly has been vital over the past few decades of movement history to enunciate the particularities of all our manifold forms of bodily being in the world, it is equally important that we now find new ways of articulating our commonalities without falling into the equally dead-end logic of totalising philosophies and programmes.

Transgender studies offer us one critical methodology for thinking through the diverse particularities of our embodied lives, as well for thinking through the commonalities we share through our mutual enmeshment in more global systems. Reactionary political movements have been very effective in telling stories about shared values—family, religion, tradition. We who work at the intersection of queer and feminist movements, we who have a different vision of our collective future, need to become equally adept in telling stories that link us in ways that advance the cause of justice, and that hold forth the promise of happy endings for all our strivings. Bringing transgender issues into women's studies, and into feminist movement building, is one concrete way to be engaged in that important work.

While it is politically necessary to include transgender issues in feminist theorising and organising, it is not intellectually responsible, nor ethically defensible, to teach transgender studies in academic women's studies without being engaged in peer-to-peer conversations with various sorts of trans- and genderqueer people. Something crucial is lost when academically based feminists fail to support transgender inclusion in the academic workplace. Genderqueer youth who have come of age after the "queer" '90s are now passing through the higher education system, and they increasingly fail to recognize the applicability of prevailing modes of feminist discourse for their own lives and experiences. How we each live our bodies in the world is a vital source of knowledge for us all, and to teach trans studies without being in dialogue with trans people is akin to teaching race studies only from a position of whiteness, or gender studies only from a position of masculinity. Why is transgender not a category targeted for affirmative action in hiring, and valued the same way that racial diversity is valued? It is past time for feminists who have imagined that transgender issues have not been part of their own concerns to take a long, hard look in the mirror. What in their own constructions of self, their own experiences of gender, prevents their recognition of transgender people as being somehow like themselves—as people engaged in parallel, intersecting, and overlapping struggles, who are not fundamentally Other?

Transgender phenomena now present queer figures on the horizon of feminist visibility. Their calls for attention are too often received, however, as an uncomfortable solicitation from an alien and unthinkable monstrosity best left somewhere outside the village gates. But justice, when we first feel its claims upon us, typically points us toward a future we can scarcely imagine. At the historical moment when racial slavery in the United States at long last became morally indefensible, and the nation plunged into civil war, what did the future of the nation look like? When greenhouse gas emissions finally become equally morally indefensible, what shape will a post-oil world take? Transgender issues make similar claims of justice upon us all, and promise equally unthinkable transformations.[5] Recognising the legitimacy of these claims will change the world, and feminism along with it, in ways we can now hardly fathom. It is about time.

NOTES

1. This essay was first delivered as a keynote address at the *Third Wave Feminism* conference at the University of Exeter, UK (25 July 2002); and in revised form at the Presidential Session plenary on "Transgender Theory" at the *National Women's Studies Association* Annual Meeting, Oakland, California (17 June 2006). Many of the ideas I present here have been worked out in greater detail elsewhere in my work (see Stryker 1994, 1998, 2004, and 2006; see also my conversation with Marysia Zalewski. For another account of the relationship between recent feminist scholarship and transgender issues, see Cressida Heyes.
2. My thoughts on the role of transgender phenomena for understanding U.S. history in general are significantly indebted to Joanne Meyerowitz (2006).
3. The concept of "articulation" is taken from Ernesto Laclau and Chantal Mouffe (93–194).
4. See Joshua Gamson on the trouble transgender presents to identity movements.
5. On monstrosity and justice, see Nikki Sullivan.

WORKS CITED

Gamson, Joshua. "Must Identity Movements Self-Destruct? A Queer Dilemma." *Social Problems* 42.3 (1995): 390–406.

Heyes, Cressida. "Feminist Solidarity after Queer Theory: The Case of Transgender." *Signs* 28.4 (2003): 1093–120.

Laclau, Ernesto, and Chantal Mouffe. *Hegemony and Socialist Strategy: Towards a Radical Democratic Politics.* 2nd ed. London: Verso, 2001.

Meyerowitz, Joanne. *How Sex Changed: A History of Transsexuality in the United States.* Cambridge: Harvard University Press, 2002.

_____. "A New History of Gender." *Trans/Forming Knowledge: The Implications of Transgender Studies for Women's, Gender, and Sexuality Studies.* University of Chicago, 17 Feb. 2006. Accessed: 27 June 2006. <http://humanities.uchicago.edu/orgs/cgs/Trans%20Conference%20Audio%20Files/Session%202_Intro_Meyerowitz.mp3>.

Stryker, Susan. "(De)Subjugated Knowledges: An Introduction to Transgender Studies." *The Transgender Studies Reader.* Ed. Susan Stryker and Stephen Whittle. New York: Routledge, 2006. 1–18.

_____. "Introduction: The Transgender Issue." *GLQ: A Journal of Lesbian and Gay Studies* 4.2 (1998): 145–58.

_____. "My Words to Victor Frankenstein Above the Village of Chamounix: Performing Transgender Rage." *GLQ: A Journal of Lesbian and Gay Studies* 1.3 (1994): 237–54.

_____. "Transgender Studies: Queer Theory's Evil Twin." *GLQ: A Journal of Lesbian and Gay Studies* 10.2 (2004): 212–15.

Sullivan, Nikki. "Transmogrification: (Un)Becoming Others." *The Transgender Studies Reader.* Ed. Susan Stryker and Stephen Whittle. New York: Routledge. 2006. 552–64.

Zalewski, Marysia. "A Conversation with Susan Stryker." *International Feminist Journal of Politics* 5.1 (2003): 118–25.

10 Debunking the Pathology of Poverty

Susan Greenbaum

The House Budget Committee's March 3, 2014 report, *The War on Poverty: 50 Years Later*,[1] states that "the single most important determinant of poverty is family structure," closely followed by a disinclination to work. The sponsor of the report, Rep. Paul Ryan, R-Wisc., claims the problem is single-parent households raising children with neither the desire nor capacity to acquire skills to support themselves as adults—creating a vicious cycle of dependency persisting across generations. He blames government-sponsored social programs for permitting the lazy among us to avoid taking responsibility for themselves and their children, and he believes the cure for this self-inflicted condition is tough love: Poor people need stronger incentives to get off the couch and find a job. . . .

Ryan traces his ideas about family structure to the 1965 Moynihan Report, written by Daniel Patrick Moynihan, then an assistant secretary in the Department of Labor and later a United States senator from New York. Moynihan argued that poverty is perpetuated by defective cultural values, an idea more generally known as the culture of poverty. That term was coined in 1959 by Oscar Lewis, an anthropologist, and was used repeatedly by Michael Harrington, a popular journalist who wrote about American poverty, but as a theory it was heavily disputed by most social scientists until the mid-1980s. With the rise of conservative politics and periodic declines in the economy, this allegedly scientific concept has repeatedly served as a convenient explanation for persistent inequality, a state of affairs that benefits the wealthy and the politicians who serve their interests. Instead of plumbing the pathologies of elite culture, recently labeled "affluenza," a sociopathic disorder based on too much privilege, most poverty research has focused on the decisions and values of single mothers in poor neighborhoods and their allegedly errant menfolk and delinquent sons.

A Cultural Plague

In his report, officially titled *The Negro Family: The Case for National Action*, Moynihan claimed that African American family values produced too many fatherless households and nurtured what he called a "tangle of pathology," a self-perpetuating, self-defeating cultural flaw responsible for persistently high rates of poverty and violent crime. Conservative columnists and politicians seized on the report, promulgated by a liberal in

Susan Greenbaum is a professor emerita of anthropology at the University of South Florida. She is the author of *Blaming the Poor: The Long Shadow of the Moynihan Report on Cruel Images about Poverty*.

Originally published March 26, 2014, on America.aljazeera.com. Reprinted courtesy of the author.

Lyndon B. Johnson's administration, as official evidence that African American culture was dangerously pathological. Civil rights leaders saw it as an attempt to blame the black community for systemic problems of racial discrimination. A wide spectrum of academic researchers criticized the report, finding errors and mistaken statistical logic; it was a hasty analysis wrapped in provocative rhetoric. Over the next decade, more evidence was brought forth that challenged Moynihan's data and assumptions (and Lewis's). By the late 1970s, the premise that poor people have a distinctive culture that causes them to fail seemed to have been rejected.

Reagan's election in 1980, however, rehabilitated the culture of poverty concept by invoking images of welfare queens and the supposed dangers of a dependent underclass. In 1984, Charles Murray, a fellow at the American Enterprise Institute, wrote a popular book called *Losing Ground,* which claimed harmful social programs and bad behavior by the poor were the main causes of the growing poverty of the era. Liberal academics countered that unemployment in deindustrialized urban areas was the main cause of poverty, though some of their cohort also conceded Moynihan's original premise, arguing that economic failure partly resulted from ineffective parenting within the underclass. Once again, cause and effect were up for grabs, and conservatives (then, as now) opted for the appealing explanation that poor people cause their own problems.

. . . Murray is a coauthor of *The Bell Curve,* published in 1994, which controversially posited a genetic link between race and IQ. His 2008 book, *Coming Apart,* argued that the white lower classes were largely abandoning marriage and family fidelity, that they too have been infected with the tangle of pathology. The steep rise in single-parent households among whites and Latinos is decried as a spreading cultural plague of bad family values, but what these trends actually confirm is the connection between a lagging economy and the ability of poor people to afford marriage.

Charting the poverty rate against other historical data shows that recessions bring steep rises in poverty and recoveries bring declines. The current rate is just over 15 percent (up from 11 percent in 2000), which is where it has been since 2009. It was also that high in 1983 and 1993, both periods of economic decline. Poverty has not returned to the extreme rates of the early 1960s (when it was over 20 percent), before the federal government enacted antipoverty programs, which played an important role in reducing poverty in the recessions that followed. Earlier peaks were short-lived. Today, though, poverty has remained at 15 percent for nearly five years. We are warned that this is the new normal, and, disturbingly, so it seems to be.

Bad Behavior from the Top

So what causes poverty? What precipitates recessions that throw people out of work and curtail vital services in cash-strapped municipalities and states? The last one, which began in 2008, resulted from bad behavior, though not by poor people. Rather, we saw fraudulent and predatory practices by the captains of finance, corrupt behavior by regulators and elected officials, and an ethos condoning exploitation at all levels of the economy, especially against the most vulnerable. These practices are also cultural—driven by the rationalized prerogatives of people with too much wealth and power—and they wreak much more havoc than the shortcomings of poor parents.

For example, the decision of many employers to short workers' wages by not paying for overtime or by altering records of time and tips is a costly cultural choice. The Economic Policy Institute determined[2] that wage theft in 2008 amounted to almost $200 million, nearly four times the haul from all types of robberies in 2009 (about $57 million). The Wall Street–caused collapse of 2008 saw 3.6 million jobs lost and up to 4 million home foreclosures, including a great many black and Latino victims of fraudulent, predatory mortgages. The wealthy perpetrators of this bad behavior have been perversely rewarded. Meanwhile, the racial wealth gap has grown enormously since 2008. Wealth inequality in the United States is greater now than at any time since 1928, and the share funneled to the top 1 percent continues to grow. . . .

The convenient fiction that poverty is self-induced and caused by bad culture has a long pedigree. . . . It is time to put an end to this canard once and for all. Until we stop blaming the wrong people and accept the fact that government can help, we will perpetuate the current dystopic state as the new normal. We need to lift the fog induced by the so-called culture of poverty and recognize that we really could wage an effective war against poverty.

NOTES

1. House Budget Committee Majority Staff (2014, March 3). *The War on Poverty: 50 Years Later*. United States House of Representatives Committee on the Budget.
2. Lafter, G. (2013, October 13). *The Legislative Attack on American Wages and Labor Standards, 2011–2012*. Economic Policy Institute.

11 | Disability and the Justification of Inequality in American History

Douglas C. Baynton

Since the social and political revolutions of the eighteenth century, the trend in Western political thought has been to refuse to take for granted inequalities between persons or groups. Differential and unequal treatment has continued, of course, but it has been considered incumbent on modern societies to produce a rational explanation for such treatment. In recent decades, historians and other scholars in the humanities have studied intensely and often challenged the ostensibly rational explanations for inequalities based on identity—in particular, gender, race, and ethnicity. Disability, however, one of the most prevalent justifications for inequality, has rarely been the subject of historical inquiry.

Disability has functioned historically to justify inequality for disabled people themselves, but it has also done so for women and minority groups. That is, not only has it been considered justifiable to treat disabled people unequally, but the *concept* of disability has been used to justify discrimination against other groups by attributing disability to them. Disability was a significant factor in the three great citizenship debates of the nineteenth and early twentieth centuries: women's suffrage, African American freedom and civil rights, and the restriction of immigration. When categories of citizenship were questioned, challenged, and disrupted, disability was called on to clarify and define who deserved, and who was deservedly excluded from, citizenship. Opponents of political and social equality for women cited their supposed physical, intellectual, and psychological flaws, deficits, and deviations from the male norm. These flaws—irrationality, excessive emotionality, physical weakness—are in essence mental, emotional, and physical disabilities, although they are rarely discussed or examined as such. Arguments for racial inequality and immigration restrictions invoked supposed tendencies to feeble mindedness, mental illness, deafness, blindness, and other disabilities in particular races and ethnic groups. Furthermore, disability figured prominently not just in arguments *for* the inequality of women and minorities but also in arguments *against* those inequalities. Such arguments took the form of vigorous denials that the groups in question actually had these disabilities; they were not disabled, the argument went, and therefore were not proper subjects for discrimination. Rarely have oppressed groups denied that disability is an adequate justification for social and political inequality. Thus, while disabled people can be considered one of

---

Douglas C. Baynton is a professor of history at the University of Iowa. His work focuses on the history of disability in the United States and its relationship with nativism, eugenics, racial stereotyping, and gender roles.

the minority groups historically assigned inferior status and subjected to discrimination, disability has functioned for all such groups as a sign of and justification for inferiority. . . .

The metaphor of the natural versus the monstrous was a fundamental way of constructing social reality in Edmund Burke's time. By the late nineteenth and early twentieth centuries, however, the concept of the natural was to a great extent displaced or subsumed by the concept of normality.[1] Since then, normality has been deployed in all aspects of modern life as a means of measuring, categorizing, and managing populations (and resisting such management). Normality is a complex concept, with an etiology that includes the rise of the social sciences, the science of statistics, and industrialization with its need for interchangeable parts and interchangeable workers. It has been used in a remarkable range of contexts and with a bewildering variety of connotations. The natural and the normal both are ways of establishing the universal, unquestionable good and right. Both are also ways of establishing social hierarchies that justify the denial of legitimacy and certain rights to individuals or groups. Both are constituted in large part by being set in opposition to culturally variable notions of disability—just as the natural was meaningful in relation to the monstrous and the deformed, so are the cultural meanings of the normal produced in tandem with disability[2]. . . .

The concept of normality in its modern sense arose in the mid-nineteenth century in the context of a pervasive belief in progress. It became a culturally powerful idea with the advent of evolutionary theory. . . .

As an evolutionary concept, normality was intimately connected to the Western notion of progress. By the mid-nineteenth century, nonwhite races were routinely connected to people with disabilities, both of whom were depicted as evolutionary laggards or throwbacks. As a consequence, the concept of disability, intertwined with the concept of race, was also caught up in ideas of evolutionary progress. Physical or mental abnormalities were commonly depicted as instances of atavism, reversions to earlier stages of evolutionary development. Down's syndrome, for example, was called mongolism by the doctor who first identified it in 1866 because he believed the syndrome to be the result of a biological reversion by Caucasians to the Mongol racial type. Teachers of the deaf at the end of the century spoke of making deaf children more like "normal" people and less like savages by forbidding them the use of sign language, and they opposed deaf marriages with a rhetoric of evolutionary progress and decline. . . .

Disability arguments were prominent in justifications of slavery in the early to mid-nineteenth century and of other forms of unequal relations between white and black Americans after slavery's demise. The most common disability argument for slavery was simply that African Americans lacked sufficient intelligence to participate or compete on an equal basis in society with white Americans. This alleged deficit was sometimes attributed to physical causes, as when an article on the "diseases and physical peculiarities of the negro race" in the *New Orleans Medical and Surgical Journal* helpfully explained, "It is the defective hematosis, or atmospherization of the blood, conjoined with a deficiency of cerebral matter in the cranium, and an excess of nervous matter distributed to the organs of sensation and assimilation, that is the true cause of that debasement of mind, which has rendered the people of Africa unable to take care of themselves." Diseases of blacks were commonly attributed to "inferior organisms and constitutional weaknesses," which were claimed to be among "the most pronounced race characteristics of the American negro." While the supposedly higher intelligence of "mulattos" compared to "pure" blacks was offered as evidence for the superiority of whites, those who argued against "miscegenation" claimed to the contrary that the products of "race-mixing" were themselves less intelligent and less healthy than members of either race in "pure" form.[3] A medical doctor, John Van Evrie of New York, avowed that the "disease and disorganization" in the "abnormal," "blotched, deformed" offspring of this "monstrous" act "could no more exist beyond a given period than any other physical degeneration, no more than tumors, cancers, or other abnormal growths or physical disease can become permanent." Some claimed greater "corporeal vigor" for "mixed offspring" but a deterioration in "moral and intellectual endowments," while still others saw greater intelligence but "frailty," "less stamina," and "inherent physical weakness."[4]

A second line of disability argument was that African Americans, because of their inherent physical and mental weaknesses, were prone to become disabled under conditions of freedom and equality. A New York medical journal reported that deafness was three times more common and blindness twice as common among free blacks in the North compared to slaves in the South. John C. Calhoun, senator from South Carolina and one of the most influential spokesmen for the slave states, thought it a powerful argument in defense of slavery that the "number of deaf and dumb, blind, idiots, and insane, of the negroes in the States that have changed the ancient relation between the races" was seven times higher than in the slave states.[5]

While much has been written about the justification of slavery by religious leaders in the South, more needs to be said about similar justifications by medical doctors. Dr. Samuel Cartwright, in 1851, for example, described two types of mental illness to which African Americans were especially subject. The first, Drapetomania, a condition that caused slaves to run away—"as much a disease of the mind as any other species of mental alienation"—was common among slaves whose masters had "made themselves too familiar with them, treating them as equals." The need to submit to a master was built into the very bodies of African Americans, in whom "we see 'genu flexit' written in the physical structure of his knees, being more flexed or bent, than any other kind of man." The second mental disease peculiar to African Americans, Dysaesthesia Aethiopis—a unique ailment differing "from every other species of mental disease, as it is accompanied with physical signs or lesions of the body"—resulted in a desire to avoid work and generally to cause mischief. It was commonly known to overseers as "rascality." Its cause, similar to that of Drapetomania, was a lack of firm governance, and it was therefore far more common among free blacks than among slaves—indeed, nearly universal among them—although it was a "common occurrence on badly-governed plantations" as well.[6]

Dr. Van Evrie also contributed to this line of thought when he wrote in the 1860s that education of African Americans came "at the expense of the body, shortening the existence" and resulted in bodies "dwarfed or destroyed" by the unnatural exertion. "An 'educated negro,' like a 'free negro,' is a social monstrosity, even more unnatural and repulsive than the latter." He argued further that, since they belonged to a race inferior by nature, *all* blacks were necessarily inferior to (nearly) *all* whites. It occasionally happened that a particular white person might not be superior to all black people because of a condition

that "deforms or blights individuals; they may be idiotic, insane, or otherwise incapable."
But these unnatural exceptions to the rule were "the result of human vices, crimes, or
ignorance, immediate or remote." Only disability might lower a white person in the scale
of life to the level of being of a marked race.[7] . . .

Daryl Michael Scott has described how both conservatives and liberals have long used
an extensive repertory of "damage imagery" to describe African Americans. Conservatives
"operated primarily from within a biological framework and argued for the innate inferiority of people of African descent" in order to justify social and political exclusion. Liberals
maintained that social conditions were responsible for black inferiority and used damage imagery to argue for inclusion and rehabilitation; but regardless of their intentions,
Scott argues, liberal damage imagery "reinforced the belief system that made whites feel
superior in the first place." Both the "contempt and pity" of conservatives and liberals—a
phrase that equally well describes historically prevalent attitudes toward disabled people—
framed Americans of African descent as defective. Scott cites the example of Charles S.
Johnson, chair of the social science department and later president of Fisk University,
who told students in a 1928 speech that "the sociologists classify Negroes with cripples,
persons with recognized physical handicaps." Like Johnson, Scott is critical of the fact that
"African Americans were often lumped with the 'defective,' 'delinquent,' and dependent
classes." This is obviously a bad place to be "lumped." Scott does not ask, however, why
that might be the case.[8] The attribution of disease or disability to racial minorities has a
long history. Yet, while many have pointed out the injustice and perniciousness of attributing these qualities to a racial or ethnic group, little has been written about why these attributions are such powerful weapons for inequality, why they were so furiously denied and
condemned by their targets, and what this tells us about our attitudes toward disability.

During the long-running debate over women's suffrage in the nineteenth and early
twentieth centuries, one of the rhetorical tactics of suffrage opponents was to point to
the physical, intellectual, and psychological flaws of women, their frailty, irrationality, and
emotional excesses. By the late nineteenth century, these claims were sometimes expressed
in terms of evolutionary progress; like racial and ethnic minorities, women were said to be
less evolved than white men, their disabilities a result of lesser evolutionary development.
Cynthia Eagle Russett has noted that "women and savages, together with idiots, criminals,
and pathological monstrosities [those with congenital disabilities] were a constant source
of anxiety to male intellectuals in the late nineteenth century."[9] What all shared was an
evolutionary inferiority, the result of arrested development or atavism.

Paralleling the arguments made in defense of slavery, two types of disability argument were used in opposition to women's suffrage: that women had disabilities that
made them incapable of using the franchise responsibly, and that because of their frailty
women would become disabled if exposed to the rigors of political participation. The
American antisuffragist Grace Goodwin, for example, pointed to the "great tempera-
mental disabilities" with which women had to contend: "woman lacks endurance in
things mental. . . . She lacks nervous stability. The suffragists who dismay England are
nervesick women." The second line of argument, which was not incompatible with the
first and often accompanied it, went beyond the claim that women's flaws made them
incapable of exercising equal political and social rights with men to warn that if women

were given those rights, disability would surely follow. This argument is most closely identified with Edward Clarke, author of *Sex in Education; or, A Fair Chance for Girls*. Clarke's argument chiefly concerned education for women, though it was often applied to suffrage as well. Clarke maintained that overuse of the brain among young women was in large part responsible for the "numberless pale, weak, neuralgic, dyspeptic, hysterical, menorraghic, dysmenorrhoeic girls and women" of America. The result of excessive education in this country was "bloodless female faces, that suggest consumption, scrofula, anemia, and neuralgia." An appropriate education designed for their frail constitutions would ensure "a future secure from neuralgia, uterine disease, hysteria, and other derangements of the nervous system."[10]

Similarly, Dr. William Warren Potter, addressing the Medical Society of New York in 1891, suggested that many a mother was made invalid by inappropriate education: "her reproductive organs were dwarfed, deformed, weakened, and diseased, by artificial causes imposed upon her during their development."[11] Dr. A. Lapthorn Smith asserted in *Popular Science Monthly* that educated women were increasingly "sick and suffering before marriage and are physically disabled from performing physiological functions in a normal manner." Antisuffragists likewise warned that female participation in politics invariably led to "nervous prostration" and "hysteria," while Dr. Almroth E. Wright noted the "fact that there is mixed up with the woman's movement much mental disorder." A prominent late nineteenth-century neurophysiologist, Charles L. Dana, estimated that enfranchising women would result in a 25 percent increase in insanity among them and "throw into the electorate a mass of voters of delicate nervous stability . . . which might do injury to itself without promoting the community's good." The answer for Clarke, Potter, and others of like mind was special education suited to women's special needs. As with disabled people today, women's social position was treated as a medical problem that necessitated separate and special care. Those who wrote with acknowledged authority on the "woman question" were doctors. As Clarke wrote, the answer to the "problem of woman's sphere . . . must be obtained from physiology, not from ethics or metaphysics."[12] . . .

Disability figured not just in arguments *for* the inequality of women and minorities, but also in arguments *against* those inequalities. Suffragists rarely challenged the notion that disability justified political inequality and instead disputed the claim that women suffered from these disabilities. Their arguments took three forms: One, women were not disabled and therefore deserved the vote; two, women were being erroneously and slanderously classed with disabled people, with those who were legitimately denied suffrage; and three, women were not naturally or inherently disabled but were *made* disabled by inequality— suffrage would ameliorate or cure these disabilities. . . .

Ethnicity also has been defined by disability. One of the fundamental imperatives in the initial formation of American immigration policy at the end of the nineteenth century was the exclusion of disabled people. Beyond the targeting of disabled people, the concept of disability was instrumental in crafting the image of the undesirable immigrant. The first major federal immigration law, the Act of 1882, prohibited entry to any "lunatic, idiot, or any person unable to take care of himself or herself without becoming a public charge." Those placed in the categories "lunatic" and "idiot" were automatically excluded. The "public charge" provision was intended to encompass people with disabilities more generally and was left to the examining officer's discretion. The criteria for excluding disabled people were steadily tightened as the eugenics movement and popular fears about the decline of the national stock gathered strength. The Act of 1891 replaced the phrase *"unable* to take care of himself or herself without becoming a public charge," with *"likely* to become a public charge." The 1907 law then denied entry to anyone judged "mentally or physically defective, such mental or physical defect being of a nature which *may affect* the ability of such alien to earn a living." These changes considerably lowered the threshold for exclusion and expanded the latitude of immigration officials to deny entry.[13]

The category of persons *automatically* excluded was also steadily expanded. In 1903, people with epilepsy were added and, in addition to those judged insane, "persons who have been insane within five years previous [or] who have had two or more attacks of insanity at any time previously." This was reduced to one "attack" in the 1917 law; the classification of "constitutional psychopathic inferiority" was also added, which inspection regulations described as including "various unstable individuals on the border line between sanity and insanity . . . and persons with abnormal sex instincts."[14] This was the regulation under which, until recently, gays and lesbians were excluded. One of the significant factors in lifting this ban, along with other forms of discrimination against gays and lesbians, was the decision by the American Psychiatric Association in 1973 to remove homosexuality from its list of mental illnesses. That is, once gays and lesbians were declared not to be disabled, discrimination became less justifiable.

Legislation in 1907 added "imbeciles" and "feeble-minded persons" to the list, in addition to "idiots," and regulations for inspectors directed them to exclude persons with "any mental abnormality whatever . . . which justifies the statement that the alien is mentally defective." These changes encompassed a much larger number of people and again granted officials considerably more discretion to judge the fitness of immigrants for American life. Fiorello H. LaGuardia, who worked his way through law school as an interpreter at Ellis Island, later wrote that "over fifty percent of the deportations for alleged mental disease were unjustified," based as they often were on "ignorance on the part of the immigrants or the doctors and the inability of the doctors to understand the particular immigrant's norm, or standard."[15]

The detection of physical disabilities was a major aspect of the immigration inspector's work. The Regulations for the medical inspection of immigrants in 1917 included a long list of diseases and disabilities that could be cause for exclusion, among them arthritis, asthma, bunions, deafness, deformities, flat feet, heart disease, hernia, hysteria, poor eyesight, poor physical development, spinal curvature, vascular disease of the heart, and varicose veins. . . .

In short, the exclusion of disabled people was central to the laws and the work of the immigration service. As the Commissioner General of Immigration reported in 1907, "The exclusion from this country of the morally, mentally, and physically deficient is the principal object to be accomplished by the immigration laws." Once the laws and procedures limiting the entry of disabled people were firmly established and functioning well, attention turned to limiting the entry of undesirable ethnic groups. Discussion on this topic often began by pointing to the general public agreement that the laws excluding disabled people had been a positive, if insufficient, step. In 1896, for example, Francis Walker noted in the *Atlantic Monthly* that the necessity of "straining out" immigrants who were "deaf, dumb, blind, idiotic, insane, pauper, or criminal" was "now conceded by men of all shades of opinion"; indeed there was a widespread "resentment at the attempt of such persons to impose themselves upon us."[16] . . .

For the more controversial business of defining and excluding undesirable ethnic groups, however, restrictionists found the *concept* of disability to be a powerful tool. That is, while people with disabilities constituted a distinct category of persons unwelcome in the United States, the charge that certain ethnic groups were mentally and physically deficient was instrumental in arguing for *their* exclusion. The belief that discriminating on the basis of disability was justifiable in turn helped justify the creation of immigration quotas based on ethnic origin. The 1924 Immigration Act instituted a national quota system that severely limited the numbers of immigrants from southern and eastern Europe, but long before that, disabilities stood in for nationality. Superintendents of institutions, philanthropists, immigration reformers, and politicians had been warning for decades before 1924 that immigrants were disproportionately prone to be mentally defective—up to half the immigrants from southern and eastern Europe were feebleminded, according to expert opinion.[17] Rhetoric about "the slow-witted Slav," the "neurotic condition of our Jewish immigrants," and, in general, the "degenerate and psychopathic types, which are so conspicuous and numerous among the immigrants," was pervasive in the debate over restriction.[18] The laws forbidding entry to the feebleminded were motivated in part by the desire to limit immigration from inferior nations, and conversely, it was assumed that the 1924 act would reduce the number of feebleminded immigrants. The issues of ethnicity and disability were so intertwined in the immigration debate as to be inseparable. . . .

Historians have scrutinized the attribution of mental and physical inferiority based on race and ethnicity, but only to condemn the slander. With their attention confined to ethnic stereotypes, they have largely ignored what the attribution of disability might also tell us about attitudes toward disabled people. Racial and ethnic prejudice is exposed while prejudice against people with disabilities is passed over as insignificant and understandable. As a prominent advocate of restriction wrote in 1930, "The necessity of the exclusion of the crippled, the blind, those who are likely to become public charges, and, of course, those with a criminal record is self evident."[19] The necessity has been treated as self-evident by historians as well, so much so that even the possibility of discrimination against people with disabilities in immigration law has gone unrecognized. In historical accounts, disability is present but rendered invisible or insignificant. While it is certain that immigration restriction rests in good part on a fear of "strangers in the land," in John Higham's phrase, American immigration restriction at the turn of the century was also clearly fueled by a fear of *defectives* in the land.

Still today, women and other groups who face discrimination on the basis of identity respond angrily to accusations that they might be characterized by physical, mental, or emotional disabilities. Rather than challenging the basic assumptions behind the hierarchy, they instead work to remove themselves from the negatively marked categories—that is, to disassociate themselves from those people who "really are" disabled—knowing that such categorization invites discrimination. For example, a recent proposal in Louisiana to permit pregnant women to use parking spaces reserved for people with mobility impairments was opposed by women's organizations. A lobbyist for the Women's Health Foundation said, "We've spent a long time trying to dispel the myth that pregnancy is a disability, for obvious reasons of discrimination." She added, "I have no problem with it being a courtesy, but not when a legislative mandate provides for pregnancy in the same way as for disabled persons."[20] To be associated with disabled people or with the accommodations accorded disabled people is stigmatizing. . . .

This common strategy for attaining equal rights, which seeks to distance one's own group from imputations of disability and therefore tacitly accepts the idea that disability is a legitimate reason for inequality, is perhaps one of the factors responsible for making discrimination against people with disabilities so persistent and the struggle for disability rights so difficult. . . .

Disability is everywhere in history, once you begin looking for it, but conspicuously absent in the histories we write. When historians do take note of disability, they usually treat it merely as personal tragedy or an insult to be deplored and a label to be denied, rather than as a cultural construct to be questioned and explored. Those of us who specialize in the history of disability, like the early historians of other minority groups, have concentrated on writing histories of disabled people and the institutions and laws associated with disability. This is necessary and exciting work. It is through this work that we are building the case that disability is culturally constructed rather than natural and timeless—that disabled people have a history, and a history worth studying. Disability, however, more than an identity, is a fundamental element in cultural signification and indispensable for *any* historian seeking to make sense of the past. It may well be that all social hierarchies have drawn on culturally constructed and socially sanctioned notions of disability. If this is so, then there is much work to do. It is time to bring disability from the margins to the center of historical inquiry.

NOTES

1. Ian Hacking, *The Taming of Chance* (Cambridge and New York: Cambridge University Press, 1990), 160–66. See also Georges Canguilhem, *The Normal and the Pathological* (New York: Zone Books, 1989); Douglas C. Baynton, *Forbidden Signs: American Culture and the Campaign against Sign Language* (Chicago: University of Chicago Press, 1996), chaps. 5–6.

2. Francois Ewald, "Norms, Discipline, and the Law," *Representations* 30 (Spring 1990): 146, 149–150, 154; Lennard Davis, *Enforcing Normalcy: Disability, Deafness, and the Body* (London: Verso, 1995); Baynton, *Forbidden Signs*, chaps. 5 and 6.

3. Samuel A. Cartwright, "Report on the Diseases and Physical Peculiarities of the Negro Race," *New Orleans Medical and Surgical Journal* 7 (May 1851): 693; George M. Fredrickson, *The Black Image in the White Mind* (New York: Harper and Row, 1971), 250–51; J. C. Nott, "The Mulatto a Hybrid," *American Journal of Medical Sciences* (July 1843), quoted in Samuel Forry, "Vital Statistics Furnished by the Sixth Census of the United States," *New York Journal of Medicine and the Collateral Sciences* 1 (September 1843): 151–53.

4. John H. Van Evrie, *White Supremacy and Negro Subordination, or Negroes a Subordinate Race* (New York: Van Evrie, Horton, & Co., 1868), 153–55; Forry, "Vital Statistics," 159; Paul B. Barringer, *The American Negro: His Past and Future* (Raleigh: Edwards & Broughton, 1900), 10.

5. Cited in Forry, "Vital Statistics," 162–63. John C. Calhoun, "Mr. Calhoun to Mr. Pakenham," in Richard K. Cralle, ed., *The Works of John C. Calhoun* (New York: D. Appleton, 1888), 5:337.

6. Cartwright, "Report," 707–10. See also Thomas S. Szasz, "The Sane Slave: A Historical Note on the use of Medical Diagnosis as Justificatory Rhetoric," *American Journal of Psychotherapy* 25 (1971): 228–39.

7. Van Evrie, *White Supremacy*, 121, 181, 221. Van Evrie notes in his preface that the book was completed "about the time of Mr. Lincoln's election" and was therefore originally an argument in favor of the continuation of slavery, but presently constituted an argument for its restoration.

8. Daryl Michael Scott, *Contempt and Pity: Social Policy and the Image of the Damaged Black Soul, 1880–1996* (Chapel Hill: University of North Carolina Press, 1997), xi–xvii; 12, 208 n. 52.

9. Cynthia Eagle Russett, *Sexual Science: The Victorian Construction of Womanhood* (Cambridge, Mass.: Harvard University Press, 1989), 63. See also Lois N. Magner, "Darwinism and the Woman Question: The Evolving Views of Charlotte Perkins Gilman," in Joanne Karpinski, ed., *Critical Essays on Charlotte Perkins Gilman* (New York: G. K. Hall, 1992), 119–20.

10. Grace Duffield Goodwin, *Anti-Suffrage: Ten Good Reasons* (New York: Duffield and Co., 1913), 91–92 (in Smithsonian Institution Archives, Collection 60 — Warshaw Collection, "Women," Box 3). Edward Clarke, *Sex in Education; or, A Fair Chance for Girls* (1873; reprint, New York: Arno Press, 1972), 18, 22, 62.

11. William Warren Potter, "How Should Girls Be Educated? A Public Health Problem for Mothers, Educators, and Physicians," *Transactions of the Medical Society of the State of New York* (1891): 48, quoted in Martha H. Verbrugge, *Able-Bodied Womanhood: Personal Health and Social Change in Nineteenth-Century Boston* (Oxford and New York: Oxford University Press, 1988), 121.

12. A. Lapthorn Smith, "Higher Education of Women and Race Suicide," *Popular Science Monthly* (March 1905), reprinted in Louise Michele Newman, ed., *Men's Ideas/Women's Realities: Popular Science, 1870–1915* (New York: Pergamon Press, 1985), 149; Almroth E. Wright quoted in Mara Mayor, "Fears and Fantasies of the Anti-Suffragists," *Connecticut Review* 7 (April 1974): 67; Charles L. Dana quoted in Jane Jerome Camhi, *Women against Women: American Anti-Suffragism, 1880–1920* (New York: Carlson Publishing Co., 1994), 18; Clarke, *Sex in Education*, 12.

13. *United States Statutes at Large* (Washington, D.C.: Government Printing Office, 1883), 22:214. *United States Statutes at Large* (Washington, D.C.: Government Printing Office, 1891), 26:1084; *United States Statutes at Large* (Washington, D.C.: Government Printing Office, 1907), 34:899. Emphases added.

14. *United States Statutes at Large* (Washington, D.C.: Government Printing Office, 1903), 32:1213; United States Public Health Service, *Regulations Governing the Medical Inspection of Aliens* (Washington, D.C.: Government Printing Office, 1917), 28–29.

15. *Statutes* (1907), 34:899; United States Public Health Service, *Regulations*, 30–31; Fiorello H. LaGuardia, *The Making of an Insurgent: An Autobiography, 1882–1919* (1948; reprint, New York: Capricorn, 1961), 65.

16. U.S. Bureau of Immigration, *Annual Report of the Commissioner of Immigration* (Washington, D.C.: Government Printing Office, 1907), 62; Francis A. Walker, "Restriction of Immigration," *Atlantic Monthly* 77 (June 1896): 822; Ellsworth Eliot, Jr., M.D., "Immigration," in Madison Grant and Charles Steward Davison, eds., *The Alien in Our Midst, or Selling Our Birthright for a Mess of Industrial Pottage* (New York: Galton Publishing Co., 1930), 101.

17. See James W. Trent, Jr., *Inventing the Feeble Mind: A History of Mental Retardation in the United States* (Berkeley: University of California Press, 1994), 166–69.

18. Thomas Wray Grayson, "The Effect of the Modern Immigrant on Our Industrial Centers" in *Medical Problems of Immigration* (Easton, Penn.: American Academy of Medicine, 1913), 103, 107–9.

19. Ellsworth Eliot, Jr., M.D., "Immigration," in Grant and Davison, *Alien in Our Midst*, 101.

20. Heather Salerno, "Mother's Little Dividend: Parking," *Washington Post* (September 16, 1997): A1.

12 | Domination and Subordination
Jean Baker Miller

What do people do to people who are different from them and why? On the individual level, the child grows only via engagement with people very different from her/himself. Thus, the most significant difference is between the adult and the child. At the level of humanity in general, we have seen massive problems around a great variety of differences. But the most basic difference is the one between women and men.

On both levels it is appropriate to pose two questions. When does the engagement of difference stimulate the development and the enhancement of both parties to the engagement? And, conversely, when does such a confrontation with difference have negative effects: When does it lead to great difficulty, deterioration, and distortion and to some of the worst forms of degradation, terror, and violence—both for individuals and for groups—that human beings can experience? It is clear that "mankind" in general, especially in our Western tradition but in some others as well, does not have a very glorious record in this regard.

It is not always clear that in most instances of difference there is also a factor of inequality—inequality of many kinds of resources, but fundamentally of status and power. One useful way to examine the often confusing results of these confrontations with difference is to ask: What happens in situations of inequality? What forces are set in motion? While we will be using the terms "dominant" and "subordinate" in the discussion, it is useful to remember that flesh and blood women and men are involved. Speaking in abstractions sometimes permits us to accept what we might not admit to on a personal level.

Temporary Inequality

Two types of inequality are pertinent for present purposes. The first might be called temporary inequality. Here, the lesser party is *socially* defined as unequal. Major examples are the relationships between parents and children, teachers and students, and, possibly, therapists and clients. There are certain assumptions in these relationships which are often not made explicit, nor, in fact, are they carried through. But they are the social structuring of the relationship.

The "superior" party presumably has more of some ability or valuable quality, which she/he is supposed to impart to the "lesser" person. While these abilities vary with the particular

Jean Baker Miller (1927–2006) was the founding director of the Jean Baker Miller Training Institute at the Wellesley Centers for Women. A practicing psychiatrist and psychoanalyst for over 40 years, Miller authored the groundbreaking 1976 work *Toward a New Psychology of Women*.

relationship, they include emotional maturity, experience in the world, physical skills, a body of knowledge, or the techniques for acquiring certain kinds of knowledge. The superior person is supposed to engage with the lesser in such a way as to bring the lesser member up to full parity; that is, the child is to be helped to become the adult. Such is the overall task of this relationship. The lesser, the child, is to be given to, by the person who presumably has more to give. Although the lesser party often also gives much to the superior, these relationships are *based in service* to the lesser party. That is their *raison d'être*.

It is clear, then, that the paramount goal is to end the relationship; that is, to end the relationship of inequality. The period of disparity is meant to be temporary. People may continue their association as friends, colleagues, or even competitors, but not as "superior" and "lesser." At least, this is the goal.

The reality is that we have trouble enough with this sort of relationship. Parents or professional institutions often tip toward serving the needs of the donor instead of those of the lesser party (for example, schools can come to serve teachers or administrators, rather than students). Or the lesser person learns how to be a good "lesser" rather than how to make the journey from lesser to full stature. Overall, we have not found very good ways to carry out the central task: to foster the movement from unequal to equal. In childrearing and education we do not have an adequate theory and practice. Nor do we have concepts that work well in such other unequal so-called "helping" relationships as healing, penology, and rehabilitation. Officially, we say we want to do these things, but we often fail.

We have a great deal of trouble deciding on how many rights "to allow" to the lesser party. We agonize about how much power the lesser party shall have. How much can the lesser person express or act on her or his perceptions when these definitely differ from those of the superior? Above all, there is great difficulty in maintaining the conception of the lesser person *as a person of as much intrinsic worth as the superior*.

A crucial point is that power is a major factor in all of these relationships. But power alone will not suffice. Power exists and it has to be taken into account, not denied. The superiors hold all the real power, but power will not accomplish *the task*. It will not bring the unequal party up to equality.

Our troubles with these relationships may stem from the fact that they exist within the context of a second type of inequality that tends to overwhelm the ways we learn to operate in the first kind. The second type molds the very ways we perceive and conceptualize what we are doing in the first, most basic kind of relationships.

The second type of inequality teaches us how to enforce inequality, but not how to make the journey from unequal to equal. Most importantly, its consequences are kept amazingly obscure — in fact they are usually denied. . . . However, the underlying notion is that this second type has determined, and still determines, the only ways we can think and feel in the first type.

Permanent Inequality

In these relationships, some people or groups of people are defined as unequal by means of what sociologists call ascription; that is, your birth defines you. Criteria may be race, sex, class, nationality, religion, or other characteristics ascribed at birth. Here, the terms of the relationships are very different from those of temporary inequality. There is, for example, no notion that superiors are present primarily to help inferiors, to impart to them their advantages and "desirable" characteristics. There is no assumption that the goal of the unequal relationship is to end the inequality; in fact, quite the reverse. A series of other governing tendencies are in force, and occur with great regularity. . . . While some of these elements may appear obvious, in fact there is a great deal of disagreement and confusion about psychological characteristics brought about by conditions as obvious as these.

Dominants

Once a group is defined as inferior, the superiors tend to label it as defective or substandard in various ways. These labels accrete rapidly. Thus, blacks are described as less intelligent than whites, women are supposed to be ruled by emotion, and so on. In addition, the actions and words of the dominant group tend to be destructive of the subordinates. All historical evidence confirms this tendency. And, although they are much less obvious, there are destructive effects on the dominants as well. The latter are of a different order and are much more difficult to recognize.

Dominant groups usually define one or more acceptable roles for the subordinate. Acceptable roles typically involve providing services that no dominant group wants to perform for itself (for example, cleaning up the dominant's waste products). Functions that a dominant group prefers to perform, on the other hand, are carefully guarded and closed to subordinates. Out of the total range of human possibilities, the activities most highly valued in any particular culture will tend to be enclosed within the domain of the dominant group; less-valued functions are relegated to the subordinates.

Subordinates are usually said to be unable to perform the preferred roles. Their incapacities are ascribed to innate defects or deficiencies of mind or body, therefore immutable and impossible of change or development. It becomes difficult for dominants even to imagine that subordinates are capable of performing the preferred activities. More importantly, subordinates themselves can come to find it difficult to believe in their own ability. The myth of their inability to fulfill wider or more valued roles is challenged only when a drastic event disrupts the usual arrangements. Such disruptions usually arise from outside the relationship itself. For instance, in the emergency situation of World War II, "incompetent" women suddenly "manned" the factories with great skill.

It follows that subordinates are described in terms of, and encouraged to develop, personal psychological characteristics that are pleasing to the dominant group. These characteristics form a certain familiar cluster: submissiveness, passivity, docility, dependency, lack of initiative, inability to act, to decide, to think, and the like. In general, this cluster includes qualities more characteristic of children than adults—immaturity, weakness, and helplessness. If subordinates adopt these characteristics, they are considered well-adjusted.

However, when subordinates show the potential for, or even more dangerously have developed, other characteristics—let us say intelligence, initiative, assertiveness—there is usually no room available within the dominant framework for acknowledgement of these characteristics. Such people will be defined as at least unusual, if not definitely abnormal.

There will be no opportunities for the direct application of their abilities within the social arrangements. (How many women have pretended to be dumb!)

Dominant groups usually impede the development of subordinates and block their freedom of expression and action. They also tend to militate against stirrings of greater rationality or greater humanity in their own members. It was not too long ago that "nigger lover" was a common appellation, and even now men who "allow their women" more than the usual scope are subject to ridicule in many circles.

A dominant group, inevitably, has the greatest influence in determining a culture's overall outlook — its philosophy, morality, social theory, and even its science. The dominant group, thus, legitimizes the unequal relationship and incorporates it into society's guiding concepts. The social outlook, then, obscures the true nature of this relationship — that is, the very existence of inequality. The culture explains the events that take place in terms of other premises, premises that are inevitably false, such as racial or sexual inferiority. While in recent years we have learned about many such falsities on the larger social level, a full analysis of the psychological implications still remains to be developed. In the case of women, for example, despite overwhelming evidence to the contrary, the notion persists that women are meant to be passive, submissive, docile, secondary. From this premise, the outcome of therapy and encounters with psychology and other "sciences" are often determined.

Inevitably, the dominant group is the model for "normal human relationships." It then becomes "normal" to treat others destructively and to derogate them, to obscure the truth of what you are doing, by creating false explanations, and to oppose actions toward equality. In short, if one's identification is with the dominant group, it is "normal" to continue in this pattern. Even though most of us do not like to think of ourselves as either believing in, or engaging in, such dominations, it is, in fact, difficult for a member of a dominant group to do otherwise. But to keep on doing these things, one need only behave "normally."

It follows from this that dominant groups generally do not like to be told about or even quietly reminded of the existence of inequality. "Normally" they can avoid awareness because their explanation of the relationship becomes so well integrated *in other terms*; they can even believe that both they and the subordinate group share the same interests and, to some extent, a common experience. If pressed a bit, the familiar rationalizations are offered: The home is "women's natural place," and we know "what's best for them anyhow."

Dominants prefer to avoid conflict — open conflict that might call into question the whole situation. This is particularly and tragically so when many members of the dominant group are not having an easy time of it themselves. Members of a dominant group, or at least some segments of it, such as white working-class men (who are themselves also subordinates), often feel unsure of their own narrow toehold on the material and psychological bounties they believe they desperately need. What dominant groups usually cannot act on, or even see, is that the situation of inequality in fact deprives them, particularly on the psychological level.

Clearly, inequality has created a state of conflict. Yet dominant groups will tend to suppress conflict. They will see any questioning of the "normal" situation as threatening; activities by subordinates in this direction will be perceived with alarm. Dominants are usually convinced that the way things are is right and good, not only for them but especially for the subordinates. All morality confirms this view, and all social structure sustains it.

It is perhaps unnecessary to add that the dominant group usually holds all of the open power and authority, and determines the ways in which power may be acceptably used.

Subordinates

What of the subordinates' part in this? Since dominants determine what is normal for a culture, it is much more difficult to understand subordinates. Initial expressions of dissatisfaction and early actions by subordinates always come as a surprise; they are usually rejected as atypical. After all, dominants *knew* that all women needed and wanted was a man around whom to organize their lives. Members of the dominant group do not understand why "they"—the first to speak out—are so upset and angry.

The characteristics that typify the subordinates are even more complex. A subordinate group has to concentrate on basic survival. Accordingly, direct, honest reaction to destructive treatment is avoided. Open, self-initiated action in its own self-interest must also be avoided. Such actions can, and still do, literally result in death for some subordinate groups. In our own society, a woman's direct action can result in a combination of economic hardship, social ostracism, and psychological isolation—and even the diagnosis of a personality disorder. Any one of these consequences is bad enough. . . .

It is not surprising then that a subordinate group resorts to disguised and indirect ways of acting and reacting. While these actions are designed to accommodate and please the dominant group, they often, in fact, contain hidden defiance and "put-ons." Folk tales, black jokes, and women stories are often based on how the wily peasant or sharecropper outwitted the rich landowner, boss, or husband. The essence of the story rests on the fact that the overlord does not even know that he has been made a fool of.

One important result of this indirect mode of operation is that members of the dominant group are denied an essential part of life—the opportunity to acquire self-understanding through knowing their impact on others. They are thus deprived of "consensual validation," feedback, and a chance to correct their actions and expressions. Put simply, subordinates won't tell. For the same reasons, the dominant group is deprived also of valid knowledge about the subordinates. (It is particularly ironic that the societal "experts" in knowledge about subordinates are usually members of the dominant group.)

Subordinates, then, know much more about the dominants than vice versa. They have to. They become highly attuned to the dominants, able to predict their reactions of pleasure and displeasure. Here, I think, is where the long story of "feminine intuition" and "feminine wiles" begins. It seems clear that these "mysterious" gifts are in fact skills, developed through long practice, in reading many small signals, both verbal and nonverbal.

Another important result is that subordinates often know more about the dominants than they know about themselves. If a large part of your fate depends on accommodating to and pleasing the dominants, you concentrate on them. Indeed, there is little purpose in knowing yourself. Why should you when your knowledge of the dominants determines your life? This tendency is reinforced by many other restrictions. One can know oneself only through action and interaction. To the extent that their range of action or interaction is limited, subordinates will lack a realistic evaluation of their capacities and problems. Unfortunately, this difficulty in gaining self-knowledge is even further compounded.

Tragic confusion arises because subordinates absorb a large part of the untruths created by the dominants; there are a great many blacks who feel inferior to whites, and women who still believe they are less important than men. This internalization of dominant beliefs is more likely to occur if there are few alternative concepts at hand. On the other hand, it is also true that members of the subordinate group have certain experiences and perceptions that accurately reflect the truth about themselves and the injustice of their position. Their own more truthful concepts are bound to come into opposition with the mythology they have absorbed from the dominant group. An inner tension between the two sets of concepts and their derivations is almost inevitable.

From a historical perspective, despite the obstacles, subordinate groups have tended to move toward greater freedom of expression and action, although this progress varies greatly from one circumstance to another. There were always some slaves who revolted; there were some women who sought greater development or self-determination. Most records of these actions are not preserved by the dominant culture, making it difficult for the subordinate group to find a supporting tradition and history.

Within each subordinate group, there are tendencies for some members to imitate the dominants. This imitation can take various forms. Some may try to treat their fellow subordinates as destructively as the dominants treat them. A few may develop enough of the qualities valued by the dominants to be partially accepted into their fellowship. Usually they are not wholly accepted, and even then only if they are willing to forsake their own identification with fellow subordinates. "Uncle Toms" and certain professional women have often been in this position. (There are always a few women who have won the praise presumably embodied in the phrase "she thinks like a man.")

To the extent that subordinates move toward freer expression and action, they will expose the inequality and throw into question the basis for its existence. And they will make the inherent conflict an open conflict. They will then have to bear the burden and take the risks that go with being defined as "troublemakers." Since this role flies in the face of their conditioning, subordinates, especially women, do not come to it with ease.

What is immediately apparent from studying the characteristics of the two groups is that mutually enhancing interaction is not probable between unequals. Indeed, conflict is inevitable. The important questions, then, become: Who defines the conflict? Who sets the terms? When is conflict overt or covert? On what issues is the conflict fought? Can anyone win? Is conflict "bad," by definition? If not, what makes for productive or destructive conflict?

PART I

SUGGESTIONS FOR FURTHER READING

Ahmed, Sara. *Strange Encounters: Embodied Others in Post-Coloniality*. Routledge, 2000.

Alba, Richard D. *Ethnic Identity: The Transformation of White American Identity*. Yale University Press, 1990.

Blazina, Chris. *Cultural Myth of Masculinity*. Praeger Publishers, 2003.

Butler, Judith. *Undoing Gender*. Routledge, 2004.

Connell, R. W. *Masculinities*, 2nd ed. University of California Press, 2005.

Crenshaw, Kimberlé, Neil Gotanda, Gary Peller, and Kendall Thomas, eds. *Critical Race Theory: The Key Writings That Formed the Movement*. The New Press, 1995.

de Beauvoir, Simone. *The Second Sex*. Alfred A. Knopf, 1952.

Dunbar-Ortiz, Roxanne. *An Indigenous Peoples' History of the United States*. Beacon Press, 2015.

Fausto-Sterling, Anne. *Sexing the Body: Gender Politics and the Construction of Sexuality*. Basic Books, 2000.

Feinberg, Leslie. *Transgender Warriors: Making History from Joan of Arc to Dennis Rodman*. Beacon Press, 1997.

Feinberg, Leslie. *Trans Liberation: Beyond Pink or Blue*. Beacon Press, 1999.

Frankenberg, Ruth. *White Women, Race Matters*. University of Minnesota Press, 1993.

Gates, Jr., Henry Louis, and Anthony Appiah. *"Race," Writing, and Difference*. University of Chicago Press, 1986.

Goldberg, David Theo. *Are We All Postracial Yet?* Polity Press, 2015.

Gould, Stephen. *The Mismeasure of Man*. W. W. Norton, 1984.

Greenbaum, Susan. *Blaming the Poor: The Long Shadow of the Moynihan Report on Cruel Images of Poverty*. Rutgers University Press, 2015.

Gregory, Steven, and Roger Sanjek, eds. *Race*. Rutgers University Press, 1994.

Hall, Stuart. *The Fateful Triangle: Race, Ethnicity, Nation*. Harvard University Press, 2017.

Haney López, Ian F. *White by Law: The Legal Construction of Race*. New York University Press, 1996.

Hubbard, Ruth. *The Politics of Women's Biology*. Rutgers University Press, 1990.

Ignatiev, Noel. *How the Irish Became White*. Routledge, 2009.

Katz, Jonathan Ned. *The Invention of Heterosexuality*. University of Chicago Press, 2007.

Kimmel, Michael. *Manhood in America*, 3rd ed. Oxford University Press, 2011.

_____. *Misframing Men: The Politics of Contemporary Masculinities*. Rutgers University Press, 2010.

Kleinman, Sherryl, Martha Copp, and Kent Sandstrom. "Making Sexism Visible: Birdcages, Martians, and Pregnant Men." *Teaching Sociology*, 34 (April 2006), pp. 126–142.

Lorber, Judith. *Paradoxes of Gender*. Yale University Press, 1995.

Lowe, Marion, and Ruth Hubbard, eds. *Women's Nature: Rationalizations of Inequality*. Pergamon Press, 1984.

Marinucci, Mimi. *Feminism Is Queer: The Intimate Connection between Queer and Feminist Theory*, 2nd ed. Zed Books Ltd., 2016.

Markus, Hazel Rose, and Paula M. L. Moya, eds. *Doing Race: 21 Essays for the 21st Century*. W. W. Norton, 2010.

Memmi, Albert. *Dominated Man*. Beacon Press, 1969.

Okamoto, Dina G. *Redefining Race: Asian American Panethnicity and Shifting Ethnic Boundaries*. Russell Sage Foundation, 2014.

Omi, Michael, and Howard Winant. *Racial Formations in the United States,* 3rd ed. Routledge, 2015.

Roberts, Dorothy. *Fatal Invention: How Science, Politics, and Big Business Re-Create Race in the Twenty-First Century.* The New Press, 2012.

Roediger, David. *Colored White: Transcending the Racial Past.* University of California Press, 2003.

_____. *The Wages of Whiteness: Race and the Making of the American Working Class.* Verso, 2007.

Sanday, Peggy R. *Female Power and Male Dominance: On the Origins of Sexual Inequality.* Cambridge University Press, 1981.

Snorton, C. Riley. *Black on Both Sides.* University of Minnesota Press, 2017.

Spence, Lester K. *Knocking the Hustle: Against the Neoliberal Turn in Black Politics.* Punctum Books, 2015.

Stryker, Susan. *Transgender History.* Seal Press, 2008.

Stryker, Susan, and Stephen Whittle, eds. *The Transgender Studies Reader.* Routledge, 2006.

Williams, Gregory Howard. *Life on the Color Line.* Dutton, 1995.

Understanding Racism, Sexism, Heterosexism, and Class Privilege

We simply do not have the luxury of building social movements that are not intersectional, nor can we believe we are doing intersectional work just by saying words.
—KIMBERLÉ CRENSHAW

In Part II, we spend time analyzing social hierarchies and how they incorporate relationships of dominance and subordination almost seamlessly into daily life. Racism, sexism, heterosexism, and class privilege are systems of advantage that provide those with the socially preferred race, sex, gender identity, sexual orientation, and class (or some intersection of these) with opportunities and rewards that are unavailable to other individuals and groups in society. These hierarchies operate in combination to create an overall system of advantage and disadvantage that enhances the life chances of some while constraining the life chances of others.

The construction of difference as deviance or deficiency (as described in the introduction to Part I) underlies the systems of oppression that determine how power, privilege, wealth, and opportunity are distributed. We are surrounded by differences every day, but our society places a value on only some of them. By valuing the characteristics and lifestyles of certain individuals or groups and devaluing those of others, society constructs some of its members as "us" and some as "other." These "others" are understood to be less deserving, less intelligent, even less human than "us." Once this happens, it is possible to distribute wealth, opportunity, and justice unequally without appearing to be unfair. The social construction of race, class, gender, and sexuality as difference—where being white, male, cisgender (i.e., having a gender identity that matches the sex assigned at birth), European, heterosexual, and prosperous confers the highest forms of status and privilege, while everyone else is considered less able and less worthy—lies at the heart of racism, sexism, heterosexism, classism, and other forms of oppression.

Words like "racism," "sexism," and "oppression" emphasize the complex, pervasive, and self-perpetuating nature of the system of beliefs, policies, practices, and attitudes that enforce relationships of subordination and domination. These words capture the specific and comprehensive nature of the systems being studied. The meaning of "oppression," for example, is explained by feminist philosopher Marilyn Frye using the metaphor of a birdcage to illustrate how a system of oppression, in this case sexism, imprisons its victims through a set of interlocking impediments to motion. "It is only when you step back," she argues, "stop looking at the wires one by one, microscopically, and take a macroscopic view of the whole cage, that you can see why the bird does not go anywhere."[1] Taken alone, none of the barriers seems very powerful or threatening; taken together, they are unyielding.

In the first selection, critical race theorist Kimberlé Crenshaw defines the concept of intersectionality and identifies its urgency. Intersectionality provides a framework for examining how racism, sexism, and classism interact to form multiple and compounding layers of oppression. "Intersectionality is an analytic sensibility," she argues, "a way of thinking about identity and its relationship to power." Crucially, it is also a tool for building transformational social movements. Intersectionality means that any combination of different forms of oppression is greater than the sum of its parts. For example, the combination of racism and sexism that black women experience can't be understood by simply adding up the effects of racism and sexism on black women, nor by looking at how sexism affects white women and racism affects black men. Intersectionality calls for an understanding of the specific and simultaneous ways in which different forms of oppression operate on specific groups.

Racism and sexism are *systems of advantage*. They are *systems*—not just isolated incidents of interpersonal prejudice—and they result in *advantages* for their beneficiaries, not just in discrimination against their victims. In the United States, racism is a system that perpetuates an interlocking system of institutions, attitudes, privileges, and rewards that work to the benefit of white people just as sexism works to the advantage of men. In Selection 2, Beverly Daniel Tatum elaborates on this definition of racism (originally offered by David Wellman in his book *Portraits of White Racism*) and discusses the resistance that some of us feel about acknowledging both the existence of racism and the advantages it bestows on people with white privilege. Once racism is defined as a system of advantage based on race, it is no longer possible to attribute racism to people of color in the United States, because they do not systematically benefit from racism; only white people do. This definition of course does not deny that people of all colors are capable of hateful and hurtful beliefs and behaviors. But Tatum reserves the term "racism" to refer specifically to the comprehensive system of advantage that works to the benefit of white people in the United States. Her metaphor comparing systemic oppression to a moving walkway at an airport allows us to see the differences between *active* racism (running on the conveyor belt), *passive* racism (standing still but carried along, receiving the advantages of a racist system), and *active antiracism* ("walking actively in the opposite direction at a speed faster than the conveyor belt"). "The relevant question is not whether all Whites are racist," she writes, "but how we can move more White people from a position of active or passive racism to one of active antiracism."

When Ta-Nehisi Coates states in Selection 3 that "race is the child of racism, not the father," he is arguing that a hierarchical system of exploitation precedes the categories of race deployed to justify that exploitation. As Morales, Omi and Winant, and other writers from Part I also argued, Coates argues that "the process of naming 'the people' has never been a matter of genealogy and physiognomy so much as one of hierarchy." Composed as a letter to his 15-year-old son in the wake of the nonindictment of the Ferguson, Missouri, police officer who killed African American teenager Michael Brown in 2014, the essay tells both a personal and a national story to explore the impact on the black body of centuries of racial plunder.

Ian Haney López further nuances our understanding of racism in Selection 4, going beyond racism viewed as hatred, implicit bias, and structural discrimination. He uses history and contemporary politics to offer a definition of *strategic* racism, in which racism is seen not as racial hatred but rather as the "strategic manipulation of racial antipathies" for political and economic gain. This concept undergirds his notion of dog-whistle politics—"coded racial appeals that carefully manipulate hostility toward nonwhites" without overtly mentioning race.

In Selection 5, Eduardo Bonilla-Silva examines the claim made by many white people in the United States today that racism is a thing of the past and that they personally do not see race or skin color (or, by extension, sex, class, disability, etc.); they just see "human beings." Bonilla-Silva and other sociologists have coined the term "color-blind racism" to refer to this new version of racial ideology. In his essay (a written version of a speech he gave at Texas A&M), Bonilla-Silva argues that, contrary to what many would like to believe, it is not racists and bigots who perpetuate the system of racial inequality in this country, but well-meaning whites as, in their everyday behavior, they simply follow "the racial script of America." In this way, Bonilla-Silva directs our attention to the ways in which white supremacy and white privilege are institutionalized in the ordinary operations of society. He spends most of his essay examining the central frames of color-blind racism that allow many who benefit from white privilege to perpetuate the racial status quo without ever having to face their responsibility for society's ongoing racism. Bonilla-Silva warns us that "[t]oday there is a sanitized, color-blind way" of justifying discrimination with "the language of liberalism" rather than racist epithets.

Angelo Ancheta, in Selection 6, asks us to consider racial relations beyond the binary of black and white, arguing that because legal paradigms, or models, depend on this dichotomous thinking, they are unable to encompass the complexity of the racialization of Asian Americans. Ancheta offers a discussion of anti-Asian violence as illustrative of the racial subordination that Asian Americans experience, emphasizing that the dynamics of immigration and nativism are essential to how race is configured in the United States.

In Selection 7, Evelyn Alsultany offers a series of vignettes to complicate simplistic notions of identity and recast ethnicity as dynamic and intersectional. As a Cuban Iraqi Muslim American woman, she describes encounters with people who refuse to see her in all her intersectional complexity: "Those who otherize me fail to see a shared humanity and those who identify with me fail to see difference."

Joan Griscom, in Selection 8, also examines the complexity of identity and intersecting modes of oppression. The gripping story she tells of a tragedy that hits a young couple becomes much more than just a story of two individuals. "The injustices they encountered," she argues, "were modes of oppression that operate at a social-structural level and affect many other people." While Alsultany focuses on interpersonal encounters, Griscom analyzes the ways in which ableism, heterosexism, and sexism shape how the law recognizes relationships and the challenges that emerge in medical crises involving caregiving and decision making.

The term "sexism" refers to the oppression of women by men in a society that is largely patriarchal. Suzanne Pharr, in Selection 9, defines "heterosexism" as involving the assumption that the world is and must be heterosexual, while it simultaneously rationalizes the existing distribution of power and privilege that flows from this assumption. She argues that economics, violence, and homophobia are the most effective weapons of sexism, and thus homophobia and heterosexism are oppressive of all women, regardless of their sexual orientation. Pharr concludes that "the only successful work against sexism must include work against homophobia."

Finally, "classism" (or "class privilege") refers to the system of advantage that continues to ensure that wealth, power, opportunity, and privilege go hand in hand. In Selection 10, Gregory Mantsios explores some of the myths about class that mislead people about their real-life chances and documents the impact of class position on daily life. Many in the United States are unaware of the full force of class privilege; the statistics in this article suggest that the class position of one's family—not hard work, intelligence, or determination—is probably the single most significant determinant of future success. This gap between people's beliefs about what it takes to succeed and the tremendous role that class privilege plays in determining who is successful provides a dramatic illustration of the effectiveness of dominant narratives both in perpetuating the current systems of advantage and in rendering their continuing operation invisible to so many. This point will be taken up again in Part VIII.

The selections in Part II offer bold and disturbing claims about unequal power and privilege. Many people in dominant groups fail to realize that they are privileged because the systems of oppression so effectively make the current distribution of privilege and power appear almost "natural." In many cases, people with privileges have enjoyed them for so long that they have simply come to take them for granted. Instead of recognizing them as special benefits, they assume that these privileges are things to which they have a right. In Selection 11, Peggy McIntosh offers the illuminating metaphor of an invisible knapsack to explain how white privilege works in powerful but often unseen ways. She points out that as a white person, she was carefully taught *not* to see her own privilege: "The pressure to avoid it is great, for in facing it I must give up the myth of meritocracy."

In other cases, privilege may be difficult to identify and acknowledge because the individual is privileged in some respects but not in others. For example, those who are privileged by virtue of their gender or sexual orientation may be disadvantaged by virtue of their perceived race, their ethnicity, or their class position. The disadvantages they experience in some areas may seem so unfair and so egregious that they are prevented from recognizing the privileges they nonetheless enjoy, take for granted, and regard as "natural" and "normal." And finally, since most people see themselves as decent and fair, those who are privileged are often reluctant to acknowledge that they have unfair advantages over others because that would require that they reevaluate their sense of who they are and what they have accomplished in their lives. Robin DiAngelo, in Selection 12, examines these very issues. Her essay uses her own experience as a white woman from a working-class background to demonstrate how racial privilege interacts with class oppression.

As should by now be clear, all of the thinkers whose work is included in Part II share the belief that the various hierarchies operate in relation to one another, forming an interlocking system of advantages and disadvantages that rationalizes and preserves the prevailing distribution of power and privilege in society. As you read these articles, try to keep an open mind about this claim. If the claim is correct, it tells us something important about our society and the entrenched forces that each of us will experience as we go about creating our own future.

NOTE

1. Marilyn Frye, "Oppression," in *The Politics of Reality: Essays in Feminist Theory* (Crossing Press, 1983), p. 5.

GUIDING QUESTIONS FOR PART II

1. In her essay "Defining Racism," Tatum rejects a "prejudice only" definition of racism. Why is that conventional definition inadequate? Tatum, Coates, Haney López, and Bonilla-Silva offer different ways of understanding racism. Why do we need these multiple perspectives on racism?

2. Crenshaw coined the term "intersectionality" (which she describes as an "analytic sensibility") to address the "profound invisibility" of black women's overlapping experiences of racism and sexism. How might this analytic sensibility inform other readings in Part II?

3. How do Griscom and Pharr complicate any singular understanding of sexism and homophobia? What other hierarchical systems do they address? Why is it so important to examine the intertwining of multiple modes of oppression?

4. How do Ancheta and Alsultany complicate binary notions of race and ethnicity or any fixed ideas about how those terms should be understood?

5. How do Coates, Alsultany, and DiAngelo use personal testimony to make a larger argument about identity, oppression, and privilege?

6. Griscom argues that the case of Sharon Kowalski and Karen Thompson reveals not just a personal tragedy but also "the power of structural discrimination, the intertwining of both our medical and legal systems." What other social institutions are implicated in the articles in Part II?

7. Tatum, Bonilla-Silva, McIntosh, Mantsios, and DiAngelo all critique the myth of meritocracy, "the myth that democratic choice is equally available to all" (McIntosh). How can an understanding of privilege help deconstruct this myth?

8. Tatum uses the metaphor of a moving walkway to explain systemic advantage and to distinguish between *active* and *passive* racism. She also offers a powerful third option for people in the dominant group: turning around on the moving walkway and choosing to be actively *anti*racist. Can you identify concrete examples of active antiracism in the readings in Part II? (Keep this question in mind as you read selections throughout this anthology.)

9. The authors in Part II all identify oppressive dynamics in mainstream society, but they also highlight ways that movements for resistance can reproduce patterns of discrimination or erasure. People of color have been marginalized in queer and feminist movements, women have been erased in immigrant and civil rights movements, trans people have been pushed aside in all of these movements, and the list goes on. "Intersectionality," Crenshaw notes, "has given many advocates a way to frame their circumstances and to fight for their visibility and inclusion." Why is intersectional analysis of identity and oppression so important for activist movements?

1 Why Intersectionality Can't Wait

Kimberlé Crenshaw

Intersectionality was a lived reality before it became a term.

Today, nearly three decades after I first put a name to the concept, the term seems to be everywhere. But if women and girls of color continue to be left in the shadows, something vital to the understanding of intersectionality has been lost.

In 1976, Emma DeGraffenreid and several other black women sued General Motors for discrimination, arguing that the company segregated its workforce by race and gender: Blacks did one set of jobs and whites did another.[1] According to the plaintiffs' experiences, women were welcome to apply for some jobs, while only men were suitable for others. This was of course a problem in and of itself, but for black women the consequences were compounded. You see, the black jobs were men's jobs, and the women's jobs were only for whites. Thus, while a black applicant might get hired to work on the floor of the factory if he were male; if she were a black female she would not be considered. Similarly, a woman might be hired as a secretary if she were white, but wouldn't have a chance at that job if she were black. Neither the black jobs nor the women's jobs were appropriate for black women, since they were neither male nor white. Wasn't this clearly discrimination, even if some blacks and some women were hired?

Unfortunately for DeGraffenreid and millions of other black women, the court dismissed their claims. Why? Because the court believed that black women should not be permitted to combine their race and gender claims into one. Because they could not prove that what happened to them was just like what happened to white women or black men, the discrimination that happened to these black women fell through the cracks.

It was in thinking about why such a "big miss" could have happened within the complex structure of anti-discrimination law that the term "intersectionality" was born. As a young law professor, I wanted to define this profound invisibility in relation to the law. Racial and gender discrimination overlapped not only in the workplace but in other arenas of life; equally significant, these burdens were almost completely absent from feminist and anti-racist advocacy. Intersectionality, then, was my attempt to make feminism, anti-racist activism, and anti-discrimination law do what I thought they should—highlight the multiple avenues through which racial and gender oppression were experienced so that the problems would be easier to discuss and understand.

Kimberlé Crenshaw is a professor of law at UCLA and Columbia Law School and is cofounder of the African American Policy Forum. Her work has been foundational in the areas of critical race studies and intersectionality.

Intersectionality is an analytic sensibility, a way of thinking about identity and its relationship to power. Originally articulated on behalf of black women, the term brought to light the invisibility of many constituents within groups that claim them as members, but often fail to represent them. Intersectional erasures are not exclusive to black women. People of color within LGBTQ movements; girls of color in the fight against the school-to-prison pipeline; women within immigration movements; trans women within feminist movements; and people with disabilities fighting police abuse—all face vulnerabilities that reflect the intersections of racism, sexism, class oppression, transphobia, able-ism and more. Intersectionality has given many advocates a way to frame their circumstances and to fight for their visibility and inclusion.

Intersectionality has been the banner under which many demands for inclusion have been made, but a term can do no more than those who use it have the power to demand. And not surprisingly, intersectionality has generated its share of debate and controversy.

Conservatives have painted those who practice intersectionality as obsessed with "identity politics." Of course, as the DeGraffenreid case shows, intersectionality is not just about identities but about the institutions that use identity to exclude and privilege. The better we understand how identities and power work together from one context to another, the less likely our movements for change are to fracture.

Others accuse intersectionality of being too theoretical, of being "all talk and no action." To that I say we've been "talking" about racial equality since the era of slavery and we're still not even close to realizing it. Instead of blaming the voices that highlight problems, we need to examine the structures of power that so successfully resist change.

Some have argued that intersectional understanding creates an atmosphere of bullying and "privilege checking." Acknowledging privilege is hard—particularly for those who also experience discrimination and exclusion. While white women and men of color also experience discrimination, all too often their experiences are taken as the only point of departure for all conversations about discrimination. Being front and center in conversations about racism or sexism is a complicated privilege that is often hard to see.

• • •

Intersectionality alone cannot bring invisible bodies into view. Mere words won't change the way that some people—the less-visible members of political constituencies—must continue to wait for leaders, decision-makers and others to see their struggles. In the context of addressing the racial disparities that still plague our nation, activists and stakeholders must raise awareness about the intersectional dimensions of racial injustice that must be addressed to enhance the lives of all youths of color.

This is why we continue the work of the #WhyWeCantWait Campaign, calling for holistic and inclusive approaches to racial justice. It is why "Say Her Name" continues to draw attention to the fact that women too are vulnerable to losing their lives at the hands of police. And it is why thousands have agreed that the tragedy in Charleston, S.C.,* demonstrates our need to sustain a vision of social justice that recognizes the ways racism,

---

*The 2015 mass shooting in which white supremacist Dylann Roof murdered nine African American churchgoers at the Emanuel African Methodist Episcopal Church.

sexism and other inequalities work together to undermine us all.[2] We simply do not have the luxury of building social movements that are not intersectional, nor can we believe we are doing intersectional work just by saying words.

NOTES

1. *DeGraffenreid* v. *GENERAL MOTORS ASSEMBLY DIV., ETC.*, 413 F. Supp. 142 (E.D. Mo. 1976).
2. The African American Policy Forum (2015, July 7). The Charleston Imperative: Why Feminism & Antiracism Must Be Linked. Retrieved from: http://www.aapf.org/recent/2015/7 /charleston

2 Defining Racism: *"Can we talk?"*
Beverly Daniel Tatum

Early in my teaching career, a White student I knew asked me what I would be teaching the following semester. I mentioned that I would be teaching a course on racism. She replied, with some surprise in her voice, "Oh, is there still racism?" I assured her that indeed there was and suggested that she sign up for my course. Years later, after exhaustive media coverage of events such as the Trayvon Martin shooting, the Ferguson unrest and the Department of Justice report on the Ferguson Police Department, the Charleston church massacre, the Walter Scott trial, the appeal to racial prejudices in electoral politics, and the bitter debates about affirmative action and immigration reform, it seems hard to imagine that anyone would still be unaware of the reality of racism in our society. But in fact, in almost every audience I address, there is someone who suggests that racism is a thing of the past. There is always someone who hasn't noticed the stereotypical images of people of color in the media, who hasn't observed the housing discrimination in their community, who hasn't read the newspaper articles about documented racial bias in lending practices among well-known banks, who isn't aware of the racial tracking pattern at the local school, who hasn't seen the reports of rising incidents of racially motivated hate crimes in America—in short, someone who hasn't been paying attention to issues of race. But if you are paying attention, the legacy of racism is not hard to see, and we are all affected by it.

The impact of racism begins early. Even in our preschool years, we are exposed to misinformation about people different from ourselves. Many of us grew up in neighborhoods where we had limited opportunities to interact with people different from our own families. When I ask my audiences, "How many of you grew up in neighborhoods where most of the people were from the same racial group as your own?" almost every hand goes up. There is still a great deal of social segregation in our communities. Consequently, most of the early information we receive about "others"—people racially, religiously, or socioeconomically different from ourselves—does not come as the result of firsthand experience. The secondhand information we do receive has often been distorted, shaped by cultural stereotypes, and left incomplete.

Some examples will highlight this process. When I was teaching at Mount Holyoke College, one of my students conducted a research project investigating preschoolers' conceptions of Native Americans.[1] Using children at a local day-care center as her participants,

Beverly Daniel Tatum is a psychologist and educator and president emerita of Spelman College. Her books include *Why Are All the Black Kids Sitting Together in the Cafeteria? And Other Conversations About Race*; *Assimilation Blues: Black Families in a White Community*; and *Can We Talk About Race? And Other Conversations in an Era of School Resegregation.*

she asked these three- and four-year-olds to draw a picture of a Native American. Most children were stumped by her request. They didn't know what a Native American was. But when she rephrased the question and asked them to draw a picture of an Indian, they readily complied. Almost every picture included one central feature: feathers. In fact, many of them also included a weapon—a knife or tomahawk—and depicted the person in violent or aggressive terms. Though this group of children, almost all of whom were White, did not live near a large Native population and probably had had little if any personal interaction with American Indians, they all had internalized an image of what Indians were like. How did they know? Cartoon images, in particular the Disney movie *Peter Pan*, were cited by the children as their number-one source of information. At the age of three, these children already had a set of stereotypes in place. Though I would not describe three-year-olds as prejudiced, the stereotypes to which they have been exposed become the foundation for the adult prejudices so many of us have.

Sometimes the assumptions we make about others come not from what we have been told or what we have seen on television or in books but rather from what we have *not* been told. The distortion of historical information about people of color leads young people (and older people, too) to make assumptions that may go unchallenged for a long time.

Consider this conversation between two White students following a discussion about the cultural transmission of racism:

"Yeah, I just found out that Cleopatra was actually a Black woman,"

"What?"

The first student went on to explain the source of her newly learned information. The second student exclaimed in disbelief, "That can't be true. Cleopatra was beautiful!"

While scholars still argue the question of Cleopatra's ancestry, what is most important in this example is what this young woman had learned about who in our society is considered beautiful and who is not. Had she conjured up images of Hollywood icon Elizabeth Taylor when she thought of Cleopatra? The new information her classmate had shared and her own deeply ingrained assumptions about who is beautiful and who is not were too incongruous to allow her to assimilate the information at that moment.

Omitted information can have similar effects. For example, another young woman, preparing to be a high school English teacher, expressed her dismay that she had never learned about any Black authors in any of her English courses. How was she to teach about them to her future students when she hadn't learned about them herself? A White male student in the class responded to this discussion with frustration in his response journal, writing, "It's not my fault that Blacks don't write books." Had one of his elementary, high school, or college teachers ever told him that there were no Black writers? Probably not. Yet because he had never been exposed to Black authors, he had drawn his own conclusion that there were none.

Stereotypes, omissions, and distortions all contribute to the development of prejudice. *Prejudice* is a preconceived judgment or opinion, usually based on limited information. I assume that we all have prejudices, not because we want them but simply because we are so continually exposed to misinformation about others. Though I have often heard students or workshop participants describe someone as not having "a prejudiced bone in his body," I usually suggest that they look again. Prejudice is one of the inescapable consequences of living in a racist society. Cultural racism—the cultural images and messages that affirm the assumed superiority of Whites and the assumed inferiority of people of color—is like smog in the air. Sometimes it is so thick it is visible, other times it is less apparent, but always, day in and day out, we are breathing it in. None of us would introduce ourselves as "smog breathers" (and most of us don't want to be described as prejudiced), but if we live in a smoggy place, how can we avoid breathing the air? If we live in an environment in which we are bombarded with stereotypical images in the media, are frequently exposed to the ethnic jokes of friends and family members, and are rarely informed of the accomplishments of oppressed groups, we will develop the negative categorizations of those groups that form the basis of prejudice.

People of color as well as Whites develop these categorizations. Even a member of the stereotyped group may internalize the stereotypical categories about his or her own group to some degree. In fact, this process happens so frequently that it has a name, *internalized oppression.* . . .

Certainly some people are more prejudiced than others, actively embracing and perpetuating negative and hateful images of those who are different from themselves. When we claim to be free of prejudice, perhaps what we are really saying is that we are not hate-mongers. But none of us is completely innocent. Prejudice is an integral part of our socialization, and it is not our fault. Just as the preschoolers my student interviewed are not to blame for the negative messages they internalized, we are not at fault for the stereotypes, distortions, and omissions that shaped our thinking as we grew up.

To say that it is not our fault does not relieve us of responsibility however. We may not have polluted the air, but we need to take responsibility, along with others, for cleaning it up. Each of us needs to look at our own behavior. Am I perpetuating and reinforcing the negative messages so pervasive in our culture, or am I seeking to challenge them? If I have not been exposed to positive images of marginalized groups, am I seeking them out, expanding my own knowledge base for myself and my children? Am I acknowledging and examining my own prejudices, my own rigid categorizations of others, thereby minimizing the adverse impact they might have on my interactions with those I have categorized? Unless we engage in these and other conscious acts of reflection and reeducation, we easily repeat the process with our children. We teach what we were taught. The unexamined prejudices of the parents are passed on to the children. It is not our fault, but it is our responsibility to interrupt this cycle.

Racism: A System of Advantage Based on Race

Many people use the terms *prejudice* and *racism* interchangeably. I do not, and I think it is important to make a distinction. In his book *Portraits of White Racism*, David Wellman argues convincingly that limiting our understanding of racism to prejudice does not offer a sufficient explanation for the persistence of racism. He defines racism as a "system of advantage based on race."[2] In illustrating this definition, he provides example after example of how Whites defend their racial advantage—access to better schools, housing, jobs—even when they do not embrace overtly prejudicial thinking. Racism cannot be fully explained as an expression of prejudice alone.

This definition of racism is useful because it allows us to see that racism, like other forms of oppression, is not only a personal ideology based on racial prejudice but a *system* involving cultural messages and institutional policies and practices as well as the beliefs and actions of individuals. In the context of the United States, this system clearly operates to the advantage of Whites and to the disadvantage of people of color. Another related definition of racism, commonly used by antiracist educators and consultants, is "prejudice plus power." Racial prejudice combined with social power—access to social, cultural, and economic resources and decision-making—leads to the institutionalization of racist policies and practices. While I think this definition also captures the idea that racism is more than individual beliefs and attitudes, I prefer Wellman's definition because the idea of systematic advantage and disadvantage is critical to an understanding of how racism operates in American society.

In addition, I find that many of my White students and workshop participants do not feel powerful. Defining racism as prejudice plus power has little personal relevance. For some, their response to this definition is the following: "I'm not really prejudiced, and I have no power, so racism has nothing to do with me." However, most White people, if they are really being honest with themselves, can see that there are advantages to being White in the United States. Despite the current rhetoric about affirmative action and "reverse racism," every social indicator, from salary to life expectancy, reveals the advantages of being White.[3]

The systematic advantages of being White are often referred to as *White privilege*. In a now well-known article, "White Privilege: Unpacking the Invisible Knapsack," Peggy McIntosh, a White feminist scholar, identified a long list of societal privileges that she received simply because she was White.[4] She did not ask for them, and it is important to note that she hadn't always noticed that she was receiving them. They included major and minor advantages. Of course she enjoyed greater access to jobs and housing. But she also was able to shop in department stores without being followed by suspicious salespeople and could always find appropriate hair-care products and makeup in any drugstore. She could send her child to school confident that the teacher would not discriminate against him on the basis of race. She could also be late for meetings and talk with her mouth full, fairly confident that these behaviors would not be attributed to the fact that she was White. She could express an opinion in a meeting or in print and not have it labeled the "White" viewpoint. In other words, she was more often than not viewed as an individual, rather than as a member of a racial group.

This article rings true for most White readers, many of whom may have never considered the benefits of being White. It's one thing to have enough awareness of racism to describe the ways that people of color are disadvantaged by it. But this new understanding of racism is more elusive. In very concrete terms, it means that if a person of color is the victim of housing discrimination, the apartment that would otherwise have been rented to that person of color is still available for a White person. The White tenant is, knowingly or unknowingly, the beneficiary of racism, a system of advantage based on race. The unsuspecting tenant is not to blame for the prior discrimination, but she benefits from it anyway.

For many Whites, this new awareness of the benefits of a racist system elicits considerable pain, often accompanied by feelings of anger and guilt. These uncomfortable emotions can hinder further discussion. We all like to think that we deserve the good things we have received and that others, too, get what they deserve. Social psychologists call this tendency a "belief in a just world."[5] Racism directly contradicts such notions of justice.

Understanding racism as a system of advantage based on race is antithetical to traditional notions of an American meritocracy. For those who have internalized this myth, this definition generates considerable discomfort. It is more comfortable simply to think of racism as a particular form of prejudice. Notions of power or privilege do not have to be addressed when our understanding of racism is constructed in that way.

The discomfort generated when a systemic definition of racism is introduced is usually quite visible in the workshops I lead. Someone in the group is usually quick to point out that this is not the definition you will find in most dictionaries. I reply, "Who wrote the dictionary?" I am not being facetious with this response. Whose interests are served by a "prejudice only" definition of racism? It is important to understand that the system of advantage is perpetuated when we do not acknowledge its existence.

Racism: For Whites Only?

Frequently someone will say, "You keep talking about White people. People of color can be racist, too." I once asked a White teacher what it would mean to her if a student or parent of color accused her of being racist. She said she would feel as though she had been punched in the stomach or called a "low-life scum." She is not alone in this feeling. The word *racist* holds a lot of emotional power. For many White people, to be called racist is the ultimate insult. The idea that this term might only be applied to Whites becomes highly problematic, for after all, can't people of color be "low-life scum" too?

Of course, people of any racial group can hold hateful attitudes and behave in racially discriminatory and bigoted ways. We can all cite examples of horrible hate crimes that have been perpetrated by people of color as well as Whites. Hateful behavior is hateful behavior no matter who does it. But when I am asked, "Can people of color be racist?" I reply, "The answer depends on your definition of racism." If one defines racism as racial prejudice, the answer is yes. People of color can and do have racial prejudices. However, if one defines racism as a system of advantage based on race, the answer is no. People of color are not racist because they do not systematically benefit from racism. And, equally important, there is no systematic cultural and institutional support or sanction for the racial bigotry of people of color. In my view, reserving the term *racist* only for behaviors committed by Whites in the context of a White-dominated society is a way of acknowledging the ever-present power differential afforded Whites by the culture and institutions that make up the system of advantage and continue to reinforce notions of White superiority. (Using the same logic, I reserve the word *sexist* for men. Though women can and do have gender-based prejudices, only men systematically benefit from sexism.)

Despite my best efforts to explain my thinking on this point, there are some who will be troubled, perhaps even incensed, by my response. To call the racially motivated acts of a person of color "acts of racial bigotry" and to describe similar acts committed by Whites as "racist" will make no sense to some people, including some people of color. To them, I respectfully say "We can agree to disagree." At moments like these, it is not agreement that is essential but clarity. Even if you don't like the definition of racism I am using, hopefully you are now clear about what it is. If I also understand how you are using the term, our conversation can continue—despite our disagreement.

Another provocative question I'm often asked is, "Are you saying all Whites are racist?" When asked this question, I again remember that White teacher's response, and I am conscious that perhaps the question I am really being asked is, "Are you saying all Whites are bad people?"

The answer to that question is of course not. However, all White people, intentionally or unintentionally do benefit from racism: A more relevant question is, "What are White people as individuals doing to interrupt racism?" For many White people, the image of a racist is a hood-wearing Klan member or a name-calling Archie Bunker figure. These images represent what might be called *active racism*, blatant, intentional acts of racial bigotry and discrimination. *Passive racism* is more subtle and can be seen in the collusion of laughing when a racist joke is told, letting exclusionary hiring practices go unchallenged, accepting as appropriate the omissions of people of color from the curriculum, and avoiding difficult race-related issues. Because racism is so ingrained in the fabric of American institutions, it is easily self-perpetuating.[6] All that is required to maintain it is to go about business as usual.

I sometimes visualize the ongoing cycle of racism as a moving walkway at the airport. Active racist behavior is equivalent to walking fast on the conveyor belt. The person engaged in active racist behavior has identified with the ideology of White supremacy and is moving with it. Passive racist behavior is equivalent to standing still on the walkway. No overt effort is being made, but the conveyor belt moves the bystanders along to the same destination as those who are actively walking. Some of the bystanders may feel the motion of the conveyor belt, see the active racists ahead of them, and choose to turn around, unwilling to go to the same destination as the White supremacists. But unless they are walking actively in the opposite direction at a speed faster than the conveyor belt—unless they are actively antiracist—they will find themselves carried along with the others.

So, not all Whites are actively racist. Many are passively racist. Some, though not enough, are actively antiracist. The relevant question is not whether all Whites are racist but how we can move more White people from a position of active or passive racism to one of active antiracism. The task of interrupting racism is obviously not the task of Whites alone. But the fact of White privilege means that Whites have greater access to the societal institutions in need of transformation. To whom much is given, much is required.

It is important to acknowledge that while all Whites benefit from racism, they do not all benefit equally. Other factors, such as socioeconomic status, gender, age, religious affiliation, sexual orientation, and mental and physical ability, also play a role in our access to social influence and power. A White woman on welfare is not privileged to the same extent as a wealthy White heterosexual man. In her case, the systematic disadvantages of sexism and classism intersect with her White privilege, but the privilege is still there. This point was brought home to me in a study conducted by one of my Mount Holyoke graduate students, Phyllis Wentworth.[7] Wentworth interviewed a group of female college students who were both older than their peers and the first members of their families to attend college about the pathways that led them to college. All of the women interviewed were White, from working-class backgrounds, and from families where women were expected to graduate from high school and get married or get a job. Several had experienced abusive relationships and other personal difficulties prior to coming to college. Yet their experiences were punctuated by "good luck" stories of apartments obtained without a deposit, good jobs offered without experience or extensive reference checks, and encouragement provided by willing mentors. While the women acknowledged their good fortune, none of them discussed their Whiteness. They had not considered the possibility that being White had worked in their favor and helped give them the benefit of the doubt at critical junctures. This study clearly showed that even under difficult circumstances, White privilege was still operating.

It is also true that not all people of color are equally targeted by racism. We all have multiple identities that shape our experience. I can describe myself as a light-skinned, well-educated, heterosexual, able-bodied, Christian African American woman raised in a two-parent middle-class family in a small, predominantly White, middle-class town. As an African American woman, I am systematically disadvantaged by race and by gender, but I systematically receive benefits in the other categories, which then mediate my experience of racism and sexism. When one is targeted by multiple isms — racism, sexism, classism, heterosexism, ableism, anti-Semitism, ageism — in whatever combination, the effect is intensified. The particular combination of racism and classism in many communities of color is life-threatening. Nonetheless, when I, the middle-class Black mother of two sons, read another story about a Black man's unlucky encounter with a White police officer's deadly force, I know that racism by itself can kill.

I was reminded of this fact once again by Ta-Nehisi Coates, author of *Between the World and Me*, when he captures the heart-wrenching pain of Dr. Jones, whose twenty-three-year-old son, Prince Jones, was killed by police during a traffic stop. Her socioeconomic success as a prominent physician and the cultural and educational advantages she was able to provide for her son throughout his life could not protect him. She said, "I spent years developing a career, acquiring assets, engaging responsibilities. And one racist act. It's all it takes."[8]

NOTES

1. C. O'Toole, "The Effect of the Media and Multicultural Education on Children's Perceptions of Native Americans" (senior thesis, Department of Psychology and Education, Mount Holyoke College, 1990).

2. For an extended discussion of this point, see David Wellman, "Prejudiced People Are Not the Only Racists in America," chap. 1 in *Portraits of White Racism* (Cambridge: Cambridge University Press, 1977), 1–44. A second edition was published in 1993. See also Eduardo Bonilla-Silva, "The Strange Enigma of Race in Contemporary America," chap. 1 in *Racism Without Racists: Color-Blind Racism and the Persistence of Racial Inequality in America*, 4th ed. (Lanham, MD: Rowman and Littlefield, 2013), 1–24.

3. For specific statistical information, see Tim Sullivan et al., *State of the Dream 2012: The Emerging Majority* (United for a Fair Economy, 2012), http://www.faireconomy.org/dream12. It measures the impacts of the past thirty years of public policy on the racial divide and offers thirty-year projections, from 2012 to 2042, based on data trends since the Reagan presidency.

4. Peggy McIntosh, "White Privilege: Unpacking the Invisible Knapsack," *Peace and Freedom,* July/August 1989, 10–12. Now available at http://nationalseedproject.org/peggy-mcintosh-s-white-privilege-papers.

5. For further discussion of the concept of "belief in a just world," see Melvin Lerner, "Social Psychology of Justice and Interpersonal Attraction," in *Foundations of Interpersonal Attraction,* ed. Ted L. Huston (New York: Academic Press, 1974), 331–351.

6. For a brief historical overview of the institutionalization of racism and sexism in our legal system, see "Part VII: How It Happened: Race and Gender Issues in U.S. Law," in *Race, Class, and Gender in the United States: An Integrated Study,* 9th ed., ed. Paula S. Rothenberg (New York: Worth Publishers, 2014). See also Daria Roithmayr, *Reproducing Racism: How Everyday Choices Lock In White Advantage* (New York: New York University Press, 2014).

7. Phyllis A. Wentworth, "The Identity Development of Non-Traditionally Aged First-Generation Women College Students: An Exploratory Study" (master's thesis, Department of Psychology and Education, Mount Holyoke College, 1994).

8. Ta-Nehisi Coates, *Between the World and Me* (New York: Penguin Random House, 2015), 144.

3 | Between the World and Me
Ta-Nehisi Coates

Son,
Last Sunday the host of a popular news show asked me what it meant to lose my body. The host was broadcasting from Washington, D.C., and I was seated in a remote studio on the far west side of Manhattan. A satellite closed the miles between us, but no machinery could close the gap between her world and the world for which I had been summoned to speak. When the host asked me about my body, her face faded from the screen, and was replaced by a scroll of words, written by me earlier that week.

The host read these words for the audience, and when she finished she turned to the subject of my body, although she did not mention it specifically. But by now I am accustomed to intelligent people asking about the condition of my body without realizing the nature of their request. Specifically, the host wished to know why I felt that white America's progress, or rather the progress of those Americans who believe that they are white, was built on looting and violence. Hearing this, I felt an old and indistinct sadness well up in me. The answer to this question is the record of the believers themselves. The answer is American history.

There is nothing extreme in this statement. Americans deify democracy in a way that allows for a dim awareness that they have, from time to time, stood in defiance of their God. But democracy is a forgiving God and America's heresies—torture, theft, enslavement—are so common among individuals and nations that none can declare themselves immune. In fact, Americans, in a real sense, have never betrayed their God. When Abraham Lincoln declared, in 1863, that the battle of Gettysburg must ensure "that government of the people, by the people, for the people, shall not perish from the earth," he was not merely being aspirational; at the onset of the Civil War, the United States of America had one of the highest rates of suffrage in the world. The question is not whether Lincoln truly meant "government of the people" but what our country has, throughout its history, taken the political term "people" to actually mean. In 1863 it did not mean your mother or your grandmother, and it did not mean you and me. Thus America's problem

Ta-Nehisi Coates is a distinguished writer in residence at the Arthur L. Carter Journalism Institute at New York University. He is the author of *The Beautiful Struggle*; *We Were Eight Years in Power*; *Between the World and Me* (2015 National Book Award); and the Marvel comic *The Black Panther*.

is not its betrayal of "government of the people," but the means by which "the people" acquired their names.

This leads us to another equally important ideal, one that Americans implicitly accept but to which they make no conscious claim. Americans believe in the reality of "race" as a defined, indubitable feature of the natural world. Racism—the need to ascribe bone-deep features to people and then humiliate, reduce, and destroy them—inevitably follows from this inalterable condition. In this way, racism is rendered as the innocent daughter of Mother Nature, and one is left to deplore the Middle Passage or the Trail of Tears the way one deplores an earthquake, a tornado, or any other phenomenon that can be cast as beyond the handiwork of men.

But race is the child of racism, not the father. And the process of naming "the people" has never been a matter of genealogy and physiognomy so much as one of hierarchy. Difference in hue and hair is old. But the belief in the preeminence of hue and hair, the notion that these factors can correctly organize a society and that they signify deeper attributes, which are indelible—this is the new idea at the heart of these new people who have been brought up hopelessly, tragically, deceitfully, to believe that they are white.

These new people are, like us, a modern invention. But unlike us, their new name has no real meaning divorced from the machinery of criminal power. The new people were something else before they were white—Catholic, Corsican, Welsh, Mennonite, Jewish—and if all our national hopes have any fulfillment, then they will have to be something else again. Perhaps they will truly become American and create a nobler basis for their myths. I cannot call it. As for now, it must be said that the process of washing the disparate tribes white, the elevation of the belief in being white, was not achieved through wine tastings and ice cream socials, but rather through the pillaging of life, liberty, labor, and land; through the flaying of backs; the chaining of limbs; the strangling of dissidents; the destruction of families; the rape of mothers; the sale of children; and various other acts meant, first and foremost, to deny you and me the right to secure and govern our own bodies.

The new people are not original in this. Perhaps there has been, at some point in history, some great power whose elevation was exempt from the violent exploitation of other human bodies. If there has been, I have yet to discover it. But this banality of violence can never excuse America, because America makes no claim to the banal. America believes itself exceptional, the greatest and noblest nation ever to exist, a lone champion standing between the white city of democracy and the terrorists, despots, barbarians, and other enemies of civilization. One cannot, at once, claim to be superhuman and then plead mortal error. I propose to take our countrymen's claims of American exceptionalism seriously, which is to say I propose subjecting our country to an exceptional moral standard. This is difficult because there exists, all around us, an apparatus urging us to accept American innocence at face value and not to inquire too much. And it is so easy to look away, to live with the fruits of our history and to ignore the great evil done in all of our names. But you and I have never truly had that luxury. I think you know.

I write you in your fifteenth year. I am writing you because this was the year you saw Eric Garner choked to death for selling cigarettes; because you know now that Renisha McBride was shot for seeking help, that John Crawford was shot down for browsing in a department store. And you have seen men in uniform drive by and murder Tamir Rice, a twelve-year-old child whom they were oath-bound to protect. And you have seen men in the same uniforms pummel Marlene Pinnock, someone's grandmother, on the side of a road. And you know now, if you did not before, that the police departments of your country have been endowed with the authority to destroy your body. It does not matter if the destruction is the result of an unfortunate overreaction. It does not matter if it originates in a misunderstanding. It does not matter if the destruction springs from a foolish policy. Sell cigarettes without the proper authority and your body can be destroyed. Resent the people trying to entrap your body and it can be destroyed. Turn into a dark stairwell and your body can be destroyed. The destroyers will rarely be held accountable. Mostly they will receive pensions. And destruction is merely the superlative form of a dominion whose prerogatives include friskings, detainings, beatings, and humiliations. All of this is common to black people. And all of this is old for black people. No one is held responsible.

There is nothing uniquely evil in these destroyers or even in this moment. The destroyers are merely men enforcing the whims of our country, correctly interpreting its heritage and legacy. It is hard to face this. But all our phrasing—race relations, racial chasm, racial justice, racial profiling, white privilege, even white supremacy—serves to obscure that racism is a visceral experience, that it dislodges brains, blocks airways, rips muscle, extracts organs, cracks bones, breaks teeth. You must never look away from this. You must always remember that the sociology, the history, the economics, the graphs, the charts, the regressions all land, with great violence, upon the body.

That Sunday, with that host, on that news show, I tried to explain this as best I could within the time allotted. But at the end of the segment, the host flashed a widely shared picture of an eleven-year-old black boy tearfully hugging a white police officer. Then she asked me about "hope." And I knew then that I had failed. And I remembered that I had expected to fail. And I wondered again at the indistinct sadness welling up in me. Why exactly was I sad? I came out of the studio and walked for a while. It was a calm December day. Families, believing themselves white, were out on the streets. Infants, raised to be white, were bundled in strollers. And I was sad for these people, much as I was sad for the host and sad for all the people out there watching and reveling in a specious hope. I realized then why I was sad. When the journalist asked me about my body, it was like she was asking me to awaken her from the most gorgeous dream. I have seen that dream all my life. It is perfect houses with nice lawns. It is Memorial Day cookouts, block associations, and driveways. The Dream is treehouses and the Cub Scouts. The Dream smells like peppermint but tastes like strawberry shortcake. And for so long I have wanted to escape into the Dream, to fold my country over my head like a blanket. But this has never been an option because the Dream rests on our backs, the bedding made from our bodies. And knowing this, knowing that the Dream persists by warring with the known world, I was sad for the host, I was sad for all those families, I was sad for my country, but above all, in that moment, I was sad for you.

That was the week you learned that the killers of Michael Brown would go free. The men who had left his body in the street like some awesome declaration of their inviolable power would never be punished. It was not my expectation that anyone would ever be punished. But you were young and still believed. You stayed up till 11 P.M. that night, waiting for the announcement of an indictment, and when instead it was announced that there was none you said, "I've got to go," and you went into your room, and I heard you crying. I came in five minutes after, and I didn't hug you, and I didn't comfort you, because I thought it would be wrong to comfort you. I did not tell you that it would be okay, because I have never believed it would be okay. What I told you is what your grandparents tried to tell me: that this is your country, that this is your world, that this is your body, and you must find some way to live within the all of it. I tell you now that the question of how one should live within a black body, within a country lost in the Dream, is the question of my life, and the pursuit of this question, I have found, ultimately answers itself.

This must seem strange to you. We live in a "goal-oriented" era. Our media vocabulary is full of hot takes, big ideas, and grand theories of everything. But some time ago I rejected magic in all its forms. This rejection was a gift from your grandparents, who never tried to console me with ideas of an afterlife and were skeptical of preordained American glory. In accepting both the chaos of history and the fact of my total end, I was freed to truly consider how I wished to live—specifically, how do I live free in this black body? It is a profound question because America understands itself as God's handiwork, but the black body is the clearest evidence that America is the work of men. I have asked the question through my reading and writings, through the music of my youth, through arguments with your grandfather, with your mother, your aunt Janai, your uncle Ben. I have searched for answers in nationalist myth, in classrooms, out on the streets, and on other continents. The question is unanswerable, which is not to say futile. The greatest reward of this constant interrogation, of confrontation with the brutality of my country, is that it has freed me from ghosts and girded me against the sheer terror of disembodiment.

4 Beyond Hate: Strategic Racism

Ian Haney López

Convict Leasing

Two themes dominate American politics today: at the forefront is declining economic opportunity; coursing underneath is race. This [work] connects the two. It explains popular enthusiasm for policies injuring the middle class in terms of "dog whistle politics": coded racial appeals that carefully manipulate hostility toward nonwhites. Examples of dog whistling include repeated blasts about criminals and welfare cheats, illegal aliens, and sharia law in the heartland. Superficially, these provocations have nothing to do with race, yet they nevertheless powerfully communicate messages about threatening nonwhites. In the last 50 years, dog whistle politics has driven broad swaths of white voters to adopt a self-defeating hostility toward government, and in the process has remade the very nature of race and racism. American politics today—and the crisis of the middle class—simply cannot be understood without recognizing racism's evolution and the power of pernicious demagoguery. . . .

. . . The Civil War and the forcible ending of slavery shattered the Southern economy, abruptly terminating a massive system of labor exploitation. In the scramble to figure out what would replace it, Southern states quickly seized on a loophole. The constitutional amendment that banned slavery provided that "neither slavery nor involuntary servitude, *except as a punishment for crime whereof the party shall have been duly convicted*, shall exist within the United States."[1] Right there in the middle of the Thirteenth Amendment was a gaping hole—one big enough to allow the reestablishment of slavery by another name. Through innumerable stratagems, the South rapidly built a criminal justice system around imprisoning blacks.[2] Fines for minor infractions suddenly morphed into jail time. Selective prosecution of blacks surged. New crimes made their way onto the books. But of course the point was not to fill jail cells; rather, it was to fuel a new form of involuntary servitude.

The heart of the system lay in leasing out convicts as laborers.[3] . . . Customers for convict labor ranged from plantations and regional industry to the great corporate titans of the age. . . .

. . . In slavery's antebellum form, humans as property were at least minimally protected because of their long-term financial value.[4] But under convict leasing, a man's value did not exceed what his employer paid the state monthly. If the laborer died in custody, the employer suffered only trivial financial inconvenience, as another convict could be readily procured at the same tariff. . . . "One dies, get another," reports historian Eric Foner, became the working motto of the system's architects.[5] . . .

Ian Haney López is the John H. Boalt professor of law at the University of California, Berkeley. His books include *White by Law: The Legal Construction of Race* and *Dog Whistle Politics*.

Convict leasing recreated a facsimile of slavery directly, with convict laborers held and exploited under the terror of the lash in fields, factories, and mines. . . .

Between circa 1870 and 1945, the manufactured connection between race and crime stood at the deadly core of white supremacy and racial exploitation in the South. . . .

Three Racisms

The terrors of convict leasing—and even the machinations of Richard Nixon—may seem located in the distant past, curious relics from a racist time but not so relevant to today. Yet convict leasing has much to teach us about our conceptions of racism, as well as about how racism operates in dog whistle politics. Currently, three understandings of racism predominate: hate, structural racism, and implicit bias. Each of these helps us understand racism, and more so when considered together. Yet none effectively explains the creation and persistence of convict leasing, or today's racial demagoguery. As I will suggest after discussing these three prevailing conceptions, convict leasing and dog whistle politics are better explained in terms of strategic racism.

The racism-as-hate model

The most common understanding of racism emphasizes discrete acts of bigotry by malicious individuals. Under this version, racism is easy to spot and clearly reprehensible. In convict leasing, for example, the racist would be the ruddy-faced, morally stunted prison warden, spewing bilious racial epithets as he mock-drowns another struggling victim. Today's skinheads, aggressive young whites whose tattoos often shout Nazi claims of racial supremacy, provide another image of the prototypical, hate-motivated racist. Recently, the number of hate groups has been spiking, posing a vicious threat to society.[6]

This model has a deep intuitive resonance, but also a distancing dynamic that makes racism seem remote. When most people think about quintessential examples of racism, they think about the angry white mobs that attacked civil rights protesters in the 1950s and 1960s, or hooded Klansmen burning crosses to terrorize black families in the night. These archetypes seem readily explicable in terms of malevolence, and so buttress the racism-as-hate conception. But when used as the sole understanding of racism, the hate model makes racism seem common in the past and rare in the present, not with standing some hate-groups' contemporary resurgence. Because very few in society today scream racial epithets or threaten racial violence, racism seems extremely unusual in the present.

This distancing helps make the hate conception popular with broad swaths of the public, and also especially preferred among conservatives. For the public at large, racism-as-hate provides self-protecting clarity: if racists are like those in the 1950s who screamed at black school children and burned crosses, then most everyone can safely conclude that they, at least, are not racists. Hollywood understands this, and rarely depicts racism other than through caricatures of ignorant bigots excreting reprehensible opinions, sparing the audience from having to grapple with a complex view of racism that might implicate their own beliefs and behavior.

Conservatives, with the important assistance of the Supreme Court, also propagate this understanding of racism, as it undercuts claims that racial discrimination remains a major social problem. By linking racism to discrete acts stemming from malice, this conception makes contemporary discrimination almost impossible to prove because showing malice inevitably requires some statement of evil intent—and those who engage in racial discrimination today typically have the wit not to shout out their prejudices. With discrimination hard to prove, its very presence comes into question. Since conservatives on the Supreme Court adopted a malice conception of racism in 1979, when using this approach the Court has rejected every claim of discrimination against non-whites brought before it. Today, the constitutional law that supposedly protects minorities defines racism solely in terms of hate, and as a result this doctrine has not found any discrimination against minorities since Jimmy Carter sat in the White House.[7] This is more than a matter of doctrine, and more than a question for individual litigants; the Court's pronouncements, especially on socially contentious issues like race, help shape what passes as commonsense.

Structural racism

Another conception of racism emphasizes structures rather than individuals. Racism under this view is woven into society's fabric; more than the cruel warden, the convict lease system itself is seen to embody racism. The idea of structural racism, also known as institutional racism, entered the American vocabulary in the late civil rights era, and a definition from that time drives the meaning home:

> When white terrorists bomb a black church and kill five black children, that is an act of *individual racism*, widely deplored by most segments of the society. But when in that same city—Birmingham, Alabama—five hundred black babies die each year because of the lack of proper food, shelter and medical facilities, and thousands more are destroyed and maimed physically, emotionally and intellectually because of conditions of poverty and discrimination in the black community, that is a function of *institutional racism*.[8]

Institutional racism stresses how past mistreatment drives current inequalities. Up through the 1940s, a Southern society built around convict leasing and debt peonage may have trapped half of all African Americans. Meanwhile, many of the government programs arising in the 1930s and 1940s—efforts that contributed to the great boom in the American middle class—were effectively available to whites only. These racially stratified differences connect across generations to vast disparities today in the average wealth of white and black families. Whereas in 2009 the typical white family had a net worth of $113,149, this outstripped the figure for African American families by 20 to 1, with the average black family owning assets of only $5,677.[9] Or put this another way: for every dollar held by whites, blacks had a lonely nickel in their pocket.[10]

Where the hate model looks for bad actors, structural racism is much more focused on outcomes. At the extreme, the question of culpable individuals drops out, and the overriding concern becomes breaking down the structures of inequality that otherwise threaten to replicate themselves indefinitely. In its focus on results, institutional racism is often understood as a radical conception of racism, since it implies a moral obligation to actually change social structures. This radical quality stems from the implications, though, and not from the analysis itself. There's nothing especially revolutionary in suggesting that social dynamics frequently continue through inertia. Indeed, insofar as it eschews identifying contemporary culprits, a structural account sometimes can be politically safer than the hate model. Structural racism is racism without racists. All that said, precisely because institutional racism implies a need to change society, it was rejected long ago by conservatives, including those on the Supreme Court who repudiated this understanding of racism in the early 1970s.

Implicit bias

Today, unconscious bias constitutes the main rival to the focus on intentional animus. This theory is especially popular among critics of the Supreme Court and among liberals more generally. They stress that almost all of us draw on racial ideas at the implicit level, sorting those we meet and forming early judgments virtually automatically, long before our conscious minds have a chance to recognize, let alone object to, the errors. Evidence for the existence of implicit bias can be readily found — indeed, experienced — in the "Implicit Association Test," available online to anyone who wishes to take it. It uses tiny differences in how quickly one pairs words like white and good, and black and bad, to detect unconscious subscriptions to notions of white superiority and black inferiority.[11] Persons first taking the test typically find the results startling. Almost all of us, of whatever color, harbor implicit biases. This burgeoning science stands as a direct refutation of the Court's understanding of racism: it shows that racial discrimination often results from unconscious thought processes, and need not stem from intentional malice, or indeed any conscious purposes at all.

Despite its strength in challenging constitutional law's singular focus on purposeful malice, spotlighting implicit bias carries three interrelated risks. These are not mistakes with the theory, but rather, errors in how unconscious bias is commonly understood. The first is the fallacious sense that "race is hardwired into our reptilian brains," as a friend evocatively but erroneously insisted. The second is that everyone favors their own race and is biased toward other races. The final inaccuracy is to suppose that, since bias is unconscious and universal, there's little anyone can do.

Rather than refer to implicit bias, I prefer to highlight what I term commonsense racism. Like the implicit bias model, this conception of racism emphasizes its unconscious quality. But rather than focusing principally on how our minds work, commonsense racism stresses the origins of racial biases in our culture and social structures. It's true that we are "hardwired" to unconsciously assign meaning to perceived *differences*. But it's false that we're automatically programmed to think in terms of *race*. Rather, notions of race come from a shared culture steeped in racial stereotypes, as well as from material arrangements like segregated cities that make race a supremely salient social category. As the race scholar john powell explains, "the unconscious is largely social. It is the environment, including our social structures and cultural meanings, that both create the negative associations and uses them in priming" our psyches.[12] It's not race our minds naturally seek out, but difference generally. Thus the fact that race comes automatically to mind reflects not our nature but our society.

In turn, precisely because implicit racial biases reflect widespread cultural stereotypes and social structures, these biases track dominant white-over-nonwhite dynamics. It's not the case that each group favors its own and dislikes others. Rather, in general all members of our society, including racial minorities, are unconsciously predisposed to hold positive associations regarding whites and negative presumptions about minorities. Despite this, we are not helpless in the face of implicit bias. One immediate solution is to self-critically reflect on how taken-for-granted ideas about race might be influencing our judgments and actions. Research in this field makes it clear that purposeful attention to race is key to avoiding racial discrimination.[13] In addition, if racial thinking arises out of stereotypes and social structures, then changing these can reduce implicit bias. Even small alterations in our milieu can shift how often unconscious racial biases are triggered, and also, whether persons are routinely encouraged to counteract the possible operation of implicit biases in their thinking.

More than angry bigotry, commonsense racism explains much of the harm race does in our society. Because race infiltrates our minds so thoroughly, even persons deeply and genuinely committed to humane engagement with others often nevertheless draw upon pernicious racial stereotypes.[14] In turn, racism gains a large degree of social power from the actions of good people in thrall to racist beliefs. Reconsider convict leasing and debt peonage. These could wreak havoc for 70 years because they made sense, as a cultural matter. Most whites didn't wrestle with whether these practices were evil, as this question never rose that high into their consciousness. Instead, the settled ideas of whites as decent folks and blacks as dangerous work animals resolved for many, at the unconscious level, the moral rightness of convict leasing. Certainly, this devilish practice could not have continued without the broad acquiescence of the white population in the South. It was simply commonsense, for many whites, that the states' law enforcement machines should feed African Americans into the maw of a brutal system of oppression and exploitation that proceeded under the motto "one dies, get another."

These three conceptions of racism—hate, structural racism, and implicit bias or commonsense racism—provide useful lenses for examining the racial complexities of convict leasing. This abhorrent system was an amalgam of hate-filled cruelty, deeply structured inequality from the slavery era that facilitated a new yet similar system of institutionalized exploitation, and unconscious racial biases that allowed many to turn a blind eye to a ghastly arrangement.

But there's something missing from this account. Convict leasing built up relatively quickly, in just a few years. Spite alone didn't do that. Hate didn't create new structures and rationales for the exploitation of black labor. Likewise, while unconscious notions of white superiority and black depravity no doubt played a role, convict leasing was not the product of anyone's id. Unconscious minds did not elaborate new criminal laws, nor devise a new form of chattel slavery even more lethal than its predecessor. Nor was convict leasing a mere continuation of past structures, unaided by contemporary actors. This was not inertia, but purposeful effort. Convict leasing constituted a carefully planned shift in the machinery of labor extraction. Southern elites systematically set about creating a new form of racial exploitation, building a system arguably more brutal, deadly, and dehumanizing than slavery itself. Today's dominant conceptions of racism do not give us a way to fathom this process. For that, we need a different understanding of racism, seeing it as sometimes cold and calculating.

Strategic Racism

Convict leasing functioned to protect the white financial interests jeopardized by slavery's end, and also was crafted to shore up white dominion over blacks in the new post-slavery world. The invention of the institution stemmed from the desire of dominant elements in society to secure their wealth, power, and status by creating a new form of slavery. The elaboration of convict leasing suggests purposeful action, not animated by hate, but instead propelled by conscious, intentional plotting. In this conception, racism emerges as the self-interested, strategic manipulation of racial antipathies. *Strategic racism refers to purposeful efforts to use racial animus as leverage to gain material wealth, political power, or heightened social standing.*[15]

This sort of racism may seem marginal, at least in the sense of being relatively rare — and so in its most calculating forms it may be. Nevertheless, the purposeful manipulation of racial ideas forms the poisonous core of racism. Indeed, this dynamic returns us to the very origins of race. How did racism first arise? Hate for different races cannot explain where racism comes from, for this would be entirely circular: racial hate cannot explain the origins of racial hate.[16] Instead, notions of race were invented, and racial hatred stimulated, to justify exploitation. In the context of colonial North America — one instance in a larger pattern of colonialism that produced the racial ideologies of the modern world — European migrants began to invent ideas about "racial differences" in order to justify their treatment of the indigenous populations on the Eastern seaboard as well as those from western Africa. These American and African populations were quite varied, organizing themselves into local nations and speaking multiple languages. At the beginning of the 1600s, before European settlement began in earnest and before the first Africans were brought to North America, the white, red, and black races did not exist. Within a century, though, these races were firmly established in cultural knowledge and social practice — with white supremacy providing a divine right to rule, and with red and black savagery justifying the expropriation of Native American land and the enslavement of African labor.[17]

For almost everyone, it is wrenching to encounter, let alone participate in, the level of intense suffering associated with driving persons from their homes or forcing people into bondage. If, however, we can convince ourselves that our victims are not like us — do not feel pain the way we do, are not intelligent and sensitive, indeed are indolent, degenerate, violent, and dangerous — then perhaps we're not doing so much harm after all; indeed, more than protecting ourselves, maybe we are helping the benighted others. And how much better, in terms of excusing our own self-interest, if it turns out that forces beyond anyone's control (and hence beyond our moral responsibility) doom these unfortunate others to subservience; if, say, God or nature fixed their insuperable character and determined their lot in life. Exploitation can be more easily justified if the exploited are placed within a fixed hierarchy — a natural or divine division of the population into the superior and inferior. Gender traditionally works this way, with basic biological distinctions supposedly justifying sharp demarcations in social roles. In different settings, caste, religion, language, ethnicity, and class, among others, all provide markers of difference sufficiently deep to justify appalling abuse. These various forms of differentiation work in discrete ways, but also share a fundamental similarity: they are the stories societies tell themselves to justify violent exploitation. In the United States, race provides such a core story, and strategic racists are the master narrators.

This is not to say that strategic racists stand completely outside the fictions they create. For however calculated their actions, racial entrepreneurs tend to reinvent existing racial ideas, rather than making them up whole cloth. Those justifying inequality do so from within already unequal societies, with extant beliefs that provide handy material for new uses. Even at the inception of racial ideology in North America, for instance, older notions of fixed differences, such as that between Christian and heathen, provided the raw materials that facilitated the evolution of distinctly modern racial ideas.[18] Likewise, in justifying convict leasing, strategic racists drew on existing ideas of racial difference created under slavery. Also, beyond drawing on available ideas, racial strategists stand within their own fictions because those seeking power typically will themselves to believe their own fabrications. Strategic racism almost always carries a strong element of self-delusion. But all that said, the principal point remains: strategic racism stands apart from other racisms insofar as its practitioners coldly set out to turn race to their advantage.

A last important point: because strategic racism is strategic, *it is not fundamentally about race*. The driving force behind strategic racism is not racial animus for its own sake or brutalizing nonwhites out of hate; it is the pursuit of power, money, and/or status. If other means of gaining these ends are ready at hand, calculating actors will use those instead of or in addition to race—just as dog whistle politicians today also often use gender, sexual orientation, and religion to whip up hysteria along those other lines too. Yes, provocateurs stimulate racial hatred intentionally, and yes they do tremendous damage to nonwhite communities. But strategic racists act out of avarice rather than animus. Their aim is to pursue their own self interest; racism is merely a route to mammon, not an end in itself.

Dog Whistle Politics as Strategic Racism

. . .

To fully understand dog whistle politics, we have to start thinking about racism as sometimes strategic. A 2006 study found that, when given a list of 40 descriptive words, members of the public were most likely to use the following terms to describe a "racist": close-minded, opinionated, stubborn, and ignorant. Here are the words the public *least* associated with racists: calm, intelligent, and wealthy.[19] This needs to change. The stereotypes that tie minorities to crime don't simply reside in minds that are shuttered, uneducated, and cantankerous. They are believed by most, and more importantly, these falsehoods are purposefully manipulated by persons otherwise cool, smart, and rich. These stereotypes form part of a strategy: a weapon in the hands of dog whistle racists seeking votes and power. They were elevated after slavery to justify convict leasing, and reinvigorated after the civil rights movement to shatter the New Deal coalition. We have learned to see racism in the spittle-laced epithets of the angry bigot. We must also learn to see racism in the coded racial entreaties promoted by calculating demagogues.

. . .

NOTES

1. US Constitution, Amendment XIII, §1. [For the full text of the Thirteenth Amendment, see "United States Constitution: Thirteenth (1865), Fourteenth (1868), and Fifteenth (1870) Amendments," in Part VII of this volume.]

2. Eric Foner, *Forever Free: The Story of Emancipation and Reconstruction* 202 (2006).

3. Douglas A. Blackmon, *Slavery by Another Name: The Re-Enslavement of Black Americans from the Civil War to World War II* (2008).

4. Stanley Engerman & Robert William Fogel, *Time on the Cross: The Economics of American Slavery* (1974).

5. Foner, 202.

6. Leonard Zeskind, *Blood and Politics: The History of the White Nationalist Movement from the Margins to the Mainstream* (2009).

7. Ian Haney López, "Intentional Blindness," 87 *New York University Law Review* 1779 (2012).

8. Stokely Carmichael & Charles V. Hamilton, *Black Power: The Politics of Liberation in America* 4 (1967). Structural and institutional racism can be distinguished: where the former can be said to refer to social structures in general, institutional racism can be understood to describe practices and ideas within particular institutions, or even the way in which practices and ideas become institutionalized. For an extended exploration of the latter understanding, see Ian Haney López, "Institutional Racism: Judicial Conduct and a New Theory of Racial Discrimination," 109 *Yale Law Journal* 1717 (2000).

9. Rakesh Kochhar, Richard Fry & Paul Taylor, "Wealth Gaps Rise to Record Highs Between Whites, Blacks and Hispanics," *Pew Research Center*, July 26, 2011.

10. For an extended discussion of structural racism, see Daria Roithmayr, *Reproducing Racism: How Everyday Choices Lock In White Advantage* (2014).

11. https://implicit.harvard.edu/.

12. john powell, *Racing to Justice: Transforming Our Conceptions of Self and Other to Build an Inclusive Society* 235 (2012).

13. Legal scholarship focused on unconscious racism prominently includes Charles Lawrence, "The Id, The Ego, and Equal Protection: Reckoning With Unconscious Racism," 39 *Stanford Law Review* 327 (1987); Linda Hamilton Krieger, "The Content of Our Categories: A Cognitive Bias Approach to Discrimination and Equal Employment Opportunity," 47 *Stanford Law Review* 1161 (1995); and Jerry Kang, "Trojan Horses of Race," 118 *Harvard Law Review* 1489 (2005).

14. See Mahzarin Banaji & Anthony G. Greenwald, *Blindspot: Hidden Biases of Good People* (2013).

15. I develop this argument in Ian Haney López, "Post-Racial Racism: Racial Stratification and Mass Incarceration in the Age of Obama," 98 *California Law Review* 1023 (2010), where I draw on Douglas Massey, *Categorically Unequal: The American Stratification System* (2008).

16. Barbara Fields, "Slavery, Race and Ideology in the United States of America," 181 *New Left Review* 95 (1990).

17. See generally Audrey Smedley, *Race in North America: Origin and Evolution of a Worldview* (1993).

18. Winthrop Jordan, *White Over Black: American Attitudes Toward the Negro, 1550–1812* (1968).

19. Samuel R. Sommers & Michael I. Norton, "Lay Theories About White Racists: What Constitutes Racism (and What Doesn't)" 9 *Group Processes & Intergroup Relations* 117, 119 (2006).

5 Color-Blind Racism

Eduardo Bonilla-Silva

For most Americans, talking about racism is talking about white supremacist organizations or Archie Bunkers. I anchor my remarks from a different theoretical shore and one that will make many of you feel quite uncomfortable. I contend that racism is, more than anything else, *a matter of group power; it is about a dominant racial group (whites) striving to maintain its systemic advantages and minorities fighting to subvert the racial status quo.* Hence, although "bigots" are part of America's (and A&M's) racial landscape, they are not the central actors responsible for the reproduction of racial inequality. If bigots are not the cogs propelling America's racial dynamics, who are they? My answer: regular white folks just following the racial script of America. Today most whites assert that they "don't see any color, just people"; that although the ugly face of discrimination is still with us, it is no longer the main factor determining minorities' life chances; and, finally, that they, like Dr. Martin Luther King, aspire to live in a society where "people are judged by the content of their character and not by the color of their skin." More poignantly, and in a curious case of group projection, many whites insist that minorities (especially blacks) are the ones responsible for our "racial problems."

But regardless of whites' "sincere fictions," racial considerations shade almost everything that happens in this country. Blacks—and dark-skinned racial minorities—lag well behind whites in virtually every relevant social indicator. For example, blacks are poorer, earn less, and are significantly less wealthy than whites. They also receive an inferior education than do whites even when they attend integrated settings. Regarding housing, blacks pay more for similar units and, because of discrimination, cannot access the totality of the housing market in any locality. In terms of social interaction, blacks receive impolite and discriminatory treatment in stores, restaurants, attempting to hail taxicabs, driving, and in a host of other commercial and social transactions. In short, blacks are, using the apt metaphor coined by Professor Derrick Bell, "at the bottom of the well."

How is it possible to have this tremendous level of racial inequality in a country where most people (whites) claim that race is no longer a relevant social factor and that "racists" are a species on the brink of extinction? More significantly, how do whites

Eduardo Bonilla-Silva is a James B. Duke professor of sociology at Duke University and the author of *Racism Without Racists: Color-Blind Racism and the Persistence of Racial Inequality in America.*

From the lecture "The Strange Enigma of Racism in Contemporary America," by Eduardo Bonilla-Silva, given March 7, 2001, at a forum on racism at Texas A&M university. Reprinted by permission of the author.

131

explain the contradiction between their professed color blindness and America's color-coded inequality? I will attempt to answer both of these questions. My main argument is that whites have developed a new, powerful ideology that justifies contemporary racial inequality and thus help maintain "systemic white privilege." I label this new ideology "color-blind racism" because this term fits quite well the language used by whites to defend the racial status quo. This ideology emerged in the 1960s concurrently with what I have labeled the "New Racism." "New Racism" practices maintain white privilege, and, unlike those typical of Jim Crow, tend to be slippery, institutional, and apparently nonracial. Post civil rights discrimination, for the most part, operates in a "now you see it, now you don't" fashion. For instance, instead of whites relying on housing covenants or on the Jim Crow signs of the past (e.g., "This is a WHITE neighborhood"), today realtors steer blacks into certain neighborhoods, individual whites use "smiling discrimination" to exclude blacks (e.g., studies by HUD and The Urban Institute), and, in some white neighborhoods, sponsorship is the hidden strategy relied upon to keep them white. Similar practices are at work in universities, banks, restaurants, and other venues.

Because the tactics for maintaining systemic white privilege changed in the 1960s, the rationalizations for explaining racial inequality changed, too. Whereas Jim Crow racism explained blacks' social standing as the product of their imputed biological and moral inferiority, color-blind racism explains it as the product of market dynamics, naturally occurring phenomena, and presumed cultural deficiencies. Below, I will highlight the central frames of color-blind racism with interview data from two projects: the 1997 Survey of College Students and the 1998 Detroit Area Study. The four central frames of color-blind racism are (1) *Abstract Liberalism*, (2) *Naturalization*, (3) *Biologization of Culture*, and (4) *Minimization of Racism*. I discuss each frame separately.

Abstract Liberalism

Whereas the principles of liberalism and humanism were not extended to nonwhites in the past, they have become the main rhetorical weapons to justify contemporary racial inequality. Whites use these principles in an *abstract* way that allows them to support the racial status quo in an apparently "reasonable" fashion. For example, Eric, a corporate auditor in his forties, opposed reparations by relying on an abstract notion of opportunity. He erupted in anger when asked if he thought reparations were due to blacks for the injuries caused by slavery and Jim Crow.

> Oh tell them to shut up, OK! I had nothing to do with the whole situation. The opportunity is there, there is no reparation involved and let's not dwell on it. I'm very opinionated about that!

After suggesting that Jews and Japanese are the only groups worthy of receiving reparations, he added,

> But something that happened three Goddamned generations ago, what do you want us to do about it now? Give them opportunity, give them scholarships, but reparations . . .

Was Eric just a white man with a "principled opposition" to government intervention? This does not seem to be the case since Eric, like most whites, makes a distinction between government spending on behalf of victims of child abuse, the homeless, and battered women (groups whom he deems as legitimate candidates for assistance) and on behalf of blacks (a group whom he deems as unworthy of assistance).

Another tenet of liberalism that whites use to explain racial matters is the Jeffersonian idea of meritocracy—"the cream rises to the top." And whites seem unconcerned by the fact that the color of the "cream" is usually white. For example, Bob, a student at Southern University, explained his opposition to the idea of providing blacks unique educational opportunities in meritocratic fashion:

> No, I would not. I think, um, I believe that you should be judged on your qualifications, your experience, your education, your background, not on your race.

Accordingly, Bob opposed affirmative action as follows:

> I oppose them mainly because, not because I am a racist, but because I think you should have the best person for the job. . . . If I was a business owner, I would want the best person in there to do the job. If I had two people, and had to choose, had to have one black to meet the quota, I think that's ridiculous.

Bob then added the following clincher: "I think [affirmative action] had a good purpose when it was instilled [sic] because it alleviated a lot of anger maybe . . . minorities felt that they were getting a foot back in the door, but I think times have changed." Bob's argumentative reasonableness is bolstered by his belief that "times have changed" and that as far as discrimination in America [is concerned], "the bigger things are already taken care of."

Another tenet of liberalism that whites employ to state their racial views is the notion of individualism. For example, Beverly, a co-owner of a small business and homemaker in her forties, stated her belief that the government has a duty to see that no one is prevented from moving into neighborhoods because of racial considerations. Yet, when asked whether the government should work to guarantee that residential integration becomes a reality, Beverly said the following:

> [Sighs] It, it, it just isn't that important. Where you decide to live is where you decide to live. If you decided to live in and can afford to live in a very upscale house, great! If you're black and you can afford that, fantastic! I mean, people have choices as to where they live. If they have the economic background or money to do this with . . . I can't envision . . . 97 percent of the black people saying, "I'm going to live in a white neighborhood 'cause it will make my life better." And I can't imagine 97 percent of the white people saying, "I'm gonna move to a black neighborhood 'cause it will make me feel better." You know, I, I, where you decide to live is your choice.

Carol, a student at SU, invoked the notion of individual choice to justify her taste for whiteness. While reviewing her romantic life in response to a question, Carol said:

> Um, there really is hardly any [laughs]. My romantic life is kinda dry [laughs]. I mean, as far as guys go, I mean, I know you're looking for um, white versus minority and. . . . I am interested in white guys, I mean, I don't want it to look like a prejudice thing or anything.

After stating her preference for "white guys," Carol had to do some major rhetorical work to avoid appearing racist. Thus, she interjected the following odd comment to save face: "if a guy comes along and he's black and like I love him, it's not gonna, I mean, I, it's not, I don't think the white–black issue's gonna make a difference, you know what I mean?"

Naturalization

The word "natural" or the phrase "That's the way it is" is often interjected when whites use this frame to normalize events or actions that could otherwise be interpreted as racially motivated (e.g., residential segregation) or even as racist (e.g., preference for whites as friends and partners). For example, Mark, a student at MU, acknowledged that: "most of my close friends don't . . . [I] also don't have that many close black friends." Mark reacted immediately to his potentially problematic confession (no black friends) by saying,

> Um . . . I don't know, I guess that circles are tight. It's not like we exclude, I don't feel like we exclude people. I don't think that we go out of our way to include people either, but it's just kinda like that. It seems like that's just the way it works out almost . . .

Later in the interview, Mark, a business major, revealed that most of the students in the business school are white males. When asked if he thought the way things were set up in the business school was racist, Mark answered the following:

> I don't really think it's racist. I just think . . . I don't know if it's a perfect example, I just think it's an example . . . or just things aren't set up in such a way where I wouldn't say it favors whites. That's just the way that happens um . . . in the business school. That's all.

Ray, another student at MU, naturalized the fact that he had no minority associates while growing up because, "they lived in different neighborhoods, they went to different schools" and "It wasn't like people were trying to exclude them . . . It's just the way things were." Hence, his response to a question about whether blacks self-segregate or are made to feel unwelcome by whites was the following:

> I would say it's a combination of the two factors. Um . . . and I don't think that . . . I don't . . . I think it's fair it's, uh . . . it's not necessarily fair to read prejudice into either half of the bargain. Um . . . I think it's just, 'em . . . I think it's like what I was saying earlier, I think people feel comfortable around people that they feel that they can identify with.

After struggling rhetorically with the implications of his argument, Ray stated that: "Ah um . . . I think, yes, things are somewhat segregated, but I think it's more, I think it's more about just people . . . feeling comfortable around each other than it is about active discrimination."

Detroit whites also used this frame widely. For instance, Bill, a manager in a manufacturing firm, explained the limited level of post 1954 school integration as a natural affair.

> Bill: I don't think it's anybody's fault. Because people tend to group with their own people. Whether it's white or black or upper-middle class or lower class or, you know, upper class, you know, Asians. People tend to group with their own. Doesn't mean if a black person moves into your neighborhood, they shouldn't go to your school? They should and you

should mix and welcome them and everything else, but you can't force people together. . . . If people want to be together, they should intermix more.

Int: OK. Hmm, so the lack of mixing is really just kind of an individual lack of desire?

Bill: Well, yeah individuals, it's just the way it is. You know, people group together for lots of different reasons: social, religious. Just as animals in the wild, you know. Elephants group together, cheetahs group together. You bus a cheetah into an elephant herd because they should mix? You can't force that [laughs].

The Biologization of Culture

Modern racial ideology no longer relies on the claim that blacks are biologically inferior to whites. Instead, it has biologized their presumed cultural practices (i.e., presented them as *fixed* features) and used that as the *rationale* for explaining racial inequality. For instance, Karen, a student at MU, agreed with the premise that blacks are poor because they lack the drive to succeed.

> I think, to some extent, that's true. Just from, like looking at the black people that I've met in my classes and the few that I knew before college that . . . not like they're—I don't want to say waiting for a handout, but to some extent, that's kind of what I'm like hinting at. Like, almost like they feel like they were discriminated against hundreds of years ago, now what are you gonna give me? Ya' know, or maybe even it's just their background, that they've never, like maybe they're first generation to be in college so they feel like just that is enough for them.

Although many white respondents used this frame as crudely as Karen, most used it in a kinder and gentler way. For example, Jay, a student at WU, answered the question on why blacks have a worse overall standing than whites as follows:

> Hmm, I think it's due to lack of education. I think because if they didn't grow up in a household that ahhh, afforded them the time to go to school and they had to go out and get jobs right away, I think it is just a cycle [that] perpetuates things, you know. I mean, some people, I mean, I can't say that blacks can't do it because, obviously, there are many, many of them [that] have succeeded in getting good jobs and all that . . .

Although Jay admitted "exceptional blacks," he immediately went back to the cultural frame to explain blacks' status.

> So it's possible that the cycle seems to perpetuate itself because it, I mean, let's say go out and get jobs and they start, they settle down much earlier than they would normally if they had gone to school and then they have kids at a young age and they—these kids have to go and get jobs and so [on].

Detroit respondents used this cultural frame too, but, in general, used it in a more crude fashion than students. For instance, Ian, a manager of information security in an automobile company in his late fifties, explained blacks' worse status compared to whites as follows:

> The majority of 'em just don't strive to do anything, to make themselves better. Again, I've seen that all the way through. "I do this today, I'm fine, I'm happy with it, I don't need anything better." Never, never, never striving or giving extra to, to make themselves better.

Minimization of Racism

Although whites and blacks believed that discrimination is still a problem in America, they dispute its salience. In general, whites believe that discrimination has all but disappeared whereas blacks believe that discrimination—old- and new-fashioned—is as American as cherry pie. For instance, Kim, a student at SU, answered a question dealing with blacks' claims of discrimination in the following manner:

> Um, I disagree. I think that um, I think that it even more like . . . it's uh . . . I mean, from what I've heard, you pretty much have to hire, you know, you have to [hire] everyone, you know? They have quotas and stuff . . .

When asked if she believes the reason why blacks lag behind whites is because they are lazy, Kim said:

> Yeah, I totally agree with that, think that um, I mean, again, I don't think, you know, they're all like that, but I mean . . . I mean, I mean . . . it's just that . . . I mean, if it wasn't that way, why would there be so many blacks living in the projects? You know, why would there be so many poor blacks? If, if they worked hard, if, if they just went out and went to college and just worked as hard as they could, they would, I mean, they, they could make it just as high as anyone else.

Detroit whites were even more likely than students to use this frame and to use it in a direct and crude manner. Sandra, a retail salesperson in her early forties, answered the question on discrimination as follows:

> I think if you are looking for discrimination, I think it's there to be found. But if you make the best of any situation, and if you don't use it as an excuse I think sometimes it's an excuse because, ah, people felt they deserved a job, ah whatever! I think if things didn't go their way I know a lot of people have a tendency to use . . . prejudice or racism as—whatever—as an excuse. I think in some ways, yes there is . . . umm . . . people who are prejudiced. It's not only blacks, it's about Spanish, or women. In a lot of ways there [is] a lot of reverse discrimination. It's just what you wanna make of it.

The policy implications of adopting this frame are extremely important. Since whites do not believe that discrimination is a normal part of America, they view race-targeted government programs as illegitimate. Thus, Henrietta, a transsexual school teacher in his fifties, answered a question on reparations as follows:

> As a person who was once reverse discriminated against, I would have to say no. Because the government does not need those programs if they, if people would be motivated to bring themselves out of the poverty level. Ah, [coughing] when we talk about certain programs, when the Irish came over, when the Italians, the Polish, and the Eastern European Jews, they all were immigrants who lived in terrible conditions too, but they had one thing in common, they all knew that education was the way out of that poverty. And they did it. I'm not saying . . . the blacks were brought over here maybe not willingly, but if they realize education's the key, that's it. And that's based on individuality.

Conclusions

I have illustrated the four central frames of color-blind racism, namely, abstract liberalism, naturalization, biologization of culture, and minimization of racism. These frames are central to *old* and *young* whites alike. They form an impregnable yet elastic ideological wall that *barricades* whites off from America's racial reality. An impregnable wall because they provide whites a safe, color-blind way to state racial views without appearing to be irrational or rabidly racist. And an elastic wall — and, hence, a stronger one — because these frames do not rely on absolutes ("All blacks are . . ." or "Discrimination ended in 1965"). Instead, color-blind racism gives room for exceptions and allows for a variety of ways of using the frames — from crude and direct to kinder and indirect — for whites to state their racial views in an angry tone ("Darned lazy blacks") or as compassionate conservatives ("Poor blacks are trapped in *their* inferior schools in *their* cycle of poverty. What a pity.").

Thus, my answers to the strange enigma of racism without "racists" is the following: America does not depend on Archie Bunkers to defend white supremacy. Modern racial ideology does not thrive on the ugliness of the past, on the language and tropes typical of slavery and Jim Crow. Today there is a sanitized, color-blind way of calling minorities "niggers," "spics," or "chinks." Today most whites justify keeping minorities out of the good things in life with the language of liberalism ("I am all for equal opportunity; that's why I oppose affirmative action!"). And today as yesterday, whites do not feel guilty about minorities' plight. Today they believe that minorities have the opportunities to succeed and that if they don't, it's because they do not try hard. And if minorities dare talk about discrimination, they are rebuked with statements such as "Discrimination ended in the sixties, man" or "You guys are hypersensitive."

6 Neither Black nor White
Angelo N. Ancheta

Race Relations in Black and White

"Are you black or are you white?" For Asian Americans the obvious answer would seem to be "neither." Yet, when questions of race relations arise, a dichotomy between black and white typically predominates. Formed largely through inequities and conflicts between blacks and whites, discourse on race relations provides minimal space to articulate experiences independent of a black–white framework. The representation of Asian Americans is especially elusive and often shifts, depending on context, between black and white.

Popular works on race suggest that expositions of Asian American experiences are peripheral, more often confined to the footnotes than expounded in the primary analyses. Studs Terkel's *Race* frames race relations through a dialogue about blacks and whites, confined almost entirely to the opinions of blacks and whites. Andrew Hacker's *Two Nations: Black and White, Separate, Hostile, Unequal* contains, as its subtitle implies, extensive discussions of inequality between blacks and whites, but only a minimal analysis of inequality among other racial groups.[1] The controversial books *The Bell Curve*, by Charles Murray and Richard Herrnstein, and *The End of Racism,* by Dinesh D'Souza, go to considerable length to expound arguments that blacks as a group are less intelligent than whites and suffer from cultural pathologies that inhibit advancement to the level of whites. When discussed at all, Asian Americans are offered as a "model minority" group, to be contrasted with blacks and likened to whites because of their higher IQ scores and cultural values stressing family, hard work, and educational achievement.

News media portrayals of racial minorities suffer from the same tendency to reduce race relations to a simple black–white equation. Popular television news shows such as ABC's *Nightline* offer recurring programming on race relations, but typically confine their analyses to black–white relations. Public opinion polls on race and civil rights usually exclude Asian Americans as subjects or as participants, or reduce them to the category of "Other." News coverage of racially charged events is most often framed by black versus white antagonisms. . . .

Public policies that reflect and reinforce race relations also approach race in terms of black and white. Historically, the major landmarks denoting both racial subordination

Angelo N. Ancheta is the director of the Katharine & George Alexander Community Law Center at Santa Clara University School of Law. His books include *Race, Rights, and the Asian American Experience.*

From *Asian American Studies Now: A Critical Reader,* edited by Jean Yu-Wen, Shen Wu, and Thomas Chen, pp. 22–34. New Brunswick: Rutgers University Press, 2010. Copyright © 2010 by Rutgers, the State University. Reprinted by permission of Rutgers University Press.

and progress in racial rights have been measured through the experiences of African Americans. Slavery and its abolition, the black codes and the Reconstruction-era constitutional amendments, Jim Crow laws and the desegregation cases culminating in *Brown v. Board of Education*, the struggles of the civil rights movement and the federal legislation of the 1960s—these are the familiar signs that have dominated the landscape of civil rights in the United States. Debates on affirmative action have occasionally shone the spotlight on Asian Americans, but almost exclusively as unintended victims of affirmative action in higher education. Problems of ongoing racial discrimination and inequality among Asian American communities are largely ignored.

Not that focusing on black experiences is unjustified. African Americans have been the largest racial minority group in the United States since the country's birth, and continue to endure the effects of racial subordination. By any social or economic measure, African Americans suffer extensive inequality because of race. In describing the African American experience, the statement of the Kerner Commission resonates as strongly today as it did in 1968: "Our nation is moving toward two societies, one black, one white—separate but unequal."[2] But to say that our nation is moving toward two separate and unequal societies, however disconcerting, is fundamentally incomplete. Underlying the Kerner Commission's statement is the assumption that our nation's cities are divisible along a single racial axis. Cleavages between black and white persist but American race relations are not an exclusively black–white phenomenon and never have been. . . .

Black and White by Analogy

Dualism is a convenient lens through which to view the world. Black or white, male or female, straight or gay—the categories help us frame reality and make sense of it. In matters of race, a black–white dichotomy has been the dominant model, based primarily on the fact that African Americans have been the largest and most conspicuous nonwhite racial group in the United States. But the legal history of the United States is punctuated by the abridgment of rights among other racial and ethnic groups such as Asian Americans, and the country's changing demographics are mandating new perspectives based on the experiences of immigrants. Still, the black–white model is the regnant paradigm in both social and legal discussions of race.

How can Asian Americans fit within a black–white racial paradigm? Historian Gary Okihiro poses the question this way: "Is yellow black or white?" Okihiro suggests that Asian Americans have been "near-blacks" in the past and "near-whites" in the present, but that "[y]ellow is emphatically neither white nor black."[3] Recognizing the dominance of the black–white paradigm in the law, Frank Wu adopts a similar view proposing that Asian Americans have been forced to fit within race relations discourse through analogy to either whites or blacks. He posits that American society and its legal system have conceived of racial groups as whites, blacks, honorary whites, or constructive (legal jargon for "implied") blacks.[4]

For most of the nation's history, Asian Americans have been treated primarily as constructive blacks. Asian Americans for decades endured many of the same disabilities of racial subordination as African Americans—racial violence, segregation, unequal access to public institutions and discrimination in housing, employment, and education. The courts even classified Asian Americans as if they were black. In the mid-nineteenth century, the California Supreme Court held in *People v. Hall* that Chinese immigrants were barred from testifying in court under a statute prohibiting the testimony of blacks, by reasoning that "black" was a generic term encompassing all nonwhites, including Chinese: "[T]he words 'Black person' . . . must be taken as contradistinguished from White, and necessarily excludes all races other than the Caucasian."[5]

Similarly, in *Gong Lum v. Rice*, decided twenty-seven years before *Brown v. Board of Education*, the United States Supreme Court upheld the constitutionality of sending Asian American students to segregated schools. Comparing its earlier rulings on the "separate but equal" doctrine, the Court stated: "Most of the cases cited arose, it is true, over the establishment of separate schools as between white pupils and black pupils, but we can not think that the question is any different or that any different result can be reached . . . where the issue is as between white pupils and the pupils of the yellow races."[6] In the eyes of the Supreme Court, yellow equaled black, and neither equaled white.

In more recent years, the inclusion of Asian Americans in civil rights laws and race-conscious remedial programs has relied on the historical parallels between the experiences of Asian Americans and African Americans. The civil rights protections available to Asian Americans are most often contingent upon the rights granted to African Americans. Civil rights laws that apply to Asian Americans, as constructive blacks, can usually trace their origins to a legislative intent to protect African Americans from racial discrimination.

The treatment of Asian Americans as "honorary whites" is more unusual. In the Reconstruction-era South, Asian Americans were initially afforded a status above blacks for a period of time during the nineteenth century; Louisiana, for example, counted Chinese as whites for census purposes before 1870.[7] The status was short-lived: the Chinese were soon reduced to constructive black status under systems of racial segregation. More contemporary race relations controversies appear to have elevated Asian Americans to the status of honorary whites, particularly in the minds of those who oppose race-conscious remedies such as affirmative action. Asian Americans are often omitted from protection in affirmative action programs as a matter of course, lumped with whites even in contexts where Asian Americans still face racial discrimination and remain underrepresented.

The rigidity of the legal system's treatment of race as either black or white is evident in civil rights litigation filed by Asian American plaintiffs in the earlier half of this century. . . . Asian Americans sought, quite unsuccessfully, to be classified as white under the law, in recognition of the social and legal stigmas attached to being categorized as black. Gong Lum, for example, argued that his daughter Martha should not have to attend the school for colored children in Mississippi because "'[c]olored' describes only one race, and that is the negro."[8] Because his daughter was "pure Chinese," Gong Lum argued that she ought to have been classified with whites rather than blacks. The Court rejected this reasoning and held that yellow was black when it came to segregation.

During the late nineteenth and early twentieth centuries, Asian Americans sought to be classified as white in attempts to become naturalized citizens.[9] Congress enacted naturalization legislation in 1790 to limit citizenship to "free white persons." After the Civil War, the law was amended to allow persons of "African nativity" or "African descent" to naturalize, but Congress rejected extending naturalization to Asian immigrants. Asian immigrants sought relief through the courts, but had little success arguing that they were white: Burmese, Chinese, Filipino, Hawaiian, Japanese, and Korean plaintiffs were all held to be nonwhite; mixed-race plaintiffs who were half-white and half-Asian were also held to be nonwhite.[10] The United States Supreme Court laid to rest any questions about the racial bar in *Ozawa v. United States,* ruling that Japanese immigrants were not white, and in *United States v. Thind,* ruling that Asian Indian immigrants were not white.[11] Asian immigrants were prohibited by statute from naturalizing through the 1940s, and the racial bar on naturalization was not repealed until 1952.

From today's vantage point, these attempts by Asian immigrants to be classified as white may seem absurd and even subordinative, because they symbolically pushed blacks down the social ladder relative to whites and Asians. But when the legal paradigm limits options to black or white and nothing else, curious and unseemly choices inevitably arise. The solution, of course, is to develop and rely on theories that comprehend the complexity of race relations, which includes discerning that the experiences of Asian Americans are not the same as the experiences of African Americans.

Racism in Context: Anti-Asian Violence

To better understand the experiences of Asian Americans, consider how racial subordination operates within a specific context: anti-Asian violence. Racial violence is not a new phenomenon, and the histories of all racial minorities include extensive violence, whether it is the genocide of Native American tribes during the expansion of the United States, the terrorism against blacks in the South, the military conquest and ongoing border violence against Latinos in the Southwest, or the attacks on Asian immigrant laborers in the West. Incidents of anti-Asian violence reveal unique themes of prejudice and discrimination that illustrate the dynamics of racism against Asian Americans.[12] . . .

The most notorious episode of recent anti-Asian violence was the killing of Vincent Chin in 1982. Chin, a twenty-seven-year-old Chinese American, was celebrating his upcoming wedding at a Detroit bar when he was approached by Ronald Ebens and Michael Nitz, two white automobile factory workers. Ebens and Nitz thought Chin was Japanese and blamed him for the loss of jobs in the automobile industry. After calling Chin a "jap," the two men chased him out of the bar. They eventually caught Chin and proceeded to beat him repeatedly with a baseball bat. Chin died from his injuries a few days later. Ebens and Nitz each pleaded guilty to manslaughter but received only probation and a fine. Ebens was later convicted of federal civil rights violations, but his conviction was overturned on appeal and he was acquitted on retrial. Neither Ebens nor Nitz spent any time in prison for the killing.

A similar incident occurred in 1989 in Raleigh, North Carolina. Jim (Ming Hai) Loo had been playing pool with several friends when he was approached by Robert Piche and his brother Lloyd Piche, who began calling Loo and his friends "chinks" and "gooks" and blaming them for the death of American soldiers in Vietnam. Once outside, Robert Piche pistol-whipped Loo on the back of the head, causing Loo to fall onto a broken bottle that pierced his brain. Loo died from his injuries two days later. Robert Piche was convicted and sentenced to thirty-seven years in prison; Lloyd Piche was sentenced to six months in prison by a state court, and sentenced to four years in prison for federal civil rights violations.

Another tragic illustration of anti-Asian violence is the multiple killings of Asian American children at the Cleveland Elementary School in Stockton, California, in 1989. Patrick Purdy used an AK-47 assault rifle to spray bullets into a crowded schoolyard, killing five children and wounding over twenty others before turning the gun on himself. Although initially labeled the product of a disturbed mind obsessed with guns and the military, the shootings were later proved to be motivated by racial hatred. A report issued by the California attorney general's office found that Purdy targeted the school because it was heavily populated by Southeast Asian children.[13]

Perpetrators who are affiliated with hate groups have been responsible for many anti-Asian crimes. During the early 1980s, when tensions erupted between Vietnamese immigrant fishermen and native-born fishermen in several coastal states, the Ku Klux Klan engaged in extensive harassment and violence against Vietnamese fishermen along the Gulf Coast of Texas. Federal litigation was required to end a pattern of threats, cross burnings, arsons, and shootings.[14] In 1990, Hung Truong, a fifteen-year-old Vietnamese boy living in Houston, was attacked by two men who were later identified as white supremacist "skinheads." After following Truong and his friends as they walked down the street, the two assailants jumped out of their car, one wielding a club, and shouted "White power." They chased Truong and proceeded to kick and beat him, even as he pleaded for his life. The two men admitted at trial that they attacked Truong because he was Vietnamese.

In August 1999, Joseph Ileto, a Filipino American postal worker, was gunned down in California's San Fernando Valley by Buford Furrow, Jr., a white supremacist who earlier the same day had riddled the North Valley Jewish Community Center with over seventy rounds from a semi-automatic weapon and wounded several individuals, including three small children. Linked to anti-Semitic and white supremacist groups, Furrow shot Ileto nine times and admitted that he had targeted Ileto because he was a "chink or spic," terms that were no doubt tied to Furrow's perception that an individual like Ileto was somehow less than fully American. Ironically, Ileto was wearing a clear symbol of membership in American society—the uniform of a U.S. Postal Service mail carrier—at the time he was killed. Pleading guilty to avoid the imposition of a federal death penalty, Furrow was ultimately sentenced to multiple life sentences without possibility of parole.[15]

More common, however, are incidents that do not involve formal hate groups and that occur in day-to-day interactions among people at work, in schools, at home, and on the street. Here are some examples, all of which occurred during 2002:

- A Japanese American man in Rancho Santa Margarita, California was attacked in his front yard by a perpetrator who threw eggs at him and shouted "You dirty Jap!" while leaving the scene.
- While stalled in traffic, a Korean American woman, along with her young son, were approached by a man who slapped the woman, asked her if she was Korean several times, and shouted: "Why don't you go fuck some Japanese bastard?,"

"What are you doing in this country?," "Go back to your country," and "Go back to where you came from."

- In a supermarket parking lot in Fort Lee, New Jersey, a Korean American woman was verbally assaulted by a couple, one of whom yelled, "Where did you learn to drive? You chink!" After confronting the couple, the woman was threatened by another customer who yelled, "Yeah, go back to your own country!" . . .
- At a business in Los Angeles, a perpetrator brandished a knife and told a South Asian American victim, "I don't like Indians or Pakistanis and if you don't go back to your country, I'll kill you." . . .
- In Beverly Hills, California, a South Asian American man working as a restaurant valet was accosted by an individual who called the man an "Indian mother fucker" and asked "Are you a terrorist?" before attempting to assault the victim.[16] . . .

Racial Themes

Without question, the examples of anti-Asian violence demonstrate that overt racism is still a serious problem for Asian Americans, just as it has been for African Americans and other racial minorities. Some types of anti-Asian violence can thus be explained by treating violence against Asian Americans and other racial minority groups as expressions of white racism. Anti-Asian violence committed by white supremacists targeting anyone who is not white fits within a binary model of race that places all racial minorities in the same category of "nonwhite."

But many incidents of anti-Asian violence suggest that more complex dynamics are at work. Members of one Asian ethnic group are often mistaken for being members of other Asian ethnic groups. Racial and ethnic slurs are interlaced with nativist anti-immigrant rhetoric. Resentment about economic competition, both foreign and domestic, is often implicated. Even hostility rooted in the United States' previous military involvement in Asian countries may be a factor. And a white–nonwhite framework cannot explain racial violence in which members of one nonwhite group victimize members of another nonwhite group. Several basic themes can be gleaned from these and other examples of violence against Asian Americans.

Racialization

One theme is the importance of *racial* categorizing in anti-Asian violence. The killing of Vincent Chin is an example of how anti-Asian violence is racialized: based on his physical appearance, Chin, a Chinese American, was taken to be a Japanese national by his killers, who had made him the focus of their anger and frustration toward Japanese competition in the automobile industry. A perpetrator who makes the race-based generalization that all Asians look alike puts every Asian American at risk, even if the specific antagonisms are targeted against a smaller subset of people.

The attribution of specific ethnic characteristics to anyone falling within the racial category of "Asian" is common in anti-Asian violence. For example, when Luyen Phan Nguyen, a Vietnamese premedical student, was killed in Coral Springs, Florida, in 1992, he was taunted with slurs at a party and later chased down by a group of men who beat and kicked him repeatedly. Among the epithets directed at Nguyen during the beating were "chink," "vietcong," and "sayonara"—three separate and distinct ethnic slurs.

Nativism and Racism

Another theme manifested by anti-Asian violence is the centrality of nativism, which John Higham defines as "intense opposition to an internal minority on the ground of its foreign (i.e., 'un-American') connections."[17] Asian Americans are equated with foreigners, or they are at least presumed to be foreign-born. Race and nativism thus intersect to produce a distinctive form of subordination of Asian Americans—what Robert Chang labels "nativistic racism."[18]

In many incidents, Asian American victims are perceived and categorized as foreigners by their assailants: Vincent Chin was transformed into a Japanese national; Jim Loo became a Vietnamese adversary; immigrant merchants were remade as foreign investors and capitalists. Even Joseph Ileto, wearing the uniform of a U.S. Postal Service mail carrier, was reduced to the position of an outsider. Anti-immigrant epithets such as "Go home!" or "Why don't you go back to your own country?" frequently accompany anti-Asian violence, along with specific racial and ethnic slurs. And under the rubric of foreign outsider, Asian Americans fall into an array of unpopular categories: economic competitor, organized criminal, "illegal alien," or just unwelcome immigrant.

Patriotic racism is a peculiar and especially deep-seated form of nativist racism. American military conflicts against the Japanese during World War II, against Koreans and Chinese during the Korean War, and against the Vietnamese during the Vietnam War have generated intense animosity against Asian Americans. During World War II, the federal government's internment of Japanese Americans, most of whom were United States citizens, reflected patriotic racism at its worst, as a formal governmental policy. Intimidation and violence against Asian Americans is still common on December 7 because of the hostility that arises on the anniversary of the bombing of Pearl Harbor by Japan. And with the ongoing war against terrorism, South Asians, coupled with Arab Americans and Muslim Americans, have been subjected to extensive harassment, intimidation, and discrimination.

Racial Hierarchies and Interracial Conflict

A related theme made evident by anti-Asian violence revolves around the intermediate position that Asian Americans appear to occupy on a social and economic ladder that places whites on top and blacks at the bottom. Black-on-Asian hate crimes often contain strong elements of cultural conflict and nativism—blacks, like whites, treat Asians as foreigners. But black-on-Asian crimes also have strains traceable to resentment over the economic achievements of Asian Americans, particularly their entrepreneurial success in the inner cities. The destruction of Korean immigrants' businesses in 1992, many located in the historically black residential area of South Central Los Angeles, reflected a growing anger against Asian American prosperity.

In this context, the "model minority" stereotype of Asian Americans becomes a two-edged sword, breeding not only incomplete and inaccurate images of Asian American success but resentment and hostility on the part of other racial groups. Racial differentiation often places Asian Americans in a middle position within the racial hierarchy of the United States—neither black nor white, and somewhere between black and white.

The Limits of Black and White

Hate violence is the most extreme form of racial subordination against Asian Americans, but it sheds light on important differences between the subordination of Asian Americans and African Americans. A binary model of race based on relations between blacks and whites cannot fully describe the complex racial matrix that exists in the U.S. In terms of representation, a black–white model ignores or marginalizes the experiences of Asian Americans, Latinos, Native Americans, Arab Americans, and other groups who have extensive histories of discrimination against them. A black–white model discounts the role of immigration in race relations and confines discussion on the impact race has had on anti-immigrant policies that affect the nation's growing Asian American and Latino populations. A black–white model also limits any analysis of the relations and tensions between racial and ethnic groups, which are increasingly significant in urban areas where racial "minorities" are now becoming majorities.

In essence a black–white model fails to recognize that the basic nature of discrimination can differ among racial and ethnic groups. Theories of racial inferiority have been applied, often with violent force, against Asian Americans, just as they have been applied against blacks and other racial minority groups. But the causes of anti-Asian subordination can be traced to other factors as well, including nativism, differences in language and culture, perceptions of Asians as economic competitors, international relations, and past military involvement in Asian countries. Recent immigration from Asian countries has elevated culture and language to prominent places on the race relations landscape, challenging even the integrity of the racial category "Asian American." And the promotion in recent years of a "model minority" racial stereotype, based on the high education levels and incomes of some Asian Americans, represents a curious and distorted form of racism, denying the existence of Asian American poverty and inequality. All of these considerations point to the need for an analysis of race that is very different from the dominant black–white paradigm. . . .

NOTES

1. Andrew Hacker, *Two Nations: Black and White, Separate, Hostile, Unequal*, rev. ed. (New York: Ballantine Books, 1995). Hacker even suggests that Asian Americans and Latinos, particularly second- and later-generation individuals, are "merging" into the white race, through intermarriage and assimilation (18–19).
2. *Report of the National Advisory Commission on Civil Disorders* (New York: Bantam, 1968), 1.

3. Gary Y. Okihiro, *Margins and Mainstreams: Asians in American History and Culture* (Seattle and London: University of Washington Press, 1994), 34.

4. Frank H. Wu, "Neither Black nor White: Asian Americans and Affirmative Action," *Boston College Third World Law Journal* 15 (Summer 1995): 225, 249–251.

5. 4 Cal. 399, 404 (1854).

6. 275 U.S. 78, 87 (1927).

7. James W. Loewen, *The Mississippi Chinese: Between Black and White* (Cambridge, Mass.: Harvard University Press, 1971).

8. *Gong Lum v. Rice*, 275 U.S. 78, 79 (1927).

9. Ian F. Haney López, *White by Law: The Legal Construction of Race* (New York and London: New York University Press, 1996).

10. Ibid., appendix A. As Haney López notes, a legal strategy arguing for whiteness rather than blackness may have had some tactical advantage at the time, because the 1870 naturalization statute employed a geographic test rather than a racial test of eligibility for blacks: the law referred to persons of "African nativity, or African descent," rather than to "black persons." More likely, though, Asian American plaintiffs sought to distinguish themselves from blacks because of the stigmas attached to being black, and sought the only available alternative—to be classified as white.

11. 260 U.S. 178 (1922); 261 U.S. 204 (1923).

12. Note, "Racial Violence against Asian Americans," *Harvard Law Review* 106 (June 1993): 1926.

13. Nelson Kempsky, *A Report to Attorney General John K. Van de Kemp on Patrick Purdy and the Cleveland School Killings* (Sauamento: California Department of Justice, Office of the Attorney General, 1989).

14. *Vietnamese Fisherman's Association v. Knights of the Ku Klux Klan*, S43 F. Supp. 198 (S.D. Tex. 1982) (permanent injunction); *Vietnamese Fisherman's Association v. Knights of the Ku Klux Klan*, 518 F. Supp. 993 (S.D. Tex. 1981) (preliminary injunction).

15. "Moving Beyond the Past," *AsianWeek*, 25 May 2000; Henry Weinstein, "Furrow Gets 5 Life Terms for Racist Rampage," *Los Angeles Times*, 27 March 2001, p. B1.

16. National Asian Pacific American Legal Consortium, *2002 Audit of Violence against Asian Pacific Americans: Tenth Annual Report* (Washington, D.C.: National Asian Pacific American Legal Consortium, 2004), 14–23.

17. John Higham, *Strangers in the Land: Patterns of American Nativism, 1860–1925* (New York: Atheneum, 1970), 4.

18. Robert S. Chang, "Toward an Asian American Legal Scholarship: Critical Race Theory, Post-Structuralism, and Narrative Space," *California Law Review* 81 (October 1993): 1241, 1255.

7 | Los Intersticios: Recasting Moving Selves

Evelyn Alsultany

Ethnicity in such a world needs to be recast so that our moving selves can be acknowledged. . . . Who am I? When am I? The questions that are asked in the street, of my identity, mold me. Appearing in the flesh, I am cast afresh, a female of color—skin color, hair texture, clothing, speech, all marking me in ways that I could scarcely have conceived of.

—MEENA ALEXANDER

I'm in a graduate class at the New School in New York City. A white female sits next to me and we begin "friendly" conversation. She asks me where I'm from. I reply that I was born and raised in New York City and return the question. She tells me she is from Ohio and has lived in New York for several years. She continues her inquiry: "Oh . . . well, how about your parents?" (I feel her trying to map me onto her narrow cartography; New York is not a sufficient answer. She analyzes me according to binary axes of sameness and difference. She detects only difference at first glance, and seeks to pigeonhole me. In her framework, my body is marked, excluded, not from this country. A seemingly "friendly" question turns into a claim to land and belonging.) "My father is Iraqi and my mother Cuban," I answer. "How interesting. Are you a U.S. citizen?"

I am waiting for the NYC subway. A man also waiting asks me if I too am Pakistani. I reply that I'm part Iraqi and part Cuban. He asks if I am Muslim, and I reply that I am Muslim. He asks me if I am married, and I tell him I'm not. In cultural camaraderie he leans over and says that he has cousins in Pakistan available for an arranged marriage if my family so desires. (My Cubanness, as well as my own relationship to my cultural identity, evaporates as he assumes that Arab plus Muslim equals arranged marriage. I can identify: he reminds me of my Iraqi relatives and I know he means well.) I tell him that I'm not interested in marriage but thank him for his kindness. (I accept his framework and respond accordingly, avoiding an awkward situation in which he realizes that I am not who he assumes I am, offering him recognition and validation for his [mis]identification.)

I am in a New York City deli waiting for my bagel to toast. The man behind the counter asks if I'm an Arab Muslim (he too is Arab and Muslim). I reply that yes, I am by part of my father. He asks my name, and I say, "Evelyn." In utter disdain, he tells me that I could

Evelyn Alsultany is Arthur F. Thurnau professor and an associate professor in the Department of American Culture at the University of Michigan, where she cofounded and is the current director of the Arab and Muslim American Studies program.

not possibly be Muslim; if I were truly Muslim I would have a Muslim name. What was I doing with such a name? I reply (after taking a deep breath and telling myself that it's not worth getting upset over) that my Cuban mother named me and that I honor my mother. He points to the fact that I'm wearing lipstick and have not changed my name, which he finds to be completely inappropriate and despicable, and says that I am a reflection of the decay of the Arab Muslim in America.

I'm on an airplane flying from Miami to New York. I'm sitting next to an Ecuadorian man. He asks me where I'm from. I tell him. He asks me if I'm more Arab, Latina, or American, and I state that I'm all of the above. He says that's impossible. I must be more of one ethnicity than another. He determines that I am not really Arab, that I'm more Latina because of the camaraderie he feels in our speaking Spanish.

I am in Costa Rica. I walk the streets and my brown skin and dark hair blend in with the multiple shades of brown around me. I love this first-time experience of blending in! I walk into a coffee shop for some café con leche, and my fantasy of belonging is shattered when the woman preparing the coffee asks me where I'm from. I tell her that I was born and raised in New York City by a Cuban mother and an Arab father. She replies, "Que eres una gringa."

I am shocked by the contextuality of identity: that my body is marked as gringa in Costa Rica, as Latina in some U.S. contexts, Arab in others, in some times and spaces not adequately Arab, or Latina, or "American," and in other contexts simply as *other*.

My body becomes marked with meaning as I enter public space. My identity fractures as I experience differing dislocations in multiple contexts. Sometimes people otherize me, sometimes they identify with me. Both situations can be equally problematic. Those who otherize me fail to see a shared humanity and those who identify with me fail to see difference; my Arab or Muslim identity negates my Cuban heritage. Identification signifies belonging or home, and I pretend to be that home for the mistaken person. It's my good deed for the day (I know how precious it can be to find a moment of familiarity with a stranger). The bridge becomes my back as I feign belonging, and I become that vehicle for others, which I desire for myself. Although it is illusory, I do identify with the humanity of the situation—the desire to belong in this world, to be understood. But the frameworks used to (mis)read my body, to disconnect me, wear on me. I try to develop a new identity. What should I try to pass for next time? Perhaps I'll just say I'm Cuban to those who appear to be Arab or South Asian. A friend suggests I say I'm an Italian from Brooklyn. I wonder if I could successfully pass for that. Ethnicity needs to be recast so that our moving selves can be acknowledged.

Author's note: I would like to thank Marisol Negrón, Alexandra Lang, María Helena Rueda, Ericka Beckman, Karina Hodoyan, Sara Rondinel, Jessi Aaron, and Cynthia María Paccacerqua for their feedback in our writing seminar at Stanford University with Mary Pratt. I would especially like to thank Mary Pratt for her invaluable feedback, and AnaLouise Keating and Gloria Anzaldúa for their thoughtful editing.

8 The Case of Sharon Kowalski and Karen Thompson: Ableism, Heterosexism, and Sexism

Joan L. Griscom

In November, 1983, Sharon Kowalski was in a head-on collision with a drunk driver, suffered a severe brain-stem injury, became paralyzed, and lost the ability to speak. Sharon was in a committed partnership with Karen Thompson. Serious conflict soon developed between Karen and Kowalski's parents, erupting in a series of lawsuits that lasted eight years. Karen fought to secure adequate rehabilitation for Sharon as well as access to friends and family of her choice. In 1985, acting under Minnesota guardianship laws, Sharon's father placed her in a nursing home without adequate rehabilitation services and prohibited Karen and others from visiting her. Karen continued to fight through the courts and the media. In 1989, Sharon was finally transferred to an appropriate rehabilitation facility, reunited with lover and friends, and, in 1991, finally allowed her choice to live with Karen.

In this article I tell the story of Sharon Kowalski and Karen Thompson. While the story shows violations of their human rights, it is more than a story of two individuals. The injustices they encountered were modes of oppression that operate at a social-structural level and affect many other people. These oppressions include ableism, discrimination against disabled persons; heterosexism, the structuring of our institutions to legitimate only heterosexual relationships; and sexism, discrimination against women. Their story shows the power of structural discrimination, the intertwining of both our medical and legal systems in ways that denied both of them the fullest quality of life.

A History of the Events

By November 1983, Sharon and Karen had lived in partnership for almost four years. Karen was thirty-six, teaching physical education at St. Cloud State University, devoutly religious, conservative. Sharon was twenty-seven, a fine athlete who had graduated from St. Cloud in physical education and just accepted a staff coaching position. She had grown up in the Iron Mine area of Minnesota, a conservative world where women are expected to marry young. Defying such expectations, she became first in her family to attend college, earning tuition working part-time in the mines. After she and Karen fell in love, they exchanged rings, bought a house together, and vowed lifetime commitment.

Joan L. Griscom (1930–2017) was a professor of women's studies at William Paterson University; she published widely on women and power, race, sexuality, disability, transgender issues, and ecology.

Reprinted by permission of the author.

After the accident Sharon lay in a coma for weeks, and doctors were pessimistic about her recovery. Karen spent hours, daily, talking to her, reading the Bible, massaging and stretching her neck, shoulders, and hands. It is essential to massage and stretch brain-injured persons in comas, for their muscles tend to curl up tightly and incur permanent damage. Early in 1984, Karen saw Sharon moving her right index finger, and found that she could indicate answers to questions by moving it. Later she began to tap her fingers, then slowly learned to write letters and words.

The Kowalski parents became suspicious of the long hours Karen was spending with her, and increasingly Karen feared they would try to exclude her from Sharon's life. After consulting a psychologist, she wrote them a letter explaining their love, in hopes they would understand her importance to Sharon. They reacted with shock, denial, and rage. As the nightmare deepened, Karen consulted a lawyer and learned she had no legal rights, unless she won guardianship. In March, 1984, she therefore filed for guardianship, and Donald Kowalski counterfiled.

Guardianship was awarded to Kowalski, but Karen was granted equal access to medical and financial information and full visitation rights. She continued to participate in both physical and occupational therapy. Sharon improved slowly; Karen made her an alphabet board, and she began to spell out answers to questions. Later she began to communicate by typewriter, and in August spoke a few words. But conflicts continued. The day after the court decision Kowalski incorrectly told Karen she did not have visitation rights, and later tried to cancel her work with Sharon's therapists. When Karen and others took Sharon out on day passes, he objected, subsequently testifying in court that he did not want her out in public. In October, Sharon was moved further away, and Kowalski filed to gain full power as guardian. Karen counterfiled to remove him as guardian.

Months elapsed while the legal battles were fought. Sharon was moved several times, regressed in her skills, and became clinically depressed. The Minnesota Civil Liberties Union (MCLU) entered the case, arguing that under the First Amendment Sharon's rights of free speech and free association were being violated. A tri-county Handicap Services Program submitted testimony of Sharon's capacity to communicate, including a long conversation in which she stated she was gay and Karen was her lover. At Sharon's request, the MCLU asked to represent her and suggested she might testify for herself. The court refused both requests, finding that Sharon lacked understanding to make decisions for herself. In July, 1985, Kowalski was awarded full guardianship. Within a day, he denied visitation to Karen, other friends, the MCLU, and disability rights groups; in two days he transferred her to a nursing home near his home with only minimal rehabilitation facilities. In August, 1985, Karen saw Sharon for what would be the last time for over three years.

As this summary indicates, the medical system failed Sharon in at least three respects. First, it failed to supply rehabilitation in the years when it was vital to her recovery. Stark in the medical record is the fact that this woman who was starting to stand and to feed herself was locked away for over three years with an implanted feeding tube, left insufficiently stretched so that muscles that had been starting to work curled back on themselves again. Second, she was deprived of the bombardment of emotional and physical stimulation needed to regenerate her cognitive faculties. Once in the nursing home, for example, she was forbidden regenerative outside excursions. Third, although medical staff often recognized Sharon's unusual response to Karen, they failed to explain to her parents its importance. Despite an urgent need for counseling to assist the parents, none, except for one court-mandated session, took place.

The failure of the medical system was consistently supported by the legal system. Initially the court ruled that Sharon must have access to a young-adult rehabilitation ward. But once Kowalski won full guardianship, he was able to move her to a nursing home without such a ward. In 1985 the Office of Health Facility Complaints investigated Sharon's right to choose visitors, a right guaranteed by the Minnesota Patient Bill of Rights, and found that indeed her right was being violated. However, the appeals court held that the Patient Bill of Rights was inapplicable, since the healthcare facility was not restricting the right of visitation, the guardian was.

The deficiencies of guardianship law are a central problem in this case. First, a guardian can restrict a person's rights, without legal recourse. As is often said, under present laws a guardian can lock up a person and throw away the key. This is a national problem, affecting the disabled, the elderly, anyone presumed incompetent. Second, guardians are inadequately supervised. Under Minnesota law, a guardian is required to have the ward tested annually for competence. Kowalski never did, and for over three years the courts did not require him to. In 1985, Karen first filed a motion to hold him in contempt for failure to arrange testing and for failure to heed Sharon's wishes for visitation. The courts routinely rejected such motions.

Between 1985 and 1988, Karen and the MCLU pursued repeated appeals to various Minnesota courts, all denied. Karen began to seek help from the media, also disability, gay/lesbian, women's, and church groups. She recognized that the legal precedents could be devastating for others, e.g., gay/lesbian couples or unmarried heterosexual couples. The reserved, closeted, conservative professor was slowly transformed into a passionate public speaker in her quest to secure freedom and rehabilitation for Sharon; and slowly she gained national attention. The alternative press responded; national groups such as the National Organization for Women were supportive; the National Committee to Free Sharon Kowalski formed, with regional chapters. Finally the mainstream media began publishing concerned articles; Karen appeared on national TV programs; state and national politicians, including Jesse Jackson, spoke out. Meanwhile Sharon remained in the nursing home, cut off from friends, physically regressed, psychologically depressed.

The first break in the case came in February, 1988. In response to a new motion from Karen, requesting that Sharon be tested for competence, testing was ordered. In January, 1989, she was moved to the Miller-Dwan Medical Center for a 60-day evaluation. Kowalski unsuccessfully argued in court against both the move and the testing. Sharon immediately expressed her wish to see Karen. On February 2, 1989, Karen visited her for the first time in three and a half years, an event which made banner headlines in the alternative press across the nation. She was, however, highly depressed, with numerous physical problems: for example, her feet had curled up so tightly that she was no longer able to stand. More significant was her cognitive ability; to this day, her short-term memory loss remains considerable.

The competency evaluation nevertheless demonstrated that she could communicate on an adult level and had significant potential for rehabilitation. The report recommended "her return to pre-morbid home environment," and added:

> We believe Sharon has shown areas of potential and ability to make rational choices in many areas of her life. She has consistently indicated a desire to return home . . . to live with Karen Thompson again.

Donald Kowalski subsequently resigned as guardian, for both financial and health reasons, and the parents stopped attending medical conferences. In June, 1989, Sharon was transferred to a long-term rehabilitation center for brain-injured young adults. Here she had extensive occupational, physical, and speech therapy. Again Karen spent hours with her and took her out on trips. She had surgery on her legs, feet, toes, left shoulder and arm to reverse the results of three years of inadequate care. She began to use a speech synthesizer and a motorized wheelchair.

Karen subsequently filed for guardianship. Medical staff testified unanimously that Sharon was capable of deciding for herself what relationships she wanted and where she wished to live. They testified that she was capable of living outside an institution and Karen was best qualified to care for her in a home environment. Witnesses for the Kowalskis opposed the petition. The judge appeared increasingly uncomfortable with the national publicity. While in 1990 he allowed Sharon and Karen to fly out to San Francisco where each received a Woman of Courage Award from the National Organization for Women, he refused Sharon permission to attend the first Disability Pride Day in Boston. He issued a gag order against Karen, which was overturned on appeal. Finally, in April, 1991, he denied Karen guardianship and awarded it to a supposedly "neutral third party," a former classmate of Sharon who lived near the Kowalski parents and had testified against Karen in a 1984 hearing. This decision raised the alarming possibility that Sharon might be returned to the inadequate facility. Karen appealed it.

In December, 1991, the appeals court reversed the judge's ruling and granted guardianship to Karen, on two bases: first, the medical testimony that Sharon was able to make her own choices; and second, the fact that the two women are "a family of affinity" that deserves respect. This is a major decision in U.S. legal history, setting important legal precedents both for disabled people and gay/lesbian families. Sharon and Karen now live together.

The Three Modes of Oppression

Sharon and Karen were denied their rights by three interacting systems of oppression: ableism, heterosexism, and sexism. Originally Karen believed that their difficulties were merely personal problems. All her life she had believed that our social institutions are basically fair, designed to support individual rights. In the book she co-authored with Julie Andrzejewski[1], she documented her growing awareness that widespread social/political forces were involved in their supposedly personal problems and that the oppression they experienced was systemic.

Ableism was rampant throughout. Sharon's inability to speak was often construed as incompetence, and her particular kinds of communication were not recognized. Quite early Karen noticed some did not speak to Sharon, some talked loudly as if she was deaf, others spoke to her as if she were a child. One doctor discussed her in her presence as if she was not there. When Karen later asked how she felt about this, she typed out "Shitty." Probably one reason she responded to Karen more than anyone was that Karen talked extensively and read to her, played music, asked questions, and constantly consulted her wishes. Although the MCLU and the Handicap Services Program submitted transcripts of long conversations with her, the courts did not accept these as evidence of competence, relying instead on testimony from people who had much less interaction with her. A major article in the St. Paul *Pioneer Press* (1987) described the Kowalskis visiting the room "where their eerily silent daughter lies trapped in her twisted body." Eerily silent? This is the person who typed out "columbine" when asked her favorite flower, answered arithmetical questions correctly, and responded to numerous questions about her life, feelings, and wishes. She also communicates nonverbally in many ways: gestures, smiles, tears, and laughter.

Thanks to ableism, Sharon was often stereotyped as helpless. The presumption of helplessness "traps" her far more severely than her "twisted body." Once a person is labeled helpless, there is no need to consult her wishes, consider her written communications, hear her testimony. When Sharon arrived at Miller-Dwan for competency testing, Karen reported with joy that staff was giving her information and allowing her choices, even if her choice was to do nothing. Most seriously, if a person is seen as helpless, then there is no potential for rehabilitation. As Ellen Bilofsky[2] has written, Sharon was presumed "incompetent until proven competent." If Karen's legal motion for competency testing had not been accepted, Sharon might have remained in the nursing home indefinitely, presumed incompetent.

Finally, ableism can lead to keeping disabled persons hidden, literally out of sight. Kowalski argued against day passes, resisted Karen's efforts to take Sharon out, and testified he would not take her to a church or shopping center because he did not wish to put her "on display . . . in her condition." Although medical staff could see that outside trips provided Sharon with pleasure and stimulation, both important for cognitive rehabilitation, they cooperated with the father in denying them. According to an article in the *Washington Post*, he once said, "What the hell difference does it make if she's gay or lesbian or straight or anything because she's laying there in diapers? . . . let the poor kid rest in peace."

Invisible in the nursing home, cut off from lover and friends, Sharon had little chance to demonstrate competence. The wonder is that after three and a half years of loss, loneliness, and lack of care, she was able to emerge from her depression and respond to her competency examiners. To retain her capacity for response, through such an experience, suggests a strong spirit.

The second mode of oppression infusing this case is heterosexism, the structuring of our institutions so as to legitimate heterosexuality only. Glaringly apparent is the failure to recognize gay/lesbian partnerships. When Karen was first to arrive at the hospital after the accident, she was not allowed access to Sharon or even any information, because she was not "family." Seeing her anguish, a Roman Catholic priest interceded, brought information, and arranged for a doctor to speak with her. Although the two women considered themselves married, in law they were not, and therefore lacked any legal rights as a couple. If heterosexual, there would have been no denial of visitation, no long nightmare of the three-and-a-half-year separation. While unmarried heterosexual partners might have trouble securing guardianship, married partners would not.

Because of heterosexism, Sharon's emotional need for her partner and Karen's rehabilitative effect on her were not honored. Because of Sharon's response, Karen was often included in the therapeutic work. Yet, prior to 1989, medical staff often refused to testify to this positive effect. Perhaps they feared condoning the same-sex relationship, perhaps they wished to stay out of the conflict. One neurologist, Dr. Keith Larson, did testify, although stipulating that he spoke as friend of the court, not as witness for Karen.

> The reason I'm here today is . . . to deliver an observation that I have agonized over and thought a great deal about, and prayed a little bit. . . . I cannot help but say that Sharon's friend, Karen, can get out of Sharon physical actions, attempts at vocalization, and longer periods of alertness and attention than can really any of our professional therapists.

Why was it necessary to "agonize" over this testimony? Pray about it? Make such a tremendous effort? Clearly, were one of the partners male, Larson would have had no difficulty. He simply would have reported that the patient responded to her partner. Some medical staff did testify positively, without effort; and after 1989, testimony from medical personnel was strong and unanimous. However, repeatedly, the courts ignored it.

Finally, heterosexism is evident in a consistent tendency to exaggerate the role of sex in same-sex relationships. Many believe that the lives of gay/lesbian people revolve around sex, though evidence from all social-psychological research is that homosexual people are no more sexually active than heterosexual people. Further, gay/lesbian sex is often perceived as sexual exploitation rather than an expression of mutual caring. The final denial of Karen's visitation rights was based on the charge that she might sexually abuse Sharon. A physician hired by the Kowalskis, Dr. William L. Wilson, leveled this charge:

> Karen Thompson has been involved in bathing Sharon Kowalski behind a closed door for a prolonged period of time. . . . Ms. Thompson has [also] alleged a sexual relationship with Sharon Kowalski that existed prior to the accident. Based on this knowledge and my best medical judgment . . . I feel that visits by Karen Thompson at this time would expose Sharon Kowalski to a high risk of sexual abuse.

Accordingly, Wilson directed the nursing home staff not to let Karen visit. Even though under statutes, Karen could have continued to visit while the court decisions were under appeal, the nursing home was obliged to obey the doctor's order.

In this instance, ableism and heterosexism merge. If they were unmarried heterosexual partners, sexual abuse probably would not have been an issue. If married, the issue would not exist. Ableism often denies disabled persons their sexuality, though a person does not lose her sexuality simply because she becomes disabled. Also, a person who loses the capacity to speak has a special need for touching. What were Sharon's sexual rights? When she was starting to emerge from the coma, she once reached out and touched Karen's breast, and later placed Karen's hand on her breast. At the time Karen did not dare ask medical advice for fear of revealing their relationship. Even to raise such questions might have exposed her to more charges of sexual abuse.

While same-sex relationships are often called "anti-family" in our heterosexist society, actually such relationships create family, in that they create stable emotional and economic units. Family, in this sense, may be defined as a kin-like unit of two or more persons related by blood, marriage, adoption, or primary commitment, who usually share the same household. Sharon and Karen considered themselves married. Karen's long pilgrimage over almost nine years testifies to an extraordinary depth of commitment. Sharon consistently said she was gay, Karen was her lover, she wanted to live with her. While marriage has historically occurred between two sexes, history cannot determine its definition. In U.S. history, marriage between black and white persons was forbidden for centuries. In 1967, when the Supreme Court finally declared miscegenation laws unconstitutional, there were still such laws in sixteen states.

Sexism is sufficiently interfused with heterosexism that they are hard to separate. Often sexism enforces a social role on women in which they are subordinated to men. Women in the Minnesota world where Sharon grew up were expected to marry young and submit to their husbands' authority, an intrinsically sexist model. According to this model, her partnership with Karen was illegitimate. Sexism also is apparent in awarding guardianship to the father. Had Sharon been a man rather than a twenty-eight-year-old "girl," such a decision might be less possible; but in a sexist society, it is appropriate to assign an adult woman to her male parent. Finally, our society devalues friendship, especially between women. Once, very early, a doctor advised Karen to forget Sharon. The gist of his remarks was that "Sharon's parents will always be her parents. They have to deal with this, but you don't. Maybe you should go back to leading your own life." Friendship between the two women was unimportant. Ableism as well as sexism is apparent in these remarks.

This case makes clear that the modes of oppression work simultaneously. Like Audre Lorde[3], I argue that "there is no hierarchy of oppression." Disability was not more important than sexuality in curtailing Sharon's freedoms; they worked together seamlessly, in her life as in the legal and medical systems. Admittedly, any individual's perspective on the case may reflect the issue most central to her or his life: e.g., the gay press, reporting the case, emphasized heterosexism, and the disability rights press emphasized ableism. Working in coalition on this case, some women were ill at ease with disability rights activists; and some disability rights groups were anxious about associating with gay/lesbian issues. But there are lesbians and gays in the disabled community, and disabled folks in women's groups. Karen experienced the inseparability of the issues once when invited to speak to a Presbyterian group. They asked her to speak only about ableism since they had already "done" gay/lesbian concerns. She tried, but found it nearly impossible; she had to censor her material, ignore basic facts, leave out crucial connections.

In each mode of oppression, one group of persons takes power over another, and this power is institutionalized. Disabled people, women, gay men and lesbians, and others are all to some degree denied their full personhood by the structures of our society. Their choices can be denied, their sexuality is controlled. On the basis of ableism, heterosexism, and sexism, both Karen Thompson's and Sharon Kowalski's opportunities for the fullest quality of life were taken from them. Sharon lost cognitive ability that might have been saved. As the Minnesota Civil Liberties Union put it, "The convicted criminal loses only his or her liberty; Sharon Kowalski has lost the right to choose whom she may see, who she may like, and who she may love." To change this picture took nearly nine years of struggle by a partner who lived out her vow of lifetime commitment and the work of many committed persons and groups.

Conclusion

Many national groups joined the struggle to provide rehabilitation for Sharon and bring her home, including disability rights activists, gays and lesbians, feminists and male supporters, and civil rights groups. In addition there were thousands of people drawn to this case by simple human rights. After all, any of us could be hit by a drunk driver, become disabled, and in the process lose our legal and medical rights. The Kowalski/Thompson case stands as a warning that in our deeply divided society, freedom is still a privilege and rights are fragile.

People living in nontraditional families need legal protection to secure legal and medical rights. Karen Thompson stresses the importance of making your relationships known to your family of birth, if possible, and informing them of your wishes in case of disability or death. Also, it is essential to execute a durable power of attorney, a document that stipulates a person to make medical and financial decisions for you, in case of need. Copies should be given to your physician. While requirements vary between states and powers of attorney are not always enforceable, they may protect your rights. Information about how to execute them may be found in your public library, in consultation with a competent lawyer, or in Appendix B of the book *Why Can't Sharon Kowalski Come Home?*

Author's note: I am indebted to Paula Rothenberg for earlier creative editing that much improved the clarity of this essay.

NOTES

1. Karen Thompson and Julie Andrzejewski. *Why Can't Sharon Kowalski Come Home?* San Francisco: Spinster/Aunt Lute, 1988. All quotations in text are from this book.
2. Ellen Bilofsky. "The Fragile Rights of Sharon Kowalski." *Health/PAC Bulletin*, 1989, *19*, 4–16.
3. Audre Lorde. "There Is No Hierarchy of Oppressions." *Interracial Books for Children Bulletin*, 1983, *14*, 9.

9 | Homophobia as a Weapon of Sexism

Suzanne Pharr

Patriarchy—an enforced belief in male dominance and control—is the ideology and sexism the system that holds it in place. The catechism goes like this: Who do gender roles serve? Men and the women who seek power from them. Who suffers from gender roles? Women most completely and men in part. How are gender roles maintained? By the weapons of sexism: economics, violence, homophobia.

Why then don't we ardently pursue ways to eliminate gender roles and therefore sexism? It is my profound belief that all people have a spark in them that yearns for freedom, and the history of the world's atrocities—from the Nazi concentration camps to white dominance in South Africa to the battering of women—is the story of attempts to snuff out that spark. When that spark doesn't move forward to full flame, it is because the weapons designed to control and destroy have wrought such intense damage over time that the spark has been all but extinguished.

Sexism, that system by which women are kept subordinate to men, is kept in place by three powerful weapons designed to cause or threaten women with pain and loss. . . .

We have to look at economics not only as the root cause of sexism but also as the underlying, driving force that keeps all the oppressions in place. In the United States, our economic system is shaped like a pyramid, with a few people at the top, primarily white males, being supported by large numbers of unpaid or low-paid workers at the bottom. When we look at this pyramid, we begin to understand the major connection between sexism and racism because those groups at the bottom of the pyramid are women and people of color. We then begin to understand why there is such a fervent effort to keep those oppressive systems (racism and sexism and all the ways they are manifested) in place to maintain the unpaid and low-paid labor.

As in most other countries, in the United States, income is unequally distributed. However, among the industrialized countries of the world, the U.S. has the most unequal distribution of income of all. (See *The State of Working America 2000/2001*, p. 388.*) What's more, over the past 30 plus years, income distribution has become even more unequal. In

*Also see World Economic Forum, The Inclusive Development Index 2018 Summary and Data Highlights.

Suzanne Pharr is an organizer, educator, and political strategist. She cofounded Southerners on New Ground (SONG) and served as director of the Highlander Research and Education Center from 1999 to 2004.

an OpEd piece distributed by Knight/Ridder/Tribune NewsService, Holly Sklar reports that poverty rates in 2001 were higher than in the 1970s and the top 5% of households got richer at the expense of everyone else. According to the U.S. Census bureau, there were 33 million poor in the U.S. in 2001 and median pretax income fell for all households except those in the top 5%. In other words, income inequality increased dramatically. In 1967, the wealthiest 5% of households had 17.5% of the income and by 2001 they had increased their share to 22.4%, while the bottom fifth had to make do with 3.5% of aggregate income, down from 4% in 1967 (September 30, 2002). And wealth is even more unequally distributed than income. According to U.S. government figures for 1997, the wealthiest 10% of U.S. families own more than 72% of the total wealth, with 39% of the total wealth concentrated in the hands of the wealthiest 1%. In contrast, the bottom 40% of the population owns less than 1%.[†]

In order for this top-heavy system of economic inequity to maintain itself, the 90 percent on the bottom must keep supplying cheap labor. A very complex, intricate system of institutionalized oppressions is necessary to maintain the status quo so that the vast majority will not demand its fair share of wealth and resources and bring the system down. Every institution—schools, banks, churches, government, courts, media, etc.—as well as individuals must be enlisted in the campaign to maintain such a system of gross inequity.

What would happen if women gained the earning opportunities and power that men have? What would happen if these opportunities were distributed equitably, no matter what sex one was, no matter what race one was born into, and no matter where one lived? What if educational and training opportunities were equal? Would women spend most of our youth preparing for marriage? Would marriage be based on economic survival for women? What would happen to issues of power and control? Would women stay with our batterers? If a woman had economic independence in a society where women had equal opportunities, would she still be thought of as owned by her father or husband?

Economics is the great controller in both sexism and racism. If a person can't acquire food, shelter, and clothing and provide them for children, then that person can be forced to do many things in order to survive. The major tactic, worldwide, is to provide unrecompensed or inadequately recompensed labor for the benefit of those who control wealth. Hence, we see women performing unpaid labor in the home or filling low-paid jobs, and we see people of color in the lowest-paid jobs available.

The method is complex: limit educational and training opportunities for women and for people of color and then withhold adequate paying jobs with the excuse that people of color and women are incapable of filling them. Blame the economic victim and keep the victim's self-esteem low through invisibility and distortion within the media and education. Allow a few people of color and women to succeed among the profitmakers so that blaming those who don't "make it" can be intensified. Encourage those few who succeed in gaining power now to turn against those who remain behind rather than to use their resources to make change for all. Maintain the myth of scarcity—that there are

[†]Wealth and income inequality have continued to grow since the time of Pharrs's writing. As of 2016, the top 1% of households owned 39.6% of the wealth, the top 10% owned 78.8%, and the bottom 40% owned less than 0.5% (Edward N. Wolff, "Household Wealth Trends in the United States, 1962 to 2016: Has Middle Class Wealth Recovered?" National Bureau of Economic Research Working Paper No. w24085, November 2017.)

not enough jobs, resources, etc., to go around—among the middle class so that they will not unite with laborers, immigrants, and the unemployed. The method keeps in place a system of control and profit by a few and a constant source of cheap labor to maintain it.

If anyone steps out of line, take her/his job away. Let homelessness and hunger do their work. The economic weapon works. And we end up saying, "I would do this or that—be openly who I am, speak out against injustice, work for civil rights, join a labor union, go to a political march, etc.—if I didn't have this job. I can't afford to lose it." We stay in an abusive situation because we see no other way to survive. . . .

Violence against women is directly related to the condition of women in a society that refuses us equal pay, equal access to resources, and equal status with males. From this condition comes men's confirmation of their sense of ownership of women, power over women, and assumed right to control women for their own means. Men physically and emotionally abuse women because they *can*, because they live in a world that gives them permission. Male violence is fed by their sense of their *right* to dominate and control, and their sense of superiority over a group of people who, because of gender, they consider inferior to them.

It is not just the violence but the threat of violence that controls our lives. Because the burden of responsibility has been placed so often on the potential victim, as women we have curtailed our freedom in order to protect ourselves from violence. Because of the threat of rapists, we stay on alert, being careful not to walk in isolated places, being careful where we park our cars, adding incredible security measures to our homes—massive locks, lights, alarms, if we can afford them—and we avoid places where we will appear vulnerable or unprotected while the abuser walks with freedom. Fear, often now so commonplace that it is unacknowledged, shapes our lives, reducing our freedom. . . .

Part of the way sexism stays in place is the societal promise of survival, false and unfulfilled as it is, that women will not suffer violence if we attach ourselves to a man to protect us. A woman without a man is told she is vulnerable to external violence and, worse, that there is something wrong with her. When the male abuser calls a woman a lesbian, he is not so much labeling her a woman who loves women as he is warning her that by resisting him, she is choosing to be outside society's protection from male institutions and therefore from wide-ranging, unspecified, ever-present violence. When she seeks assistance from woman friends or a battered women's shelter, he recognizes the power in woman bonding and fears loss of her servitude and loyalty: the potential loss of his control. The concern is not affectional/sexual identity: the concern is disloyalty and the threat is violence.

The threat of violence against women who step out of line or who are disloyal is made all the more powerful by the fact that women do not have to do anything—they may be paragons of virtue and subservience—to receive violence against our lives: the violence still comes. It comes because of the woman-hating that exists throughout society. Chance plays a larger part than virtue in keeping women safe. Hence, with violence always a threat to us, women can never feel completely secure and confident. Our sense of safety is always fragile and tenuous.

Many women say that verbal violence causes more harm than physical violence because it damages self-esteem so deeply. Women have not wanted to hear battered women say that the verbal abuse was as hurtful as the physical abuse: to acknowledge that truth would be tantamount to acknowledging that *virtually every woman is a battered woman.* It is difficult to keep strong against accusations of being a bitch, stupid, inferior, etc., etc. It is especially difficult when these individual assaults are backed up by a society that shows women in textbooks, advertising, TV programs, movies, etc. as debased, silly, inferior, and sexually objectified, and a society that gives tacit approval to pornography. When we internalize these messages, we call the result "low self-esteem," a therapeutic individualized term. It seems to me we should use the more political expression: when we internalize these messages, we experience *internalized sexism,* and we experience it in common with all women living in a sexist world. The violence against us is supported by a society in which woman-hating is deeply imbedded.

In "Eyes on the Prize," a 1987 Public Television documentary about the Civil Rights Movement, an older white woman says about her youth in the South that it was difficult to be anything different from what was around her when there was no vision for another way to be. Our society presents images of women that say it is appropriate to commit violence against us. Violence is committed against women because we are seen as inferior in status and in worth. It has been the work of the women's movement to present a vision of another way to be.

Every time a woman gains the strength to resist and leave her abuser, we are given a model of the importance of stepping out of line, of moving toward freedom. And we all gain strength when she says to violence, "Never again!" Thousands of women in the last fifteen years have resisted their abusers to come to this country's 1100 battered women's shelters. There they have sat down with other women to share their stories, to discover that their stories again and again are the same, to develop an analysis that shows that violence is a statement about power and control, and to understand how sexism creates the climate for male violence. Those brave women are now a part of a movement that gives hope for another way to live in equality and peace.

Homophobia works effectively as a weapon of sexism because it is joined with a powerful arm, heterosexism. Heterosexism creates the climate for homophobia with its assumption that the world is and must be heterosexual and its display of power and privilege as the norm. Heterosexism is the systemic display of homophobia in the institutions of society. Heterosexism and homophobia work together to enforce compulsory heterosexuality and that bastion of patriarchal power, the nuclear family. The central focus of the rightwing attack against women's liberation is that women's equality, women's self-determination, women's control of our own bodies and lives will damage what they see as the crucial societal institution, the nuclear family. The attack has been led by fundamentalist ministers across the country. The two areas they have focused on most consistently are abortion and homosexuality, and their passion has led them to bomb women's clinics and to recommend deprogramming for homosexuals and establishing camps to quarantine people with AIDS. To resist marriage and/or heterosexuality is to risk severe punishment and loss.

It is not by chance that when children approach puberty and increased sexual awareness they begin to taunt each other by calling these names: "queer," "faggot," "pervert." It is at puberty that the full force of society's pressure to conform to heterosexuality and prepare for marriage is brought to bear. Children know what we have taught them, and we have given clear messages that those who deviate from standard expectations are to be made to get back in line. The best controlling tactic at puberty is to be treated as an outsider, to be ostracized at a time when it feels most vital to be accepted. Those who are different must be made to suffer loss. It is also at puberty that misogyny begins to be more apparent, and girls are pressured to conform to societal norms that do not permit them to realize their full potential. It is at this time that their academic achievements begin to decrease as they are coerced into compulsory heterosexuality and trained for dependency upon a man, that is, for economic survival.

There was a time when the two most condemning accusations against a woman meant to ostracize and disempower her were "whore" and "lesbian." The sexual revolution and changing attitudes about heterosexual behavior may have led to some lessening of the power of the word *whore*, though it still has strength as a threat to sexual property and prostitutes are stigmatized and abused. However, the word *lesbian* is still fully charged and carries with it the full threat of loss of power and privilege, the threat of being cut asunder, abandoned, and left outside society's protection.

To be a lesbian is to be *perceived* as someone who has stepped out of line, who has moved out of sexual/economic dependence on a male, who is woman-identified. A lesbian is perceived as someone who can live without a man, and who is therefore (however illogically) against men. A lesbian is perceived as being outside the acceptable, routinized order of things. She is seen as someone who has no societal institutions to protect her and who is not privileged to the protection of individual males. Many heterosexual women see her as someone who stands in contradiction to the sacrifices they have made to conform to compulsory heterosexuality. A lesbian is perceived as a threat to the nuclear family, to male dominance and control, to the very heart of sexism.

Gay men are perceived also as a threat to male dominance and control, and the homophobia expressed against them has the same roots in sexism as does homophobia against lesbians. Visible gay men are the objects of extreme hatred and fear by heterosexual men because their breaking ranks with male heterosexual solidarity is seen as a damaging rent in the very fabric of sexism. They are seen as betrayers, as traitors who must be punished and eliminated. In the beating and killing of gay men we see clear evidence of this hatred. When we see the fierce homophobia expressed toward gay men, we can begin to understand the ways sexism also affects males through imposing rigid, dehumanizing gender roles on them. The two circumstances in which it is legitimate for men to be openly physically affectionate with one another are in competitive sports and in the crisis of war. For many men, these two experiences are the highlights of their lives, and they think of them again and again with nostalgia. War and sports offer a cover of all-male safety and dominance to keep away the notion of affectionate openness being identified with homosexuality. When gay men break ranks with male roles through bonding and affection outside the arenas of war and sports, they are perceived as not being "real men," that is, as being identified with women, the weaker sex that must be dominated and that over the centuries has been the object of male hatred and abuse. Misogyny gets transferred to gay men with a vengeance and is increased by the fear that their sexual identity and behavior will bring down the entire system of male dominance and compulsory heterosexuality.

If lesbians are established as threats to the status quo, as outcasts who must be punished, homophobia can wield its power over all women through lesbian baiting. Lesbian baiting is an attempt to control women by labeling us as lesbians because our behavior is not acceptable, that is, when we are being independent, going our own way, living whole lives, fighting for our rights, demanding equal pay, saying no to violence, being self-assertive, bonding with and loving the company of women, assuming the right to our bodies, insisting upon our own authority, making changes that include us in society's decision-making; lesbian baiting occurs when women are called lesbians because we resist male dominance and control. And it has little or nothing to do with one's sexual identity.

To be named as lesbian threatens all women, not just lesbians, with great loss. And any woman who steps out of role risks being called a lesbian. To understand how this is a threat to all women, one must understand that any woman can be called a lesbian and there is no real way she can defend herself: there is no way to credential one's sexuality. ("The Children's Hour," a Lillian Hellman play, makes this point when a student asserts two teachers are lesbians and they have no way to disprove it.) She may be married or divorced, have children, dress in the most feminine manner, have sex with men, be celibate—but there are lesbians who do all those things. *Lesbians look like all women and all women look like lesbians.* There is no guaranteed method of identification, and as we all know, sexual identity can be kept hidden. (The same is true for men. There is no way to prove their sexual identity, though many go to extremes to prove heterosexuality.) Also, women are not necessarily born lesbian. Some seem to be, but others become lesbians later in life after having lived heterosexual lives. Lesbian baiting of heterosexual women would not work if there were a definitive way to identify lesbians (or heterosexuals).

We have yet to understand clearly how sexual identity develops. And this is disturbing to some people, especially those who are determined to discover how lesbian and gay identity is formed so that they will know where to start in eliminating it. (Isn't it odd that there is so little concern about discovering the causes of heterosexuality?) There are many theories: genetic makeup, hormones, socialization, environment, etc. But there is no conclusive evidence that indicates that heterosexuality comes from one process and homosexuality from another.

We do know, however, that sexual identity can be in flux, and we know that sexual identity means more than just the gender of people one is attracted to and has sex with. To be a lesbian has as many ramifications as for a woman to be heterosexual. It is more than sex, more than just the bedroom issue many would like to make it: it is a woman-centered life with all the social interconnections that entails. Some lesbians are in long-term relationships, some in short-term ones, some date, some are celibate, some are married to men, some remain as separate as possible from men, some have children by men, some by alternative insemination, some seem "feminine" by societal standards, some "masculine," some are doctors, lawyers and ministers, some laborers, housewives and writers: what all share in common is a sexual/affectional identity that focuses on women in its attractions and social relationships.

If lesbians are simply women with a particular sexual identity who look and act like all women, then the major difference in living out a lesbian sexual identity as opposed to a heterosexual identity is that as lesbians we live in a homophobic world that threatens and imposes damaging loss on us *for being who we are,* for choosing to live whole lives.

Homophobic people often assert that homosexuals have the choice of not being homo-sexual; that is, we don't have to act out our sexual identity. In that case, I want to hear heterosexuals talk about their willingness not to act out their sexual identity, including not just sexual activity but heterosexual social interconnections and heterosexual privilege. It is a question of wholeness. It is very difficult for one to be denied the life of a sexual being, whether expressed in sex or in physical affection, and to feel complete, whole. For our loving relationships with humans feed the life of the spirit and enable us to overcome our basic isolation and to be interconnected with humankind.

If, then, any woman can be named a lesbian and be threatened with terrible losses, what is it she fears? Are these fears real? Being vulnerable to a homophobic world can lead to these losses:

- *Employment.* The loss of job leads us right back to the economic conection to sexism. This fear of job loss exists for almost every lesbian except perhaps those who are self-employed or in a business that does not require societal approval. Consider how many businesses or organizations you know that will hire and protect people who are openly gay or lesbian.

- *Family.* Their approval, acceptance, love.

- *Children.* Many lesbians and gay men have children, but very, very few gain custody in court challenges, even if the other parent is a known abuser. Other children may be kept away from us as though gays and lesbians are abusers. There are written and unwritten laws prohibiting lesbians and gays from being foster parents or from adopting children. There is an irrational fear that children in contact with lesbians and gays will become homosexual through influence or that they will be sexually abused. Despite our knowing that 95 percent of those who sexually abuse children are heterosexual men, there are no policies keeping heterosexual men from teaching or working with children, yet in almost every school system in America, visible gay men and lesbians are not hired through either written or unwritten law.

- *Heterosexual privilege and protection.* No institutions, other than those created by lesbians and gays—such as the Metropolitan Community Church, some counseling centers, political organizations such as the National Gay and Lesbian Task Force, the National Coalition of Black Lesbians and Gays, the Lambda Legal Defense and Education Fund, etc.—affirm homosexuality and offer protection. Affirmation and protection cannot be gained from the criminal justice system, mainline churches, educational institutions, the government.

- *Safety.* There is nowhere to turn for safety from physical and verbal attacks because the norm presently in this country is that it is acceptable to be overtly homophobic. Gay men are beaten on the streets; lesbians are kidnapped and "deprogrammed." The National Gay and Lesbian Task Force, in an extended study, has documented violence against lesbians and gay men and noted the inadequate response of the criminal justice system. One of the major differences between homophobia/heterosexism and racism and sexism is that because of the Civil Rights Movement and the women's movement racism and sexism are expressed more covertly (though with great harm); because there has not been a major, visible lesbian and gay movement, it is permissible to be overtly homophobic in any institution or public forum. Churches spew forth homophobia in the same way they did racism prior to the Civil Rights Movement. Few laws are in place to protect lesbians and gay men, and the criminal justice system is wracked with homophobia.

- *Mental health.* An overtly homophobic world in which there is full permission to treat lesbians and gay men with cruelty makes it difficult for lesbians and gay men to maintain a strong sense of well-being and self-esteem. Many lesbians and gay men are beaten, raped, killed, subjected to aversion therapy, or put in mental institutions. The impact of such hatred and negativity can lead one to depression and, in some cases, to suicide. The toll on the gay and lesbian community is devastating.

- *Community.* There is rejection by those who live in homophobic fear, those who are afraid of association with lesbians and gay men. For many in the gay and lesbian community, there is a loss of public acceptance, a loss of allies, a loss of place and belonging.

- *Credibility.* This fear is large for many people: the fear that they will no longer be respected, listened to, honored, believed. They fear they will be social outcasts.

The list goes on and on. But any one of these essential components of a full life is large enough to make one deeply fear its loss. A black woman once said to me in a workshop, "When I fought for Civil Rights, I always had my family and community to fall back on even when they didn't fully understand or accept what I was doing. I don't know if I could have borne losing them. And you people don't have either with you. It takes my breath away."

What does a woman have to do to get called a lesbian? Almost anything, sometimes nothing at all, but certainly anything that threatens the status quo, anything that steps out of role, anything that asserts the rights of women, anything that doesn't indicate submission and subordination. Assertiveness, standing up for oneself, asking for more pay, better working conditions, training for and accepting a non-traditional (you mean a man's?) job, enjoying the company of women, being financially independent, being in control of one's life, depending first and foremost upon oneself, thinking that one can do whatever needs to be done, but above all, working for the rights and equality of women.

In the backlash to the gains of the women's liberation movement, there has been an increased effort to keep definitions man-centered. Therefore, to work on behalf of women must mean to work against men. To love women must mean that one hates men. A very effective attack has been made against the word *feminist* to make it a derogatory word. In current backlash usage, *feminist* equals *man-hater* which equals *lesbian.* This formula is created in the hope that women will be frightened away from their work on behalf of women. Consequently, we now have women who believe in the rights of women and work for those rights while from fear deny that they are feminists, or refuse to use the word because it is so "abrasive."

So what does one do in an effort to keep from being called a lesbian? She steps back into line, into the role that is demanded of her, tries to behave in such a way that doesn't threaten the status of men, and if she works for women's rights, she begins modifying that work. When women's organizations begin doing significant social change work, they inevitably are lesbian-baited; that is, funders or institutions or community members tell us that they can't work with us because of our "man-hating attitudes" or the presence of lesbians. We are called too strident, told we are making enemies, not doing good. . . .

In my view, homophobia has been one of the major causes of the failure of the women's liberation movement to make deep and lasting change. (The other major block has been racism.) We were fierce when we set out but when threatened with the loss of heterosexual privilege, we began putting on brakes. Our best-known nationally distributed women's magazine was reluctant to print articles about lesbians, began putting a man on the cover several times a year, and writing articles about women who succeeded in a man's world. We worried about our image, our being all right, our being "real women" despite our work. Instead of talking about the elimination of sexual gender roles, we stepped back and talked about "sex role stereotyping" as the issue. Change around the edges for middle-class white women began to be talked about as successes. We accepted tokenism and integration, forgetting that equality for all women, for all people—and not just equality of white middle-class women with white men—was the goal that we could never put behind us.

But despite backlash and retreats, change is growing from within. The women's liberation movement is beginning to gain strength again because there are women who are talking about liberation for all women. We are examining sexism, racism, homophobia, classism, anti-Semitism, ageism, ableism, and imperialism, and we see everything as connected. This change in point of view represents the third wave of the women's liberation movement, a new direction that does not get mass media coverage and recognition. It has been initiated by women of color and lesbians who were marginalized or rendered invisible by the white heterosexual leaders of earlier efforts. The first wave was the 19th and early 20th century campaign for the vote; the second, beginning in the 1960s, focused on the Equal Rights Amendment and abortion rights. Consisting of predominantly white middle-class women, both failed in recognizing issues of equality and empowerment for all women. The third wave of the movement, multi-racial and multi-issued, seeks the transformation of the world for us all. We know that we won't get there until everyone gets there; that we must move forward in a great strong line, hand in hand, not just a few at a time.

We know that the arguments about homophobia originating from mental health and Biblical/religious attitudes can be settled when we look at the sexism that permeates religious and psychiatric history. The women of the third wave of the women's liberation movement know that *without the existence of sexism, there would be no homophobia.*

Finally, we know that as long as the word *lesbian* can strike fear in any woman's heart, then work on behalf of women can be stopped; the only successful work against sexism must include work against homophobia.

10 Class in America

Gregory Mantsios

In the fall of 2011, a band of young activists occupied Zuccotti Park, a relatively small patch of property in New York City's financial district. In the process, they captured media attention; added the phrase "one-percenter" to our lexicon; and sparked anti-corporate protests around the world. Though short-lived, the Occupy Wall Street movement changed the national and international discourse on capitalism and class privilege. It laid the groundwork for a relatively obscure, self-described democratic socialist senator from Vermont — Bernie Sanders — to put the subject of class and economic inequality front and center in a national campaign for the Presidency of the United States. Others have taken up the discussion. Massachusetts Senator Elizabeth Warren has made the question of inequality a centerpiece of her political efforts. And in the 2018 mid-term election, a group of young and progressive candidates — with strong ideas about economic justice — flipped the Congress from Red to Blue, posing a significant challenge to the hard-core capitalist, pro-business administration of Donald Trump.

Yet these efforts to confront the class divide in America remain an aberration — one limited to the left wing of the Democratic Party and anti-establishment groupings. For the most part, Americans don't like to talk about class. We don't speak about class privileges, or class oppression, or the class nature of society. These terms are not part of our everyday vocabulary, and in most circles this language is associated with the language of the rhetorical fringe. Unlike people in most other parts of the world, we shrink from using words that classify along economic lines or that point to class distinctions: Phrases like "working class," "upper class," "capitalist class," and "ruling class" are rarely uttered by Americans.

Avoidance of class-laden vocabulary crosses class boundaries. There are few among the poor who speak of themselves as lower class; instead, they refer to their race, ethnic group, or geographic location. Workers are more likely to identify with their employer, industry, or occupational group than with other workers, or with the working class. Neither are those at the upper end of the economic spectrum likely to use the word "class."[1] In her study of 38 wealthy and socially prominent women, Susan Ostrander asked participants if they considered themselves members of the upper class. One participant responded, "I hate to use the word 'class.' We are responsible, fortunate people, old families, the people who have something." Another said, "I hate [the term] upper class. It is so non-upper class to use it. I just call it 'all of us'—those who are well-born."[2]

It is not that Americans, rich or poor, aren't keenly aware of class differences — those quoted above obviously are; it is that class is usually not in the domain of public

Gregory Mantsios is founder and director of the Murphy Institute for Worker Education and Labor Studies at the City University of New York. He is the author of *A New Labor Movement for the New Century*.

conversation. Class is not discussed or debated in public because class identity has been stripped from popular culture. The institutions that shape mass culture and define the parameters of public debate have avoided class issues. In politics, in primary and second-ary education, and in the mass media, formulating issues in terms of class has been consid-ered culturally unacceptable, unnecessarily combative, and even un-American. (See my essay "Media Magic: Making Class Invisible," in Part VIII of this volume.)

There are, however, two notable exceptions to this phenomenon. First, it is acceptable in the United States to talk about "the middle class." Interestingly enough, the term mid-dle class appears to be acceptable precisely because it mutes class differences. References to the middle class by politicians, for example, are designed to encompass and attract the broadest possible constituency. Not only do references to the middle class gloss over differ-ences, but they also avoid any suggestion of conflict or injustice.

This leads us to a second exception to the class-avoidance phenomenon. We are, on occa-sion, presented with glimpses of the upper class and the lower class (the language used is "the wealthy" and "the poor"). In the media, these presentations are designed to satisfy some real or imagined voyeuristic need of "the ordinary person." As curiosities, the ground-level view of street life and trailer parks and the inside look at the rich and the famous serve as unique models, one to avoid and one to emulate. In either case, the two sets of lifestyles are presented as though they have no causal relation to each other: There is nothing to suggest that our economic system allows people to grow wealthy *at the expense of* those who are not.

Similarly, when politicians and social commentators draw attention to the plight of the poor, they do so in a manner that obscures the class structure and denies any sense of exploitation. Wealth and poverty are viewed as one of several natural and inevitable states of being: Differences are only differences. One may even say differences are the American way, a reflection of American social diversity.

We are left with one of two possible explanations for why Americans usually don't talk about class: Either class distinctions are not relevant to U.S. society, or we mistakenly hold a set of beliefs that obscure the reality of class differences and their impact on people's lives.

Let's look at four common, albeit contradictory, beliefs about class in America that have persisted over time.

Myth 1: We are a middle-class nation. Despite some variations in economic status, most Americans have achieved relative affluence in what is widely recognized as a con-sumer society.

Myth 2: Class really doesn't matter in the United States. Whatever differences do exist in economic standing, they are—for the most part—irrelevant. Our democracy provides for all regardless of economic class: Rich or poor, we are all equal in the eyes of the law.

Myth 3: We live in a land of upward mobility. The American public as a whole is steadily moving up the economic ladder and each generation propels itself to greater eco-nomic well-being.

Myth 4: Everyone has an equal chance to succeed. Success in the United States requires no more than hard work, sacrifice, and perseverance: "In America, anyone can become a billionaire; it's just a matter of being in the right place at the right time."

In trying to assess the legitimacy of these beliefs, we want to ask several important questions. Are there significant class differences among Americans? If these differences do exist, are they getting bigger or smaller? Do class differences have a significant impact on the way we live? How much upward mobility is there in the United States? Finally, does everyone in the United States really have an equal opportunity to succeed and an equal voice in our democracy?

The Economic Spectrum

For starters, let's look at difference. An examination of available data reveals that variations in economic well-being are, in fact, dramatic. Consider the following:

- The richest 20 percent of Americans hold nearly 90 percent of the total household wealth in the country. The wealthiest 1 percent of the American population holds 40 percent of the total national wealth. The 1 percent now own a higher share of wealth than at any other point in the last fifty years.[3]
- There are 424,870 Americans—less than one-fifth of 1 percent of the adult population—who earn more than $1 million annually.[4] There are over 500 billionaires in the United States today, 40 of them worth over $10 billion each.[5] It would take the typical American male worker earning $52,146 (the median income in the United States for men)—and spending absolutely nothing at all—a total of 191,769 years (or over 2,500 lifetimes) to earn $10 billion. It would take the typical American female worker at a median income of $41,977 over 238,225 years (or over 2,900 lifetimes).[6]

Affluence and prosperity are clearly alive and well in certain segments of the U.S. population. However, this abundance is in sharp contrast to the poverty that persists in America. At the other end of the spectrum:

- More than 12 percent of the American population—that is, approximately 1 of every 8 people in this country—live below the official poverty line (calculated at $12,488 for an individual and $25,094 for a family of four).[7] In 2017, there were more than 39 million people living below the poverty line in the United States.[8]
- An estimated 552,830 people are homeless, of whom 111,492 (about 20%) are children.[9]
- According to 2017 data from the U.S. Census Bureau, more than 1 out of every 6 children under the age of 18 live in poverty.[10]

Reality 1: The contrast between rich and poor is sharp, and with one-third of the American population living at one extreme or the other, it is difficult to argue that we live in a classless society.

While those at the bottom of the economic ladder have fared poorly relative to those at the top, so too have those in the middle—and their standing relative to the top has been declining as well.

- The middle fifth of the population holds less than 3 percent of the national *wealth*.[11]
- The share of wealth held by the middle fifth in 1962 was 5.4 percent of the total. Today's share held by the middle sector is 44 percent less than what it was almost 6 decades ago.[12]

Reality 2: The middle class in the United States holds a very small share of the nation's wealth and that share has declined steadily.

The gap between rich and poor—and between the rich and the middle class—leaves the vast majority of the American population at a distinct disadvantage.

- Eighty percent of the population—that is, four out of every five Americans, is left sharing a little more than 10 percent of the nation's wealth.[13]
- The income gap between the very rich (top 1 percent) and everyone else (the 99 percent) has widened sharply over the last 40 years, with incomes of the top 1% rising at a much faster rate. Between 1979 and 2015, before-tax incomes of the top 1% rose 233%; in contrast, incomes of the middle 60% rose only 32%.[14]

This level of inequality is neither inevitable nor universal. The inequality between rich and poor in a country is generally measured by a statistic called the Gini coefficient, which provides a mathematical ratio and scale that allows comparisons between countries of the world. According to the World Economic Forum's Inclusive Development Index 2018, the United States ranked 98th out of 106 countries studied—that is, 97 countries (including almost all the industrialized nations of the world) had a more equal distribution of wealth than the United States.[15]

The numbers and percentages associated with economic inequality are difficult to fully comprehend. To help his students visualize the distribution of income, the well-known economist Paul Samuelson asked them to picture an income pyramid made of children's blocks, with each layer of blocks representing $1,000. If we were to construct Samuelson's pyramid today, the peak of the pyramid would be much higher than the Eiffel Tower, yet almost all of us would be within 6 feet of the ground.[16] In other words, a small minority of families takes the lion's share of the national income, and the remaining income is distributed among the vast majority of middle-income and low-income families. Keep in mind that Samuelson's pyramid represents the distribution of income, not wealth (accumulated resources). The distribution of wealth is skewed even further. Ten billion dollars of wealth would reach more than 1,000 times the height of the Eiffel Tower.[17]

Reality 3: Middle- and lower-income earners—what many in other parts of the world would refer to as the working class—share a miniscule portion of the nation's wealth. For the most part, the real class divide in the United States is between the very wealthy and everyone else—and it is a divide that is staggering.

American Lifestyles

The late political theorist/activist Michael Harrington once commented, "America has the best-dressed poverty the world has ever known."[18] Clothing disguises much of the poverty in the United States, and this may explain, in part, the country's middle-class image. With increased mass marketing of "designer" clothing and with shifts in the nation's economy from blue-collar (and often better-paying) manufacturing jobs to white-collar and pink-collar jobs in the service sector, it is becoming increasingly difficult to distinguish class differences based on appearance.[19] The dress-down environment prevalent in the high-tech industry (what American Studies scholar Andrew Ross refers to as the "no-collar movement") has reduced superficial distinctions even further.[20]

Beneath the surface, there is another reality. Let's look at some "typical" and not-so-typical lifestyles.

American Profile 1

Name:	Harold S. Browning
Father:	Manufacturer, industrialist
Mother:	Prominent social figure in the community
Principal child-rearer:	Nanny
Primary education:	An exclusive private school on Manhattan's Upper East Side
	Note: A small, well-respected primary school where teachers and administrators have a reputation for nurturing student creativity and for providing the finest educational preparation
	Ambition: "To become President"
Supplemental tutoring:	Tutors in French and mathematics
Summer camp:	Sleep-away camp in northern Connecticut
	Note: Camp provides instruction in the creative arts, athletics, and the natural sciences
Secondary education:	A prestigious preparatory school in Westchester County
	Note: Classmates included the sons of ambassadors, doctors, attorneys, television personalities, and well-known business leaders
	Supplemental education: Private SAT tutor
	After-school activities: Private riding lessons
	Ambition: "To take over my father's business"
	High-school graduation gift: BMW
Family activities:	Theater, recitals, museums, summer vacations in Europe, occasional winter trips to the Caribbean
	Note: As members of and donors to the local art museum, the Brownings and their children attend private receptions and exhibit openings at the invitation of the museum director

Higher education:	An Ivy League liberal arts college in Massachusetts *Major:* Economics and political science *After-class activities:* Debating club, college newspaper, swim team *Ambition:* "To become a leader in business"
First full-time job (age 23):	Assistant manager of operations, Browning Manufacturing, Inc. (family enterprise, specializing in power cords for laptops)
Subsequent employment:	3 years—Executive assistant to the president, Browning Manufacturing *Responsibilities included:* Purchasing (materials and equipment), personnel, and distribution networks 4 years—Advertising manager, Lackheed Manufacturing (home appliances) 3 years—Director of marketing and sales, Comerex, Inc. (business machines)
Current employment (age 38):	Executive vice president, SmithBond and Co. (digital instruments) *Typical daily activities:* Review financial reports and computer printouts, dictate memoranda, lunch with clients, initiate conference calls, meet with assistants, plan business trips, meet with associates *Transportation to and from work:* Chauffeured company limousine *Annual salary:* $480,804 *Ambition:* "To become chief executive officer of the firm, or one like it, within the next five to ten years"
Current residence:	Eighteenth-floor condominium on Manhattan's Upper West Side, eleven rooms, including five spacious bedrooms and terrace overlooking river *Interior:* Professionally decorated and accented with elegant furnishings, valuable antiques, and expensive artwork *Note:* Building management provides doorman and elevator attendant; family employs au pair for children and maid for other domestic chores

Second residence:	Farm in northwestern Connecticut, used for weekend retreats and for horse breeding (investment/hobby) *Note:* To maintain the farm and cater to the family when they are there, the Brownings employ a part-time maid, groundskeeper, and horse breeder

Harold Browning was born into a world of nurses, maids, and governesses. His world today is one of airplanes and limousines, five-star restaurants, and luxurious living accommodations. The life and lifestyle of Harold Browning is in sharp contrast to that of Bob Farrell.

American Profile 2

Name:	Bob Farrell
Father:	Machinist
Mother:	Retail clerk
Principal child-rearer:	Mother and sitter
Primary education:	A medium-size public school in Queens, New York, characterized by large class size, outmoded physical facilities, and an educational philosophy emphasizing basic skills and student discipline *Ambition:* "To become President"
Supplemental tutoring:	None
Summer camp:	YMCA day camp *Note:* Emphasis on team sports, arts and crafts
Secondary education:	Large regional high school in Queens *Note:* Classmates included the sons and daughters of carpenters, postal clerks, teachers, nurses, shopkeepers, mechanics, bus drivers, police officers, salespersons *Supplemental education:* SAT prep course offered by national chain *After-school activities:* Basketball and handball in school park *Ambition:* "To make it through college" *High-school graduation gift:* $500 savings bond

Family activities:	Family gatherings around television set, softball, an occasional trip to the movie theater, summer Sundays at the public beach
Higher education:	A two-year community college with a technical orientation *Major:* Electrical technology *After-school activities:* Employed as a part-time bagger in local supermarket *Ambition:* "To become an electrical engineer"
First full-time job (age 19):	Service-station attendant *Note:* Continued to take college classes in the evening
Subsequent employment:	Mail clerk at large insurance firm; manager trainee, large retail chain
Present employment (age 38):	Assistant sales manager, building supply firm *Typical daily activities:* Demonstrate products, write up product orders, handle customer complaints, check inventory *Transportation to and from work:* City subway *Annual salary:* $48,261 *Additional income:* $6,100 from evening and weekend work as salesman in local men's clothing store *Ambition:* "To open up my own business"
Current residence:	The Farrells own their own home in a working-class neighborhood in Queens, New York

Bob Farrell and Harold Browning live very differently: One is very privileged, the other much less so. The differences are class differences, which have a profound impact on the way they live. They are differences between playing a game of handball in the park and taking riding lessons at a private stable; watching a movie on television and going to the theater; and taking the subway to work and being driven in a limousine. More important, the difference in class determines where they live, who their friends are, how well they are educated, what they do for a living, and what they come to expect from life.

Yet, as dissimilar as their lifestyles are, Harold Browning and Bob Farrell have some things in common: they live in the same city, they work long hours, and they are highly motivated. More importantly, they are both white males.

Let's look at someone else who works long and hard and is highly motivated. This person, however, is black and female.

American Profile 3

Name:	Cheryl Mitchell
Father:	Janitor
Mother:	Waitress
Principal child-rearer:	Grandmother
Primary education:	Large public school in Ocean Hill-Brownsville, Brooklyn, New York
	Note: Rote teaching of basic skills and emphasis on conveying the importance of good attendance, good manners, and good work habits; school patrolled by security guards
	Ambition: "To be a teacher"
Supplemental tutoring:	None
Summer camp:	None
Secondary education:	Large public school in Ocean Hill-Brownsville
	Note: Classmates included sons and daughters of hairdressers, groundskeepers, painters, dressmakers, dishwashers, domestics
	Supplemental education: None
	After-school activities: Domestic chores, part-time employment as babysitter and housekeeper
	Ambition: "To be a social worker"
	High-school graduation gift: Corsage
Family activities:	Church-sponsored socials
Higher education:	One semester of local community college
	Note: Dropped out of school for financial reasons
First full-time job (age 17):	Counter clerk, local bakery
Subsequent employment:	File clerk with temporary-service agency, supermarket checker
Current employment (age 38):	Nurse's aide at a municipal hospital
	Typical daily activities: Make up hospital beds, clean out bedpans, weigh patients and assist them to the bathroom, take temperature readings, pass out and collect food trays, feed patients who need help, bathe patients, and change dressings
	Annual salary: $25,696
	Ambition: "To get out of the ghetto"

| **Current residence:** | Three-room apartment in the South Bronx, needs painting, has poor ventilation, is in a high-crime area
Note: Cheryl Mitchell lives with her four-year-old son and her elderly mother |

When we look at Cheryl Mitchell, Bob Farrell, and Harold Browning, we see three very different lifestyles. We are not looking, however, at economic extremes. Cheryl Mitchell's income as a nurse's aide puts her above the government's official poverty line.[21] Below her on the income pyramid are 39 million poverty-stricken Americans. Far from being poor, Bob Farrell has an annual income ($54,361) as an assistant sales manager that puts him above the median income level—that is, more than 50 percent of the U.S. population earns less money than Bob Farrell.[22] And while Harold Browning's income puts him in a high-income bracket, he stands only a fraction of the way up Samuelson's income pyramid. Well above him are the 424,870 Americans whose annual incomes exceed $1 million. Yet Harold Browning spends more money on his horses than Cheryl Mitchell earns in a year.

Reality 4: Even ignoring the extreme poles of the economic spectrum, we find enormous class differences in the lifestyles among the haves, the have-nots, and the have-littles.

Class affects more than lifestyle and material well-being. It has a significant impact on our physical and mental well-being as well. Researchers have found an inverse relationship between social class and health. Lower-class standing is correlated with higher rates of infant mortality, eye and ear disease, arthritis, physical disability, diabetes, nutritional deficiency, respiratory disease, mental illness, and heart disease.[23] In all areas of health, poor people do not share the same life chances as those in the social class above them. Furthermore, low income correlates with a lower quality of treatment for illness and disease. The results of poor health and poor treatment are borne out in the life expectancy rates within each class. Researchers have found that the higher one's class standing is, the higher one's life expectancy is. Conversely, they have also found that within each age group, the lower one's class standing, the higher the death rate; in some age groups, the figures are as much as two and three times higher.[24]

It's not just physical and mental health that is so largely determined by class. The lower a person's class standing is, the more difficult it is to secure housing; the more time is spent on the routine tasks of everyday life; the greater is the percentage of income that goes to pay for food, health care (which accounts for 23 percent of spending for low-income families)[25] and other basic necessities; and the greater is the likelihood of crime victimization.[26]

Class and Educational Attainment

School performance (grades and test scores) and educational attainment (level of schooling completed) also correlate strongly with economic class. Furthermore, despite some efforts to make testing fairer and schooling more accessible, current data suggest that the level of inequity is staying the same or getting worse.

In his study for the Carnegie Council on Children in 1978, Richard De Lone examined the test scores of over half a million students who took the College Board exams (SATs). His findings were consistent with earlier studies that showed a relationship between class and scores on standardized tests; his conclusion: "the higher the student's social status, the higher the probability that he or she will get higher grades."[27] Today, more than 40 years after the release of the Carnegie report, College Board surveys reveal data that are no different: test scores still correlate with family income.

Average Combined Scores by Income (600 to 2400 scale)[28]	
Family Income	**Mean Score**
More than $200,000	1717
About $140,001 to $200,000	1623
About $100,001 to $140,000	1582
About $80,001 to $100,000	1545
About $60,001 to $80,000	1497
About $40,001 to $60,000	1454
About $20,000 to $40,000	1394
Less than $20,000	1314

These figures are based on the test results of 978,163 SAT test takers in 2016.

In another study conducted 40 years ago, researcher William Sewell showed a positive correlation between class and overall educational achievement. In comparing the top quartile (25 percent) of his sample to the bottom quartile, he found that students from upper-class families were twice as likely to obtain training beyond high school and four times as likely to attain a postgraduate degree. Sewell concluded: "Socioeconomic background . . . operates independently of academic ability at every stage in the process of educational attainment."[29]

Today, the pattern persists. There are, however, two significant changes. On the one hand, the odds of getting into college have improved for the bottom quartile of the population, although they still remain relatively low compared to the top. On the other hand, the chances of completing a 4-year college degree for those who are poor are extraordinarily low compared to the chances for those who are rich. Researchers estimate college completion is 10 times more likely for the top 25 percent of the population than it is for the bottom 25 percent.[30]

Reality 5: From cradle to grave, class position has a significant impact on our well-being. Class accurately predicts chances for survival, educational achievement, and economic success.

Media-induced excitement over big payoff reality shows, celebrity salaries, and multimillion-dollar lotteries suggests that we in the United States live in a "rags to riches" society. So too does news about dot-com acquisitions and initial public offerings (IPOs) that provide enormous windfalls to young company founders. But rags-to-riches stories notwithstanding, the evidence suggests that "striking it rich" is extremely rare and that class mobility in general is uncommon and becoming increasingly so.

One study showed that 79 percent of families remained in the same quintile (fifth) of income earners or moved up or down only one quintile. (Of this group, most families did not move at all).[31] Another study showed that fewer than one in five men surpass the economic status of their fathers.[32] Several studies have shown that there is less class mobility in the United States than in most industrialized democracies in the world. One such study placed the United States in a virtual tie for last place.[33] Why does the United States occupy such a low position on the mobility scale? Several explanations have been offered: The gap between rich and poor in the United States is greater; the poor are poorer in the United States and have farther to go to get out of poverty; and the United States has a lower rate of unionization than other industrialized nations.

The bottom line is that very affluent families transmit their advantages to the next generation and poor families stay trapped.[34] For those whose annual income is in six figures, economic success is due in large part to the wealth and privileges bestowed on them at birth. Over 66 percent of the consumer units with incomes of $100,000 or more have inherited assets. Of these units, over 86 percent reported that inheritances constituted a substantial portion of their total assets.[35]

Economist Harold Wachtel likens inheritance to a series of Monopoly games in which the winner of the first game refuses to relinquish his or her cash and commercial property for the second game. "After all," argues the winner, "I accumulated my wealth and income by my own wits." With such an arrangement, it is not difficult to predict the outcome of subsequent games.[36]

Reality 6: All Americans do not have an equal opportunity to succeed, and class mobility in the United States is lower than that of the rest of the industrialized world. Inheritance laws provide built-in privileges to the offspring of the wealthy and add to the likelihood of their economic success while handicapping the chances for everyone else.

One would think that increases in worker productivity or a booming economy would reduce the level of inequality and increase class mobility. While the wages of workers *may* increase during good times—that is, relative to what they were in the past—the economic advantages of higher productivity and a booming economy go disproportionately to the wealthy, a factor that adds still further to the level of inequality. For example, during the period 1979 to 2017, the U.S. economy expanded and productivity (output per hours worked) increased by more than 70 percent. During that same period, however, hourly compensation for production and non-supervisory workers grew by only 11 percent. The top 1 percent of earners, however, saw gains in compensation of over 157 percent, while earnings of the top 0.1 percent increased by more than 343 percent.[37] Observing similar patterns in U.S. economic history, one prominent economist described economic growth in the United States as a "spectator sport for the majority of American families."[38] Economic decline, on the other hand, is much more "participatory," with layoffs and cuts in public services hitting middle- and lower-income families hardest—families that rely on public services (e.g., public schools, transportation) and have fewer resources to fall back on during difficult economic times.

Reality 7: Inequality in the United States is persistent in good times and bad.

While most Americans rely on their wages or salaries to make ends meet, the rich derive most of their wealth from such income-producing assets as stocks, bonds, business equity, and non-home real estate. This type of wealth is even more highly concentrated than wealth in general. Over 84 percent of all stocks in the U.S., for example, are owned by the wealthiest 10 percent of Americans.[39] This makes the fortunes of the wealthy (whether they are corporate executives, investment bankers, or not) closely tied to the fortunes of corporate America and the world of finance. While defenders of capitalism and the capitalist class argue that what's good for corporate America is good for all of America, recent economic experience has raised more doubts than ever about this. Putting aside illegal manipulation of the financial system, the drive to maximize corporate profit has led to job destruction (as companies seek cheaper labor in other parts of the world and transfer investments off shore); deregulation (e.g., so environmental protections don't inhibit corporate profit); and changes in tax policy that favor corporations (through loopholes) and those who rely on corporate profit for their wealth (by taxing their capital gains at lower rates).

Reality 8: The privileges that accrue to the wealthy are tied to the worlds of capital and finance—worlds whose good fortune [is] often the misfortune of the rest of the population.

Government is often portrayed as the spoiler of Wall Street—and at times it is. There are certainly examples of the government imposing fines for environmental violations, establishing regulations that protect consumers and workers, restrict corporate conduct, etc. But government as the "great equalizer" often isn't what it appears to be. In 2010, for example, when the federal government concluded a fraud case against a major investment bank (Goldman Sachs), it touted the case as one of the largest settlements in U.S. history— a whopping $550 million dollars. It turns out that $550 million was less than 4 percent of what the bank paid its executives in bonuses that year.

Similarly, changes in policy that reduce taxes are often touted as vehicles for leveling the playing field and bringing economic relief to the middle class. But at best, these do little or nothing to help middle- and low-income families. More often than not, they increase the level of inequality by providing disproportionate tax benefits to the wealthy while reducing public budgets and increasing the costs of such public services as transportation and college tuition. For example, changes in tax policy over the last five decades—especially those during the 1980s—have favored the wealthy: Federal taxes for the wealthiest 0.1 percent have fallen from 51 to 26 percent over the last 50 years, while the rate for middle income earners has risen from 14 to 16 percent.[40]

It's not just that economic resources are concentrated in the hands of a few; so too are political resources. And it is the connection between wealth and political power that allows economic inequality to persist and grow. Moreover, as the costs of political influence rise, so does the influence of the "monied" class. Running for public office has always been an expensive proposition, but it's become increasingly so: It now costs, on average, $1.5 million in campaign funds to win a seat in the House of Representatives and $10.4 million to win a seat in the U.S. Senate.[41] Wealthy individuals who want to make public policy often underwrite their own campaigns.* The average wealth of U.S. senators, for example, is $11 million.[42]

High-priced lobbyists also ensure that the interests of the wealthy and of corporate America are well represented in the halls of government. Not surprisingly, organizations that track the connection between political contributions and votes cast by public officials find a strong correlation between money and voting.[43] It's not that the power of the economic elite is absolute; it's not. The power of the wealthy is often mitigated by social movements and by grassroots organizations that advocate on behalf of the poor and working class. The Occupy Wall Street movement—like movements that came before it—changed not only the public debate, but led to policy reforms as well. The power of the rich, however, remains so disproportionate that it severely undermines our democracy. Over three-quarters of a century ago, such an assault on democratic principles led Supreme Court Justice Louis Brandeis to observe, "We can have democracy in this country or we can have great wealth concentrated in the hands of a few, but we can't have both." Talking about the power elite or the ruling class may put people off, but there is no doubt that the interests of the wealthy predominate in American politics.

Reality 9: Wealth and power are closely linked. The economic elite have a grossly disproportionate amount of political power—more than enough power to ensure that the system that provides them such extraordinary privileges perpetuates itself.

Spheres of Power and Oppression

When we look at society and try to determine what it is that keeps most people down—what holds them back from realizing their potential as healthy, creative, productive individuals—we find institutional forces that are largely beyond individual control. Class domination is one of these forces. People do not choose to be poor or working class; instead, they are limited and confined by the opportunities afforded or denied them by a social and economic system. The class structure in the United States is a function of its economic system: capitalism, a system that is based on private rather than public ownership and control of commercial enterprises. Under capitalism, these enterprises are governed by the need to produce a profit for the owners, rather than to fulfill societal needs. Class divisions arise from the differences between those who own and control corporate enterprise and those who do not.

Racial and gender domination are other forces that hold people down. Although there are significant differences in the way capitalism, racism, and sexism affect our lives, there are also a multitude of parallels. And although class, race, and gender act independently of each other, they are at the same time very much interrelated.

On the one hand, issues of race and gender cut across class lines. Women experience the effects of sexism whether they are well-paid professionals or poorly paid clerks. As women, they are not only subjected to stereotyping and sexual harassment, they face discrimination and are denied opportunities and privileges that men have. Similarly, a wealthy black man faces racial oppression, is subjected to racial slurs, and is denied

---

*Over the course of three elections, Michael Bloomberg spent more than $261 million of his own money to become mayor of New York City. He spent $102 million in his last mayoral election alone—more than $172 per vote.

opportunities because of his color. Regardless of their class standing, women and members of minority races are constantly dealing with institutional forces that hold them down precisely because of their gender, the color of their skin, or both.

On the other hand, the experiences of women and minorities are differentiated along class lines. Although they are in subordinate positions vis-à-vis white men, the particular issues that confront women and people of color may be quite different, depending on their position in the class structure.

Power is incremental and class privileges can accrue to individual women and to individual members of a racial minority. While power is incremental, oppression is cumulative, and those who are poor, black, and female are often subject to all of the forces of class, race, and gender discrimination simultaneously. This cumulative situation is what is sometimes referred to as the double and triple jeopardy of women and people of color.

Chances of Being Poor in America[44]					
White male/ female	White female head*	Hispanic male/female	Hispanic female head*	Black male/ female	Black female head*
1 in 11	1 in 5	1 in 5	1 in 3	1 in 5	1 in 3

*Persons in families with female householder, no husband present.

Furthermore, oppression in one sphere is related to the likelihood of oppression in another. If you are black and female, for example, you are much more likely to be poor or working class than you would be as a white male. Census figures show that the incidence of poverty varies greatly by race and gender.

In other words, being female and being nonwhite are attributes in our society that increase the chances of poverty and of lower-class standing.

Reality 10: Racism and sexism significantly compound the effects of class in society.

None of this makes for a very pretty picture of our country. Despite what we like to think about ourselves as a nation, the truth is that the qualities of our lives and the opportunities for success are highly circumscribed by our race, our gender, and the class we are born into. As individuals, we feel hurt and angry when someone is treating us unfairly; yet as a society we tolerate unconscionable injustice. A more just society will require a radical redistribution of wealth and power. We can start by reversing the current trends that polarize us as a people and adopt policies and practices that narrow the gaps in income, wealth, power, and privilege. That will only come about with sustained pressure from below: mass movements, electoral victories, and strong organizations and institutions advocating for a more just and equitable society.

NOTES

1. See Jay MacLead, *Ain't No Makin' It: Aspirations and Attainment in a Lower-Income Neighborhood* (Boulder, CO: Westview Press, 1995); Benjamin DeMott, *The Imperial Middle* (New York: Morrow, 1990); Ira Katznelson, *City Trenches: Urban Politics and Patterning of Class in the United States* (New York: Pantheon Books, 1981); Charles W. Tucker,

"A Comparative Analysis of Subjective Social Class: 1945–1963," *Social Forces*, no. 46 (June 1968): 508–514; Robert Nisbet, "The Decline and Fall of Social Class," *Pacific Sociological Review* 2 (Spring 1959): 11–17; and Oscar Glantz, "Class Consciousness and Political Solidarity," *American Sociological Review* 23 (August 1958): 375–382.

2. Susan Ostrander, "Upper-Class Women: Class Consciousness as Conduct and Meaning," in *Power Structure Research*, ed. G. William Domhoff (Beverly Hills, CA: Sage Publications, 1980), 78–79. Also see Stephen Birmingham, *America's Secret Aristocracy* (Boston: Little Brown, 1987).

3. Wolff, E., "Household Wealth Trends in the United States, 1962 to 2016: Has Middle Class Wealth Recovered?" National Bureau of Economic Research Working Paper No. w24085 (November 2017).

4. The number of individuals filing tax returns with a gross adjusted income of $1 million or more in 2016 was 424,870 ("Tax Stats at a Glance," Internal Revenue Service, U.S. Treasury Department, available at https://www.irs.gov/pub/irs-soi/18taxstatscard.pdf). The adult population (18 years and over) of the United States in 2016 was 244,807,000 (U.S. Census Bureau, Current Population Survey, Annual Social and Economic Supplement, 2016, available at https://www.census.gov/content/census/en/data/tables/2016/demo/age-and-sex/2016-age-sex-composition.html).

5. *Forbes.* "The World's Billionaires List: United States," accessed March 4 2019, https://www.forbes.com/billionaires/list/6/#version:static_country:United%20States.

6. The median income in 2017 as reported in Jessica Semega, Kayla Fontenot, and Melissa Kollar, "Income and Poverty in the United States: 2017," Report Number P60-263, September 12, 2018 (available at https://www.census.gov/data/tables/2018/demo/income-poverty/p60-263.html). Lifetimes based on CDC calculation for male and female life expectancy in 2015 (available at https://www.cdc.gov/nchs/data/nvsr/nvsr67/nvsr67_07-508.pdf).

7. Based on information collected in the 2018 Current Population Survey Annual Social and Economic Supplements (CPS ASEC) conducted by the U.S. Census Bureau. Jessica Semega, Kayla Fontenot, and Melissa Kollar, "Income and Poverty in the United States: 2017," Report Number P60-263, September 12, 2018 (available at https://www.census.gov/data/tables/2018/demo/income-poverty/p60-263.html).

8. Ibid.

9. Meghan Henry, Anna Mahathey, Tyler Morrill, Anna Robinson, Azim Shivji, and Rian Watt, "The 2018 Annual Homeless Assessment Report (AHAR) to Congress, Part 1: Point-in-Time Estimates of Homelessness," U.S. Department of Housing and Urban Development: Office of Community Planning and Development (December 2018).

10. Jessica Semega, Kayla Fontenot, and Melissa Kollar, "Income and Poverty in the United States: 2017," Report Number P60-263, September 12, 2018 (available at https://www.census.gov/data/tables/2018/demo/income-poverty/p60-263.html).

11. Edward N. Wolff, "Household Wealth Trends in the United States, 1962 to 2016: Has Middle Class Wealth Recovered?" National Bureau of Economic Research Working Paper No. w24085 (November 2017).

12. Ibid.

13. Economic Policy Institute, "Wealth Holdings Remain Unequal in Good and Bad Times," *The State of Working America* (Washington, DC: Economic Policy Institute, 2001), accessed September 25, 2011, http://www.stateofworkingamerica.org/files/files/Figure%20B_wealth_dis_byclass.xlsx.

14. Chad Stone, Danilo Trisi, Arloc Sherman, and Roderick Taylor, "A Guide to Statistics on Historical Trends in Income Inequality." Center on Budget and Policy: Policy Futures (December 2018).

15. World Economic Forum (2018). The Inclusive Development Index 2018 Summary and Data Highlights.

16. Paul Samuelson, *Economics*, 10th ed. (New York: McGraw-Hill, 1976), 84.

17. Calculated at 1.5 inches per children's block and 1,050 feet for the height of the Eiffel Tower.

18. Michael Harrington, *The Other America* (New York: Macmillan, 1962), 12–13.

19. Stuart Ewen and Elizabeth Ewen, *Channels of Desire: Mass Images and the Shaping of American Consciousness* (New York: McGraw-Hill, 1982).

20. Andrew Ross, *No-Collar: The Humane Workplace and Its Hidden Costs* (New York: Basic Books, 2002).

21. Based on a poverty threshold for a three-person household in 2017 of $19,730, as reported in Jessica Semega, Kayla Fontenot, and Melissa Kollar, "Income and Poverty in the United States: 2017," Report Number P60-263, September 12, 2018 (available at https://www.census.gov/data /tables/2018/demo/income-poverty/p60-263.html).

22. The median income in 2017 was $52,751 for men working full time, year round, $42,448 for women, and $60,309 for households, as reported in Jessica Semega, Kayla Fontenot, and Melissa Kollar, "Income and Poverty in the United States: 2017," Report Number P60-263, September 12, 2018 (available at https://www.census.gov/data/tables/2018/demo/income -poverty/p60-263.html).

23. U.S. Government Accountability Office, *Poverty in America: Economic Research Shows Adverse Impacts on Health Status and Other Social Conditions* (Washington, DC: U.S. Government Accountability Office, 2007), 9–16; see also E. Pamuk, D. Makuc, K. Heck, C. Reuben, and K. Lochner, *Health, United States, 1998: Socioeconomic Status and Health Chartbook* (Hyattsville, MD: National Center for Health Statistics, 1998), 145–159; Vincente Navarro, "Class, Race, and Health Care in the United States," in *Critical Perspectives in Sociology*, 2nd ed., ed. Bersh Berberoglu (Dubuque, IA: Kendall/Hunt, 1993), 148–156; Melvin Krasner, *Poverty and Health in New York City* (New York: United Hospital Fund of New York, 1989). See also U.S. Department of Health and Human Services, "Health Status of Minorities and Low Income Groups, 1985"; and Dan Hughes, Kay Johnson, Sara Rosenbaum, Elizabeth Butler, and Janet Simons, *The Health of America's Children* (The Children's Defense Fund, 1988).

24. Pamuk et al., *Health, United States, 1998*; Kenneth Neubeck and Davita Glassberg, *Sociology: A Critical Approach* (New York: McGraw-Hill, 1996), 436–438; Aaron Antonovsky, "Social Class, Life Expectancy, and Overall Mortality," in *The Impact of Social Class* (New York: Thomas Crowell, 1972), 467–491. See also Harriet Duleep, "Measuring the Effect of Income on Adult Mortality Using Longitudinal Administrative Record Data," *Journal of Human Resources* 21, no. 2 (Spring 1986); and Paul Farmer, *Pathologies of Power: Health, Human Rights, and the New War on the Poor* (Berkeley: University of California Press, 2005).

25. Patricia Ketsche, Sally Wallace, and Kathleen Adams, "Hidden Health Care Costs Hit Low-Income Families the Hardest," Georgia State University, September 21, 2011 http://www.gsu.edu/news/54728.html.

26. Pamuk et al., *Health, United States, 1998*, figure 20; Dennis W. Roncek, "Dangerous Places: Crime and Residential Environment," *Social Forces* 60, no. 1 (September 1981), 74–96. See also Steven D. Levitt, "The Changing Relationship Between Income and Crime Victimization," *Economic Policy Review* 5, no. 3 (September 1999).

27. Richard De Lone, *Small Futures* (New York: Harcourt Brace Jovanovich, 1978), 14–19.

28. College Board, "2017 College-Bound Seniors Total Group Profile Report" (available at https://reports.collegeboard.org/pdf/total-group-2016.pdf).

29. William H. Sewell, "Inequality of Opportunity for Higher Education," *American Sociological Review* 36, no. 5 (1971): 793–809.

30. Thomas G. Mortenson, "Family Income and Educational Attainment, 1970 to 2009," *Postsecondary Education Opportunity*, no. 221 (November 2010).
31. Derived from David Leonhardt, "A Closer Look at Income Mobility," *New York Times*, May 14, 2005; and Katharine Bradbury and Jane Katz, "Trends in U.S. Family Income Mobility 1969–2006," Federal Reserve Bank of Boston, 2009.
32. De Lone, *Small Futures*, 14–19. See also Daniel McMurrer, Mark Condon, and Isabel Sawhill, "Intergenerational Mobility in the United States," (Washington DC: Urban Institute, 1997), http://www.urban.org/publications/406796.html?; and Bhashkar Mazumder, "Earnings Mobility in the U.S.: A New Look at Intergenerational Inequality," Federal Reserve Bank of Chicago Working Paper no. 2001-18, March 21, 2001. doi: 10.2139/ssrn.295559.
33. Miles Corak, "Do Poor Children Become Poor Adults? Lessons from a Cross-Country Comparison of Generational Earnings Mobility" (Bonn, Germany: IZA, 2006). Available at http://repec.iza.org/dp1993.pdf.
34. Jason DeParle, "Harder for Americans to Rise From Lower Rungs," *New York Times*, January 4, 2012.
35. Howard Tuchman, *Economics of the Rich* (New York: Random House, 1973), 15. See also Greg Duncan, Ariel Kalil, Susan Mayer, Robin Tepper, and Monique Payne, "The Apple Does Not Fall Far From the Tree," in *Unequal Chances: Family Background and Economic Success*, ed. Samuel Bowles, Herbert Gintis, and Melissa Groves (Princeton, NJ: Princeton University Press, 2008), 23–79; Bhashkar Mazumder, "The Apple Falls Even Closer to the Tree Than We Thought," in Bowles, et. al., 80–99. For more information on inheritance, see Samuel Bowles and Herbert Gintis, "The Inheritance of Inequality," *Journal of Economic Perspectives* 16, no. 3 (Summer 2002): 2–30; and Tom Hertz, *Understanding Mobility in America*, Center for American Progress, available at http://www.americanprogress.org/wp-content /uploads/kf/hertz_mobility_analysis.pdf?.
36. Howard Wachtel, *Labor and the Economy* (Orlando, FL: Academic Press, 1984), 161–162.
37. Gould, Elise. "State of Working America Wages 2018." *Economic Policy Institute*, 19 Feb. 2019, www.epi.org/publication/state-of-american-wages-2018/.
38. Alan Blinder, quoted by Paul Krugman, in "Disparity and Despair," *U.S. News and World Report*, March 23, 1992, 54.
39. Wolff, E., "Household Wealth Trends in the United States, 1962 to 2016: Has Middle Class Wealth Recovered?" National Bureau of Economic Research Working Paper No. w24085 (November 2017).
40. The National Economic Council, "The Buffett Rule: A Basic Principle of Tax Fairness," White House, April 2012, citing Internal Revenue System Statistics of Income 2005 Public Use File, National Bureau of Economic Research TAXISM, and CEA calculations. Available at http://www.whitehouse.gov/sites/default/files/Buffett_Rule_Report_Final.pdf. Also cited in *The New York Times* editorial "Mr. Obama and the 'Buffett Rule,'" April 10, 2012. Available at http://www.nytimes.com/2012/04/11/opinion/mr-obama-and-the-buffett-rule.html?_r=0.
41. Campaign Finance Institute, "2016 Federal Election" (accessed March 5, 2017, available at http://www.cfinst.org/pdf/federal/2016Report/pdf/CFI_Federal-CF_16_Table2-01.pdf).
42. 2015 figures from "Average Wealth of Members of Congress," Center for Responsive Politics (available at https://www.opensecrets.org/personal-finances/top-net-worth).
43. See Larry Bartels, *Unequal Democracy: The Political Economy of the New Gilded Age* (Princeton, NJ: Princeton University Press, 2008), chapter 9; see also MAPLight.org (MAPLight tracks political contributions and their impact on the votes of public officials).
44. Based on 2017 data from Historical Poverty Tables: People and Families—1959 to 2017 (Table 2. Poverty Status of People by Family Relationship, Race, and Hispanic Origin: 1959 to 2017), last revised August, 28, 2019 (available at www.census.gov/data/tables/time-series/demo/income-poverty/historical-poverty-people.html).

11 White Privilege: Unpacking the Invisible Knapsack

Peggy McIntosh

Through work to bring materials from Women's Studies into the rest of the curriculum, I have often noticed men's unwillingness to grant that they are over-privileged, even though they may grant that women are disadvantaged. They may say they will work to improve women's status, in the society, the university, or the curriculum, but they can't or won't support the idea of lessening men's. Denials which amount to taboos surround the subject of advantages which men gain from women's disadvantages. These denials protect male privilege from being fully acknowledged, lessened or ended.

Thinking through unacknowledged male privilege as a phenomenon, I realized that since hierarchies in our society are interlocking, there was most likely a phenomenon of white privilege which was similarly denied and protected. As a white person, I realized I had been taught about racism as something which puts others at a disadvantage, but had been taught not to see one of its corollary aspects, white privilege, which puts me at an advantage.

I think whites are carefully taught not to recognize white privilege, as males are taught not to recognize male privilege. So I have begun in an untutored way to ask what it is like to have white privilege. I have come to see white privilege as an invisible package of unearned assets which I can count on cashing in each day, but about which I was "meant" to remain oblivious. White privilege is like an invisible weightless knapsack of special provisions, maps, passports, codebooks, visas, clothes, tools and blank checks.

Describing white privilege makes one newly accountable. As we in Women's Studies work to reveal male privilege and ask men to give up some of their power, so one who writes about having white privilege must ask, "Having described it, what will I do to lessen or end it?"

After I realized the extent to which men work from a base of unacknowledged privilege, I understood that much of their oppressiveness was unconscious. Then I remembered the frequent charges from women of color that white women whom they encounter are oppressive. I began to understand why we are justly seen as oppressive, even when we

---

Peggy McIntosh is a feminist scholar and founder of the National SEED (Seeking Educational Equity and Diversity) Project on Inclusive Curriculum.

This article first appeared in *Peace and Freedom Magazine*, July/August, 1989, pp. 10–12, a publication of the Women's International League for Peace and Freedom, Philadelphia, PA. Reprinted by permission. Copyright ©1989. Anyone who wishes to reproduce more than 35 copies of this article must apply to the author, Dr. Peggy McIntosh, at mmcintosh@wellesley.edu. This article may not be electronically posted except by the National SEED Project.

don't see ourselves that way. I began to count the ways in which I enjoy unearned skin privilege and have been conditioned into oblivion about its existence.

My schooling gave me no training in seeing myself as an oppressor, as an unfairly advantaged person, or as a participant in a damaged culture. I was taught to see myself as an individual whose moral state depended on her individual moral will. My schooling followed the pattern my colleague Elizabeth Minnich has pointed out: whites are taught to think of their lives as morally neutral, normative, and average, and also ideal, so that when we work to benefit others, this is seen as work which will allow "them" to be more like "us."

I decided to try to work on myself at least by identifying some of the daily effects of white privilege in my life. I have chosen those conditions which I think in my case *attach somewhat more to skin-color privilege* than to class, religion, ethnic status, or geographical location, though of course all these other factors are intricately intertwined. As far as I can see, my African American co-workers, friends and acquaintances with whom I come into daily or frequent contact in this particular time, place, and line of work cannot count on most of these conditions.

1. I can if I wish arrange to be in the company of people of my race most of the time.
2. If I should need to move, I can be pretty sure of renting or purchasing housing in an area which I can afford and in which I would want to live.
3. I can be pretty sure that my neighbors in such a location will be neutral or pleasant to me.
4. I can go shopping alone most of the time, pretty well assured that I will not be followed or harassed.
5. I can turn on the television or open to the front page of the paper and see people of my race widely represented.
6. When I am told about our national heritage or about "civilization," I am shown that people of my color made it what it is.
7. I can be sure that my children will be given curricular materials that testify to the existence of their race.
8. If I want to, I can be pretty sure of finding a publisher for this piece on white privilege.
9. I can go into a music shop and count on finding the music of my race represented, into a supermarket and find the staple foods which fit with my cultural traditions, into a hairdresser's shop and find someone who can cut my hair.
10. Whether I use checks, credit cards, or cash, I can count on my skin color not to work against the appearance of financial reliability.
11. I can arrange to protect my children most of the time from people who might not like them.
12. I can swear, or dress in secondhand clothes, or not answer letters, without having people attribute these choices to the bad morals, the poverty, or the illiteracy of my race.
13. I can speak in public to a powerful male group without putting my race on trial.
14. I can do well in a challenging situation without being called a credit to my race.
15. I am never asked to speak for all the people of my racial group.

16. I can remain oblivious of the language and customs of persons of color who constitute the world's majority without feeling in my culture any penalty for such oblivion.
17. I can criticize our government and talk about how much I fear its policies and behavior without being seen as a cultural outsider.
18. I can be pretty sure that if I ask to talk to "the person in charge," I will be facing a person of my race.
19. If a traffic cop pulls me over or if the IRS audits my tax return, I can be sure I haven't been singled out because of my race.
20. I can easily buy posters, postcards, picture books, greeting cards, dolls, toys, and children's magazines featuring people of my race.
21. I can go home from most meetings of organizations I belong to feeling somewhat tied in, rather than isolated, out-of-place, outnumbered, unheard, held at a distance, or feared.
22. I can take a job with an affirmative action employer without having co-workers on the job suspect that I got it because of my race.
23. I can choose public accommodation without fearing that people of my race cannot get in or will be mistreated in the places I have chosen.
24. I can be sure that if I need legal or medical help, my race will not work against me.
25. If my day, week, or year is going badly, I need not ask of each negative episode or situation whether it has racial overtones.
26. I can choose blemish cover or bandages in "flesh" color and have them more or less match my skin.

I repeatedly forgot each of the realizations on this list until I wrote it down. For me white privilege has turned out to be an elusive and fugitive subject. The pressure to avoid it is great, for in facing it I must give up the myth of meritocracy. If these things are true, this is not such a free country; one's life is not what one makes it; many doors open for certain people through no virtues of their own.

In unpacking this invisible knapsack of white privilege, I have listed conditions of daily experience which I once took for granted. Nor did I think of any of these perquisites as bad for the holder. I now think that we need a more finely differentiated taxonomy of privilege, for some of these varieties are only what one would want for everyone in a just society, and others give license to be ignorant, oblivious, arrogant and destructive.

I see a pattern running through the matrix of white privilege, a pattern of assumptions which were passed on to me as a white person. There was one main piece of cultural turf; it was my own turf, and I was among those who could control the turf. *My skin color was an asset for any move I was educated to want to make.* I could think of myself as belonging in major ways, and of making social systems work for me. I could freely disparage, fear, neglect, or be oblivious to anything outside of the dominant cultural forms. Being of the main culture, I could also criticize it fairly freely.

In proportion as my racial group was being made confident, comfortable, and oblivious, other groups were likely being made inconfident, uncomfortable, and alienated.

Whiteness protected me from many kinds of hostility, distress, and violence, which I was being subtly trained to visit in turn upon people of color.

For this reason, the word "privilege" now seems to me misleading. We usually think of privilege as being a favored state, whether earned or conferred by birth or luck. Yet some of the conditions I have described here work to systematically overempower certain groups. Such privilege simply *confers dominance* because of one's race or sex.

I want, then, to distinguish between earned strength and unearned power conferred systemically. Power from unearned privilege can look like strength when it is in fact permission to escape or to dominate. But not all of the privileges on my list are inevitably damaging. Some, like the expectation that neighbors will be decent to you, or that your race will not count against you in court, should be the norm in a just society. Others, like the privilege to ignore less powerful people, distort the humanity of the holders as well as the ignored groups.

We might at least start by distinguishing between positive advantages which we can work to spread, and negative types of advantages which unless rejected will always reinforce our present hierarchies. For example, the feeling that one belongs within the human circle, as Native Americans say, should not be seen as privilege for a few. Ideally it is an *unearned entitlement*. At present, since only a few have it, it is an unearned advantage for them. This paper results from a process of coming to see that some of the power which I originally saw as attendant on being a human being in the U.S. consisted in *unearned advantage* and *conferred dominance*.

I have met very few men who are truly distressed about systemic, unearned male advantage and conferred dominance. And so one question for me and others like me is whether we will be like them, or whether we will get truly distressed, even outraged, about unearned race advantage and conferred dominance and if so, what we will do to lessen them. In any case, we need to do more work in identifying how they actually affect our daily lives. Many, perhaps most, of our white students in the U.S. think that racism doesn't affect them because they are not people of color; they do not see "whiteness" as a racial identity. In addition, since race and sex are not the only advantaging systems at work, we need similarly to examine the daily experience of having age advantage, or ethnic advantage, or physical ability, or advantage related to nationality, religion, or sexual orientation.

Difficulties and dangers surrounding the task of finding parallels are many. Since racism, sexism, and heterosexism are not the same, the advantaging associated with them should not be seen as the same. In addition, it is hard to disentangle aspects of unearned advantage which rest more on social class, economic class, race, religion, sex and ethnic identity than on other factors. Still, all of the oppressions are interlocking, as the Combahee River Collective Statement of 1977 continues to remind us eloquently.

One factor seems clear about all of the interlocking oppressions. They take both active forms which we can see and embedded forms which as a member of the dominant group one is taught not to see. In my class and place, I did not see myself as a racist because I was taught to recognize racism only in individual acts of meanness by members of my group, never in invisible systems conferring unsought racial dominance on my group from birth.

Disapproving of the systems won't be enough to change them. I was taught to think that racism could end if white individuals changed their attitudes. [But] a "white" skin in the United States opens many doors for whites whether or not we approve of the way dominance has been conferred on us. Individual acts can palliate, but cannot end, these problems.

To redesign social systems we need first to acknowledge their colossal unseen dimensions. The silences and denials surrounding privilege are the key political tool here. They keep the thinking about equality or equity incomplete, protecting unearned advantage and conferred dominance by making these taboo subjects. Most talk by whites about equal opportunity seems to me now to be about equal opportunity to try to get into a position of dominance while denying that *systems* of dominance exist.

It seems to me that obliviousness about white advantage, like obliviousness about male advantage, is kept strongly inculturated in the United States so as to maintain the myth of meritocracy, the myth that democratic choice is equally available to all. Keeping most people unaware that freedom of confident action is there for just a small number of people props up those in power, and serves to keep power in the hands of the same groups that have most of it already.

Though systemic change takes many decades, there are pressing questions for me and I imagine for some others like me if we raise our daily consciousness on the perquisites of being light-skinned. What will we do with such knowledge? As we know from watching men, it is an open question whether we will choose to use unearned advantage to weaken hidden systems of advantage, and whether we will use any of our arbitrarily-awarded power to try to reconstruct power systems on a broader base.

12 | My Class Didn't Trump My Race: Using Oppression to Face Privilege

Robin J. DiAngelo

I was born to working class parents; my father was a construction worker and my mother was a switchboard operator. When I was 2, my parents divorced and my mother began to raise us on her own; at that point we entered into poverty. I have never understood people who say, "we were poor but we didn't know it because we had lots of love." Poverty hurts. It isn't romantic, or some form of "living simply." Poor people are not innocent and child-like. The lack of medical and dental care, the hunger, and the ostracization, are concrete. The stress of poverty made my household much more chaotic than loving.

We were evicted frequently, and moved four to five times a year. There were periods when oatmeal was the only food in our house. I had no health or dental care during my childhood, and today all of my front teeth are filled because by the time I was 10 they were rotten. If we got sick, my mother would beat us, screaming that we could not get sick because she could not afford to take us to the doctor. We occasionally had to live in our car, and I was left with relatives for 8 months while my mother tried to secure housing for us. My teacher once held my hands up to my fourth-grade class as an example of poor hygiene and with the class as her audience, told me to go home and tell my mother to wash me.

I used to stare at the girls in my class and ache to be like them; to have a father, to wear pretty clothes, to go to camp, to be clean and get to sit with them. I knew we didn't have enough money and that meant that I couldn't join them in school or go to their houses or have the same things they had. But the moment the real meaning of poverty crystallized for me came when we were visiting another family. As we were leaving I heard one of their daughters ask her mother, "What is wrong with them?" I stopped, riveted. I too, wanted to know. Her mother held her finger to her lips and whispered, "Shhh, they're *poor*." This was a revelatory moment for me. The shock came not just in the knowledge that we were poor, but that it was exposed. There was something wrong with us, indeed, and it was something that was obvious to others and that we couldn't hide, something shameful that could be seen but should not be named. It took me many years to gain a structural analysis of class that would help shift this sense of shame.

I begin this narrative with my class background because it so deeply informs my understanding of race. From an early age I had the sense of being an outsider; I was acutely

---

Robin DiAngelo, a writer and racial justice consultant, is the author of *White Fragility: Why It's So Hard to Talk to White People About Racism*.

aware that I was poor, that I was dirty, that I was not normal, and that there was something "wrong" with me. But I also knew that I was *not* Black. We were at the lower rungs of society, but there was always someone on the periphery, just below us. I knew that "colored" people existed and that they should be avoided. I can remember many occasions when I reached for candy or uneaten food laying on the street and was admonished by my grandmother not to touch it because a "colored person" may have touched it. The message was clear to me; if a colored person touched something it became dirty. The irony here is that the marks of poverty were clearly visible on me: poor hygiene, torn clothes, homelessness, hunger. Yet through comments such as my grandmother's, a racial Other was formed in my consciousness, an Other through whom I became clean. Race was the one identity that aligned me with the other girls in my school.

I left home as a teenager and struggled to survive. As I looked at what lay ahead, I could see no path out of poverty other than education. The decision to take that path was frightening for me; I had never gotten the message that I was smart and academia was a completely foreign social context. But once I was in academia, I understood that a college degree is not conferred upon those who are smarter or who try harder than others, it comes through a complex web of intersecting systems of privileges that include internal expectations as well as external resources. In academia, racism, a key system that I benefit from, helped to mediate my class-based disadvantages. . . .

Since those early days, I have led dialogues on race with police officers, social workers, teachers, and in both the private and government sectors. I recently completed my dissertation on how White student teachers reproduce racism in interracial dialogues about race. As I look at the world now, I see racism as ever-present and multidimensional. I realize that poor and working class White people don't necessarily have any less racism than middle or upper class White people, our racism is just conveyed in different ways and we enact it from a different social location than the middle or upper classes.

As I reflect back on the early messages I received about being poor and being White, I now realize that my grandmother and I *needed* people of color to cleanse and realign us with the dominant White culture that our poverty had separated us from. I now ask myself how the classist messages I internalized growing up lead me to collude in racism. For example, as a child who grew up in poverty, I received constant reminders that I was stupid, lazy, dirty, and a drain on the resources of hardworking people. I internalized these messages, and they work to silence me. Unless I work to uproot them, I am less likely to trust my own perceptions or feel like I have a "right" to speak up. I may not attempt to interrupt racism because the social context in which it is occurring intimidates me. My fear on these occasions may be coming from a place of internalized class inferiority, but in practice my silence colludes with racism and ultimately benefits me by protecting my White privilege and maintaining racial solidarity with other White people. This solidarity connects and realigns me with White people across other lines of difference, such as the very class locations that have silenced me in the first place. I am also prone to use others to elevate me, as in the example with my grandmother. So although my specific class background mediated the way I learned racism and how I enact it, in the end it still socialized me to collude with the overall structure.

It is my observation that class dictates proximity between Whites and people of color. Poor Whites are most often in closest proximity to people of color because they tend to share poverty. I hear the term "White trash" frequently. It is not without significance that this is one of the few expressions in which race is named for Whites. I think the proximity of the people labeled as White trash to people of color is why; race becomes marked or "exposed" by virtue of a closeness to people of color. In a racist society, this closeness both highlights and pollutes Whiteness. Owning class people also have people of color near them because people of color are often their domestics and gardeners—their servants. But they do not interact socially with people of color in the same way that poor Whites do. Middle class Whites are generally the furthest away from people of color. They are the most likely to say that, "there were no people of color in my neighborhood or school. I didn't meet a Black person until I went to college" (often adding, "so I was lucky because I didn't learn anything about racism"). Looking specifically at how class shaped my racial identity has been very helpful to me in attempting to unravel the specific way I manifest my internalized racial superiority.

I am no longer poor. Although I still carry the marks of poverty, those marks are now only internal. But these marks limit me in more than what I believe I deserve or where I think I belong; they also interfere with my ability to stand up against injustice, for as long as I believe that I am not as smart or as valuable as other White people, I won't challenge racism. I believe that in order for Whites to unravel our internalized racial dominance, we have two interwoven tasks. One is to work on our own internalized oppression—the ways in which we impose limitations on ourselves based on the societal messages we receive about the inferiority of the lower status groups we belong to. The other task is to face the internalized dominance that results from being socialized in a racist society—the ways in which we consciously or unconsciously believe that we are more important, more valuable, more intelligent, and more deserving than people of color. I cannot address the interwoven complexity of other White people's social locations. However, after years facilitating dialogues on race with thousands of White people from a range of class positions (as well as varied gender, sexual orientation, religious, and ability positions), and bearing witness to countless stories and challenges from people of color about my own racism and that of other Whites, I have come to see some very common patterns of internalized dominance. These patterns are shared across other social positions due to the bottom line nature of racism: Regardless of one's other locations, White people know on some level that being White in this society is "better" than being a person of color, and this, along with the very real doors Whiteness opens, serves to mediate the oppression experienced in those other social locations. In the next section of this article, I will identify several of these patterns of internalized dominance that are generally shared among Whites.

We Live Segregated Lives

Growing up in segregated environments (schools, workplaces, neighborhoods, media images, historical perspectives, etc.), we are given the message that our experiences and perspectives are the only ones that matter. We receive this message day in and day out, and it is not limited to a single moment, it is a *relentless experience*. Virtually all of our teachers, history books, role models, movie and book characters, are White like us. Further, as White people, we are taught not to feel any loss about the absence of people of color in our lives. In fact, the absence of people of color is what defines our schools and neighborhoods as "good." And we get this message regardless of where we are oppressed in other areas of our lives. Because we live primarily segregated lives in a White-dominated society, we receive little or no authentic information about racism and are thus unprepared to think critically or complexly about it. Although segregation is often mediated somewhat for poor urban (and other) Whites who may live near and have friendships with people of color on the microlevel, segregation is still operating on the macrolevel and informing our collective perspectives and what is deemed the most valuable or "official" knowledge.

Whites from the lower classes who may have more integrated lives on the microlevel still receive the message that achievement means moving out of poverty and away from the neighborhoods and schools that define us. Upward mobility is the great class goal in the United States, and the social environment gets tangibly Whiter the higher up one goes, whether it be in academia or management. Whiter environments, in turn, are marked as the most socially and economically valuable. Reaching towards the most valuable places in society thus entails leaving people of color behind. . . .

We Are Raised to Value the Individual and to See Ourselves as Individuals, Rather Than as Part of a Socialized Group

Individuality allows us to present ourselves as having "just arrived on the scene," unique and original, outside of socialization and unaffected by the relentless racial messages we receive. This also allows us to distance ourselves from the actions of our group and demand that we be granted the benefit of the doubt (because we are individuals) in all cases. Thus we get very irate when we are "accused" of racism, because as individuals, we are "different" from other White people and expect to be seen as such. We find intolerable any suggestion that our behavior or perspectives are typical of our group as a whole, and this ensures that we cannot deepen our understanding of racism.

Seeing ourselves as individuals erases our history and hides the way in which wealth has accumulated over generations and benefits us, *as a group*, today. Further, being an individual is a privilege only afforded to White people. By focusing on ourselves as individuals, Whites are able to conceptualize the racist patterns in our behavior as "just our personality" and not connected to intergroup dynamics. For example, I might be an extrovert and cut people off when I am engaged in a discussion. I can say, "that is just my personality, I do that to everyone. That is how we talked at the dinner table in my family." But the moment I cut off a person of color, it becomes racism because the history and the impact of that behavior for both of us is different. The freedom to remain oblivious to that fact, with no sense that this obliviousness has any consequences of importance, is White privilege (racism).

If we use the line of reasoning that we are all individuals and social categories such as race, class, and gender don't matter and are just "labels" that stereotype us, then it follows that we all end up in our own "natural" places. Those at the top are merely a collection of individuals who rose under their own individual merits, and those at the bottom are there due to individual lack. Group membership is thereby rendered inoperative and racial disparities are seen as essential rather than structural. Thus the discourse of individuality is not only connected to the discourse of meritocracy, but also with the Darwinism of the "bell curve." It behooves those of us oppressed in other places to understand group membership, for the discourse of individuality may benefit us in terms of racial privilege but ultimately holds all of our oppressions in place. . . .

We Feel That We Should Be Judged by Our Intentions Rather Than the Effects of Our Behavior

A common White reasoning is that as long as we didn't intend to perpetuate racism, then our actions don't count as racism. We focus on our intentions and discount the impact, thereby invalidating people of color's experiences and communicating that the effects of our behavior on them are unimportant. We then spend great energy explaining to people of color why our behavior is not racism at all. This invalidates their perspectives while enabling us to deny responsibility for making the effort to understand enough about racism to see our behavior's impact in both the immediate interaction and the broader, historical context.

We Believe That if We Can't Feel Our Social Power, Then We Don't Have Any

White social power is so normalized that it is outside of our conscious awareness. Yet we often expect that power is something that one can feel, rather than something one takes for granted. The issue of social power is where a lower class location often becomes confused with a lack of racial privilege. For example, in discussions on race I often hear White working class men protest that they don't have any social power. They work long and grueling hours, often in jobs in which they have no long-term security, and come home feeling beaten and quite disempowered. These men can often not relate to the concept of holding social power. But if being able to feel racial privilege is required before Whites can acknowledge its reality, we will not be able to see (and thus change) it. The key to recognizing power is in recognizing normalcy—what is not attended to or in need of constant navigation. These men are indeed struggling against social and economic barriers, but race is simply not one of them; in fact, race is a major social current running in their direction and not only moving them along, but helping them navigate their other social struggles. Not feeling power is not necessarily aligned with how others perceive or respond to us, or our relationship to social and institutional networks.

We Think It Is Important Not to Notice Race

The underlying assumption of a colorblind discourse is that race is a defect and it is best to pretend that we don't notice it. But if we pretend we don't notice race, we cannot notice racism. If we don't notice racism, we can't understand or interrupt it in ourselves or others. We have to start being honest about the fact that we do notice race (when it isn't White) and then pay attention to what race means in our everyday lives. White people and people of color do not have the same racial experience, and this has profound and tangible consequences that need to be understood if we want to stop colluding with racism. . . .

Racism Has Been Constructed as Belonging to Extremists and Being Very Bad

Racism is a deeply embedded, multidimensional, and internalized system that all members of this society are shaped by. Yet dominant culture constructs racism as primarily in the past and only currently occurring as isolated acts relegated to individual bad people (usually living somewhere in the South, or "old"). Although many White people today sincerely believe that racism is a bad thing, our abhorrence of racism coupled with a superficial conceptualization of it causes us to be highly defensive about any suggestion that we perpetuate it. Many Whites (and liberal Whites in particular) think that we can deal with racism in our heads (and without ever interacting with people of color) by deciding that we have not been affected because we don't want to have been affected.

A superficial understanding of racism coupled with a desire to distance ourselves from being perceived as "bad" is further complicated by resentments we may feel about places in our lives where we suffer from other forms of social injustice. It is often very difficult for Whites who have not been validated for the oppression they experience elsewhere to keep their attention on a form of oppression from which they benefit. But I have found that when I explore how classism and other oppressions I experience set me up to participate in racism, I am more able to interrupt the manifestation of both in my life. By placing racism in the center of my analysis, I have been able to begin to unravel my other group socializations and how they work together to support social hierarchies.

Interrupting Internalized Dominance

I have found that a key to interrupting my internalized racial dominance is to defer to the knowledge of people whom I have been taught, in countless ways, are less knowledgeable and less valuable than I am. I must reach for humility and be willing to *not know*. I may never fully understand the workings of racism, as I have been trained my entire life to perpetuate racism while denying its reality. I do not have to understand racism for it to be real, and my expectation that I could is part of my internalized dominance. Reaching for racial humility as a White person is not the same for me as being mired in class shame.

My class position is only one social location from which I learned to collude with racism. For example, I have also asked myself how I learned to collude with racism as a Catholic and a woman. How did it shape my sense of racial belonging, of racial *correctness*, to be presented with God, the ultimate and universal authority, as White? How did the active erasure of Jesus' race and ethnicity shape my racial consciousness? How did the universalization of Catholicism as the true religion for all peoples of the world engender racial superiority within me when all the authorities within that religion were White like myself?

At the same time, how did my conditioning under Catholicism not to question authority lead me to silently collude with the racism of other Whites?

As a White woman, how did I internalize racial superiority through the culture's representation of White women as the embodiment of ultimate beauty? What has it meant for me to have a key signifier of female perfection—Whiteness—available to me? How have images of White women in the careers deemed valuable for woman shaped my goals? How has mainstream feminism's articulation of White women's issues as universal women's issues shaped what I care about? At the same time, what has it meant to live under patriarchy and to be taught that as a woman I am less intelligent, that I should not speak up, that I should defer to others, and at all times be nice and polite? How have all of these messages ultimately set me up to collude in the oppression of people of color? By asking questions such as these I have been able to gain a much deeper and more useful analysis of racism, and rather than finding that centering racism denies my other oppressions, I find that centering racism has been a profound way to address the complexity of all my social locations.

PART II

SUGGESTIONS FOR FURTHER READING

Allison, Dorothy. *Skin: Talking About Sex, Class, and Literature*, 2nd ed. Open Road Integrated Media, 2013.

Anderson, Carol. *White Rage: The Unspoken Truth of Our Racial Divide*. Bloomsbury, 2017.

Anderson, Kristin. *Benign Bigotry: The Psychology of Subtle Prejudice*. Cambridge University Press, 2010.

Baird, Robert M., and Stuart E. Rosenbaum, eds. *Bigotry, Prejudice, and Hatred*, 2nd ed. Prometheus Press, 1999.

Bonilla-Silva, Eduardo. *Racism Without Racists: Color-Blind Racism and the Persistence of Racial Inequality in the U.S.*, 5th ed. Rowman & Littlefield, 2017.

_____. *White Supremacy and Racism in the Post–Civil Rights Era*. Rienner, 2001.

Brandt, Eric, ed. *Dangerous Liaisons: Blacks, Gays, and the Struggle for Equality*. New Press, 1999.

Brown, Michael K., et al. *Whitewashing Race in America: The Myth of a Color-Blind Society*. University of California Press, 2005.

Chang, Jeff. *Who We Be: A Cultural History of Race in Post–Civil Rights America*. St. Martin's Press, 2014.

Coates, Ta-Nehisi. *Between the World and Me*. Spiegel & Grau, 2015.

Cose, Ellis. *The Rage of a Privileged Class*. HarperCollins, 1994.

Crenshaw, Kimberlé Williams. "Mapping the Margins: Intersectionality, Identity Politics, and Violence Against Women of Color." In *The Feminist Philosophy Reader*, Alison Bailey and Chris Cuomo, eds., 279–309. McGraw-Hill, 2008.

Currah, Paisley, Richard M. Juang, and Shannon Price Minter, eds. *Transgender Rights*. University of Minnesota Press, 2006.

D'Emilio, John, and Estelle B. Freedman. *Intimate Matters: A History of Sexuality in America*, 3rd ed. University of Chicago Press, 2012.

DeMott, Benjamin. *The Trouble with Friendship: Why Americans Can't Think Straight About Race*. Atlantic Monthly Press, 1995.

Dusky, Lorraine. *Still Unequal: The Shameful Truth About Women and Justice in America*. Crown Books, 1996.

Dyer, Richard. *White*. Routledge, 1997.

Faludi, Susan. *Backlash: The Undeclared War Against American Women*, 15th anniversary ed. Broadway, 2006.

_____. *Stiffed: The Betrayal of the American Man*. HarperPerennial, 2000.

Feagin, Joe R. *Racist America: Roots, Realities, and Future Reparations*. Routledge, 2000.

Freedman, Estelle B., ed. *The Essential Feminist Reader*. Modern Library, 2007.

Glenn, Evelyn Nakano. *Unequal Freedom: How Race and Gender Shaped American Citizenship and Labor*. Harvard University Press, 2004.

Haney López, Ian. *Dog Whistle Politics: How Coded Racial Appeals Have Reinvented Racism and Wrecked the Middle Class*. Oxford University Press, 2014.

Harris, Leonard. *Racism*. Humanities Books, 1999.

Ignatiev, Noel. *How the Irish Became White*. Routledge, 2008.

Incite! Women of Color Against Violence, eds. *The Color of Violence: The Incite! Anthology*. South End Press, 2006.

Johnson, Allan G. *Privilege, Power, and Difference*, 2nd ed. McGraw-Hill, 2005.

Jones, Alethia, and Virginia Eubanks, eds., with Barbara Smith. *Ain't Gonna Let Nobody Turn Me Around: Forty Years of Movement Building with Barbara Smith*. SUNY Press, 2014.

Kadi, Joanne. *Thinking Class: Sketches from a Cultural Worker*. South End Press, 1996.

Katznelson, Ira. *When Affirmative Action Was White: An Untold History of Racial Inequality in Twentieth-Century America*. W. W. Norton, 2005.

Kimmel, Michael. *The Gendered Society*, 6th ed. Oxford University Press, 2016.

Lareau, Annette. *Unequal Childhoods: Class, Race, and Family Life*, 2nd ed. University of California Press, 2011.

Lee, Erika. *The Making of Asian America: A History*. Simon and Schuster, 2015.

Lipsitz, George. *The Possessive Investment in Whiteness*, rev. ed. Temple University Press, 2006.

Marable, Manning. *Race, Reform, and Rebellion: The Second Reconstruction in Black America, 1945–2006*, 3rd ed. University Press of Mississippi, 2007.

Perry, Barbara. *In the Name of Hate: Understanding Hate Crimes*. Routledge, 2001.

Pharr, Suzanne. *Homophobia as a Weapon of Sexism*. Chardon Press, 1988.

Rhode, Deborah L. *Speaking of Sex: The Denial of Gender Inequality*. Harvard University Press, 1997.

Ronai, Carol R., et al. *Everyday Sexism in the Third Millennium*. Routledge, 1997.

Shipler, David K. *A Country of Strangers: Blacks and Whites in America*. Knopf, 1997.

Sue, Derald Wing. *Microaggressions in Everyday Life: Race, Gender, and Sexual Orientation*. John Wiley & Sons, 2010.

Tatum, Beverly Daniel. *Why Are All the Black Kids Sitting Together in the Cafeteria? And Other Conversations About Race*, rev. ed. Basic Books, 2017.

Williams, Lena. *It's the Little Things, the Everyday Interactions That Get Under the Skin of Blacks and Whites*. Harcourt, 2000.

PART

III

Citizenship and Immigration: Constructing Nationality, Borders, and Belonging

The psychological borderlands, the sexual borderlands, and the spiritual borderlands are not particular to the Southwest. In fact the Borderlands are physically present wherever two or more cultures edge each other, where people of different races occupy the same territory, where under, lower, middle and upper classes touch, where the space between two individuals shrinks with intimacy.

—GLORIA ANZALDÚA, *BORDERLANDS / LA FRONTERA: THE NEW MESTIZA*

In Part I, we discussed how race, class, gender, and sexuality are social constructions with real material consequences. In Part II, we focused on the systems of oppression attached to these categories of identity. In Part III, we examine notions like "American," "citizen," "borders," and "belonging" as shifting and malleable categories that also have been deployed to justify inequality, exploitation, and exclusion. Citizenship is a legal designation, but social narratives produce the *meanings* of "citizen" as a shared identity that can offer—or deny—a sense of belonging. The meaning of "citizen" has never been fixed but is rather a site of ongoing contest and struggle.

The 1790 Naturalization Act—one of the very first laws passed by a young U.S. Congress on the matter—restricted naturalized citizenship to those who were "free" and "white." This racial demarcation endured for more than one hundred and fifty years. Numerous other policies, practices, and discourses have narrowed and expanded the definition of "American" over the years, based on race, class, religion, gender, sexuality, ability, place of origin, and many other categories. The authors in Part III each examine a different aspect of how citizenship has been constructed for the benefit and detriment of different groups, by giving or withholding a sense of identity and belonging.

Chicana feminist writer Gloria Anzaldúa challenges the idea of "border" as a fixed line demarcating a national boundary and offers instead the notion of "borderlands," referring to an entire border region as well as to cultural, economic, psychological, sexual, and spiritual points of conflict and connection. The rhetoric of "border security" has dominated the U.S. political landscape for several years, but debates about borders are part of a larger struggle over who is included in notions of what it means to be an American. "The border" represents the geographic boundaries of our nation, but these debates also represent the boundaries of who is included in our picture of ourselves as a society.

In announcing his bid for the presidency in June 2015, candidate Donald Trump associated Mexican immigrants with crime and declared, "I will build a great, great wall on our southern border."[1] Even before becoming a candidate he called for "a total and complete shutdown of Muslims entering the United States,"[2] and he introduced an executive order to that effect in the first days of his presidency. While such gestures came to be central in his candidacy and presidency, and his reliance on white nationalist discourses marks a particular intensification of racialized notions of the United States as a white and Christian nation, Trump is by no means the first U.S. leader to deploy anti-immigrant rhetoric or enact anti-immigrant policies. Immigrant rights activists referred to Trump's immediate predecessor, Barack Obama, as the "Deporter in Chief" because of the 2.5 million deportations under his watch (even as he issued an executive order offering some protections for certain undocumented immigrants who arrived in the United States as children).[3] George W. Bush, in the aftermath of 9/11, created a machinery of immigration enforcement—including the Department of Homeland Security and, under its control, a new law enforcement agency called Immigration and Customs Enforcement (ICE)—that helped make those record numbers possible under Obama. In 1996, Bill Clinton signed into law the Illegal Immigration Reform and Immigrant Responsibility Act, which intensified immigration enforcement measures (including detention and deportation), made it more difficult to seek asylum, and criminalized undocumented immigrants in new ways.[4] As Aviva Chomsky writes, "Whether halting the entry of refugees or persons with visas from particular countries, hiring thousands of new ICE and Border Patrol agents, promising to build a 'great, great wall,' denying federal money to sanctuary cities, or publishing lists of crimes committed by immigrants, Trump's immigration policies follow in the footsteps but also intensify those of his predecessors, and continue to create fear, justify exploitation, and rationalize authoritarianism."[5]

Understanding the complexities of contemporary debates over immigration and citizenship requires grappling with our history and our national mythologies. "They keep coming," intoned an ominous voice-over in a 1994 presidential campaign ad featuring a loop of a few seconds of grainy footage of migrants running across a freeway ostensibly near the border with Mexico. "We are a country of immigrants" is often the counternarrative from supporters of immigrant rights. Both slogans generate a simplistic narrative that the authors in Part III complicate. "They keep coming" invokes hordes of threatening (and racialized) outsiders, covers up our history of Manifest Destiny and genocide, and justifies harsh policies to "crack down" and "stem the flow." It paints a false picture of "too lenient" policies in an excessively welcoming nation. "We are a country of immigrants" is indeed an important counternarrative, but it also generates a "too generous" image of our national policy and simultaneously erases the many groups who did not come here as immigrants seeking a better life. Indigenous peoples were in North America for thousands of years before Europeans arrived; Africans were forcibly brought to the Americas and enslaved; Mexican Americans were first swept into the United States by the 1848 Treaty of Guadalupe Hidalgo that ended the U.S.-instigated war with Mexico, leading many immigrant activists to say, "We didn't cross the border, the border crossed us."[6] The "country of immigrants" counternarrative imagines a history of U.S. friendliness to the tired, the poor, and the huddled masses, but covers up the fact that America's welcome has always been racialized and contingent.

In Selection 1, Ian Haney López identifies racial restrictions in U.S. citizenship laws as well as many ways in which those restrictions have intersected with class and gender. Racialized notions of who is (or can become) an American are explicit in our earliest laws governing immigration, naturalization, and birthright citizenship, yet these categories have also proved malleable and mutually contradictory. Under the English common law principle of *jus soli* ("law of the soil"), citizenship is determined by one's place of birth; nonetheless, American law denied birthright citizenship to people of color for more than a century, even after the Fourteenth Amendment stated the principle unambiguously. Even something as clear-cut in its racism as the 1790 naturalization restriction to free white persons was also subject to interpretation, since "white" does not have an actual legal or biological definition. In one moment, for example, immigrants from India were granted the right to naturalize, and in another moment, judges decided that Indian Americans were evidently not white and thus ineligible for citizenship. Overnight, naturalized immigrants were stripped of their citizenship status (see excerpts from the ruling in *U.S. v. Thind,* in Part VII of this volume). Also stripped of citizenship under U.S. law were American-born women who married "aliens ineligible for citizenship" (that is, nonwhite immigrants). According to Haney López, "The laws governing the racial composition of this country's citizenry are inseverably bound up with and exacerbated by sexism."

In Selection 2, Angelica Quintero tracks the often contradictory ebbs and flows of U.S. immigration policies from the nineteenth century through the first months of the Trump administration. Quintero notes that, in addition to racialized exclusions (sometimes inflected with religion) that targeted Asian immigrants as well as southern and eastern Europeans, "[t]he poor, the sick and those espousing certain political beliefs were [also] barred from entry" under other laws. She examines not only government policies and demographic trends but also patterns of violence against those "perceived as un-American," revealing that constructions of belonging can have life-and-death consequences.

Aviva Chomsky deconstructs the mythology of "We are a country of immigrants" in Selection 3 by illuminating the narrative of race embedded in the "invisible underside" of the mythology: "the imperial narrative of conquest and dispossession . . . upon which the new 'country of [white] immigrants' was built." She analyzes conquest, war, and labor exploitation to lay the groundwork for understanding the state of being "undocumented" as a political construction. The nation's policies at different political moments have created (and at times criminalized) an undocumented population. "We created illegal immigration," Chomsky argues, "by fostering a global system that bases the prosperity for the few on the exploitation of the many and enforcing it, in the modern era, through borders and exclusive citizenship."

In Selection 4, Jaclyn Granick and Britt Tevis show the intersections between nativism and antisemitism, connecting nineteenth-century policies to World War I and World War II and finally to a mass shooting at a Pittsburgh synagogue in 2018. They focus on intersections of oppression but also activist coalitions across differences as they chronicle the efforts of Jewish lawyers to support not only Jewish immigrants and refugees but also Asian immigrants during Chinese exclusion (see excerpts from the Chinese Exclusion Act in Part VII of this volume) and Muslim immigrants under President Trump's travel ban.

In Selection 5, Moustafa Bayoumi chronicles the experiences of Muslim and Arab Americans being deemed suspicious and threatening in the period immediately following the terrorist attacks of September 11, 2001. Bayoumi places this discussion in a historical context, tracing the ways that Muslim communities have been perceived over time as well as how other racialized groups have been designated "a problem." He analyzes the ways in which "young Arab and Muslim Americans are forging their lives as the newest minorities in the American imagination," arguing that "the human drama of their predicament has now become a part of what it means to be an American."

Selections 6 and 7 are autobiographical poems that provide insight into the complicated experiences that drive people to leave their homes and come to a new country, one that is not necessarily welcoming but that seems safer than the places they fled. Both pieces also remind the reader that these issues are transnational and that the United States is implicated in the conditions that create refugees and drive migration. In the poem "Cookies," Bao Phi weaves together his family's traumatic experiences in the Vietnam War, his own memories as a child who fled the war and ended up in Minnesota, and his young daughter's effort to understand war. *"And that's why I am here and you are here,"* he says, struggling for the words to explain unexplainable histories and their consequences: *"And that is why sometimes other people look at us and they don't know why we are here and sometimes that makes us feel like we don't know, either."* The ongoing impact of intergenerational trauma influences their sense of belonging (or not belonging) in the "host" country, even for the U.S.-born descendants of refugees. In "Second Attempt Crossing," Javier Zamora tells a personal story about fleeing El Salvador, crossing the U.S. border unaccompanied, and being protected by someone who was himself fleeing danger. His testimony challenges several myths about people crossing the border, including unaccompanied youth. The young man who protects a 9-year-old Zamora has been inducted into a Salvadoran gang that he now flees. The enduring consequences of these experiences are both traumatizing and life affirming ("your brown arms that shielded me then, / that shield me now, from La Migra"). Both Phi and Zamora escape danger in their home countries, but Phi's family arrives as refugees with some legal standing and Zamora enters the United States as an undocumented child threatened by immigration enforcement agents.

In Selection 8, Mireya Navarro explores some of the complexities involved in articulating a Latino/a or Hispanic racial/ethnic identity. The category "Hispanic" was created by the U.S. government and first appeared in the census in 1980, providing a good example of how race/ethnicity is socially constructed. Currently, the census asks respondents to select a *race* by choosing one or more categories from more than a dozen options (plus the write-in "some other race"). In addition, respondents are given the option of choosing "Hispanic" as their *ethnicity*. But what is the basis for assigning or choosing this ethnic identity? Language, skin color, shared culture, national origin? There is significant diversity among Americans who might choose the government term "Hispanic." Many Mexican Americans reject the term "Hispanic" and prefer to be identified as "Latino/a" or "Chicano/a." The term "Hispanic" is associated with predominantly white Spain, whereas "Latino/a" is a more political term, generated from the grassroots, that articulates a cultural connection to Latin America.[7] The term "Chicano/a" more specifically evokes the connection with Indigenous peoples of the Americas and also emphasizes the U.S.–Mexico borderlands region that Gloria Anzaldúa names. More recently, writers and activists have created new spellings to challenge the gender binary embedded in Spanish, offering "Latinx" and "Chicanx" as terms that embrace people across the gender spectrum, including women, men, and nonbinary people.[8]

There is an important difference between terms of solidarity chosen by people about themselves and bureaucratic terms devised and authorized mainly by people outside the group being labeled. For the most part, it has been our largely white power structure that has created and applied racial/ethnic categories, with the result that people of color from very different ethnic backgrounds have often been lumped together regardless of important cultural, social, and economic differences associated with their backgrounds and places of origin. People born in Puerto Rico, Mexico, and Spain may all be grouped together as "Hispanics," flattening significant differences among them. In Selection 9, Christina M. Greer looks at distinctions of race and ethnicity in black communities. People from Ethiopia, Namibia, and Haiti are categorized as "black," but this categorization leaves out vastly different histories and heritages. Greer shows the complexity of racial formation by focusing on the relationships between native-born black Americans and immigrants from the African diaspora.

In Selection 10, Noy Thrupkaew examines the unique situations and challenges faced by various populations categorized as "Asian Americans." She critiques the construction of Asian Americans as a "model minority," even though it might sound like a *positive* stereotype. Quoting Frank Wu, Thrupkaew suggests that the model minority myth is deployed by political conservatives who use it to rationalize and obscure the unequal distribution of wealth, opportunity, and privilege in this country. By idealizing the success of some Asian Americans — and tapping into the equally misleading myth of meritocracy — conservatives imply that African Americans and Latinos/as who do not succeed do not work hard enough. In reality, many Southeast Asians in the United States (largely from Cambodia, Laos, and Vietnam) have extremely high rates of poverty, but the model minority myth ignores this reality and allows their true situation to go unrecognized and their needs to go unmet. The mythology simultaneously erases the complexity and the struggles of Asian Americans and pits communities of color against each other. Thrupkaew cites activists who call for coalition-building over divide-and-conquer strategies: "Disadvantaged people share a lot in common . . . and we have to help each other."

Instead of border walls between countries and horizontal hostility between communities, the authors in this part embrace an intersectional approach to borderlands and belonging. These writers propose that we must know our history, understand its relevance today, and engage with the complexity of individual, community, national, and transnational identities. Once we do that, it becomes harder to build physical or figurative walls between us or to tolerate the existence of such walls in our world.

NOTES

1. "Donald Trump Announces a Presidential Bid." *Washington Post*, June 16, 2015.

2. Jenna Johnson, "Trump calls for 'total and complete shutdown of Muslims entering the United States,'" *The Washington Post*, December 7, 2015.

3. https://www.migrationpolicy.org/article/obama-record-deportations-deporter-chief-or-not.

4. Donald Kerwin, "From IIRIRA to Trump: Connecting the Dots to the Current US Immigration Policy Crisis," *Journal on Migration and Human Security*, 2018, Vol. 6(3) 192–204.

5. Aviva Chomsky, "Clinton and Obama Laid the Groundwork for Donald Trump's War on Immigrants," *The Nation*, April 25, 2017.

6. Josue David Cisneros, *The Border Crossed Us: Rhetorics of Borders, Citizenship, and Latina/o Identity*. University of Alabama Press, 2014.

7. Ramón A. Gutierrez, "What's in a Name? The History and Politics of Hispanic and Latino Panethnicities," in *The New Latino Studies Reader: A Twenty-first Century Perspective*, Ramón A. Gutierrez and Tomás Almaguer (eds.). University of California Press, 2016, p. 38.

8. Raquel Reichard, "Latino/a vs. Latinx vs. Latine: Which Word Best Solves Spanish's Gender Problem?" *Latina Magazine*, March 30, 2017.

GUIDING QUESTIONS FOR PART III

1. Part III begins with an essay about racial restrictions in citizenship laws, but race is not the only category of identity that has played a role in notions of U.S. citizenship and belonging. Identify some of the ways in which racism intersects with sexism, nativism, antisemitism, or economic exploitation in the readings in this part (and in current events) in relation to issues of citizenship and belonging.

2. Ian Haney López argues that the composition of our citizenry "reflects the conscious design of U.S. immigration and naturalization laws." As you read the selections in this part, consider the motives, methods, and consequences of U.S. policies around immigration and citizenship. What factors have shaped the "conscious design" of our laws, from our founding until the present? How have specific historical events and movements influenced those policies?

3. Angelica Quintero argues that the United States has always had a "love–hate relationship" with immigrants. What are some of the tensions and contradictions in U.S. rhetoric and policies around immigration that Quintero identifies in U.S. history or that you see in other Part III essays or in current events?

4. According to Aviva Chomsky, more stringent border enforcement policies have actually *increased* the number of unauthorized immigrants in the United States. How does she explain this seeming contradiction?

5. How do Navarro, Greer, and Thrupkaew complicate questions of racial, ethnic, and national identity in their articles?

6. Throughout the readings in Part III, how do the authors portray the role of violence?

7. How do some of the authors address the lasting impact of 9/11?

8. How does Thrupkaew deconstruct the myth of the "model minority"? How are social myths (e.g., stereotypes about which groups are "hard-working" and which are "lazy") related to maintaining dominant power structures? How do the other authors in this part dismantle other myths?

9. How do the personal stories (particularly in the two poems in this part, by Phi and Zamora) illuminate issues raised in other selections that rely more upon history, law, and statistics? How do Phi, Zamora, and Bayoumi address notions of fear and belonging?

10. What possibilities for activism and coalition emerge from the readings? What examples of activism and coalition can you identify in your communities?

1 Racial Restrictions in the Law of Citizenship

Ian Haney López

The racial composition of the U.S. citizenry reflects in part the accident of world migration patterns. More than this, however, it reflects the conscious design of U.S. immigration and naturalization laws.

Federal law restricted immigration to this country on the basis of race for nearly one hundred years,* roughly from the Chinese exclusion laws of the 1880s until the end of the national origin quotas in 1965.[1] The history of this discrimination can briefly be traced. Nativist sentiment against Irish and German Catholics on the East Coast and against Chinese and Mexicans on the West Coast, which had been doused by the Civil War, reignited during the economic slump of the 1870s. Though most of the nativist efforts failed to gain congressional sanction, Congress in 1882 passed the Chinese Exclusion Act, which suspended the immigration of Chinese laborers for ten years.[2] The Act was expanded to exclude all Chinese in 1884, and was eventually implemented indefinitely.[3] In 1917, Congress created "an Asiatic barred zone," excluding all persons from Asia.[4] During this same period, the Senate passed a bill to exclude "all members of the African or black race." This effort was defeated in the House only after intensive lobbying by the NAACP.[5] Efforts to exclude the supposedly racially undesirable southern and eastern Europeans were more successful. In 1921, Congress established a temporary quota system designed "to confine immigration as much as possible to western and northern European stock," making this bar permanent three years later in the National Origin Act of 1924.[6] With the onset of the Depression, attention shifted to Mexican immigrants. Although no law explicitly targeted this group, federal immigration officials began a series of round-ups and mass deportations of people of Mexican descent under the general rubric of a "repatriation campaign." Approximately 500,000 people were forcibly returned to Mexico during the Depression, more than half of them U.S. citizens.[7] This pattern was repeated in the 1950s, when Attorney General Herbert Brownell launched a program to expel Mexicans. This effort, dubbed "Operation Wetback," indiscriminately deported more than one million citizens and noncitizens in 1954 alone.[8]

Racial restrictions on immigration were not significantly dismantled until 1965, when Congress in a major overhaul of immigration law abolished both the national origin system and the Asiatic Barred Zone.[9] Even so, purposeful racial discrimination in immigration law

---

*See Part VII in this volume for excerpts from four documents mentioned in this selection: the Chinese Exclusion Act, *Dred Scott* v. *Sandford*, the Fourteenth Amendment, and *Elk* v. *Wilkins*.

Ian Haney López is the John H. Boalt professor of law at the University of California, Berkeley. His books include *White by Law: The Legal Construction of Race* and *Dog Whistle Politics*.

---

by Congress remains constitutionally permissible, since the case that upheld the Chinese Exclusion Act to this day remains good law.[10] Moreover, arguably racial discrimination in immigration law continues. For example, Congress has enacted special provisions to encourage Irish immigration, while refusing to ameliorate the backlog of would-be immigrants from the Philippines, India, South Korea, China, and Hong Kong, backlogs created in part through a century of racial exclusion.[11] The history of racial discrimination in U.S. immigration law is a long and continuing one.

As discriminatory as the laws of immigration have been, the laws of citizenship betray an even more dismal record of racial exclusion. From this country's inception, the laws regulating who was or could become a citizen were tainted by racial prejudice. Birthright citizenship, the automatic acquisition of citizenship by virtue of birth, was tied to race until 1940. Naturalized citizenship, the acquisition of citizenship by any means other than through birth, was conditioned on race until 1952. Like immigration laws, the laws of birthright citizenship and naturalization shaped the racial character of the United States.

Birthright Citizenship

Most persons acquire citizenship by birth rather than through naturalization. . . .

The U.S. Constitution as ratified did not define the citizenry, probably because it was assumed that the English common law rule of *jus soli* would continue.[12] Under *jus soli*, citizenship accrues to "all" born within a nation's jurisdiction. Despite the seeming breadth of this doctrine, the word "all" is qualified because for the first one hundred years and more of this country's history it did not fully encompass racial minorities. This is the import of the *Dred Scott* decision.[13] Scott, an enslaved man, sought to use the federal courts to sue for his freedom. However, access to the courts was predicated on citizenship. Dismissing his claim, the United States Supreme Court in the person of Chief Justice Roger Taney declared in 1857 that Scott and all other Blacks, free and enslaved, were not and could never be citizens because they were "a subordinate and inferior class of beings." The decision protected the slaveholding South and infuriated much of the North, further dividing a country already fractured around the issues of slavery and the power of the national government. *Dred Scott* was invalidated after the Civil War by the Civil Rights Act of 1866, which declared that "All persons born . . . in the United States and not subject to any foreign power, excluding Indians not taxed, are declared to be citizens of the United States."[14] *Jus soli* subsequently became part of the organic law of the land in the form of the Fourteenth Amendment: "All persons born or naturalized in the United States, and subject to the jurisdiction thereof, are citizens of the United States and of the state wherein they reside."[15]

Despite the broad language of the Fourteenth Amendment—though in keeping with the words of the 1866 act—some racial minorities remained outside the bounds of *jus soli* even after its constitutional enactment. In particular, questions persisted about the citizenship status of children born in the United States to noncitizen parents, and about the status of Native Americans. The Supreme Court did not decide the status of the former until 1898, when it ruled in *U.S. v. Wong Kim Ark* that native-born children of aliens, even those permanently barred by race from acquiring citizenship, were birthright citizens of the United States.[16] On the citizenship of the latter, the Supreme Court answered negatively in 1884, holding in *Elk v. Wilkins* that Native Americans owed allegiance to their tribe and so did not acquire citizenship upon birth.[17] Congress responded by granting Native Americans citizenship in piecemeal fashion, often tribe by tribe. Not until 1924 did Congress pass an act conferring citizenship on all Native Americans in the United States.[18] Even then, however, questions arose regarding the citizenship of those born in the United States after the effective date of the 1924 act. These questions were finally resolved, and *jus soli* fully applied, under the Nationality Act of 1940, which specifically bestowed citizenship on all those born in the United States "to a member of an Indian, Eskimo, Aleutian, or other aboriginal tribe."[19] Thus, the basic law of citizenship, that a person born here is a citizen here, did not include all racial minorities until 1940.

Unfortunately, the impulse to restrict birthright citizenship by race is far from dead in this country. Bill Ong Hing writes, "The discussion of who is and who is not American, who can and cannot become American, goes beyond the technicalities of citizenship and residency requirements; it strikes at the very heart of our nation's long and troubled legacy of race relations."[20] As this troubled legacy reveals, the triumph over racial discrimination in the laws of citizenship and alienage came slowly and only recently. In the campaign for the "control of our borders," we are once again debating the citizenship of the native-born and the merits of *Dred Scott.*[21]

Naturalization

Although the Constitution did not originally define the citizenry, it explicitly gave Congress the authority to establish the criteria for granting citizenship after birth. Article I grants Congress the power "To establish a uniform Rule of Naturalization."[22] From the start, Congress exercised this power in a manner that burdened naturalization laws with racial restrictions that tracked those in the law of birthright citizenship. In 1790, only a few months after ratification of the Constitution, Congress limited naturalization to "any alien, being a free white person who shall have resided within the limits and under the jurisdiction of the United States for a term of two years."[23] This clause mirrored not only the de facto laws of birthright citizenship, but also the racially restrictive naturalization laws of several states. At least three states had previously limited citizenship to "white persons": Virginia in 1779, South Carolina in 1784, and Georgia in 1785.[24] Though there would be many subsequent changes in the requirements for federal naturalization, racial identity endured as a bedrock requirement for the next 162 years. In every naturalization act from 1790 until 1952, Congress included the "white person" prerequisite.[25]

The history of racial prerequisites to naturalization can be divided into two periods of approximately eighty years each. The first period extended from 1790 to 1870, when only Whites were able to naturalize. In the wake of the Civil War, the "white person" restriction on naturalization came under serious attack as part of the effort to expunge

Dred Scott. Some congressmen, Charles Sumner chief among them, argued that racial barriers to naturalization should be struck altogether. However, racial prejudice against Native Americans and Asians forestalled the complete elimination of the racial prerequisites. During congressional debates, one senator argued against conferring "the rank, privileges, and immunities of citizenship upon the cruel savages who destroyed [Minnesota's] peaceful settlements and massacred the people with circumstances of atrocity too horrible to relate."[26] Another senator wondered "whether this door [of citizenship] shall now be thrown open to the Asiatic population," warning that to do so would spell for the Pacific coast "an end to republican government there, because it is very well ascertained that those people have no appreciation of that form of government; it seems to be obnoxious to their very nature; they seem to be incapable either of understanding or carrying it out."[27] Sentiments such as these ensured that even after the Civil War, bars against Native American and Asian naturalization would continue.[28] Congress opted to maintain the "white person" prerequisite, but to extend the right to naturalize to "persons of African nativity, or African descent."[29] After 1870, Blacks as well as Whites could naturalize, but not others.

During the second period, from 1870 until the last of the prerequisite laws were abolished in 1952, the White-Black dichotomy in American race relations dominated naturalization law. During this period, Whites and Blacks were eligible for citizenship, but others, particularly those from Asia, were not. Indeed, increasing antipathy toward Asians on the West Coast resulted in an explicit disqualification of Chinese persons from naturalization in 1882.[30] The prohibition of Chinese naturalization, the only U.S. law ever to exclude by name a particular nationality from citizenship, was coupled with the ban on Chinese immigration discussed previously. The Supreme Court readily upheld the bar, writing that "Chinese persons not born in this country have never been recognized as citizens of the United States, nor authorized to become such under the naturalization laws."[31] While Blacks were permitted to naturalize beginning in 1870, the Chinese and most "other non-Whites" would have to wait until the 1940s for the right to naturalize.[32]

World War II forced a domestic reconsideration of the racism integral to U.S. naturalization law. In 1935, Hitler's Germany limited citizenship to members of the Aryan race, making Germany the only country other than the United States with a racial restriction on naturalization.[33] The fact of this bad company was not lost on those administering our naturalization laws. "When Earl G. Harrison in 1944 resigned as United States Commissioner of Immigration and Naturalization, he said that the only country in the world, outside the United States, that observes racial discrimination in matters relating to naturalization was Nazi Germany, 'and we all agree that this is not very desirable company.'"[34] Furthermore, the United States was open to charges of hypocrisy for banning from naturalization the nationals of many of its Asian allies. During the war, the United States seemed through some of its laws and social practices to embrace the same racism it was fighting. Both fronts of the war exposed profound inconsistencies between U.S. naturalization law and broader social ideals. These considerations, among others, led Congress to begin a process of piecemeal reform in the laws governing citizenship.

In 1940, Congress opened naturalization to "descendants of races indigenous to the Western Hemisphere."[35] Apparently, this "additional limitation was designed 'to more fully cement' the ties of Pan-Americanism" at a time of impending crisis.[36] In 1943, Congress replaced the prohibition on the naturalization of Chinese persons with a provision explicitly granting them this boon.[37] In 1946, it opened up naturalization to persons from the Philippines and India as well.[38] Thus, at the end of the war, our naturalization law looked like this:

The right to become a naturalized citizen under the provisions of this Act shall extend only to—

1. white persons, persons of African nativity or descent, and persons of races indigenous to the continents of North or South America or adjacent islands and Filipino persons or persons of Filipino descent;
2. persons who possess, either singly or in combination, a preponderance of blood of one or more of the classes specified in clause (1);
3. Chinese persons or persons of Chinese descent; and persons of races indigenous to India; and
4. persons who possess, either singly or in combination, a preponderance of blood of one or more of the classes specified in clause (3) or, either singly or in combination, as much as one-half blood of those classes and some additional blood of one of the classes specified in clause (1).[39]

This incremental retreat from a "Whites only" conception of citizenship made the arbitrariness of U.S. naturalization law increasingly obvious. For example, under the above statute, the right to acquire citizenship depended for some on blood-quantum distinctions based on descent from peoples indigenous to islands adjacent to the Americas. In 1952, Congress moved towards wholesale reform, overhauling the naturalization statute to read simply that "[t]he right of a person to become a naturalized citizen of the United States shall not be denied or abridged because of race or sex or because such person is married."[40] Thus, in 1952, racial bars on naturalization came to an official end.[41]

Notice the mention of gender in the statutory language ending racial restrictions in naturalization. The issue of women and citizenship can only be touched on here, but deserves significant study in its own right.[42] As the language of the 1952 Act implies, eligibility for naturalization once depended on a woman's marital status. Congress in 1855 declared that a foreign woman automatically acquired citizenship upon marriage to a U.S. citizen, or upon the naturalization of her alien husband.[43] This provision built upon the supposition that a woman's social and political status flowed from her husband. As an 1895 treatise on naturalization put it, "A woman partakes of her husband's nationality; her nationality is merged in that of her husband; her political status follows that of her husband."[44] A wife's acquisition of citizenship, however, remained subject to her individual qualification for naturalization—that is, on whether she was a "white person."[45] Thus, the Supreme Court held in 1868 that only "white women" could gain citizenship by marrying a citizen.[46] Racial restrictions further complicated matters for noncitizen women in that naturalization was denied to those married to a man racially ineligible for citizenship, irrespective of the woman's own qualifications, racial or otherwise.[47] The automatic naturalization of a woman upon her marriage to a citizen or upon the naturalization of her husband ended in 1922.[48]

The citizenship of American-born women was also affected by the interplay of gender and racial restrictions. Even though under English common law a woman's nationality was unaffected by marriage, many courts in this country stripped women who married noncitizens of their U.S. citizenship.[49] Congress recognized and mandated this practice in 1907, legislating that an American woman's marriage to an alien terminated her citizenship.[50] Under considerable pressure, Congress partially repealed this act in 1922.[51] However, the 1922 act continued to require the expatriation of any woman who married a foreigner racially barred from citizenship, flatly declaring that "any woman citizen who marries an alien ineligible to citizenship shall cease to be a citizen."[52] Until Congress repealed this provision in 1931,[53] marriage to a non-White alien by an American woman was akin to treason against this country: either of these acts justified the stripping of citizenship from someone American by birth. Indeed, a woman's marriage to a non-White foreigner was perhaps a worse crime, for while a traitor lost his citizenship only after trial, the woman lost hers automatically.[54] The laws governing the racial composition of this country's citizenry came inseverably bound up with and exacerbated by sexism. . . .

NOTES

1. U.S. COMMISSION ON CIVIL RIGHTS, THE TARNISHED GOLDEN DOOR: CIVIL RIGHTS ISSUES IN IMMIGRATION 1–12 (1990).
2. Chinese Exclusion Act, ch. 126, 22 Stat. 58 (1882). *See generally* Harold Hongju Koh, *Bitter Fruit of the Asian Immigration Cases*, 6 CONSTITUTION 69 (1994). For a sobering account of the many lynchings of Chinese in the western United States during this period, *see* John R. Wunder, *Anti-Chinese Violence in the American West, 1850–1910*, LAW FOR THE ELEPHANT, LAW FOR THE BEAVER: ESSAYS IN THE LEGAL HISTORY OF THE NORTH AMERICAN WEST 212 (John McLaren, Hamar Foster, and Chet Orloff eds., 1992). Charles McClain, Jr., discusses the historical origins of anti-Chinese prejudice and the legal responses undertaken by that community on the West Coast. Charles McClain, Jr., *The Chinese Struggle for Civil Rights in Nineteenth Century America: The First Phase, 1850–1870*, 72 CAL. L. REV. 529 (1984). For a discussion of contemporary racial violence against Asian Americans, *see* Note, *Racial Violence against Asian Americans*, 106 HARV. L. REV. 1926 (1993); Robert Chang, *Toward an Asian American Legal Scholarship: Critical Race Theory, Post-Structuralism, and Narrative Space*, 81 CAL. L. REV. 1241, 1251–58 (1993).
3. Act of July 9, 1884, ch. 220, 23 Stat. 115; Act of May 5, 1892, ch. 60, 27 Stat. 25; Act of April 29, 1902, ch. 641, 32 Stat. 176; Act of April 27, 1904, ch. 1630, 33 Stat. 428.
4. Act of Feb. 5, 1917, ch. 29, 39 Stat. 874.
5. U.S. COMMISSION ON CIVIL RIGHTS, *supra*, at 9.
6. *Id. See* Act of May 19, 1921, ch. 8, 42 Stat. 5; Act of May 26, 1924, ch. 190, 43 Stat. 153.
7. U.S. COMMISSION ON CIVIL RIGHTS, *supra*, at 10.
8. *Id.* at 11. See *generally* JUAN RAMON GARCIA, OPERATION WETBACK: THE MASS DEPORTATION OF MEXICAN UNDOCUMENTED WORKERS IN 1954 (1980).
9. Act of Oct. 2, 1965, 79 Stat. 911.
10. Chae Chan Ping v. United States, 130 U.S. 581 (1889). The Court reasoned in part that if "the government of the United States, through its legislative department, considers the presence of foreigners of a different race in this country, who will not assimilate with us, to be dangerous

to its peace and security, their exclusion is not to be stayed." For a critique of this deplorable result, *see* Louis Henkin, *The Constitution and United States Sovereignty: A Century of Chinese Exclusion and Its Progeny*, 100 HARV. L. REV. 853 (1987).

11. For efforts to encourage Irish immigration, *see, e.g.*, Immigration Act of 1990, § 131, 104 Stat. 4978 (codified as amended at 8 U.S.C. § 1153 (c) [1994]). Bill Ong Hing argues that Congress continues to discriminate against Asians. "Through an examination of past exclusion laws, previous legislation, and the specific provisions of the Immigration Act of 1990, the conclusion can be drawn that Congress never intended to make up for nearly 80 years of Asian exclusion, and that a conscious hostility towards persons of Asian descent continues to pervade Congressional circles." Bill Ong Hing, *Asian Americans and Present U.S. Immigration Policies: A Legacy of Asian Exclusion*, ASIAN AMERICANS AND THE SUPREME COURT: A DOCUMENTARY HISTORY 1106, 1107 (Hyung-Chan Kim ed., 1992).

12. CHARLES GORDON AND STANLEY MAILMAN, IMMIGRATION LAW AND PROCEDURE § 92.03[1][b] (rev. ed. 1992).

13. Dred Scott v. Sandford, 60 U.S. (19 How.) 393 (1857). For an insightful discussion of the role of *Dred Scott* in the development of American citizenship, *see* JAMES KETTNER, THE DEVELOPMENT OF AMERICAN CITIZENSHIP, 1608–1870, at 300–333 (1978); *see also* KENNETH L. KARST, BELONGING TO AMERICA: EQUAL CITIZENSHIP AND THE CONSTITUTION 43–61 (1989).

14. Civil Rights Act of 1866, ch. 31, 14 Stat. 27.

15. U.S. Const. amend. XIV.

16. 169 U.S. 649 (1898).

17. 112 U.S. 94 (1884).

18. Act of June 2, 1924, ch. 233, 43 Stat. 253.

19. Nationality Act of 1940, § 201(b), 54 Stat. 1138. *See generally* GORDON AND MAILMAN, *supra*, at § 92.03[3][e].

20. Bill Ong Hing, *Beyond the Rhetoric of Assimilation and Cultural Pluralism: Addressing the Tension of Separatism and Conflict in an Immigration-Driven Multiracial Society*, 81 CAL. L. REV. 863, 866 (1993).

21. Gerald Neuman warns against amending the Citizenship Clause. Gerald Neuman, *Back to Dred Scott?* 24 SAN DIEGO L. REV. 485, 500 (1987). *See also* Note, *The Birthright Citizenship Amendment: A Threat to Equality*, 107 HARV. L. REV. 1026 (1994).

22. U.S. Const. art. I, sec. 8, cl. 4.

23. Act of March 26, 1790, ch. 3, 1 Stat. 103.

24. KETTNER, *supra*, at 215–16.

25. One exception exists. In revisions undertaken in 1870, the "white person" limitation was omitted. However, this omission is regarded as accidental, and the prerequisite was reinserted in 1875 by "an act to correct errors and to supply omissions in the Revised Statutes of the United States." Act of Feb. 18, 1875, ch. 80, 18 Stat. 318. *See* In re Ah Yup, 1 F.Cas. 223 (C.C.D.Cal. 1878) ("Upon revision of the statutes, the revisors, probably inadvertently, as Congress did not contemplate a change of the laws in force, omitted the words 'white persons.'").

26. Statement of Senator Hendricks, 59 CONG. GLOBE, 42nd Cong., 1st Sess. 2939 (1866). *See also* John Guendelsberger, *Access to Citizenship for Children Born Within the State to Foreign Parents*, 40 AM. J. COMP. L. 379, 407–9 (1992).

27. Statement of Senator Cowan, 57 CONG. GLOBE, 42nd Cong., 1st Sess. 499 (1866). For a discussion of the role of anti-Asian prejudice in the laws governing naturalization, *see generally*

Elizabeth Hull, *Naturalization and Denaturalization*, ASIAN AMERICANS AND THE SUPREME COURT: A DOCUMENTARY HISTORY 403 (Hyung-Chan Kim ed., 1992)

28. The Senate rejected an amendment that would have allowed Chinese persons to naturalize. The proposed amendment read: "That the naturalization laws are hereby extended to aliens of African nativity, and to persons of African descent, and to persons born in the Chinese empire." BILL ONG HING, MAKING AND REMAKING ASIAN AMERICA THROUGH IMMIGRATION POLICY, 1850–1990, at 239 n.34 (1993).

29. Act of July 14, 1870, ch. 255, § 7, 16 Stat. 254.

30. Chinese Exclusion Act, ch. 126, § 14, 22 Stat. 58 (1882).

31. Fong Yue Ting v. United States, 149 U.S. 698, 716 (1893).

32. Neil Gotanda contends that separate racial ideologies function with respect to "other non-Whites," meaning non-Black racial minorities such as Asians, Native Americans, and Latinos. Neil Gotanda, *"Other Non-Whites" in American Legal History: A Review of* Justice at War, 85 COLUM. L. REV. 1186 (1985). Gotanda explicitly identifies the operation of this separate ideology in the Supreme Court's jurisprudence regarding Asians and citizenship. Neil Gotanda, *Asian American Rights and the "Miss Saigon Syndrome,"* ASIAN AMERICANS AND THE SUPREME COURT: A DOCUMENTARY HISTORY 1087, 1096–97 (Hyung-Chan Kim ed., 1992).

33. Charles Gordon, *The Racial Barrier to American Citizenship*, 93 U. PA. L. REV. 237, 252 (1945).

34. MILTON KONVITZ, THE ALIEN AND THE ASIATIC IN AMERICAN LAW 80–81 (1946) (citation omitted).

35. Act of Oct. 14, 1940, ch. 876, § 303, 54 Stat. 1140.

36. Note, *The Nationality Act of 1940*, 54 HARV. L. REV. 860, 865 n.40 (1941).

37. Act of Dec. 17, 1943, ch. 344, § 3, 57 Stat. 600.

38. Act of July 2, 1946, ch. 534, 60 Stat. 416.

39. *Id.*

40. Immigration and Nationality Act of 1952, ch. 2, § 311, 66 Stat. 239 (codified as amended at 8 U.S.C. 1422 [1988]).

41. Arguably, the continued substantial exclusion of Asians from immigration, not remedied until 1965, rendered their eligibility for naturalization relatively meaningless. "[T]he national quota system for admitting immigrants which was built into the 1952 Act gave the grant of eligibility a hollow ring." Chin Kim and Bok Lim Kim, *Asian immigrants in American Law: A Look at the Past and the Challenge Which Remains*, 26 AM. U. L. REV. 373, 390 (1977).

42. *See generally* Ursula Vogel, *Is Citizenship Gender-Specific?* THE FRONTIERS OF CITIZENSHIP 58 (Ursula Vogel and Michael Moran eds., 1991).

43. Act of Feb. 10, 1855, ch. 71, § 2, 10 Stat. 604. Because gender-based laws in the area of citizenship were motivated by the idea that a woman's citizenship should follow that of her husband, no naturalization law has explicitly targeted unmarried women. GORDON AND MAILMAN, *supra*, at § 95.03[6] ("An unmarried woman has never been [statutorily] barred from naturalization.").

44. PRENTISS WEBSTER, LAW OF NATURALIZATION IN THE UNITED STATES OF AMERICA AND OTHER COUNTRIES 80 (1895).

45. Act of Feb. 10, 1855, ch. 71, § 2, 10 Stat. 604.

46. Kelly v. Owen, 74 U.S. 496, 498 (1868).

47. GORDON AND MAILMAN, *supra* at § 95.03[6].

48. Act of Sept. 22, 1922, ch. 411, § 2, 42 Stat. 1011.

49. GORDON AND MAILMAN, *supra* at § 100.03[4][m].

50. Act of March 2, 1907, ch. 2534, § 3, 34 Stat. 1228. This act was upheld in MacKenzie v. Hare, 239 U.S. 299 (1915) (expatriating a U.S.-born woman upon her marriage to a British citizen).

51. Act of Sept. 22, 1922, ch. 411, § 3, 42 Stat. 1021.

52. *Id.* The Act also stated that "[n]o woman whose husband is not eligible to citizenship shall be naturalized during the continuance of the marriage."

53. Act of March 3, 1931, ch. 442, § 4(a), 46 Stat. 1511.

54. The loss of birthright citizenship was particularly harsh for those women whose race made them unable to regain citizenship through naturalization, especially after 1924, when the immigration laws of this country barred entry to any alien ineligible to citizenship. Immigration Act of 1924, ch. 190, § 13(c), 43 Stat. 162. *See, e.g.,* Ex parte (Ng) Fung Sing, 6 F.2d 670 (W.D.Wash. 1925). In that case, a U.S. birthright citizen of Chinese descent was expatriated because of her marriage to a Chinese citizen, and was subsequently refused admittance to the United States as an alien ineligible to citizenship.

2 | America's Love-Hate Relationship with Immigrants

Angelica Quintero

Oddly for a nation made up mostly of immigrants, the United States has always had a problem with immigration. Long before President Trump was quoted saying, "Why are we having all these people from shithole countries come here?" generations of Americans have advocated limiting immigration to the country.

In the 1800s, the Irish were a favorite target, and newspaper want ads commonly included the phrase "No Irish need apply." Later in the 19th century, anti-immigration sentiment was codified in federal laws that singled out Asians. Subsequent federal laws targeted Italians and southern Europeans.

Scholars have identified three waves of immigration: the first era, the second era and the current era. As the U.S. once again debates who should be let into the country, perhaps it's time to review major immigration laws passed from 1870 to the present day. Some tried to bring order to the immigration process. Others aimed to keep out those perceived as un-American.

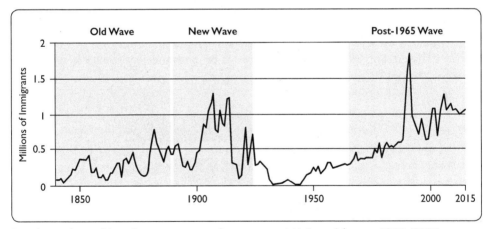

Total number of immigrants granted permanent U.S. residency, 1840–2015

Sources: Pew Research Center, U.S. Department of Homeland Security

Angelica Quintero is a multimedia journalist from the University of Miami. Her work has appeared in the *Los Angeles Times*, *National Geographic*, and *Diario Las Américas*.

FIRST ERA: The "Free White Persons" and Asian "Coolies"

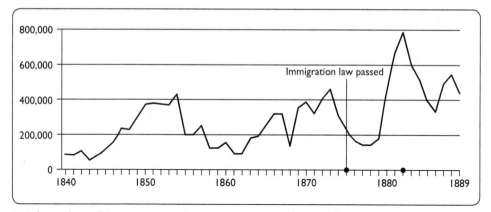

Total number of immigrants granted permanent U.S. residency, 1840–1889

Sources: Pew Research Center, U.S. Department of Homeland Security

Poor and unskilled immigrants from Northern Europe and Asia poured into the United States in the mid-1800s. Most of the European immigrants were German and Irish, and under the law they were considered "free white persons" able to achieve citizenship.

Citizenship wasn't an option for the growing numbers of Chinese and Asian immigrants settling on the West Coast. A cheap source of labor for mines, farms and railways, the Chinese were called "coolies." The word originally meant "unskilled laborer," but became a slur hurled at workers who labored for low wages or came to the U.S. as indentured laborers. Chinese women were largely assumed to be prostitutes.

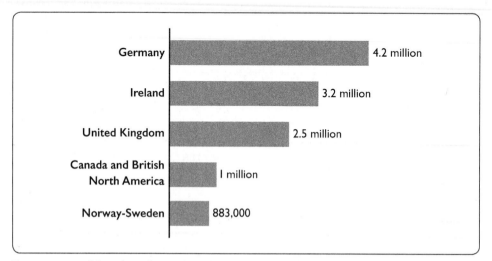

Top sources of immigration, 1840–1889

Sources: Pew Research Center, U.S. Department of Homeland Security

In Los Angeles, the backlash against Asians culminated in 1871 with the Chinese Massacre. A mob of more than 500 white men killed at least 18 Chinese men and boys near downtown. No one was ever convicted of the killings.

The growing animus against Asians across the country led to discriminatory laws that would remain on the books for decades.

Major Immigration Laws [1840–1889]

1870 Naturalization Act

- Allowed African immigrants and those of African descent to become U.S. citizens. Other nonwhites remained unable to obtain citizenship.

1875 Asian Exclusion Act

- Established federal regulation of immigration.
- Prohibited bringing Asians into the U.S. without their consent and supplying Asians for labor.

1882 Chinese Exclusion Act*

- The first law to limit immigration based on a specific ethnicity.
- Prohibited "skilled and unskilled laborers and Chinese employed in mining" from coming to the U.S. for 10 years. Prohibited state and federal courts from granting citizenship to Chinese immigrants (those courts had such power at the time). The act was extended repeatedly over the decades but repealed in 1943 during World War II to maintain a military alliance with China.

SECOND ERA: Southern Europeans Not Welcome

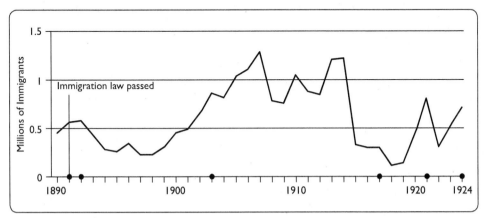

Total number of immigrants granted permanent U.S. residency, 1890–1924

Sources: Pew Research Center, U.S. Department of Homeland Security

*An excerpt from the Chinese Exclusion Act is in Part VII of this volume.

During the next wave of immigration, from the late 1800s to the 1920s, immigration laws continued to target Asians, but also tried to discourage immigration from Southern and Eastern Europe.

Roger Waldinger, a UCLA distinguished professor of sociology, said the laws passed during this era "set a low limit on total immigration from the Eastern Hemisphere and virtually stopped migration from Asia."

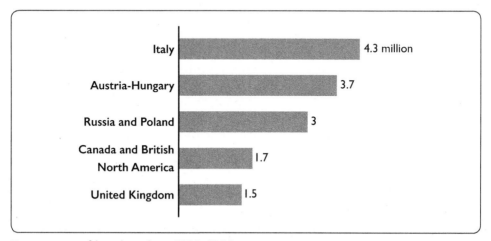

Top sources of immigration, 1890–1924

Sources: Pew Research Center, U.S. Department of Homeland Security

The poor, the sick and those espousing certain political beliefs were barred from entry into the U.S. under other new laws. Laws discouraging immigration from Southern Europe — mainly from Italy — reflected widespread anti-Catholic sentiment. Italians were frequent targets of abuse and one of the most infamous mass lynchings in U.S. history occurred in New Orleans, where 11 Italians were attacked and killed by a mob in 1891.

After World War I, immigration decreased dramatically with the passage of more restrictive legislation. Permanent residency status grants went from 1.2 million in 1914 to a little more than 110,000 in 1918.

Major Immigration Laws [1890–1924]

1891 Immigration Act

- Established a federal Bureau of Immigration and allowed deportation of immigrants in the country illegally or excluded by previous laws.

- Prohibited bringing people to the U.S. unlawfully. Banned a wide variety of individuals, including polygamists, paupers, idiots and "persons suffering from a loathsome or a dangerous contagious disease."

1892 *Geary Act*

- Extended the Chinese Exclusion Act for 10 more years.
- Required people of Chinese ancestry, whether immigrants or U.S.-born, to obtain identification papers and carry them at all times or else face prison or deportation.

1903 *Anarchist Exclusion Act*

- Banned anarchists, beggars and importers of prostitutes, among others, from entering the country following the assassination of President William McKinley by a self-proclaimed anarchist.

1917 *Asian Barred Zone Act*

- Required a literacy test for all immigrants over 16 in an effort to stop "unskilled" immigration.
- Prohibited Asians, except for Filipinos and Japanese, from immigrating to the U.S.

1921 *Emergency Quota Act*

- Created the first numerical quotas for immigration based on nationality.
- The quotas discouraged immigration from Eastern and Southern Europe, whose people were considered un-American because of their political and religious affiliations. The annual immigration cap was set at 350,000 people.

1924 *Labor Appropriation Act*

- Established the U.S. Border Patrol to combat illegal immigration and smuggling along the borders. Previously, another agency, the U.S. Immigration Service, had been combating illegal immigration of Chinese crossing the Mexico-U.S. border.

1924 *Johnson–Reed Act*

- Established a quota system based on country of origin. Northern European immigrants had better chances at being allowed to stay than any other groups.
- Prohibited Japanese immigrants from the country. Scaling back earlier immigration caps, the act limited annual immigration to 165,000.

CURRENT ERA: Secure the Border and Build the Wall

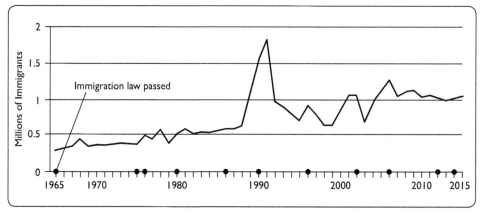

Total number of immigrants granted permanent U.S. residency, 1965–2015

Sources: Pew Research Center, U.S. Department of Homeland Security

The immigration control system in place today began to take shape with passage of the Hart–Celler Act in 1965, which eliminated the quota system based on national origin.

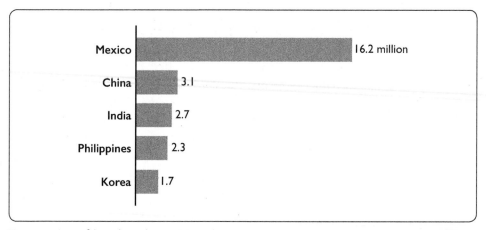

Top sources of immigration, 1965–2015

Sources: Pew Research Center, U.S. Department of Homeland Security

Reflecting larger, global conditions, later laws addressed refugees, border security or illegal immigration. The most far-reaching legislation was the Immigration Reform and Control Act of 1986, a law that, depending on the point of view, is hailed as groundbreaking or denounced as a huge mistake. In addition to immigration laws passed by Congress, two executive actions by President Obama also prompted praise and criticism.

Major Immigration Laws and Executive Actions [1965–2015]

1965 Immigration and Nationality Act (Hart-Celler Act)

▪ Dramatically changed immigration policy by eliminating the quota system based on national origin. The law placed an emphasis on admitting skilled workers and family reunification. There were no limits on the number of immediate family members of U.S. citizens admitted per year.

▪ The number of visas granted annually was set at 170,000 for Eastern Hemisphere countries. By 1968, Western Hemisphere countries had a limit of 120,000 visas per year.

1975 Indochina Migration and Refugee Assistance Act

▪ Defined for the first time the term "refugee" and designated money to move Cambodian and South Vietnamese people to the U.S. after the Vietnam War.

1980 The Refugee Act

▪ Created the Federal Refugee Resettlement Program to help resettle refugees.

▪ The total number of visas given annually, not including admission for refugees, was set at 270,000, a reduction from the 1965 law.

1986 Immigration Reform and Control Act (Simpson–Mazzoli Act)

▪ One of the most sweeping immigration laws in the nation's history, allowing permanent residency to workers who had lived in the U.S. illegally since 1982 or worked in certain agricultural jobs. The law gave almost 3 million people legal status, denounced by many as "amnesty."

▪ Called for stricter border enforcement and sanctions on employers hiring people in the country illegally (critics have long said the sanctions lacked teeth and have been applied unevenly). Protected children of those legalized by the act from being deported. Created a visa for temporary, seasonal agricultural workers, and the annual immigration ceiling rose to 540,000.

1990 Immigration Act

▪ Directed the attorney general to provide "temporary protected status" to immigrants from countries experiencing armed conflicts, natural disasters or other "extraordinary temporary conditions."

▪ Placed a permanent worldwide annual cap of 675,000 visas per year after 1995. Created visas for highly skilled and temporary workers and revised the grounds for deportation based on political and ideological beliefs, among other reasons.

1996 *Illegal Immigration Reform and Immigrant Responsibility Act*

- Beefed up border security in various ways, most notably by authorizing construction of barriers along parts of the U.S.–Mexico border. Increased immigration enforcement actions, which resulted in more deportations.

2002 *Homeland Security Act*

- Created the Department of Homeland Security in the wake of the Sept. 11, 2001, terrorist attacks.
- Created an electronic data system to maintain information on the admission of immigrants and on possible grounds for removal from the country.

2006 *Secure Fence Act*

- Authorized the construction of nearly 700 miles of fencing along the southern U.S. border.

2012 *Deferred Action for Childhood Arrivals (DACA)*

- An executive action, not a law, that shielded more than 752,000 young adults from deportation.
- Granted two-year work permits to those between ages 15 and 30 who were brought to the U.S. illegally as children.

2014 *Deferred Action for Parents of Americans and Lawful Permanent Residents (DAPA)*

- An executive action, not a law, that sought to remove the threat of deportation for more than 4 million immigrant parents of children who are U.S. citizens or lawful permanent residents.
- Implementation of DAPA was initially blocked by a federal judge. In June [2017] the Trump administration announced it was ending the program.

Immigration Under the Trump Presidency

President Trump, who made cracking down on illegal immigration a centerpiece of his campaign, has stepped up deportation efforts and continues to call for a wall on the U.S.-Mexico border.

In a series of executive actions, Trump has also tried to temporarily halt refugee resettlement and bar travel from six Muslim-majority countries. The motivation driving these efforts, Trump says, is national security.

Trump's executive actions continue to be challenged in the courts, and how those cases will be resolved is anybody's guess.

But one thing is certain. The nation's demographics will continue to change and immigration, no doubt, will remain part of the national conversation.

According to Pew Research Center studies, in less than 40 years, there will be no ethnic majority group in the U.S., and by 2065, Asians are projected to become the largest immigrant group.

Executive Orders 2017

1/25/2017: *Executive order*

- President Trump ordered an overhaul of immigration law enforcement, stripping away most restrictions on who should be deported. Under the new guidelines, up to 8 million people in the country illegally could be targeted for deportation, according to calculations by the Los Angeles Times.

1/27/2017: *Executive order (first travel ban)*

- President Trump signed an executive order banning travelers from seven predominantly Muslim countries from entering the U.S. for 90 days and stopping the admission of Syrian refugees indefinitely.
- Federal courts put the order on hold.

3/6/2017: *Executive order (revised travel ban)*

- The Trump administration revised the travel ban, limiting it to six countries, among other changes. Even so, federal judges in Hawaii and Maryland still stopped it from taking effect.
- On June 26 the Supreme Court allowed much of Trump's revised travel ban to take effect. The ruling cleared the way for a ban on foreign arrivals from six Muslim-majority countries to take effect, but it also carved out exemptions for those with "bona fide relationships" with Americans or U.S. entities, including spouses, other close family members, employers and universities. A court battle continues over how to define close family members.

8/2/2017: *Expressing support for curtailing legal immigration*

- On Aug. 2, Trump endorsed a bill that, in a departure from the 1965 Hart–Celler Act, would create an immigration system based on merit and skills instead of family connections. Introduced by two Republican senators, Tom Cotton of Arkansas and David Perdue of Georgia, the bill is called the Reforming American Immigration for Strong Employment (RAISE) Act. It's estimated the measure would cut legal immigration by half.

3 | Undocumented: How Immigration Became Illegal

Aviva Chomsky

. . . Many politicians and others who see immigration control as an issue of security and sovereignty imagine that hordes of poor people of color are seeking to appropriate the resources of this land that we now call the United States. This formulation of the problem is a precise reversal of the actual European settlement of the country, from the perspective of the Native Americans.

It is also a mirror image of the United States' relationship with the countries—primarily Mexico, Central America, and other Latin American countries—from which the undocumented come. In every case, the products and profits accumulated in the sending countries are a major source of the abundance and affluence in the United States. A quick review of any supermarket or clothing or electronics store reveals the Third World and often Latin American origins of many of the products we consume. More invisible are the mines, oil wells, multinationals, and profits behind the products. But the flow of resources is undeniable.

The history that is drummed into the heads of US schoolchildren insists that the "country of immigrants" was founded and built by Europeans. The invisible underside of this narrative is the imperial narrative of conquest and dispossession that continued until the end of the nineteenth century and upon which the new "country of [white] immigrants" was built.

The country-of-immigrants narrative is very much a narrative of race. Immigrants were conceived as white Europeans (the only people allowed to naturalize), and their presence and comfort depended upon the labor of people who were legally excluded from the polity. Throughout the nineteenth and much of the twentieth centuries, Mexicans, like African Americans prior to 1868, were accepted as a necessary evil for their labor and considered unthreatening to the white nature of the country that viewed them as exploitable workers rather than as potential citizens. The history of reliance on Mexican labor coupled with the refusal to grant rights to Mexican workers is a long one indeed.

The Treaty of Guadalupe Hidalgo and the Gadsden Purchase (La Mesilla Purchase of 1853) offered US citizenship to Mexican citizens resident in the territories newly taken. By specifying "Mexican citizens," the laws excluded the Native American population

---

Aviva Chomsky is a professor of history and coordinator of Latin American studies at Salem State University, in Massachusetts. Her books include *Undocumented* and *They Take Our Jobs! And Twenty Other Myths about Immigration.*

resident in the area. And by offering citizenship to Mexicans at a time when citizenship was restricted to whites, the laws implied that Mexicans would be considered white. In the midcentury, then, "it was possible . . . to be both white *and* Mexican in the United States."[1] However, as Katherine Benton-Cohn explains in her detailed study of four Arizona border towns, Mexican nationality became racialized as nonwhite during the nineteenth century through work. Where Mexicans were workers, rather than landholders, they came to be legally defined as racially Mexican and disqualified from citizenship.

"Where Mexicans owned ranches and farms, racial categories were blurry and unimportant. But in the industrial copper-mining town of Bisbee, Mexican workers were segregated economically by their lower pay ('Mexican wage') and geographically by new town-planning experiments. To most non-Mexican residents of Bisbee, Mexicans were peon workers or potential public charges, not neighbors or business partners, not co-workers or co-worshipers, and certainly not potential marriage partners." In these areas, where Mexicans became defined as racially Mexican through their laboring status, "'American' increasingly equaled 'white,' and so 'Mexican' came to mean the opposite of both."[2]

Nicolas De Genova notes the "longstanding equation of Mexican migration with a presumably temporary, disposable (finally, deportable) labor migration predominated by men (who were predominantly single or left wives and children behind)."[3] The 1911 Dillingham US Immigration Commission argued that "while [Mexicans] are not easily assimilated, this is of no very great importance as long as most of them return to their native land. In the case of the Mexican, he is less desirable as a citizen than as a laborer."[4] "One way or the other, then," De Genova concludes, "US policy would ensure that 'most of them' proved to be sojourners."[5]

The laws that restricted citizenship to whites did not restrict the right to work to whites. On the contrary, Congress has repeatedly created new categories of nonwhite people who were specifically cast as workers. (Slave laborers comprised the original worker-but-not-potential-citizen category.) Deportability became a crucial factor in cementing the association between Mexican-ness as a race and legal status as a temporary worker. The threat of deportation worked to institutionalize the fragile character of Mexicans' claims to rights in the land where they came, invited, to work. It could be used to accommodate the changing needs of employers, and it could also be used to discourage union organizing or other forms of social protest.[6] Until the 1960s, racial justifications seemed sufficient for legal discrimination against Mexicans.

Making Immigration Illegal

After the 1960s, when race was finally rejected as a rationale for excluding people from access to public spaces, citizenship, or entry into the United States, new forms of legal and legalized exclusion took its place. The last two major immigration reforms, in 1965 and 1986, turned Mexican migrant workers into "illegal" workers and used that legal status to justify discrimination. They also, paradoxically, helped to greatly increase both the immigrant and the undocumented population.

The 1965 law is generally seen as a civil rights triumph. One typical account explains that it "ended discrimination" and "represented a significant watershed in US immigration history and particularly in its explicit reversal of decades of systematically exclusive and restrictive immigration policies." Immigration scholars agree that the climate of the civil rights movement of the 1960s set the context for the 1965 immigration reform.[7]

Despite this generous interpretation, the 1965 law was actually "distinctly and unequivocally restrictive" when it came to Mexican migrants.[8] Through the 1950s and early 1960s, hundreds of thousands of Mexicans were crossing the border as braceros or alongside the braceros each year. Then the Bracero Program was ended and Mexican immigration was suddenly capped. By 1976, a cap of twenty thousand immigrant visas a year was enforced. The seasonal, circular migration of Mexicans over many decades that had attracted little national attention suddenly became "a yearly and highly visible violation of American sovereignty by hostile aliens who were increasingly framed as invaders and criminals."[9]

If the new restrictions were intended to lower migration from Latin America, they failed miserably. Instead, all types of immigration from Latin America rose after 1965: temporary and permanent, legal and illegal. Legal immigration from Latin America grew from about 450,000 between 1950 and 1960 to over 4 million between 1990 and 2000, while the number of undocumented Latin Americans living long term in the United States grew from almost none in 1965 to close to 10 million in the first decade of the new century.[10]

Further "unintended consequences" flowed from the greatly increased border enforcement of the 1990s and 2000s. As border crossing became more difficult, more dangerous, and more expensive, seasonal migrants began to change their patterns and stay on in the United States, sometimes bringing their families as well. The undocumented population grew rapidly in those decades, not because more immigrants were arriving, but because fewer were leaving. . . .

Starting in 1990, a series of laws made life even more difficult for noncitizens, including green-card holders (legal permanent residents). Family reunification privileges favored citizens over legal permanent residents. In 1996, legal permanent residents were barred from receiving most social services, while the Antiterrorism and Effective Death Penalty Act made noncitizens deportable for a wide range of crimes, even if they had been committed in a distant past. Then, in 2001, the USA-PATRIOT Act made deportation and arrest possible for virtually any noncitizen, based only upon the US Attorney General's decision.[11] . . .

Structural Causes of Increased Migration

While US legislative changes played a large role in increasing both documented and undocumented immigration, the enormous political and economic convulsions that wracked Latin America in the post-1905 era and the shifts in the global economy were also important. Political movements for social change were crushed as a wave of extraordinarily repressive right-wing dictatorships spread through the continent. Supply-side economics and structural adjustment programs tore apart social safety networks and spurred export-oriented extraction and production. . . . Meanwhile, both consumption and inequality shot up in the United States, creating massive demand for cheap immigrant workers. . . .

Even as US politicians railed about illegal immigration and border control, they pursued policies that served to increase migrant flows. . . .

Over the past century, the United States has consistently promoted export-oriented economies in Latin America based on foreign investment. It has opposed and overthrown Latin American governments that have tried to take control of or redistribute their countries' resources. During recent decades, US policies promoting neoliberal austerity measures and market fundamentalism have had noxious effects on Latin American society. They undermine subsistence agriculture, employment, and the social safety network, while increasing structural and individual violence in Latin America. The United States has used international institutions, military interventions, trade agreements, and corporate privilege to arrive at a situation in which it, with 4 percent of the world's population, consumes between 25 percent and 50 percent of the planet's major resources, while simultaneously creating an enormous demand for low-wage, informal, and seasonal labor. Thus, the United States continues to set the stage for large migrations from Latin America.[12] . . .

Deliberate US policies, from invasions and occupations to military aid to loans and investments, have created the Latin American polities and economies and the disparities that are now the roots of today's migrations. Attempts to seal the border only reinforce the very inequalities that contribute to migration.

Challenging Discrimination

The campaigns to strengthen immigration law and make it harsher are fairly well known and have been related to the successive punitive measures against undocumented immigrants since the 1980s. But organizations that defended the rights of immigrants and, in particular, the undocumented also grew in the last decades of the twentieth century.[13]

While nativism has been part of US society and culture since the country was founded, specifically anti-*undocumented* sentiment and movements date to the post-1965 and especially the post-1986 period. The Republican Party first mentioned immigration enforcement in its 1980 national platform and in 1984 first "affirmed the right of the United States to control its boundaries and voiced concern about illegal immigration." The Democratic Party first mentioned illegal immigration in its 1996 platform.[14] Popular movements for the defense of the rights of the undocumented also grew [during] this period.

Mexican American rights organizations like LULAC [League of United Latin American Citizens] have taken mixed stances on the undocumented and even on immigrants in general over the course of the twentieth century. Mexican Americans sought to claim their rights by demonstrating their patriotism and distancing themselves from new arrivals, even as their communities, friends, and families included both documented and undocumented new immigrants.[15] Even the United Farm Workers union, made up primarily of immigrants, was hesitant to defend the rights of the undocumented.

However, Mexican American rights, immigrant rights, and the rights of the undocumented have also been intertwined. The Chicano movement of the 1960s and '70s rejected the emphasis on patriotism and assimilation of earlier generations, and insisted on a cultural nationalism that united people of Mexican origin, regardless of status. (The movement adopted the name Chicano to emphasize the indigenous roots of Mexicans and the difference in their historical experience from that of European immigrants.) "Chicano families became the new underground railroad," explained Alma Martinez evocatively, referring to the ties that bound US-born Chicanos to new, including undocumented, immigrants.[16] Even as politicians and the media raised their voices against the undocumented, networks and organizations grew to defend their rights.

In the 1980s, growing numbers of Central American refugees joined the ranks of what had previously been primarily a Mexican phenomenon. The sanctuary movement, growing primarily out of Central American refugee organizations and Anglo religious congregations, sought to aid Salvadoran and Guatemalan refugees in the United States without legal status. Some organizations were made up of refugees themselves, like the Central American Refugee Center (CARECEN, later changed to Central American Resource Center), founded in 1983. These and other organizations concerned with the rights of Salvadoran (and to a lesser extent, Guatemalan) refugees were the first to bring the question of the rights of the undocumented into the public sphere. They also emphasized how US intervention was behind much of the violence that was causing people to flee Central America. . . .

The First Comprehensive Reform

The 1986 Immigration Reform and Control Act (IRCA) was comprehensive in the same way that twenty-first-century proposals for comprehensive reform were. It combined enforcement—in the form of employer sanctions and increased border security—with legalization or amnesty. The rationale was that by legalizing some of the undocumented population, encouraging others to leave (through employer sanctions that would make it more difficult for them to work), and making it more difficult for further undocumented people to enter the country, the numbers of the undocumented should be significantly reduced.

IRCA had complicated implications for the undocumented. For those who could document presence since 1982 or eligibility for Special Agricultural Worker Status, the chance to obtain legal status was priceless. . . . The employer sanctions provisions of the law, however, created a new system for marginalizing and discriminating against the undocumented. By offering legal status to some, but not all of the undocumented, IRCA (like the DREAM Act and DACA) invited even more pernicious racism against those it left out.

The National Network for Immigrant and Refugee Rights was established in 1986, growing out of a coalition that coalesced in 1985 to organize a National Day of Justice for Immigrants and Refugees in opposition to legislative proposals for employer sanctions for the hiring of undocumented workers, which was incorporated in the 1986 IRCA. Following the passage of the law, new organizations like the New York Immigrant Coalition and the Massachusetts Immigrant and Refugee Advocacy Coalition formed both to help undocumented immigrants gain legal status and to challenge discriminatory aspects of the enforcement of employer sanctions (and sometimes the notion of employer sanctions itself). . . .

The AFL-CIO supported employer sanctions in 1986. But as Jeff Stansbury wrote a few years later, "The IRCA is not a border-control law," rather, it is "a worker-control law." In the words of Asian Law Caucus staff attorney Bill Tamayo, "The new law has codified the existence of a cheap and highly exploitable class of labor, largely non-white and non-English-speaking, with little rights, if any." And employers lost no time in using the law as a weapon against workers who tried to organize unions.[17] In 2000, the AFL-CIO reversed its stance and called for a repeal of employer sanctions.[18] AFL-CIO executive vice president Linda Chavez-Thompson explained, "Employers often knowingly hire workers who are undocumented, and then when workers seek to improve working conditions employers use the law to fire or intimidate workers."[19] . . .

The Anti-Immigrant 1990s

In the 1990s, explicitly anti-undocumented or anti-illegal mobilization took off, especially in California, where Proposition 13 in 1978 had decimated state finances. Under Governor Pete Wilson, "illegal" immigrants became a convenient scapegoat.[20] Proposition 187 in 1994 was the first of many state- and nationwide efforts to impose austerity on the backs of the most vulnerable. Nicknamed "Save Our State," it sought primarily to bar the undocumented from receiving public services. . . .

Many of Proposition 187's provisions were never enacted, being tied up or rejected in the courts. However, as California goes, so goes the nation. After the Democrat Bill Clinton became president in 1993, Wilson connected anti-immigrant with anti-Washington bombast, claiming that the federal government had failed to protect the country's borders. Wilson's attacks helped to push Clinton to the right on border enforcement, as Clinton sought to woo California's apparently increasingly anti-immigrant electorate.[21]

Anti-"illegal" rhetoric mirrored and intertwined with a growing anti-black, anti–civil rights backlash in multiple ways. It replaced explicitly racialized language with a two-pronged attack against people of color. First, starting with the 1980 election, conservatives "repeatedly raised the issue of welfare, subtly framing it as a context between hardworking blue-collar whites and poor blacks who refused to work."[22] Second was rhetoric about law and order.[23] . . .

By the end of 1993, "politicians began tripping over one another to take a tough stance on boundary enforcement and unauthorized migration."[24] In 1994, President Clinton implemented Operation Gatekeeper to bring the border "under control" and undercut Pete Wilson's protagonism by taking the lead on border enforcement as the elections approached.[25] In 1996, Clinton pressed for punitive Welfare Reform and Immigration Reform laws that enacted federally much of what California had tried to do at the state level. With these laws, Clinton made both welfare reform and law and order centerpieces of the Democratic Party program, and linked the anti-black and the anti-immigrant aspects of these policies. In the panic following the 9/11 attacks, the USA-PATRIOT Act of 2001 and the subsequent creation of the Department of Homeland Security in 2003 strengthened both institutional controls against potential and current immigrants, as well as the ideological climate of anti-immigrant sentiment.

Joseph Nevins argues that the government's increasing attention to border enforcement in the 1990s actually served to *create* the supposed immigration crisis. Through its sensationalist rhetoric and justifications, as well as its ostentatious enforcement policies, the state helped to convince the population that such a crisis indeed existed.[26] . . .

"Comprehensive" Versus "Enforcement Only" in the New Century

In January 2004, president and candidate George W. Bush had lauded the country's immigrant history in a speech whose audience included representatives of LULAC and other Hispanic organizations. Bush acknowledged the country's need for migrant workers and expressed great sympathy for the undocumented. . . .

. . . Bush proposed offering temporary legal status to all undocumented workers in the country. Although he emphasized that the status would be temporary—initially for three years, but renewable—he also emphasized that those who wanted to apply for citizenship should also be allowed to do so.[27]

Several congressional proposals for so-called comprehensive immigration reform were launched in the first decade of the new century. . . .

While these comprehensive approaches stalled, the House passed an extraordinarily punitive piece of legislation that epitomized what came to be called the enforcement-only approach, H.R. 4437, the Border Protection, Antiterrorism, and Illegal Immigration Control Act of 2005. This vote became a catalyst for a new level of immigrant rights mobilization, the huge demonstrations in the spring and especially on May 1, 2006. . . .

New Protests in the New Century

. . ."In a short span of twelve weeks between mid-February and early May 2006, an estimated 3.7 million to 5 million people took to the streets in over 160 cities across the United States to rally for immigrant rights."[28] The protests were also unique in being carried out within the political system but primarily by people legally excluded from the polity—the undocumented. . . .

The culmination of these many protests was on May 1, when a coordinated day-without-an-immigrant protest brought walkouts and business closings throughout the country to illustrate the importance of immigrants to the economy and their role in citizens' daily lives.

Another thing the immigrant and undocumented communities had in their favor were the reformers in the labor movement who pushed for more pro-immigrant, and pro-undocumented positions. In the fall of 2003, the AFL-CIO, UNITE-HERE, and the SEIU sponsored the first Immigrant Workers Freedom Ride. Undocumented immigrant workers took off from 101 cities around the United States, headed for Washington, DC, where they lobbied and demanded legislative change, and to New York, where they held public rallies.[29] One study suggests that the Immigrant Workers Freedom Ride three years earlier helped bring groups together and lay the groundwork for the 2006 mobilizations.[30]

To the extent that the protests aimed to prevent H.R. 4437 from becoming law, they succeeded: the Senate declined to consider the proposal and, in fact, passed its own, comprehensive reform bill later in May 2006 (which was then rejected by the House). . . .

Consulting Firms and the Cultural Battle

Rinku Sen argues that despite the successes of 2006, a cultural battle for the rights of the undocumented was lost in the rise of xenophobia after 9/11. Fox News, talk radio, reality TV, and other media and entertainment sources offer the public epic battles between "criminal aliens" and beleaguered law enforcement in what Sen calls a "racialized cultural fight over the nation's identity."[31] Sen especially critiques the immigrants' rights organizations that have sought and followed the advice of consultants and "mainstreamed" their messages so as to tacitly accept, rather than challenge, common anti-immigrant sentiments. Many large organizations have relied on consulting firms like Westen Strategies that use surveys and focus groups to determine what messages will resonate with different sectors of the American public.

The firm's founder, psychologist Drew Westen, urged advocates to concede to the public's antipathy for immigrants considered illegal, rather than to challenge that stance. Advocates should aim for the center, he argued, by avoiding talk of immigrants' rights and instead relying on some key phrases that would resonate with those less sympathetic. His surveys found that the phrases "comprehensive immigration reform" and "fixing a broken immigration system" went over especially well with these centrist voters. An effective message, Westen discovered, begins with "taking tough measures to secure our borders," continues with "cracking down on illegal employers," and finally ends with "requiring those who came here without our permission to get in line, work hard, obey our laws, and learn our language."[32] His firm works with and has been commissioned by major immigrants' rights organizations like the Center for American Progress and Reform Immigration for America. Indeed, Westen's key phrases began to enter every politician's immigration proposals. . . .

A few advocates and organizations opposed the focus-group approach. Oscar Chacón, executive director of the National Alliance of Latin American and Caribbean Communities, or NALAAC, rejected the "comprehensive" consensus arguing that "this is oppressive language—punitive and restrictive." The 2008 Democracy Corps report was "nothing but an effort by D.C. groups to justify their views with a public opinion survey." The Democrats were "accept[ing] more and more of the premises of the anti-immigrant lobby." "We should be trying to change the way people think about the situation . . . instead of finding a way to make anti-immigrant sentiments tolerable," Chacón urged.[33]

Once Obama took office, the idea of a comprehensive reform died a quiet death. The Obama administration moved instead on the enforcement side, promoting and imposing the Secure Communities and E-Verify programs. Secure Communities, a Bush-era program that empowered local police forces to share data on arrests with ICE, grew from a small, voluntary pilot program to one Obama insisted would be imposed nationwide by 2013. E-Verify likewise grew from a small-scale, voluntary program to one required for companies holding government contracts—about 170,000 of them, employing some 4 million workers—and encouraged for all.[34]

The immigrant rights organizations that had worked for Obama were disappointed when the first years of his presidency seemed to pander to the anti-immigrant right rather than pay them back for their support of his candidacy. . . .

Can We Abandon "Enforcement"?

The more that US authorities have tried to control or stop Mexican border crossing over the course of the twentieth century, the more people have come. . . .

The past few decades have demonstrated that the more the United States tries to militarily control the border, the more out of control it gets. The huge growth in organized crime, drug smuggling, drug and smuggling cartels, kidnappings, and violent and unnecessary death at the border is the *result* of misguided policies attempting to impose control.

Supporters of the idea of border control often argue that without draconian measures to deter migrants, floods of Mexicans and other Latin Americans would overwhelm the border and the country. They forget, perhaps, that during the many decades in which the border was relatively open, there were no floods. The number of undocumented immigrants in the United States began its precipitous rise *after* the country began to try to seal the border, in large part because instead of leaving after a season of work, migrants felt compelled to stay, since they realized that returning would be difficult.

Recent trends demonstrate the extent to which structural factors still govern migrant flows. The slowing and even reversal of migration from Mexico and the concomitant rise in numbers migrating from Central America, particularly from Honduras, suggest that factors other than border policies are the ones that really affect migrant streams. Border policies can shape *where* people try to cross, how much it will cost, and how many will die in the process, but they seem to have little effect on the numbers of people crossing.

Deeper Questions

If the United States can't close the border, and if comprehensive immigration reform is such a flawed approach, what can we do?

By now, we have become accustomed to the notion that controlling the border is a basic prerequisite for security, safety, and sovereignty. So accustomed, that we rarely question this idea.

. . . The entire immigration apparatus is based on the presumption that we know where people belong and we need to legislate their mobility.

It's also based on some unquestioned assumptions about *countries*. It is not OK for a public park, a town, a county, or a state to discriminate regarding who is allowed to enter its space. But it's OK for a country to do that. It's not OK to treat people differently based on their religion, race, gender, or many other characteristics. But it's OK to treat people differently based on where they were born or their nationality (which is generally determined by where a person is born). US immigration laws do just that: discriminate, on the basis of nationality, regarding who is allowed to be where.

If we really want to address the problem of undocumentedness, or so-called "illegal" immigration, we need to look more in depth at why the United States made some immigration illegal to begin with. I hope that I have shown that the drive to illegalize immigration was wrongheaded from the start. It's just the latest stage in a centuries-long process of legislated inequality, a process both global and domestic.

Rather than what currently passes for comprehensive reform, some organizations are pushing for what they call a "cultural strategy" that challenges the nationalist—and racist—underpinnings of popular views of immigrants. The new generation of undocumented youth—the DREAMers . . .—has taken this approach. Rinku Sen emphasizes that their goal goes beyond gaining their own access to citizenship: the bigger aim is to challenge the anti-immigrant culture. "Young, savvy with social media, and artistically inclined, DREAMers have compensated for their lack of political power by telling their stories in many forms and venues." With their stories, they sought to reframe the entire debate.[35]

The Applied Research Center launched its Drop-the-I-Word (i.e., illegal) campaign in 2010 in another attempt to challenge the terms of the mainstream debate about immigration that directly contradicted Westen's advice. Arguing that the very term "illegal" (or "illegal immigrant") "opens the door to racial profiling and violence and prevents truthful, respectful debate on immigration," and that "no human being is illegal," supporters challenged politicians, the media, and others to stop using it.[36] By 2013, numerous mainstream news outlets had shifted their usage. "Illegal immigrant isn't always accurate because it implies that somebody illegally immigrated when it fact a lot of people who are here illegally are here because their documentation expired after they came," the Associated Press explained when its new style guide recommended against using the term.[37] The *New York Times* and *Los Angeles Times* soon followed suit.[38] . . .

At my own university, Salem State, in Massachusetts, a group supporting undocumented students engaged in a similar debate a few years ago. Should the university openly admit and support students who were undocumented? Or should it quietly open some back doors? One local high school guidance counselor cautioned us that the anti-immigrant climate at her school was so virulent that she preferred to counsel students individually and would not recommend that we hold a public event at her school. A faculty member worried that if we raised the issue publicly, it would imperil our undocumented students. Another retorted: "Do you know of any historical example where social change has come about by people keeping quiet?"

That question has stayed with me over the years and seems to surface again and again. . . . There are those who truly believe that the best way to help the undocumented is through backroom deals that may bring some benefits for some people without addressing the larger structural issues of unequal international relations, an economy based on the use of labor kept cheap through legal marginalization, restrictive immigration policies, discrimination, and inequality before the law. History shows, though, that whether we are trying to change foreign policy, domestic and global economic structures, or laws that discriminate, Frederick Douglass was closer to the truth when he argued that change "must be a struggle. Power concedes nothing without a demand. It never did and it never will."[39]

Although the cultural strategy is a very important way to raise awareness and open a real debate about immigration policy, we also need to address the root global and economic factors that have contributed to today's problems. In the most immediate terms, we as a society created illegal immigration by making immigration illegal. In larger terms, we created illegal immigration by fostering a global system that bases the prosperity for the few on the exploitation of the many and enforcing it, in the modern era, through borders and exclusive citizenship. It's up to us to change it.

NOTES

1. Katherine Benton-Cohen, *Borderline Americans: Racial Division and Labor War in the Arizona Borderlands* (Cambridge, MA: Harvard University Press, 2009), 7.
2. Ibid., 8–9.
3. Nicholas De Genova, *Working the Boundaries: Race, Space, and "Illegality" in Mexican Chicago* (Durham, NC: Duke University Press, 2005), 91–92.
4. Ibid., 92, quoting Kitty Calavita, *Inside the State: The Bracero Program, Immigration, and the I.N.S.* (New York: Routledge, 1992), 180.
5. De Genova, *Working the Boundaries*, 93.
6. Ibid., 224.
7. Marc Georges Pufong, "Immigration and Nationality Act Amendments of 1965," in *The Encyclopedia of American Civil Liberties*, vol. 1, ed. Paul Finkelman (New York: Taylor and Francis, 2006), 796–97.
8. De Genova, *Working the Boundaries*, 230.
9. Douglas S. Massey and Karen A. Pren, "Unintended Consequences of US Immigration Policy: Explaining the Post-1965 Surge from Latin America," *Population and Development Review* 38, no. 1 (March 2012): 4, http://www.princeton.edu/coverstories/Massey_LatinAmericaImmigrationSurge/Unintended=Consequences.pdf.
10. Ibid., 2.
11. Ibid., 19–20.
12. See David Bacon, *Illegal People: How Globalization Creates Migration and Criminalizes Immigrants* (Boston: Beacon Press, 2008), and David Bacon, *The Right to Stay Home* (Boston: Beacon Press, 2013), for further discussion of how US policies foster out-migration. For US policy in Latin America more generally, see Greg Grandin, *Empire's Workshop: Latin America, the United States, and the Rise of the New Imperialism* (New York: Henry Holt, 2006).
13. I would like to thank Oscar Chacón of NALAAC for sharing his thoughts on the history of these various immigration reform agendas and allowing me to incorporate his ideas in this section.
14. Joseph Nevins, *Operation Gatekeeper and Beyond: The War on 'Illegals' and the Remaking of the US–Mexico Boundary*, 2nd ed. (New York: Routledge, 2010), 140.
15. David G. Gutiérrez, *Walls and Mirrors; Mexican Americans, Mexican Immigrants, and the Politics of Ethnicity* (Berkeley: University of California Press, 1995).
16. Alma Martínez, "Pancho Villa's Head: The Mexican Revolution and the Chicano Dramatic Imagination," Pomona College Oldenborg Lunch Series, April 25, 2013.
17. Jeff Stansbury, "L.A. Labor and the New Immigrants," *Labor Research Review* 1, no. 13 (1989): 22.
18. See Nancy Cleeland, "AFL-CIO Calls for Amnesty for Illegal US Workers," *Los Angeles Times*, February 17, 2000.

19. "AFL-CIO: End Sanctions," *Migration News* 7, no. 3 (March 2000), http://migration.ucdavis. edu/mn/more.php?id=2037_0_2_0.

20. See Nevins, *Operation Gatekeeper and Beyond*, 105.

21. Nevins, *Operation Gatekeeper and Beyond*, 108.

22. Michelle Alexander, *The New Jim Crow: Mass Incarceration in the Age of Colorblindness* (New York: New Press, 2010), 47.

23. Ibid., 42.

24. Nevins, *Operation Gatekeeper and Beyond*, 110.

25. Ibid., 4, quoting US Border Patrol, "Border Patrol Strategic Plan: 1994 and Beyond," 1994, 114.

26. Nevins, *Operation Gatekeeper and Beyond*, 12.

27. Text of Bush immigration speech, January 7, 2004, available on a number of websites, including [https://georgewbush-whitehouse.archives.gov/news/releases/2004/01/20040107-3.html].

28. Irene Bloemraad, Kim Voss, and Taeku Lee, "The Protests of 2006: What They Were, How Do We Understand Them, Where Do They Go?," in *Rallying for Immigrant Rights: The Fight for Inclusion in 21st Century America*, ed. Kim Voss and Irene Bloemraad (Berkeley: University of California Press, 2011), 3–4.

29. See Sarah Anne Wright, "'Freedom Ride' 'Focuses Attention on Immigrants' Rights," *Seattle Times*, September 21, 2003. See also Randy Shaw, "Building the Labor-Clergy-Immigrant Alliance," in *Rallying for Immigrant Rights*, ed. Voss and Bloemraad, 82–100.

30. Shaw, "Building the Labor-Clergy-Immigrant Alliance."

31. Rinku Sen, "Immigrants Are Losing the Policy Fight. But That's Beside the Point," *Colorlines*, September 17, 2012, http://colorlines.com/archives/2012/09/immigrants_are_losing_the_ political_fight_but_thats_beside_the_point.html.

32. Drew Westen, "Immigrating from Facts to Values: Political Rhetoric in the US Immigration Debate," Migration Policy Institute, 2009, http://www.migrationpolicy.org/pubs/TCM-politicalrhetoric-Westen.pdf.

33. Gabriel Thompson, "How the Right Made Racism Sound Fair—and Changed Immigration Politics," *Colorlines*, September 13, 2011, http://colorlines.com/archives/2011/09/how_the_ right_made__racist_rhetoric_sound_neutral—and_shaped_immigration_politics.html.

34. Spencer S. Hsu, "Obama Revives Bush Idea of Using E-Verify to Catch Illegal Contract Workers," *Washington Post*, July 9, 2009.

35. Sen, "Immigrants Are Losing the Policy Fight."

36. The campaign is described on the *Colorlines* website, http://colorlines.com/droptheiword/.

37. Craig Kopp, "Associated Press Recommends Media Stop Using 'Illegal Immigrant,'" WUSF News, April 12, 2013, http://wusfnews.wusf.usf.edu/post/ associated-press-recommends-media-stop-using-illegal-immigrant.

38. Adam Clark Estes, "*L.A. Times* Ban on 'Illegal Immigrant' Puts Everybody Else on the Spot," *Atlantic Wire*, May 1, 2013, http://www.theatlanticwire.com/politics/2013/05/new-la-times-ban-illegal-immigrant-puts-everybody-else-spot/64795/.

39. Frederick Douglass, "West India Emancipation," August 3, 1857. Reproduced at http://www. blackpast.org/?q=1857-frederick-douglass-if-there-no-struggle-there-no-progress.

4 There Are Deep Ties Between Nativism and Anti-Semitism

Jaclyn Granick and Britt Tevis

On Saturday [October 27, 2018], a shooter opened fire inside a synagogue in the heart of a heavily Jewish neighborhood in Pittsburgh. The attack occurred during Shabbat services and during a bris, a celebration of a newborn life.

Immediately before the massacre, the alleged killer tweeted about HIAS, an organization once known as the Hebrew Sheltering and Immigrant Aid Society that dates back to the late 19th century. "HIAS likes to bring invaders that kill our people," he wrote. It doesn't take a deep understanding of American anti-Semitism to know that to him, "our people" did not include Jewish Americans, even though Jews have lived in America since before the founding of the United States and the congregation he attacked has been convening to pray since the Civil War. (The congregation also had no particular ties to HIAS.)

Why, then, did this white-nationalist xenophobe gun down local Jews to protest HIAS? The massacre reflects a stark reality with deep roots in American history: Anti-Semitism, nativism and anti-immigrant sentiments have long been inextricably intertwined. Themselves targeted for exclusion from the country, some Jewish Americans worked through HIAS to make America more welcoming for all immigrants, making the organization a target for those blended prejudices. In Pittsburgh, as in all Jewish communities throughout time, there is no consensus among members on pressing issues such as immigration. But the synagogue wasn't targeted because it had ties to HIAS—it was targeted because those who spew hate take it out on the most readily available Jews.

HIAS was founded in the last decades of the 19th century by Jewish communal leaders to assist Jews from Eastern Europe in making their way in the United States. Its most prominent leaders were lawyers—Max J. Kohler, Leon Sanders and Benjamin Levinson—who would go to Ellis Island to advocate for Jews who had been marked for exclusion for reasons beyond the rule of law.

While primarily focused on Jews, the organization's commitment to aiding non-Jews in need of legal representation also quickly became evident. Understanding anti-Chinese sentiments as synonymous with anti-Jewish bigotry, Kohler repeatedly represented

Jaclyn Granick is a junior research fellow in Jewish studies at the University of Oxford and is writing a book on American Jewish humanitarianism. She lived in Pittsburgh from 2011 to 2014.

Britt Tevis is a lecturer at Deakin Law School and is writing a book on late nineteenth- and early twentieth-century American Jewish lawyers.

people of Chinese descent charged under the Chinese Exclusion Act, even arguing cases in front of the U.S. Supreme Court. HIAS thought of itself as a very American organization, visualizing and working toward a country that was welcoming and open to all immigrants.

As World War I drew to a close, Europe was faced with a massive refugee crisis. A power vacuum following the Russian Revolution and the collapse of the German and Austro-Hungarian empires led to tremendous violence, including pogroms in Ukraine in which more than 200,000 Jews were killed. Jews were among the refugees who sought safe places to live, but they found few places to go because of "wartime" limits on migration that were never lifted. As it had done before the war, HIAS came to the rescue of these hundreds of thousands of Jewish refugees.

The war spurred HIAS to become an international refugee organization as U.S. border control moved from Ellis Island to U.S. consulates abroad. HIAS came to view itself as something like an American Red Cross for Jews. The Red Cross had also begun working abroad under a broad mandate due to the war. But it was guided by American Christian thinking and closely linked with U.S. state power. By default, the Red Cross tended to serve Christians and only sporadically cooperated with Jewish organizations or made efforts to reach out to Jewish war victims.

Publicly, HIAS also cooperated with the State Department as it helped Jewish immigrant hopefuls try to arrange safe passage to the United States. But behind closed doors, HIAS lawyers frequently clashed with State Department officials and the Labor Department over the latter's implementation of immigration policies. Further, government employees, couching anti-Semitic tropes in diplomatic language, considered Jewish immigrants "inferior" and fought to keep them out.

Why? Because anti-Semitism runs deep in the United States, and it has sinister ties to anti-immigrant sentiment. From the late 19th century onward, U.S. Public Health Service officers on Ellis Island deployed racialized conceptions of health that also led to the exclusion of Jews and other would-be immigrants. For example, favus, a scalp disease, was commonly associated with Eastern European Jews, and fears of typhus were used to justify diplomats' exclusionary, anti-Semitic stance after World War I.

More often, immigration officers excluded Jews by determining that they were "likely to become public charges," a rule that the Department of Homeland Security recently announced it would reinstate.[1] The U.S. government had banned immigrants it thought would be likely to depend on charitable organizations or government programs upon entry; Congress, however, left the definition of "likely to become a public charge" undefined, thereby enabling immigration inspectors to deploy the classification at will to keep out whomever they identified as undesirable.

And so HIAS battled back as best it could.

It could not stop the tide of public opinion that fueled passage of laws in 1921 and 1924 that set explicit immigration quotas that aimed to prevent Southern and Eastern European immigration. These laws were clearly intended to keep Jews out. Sen. David Reed (R-Pa.), who sponsored the 1924 law, complained on the Senate floor about "sick and starving" Southern European and Jewish immigrants whom he viewed as "less capable of contributing to the American economy, and [less able] to adapt to American culture."

These laws significantly limited HIAS's capacity to help Jewish immigrants in the United States and made it nearly impossible to save Jewish refugees from Nazism a decade later.

The Holocaust did little to change anti-immigrant or anti-Jewish sentiments in the United States. In 1939, the country infamously turned away passengers on the SS *St. Louis* fleeing Nazi Germany, many of whom were children. Some, out of sheer desperation, resorted to illegal entry.[2]

But HIAS persisted in its efforts to aid those who entered the United States as refugees. And in the wake of the 1965 immigration law abolishing the quota system, it expanded its services to help non-Jewish newcomers. This is why HIAS lawyers could be found at airports assisting immigrants after President Trump enacted the "Muslim ban."[3]

The anti-Semitism that drove the immigration policy of the early 20th century never faded from American life. Nor did its connection to anti-immigrant sentiment. These feelings are why bombs were sent . . . to George Soros, often the victim of anti-Semitic caricatures, and why he has been outlandishly charged with funding the caravan of Central American asylum seekers . . . heading toward the United States.

And that sentiment is what compelled a shooter ranting about HIAS to massacre Jews who were part of a congregation that dates to the 1800s and is located in a city where HIAS has no offices or presence. This hateful anti-Semitic, anti-immigrant mind-set links all Jews together, conflating them wherever they are and whatever they do. As has been true throughout history, the Jews who ended up victims Saturday were simply those nearest at hand.

NOTES

1. Torrie Hester et al. "Now the Trump Administration Is Trying to Punish Legal Immigrants for Being Poor." *The Washington Post*, 9 Aug. 2018

2. Libby Garland. *After They Closed the Gates: Jewish Illegal Immigration to the United States, 1921–1965.* University of Chicago Press, 2018.

3. Gabe Cahn. "HIAS Returns to Court to Challenge Muslim Ban 3.0." *HIAS*, 16 Oct. 2017.

5 How Does It Feel to Be a Problem?

Moustafa Bayoumi

How does it feel to be a problem? Just over a century ago, W. E. B. Du Bois asked that very question in his American classic *The Souls of Black Folk*, and he offered an answer. "Being a problem is a strange experience," he wrote, "peculiar even," no doubt evoking the "peculiar institution" of slavery. Du Bois composed his text during Jim Crow, a time of official racial segregation that deliberately obscured to the wider world the human details of African-American life. Determined to pull back "the veil" separating populations, he showed his readers a fuller picture of the black experience, including "the meaning of its religion, the passion of its human sorrow, and the struggle of its greater souls."

A century later, Arabs and Muslim Americans are the new "problem" of American society, but there have of course been others. Native Americans, labeled "merciless Indian savages" by the Declaration of Independence, were said to be beyond civilization and able to comprehend only the brute language of force. With the rise of Catholic immigration to the country in the nineteenth century, Irish and Italian Americans were attacked for their religion. They suffered mob violence and frequent accusations of holding papal loyalties above republican values. During World War I, German Americans were loathed and reviled, sauerkraut was redubbed "liberty cabbage," and several states banned the teaching of German, convinced that the language itself promoted un-American values. Between the world wars, anti-Semitism drove Jewish Americans out of universities and jobs and fueled wild and pernicious conspiracy theories concerning warfare and world domination. Japanese Americans were herded like cattle into internment camps during World War II (as were smaller numbers of German, Italian, Hungarian, and Romanian Americans). Chinese Americans were commonly suspected of harboring Communist sympathies during the McCarthy era, frequently losing careers and livelihoods. And Hispanic Americans have long been seen as outsider threats to American culture, even though their presence here predates the formation of the present-day United States.

But since the terrorist attacks of September 11 and the wars in Afghanistan and Iraq, Arabs and Muslims, two groups virtually unknown to most Americans prior to 2001, now hold the dubious distinction of being the first new communities of suspicion after the hard-won victories of the civil-rights era. . . .

Moustafa Bayoumi is a professor of English at Brooklyn College and a columnist for *The Guardian*. His books include *How Does It Feel To Be a Problem?: Being Young and Arab in America* and *This Muslim American Life: Dispatches from the War on Terror*.

In this rocky terrain, young Arab and Muslim Americans are forging their lives as the newest minorities in the American imagination. In their circumstances and out of their actions, they are also shaping the contours of a future American society. And though they don't always succeed in their efforts, the human drama of their predicament has now become a part of what it means to be an American.

The burning question really is whether American society will treat them as equals. The answer is not entirely clear. Simply put, the general public seems divided about the Arabs and Muslims in our midst. On the one hand, the last few years have seen a spirit of inclusion and desire for mutual cooperation spread across the country. Arab and Muslim organizations have matured in this environment, as they engage the general public more openly and fully than before, and the results are evident. Islam is increasingly understood as an American religion — in 2006 the first American Muslim, Keith Ellison, was elected to Congress — and Arab Americans are now frequently acknowledged to be an integral part of the United States. Despite an unwarranted controversy, the first dual-language Arabic–English New York City public high school opened its doors in Brooklyn in 2007. Arabs and Muslims are successfully integrating themselves into the institutional framework of American society.

Yet too many people continue to see Arabs and Muslims in America — particularly the young generation — through narrowed eyes, as enemies living among us. Key members of the political class, an often shrill news media, and a law-enforcement establishment that succumbs to ethnic and religious profiling lead the charge, and Muslims and Arabs are scrutinized for sedition at every turn. Even the most mundane facts of their lives, such as visiting mosques and *shisha* cafés, are now interpreted as something sinister and malevolent. On any given day, popular feelings seem to swing wildly between these poles of fear and acceptance, illustrating what the sociologist Louise Cainkar has called "the apparent paradox of this historical moment: [where] repression and inclusion may be happening at the same time."

It's a strange place to inhabit, and it reveals not only the bifurcated nature of contemporary American society but also the somewhat precarious condition of Arab and Muslim Americans. Because their situation here is ultimately dependent less on what happens on the home front and more on what happens in the Middle East, Muslim and Arab Americans know that their own domestic security and their ability to live full American lives turn on the winds of global conflicts and on America's posture in the world and its policies abroad.

In *The Souls of Black Folk*, W. E. B. Du Bois observed that the treatment of African Americans stands as "a concrete test of the underlying principles of the great republic." In fact, the same can be said about Arabs and Muslims today. However, the principles currently at stake revolve not only around issues of full equality and inclusion, but fundamentally around the consequences that American foreign policy has on domestic civil rights. This condition is not new, and the history is important to remember.

• • •

Islam was practiced in this land centuries ago. As far back as the colonial era, many West African Muslims were sold into slavery, making Muslim-American history older than the republic itself. Mustapha, historians tell us, was actually a fairly common name among slaves in colonial South Carolina. For their part, Arabs have been arriving on these shores since the latter part of the nineteenth century, when mostly Christian Arabs from Mount Lebanon packed up their belongings and landed on Ellis Island with an average of $31.85 in their pockets, more than the $12.26 that Polish immigrants carried or the $21.32 of the Greeks. The migrations of both Arabs and Muslims have ebbed and flowed over the years for many reasons, primarily because of the vicissitudes of American immigration law.

In the late nineteenth century, a few years after they began arriving in the United States, Arab Americans established themselves on Washington Street in Lower Manhattan (dubbed "Little Syria"), where they opened stores, published lots of newspapers, lived closely, fought among themselves, and worried about being too different from other Americans or about becoming too American. (The move to Brooklyn happened mostly in the 1940s, with the construction of the Brooklyn Battery Tunnel, which razed much of Little Syria.) The early community thrived mostly as pack peddlers who, after stocking up on jewelry and notions from the stores on Washington Street, would then set off to sell their Holy Land wares, criss-crossing the country, often on foot.

The Washington Street shops spawned a certain amount of nineteenth-century exotic curiosity. An 1892 *New York Tribune* article noted that in them were boxes piled high with gossamer silks, olivewood trinkets, and luxurious satins. "In the midst of all this riot of the beautiful and odd," the article says, "stands the dealer, the natural gravity of his features relaxed into a smile of satisfaction at the wonder and delight expressed by his American visitor. But the vision ends, and with many parting 'salaams' one goes back to the dust and dirt, the noise and bustle" of Washington Street.

The early Arab-American community also encountered ethnic bigotry typical of the period. An 1890 *New York Times* article, for example, manages to illustrate this in a few words, while insulting a few others along the way. "The foreign population in the lower part of this city has of late years been increased by the Arabic-speaking element from the Lebanon, in Syria," it begins. "In clannishness and outlandish manners these people resemble the Chinese and what are called the Diego Italians. Nearly all of them are Maronite [Christians], and in many respects they are inferior to the Chinese and Italians, who do possess a certain amount of self-respect and are willing to work honestly and work hard for a living." The comments seem antiquarian today ("Diego Italians"?), but what we find here, between exoticism and chauvinism, is precisely the nation's early-twentieth-century spirit, which welcomed and reviled foreigners simultaneously. (Like any ethnic story, really, Arab-American history reveals as much or more about *American* culture as it does about immigrant ethnic mores.)

The second phase of Arab-American history dates from around 1909 until 1944. During this period the main issue plaguing the Arab-American community, beside the growing unrest in Palestine, was whether Arabs could naturalize as American citizens. According to the citizenship laws of the period (and until 1952), only "free white persons" could qualify for naturalization, and laws were passed explicitly to bar "Asiatics" from American citizenship. Confronted with this reality, the Arab-American community from across the nation mobilized to prove that they were indeed "free white people," and a series of court rulings eventually affirmed that position. A close examination of these years similarly reveals much less about the genetic makeup of Arabs and much more about America's domestic racial politics between the wars.

When an immigration judge ruled in 1942 that the Yemeni Ahmed Hassan—perhaps the first Arab Muslim to face the court (the others had been Arab Christians)—could not petition for citizenship, the community faced a setback. "Arabs are not white persons within the meaning of the [Immigration] Act," wrote Judge Arthur Tuttle, who heard Hassan's petition, citing Hassan's Muslim background as proof of his racial difference. "Apart from the dark skin of the Arabs," he explained, "it is well known that they are a part of the Mohammedan world and that a wide gulf separates their culture from that of the predominately [sic] Christian peoples of Europe."

Yet less than a year and a half later, the court changed its mind. In 1944, Mohamed Mohriez, "an Arab born in Sanhy, Badan, Arabia," who had been in the United States since 1921, succeeded in his case. Why the change? District Judge Charles E. Wyzanski explained. The "vital interest [of the United States] as a world power" required granting Mohriez's petition, wrote the judge, because it was now necessary "to promote friendlier relations between the United States and other nations and so as to fulfill the promise that we shall treat all men as created equal." Part of these warmer ties included a controversial aid package made in February 1943 under the Lend-Lease Act to Saudi Arabia, as the United States was now eager to secure access to [that] kingdom's massive oil reserves. In other words, as the United States assumed its leadership role on the world stage, the domestic understandings of America's racial-classification system and where Arabs fit within it altered alongside. The exigencies of international politics changed the supposedly immutable facts of the Arab "race," all within the span of seventeen months.

The decision was significant, but it had little effect on the Arab-American community, since immigration was still mostly a closed door until 1965. But when the immigration laws changed again in that year, abandoning the quota system that had favored European immigrants, the community grew substantially with new arrivals. . . . This is also a period when two other important things were happening in the United States: the civil-rights movement and, after 1967, the deepening role of the United States in the Middle East in the wake of the 1967 Arab-Israeli War. Now, unlike in the earlier periods of Arab-American history, it will be American foreign policy and its designs on the Middle East— and not America's domestic ethnic or racial hierarchies—that define the parameters of Arab American life. . . .

• • •

At least since the Second World War and especially since 1967, the United States has become progressively intertwined in the affairs of the Middle East. ("Whoever controls the Middle East controls access to three continents," counseled British ambassador Sir Oliver Franks to American officials in 1950.) But that involvement has been far from benign. For several long decades and through a series of security pacts, arms sales, military engagements, covert actions, and overt wars, the United States has followed a course that supported one dictatorial regime after another, sought control of the natural resources of the region, attempted to forge client states amenable to U.S. interests, and, with the cooperation of native elites, engaged in a policy of neorealist stability at the expense of the aspirations of the vast majority of people who live in the region. . . .

One can debate whether this history since 1967 constitutes an "imperial" or "hegemonic" posture of the United States concerning the Middle East. . . . But since the terrorist attacks of 2001, things have taken a decidedly imperial turn, culminating now in the direct military occupation of a major Arab country, an adventure labeled a "colonial war in the postcolonial age,"* by former national security adviser Zbigniew Brzezinski. And the political theorists of empire have repeatedly cautioned that the consequences of imperialism can reach far beyond the colony.

In the middle book of *The Origins of Totalitarianism*, titled *Imperialism*, Hannah Arendt explores the political history and implications of imperial rule, noting its bases of authority and actions in the world. She draws attention precisely to many of those pursuits and tactics of imperialism that confront us today: the establishment of penal colonies, the horrors of conquest, wild profiteering, colonial lawlessness, arbitrary and exceptional exercises of power, and the growth of racism along with its political exploitation. Arendt and others also have warned that in the long run imperialism tends not to be exercised solely in some blank, foreign space "out there" but has the dangerous capacity to return home and undermine the nation. She borrows this observation in part from the historian of the British Empire J. A. Hobson, who observed long ago that imperialism corrodes a nation's psyche and endangers its republican institutions. Arendt labels her caution the "boomerang effects" of imperialism.

The current erosion of domestic civil rights in the age of terror ought to be viewed through this lens. This is not only about the ways that torture has been normalized into American culture or how the moral questions raised by maintaining the penal colony at Guantánamo Bay cost the Republic's soul dearly. It is also about the specific ways that imperialism is boomeranging back directly to the home front. With the passage of the Military Commissions Act, for example, the concept of indefinite detentions—even of United States citizens—has now been enshrined into law. The government claims a national security exception in key legal cases and further employs the use of "secret evidence." Warrantless wiretapping is now legal and pervasive. The government's use of all these instruments of law has been detailed by others, most notably by the *Boston Globe's* Charlie Savage in his book *Takeover: The Return of the Imperial Presidency and the Subversion of American Democracy*. But each of them has been used before the "war on terror" on certain members of the Arab-American community, as the United States sought to impose its will over the Arab region. What we are currently living through is the slow creep of imperial high-handedness into the rest of American society, performed in the name of national security and facilitated through the growth of racist policies. This fact alone menaces the foundations of American society far beyond what has happened to Arab- and Muslim-American communities. "It is indeed a nemesis of Imperialism," writes Hobson, "that the arts and crafts of tyranny, acquired and exercised in our unfree Empire, should be turned against our liberties at home." . . .

---

*Ed.: Referring to the 2003 invasion of Iraq.

6 | Cookies
Bao Phi

For the holidays, our Lutheran sponsors used to give us a blue cookie tin. Within lay two layers of small hard cookies separated by little white paper cups with frilly edges. My five siblings and I, we'd fight over the round ones with sugar sprinkles. For Christmas my sister gave my daughter a box of shortbread cookies shaped like Scottish terriers. She wanted to share them with me, and they tasted so much like those cookies from our childhood I had to close my eyes and look away. Her five-year-old eyes track some commercial in which white men are playing at battle and she asks me about war. I want to tell her that her grandpa once told me how one of his friends on the front lines got hit in the side with a rocket while crawling out of a foxhole, and he had to pick up smoking pieces of him and put him into a cookie tin to send the remains to his family. I want to say that one of the few things my father showed me from Vietnam was a black-and-white photo of him and his brother; one day I will have to find a way to tell her how he was killed. Or my father will tell her, if he can bear to tell it in English. I want to say *I am made of war and that means so are you.* I want to say *I was born inside a halo of gunpowder. No—a silhouette of a circle left by an exploding bomb. No—a snake eating itself.* But instead I take a deep breath and begin to tell her, *Your Ông nội, he fought in a war, along with many others, and like many others he didn't want to. And that's why I am here and you are here. And that is why sometimes other people look at us and they don't know why we are here and sometimes that makes us feel like we don't know, either.* And like so many other times, I don't know how to end these truest of stories. At the end I say nothing; I just look into her eyes, wishing I could say *surviving all of this makes you tough.*

Bao Phi is the author of two volumes of poetry, *Sông I Sing* and *Thousand Star Hotel*, and the award-winning children's book *A Different Pond*.

7 Second Attempt Crossing

Javier Zamora

Editor's Note: Born in 1990 in the small fishing town of La Herradura, El Salvador, Javier Zamora migrated alone to the United States at the age of nine. His parents had fled to the U.S. when he was a small child (his father when he was just one year old, his mother when he was four), as part of the wave of migration during and after the Salvadoran civil war of 1980–1992. Zamora's first volume of poetry, *Unaccompanied*, explores his harrowing journey and the lasting impact of migration and a civil war in which the Salvadoran military government received significant U.S. funding.

Second Attempt Crossing

for Chino

In the middle of that desert that didn't look like sand
    and sand only,
in the middle of those acacias, whiptails, and coyotes, someone yelled
    "¡La Migra!"[1] and everyone ran.
In that dried creek where forty of us slept, we turned to each other,
    and you flew from my side in the dirt.

Black-throated sparrows and dawn
    hitting the tops of mesquites.
Against the herd of legs,

    you sprinted back toward me,
I jumped on your shoulders,
    and we ran from the white trucks, then their guns.

I said, "freeze, Chino, ¡pará por favor!"[2]

    So I wouldn't touch their legs that kicked you,
you pushed me under your chest,
    and I've never thanked you.

Javier Zamora is a Salvadoran American poet and activist. His work explores borderland politics, race, and the ways in which immigration and the Salvadoran civil war have impacted his family. He is a 2018–2019 Radcliffe Fellow at Harvard University.

Beautiful *Chino*—

>the only name I know to call you by—
farewell your tattooed chest: the M,
>the S, the 13.[3] Farewell
the phone number you gave me
>when you went east to Virginia,
and I went west to San Francisco.

>You called twice a month,
then your cousin said the gang you ran from
>in San Salvador
found you in Alexandria. Farewell
>your brown arms that shielded me then,
that shield me now, from La Migra.

NOTES

1. Immigration police.
2. "stop please!"
3. MS-13 is a transnational gang that originated in Los Angeles in the early 1980s. The tattoo denotes that Chino was inducted into the gang, from which he later fled.

8 For Many Latinos, Racial Identity Is More Culture Than Color

Mireya Navarro

Every decade, the Census Bureau spends billions of dollars and deploys hundreds of thousands of workers to get an accurate portrait of the American population. Among the questions on the census form is one about race, with 15 choices, including "some other race."

More than 18 million Latinos checked this "other" box in the 2010 census, up from 14.9 million in 2000. It was an indicator of the sharp disconnect between how Latinos view themselves and how the government wants to count them. Many Latinos argue that the country's race categories—indeed, the government's very conception of identity—do not fit them.

The main reason for the split is that the census categorizes people by race, which typically refers to a set of common physical traits. But Latinos, as a group in this country, tend to identify themselves more by their ethnicity, meaning a shared set of cultural traits, like language or customs.

So when they encounter the census, they see one question that asks them whether they identify themselves as having Hispanic ethnic origins and many answer it as their main identifier. But then there is another question, asking them about their race, because, as the census guide notes, "people of Hispanic, Latino or Spanish origin may be of any race," and more than a third of Latinos check "other."

This argument over identity has gained momentum with the growth of the Latino population, which in 2010 stood at more than 50 million. Census Bureau officials have acknowledged that the questionnaire has a problem and say they are wrestling with how to get more Latinos to pick a race. In 2010, they tested different wording in questions and last year [2011] they held focus groups, with a report on the research scheduled to be released by this summer.

Some experts say officials are right to go back to the drawing table. "Whenever you have people who can't find themselves in the question, it's a bad question," said Mary C. Waters, a sociology professor at Harvard who specializes in the challenges of measuring race and ethnicity.

Mireya Navarro joined the Brennan Center for Justice as a media strategist after a 27-year career as a staff writer for the *New York Times*. She has especially focused on social justice and was on the writing team that won a Pulitzer Prize in 2001 for the series "How Race is Lived in America."

The problem is more than academic—the census data on race serves many purposes, including determining the makeup of voting districts, and monitoring discriminatory practices in hiring and racial disparities in education and health. When respondents do not choose a race, the Census Bureau assigns them one, based on factors like the racial makeup of their neighborhood, inevitably leading to a less accurate count.

Latinos, who make up close to 20 percent of the American population, generally hold a fundamentally different view of race. Many Latinos say they are too racially mixed to settle on one of the government-sanctioned standard races—white, black, American Indian, Alaska native, native Hawaiian, and a collection of Asian and Pacific Island backgrounds.

Some regard white or black as separate demographic groups from Latino. Still others say Latinos are already the equivalent of another race in this country, defined by a shared set of challenges.

"The issues within the Latino community—language, immigration status—do not take into account race," said Peter L. Cedeño, 43, a lawyer and native New Yorker born to Dominican immigrants. "We share the same hurdles."

At a time when many multiracial Americans are proudly asserting their mixed-race identity, many Latinos, an overwhelmingly blended population with Indian, European, African and other roots, are sidestepping or ignoring questions of race.

Erica Lubliner, who has fair skin and green eyes—legacies of her Jewish father and her Mexican mother—said she was so "conflicted" about the race question on the census form that she left it blank.

Ms. Lubliner, a recent graduate of the medical school at the University of California, Los Angeles, in her mid-30s, was only 9 when her father died, and she grew up steeped in the language and culture of her mother. She said she has never identified with "the dominant culture of white." She believes her mother is a mix of white and Indian. "Believe me, I am not a confused person," she said. "I know who I am, but I don't necessarily fit the categories well."

Alejandro Farias, 23, from Brownsville, Tex., a supervisor for a freight company, sees himself simply as Latino. His ancestors came from the United States, Mexico and Portugal. When pressed, he checked "some other race."

"Race to me gets very confusing because we have so many people from so many races that make up our genealogical tree," he said.

Yet race matters. How Latinos identify themselves—and how the census counts them—affects the political clout of Latinos and other minority groups. Some studies have found that African-Latinos tend to be significantly more supportive of government-sponsored health care and much less supportive of the death penalty than Latinos who identify as white, a rift that is also found in the broader white and black populations.

This racial effect "weakens the political effectiveness of Latinos as a group," said Gary M. Segura, a political science professor at Stanford who has conducted some of the research.

A majority of Latinos identify themselves as white. Among them is Fiordaliza A. Rodriguez, 40, a New York lawyer who says she considers herself white because "I am light-skinned" and that is how she is viewed in her native Dominican Republic.

But she says there is no question that she is seen as different from the white majority in this country. Ms. Rodriguez recalled an occasion in a courtroom when a white lawyer assumed she was the court interpreter. She surmised the confusion had to do with ethnic stereotyping, "no matter how well you're dressed."

Some of the latest research, however, shows that many Latinos—like Irish and Italian immigrants before them—drop the Latino label to call themselves simply "white." A study published last year in the *Journal of Labor Economics* found that the parents of more than a quarter of third-generation children with Mexican ancestry do not identify their children as Latino on census forms.

Most of this ethnic attrition occurs among the offspring of parents or grandparents married to non-Mexicans, usually non-Hispanic whites. These Latinos tend to have high education, high earnings and high levels of English fluency. That means that many successful Latinos are no longer present in statistics tracking Latino economic and social progress across generations, hence many studies show little or no progress for third-generation Mexican immigrants, said Stephen J. Trejo, an economist at the University of Texas at Austin and co-author of the study.

And a more recent study by University of Southern California researchers found that more than two million people, or 6 percent of those who claimed any type of Latin American ancestry on census surveys, did not ultimately identify as Latino or Hispanic. The trend was more prevalent among those of mixed parentage who spoke only English and who identified as white, black or Asian when asked their race.

James Paine, whose father is half Mexican-American, said it never occurred to him to claim a Latino identity. Mr. Paine, 25, the owner of a real estate investment management company in La Jolla, Calif., spent summers with his Mexican-American aunt and attends his father's big family reunions every year (his mother is white of Irish and French descent). But he says he does not speak Spanish or live in a Latino neighborhood.

"If the question is 'What's your heritage?' I'd say Irish-Mexican," he said. "But the question is 'What are you?' and the answer is I'm white."

On the other side of the spectrum are black Latinos, who say they feel the sting of racism much the same as other blacks. A sense of racial pride has been emerging among many black Latinos who are now coming together in conferences and organizations.

Miriam Jimenez Roman, 60, a scholar on race and ethnicity in New York, says that issues like racial profiling of indigenous-looking and dark-skinned Latinos led her to appear in a 30-second public service announcement before the 2010 census encouraging Latinos of African descent to "check both: Latino and black." "When you sit on the subway, you just see a black person, and that's really what determines the treatment," she said. The 2010 census showed 1.2 million Latinos who identified as black, or 2.5 percent of the Hispanic population.

Over the decades, the Census Bureau has repeatedly altered how it asks the race question, and on the 2010 form, it added a sentence spelling out that "Hispanic origins are not races." The change helped steer 5 percent more Latinos away from "some other race," with the vast majority of those choosing the white category.

Still, critics of the census questionnaire say the government must move on from racial distinctions based on 18th-century binary thinking and adapt to Americans' sense of self.

But Latino political leaders say the risk in changing the questions could create confusion and lead some Latinos not to mark their ethnicity, shrinking the overall Hispanic numbers.

Ultimately, said Angelo Falcon, president of the National Institute for Latino Policy and chairman of the Census Advisory Committee on the Hispanic Population, this is not just a tussle over identity, it is a political battle, too.

"It comes down to what yields the largest numbers for which group," he said.

9 Black Ethnics: Race, Immigration, and the Pursuit of the American Dream

Christina M. Greer

A Theory of Black Elevated Minority Status

Before Barack Obama exploded onto the national political scene in 2004, the Republicans, as some may remember, were giddy with excitement over their own special potential candidate for the presidency. In 1992, Colin Powell's name was being thrown around as a possible running mate for then president George H. W. Bush, and in 1995, his name was mentioned as a possible GOP presidential candidate. Powell seemed to have stepped out of a GOP's dream. He was a general in the US Army, and for many whites, he transcended race. Not only had he been quoted on the record as saying, "I ain't that black" (Gates 1997: 84), but he seemed to be the antithesis of Jesse Jackson, the most recent serious black candidate for a party's nomination. Jackson had run for the Democratic nomination for presidency in 1984 and 1988 and was what many in white America viewed as a quintessential African American: descendant of US slavery and the South, a student of the Baptist preaching tradition, a product of a broken home, and a social agitator.[1] General Powell, for many, was a product of arguably one of the most established institutions of American patriotism. He was fair skinned, "articulate," a product of the US military, and a leader in what many viewed as a successful Gulf War. But Powell possessed something else that made him *special*: In the eyes of some of his supporters, he was not African American. For many, it was his Jamaican heritage that made him different, that explained his discipline, professional excellence, and supreme intellect.

Fast forward to 2008, when Barack Obama, the son of a man from Kenya and a woman from Kansas, captivated the hearts of so many Americans. Many of the same conversations began linking Obama and Powell as an ideal presidential candidate, despite not being *really* African American—that is, not a descendant of US slavery and therefore possessing a different relationship with America. I wondered if Obama would have been as attractive to American voters, white voters in particular, if his background were that of a man from Detroit and a woman from Duluth, or a man from Newark

---

Christina M. Greer is an associate professor of political science at Fordham University, where she focuses on American, ethnic, urban, and presidential politics. She is a frequent political commentator; produces and hosts *The Aftermath with Christina Greer*, a series of political commentary videos; and cohosts the podcast FAQ-NYC.

and a woman from Nebraska, or a man from Oakland and a woman from Omaha. You see where I am going with this line of thought. The subtle but significant message of his non–African American heritage was a variable both black and white voters initially discussed, debated, and ultimately digested. Many voters saw Obama as black, whether his dad was from Kenya or Kentucky. For some voters, when presented with ethnic diversity, Obama's lack of "authenticity" complicated their sense of racial attachment. For others, though, the comparisons to Jesse Jackson were endless. Whereas Jackson was portrayed as obsessed with race and racial politics, specifically black politics, Obama was presented as a "postracial" candidate. Obama had a racial identity that linked him to the black population, but he was different. For many, he did not have the same "racial baggage" as ninth-generation African Americans—the Jesse Jacksons of the world—thus begging the question, what does racial identity and ethnic distinction mean for blacks living in America? . . .

The Blurred Color Line

. . . Over one hundred years ago, caste systems were recognized as "natural" ways of organizing individuals in American society. Rigid castelike systems no longer exist in the United States, but a new type of caste system threatens the country today. It is not one imposed by overt white power subjugating people of color into slave and indentured servant positions; rather, the new caste system that now threatens American democracy comes from within the deeply seated mind-sets of those who were once held in subservient positions. This mind-set is even shared by newly arriving immigrants who possess a knowledge of America's past practices and who strive to position themselves as far from the "bottom" caste as possible. The modern-day caste struggle is most poignantly played out in some of the interactions between native-born black Americans and their black ethnic counterparts who understand the continued burden of the color line and the weight of race in the United States. . . .

At the core, all discussions of race and ethnicity for blacks in America must emphasize the duality that exists for these diverse groups of blacks. Afro-Caribbean and African immigrants living in America have experienced forms of oppression, racism, and subjugation as blacks, even by blacks. For example, residential segregation of blacks has often swiftly introduced black immigrant ethnic groups to the inequities still faced by blacks in the United States. However, this forced integration of native-born blacks and foreign-born blacks, due to segregation, has also produced tensions, mistrust, and competition among black groups (Kasinitz, Battle, and Miyares 2001; Massey and Denton 1988). The historically racist black-white paradigm has extended to black immigrants in many ways. However, this black-white paradigm has also manifested itself in more positive ways for foreign-born blacks. The historical racism and oppression in the United States seems to have either placed Afro-Caribbean and African populations with black Americans, both literally and symbolically, or have treated Afro-Caribbean and African immigrants as different, that is, harder working, smarter, and/or "better" than native-born blacks, what Rogers (2006) defines as "good blacks."

The understanding of race for black newcomers is that racial formation and construction is a largely unique phenomenon applicable to the United States. New immigrants may not easily or readily accept or adhere to the racial categories ascribed to them upon their arrival in the country and therefore cannot (or should not) be expected to automatically accept or identify with the larger black American racial category or group as a whole. Studies have documented Afro-Caribbean populations expressing disillusionment with assimilation in the United States and thereby becoming "black Americans" as opposed to just "Americans," like their white immigrant counterparts (Rogers 2000; Waters 1994; Foner 1987).[2] . . . Once black immigrants arrive in the United States, they become black American, not just American. The concepts of race, identity, and national origin have created a complex set of issues for the individual and for the larger group. . . .

Many immigrant groups share similar obstacles when arriving in the United States. Some scholars have argued that African and Caribbean immigrants may have more in common with other immigrants from across the globe than with native-born black Americans (Portes and Rumbaut 2001). First-generation black immigrants in the United States have faced overwhelming pressures to identify only as "blacks" (Kasinitz 1992; Foner 1987). In fact, they have been described as "invisible immigrants" (Bryce-Laporte 1972), because rather than being contrasted with other immigrants (for example, evaluating Jamaican successes as compared with Chinese), they have been compared most often to black Americans.[3] Because racial phenotype seems to link black ethnics into one racial group, can and will substantive coalitions form? Black groups are clearly grouped together in the United States. However, whether their fates are ultimately linked is part of a larger and constantly changing black ethnic puzzle.

Linked Fates and Coalition Building

Over the past several decades, significant strides have been made by blacks achieving educational success, attaining occupational advancements, and being incorporated into the middle class. However, dark skin is still correlated with poverty in the United States and throughout the globe (Segura and Rodrigues 2006); therefore, class position, societal status, and opportunities for political and economic advancement are in many ways racially assigned in the United States. Race is obviously a physical characteristic that has been used in this country to distinguish a certain group of people with similar phenotypes. This color distinction has led to widespread discrimination and inequities, as Rogers (2006) analyzed, thus lumping phenotypically similar individuals together based on outward identity, without accounting for the existence of differing self-identifications and belief systems.

The racial socialization of people of African descent living in the United States has had distinguishing effects on black populations, one of a "blended" cultural heritage (Larkey, Hecht, and Martin 1993) that emphasizes and connects to African ancestry and representation, as well as subjugation in American culture (Anglin and Whaley 2006). Due to shared skin color with native-born populations, foreign-born black phenotype serves as a basis for discrimination in America (Deaux et al. 2007).

New black immigrants also discover the inequities present in America and the subsequent negotiations with race and identity that directly affect their pursuits of becoming "American" without the mandatory modifier "black." For foreign-born blacks, their American status has a permanent "black" modifier attached to it. The permanent prefix aids in preventing native-born and foreign-born populations from attaining the same American incorporation experienced by . . . nonblack immigrants. Black racial classification has affected first- and second-generation black ethnics in that they did not experience the same processes of assimilation as previous white immigrant populations (Waters 1998; Kinder and Sanders 1996) . . . . Thus, black immigrants seek ways to reduce and possibly diminish the negative effects of the minority status imposed on their American status. It is because of this linking of black immigrants to native-born blacks that in-group fighting and competition decreases opportunities for substantive coalition building. As Afro-Caribbean and African black populations are occasionally promoted to elevated minority status over native-born black populations by whites, coalitional efforts are severely jeopardized and undermined within the larger black group. In that, one group is promoted and their interests are advanced at the expense and exclusion of others.[4] . . .

All of the Blacks Are American. All of the Immigrants Are Latino. But Some of Us Are . . . ?

Black Americans have largely been categorized in comparison to whites, based on region, political affiliation, class, and education levels. Segura and Rodrigues (2006: 376) argued that the "historical construction of a racial dynamic that is almost exclusively binary, i.e., black and white . . . [and] racial and ethnic interactions between Anglos and other minority groups are assumed to mimic—to some degree—the black-white experience." Simply put, Segura and Rodrigues argued that the "black-white paradigm is no longer sufficient to provide genuine understanding of the political circumstances and experiences of all nonwhite groups" (ibid.: 391). . . .

Several nonblack and nonwhite immigrant groups have expressed feelings of an "in-between" status in which they are "not Black but not White" (Perlmann and Waldinger 1997: 905) or "native born, and not black" (Cordero-Guzman, Smith, and Grosfoguel 2001: 6; Smith 1996). This in-between status for nonblack and nonwhite immigrants extends to black immigrants as well, thereby creating a complex duality in defining race, place, and status in American society.[5] Relationships pertaining to electoral behaviors, partisanship, group mobilization, and other group politics cannot necessarily easily translate into similar black immigrant experiences and relationships with whites and other nonblack populations (Leighley and Vedlitz 1999). According to the US census, the face of black America now includes over 1.5 million immigrants from African nations and over 3.5 million black immigrants from the Caribbean, representing close to 10 percent of the total black population (US Census Bureau 2010).

How blacks in America imagine and create black ethnic coalitions directly relates to how scholars can apply these multifaceted relationships to numerous other ethnic communities. The physical characteristics that seem to link native-born and immigrant blacks and the inequities of resources that continue to affect black peoples in America have led to what Bobo and Hutchings (1996) label as in-group superiorities, elements of ethnocentrism, and overall group hostilities. The limited access to larger political and economic goals creates intraracial tensions and resentments between native-born and newcomer populations. However, the competition among black groups jockeying for anything but last place in the social order has also created a link, bond, or even an understanding of the role of blackness in American society. Descriptive representation—that is, shared characteristics along racial and ethnic (and gender) lines—helps promote feelings of "solidarity, familiarity, and self-esteem among members of that respective group" (Junn and Masuoka 2008: 731; see also Dovi 2002; Mansbridge 2003; Pitkin 1967). The jockeying for economic and political placement in civil society is intraracial (between black ethnic groups) as well as extraracial (between other minority, immigrant, and ethnic groups). It is because of the systemic racism that has occurred, and (to the surprise of many black immigrants) still occurs, that a sense of black racial alliance can be measured. . . .

NOTES

1. This label was applied to Jackson for his many protests pertaining to civil rights, equal rights, corporate divestment from South Africa, housing equity, etc.
2. There is a host of literature that outlines how Jewish, Italian, Irish, and other white ethnic populations became "white." However, although their paths to incorporation may have begun with an identification with blacks during the early stages of assimilation, these immigrant groups were able to transcend ethnicity and identify racially, thus shedding light on the fluidity of ethnicity and the permanence of race. Whites are grouped into a homogeneous category. Sipress (1997:181) comments: "The 'whitening' of Irish-Americans provides an example of a marginal social group that embraced a racial identity to advance its own interests." The "whitening" of the Irish race is discussed by Ignatiev (1995: 1), who notes that "whites" are "those who partake of the privileges of the white skin in this society. Its most wretched members share a status higher, in certain respects, than that of the most exalted persons excluded from it." Similar assimilation tactics were used by Italian and Jewish immigrants in the nineteenth and twentieth centuries as well (Fears 2003). These ethnic groups often used party politics and coalition building to bridge the cultural divide (Logan 2003). However, the political inclusion, participation, and ultimate assimilation of Irish, Italian, and Jewish immigrants has also been largely due to the color line in America. Whereas these immigrants were not considered white at some point in time, the color line shifted, and inclusion followed suit. [For a discussion of such a shift in the color line, see "How Jews Became White Folks, and What That Says About Race in America," by Karen Brodkin, in Part I of this volume.]
3. Multiracial coalitions primarily focus on the issues of racial and ethnic equality (Hochschild and Rogers 2000). However, this emphasis on equality in the face of diverse histories and negotiations with assimilation and incorporation often lead[s] to groups fragmenting into competitive factions. Thus, biracial and multiracial coalitions are thought to be unattainable due to past political disagreements, individual attitudes about other groups, and fears among minority groups within the larger group (Tedin and Murray 1994). Intraracial distrust exists among black ethnic populations and has thus contributed to ethnic factions and decreased rates of collective actions (Okamoto 2003). However, possibilities for coalition building will still be greater among groups with a shared racial classification even if cross-racial migratory narratives may appear more similar. See also Hochschild, Weaver, and Burch 2012.

4. Betancur and Gills (2000) also argue that coalitional efforts are undermined when influential leaders advance only the interests of one group to the exclusion of others. This is most clearly demonstrated in Miami when observing the NAACP and the loss of significant numbers of members of Haitian descent. The defection of Haitian members from the NAACP as well as the National Urban League signaled a disconnect between the black American leadership and predominantly black American membership within these two organizations, and a small but growing population who felt their needs and wants (i.e., increased attention to international issues, specifically issues affecting Haitians both in Haiti and in Florida) were not being addressed by the organization elite.

5. Okamoto (2003) argued that the construction of pan-ethnic boundaries and a pan-ethnic identity affect collective action efforts. Similarly, Padilla (1985) stated that differences in language, culture, and immigration histories also affect organizing capabilities and understandings of a common fate.

REFERENCES

Anglin, Deidre M., and Arthur L. Whaley. 2006. Racial/Ethnic Self-labeling in Relation to Group Socialization and Identity in African-Descended Individuals. *Journal of Language and Social Psychology* 25, no. 4 (December): 457–63.

Betancur, John Jairo, and Doug Gills. 2000. *The Collaborative City: Opportunities and Struggles for Blacks and Latinos in U.S. Cities.* Garland Reference Library of Social Science, vol. 1461. New York: Garland.

Bobo, Lawrence, and Vincent L. Hutchings. 1996. Perceptions of Racial Group Competition: Extending Blumer's Theory of Group Position to a Multiracial Social Context. *American Sociological Review* 61, no. 6 (December): 951–72.

Bryce-Laporte, Roy Simon. 1972. Black Immigrants: The Experience of Invisibility and Inequality. *Journal of Black Studies* 3 (September): 29–56.

Cordero-Guzmán, Héctor R., Robert C. Smith, and Ramón Grosfoguel. 2001. *Migration, Transnationalization, and Race in a Changing New York.* Philadelphia: Temple University Press.

Deaux, Kay, Nida Bikmen, Alwyn Gilkes, Ana Ventuneac, Yvanne Joseph, Yasser Payne, and Claude Steele. 2007. Becoming American: Stereotype Threat Effects in Afro-Caribbean Immigrant Groups. *Social Psychology Quarterly* 70, no. 4: 384–404.

Dovi, Suzanne. 2002. Preferable Descriptive Representatives: Will Just Any Woman, Black, or Latino Do? *American Political Science Review* 96, no. 4 (December): 729–43.

Fears, Darryl. 2003. Disparity Marks Black Ethnic Groups, Report Says. *Washington Post*, March 9.

Foner, Nancy. 1987. The Jamaicans: Race and Ethnicity among Migrants in New York City. In *New Immigrants in New York*, ed. Nancy Foner. New York: Columbia University Press.

Gates, Henry L. 1997. *Thirteen Ways of Looking at a Black Man.* New York: Vintage Books.

Hochschild, J., and R. Rogers. 2000. Race Relations in a Diversifying Nation. In *New Directions: African Americans in a Diversifying Nation*, edited by James S. Jackson. Ann Arbor: University of Michigan.

Ignatiev, Noel. 1995. *How the Irish Became White.* New York: Routledge.

Junn, Jane, and Natalie Masuoka. 2008. Asian American Identity: Shared Racial Status and Political Context. *Perspectives on Politics* 6, no. 4: 729–40.

Kasinitz, Philip. 1992. *Caribbean New York: Black Immigrants and the Politics of Race.* Ithaca, NY: Cornell University Press.

Kasinitz, Philip, Juan Battle, and Ines Miyares. 2001. Fade to Black?: The Children of West Indian Immigrants in South Florida. In *Ethnicities: Coming of Age in Immigrant America*, edited by Alejandro Portes and Ruben Rumbaut, 267–300. Berkeley: Russell Sage Foundation and the University of California Press.

Kinder, Donald R., and Lynn M. Sanders. 1996. *Divided by Color: Racial Politics and Democratic Ideals.* Chicago: University of Chicago Press.

Larkey, L. K., M. L. Hecht, and Judith Martin. 1993. What's in a Name? African American Ethnic Identity Terms and Self-Determination. *Journal of Language and Social Psychology* 12, no. 4: 302–17.

Leighley, Jan E., and Arnold Vedlitz. 1999. Race, Ethnicity, and Political Participation: Competing Models and Contrasting Explanations. *Journal of Politics* 61, no. 4 (November): 1092–1114.

Logan, John R. 2003, July. How Race Counts for Hispanic Americans. Retrieved June 15, 2006, from http://mumford1.dyndns.org/cen2000/BlackLatinoReport/BlackLatino01.htm.

Mansbridge, Jane. 2003. Rethinking Representation. *American Political Science Review* 97, no. 4: 515–28.

———. 1999. Should Blacks Represent Blacks and Women Represent Women? A Contingent "Yes." *Journal of Politics* 61, no. 3 (August): 628–57.

Massey, Douglas S., and Nancy A. Denton. 1988. The Dimensions of Residential Segregation. *Social Forces* 67, no. 2: 281–315.

Padilla, Felix. 1985. *Latino Ethnic Consciousness: The Case of Mexican Americans and Puerto Ricans in Chicago.* Notre Dame, IN: University of Notre Dame Press.

Perlmann, Joel, and Roger Waldinger. 1997. Second Generation Decline? Children of Immigrants, Past and Present—A Reconsideration. *International Migration Review* 31, no. 4 (Winter): 893–922.

Pitkin, Hanna. 1967. *The Concept of Political Representation.* Berkeley: University of California Press.

Portes, Alejandro, and Rubén G. Rumbaut. 2001. *Legacies: The Story of the Immigrant Second Generation.* New York: Russell Sage Foundation.

Portes, Alejandro, and Alex Stepick. 1993. *City on the Edge: The Transformation of Miami.* Berkeley: University of California Press.

Rogers, Reuel Reuben. 2006. *Afro-Caribbean Immigrants and the Politics of Incorporation: Ethnicity, Exception, or Exit.* New York: Cambridge University Press.

———. 2000. Afro-Caribbean Immigrants, African Americans, and the Politics of Group Identity. In *Black and Multiracial Politics in America*, edited by Yvette M. Alex-Assensoh and Lawrence J. Hanks, 15–59. New York: New York University Press.

Segura, Gary M., and Helena Alves Rodrigues. 2006. Comparative Ethnic Politics in the United States: Beyond Black and White. *Annual Review of Political Science* 9: 375–95.

Sipress, Joel M. 1997. Relearning Race: Teaching Race as a Cultural Construction. *History Teacher* 30, no. 2 (February): 175–85.

Smith, Robert C. 1996. Mexicans in New York City: Membership and Incorporation of New Immigrant Groups. In *Latinos in New York: Communities in Transition*, edited by Gabriel Haslip-Viera and Sherrie L. Baver. Notre Dame, IN: University of Notre Dame Press.

Tedin, Kent L., and Richard W. Murray. 1994. Support for Biracial Political Coalitions among Blacks and Hispanics. *Social Science Quarterly* 75, no. 4: 772–89.

Waters, Mary C. 1998. Multiple Ethnic Identity Choices. In *Beyond Pluralism: The Conception of Groups and Group Identities in America*, edited by Wendy F. Katkin, Ned Landsman, and Andrea Tyree, 28–46. Urbana: University of Illinois Press.

———. 1994. Ethnic and Racial Identities of Second-Generation Black Immigrants in New York City. *International Migration Review* 28, no. 4 (Winter): 795–820.

10 The Myth of the Model Minority

Noy Thrupkaew

Mali Keo fled Cambodia with her husband and four children in 1992. Several years later, she was still haunted by searing memories of "the killing fields," the forced-labor camps where millions of Cambodians died, victims of Communist despot Pol Pot's quest for a perfect agrarian society. Because of the brutal beatings she suffered at the hands of Pol Pot's Khmer Rouge, she was still wracked with physical pain as well. Traumatized and ailing, uneducated, unskilled, and speaking very little English, Mali Keo (a pseudonym assigned by researchers) could barely support her children after her husband abandoned the family.

And now she may not even have public assistance to fall back on, because the 1996 welfare-reform act cut off most federal benefits to immigrants and subsequent amendments have not entirely restored them. In what was supposed to be the land of her salvation, Mali Keo today is severely impoverished. Living in a hard-pressed neighborhood of Philadelphia, she struggles with only mixed success to keep her children out of trouble and in school.

The Southeast Asia Resource Action Center (SEARAC), an advocacy group in Washington, estimates that more than 2.2 million Southeast Asians now live in the United States. They are the largest group of refugees in the country and the fastest-growing minority. Yet for most policy makers, the plight of the many Mali Keos has been overshadowed by the well-known success of the Asian immigrants who came before and engendered the myth of the "model minority." Indeed, conservatives have exploited this racial stereotype—arguing that Asians fare well in the United States because of their strong "family values" and work ethic. These values, they say, and not government assistance, are what all minorities need in order to get ahead.

Paradoxically, Southeast Asians—supposedly part of the model minority—may be suffering most from the resulting public policies. They have been left in the hands of underfunded community-assistance programs and government agencies that, in one example of well-intentioned incompetence, churn out forms in Khmer and Lao for often illiterate populations. But fueled by outrage over bad services and a fraying social safety-net, Southeast Asian immigrants have started to embrace that most American of activities,

---

Noy Thrupkaew is an independent journalist who researches human trafficking and labor exploitation. She has reported from Burma, Thailand, Cambodia, Vietnam, Iran, Morocco, and Cuba, and written for outlets including *The New York Times*, *The Washington Post*, *The Guardian*, *National Geographic*, *The Nation*, Radio Netherlands, Reveal Radio, and *Marie Claire*.

Reprinted with permission from *The American Prospect*, vol. 13, no. 7, April 8, 2002. The American Prospect, 11 Beacon Street, Suite 1120, Boston, MA 02108. All rights reserved.

political protest—by pushing for research on their communities, advocating for their rights, and harnessing their political power.

The model-minority myth has persisted in large part because political conservatives are so attached to it. "Asian Americans have become the darlings of the right," said Frank Wu, a law professor at Howard University and the author of *Yellow: Race beyond Black and White*. "The model-minority myth and its depiction of Asian-American success tells a reassuring story about our society working."

The flip side is also appealing to the right. Because Asian Americans' success stems from their strong families and their dedication to education and hard work, conservatives say, then the poverty of Latinos and African Americans must be explained by their own "values": They are poor because of their nonmarrying, school-skipping, and generally lazy and irresponsible behavior, which government handouts only encourage.

The model-minority myth's "racist love," as author Frank Chin terms it, took hold at a sensitive point in U.S. history: after the 1965 Watts riots and the immigration reforms of that year, which selectively allowed large numbers of educated immigrants into the United States. Highly skilled South and East Asian nurses, doctors, and engineers from countries like India and China began pouring into the United States just as racial tensions were at a fever pitch.

Shortly thereafter, articles like "Success Story of One Minority in the U.S.," published by *U.S. News & World Report* in 1966, trumpeted: "At a time when it is being proposed that hundreds of billions be spent to uplift Negroes and other minorities, the nation's 300,000 Chinese Americans are moving ahead on their own, with no help from anyone else." *Newsweek* in 1971 had Asian Americans "outwhiting the whites." And *Fortune* in 1986 dubbed them a "superminority." As Wu caricatures the model-minority myth in his book:

> Asian Americans vindicate the American Dream. . . . They are living proof of the power of the free market and the absence of racial discrimination. Their good fortune flows from individual self-reliance and community self-sufficiency, not civil-rights activism or government welfare benefits.

A closer look at the data paints another picture, however. If Asian-American households earn more than whites, statistics suggest, it's not because their individual earnings are higher but because Asian Americans live in larger households, with more working adults. In fact, a recent University of Hawaii study found that "most Asian Americans are overeducated compared to whites for the incomes they earn"—evidence that suggests not "family values" but market discrimination.

What most dramatically skews the data, though, is the fact that about half the population of Asian (or, more precisely, Asian–Pacific Islander) Americans is made up of the highly educated immigrants who began arriving with their families in the 1960s. The plight of refugees from Cambodia, Laos, and Vietnam, who make up less than 14 percent of Asian Americans, gets lost in the averaging. Yet these refugees, who started arriving in the United States after 1975, differ markedly from the professional-class Chinese and Indian immigrants who started coming 10 years earlier. The Southeast Asians were fleeing wartime persecution and had few resources. And those disadvantages have had devastating effects on their lives in the United States. The most recent census data available show that 47 percent of Cambodians, 66 percent of Hmong (an ethnic group that lived in the mountains of Laos), 67 percent of Laotians, and 34 percent of Vietnamese were impoverished in 1990—compared with 10 percent of all Americans and 14 percent of all Asian Americans. Significantly, poverty rates among Southeast Asian Americans were much higher than those of even the "nonmodel" minorities: 21 percent of African Americans and 23 percent of Latinos were poor.

Yet despite the clear inaccuracies created by lumping population[s] together, the federal government still groups Southeast Asian refugees under the overbroad category of "Asian" for research and funding purposes. "We've labored under the shadow of this model myth for so long," said Ka Ying Yang, SEARAC's executive director. "There's so little research on us, or we're lumped in with all other Asians, so people don't know the specific needs and contributions of our communities."

To get a sense of those needs, one has to go back to the beginning of the Southeast Asian refugees' story and the circumstances that forced their migration. In 1975, the fall of Saigon sent shock waves throughout Southeast Asia, as communist insurgents toppled U.S.-supported governments in Vietnam and Cambodia. In Laos, where the CIA had trained and funded the Hmong to fight Laotian and Vietnamese communists as U.S. proxies, the communists who took over vowed to purge the country of ethnic Hmong and punish all others who had worked with the U.S. government.

The first refugees to leave Southeast Asia tended to be the most educated and urban, English-speakers with close connections to the U.S. government. One of them was a man who wishes to be identified by the pseudonym John Askulraskul. He spent two years in a Laotian re-education camp—punishment for his ability to speak English, his having been educated, and, most of all, his status as a former employee of the United States Agency for International Development (USAID).

"They tried to brainwash you, to subdue you psychologically, to work you to death on two bowls of rice a day," Askulraskul told me recently.

After being released, he decided to flee the country. He, his sister, and his eldest daughter, five and a half years old, slipped into the Mekong River with a few others. Clinging to an inflated garbage bag, Askulraskul swam alongside their boat out of fear that his weight would sink it.

After they arrived on the shores of Thailand, Askulraskul and his daughter were placed in a refugee camp, where they waited to be reunited with his wife and his two other daughters.

It was not to be.

"My wife tried to escape with two small children. But my daughters couldn't make it"—he paused, drawing a ragged breath—"because the boat sank."

Askulraskul's wife was swept back to Laos, where she was arrested and placed in jail for a month. She succeeded in her next escape attempt, rejoining her suddenly diminished family.

Eventually, with the help of his former boss at USAID, they moved to Connecticut, where Askulraskul found work helping to resettle other refugees. His wife, who had been an elementary-school teacher, took up teaching English as a second language (ESL) to Laotian refugee children. His daughter adjusted quickly and went to school without incident.

Askulraskul now manages a project that provides services for at-risk Southeast Asian children and their families. "The job I am doing now is not only a job," he said. "It is part of my life and my sacrifice. My daughter is 29 now, and I know raising kids in America is not easy. I cannot save everybody, but there is still something I can do."

Like others among the first wave of refugees, Askulraskul considers himself one of the lucky ones. His education, U.S. ties, and English-language ability—everything that set off the tragic chain of events that culminated in his daughters' deaths—proved enormously helpful once he was in the United States.

But the majority of refugees from Southeast Asia had no such advantages. Subsequent waves frequently hailed from rural areas and lacked both financial resources and formal schooling. Their psychological scars were even deeper than the first group's, from their longer years in squalid refugee camps or the killing fields. The ethnic Chinese who began arriving from Vietnam had faced harsh discrimination as well, and the Amerasians—the children of Vietnamese women and U.S. soldiers—had lived for years as pariahs.

Once here, these refugees often found themselves trapped in poverty, providing low-cost labor, and receiving no health or other benefits, while their lack of schooling made decent jobs almost impossible to come by. In 1990, two-thirds of Cambodian, Laotian, and Hmong adults in America had less than a high-school education—compared with 14 percent of whites, 25 percent of African Americans, 45 percent of Latinos, and 15 percent of the general Asian-American population. Before the welfare-reform law cut many of them off, nearly 30 percent of Southeast Asian Americans were on welfare—the highest participation rate of any ethnic group. And having such meager incomes, they usually lived in the worst neighborhoods, with the attendant crime, gang problems, and poor schools.

But shouldn't the touted Asian dedication to schooling have overcome these disadvantages, lifting the refugees' children out of poverty and keeping them off the streets? Unfortunately, it didn't. "There is still a high number of dropouts for Southeast Asians," Yang said. "And if they do graduate, there is a low number going on to higher education."

Their parents' difficulty in navigating American school systems may contribute to the problem. "The parents' lack of education leads to a lack of role models and guidance. Without those things, youth can turn to delinquent behavior and in some very extreme cases, gangs, instead of devoting themselves to education," said Narin Sihavong, director of SEARAC's Successful New Americans Project, which interviewed Mali Keo. "This underscores the need for Southeast Asian school administrators or counselors who can be role models, ease the cultural barrier, and serve as a bridge to their parents."

"Sometimes families have to choose between education and employment, especially when money is tight," said Porthira Chimm, a former SEARAC project director. "And unfortunately, immediate money concerns often win out."

The picture that emerges—of high welfare participation and dropout rates, low levels of education and income—is startlingly similar to the situation of the poorest members of "nonmodel" minority groups. Southeast Asians, Latinos, and African Americans also have in common significant numbers of single-parent families. Largely as a result of the killing fields, nearly a quarter of Cambodian households are headed by single women. Other Southeast Asian families have similar stories. Sihavong's mother, for example, raised him and his five siblings on her own while his father was imprisoned in a Laotian re-education camp.

No matter how "traditional" Southeast Asians may be, they share the fate of other people of color when they are denied access to good education, safe neighborhoods, and jobs that provide a living wage and benefits. But for the sake of preserving the model-minority myth, conservative policy makers have largely ignored the needs of Southeast Asian communities.

One such need is for psychological care. Wartime trauma and "lack of English proficiency, acculturative stress, prejudice, discrimination, and racial hate crimes" place Southeast Asians "at risk for emotional and behavioral problems," according to the U.S. surgeon general's 2001 report on race and mental health. One random sample of Cambodian adults found that 45 percent had post-traumatic stress disorder and 51 percent suffered from depression.

John Askulraskul's past reflects trauma as well, but his education, English-language ability, and U.S. connections helped level the playing field. Less fortunate refugees need literacy training and language assistance. They also need social supports like welfare and strong community-assistance groups. But misled by the model-minority myth, many government agencies seem to be unaware that Southeast Asians require their services, and officials have done little to find these needy refugees or accommodate them. Considering that nearly two-thirds of Southeast Asians say they do not speak English very well and more than 50 percent live in linguistically isolated ethnic enclaves, the lack of outreach and translators effectively denies them many public services.

The problem extends beyond antipoverty programs, as Mali Keo's story illustrates. After her husband left her, she formed a relationship with another man and had two more children. But he beat the family for years, until she asked an organization that served Cambodian refugees to help her file a restraining order. If she had known that a shelter was available, she told her interviewer, even one without Khmer-speaking counselors, she would have escaped much earlier.

Where the government hasn't turned a blind eye, it has often wielded an iron fist. The welfare-reform law of 1996, which cut off welfare, SSI, and food-stamp benefits for most noncitizens—even those who are legal permanent residents—sent Southeast Asian communities into an uproar. Several elderly Hmong in California committed suicide, fearing that they would become burdens to their families. Meanwhile, the lack of literacy programs prevented (and still does prevent) many refugees from passing the written test that would gain them citizenship and the right to public assistance.

"We achieved welfare reform on the backs of newcomers," Frank Wu said. "People said that 'outsiders' don't have a claim to the body politic, and even liberals say we should care for 'our own' first." Few seemed to ask the question posed by sociologist Donald Hernandez: "What responsibility do we have to ensure a basic standard of living for immigrants who have fled their countries as a result of the American government's economic, military, and political involvement there?"

But welfare reform also had a second effect. "It was such a shocking event, it completely galvanized the Southeast Asian community," said Karen Narasaki, executive director of the National Asian Pacific American Legal Consortium. "In different Asian cultures, you have 'the crab who crawls out of the bucket gets pulled back' [and] 'the nail that sticks out gets pounded down.' But in the United States, 'the squeaky wheel gets the grease,' and people had to learn that."

The learning process has been a difficult one. At first, because of their past negative experiences with the United States and their homeland governments, many Southeast Asians feared political involvement. Many saw themselves as noncitizens and second-class "outsiders" with a precarious standing in the United States. But as they have grown more familiar with this country, even noncitizens have started to think of themselves less as refugees in a temporary home and more as "new Americans" who are entitled to shape their destinies through political engagement.

The energy for this new activism grew out of the mutual-assistance associations (MAAs) that have taken root in various Southeast Asian communities. Primarily staffed by people like Askulraskul—the more successful members of the ethnic groups they serve—MAAs form the backbone of support for Southeast Asians, providing, among many other things, child care, job training, school liaisons, and assistance with navigating government bureaucracies.

But the MAAs are facing problems of their own. The funding they used to get from the federal Office of Refugee Resettlement is dwindling. In 1996 new federal guidelines mandated that these funds go exclusively to organizations serving the most recent refugees. (In response, several Southeast Asian MAAs have tried to stay afloat by offering their services to newer refugees from places like Ethiopia and Iraq.) As for outside funding, only 0.3 percent of all philanthropic aid goes to groups that work specifically with Asian-American populations, according to the 1998 edition of *Foundation Giving*. "A lot of people in philanthropy think [that Asians] are doing so well, they don't need help," Narasaki said.

Despite these problems, MAAs and national advocacy organizations like SEARAC have won limited restorations of benefits and food stamps for immigrants. And a significant victory came in 2000, when legislation sponsored by Minnesota Senator Paul Wellstone was adopted: It will allow Hmong veterans—or their widows—from America's "secret war" in Laos to take the U.S. citizenship test in Hmong, with a translator.

One key to the MAAs' success is their networking with other minority-advocacy groups, says Sandy Dang, executive director of Asian American LEAD, an organization based in Washington, that provides a range of services for Vietnamese Americans, including ESL classes, youth mentoring, and parent-support groups.

When Dang founded the organization, she didn't know how to write grant proposals, so she asked the director of a nearby youth center for Latin Americans to provide guidance. "The Latino organizations have a lot of empathy for people starting out," she said. "They understand the refugee-immigrant experience.

"Disadvantaged people share a lot in common," Dang continued, "and we have to help each other. People who are empowered in this country like to play us off each other, like with the model-minority myth. They need the poor and disadvantaged to fight each other. Because if we unite, we can make it difficult for them."

Southeast Asians are disproving the model-minority myth not just with their difficult lives but with their growing insistence that it takes more than "traditional values" and "personal responsibility" to survive in this country. It takes social supports and participation in the legacy of civil rights activism as well.

The refugees and their children are forging their identities as new Americans and are starting to emerge as a political force. At first, Yang said, "we had no time to think about anything else but our communities—and no one was thinking about us. But now we know that what we were grappling with [affects both] me and my neighbor, who might be poor black, Latino, or Asian. We are no longer refugees, we are Americans. And we know what being 'successful' is: It's being someone who is truly aware of the meaning of freedom to speak out."

PART III

SUGGESTIONS FOR FURTHER READING

Ancheta, Angelo N. *Race, Rights, and the Asian American Experience*. Rutgers University Press, 2006.

Cacho, Lisa Marie. *Social Death: Racialized Rightlessness and the Criminalization of the Unprotected*. New York University Press, 2012.

Canaday, Margot. *The Straight State: Sexuality and Citizenship in Twentieth-Century America*. Princeton University Press, 2009.

Chang, Grace. *Disposable Domestics: Immigrant Women Workers in the Global Economy*, 2nd ed. Haymarket Books, 2016.

Chávez, Karma R. *Queer Migration Politics: Activist Rhetoric and Coalitional Possibilities*. University of Illinois Press, 2013.

Chomsky, Aviva. *Undocumented: How Immigration Became Illegal*. Beacon Press, 2016.

Foner, Nancy. *New Immigrants in New York*. Columbia University Press, 2001.

Fox, Geoffrey F. *Hispanic Nation: Culture, Politics, and the Constructing of Identity*. University of Arizona Press, 1997.

Glenn, Evelyn Nakano. *Unequal Freedom: How Race and Gender Shaped American Citizenship*. Harvard University Press, 2014.

Greer, Christina. *Black Ethnics: Race, Immigration, and the Pursuit of the American Dream*. Oxford University Press, 2013.

Lee, Erika, and Judy Yung. *Angel Island: Immigrant Gateway to America*. Oxford University Press, 2010.

Lee, Jennifer, and Min Zhou. *The Asian American Achievement Paradox*. Russell Sage Foundation, 2015.

Lee, Stacey J. *Unraveling the "Model Minority" Stereotype: Listening to Asian American Youth*, 2nd ed. Teachers College Press, 2009.

Luibheid, Eithne, and Lionel Cantú, eds. *Queer Migrations: Sexuality, U.S. Citizenship, and Border Crossings*. University of Minnesota Press, 2005.

Macías-Rojas, Patrisia. *From Deportation to Prison: The Politics of Immigration Enforcement in Post-Civil Rights America*. New York University Press, 2016.

Morales, Ed. *Living in Spanglish: The Search for Latino Identity in America*. New York: St. Martin's Press, 2003.

Ngai, Mae M. *Impossible Subjects: Illegal Aliens and the Making of Modern America*. Princeton University Press, 2005.

Pastor, Manuel. *State of Resistance: What California's Dizzying Descent and Remarkable Resurgence Mean for America's Future*. The New Press, 2018.

Pedraza, Silvia, and Rubén G. Rumbaut. *Origins and Destinies: Immigration, Race, and Ethnicity in America*. Wadsworth, 1995.

Pinder, Sherrow O. *The Politics of Race and Ethnicity in the United States: Americanization, De-Americanization, and Racialized Ethnic Groups*. Palgrave Macmillan, 2010.

Portes, Alejandro, and Rubén G. Rumbaut. *Legacies: The Story of the Immigrant Second Generation*. University of California Press, 2001.

Prashad, Vijay. *The Karma of Brown Folk*. University of Minnesota Press, 2001.

Prashad, Vijay. *Uncle Swami: South Asians in America Today*. The New Press, 2012.

Roediger, David R. *Working Toward Whiteness: How America's Immigrants Became White: The Strange Journey from Ellis Island to the Suburbs.* Basic Books, 2005.

Schmid, Carol L. *The Politics of Language: Conflict, Identity, and Cultural Pluralism in Comparative Perspective.* Oxford University Press, 2001.

Schmidt, Ronald, Sr. *Language Policy and Identity Politics in the United States.* Temple University Press, 2000.

Smith, Andrea. *Conquest: Sexual Violence and American Indian Genocide.* South End Press, 2005.

Sniderman, Paul M., and Thomas Piazza. *Black Pride, Black Prejudice.* Princeton University Press, 2002.

Suárez-Orozco, Marcelo M., and Mariela M. Páez, eds. *Latinos: Remaking America.* University of California Press, 2008.

Treitler, Vilna Bashi. *The Ethnic Project: Transforming Racial Fiction into Ethnic Factions.* Stanford University Press, 2013.

Tuan, Mia. *Forever Foreigners or Honorary Whites? The Asian Ethnic Experience Today.* Rutgers University Press, 1999.

Villalón, Roberta. *Violence Against Latina Immigrants: Citizenship, Inequality and Community.* New York University Press, 2010.

Waldinger, Roger. *Strangers at the Gates: New Immigrants in Urban America.* University of California Press, 2001.

PART
IV

Discrimination in Everyday Life

Today, the political fanfare and the vehement, racialized rhetoric regarding crime and drugs are no longer necessary. Mass incarceration has been normalized, and all of the racial stereotypes and assumptions that gave rise to the system are now embraced (or at least internalized) by people of all colors, from all walks of life, and in every major political party. . . . It is simply taken for granted that, in cities like Baltimore and Chicago, the vast majority of young black men are currently under the control of the criminal justice system or branded criminals for life. This extraordinary circumstance—unheard of in the rest of the world—is treated here in America as a basic fact of life, as normal as separate water fountains were just a half century ago.
—MICHELLE ALEXANDER

The systems of oppression we have been studying—racism, sexism, heterosexism, and class privilege—express themselves in everyday life in a variety of ways. Sometimes they are reflected in the attitudes that people carry with them into the workplace or the community. Sometimes they emerge in racist, sexist, or homophobic utterances that reach us across the playground or through social media. Sometimes they erupt in acts of harassment or even in violence against targeted groups (all too often, fatal violence). They are also deeply embedded in the discriminatory policies and practices of government and business. As the writers in Part IV demonstrate, discrimination is more than just overt individual acts of interpersonal hostility. The selections in this part also reveal the pervasive underlying patterns of institutional and structural oppression and discrimination, often carefully masked as neutral policies. As Michelle Alexander notes in Selection 3, extraordinary disparities are often treated "as a basic fact of life, as normal as separate water fountains were just a half century ago." Alexander and the other writers in this part seek to challenge that sense of normality and to open our eyes to everyday discrimination.

Selection 1 is an excerpt from a report issued by the U.S. Commission on Civil Rights on diverse forms of discrimination in U.S. society. It offers some categories and distinctions that will prove useful in thinking about the selections that follow. According to this report, discrimination can take many forms, some easier to see than others. It can exist at the level of *individual* attitudes and behavior, as when guidance counselors make racist, classist, or sexist assumptions about students or when real estate agents steer clients of color away from white neighborhoods; or it can be carried out through the routine application of the rules, policies, and practices of *organizations* when they unfairly exclude certain applicants and favor others; and it can be carried out through the day-to-day, unexamined practices of schools, government agencies, the media, and manifold other institutions, resulting in *structural* discrimination—that is, discrimination pervasive enough to be regarded as part of the basic structure of our society. "Structural discrimination" is not just pervasive, but it is also an interlocking system in which discrimination in one area—for example, education—leads to discrimination in other areas, such as employment and housing, creating a cycle of discrimination and disadvantage from which it is difficult to break free.

As the selections in Part IV make clear, discrimination of every type is a fact of life in every area of contemporary U.S. society. Why, then, would anyone believe that racism and sexism are largely things of the past? Perhaps this belief is based on the mistaken notion that whether a word, an act, a rule, or a policy is discriminatory can be determined by examining the stated motives of individuals or institutions rather than by seeing and understanding the effects on those who are impacted. In Part II, authors Beverly Daniel Tatum, Ian Haney López, and Eduardo Bonilla-Silva laid the groundwork for a more complex understanding of systems of advantage and disadvantage. As Haney-López wrote, discrimination is not merely found in the "spittle-laced epithets of the angry bigot." He highlights "strategic racism," the calculated deployment of coded racial appeals for political gain. As the members of the U.S. Civil Rights Commission reiterate in Selection 1, even superficially "gender-neutral" or "color blind" organizational practices can place women of all races and men of color at a disadvantage. Even those of us who firmly believe we are not bigots can reinforce heterosexism, racism, sexism, and class privilege through our unconscious mindsets and automatic behaviors and in the operation of our workplaces and community spaces. Interlocking systems of oppression and the advantages and disadvantages they create are part of our history and part of everyday life. Learning to recognize discrimination is an essential prerequisite for acting to end it.

In Selection 2, Vann R. Newkirk II addresses patterns of voter suppression that have had and continue to have a profound impact on U.S. elections. Ostensibly race-neutral policies—including voter purges, voter ID laws, and polling place changes—all have a disparate impact on people of color and poor people, a disparate impact that can often be seen as the conscious goal of the officials behind the policies. Newkirk cites the Supreme Court's 2013 decision in *Shelby County v. Holder* (excerpted in Part VII of this volume), which blocked a key provision of the 1965 Voting Rights Act, as a catalyst for many of these changes. He compares Jim Crow voting roadblocks of the past to these contemporary policies, which he argues have increasingly jeopardized the political rights of people of color.

In Selection 3, Michelle Alexander—also invoking contemporary manifestations of the Jim Crow past (in an excerpt from her groundbreaking book, *The New Jim Crow: Mass*

Incarceration in the Age of Colorblindness)—examines mass incarceration and the lasting harm of "the prison label." Alexander argues that "the role of the criminal justice system in creating and perpetuating racial hierarchy in the United States" reveals a "hidden under-world of legalized discrimination and permanent social exclusion." Her analysis reveals that the criminal justice system produces widespread everyday discrimination that most Americans can pretend either does not exist or is fully justified.

Several of the subsequent readings address complex forms of criminalization in everyday life. In Selection 4, P. R. Lockhart dissects everyday racial discrimination through recent "Living While Black" incidents caught on video—white people calling 911 on African Americans engaged in activities ranging from sitting in a Starbucks to napping in their college residence hall. Lockhart draws connections between historical and contemporary forms of criminalization, and between state authorities and bystanders: "From the use of slave patrols to lynching to legal segregation, and in modern iterations like stop and frisk, racial profiling has long been used to maintain white authority by singling out the presence and behavior of people of color—especially African Americans—as requiring punishment. These systems rely on the participation of bystanders and observers to alert authorities to those deemed 'suspicious.'"

In Selection 5, Joey Mogul, Andrea Ritchie, and Kay Whitlock focus on the criminalization of queer sexualities, excavating important historical and present-day patterns of policing "the borders of the gender binary." Despite extensive evidence of abuses, the authors point out that "resistance to abusive policing of LGBT people has largely been absent from the agendas of national mainstream LGBT organizations." Their analysis reveals intersections between sexuality, class, homelessness, youth, and race. They call upon "LGBT, police accountability, and civil rights movements" to pay more attention to the subtle, institutionalized, and outright violent policing of queer identities.

The next selection provides a harrowing example of such oppression and victimization. Sabrina Rubin Erdeley analyzes CeCe McDonald's experiences of being targeted first by street violence and then by the legal system when she was convicted and imprisoned for defending herself against a violent transphobic and racist assault. The article focuses on not only the discrimination faced by McDonald, but also her resilience and resistance.

In Selection 7, Raven E. Heavy Runner describes his experiences as a Native queer youth facing homophobic harassment in school, danger on the street, and antigay religious practices. He finds a road back to wholeness when he connects with a community of queer Natives, rejects his past indoctrinations, and learns about the honored place that Two-Spirit people have had in Indigenous Nations.

The next three selections focus on the complex (and often traumatic) experiences of immigrants in the United States. In Selection 8, Mohammad, a young, queer Iranian American without legal papers, reveals intersections between nationality, ethnicity, immigration status, and sexuality. He immigrated to this country as a child, and his family had legal status until a bureaucratic error rendered them undocumented. He finds himself in legal limbo, unable to secure papers in the United States but unable as a queer person to live safely in Iran (a country he left at age three). In Selection 9, Samantha Artiga and Petry Ubri analyze the daily challenges faced by immigrant families in the current moment, including toxic levels of stress. They discuss the health implications of increased fear and anxiety, even for immigrant families with lawful status, "with particularly pronounced effects for Latinos and Muslims."

Selection 10 tells the story of Aura Hernández, who fled domestic violence in Guatemala, only to be sexually assaulted by a U.S. border patrol agent. A decade later, despite "her regular attendance at ICE check-ins, her thriving family and diligent work life," she faces threats of detention and deportation. The title of the article quotes her perspective on these experiences: "They treat me like I'm a criminal, but they are the criminals."

The next two selections also address sexualized violence. Yolonda Wilson brings an intersectional and historical lens to the Me Too movement by tracing the ways that black women's bodies have been violated throughout U.S. history and into the present. She examines not only rape but also other forms of violence against black women, such as public strip searches, forced nudity, and medical abuses. Her argument has important implications for social movements for change. "Race and gender converge in black women's lives and have created the social conditions under which black women are coerced and expected to suffer the exposure of intimate body parts, or else face punishment," she writes. "If movements like #MeToo are serious about combating sexual violence, then they have to also understand these practices as sexual violence."

In Selection 12, Chris Linder and Jessica Harris call for power-conscious and intersectional approaches to ending campus sexual violence. They urge campus advocates to learn the history of rape and racism and to apply intersectional perspectives when designing campus programs, cautioning that "seemingly identity-neutral approaches effectively make the experiences of any victim who is not a white, cisgender, heterosexual woman invisible."

Selection 13 examines environmental racism, comparing the devastating impact of policies and politics in Standing Rock, South Dakota, and Flint, Michigan. The authors argue: "Linking the politics surrounding the Dakota Access Pipeline project to Flint, Michigan's lead-poisoning crisis is critical for understanding how race and class inform presumed social risk, vulnerability to premature death, and access to democratic decision-making." Ultimately, the authors call for comparative analysis and coalition building in addressing critical issues such as democratic participation and access to clean water.

The final selection is a call for healing from Sikh American musician and educator Sonny Singh, who offers testimony of post-9/11 harassment and discrimination, from verbal and physical assaults to being arrested for posting concert flyers. He writes, "as I cope with the trauma of bigotry, I struggle in a very personal way to remain hopeful." Singh finds hope in the transformative and healing power of sharing his story, through music, teaching, and writing.

GUIDING QUESTIONS FOR PART IV

1. The opening selection in Part IV, "The Problem: Discrimination," describes multiple forms of discrimination: individual, organizational, and structural. Identify some examples of organizational and structural discrimination in other readings in Part IV. Why is it important to extend our analysis beyond individual and interpersonal forms of discrimination?

2. Michelle Alexander describes a system of *racialized* mass incarceration in an age of *colorblind* rhetoric. What are the mechanisms that make this seeming paradox possible? As you read the articles in Part IV, identify other examples of discrimination masked in neutral-seeming policies.

3. In Selection 10, Aura Hernández describes her harrowing experiences with the U.S. immigration system by saying, "They treat me like I'm a criminal, but they are the criminals." What are some of the different forms of criminalization discussed in the readings in Part IV? What groups are constructed as "criminal" in our society? Who decides? What are the consequences for the people and communities so labeled?

4. Identify examples of intersectionality in the readings in Part IV. Where do you see multiple forms of identity and multiple forms of discrimination coming together? How do these examples complicate efforts to divide discrimination into discrete categories?

5. What are some of the different forms of violence analyzed in the readings in Part IV? What rhetorics or rationales are used to justify or ignore certain forms of violence?

6. The readings in Part IV all address contemporary discrimination in the United States, but many of them also address histories of oppression and resistance. Why do the authors think it's important to frame their stories with historical analysis? Why do we need to learn these histories?

7. What concrete examples of resistance appear in the readings in Part IV, and what strategies for change are discussed in these readings?

8. Have you experienced discrimination in your life? Which concepts from the readings help you understand the historical and ideological contexts for your personal experience? Do you feel like you have the tools you need to challenge discrimination? What social changes are needed to ensure that individuals and institutions are held accountable for the effects of their discrimination and to prevent such injustice in the future?

1

The Problem: Discrimination

U.S. Commission on Civil Rights

Making choices is an essential part of everyday life for individuals and organizations. These choices are shaped in part by social structures that set standards and influence conduct in such areas as education, employment, housing, and government. When these choices limit the opportunities available to people because of their race, sex, or national origin, the problem of discrimination arises.

Historically, discrimination against minorities and women was not only accepted but it was also governmentally required. The doctrine of white supremacy used to support the institution of slavery was so much a part of American custom and policy that the Supreme Court in 1857 approvingly concluded that both the North and the South regarded slaves "as beings of an inferior order, and altogether unfit to associate with the white race, either in social or political relations; and so far inferior, that they had no rights which the white man was bound to respect."[1] White supremacy survived the passage of the Civil War amendments to the Constitution and continued to dominate legal and social institutions in the North as well as the South to disadvantage not only blacks,[2] but other racial and ethnic groups as well—American Indians, Alaskan Natives, Asian [Americans] and Pacific Islanders and Hispanics.[3]

While minorities were suffering from white supremacy, women were suffering from male supremacy. Mr. Justice Brennan has summed up the legal disabilities imposed on women this way:

> [T]hroughout much of the 19th century the position of women in our society was, in many respects, comparable to that of blacks under the pre–Civil War slave codes. Neither slaves nor women could hold office, serve on juries, or bring suit in their own names, and married women traditionally were denied the legal capacity to hold or convey property or to serve as legal guardians of their own children.[4]

In 1873 a member of the Supreme Court proclaimed, "Man is, or should be, woman's protector and defender. The natural and proper timidity and delicacy which belongs to the female sex evidently unfits it for many of the occupations of civil life."[5] Such romantic paternalism has alternated with fixed notions of male superiority to deny women in law and in practice the most fundamental of rights, including the right to vote, which was not granted until 1920;[6] the Equal Rights Amendment has yet to be ratified.[7]

White and male supremacy are no longer popularly accepted American values. The blatant racial and sexual discrimination that originated in our conveniently forgotten past, however, continues to manifest itself today in a complex interaction of attitudes and actions of individuals, organizations, and the network of social structures that make up our society.

From *Affirmative Action in the 1980s.* U.S. Commission on Civil Rights 65 (January 1981): 9–15.

Individual Discrimination

The most common understanding of discrimination rests at the level of prejudiced individual attitudes and behavior. Although open and intentional prejudice persists, individual discriminatory conduct is often hidden and sometimes unintentional.[8] Some of the following are examples of deliberately discriminatory actions by consciously prejudiced individuals. Some are examples of unintentionally discriminatory actions taken by persons who may not believe themselves to be prejudiced but whose decisions continue to be guided by deeply ingrained discriminatory customs.

- Personnel officers whose stereotyped beliefs about women and minorities justify hiring them for low level and low paying jobs exclusively, regardless of their . . . experience or qualifications for higher level jobs.[9]
- Administrators, historically white males, who rely on "word-of-mouth" recruiting among their friends and colleagues, so that only their friends and protégés of the same race and sex learn of potential job openings.[10]
- Employers who hire women for their sexual attractiveness or potential sexual availability rather than their competence, and employers who engage in sexual harassment of their female employees.[11]
- Teachers who interpret linguistic and cultural differences as indications of low potential or lack of academic interest on the part of minority students.[12]
- Guidance counselors and teachers whose low expectations lead them to steer female and minority students away from "hard" subjects, such as mathematics and science, toward subjects that do not prepare them for higher paying jobs.[13]
- Real estate agents who show fewer homes to minority buyers and steer them to minority or mixed neighborhoods because they believe white residents would oppose the presence of black neighbors.[14]
- Families who assume that property values inevitably decrease when minorities move in and therefore move out of their neighborhoods if minorities do move in.[15]
- Parole boards that assume minority offenders to be more dangerous or more unreliable than white offenders and consequently more frequently deny parole to minorities than to whites convicted of equally serious crimes.[16]

These contemporary examples of discrimination may not be motivated by conscious prejudice. The personnel manager is likely to deny believing that minorities and women can only perform satisfactorily in low level jobs and at the same time allege that other executives and decision makers would not consider them for higher level positions. In some cases, the minority or female applicants may not be aware that they have been discriminated against—the personnel manager may inform them that they are deficient in experience while rejecting their applications because of prejudice; the white male administrator who recruits by word-of-mouth from his friends or white male work force excludes minorities and women who never learn of the available positions. The discriminatory results these activities cause may not even be desired. The guidance counselor may honestly believe there are no other realistic alternatives for minority and female students.

Whether conscious or not, open or hidden, desired or undesired, these acts build on and support prejudicial stereotypes, deny their victims opportunities provided to others, and perpetuate discrimination, regardless of intent.

Organizational Discrimination

Discrimination, though practiced by individuals, is often reinforced by the well-established rules, policies, and practices of organizations. These actions are often regarded simply as part of the organization's way of doing business and are carried out by individuals as just part of their day's work.

Discrimination at the organizational level takes forms that are similar to those on the individual level. For example:

- Height and weight requirements that are unnecessarily geared to the physical proportions of white males and, therefore, exclude females and some minorities from certain jobs.[17]

- Seniority rules, when applied to jobs historically held only by white males, make more recently hired minorities and females more subject to layoff—the "last hired, first fired" employee—and less eligible for advancement.[18]

- Nepotistic membership policies of some referral unions that exclude those who are not relatives of members who, because of past employment practices, are usually white.[19]

- Restrictive employment leave policies, coupled with prohibitions on part-time work or denials of fringe benefits to part-time workers, that make it difficult for the heads of single parent families, most of whom are women, to get and keep jobs and meet the needs of their families.[20]

- The use of standardized academic tests or criteria, geared to the cultural and educational norms of the middle-class or white males, that are not relevant indicators of successful job performance.[21]

- Preferences shown by many law and medical schools in the admission of children of wealthy and influential alumni, nearly all of whom are white.[22]

- Credit policies of banks and lending institutions that prevent the granting of mortgage monies and loans in minority neighborhoods, or prevent the granting of credit to married women and others who have previously been denied the opportunity to build good credit histories in their own names.[23]

Superficially "color-blind" or "gender-neutral," these organizational practices have an adverse effect on minorities and women. As with individual actions, these organizational actions favor white males, even when taken with no conscious intent to affect minorities and women adversely, by protecting and promoting the status quo arising from the racism and sexism of the past. If, for example, the jobs now protected by "last hired, first fired" provisions had always been integrated, seniority would not operate to disadvantage minorities and women. If educational systems from kindergarten through college had not historically favored white males, many more minorities and women would hold advanced degrees and thereby be included among those involved in deciding what academic tests should test for. If minorities had lived in the same neighborhoods as whites, there would be no minority neighborhoods to which mortgage money could be denied on the basis of their being minority neighborhoods.

In addition, these barriers to minorities and women too often do not fulfill legitimate needs of the organization, or these needs can be met through other means that adequately maintain the organization without discriminating. Instead of excluding all women on the assumption that they are too weak or should be protected from strenuous work, the organization can implement a reasonable test that measures the strength actually needed to perform the job or, where possible, develop ways of doing the work that require less physical effort. Admissions to academic and professional schools can be decided not only on the basis of grades, standardized test scores, and the prestige of the high school or college from which the applicant graduated, but also on the basis of community service, work experience, and letters of recommendation. Lending institutions can look at the individual and his or her financial ability rather than the neighborhood or marital status of the prospective borrower.

Some practices that disadvantage minorities and women are readily accepted aspects of everyday behavior. Consider the "old boy" network in business and education built on years of friendship and social contact among white males, or the exchanges of information and corporate strategies by business acquaintances in racially or sexually exclusive country clubs and locker rooms paid for by the employer.[24] These actions, all of which have a discriminatory impact on minorities and women, are not necessarily acts of conscious prejudice. Because such actions are so often considered part of the "normal" way of doing things, people have difficulty recognizing that they are discriminating and therefore resist abandoning these practices despite the clearly discriminatory results. Consequently, many decision makers have difficulty considering, much less accepting, nondiscriminatory alternatives that may work just as well or better to advance legitimate organizational interests but without systematically disadvantaging minorities and women.

This is not to suggest that all such discriminatory organizational actions are spurious or arbitrary. Many may serve the actual needs of the organization. Physical size or strength at times may be a legitimate job requirement; sick leave and insurance policies must be reasonably restricted; educational qualifications are needed for many jobs; lending institutions cannot lend to people who cannot reasonably demonstrate an ability to repay loans. Unless carefully examined and then modified or eliminated, however, these apparently neutral rules, policies, and practices will continue to perpetuate age-old discriminatory patterns into the structure of today's society.

Whatever the motivation behind such organizational acts, a process is occurring, the common denominator of which is unequal results on a very large scale. When unequal outcomes are repeated over time and in numerous societal and geographical areas, it is a clear signal that a discriminatory process is at work.

Such discrimination is not a static, one-time phenomenon that has a clearly limited effect. Discrimination can feed on discrimination in self-perpetuating cycles.[25]

- The employer who recruits job applicants by word-of-mouth within a predominantly white male work force reduces the chances of receiving applications from minorities and females for open positions. Since they do not apply, they are not hired. Since they are not hired, they are not present when new jobs become available. Since they are not aware of new jobs, they cannot recruit other minority or female applicants. Because there are no minority or female employees to recruit others, the employer is left to recruit on his own from among his predominantly white and male work force.[26]

- The teacher who expects poor academic performance from minority and female students may not become greatly concerned when their grades are low. The acceptance of their low grades removes incentives to improve. Without incentives to improve, their grades remain low. Their low grades reduce their expectations, and the teacher has no basis for expecting more of them.[27]

- The realtor who assumes that white home owners do not want minority neighbors "steers" minorities to minority neighborhoods. Those steered to minority neighborhoods tend to live in minority neighborhoods. White neighborhoods then remain white, and realtors tend to assume that whites do not want minority neighbors.[28]

- Elected officials appoint voting registrars who impose linguistic, geographic, and other barriers to minority voter registration. Lack of minority registration leads to low voting rates. Lower minority voting rates lead to the election of fewer minorities. Fewer elected minorities leads to the appointment of voting registrars who maintain the same barriers.[29]

Structural Discrimination

Such self-sustaining discriminatory processes occur not only within the fields of employment, education, housing, and government but also between these structural areas. There is a classic cycle of structural discrimination that reproduces itself. Discrimination in education denies the credentials to get good jobs. Discrimination in employment denies the economic resources to buy good housing. Discrimination in housing confines minorities to school districts providing inferior education, closing the cycle in a classic form.[30]

With regard to white women, the cycle is not as tightly closed. To the extent they are raised in families headed by white males, and are married to or live with white males, white women will enjoy the advantages in housing and other areas that such relationships to white men can confer. White women lacking the sponsorship of white men, however, will be unable to avoid gender-based discrimination in housing, education, and employment. White women can thus be the victims of discrimination produced by social structures that is comparable in form to that experienced by minorities.

This perspective is not intended to imply that either the dynamics of discrimination or its nature and degree are identical for women and minorities. But when a woman of any background seeks to compete with men of any group, she finds herself the victim of a discriminatory process. Regarding the similarities and differences between the discrimination experienced by women and minorities, one author has aptly stated:

> [W]hen two groups exist in a situation of inequality, it may be self-defeating to become embroiled in a quarrel over which is more unequal or the victim of greater oppression. The more salient question is how a condition of inequality for both is maintained and perpetuated—through what means is it reinforced?[31]

The following are additional examples of the interaction between social structures that affect minorities and women:

- The absence of minorities and women from executive, writing, directing, news reporting, and acting positions in television contributes to unfavorable stereotyping on the screen, which in turn reinforces existing stereotypes among the public and creates psychological roadblocks to progress in employment, education, and housing.[32]

- Living in inner-city high crime areas in disproportionate numbers, minorities, particularly minority youth, are more likely to be arrested and are more likely to go to jail than whites accused of similar offenses, and their arrest and conviction records are then often used as bars to employment.[33]

- Because of past discrimination against minorities and women, female and minority-headed businesses are often small and relatively new. Further disadvantaged by contemporary credit and lending practices, they are more likely than white male–owned businesses to remain small and be less able to employ full-time specialists in applying for government contracts. Because they cannot monitor the availability of government contracts, they do not receive such contracts. Because they cannot demonstrate success with government contracts, contracting officers tend to favor other firms that have more experience with government contracts.[34]

Discriminatory actions by individuals and organizations are not only pervasive, occurring in every sector of society, but also cumulative with effects limited neither to the time nor the particular structural area in which they occur. This process of discrimination, therefore, extends across generations, across organizations, and across social structures in self-reinforcing cycles, passing the disadvantages incurred by one generation in one area to future generations in many related areas.[35]

These interrelated components of the discriminatory process share one basic result: the persistent gaps seen in the status of women and minorities relative to that of white males. These unequal results themselves have real consequences. The employer who wishes to hire more minorities and women may be bewildered by charges of racism and sexism when confronted by what appears to be a genuine shortage of qualified minority and female applicants. The guidance counselor who sees one promising minority student after another drop out of school or give up in despair may be resentful of allegations of racism when there is little he or she alone can do for the student. The banker who denies a loan to a female single parent may wish to do differently, but believes that prudent fiscal judgment requires taking into account her lack of financial history and inability to prove that she is a good credit risk. These and other decision makers see the results of a discriminatory process repeated over and over again, and those results provide a basis for rationalizing their own actions, which then feed into that same process.

When seen outside the context of the interlocking and intertwined effects of discrimination, complaints that many women and minorities are absent from the ranks of qualified job applicants, academically inferior and unmotivated, poor credit risks, and so forth, may appear to be justified. Decision makers like those described above are reacting to real social problems stemming from the process of discrimination. But many too easily fall prey to stereotyping and consequently disregard those minorities and women who have the necessary skills or qualifications. And they erroneously "blame the victims" of discrimination,[36] instead of examining the past and present context in which their own actions are taken and the multiple consequences of these actions on the lives of minorities and women.

The Process of Discrimination

Although discrimination is maintained through individual actions, neither individual prejudices nor random chance can fully explain the persistent national patterns of inequality and underrepresentation. Nor can these patterns be blamed on the persons who are at the bottom of our economic, political, and social order. Overt racism and sexism as embodied in popular notions of white and male supremacy have been widely repudiated, but our history of discrimination based on race, sex, and national origin has not been readily put aside. Past discrimination continues to have present effects. The task today is to identify those effects and the forms and dynamics of the discrimination that produced them.

Discrimination against minorities and women must now be viewed as an interlocking process involving the attitudes and actions of individuals and the organizations and social structures that guide individual behavior. That process, started by past events, now routinely bestows privileges, favors, and advantages on white males and imposes disadvantages and penalties on minorities and women. This process is also self-perpetuating. Many normal, seemingly neutral, operations of our society create stereotyped expectations that justify unequal results; unequal results in one area foster inequalities in opportunity and accomplishment in others; the lack of opportunity and accomplishment confirms the original prejudices or engenders new ones that fuel the normal operations generating unequal results.

As we have shown, the process of discrimination involves many aspects of our society. No single factor sufficiently explains it, and no single means will suffice to eliminate it. Such elements of our society as our history of *de jure* discrimination, deeply ingrained prejudices,[37] inequities based on economic and social class,[38] and the structure and function of all our economic, social, and political institutions[39] must be continually examined in order to understand their part in shaping today's decisions that will either maintain or counter the current process of discrimination.

It may be difficult to identify precisely all aspects of the discriminatory process and assign those parts their appropriate importance. But understanding discrimination starts with an awareness that such a process exists and that to avoid perpetuating it, we must carefully assess the context and consequences of our everyday actions. . . .

NOTES

1. Dred Scott v. Sandford, 60 U.S. (19 How.) 393, 408 (1857). [See excerpts from *Dred Scott v. Sandford* in Part VII of this volume.]
2. For a concise summary of this history, see U.S. Commission on Civil Rights, *Twenty Years After Brown*, pp. 4–29 (1975); *Freedom to the Free: 1863, Century of Emancipation* (1963).
3. The discriminatory conditions experienced by these minority groups have been documented in the following publications by the U.S. Commission on Civil Rights: *The Navajo Nation: An American Colony* (1975); *The Southwest Indian Report* (1973); *The Forgotten Minority: Asian Americans in New York City* (State Advisory Committee Report 1977); *Success of Asian Americans: Fact or Fiction?* (1980); *Stranger in One's Land* (1970); *Toward Quality Education for Mexican Americans* (1974); *Puerto Ricans in the Continental United States: An Uncertain Future* (1976).
4. Frontiero v. Richardson, 411 U.S. 677, 684–86 (1973), citing L. Kanowitz, *Women and the Law: The Unfinished Revolution*, pp. 5–6 (1970), and G. Myrdal, *An American Dilemma* 1073 (20th Anniversary Ed., 1962). Justice Brennan wrote the opinion of the Court, joined by Justices Douglas, White, and Marshall. Justice Stewart concurred in the judgment. Justice Powell, joined by Chief Justice Burger and Justice Blackmun, wrote a separate concurring opinion. Justice Rehnquist dissented. See also H. M. Hacker, "Women as a Minority Group," *Social Forces*, vol. 30 (1951), pp. 60–69; W. Chafe, *Women and Equality: Changing Patterns in American Culture* (New York: Oxford University Press, 1977).
5. Bradwell v. State, 83 U.S. (16 Wall) 130, 141 (1873) (Bradley, J., concurring), quoted in *Frontiero, supra* note 4. [See excerpts from *Bradwell v. Illinois* in Part VII of this volume.]
6. U.S. Const. amend. XIX. [The full text of the Nineteenth Amendment is in Part VII of this volume.]
7. See U.S. Commission on Civil Rights, *Statement on the Equal Rights Amendment* (December 1978). [See "The Equal Rights Amendment," in Part VII of this volume.]
8. See, e.g., R. K. Merton, "Discrimination and the American Creed," in R. K. Merton, *Sociological Ambivalence and Other Essays* (New York: The Free Press, 1976), pp. 189–216. In this essay on racism, published for the first time more than 30 years ago, Merton presented a typology which introduced the notion that discriminatory actions are not always directly related to individual attitudes of prejudice. Merton's typology consisted of the following: Type I—the unprejudiced nondiscriminator; Type II—the unprejudiced discriminator; Type III—the prejudiced nondiscriminator; Type IV—the prejudiced discriminator. In the present context, Type II is crucial in its observation that discrimination is often practiced by persons who are not themselves prejudiced, but who respond to, or do not oppose, the actions of those who discriminate because of prejudiced attitudes (Type IV). See also D. C. Reitzes, "Prejudice and Discrimination: A Study in Contradictions," in *Racial and Ethnic Relations*, ed. H. M. Hughes (Boston: Allyn and Bacon, 1970), pp. 56–65.
9. See R. M. Kanter and B. A. Stein, "Making a Life at the Bottom," in *Life in Organizations, Workplaces as People Experience Them*, ed. Kanter and Stein (New York: Basic Books, 1976), pp. 176–90; also L. K. Howe, "Retail Sales Worker," ibid., pp. 248–51; also R. M. Kanter, *Men and Women of the Corporation* (New York: Basic Books, 1977).
10. See M. S. Granovetter, *Getting a Job: A Study of Contracts and Careers* (Cambridge: Harvard University Press, 1974), pp. 6–11; also A. W. Blumrosen, *Black Employment and the Law* (New Brunswick, N.J.: Rutgers University Press, 1971), p. 232.
11. See U.S. Equal Employment Opportunity Commission, "Guidelines on Discrimination Because of Sex," 29 C.F.R. §1604.4 (1979); L. Farley, *Sexual Shakedown: The Sexual Harassment of Women on the Job* (New York: McGraw-Hill, 1978), pp. 92–96, 176–79; C. A. Mackinnon, *Sexual Harassment of Working Women* (New Haven: Yale University Press, 1979), pp. 25–55.

12. See R. Rosenthal and L. F. Jacobson, "Teacher Expectations for the Disadvantaged," *Scientific American*, 1968 (b) 218, 219–23; also D. Bar Tal, "Interactions of Teachers and Pupils," in *New Approaches to Social Problems*, ed. I. H. Frieze, D. Bar Tal, and J. S. Carrol (San Francisco: Jossey Bass, 1979), pp. 337–58; also U.S. Commission on Civil Rights, *Teachers and Students, Report V: Mexican American Education Study. Differences in Teacher Interaction with Mexican American and Anglo Students* (1973), pp. 22–23.

13. Ibid.

14. U.S. Department of Housing and Urban Development, "Measuring Racial Discrimination in American Housing Markets: The Housing Market Practices Survey" (1979); D. M. Pearce, "Gatekeepers and Home Seekers: Institutional Patterns in Racial Steering," *Social Problems*, vol. 26 (1979), pp. 325–42; "Benign Steering and Benign Quotas: The Validity of Race Conscious Government Policies to Promote Residential Integration," 93 *Harv. L. Rev.* 938, 944 (1980).

15. See M. N. Danielson, *The Politics of Exclusion* (New York: Columbia University Press, 1976), pp. 11–12; U.S. Commission on Civil Rights, *Equal Opportunity in Suburbia* (1974).

16. See L. L. Knowles and K. Prewitt, eds., *Institutional Racism in America* (Englewood Cliffs, N.J.: Prentice Hall, 1969), pp. 58–77, and E. D. Wright, *The Politics of Punishment* (New York: Harper and Row, 1973). Also, S. V. Brown, "Race and Parole Hearing Outcomes," in *Discrimination in Organizations*, ed. R. Alvarez and K. G. Lutterman (San Francisco: Jossey Bass, 1979), pp. 355–74.

17. Height and weight minimums that disproportionately exclude women without a showing of legitimate job requirement constitute unlawful sex discrimination. *See* Dothard v. Rawlinson, 433 U.S. 321 (1977); Bowe v. Colgate Palmolive Co., 416 F.2d 711 (7th Cir. 1969). Minimum height requirements used in screening applicants for employment have also been held to be unlawful where such a requirement excludes a significantly higher percentage of Hispanics than other national origin groups in the labor market and no job relatedness is shown. See Smith v. City of East Cleveland, 520 F.2d 492 (6th Cir. 1975).

18. U.S. Commission on Civil Rights, *Last Hired, First Fired* (1976); Tangren v. Wackenhut Servs., Inc., 480 F. Supp. 539 (D. Nev. 1979).

19. U.S. Commission on Civil Rights, *The Challenge Ahead, Equal Opportunity in Referral Unions* (1977), pp. 84–89.

20. A. Pifer, "Women Working: Toward a New Society," pp. 13–34, and D. Pearce, "Women, Work and Welfare: The Feminization of Poverty," pp. 103–24, both in K. A. Fernstein, ed., *Working Women and Families* (Beverly Hills: Sage Publications, 1979). Disproportionate numbers of single-parent families are minorities.

21. See Griggs v. Duke Power Company, 401 U.S. 424 (1971); U.S. Commission on Civil Rights, *Toward Equal Educational Opportunity: Affirmative Admissions Programs at Law and Medical Schools* (1978), pp. 10–12; I. Berg, *Education and Jobs: The Great Training Robbery* (Boston: Beacon Press, 1971), pp. 58–60.

22. See U.S. Commission on Civil Rights, *Toward Equal Educational Opportunity: Affirmative Admissions Programs at Law and Medical Schools* (1978), pp. 14–15.

23. See U.S. Commission on Civil Rights, *Mortgage Money: Who Gets It? A Case Study in Mortgage Lending Discrimination in Hartford, Conn.* (1974); J. Feagin and C. B. Feagin, *Discrimination American Style, Institutional Racism and Sexism* (Englewood Cliffs, N.J.: Prentice Hall, 1976), pp. 78–79.

24. See *Club Membership Practices by Financial Institutions: Hearing before the Comm. on Banking, Housing and Urban Affairs, United States Senate*, 96th Cong., 1st Sess. (1979). The Office of Federal Contract Compliance Programs of the Department of Labor has proposed a rule that would make the payment or reimbursement of membership fees in a private club

that accepts or rejects persons on the basis of race, color, sex, religion, or national origin a prohibited discriminatory practice. 45 Fed. Reg. 4954 (1980) (to be codified in 41 C.F.R. §60–1.11).

25. See U.S. Commission on Civil Rights, *For All the People . . . By All the People* (1969), pp. 122–23.
26. See note 10.
27. See note 12.
28. See notes 14 and 15.
29. See Statement of Arthur S. Flemming, Chairman, U.S. Commission on Civil Rights, before the Subcommittee on Constitutional Rights of the Committee on the Judiciary of the U.S. Senate on S.407, S.903, and S.1279, Apr. 9, 1975, pp. 15–18, based on U.S. Commission on Civil Rights, *The Voting Rights Act: Ten Years After* (January 1975).
30. See, e.g., U.S. Commission on Civil Rights, *Equal Opportunity in Suburbia* (1974).
31. Chafe, *Women and Equality*, p. 78.
32. U.S. Commission on Civil Rights, *Window Dressing on the Set* (1977).
33. See note 16; Gregory v. Litton Systems, Inc., 472 F.2d 631 (9th Cir. 1972); Green v. Mo.-Pac. R.R., 523 F.2d 1290 (8th Cir. 1975).
34. See U.S. Commission on Civil Rights, *Minorities and Women as Government Contractors*, pp. 20, 27, 125 (1975).
35. See, e.g., A. Downs, *Racism in America and How to Combat It* (U.S. Commission on Civil Rights, 1970); "The Web of Urban Racism," in *Institutional Racism in America*, ed. Knowles and Prewitt (Englewood Cliffs, N.J.: Prentice Hall, 1969), pp. 134–76. Other factors in addition to race, sex, and national origin may contribute to these interlocking institutional patterns. In *Equal Opportunity in Suburbia* (1974), this Commission documented what it termed "the cycle of urban poverty" that confines minorities in central cities with declining tax bases, soaring educational and other public needs, and dwindling employment opportunities, surrounded by largely white, affluent suburbs. This cycle of poverty, however, started with and is fueled by discrimination against minorities. *See also* W. Taylor, *Hanging Together, Equality in an Urban Nation* (New York: Simon & Schuster, 1971).
36. The "self-fulfilling prophecy" is a well-known phenomenon. "Blaming the victim" occurs when responses to discrimination are treated as though they were the causes rather than the results of discrimination. *See* Chafe, *Women and Equality*, pp. 76–78; W. Ryan, *Blaming the Victim* (New York: Pantheon Books, 1971).
37. See, e.g., J. E. Simpson and J. M. Yinger, *Racial and Cultural Minorities* (New York: Harper and Row, 1965), pp. 49–79; J. M. Jones, *Prejudice and Racism* (Reading, Mass.: Addison Wesley, 1972), pp. 60–111; M. M. Tumin, "Who Is Against Desegregation?" in *Racial and Ethnic Relations*, ed. H. Hughes (Boston: Allyn and Bacon, 1970), pp. 76–85; D. M. Wellman, *Portraits of White Racism* (Cambridge: Cambridge University Press, 1977).
38. See, e.g., D. C. Cox, *Caste, Class and Race: A Study in Social Dynamics* (Garden City, N.Y.: Doubleday, 1948); W. J. Wilson, *Power, Racism and Privilege* (New York: Macmillan, 1973).
39. H. Hacker, "Women as a Minority Group," *Social Forces*, vol. 30 (1951), pp. 60–69; J. Feagin and C. B. Feagin, *Discrimination American Style*; Chafe, *Women and Equality*; J. Feagin, "Indirect Institutionalized Discrimination," *American Politics Quarterly*, vol. 5 (1977), pp. 177–200; M. A. Chesler, "Contemporary Sociological Theories of Racism," in *Towards the Elimination of Racism*, ed. P. Katz (New York: Pergamon Press, 1976); P. Van den Berghe, *Race and Racism: A Comparative Perspective* (New York: Wiley, 1967); S. Carmichael and C. Hamilton, *Black Power* (New York: Random House, 1967); Knowles and Prewitt, *Institutional Racism in America*; Downs, *Racism in America and How to Combat It*.

2 | The Georgia Governor's Race Has Brought Voter Suppression into Full View

Vann R. Newkirk II

Editor's Note: Update—Newkirk's essay appeared on election day, November 6, 2018. It took ten days for the race to be resolved, when Georgia gubernatorial candidate Stacey Abrams acknowledged that Brian Kemp had received more votes, while also stating that "eight years of systemic disenfranchisement, disinvestment and incompetence had its desired effect on the electoral process in Georgia." Abrams came within 55,000 votes of being elected the nation's first black woman governor.

The Georgia governor's race is balanced on a knife's edge. Local polls have the Democratic nominee Stacey Abrams and her GOP opponent, Georgia Secretary of State Brian Kemp, virtually tied.[1] Abrams's team in particular will scramble to make sure every provisional ballot is completed, that every person who faced challenges to registration is able to participate, that all absentee and vote-by-mail ballots are counted, and that every allegation of intimidation or unfair practices on Election Day is investigated. In a race in which a December runoff is a distinct possibility if neither candidate can secure 50 percent support, every single vote matters.[2]

But no matter the outcome, it's clear that voter rights and suppression will be one of the major stories of the 2018 election in Georgia. The state has become the battleground for something deeper than the ideas of the candidates themselves; it's now emblematic of a larger struggle over voting rights that has changed party politics markedly over the past five years. The true nature of voter suppression as an accumulation of everyday annoyances, legal barriers, and confusion has come into full view. Today, voter suppression is a labyrinth, not a wall.

That labyrinth has been under construction for years. Kemp has embarked on what his opponents and critics say is a series of naked attempts to constrict the electorate. Since 2010, his office reports that it has purged upwards of 1.4 million voters from the rolls, including more than 660,000 Georgians in 2017 and almost 90,000 this year.[3] Many of those voters found their registration canceled because they had not voted in the previous election. Additionally, under an "exact match" law passed by the state legislature that requires handwritten voter registrations to be identical to personal documents, 53,000 people had their registrations

Vann R. Newkirk II is a staff writer at *The Atlantic*, where he covers politics and policy. Newkirk is also a cofounder of and contributing editor for Seven Scribes, a website and community dedicated to promoting young writers and artists of color.

moved to "pending" status because of typos or other errors before a district court enjoined the policy. More than 80 percent of those registrations belonged to black voters.

Most of these maneuvers have rather small effects in a vacuum, and it's difficult to track the effects of any one policy on the outcomes of elections. For example, Georgia's early-voting period featured a record-shattering 2 million votes cast, a number that dwarfs the thousands of people who could have faced disenfranchisement under the exact-match law.[4] But much of the research on election law and voter turnout shows that it's the combination of major policies and minor barriers—like polling-place changes, long lines at the polls, and small bureaucratic hurdles—that have real and measurable impacts on turnout.

According to a new working paper from the Harvard University professor Desmond Ang, protections against those accumulative assaults against democracy have all but been erased in the past five years.[5] Ang studied the effects of a provision in the Voting Rights Act (VRA) that required the federal preclearance of election laws in places where Jim Crow had kept black people from voting, a requirement that was expanded in 1975 to some states and districts outside the Deep South. As originally envisioned, preclearance forced districts with significant proportions of minority voters and low minority turnout to submit all changes to election laws for federal approval. The federal litmus test approved new provisions only if they were found not to decrease minority turnout relative to the status quo. Thus, the VRA was not only a protective shield against scorched-earth Jim Crow policies—it was also intended to guard against more subtle restrictions, all while promoting higher minority turnout as an explicit goal.

Ang found that in the districts covered by preclearance from 1975 to 2013, federal oversight was a major factor in sustained increases in minority turnout relative to counties not covered by the VRA. And that doesn't include counties and states that had more explicit anti-black laws, like poll taxes, that the VRA outlawed. Ang's findings indicate that the act of continued federal monitoring alone was responsible for a good deal of minority turnout across the country. "The estimated gains in voter turnout are large—ranging from 4 to 8 percentage points—and lasting—having persisted for 40 years," Ang writes.

"The fact that the VRA was successful means that these places couldn't have been putting in discriminatory measures all the way from when they fell under coverage . . . until 2013," Ang told me. "I think that the whole rationale behind preclearance was this idea that there are essentially infinite margins on which you can discriminate."

The Justice Department and the U.S. Congress in the 1960s and '70s predicted that southern election officials would employ clever incremental policies that, over time, would bring back Jim Crow—and cloak it in an even thicker aura of legitimacy than it existed under before. Ang cites a Jim Crow–era official in Mississippi who said: "What those smart fellows [at the Justice Department] don't realize is that we can still get to these darkies in a whole lot of subtle ways."

But the Supreme Court's decision in *Shelby County v. Holder* in 2013 reversed the federal doctrine of proactiveness when it effectively ended preclearance.[*] Since that decision, Ang has tracked what appears to be the beginning of a troubling trend. Minority turnout in the past two federal elections has plummeted, specifically in the counties in which preclearance was once a first step for creating new election laws. The data don't yet exist to confirm causality between *Shelby County* and the recent dips in turnout, but Ang writes

---

[*] See an excerpt from *Shelby County v. Holder* in Part VII of this volume.

that the numbers imply that "recently enacted election laws may have negated many of the gains made under preclearance."

Included in those recently enacted laws are most of Kemp's most controversial policies. In late October, U.S. District Court Judge Leigh Martin May enjoined the exact-match law, a policy that allowed election officials to reject absentee ballots because of signature mismatches.[6] On Kemp's watch, Georgia has lost almost a tenth of its polling places since 2012, with the majority of closings occurring in poor counties and those with significant African American populations.[7] NYU's Brennan Center for Justice finds that Georgia—along with Florida and North Carolina—has increased its voter-purge rates since the *Shelby County* decision.

And Georgia is merely representative of a nationwide trend. Kemp's Kansan counterpart, Kris Kobach—who is also administering his own election—has been held in contempt of court for his attempts to disenfranchise Latino voters in the state[8]; has rejected thousands of registrations and ballots; and has overseen the curious relocation of the polling place in Dodge City to a location outside of the city, a move that will force the city's Hispanic majority to travel far in order to vote.[9] In North Dakota, courts have upheld a voter-ID law that could disproportionately affect the state's American Indian voters, a crucial constituency for Democratic Senator Heidi Heitkamp.[10]

"Because it looks clinical and bureaucratic, we don't pay attention to it," says Carol Anderson, an African American–studies professor at Emory University and the author of *One Person, No Vote*, an exhaustive review of modern voter-suppression efforts.

"These states have been really good about making Jim Crow 2.0 seem reasonable," Anderson told me. "This is massive disenfranchisement that is slow and corrosive. We don't see it the way we see cross burnings and riots and beatings. What instead happens is you frustrate people out of their basic right."

As Anderson told me, the thing about the suppression-by-frustration regime is that it provides dozens of potential exit points for voters burdened by bureaucracy. "You have to punch a clock to go to work," she said. "If you go to the polls on Tuesday and your name's not on the rolls, now what are you going to do? So you're either going to go to work anyway because you can't afford to lose pay, or you're going to have to take some vacation leave." Include in that calculus the process of obtaining identification in the first place, the potentially long lines on Election Day, and the fact that provisional ballots for people with discrepancies can require even more paperwork and time off, and the true costs of voting become clear.

On Election Day, it's worth remembering just how Jim Crow elections worked. Yes, black people were lynched for attempting to vote—a history particularly salient in Georgia. The extralegal components of the system were real and dangerous, and they claimed countless lives.

But Jim Crow states were also administrative states, and the bureaucracies they developed came about as a result of a drive among powerful white politicians to discriminate within the bounds of federal law. That meant poll taxes and literacy tests, which were originally perfectly legal. It also meant recitations of preambles, long walks to county registrars, and frustration even among black people who somehow managed to register and vote. It meant all-white primaries and at-large districts and intense gerrymandering.

It relied on obsessive tinkering along the margins to come up with a system that was de jure passable under the Constitution, but in the aggregate became a de facto impossible impediment for black people voting in any real numbers. In order to build their regime, southern officials needed to build mazes.

Those are important considerations for this election, and for elections to come. Regardless of the outcomes of individual races—and even perhaps because of them, if Republicans face major losses—the incentives for disenfranchising black and Latino voters may only be increasing as their share of the electorate increases, and as they steadily back Democratic candidates. And that's as the main tool for protecting voters, the VRA, has been rendered partially inert. In places like Georgia, the rudiments of a labyrinth appear to already be in place.

NOTES

1. Wheeler, Lydia. "Poll: Abrams and Kemp Tied in Georgia Governor's Race." *The Hill*, 2 Nov. 2018, thehill.com/homenews/campaign/414503-poll-abrams-and-kemp-tied-in-georgia-governors-race.

2. Strauss, Daniel. "Abrams, Kemp Prepare for Overtime in Georgia Governor's Race." *Politico*, 5 Nov. 2018, www.politico.com/story/2018/11/05/georgia-governor-2018-elections-midterms-abrams-kemp-960750.

3. Niesse, Mark. "Georgia Cancels Fewer Voter Registrations after Surge Last Year." *The Atlanta Journal-Constitution*, 17 Oct. 2018, www.ajc.com/news/local-govt--politics/georgia-cancels-fewer-voter-registrations-after-surge-last-year/fqT1bcSzGu33UEpTMDzMVK/.

4. Enamorado, Ted. "Georgia's 'Exact Match' Law Could Potentially Harm Many Eligible Voters." *The Washington Post*, 20 Oct. 2018, www.washingtonpost.com/news/monkey-cage/wp/2018/10/20/georgias-exact-match-law-could-disenfranchise-3031802-eligible-voters-my-research-finds/?noredirect=on&utm_term=.2d81f47280d4.

5. Ang, Desmond. Harvard Kennedy School, 2018, research.hks.harvard.edu/publications/getFile.aspx?Id=1714.

6. Estep, Tyler. "Federal Judge to Order Ga. Counties to Stop Absentee Ballot Rejections." *The Atlanta Journal-Constitution*, 24 Oct. 2018, www.ajc.com/news/local-govt--politics/breaking-judge-proposes-injunction-absentee-ballot-rejections/drBFCpDG2Kmn1kJwQxItMJ/.

7. Niesse, Mark, et al. "Voting Precincts Closed Across Georgia Since Election Oversight Lifted." *The Atlanta Journal-Constitution*, 31 Aug. 2018, www.ajc.com/news/state-regional-govt-politics/voting-precincts-closed-across-georgia-since-election-oversight-lifted/bBkHxptlim0Gp9pKu7dfrN/.

8. Foran, Clare. "Kris Kobach Found in Contempt of Court by Federal Judge." CNN, 19 Apr. 2018, www.cnn.com/2018/04/19/politics/kris-kobach-contempt-of-court/index.html.

9. Smith, Mitch. "To Cast Their Ballots, These Voters Will Have to Get Out of Dodge." *The New York Times*, 26 Oct. 2018, www.nytimes.com/2018/10/26/us/dodge-city-kansas-voting.html.

10. "North Dakota Voter ID Law Could Keep Rural Native Americans From Voting." *Here & Now*. Boston University, WBUR, Boston, 23 Oct. 2018.

3 | The New Jim Crow: Mass Incarceration in the Age of Colorblindness

Michelle Alexander

It was no ordinary Sunday morning when presidential candidate Barack Obama stepped to the podium at the Apostolic Church of God in Chicago. It was Father's Day. Hundreds of enthusiastic congregants packed the pews at the overwhelmingly black church eager to hear what the first black Democratic nominee for president of the United States had to say.

The message was a familiar one: black men should be better fathers. Too many are absent from their homes. For those in the audience, Obama's speech was an old tune sung by an exciting new performer. His message of personal responsibility, particularly as it relates to fatherhood, was anything but new; it had been delivered countless times by black ministers in churches across America. The message had also been delivered on a national stage by celebrities such as Bill Cosby and Sidney Poitier. And the message had been delivered with great passion by Louis Farrakhan, who more than a decade earlier summoned one million black men to Washington, D.C., for a day of "atonement" and recommitment to their families and communities.

The mainstream media, however, treated the event as big news, and many pundits seemed surprised that the black congregants actually applauded the message. For them, it was remarkable that black people nodded in approval when Obama said: "If we are honest with ourselves, we'll admit that too many fathers are missing—missing from too many lives and too many homes. Too many fathers are MIA. Too many fathers are AWOL. They have abandoned their responsibilities. They're acting like boys instead of men. And the foundations of our families are weaker because of it. You and I know this is true everywhere, but nowhere is this more true than in the African American community."

The media did not ask—and Obama did not tell—where the missing fathers might be found.

The following day, social critic and sociologist Michael Eric Dyson published a critique of Obama's speech in *Time* magazine. He pointed out that the stereotype of black men being poor fathers may well be false. Research by Boston College social psychologist Rebekah Levine Coley found that black fathers not living at home are more likely to keep in contact with their children than fathers of any other ethnic or racial group. Dyson chided Obama for evoking a black stereotype for political gain, pointing out that "Obama's words may have been spoken to black folk, but they were aimed at those whites still on the fence about whom to send to the White House."[1] Dyson's critique was a fair one, but like

---

Michelle Alexander is a civil rights lawyer, advocate, and legal scholar. She has taught at Stanford Law School and directed the ACLU of Northern California's Racial Justice Project.

other media commentators, he remained silent about where all the absent black fathers could be found. He identified numerous social problems plaguing black families, such as high levels of unemployment, discriminatory mortgage practices, and the gutting of early-childhood learning programs. Not a word was said about prisons.

The public discourse regarding "missing black fathers" closely parallels the debate about the lack of eligible black men for marriage. The majority of black women are unmarried today, including 70 percent of professional black women.[2] "Where have all the black men gone?" is a common refrain heard among black women frustrated in their efforts to find life partners.

The sense that black men have disappeared is rooted in reality. The U.S. Census Bureau reported in 2002 that there are nearly 3 million more black adult women than men in black communities across the United States, a gender gap of 26 percent.[3] In many urban areas, the gap is far worse, rising to more than 37 percent in places like New York City. The comparable disparity for whites in the United States is 8 percent.[4] Although a million black men can be found in prisons and jails, public acknowledgment of the role of the criminal justice system in "disappearing" black men is surprisingly rare. Even in the black media—which is generally more willing to raise and tackle issues related to criminal justice—an eerie silence can often be found.[5]

Ebony magazine, for example, ran an article in December 2006 entitled "Where Have the Black Men Gone?" The author posed the popular question but never answered it.[6] He suggested we will find our black men when we rediscover God, family, and self-respect. A more cynical approach was taken by Tyra Banks, the popular talk show host, who devoted a show in May 2008 to the recurring question, "Where Have All the Good Black Men Gone?" She wondered aloud whether black women are unable to find "good black men" because too many of them are gay or dating white women. No mention was made of the War on Drugs or mass incarceration.

The fact that Barack Obama can give a speech on Father's Day dedicated to the subject of fathers who are "AWOL" without ever acknowledging that the majority of young black men in many large urban areas are currently under the control of the criminal justice system is disturbing, to say the least. What is more problematic, though, is that hardly anyone in the mainstream media noticed the oversight. One might not expect serious analysis from Tyra Banks, but shouldn't we expect a bit more from the *New York Times* and CNN? Hundreds of thousands of black men are unable to be good fathers for their children, not because of a lack of commitment or desire but because they are warehoused in prisons, locked in cages. They did not walk out on their families voluntarily; they were taken away in handcuffs, often due to a massive federal program known as the War on Drugs.

More African American adults are under correctional control today—in prison or jail, on probation or parole—than were enslaved in 1850, a decade before the Civil War began.[7] The mass incarceration of people of color is a big part of the reason that a black child born today is less likely to be raised by both parents than a black child born during slavery.[8] The absence of black fathers from families across America is not simply a function of laziness, immaturity, or too much time watching Sports Center. Thousands of black men have disappeared into prisons and jails, locked away for drug crimes that are largely ignored when committed by whites.

The clock has been turned back on racial progress in America, though scarcely anyone seems to notice. All eyes are fixed on people like Barack Obama and Oprah Winfrey, who have defied the odds and risen to power, fame, and fortune. For those left behind, especially those within prison walls, the celebration of racial triumph in America must seem a tad premature. More black men are imprisoned today than at any other moment in our nation's history. More are disenfranchised today than in 1870, the year the Fifteenth Amendment was ratified prohibiting laws that explicitly deny the right to vote on the basis of race.[9] Young black men today may be just as likely to suffer discrimination in employment, housing, public benefits, and jury service as a black man in the Jim Crow era — discrimination that is perfectly legal, because it is based on one's criminal record.

This is the new normal, the new racial equilibrium.

The launching of the War on Drugs and the initial construction of the new system required the expenditure of tremendous political initiative and resources. Media campaigns were waged; politicians blasted "soft" judges and enacted harsh sentencing laws; poor people of color were vilified. The system now, however, requires very little maintenance or justification. In fact, if you are white and middle class, you might not even realize the drug war is still going on. Most high school and college students today have no recollection of the political and media frenzy surrounding the drug war in the early years. They were young children when the war was declared, or not even born yet. Crack is out; terrorism is in.

Today, the political fanfare and the vehement, racialized rhetoric regarding crime and drugs are no longer necessary. Mass incarceration has been normalized, and all of the racial stereotypes and assumptions that gave rise to the system are now embraced (or at least internalized) by people of all colors, from all walks of life, and in every major political party. We may wonder aloud "where have the black men gone?" but deep down we already know. It is simply taken for granted that, in cities like Baltimore and Chicago, the vast majority of young black men are currently under the control of the criminal justice system or branded criminals for life. This extraordinary circumstance — unheard of in the rest of the world — is treated here in America as a basic fact of life, as normal as separate water fountains were just a half century ago . . . .

How It Works

Precisely how the system of mass incarceration works to trap African Americans in a virtual (and literal) cage can best be understood by viewing the system as a whole . . . . Only when we view the cage from a distance can we disengage from the maze of rationalizations that are offered for each wire and see how the entire apparatus operates to keep African Americans perpetually trapped.

This, in brief, is how the system works: The War on Drugs is the vehicle through which extraordinary numbers of black men are forced into the cage. The entrapment occurs in three distinct phases . . . . The first stage is the roundup. Vast numbers of people are swept into the criminal justice system by the police, who conduct drug operations primarily in poor communities of color. They are rewarded in cash — through drug forfeiture laws and federal grant programs—for rounding up as many people as possible, and they operate unconstrained by constitutional rules of procedure that once were considered inviolate. Police can stop, interrogate, and search anyone they choose for drug investigations, provided they get "consent." Because there is no meaningful check on the exercise of police discretion, racial biases are granted free rein. In fact, police are allowed to rely on race as a factor in selecting whom to stop and search (even though people of color are no more likely to be guilty of drug crimes than whites)—effectively guaranteeing that those who are swept into the system are primarily black and brown.

The conviction marks the beginning of the second phase: the period of formal control. Once arrested, defendants are generally denied meaningful legal representation and pressured to plead guilty whether they are or not. Prosecutors are free to "load up" defendants with extra charges, and their decisions cannot be challenged for racial bias. Once convicted, due to the drug war's harsh sentencing laws, drug offenders in the United States spend more time under the criminal justice system's formal control—in jail or prison, on probation or parole—than drug offenders anywhere else in the world. While under formal control, virtually every aspect of one's life is regulated and monitored by the system, and any form of resistance or disobedience is subject to swift sanction. This period of control may last a lifetime, even for those convicted of extremely minor, nonviolent offenses, but the vast majority of those swept into the system are eventually released. They are transferred from their prison cells to a much larger, invisible cage.

The final stage has been dubbed by some advocates as the period of invisible punishment.[10] This term, first coined by Jeremy Travis, is meant to describe the unique set of criminal sanctions that are imposed on individuals after they step outside the prison gates, a form of punishment that operates largely outside of public view and takes effect outside the traditional sentencing framework. These sanctions are imposed by operation of law rather than decisions of a sentencing judge, yet they often have a greater impact on one's life course than the months or years one actually spends behind bars. These laws operate collectively to ensure that the vast majority of convicted offenders will never integrate into mainstream, white society. They will be discriminated against, legally, for the rest of their lives—denied employment, housing, education, and public benefits. Unable to surmount these obstacles, most will eventually return to prison and then be released again, caught in a closed circuit of perpetual marginality.

In recent years, advocates and politicians have called for greater resources devoted to the problem of "prisoner re-entry," in view of the unprecedented numbers of people who are released from prison and returned to their communities every year. While the terminology is well intentioned, it utterly fails to convey the gravity of the situation facing prisoners upon their release. People who have been convicted of felonies almost never truly reenter the society they inhabited prior to their conviction. Instead, they enter a separate society, a world hidden from public view, governed by a set of oppressive and discriminatory rules and laws that do not apply to everyone else. They become members of an undercaste—an enormous population of predominately black and brown people who, because of the drug war, are denied basic rights and privileges of American citizenship and are permanently relegated to an inferior status. This is the final phase, and there is no going back.

Nothing New?

Some might argue that as disturbing as this system appears to be, there is nothing particularly new about mass incarceration; it is merely a continuation of past drug wars and biased law enforcement practices. Racial bias in our criminal justice system is simply an old problem that has gotten worse, and the social excommunication of "criminals" has a long history; it is not a recent invention. There is some merit to this argument.

Race has always influenced the administration of justice in the United States. Since the day the first prison opened, people of color have been disproportionately represented behind bars. In fact, the very first person admitted to a U.S. penitentiary was a "light skinned Negro in excellent health," described by an observer as "one who was born of a degraded and depressed race, and had never experienced anything but indifference and harshness."[11] Biased police practices are also nothing new, a recurring theme of African American experience since blacks were targeted by the police as suspected runaway slaves. And every drug war that has ever been waged in the United States—including alcohol prohibition—has been tainted or driven by racial bias.[12] Even postconviction penalties have a long history. The American colonies passed laws barring criminal offenders from a wide variety of jobs and benefits, automatically dissolving their marriages and denying them the right to enter contracts. These legislatures were following a long tradition, dating back to ancient Greece, of treating criminals as less than full citizens. Although many collateral sanctions were repealed by the late 1970s, arguably the drug war simply revived and expanded a tradition that has ancient roots, a tradition independent of the legacy of American slavery.

In view of this history and considering the lack of originality in many of the tactics and practices employed in the era of mass incarceration, there is good reason to believe that the latest drug war is just another drug war corrupted by racial and ethnic bias. But this view is correct only to a point.

In the past, the criminal justice system, as punitive as it may have been during various wars on crime and drugs, affected only a relatively small percentage of the population. Because civil penalties and sanctions imposed on ex-offenders applied only to a few, they never operated as a comprehensive system of control over any racially or ethnically defined population. Racial minorities were always overrepresented among current and ex-offenders, but as sociologists have noted, until the mid-1980s, the criminal justice system was marginal to communities of color. While young minority men with little schooling have always had relatively high rates of incarceration, "before the 1980s the penal system was not a dominant presence in the disadvantaged neighborhoods."[13]

Today, the War on Drugs has given birth to a system of mass incarceration that governs not just a small fraction of a racial or ethnic minority but entire communities of color. In ghetto communities, nearly everyone is either directly or indirectly subject to the new caste system. The system serves to redefine the terms of the relationship of poor people of color and their communities to mainstream, white society, ensuring their subordinate and marginal status. The criminal and civil sanctions that were once reserved for a tiny minority are now used to control and oppress a racially defined majority in many communities, and the systematic manner in which the control is achieved reflects not just a difference in scale. The nature of the criminal justice system has changed. It is no longer concerned primarily with the prevention and punishment of crime, but rather with the management and control of the dispossessed. Prior drug wars were ancillary to the prevailing caste system. This time the drug war *is* the system of control.

If you doubt that this is the case, consider the effect of the war on the ground, in specific locales. Take Chicago, Illinois, for example. Chicago is widely considered to be one of America's most diverse and vibrant cities. It has boasted black mayors, black police chiefs, black legislators, and is home to the nation's first black president. It has a thriving economy, a growing Latino community, and a substantial black middle class. Yet as the Chicago Urban League reported in 2002, there is another story to be told.[14]

If Martin Luther King Jr. were to return miraculously to Chicago, some forty years after bringing his Freedom Movement to the city, he would be saddened to discover that the same issues on which he originally focused still produce stark patterns of racial inequality, segregation, and poverty. He would also be struck by the dramatically elevated significance of one particular institutional force in the perpetuation and deepening of those patterns: the criminal justice system. In the few short decades since King's death, a new regime of racially disparate mass incarceration has emerged in Chicago and become the primary mechanism for racial oppression and the denial of equal opportunity.

In Chicago, like the rest of the country, the War on Drugs is the engine of mass incarceration, as well as the primary cause of gross racial disparities in the criminal justice system and in the ex-offender population. About 90 percent of those sentenced to prison for a drug offense in Illinois are African American.[15] White drug offenders are rarely arrested, and when they are, they are treated more favorably at every stage of the criminal justice process, including plea bargaining and sentencing.[16] Whites are consistently more likely to avoid prison and felony charges, even when they are repeat offenders.[17] Black offenders, by contrast, are routinely labeled felons and released into a permanent racial undercaste.

The total population of black males in Chicago with a felony record (including both current and ex-felons) is equivalent to 55 percent of the black adult male population and an astonishing 80 percent of the adult black male workforce in the Chicago area.[18] This stunning development reflects the dramatic increase in the number and race of those sent to prison for drug crimes. From the Chicago region alone, the number of those annually sent to prison for drug crimes increased almost 2,000 percent, from 469 in 1985 to 8,755 in 2005.[19] That figure, of course, does not include the thousands who avoid prison but are arrested, convicted, and sentenced to jail or probation. They, too, have criminal records that will follow them for life. More than 70 percent of all criminal cases in the Chicago area involve a class D felony drug possession charge, the lowest-level felony charge.[20] Those who do go to prison find little freedom upon release.

When people are released from Illinois prisons, they are given as little as $10 in "gate money" and a bus ticket to anywhere in the United States. Most return to impoverished neighborhoods in the Chicago area, bringing few resources and bearing the stigma of their prison record.[21] In Chicago, as in most cities across the country, ex-offenders are banned or severely restricted from employment in a large number of professions, job categories, and fields by professional licensing statutes, rules, and practices that discriminate against potential employees with felony records. According to a study conducted by the DePaul

University College of Law in 2000, of the then ninety-eight occupations requiring licenses in Illinois, fifty-seven placed stipulations and/or restrictions on applicants with a criminal record.[22] Even when not barred by law from holding specific jobs, ex-offenders in Chicago find it extraordinarily difficult to find employers who will hire them, regardless of the nature of their conviction. They are also routinely denied public housing and welfare benefits, and they find it increasingly difficult to obtain education, especially now that funding for public education has been hard hit, due to exploding prison budgets.

The impact of the new caste system is most tragically felt among the young. In Chicago (as in other cities across the United States), young black men are more likely to go to prison than to college.[23] As of June 2001, there were nearly 20,000 more black men in the Illinois state prison system than enrolled in the state's public universities.[24] In fact, there were more black men in the state's correctional facilities that year *just on drug charges* than the total number of black men enrolled in undergraduate degree programs in state universities.[25] To put the crisis in even sharper focus, consider this: just 992 black men received a bachelor's degree from Illinois state universities in 1999, while roughly 7,000 black men were released from the state prison system the following year just for drug offenses.[26] The young men who go to prison rather than college face a lifetime of closed doors, discrimination, and ostracism. Their plight is not what we hear about on the evening news, however. Sadly, like the racial caste systems that preceded it, the system of mass incarceration now seems normal and natural to most, a regrettable necessity. . . .

NOTES

1. Michael Eric Dyson, "Obama's Rebuke of Absentee Black Fathers," *Time*, June 19, 2008.
2. Sam Roberts, "51% of Women Now Living with a Spouse," *New York Times*, Jan 16, 2007.
3. See Jonathan Tilove, "Where Have All the Men Gone? Black Gender Gap Is Widening," *Seattle Times*, May 5, 2005, and Jonathan Tilove, "Where Have All the Black Men Gone?" *Star-Ledger* (Newark), May 8, 2005.
4. Ibid.
5. Cf. Salim Muwakkil, "Black Men: Missing," *In These Times*, June 16, 2005.
6. G. Garvin, "Where Have the Black Men Gone?" *Ebony*, Dec. 2006.
7. One in eleven black adults was under correctional supervision at year end 2007, or approximately 2.4 million people. See Pew Center on the States, *One in 31: The Long Reach of American Corrections* (Washington, DC: Pew Charitable Trusts, 2009). According to the 1850 Census, approximately 1.7 million adults (ages 15 and older) were slaves.
8. See Andrew J. Cherlin, *Marriage, Divorce, Remarriage*, rev. ed. (Cambridge, MA: Harvard University Press, 1992), 110.
9. See Glenn C. Loury, *Race, Incarceration, and American Values* (Cambridge, MA: MIT Press, 2008), commentary by Pam Karlan.
10. See Marc Mauer and Meda Chesney-Lind, eds., *Invisible Punishment: The Collateral Consequences of Mass Imprisonment* (New York: The New Press, 2002); and Jeremy Travis, *But They All Come Back: Facing the Challenges of Prisoner Reentry* (Washington, DC: Urban Institute Press, 2005).
11. Negley K. Teeters and John D. Shearer, *The Prison at Philadelphia, Cherry Hill: The Separate System of Prison Discipline, 1829–1913* (New York: Columbia University Press, 1957), 84.

12. See David Musto, *The American Disease: Origins of Narcotics Control*, 3rd ed. (New York: Oxford University Press, 1999), 4, 7, 43–44, 219–20, describing the role of racial bias in earlier drug wars; and Doris Marie Provine, *Unequal Under Law: Race in the War on Drugs* (Chicago: University of Chicago Press, 2007), 37–90, describing racial bias in alcohol prohibition, as well as other drug wars.
13. Mary Pattillo, David F. Weiman, and Bruce Western, *Imprisoning America: The Social Effect of Mass Incarceration* (New York: Russell Sage Foundation, 2004), 2.
14. Paul Street, *The Vicious Circle: Race, Prison, Jobs, and Community in Chicago, Illinois, and the Nation* (Chicago: Chicago Urban League, Department of Research and Planning, 2002).
15. Street, *Vicious Circle*, 3.
16. Alden Loury, "Black Offenders Face Stiffest Drug Sentences," *Chicago Reporter*, Sept. 12, 2007.
17. Ibid.
18. Street, *Vicious Circle*, 15.
19. Donald G. Lubin et al., *Chicago Metropolis 2020: 2006 Crime and Justice Index*, (Washington, DC: Pew Center on the States, 2006), 5, www.pewcenteronthestates.org/report_detail.aspx?id=33022.
20. Report of the Illinois Disproportionate Justice Impact Study Commission, Dec. 2010, available at www.centerforhealthandjustice.org/DJIS_ExecSumm_FINAL.pdf.
21. Lubin et al., *Chicago Metropolis 2020*, 37.
22. Ibid., 35.
23. Ibid., 3; see also Bruce Western, *Punishment and Inequality in America* (New York: Russell Sage Foundation, 2006), 12.
24. Street, *Vicious Circle*, 3.
25. Ibid.
26. Ibid.

4 Living While Black and the Criminalization of Blackness

P. R. Lockhart

On April 12, Rashon Nelson and Donte Robinson entered a Philadelphia Starbucks to meet with a business partner. But after waiting less than 10 minutes for him, they found themselves surrounded by police, facing charges of trespassing and creating a disturbance.[1]

Their crime? Asking to use the restroom and sitting inside before placing an order.

That was all it took for the store's manager to call the police, telling a 911 dispatcher that there were "two gentlemen in my cafe that are refusing to make a purchase or leave." Police arrived shortly thereafter, and the two men, both black, were put in handcuffs.

Robinson later told *Good Morning America* that his first thought when he saw the police officers was, "They can't be here for us."[2] Nelson told the Associated Press that he feared for his life.[3]

"Anytime I'm encountered by cops, I can honestly say it's a thought that runs through my mind," Nelson added. "You never know what's going to happen."

What happened to Nelson and Robinson, and the social media outcry that followed, prompted Starbucks to shut down all 8,000 company-owned stores for a day of anti-bias training.[4] Beyond that, the incident began a wave of stories sharing a common framework: A black or brown person, doing something innocuous or nothing at all, prompts a suspicious white person to call the police.

It's created a seemingly endless stream of stories involving calls to police or 911 on people of color: A black child who mowed part of the wrong yard[5], a black family eating at Subway[6], an 8-year-old girl selling bottled water[6], a woman using the private pool in her gated community[8], a trio of filmmakers staying in an Airbnb[9], or a group of black women on a golf course.[10] These are just some examples of a person or group being forced to defend their presence.

These stories and others have been published so frequently that they've formed a new news genre: "Living While Black," a phrase that encompasses the myriad ways black people are viewed with suspicion, profiled, and threatened with responses from police for minor infractions, or less.

Collectively, they illustrate the ways people of color are subjected to arbitrary social expectations, and how violating those expectations is punishable. Decades after the collapse of legal segregation, they also show that spaces like clothing stores, coffee shops, neighborhoods, and universities remain strongly controlled along racial lines.

P. R. Lockhart writes about race: how it intersects with gender, sexuality, and economic status, how it influences social justice movements, and how communities of color interact with and are affected by policy and politics. Before joining Vox, Lockhart covered race and politics for *Mother Jones*.

In many ways, the recent wave of Living While Black incidents highlights issues that go beyond the circumstances that fuel any single story. They speak to the intensification of racial tension in a political climate that has emboldened whites frustrated with a perceived loss of power and fueled fear and anxiety in communities of color.

The incidents also speak to the persistence of residential segregation and isolation, particularly of whites, and how that isolation simultaneously maintains and heightens white mistrust of nonwhite groups.[11] And with many of these calls leading to requests for police intervention, they highlight the use of law enforcement to "manage" the behavior of African Americans. That's fraught with menace because of the racial disparities in police use of force that make people of color more likely to encounter violence or harassment.[12]

Much like the rise of Black Lives Matter and the videos of police violence that accompanied it, Living While Black offers evidence in real time that America is still grappling with long-held racial divisions. As the incidents continue, the deluge of footage is sparking a discussion about race and racism that focuses on the ways individual behavior can play into larger acts of systemic racism. It's an important discussion driven by unfortunate circumstances. But it's also a very old issue.

Racial Profiling Isn't New, but Living While Black Is Calling New Attention to It

At its core, Living While Black is about racial profiling, the concept that a person's race or ethnicity makes them an object of suspicion and heightened scrutiny from law enforcement. From the use of slave patrols to lynching to legal segregation, and in modern iterations like stop and frisk, racial profiling has long been used to maintain white authority by singling out the presence and behavior of people of color—especially African Americans—as requiring punishment. These systems rely on the participation of bystanders and observers to alert authorities to those deemed "suspicious."

So on one hand, what we are seeing now isn't new. . . . But the current Living While Black incidents—captured on video and spread on social media—do make it easier for the broader public to see these calls to police. This phenomenon is similar to the spread of video documenting police violence and misconduct. By putting these incidents on camera, they serve as evidence, providing a digital record for those affected by profiling and a way of alerting a wider audience to the ways in which black behavior continues to be criminalized and subject to policing.

Robin DiAngelo, a sociologist and the author of *White Fragility: Why It's So Hard for White People to Talk About Racism*, says these videos make it much more difficult for white people to deny that profiling has occurred.[*] "These incidents have always happened, but white people do not always believe it because it doesn't happen to us," DiAngelo told me. "The only real difference we have now is that we are able to record it in a way that makes it undeniable."

---

[*] Robin DiAngelo's article "My Class Didn't Trump My Race: Using Oppression to Face Privilege" appears in Part II of this volume.

In doing so, the incidents highlight just how quickly a misplaced assumption or feeling uncomfortable can lead a white person to call the police. They also show how black people are continually asked to justify their presence in spaces where they are seen as not being the norm.

Take, for example, the story of Lolade Siyonbola, a black graduate student at Yale who woke from a nap in a dorm common room in May to questions from police.[13] A white classmate had called 911, saying that she wasn't sure if Siyonbola belonged in the dorm. When police officers arrived, Siyonbola unlocked her dorm room to prove her residence, but she was still asked for ID.

"I deserve to be here. I pay tuition like everybody else," Siyonbola told police officers in a video posted to Facebook.[14] "I'm not going to justify my existence here."

The request to "justify my existence," and the frustration that this sort of request creates, lies at the core of these incidents. Academics have noted that people of color, especially black people, are often asked to provide justification and proof when they enter spaces where they are in the minority. Yale sociologist Elijah Anderson explains that there is a difference between "white spaces," where black people are often not present or exist in a limited number, and "black spaces," communities and spaces occupied by larger numbers of black people.[15]

Anderson notes that commonly held stereotypes of black people as being criminal and black behavior as being deviant strongly shape how they are viewed by others. As a result, black people in these "white spaces" are forced to justify their presence, and face consequences when that justification isn't accepted by others.

"In the minds of many of their detractors, to scrutinize and stop black people is to prevent crime and protect the neighborhood," he explained in "The White Space," a 2015 paper published in *Sociology of Race and Ethnicity*. "Thus, for the black person, particularly young males, virtually every public encounter results in a degree of scrutiny that a 'normal,' white person would certainly not need to endure."

Research has shown that black people are often subjected to heightened scrutiny and suspicion, which begins in childhood. In 2014, researcher Phillip Goff found that by the age of 10, black boys begin to be seen as less innocent than their white peers.[16] And a Georgetown study released in 2017 found that black girls as young as 5 are already perceived as more adult-like and less innocent than white girls of the same age.[17]

It tracks with other data examining attitudes about race. A series of studies published by the American Psychological Association in 2017 have shown that black men are more often associated with violence than white men[18], and a 2015 study from researchers at the University of California Los Angeles found that just mentioning a "black-sounding" name is enough to conjure a mental image that is larger and more threatening than a "white-sounding" one.[19]

It's likely that the Living While Black incidents we hear about now reflect this sort of implicit, fear-driven, stereotype-laden thinking. But these incidents may also point to something else—like a more explicit desire to preserve racial hierarchies by casting people of color as deviants who can be removed at any moment. . . .

How Living While Black Collides with Policing

If the recent spate of incidents has sparked a conversation about why black people are met with so much suspicion in public, it's important to ask why callers want police to respond to situations where they aren't really needed. . . .

You don't need to look far for examples of how this can quickly take a turn for the worse. In 2015, white residents in McKinney, Texas, called police with a noise complaint against a group of black high schoolers holding a pool party. [20] One adult allegedly told the teenagers to return to "Section 8 [public] housing." When police arrived, a black girl was violently slammed to the ground and pinned by an officer. Residents later posted signs thanking the officers for "keeping us safe."[21]

In 2014, John Crawford was fatally shot by police inside an Ohio Walmart after a man called 911, telling the dispatcher that Crawford was pointing a gun at people.[22] Crawford was holding a BB gun [from the Walmart], and video footage later showed that he was not brandishing the weapon.[23]

In early July [2018], four black teenagers were detained by Minnesota police officers, including one officer who drew his weapon, after a woman called the police saying that the boys had knives and assaulted a white man in the park.[24] The call was quickly shown to be false after police found no weapons.

Data from the Department of Justice has shown that people of color call the police less often than white people.[25] Experts note that this difference is driven by a crucial perception: While white people see police as a force that will protect them, communities of color see a force that is more likely to do the opposite.

There's a real reason for that. In addition to studies that reveal racial disparities in police use of force, data collected by the Guardian shows that black Americans are more likely than whites to be shot by police, when controlling for population.[26]

High-profile incidents of police violence can further erode trust in law enforcement, and that trust can be difficult to regain.[27] A 2016 study from a group of sociologists at Yale, Harvard, and Oxford found that after the 2004 police beating of Frank Jude in Milwaukee, residents made 17 percent fewer 911 calls the next year.[28] And those numbers remained low even after the officers involved in the incident had been punished. Researchers found similar results after high-profile incidents of police brutality in other predominantly black communities. Those changes didn't happen in white communities.

A deterioration in trust can happen even when a fatal police shooting isn't involved. In 2013, political scientists Amy Lerman and Vesla Weaver examined the potential effects 311 non-emergency calls have on communities.[29] Analyzing some 3 million 311 call records and 1.2 million police stops in New York City, they found that many of these calls, which are usually used to lodge complaints about minor issues like noise disturbances, were more likely to occur in low-income and minority neighborhoods.

While 311 data does not include information about the race of the caller, a recent report from BuzzFeed found that census tracts in gentrifying parts of New York City yielded more 311 calls than non-gentrifying ones, suggesting that these calls increase when the white population in a neighborhood increases.[30]

Lerman and Weaver noted that how police handled these cases had a significant effect on perceptions of local institutions. "When police search a higher number of citizens or deploy more force in their stops of community members, people become much less likely" to interact with their local government. "Thus, the relationship turns on the quality of policing, not merely the quantity."

Paul Butler, a professor at Georgetown Law and the author of *Chokehold: Policing Black Men*, told me that one reason unnecessary 911 calls are so dangerous is that they put African Americans in unnecessary interactions with law enforcement. "When the police are called on African Americans, it has a very negative impact on those black people, even if they are not arrested, or beat up, or killed," he said. "You're required to justify your existence and your presence in a white space. It makes you feel like less of a citizen and less of a human being. It's impossible to overstate the adverse consequences." . . .

The Tensions in This Phenomenon Reveal Anxiety Among White People

Living While Black is, of course, taking place in a wider context. Four years ago, Black Lives Matter and the Movement for Black Lives sparked a national conversation about race and policing that laid the groundwork for the use of video and social media seen in Living While Black and increased knowledge of how policing affects black communities. But this new wave of videos is getting so much attention as heightened concerns about the treatment of immigrant communities, the rise of emboldened white supremacists [31], and an increase in hate crimes share the spotlight.[32]

The story of Living While Black isn't just about black people. It's also about white people, their anxieties, and what that anxiety means for black people simply trying to navigate daily life.

Polling shows that white people's thoughts about race aren't accurate. They are overly optimistic about the progress of other groups; a 2017 Yale study, for example, found that white Americans dramatically overestimate the level of economic equality between black and white people, and other forms of racial equality in the US.[33]

Polling also shows that whites believe they face as much, or even more discrimination than black Americans and other racial groups. In fact, according to a 2016 poll from the Public Religion Research Institute, 57 percent of whites and 66 percent of those identified as "white working class" in the poll, said that "discrimination against whites is as big a problem today as discrimination against blacks and other minorities."[34] A recent PRRI study found that roughly one-third of Americans and half of Republicans believe America's growing racial diversity will have a negative impact on American society.[35]

Perhaps it's because many of those within this group are experiencing the feeling of being left behind, in part, because of the slow steady ascension of people of color. Arlie Hochschild, a sociologist and author of *Strangers in Their Own Land*, describes certain white Americans as feeling like they are standing in [a] line that leads up a hill toward the endpoint, prosperity.[36] But faced with globalization and income stagnation, they see marginalized people "cutting" the line with the help of programs like affirmative action or anti-discrimination laws. This also introduces more black and brown people into previously white-only spaces.

As Yale psychologist Jennifer Richeson recently [said], this zero-sum framing can play a powerful role in whites' political behavior, even if it doesn't acknowledge that whites as a group still hold significant societal advantages.[37] It isn't much of a stretch to suggest that these attitudes likely fuel heightened distrust and animosity toward people of color. These anxieties, cranked up to an extreme in declarations that racial progress would result in so-called "white genocide," create an even more dire perception of nonwhites and the way demographic change is affecting the country.[38]

But there's another issue here too: Whites are rarely discussed as a racial group. . . .

That failure to truly grapple with race helps reinforce a defensive understanding of race and its continued consequences. It's part of why so many of the people calling police on a black person react to criticism with a simple response: "I'm not a racist."

Take, for example, Linda Krakora, an Ohio woman whose husband called police after Reggie Fields, a black 12-year-old, mowed a small patch of their grass.[39] When a Facebook video of the incident [went] viral, Krakora quickly defended herself and her family from accusations of racism, noting that she lived in a predominantly black community.[40]

Another example lies in McKinney, the site of the aforementioned pool party in 2015. When the Atlantic's Olga Khazan visited the town this year, she noted that several community members openly declined to discuss the incident.[41] Those who did were often defensive when questioned about the role that race might have played in the encounter. "[Police] were called not because there were black people in the pool," George Fuller, the mayor of McKinney, told Khazan. "They came . . . because there were people trespassing, destroying property, and smoking dope." (Khazan noted that police reports and 911 calls from the incident made no mention of drugs.)

DiAngelo told me that these defenses posit a "good-bad binary," a framing that positions racism as an intentional act exclusively done by bad people. "It exempts virtually all white people from the system that we're in," she said. "As long as we think nice people can't be racist, we're going to protect the system."

That failure to acknowledge the depths and breadth of racism also makes it harder to acknowledge the ways that nonwhite groups are exposed to harm by actions like calling the police. In the short term, the problem highlighted by Living While Black can be solved by white people calling the police less. But addressing the underlying issues will require much more than that.

NOTES

1. Stewart, Emily. "Two Black Men Were Arrested in a Philadelphia Starbucks for Doing Nothing." Vox, 15 Apr. 2018, www.vox.com/identities/2018/4/14/17238494/what-happened-at-starbucks-black-men-arrested-philadelphia.

2. @GMA. "FULL INTERVIEW: 'This is something that has been going on for years…everyone is blind to it.' Rashon Nelson & Donte Robinson, the 2 black men arrested at a Starbucks in Philadelphia, speak out exclusively to @RobinRoberts: abcn.ws/2Hf4Qb5." Twitter, 19 Apr. 2018, 4:47 a.m., twitter.com/GMA/status/986934358563946496.

3. Whack, Errin Haines. "2 Black Men Arrested at Starbucks Get an Apology from Police." *AP News*, 19 Apr. 2018, apnews.com/45547c3ae5324b679e982c4847ee1378.

4. Stewart, Emily. "What Starbucks Is Teaching Its Employees During Anti-Bias Training." *Vox*, 29 May 2018, www.vox.com/identities/2018/5/29/17405338/starbucks-racial-bias-training-why-closed.

5. Lockhart, P.R. "A White Neighbor Called Police on a Kid Mowing a Lawn. Later, They Called as He Played in a Yard." *Vox*, 9 July 2018, www.vox.com/identities/2018/7/2/17527382/reggie-fields-racial-profiling-911-police.

6. Edwards, Breanna. "#EatingOutWhileBlack: Subway Employee Calls 911 on Black Family Because She Thought They Would Rob Her." *The Root*, 7 May 2018, www.theroot.com/eatingoutwhileblack-subway-employee-calls-911-on-blac-1827358215.

7. Murdock, Sebastian. "White Woman Threatened To Call Cops On 8-Year-Old Girl Selling Water." *Huffpost*, 26 June 2018, www.huffpost.com/entry/white-woman-sees-black-girl-selling-water-allegedly-calls-police_n_5b2e94a5e4b00295f15cf35f?guccounter=1.;

8. Zraick, Karen. "Man Labeled 'ID Adam' Is Fired After Calling the Police on a Black Woman at Pool." *The New York Times*, 6 July 2018, www.nytimes.com/2018/07/06/us/pool-racial-profiling-white-man.html.

9. "Black Filmmakers Say They Were Swarmed by Police after Checking out of Airbnb." *CBS News*, 8 May 2018, www.cbsnews.com/news/black-filmmakers-swarmed-by-police-after-checking-out-of-airbnb-in-california/.;

10. Marco, Tony, and Lauren DelValle. "A Group of Black Women Say a Golf Course Called the Cops on Them for Playing Too Slow." *CNN*, 25 Apr. 2018, www.cnn.com/2018/04/25/us/black-women-golfers-pennsylvania-trnd/index.html.

11. Klein, Ezra. "White Threat in a Browning America." *Vox*, 30 July 2018, www.vox.com/policy-and-politics/2018/7/30/17505406/trump-obama-race-politics-immigration.

12. Lopez, German. "There Are Huge Racial Disparities in How US Police Use Force." *Vox*, 14 Nov. 2018, www.vox.com/identities/2016/8/13/17938186/police-shootings-killings-racism-racial-disparities.

13. Griggs, Brandon. "A Black Yale Graduate Student Took a Nap in Her Dorm's Common Room. So a White Student Called Police." *CNN*, 12 May 2018, www.cnn.com/2018/05/09/us/yale-student-napping-black-trnd/index.html.

14. Siyonbola, Lolade. Cops called on black Yale student. *Facebook*, 7 May 2018, 10:56 p. m., https://www.facebook.com/loladeskentele/videos/10156361381958832/.

15. Anderson, Elijah. "The White Space." *Sociology of Race and Ethnicity*, vol. 1, no. 1, 2015, pp. 10–21., doi: 10.1177/2332649214561306.

16. Goff, Phillip Atiba, et al. "The Essence of Innocence: Consequences of Dehumanizing Black Children." *Journal of Personality and Social Psychology*, vol. 106, no. 4, 2014, pp. 526–545. *American Psychological Association*, APA PsycNET, doi:10.1037/a0035663.

17. Epstein, Rebecca, et al. *Girlhood Interrupted: The Erasure of Black Girls' Childhood.* Georgetown Law Center on Poverty and Inequality, 2017. www.law.georgetown.edu/poverty-inequality-center/wp-content/uploads/sites/14/2017/08/girlhood-interrupted.pdf.

18. Lopez, German. "Study: People See Black Men as Larger and More Threatening Than Similarly Sized White Men." *Vox*, 17 Mar. 2017, www.vox.com/identities/2017/3/17/14945576/black-white-bodies-size-threat-study.

19. Lopez, German. "A Depressing Study of How People Respond to Stereotypically Black and White Names." *Vox*, 9 Oct. 2015, www.vox.com/2015/10/9/9482537/implicit-bias-names.

20. Lopez, Geman. "The McKinney, Texas, Pool Party Shows Racial Segregation Is Still Alive in America." *Vox*, 8 June 2015, www.vox.com/2015/6/8/8747011/mckinney-texas-segregation.

21. @ZANews16. "Pool just put up this sign supporting McKinney PD & thanking officers for their response Friday." Twitter, 7 June 2015, 3:15 p.m., twitter.com/ZANews16/status/607672344618758144?ref_src=twsrc%5Etfw&.

22. Lind, Dara, and German Lopez. "Video: John Crawford Didn't Seem To Aim Toy Gun at Anyone Before Police Shot at Him." *Vox*, 24 Sept. 2014, www.vox.com/2014/9/24/6839953/video-john-crawford-walmart-police-beavercreek-ohio-toy-gun.

23. "911 Caller in John Crawford III Case may Face Prosecution." *YouTube*, uploaded by WPCO.com | 9 On Your Side, 7 Apr. 2016, www.youtube.com/watch?v=6y7WC39d-To.

24. Perez, Maria. "Viral Video of Black Teens in Handcuffs Is Investigated by Police after False 911 Call." *Newsweek*, 12 July 2018, www.newsweek.com/racial-slurs-911-call-minneapolis-park-police-minnesota-1021321.

25. Durose, Matthew and Lynn Langton. "Requests for Police Assistance, 2011." NCJ 242938, U.S. Department of Justice, September 2013. Available at www.bjs.gov/content/pub/pdf/rpa11.pdf.

26. *The Counted: People killed by police in the US*, The Guardian, 2016, www.theguardian.com/us-news/ng-interactive/2015/jun/01/the-counted-police-killings-us-database.

27. Lopez, German. "Police Officer Chokes Black Man Following Verbal Dispute at Waffle House." *Vox*, 10 May 2018, www.vox.com/identities/2018/5/10/17340008/anthony-wall-police-waffle-house-video.

28. Desmond, Matthew, et al. "Police Violence and Citizen Crime Reporting in the Black Community." *American Sociological Review*, 2016, pp. 1–20., doi:10.1177/0003122416663494.;

29. Lerman, Amy E., and Vesla Weaver. "Staying out of Sight? Concentrated Policing and Local Political Action." *The ANNALS of the American Academy of Political and Social Science*, vol. 651, no. 1, 2013, pp. 202–219., doi:10.1177/0002716213503085.

30. Vo, Lam Thuy. "They Played Dominoes Outside Their Apartment For Decades. Then The White People Moved In And Police Started Showing Up." *BuzzFeed News*, 29 June 2018, www.buzzfeednews.com/article/lamvo/gentrification-complaints-311-new-york.

31. Coaston, Jane. "Self-Described Nazis and White Supremacists Are Running as Republicans Across the Country. The GOP Is Terrified." *Vox*, 9 July 2018, www.vox.com/2018/7/9/17525860/nazis-russell-walker-arthur-jones-republicans-illinois-north-carolina-virginia.;

32. Lopez, German. "A New FBI Report Says Hate Crimes—Especially Against Muslims—Went Up in 2016." *Vox*, 13 Nov. 2017, www.vox.com/identities/2017/11/13/16643448/fbi-hate-crimes-2016.;

33. Kraus, Michael W., et al. "Americans Misperceive Racial Economic Equality." *Proceedings of the National Academy of Sciences*, vol. 114, no. 39, 10 Aug. 2017, pp. 10324–10331, doi:10.1073/pnas.1707719114.

34. Cooper, Betsy, et al. "How Immigration and Concerns about Cultural Change Are Shaping the 2016 Election | PRRI/Brookings Survey." *PRRI*, 23 June 2016, www.prri.org/research/prri-brookings-poll-immigration-economy-trade-terrorism-presidential-race/.

35. Vandermaas-Peeler, Alex, et al. "American Democracy in Crisis: The Challenges of Voter Knowledge, Participation, and Polarization." *PRRI*, 17 July 2018, www.prri.org/research/american-democracy-in-crisis-voters-midterms-trump-election-2018/.

36. Hochschild, Arlie Russell. *Strangers in Their Own Land: Anger and Mourning on the American Right*. The New Press, 2016.

37. Klein, Ezra. "White Threat in a Browning America." *Vox*, 30 July 2018, www.vox.com/policy-and-politics/2018/7/30/17505406/trump-obama-race-politics-immigration.

38. Coaston, Jane. "The Scary Ideology Behind Trump's Immigration Instincts." *Vox*, 6 Nov. 2018, www.vox.com/2018/1/18/16897358/racism-donald-trump-immigration.

39. Lockhart, P.R. "A White Neighbor Called Police on a Kid Mowing a Lawn. Later, They Called as He Played in a Yard." *Vox*, 9 July 2018, www.vox.com/identities/2018/7/2/17527382/reggie-fields-racial-profiling-911-police.

40. Alcorn, Chauncey. "White Ohio Family That Called 911 on Black Boy Mowing Lawn Calls Police on Him Again July 4." *Mic*, 6 July 2018, www.mic.com/articles/190120/white-ohio-family-that-called-911-on-black-boy-mowing-lawn-calls-police-on-him-again-july-4#. Chy52V7ho.

41. Khazan, Olga. "After the Police Brutality Video Goes Viral." *The Atlantic*, 23 July 2018, www.theatlantic.com/politics/archive/2018/07/after-the-police-brutality-video-goes-viral/564863/.

5

The Ghosts of Stonewall: Policing Gender, Policing Sex

Joey L. Mogul, Andrea J. Ritchie, and Kay Whitlock

Our entire movement started from fighting police violence, and we're still fighting police violence. In many ways, it's gotten worse.

—Imani Henry, founder of TransJustice[1]

On a hot August night in 1966, "drag queens" and gay "hustlers" at the Compton Cafeteria in the Tenderloin District of San Francisco rose up and fought back when police tried to arrest them for doing nothing more than being out.[2] The late 1960s saw frequent police raids, often accompanied by brutality, on gay establishments across the country, which were meeting with increasing resistance. The previous five years had also seen uprisings in Watts, Detroit, Chicago, and Newark and dozens of other cities, in many cases sparked by incidents of widespread racial profiling and abuse of people of color by police.[3]

It was against this backdrop that, in the early morning hours of Saturday, June 28, 1969, police raided the Stonewall Inn in New York City. Claiming to be enforcing liquor laws, they began arresting employees and patrons of the private lesbian and gay establishment. Police action, which included striking patrons with billy clubs while spewing homophobic abuse, sparked outrage among those present. Led by people described by many as drag queens and butch lesbians, bar patrons, joined by street people, began yelling "Gay Power!" and throwing shoes, coins, and bricks at the officers. Over the next several nights, police and queers clashed repeatedly in the streets of the West Village. One report described the impacts of the police response to the uprising as follows:

> At one point, Seventh Avenue . . . looked like a battlefield in Vietnam. Young people, many of them queens, were lying on the sidewalk bleeding from the head, face, mouth, and even the eyes. Others were nursing bruised and often bleeding arms, legs, backs, and necks.[4]

Joey L. Mogul is a partner at the People's Law Office in Chicago, representing survivors of abuse and misconduct in civil rights cases and defendants in criminal and capital cases. Mogul also directs the Civil Rights Clinic at DePaul University College of Law.

Andrea J. Ritchie is a police-misconduct attorney, advocate against police violence, and Researcher-in-Residence on Race, Gender, Sexuality, and Criminalization at the Social Justice Institute of the Barnard Center for Research on Women.

Kay Whitlock is a writer and activist who focuses on racial, gender, queer, and economic justice. She is the cofounder and coeditor of the weekly Criminal Injustice series published on CriticalMassProgress.com. With Mogul and Ritchie, Whitlock coauthored *Queer (In)Justice: The Criminalization of LGBT People in the United States*.

Excerpt from *Queer (In)Justice*, by Joey Mogul, Kay Whitlock, and Andrea Ritchie. Copyright © 2011 by Katherine Whitlock, Joey L. Mogul, and Andrea J. Ritchie. Reprinted by permission of Beacon Press, Boston.

The Stonewall Uprising, as the rebellion against the raids came to be known, has been mythically cast as the "birthplace" of the modern LGBT rights movement in the United States, although in reality it was but one of its primary catalysts. In the weeks that followed, the Gay Liberation Front, inspired by contemporaneous movements such as the women's liberation movement, the Black Panthers, and the Young Lords, was formed.[5] Spontaneous resistance to police raids on gay bars and bathhouses blossomed in the ensuing decade. The 1970 protest march commemorating the one-year anniversary of the raid on the Stonewall Inn grew into an annual worldwide celebration of gay pride.

Fast forward three decades to March 2003, when the Power Plant, a private club in the Highland Park area of Detroit, frequented primarily by African American gay men, lesbians, and transgender women, was filled to capacity. Around 3:00 a.m., between 50 and 100 officers from the Wayne County Sheriff's Department dressed in black clothing, with guns drawn and laser sights on, suddenly cut the lights and stormed the premises, shouting orders for everyone to "hit the floor." Over 350 people in the club at that time were handcuffed, forced to lie face down on the floor, and detained for up to twelve hours, left to "sit in their own and others' urine and waste." Some were kicked in the head and back, slammed into walls, and verbally abused. Officers on the scene were heard saying things like "it's a bunch of fags" and "those fags in here make me sick." As at Stonewall, the officers claimed to be enforcing building and liquor codes. The sheriff's department said they were responding to complaints from neighbors and concerns for public safety. They had obtained a warrant to search the premises, but rather than execute it during the daytime against only the owner of the establishment, they chose to wait until the club was full, and then unjustifiably arrested over 300 people, citing them for "loitering inside a building," an offense carrying a maximum fine of $500. Vehicles within a three-block radius of the club were also ticketed and towed, despite the fact that some of the car owners had never even entered the club that night.[6]

The policing of queer sexualities has been arguably the most visible and recognized point of contact between LGBT people and the criminal legal system. From the images that form the opening sequence of *Milk*—the 2008 biopic about gay San Francisco supervisor Harvey Milk—of groups of white gay men hiding from cameras as they are rounded up by police in the 1950s, to the historic clashes with police of the late 1960s and early 1970s, police repression and resistance to it are central themes of gay life in the United States. Groundbreaking gay rights organizations such as the Mattachine Society and the Daughters of Bilitis have expressed strong concern about bar raids and police harassment.[7] A study conducted by the National Gay Task Force (now the NGLTF [and since renamed The National LGBTQ Task Force]) in the mid-eighties found that 23 percent of gay men and 13 percent of lesbians reported having been harassed, threatened with violence, or physically attacked by police because of their sexual orientation.[8] It remains a daily occurrence for large numbers of LGBT people. According to reports made to the National Coalition of Anti-Violence Programs (NCAVP) in 2008, law enforcement officers were the third-largest category of perpetrators of anti-LGBT violence.[9] Incidences of reported police violence against LGBT people increased by 150 percent between 2007 and 2008, and the number of law enforcement officers reported to have engaged in abusive treatment of LGBT people increased by 11 percent.[10] In 2000, the NCAVP stated that 50 percent of bias-related violence reported by transgender women in San Francisco was committed by police and private security officers.[11]

As demonstrated by the Power Plant incident, in many ways, policing of queers has not changed significantly since the days when it sparked outrage and resistance from LGBT communities, although its focus has narrowed to some degree. According to the New York City Anti-Violence Project, "Young queer people of color, transgender youth, homeless and street involved youth are more vulnerable to police violence . . . AVP's data analysis also reveals that transgender individuals are at a greater risk of experiencing police violence and misconduct than non trans people."[12] The National Center for Lesbian Rights (NCLR) and Transgender Law Center reported in 2003 that one in four transgender people in San Francisco had been harassed or abused by the police.[13] Far from fading into the annals of LGBT history, police violence against queers is alive and well.

Yet with the exception of sodomy law enforcement, since the mid 1970s resistance to abusive policing of LGBT people has largely been absent from the agendas of national mainstream LGBT organizations, particularly as police have increasingly narrowed their focus to segments of LGBT communities with little power or voice inside and outside such groups. Similarly, while mainstream police accountability and civil rights organizations have called for accountability in a limited number of cases involving LGBT individuals, policing of gender and queer sexualities has not been central to their analysis of the issue. It is essential to bring the persistent police violence experienced by LGBT people to the fore of these movements to ensure the ghosts of Stonewall do not continue to haunt for years to come. . . .

Policing Gender

Queer encounters with police are not limited to those driven by efforts to punish deviant sexualities. Sylvia Rivera, one of the veterans of the Stonewall Uprising, described the treatment of transgender women at the time: "When drag queens were arrested, what degradation there was! . . . We always felt that the police were the real enemy . . . . We were disrespected. A lot of us were beaten up and raped."[14]

Law enforcement officers have fairly consistently and explicitly policed the borders of the gender binary. Historically and up until the 1980s, such policing took the form of enforcement of sumptuary laws, which required individuals to wear at least three articles of clothing conventionally associated with the gender they were assigned at birth, and subjected people to arrest for impersonating another gender.[15] . . .

Currently, gender is often directly policed through arbitrary and violent arrests of transgender and gender-nonconforming people for using the "wrong" restroom—even though there is generally no law requiring individuals who use bathrooms designated as for men or women to have any particular set of characteristics. As Franke notes, sumptuary laws and bathroom signs serve similar functions, creating and reinforcing an "official symbolic language of gendered identity that rightfully belongs to either sex. 'Real women' and 'real men' conform to the norms; the rest of us are deviants. Curiously, in life and in law, bathrooms seem to be the site where one's sexual authenticity is tested."[16] . . .

Beyond bathrooms, gender policing takes place through routine harassment. Verbal abuse of transgender and gender-nonconforming people is commonplace. According to a Los Angeles study of 244 transgender women, 37 percent of respondents reported experiencing verbal abuse from a police officer on at least one occasion.[17] It also takes place through arrests of individuals who carry identification reflecting the "wrong" gender. Such policing draws on and reinforces the criminalizing archetype of transgender and gender-nonconforming people as intrinsically dishonest and deceptive. It often extends to routinely subjecting transgender and gender-nonconforming people to inappropriate, invasive, and unlawful searches conducted for the purpose of viewing or touching individuals' genitals, either to satisfy law enforcement officers' curiosity, or to determine a person's "real" gender. Jeremy Burke, a white transgender man arrested in San Francisco in 2002, was kicked and beaten, and forcibly strip-searched by several female officers, then placed naked and handcuffed in a holding tank. A dress was later thrown into the cell, which Burke refused to wear. An officer subsequently forced Burke to display his genitalia, justifying police actions by saying, "The boss doesn't know where to put you," and then taunting him further, stating, "That's the biggest clit I ever saw."[18]

Gender nonconformity is also often punished in and of itself, through physical violence, drawing on a toxic amalgam of queer criminalizing archetypes. Controlling narratives framing women of African descent as masculine and women of color as sexually degraded are also at play, dictating punishment for failure to conform to racialized gender norms. For instance, Black lesbians frequently report being punched in the chest by officers who justify their violence by saying something along the lines of, "You want to act like a man, I'll treat you like a man."[19] A Latina lesbian arrested at a demonstration in New York City in 2003 reported that an officer walked her by cells holding men and told her, "You think you're a man, we'll put you in there and see what happens." A Black lesbian in Atlanta reported being raped by a police officer who told her the world needed "one less dyke."[20]

At other times, gender policing is subtler. Gender nonconformity in appearance or expression gives rise to police presumptions of disorder, violence, and mental instability, among other qualities. Such presumptions are heightened when synergistically reinforced by equally powerful stereotypes based on race, class, or both. In routine daily interactions, police can be described as succumbing to "classification anxiety."[21] When officers feel challenged in engaging in the rigid classification of individuals as male and female, gay and straight, an individual's mere presence in public spaces is experienced as a disruption of the social order. Queer, transgender, and gender-nonconforming people are threatening because they place in question "identities previously conceived as stable, unchallengeable, grounded and 'known,'" which serve as critical tools of heterosexist culture.[22] As a transgender woman said, "If people can't put a label on you they get confused . . . people have to know who you are. You categorize in your mind. One of the first things you do is determine sex—if you can't do that, it blows the whole system up."[23] Where law enforcement officers experience classification anxiety, the consequences are widespread harassment, abuse, and arbitrary arrest.

● ● ●

In Feinberg's words, "Even where the laws are not written down, police are empowered to carry out merciless punishment for sex and gender difference."[24] Beyond the daily violence and humiliation law enforcement officers mete out on the streets, police also serve as a first point of contact with the criminal legal system, thereby playing a critical role in shaping how queers will be treated within it. Alternately determining whether queers will be seen as victims or suspects, fueling archetype-driven prosecutions, and driving incarceration and punishment, policing of queers continues to warrant concerted attention on the part of LGBT, police accountability, and civil rights movements.

NOTES

1. Imani Henry, founder of TransJustice, an organizing initiative of the Audre Lorde Project, www.alp.org.
2. For more information, see www.comptonscafeteriariot.org/main.html.
3. Urvashi Vaid, *Virtual Equality: The Mainstreaming of Gay & Lesbian Liberation*, (New York: Anchor Books, 1995), 55–56; and Michael Bronski, "Stonewall Was a Riot," ZNet, June 10, 2009, www.zmag.org/znet/viewArticle/21666 (accessed July 14, 2009).
4. Leigh W. Rutledge, *The Gay Decades: From Stonewall to the Present: The People and Events That Shaped Gay Lives* (New York: Penguin, 1992), 3.
5. Bronski, "Stonewall Was a Riot."
6. Amnesty International, *Stonewalled: Police Abuse and Misconduct against Lesbian, Gay, Bisexual and Transgender People in the U.S.* (New York: Amnesty International USA, 2005), 30; and Jeff Montgomery, executive director, Triangle Foundation, to Don Cox, chief of staff, Wayne County Sheriff's Department, March 11, 2003 (on file with coauthor Ritchie).
7. Bronski, "Stonewall Was a Riot."
8. Kevin Berrill, "Criminal Justice Subcommittee: Hearing on Police Practices—Testimony Submitted by Kevin Berrill, Violence Project Director of the National Gay Task Force," November 28, 1983 (on file with coauthors).
9. National Coalition of Anti-Violence Programs, *Anti-Lesbian, Gay, Bisexual and Transgender Violence in 2008* (2009), 13, 15.
10. National Coalition of Anti-Violence Programs, *Anti-Lesbian, Gay, Bisexual and Transgender Violence in 2007* (2008), 3. See also NCAVP, *Anti-LGBT Violence in 2008*, 5. It should be noted that these figures likely fall far short of reflecting the totality of police violence against LGBT people. NCAVP's member organizations' primary focus is on collecting data on anti-LGBT violence broadly defined, rather than specifically on police misconduct against queers. It should also be noted that in 2007 the NCAVP reported a 133 percent increase in reported cases of false arrest or "entrapment" of queers by police.
11. National Coalition of Anti-Violence Programs, *Anti-Lesbian, Gay, Bisexual and Transgender Violence in 2000* (2001), 47.
12. NCAVP, *Anti-LGBT Violence in 2007*, 40.
13. Shannon Minter and Christopher Daley, *Trans Realities: A Legal Needs Assessment of San Francisco's Transgender Communities*, National Center for Lesbian Rights, Transgender Law Center (2003).
14. Leslie Feinberg, " 'I'm glad I was in the Stonewall Riot': Leslie Feinberg Interviews Sylvia Rivera," *Workers' World*, July 2, 1998.

15. Gwen Smith, "Transsexual Terrorism," *Washington Blade*, October 3, 2003. See also Elaine Craig, "Transphobia and the Relational Production of Gender," *Hastings Women's Law Journal* 18 (2007): 162.

16. Franke, "Central Mistake," 69, 57. See also Amnesty, *Stonewalled*, 20.

17. Reback et al., *The Los Angeles Transgender Health Study: Community Report* (Los Angeles: University of California at Los Angeles, 2001). See also Amnesty, *Stonewalled*, 48–52.

18. R. Gierach, "Transgender Sues San Francisco Law Enforcement for Brutality," *Lesbian News* 28, no. 2 (September 2002): 16.

19. Andrea Ritchie, "Law Enforcement Violence against Women of Color," in *The Color of Violence: The INCITE! Anthology* (Cambridge, MA: South End, 2006).

20. Amnesty, *Stonewalled*, 41.

21. See Leslie Pearlman, "Transsexualism as Metaphor: The Collision of Sex and Gender," *Buffalo Law Review* 43 (1995): 835, 844.

22. Marjorie Garber, *Vested Interests: Cross-Dressing and Cultural Anxiety* (New York: Harper Perennial, 1992).

23. Annie Woodhouse, *Fantastic Women: Sex, Gender and Transvestism* (Rutgers, NJ: Rutgers University Press, 1989), xiii.

24. Feinberg, *Trans Liberation*, 11.

6 The Transgender Crucible

Sabrina Rubin Erdely

This article contains accounts of different forms of violence and assault, including transphobic, racist, and sexual violence.—Editor

A dozen eggs, bacon, maybe some biscuits: CeCe McDonald had a modest shopping list in mind, just a few things for breakfast the next day. It was midnight, the ideal time for a super-market run. Wearing a lavender My Little Pony T-shirt and denim cutoffs, CeCe grabbed her purse for the short walk to the 24-hour Cub Foods. She preferred shopping at night, when the darkened streets provided some relief from the stares, whispers and insults she encountered daily as a transgender woman. CeCe, 23, had grown accustomed to snickers and double takes—and was practiced in talking back to strangers who'd announce, "That's a man!" But such encounters were tiring; some days a lady just wanted to buy her groceries in peace.

And so it was that on a warm Saturday night in June 2011, CeCe and four friends, all African-Americans in their twenties, found themselves strolling the tree-lined streets of her quiet working-class Longfellow neighborhood in Minneapolis, toward a commercial strip. Leading the way was CeCe's roommate Latavia Taylor and two purse-carrying gay men—CeCe's makeshift family, whom she called "cousin" and "brothers"—with CeCe, a fashion student at a local community college, and her lanky boyfriend trailing behind. They were passing the Schooner Tavern when they heard the jeering.

"Faggots."

Gathered outside the dive bar were a handful of cigarette-smoking white people, looking like an aging biker gang in their T-shirts, jeans and bandannas, motorcycles parked nearby. Hurling the insults were 47-year-old Dean Schmitz, in a white button-down and thick silver chain, and his 40-year-old ex-girlfriend Molly Flaherty, clad in black, drink in hand. "Look at that boy dressed as a girl, tucking his dick in!" hooted Schmitz, clutching two beer bottles freshly fetched from his Blazer, as CeCe and her friends slowed to a stop. "You niggers need to go back to Africa!"

Chrishaun "CeCe" McDonald stepped in front of her friends, a familiar autopilot kicking in, shunting fury and fear to a distant place while her mouth went into motion. "Excuse me. We are people, and you need to respect us," CeCe began in her lisping delivery, one acrylic-nailed finger in the air, her curtain of orange microbraids swaying. With

Sabrina Rubin Erdely is a feature writer and investigative journalist who focuses on crime, health, and other social issues. She is a contributing editor at *Rolling Stone* and has also taught writing at the University of Pennsylvania and Temple University.

her caramel skin, angled jaw and square chin, friends called her "CeCe" for her resemblance to the singer Ciara; even her antagonist Flaherty would later describe CeCe as "really pretty." "We're just trying to walk to the store," CeCe continued, raising her voice over the blare of Schmitz and Flaherty's free-associating invective: "bitches with dicks," "faggot-lovers," "niggers," "rapists." The commotion was drawing more patrons out of the bar—including a six-foot-eight, 310-pound biker in leather chaps—and CeCe's boyfriend, Larry Thomas, nervously called to Schmitz, "Enjoy your night, man—just leave us alone." CeCe and her friends turned to go. Then Flaherty glanced at Schmitz and laughed.

"I'll take all of you bitches on!" Flaherty hollered, and smashed CeCe in the side of her face with a glass tumbler.

Just like that, a mundane walk to the store turned into a street brawl, in a near-farcical clash of stereotypes. Pandemonium erupted as CeCe and Flaherty seized each other by the hair; the bikers swung fists and hurled beer bottles, hollering "beat that faggot ass!"; and CeCe's friends flailed purses and cracked their studded belts as whips. When the two sides separated, panting and disoriented, Flaherty was curled up amid the broken glass screaming, mistakenly, that she'd been knifed, and CeCe stood over her, her T-shirt drenched with her own blood. Touching her cheek, CeCe felt a shock of pain as her finger entered the open wound where Flaherty's glass had punctured her salivary gland. Purse still over her shoulder, CeCe fast-walked from the scene. She'd made it more than a half-block away when she heard her friends calling, "Watch your back!"

CeCe whirled around to see Schmitz heading toward her: walking, then running, his face a twist of wild, unrestrained hatred. CeCe felt terror burst out from that remote place where she normally locked it away. She didn't know that Schmitz's veins were pounding with cocaine and meth. She didn't know of his lengthy rap sheet, including convictions for assault. Nor did she know that under Schmitz's shirt, inked across his solar plexus, was a four-inch swastika tattoo. All CeCe needed to see was the look on his face to know her worst fears were coming true: Her young life was about to end as a grim statistic, the victim of a hate crime.

"Come here, bitch!" Schmitz roared as he closed in. CeCe pedaled backward, blood dripping from her slashed face.

"Didn't y'all get enough?" CeCe asked, defiant and afraid, while her hand fished into her large handbag for anything to protect herself. Her fingers closed on a pair of black-handled fabric scissors she used for school. She held them up high as a warning, their five-inch blades glinting in the parking-lot floodlights. Schmitz stopped an arm's length away, raising clenched fists and shuffling his feet in a boxing stance. His eyes were terrible with rage.

"Bitch, you gonna stab me?" he shouted. They squared off for a tense moment: the furious white guy, amped up on meth, Nazi tattoo across his belly; the terrified black trans woman with a cartoon pony on her T-shirt; the scissors between them. CeCe saw Schmitz lunge toward her and braced herself for impact. Their bodies collided, then separated. He was still looking at her.

"Bitch—you stabbed me!"

"Yes, I did," CeCe announced, even as she wondered if that could possibly be true; in the adrenaline of the moment, she'd felt nothing. Scanning Schmitz over, she saw no sign of injury—though in fact he'd sustained a wound so grisly that CeCe would later recall to police that the button-down shirt Schmitz wore that night was not white but "mainly red.

Like one of them Hawaiian shirts." CeCe waited until he turned to rejoin his crowd. Then she and Thomas ran arm in arm down the block toward the nearly empty Cub Foods parking lot, where they waited for police to arrive.

They didn't see the scene unfolding behind them: how Schmitz took a few faltering steps, uttered, "I'm bleeding," then lifted his shirt to unleash a geyser of blood. CeCe had stabbed him in the chest, burying the blade almost three and a half inches deep, slicing his heart. Blood sprayed the road as Schmitz staggered, collapsed and, amid his friends' screams, died. When CeCe and Thomas waved down a police car minutes later, she was promptly handcuffed and arrested.

• • •

Given the swift political advances of the transgender movement, paired with its new pop-culture visibility, you'd be forgiven for believing that to be gender-nonconforming today is to be accepted, celebrated, even trendy—what with trans models in ads for American Apparel and Barneys; Facebook's more than 50 gender options for users to choose from; and Eurovision song-contest winner Conchita Wurst, who accepted the trophy in an evening gown and a full beard. When this spring Secretary of Defense Chuck Hagel recommended a review of the military's ban on allowing trans people to serve openly—by one estimate, trans people are as much as twice as likely as the general U.S. population to serve in the armed forces—his announcement seemed to herald a new era of recognition. But the appearance of tolerance belies the most basic day-to-day reality: No community living in America today is as openly terrorized as transgender women, especially trans women of color . . . .

"Just being trans out on the street is cause for our lives to be in danger," says trans actress Laverne Cox, who says she envisioned her *Orange Is the New Black* character, Sophia Burset, as a homage to CeCe McDonald. "So many times I've been walking on the street as a trans woman and been harassed, called a man – one time I was kicked," she adds. "Any of them could have escalated into someone doing me harm. I very easily could be CeCe."

Living with a gender identity different from one's birth anatomy (a phenomenon thought to affect as many as one in 10,000 people) means that trans women live with constant anxiety of being recognized as trans—"getting spooked" or "getting clocked"—because reactions can be harsh to the extreme. Though transgender people make up perhaps 10 percent of the LGBT community, they account for a shocking proportion of its hate-crime statistics, with trans people nearly twice as likely to be threatened as their LGB peers. And trans people all too often meet with violent deaths: Of the 25 reported anti-LGBT homicides in 2012, according to the National Coalition of Anti-Violence Programs, transgender people accounted for more than half of the victims. All of those trans homicide victims were trans women of color.

Highlighting the danger, transgender murders tend to be gruesome, often involving torture and mutilation, as in the 2012 California murder of 37-year-old Brandy Martell, who was shot in the genitals; or the brutal hatchet slaying last July in Philadelphia of 31-year-old Diamond Williams, whose body was hacked to pieces and strewn in an overgrown lot. After Williams' alleged killer reportedly confessed that he'd killed Williams, a prostitute he'd solicited, when he'd realized she was trans—commonly known as the "trans panic defense"—online commenters were quick to agree "the cross-dresser had it coming": that Williams' transgender status was an act of duplicity whose logical punishment was death. "It's socially sanctioned to say that," says Cox. "If a guy is even attracted to her, then she has to die. What is that?" And when these cases go unresolved, as they often do—like last summer's vicious Harlem beating death of 21-year-old Islan Nettles, reportedly after a cat-calling admirer turned vengeful—the lack of resolution seems a further reminder to trans women of their own disposability. It's telling that the closest thing the trans community has to a long-running Pride event is Transgender Day of Remembrance, a day of mourning for victims of violence.

"It takes a toll. This life is not an easy life," says trans woman Anya Stacy Neal. "Trust me, if this was a choice, I would have packed it up a long time ago."

As the sisterhood is picked off one by one, each gets a chilling vision of her own fate. "You rarely hear of a trans woman just living a long life and then dying of old age," says CeCe today, seated at a friend's Minneapolis dining-room table with her legs crossed lady-like at the knee. Wearing a striped cardigan that she opens to reveal, laughing, a T-shirt reading it's all about me, CeCe's an animated run-on talker with a lip ring and a warm, open nature, whose cadences recall the church days of her youth, mouth opening wide to flash a tongue stud. "You never hear, 'She passed on her own, natural causes, old age,' no, no, no," she continues, ticking off on her fingers. "She's either raped and killed, she's jumped and killed, stalked and killed—or just killed." Which is why, amid all the death and sorrow, CeCe, whose jagged life experience embodies the archetypal trans woman's in so many ways, has become an LGBT folk hero for her story of survival—and for the price she paid for fighting back . . . .

From earliest childhood CeCe had felt at odds with her boy's body, boyish clothes and boy's name (a name that she still can't discuss without anguish). She'd always felt such an irrepressible girlishness. In grade school she walked with graceful wrists and swishing hips, to the consternation of her family. CeCe was the oldest of seven, raised on Chicago's gritty South Side by a single mother; a dozen family members crammed under one roof, where no one could fail to notice young CeCe sashaying in her mother's heels. "You need to pray that out of you," her religious family instructed, and at night, CeCe tearfully pleaded with God to take away her sinful attraction to boys. Better yet, she prayed to awaken a girl, in the body He had surely meant for her.

She redoubled her prayers as other kids began to mock her femininity, and their taunts turned violent. CeCe was chased through the neighborhood, beaten up and, around seventh grade, attacked by five high schoolers yelling "kill that faggot," who kicked her in the mouth so savagely that her incisor tore through the skin above her lip. Such bullying is the norm for transgender kids, nearly nine out of 10 of whom are harassed by peers, and 44 percent of whom are physically assaulted. But no number of beatings could change CeCe. In school she'd dash into the girls' bathroom when the coast was clear, frightened of being seen in the boys' room sitting down to pee. She joined the cheerleading squad—gleefully doing splits at basketball games—coming to class in her mom's blouse or platform shoes, though she'd change back into boy clothes before returning home, fearful of her family's wrath, and of losing the love of her mother, who was trying to persuade CeCe onto a more traditional path.

"It kind of scared me," says mom Christi McDonald of CeCe's femininity. "I know it's a cruel world, and if you're different it's hard for people to accept you." Christi bought CeCe baggy jeans and dropped hints about cute girls, just as when CeCe was smaller Christi had urged her to draw pictures of Superman instead of sketching dresses. "I kept questioning him, 'Why are you doing this?'" Christi says, adjusting her pronouns to add, "I just wanted a peaceful life for her."

CeCe had always tried staying in her mom's good graces by being a responsible, diligent child, constantly neatening the house, making the beds and whipping up recipes inspired by cooking shows, but nonetheless she felt her mother grow distant. CeCe was unable to find sanctuary with her family, and tensions grew in the crowded three-bedroom house. One day, an uncle found an undelivered love note she'd written to a boy and, CeCe says, knocked her to the kitchen floor and choked her. She ran away from home, never to return. She was 14.

She crashed with friends before taking up residence in a glorified drug den where other runaways congregated. CeCe tried to see the bright side of her family's rejection: She was finally free to be herself. The first time she tried on a bra and panties, she felt a shiver of recognition that she was headed in the right direction. Instead, she fell right through a trapdoor. She'd reached a crucial point in the too-typical trans woman's narrative, in which, cut loose at a young age from family, she falls directly into harm's way. Up to 40 percent of U.S. homeless youth are LGBT. Adrift without money, shelter, education or a support system, they're exposed to myriad dangers. According to one study, 58 percent of LGBT homeless youth are sexually assaulted (compared with 33 percent of their hetero peers). Drug and alcohol use is rampant. CeCe grew up fast. "Honey, I think there's not too much in this world that I haven't heard or seen or done," she tells me. "And a lot of that is sad."

She learned to sell crack and marijuana. Out in the streets, her appearance in girls' clothing was met with outbursts of violence, as when a man once threw an empty 40-ounce bottle at her head, knocking her unconscious; another time, a stranger pulled a knife. Even more traumatic, a handsome man lured CeCe into his home with an invitation to smoke weed—"I was like, 'Oh, my goodness, this is so cool.' Very naive, thinking everybody is good"—then pushed her face-forward onto his bed and anally raped her. The assault changed CeCe profoundly, crystallizing how expendable she was in the eyes of the world. Never had she felt so degraded, and so certain no one would care. Living in poverty and unpredictability so extreme that she sometimes found herself sleeping on park benches and eating grass to fill her belly, CeCe decided to offer herself in the one last arena where she felt she had worth.

At 15, CeCe was a child prostitute working the strip off Belmont Avenue in Boystown, climbing into men's cars to earn up to $1,000 on a Saturday night. In choosing the sex trade, CeCe was heading down a well-worn path. Studies of urban transgender women have found that upward of 50 percent had engaged in sex work. It's a risky job, in which the threat of violence is only one hazard. Transgender women are considered the fastest-growing HIV-positive population in the country, with a meta-analysis showing that nearly 28 percent of trans women in America have the virus. Bearing the highest risk are trans women in sex work, who are four times more likely to be living with HIV than other female sex workers . . . .

"I became this soulless drone," says CeCe. She entertained a dim hope she'd get AIDS and die. She was tired of internalizing hostility and worthlessness, mentally exhausted from constantly scanning for danger. Such daily burdens take a heavy toll: Though the suicide-attempt rate in the general population is estimated to be 4.6 percent, the National Transgender Discrimination Survey found that an extraordinary 41 percent of trans respondents had attempted suicide, with the rate soaring to 64 percent for sexual-assault victims. The first time CeCe attempted suicide, it was with pills washed down with a bottle of NyQuil. The second time, she crushed up a pile of pills and drank it down with juice. Asked how many times she tried to kill herself, CeCe has to think for a long moment; it's hard to sort out, since her late teens were basically an extended death wish. So much so that when one night a man on a street corner pointed a gun at her, shouting, "Faggot, I'll kill you," CeCe just looked at him and said, "Shoot me."

Surely it would have been far easier for CeCe if she'd given up, renounced her womanhood and opted to live life as a gay man. And yet even in her darkest despair, CeCe never considered retreat an option. If she was going to continue living, it was going to be as a lady. For her there was no decision-making; she felt she couldn't "choose" to be a man, because she'd never been male to begin with . . . .

[In 2006, CeCe took a Greyhound bus to the Twin Cities,] hoping to escape her Chicago misery and start anew. Instead she'd been floundering, in and out of shelters, flirting with coke and meth addictions, jailed for shoplifting and other misdemeanors, and hospitalized for suicidal ideation. But she'd also started visiting a drop-in youth center, where she learned how to regain control of her life bit by bit. "CeCe caught my attention right away," says her case manager Abby Beasley. "Her energy, she's just so bubbly, laughing constantly, just a real loving person. I put more work into her than I did anybody else, trying to help her stabilize her life."

Education was a first step: CeCe earned her GED, then enrolled in Minneapolis Community and Technical College, focusing on fashion design. Estrogen came next. A doctor diagnosed CeCe with gender dysphoria—determining that there was an incongruity between her biological sex and her gender identity—after which she started wearing a hormone patch on her hip, the cost covered by state medical assistance. CeCe watched with amazement as over the following months she developed smooth skin, fuller hips and, most fulfilling of all, breasts. Finally seeing her outer self match her inner self "was definitely something like a relief," she remembers. In an important move for CeCe, she called her mother to re-establish ties after years of separation. "Are those real?" Christi exclaimed when she finally got her first glimpse of CeCe post-hormones, and CeCe laughed in reply.

A legal name change tied a ribbon on CeCe's transition, a bureaucratic process that yielded a government ID identifying her by her carefully chosen new name: Chrishaun Reed Mai'luv McDonald. It was a name she liked for its mystique and personality; Chrishaun was also her aunt's name, keeping her tethered just a little bit to her past.

Secure in her identity at last, CeCe felt something free up within herself. And with confidence also came a new ability to stand up to street harassment; for perhaps the first time, she felt herself truly worth defending. "It's not OK that you called me a tranny," she'd lecture a surprised heckler. "You're gonna apologize, and then you're gonna go home and think about why you turned my pretty smile into an ugly mug." Satisfied, she'd coolly walk on, her self-respect growing with each small triumph.

"She looked like someone who knew where she was heading in life," says Larry Thomas, who caught sight of CeCe at a corner store and, knowing full well she was trans, gave her his phone number—thus beginning, in fits and starts, that thing that eludes so many trans women: an actual in-the-daylight relationship. Thomas was a straight man who usually kept his "flings" with trans women on the down-low. But CeCe began occupying much of his time, and she started to wonder if she wasn't doomed to live a lonely life after all.

Then came more good fortune, when in May 2011, after a decade of couch-surfing homelessness, CeCe moved into the very first apartment of her own. It was a two-bedroom oasis she shared with a roommate. Though still unemployed—CeCe paid her rent with general assistance and SSI—she was certain now that she was a college student with a permanent address, that remaining piece of the puzzle would be forthcoming.

"I was feeling really accomplished," remembers CeCe wistfully as she stands on the sidewalk looking up at the weather-beaten three-story brick apartment building on an early spring day. She tries flashing her patented wide smile, but it evaporates. We're taking a tour through her old neighborhood, and in skinny jeans, cropped jacket and a colorful head scarf, CeCe points at the second-floor window where she once lived, so full of potential and promise—a period that lasted for a single, shining month . . . .

● ● ●

In a police interrogation room hours after the stabbing, CeCe had given a full confession. "I was only trying to defend myself," CeCe sobbed. Police interviews with nearly a dozen witnesses would paint a consistent picture of the events of that night: Dean Schmitz and Molly Flaherty started the confrontation, Flaherty had triggered the fight by breaking a glass on CeCe's face, and Schmitz had pursued CeCe when she'd tried to escape—all precisely the way CeCe recounted in her confession. But no witness had seen exactly how the stabbing had transpired. "I didn't jab him; I didn't force the scissors into him; he was coming after me," CeCe insisted to detectives. "He ran into the scissors." And yet in Hennepin County Jail, CeCe was shocked to learn she was charged with second-degree murder. She faced up to 40 years in prison.

Dressed in orange scrubs, CeCe would cry and stare at the white brick walls of her cell for hours on end, her thoughts a tangle. There was the horrific knowledge that someone had died by her hand. And there was the agony that the life she'd been trying so hard to build had been decimated in an instant. "There wasn't a moment when I wasn't in pain mentally and spiritually, and even beating myself up for defending myself," CeCe says. She had nothing but time to obsess because she was locked alone in her cell for 23 hours a day. The jail had determined that for her own safety, she be held in solitary confinement.

Trans women have a difficult time behind bars, where they show up in disproportionate numbers; one survey found 16 percent of trans women had been to jail, compared to 2.7 percent of the general population. Once in prison they pose a dilemma, because, as a study of seven California prisons revealed, 59 percent of transgender inmates reported being sexually abused, compared to 4.4 percent of the general inmate population. A common solution, then, is to put them in solitary. For CeCe, who'd previously spent short stints in men's jails, the brain-racking isolation was a form of confinement she'd never known before. "There's no room for sanity," she says of her subsequent mental collapse. When her former caseworker Abby Beasley visited, Beasley was shocked at the sight of CeCe on the other side of the glass, scared and shaken, her left cheek swollen to the size of a golf ball.

"Whatever you can do to help me, please," CeCe begged.

Beasley notified the Trans Youth Support Network, a Minneapolis organization, which secured CeCe a pro bono lawyer. The case immediately galvanized the local trans and queer community, who saw CeCe's attack as something that could easily have happened to any of them, and hailed her as a hero. "CeCe was attacked in a racist, transphobic incident that could have killed her," says Billy Navarro Jr. of the Minnesota Transgender Health Coalition, who helped found the Free CeCe campaign. "And then how is she treated? She is prosecuted for having the audacity to survive."

Her support base grew after the Florida shooting death of Trayvon Martin, which stoked a national debate over race, self-defense and justice. CeCe's supporters argued that unlike George Zimmerman, who would be acquitted of all charges, CeCe had been faced with an actual threat, against which she had stood her ground. But they feared the justice system would view CeCe, as a black trans woman, unkindly. A petition advocating for CeCe's release gathered more than 18,000 signatures from across the country. As supporters in FREE CECE T-shirts held rallies outside the jail and packed the courthouse for each hearing, defense lawyer Hersch Izek set about building a case . . . .

The months leading to trial saw the judge's rulings laying waste to CeCe's defense case. Evidence of Schmitz's swastika tattoo was deemed inadmissible, since CeCe never saw the tattoo—it had no bearing on her mindset at the time of the killing—and because, Judge Daniel Moreno wrote, "the tattoo does not establish that [Schmitz] intended to threaten, fight or kill anyone." Schmitz's prior assault convictions were deemed irrelevant, and the judge would allow only limited testimony about the toxicology report showing Schmitz was high on meth, feeding his aggression. The defense's bid to include expert testimony about the lives of transgender women also failed. "The idea was to show the violence transgender individuals face, to bolster the self-defense claim," says Izek. "We'd have to be educating the jury about what it meant to be transgender. That would be difficult. Most wouldn't even know what that meant."

Seated at the defense table with a headache on the morning of the trial, May 2nd, 2012, CeCe looked at the mostly white jury staring back at her. She knew those expressions all too well. She'd been intent on seeing her case through, but glancing at those tasked with deciding her fate, she gave up. "These people weren't going to let me win," she says. She accepted a deal and pleaded guilty to second-degree manslaughter. Her supporters in the courtroom cried as the judge led her through her admission of guilt. CeCe tried her best to choke back tears as she was led from the courtroom, overwhelmed by what was next for her: A 41-month sentence in a state men's prison . . . .

• • •

CeCe was released from the Minnesota Correctional Facility in St. Cloud in January after 19 months, her sentence reduced for good behavior and for the 275 days she'd served prior to trial. While in prison she'd been intent on staying positive and grateful for having continued access to her hormones, and having her own cell with a TV, where she'd escape the hypermasculinity of her fellow inmates for *Sex and the City* marathons on E!. She says she never encountered violence, kept mostly to herself and even made a couple of friends. Mostly, she tried to work on recovering, and on remaining sane. When she was notified that Molly Flaherty was being prosecuted for attacking her, CeCe declined to testify, viewing it as a pointless act of vengeance potentially bad for her own mental health. (Flaherty pleaded guilty to third-degree assault and was sentenced to six months in jail.) "It's easy, especially for a person who's been through so much, to be a cruel and coldhearted person. But I chose not to be," CeCe says . . . .

"My story wouldn't have been important had I been killed. Because it's like nobody cares," CeCe says forcefully at her dining-room table, as day turns to evening. A shiny, sickle-shaped scar cuts across the jawbone of her left cheek, a permanent reminder of her tragic walk to the supermarket. "But fortunately for me, I'm a survivor. I'm not gonna beat myself up for being a woman, I'm not gonna beat myself up for being trans, I'm not gonna beat myself up for defending myself." She smacks her lips for punctuation. "Cause I am a survivor." . . .

7 First Nations, Queer and Education

Raven E. Heavy Runner

It was a clear day and Elk meat was boiling on the fire outside the tipi. I sat inside a tipi somewhere in Saskatchewan, asking a *Medawin* (an Anishinabe medicine person) elder what she thought of Two-Spirit people. She believed that when we died we really didn't die. We traveled toward the stars to be with our people. Yet some needed to return to Earth to learn more. As life was getting ready to be formed during conception and the spiritual entity entered into the child, usually it was a female spirit that entered a female child, and a male spirit that entered a male child. Some of us were so excited to get back to our people that we didn't look at which body we entered into and didn't realize until later.

Sherman Alexie, noted author, came to my class at Haskell Indian Nations University and talked about how homophobia was rampant in the Native community where for centuries Queer Natives had a *place* in society. This homophobia, I believe, is what European education taught the Native People. Sadly, we learned this lesson well. For as I went through school I heard on the playgrounds: queerbait, faggot, gay, cocksucker, and the list goes on. Throughout grade school, I was teased and harassed. I had realized very young that I was attracted to people of my same sex and got into lots of trouble when others found my misplaced notebook with "Raven & Ed 4ever" written on the inside cover. I am sure they noticed that I wasn't the burly, studly Native male. As my schoolmates and I approached seventh and then eighth grade, the pressure to conform to gender roles became more intense. Jokes about sex and sexuality abounded. My best friend was a sixteen-year-old lean and mean bull dyke. I was thirteen and very skinny. Guys would try to mess with us and she would kick ass and totally intimidate them. So they stayed clear of us when we were together, but she didn't go to school and therefore my bodyguard wasn't with me as I walked the halls each day. It was like walking down some dark alley with the potential for danger around every corner. I felt like a Jewish person in Nazi Germany. Wondering whether I would be spit on, kicked, stopped, and harassed. I loved learning and excelled in learning. I knew I was smart. Smart enough to not want to subject myself to the approaching high school years of terror and humiliation.

At age fourteen, I ran away with my lesbian friend. We came to Seattle and hung around on the streets. It wasn't, long before I began sex work in order to survive. My education

---

Raven E. Heavy Runner is a member of the Blackfeet Tribe of Montana. His experiences attending a Bureau of Indian Affairs boarding school, living on the streets, and serving in the U.S. Army have contributed to his passion for ending homophobia within Native American communities. A social worker and oral historian, he chaired the Northwest Two-Spirit Society for over 15 years and sits on several other Native boards.

---

during my high school years consisted of negotiating for my next meal. I learned that time meant money and, honey, if you didn't have the money you didn't have my time. I learned other people's bodies, but lost touch with my own. I learned that beef wasn't the only meat on the market and that the police weren't always there to protect and serve. I learned that I didn't like what I saw happening to me. I learned that drugs made it all go away. I learned if my friends took enough drugs that they would go away, too.

I was eighteen when I talked with some social workers. They wanted to help the street kids obtain various services, and seemed benign and friendly. Within a couple of months I completed my GED and was in college. College was very different from high school. I went to a community college on the reservation and did very well. A year later I went to the University of Montana. I had been raised fundamentalist Christian and hadn't embraced it for years. That year I began attending church while in school and hung out with the Christian crowd. There were no other Natives in this group and because of the color lines in many religions I felt separate from other Natives. Some of the Christian college youth were high school heroes and scholars. One of them, a football star from Nebraska. We often learned about each other at Bible Study in the University cafeteria rooms. Questions about where we went to high school would come up and finally I told them where I had been. Well we all got down on our knees and they prayed that this spirit of homosexuality would leave me. It wasn't until years later when I sat with that *Medawin* elder that I realized that if what she had said was true, then if the spirit of homosexuality left me then my own spirit would too, for they were inexplicably intertwined. I had prayed that God take the spirit of homosexuality from me: Then I had prayed, fasted, and cried some more. I just wanted to die. It took me a couple of years before I saw the light and decided to leave.

I heard about a group of Queer Natives from all over North America who were getting together. They were learning ceremonies and teaching them to each other. This for me was the essential educational experience. I began attending these gatherings and learning what had been lost during the years of European oppressive pedagogy. I learned that Natives had historically honored the path that the Creator had made for Two-Spirit people. Within these Native communities, Two-Spirits had filled many roles. These roles included healers, spiritual intermediaries, storytellers, matchmakers, historians, teachers, artists, husbands, wives, civil counselors, diplomats, and many more. Their names differed from Nation to Nation and their status was by no means monolithic. Each Nation attributed differing statuses to their Two-Spirit members. During my education at these gatherings I carried many questions with me.

I recently graduated with a bachelor's degree in social work, but during the summer between my junior and senior years of college I did research on the self-esteem of Native Two-Spirits. I passed out a questionnaire to Two-Spirits and got responses back from Canada and the United States. I found that how educated a Queer Native was didn't impact their self-esteem. Interestingly, their self-esteem was tied to their spirituality. If their spirit lived, so did they.

8 Queer and Undocumented
Mohammad

"Get in line!" they like to say without realizing that many of us were at some point in this infamous line. My family immigrated to the United States from Iran when I was just three years old. At the time my dad was accepted by a university on a student visa to get his doctoral degree. After three years he completed his studies and applied for something called Optional Practical Training (OPT), essentially allowing him to extend his stay for twelve months. During that time, he would be able to continue to work and study in the same field in which he received his PhD.

While still under the OPT program, my dad secured sponsorship from a job and applied for a change of status from OPT to an H-1B visa. The university's immigration attorney handled all of the paperwork. My parents paid the required fee and they were told that everything was set to go, or so they thought. Until this point, we still had legal status, we were still "in line." Eventually a letter came from the Immigration and Naturalization Service (INS) stating that the application was rejected because the fee that had been enclosed hadn't been for the right amount. Apparently INS had raised its fee the previous year and it was now $20 more than we were instructed by the attorney to provide.

My parents immediately hired an attorney who was independent from the university but that attorney failed to inform my parents that they only had sixty days to appeal the decision. The attorney failed to take any measures to protect our status or to inform us of what could be done. And so we lost legal status,

I now find myself in a constant state of limbo. I am currently enrolled in the Social Work program at my college, and I have always volunteered within the local community. I have been offered several jobs that I have had to unfortunately decline.

I can't see myself living anywhere else other than America. All my childhood memories are from America and it is the only home I have known. Apart from that, I also happen to be gay. If one is at all up to date on their current events, I am sure you know how unfriendly a place Iran is for anyone who happens to be LGBTQ (Lesbian, Gay, Bisexual, Trans, Queer).

Iran is one of the countries that not only punishes people for being gay, but also kills them. Mahmoud Asgari (16) and Ayaz Marhoni (18) are two teenagers who were killed for

Mohammad was 22 when his story appeared in the 2012 collection *Papers*. The undocumented youth in this collection used only their first names when telling their stories of growing up in the United States without papers.

Excerpt from *Papers: Stories by Undocumented Youth*, edited by José Manuel, Cesar Pineda, Anne Galisky, and Rebecca Shine. Illustrated by Julio Salgado. Published by Graham Street Productions, 2012. Used with permission.

no reason other than being gay. In addition to the outright intolerance towards homosexuality, it is the view of the Iranian clerics that the cure to homosexuality is a sex-change operation. Going back to Iran is not an option for me.

The only difference I see between myself and the next American is $20, two strong cases of legal malpractice, and a piece of paper.

9 Living in an Immigrant Family in America: How Fear and Toxic Stress Are Affecting Daily Life, Well-Being, and Health

Samantha Artiga and Petry Ubri

Immigration policy has been and continues to be a controversial topic in the U.S. Over the course of the election and since taking office, President Trump has intensified national debate about immigration as he has implemented policies to enhance immigration enforcement and restrict the entry of immigrants from selected countries the Administration believes may pose a threat to the country. The climate surrounding these policies and this debate potentially affect 23 million noncitizens in the U.S., including both lawfully present and undocumented immigrants, many of whom came to the U.S. seeking safety and improved opportunities for their families.[1] They also have implications for the over 12 million children who live with a noncitizen parent who are predominantly U.S-born citizen children.[2] We conducted focus groups with 100 parents from 15 countries and 13 interviews with pediatricians to gain insight into how the current environment is affecting the daily lives, well-being, and health of immigrant families, including their children. Key findings include:

Immigrant families, including those with lawful status, are experiencing resounding levels of fear and uncertainty. Fears affected participants across backgrounds and locations, with particularly pronounced effects for Latinos and Muslims. Undocumented parents fear being deported and separated from their children while many of those with lawful status feel uncertain about their status and worry they may lose their status or permission to remain in the U.S. These feelings of uncertainty escalated after rescission of the Deferred Action for Child Arrivals (DACA) program in September 2017. Parents said that although they try to shield their children from these issues, many children are hearing

Samantha Artiga serves as director of the Disparities Policy Project at the Kaiser Family Foundation and as associate director for the Foundation's Program on Medicaid and the Uninsured.

Petry Ubri is a policy analyst with the Kaiser Family Foundation's Program on Medicaid and the Uninsured where she works on projects related to insurance coverage and access to care.

about them at school and fear potentially losing their parents to deportation or having to leave the U.S., the only home many have ever known.

> " . . . we wake up every day with the fear of being deported, of the separation of our families, to have to leave the kids."—Latino Parent, Boston, Massachusetts

> "Uncomfortable and unstable; we feel that in any moment a new rule could be issued leading to expelling us and sending us back."—Arabic-speaking Parent, Anaheim, California

Parents and pediatricians said that racism and discrimination, including bullying of children, have significantly increased since the election. Many felt that Latinos and Muslims have been the primary targets of increased racism and discrimination. They also noted that the increased bullying of children in schools extends beyond immigrants to children of color, regardless of their immigration status.

> "They get bullied . . . told things like, 'now you and your family will have to leave.' . . . And so, even though those kids don't actually have to worry about their immigration status, I think obviously a child, they don't know the details of how the system works."—Pediatrician, Pennsylvania

Daily life has become more difficult for immigrant families due to increased fear and uncertainty. Some parents said that it is harder to find employment in the current environment, further increasing financial strains on families. Increased fears also are affecting some families' daily routines. Some parents, particularly those who are undocumented or who have an undocumented family member, said they are only leaving the house when necessary, such as for work; limiting driving; and no longer participating in recreational activities, like visiting their local park. As a result, they and their children are spending long hours in the house behind locked doors. Parents also indicated that they and their children are increasingly fearful of interacting with police or authorities.

> "Before, there were many kids in the parks . . . but now . . . the kids spend more time inside these days, because we are afraid of being deported."—Latino Parent, Boston, Massachusetts

> "My spouse does not go out of the house . . . The last thing she wants is to get stopped and that they start asking her questions . . . "—Latino Parent, San Diego, California

Most parents said they are continuing to access health care for their children and maintaining their children's Medicaid and CHIP coverage, but there were some reports of changes in health care use and decreased participation in programs. Parents note that they highly prioritize their children's health and generally view hospitals and doctors' offices as safe spaces. However, there were some reports of changes in health care use, including decreased use of some care, and decreased participation in Medicaid and CHIP and other programs due to increased fears.

> "The thing is . . . if you are at the hospital you are safe. They can't go into a hospital, a school or a church . . . because it is a sanctuary."—Latino Parent, Chicago, Illinois

Increased fears are having significant negative effects on the health and well-being of children that have lifelong consequences. Parents and pediatricians reported that children are manifesting fears in many ways. They described behavioral changes, such as problems sleeping and eating; psychosomatic symptoms, such as headaches and stomach-aches; and mental health issues, such as depression and anxiety. Parents and pediatricians also felt that fears are negatively affecting children's behavior and performance in school. Pediatricians uniformly expressed significant concerns about the long-term health consequences of the current environment for children. They pointed to longstanding research on the damaging effects of toxic stress on physical and mental health over the lifespan. They also expressed concerns about negative effects on children's growth and development, and felt that the current environment is compounding social and environmental challenges that have negative impacts on health.

> "When you're worried every day that your parents are going to be taken away or that your family will be split up, that really is a form of toxic stress . . . we know that it's going to have long-term implications for heart disease, for health outcomes for these children in adulthood." — Pediatrician, Minnesota

Together these findings show that immigrant families across different backgrounds and locations are feeling increased levels of fear and uncertainty amid the current climate, and that these feelings extend to those with lawful status. The findings show that these fears are having broad effects on the daily lives and routines of some immigrant families. In addition, they point to long-term consequences for children in immigrant families, including poorer health outcomes over the lifespan, compromised growth and development, and increased challenges across social and environmental factors that influence health.

NOTES

1. Kaiser Family Foundation, *Health Coverage and Care for Immigrants*, (Washington, DC: Kaiser Family Foundation, December 2017), https://www.kff.org/disparities-policy/fact-sheet/health-coverage-of-immigrants.
2. Ibid.

10 | "They Treat Me Like a Criminal, but They Are the Criminals"

Laura Gottesdiener, Malav Kanuga, and Cinthya Santos-Briones

This article contains accounts of different forms of violence, including sexual assault.—Editor

On a Tuesday afternoon in March [2018], Aura Hernández drew a bath for her daughter, Camila Guadalupe, in a makeshift bathroom tucked inside the basement of a Manhattan church. The water was warm, but the toddler shivered as she stood inside her inflatable hot-pink tub. Hernández smiled at the girl and chuckled. "You know how it feels—the first time in a new place," she said. "Everything is different. It's an adjustment." Indeed, everything was different, both for mother and daughter. One day earlier, the pair had moved into the Fourth Universalist Society of New York, a 120-year-old English Gothic church across the street from Central Park. They had made the dramatic move in an attempt to find safety and to avoid Hernández's scheduled deportation to Guatemala. . . .

Hernández bent down to lather Camila's hair with shampoo, moving gently but efficiently so as to shorten her daughter's discomfort. The 15-month-old's pudgy legs wobbled, but she kept her balance. At last, Hernández wrapped the shivering girl in a towel and navigated the trek from the basement to the second floor. There, she placed Camila gently in her crib and, satisfied that the child was resting, began to explain why she had decided to go to extreme lengths to fight her deportation.

Hernández had come to the United States over a decade ago, she said, fleeing deadly domestic violence. But when she arrived, one of the supervisory agents in a Customs and Border Protection (CBP) station in Texas pulled her aside and threatened to indefinitely detain her 9-year-old nephew, with whom she'd traveled, unless she followed the agent into a private office. Once there, he sexually assaulted her—and vowed to hunt her down if she ever revealed what had transpired.

Laura Gottesdiener is an independent journalist whose work focuses on immigration, U.S. militarism, territorial struggles, and human rights. Her articles have been published in *Al Jazeera*, *Mother Jones*, *The Nation*, and other outlets.

Malav Kanuga is an urban anthropologist and founding editor of Common Notions, an independent book publishing and programming house. His research focuses on historical and contemporary struggles around space, culture, and urban life from an international and postcolonial perspective.

Cinthya Santos-Briones is a Mexican documentary photographer and photojournalist based in New York City. She is a Magnum Foundation Fellow and an En Foco Fellow. Her work has been published in the *New York Times*, *PDN*, *La Jornada*, *Vogue*, *Buzzfeed*, and elsewhere.

For many years, Hernández said, she was so traumatized by the experience that she stayed quiet. But recently—under the threat of being detained by the same immigration system in which she'd been sexually abused, and then deported back to a country in which her life is still in danger—she has decided to break her silence. In so doing, she has joined the scores of women from across the United States and the world who have come forward in recent months to tell their stories of rape, sexual assault, and sexual harassment. These women include Hollywood actresses and hotel cleaners, journalists and farmworkers, and their abusers were almost invariably men who had power over them: A-list producers and shift managers, network executives and farm owners.

But largely missing from the #MeToo movement are the stories of women who have been sexually abused by members of the largest law-enforcement agency in the United States: Customs and Border Protection. In such circumstances, the power differential is extreme: The men, often armed, are federal agents tasked with hunting down, capturing, and detaining these women; the women are unarmed civilians who have often survived gender-based violence in their home countries or along the dangerous journey to the US border. And because they are undocumented, speaking out, even many years later, means risking deportation—leading to widespread impunity for abuse by border agents.

But as she sat in her new church bedroom, Hernández said she was determined to go public with her story—to demand justice for herself and for other undocumented women who have suffered similar abuse. She was adamant that the system that allowed her to be victimized while she was fleeing for her life would not be allowed to separate her from Camila and her other child, a son named Victor Daniel. And she was committed to doing whatever it takes to protect the little girl sleeping in a crib just a few feet away.

"I'm here," she said, "because I'm never going to let anything like what happened to me happen to my daughter."

The story of how Hernández wound up in Texas, trapped in a room with a border agent, begins thousands of miles away in Guatemala. It was the summer of 2005; she was 24, and facing such life-threatening violence that she felt her only choice was to go north, to a place, she'd heard, where domestic abuse wasn't tolerated. "I never wanted to leave my country," Hernández said. "I was forced to flee."

She did this by bus, car, and foot—across parts of her own country and the length of Mexico. For the very last leg, she floated across the Rio Grande River in a red inflatable raft. The trip took two arduous weeks, but when she finally arrived in Texas, she was there for barely 30 minutes before she was apprehended by border agents and driven to the nearby CPB station.

This facility, located in Rio Grande City, is part of a sprawling web of detention centers that have sprung up along the US-Mexico border in recent years to hold immigrants and asylum seekers when they first arrive in the United States. While they look innocuous enough in pictures—like a low-slung suburban bank—lawyers and advocates say these border-region facilities are among the most secretive and least regulated of all jails or detention centers in the nation. The National Immigration Law Center has spent years in litigation simply trying to access surveillance footage from inside some of these places. When video stills from one CBP center in Arizona were finally made public, the law center denounced the "deplorable and unconstitutional" conditions depicted in the images.

In a series of interviews with *The Nation*, Hernández has described her own experience in the Rio Grande City station as degrading and inhumane. It began in a cell that was completely bare, save for concrete benches, where Hernández waited for hours with her nephew and a few other women as CBP officers called the immigrants out one by one to record their personal information. There was no toilet, food, or water, and the whole facility was freezing. "It was so cold, it burned," Hernández recalled.

"They treated us like animals," she added. "They called us 'illegals, illegals, illegals.'" At last, Hernández and her nephew were called to a crescent-shaped desk to share their information. It was there, Hernández said, that they encountered a supervisory Border Patrol agent with dark hair and a medium build who eyed her up and down and began "saying obscenities" to her. "What beautiful breasts!" she recalled him telling her. "They're so big." As he leered, one of his colleagues—a fat white man, Hernández recalled—began to laugh.

As an abuse survivor, Hernández had an acute sense for when a situation was on the verge of going wrong. "I felt like my heart was going to jump out of my chest," she said. Yet she continued to answer the agent's questions, even as he derisively asked her whether she had a husband. She told him she had fled domestic violence—a response that might have evoked sympathy. Instead, after a few more questions, the supervisory agent told Hernández he needed more information from her "in private."

Years later, Hernández says she still remembers what happened next "as if it were yesterday": the fat officer laughing even harder than before, as if he knew what "in private" meant; the dark-haired officer denying her efforts to bring her nephew with her and instead shooing the boy back to their cell; the officer's threatening suggestion that perhaps she wasn't really the boy's aunt, that perhaps she was actually engaged in trafficking children. "He told me, 'If you ever want the boy to get out of here, you'll cooperate with me,'" she recalled.

For Hernández, the threat carried weight: During the hours in which she was detained, she said, she had seen the agent personally signing other immigrants' paperwork just before they were released. So she complied, following the agent into a small office with a desk and a filing cabinet and the window shades pulled low. It was there, she said, that the officer sexually abused her.

In a statement responding to Hernández's allegations, a Customs and Border Protection spokesperson said: "A full investigation by [the] US Immigration and Customs Enforcement Office of Professional Responsibility, the US Attorney's Office, and local law enforcement, was conducted and the allegations against the border patrol agent were found to be unsubstantiated." The agency refused a request to provide documentation of these investigations.

Nonetheless, lawyers and experts say there is a widespread pattern of sexual abuse perpetrated against immigrants in the custody of the Department of Homeland Security. Over a recent two-year period, immigrants filed, on average, more than one complaint every single day of sexual abuse or assault inside DHS facilities. According to this data, obtained by the group Freedom for Immigrants, less than 3 percent of these complaints were even investigated.[1] (Meanwhile, under the Trump administration, the Immigration and Customs Enforcement agency, or ICE, has gained provisional approval to begin destroying its sexual-assault records after 20 years.)

Denise Gilman, the director of the immigration clinic at the University of Texas School of Law, says Border Patrol jails like the one where Hernández was held are among the most unaccountable of all DHS facilities. "These facilities are sort of a black hole," she said, highlighting how immigrants who dare to report abuse can face many forms of retaliation, including immediate deportation.

Still, the accusations abound. Last year, the American Civil Liberties Union filed claims on behalf of two teenage Guatemalan sisters who asked border agents for help after crossing the border, only to be taken to a CBP field office and then sexually assaulted, one after the other, in a closet.[2] In 2014, human-rights groups filed a complaint on behalf of more than 100 children who suffered abuse in CBP custody; a quarter of the children said they were the victims of physical or sexual assault.

That same year, a border agent apprehended two girls and a woman traveling from Honduras. He sexually assaulted and attempted to kill the woman and her 14-year-old daughter, then kidnapped the other girl and raped her in his apartment. Around the same time, James Tomsheck, then chief of internal affairs at Customs and Border Protection, e-mailed the head of CBP to report a "disturbing" number of sexual-abuse cases "that appear to exist in disproportionate numbers in our workforce."

Few of these reports ever result in prosecution. But a rare case that was successfully prosecuted in 2002 shows the risks and retaliation that migrant women in the border region can face.[3] In 2000, a Salvadoran woman named Blanca Amaya-Flores was apprehended by border agents in Arizona and then driven by one of the agents, Dennis Johnson, out into the desert. His co-workers watched them leave. Once they were alone, Johnson forced her to perform oral sex on him while she was naked and restrained by handcuffs. He then dropped her off in the middle of the night a few blocks from the border and pointed her in the direction of Mexico.

To this day, Hernández has said that she does not like to discuss publicly the specific details of the sexual abuse she experienced in detention. But what she does say is that when it was all over, the CBP agent issued a barely veiled threat. "He said, 'I know I'll never hear anything about this because I have all of your information. And if you ever speak about this, I will find you,'" she recalled. "This is why I didn't say anything, why I stayed silent."

Once back in her cell, Hernández said, she was so disgusted that she couldn't stop gagging. She was overwhelmed by the urge to vomit, but she had nothing in her stomach to throw up, as the detainees had been denied food and water for many hours. "My nephew kept asking me, 'What's wrong? What's wrong?'" she recalled. But she didn't tell the boy anything. Instead, she remained silent even as the officer walked by the partial glass wall of their cell and, seeing her dry-heaving, laughed.

In the days that followed, Hernández and her nephew were left alone—too alone—stuck in detention as all the other members of their group were released. They stayed until new border agents arrived with another group of captured immigrants, and one of the agents asked why Hernández and her nephew were still in the cell when their paperwork had already been processed. Hernández recalled another agent saying that her release was up to the supervisory agent—the very man, she said, who had sexually abused her. Under pressure from the new agents, she and her nephew were allowed to leave their cell, and then one of the new agents loaded them into a truck and drove them away in the summer heat.

Where is he taking us? Hernández wondered. *What is going to happen next?*

To her relief, they arrived about 15 minutes later at a small bus station, where the agent handed her a few pieces of paper written in English. According to government documents reviewed by *The Nation*, one of those papers was a notice to appear in a Texas courtroom, and it was signed by the same supervisory agent who Hernández says sexually abused her.

• • •

For nearly a decade, Hernández stayed silent about her experience with Customs and Border Protection. When she first arrived in New York State to join family members, she hid her paperwork away in a drawer—and tried to bury the memories of what had happened. . . .

Yet the trauma leached into all aspects of her world. Hernández has described herself in this period as timid and unassertive, which she attributes to the violence she suffered in Guatemala and the abuse while in custody in Texas. If someone told her to do something, she'd do it—even if she disagreed. On her first date with her husband, she told the waiter she'd eat whatever he was eating. "I barely spoke," she said. "It was like I was delayed, almost like a child, because of all the trauma."

Still, she managed to create a fragile equilibrium for herself—until, in the fall of 2012, on her way to church, she mistakenly drove down a street that was one-way on Sundays and was stopped by a police officer who reported her to ICE. Suddenly, she faced the very real possibility of deportation. This would mean returning to Guatemala, from which she'd fled for her life nearly a decade earlier and which, over the ensuing years, had become only more dangerous. By 2012, violence was proliferating across the country. The femicide rate was among the highest in the world—and the conviction rate for the women's killers was between only 1 and 2 percent.

But Hernández's first fear was closer to home: She was terrified of being sent back to a US detention facility, convinced she'd see the same agent who had abused her in Texas. Hernández was overcome with distress from the moment the police officer pulled her over and she saw his blue uniform—the same color the agent's had been. "They wanted to send me to the place that was the nightmare of my entire life," she said.

A therapist who treated her at the time diagnosed her with acute post-traumatic-stress disorder, writing: "Because of the mistreatment at the hands of an American citizen, Aura is suffering from nightmares, flashbacks, body memories, extreme anxiety, and panic attacks."

As her agony began to alarm her family, Hernández eventually worked up the courage to break her silence, sharing the story of what had happened to her with them. (*The Nation* has spoken with several members of Hernández's family as well as the therapist, all of whom confirmed that she told them shortly after the police stop that she had been sexually abused while detained in Texas.) But while her secret was out, a larger problem remained: What was she going to do?

Among the many lessons of the #metoo moment, one of the more pronounced has been just how hard it is for women—even the most powerful and well-resourced—to wrest any kind of accountability from the people who violate and harass them. For women who are poor, disenfranchised, and undocumented, as Hernández was, the possibility of redress slips to almost zero. Nonetheless, when Hernández contacted a lawyer to help with her immigration case, he offered an unusual suggestion: He said that the abuse she had suffered in CBP custody could make her eligible for something called a "U visa," a special visa offered to victims of certain crimes who cooperate with law enforcement in the investigation or prosecution of that criminal activity. Hernández agreed to try and, shortly after, found herself sitting in her lawyer's office in front of multiple DHS internal-affairs investigators.

This meeting was not easy for Hernández. "I felt fear, terrible fear," she recalled. "I felt like they were going to tell me, 'I don't believe you. I don't believe you.'" But she spoke out anyway, denouncing the agent who had abused her by name and recounting what had transpired.

What happened next was… nothing. As is so often the case for women in Hernández's position, the Department of Homeland security declined to certify her petition for a U visa. "It's very hard to get these certifications," explained Barbara Hines, the founder of the immigration clinic at the University of Texas Law School. In many sexual-abuse cases, she said, "the authorities say it was consensual, or pretend it didn't happen, or transfer the agent, or deport the woman as fast as they can."

Without the certification, Hernández's lawyer was unable to file the U-visa petition. Her case stalled and, with it, any hopes for accountability from the DHS as well as a chance to solidify her immigration status. Still, Hernández was allowed to continue living in the United States by attending regular ICE check-ins; she also received a work permit and a driver's license. As time passed, her life stabilized and, thanks to professional counseling and family support, she grew more assertive and outspoken. In late 2016, she gave birth to her daughter.

And then Donald Trump took office, and with him an administration that made a priority of deporting all immigrants without status. Despite her regular attendance at ICE check-ins, her thriving family and diligent work life, Hernández was one of these targeted immigrants—a fact she learned at an ICE check-in in late 2017 as she held Camila in her arms. She was enraged. After five years of fighting her immigration case, after reliving her abuse and reporting her attacker to the authorities, she was being told that some unnamed supervisor had said it was time for her to go—that very day.

"They treat me like I'm a criminal, but they are the criminals," she said. "After everything they've done to me, how can they say that I'm the criminal?"

So, rather than given in, she pushed back, mounting such a fierce protest that the immigration officer agreed to postpone her deportation until March 1. With this reprieve, she scrambled to find a new lawyer, who submitted an asylum petition based on the domestic violence she had suffered in Guatemala and resumed work on the U-visa route. But as the clock ticked, it became clear to Hernández that legal maneuvers would not resolve the situation in time. She decided to keep fighting her case from sanctuary.

On March 29, Holy Thursday, Aura Hernández stood inside the sanctuary of the Fourth Universalist Society and, in front of a throng of cameras, declared, "I am not going to keep silent any longer. I'm asking all of you not to keep quiet, to defend your rights and the rights of our children."

Directly in front of her, resting on a table, was the Unitarian Universalism chalice: a burning flame inside a cup encircled by two metal rings. The church's senior minister, Schuyler Vogel, explained that the symbol was used throughout World War II as a secret code showing the persecuted where they could find safety. Behind Hernández stood a poster, drawn the night before by her son, reading "Please Don't Deport My Mommy."

Away from the limelight, Hernández and her daughter have been settling into their new life in the church, without any idea of when they can leave. Hernández's 10-year-old son visits at every opportunity, and the two of them play basketball and soccer in the gymnasium in the basement, carefully avoiding tripping over Camila as she crawls across the court.

The church's congregation and leaders have also begun adjusting to the family's stay. A year ago, two swastikas were carved into the building's heavy wood doors after the members voted to make it a sanctuary space. But rather than shrink from the responsibility, the church and its congregation have rallied to help Hernández. Many have volunteered to bring her food, keep her company, and support her nonstop efforts to call attention to her story.

In recent weeks, these efforts have included Skyped-in appearances at conferences and in classrooms, as well as countless interviews and an address to a group of middle-school students who visited her in the church. She also wrote a speech to be read aloud at a Washington, DC, protest against sexual violence by immigration authorities, and she coached her son to speak on her behalf at a march outside Trump Tower in New York City as well as at a recent sanctuary symposium in Washington Heights. Her most recent action has been to help organize a Mother's Day march to demand freedom for herself and all the other immigrants who have been forced to take sanctuary to avoid deportation and separation from their families.

So far, despite repeatedly denouncing the border agent for sexual abuse, she hasn't received the type of justice that other women have won through the #MeToo movement. But she's resolved to keep fighting. After all, despite the odds, a handful of women have successfully denounced immigration authorities in recent years for perpetrating sexual abuse. In March, Salvadoran immigrant Laura Monterrosa was finally released from detention in Texas after publicly accusing a female guard of sexually assaulting her.[4] In 2010, a Guatemalan woman reported surviving an attempted rape by a Corrections Corporation of America guard named Donald Dunn. (The company has since been renamed CoreCivic.) The complaint spiraled into a massive sexual-abuse scandal as a slew of other women came forward, and Dunn was jailed after pleading guilty to assault charges. And in 2002, Blanca Amaya-Flores, the Salvadoran woman who was sexually assaulted by border agent Dennis Johnson, saw him convicted of sexual assault and kidnapping and sentenced to seven years in prison.

"It's not just me—there are so many women who have suffered this and stay silent because of fear, like I was afraid," Hernández said a few days after she had taken sanctuary. As Camila toddled around the room, Hernández paused for a moment to reflect on how dramatically her life had changed—not only because of her need to take sanctuary, but also because of her own transformation.

"In the past, I wouldn't have said a single word about any of this to you—not a single word of this," she said. "But now, I say that if there's anything I can offer with my experience, I'll do it. Anything—you understand?—to put an end to so much evil and injustice."

NOTES

1. Merton, Rebecca, and Christina Fialho. "Re: Sexual Abuse, Assault, and Harassment in U.S. Immigration Detention Facilities." Received by Homan, Thomas D., et. al., 11 Apr. 2017. Available at: www.endisolation.org/wp-content/uploads/2017/05/CIVIC_SexualAssault_Complaint.pdf.
2. "ACLU of Northern California Files Claims Against Customs and Border Protection for Sexual Assault." The American Civil Liberties Union, 22 Mar. 2017, www.aclu.org/news/aclu-northern-california-files-claims-against-customs-and-border-protection-sexual-assault.
3. *State of Arizona v. Dennis Johnson*, Case 351 F.3d 988, U.S. Court of Appeals for the Ninth Circuit. Entered 16 Dec. 2003. *Justia*, law.justia.com/cases/federal/appellate-courts/F3/351/988/526002/.
4. Muñoz, Claudia. "BREAKING: Laura Monterrosa Released from Immigrant Detention Center in Texas." *Grassroots Leadership*, 17 Mar. 2018, grassrootsleadership.org/releases/2018/03/breaking-laura-monterrosa-released-immigrant-detention-center-texas.

11 | Why Black Women's Experiences of #MeToo Are Different

Yolonda Wilson

This article contains accounts of different forms of sexual violence.—Editor

In April, a 25-year-old black woman named Chikesia Clemons was violently arrested by police at a Waffle House restaurant in Alabama.[1]

A video of the arrest that went viral shows police pulling Clemons from her chair and throwing her to the floor. In the process, her breasts are exposed and her dress rides up in the back. When she attempts to cover her breasts, the two officers on top of her threaten to break her arm for "resisting."

Clemons' experience is not unique. In the U.S., black women are not afforded the same regard for bodily privacy as white women.

Another example: In an investigation of the Baltimore City Police Department, the Department of Justice found that the Baltimore Police Department frequently engaged in unjustified strip searches of African-Americans.[2] In one instance, Baltimore police conducted a strip search of a black woman, including an anal cavity search, on a sidewalk in broad daylight and in full public view.[3] The woman's pleas to not be forced to disrobe in public were ignored. Her offense? A broken headlight.

While the #MeToo movement has been successful in bringing down several high-profile assailants, critics continue to argue that it has been monopolized by middle- and upper-class white women, particularly white Hollywood actresses.[4] This, despite the fact that a black woman, Tarana Burke, created the Me Too campaign more than a decade ago.[5] These criticisms reflect the fact that black women have experienced sexual violence differently than white women.

As a philosopher of race and gender who has written about sexual harassment, I offer historical context on the ways that black women experience sexual abuse, often by the authority of the state, as a way to think about black women's contemporary experiences as the kinds of experiences that #MeToo should address.[6]

Yolonda Wilson is an assistant professor of philosophy at Howard University. She specializes in bioethics as it intersects with social/political philosophy, feminist philosophy, and race.

History of Black Women's Bodies on Display

As early as the 17th century, European men wrote travel narratives about their trips to West Africa to capture, enslave and trade African people.[7] Their writings offer a window into how they perceived African women and what they thought primarily European male readers would find titillating.

In particular, their descriptions of West African women's style of dance played a role in shaping European perceptions of black women's sexual immorality and availability.

These travel accounts were the popular media of their day and offered some of the first reports of continental Africa to average Europeans. For example, Frenchman Jean Barbot wrote of African men and women "knocking bellies together very indecently" while "uttering some dirty mysterious words." Meanwhile, naval officer Abraham Duqesne characterized African women as desiring the "caresses of white men."

Because African women differed from European women both in attire and bodily movement, European travel writers regarded African women as sexually available and immoral. European settlers carried these attitudes to the United States where enslaved black women were subjected to violent sexual abuse and forced nudity as routine social practice, in ways that would have been unthinkable toward white women.[8]

Sexual Violence and the Father of Gynecology

By the 19th century, treating black and white women differently was firmly entrenched in society. Nowhere was this more evident than in the practice of J. Marion Sims, the physician widely regarded by gynecologists as the "father of modern gynecology."[9] The convention of the period was for physicians to conduct gynecological examinations of white women with averted gazes while the patients remained as clothed as possible.

However, Sims also conducted medical experiments on enslaved black women that ultimately resulted in a technique to repair vesicovaginal fistula, an opening that can develop between the vaginal wall and the bladder or large intestine, sometimes as a result of childbirth.[10] The enslaved black women were stripped completely naked and examined on all fours, as Sims and other physicians took turns using a specially created speculum that enabled full viewing of the vagina. Private citizens were also allowed to watch these experiments and they, too, were invited to witness the full exposure of enslaved women's vaginas.

Sims conducted his experiments without anesthesia, despite the fact that ether was known and in use by the time he performed later surgeries.[11] Black women were denied anesthesia on the grounds that black people did not feel pain in the same ways that white people felt pain, a perception that still exists today.[12] For example, one study found that when people viewed images of blacks receiving painful stimuli, like needle pricks, they responded with less empathy than when they viewed similar images of white people in pain.

Sexual Violence in a Court of Law

In New York in 1925, another historical example shows how black women's exposed bodies have been treated with indifference. Kip Rhinelander, a member of New York's high society, was set to wed Alice Beatrice Jones, a working-class biracial woman.[13] Their union drew national attention.

Although New York did not legally prohibit interracial marriage as other statesdid at that time, society strongly disapproved of interracial marriage.[14]

Once their marriage was made public, Kip filed for divorce on the grounds of fraud. The salient question in the divorce hearing was whether Kip knew that Alice was black at the time of their marriage.

In order to answer that question, Alice's attorney suggested that Alice bare her breasts in front of the all-white male jury, judge and attorneys in order to prove her racial identity. By viewing the shading of her areolas and legs, he said, the jurors could assess whether Kip – who had admitted to premarital sex with her – should have known her racial identity.

The judge directed Alice to follow through. Neither Alice Rhinelander's tears nor her connection to a prominent white family could save her from the indignity of forced nudity in front of strangers. Ultimately, the jury decided that Alice was, in fact, "of colored blood" and that she did not conceal or misrepresent her racial identity.

The Past Is Present

The hostility to black women's bodily privacy and dignity in these examples isn't accidental. Rather, it is part of the history of how black women have been cast in U.S. society.

In the Sims and Rhinelander examples, the legal status of enslavement and weight of the court validated the coercive display of black women's bodies. The Department of Justice found that the Baltimore police used the weight of their badges to force compliance with public strip searches. Likewise, in the Waffle House example, although Clemons' initial exposure may not have been intentional, the police responded to her cries and her attempts to cover herself by using their authority to threaten her with further harm.

This is a unique form of sexual violence experienced by black women. The convergence of race and gender in black women's lives has created the social conditions in which black women are coerced and often expected, under threat of punishment by the government, to suffer the exposure of intimate body parts.

Race and gender converge in black women's lives and have created the social conditions under which black women are coerced and expected to suffer the exposure of intimate body parts, or else face punishment. If movements like #MeToo are serious about combating sexual violence, then they have to also understand these practices as sexual violence.

NOTES

1. Sheets, Connor. "Outrage Growing Over Black Woman's Arrest in Alabama Waffle House by White Police Officers." *Advance Local*, 22 Apr. 2018, www.al.com/news/birmingham/2018/04/outrage_growing_over_black_wom.html.

2. *Investigation of the Baltimore City Police Department*, U.S. Department of Justice, Civil Rights Division, 10 Aug. 2016. Available at www.justice.gov/crt/file/883296/download.

3. Adams, Genetta M. "The 7 Most Outrageous and Racist Acts Found in DOJ's Report on Baltimore Police Department." *The Root*, 11 Aug. 2016, www.theroot.com/the-7-most-outrageous-and-racist-acts-found-in-doj-s-re-1790856365.

4. White, Gillian B. "The Glaring Blind Spot of the 'Me Too' Movement." *The Atlantic*, 22 Nov. 2017, www.theatlantic.com/entertainment/archive/2017/11/the-glaring-blind-spot-of-the-me-too-movement/546458/.

5. Garcia, Sandra E. "The Woman Who Created #MeToo Long Before Hashtags." *The New York Times*, 20 Oct. 2017, www.nytimes.com/2017/10/20/us/me-too-movement-tarana-burke.html.

6. Wilson, Yolonda Y. "How Might We Address the Factors That Contribute to the Scarcity of Philosophers Who Are Women and/or of Color?" *Hypatia: A Journal of Feminist Philosophy*, vol. 32, no. 4, 9 Sept. 2017, pp. 853–861. *Wiley Online Library*, doi:10.1111/hypa.12353.

7. Thompson, Katrina Dyonne. "'Some Were Wild, Some Were Soft, Some Were Tame, and Some Were Fiery': Female Dancers, Male Explorers, and the Sexualization of Blackness, 1600–1900." *Black Women, Gender Families*, vol. 6, no. 2, 2012, pp. 1–28. *JSTOR*, doi:10.5406/blacwomegendfami.6.2.0001.

8. Feimster, Crystal N. "When Black Women Reclaimed Their Bodies." *Slate*, 2 Feb. 2018, slate.com/human-interest/2018/02/how-formerly-enslaved-black-women-fought-for-human-dignity-and-sexual-justice.html.

9. Zhang, Sarah. "The Surgeon Who Experimented on Slaves." *The Atlantic*, 18 Apr. 2018, www.theatlantic.com/health/archive/2018/04/j-marion-sims/558248/.

10. Washington, Harriet A. *Medical Apartheid: The Dark History of Medical Experimentation on Black Americans from Colonial Times to the Present.* Anchor, 2008.

11. Domonoske, Camila. "'Father of Gynecology,' Who Experimented on Slaves, No Longer on Pedestal in NYC." *NPR*, 17 Apr. 2018, www.npr.org/sections/thetwo-way/2018/04/17/603163394/-father-of-gynecology-who-experimented-on-slaves-no-longer-on-pedestal-in-nyc.

12. "Study: Whites Think Black People Feel Less Pain." *Tell Me More.* NPR, 11 June 2013.

13. Onwuachi-Willig, Angela. "A Beautiful Lie: Exploring Rhinelander v. Rhinelander as a Formative Lesson on Race, Identity, Marriage, and Family." *California Law Review*, vol. 95, no. 6, Dec. 2007, pp. 2393–2458., doi:10.15779/Z38P98N.

14. Pascoe, Peggy. *What Comes Naturally: Miscegenation Law and the Making of Race in America.* Oxford University Press, 2009.

12 Power-Conscious Approaches to Campus Sexual Violence

Chris Linder and Jessica C. Harris

Feminists have long advocated that sexual violence is more about power than about sex, yet few people understand what this means. Further, when mainstream feminist movements (i.e., white, middle-class, educated, cisgender women) highlight that power is integral to understanding sexual violence, that usually (re)centers power connected with only sexist oppression. While misogyny, patriarchy and sexism contribute to sexual violence, we argue that the root of sexual violence is deeper than the sum of these sexist systems.

The root cause of sexual violence is oppression, in all of its manifestations, including racism, cissexism, heterosexism, ableism *and* sexism. Oppression results from people abusing power or lacking consciousness about how power influences their own and others' experiences. For these reasons, we advocate a power-conscious approach to addressing sexual violence.

What does "power conscious" mean? Simply put, it means paying attention to power dynamics at work in individual, institutional and cultural systems of oppression. Developing power consciousness means that we ask:

- Who is missing in this discussion? Who is centered? Why? . . .
- Who has the power — both formal and informal — in this system?
- How do social identities influence who is heard and who is ignored and silenced?
- Who benefits from this system? Who does not?

• • •

College campuses are mostly made up of the same people who make up our larger communities, so racism and classism are showing up in our campus accountability systems, as well. Campus police, campus judicial systems and even victim advocacy services are not immune from failing to consider the ways people from historically minoritized communities may not experience campus systems the same as students with mostly dominant identities.

So, what do we do? Below, we offer three specific recommendations for approaching sexual violence from a power-conscious perspective.

Chris Linder is an assistant professor of higher education at the University of Utah, where her scholarship focuses on sexual violence and student activism. She is the author of *Sexual Violence on Campus: Power-Conscious Approaches to Awareness, Prevention, and Response*.

Jessica C. Harris is an assistant professor of higher education and organizational change at the University of California, Los Angeles. She and Linder coedited the volume *Intersections of Identity and Sexual Violence on Campus: Centering Minoritized Students' Experiences*.

Learn the history of rape and racism. Ahistoricism, or failing to understand or account for the history and context of an issue or topic, leads to incomplete and ineffective strategies for dealing with sexual violence. For example, sexual violence law is fundamentally racialized.[1]

Early sexual violence laws in America were rooted in property law. White men were the only people who could file charges of rape, as rape was considered a property crime — something that reduced the value of a man's daughter, essentially his "property." Additionally, in the time period after the Civil War, white men falsely accused black men as perpetrators of sexual violence directed toward white women to maintain white men's power and dominance.[2]

More recent sexual violence laws, specifically, the Violence Against Women Act, emerged during the "tough on crime" era of the 1980s and '90s, which was also highly racialized. People in that era sought to address drug abuse, but drug laws and enforcement focused primarily on poor communities and communities of color, contributing to the continuation of portraying men of color as criminals.[3]

Given the racialized history of sexual violence law and the current context of racism in legal and policy systems, administrators and educators on college campuses should consider community accountability processes as an option for addressing sexual violence. Community accountability, as described by the INCITE! women of color against violence collective, means that communities stop relying on systems that perpetuate violence toward them and start relying on each other to hold perpetrators of violence accountable and work to transform perpetrator behavior.[4] Community accountability is not appropriate in all cases and must be carefully implemented under the leadership of people with a significant understanding of it (specifically, women of color, who created it).

Further, in cases where campus adjudication systems are used, people involved in those systems must be educated about the role of oppression in legal and policy response, as well as the history of the intersections of oppression and sexual violence. A deeper understanding of history may lead to more equitable outcomes in campus adjudication systems.

Employ an intersectional, identity-conscious perspective. Foundational intersectionality scholar Kimberlé Crenshaw provides a number of examples to illustrate centering women of color and poor women in interpersonal-violence work.[5] Crenshaw helps us understand that, by centering the most marginalized people in efforts to address interpersonal violence, no one is left out. When white, cisgender, heterosexual women at elite institutions of higher education are centered in sexual violence work (as they are now), they are the only ones to benefit. However, when marginalized populations are at the center of antioppression work, strategies are more comprehensive, resulting in more effectively dealing with interpersonal violence.

That being said, incorporating intersectionality into student affairs practice does not mean that every program has to be for every student. There is no such thing as an "all-inclusive" program. In fact, this is dangerously close to the concept of "color blindness," or the notion that one does not "see" color when discussing race. In addition to the ableist nature of the term "color blindness," using an "identity-neutral" approach to any issue effectively (re)centers people with dominant identities, who are treated as the norm or default.[6]

Related to campus sexual violence, seemingly identity-neutral approaches effectively make the experiences of any victim who is not a white, cisgender, heterosexual woman invisible. Designing programs that specifically center the experiences of men survivors, trans and queer survivors, survivors of color, and survivors with disabilities (re)centers their experiences in the conversation. Doing so will result in better-informed providers and more empowered survivors. This also frees up space to develop programs specifically for white, cis, hetero women, whose experiences are distinct in and of their own—just not the *only* experiences, as currently portrayed.

Focus on perpetrators. We are working on a research project examining the ways sexual violence is portrayed in campus newspapers. An initial review of the data reveals that perpetrators are invisible in most articles about sexual violence. Language used throughout newspaper articles often implies that sexual violence just "happens," as though there is no actor or explanation for it.

By making perpetrators invisible, we ignore important power dynamics at play. Perpetrators—not alcohol, not being at the wrong place at the wrong time, not miscommunication—are *solely* responsible for sexual violence. Failing to acknowledge this ignores the power that perpetrators wield, placing responsibility for ending sexual violence on the wrong people: potential victims, bystanders and advocates.

Campus administrators and educators should work to ensure that perpetrators are made more visible in discussions of sexual violence prevention. For example, rather than only focusing on teaching potential victims how to avoid being assaulted, we should spend more resources teaching people not to rape. Focusing on perpetrators as the cause of sexual violence may contribute to increased community accountability for their actions. People will begin to see the perpetrator—not alcohol or miscommunication—as the key problem.

NOTES

1. Donat, Patricia L. N., and John D'Emilio. "A Feminist Redefinition of Rape and Sexual Assault: Historical Foundations and Change."*Journal of Social Issues*, vol. 48, no. 1, 1992, pp. 9–22. *Wiley Online Library*, The Society for the Psychological Study of Social Issues, doi:10.1111/j.1540-4560.1992.tb01154.x.

2. Freedman, Estelle B. *Redefining Rape: Sexual Violence in the Era of Suffrage and Segregation.* Harvard University Press, 2015.

3. Alexander, Michelle. *The New Jim Crow: Mass Incarceration in the Age of Colorblindness.* The New Press, 2012.

4. "Community Accountability." INCITE!, Allied Media Projects, 22 Feb. 2019, incite-national. org/community-accountability/.

5. Crenshaw, Kimberlé. "The Urgency of Intersectionality." TED, Oct. 2016, www.ted.com/talks/ kimberle_crenshaw_the_urgency_of_intersectionality.

6. Annamma, Subini Ancy, et al. "Dis/Ability Critical Race Studies (DisCrit): Theorizing at the Intersections of Race and Dis/Ability." *Race Ethnicity and Education*, vol. 16, no. 1, 2013, pp. 1–31. *Taylor & Francis Online*, doi:10.1080/13613324.2012.730511.

13 Standing Rock, Flint, and the Color of Water

Christopher F. Petrella with Ameer Loggins

While much attention has rightly been paid to those who are courageously protecting water resources and sacred land on North Dakota's Standing Rock Sioux Reservation, few mainstream commentators have situated Standing Rock as part of a larger political struggle for self-determination and survival. Linking the politics surrounding the Dakota Access Pipeline project to Flint, Michigan's lead-poisoning crisis[1] is critical for understanding how race and class inform presumed social risk, vulnerability to premature death, and access to democratic decision-making.

In the case of the Dakota Access Pipeline, the Army Corps of Engineers Nationwide Permit No. 12 (NWP12) has fast-tracked construction—circumventing the democratic will of members of the Standing Rock Sioux community—by exempting the project from certain environmental inspections.[2] Similarly, the application of Michigan's Emergency Manager Law (EML) to Flint—a majority black city—authorized the state's governor unilaterally to appoint unelected officials to make decisions about how and where to source cheap water for the municipality. This sourcing resulted in widespread lead poisoning.[3]

Both NWP12 (a provision strongly supported by the oil industry and its lobbyists) and Michigan's EML (legislation passed with bipartisan support) constitute policies that pervert the democratic process. Both serve the interests of wealthy white men and thwart the decision-making capacities of communities of color. These policies beg larger questions: *What is the color of democracy?*[4] *Who is presumed to be capable of self-governance? And which types of communities have the right to avoid public health risks and increased vulnerability to premature death?*[5]

Since March [of 2016], thousands of tribal nations and non-indigenous allies from across the country have gathered at the Standing Rock Sioux Reservation to protect land and water that could be destroyed and/or contaminated by the proposed Dakota Access Pipeline.[6] Many members of the tribe oppose the pipeline's construction near their reservation on the grounds that it threatens their public health and welfare, water supply, cultural resources, and sacred sites. If completed, the $3.7 billion pipeline fabricated by Texas-based Energy Transfer Partners would span nearly 1,200 miles from North Dakota to Illinois and would transport at least 470,000 barrels of crude oil per day.

Christopher F. Petrella is a lecturer in American cultural studies at Bates College. His work explores the intersections of race, state, and criminalization. He has a Ph.D. in African diaspora studies from the University of California, Berkeley.

Ameer Loggins is a Ph.D. candidate in African diaspora studies at the University of California, Berkeley. His work examines black representation in media.

Christopher F. Petrella & Ameer Loggins, "Standing Rock, Flint, and the Color of Water ," *Black Perspectives,* November 2, 2016. Copyright © 2016 by African American Intellectual History Society. Used with permission.

Members of the Standing Rock Sioux Tribe have argued that under federal law the U.S. government should have consulted with them about the pipeline in the early stages of project development—and did not.[7] Last July, the Standing Rock Sioux and the non-profit Earthjustice sued the U.S. Army Corps of Engineers in federal court, contending that the agency had wrongly approved the pipeline without reasonable consultation. The tribe has also argued that because the Dakota Access Pipeline would cross right under the Missouri River at Lake Oahe—the reservation's main source of drinking water—a leak or oil spill could prove disastrous.

According to the National Institutes of Health, safe drinking water is presently "unavailable in 13 percent of American Indian/Alaska Native homes on reservations, compared with 1 percent of the overall U.S. population."[8] Moreover, the tribe points out that the pipeline's original path was supposed to go farther north, near Bismarck, but state and federal officials rejected that route out of concern that a leak might harm the state capital's drinking water.[9]

According to federal pipeline regulators the Bismarck route would have traversed land considered a "high consequence area," a designation reserved for zones determined to have "the most significant adverse consequences in the event of a pipeline spill."

This is significant for the following reason:

> Originally, the pipeline was supposed to cross the Missouri near Bismarck, but authorities worried that an oil spill there would have wrecked the state capital's drinking water. So they moved the crossing to half a mile from the reservation, across land that was taken from the tribe in 1958, without their consent. The tribe says the government hasn't done the required consultation with them—if it had, it would have learned that building the pipeline there would require digging up sacred spots and old burial grounds.[*]

● ● ●

To be sure, the language of "high consequence areas," serves as a politically vacuous euphemism for high consequence lives, people, and bodies. These raced and classed demographic realities beg the questions: *Whose lives matter?*[10] *Whose historic use of land and water matter? And whose health matters?*

One could ask the same questions of Flint, Michigan.

Whereas members of the Standing Rock Sioux Tribe were not consulted in the initial stages of the Dakota Access Pipeline planning process, many citizens of Flint, Michigan—a majority-black city—were subjected to a lead-tainted water supply and stripped of their civic power, representative government, and legal recourse in an effort to save the city from financial default.

Residents of Flint, 57 percent of whom are black and 42 percent of whom live below the poverty line, were deprived of the basic right to govern their city from 2011–2015 by Michigan's Emergency Manager Law (EML).[11] The provision empowers the governor with the authority to appoint unelected officials to control any city determined to be in "fiscal crisis." The emergency manager has the power to "renegotiate contracts, liquidate assets, suspend local government [and] unilaterally draft policy."

---

[*] Bill McKibben, "A Pipeline Fight and America's Dark Past," *The New Yorker*, September 6, 2016.

In 2013, Flint residents filed a lawsuit challenging the constitutionality of Michigan's EML on the basis that most appointments have come in cities in which most of the residents are people of color. A federal appeals court upheld the state's EML in 2016 by arguing that citizens have "no fundamental right" to elect local government officials. The court also found that the law appeared to be applied with colorblind intentions and was "facially entirely neutral with respect to race." The outcome of these policies, however, strongly suggests otherwise. In theory, emergency financial managers are supposed to assist municipalities based on an unbiased evaluation of their financial circumstances—but majority-white communities facing similar fiscal challenges have not been subject to the same levels of unwanted political imposition.

Ideologically, the EML law rests on the assumption that residents of predominantly-black cities are ill-equipped to manage their own local democracies, as six unelected managers have been assigned to govern Flint over the past 13 years. One should ask if the same *in loco parentis* form of governance would be applied to majority-white cities in Michigan with the same zeal? To date, Allen Park, Michigan seems to be the singular majority-white city in the state to have come under the supervision of an emergency manager.

A similar question could be posed to the U.S. Army Corps of Engineers and political leaders in North Dakota's capital of Bismarck: would an oil pipeline of great economic significance ever be allowed to traverse a local water source in a relatively affluent city that is 95 percent white?

Though it would be wrong to suggest that Standing Rock is the new Flint, the struggles over access to democratic decision-making power are strikingly similar, as is the raced and classed (in)ability to eschew exposure to environmental health-risks and vulnerability to premature death.

The political battles at Standing Rock and in Flint are not just about clean water. Rather, access to clean water serves as a powerful litmus test for evaluating access to full and non-negotiable democratic participation.[17] The fight over the color of water—that is, its racialized policy antecedents—provides a deep challenge to the parameters and possibilities of self-determination and survival in a political space hostile to communities of color. The truth is that the very assumptions of social worth undergirding the decision to divert the Dakota Access Pipeline from Bismarck to Standing Rock are the very same assumptions that inform the decision to source Flint water from a polluted river.

Linking these battles over political recognition, entrance to democratic participation, and access to basic public goods such as clean drinking water brings into relief the necessity of coalition-building and the acknowledgment of shared interests.[13] We must contest these race- and class-based injustices from Flint to Standing Rock and beyond.

NOTES

1. Kennedy, Merrit. "Lead-Laced Water In Flint: A Step-By-Step Look At The Makings Of A Crisis." *NPR*, 20 Apr. 2016, www.npr.org/sections/thetwo-way/.

2. Horn, Steve. "Documents: How Big Oil Pushed to Make Dakota Access-Style Permitting a New Normal." *Huffpost*, 6 Dec. 2017, www.huffpost.com/entry/documents-how-big-oil-pus_b_11922862.

3. Vasilogambros, Matt. "Upholding Michigan's Emergency Manager Law." *The Atlantic*, 12 Sept. 2016, www.theatlantic.com/news/archive/2016/09/michigan-emergency-manager-law/499658/.

4. Rickford, Russell. "Managed Democracy and the Illusion of Politics." *Black Perspectives*, African American Intellectual History Society, 23 Oct. 2016, www.aaihs.org/managed-democracy-and-the-illusion-of-politics/.

5. Rankine, Claudia. "'The Condition of Black Life Is One of Mourning." *The New York Times*, 22 June 2015, www.nytimes.com/2015/06/22/magazine/the-condition-of-black-life-is-one-of-mourning.html?_r=0.

6. Skalickey, Sue, and Monica Davey. "Tension Between Police and Standing Rock Protesters Reaches Boiling Point." *The New York Times*, 28 Oct. 2016, www.nytimes.com/2016/10/29/us/dakota-access-pipeline-protest.html.

7. Carpenter, Kristen A., and Angela R. Riley. "Standing Tall." *Slate*, 23 Sept. 2016, slate.com/news-and-politics/2016/09/why-the-sioux-battle-against-the-dakota-access-pipeline-is-such-a-big-deal.html.

8. "2009: Many Reservation Homes Lack Clean Drinking Water." *Native Voices*, U.S. National Library of Medicine, www.nlm.nih.gov/nativevoices/timeline/616.html.

9. McBride, Jessica. "Dakota Access Pipeline Maps & Routes: Where Would It Go?" *Heavy*, 10 Sept. 2016, heavy.com/news/2016/09/dakota-access-pipeline-map-route-protests-dogs-state-north-dakota-illinois-south-iowa-counties-standing-rock-native-american-jill-stein/.

10. Joseph, Peniel. "The Radical Democracy of the Movement for Black Lives." *Black Perspectives*, African American Intellectual History Society, 18 Sept. 2016, www.aaihs.org/joseph-the-radical-democracy-of-the-movement-for-black-lives/.

11. Hakala, Josh. "How Did We Get Here? A Look Back at Michigan's Emergency Manager Law." *Michigan Radio*, NPR, 3 Feb. 2016, www.michiganradio.org/post/how-did-we-get-here-look-back-michigans-emergency-manager-law.

12. Delmont, Matt. "Policy ad Possibility in the Movement for Black Lives Platform." *Black Perspectives*, African American Intellectual History Society, 17 Sept. 2016, www.aaihs.org/policy-and-possibility-in-the-movement-for-black-lives-platform/.

13. Rickford, Russell. "Rebuilding the Robesonian Labor Movement." *Black Perspectives*, African American Intellectual History Society, 10 Sept. 2016, www.aaihs.org/rebuilding-the-robesonian-labor-movement/.

14 Healing the Trauma of Post-9/11 Racism One Story (and Melody) at a Time

Sonny Singh

Once the term terrorist attack was all over the headlines on September 11, 2001, some-thing inside my 21-year-old, fresh-out-of-college self was dreadfully certain of what was coming next. Before I even had a chance to begin processing and mourning the horrific loss of thousands of lives in New York City, I was getting calls from even the most apoliti-cal of my extended family members, urging me to be careful and "keep a low profile," to not leave my house unless I absolutely had to. No one in my family talked much about racism when I was growing up, but suddenly it was clear that while many in my Sikh family might not share my anti-oppression, leftist politics on paper, they sure as hell knew what it meant to be a target.

For those in the U.S. Sikh community who weren't already dreading the racist back-lash immediately after 9/11, the murder of Balbir Singh Sodhi on September 15, 2001, in Phoenix, Arizona (my hometown), surely shook them to the core. Quickly U.S. flags were being distributed at gurdwaras throughout the country, stickers with slogans like "Sikhs love America" in red, white, and blue emerged on car bumpers. Suddenly we became "Sikh Americans," a term seldom used before 9/11.

It's almost ten years later, and I still walk the streets and ride the subway with a hyper-vigilance built up through a lifetime of being targeted because of my brown skin, turban, and beard. In my daily life in New York City, where I have lived since 2003, I experience some form of explicit harassment from strangers at least once a week, on average. Some times several separate incidents in one day. Yes, in New York City, the most diverse city on the planet.

Most commonly, someone will call me a terrorist or "Osama" either directly to my face or to someone they are with, with the intention of me hearing it. And it doesn't stop there.

A few months ago on my first day teaching in a high school in the Bronx, a student walking by me said to his friends, "Look, an Iraqi! He's gonna blow up the school!" and they all burst into laughter.

Last month at the laundromat across the street from my Brooklyn apartment, I found my wet clothes thrown out of the dryers I was using and scattered on the grimy floor.

In 2007, four police cars surrounded me while I was putting up flyers for my band's concert in Williamsburg, Brooklyn (a neighborhood where every street pole is covered

Sonny Singh is a musician, writer, and activist working toward social and economic justice. He has designed and led workshops on issues related to oppression and strategies for creating social jus-tice, and he trains educators on racial justice.

Originally published in *Asian American Literary Review*, September 11, 2011. Reprinted by permission of the author.

with concert flyers). I was handcuffed and arrested and spent 16 hours in jail, where the white cop who arrested me forced me to take off my turban "for my own safety."

In 2006, a stranger ripped off my turban (dastar) while I was riding the subway, which had also happened to me in the fifth grade. I wrote these words after the incident:

> I get off at Smith and 9th Street with my dirty dastar in my hands, not knowing what to do. My eyes fill with tears immediately. I feel naked and exposed, so small, so humiliated, and so, so alone. Why did he do that? Why? Was it fun for him? Did he impress his friends? Does it make him feel like he has more power than someone else—someone who looks like an immigrant, a foreigner, bin Laden?
>
> I get to a corner of the platform and break down in despair, remembering fifth grade vividly, feeling so angry and exhausted from living in this country. The twenty-something years of this shit is going through me at once—the slurs, the obnoxious stares, the go-back-to-your-countries, the threats, the towel/rag/tomato/condom/tumor heads, all of it. But somehow pulling off my turban hurts more than anything. Maybe it's the symbolism of my identity wrapped up in this one piece of cloth that, like my brown skin, I wear every day.

I am an activist, an educator, and a musician. I dedicate my life to raising consciousness about oppression and injustice in the world and helping people see that change is possible. The music I make is often joyful and celebratory, embodying a hopeful spirit that is so needed in these times.

Yet simultaneously, as I cope with the trauma of bigotry, I struggle in a very personal way to remain hopeful. This is actually the first time I am using that word, trauma, in writing to refer to my experience. Being stared at with contempt and called derogatory names as I walk down the street is my status quo. It is an exhausting status quo. As I get older, it is becoming harder to avoid the emotional toll that a few decades of racist harassment has taken on me. In this post-9/11 climate, there is no "post-" in sight to the trauma of racism.

The reality seems especially bleak in the last year with the right-wing rage that has taken the U.S. by storm with a very clear enemy: Muslims. The hateful fear-mongering perpetuated by pundits and politicians on the evening news has real life consequences indicated by a rise in hate crimes as well as bullying in schools. From Quran Burning days to Stop Islamization of America rallies, Muslim-bashing is becoming an increasingly mainstream phenomenon. As always, the outward appearance of Sikhs makes us especially vulnerable. Just last week, two elderly Sikh men were shot, one of them killed, while going on an afternoon walk in their suburban Sacramento neighborhood.

Trauma upon trauma.

A decade of fear.

How will I, and we, heal?

Every time I step onto a stage and perform, wearing my turban proudly, I am breaking down the barriers and insecurities and anxieties that the trauma of racism has caused me. As my air creates melody through my trumpet and my voice, I am no longer afraid. As a crowd of a hundred or a thousand bursts into joyous dance and celebration the moment I play my first note, everything and anything feels possible.

As an educator, when I share my own experiences of being bullied and harassed with students, I witness transformation happening. When I refuse to separate myself and my experiences from the content I am teaching, I feel empowered and confident in who I am.

I witness students coming to a deeper understanding of their own prejudices and working to change them.

After my turban was pulled off on the subway several years ago, the only thing I could do was write. I went home, devastated, and wrote furiously. I emailed what I wrote to some of my closest friends and then eventually cleaned it up and had it published on a racial justice blog. By documenting what happened to me and sharing it, I began my healing process.

In all of these cases, I am sharing my story, whether through a melody, in a classroom, or on a blog. And as I share my post-9/11/01 story here in 2011 with these words, I feel a profound sense of hope that may not be rooted in a logical, physical reality, but perhaps in a deeper reality that connects us all and is a foundation for our belief in liberation and justice. Even in the worst of circumstances, remaining hopeful is a necessity to our survival as people traumatized by oppression. We Sikhs call this chardi kala—a spirit of revolutionary eternal optimism. Our collective struggles for dignity and social justice are not only necessary to tear down systemic inequalities, but also to heal our own personal wounds as oppressed people, always remaining in the chardi kala spirit.

Alexander, Michelle. *The New Jim Crow: Mass Incarceration in the Age of Colorblindness*. The New Press, 2012.

Anderson, Carol. *One Person, No Vote: How Voter Suppression Is Destroying Our Democracy*. Bloomsbury Publishing, 2018.

Anderson, Kristin J. *Benign Bigotry: The Psychology of Subtle Prejudice*. Cambridge University Press, 2010.

Beydoun, Khaled A. *American Islamophobia: Understanding the Roots and Rise of Fear*. University of California Press, 2018.

Gay, Roxanne, ed. *Not That Bad: Dispatches from Rape Culture*. Harper Perennial, 2018.

Gold, Jodi, and Susan Villari. *Just Sex: Students Rewrite the Rules on Sex, Violence, Equality and Activism*. Rowman & Littlefield Publishers, 1999.

Goluboff, Risa. *Vagrant Nation: Police Power, Constitutional Change, and the Making of the 1960s*. Oxford University Press, 2016.

Mogul, Joey, Beth Ritchie, and Kay Whitlock. *Queer (In)Justice: The Criminalization of LGBT People in the United States*. Beacon Press, 2012.

Nadal, Kevin L. *That's So Gay!: Microaggressions and the Lesbian, Gay, Bisexual, and Transgender Community*. American Psychological Association (APA), 2013.

Scarce, Michael. *Male on Male Rape: The Hidden Toll of Stigma and Shame*. Basic Books, 2001.

Sethi, Arjun S. *American Hate: Survivors Speak Out*. The New Press, 2018.

Sue, Derald W. *Microaggressions in Everyday Life: Race, Gender, and Sexual Orientation*. Wiley, 2010.

Whitlock, Kay, and Michael Bronski. *Considering Hate: Violence, Goodness, and Justice in American Culture and Politics*. Beacon, 2015.

PART
V

The Economics of Race, Class, and Gender

The horror of class stratification, racism, and prejudice is that some people begin to believe that the security of their families and communities depends on the oppression of others, that for some to have good lives there must be others whose lives are truncated and brutal. It is a belief that dominates this culture.

—Dorothy Allison

We live in an economic system that requires us to disconnect from each other despite the fact that we are ultimately interconnected.

—Ai-jen Poo

In the United States, we tend to obscure the distinction between rich and poor, instead proclaiming ourselves all "middle class," but economic divisions are real, and the gap between rich and poor in this country is growing at an alarming rate. In fact, late in 2017, the wealth gap between upper- and lower-income families was the highest ever recorded.[1] In Part V we attempt to deepen our understanding of race, class, gender, and sexuality by turning our attention to the economic realities faced by most people in their daily lives.

In the opening selection, Dorothy Allison offers a complex and intersectional analysis of economic and social class through her own multiple identities as a white queer woman, a survivor of childhood violence, a writer of fiction, and someone born into poverty. Allison places the question of class at the center of her story while also emphasizing that "class, gender, sexual preference, and prejudice—racial, ethnic, and religious—form an intricate lattice that restricts and shapes our lives."

In Selection 2, Holly Sklar provides a dramatic and thought-provoking overview of economic inequality and other forms of injustice in a country supposedly founded upon articulated ideals of equality and fairness. She explores the ironies of that mythology through wide-ranging statistics relating to wages, wealth, tax breaks for millionaires, student debt, public school funding, violence, incarceration, discrimination, and more.

The 1990s saw significant economic growth in the United States, but at the start of the twenty-first century, many workers' pensions and 401K plans vanished overnight, and the proportion of Americans living in poverty rose significantly. The "Great Recession," which officially began in late 2007, only worsened these trends, and the repercussions are still being felt today. The economic story of the twenty-first century continues to be a persistent increase in the gap between rich and poor, a gap that has been widening slowly but steadily since 1973. Selections 3 through 7 report on the most recent rise in this gap and paint a bleak picture of how families are faring on average in this economy. In Selection 3, Jillian Olinger examines the lasting consequences of the recession by focusing on the subprime and foreclosure crisis and its disproportionate impact on communities of color. Even a decade later, she argues, "[t]he racial wealth gap continues to drive inequality in opportunity for Americans across the country, ensuring the crisis continues, and our national economy suffers because of it." In Selection 4, Barbara Ehrenreich and John Ehrenreich also address the recession, focusing on how it laid bare the deep inequities in our society and helped give rise to the Occupy Wall Street movement. They discuss the long history of unequal wealth distribution but point out that "it took the crash and its grim economic aftermath to awaken the 99% to a widespread awareness of shared danger."

In Selection 5, Alexandra Bastien examines the "criminalization of poverty" through court-imposed fees and fines. "These fees play an integral role in wealth and income inequality," Bastien argues, "and contribute to the growing racial wealth gap in our country where Black and Latino households, on average, own less than 1/13 and 1/10, respectively, of the average wealth of white households." She concludes with a list of concrete strategies that can help put an end to these pervasive practices whereby municipalities turn poor people into sources of revenue.

In Selection 6, Douglas Massey analyzes the economic consequences of constructions of race, arguing that the U.S. immigration enforcement apparatus has "become a central race-making institution for Latinos." Like Aviva Chomsky (Selection 2 in Part III), Massey identifies several ways that U.S. policies have "manufactured a large population of undocumented migrants." The rise of the "Latino threat narrative," increased xenophobia, and an aggressive war on immigrants all combine to create a class of exploited workers (both with and without documents) lacking full legal protections. "After occupying an intermediate position between blacks and whites in the American status hierarchy," he argues, "after 1990 Latinos increasingly joined African Americans at the bottom of the socioeconomic distribution to comprise a new American underclass."

In Selection 7, Linda Burnham offers an intersectional discussion of how the gender gap and the racial gap in wages affect African American women, who are both unemployed at higher rates than other women and overrepresented among low-wage workers. The material in this selection documents a persistent wage gap over many years and suggests that racism and sexism, not ability or qualifications, have determined which jobs women and men do and how much worth is attached to their work.

In Selection 8, Ai-jen Poo addresses the racism and sexism that affect the working lives of domestic workers, whose vital labor has been devalued in our economic system. She also asks deeper questions about our society's values: "What does it say about this nation that this workforce — that provides such a crucial type of care — is the least valued and most invisible?" Poo also describes feminist organizing strategies that build from this platform of "women's work" as a way to not only protect the rights of domestic workers but also "structurally recalibrate to what is important in life." Ultimately she argues for "a more sustainable system that adequately supports our basic human needs."

In sharp contrast to the reality that the articles in this section describe (often in statistical detail), the mythology of the American Dream continues to assure us that hard work and ability, not family background and connections, are the key to success. As we have already seen, the dramatic increase in American inequality has made the gap between the rich and the middle class wider, and hence more difficult to cross, than it was in the past. Unequal treatment starts well before a student ever thinks of pursuing any higher education. Selection 9 reports on the inequalities of public school funding across the country, inequalities that are rooted in the reliance on property taxes. Wealthy and white school districts receive significantly more funding than do poor districts and districts with large numbers of students of color, a pattern established by historical funding decisions and reinforced by more recent court rulings.

In Selection 10, Tracie McMillan looks at hunger inequality and finds that "in the United States more than half of hungry households are white, and two-thirds of those with children have at least one working adult—typically in a full-time job." Declining wages across color lines help to explain why one-sixth of Americans do not have enough to eat. In Selection 11, Ed Pilkington views economic inequality from a different angle, through a discussion of how gender expression and self-determination can be shaped by material realities and access to resources.

Finally, Selection 12 — Alejandro Reuss's sobering article "Cause of Death: Inequality" — explores the relationship between socioeconomic status and poor health and finds that life expectancy, chronic disease, death by injury, and generally poor health are highly correlated with low income and low status. Inequality, he concludes, quite literally ills.

NOTE

1. Rakesh Kochhar and Anthony Cilluffo, "How Wealth Inequality Has Changed in the U.S. Since the Great Recession, by Race, Ethnicity and Income," Pew Research Center, November 1, 2017. https://www.pewresearch.org/fact-tank/2017/11/01/how-wealth-inequality-has-changed-in-the-u-s-since-the-great-recession-by-race-ethnicity-and-income/.

GUIDING QUESTIONS FOR PART V

1. In Part II, Gregory Mantsios identified four class myths that he countered with several realities. How do the authors in Part V deconstruct some of these myths? Do they identify and challenge any other mythologies of class in America?

2. The myth of meritocracy tells us that success is the deserved result of merit and hard work. How do the readings in this part reveal the legal, historical, institutional, and structural elements of economic success (and economic struggles)?

3. Dorothy Allison writes, "class, gender, sexual preference, and prejudice—racial, ethnic, and religious—form an intricate lattice that restricts and shapes our lives." How does her essay reveal the ways in which that lattice operates in her life? How do intersections of identity operate in some of the other articles in this part? How have intersections of identity shaped your own economic life?

4. Several articles in this part focus on contemporary statistics, but many of them also speak to the legal and historical roots of present-day economic realities. Which policies, court cases, and other historical factors mentioned in these readings are particularly relevant today?

5. Douglas Massey argues that our immigration enforcement system has become "a central race-making institution for Latinos, on a par with the criminal justice system for African Americans." What does he mean by this comparison? What does he mean by a "race-making institution"? How does the "making" of race impact class?

6. Ai-jen Poo argues, "The upside-down concentration of the world's resources and wealth in the hands of a small minority at the expense of the vast majority is in fact unsustainable for everyone." What might a more sustainable system look like? What strategies might we use to bring about such a system?

7. Identify some of the strategies for change or movements for resistance discussed in the readings in Part V. What are the strengths and limitations of these efforts? Which efforts do you think will have a lasting impact? Why?

1 Imagine a Country

Holly Sklar

Imagine a country living history in reverse.

The average worker's wage buys less today than it did in the 1970s.[1]

The minimum wage buys less than it did in the 1950s.

Income inequality has roared back to the 1920s.

It's not Ireland.

Imagine a country where the richest family derives its fortune from the nation's largest employer—a company famous for paying poverty wages.

Imagine a country where one out of four children is born into poverty, and wealth is being redistributed upward. Since the 1970s, the richest 1 percent of households has nearly doubled its share of the nation's wealth. The top 1 percent has more wealth than the bottom 90 percent of households combined.

It's not Mexico.

Imagine a country where none of the nation's income growth goes to the bottom 90 percent of people.

Between 1973 and 2010, all of the nation's income growth went to the top 10 percent. Income for the bottom 90 percent declined, adjusted for inflation.

It wasn't always like that. Between 1947 and 1973, the richest 10 percent got 32 percent of the nation's growth. The bottom 90 percent shared 68 percent of the nation's income growth.

Imagine a country where, by 2007, the richest 1 percent had increased their share of the nation's income to the second-highest level on record, nearly tying the record set in 1928—on the eve of a great depression.

Not coincidentally, the nation experienced its worst economic downturn since the great depression—from December 2007 until June 2009, when the economy began growing again but unemployment, underemployment and foreclosures remained high.

Imagine a country where in 2010—the first year of economic recovery after a "great recession"—93 percent of all the nation's income growth went to the richest 1 percent.

Imagine a country where more and more jobs are keeping people in poverty instead of out of poverty.

Holly Sklar is the founder and CEO of Business for a Fair Minimum Wage, a national network of business owners, executives, and business organizations that believe a fair minimum wage makes good business sense. Sklar serves on the board of directors of the American Sustainable Business Council and is the coauthor of *Raise the Floor: Wages and Policies That Work for All of Us* and *Streets of Hope: The Fall and Rise of an Urban Neighborhood.*

Revised and updated July 22, 2012. © 2012 by Holly Sklar. Permission granted by the author.

Imagine a country where healthcare aides can't afford to take sick days. Where farm workers and security guards turn to overwhelmed food banks to help feed their families, and homelessness is rising among working families.

Imagine a country where some are paid so little their children go without necessities — while others are paid so much their grandchildren could live in luxury without having to work at all.

Imagine a country ranked number 42 — between Uruguay and Cameroon — in the list of nations from greatest to least inequality in family income distribution. More than ninety countries are less unequal.

It's not Argentina.

Imagine a country where taxes were cut so much that the nation's richest bosses pay lower effective rates than workers. The nation's 400 richest taxpayers paid an average federal tax rate of 19.9 percent in 2009 — down from 29.9 percent in 1995.

As a *Reuters* columnist observed, "The top 400 paid an average income tax rate of 19.9 percent, the same rate paid by a single worker who made $110,000 in 2009. The top 400 earned five times that much every day."

Imagine a country that gave tax breaks to millionaires while millions of people went without health insurance and the infrastructure built by earlier generations of taxpayers fell apart.

Imagine a country giving nearly a trillion dollars in tax breaks to millionaires and billionaires since 2001 while going into massive debt with other countries.

It's not Greece.

Imagine a country where worker productivity went up, but workers' wages went down.

In the words of the national labor department, "As the productivity of workers increases, one would expect worker compensation [wages and benefits] to experience similar gains." That's what happened between 1947 and 1973. But between 1973 and 2011, productivity grew 80 percent and the average worker wage fell 7 percent adjusted for inflation.

Imagine a country where minimum wage raises have been so little, so late that minimum wage workers earned less in 2012, adjusted for inflation, than they did in 1956.

The national minimum wage reached its peak value back in 1968, when it was $10.55 an hour, adjusted for inflation in 2012 dollars. At the $7.25 minimum wage in effect since 2009, today's full-time minimum wage retail worker, security guard, child care worker or health aide makes just $15,080 a year. Last century's 1968 minimum wage worker made $21,944 a year, adjusted for inflation.

Imagine a country where the minimum wage has become a poverty wage instead of an anti-poverty wage. The minimum wage has lagged so far behind necessities that keeping a roof overhead is a constant struggle and family health coverage would cost nearly all the annual income of a full-time worker at minimum wage.

Imagine a country with poverty rates higher than they were in the 1970s. Imagine a country that sets the official poverty line well below the actual cost of minimally adequate housing, healthcare, food and other necessities. On average, households need more than double the official poverty threshold to meet basic needs.

Imagine a country where some of the worst CEOs make millions more in a year than the best CEOs of earlier generations made in their lifetimes.

In 1980, CEOs of major corporations made an average 45 times the pay of average full-time workers. In 1991, when CEOs made 140 times as much as workers, a prominent pay expert said the CEO "is paid so much more than ordinary workers that he hasn't got the slightest clue as to how the rest of the country lives."

In 2003, a leading business magazine put a pig in a pinstriped suit on the cover and headlined its CEO pay roundup, "Have they no shame? Their performance stank last year, yet most CEOs got paid more than ever." The story began with a quote from George Orwell's *Animal Farm*: "But the pigs were so clever that they could think of a way round every difficulty." In 2011, CEOs at major corporations made 259 times the pay of average full-time workers.

Imagine a country where corporate profits are high and workers' wages are low. The nation's biggest bank explained it this way in 2011: "Reductions in wages and benefits explain the majority of the net improvement in [profit] margins . . . US labor compensation is now at a 50-year low relative to both company sales and US GDP."

It's not England.

Imagine a country where wages have fallen despite greatly increased education. Since 1973, the share of workers without a high school degree has plummeted and the percentage with at least four years of college has more than doubled.

Imagine a country where wages have fallen way behind the costs of major expenses like housing, health and college. Between 1970 and 2009, adjusted for inflation, rent and utilities rose 41 percent, health expenditures rose 50 percent, public college rose 80 percent and private college rose 113 percent.

Imagine a country where the wages of young college graduates (age 21–24) fell 5.4 percent between 2000 and 2011. But, as the College Board reports, "Over the decade from 2000–01 to 2010–11, total borrowing per full-time equivalent student for undergraduate and graduate students combined increased by 57% in inflation-adjusted dollars. Undergraduate borrowing increased by 56% per FTE student."

Students from lower-income families receive smaller grants from colleges and universities than students from upper-income families.

Imagine a country where households headed by persons under age 55 had much lower median net worth (assets minus debt) in 2010 than in 1989, adjusted for inflation.

Imagine a country where more and more two-paycheck households are struggling to afford a home, college, healthcare and retirement once normal for middle-class households with one paycheck. Middle-class households are a medical crisis, outsourced job or busted pension away from bankruptcy.

Households tried to prop themselves up in the face of falling real wages by maxing out work hours, credit cards and home equity loans. Consumer spending makes up about 70 percent of the economy. An economy fueled by rising debt rather than rising wages is a house of cards.

Imagine a country where underpaid workers are bailing out banks and corporations run by overpaid, undertaxed bosses who milked their companies and country like cash cows and crashed the world economy.

Imagine a country where "too big to fail" banks are bigger than before the financial meltdown. The assets of the five biggest banks were equal to 56 percent of the nation's economy in 2011. That's up from 43 percent in 2006.

It's not Germany.

Imagine a country where more workers are going back to the future of sweatshops and day labor. Corporations are replacing full-time jobs with disposable "contingent workers." They include temporary employees, on-call workers, contract workers, freelancers and "leased" employees—some of them fired and then "rented" back at a large discount by the same company—and involuntary part-time workers, who want permanent full-time work.

How do workers increasingly forced to migrate from job to job, at low and variable wage rates, without health insurance or paid vacation, much less a pension, care for themselves and their families, pay for college, save for retirement, plan a future, build strong communities?

Imagine a country, which negotiated "free trade" agreements, helping corporations trade freely on cheap labor at home and abroad.

Imagine a country becoming a nation of Scrooge-Marts and outsourcers—with an increasingly low-wage, underemployed workforce instead of a growing middle class.

It's not Canada.

Imagine a country where polls show most workers would join a union if they could, but for decades, employers have routinely violated workers' rights to organize.

A leading business magazine observed in 2004, "While labor unions were largely responsible for creating the broad middle class after World War II . . . that's not the case today. Most . . . employers fiercely resist unionization, which, along with other factors, has helped slash union membership to just 13% of the workforce, vs. a midcentury peak of more than 35%."

By 2011, the union membership rate was just 11.8 percent. Full-time workers who were union members had median 2011 weekly earnings of $938 compared with just $729 for workers not represented by unions.

It's not South Korea

Imagine a country where nearly two thirds of women with children under age 6 and more than three-fourths of women with children ages 6–17 are in the labor force, but paid family leave and affordable childcare and after-school programs are scarce. Apparently, kids are expected to have three parents: Two parents with jobs to pay the bills, and another parent to be home in mid-afternoon when school lets out—as well as all summer.

Imagine a country where women working full time earn 77 cents for every dollar men earn. Women don't pay 77 cents on a man's dollar for their education, rent, food or healthcare. The gender wage gap has closed just 13 cents since 1955, when women earned 64 cents for every dollar earned by men. There's still another 23 cents to go.

The average female high school graduate who works full time, year round from ages 25 to 64 will earn about $383,000 less than the average male high school graduate. The gap widens to $654,000 for full-time workers with Bachelor's degrees and $824,000 for workers with Master's degrees. The gap shrinks to $609,000 for those with PhDs. But it balloons for full-time workers with professional degrees: women will earn $1,023,000 less than men in the course of their careers.

Imagine a country where childcare workers, mostly women, typically make less than baggage porters and bellhops and much less than animal trainers and pest control workers.

Out of nearly 800 occupations surveyed by the labor department, only 20 have lower median hourly wages than childcare workers.

Imagine a country where women are 47 percent of the nation's labor force but just 4 percent of the CEOs and 14 percent of the executive officers at the largest 500 companies. Never mind that companies with a higher share of women in their senior management teams financially outperform companies with lower representation.

Imagine a country where discrimination against women is pervasive from the bottom to the top of the pay scale, and it's not because women are on the "mommy track." The words of a leading business magazine still ring true, "At the same level of management, the typical woman's pay is lower than her male colleague's—even when she has the exact same qualifications, works just as many years, relocates just as often, provides the main financial support for her family, takes no time off for personal reasons, and wins the same number of promotions to comparable jobs."

Imagine a country where instead of rooting out discrimination, many policy makers blame women for their disproportionate poverty. If women earned as much as similarly qualified men, poverty in single-mother households would be cut in half.

It's not Japan.

Imagine a country where violence against women remains common. "Females made up 70% of victims killed by an intimate partner in 2007, a proportion that has changed very little since 1993," the department of justice reports. In 2007, 24 percent of female homicide victims were killed by a spouse or ex-spouse; 21 percent were killed by a boyfriend or girlfriend; and 19 percent were killed by another family member. Researchers say, "Men commonly kill their female partners in response to the woman's attempt to leave an abusive relationship."

The country has no equal rights amendment.

It's not Pakistan.

Imagine a country whose school system is rigged in favor of the already privileged, with lower caste children tracked by race and income into the most deficient and demoralizing schools and classrooms. Public school budgets are heavily determined by private property taxes, allowing higher income districts to spend more than poorer ones.

In rich districts, kids take modern libraries, laboratories and computers for granted. In poor districts, they are rationing out-of-date textbooks and toilet paper. Rich schools often look like country clubs—with manicured sports fields and swimming pools. In poor districts, schools often look more like jails—with concrete grounds and grated windows. College prep courses, art, music, physical education, field trips and foreign languages are often considered necessities for the affluent, luxuries for the poor.

It's not India.

Imagine a country whose constitution once counted black slaves as worth three-fifths of whites. Today, black per capita income is about three-fifths of whites'.

Imagine a country where racial disparities take their toll from birth to death. The black infant mortality rate is more than double that of whites. Black life expectancy is more than four years less. The official black unemployment rate is about twice that of whites and the black poverty rate is about triple that of whites.

Imagine a country where the government subsidized decades of segregated suburbanization for whites while the inner cities left to people of color were treated as outsider cities — separate, unequal and disposable. Studies have documented continuing discrimination in housing, education, employment, banking, insurance, healthcare and criminal justice.

Imagine a country where the typical white household has more than six times the net worth of the typical household of color. In 2010, median household net worth — including home equity — was $130,600 for white households and just $20,400 for households of color.

It's not South Africa.

Imagine a country that doesn't count you as unemployed just because you're unemployed. To be counted in the official unemployment rate you must be actively searching for work. The government doesn't count people as "unemployed" if they are so discouraged from long and fruitless job searches they have given up looking. It doesn't count as "unemployed" those who couldn't look for work in the past month because they had no childcare, for example. If you need a full-time job, but you're working part-time — whether 1 hour or 34 hours weekly — because that's all you can find, you're counted as employed.

A leading business magazine observed, "Increasingly the labor market is filled with surplus workers who are not being counted as unemployed."

Imagine a country where there is a shortage of jobs, not a shortage of work. Millions of people need work and urgent work needs people — from staffing schools, libraries, health centers and fire stations, to creating affordable housing, to repairing bridges and building mass transit, to cleaning up pollution and converting to renewable energy.

It's not Spain.

Imagine a country with full prisons instead of full employment. The jail and prison population has more than quadrupled since 1980. In 1980, one in every 453 residents was incarcerated. In 2010, the figure was one in every 137. The figures are even grimmer when it comes to people in prison or jail or on probation or parole: one in every 44 people (including children) is under some form of correctional control.

Imagine a country that is Number One in the world when it comes to locking up its own people. It has less than 5 percent of the world's population, but 23 percent of the world's incarcerated population.

Imagine a country where prison is a growth industry. State governments spend an average $29,000 a year to keep someone in prison, while cutting cost-effective programs of education, job training, employment, community development, and mental illness and addiction treatment to keep them out. In the words of a national center on institutions and alternatives, this nation has "replaced the social safety net with a dragnet."

A leading magazine reported in a piece titled "Incarceration Nation" that state expenditures for prisons rose at six times the rate of spending on higher education in the past 20 years. In 2011, the nation's largest state spent $9.6 billion on prisons and $5.7 billion on state colleges and universities. The article noted that since 1980, the state "built one college campus and 21 prisons. A college student costs the state $8,667 per year; a prisoner costs it $45,006 a year."

It's not China.

Imagine a country that imprisons black people at a rate much higher than South Africa did under apartheid. One out of ten black men ages 30–34 were locked up in prisons or jails compared to one out of 61 white men in the same age group in 2010. The overall incarceration rate for black women is three times higher than for white women.

Meanwhile, one out of seven black men and women were unemployed according to the official count in mid 2012 compared to one out of fourteen white men and women. Remember, to be counted in the official unemployment rate you must be actively looking for a job and not finding one. "Surplus" workers are increasingly being criminalized.

Imagine a country whose justice department observed, "The fact that the legal order not only countenanced but sustained slavery, segregation, and discrimination for most of our Nation's history—and the fact that the police were bound to uphold that order—set a pattern for police behavior and attitudes toward minority communities that has persisted until the present day." Racial profiling and "driving while black" are well-known terms.

Imagine a country where from first arrest to third strikes resulting in lifetime sentences—often for nonviolent petty crimes—blacks and Latinos are arrested and imprisoned in massively disproportionate numbers.

Imagine a country waging a racially biased "War on Drugs." Although blacks and whites engage in drug offenses at comparable rates, a human rights group reports, blacks are ten times more likely than whites to enter prison for drug offenses. Between 1999 and 2007, 80 percent or more of all drug arrests were for possession, not sales.

A study in a prominent medical journal found that drug and alcohol rates were slightly higher for pregnant white women than pregnant black women, but black women were about ten times more likely to be reported to authorities by private doctors and public health clinics—under a mandatory reporting law. Poor women were also more likely to be reported.

It is said that truth is the first casualty in war, and the "War on Drugs" is no exception. Contrary to stereotype, "The typical cocaine user is white, male, a high school graduate employed full time and living in a small metropolitan area or suburb," says the nation's former drug czar. A leading newspaper reported that law officers and judges say, "Although it is clear that whites sell most of the nation's cocaine and account for 80% of its consumers, it is blacks and other minorities who continue to fill up [the] courtrooms and jails, largely because, in a political climate that demands that something be done, they are the easiest people to arrest." They are the easiest to scapegoat.

It's not Australia.

Imagine a country that ranks first in the world in wealth and military power, and just 48th in infant mortality, a little better than Croatia and behind countries such as Cuba and South Korea. If the government were a parent, it would be guilty of child abuse. Thousands of children die preventable deaths.

Imagine a country where healthcare is managed for healthy profit. Between 1999 and 2011, the average cost of insurance premiums more than doubled. Other industrialized countries have universal health coverage. But in this nation, one out of five people under age 65 had no health insurance, public or private, at any time in 2010.

"The absence of health insurance is hazardous to your health," says the Institute of Medicine. "Uninsured people, children as well as adults, suffer worse health and die sooner than those with insurance."

Lack of health insurance typically means lack of preventive healthcare and delayed or second-rate treatment. The uninsured are at much higher risk for chronic disease and disability, and uninsured adults have a 25 percent greater chance of dying (adjusting for demographic, socioeconomic and health characteristics). Uninsured women with breast cancer have a 30 percent to 50 percent higher risk of dying than insured women, for example. Severely injured car crash victims who are uninsured receive less care in the hospital and have a 39 percent higher mortality rate than privately insured patients.

Imagine a country where healthcare is literally a matter of life and death, but every day more than 2000 babies are born without health insurance. The country's northern neighbor, which has universal healthcare, has a life expectancy that is three years longer.

Imagine a country where many descendants of its first inhabitants live on reservations strip-mined of natural resources and have a higher proportion of people in poverty than any other ethnic group.

Imagine a country where centuries of plunder and lies are masked in expressions like "Indian giver." Where the military still dubs enemy territory, "Indian country." The 2011 military operation that killed the nation's No. 1 enemy was called Operation Geronimo.

Imagine a country that has less than 5 percent of the world's population and less than 3 percent of the world's proven oil reserves, but consumes 25 percent of the world's oil. The nation's federal spending on clean energy—including research, development and usage subsidies—rose sharply to $44 billion in 2009, and then plummeted in the years after to $16 billion in 2012, with more decreases expected.

Imagine a country whose per capita carbon dioxide emissions from the consumption of energy are nearly two times that of manufacturing powerhouse Germany, three times that of China and 12 times that of India. It has long obstructed international action against catastrophic climate change and continues subsidizing fossil fuels such as the oxymoronic "clean coal."

It's not Brazil.

Imagine a country whose senate and house of representatives are not representative of the nation. They are overwhelmingly white and male, and increasingly millionaire. Forty-two percent of house members were millionaires in 2010, according to financial disclosure records that don't even include the value of their homes or other non–income producing property. In the 100-member senate in 2010, there were 67 millionaires and no women of color. If the senate reflected the population, only one senator would be a millionaire.

Imagine a country that's ranked just number 79—between Morocco and Turkmenistan—when it comes to the percentage of women in national legislative bodies. Just 17 percent of its senate and house of representatives were women in 2012.

If the 100-member senate reflected the population it would have 51 women and 49 men—including 64 whites, 16 Latinos, 13 blacks, 5 Asian and Pacific Islanders, and 1 Native American and 1 other. Instead, it has 17 women and 83 men—including 96 whites, 2 Latinos, 2 Asians and no blacks or Native Americans.

Imagine a country that made it easier for billionaires and corporations to pour money into elections while making it harder for people to vote.

Imagine a country whose leaders misused a fight against terrorism as camouflage for trampling the bill of rights and undermining democracy. The most fundamental civil liberties, including the right of citizens not to be thrown into prison indefinitely or assassinated on the secret word of government officials, were tossed aside.

Imagine a country that leads the world in arms exports and accounts for 41 percent of world military spending. The next highest country accounts for 8 percent.

In this same country, a five-star general who became president had warned in 1961, "In the councils of government, we must guard against the acquisition of unwarranted influence, whether sought or unsought, by the military-industrial complex . . . We must never let the weight of this combination endanger our liberties or democratic processes. We should take nothing for granted. Only an alert and knowledgeable citizenry can compel the proper meshing of the huge industrial and military machinery of defense with our peaceful methods and goals, so that security and liberty may prosper together."

It's not Russia.

It's the United States.

The words of Dr. Martin Luther King Jr. call down to us today:

"A true revolution of values will soon cause us to question the fairness and justice of many of our past and present policies. We are called to play the Good Samaritan on life's roadside; but . . . one day the whole Jericho road must be transformed so that men and women will not be beaten and robbed as they make their journey through life. . . .

"A true revolution of values will soon look uneasily on the glaring contrast of poverty and wealth. . . . There is nothing but a lack of social vision to prevent us from paying an adequate wage to every American citizen whether he be a hospital worker, laundry worker, maid or day laborer."

EDITOR'S NOTE

1. The trends and general features of economic inequality described by Sklar continue today, though many of the specific statistics have changed. For more recent statistics, see Gregory Mantsios, "Class in America," in Part II in this volume, as well as the Pew Center for Research (www.pewresearch.org) and the other websites listed in Suggestions for Further Reading at the end of Part V. You can also find relevant data in the following articles:

   - Chad Stone, et al., "A Guide to Statistics on Historical Trends in Income Inequality." Center on Budget and Policy Priorities, December 11, 2018. Available at www.cbpp.org/research/poverty-and-inequality/a-guide-to-statistics-on-historical-trends-in-income-inequality.

   - David Cooper, "The Federal Minimum Wage Has Been Eroded by Decades of Inaction." The Economic Policy Institute, July 25, 2016. Available at https://www.epi.org/publication/the-federal-minimum-wage-has-been-eroded-by-decades-of-inaction/.

   - Drew Desilver, "For Most U.S. Workers, Real Wages Have Barely Budged in Decades." The Pew Research Center, August 7, 2018. Available at www.pewresearch.org/fact-tank/2018/08/07/for-most-us-workers-real-wages-have-barely-budged-for-decades.

   - Christopher Ingraham, "The Richest 1 Percent Now Owns More of the Country's Wealth Than at Any Time in the Past 50 Years." *The Washington Post*. December 6, 2017. Available at https://www.washingtonpost.com/news/wonk/wp/2017/12/06/the-richest-1-percent-now-owns-more-of-the-countrys-wealth-than-at-any-time-in-the-past-50-years.

   - Brian Thompson, "The Racial Wealth Gap: Addressing America's Most Pressing Epidemic." *Forbes*, February 18, 2018. Available at https://www.forbes.com/sites/brianthompson1/2018/02/18/the-racial-wealth-gap-addressing-americas-most-pressing-epidemic/#404a9f077a4.

SELECTED SOURCES

Bloomberg Businessweek, "Big Banks: Now Even Too Bigger to Fail," April 19, 2012.

Anthony P. Carnevale, et al., *The College Payoff: Education, Occupations, Lifetime Earnings*, Georgetown University Center on Education and the Workforce, 2011.

Catalyst, New York, reports on women in business.

Center for American Women and Politics, Rutgers University, New Jersey.

Center for Responsive Politics, OpenSecrets.org.

Ira J. Chasnoff, et al., "The Prevalence of Illicit-Drug or Alcohol Use During Pregnancy and Discrepancies in Mandatory Reporting," *New England Journal of Medicine*, April 26, 1990.

Children's Defense Fund, Washington, DC.

CIA World Factbook, Country Comparisons.

Citizens for Tax Justice, Washington, DC.

College Board Advocacy & Policy Center, *Trends in Student Aid 2011*.

Congressional Budget Office.

Michelle Conlin and Aaron Bernstein, "Working . . . and Poor," *Business Week*, May 31, 2004.

Graef S. Crystal, *In Search of Excess: The Overcompensation of American Executives* (New York: Norton, 1992/1991).

Economic Policy Institute, Washington, DC.

President Dwight D. Eisenhower, Farewell Radio and Television Address to the American People, January 17, 1961.

Anne B. Fisher, "When Will Women Get To The Top?" *Fortune*, September 21, 1992.

Forbes, annual reports on CEO compensation.

Human Rights Watch, *Decades of Disparity: Drug Arrests and Race in the United States* (2009) and *Targeting Blacks* (2008).

Institute for Women's Policy Research, *The Gender Wage Gap: 2011*, March 2012.

Institute of Medicine, National Academy of Sciences, *America's Uninsured Crisis* (2009) and other reports on the consequences of lack of health insurance.

International Centre for Prison Studies, King's College, London, UK.

Inter-Parliamentary Union, Women in National Parliaments, May 31, 2012.

David Cay Johnston, "The fortunate 400," *Reuters*, June 6, 2012.

J.P. Morgan, *Eye on the Market*, July 11, 2011.

Henry J. Kaiser Family Foundation reports on health insurance costs.

Martin Luther King Jr. *Where Do We Go From Here: Chaos or Community?* (Harper & Row, 1967).

Jonathan Kozol, *The Shame of the Nation: The Restoration of Apartheid Schooling in America* (New York: Crown, 2005) and *Savage Inequalities: Children in America's Schools* (Crown, 1991).

Peter Medoff and Holly Sklar, *Streets of Hope: The Fall and Rise of an Urban Neighborhood* (Boston: South End Press, 1994).

National Center for Public Policy and Higher Education, *Measuring Up 2008: The National Report Card on Higher Education*.

National Center on Institutions and Alternatives.

Emmanuel Saez, "Striking it Richer: The Evolution of Top Incomes in the United States," updated March 2012, and updated data tables for 1913-2010.

Sentencing Project, Washington, DC, reports on incarceration trends and racial disparity in criminal justice.

Holly Sklar, Laryssa Mykyta and Susan Wefald, *Raise The Floor: Wages and Policies That Work For All Of Us* (Boston: South End Press, 2002).

Stockholm International Peace Research Institute, data on world military expenditures and arms transfers.

Jerry Useem, "Have They No Shame?" *Fortune*, April 28, 2003 on CEO pay.

U.S. Census Bureau.

U.S. Centers for Disease Control and Prevention, National Center for Health Statistics.

U.S. Department of Education.

U.S. Department of Justice, Bureau of Justice Statistics.

U.S. Department of Justice, *Female Victims of Violence*, revised October 23, 2009.

U.S. Department of Labor, Bureau of Labor Statistics.

U.S. Energy Information Administration, International Energy Statistics.

U.S. Federal Reserve Board, Survey of Consumer Finances.

U.S. Internal Revenue Service, "The 400 Individual Income Tax Returns Reporting the Highest Adjusted Gross Incomes Each Year, 1992–2009," June 2012.

U.S. Senate, Health, Education, Labor and Pensions Committee, *Saving the American Dream*, September 1, 2011.

Hubert Williams and Patrick V. Murphy, "The Evolving Strategy of Police: A Minority View," *Perspectives on Policing*, U.S. Department of Justice, 1990.

Fareed Zakaria, "Incarceration Nation," *Time*, April 2, 2012.

2 A Question of Class
Dorothy Allison

The first time I heard, "They're different than us, don't value human life the way we do," I was in high school in Central Florida. The man speaking was an army recruiter talking to a bunch of boys, telling them what the army was really like, what they could expect overseas. A cold angry feeling swept over me. I had heard the word *they* pronounced in that same callous tone before. *They*, those people over there, those people who are not us, they die so easily, kill each other so casually. They are different. *We*, I thought. *Me*.

When I was six or eight back in Greenville, South Carolina, I had heard that same matter-of-fact tone of dismissal applied to me. "Don't you play with her. I don't want you talking to them." Me and my family, we had always been *they*. Who am I? I wondered, listening to that recruiter. Who are my people? We die so easily, disappear so completely— we/they, the poor and the queer. I pressed my bony white trash fists to my stubborn lesbian mouth. The rage was a good feeling, stronger and purer than the shame that followed it, the fear and the sudden urge to run and hide, to deny, to pretend I did not know who I was and what the world would do to me.

My people were not remarkable. We were ordinary, but even so we were mythical. We were the *they* everyone talks about—the ungrateful poor. I grew up trying to run away from the fate that destroyed so many of the people I loved, and having learned the habit of hiding, I found I had also learned to hide from myself. I did not know who I was, only that I did not want to be *they*, the ones who are destroyed or dismissed to make the "real" people, the important people, feel safer. By the time I understood that I was queer, that habit of hiding was deeply set in me, so deeply that it was not a choice but an instinct. Hide, hide to survive, I thought, knowing that if I told the truth about my life, my family, my sexual desire, my history, I would move over into that unknown territory, the land of they, would never have the chance to name my own life, to understand it or claim it.

Why are you so afraid? my lovers and friends have asked me the many times I have suddenly seemed a stranger, someone who would not speak to them, would not do the things they believed I should do, simple things like applying for a job, or a grant, or some award they were sure I could acquire easily. Entitlement, I have told them, is a matter of feeling like we rather than they. You think you have a right to things, a place in the world,

Dorothy Allison is a feminist writer and speaker whose award-winning poetry, short stories, essays, memoir, and novels deal with LGBTQ, gender, and class issues. Her novel *Bastard Out of Carolina*, a 1992 National Book Award finalist, has been translated into more than a dozen languages and adapted for the stage and screen.

and it is so intrinsically a part of you that you cannot imagine people like me, people who seem to live in your world, who don't have it. I have explained what I know over and over, in every way I can, but I have never been able to make clear the degree of my fear, the extent to which I feel myself denied: not only that I am queer in a world that hates queers, but that I was born poor into a world that despises the poor. The need to make my world believable to people who have never experienced it is part of why I write fiction. I know that some things must be felt to be understood, that despair, for example, can never be adequately analyzed; it must be lived. But if I can write a story that so draws the reader in that she imagines herself like my characters, feels their sense of fear and uncertainty, their hopes and terrors, then I have come closer to knowing myself as real, important as the very people I have always watched with awe.

I have known I was a lesbian since I was a teenager, and I have spent a good twenty years making peace with the effects of incest and physical abuse. But what may be the central fact of my life is that I was born in 1949 in Greenville, South Carolina, the bastard daughter of a white woman from a desperately poor family, a girl who had left the seventh grade the year before, worked as a waitress, and was just a month past fifteen when she had me. That fact, the inescapable impact of being born in a condition of poverty that this society finds shameful, contemptible, and somehow deserved, has had dominion over me to such an extent that I have spent my life trying to overcome or deny it. I have learned with great difficulty that the vast majority of people believe that poverty is a voluntary condition.

I have loved my family so stubbornly that every impulse to hold them in contempt has sparked in me a countersurge of pride—complicated and undercut by an urge to fit us into the acceptable myths and theories of both mainstream society and a lesbian-feminist reinterpretation. The choice becomes Steven Spielberg movies or Erskine Caldwell novels, the one valorizing and the other caricaturing, or the patriarchy as villain, trivializing the choices the men and women of my family have made. I have had to fight broad generalizations from every theoretical viewpoint.

Traditional feminist theory has had a limited understanding of class differences and of how sexuality and self are shaped by both desire and denial. The ideology implies that we are all sisters who should only turn our anger and suspicion on the world outside the lesbian community. It is easy to say that the patriarchy did it, that poverty and social contempt are products of the world of the fathers, and often I felt a need to collapse my sexual history into what I was willing to share of my class background, to pretend that my life both as a lesbian and as a working-class escapee was constructed by the patriarchy. Or conversely, to ignore how much my life was shaped by growing up poor and talk only about what incest did to my identity as a woman and as a lesbian. The difficulty is that I can't ascribe everything that has been problematic about my life simply and easily to the patriarchy, or to incest, or even to the invisible and much-denied class structure of our society.

. . .

The first time I read the Jewish lesbian Irena Klepfisz's poems[1] I experienced a frisson of recognition. It was not that my people had been "burned off the map" or murdered as hers had. No, we had been encouraged to destroy ourselves, made invisible because we did not fit the myths of the noble poor generated by the middle class. Even now, past forty and stubbornly proud of my family, I feel the draw of that mythology, that romanticized, edited version of the poor. I find myself looking back and wondering what was real, what was true. Within my family, so much was lied about, joked about, denied, or told with deliberate indirection, an undercurrent of humiliation or a brief pursed grimace that belied everything that had been said. What was real? The poverty depicted in books and movies was romantic, a backdrop for the story of how it was escaped.

The poverty portrayed by left-wing intellectuals was just as romantic, a platform for assailing the upper and middle classes, and from their perspective, the working-class hero was invariably male, righteously indignant, and inhumanly noble. The reality of self-hatred and violence was either absent or caricatured. The poverty I knew was dreary, deadening, shameful, the women powerful in ways not generally seen as heroic by the world outside the family.

My family's lives were not on television, not in books, not even comic books. There was a myth of the poor in this country, but it did not include us, no matter how hard I tried to squeeze us in. There was an idea of the good poor—hard-working, ragged but clean, and intrinsically honorable. I understood that we were the bad poor: men who drank and couldn't keep a job; women, invariably pregnant before marriage, who quickly became worn, fat, and old from working too many hours and bearing too many children; and children with runny noses, watery eyes, and the wrong attitudes. My cousins quit school, stole cars, used drugs, and took dead-end jobs pumping gas or waiting tables. We were not noble, not grateful, not even hopeful. We knew ourselves despised. My family was ashamed of being poor, of feeling hopeless. What was there to work for, to save money for, to fight for or struggle against? We had generations before us to teach us that nothing ever changed, and that those who did try to escape failed.

. . .

When I was five, Mama married the man she lived with until she died. Within the first year of their marriage Mama miscarried, and while we waited out in the hospital parking lot, my stepfather molested me for the first time, something he continued to do until I was past thirteen. When I was eight or so, Mama took us away to a motel after my stepfather beat me so badly it caused a family scandal, but we returned after two weeks. Mama told me that she really had no choice: she could not support us alone. When I was eleven I told one of my cousins that my stepfather was molesting me. Mama packed up my sisters and me and took us away for a few days, but again, my stepfather swore he would stop, and again we went back after a few weeks. I stopped talking for a while, and I have only vague memories of the next two years.

My stepfather worked as a route salesman, my mama as a waitress, laundry worker, cook, or fruit packer. I could never understand, since they both worked so hard and such long hours, how we never had enough money, but it was also true of my mama's brothers and sisters who worked hard in the mills or the furnace industry. In fact, my parents did better than anyone else in the family. But eventually my stepfather was fired and we hit bottom—nightmarish months of marshals at the door, repossessed furniture, and rubber checks. My parents worked out a scheme so that it appeared my stepfather had abandoned us, but instead he went down to Florida, got a new job, and rented us a house. He returned with a U-Haul trailer in the dead of night, packed us up, and moved us south.

. . .

I was only thirteen. I wanted us to start over completely, to begin again as new people with nothing of the past left over. I wanted to run away from who we had been seen to be, who we had been. That desire is one I have seen in other members of my family. It is the first thing I think of when trouble comes—the geographic solution. Change your name, leave town, disappear, make yourself over. What hides behind that impulse is the conviction that the life you have lived, the person you are, is valueless, better off abandoned, that running away is easier than trying to change things, that change itself is not possible. Sometimes I think it is this conviction—more seductive than alcohol or violence, more subtle than sexual hatred or gender injustice—that has dominated my life and made real change so painful and difficult.

Moving to Central Florida did not fix our lives. It did not stop my stepfather's violence, heal my shame, or make my mother happy. Once there, our lives became controlled by my mother's illness and medical bills. She had a hysterectomy when I was about eight and endured a series of hospitalizations for ulcers and a chronic back problem. Through most of my adolescence she superstitiously refused to allow anyone to mention the word cancer. When she was not sick, Mama and my stepfather went on working, struggling to pay off what seemed an insurmountable load of debts.

By the time I was fourteen, my sisters and I had found ways to discourage most of our stepfather's sexual advances. We were not close, but we united against him. Our efforts were helped along when he was referred to a psychotherapist after he lost his temper at work, and was prescribed drugs that made him sullen but less violent. We were growing up quickly, my sisters moving toward dropping out of school while I got good grades and took every scholarship exam I could find. I was the first person in my family to graduate from high school, and the fact that I went on to college was nothing short of astonishing.

We all imagine our lives are normal, and I did not know my life was not everyone's. It was in Central Florida that I began to realize just how different we were. The people we met there had not been shaped by the rigid class structure that dominated the South Carolina Piedmont. The first time I looked around my junior high classroom and realized I did not know who those people were—not only as individuals but as categories, who their people were and how they saw themselves—I also realized that they did not know me. In Greenville, everyone knew my family, knew we were trash, and that meant we were supposed to be poor, supposed to have grim low-paid jobs, have babies in our teens, and never finish school. But Central Florida in the 1960s was full of runaways and immigrants, and our mostly white working-class suburban school sorted us out not by income and family background but by intelligence and aptitude tests. Suddenly I was boosted into the college-bound track, and while there was plenty of contempt for my inept social skills, pitiful wardrobe, and slow drawling accent, there was also something I had never experienced before: a protective anonymity, and a kind of grudging respect and curiosity about who I might become. Because they did not see poverty and hopelessness as a foregone conclusion for my life, I could begin to imagine other futures for myself.

In that new country, we were unknown. The myth of the poor settled over us and glamorized us. I saw it in the eyes of my teachers, the Lions Club representative who paid for my new glasses, and the lady from the Junior League who told me about the scholarship I had won. Better, far better, to be one of the mythical poor than to be part of the *they* I had known before. I also experienced a new level of fear, a fear of losing what had never before been imaginable. Don't let me lose this chance, I prayed, and lived in terror that I might suddenly be seen again as what I knew myself to be.

. . .

My aunt Dot used to joke, "There are two or three things I know for sure, but never the same things and I'm never as sure as I'd like." What I know for sure is that class, gender, sexual preference, and prejudice—racial, ethnic, and religious—form an intricate lattice that restricts and shapes our lives, and that resistance to hatred is not a simple act. Claiming your identity in the cauldron of hatred and resistance to hatred is infinitely complicated, and worse, almost unexplainable.

I know that I have been hated as a lesbian both by "society" and by the intimate world of my extended family, but I have also been hated or held in contempt (which is in some ways more debilitating and slippery than hatred) by lesbians for behavior and sexual practices shaped in large part by class. My sexual identity is intimately constructed by my class and regional background, and much of the hatred directed at my sexual preferences is class hatred—however much people, feminists in particular, like to pretend this is not a factor. The kind of woman I am attracted to is invariably the kind of woman who embarrasses respectably middle-class, politically aware lesbian feminists. My sexual ideal is butch, exhibitionistic, physically aggressive, smarter than she wants you to know, and proud of being called a pervert. Most often she is working class, with an aura of danger and an ironic sense of humor. There is a lot of contemporary lip service paid to sexual tolerance, but the fact that my sexuality is constructed within, and by, a butch/femme and leather fetishism is widely viewed with distaste or outright hatred.

. . .

. . . [I]t was not my sexuality, my lesbianism, that my family saw as most rebellious; for most of my life, no one but my mama took my sexual preference very seriously. It was the way I thought about work, ambition, and self-respect. They were waitresses, laundry workers, counter girls. I was the one who went to work as a maid, something I never told any of them. They would have been angry if they had known. Work was just work for them, necessary. You did what you had to do to survive. They did not so much believe in taking pride in doing your job as in stubbornly enduring hard work and hard times. At the same time, they held that there were some forms of work, including maid's work, that were only for Black people, not white, and while I did not share that belief, I knew how intrinsic it was to the way my family saw the world. Sometimes I felt as if I straddled cultures and belonged on neither side. I would grind my teeth at what I knew was my family's unquestioning racism while continuing to respect their pragmatic endurance. But more and more as I grew older, what I felt was a deep estrangement from their view of the world, and gradually a sense of shame that would have been completely incomprehensible to them.

"Long as there's lunch counters, you can always find work," I was told by my mother and my aunts. Then they'd add, "I can get me a little extra with a smile." It was obvious there was supposed to be nothing shameful about it, that needy smile across a lunch counter, that rueful grin when you didn't have rent, or the half-provocative, half-pleading way my mama could cajole the man at the store to give her a little credit. But I hated it, hated the need for it and the shame that would follow every time I did it myself. It was begging, as far as I was concerned, a quasi-prostitution that I despised even while I continued to rely on it. After all, I needed the money.

"Just use that smile" my girl cousins used to joke, and I hated what I knew they meant. After college, when I began to support myself and study feminist theory, I became more contemptuous rather than more understanding of the women in my family. I told myself that prostitution is a skilled profession and my cousins were never more than amateurs. There was a certain truth in this, though like all cruel judgments rendered from the outside, it ignored the conditions that made it true. The women in my family, my mother included, had sugar daddies, not Johns, men who slipped them money because they needed it so badly. From their point of view they were nice to those men because the men were nice to them, and it was never so direct or crass an arrangement that they would set a price on their favors. Nor would they have described what they did as prostitution. Nothing made them angrier than the suggestion that the men who helped them out did it just for their favors. They worked for a living, they swore, but this was different.

. . .

When the women in my family talked about how hard they worked, the men would spit to the side and shake their heads. Men took real jobs—harsh, dangerous, physically daunting work. They went to jail, not just the cold-eyed, careless boys who scared me with their brutal hands, but their gentler, softer brothers. It was another family thing, what people expected of my mama's people, mine. "His daddy's that one was sent off to jail in Georgia, and his uncle's another. Like as not, he's just the same," you'd hear people say of boys so young they still had their milk teeth. We were always driving down to the county farm to see somebody, some uncle, cousin, or nameless male relation. Shaven-headed, sullen, and stunned, they wept on Mama's shoulder or begged my aunts to help. "I didn't do nothing, Mama," they'd say, and it might have been true, but if even we didn't believe them, who would? No one told the truth, not even about how their lives were destroyed.

One of my favorite cousins went to jail when I was eight years old, for breaking into pay phones with another boy. The other boy was returned to the custody of his parents. My cousin was sent to the boys' facility at the county farm. After three months, my mama took us down there to visit, carrying a big basket of fried chicken, cold cornbread, and potato salad. Along with a hundred others we sat out on the lawn with my cousin and watched him eat like he hadn't had a full meal in the whole three months. I stared at his near-bald head and his ears marked with fine blue scars from the carelessly handled razor. People were laughing, music was playing, and a tall, lazy, uniformed man walked past us chewing on toothpicks and watching us all closely. My cousin kept his head down, his face hard with hatred, only looking back at the guard when he turned away.

"Sons-a-bitches," he whispered, and my mama shushed him. We all sat still when the guard turned back to us. There was a long moment of quiet, and then that man let his face relax into a big wide grin.

"Uh-huh," he said. That was all he said. Then he turned and walked away. None of us spoke. None of us ate. He went back inside soon after, and we left. When we got back to the car, my mama sat there for a while crying quietly. The next week my cousin was reported for fighting and had his stay extended by six months.

My cousin was fifteen. He never went back to school, and after jail he couldn't join the army. When he finally did come home we never talked, never had to. I knew without asking that the guard had had his little revenge, knew too that my cousin would break into another phone booth as soon as he could, but do it sober and not get caught. I knew without asking the source of his rage, the way he felt about clean, well-dressed, contemptuous people who looked at him like his life wasn't as important as a dog's. I knew because I felt it too. That guard had looked at me and Mama with the same expression he used on my cousin. We were trash. We were the ones they built the county farm to house and break. The boy who was sent home was the son of a deacon in the church, the man who managed the hardware store.

As much as I hated that man, and his boy, there was a way in which I also hated my cousin. He should have known better, I told myself, should have known the risk he ran. He should have been more careful. As I grew older and started living on my own, it was a litany I used against myself even more angrily than I used it against my cousin. I knew who I was, knew that the most important thing I had to do was protect myself and hide my despised identity, blend into the myth of both the good poor and the reasonable lesbian. When I became a feminist activist, that litany went on reverberating in my head, but by then it had become a groundnote, something so deep and omnipresent I no longer heard it, even when everything I did was set to its cadence.

By 1975 I was earning a meager living as a photographer's assistant in Tallahassee, Florida. But the real work of my life was my lesbian-feminist activism, the work I did with the local women's center and the committee to found a women's studies program at Florida State University. Part of my role, as I saw it, was to be a kind of evangelical lesbian feminist, and to help develop a political analysis of this woman-hating society. I did not talk about class, except to give lip service to how we all needed to think about it, the same way I thought we all needed to think about racism. I was a determined person, living in a lesbian collective—all of us young and white and serious—studying each new book that purported to address feminist issues, driven by what I saw as a need to revolutionize the world.

Years later it's difficult to convey just how reasonable my life seemed to me at that time. I was not flippant, not consciously condescending, not casual about how tough a struggle remaking social relations would be, but like so many women of my generation, I believed absolutely that I could make a difference with my life, and I was willing to give my life for the chance to make that difference. I expected hard times, long slow periods of self-sacrifice and grinding work, expected to be hated and attacked in public, to have to set aside personal desire, lovers, and family in order to be part of something greater and more important than my individual concerns. At the same time, I was working ferociously to take my desires, my sexuality, my needs as a woman and a lesbian more seriously. I believed I was making the personal political revolution with my life every moment, whether I was scrubbing the floor of the childcare center, setting up a new budget for the women's lecture series at the university, editing the local feminist magazine, or starting a women's bookstore. That I was constantly exhausted and had no health insurance, did hours of dreary unpaid work and still sneaked out of the collective to date butch women my housemates thought retrograde and sexist never interfered with my sense of total commitment to the feminist revolution. I was not living in a closet: I had compartmentalized my own mind to such an extent that I never questioned why I did what I did. And I never admitted what lay behind all my feminist convictions—a class-constructed distrust of change, a secret fear that someday I would be found out for who I really was, found out and thrown out. If I had not been raised to give my life away, would I have made such an effective, self-sacrificing revolutionary?

The narrowly focused concentration of a revolutionary shifted only when I began to write again. The idea of writing stories seemed frivolous when there was so much work to be done, but everything changed when I found myself confronting emotions and ideas that could not be explained away or postponed until after the revolution. The way it happened was simple and unexpected. One week I was asked to speak to two completely different groups: an Episcopalian Sunday school class and a juvenile detention center. The Episcopalians were all white, well-dressed, highly articulate, nominally polite, and obsessed with getting me to tell them (without their having to ask directly) just what it was that two women did together in bed. The delinquents were all women, 80 percent Black and Hispanic, wearing green uniform dresses or blue jeans and workshirts, profane, rude, fearless, witty, and just as determined to get me to talk about what it was that two women did together in bed.

I tried to have fun with the Episcopalians, teasing them about their fears and insecurities, and being as bluntly honest as I could about my sexual practices. The Sunday school teacher, a man who had assured me of his liberal inclinations, kept blushing and stammering as the questions about my growing up and coming out became more detailed. I stepped out into the sunshine when the meeting was over, angry at the contemptuous attitude implied by all their questioning, and though I did not know why, so deeply depressed I couldn't even cry.

The delinquents were another story. Shameless, they had me blushing within the first few minutes, yelling out questions that were part curiosity and partly a way of boasting about what they already knew. "You butch or femme?" "You ever fuck boys?" "You ever want to?" "You want to have children?" "What's your girlfriend like?" I finally broke up when one very tall, confident girl leaned way over and called out, "Hey, girlfriend! I'm getting out of here next weekend. What you doing that night?" I laughed so hard I almost choked. I laughed until we were all howling and giggling together. Even getting frisked as I left didn't ruin my mood. I was still grinning when I climbed into the waterbed with my lover that night, grinning right up to the moment when she wrapped her arms around me and I burst into tears.

That night I understood, suddenly, everything that had happened to my cousins and me, understood it from a wholly new and agonizing perspective, one that made clear how brutal I had been to both my family and myself. I grasped all over again how we had been robbed and dismissed, and why I had worked so hard not to think about it. I had learned as a child that what could not be changed had to go unspoken, and worse, that those who cannot change their own lives have every reason to be ashamed of that fact and to hide it. I had accepted that shame and believed in it, but why? What had I or my cousins done to deserve the contempt directed at us? Why had I always believed us contemptible by nature? I wanted to talk to someone about all the things I was thinking that night, but

I could not. Among the women I knew there was no one who would have understood what I was thinking, no other working-class woman in the women's collective where I was living. I began to suspect that we shared no common language to speak those bitter truths.

In the days that followed I found myself remembering that afternoon long ago at the county farm, that feeling of being the animal in the zoo, the thing looked at and laughed at and used by the real people who watched us. For all his liberal convictions, that Sunday school teacher had looked at me with the eyes of my cousin's long-ago guard. I felt thrown back into my childhood, into all the fears I had tried to escape. Once again I felt myself at the mercy of the important people who knew how to dress and talk, and would always be given the benefit of the doubt, while my family and I would not.

I experienced an outrage so old I could not have traced all the ways it shaped my life. I realized again that some are given no quarter, no chance, that all their courage, humor, and love for each other is just a joke to the ones who make the rules, and I hated the rule-makers. Finally, I recognized that part of my grief came from the fact that I no longer knew who I was or where I belonged. I had run away from my family, refused to go home to visit, and tried in every way to make myself a new person. How could I be working class with a college degree? As a lesbian activist? I thought about the guards at the detention center. They had not stared at me with the same picture-window emptiness they turned on the girls who came to hear me, girls who were closer to the life I had been meant to live than I could bear to examine. The contempt in their eyes was contempt for me as a lesbian, different and the same, but still contempt.

While I raged, my girlfriend held me and comforted me and tried to get me to explain what was hurting me so bad, but I could not. She had told me so often about her awkward relationship with her own family, the father who ran his own business and still sent her checks every other month. She knew almost nothing about my family, only the jokes and careful stories I had given her. I felt so alone and at risk lying in her arms that I could not have explained anything at all. I thought about those girls in the detention center and the stories they told in brutal shorthand about their sisters, brothers, cousins, and lovers. I thought about their one-note references to those they had lost, never mentioning the loss of their own hopes, their own futures, the bent and painful shape of their lives when they would finally get free. Cried-out and dry-eyed, I lay watching my sleeping girlfriend and thinking about what I had not been able to say to her. After a few hours I got up and made some notes for a poem I wanted to write, a bare, painful litany of loss shaped as a conversation between two women, one who cannot understand the other, and one who cannot tell all she knows.

It took me a long time to take that poem from a raw lyric of outrage and grief to a piece of fiction that explained to me something I had never let myself see up close before — the whole process of running away, of closing up inside yourself, of hiding. It has taken me most of my life to understand that, to see how and why those of us who are born poor and different are so driven to give ourselves away or lose ourselves, but most of all, simply to disappear as the people we really are. By the time that poem became the story "River of Names,"[2] I had made the decision to reverse that process: to claim my family, my true history, and to tell the truth not only about who I was but about the temptation to lie.

By the time I taught myself the basics of storytelling on the page, I knew there was only one story that would haunt me until I understood how to tell it—the complicated, painful story of how my mama had, and had not, saved me as a girl. Writing *Bastard Out of Carolina*[3] became, ultimately, the way to claim my family's pride and tragedy, and the embattled sexuality I had fashioned on a base of violence and abuse.

. . .

It is only as the child of my class and my unique family background that I have been able to put together what is for me a meaningful politics, to regain a sense of why I believe in activism, why self-revelation is so important for lesbians. There is no all-purpose feminist analysis that explains the complicated ways our sexuality and core identity are shaped, the way we see ourselves as parts of both our birth families and the extended family of friends and lovers we invariably create within the lesbian community. For me, the bottom line has simply become the need to resist that omnipresent fear, that urge to hide and disappear, to disguise my life, my desires, and the truth about how little any of us understand—even as we try to make the world a more just and human place. Most of all, I have tried to understand the politics of *they*, why human beings fear and stigmatize the different while secretly dreading that they might be one of the different themselves. Class, race, sexuality, gender—and all the other categories by which we categorize and dismiss each other—need to be excavated from the inside.

The horror of class stratification, racism, and prejudice is that some people begin to believe that the security of their families and communities depends on the oppression of others, that for some to have good lives there must be others whose lives are truncated and brutal. It is a belief that dominates this culture. It is what makes the poor whites of the South so determinedly racist and the middle class so contemptuous of the poor. It is a myth that allows some to imagine that they build their lives on the ruin of others, a secret core of shame for the middle class, a goad and a spur to the marginal working class, and cause enough for the homeless and poor to feel no constraints on hatred or violence. The power of the myth is made even more apparent when we examine how, within the lesbian and feminist communities where we have addressed considerable attention to the politics of marginalization, there is still so much exclusion and fear, so many of us who do not feel safe.

I grew up poor, hated, the victim of physical, emotional, and sexual violence, and I know that suffering does not ennoble. It destroys. To resist destruction, self-hatred, or lifelong hopelessness, we have to throw off the conditioning of being despised, the fear of becoming the *they* that is talked about so dismissively, to refuse lying myths and easy moralities, to see ourselves as human, flawed, and extraordinary. All of us—extraordinary.

NOTES

1. *A Few Words in the Mother Tongue: Poems, Selected and New* (Eighth Mountain Press: Portland, Oregon, 1990).
2. *Trash* (Firebrand Books: Ithaca, New York, 1988).
3. Dutton: New York, 1992.

3 The Subprime and Foreclosure Crisis: Ten Years Later

Jillian Olinger

This past month marked the ten-year anniversary of the onset of the Great Recession. Beginning in September 2007, and continuing at a breathtaking pace, Lehman Brothers collapsed, setting off a chain reaction during which American International Group (AIG) came to the brink of failure, disruptions requiring the Federal Reserve and Treasury Department to take unprecedented steps to provide liquidity and support to a rapidly (and globally) destabilizing financial sector;[1] Fannie Mae and Freddie Mac were placed in conservatorship as their books of business reflected severe damage from deteriorating housing market conditions; and Congress passed the Emergency Economic Stabilization Act of 2008, which included a $700 billion Troubled Asset Relief Program.

The pain—even trauma[2]—inflicted on American households and workers as a result of this crisis cannot be overstated. With time, effort, and the installment of new rules and protections, many have been able to bounce back,[3] and the intensity of the crisis may be fading from our collective consciousness. The national unemployment rate peaked at 10% in October 2009 (and was significantly higher for workers of color);[4] today, it is 4.4%.[5] In 2009, a stunning 3 million homes had been foreclosed on in communities across the country.[6] Today, approximately 483,000 homes are in some stage of the foreclosure process.[7]

And yet, for too many Americans—especially people of color—this crisis has not ebbed. For some, and in many communities, it has instead grown. Recovery has been, and continues to be, extremely uneven. For example, analysis shows that Black median wealth never recovered from the 2001 recession, and Latino wealth has not recovered from the Great Recession. In contrast, white wealth was left untouched by the 2001 recession and rebounded after only two years from the Great Recession.[8]

Racial Wealth Gap Reaches Startling New Levels

Research shows that the average wealth of white families has grown 84% over the past 30 years, which is 1.2 times the rate of growth for Latino households, and three times the rate of Black households. It is projected that by the year 2043, when people of color

Jillian Olinger spent 11 years as a public policy and planning analyst and director of the Division of Housing and Civic Engagement at the Kirwan Institute for the Study of Race and Ethnicity at Ohio State University. Her research on policy making and community development decisions is directed toward the goal of safe and affordable housing for people of all demographics.

will become the majority of the population, the wealth divide will have doubled from $500,000 in 2013 to over $1 million.[9] By this measure, it will take 228 years to resolve this inequality for Black families, just 17 years shorter than the span of slavery. . . . [I]t will take Latino families 84 years to reach the same amount of wealth that white families have today. . . .*

The Great Recession drained more than $17 trillion in wealth from American families. Black and Hispanic families lost a shocking 66% and 53% of their household wealth, respectively, harming their ability to save and invest in the future of their families, their communities, and our nation's economy. Without wealth, households have no foundation on which to build and leverage their hopes, for example for retirement, college savings, moving to take advantage of a new job opportunity, or opening a small business. The racial wealth gap continues to drive inequality in opportunity for Americans across the country, ensuring the crisis continues, and our national economy suffers because of it: the nation's median wealth decreased nearly 20% from 1983 to 2013 because of the growing racial wealth gap.[10]

Affordable Housing Crisis Continues Unabated

While an affordable housing crisis has been plaguing low-income households for generations, its reach has now ensnared many middle-income households—renter and owner alike. Foreclosures, tighter credit and housing markets, and economic challenges for workers have created tremendous housing burdens.[11] Today, a staggering one in five of all renting American households spends at least 30% of its income on housing.[12] The burden is more pronounced for renters of color: nearly 60% of Black renters and 57% of Latino renters spend more than 30% of their incomes on housing.[13] In nearly every state, rents (up 4% since 2007 nationally) have far outpaced growth in incomes (down 7% nationally) since before the recession.[14] Increasingly tenuous housing situations compounded by growing income volatility for our lowest income households have facilitated a growth in homelessness in our tightest housing markets.[15] . . .

Threats to Federal Protections Place American Households at Risk of Another Fallout

Under the Trump Administration, threats to consumer protections have been repeatedly launched. In the aftermath of the subprime and foreclosure crisis, the federal government undertook prudent financial regulations to reinstate soundness to a financial system that had undergone substantial—and as we now know, devastating—deregulation. One key outcome of these efforts (known as the Dodd–Frank Wall Street Reform and Consumer

---

*For a detailed picture of U.S. wealth gaps at the time of this writing, see "How Wealth Inequality Has Changed in the U.S. Since the Great Recession, by Race, Ethnicity and Income," a Pew Research Center report by Rakesh Kochhar and Anthony Cilluffo (http://www.pewresearch.org/fact-tank/2017/11/01/how-wealth-inequality-has-changed-in-the-u-s-since-the-great-recession-by-race-ethnicity-and-income/).

Protection Act) was the creation of a new agency tasked with consumer protections, the Consumer Financial Protection Bureau (CFPB). In its first five years alone, the CFPB has returned nearly $12 billion to millions of victims of financial wrongdoing across the country.[16] It has written stronger rules governing mortgages, prepaid cards, payday loans, credit cards, student loans, auto loans, and more. Indeed, for every $1 of funding, the agency has returned $5 to victims of financial predation.[17] The CFPB is a critical antidote to the harms visited on vulnerable communities of color at the height of the subprime crisis. It must be protected.

Implicit Racial Biases Influence Our Financial Decision-Making, Arbitrarily Harming Borrowers of Color

Research is demonstrating how a broad range of implicit, invisible barriers affect very real and critical decisions in the housing landscape. Generations of racialized laws, policies, and practices (i.e., structural racialization) have imposed a racial bias on our collective normative values over time. Our minds are wired to automatically piece together information to make sense of the world around us. As part of this automatic process, people unconsciously internalize the patterns of inequity in our society in the form of implicit racial bias, or those attitudes or stereotypes that affect our behavior and decision-making without our conscious awareness. This translates to a pervasive implicit association of race with risk, or more precisely, blackness with risk, and whiteness with security and safety.[18] One example of this can be found in our credit scoring practices. Research consistently documents that current industry standards of credit scoring disadvantage borrowers of color, and that more promising practices of determining risk exist. For example, studies conducted by Experian have found the inclusion of utility payments in a credit scoring model could cut the number of borrowers considered subprime in half.[19] Importantly, this inclusion could be achieved without loosening credit standards. . . .

Predatory Practices on the Rise Again: Land Contracts and FinTech Highlight Emerging Gaps in Regulation

Homeownership remains a worthy goal of Americans across the country, and yet, thousands find themselves locked out of it (for example, due to stagnant incomes, or outdated credit scoring models). Recognizing a market ripe for exploitation, large-scale investors have swooped in with high-interest, seller-financed deals that work as installment plans for housing. These too-good-to-be-true instruments—which are unevenly regulated—are known as "land contracts" and while these instruments are not new, they have always been predatory and designed to fail. In these contracts, the owner of the property promises to convey legal title of the home to the buyer after successful completion of payments towards the full purchase price of the home, often 30 years. During this time, the buyer is responsible for all aspects of "homeownership" and should the buyer at any time default on payments, the seller retains the right to cancel the contract, keep all payments, and evict the buyer. Historically, land contracts were the province of individual sellers, who owned one or two investment properties and who targeted redlined communities of color. Today, the exploitative nature of these instruments has taken on new urgency as large-scale investors buy up large numbers of foreclosed homes . . . and market them to locked-out, would-be homeowners. Analysis finds problems or abuses with these instruments in 80% of states.[20] This practice not only depletes the precious resources of would-be homeowners (with little or no room for redress), it also stymies the revitalization of neighborhoods devastated by the foreclosure crisis.

A second emerging industry to keep an eye on is the rise of "FinTech." FinTech firms have been able to exploit a regulatory vacuum because they are not deemed "traditional banking entities" (and thus are not subject to oversight by the FDIC, for example). FinTech operates in much the same way that predatory payday lending does for individual consumers. This "fledgling" industry (representing an estimated $25 billion a year in loans)[21] promises faster loan application and approval processes, which is surely appealing, than traditional small business lending is able to offer. But as the subprime crisis revealed—when it comes to our financial system, faster is almost never better, especially when it comes at the expense of consumer protections. These firms have been found to violate the standards of fairness in lending, which includes straightforward and honest disclosure about the terms of the loan. Already, some firms have been brought to task for failing to deliver on promises of improved consumer outcomes,[22] hiding "junk fees," charging interest rates that run into the hundreds, changing the terms of the agreement, automatically debiting payments from consumer accounts (with no recourse for suspending the debit), or initiating prepayment penalties.[23] FinTech poses grave civil rights concerns. As they stand now, non-depository FinTech firms are beyond the reach of the Community Reinvestment Act, which opens the door to "digital (reverse) redlining." . . . And because FinTech firms operate online, they can simply avoid setting up shop in unfriendly states, thereby avoiding any interest rate caps put in place by that state, and yet still market their products nationwide.

Advocates across the country continue to grapple with the challenges of pursuing financial justice, especially when it comes to making meaningful inroads on closing the racial wealth gap. . . . [R]ecent developments with online lending and new predatory, minimally regulated instruments such as land contracts, mean that tracking consumer protections and outcomes is all the more challenging. Meanwhile, households continue to struggle to make ends meet, to secure a financial foothold that will provide opportunity for them today, and the next generation. . . . For white households, reaching the "middle class" brings with it far different opportunities than it does for Black and Latino households. Indeed, "first-generation, even second-generation African-American and Latino households have professional jobs and are making 'middle-income money'—but they have the wealth of a white high-school dropout."[24] Middle-class status *should* mean financial stability, and the ability to weather economic shocks and invest in the future. For far too many Americans, this is simply not the case. This stark reality forces us to question our assumptions about housing and its purpose, and its role in pursuing the American Dream. This is no small task, ideologically or practically: "For the oppressed, housing is always in crisis. . . . Discrete moments when housing crises become acute tend to be interpreted away as exceptions to a fundamentally sound system. But this is an ideological distortion. Housing crisis is not the result of the system breaking down, but of the system working as it intended."[25] The Subprime Crisis of 2007, and subsequent Great Recession, showed us many things about our housing and finance markets. It remains to be seen whether we have, in fact, internalized those lessons.

REFERENCES

1. Janet Yellen (August 25, 2017). "Financial Stability a Decade after the Onset of the Crisis." Remarks at *Fostering a Dynamic Global Recovery*. Federal Reserve Bank of Kansas City Symposium. Jackson Hole, WY. https://www.federalreserve.gov/newsevents/speech/yellen20170825a.htm

2. *See* Cagney, K. A., Browning, C. R., Iveniuk, J., and English, N. (2014). "The onset of depression during the great recession: foreclosure and older adult mental health." *American Journal of Public Health*, 104(3), 498-505. *See also* Mehta, Kaushal, et al. (2015). "Depression in the US population during the time periods surrounding the great recession." *The Journal of Clinical Psychiatry* 76.4: e499-504. *See* Ross, Lauren M. and Gregory D. Squires (2011). "The Personal Costs of Subprime Lending and the Foreclosure Crisis: A Matter of Trust, Insecurity, and Institutional Deception." *Social Science Quarterly* 92.1.

3. For analysis on the racial and spatial unevenness of the foreclosure crisis, *see* Hall, Matthew, Kyle Crowder, and Amy Spring (2015). "Variations in housing foreclosures by race and place, 2005–2012." *The Annals of the American Academy of Political and Social Science* 660.1: 217-237.

4. US Bureau of Labor Statistics. (February 2012). "The Recession of 2007-2009." Available at https://www.bls.gov/spotlight/2012/recession/pdf/recession_bls_spotlight.pdf

5. August 2017. US Bureau of Labor Statistics.

6. Les Christie (January 14, 2010). "Record 3 million households hit with foreclosure in 2009," CNNMoney.

7. Realtytrac. "US Real Estate Statistics & Foreclosure Trends Summary." Available at http://www.realtytrac.com/statsandtrends

8. Jamiles Lartey (September 13, 2017). "Median wealth of black Americans 'will fall to zero by 2053,' warns new report." *The Guardian*. Available at https://www.theguardian.com/inequality/2017/sep/13/median-wealth-of-black-americans-will-fall-to-zero-by-2053-warns-new-report

9. Collins, Chuck, Dedrick Asante-Muhammed et al. (2016). "The Ever Growing Gap." CFED & Institute for Policy Studies.

10. Collins, Chuck, Dedrick Asante-Muhammed, et al. (November 2015). "The Road to Zero: How the Racial Wealth Divide is Hollowing Out America's Middle Class." Prosperity Now and Institute for Social Policy. Available at http://www.ips-dc.org/wp-content/uploads/2017/09/The-Road-to-Zero-Wealth_FINAL.pdf

11. Shapiro, Thomas M., et al. (May 2015). "The Racial Wealth Gap Increases Fourfold." IASP Research and Policy Brief.

12. Joint Center for Housing Studies of Harvard University (2015). "The State of the Nation's Housing 2015." Available at http://www.jchs.harvard.edu/sites/jchs.harvard.edu/files/jchs-sonhr-2015-full.pdf

13. Wiedrick, Kasey et al. (November 2017). "On Track or Left Behind? Findings from the 2017 *Prosperity Now Scorecard*." Prosperity Now. Available at https://prosperitynow.org/files/PDFs/2017_Prosperity_Now_Scorecard_Homeownership_Housing.pdf

14. Alicia Mazzara (September 18, 2015). "New Census Data Show Rising Rents, Weak Income Growth." Center on Budget and Policy Priorities. Available at http://www.cbpp.org/blog/new-census-data-show-rising-rentsweak-income-growth

15. Been, Vicki and Ingrid Gould Ellen (April 2012). "Challenges Facing Housing Markets in the Next Decade." Furman Center for Real Estate and Urban Policy. Available at https://www.urban.org/sites/default/files/publication/25341/412556-Challenges-Facing-Housing-Markets-in-the-Next-Decade-Developing-a-Policy-Relevant-Research-Agenda.PDF

16. Tom Caiazza (March 28, 2017). "With the CFPB Under Threat, CAP Brief Shows How Critical the Agency Is in Protecting Vulnerable Communities from Predatory Practices." Center for American Progress. Available at https://www.americanprogress.org/press/release/2017/03/28/429300/release-cfpb-threat-cap-brief-shows-critical-agency-protecting-vulnerable-communities-predatory-practices/

17. Gregg Gelzinis et al. (March 27, 2017). "The Importance of Dodd–Frank, in 6 Charts." Center for American Progress. Available at https://www.americanprogress.org/issues/economy/news/2017/03/27/429256/importance-dodd-frank-6-charts/

18. Olinger, Jillian and Kelly Capatosto (December 2016). "Challenging Race as Risk: Implicit Bias in Housing." Kirwan Institute for the Study of Race and Ethnicity. Available at http://kirwaninstitute.osu.edu/my-product/challenging-race-as-risk-implicit-bias-in-housing/

19. James H. Carr (April 9, 2015). "Outdated Credit Scoring Models Shut Minorities Out of Housing Market." *Forbes*. Available at https://www.forbes.com/sites/janetnovack/2015/04/09/outdated-credit-scoring-models-shut-minorities-out-of-housing-market/#35f263ddcecd

20. Matthew Goldstein and Alexandria Stevenson (July 7, 2017). "How a Home Bargain Became a 'Pain in the Butt,' and Worse." *The New York Times DealBook*. Available at https://www.nytimes.com/2017/07/07/business/dealbook/how-a-home-bargain-became-a-pain-in-the-butt-and-worse.html

21. Liz Farmer (May 2015). "Are Predatory Business Loans the Next Credit Crisis?" *Governing*. Available at http://www.governing.com/topics/finance/gov-predatory-business-loans-crisis.html

22. The CFPB has ordered Flurish, Inc., doing business as LendUp, to provide more than 50,000 consumers with approximately $1.83 million in refunds. The company will also pay a civil penalty of $1.8 million. *See* https://www.consumerfinance.gov/about-us/newsroom/lendup-enforcement-action/

23. Tammy Forrest and Kevin Brennan (January 26, 2017). "As Banks Lend Less to Small Businesses, Online Predatory Lending Practices Rise." *The Metropreneur*. Available at http://themetropreneur.com/columbus/as-banks-lend-less-to-small-businesses-online-predatory-lending-practices-rise/

24. Supra n. 10.

25. Madden, David and Peter Marcuse (2016). *In Defense of Housing*. New York: Maple Press.

4 The Making of the American 99% and the Collapse of the Middle Class

Barbara Ehrenreich and John Ehrenreich

Class happens when some men, as a result of common experiences (inherited or shared), feel and articulate the identity of their interests as between themselves, and as against other men whose interests are different from (and usually opposed to) theirs.
—E. P. THOMPSON, *THE MAKING OF THE ENGLISH WORKING CLASS*

The "other men" (and of course women) in the current American class alignment are those in the top 1% of the wealth distribution—the bankers, hedge-fund managers, and CEOs targeted by the Occupy Wall Street movement. They have been around for a long time in one form or another, but they only began to emerge as a distinct and visible group, informally called the "super-rich," in recent years.

Extravagant levels of consumption helped draw attention to them: private jets, multiple 50,000 square-foot mansions, $25,000 chocolate desserts embellished with gold dust. But as long as the middle class could still muster the credit for college tuition and occasional home improvements, it seemed churlish to complain. Then came the financial crash of 2007–2008, followed by the Great Recession, and the 1%—to whom we had entrusted our pensions, our economy, and our political system—stood revealed as a band of feckless, greedy narcissists, and possibly sociopaths.

Still, until a few months ago, the 99% was hardly a group capable of (as Thompson says) articulating "the identity of their interests." It contained, and still contains, most "ordinary" rich people, along with middle-class professionals, factory workers, truck drivers, and miners, as well as the much poorer people who clean the houses, manicure the fingernails, and maintain the lawns of the affluent.

Barbara Ehrenreich is a journalist and activist who focuses on social injustice and inequality. She studied chemistry, physics, and molecular and cell biology before becoming involved in the women's health movement in 1970. In 2011 she initiated the Economic Hardship Reporting Project with the goal of improving journalism on poverty. She is the author of 14 books, including *Nickel and Dimed: On (Not) Getting By in America* and *Natural Causes*.

John Ehrenreich is a clinical psychologist and writer interested in social policy and the American right. Now a professor of psychology at the State University of New York, he was a leader in the anti–Vietnam War movement in New York in the 1960s and has traveled around the world as an expert consultant on psychosocial support for humanitarian workers.

It was divided not only by these class differences, but most visibly by race and ethnicity—a division that has actually deepened since 2008. African-Americans and Latinos of all income levels disproportionately lost their homes to foreclosure in 2007 and 2008, and then disproportionately lost their jobs in the wave of layoffs that followed. On the eve of the Occupy movement, the black middle class had been devastated. In fact, the only political movements to have come out of the 99% before Occupy emerged were the Tea Party movement and, on the other side of the political spectrum, the resistance to restrictions on collective bargaining in Wisconsin.

But Occupy could not have happened if large swaths of the 99% had not begun to discover some common interests, or at least to put aside some of the divisions among themselves. For decades, the most stridently promoted division within the 99% was the one between what the right calls the "liberal elite"—composed of academics, journalists, media figures, etc.—and pretty much everyone else.

As *Harper's Magazine* columnist Tom Frank has brilliantly explained, the right earned its spurious claim to populism by targeting that "liberal elite," which supposedly favors reckless government spending that requires oppressive levels of taxes, supports "redistributive" social policies and programs that reduce opportunity for the white middle class, creates ever more regulations (to, for instance, protect the environment) that reduce jobs for the working class, and promotes kinky countercultural innovations like gay marriage. The liberal elite, insisted conservative intellectuals, looked down on "ordinary" middle- and working-class Americans, finding them tasteless and politically incorrect. The "elite" was the enemy, while the super-rich were just like everyone else, only more "focused" and perhaps a bit better connected.

Of course, the "liberal elite" never made any sociological sense. Not all academics or media figures are liberal (Newt Gingrich, George Will, Rupert Murdoch). Many well-educated middle managers and highly trained engineers may favor latte over Red Bull, but they were never targets of the right. And how could trial lawyers be members of the nefarious elite, while their spouses in corporate law firms were not?

A Greased Chute, Not a Safety Net

"Liberal elite" was always a political category masquerading as a sociological one. What gave the idea of a liberal elite some traction, though, at least for a while, was that the great majority of us have never knowingly encountered a member of the actual elite, the 1% who are, for the most part, sealed off in their own bubble of private planes, gated communities, and walled estates.

The authority figures most people are likely to encounter in their daily lives are teachers, doctors, social workers, and professors. These groups (along with middle managers and other white-collar corporate employees) occupy a much lower position in the class hierarchy. They made up what we described in a 1976 essay as the "professional managerial class." As we wrote at the time, on the basis of our experience of the radical movements of the 1960s and 1970s, there have been real, longstanding resentments between the working-class and middle-class professionals. These resentments, which the populist right cleverly deflected toward "liberals," contributed significantly to that previous era of rebellion's failure to build a lasting progressive movement.

As it happened, the idea of the "liberal elite" could not survive the depredations of the 1% in the late 2000s. For one thing, it was summarily eclipsed by the discovery of the actual Wall Street–based elite and their crimes. Compared to them, professionals and managers, no matter how annoying, were pikers. The doctor or school principal might be overbearing, the professor and the social worker might be condescending, but only the 1% took your house away.

There was, as well, another inescapable problem embedded in the right-wing populist strategy: even by 2000, and certainly by 2010, the class of people who might qualify as part of the "liberal elite" was in increasingly bad repair. Public-sector budget cuts and corporate-inspired reorganizations were decimating the ranks of decently paid academics, who were being replaced by adjunct professors working on bare subsistence incomes. Media firms were shrinking their newsrooms and editorial budgets. Law firms had started outsourcing their more routine tasks to India. Hospitals beamed X-rays to cheap foreign radiologists. Funding had dried up for nonprofit ventures in the arts and public service. Hence the iconic figure of the Occupy movement: the college graduate with tens of thousands of dollars in student loan debts and a job paying about $10 a hour, or no job at all.

These trends were in place even before the financial crash hit, but it took the crash and its grim economic aftermath to awaken the 99% to a widespread awareness of shared danger. In 2008, the intention of "Joe the Plumber" to earn a quarter-million dollars a year still had some faint sense of plausibility. A couple of years into the recession, however, sudden downward mobility had become the mainstream American experience, and even some of the most reliably neoliberal media pundits were beginning to announce that something had gone awry with the American dream.

Once-affluent people lost their nest eggs as housing prices dropped off cliffs. Laid-off middle-aged managers and professionals were staggered to find that their age made them repulsive to potential employers. Medical debts plunged middle-class households into bankruptcy. The old conservative dictum—that it was unwise to criticize (or tax) the rich because you might yourself be one of them someday—gave way to a new realization that the class you were most likely to migrate into wasn't the rich, but the poor.

And here was another thing many in the middle class were discovering: the downward plunge into poverty could occur with dizzying speed. One reason the concept of an economic 99% first took root in America rather than, say, Ireland or Spain is that Americans are particularly vulnerable to economic dislocation. We have little in the way of a welfare state to stop a family or an individual in free-fall. Unemployment benefits do not last more than six months or a year, though in a recession they are sometimes extended by Congress. At present, even with such an extension, they reach only about half the jobless. Welfare was all but abolished 15 years ago, and health insurance has traditionally been linked to employment.

In fact, once an American starts to slip downward, a variety of forces kick in to help accelerate the slide. An estimated 60% of American firms now check applicants' credit ratings, and discrimination against the unemployed is widespread enough to have begun to warrant Congressional concern. Even bankruptcy is a prohibitively expensive, often crushingly difficult status to achieve. Failure to pay government-imposed fines or fees can even lead, through a concatenation of unlucky breaks, to an arrest warrant or a criminal record.* Where other once-wealthy nations have a safety net, America offers a greased chute, leading down to destitution with alarming speed.

Making Sense of the 99%

The Occupation encampments that enlivened approximately 1,400 cities this fall provided a vivid template for the 99%'s growing sense of unity. Here were thousands of people—we may never know the exact numbers—from all walks of life, living outdoors in the streets and parks, very much as the poorest of the poor have always lived: without electricity, heat, water, or toilets. In the process, they managed to create self-governing communities.

General assembly meetings brought together an unprecedented mix of recent college graduates, young professionals, elderly people, laid-off blue-collar workers, and plenty of the chronically homeless for what were, for the most part, constructive and civil exchanges. What started as a diffuse protest against economic injustice became a vast experiment in class building. The 99%, which might have seemed to be a purely aspirational category just a few months ago, began to will itself into existence.

Can the unity cultivated in the encampments survive as the Occupy movement evolves into a more decentralized phase? All sorts of class, racial, and cultural divisions persist within that 99%, including distrust between members of the former "liberal elite" and those less privileged. It would be surprising if they didn't. The life experience of a young lawyer or a social worker is very different from that of a blue-collar worker whose work may rarely allow for biological necessities like meal or bathroom breaks. Drum circles, consensus decision-making, and masks remain exotic to at least the 90%. "Middle class" prejudice against the homeless, fanned by decades of right-wing demonization of the poor, retains much of its grip.

Sometimes these differences led to conflict in Occupy encampments—for example, over the role of the chronically homeless in Portland or the use of marijuana in Los Angeles—but amazingly, despite all the official warnings about health and safety threats, there was no "Altamont moment": no major fires and hardly any violence. In fact, the encampments engendered almost unthinkable convergences: people from comfortable backgrounds learning about street survival from the homeless, a distinguished professor of political science discussing horizontal versus vertical decision making with a postal worker, military men in dress uniforms showing up to defend the occupiers from the police.

Class happens, as Thompson said, but it happens most decisively when people are prepared to nourish and build it. If the "99%" is to become more than a stylish meme, if it's to become a force to change the world, eventually we will undoubtedly have to confront some of the class and racial divisions that lie within it. But we need to do so patiently, respectfully, and always with an eye to the next big action—the next march, or building occupation, or foreclosure fight, as the situation demands.

---

*For an extended discussion of this issue, see "Ending the Debt Trap: Strategies to Stop the Abuse of Court-Imposed Fines and Fees," by Alexandra Bastien (the next selection in Part V of this volume).

5 Ending the Debt Trap: Strategies to Stop the Abuse of Court-Imposed Fines and Fees

Alexandra Bastien

In 2014, Michael Brown, an unarmed African American teenager, was shot and killed by a police officer in Ferguson, Missouri. The U.S. Department of Justice's investigation of the incident awakened the nation to the long-standing practice of local courts and police departments criminalizing the activities of low-income people and people of color in order to generate revenue. Ferguson police routinely and disproportionately charged African Americans fines and fees for parking violations, traffic violations, housing code infractions, and more. These charges did not promote public safety—the local justice system instead employed this tactic to fund its activities by using residents as a cash source. If the fines and fees charged to residents were not paid, the threat of jail loomed over them.

The inequitable treatment of low-income residents and people of color was happening not only in Ferguson, but also around the nation—and it continues in many places today. . . . While "debtors' prisons" are technically outlawed, courts and police departments have used loopholes in laws to place people in jail for the nonpayment of fines and fees. More than $50 billion in debt from fines and fees is currently being held by approximately 10 million people because of their involvement in the criminal justice system.[1] Much of this debt is not collected because low-income people simply do not have the money to pay it; this, in turn, causes state governments to spend more on the expense of trying to collect on fines and fees than what they actually take in. . . .

. . . Since 2010, 48 states have increased civil and/or criminal fees assessed on defendants. The growth of these user fees is linked to an inequitable and regressive tax code that often requires little in local and state taxes from businesses and the wealthy.

. . . These fees play an integral role in wealth and income inequality, and contribute to the growing racial wealth gap in our country where Black and Latino households, on average, own less than 1/13 and 1/10, respectively, of the average wealth of White households.[2] . . .

Alexandra Bastien is a senior associate at PolicyLink, where she works to advance policy solutions pertaining to wealth inequality across the nation. She conducts research, provides technical expertise, and develops programs and strategies related to asset building and equitable economic development.

The Criminalization of Poverty

Despite a U.S. Supreme Court ruling in 1983 that prohibited the practice of imprisonment for nonpayment of court fines and/or fees, this practice is still all too common due to loopholes in the law.[3] These loopholes allow courts to incarcerate defendants by holding them in contempt of court if they do not have the cash on hand to immediately pay a fine. . . .

As the costs of a growing incarcerated population put pressure on states and municipalities to raise revenue, the option of increasing fines, fees, and bail became more attractive.[4] The law requires that judges consider a defendant's ability to pay before determining that his or her nonpayment of a fine or fee is willful. However, these hearings are often not held and, when they are, there is no consistent standard of how the defendant's actual ability to pay is evaluated.[5] Some judges may ask a defendant if he or she smokes. If the answer is yes, they are considered able to pay because they have purchased cigarettes.[6] Other examples include similar questions to defendants with tattoos[7] or a manicure.[8] . . . [T]he defendant, unable to pay the fine on the spot, may be placed on supervision, on probation, or in jail.[9] All of these punishments come with yet more fees attached.[10]

In almost every state, defendants are charged fees, including room and board, during the time they spend in jail or prison (referred to as "pay-to-stay" fees). These fees can accumulate daily while a defendant waits for weeks[11] or, in larger cities like Chicago, months before their arraignment or trial.[12] . . . Even when a person is found not guilty, or if charges are dropped, he or she may still be liable for the fees incurred during the stay and for the cost of a public defender.

A Disproportionate Impact on Low-Income People and People of Color

Accumulated debt follows low-income people and often leads to discrimination in securing housing and obtaining jobs, because many landlords and employers perform credit checks on candidates. Even in cities and states that have adopted ban-the-box policies that forbid employers from asking a person about their criminal history until a designated time after initial screening, credit checks still show outstanding debt that is related to a criminal charge, providing a loophole to housing and employment anti-discrimination laws.[13] Additionally, when a person with unpaid debt does find employment, their wages and taxes can be subject to garnishment. . . . In addition to garnishing wages, unpaid fines and fees can be prohibitive for low-income people seeking other public supports that might help them achieve a certain level of economic stability. . . . This creates a cycle of instability that does not serve the original purpose of the fine.

Criminal debt cannot be discharged under bankruptcy protections, and there is no statute of limitation on collections.[14] Therefore, collections actions against a defendant can remain active indefinitely. For formerly incarcerated low-income people, unpaid fees can be considered a parole violation, making them ineligible for public benefits, including food and housing assistance, and can lead to being charged for new offenses based on this debt.[15]

Decriminalization efforts for a range of offenses have helped reduce some inequities in the criminal justice system, and have been a positive policy change in many regards. However, efforts to decriminalize some misdemeanors into "fine-only offenses" have, ironically, fed the practice of issuing fines and fees. . . .

In a 2016 Priceonomics analysis, author Dan Kopf noted that "The use of fines as a source of revenue is not a socioeconomic problem, but a racial one."[16] He found that cities with large African American populations relied more heavily on fines and fees than cities with smaller populations of color.[17] In Philadelphia, a 15-year study of the use of criminal justice fees found that fees were significantly more likely to be imposed on African Americans than on Whites.[18] People of color, particularly African American men, are more than twice as likely[19] to be stopped and cited for infractions like marijuana possession or moving violations,[20] yet they have only about a third as much available cash on average [as] White Americans across income levels,[21] which seriously limits their ability to pay fees without a payment plan or other accommodation. A recent study in New Orleans found that in 2015, Black residents were 1.5 times more likely to be jailed for nonpayment of fees than White residents.[22] . . .

Lower Economic Prospects for Youth

The justice system is also actively steering youth and their families into periods of financial hardship that can have lasting consequences. Over 20 states charge court-involved youth fees for investigations, monitoring, and the use of a public defender.[23]

Youth with records can carry over court-imposed debt from childhood into adulthood. A juvenile record is not automatically sealed or expunged upon release or upon the young person turning 18, which can limit his or her ability to get a job,[24] be accepted into college, and receive financial aid.[25] . . . Juvenile court debt undermines family financial stability when it is needed most. It pushes families that are already struggling further into debt, which works against the stated goal of juvenile court, that of rehabilitation.

In some states, the debt incurred during juvenile detention is applied to parents, with the threat of wage and tax garnishment if it goes unpaid.[26] For example, a mother in Michigan was jailed for her failure to pay her child's court fees. Unable to pay the $104 monthly fee for her son's detention, she herself was jailed and charged a total of $144 for her booking and drug test.[27] . . .

Finally, the racial disparities previously discussed continue to carry through into the juvenile system. Children of color are more likely than White children to be profiled and targeted by police,[28] and are more likely to incur court debt because they are pushed deeper into the system. The further interactions with the system, in terms of length of stay, amount of time on probation, and supervision, all incur additional fees throughout the process. . . .

Ineffective Revenue Strategy

At first glance, it may seem practical for cash-strapped governments to turn to fines and fees to augment their budgets. However, a deeper analysis of the practice has shown that, in many cases, using fines and fees actually costs the government more money than it receives. Increased government expenditures often arise because of the administration and processing of fee assessments, additional courtroom time, increased jail populations, and costly collection efforts.[29] . . .

In Florida, the state began raising revenue through fines and fees, but estimates show that the state recouped only about 20 percent of its debt from those charged.[30] In Riverside County, California, raising court fees raised less than 1 percent of what it hoped to generate.[31] Because low-income people who are unable to pay these debts are often imprisoned as punishment, municipalities are effectively *increasing* the budgetary costs to the criminal justice system. . . .

Promising Practices

In light of the damaging and inefficient court practices described above, several local and state governments have enacted reforms that can help reduce the over-reliance on revenue from fines and fees assessed on low-income populations[:] . . .

. . .

Require "Ability-to-Pay" Hearings for All Defendants: Some states now require "ability-to-pay" hearings to bring more uniformity and fairness to assessing whether a defendant is actually able to pay assessed fines and/or fees for minor offenses. . . .

. . .

Offer Flexible, Penalty-Free Payment Plans: Iowa passed legislation in 2016 that allowed an individual with overdue court debt to enter payment plans before his driver's license was suspended for nonpayment. Previously, the license had to be suspended before a payment plan was an option. . . .

Enact Amnesty Periods: In 2011, California enacted a law that relieved a noncustodial parent of child-support obligations during the time the person was incarcerated. This prevented the accrual of additional penalties and fees when a person was unable to earn income. . . .[32]

Cease Warrant Issuance for Unpaid Debt: The reforms to the fines and fees practices introduced by the Supreme Court of Ohio in 2015 . . . protect Ohio residents from the risk of incarceration for unpaid debt, and saved court resources and staff time by reducing costs and jail populations.

. . .

Place Caps on Allowable Revenue from Fines and Fees: Following the U.S. Department of Justice report on unfair policing practices in Ferguson, Missouri, in 2015, the state of Missouri passed a law that limits a municipality's ability to raise more than 12.5 percent of its annual revenue from traffic tickets.[33]

Eliminate Debt for Juveniles: In 2015, Washington State limited municipalities' ability to charge fees to juveniles. The statute eliminates nonrestitution fines and fees and "prohibits cities, towns, and counties from imposing financial obligations for juvenile offenses unless specifically authorized by statute."[34]

. . .

Connect Indigent Defendants to Workforce Development Programs: A 2008 pilot program in Suffolk County, Massachusetts, reduced court debt for indigent defendants who completed job training, mental health, and/or addiction programs, where applicable. . . .[35]

. . .

Provide Relief for Indigent Defendants: In settling a lawsuit in which a woman was arrested for unpaid traffic tickets, Montgomery, Alabama, agreed to a "presumption of indigence" for defendants whose income is at or below 125 percent of the federal poverty level. This policy was designed to make clear that unpaid debt from impoverished individuals is not the same as "willful" nonpayment worthy of punishment.[36]

Provide Free Public Defender Services for Debt Hearings: Montgomery, Alabama, now provides public defenders in administrative hearings on outstanding debt.[37] Previously, this right did not apply because debt assessment hearings are civil rather than criminal. . . .

. . .

Eliminate Bail for Minor Crimes: In 2017, the New Orleans City Council voted unanimously to allow indigent defendants charged with minor offenses to be released without bail in its municipal court system. . . .[38]

. . .

Conclusion

Governments across the nation are finding themselves to be predatory financial actors in low-income communities and communities of color. They should properly assess how deep the economic impact has been, and address the harm that has been done to the communities they serve. State and local courts should revise their practices to reflect a new understanding of "equality and justice for all" by incorporating the tools and lessons that have emerged to stop the widespread practices that have led to the criminalization of poverty.

State governments should implement strong policies that remove local incentives to funnel low-income people through the justice system for the sake of revenue, and ensure that moving forward all people can fully participate and prosper in a fair and just society— one in which the judicial system does not penalize or criminalize poverty. The fight to achieve these changes does not rest solely on advocates focused on criminal justice reform. Economic security advocates, anti-poverty groups, and the asset-building field must join the call for an end to wealth stripping taking place in communities across the country, especially communities of color, and there must be an end to the caging of human beings for the sake of profit.

NOTES

1. Lauren-Brooke Eisen, *Charging Inmates Perpetuates Mass Incarceration* (New York, NY: Brennan Center For Justice at New York University School of Law, 2015), https://www. brennancenter.org/sites/default/files/blog/Charging_Inmates_Mass_Incarceration.pdf.

2. Rakesh Kochhar and Richard Fry, "Wealth Inequality Has Widened along Racial, Ethnic Lines Since End of Great Recession," Facttank, Pew Research Center, December 12, 2014, http://www.pewresearch.org/fact-tank/2014/12/12/racial-wealthgaps-great-recession/.

3. *Bearden v. Georgia*, 461 US 660, 103 S. Ct. 2064, 76 L. Ed. 2d 221 (1983) (holding that a person could only be jailed for nonpayment of court fines if the state shows that the nonpayment is "willful").

4. Jason Furman and Sandra Black, "Fines, Fees, and Bail: An Overlooked Part of the Criminal Justice System That Disproportionately Impacts the Poor," *The Huffington Post* (blog), December 3, 2015, http://www.huffingtonpost.com/jasonfurman/fincs-fees-and-bail-an-ov_b_8702912.html.

5. Jessica Eaglin, "Improving Economic Sanctions in the States," *Minnesota Law Review* 99 (2015): 1855.

6. Emily Green, "Sentenced to a Life in Debt," *Street Roots News*, June 7, 2016.

7. Joseph Shapiro, "As Court Fees Rise, the Poor Are Paying the Price," *All Things Considered* (NPR), May 19, 2014.

8. Green, "Sentenced to a Life in Debt."

9. Kendall Taggart and Alex Campbell, "Their Crime: Being Poor. Their Sentence: Jail." *BuzzFeed News*, October 7, 2015.

10. Shapiro, "As Court Fees Rise, the Poor are Paying the Price."

11. Nick Pinto, "The Bail Trap," *New York Times Magazine*, August 15, 2015.

12. Elliot Hannon, "Chicago Justice System Is So Bad Inmates Spent 218 Years Longer in Jail Than Actually Sentenced," Slate, June 8, 2016.

13. Alicia Bannon, Mitali Nagrecha, and Rebekah Diller 2010, *Criminal Justice Debt: A Barrier to Reentry*, (New York, NY: Brennan Center for Justice at New York University School of Law, 2010), 27, https://www.brennancenter.org/publication/criminaljustice-debt-barrier-reentry.

14. Rebecca Vallas and Roopal Patel, "Sentenced to a Life of Criminal Debt: A Barrier to Reentry and Climbing out of Poverty," *Journal of Poverty Law and Policy* 46 (2012): 133.

15. Bannon, Nagrecha, and Diller, "Criminal Justice Debt: A Barrier to Reentry," 27.

16. Dan Kopf, "The Fining of Black America," Priceonomics, June 24, 2016, https://priceonomics.com/the-fining-of-blackamerica/.

17. Ibid.

18. Jessica Eaglin and Danyelle Solomon, *Reducing Racial and Ethnic Disparities in Jails: Recommendations for Local Practice* (New York, NY: Brennan Center for Justice at New York University School of Law, 2015), https://www.brennancenter.org/publication/reducing-racial-and-ethnic-disparities-jailsrecommendations-local-practice.

19. "Race & Bail in America," Pretrial Justice Institute, http://projects.pretrial.org/racialjustice/, accessed February 22, 2017.

20. Alexandra Natapoff, "Misdemeanor Decriminalization," *Vanderbilt Law Review* 68 (2015): 1076-1077.

21. Paul Kiel and Annie Waldman, "The Color of Debt: How Collection Suits Squeeze Black Neighborhoods," *ProPublica*, October 8, 2015, https://www.propublica.org/article/debt-collectionlawsuits-squeeze-black-neighborhoods.

22. Mathilde Laisne, Jon Wool, and Christian Henrichson. *Past Due: Examining the Costs and Consequences of Charging for Justice in New Orleans* (New York: Vera Institute of Justice, 2017).

23. Ibid.

24. Kate Weisburd, "High Cost, Young Age: Sentencing Youth to a Life of Debt," *The Huffington Post* (blog), June 9, 2014, http://www.huffingtonpost.com/kate-weisburd/youth-juvenile-debt_b_5118950.html.

25. Marsha Weissman, Alan Rosenthal, Patricia Warth, Elaine Wolf, and Michael Messina-Yauchzy 2010, *The Use of Criminal History Records in College Admissions: Reconsidered* (New York, NY: Center for Community Alternatives, 2010), 4, http://www.communityalternatives.org/pdf/Reconsidered-criminalhist-recs-in-college-admissions.pdf.

26. Birckhead, "The New Peonage," 1605.

27. Sarah Alexander, Yelena Konanova, and Deuel Ross, *In for a Penny: The Rise of America's New Debtors' Prisons* (New York, NY: American Civil Liberties Union, 2010), 35-36, https://www.aclu.org/files/assets/InForAPenny_web.pdf.

28. Neelum Arya and Ian Augarten, *Critical Condition: African-American Youth in the Criminal Justice System* (Washington, DC: Campaign for Youth Justice, September 2008), http://campaignforyouthjustice.org/documents/AfricanAmericanBrief.pdf.

29. Council of Economic Advisers, *Fines, Fees, and Bail: Payments in the Criminal Justice System that Disproportionately Impact the Poor* [Issue Brief] (Washington, DC: Council of Economic Advisers, December 2015), 6.

30. Furman and Black, "Fines, Fees, and Bail: An Overlooked Part of the Criminal Justice System That Disproportionately Impacts the Poor."

31. Bernadette Rabuy and Daniel Kopf, *Detaining the Poor: How money bail perpetuates an endless cycle of poverty and jail time* (Northampton, MA: Prison Policy Initiative, 2016), https://www.prisonpolicy.org/reports/incomejails.html.

32. Leora Gershenzon,. "Child Support: Suspension of Order: Bill Analysis, http://www.leginfo.ca.gov/pub/15-16/bill/asm/ab_0601-0650/ab_610_cfa_20150903_194321_asm_floor.html.

33. Mitch Smith, "Missouri Lawmakers Limit Revenue from Traffic Fines in St. Louis Area," *New York Times*, May 8, 2015.

34. Nicole Porter, *The State of Sentencing 2015: Developments in Policy and Practice* (Washington, DC: The Sentencing Project, 2016), http://sentencingproject.org/wp-content/uploads/2016/02/State-of-Sentencing-2015.pdf.

35. Vallas and Patel, "Sentenced to a Life of Criminal Debt: A Barrier to Reentry and Climbing out of Poverty," 140.

36. "State Bans on Debtors' Prisons and Criminal Justice Debt," *Harvard Law Review* (Note), February 10, 2016, 1030.

37. Ibid.

38. Kevin Litten, "New Orleans City Council Votes to End Jailing of Indigent Offenders on Minor Crimes," *The Times-Picayune*, January 12, 2017, http://www.nola.com/politics/index.ssf/2017/01/city_council_bail_overhaul.html.

6 | Immigration Enforcement as a Race-Making Institution

Douglas S. Massey

With 50.5 million persons in 2010, Latinos constitute the largest minority group in the United States, representing 16.3% of the population compared with just 12.6% for African Americans. Mexicans alone numbered 31.8 million persons in 2010 and made up 10.3% of the U.S. population (Ennis, Ríos-Vargas, and Albert 2011). Although fertility will play a large role in population growth moving forward, through 2008 the main source of Latino increase was immigration (Pew Hispanic Center 2011). . . .

. . . Whereas Latino immigrants from the Caribbean are overwhelmingly legal residents or U.S. citizens, 58% of all Mexican immigrants present in the United States in 2010 were unauthorized, compared with 57% of those born in El Salvador, 71% of those from Guatemala, and 77% of those from Honduras. Even considering *all* persons of Mexican, Salvadoran, Guatemalan, and Honduran origin, the shares unauthorized stood 21%, 38%, 50%, and 51%, respectively, in 2010 (Massey and Pren 2012a). Illegality has thus become a fundamental condition of life for sizeable shares of Mexicans and Central Americans living in the United States. . . .

Although the racialization of Latinos goes back to 1848, when the Treaty of Guadalupe Hidalgo brought some 50,000 Mexicans into the United States, the contemporary era of racial formation can be traced back to the 1960s, when the United States adopted a new set of immigration policies that made it difficult for Mexicans and other Latin Americans to enter the country legally (Massey and Pren 2012a). Although the number of Latino arrivals changed little in subsequent years, after 1965 their composition shifted dramatically from documented to undocumented (Massey, Durand, and Pren 2009). . . .

Between 1965 and 2000 a new "Latino threat narrative" came to dominate public debate and media coverage of Latinos in the United States (Chavez 2001, 2008) and U.S. policy makers responded by launching what Rosen has called a "war on immigrants" (Rosen 1995). This "war" involved an unprecedented militarization of the Mexico-U.S. border, a massive expansion of the immigrant detention system, and a return to mass deportations for the first time since the 1930s (Massey and Sánchez 2010). Government repression accelerated markedly after September 11, 2001 as the war on immigrants was

Douglas S. Massey is a professor of sociology and public affairs at Princeton University, where his research focuses on migration, race and housing, discrimination, education, urban poverty, stratification, and Latin America. His books include *Brokered Boundaries: Creating Immigrant Identity in Anti-Immigrant Times* (coauthored with Magaly Sánchez).

increasingly conflated with the war on terror (Massey and Sánchez 2010; Massey and Pren 2012b). By 2010, America's immigration enforcement apparatus had become a central race-making institution for Latinos, on a par with the criminal justice system for African Americans. . . .

Prior to 1965, it was relatively easy for Latin Americans to enter the United States in legal status, as there were no numerical limits placed on immigrants from the Western Hemisphere. Mexico, in particular, also benefitted from a generous bilateral guest worker agreement known as the Bracero Program that in its 22 year history brought nearly five million Mexican workers into the United States on temporary work visas (Massey, Durand, and Malone 2002; Calavita 1992). . . .

During the late 1950s and early 1960s the total annual inflow of migrants from Mexico alone fluctuated around half a million persons per year, all in legal status. At the end of 1964, however, the United States unilaterally terminated the Bracero Program over Mexican protests; and in 1965 congress passed amendments to the Immigration and Nationality Act that placed a first-ever cap of 120,000 total immigrants from the Western Hemisphere. Additional amendments enacted in 1976 put each country in the hemisphere under an annual quota of just 20,000 immigrant visas (Zolberg 2006).

. . . Despite the curtailment of avenues for legal entry, however, the demand for Mexican workers did not change and Mexicans continued to flow to the jobs they had traditionally held (Massey, Durand, and Malone 2002; Massey and Pren 2012a).

The inevitable result of curtailing opportunities for legal entry from Mexico was a sharp rise in undocumented migration [see Figure 1] . . . .

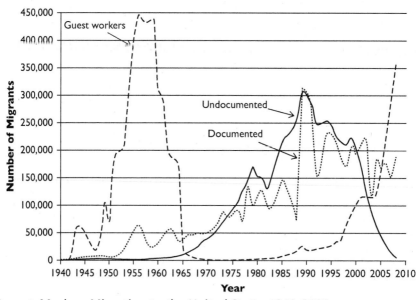

Figure 1 Mexican Migration to the United States 1940–2008

Source: Author's compilation of data from the Office of Immigration Statistics, U.S. Department of Homeland Security and predecessor agencies.

Owing to U.S. policy shifts between the early 1960s and the early 1980s, therefore, Mexican immigration was transformed from an overwhelmingly legal flow to one that was substantially illegal. . . .

The other major surge in undocumented migration from Latin America came during the 1980s, with the U.S. Contra intervention in Nicaragua and the broader prosecution of the Cold War within Central America. Research clearly indicates that outflows from Central America during the 1980s were driven by the U.S.-sponsored Contra intervention (Lundquist and Massey 2005) as well as the violence and the economic dislocations it produced (Stanley 1987; Jones 1989; Funkhouser 1992; Morrison and May 1994; Alvarado and Massey 2010). Owing to the restrictions imposed in 1965, however, there were few avenues by which refugees from Central America could enter the United States in legal status and, not surprisingly, most ended up coming as undocumented migrants, either moving through Mexico to cross the border without authorization of entering as tourists and overstaying their visas.

. . . Whereas the Nicaraguan Adjustment and Central American Relief Act offered an easy pathway to legal status for Nicaraguans, it grudgingly offered only temporary protected status to other Central Americans. Whereas Nicaraguans had the good fortune of fleeing a left-wing regime at odds with the United States, those from Guatemala, El Salvador, and Honduras had the bad luck to come from nations dominated by right-wing regimes allied with the United States. As a result, although most Central Americans were at some point undocumented, Nicaraguans were able to adjust to documented status whereas other Central Americans ended up languishing in temporary protected status until it was finally revoked with the end of the Cold War, pushing them into undocumented status.

Once again, U.S. policies had manufactured a large population of undocumented migrants. After Mexico, which accounted for an estimated 62% of undocumented migrants present in the United States as of January 1, 2010, the next largest contributors were El Salvador (6%), Guatemala (5%), and Honduras (3%) (Hoefer, Rytina, and Baker 2010). All told, three-quarters of all undocumented migrants come from Mexico or Central America, and no other nation makes up more than 2% of the total. When most Americans visualize an "illegal immigrant," they see a Mexican and, if not a Mexican in particular, certainly a Latino (Lee and Fiske 2006). Adding in Latino migrants from the Caribbean, South America, and Panama, we find that Latin Americans comprise more than 80% of the total unauthorized population. It is doubtful, of course, whether the average Anglo-American can distinguish between a Mexican, a Salvadoran, a Dominican, or a Colombian and many simply get categorized as "Mexican," which has become the default Latino identity in the American mind (Lee and Fiske 2006).

Rise of the Latino Threat Narrative

Throughout U.S. history, immigrants have periodically served as scapegoats for America's problems, being blamed for joblessness, low wages, and high social spending while being framed as threats to national security owing to their supposed moral deficits, suspect ideologies, and subversive intentions (Higham 1955; Zolberg 2006; Schrag 2010).

Anti-immigrant hostility rises during periods of economic dislocation, ideological conflict, and political uncertainty (Massey 1999; Meyers 2004). The 1970s and 1980s were such a period, as the long postwar economic boom faltered, the New Deal Coalition unraveled, and the Cold War reached its apex. After a brief respite during the 1990s, when the economy rebounded and the Cold War receded, the conditions for popular xenophobia returned with a vengeance with the bursting of the stock market bubble in 2000, the terrorist attacks in 2001, and the collapse of the economy in 2008 (Massey and Sánchez 2010).

Under these circumstances, anti-immigrant hostility is only to be expected; but since 1965 portrayals of Latin American immigrants as a threat to American society have been greatly facilitated by the fact that a rising share of Latino immigrants are present in the country illegally and thus readily framed as lawbreakers, criminals, and terrorists. The growing predominance of undocumented migrants among Latin Americans has contributed to the rise of what Chavez (2008) has called the "Latino threat narrative." . . .

Immigrants clearly perceive the rising hostility against them. By 2006, 70% of Latino immigrants had come to view anti-Hispanic discrimination as a major problem in the United States, 68% worried about being deported themselves, and 35% knew someone who had been deported (Kohut and Suro 2006). Half of all Latino immigrants interviewed in 2010 felt that Americans were less accepting of immigrants than they had been five years earlier (Lopez, Morin, and Taylor 2010). Whereas only 47% of Latinos saw discrimination against them as a major problem in American society in 2002, by 2010 the share had risen to 61%, and another 24% viewed it as at least a minor problem, bringing the total seeing discrimination as problematic to 85% (Lopez, Morin, and Taylor 2010). . . .

Prosecuting the War on Immigrants

In sum, over the past several decades the repressive power of the state has increasingly been directed against immigrants, documented as well as undocumented. Although the escalation of anti-immigrant repression is apparent at the state and local levels, it is most clearly reflected in federal statistics. Figure 2 shows trends in the budget of the U.S. Border Patrol, the number of Border Patrol Agents, and the number of deportations from the United States (U.S. Office of Immigration Statistics 2012). Each series has been divided by its value in 1986 to indicate the factor by which the enforcement effort has increased since then. . . .

Building a New Underclass

Paradoxically, the effect of increased immigration enforcement was actually to *increase* the net inflow of undocumented migrants and to spread them more widely throughout the nation (Massey, Durand, and Malone 2002; Massey 2008; Massey, Rugh, and Pren 2010). Once they had experienced the costs and risks of undocumented border crossing, migrants declined to repeat the experience and remained north of the border rather than returning home, bringing about a pronounced decline in levels of out-migration (Redburn, Reuter,

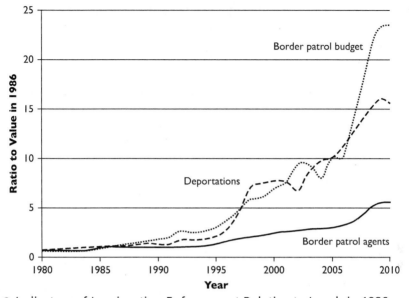

Figure 2 Indicators of Immigration Enforcement Relative to Levels in 1986

Source: Author's compilation of data from the Office of Immigration Statistics, U.S. Department of Homeland Security and predecessor agencies.

and Majmundar 2011). With the full-scale militarization of the border in San Diego and the erection of a steel wall from the Pacific Ocean to the peaks of the Sierra Madre, in-migrants were diverted away from California toward new crossing points along the border with Arizona and to new destinations throughout the United States. . . . Mexican migration was thus transformed from a largely circular movement of male workers going to three states into a settled population of families living in 50 states (Massey, Durand, and Pren 2009). By 2010, more Latinos were living in undocumented status in more places than at any point in American history (Massey 2011; Massey and Pren 2012a).

As a result of U.S. actions over the past several decades, never before have so many U.S. residents lacked basic legal protections. Undocumented migrants currently constitute a third of all foreigners present in the United States, more than 40% of those from Latin America, and large majorities of those from Mexico and Central America; and because undocumented migrants generally inhabit households containing family members who are not undocumented, the share of people touched by illegal migration is actually much larger. According to estimates by Passel (2006), about a quarter of all persons living in households that contain undocumented migrants are themselves U.S. citizens. . . .

Net undocumented migration appears now to have dropped to zero not because of U.S. enforcement efforts, but owing to a collapsed U.S. economy, declining population growth in Mexico, and generally favorable economic conditions throughout Latin America (Wasem 2011; Redburn, Reuter, and Majmundar 2011). In the past decade, however, the falling number of undocumented migrants has been offset by a rising number of tempo-rary workers. With little fanfare or public awareness, mass guest worker recruitment has returned to the United States, bringing annual entries up to levels last seen in the 1950s (Massey and Pren 2012b). Although only a tiny fraction of Mexicans who entered the United States in 2010 were unauthorized, most of those who entered with documents nonetheless did not possess full labor rights. . . .

. . . With more people occupying ever more vulnerable and exploitable positions in the U.S. labor market, the socioeconomic status of Latinos generally declined over the past several decades. After occupying an intermediate position between blacks and whites in the American status hierarchy, after 1990 Latinos increasingly joined African Americans at the bottom of the socioeconomic distribution to comprise a new American underclass (Massey 2007). In the absence of meaningful immigration reform and a curtailment of repression against immigrants, this population can only be expected to see its problems proliferate and multiply.

Figure 3 illustrates the decline in Latino socioeconomic status by showing trends in median personal income earned by white, black, and Latino males from 1972 through 2010 (in constant dollars). . . .

The foregoing figures, of course, do not control for human capital and other character-istics of white, black, and Latino workers, and some have argued that the deterioration in the relative economic standing of Latinos reflects the declining quality of successive immi-grant cohorts, especially for Mexicans (Borjas 1995, 1999). . . . According to Massey and Gelatt (2010), what changed over time was not so much the characteristics of immigrants, as how various forms of human capital were rewarded in the U.S. labor market. . . .

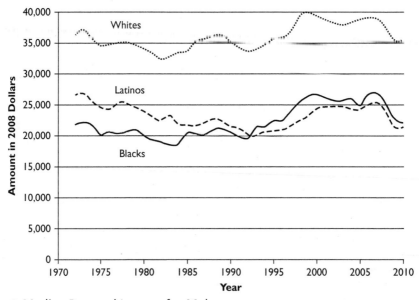

Figure 3 Median Personal Income for Males

Source: Author's compilation of data from the U.S. Census Bureau.

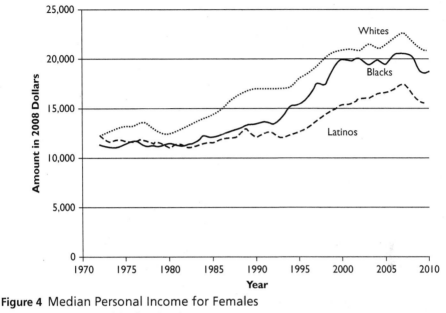

Figure 4 Median Personal Income for Females

Source: Author's compilation of data from the U.S. Census Bureau.

In the early 1970s, all women earned relatively low incomes—both absolutely and compared with men; but things began to change in 1980, when the incomes of white women began to rise steadily, going from a little over $12,000 in that year to peak at almost $23,000 in 2007. Although the upturn for black women lagged behind that of white women, beginning around 1985 their incomes also began to rise and this increase accelerated during the 1990s to narrow the black-white gap substantially, with black female income peaking at almost $21,000 in 2007. In contrast, the income of Latinas remained flat until 1993 and then rose at a slower rate than either white or black women, so that by 2010 the Latina-white gap was wider than it had ever been. Whereas white and Latina women earned roughly the same incomes in 1972, by 2010 Latinas earned a quarter less than whites [see Figure 4].

The shifting fortunes of Latinos and African Americans in U.S. labor markets are clearly reflected in U.S. poverty statistics. Figure 5 shows trends in the poverty rate for white, black, and Latino families from 1972 to 2010. Once again Latinos occupied a middle position in the distribution of poverty until 1994, when black and Latino poverty rates converged to identical levels. From then until 2000 black and Latino families shared the same poverty trajectory, but then black poverty rates rose above those of Latinos until 2008 when the onset of the Great Recession brought them back together at around 24% in 2010, some 3.4 times greater than the rate of 7% among white families.

In sum, the . . . data clearly suggest that something happened over the course of the 1990s to undermine earnings among Latinos living in the United States. . . .

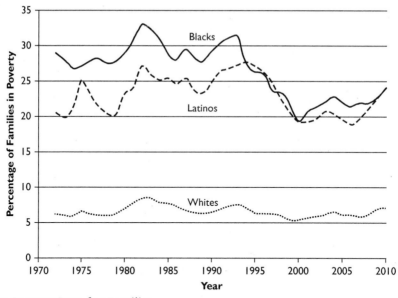

Figure 5 Poverty Rate for Families

Source: Author's compilation of data from the U.S. Census Bureau.

The deterioration in the labor market position of Hispanics relative to blacks was accompanied by a similar reversal of fortune in U.S. housing markets. Whereas in 1989 Hispanics were 19% *less likely* than blacks to experience adverse treatment in America's rental housing markets, in 2000 they were 8% *more likely* to suffer discrimination. In addition, although the incidence of discriminatory treatment fell for both groups in the sales market, the decline for Hispanics was much smaller. As a result, whereas blacks in 1989 were twice as likely as Hispanics to experience discrimination in home sales, by 2000 Hispanics were 18% *more likely* than blacks to experience it (Turner et al. 2002). Consistent with these data, in their audit of rental housing in the San Francisco Bay area, Purnell, Idsardi, and Baugh (1999) documented extensive "linguistic profiling" that excluded speakers of Chicano English from access to housing. In addition, several state and local initiatives have sought to mandate discrimination on the basis of legal status by forbidding real estate agents from renting or selling homes to those present without authorization (Hopkins 2010). . . .

The effect of the [housing] crisis on Latino wealth is indicated in Figure 6, which shows trends in median net wealth for black and Latino households. Historically both groups have been characterized by low levels of wealth, which prior to 2000 averaged between just $6,000 and $10,000 compared with a range of $70,000 and $80,000 for white households (not shown). Beginning in 2001 the net wealth of Latino and black households began to rise as the housing boom began to reach into neighborhoods where they were located and both groups were targeted for extensive subprime mortgage lending. Given that Latinos were disproportionately living in states affected by the boom, their net wealth rose faster and higher than blacks to peak at $24,000 in 2007 compared with just $14,000

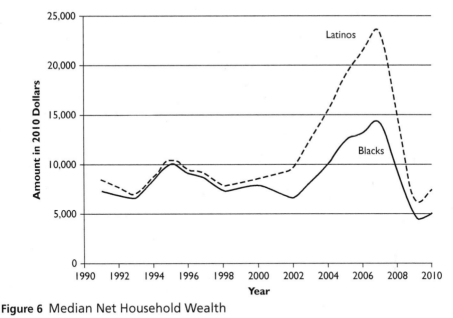

Figure 6 Median Net Household Wealth

Source: Author's compilation of data from the U.S. Census Bureau.

for African Americans. With the collapse of housing prices, however, both groups ended up much at the same place, with a net worth of just $6,000 for the former and $5,000 for the latter by 2009. Latinos, however, experienced the greatest decline in net wealth of any major group, with a drop of 73% between peak and trough.

Immigration Reform as Social Justice

Over the past four decades, the immigration enforcement system of the United States has become increasingly important as a major race-making institution in much the same way that the criminal justice system did for African Americans over the same period. In both cases, there were massive increases in arrests, incarcerations, and in the case of immigrants, apprehensions and deportations, combined with huge increases in the relevant agency budgets. The immigrant detention system is now the fastest growing component of America's prison industrial complex. In 2011, for example, some 429,000 immigrants were incarcerated and awaiting trial or deportation, 397,000 were expelled from the United States, and 328,000 were apprehended at the Mexico-U.S. border (American Civil Liberties Union 2012; U.S. Office of Immigration Statistics 2012). As a result, . . . the number incarcerated among Latinos is rapidly rising relative to African Americans. Whereas the ratio of Latino to black prisoners in state and federal penal institutions averaged between 0.34 and 0.39, after 2001 it rose steadily to peak at around 0.59 in 2010. At this rate of change, Latinos will surpass African Americans as the largest prison population around two decades from now.

Whereas among African Americans, the prison industrial complex created a large population of current and ex-felons who suffer a variety of forms of exclusion and discrimination (Pager 2007; Pettit 2012), among Latinos it has generated a population not simply of current and ex-felons, but a larger population of marginalized, repressed, and eminently exploitable undocumented migrants. Despite all their well-documented disadvantages, however, black felons at least retain basic social and economic rights as American citizens, whereas undocumented migrants under current circumstances have virtually no rights at all and are subject to arrest, incarceration without representation, and summary deportation without trial or benefit of counsel. Even documented migrants may now be arrested, detailed, and deported on the say-so of low level Justice Department officials and they have been declared by congress to be deportable ex post facto for crimes they earlier committed (see Legomsky 2000).

The situation is especially dire in the case of Mexicans, the nation's largest immigrant group and the second largest minority after African Americans. At present, nearly 60% of all persons born in Mexico are illegally present; and among those who do hold legal residence papers, two-thirds first entered the United States without documents, thus rendering them legally deportable under current law (Massey and Malone 2003). These figures imply that nearly a quarter (23%) of all persons of Mexican origin living in the United States are currently undocumented, while another 8% are formerly undocumented, putting roughly a third of all Mexican Americans at serious risk of deportation. . . .

REFERENCES

Alvarado, Steven E., and Douglas S. Massey. 2010. "In Search of Peace: Structural Adjustment, Violence, and International Migration." *Annals of the American Academy of Political and Social Science* 630(1): 294-321.

American Civil Liberties Union. 2012. *Immigration Detention*. Retrieved from ACLU Website November 22, 2012 at http://www.aclu.org/immigrants-rights/detention.

Borjas, George J. 1995. "Assimilation and Changes in Cohort Quality Revisited: What Happened to Immigrant Earnings in the 1980s?" *Journal of Labor Economics* 13:201-245.

_____. 1999. *Heaven's Door: Immigration Policy and the American Economy*. Princeton, NJ: Princeton University Press.

Calavita, Kitty. 1992. *Inside the State: The Bracero Program, Immigration, and the INS*. New York: Routledge.

Chavez, Leo R. 2001. *Covering Immigration: Population Images and the Politics of the Nation*. Berkeley: University of California Press.

_____. 2008. *The Latino Threat: Constructing Immigrants, Citizens, and the Nation*. Stanford, CA: Stanford University Press.

Ennis, Sharon R., Merarys Ríos-Vargas, and Nora G. Albert. 2011. *The Hispanic Population: 2010*. 2010 Census Briefs, U.S. Bureau of the Census, Washington, DC.

Funkhouser, Edward. 1992. "Migration from Nicaragua: Some Recent Evidence." *World Development* 20: 1209-18.

Higham, John. 1955. *Strangers in the Land: Patterns of American Nativism, 1860-1925*. New Brunswick, NJ, Rutgers University Press, 1955.

Hoefer, Michael, Nancy Rytina, and Bryan C. Baker. 2011. "Estimates of the Unauthorized Immigrant Population Residing in the United States: January 2010." Washington, DC: Office of Immigration Statistics, US Department of Homeland Security, https://www.dhs.gov/xlibrary/ assets/statistics/publications/ois_ill_pe_2010.pdf.

Hopkins, Daniel J. 2010. "Politicized Places: Explaining Where and When Immigrants Provoke Local Opposition." *American Political Science Review* 104:40–60.

Jones, Richard C. 1989. "Causes of Salvadoran Migration to the United States." *The Geographical Review* 79:183-94.

Kohut, Andrew, and Roberto Suro. 2006. *America's Immigration Quandary: No Consensus on Immigration Problem or Proposed Fixes.* Washington, DC. Pew Research Center for the People and the Press and Pew Hispanic Center.

Lee, Tiane L., and Susan T. Fiske. 2006. "Not an Outgroup, Not Yet an Ingroup: Immigrants in the Stereotype Content Model." *International Journal of Intercultural Relations* 30:751-68.

Legomsky, Stephen H. 2000. "Fear and Loathing in Congress and the Courts: Immigration and Judicial Review." *Texas Law Review* 78:1612-20.

Lopez, Mark Hugo, Rich Morin, and Paul Taylor. 2010. *Illegal Immigration Backlash Worries, Divides Latinos.* Washington, DC: Pew Hispanic Center.

Lundquist, Jennifer H., and Douglas S. Massey. 2005. "The Contra War and Nicaraguan Migration to the United States." *Journal of Latin American Studies* 37:29-53.

Massey, Douglas S. 1999. "International Migration at the Dawn of the Twenty-First Century: The Role of the State." *Population and Development Review* 25:303-23.

———. 2007. *Categorically Unequal: The American Stratification System.* New York: Russell Sage Foundation.

———. 2008. *New Faces in New Places: The Changing Geography of American Immigration.* New York: Russell Sage Foundation.

———. 2011. "Epilogue: The Past and Future of Mexico-U.S. Migration." Pp. 241-265 in *Beyond la Frontera: The History of Mexico-U.S. Migration,* edited by Mark Overmyer-Velázquez. New York: Oxford University Press.

Massey, Douglas S., Jorge Durand, and Nolan J. Malone. 2002. *Beyond Smoke and Mirrors: Mexican Immigration in an Age of Economic Integration.* New York: Russell Sage Foundation.

Massey, Douglas S., Jorge Durand, and Karen A. Pren. 2009. "Nuevos Escenarios de la Migración México-Estados Unidos: Las Consecuencias de la Guerra Antiinmigrante." *Papeles de Población* 61:101-28.

Massey, Douglas S., and Julia Gelatt. 2010. "What Happened to the Wages of Mexican Immigrants? Trends and Interpretations." *Latino Studies* 8:328-54.

Massey, Douglas S., and Nolan J. Malone. 2003. "Pathways to Legalization." *Population Research and Policy Review* 21:473-504.

Massey, Douglas S., and Karen A. Pren. 2012a. "Unintended Consequences of US Immigration Policy: Explaining the Post-1965 Surge from Latin America." *Population and Development Review* 38:1-29.

———. 2012b. "Origins of the New Latino Underclass." *Race and Social Problems* 4(1): 5-17.

Massey, Douglas S., Jacob S. Rugh, and Karen A. Pren. 2010. "The Geography of Undocumented Mexican Migration." *Mexican Studies/Estudios Mexicanos* 26:120-52.

Massey, Douglas S., and Magaly Sánchez R. 2010. *Brokered Boundaries: Creating Immigrant Identity in Anti-Immigrant Times.* New York: Russell Sage Foundation.

Meyers, Eytan. 2004. *International Immigration Policy: A Theoretical and Comparative Analysis.* London: Palgrave Macmillan.

Morrison, Andrew R., and Rachel A. May. 1994. "Escape from Terror: Violence and Migration in Post-Revolutionary Guatemala." *Latin American Research Review* 29:111-32.

Pager, Devah. 2007. *Marked: Race, Crime, and Finding Work in an Era of Mass Incarceration.* Chicago, IL: University of Chicago Press.

Passel, Jeffrey. 2006. *The Size and Characteristics of the Unauthorized Migrant Population in the U.S.: Estimates Based on the March 2005 Current Population Survey.* Washington, DC: Pew Hispanic Center.

Pettit, Becky. 2012. *Invisible Men: Mass Incarceration and the Myth of Black Progress.* New York: Russell Sage Foundation.

Pew Hispanic Center. 2011. *The Mexican-American Boom: Births Overtake Immigration.* Washington, DC: Pew Hispanic Center.

Purnell, Thomas, William Idsardi, and John Baugh. 1999. "Perceptual and Phonetic Experiments on American English Dialect Identification." *Journal of Language and Social Psychology* 18:10-30.

Redburn, Steve, Peter Reuter, and Malay Majmundar. 2011. *Budgeting for Immigration Enforcement: A Path to Better Performance.* Washington, DC: National Academies Press.

Rosen, Jeffrey. 1995. "The War on Immigrants: Why the Courts Can't Save Us." *The New Republic*, January 30. Accessed on June 8, 2011 at http://www.tnr.com/article/politics/the-war-immigrants.

Schrag, Peter. 2010. *Not Fit for Our Society: Immigration and Nativism in America.* Berkeley: University of California Press.

Stanley, William D. 1987. "Economic Migrants or Refugees from Violence? A Time-Series Analysis of Salvadoran Migration to the United States." *Latin American Research Review* 22:132-154.

Turner, Margery A., Stephen L. Ross, George C. Galster, and John Yinger. 2002. *Discrimination in Metropolitan Housing Markets: National Results from Phase I.* Washington, DC: U.S. Department of Housing and Urban Development.

U.S. Office of Immigration Statistics. 2012. *The 2011 Yearbook of Immigration Statistics.* Washington, DC: U.S. Office of Immigration Statistics. http://www.dhs.gov/files/statistics/publications/yearbook.shtm

Wasem, Ruth E. 2011. *Unauthorized Aliens Residing in the United States: Estimates Since 1986.* Washington, DC: Congressional Research Service.

Zolberg, Aristide R. 2006. *A Nation by Design: Immigration Policy in the Fashioning of America.* New York: Russell Sage Foundation.

7 Gender and the Black Jobs Crisis
Linda Burnham

Introduction

Ten million African American women wake up and go to work every day.[1] They prepare and serve food at the fast-food chains. They staff the registers at the big-box stores. They tend to the needs of patients in nursing facilities or provide homecare to elders. Often enough, when they're done with one job for the day, they hop a bus and go on to a second. The moms among them start their long days extra early, getting the kids ready for school or dropping them off at daycare. They worry incessantly whether patched-together childcare arrangements will hold up. Yet, at the end of the week, their paychecks are so meager that even the most frugal are desperate to make ends meet. Instead of supporting the lives and aspirations of African American women who are part of the low-wage workforce, the U.S. economy is brutalizing them.

The core of the jobs crisis facing African American women is low wages. African American women are working, and working hard. They participate in the workforce at slightly higher rates than women of every other race or ethnicity, but, in too many cases, their hard work goes unrewarded. Low wages trap black women, together with their families and communities, in cycles of economic distress, with reverberant and widespread social consequences.

There are five key elements of the jobs crisis facing African American women:

1. African American women are overrepresented among low-wage workers, including those workers earning at or below minimum wage.
2. African American women are impacted by both the gender gap and the racial gap in wages.
3. African American women are unemployed at higher rates and for longer periods than other women.
4. African American women were especially hard hit by the most recent recession and have lagged behind in the recovery.
5. African American women in the labor force are far more likely to be single heads of household than are women of other races and ethnicities.

Linda Burnham is an activist and writer whose work focuses on women's rights, racial justice, and national politics. She is the coauthor of *Home Economics: The Invisible and Unregulated World of Domestic Work*. In 1990 she cofounded the Women of Color Resource Center and served as its executive director for 18 years.

Originally published in *Souls: A Critical Journal of Black Politics, Culture, and Society*, Volume 18, Issue 1, pp. 126–134, 2016. Copyright © 2016 by Taylor & Francis. Reprinted by permission of the University of Illinois–Chicago, www.uic.edu.

Overrepresentation Among Low-Wage Workers[2]

Women are significantly overrepresented in low-wage occupations and sectors of the economy, contributing to the gender gap in wages. Even within low-wage occupations, women's wages are lower than those of men in the same job categories. African Americans are also significantly overrepresented in low-wage occupations and sectors of the economy, contributing to the racial gap in wages. African American women's economic profile is fundamentally shaped by the confluence of these two persistent trends.

Key sectors of the economy in which both women and African Americans are highly concentrated include service and sales. Occupations for which both women and African Americans form a disproportionately high segment of the workforce include health support occupations, fast food, and retail sales.

For example, African Americans constitute 11.4 percent of the employed civilian labor force, but 16.2 percent of those employed in service occupations. Women make up 46.9 percent of the labor force but are 56.7 percent of those employed in the service sector.[3] The service sector, with median weekly earnings of $508 ($470 for women; $588 for men), compensates workers at a lower rate than any other sector of the economy.[4]

The workforce in some cleaning and caretaking jobs, stereotypically considered women's work, is over 80 percent female. Black workers are concentrated in some of these jobs at double, or even triple, the rate of their share of the employed. Those occupations in which both women and African Americans are significantly overrepresented are especially likely to confer low wages.

Women and African Americans are highly concentrated in healthcare support occupations, with a workforce that is 87.6 percent female and 25.7 percent black. Wages within this group of occupations vary but are particularly low for jobs with higher proportions of African Americans. For example, nursing, psychiatric, and home health aides, taken together as a group, earn $11.87 per hour, bringing full-time, year-round workers just over the poverty threshold for a family of four, while home health aides, considered alone, earn just $10.60 an hour.[5] [See Table 1.]

Home health aides and personal care aides are among the fastest growing occupations, responsive to the aging of the boomer generation. These occupations are projected to grow by nearly 50 percent between 2012 and 2022, and we can expect that they will be major areas of job growth for black women.[6] Only 40 percent of home health aides and personal care aides are employed full-time year-round, and wages hover around ten dollars an hour. As a result, more than half of homecare workers rely on some form of public assistance: Medicaid, food stamps, or housing assistance.[7] Black women working as nannies, housecleaners, and elder caregivers in the private-pay market are paid just as poorly, are rarely paid for overtime, and are frequently required to take on tasks well beyond the scope of the work they were originally hired to perform.[8] Raising the level of compensation for healthcare support occupations and domestic work is critical to improving the job picture for black women.

Jobs that combine food preparation and serving, including fast food jobs, have the distinction of being both the lowest paid of major U.S. occupations, with median hourly wages of $9.08, and among the largest, accounting for more than three million workers. African Americans are overrepresented at the low end of the food service sector, making

TABLE 1	Concentration of Women and African Americans in Low-Wage Occupations			
Occupation	Women as % of Total Employed	Blacks as % of Total Employed	Mean Hourly Wage (2013)	Mean Annual Wage (2013)
Employed persons 16 years or over	46.9	11.4		
Food preparation and serving workers, including fast food	61.9	20.5	9.08	18,880
Cashiers	72.2	18.3	9.82	20,420
Personal care aides	83.9	23.0	10.09	20,990
Childcare workers	95.5	15.9	10.33	21,490
Home health aides			10.60	22,050
Maids and housekeeping	88.6	16.8	10.64	22,130
Food servers, non-restaurant	61.9	23.5	10.77	22,400
Nursing, psychiatric, and home health aides	88.5	35.9	11.87	24,700

Wage data from Bureau of Labor Statistics, "Occupational Employment and Wages, May 2013."

Data for women and black workers as percentage of occupation from Bureau of Labor Statistics, "Employed persons by detailed occupation, sex, race and Hispanic or Latino ethnicity."

up nearly double their share of the employed among fast-food workers (20.5 percent) and an even higher proportion of non-restaurant food servers (23.5 percent), occupations in which the workforce is 62 percent female.[9]

At $9.82 an hour, cashiers are the lowest paid workers in sales. Here again, in a low-wage occupation that employs more than three million workers, we find a high concentration of female workers (72.2 percent) and a substantial overrepresentation of African Americans (18.3 percent). [In contrast, at the other end of the sales spectrum, wholesale and manufacturing sales representatives earn over $33 an hour; 30 percent of them are women, and 5 percent are African American.][10] Within retail sales, documented racial discrimination in hiring, promotions, and scheduling puts African American women at a further disadvantage.[11]

Not only are these occupations low-wage, many of them pay at or below minimum wage. Nearly two-thirds of workers paid at or below minimum wage are in service occupations (63.6 percent) and nearly half (46.7 percent) are in jobs related to food preparation and serving.[12] African American women's overrepresentation among minimum wage workers is tied to their disproportionate presence in these occupations. Black women are 7.4 percent of wage and salary workers earning hourly wages, but 10.1 percent of those earning minimum wage.[13]

In light of the concentration of black women in low-wage jobs, it comes as no surprise that their earnings trail those of every other demographic group, with the exception of Hispanic women. In the fourth quarter of 2014, the median weekly earnings of black women who were full-time wage and salary workers amounted to 90 percent of those earned by black men but only 82 percent and 66 percent of the earnings of white women and white men respectively. Further, black women are the only group whose median weekly fourth-quarter earnings dropped from 2013 to 2014, sliding from $621 to $602.[14]

While the jobs crisis for black women is, first and foremost, a crisis of wages, low-wage jobs are also characterized by a near-complete absence of benefits, unpredictable or on-demand scheduling, and extremely limited avenues for advancement.

High Rates of Unemployment

High unemployment rates compound the wage crisis for African American women, a long established and persistent problem made worse by the Great Recession. During the recession, jobs were stripped from black men and women and their rates of unemployment ratcheted up alarmingly. Moreover, the vaunted recovery has not been experienced equally across racial groups. The unemployment rate for blacks, already considerably higher than the rates for other racial groups, increased disproportionately, was slower to fall, and has yet to return to the pre-recession rate. [See Table 2.]

In December 2009, six months into the recovery, black women were unemployed at a rate nearly five percentage points higher than before the recession began, and the rate was still climbing. It peaked at 14.8 percent in July 2011, two years into what was, for some, the recovery before beginning to descend. At the end of 2014, it was still three points higher than it was pre-recession. The unemployment rate for black men peaked at just over 20 percent in March 2010, far higher than the peak rate for any other group. To put this in some perspective, white women's unemployment rate, at its recessionary height of 7.7 percent, never reached the 2007 pre-recession low for black men.[15] In the purportedly recovered economy of 2011, black unemployment stood at 15.8 percent, double the rate for whites (7.9 percent) and significantly higher than the rate for Hispanics (11.5 percent). Blacks remained unemployed, on average, for seven weeks longer than whites, and black women made up a larger share of the black unemployed (46.9 percent) than white and

TABLE 2 Unemployment in the Recession and Recovery				
Unemployment Rate	**Dec. 2007**	**Dec. 2009**	**Dec. 2011**	**Dec. 2014**
Black women	6.8	11.5	13.2	9.8
Black men	8.4	16.7	15.2	11
White women	3.6	6.8	6.3	4.1
White men	4.1	9.6	7.3	4.4

BLS Data Series from Current Population Survey, Unemployment Rate 20 years and over, 2005–2015.

Hispanic women did in their racial or ethnic groups.[16] Racially disparate patterns in the rates and duration of unemployment attest to the persistence of racial bias in hiring and retention, lending credibility to the conventional wisdom that black workers are the last hired and first fired.

Race, Household Type, and Poverty

African American women are far more likely than the women of every other race or ethnicity to be single-earner heads of household. These households are vulnerable to poverty, especially when children are present. Black women are three to four times as likely as white and Asian women to be the heads of household with children under the age of 18. Seventeen percent of black households are headed by women with children, as compared to 4.7 percent of white and 4.1 percent of Asian households.[17] [See Table 3.]

Black women are not only far more likely than other women to be single heads of household, but, within this household type, they experience poverty at nearly twice the rate of white women and three times that of Asian women [see Table 4]. More than

TABLE 3 Single Householder, No Spouse Present, as Percentage of Household Types

Race/Ethnicity	Women	Women with Children	Men
Black	30.1	17.4	6.3
American Indian/Alaska Native	21.4	12.3	8.9
Hispanic	19.2	12.1	9.1
Native Hawaiian/Pacific Islander	17	9.8	8.7
Asian	9.5	4.1	4.7
Non-Hispanic White	9.2	4.7	4.0

U.S. Census Bureau, *Households and Families: 2010*, Table 3: "Household Types by Race and Hispanic Origin: 2010."

TABLE 4 Single Female Householders Living in Poverty

Race/Ethnicity	% of Single Female Householders in Poverty
Black	42.5
Hispanic	41.6
White	22.9
Asian	13.7

U.S. Census Bureau, Current Population Reports, September 2014. *Income and Poverty in the United States*, 2013.

40 percent of black single female householders live in poverty.[18] Dual-earner families have more spending power than single-earner families, as well as the cushion of a partner's income in times of unemployment. Given that female-headed households are a more common household type among African Americans than are wife-husband households, that safety net is unavailable to black women. As economic fortunes have polarized, so too has marriage stability. People earning little are far less likely to marry than those higher up the income ladder, and the marriages of those who do are less stable.[19]

The combination of low wages, high levels of unemployment, high likelihood of living in single-earner households, and minimal accumulation of wealth and assets has a devastating impact on the economic well-being of African American women, their families, and their communities. A focus on the gender gap undifferentiated by race obscures the realities black women face, as does a focus on racial disparities undifferentiated by gender.

Black LGBTQ Workers

LGBTQ workers who are black face added dimensions of gender bias and disadvantage in the labor force. Reliable data about black workers who are LGBTQ is scarce, but studies confirm both high levels of employment discrimination based on race, gender identity, and sexual orientation and high levels of poverty, particularly among black lesbians and transgender individuals. Unprotected from job discrimination in many states and lacking access to the multiple benefits that accrue to married couples and state-recognized family forms, LGBTQ workers in general face particular challenges in the labor force. At the same time, both the gender gap and the racial gap in wages and income are salient within the LGBTQ community.

Black lesbian couples earn about $5000 less per year than black male couples, but white lesbian couples out-earn their black counterparts by $21,000 and white male couples out-earn black male couples by $23,000.[20] [See Table 5.] Poverty rates are also far higher for black lesbian and gay couples than they are for either heterosexual couples or for white same-sex couples [see Table 6]. At 21.1 percent, the poverty rate for black lesbian couples is more than five times the rate for white heterosexual couples and close to eight times higher than the rate for white male couples.[21]

TABLE 5 Median Income of Same-Sex Couples by Gender and Race

Same-Sex Couples	Median Annual Household Income
Black female	$39,000
Black male	44,000
White female	60,000
White male	67,000

Black Same-Sex Households in the United States: A Report from the 2000 Census.

TABLE 6 Poverty Rates for Heterosexual and Same-Sex Couples by Race and Ethnicity

	Married Heterosexual	Male Same-Sex Couples	Female Same-Sex Couples
African American	9.3	14.4	21.1
American Indian/Alaska Native	12.9	19.1	13.7
Hispanic	16.7	9.2	19.1
White	4.1	2.7	4.3
Asian/Pacific Islander	9.1	4.5	11.8

Albelda, *Poverty in the Lesbian, Gay and Bisexual Community.*

Transgender people report exceedingly high rates of gender discrimination in hiring, gender harassment at work, high unemployment, and low wages. In a national survey, black transgender people reported an unemployment rate of 26 percent, high rates of job loss or no-hires due to gender bias, and extremely high incidence of harassment on the job. Not surprisingly, earnings suffer for transgender individuals who are black. Thirty-four percent reported annual incomes of under $10,000, which is twice the rate of extreme poverty among transgender people in general and four times the rate for black people.[22]

Conclusion

To impact the lives of African American women and LGBTQ individuals who work for low wages—along with the fortunes of the families and communities that depend on their income—we need a multi-pronged short-term and long-term advocacy and organizing strategy that raises wages and provides benefits for the occupations in which African American women are highly concentrated, targets gender and race bias in hiring, promotion, and firing, and begins to close the gender and race wage gaps. In short, we need a labor compact that rewards rather than punishes black women for their contributions to the U.S. economy.

NOTES

1. 9.4 million black female workers were in the civilian labor force in 2010. 10.7 million are projected to be part of the workforce in 2018. *Civilian Labor Force and Participation Rates with Projections 1980–2018*, Statistical Abstract of the United States 2012, U.S. Census Bureau, 2012.
2. Low-wage workers are those workers whose hourly wage rates are so low that, even if they worked full-time, year-round, their annual earnings would fall below the poverty threshold for a family of four. Poverty threshold for family of four: $24,250—2015, $23,850—2014, $23,550—2013. http://www.census.gov/hhes/www/poverty/data/threshld/, http://aspe.hhs.gov/poverty/15poverty.cfm#thresholds, accessed March 18, 2015.

3. U.S. Bureau of Labor Statistics, "Employed Persons by Detailed Occupation, Sex, Race, and Hispanic or Latino Ethnicity," Current Population Survey Data 2014, U.S. Department of Labor, http://www.bls.gov/cps/cpsaat11.htm, accessed March 18, 2015.

4. U.S. Bureau of Labor Statistics, "Usual Weekly Earnings of Wage and Salary Workers, Fourth Quarter 2014," U.S. Department of Labor, http://www.bls.gov/news.release/pdf/wkyeng.pdf, accessed March 18, 2015.

5. U.S. Bureau of Labor Statistics, "Occupational Employment and Wages—May 2013," http://www.bls.gov/news.release/pdf/ocwage.pdf, accessed March 3, 2015.

6. U.S. Bureau of Labor Statistics, *Occupational Outlook Handbook*, U.S. Department of Labor, http://www.bls.gov/ooh/fastest-growing.htm, accessed March 18, 2015.

7. Paraprofessional Healthcare Institute (PHI), *Paying the Price: How Poverty Wages Undermine Home Care in America*, February 2015, http://phinational.org/research-reports/paying-price-how-poverty-wages-undermine-home-care-america, accessed March 18, 2015.

8. Linda Burnham and Nick Theodore, *Home Economics: The invisible and unregulated world of domestic work*, National Domestic Workers Alliance, November 2010.

9. U.S. Bureau of Labor Statistics, "Occupational Employment and Wages—May 2013."

10. U.S. Bureau of Labor Statistics, "Occupational Employment and Wages—May 2013."

11. Stephanie Luce and Naoki Fujita, *Discounted Jobs: How Retailers Sell Workers Short*, Murphy Institute at City University of New York and Retail Action Project, 2012.

12. U.S. Bureau of Labor Statistics, *Characteristics of Minimum Wage Workers, 2013*, Table 4, BLS Report 1048, U.S. Department of Labor, March 2014.

13. U.S. Bureau of Labor Statistics, *Characteristics of Minimum Wage Workers, 2013*, Table 1.

14. U.S. Bureau of Labor Statistics, "Usual Weekly Earnings of Wage and Salary Workers," Table 2.

15. Author's analysis of labor force statistics from the Current Population Survey, 2005–2015.

16. U.S. Department of Labor, *The African American Labor Force in the Recovery*, February 29, 2012.

17. Daphne Lofquist, Terry Lugaila, Martin O'Connell, and Sarah Feliz, *Households and Families: 2010*, Table 3, U.S. Census Bureau, April 2012.

18. Carmen DeNavas-Walt and Bernadette D. Proctor, *Income and Poverty in the U.S.. 2013*, U.S. Census Bureau, September 2014.

19. Stephanie Coontz, "The New Instability," *New York Times*, July 26, 2014, http://www.nytimes.com/2014/07/27/opinion/sunday/the-new-instability.html, accessed April 1, 2015.

20. Alain Dang and Somjen Frazer, *Black Same-Sex Households in the United States: A Report from the 2000 Census*, National Gay and Lesbian Task Force and National Black Justice Coalition, Second Edition: December 2005.

21. Randy Albelda, M.V. Lee Badgett, Alyssa Schneebaum, and Gary J. Gates, *Poverty in the Lesbian, Gay and Bisexual Community*, Center for Social Policy Publications, Paper 4, The Williams Institute, 2009.

22. National Justice Coalition, National Center for Transgender Equality, and National Gay and Lesbian Task Force, *Injustice at Every Turn: A Look at Black Responses to the National Transgender Discrimination Survey*, http://nbjc.org/sites/default/files/trans-adjustment-web.pdf, accessed April 1, 2015.

8 | Domestic Workers Bill of Rights: A Feminist Approach for a New Economy

Ai-jen Poo

Editor's Note: After a six-year grassroots campaign waged by Domestic Workers United, the New York State legislature passed the Domestic Workers Bill of Rights in 2010. Similar measures subsequently passed in Hawaii, California, Massachusetts, Oregon, Connecticut, Illinois, and Nevada. In 2018, Seattle, Washington, became the first city to pass a Domestic Workers Bill of Rights.

Several years ago, my grandfather had a stroke that left him paralyzed on the left side of his body. My grandmother, while in good health, was over 70 and unable to help him move around, bathe or meet many of his basic needs. So like thousands of other families, they hired a home attendant. The first time I met Ms. Li was a couple of years after she was hired. A second stroke had put my grandfather back in the hospital in critical condition. I remember entering the hospital room to visit him. Ms. Li sat at the side of his bed with a small plastic comb in her hand, slowly combing back his thin grey hair. His eyes were closed, and his expression peaceful and light. I turned to greet my grandmother, who said quietly, "He asks for her to comb his hair. It puts him at ease." Apparently, every morning at home for the last two years, she patiently combed his hair after bathing him. At that moment, it was clear to me that there are few greater gifts than being cared for by another person. It is rooted in the interconnectedness of humanity; we rely on one another, particularly when we face the uncertainty of life.

We live in an economic system that requires us to disconnect from each other despite the fact that we are ultimately interconnected. In fact, many forms of necessary labor are erased and devalued in our current system, particularly work that has historically been associated with women and women of color. The domestic work industry provides a clear window into this reality. Domestic worker organizing not only seeks to address the systemic problems facing the workforce, but also points to ways we can reshape the economy, toward a more sustainable system that adequately supports our basic human needs.

Ai-jen Poo is an activist, thought leader, and social innovator. Her work has led to advocacy movements and legislation aimed at protecting domestic workers, the aging population, and caregivers. She serves as the executive director of the National Domestic Workers Alliance and the codirector of Caring Across Generations.

Published on S&F Online: The Scholar and Feminist Online. Published by The Barnard Center for Research on Women — Issue 8.1: Fall 2009. Republished with permission of the author.

A World of Work in the Home

The estimated 2.5 million women who labor as domestic workers in the United States make it possible for their employers to go to work every day by caring for the most precious elements of their employers' lives: their families and homes. Essentially, domestic workers produce the labor power of the families they work for. Those families go to work knowing that they can return to a clean home, to clean clothes to wear, and to elderly parents and children who will have their basic needs met. In fact, domestic workers have to play the role of nurses, art teachers, counselors, tutors, assistants, and nutritionists. Yet, because this work has historically been associated with the unpaid work of women in the home or with the poorly paid work of Black and immigrant women, it remains undervalued and virtually invisible to public consciousness.

In New York, over 200,000 women of color leave their homes several hours before everyone else, often in the dark, in order to arrive at their employers' homes before they leave for work. Many arrive early to prepare children for school and walk them to their buses. Some even live in their employers' homes, prepare breakfast and pack lunches for the entire household. Because women's work in the home has never been factored into national labor statistics, it is difficult to quantify the economic contributions of this workforce. However, if domestic workers across the city went on strike, almost every industry would be impacted. Doctors, lawyers, bankers, professors, small business owners, civil sector employees and media executives would all be affected. The urban economy would be paralyzed.

Most domestic workers are immigrant women of color from the global South who bear enormous pressure to support families both in the U.S. and abroad. In a recent survey conducted by DataCenter and Domestic Workers United, researchers found that 98% of domestic workers are foreign born and that 59% are the primary income earners for their families. Domestic work remains one of the few professions available to immigrant women in major cities. For this reason, it tends to draw in migrants from poor countries in search of work in our cities' growing informal service sectors. Many urban immigrant communities rely on the income of domestic workers for their economic survival.

The pressure to support their families economically is compounded by domestic workers' responsibilities to provide care for their own families and homes. The more hours they work, the fewer hours they have to spend with their own children: making nutritious meals, helping them with homework, or reading them a bedtime story. If you are working as a domestic worker in the United States, your own family will often be left without the care they need and deserve.

Long hours are just the beginning. While some employers treat their employees with dignity and respect, others use their power to compel their employees to work as many hours as possible for as little as possible. The power imbalance between domestic workers and employers is severe. The employers are commonly of a privileged class, race, and immigration status with respect to the women they hire to care for their homes and families. Most workplaces have one lone worker. The workplace is their employers' private homes—often seen as a "man's castle"—a place where the government has no business or authority. Advocates often compare the industry to the "Wild West" because it seems to function above the law. Employers can utilize sexual and gender-based harassment to instill fear, as well as exploit workers' immigration status to establish control in the workplace. Considering the prevalence of domestic violence, despite generations of organizing and advocacy on the part of the women's movement, one can imagine what is possible behind closed doors.

"Maria" worked as a caregiver for a child with a disability. A Central American woman in her mid-sixties, she came to the United States to support her family, including her diabetic son whose insulin she could not afford. In addition to constant care for a child with a disability, she was responsible for doing the cooking, cleaning, and ironing for the entire household. Maria worked 18 hours per day, six days per week for under $3 per hour. She lived in the basement of her employer's home where a broken sewage system flooded the floor by her bed. She had to collect cardboard and wood from the street during the day so she could use them as stepping stones to her bed at night. After three years working under these terrible conditions, Maria was fired without notice or severance pay. Working as a domestic worker in the United States often means working in unhealthy conditions, facing constant fear of firing, of deportation, of harassment and of abuse.

Domestic work is one [of] our nation's oldest professions, so one should be able to assume that labor laws and other measures would protect the basic rights of the workforce. Instead, domestic workers have been explicitly excluded from labor laws since the New Deal. The exclusion of domestic workers—most of whom were African American women in the South at the time those labor laws were passed—is rooted in the legacy of slavery. It reminds us that Jim Crow is alive and well in the labor laws. In many states, domestic workers are excluded from the definition of "employee." Eight decades after the passage of this nation's foundational labor protections, domestic workers are still struggling to assert basic worker rights like time off and overtime pay.

Organizing for Dignified Work

Since 2000, Domestic Workers United (DWU) has organized Caribbean, Latina and African nannies, housekeepers, and elderly caregivers in New York. They are fighting for power, respect and fair labor standards, and their work helps to build a broader movement for social change. DWU helped organize public pressure for justice for workers like Maria who have been mistreated by their employers. DWU organized demonstrations at Maria's employer's businesses and worked with the CUNY Immigrant and Refugee Rights Clinic to file a successful lawsuit against her employer for unpaid wages. Using this combination of legal pressure and direct action, DWU has helped to recover over $450,000 in stolen wages for workers like Maria.

For the past 5 years, DWU has been waging a campaign to pass the "Domestic Workers Bill of Rights," statewide legislation that would establish basic labor standards for more than 200,000 domestic workers in New York State. These standards would include: notice of termination, a minimum of one day off per week, paid holidays, vacation and sick days and protection from discrimination. The coalition of domestic workers organizations led by DWU has gained tremendous support from labor unions, progressive employers, clergy, academics, student, community and women's organizations. The effort has raised the profile of the workforce considerably. However, the challenges to legislative change are great.

Some legislators have argued, in order to achieve days off and benefits domestic workers must form a union and collectively bargain "like other workers have to do." A few legislators have claimed that they cannot enact a law with these types of provisions because it would provide "special protections" for domestic workers that other workers do not receive by law. However, DWU has argued that the decentralized nature of this industry "wires" it for abuse, and makes it impossible to engage in collective bargaining. There is no collective workforce because workers are isolated as individuals in scattered, unmarked separate homes; and there isn't a central employer with whom to bargain. When one worker bargains with her employer, termination is the standard result. Employers simply seek to hire someone else. In the context of such intensified inequality and the nature of the industry itself, the National Labor Relations Act (the New Deal policy that provides the current framework for collective bargaining in the U.S.) would fail domestic workers, even if they were not excluded. These dynamics make every domestic worker vulnerable to conditions of indentured servitude.

But the Domestic Workers Bill of Rights is not just a campaign to address the impracticality of collective bargaining for the domestic work labor force. The Bill of Rights exposes our moral responsibility to value their work because it makes all other work possible, and it calls for an expansion of the practical role of the government in establishing and enforcing labor standards for all workers. Domestic workers have always been treated as a "special class" of workers; they have been "specially" excluded and undervalued as workers. What does it say about this nation that this workforce—that provides such a crucial type of care—is the least valued and most invisible?

In fact, the work that has historically been associated with women has made it possible for us to be where we are today. Challenging the government to account for this work and to provide appropriate protections points to the necessity for a feminist lens. It is only with this lens that we adequately account for the full reality of our economic system. Everyone needs the care of others at one point or another in their lives. We rely on others to care for us when we are children, in times of need and when we age. Even while institutional sexism devalues this work and tries to render these workers invisible, we all have a relationship to this kind of care-giving labor.

Our common experiences—in giving and receiving care—gives us an opportunity to take action in our common interest towards institutional change. As we emerge from one of the greatest economic crises of our time, we will need models that help us redefine the role of government, and its relationship to the economy. The Bill of Rights points to a new relationship between government and this industry—a relationship that is more proactive and reflective of the economic realities and needs we all face.

Lessons for a New Economy

Organizing with a feminist approach, DWU organizers have utilized everyone's connection to and reliance upon "women's work" as the basis for organizing. They have made the stories of domestic workers central. They tell the story of the work they do and the pride they feel for the work. They also tell the stories of the profound vulnerability and abuses they face. DWU has brought children who were raised by domestic workers and employers who rely on domestic workers together with domestic workers and their own children. The power of their collective stories—as workers and as people who have been the beneficiaries of their caring labor—demonstrate the power and significance of domestic work. The campaign has created the space for everyone to take action from this place of interdependence. They model a world where, in the words of DWU, "all work is valued equally."

Domestic Workers United is a part of a growing national movement of domestic worker resistance. They helped to organize the first national meeting of domestic workers organizations in 2007. After an historic exchange about organizing strategies, domestic worker organizations from around the country decided to form the National Domestic Workers Alliance as a vehicle for domestic workers to build power and raise their voice as a national force for change. Two years later, the Alliance has doubled in size. The Alliance has established a National Training Institute for domestic workers. It is leading campaigns at the state, national and international levels to enforce existing labor laws and to establish new labor standards for domestic workers. In 2010, California domestic worker organizations will be launching their campaign for the California Domestic Workers Bill of Rights. State by state, workers are asserting their rights as workers, and they are challenging the government to take responsibility for mediating their vulnerability to exploitation.

Understanding the power of Ms. Li and Maria's work can help us to structurally recalibrate to what is important in life. Some people will pay more for a pair of shoes than they pay their domestic workers for a week of work. The historic exclusions of domestic workers reinforce this system of values. Similarly, the legislature has waited five years to pass basic legislation to improve the lives of over 200,000 women. There is no organized opposition to the bill, nor is there a significant cost to the State of New York, but the bill has not yet become a legislative priority. The legislature has not yet understood that what seems like a measure that's specific to domestic workers, actually touches all of us. A recalibration is needed, and it must be institutionalized in the form of policy.

The upside-down concentration of the world's resources and wealth in the hands of a small minority at the expense of the vast majority is in fact unsustainable for everyone. Domestic worker policy demands that we recognize and value the basic care that we all require to live and provides a model for reshaping our economy to serve our collective human needs. We will need this kind of balance and systemic equity if we are going to sustain ourselves through the changes and uncertainty to come.

9

Why America's Schools Have a Money Problem

NPR*

Let's begin with a choice.

Say there's a check in the mail. It's meant to help you run your household. You can use it to keep the lights on, the water running and food on the table. Would you rather that check be for $9,794 or $28,639?

It's not a trick question. It's the story of America's schools in two numbers.

That $9,794 is how much money the Chicago Ridge School District in Illinois spent per child in 2013 (the number has been adjusted by *Education Week* to account for regional cost differences).[1] It's well below that year's national average of $11,841.

Ridge's two elementary campuses and one middle school sit along Chicago's southern edge. Roughly two-thirds of its students come from low-income families, and a third are learning English as a second language.

Here, one nurse commutes between three schools, and the two elementary schools share an art teacher and a music teacher. . . .

"We don't have a lot of the extra things that other districts may have, simply because we can't afford them," says Ridge Superintendent Kevin Russell.

One of those other districts sits less than an hour north, in Chicago's affluent suburbs, nestled into a warren of corporate offices: Rondout School, the only campus in Rondout District 72.

It has 22 teachers and 145 students, and spent $28,639 on each one of them.

What does that look like?

Class sizes in Rondout are small, and every student has an individualized learning plan. Nearly all teachers have a decade of experience and earn, on average, more than $90,000. Kids have at least one daily break for "mindful movement," and lunch is cooked on-site, including a daily vegetarian option.

. . .

Why does Rondout have so much and Ridge so little?

. . .

The simple answer is that many of Rondout's neighbors are successful businesses. They pay local taxes, and those taxes help pay for local schools. Ridge simply has less to work with—fewer businesses, lower property values.

*This selection is the work of NPR Ed Team senior editor Cory Turner in collaboration with Rheema Khrais, Tim Lloyd, Alexandra Olgin, Laura Isensee, Becky Vevea, and Dan Carsen.

More broadly: "You've got highly segregated rich and poor towns," says Bruce Baker of Rutgers University, who studies how states pay for their public schools.[2] "[They] raise vastly different amounts of local revenue based on their local bases, and [Illinois] really doesn't put much effort into counterbalancing that."

To be fair, Illinois gives more money to Ridge than it does to Rondout. It's just not nearly enough to level the playing field.

This tale of two schools isn't specific to Illinois. It plays out across the U.S., with kids the same age, in the same grade attending schools that try to educate them with wildly different resources. On average, New York, Alaska, and Wyoming each spent more than $17,000 per student in 2013, while California, Oklahoma and Nevada spent roughly half that.

. . .

Here's one cause for alarm: The achievement gap between this nation's wealthiest and poorest students is growing dramatically, not shrinking.[3]

We'll begin . . . with a question . . . :

"How do we pay for our schools?"

And the answer starts with Satan.

Yes, that Satan.

. . .

In 1647, Massachusetts Bay colonists were worried. New neighbors were arriving, and many could not read. Puritans considered literacy key to the survival of their faith: Teach every child to read so that every child can read the Bible.

And so the colony created a remarkable new law. It began, "It being one chief project of that old deluder, Satan, to keep men from the knowledge of the Scriptures . . . " and ended with a mandate: that towns of more than 50 families hire a teacher. The law also required that the teacher's wages be paid for "either by the parents or masters of such children, or by the inhabitants in general."

"This law reflected the idea that the local community was responsible for the well-being of all children, not just out of a sense of altruism but because the whole community depended on it," says Ben Justice, a professor of education history at Rutgers.

Fast forward 369 years, give or take a few months.

Today, our school funding system is infinitely more complex, but still based on that one, powerful idea — that education is a public good, and paying for it could be considered a public obligation.

In the U.S., school funding comes from a combination of three sources. The balance varies from state to state but, on average, looks like this: 45 percent local money, 45 percent from the state and 10 percent federal.[4]

Which brings us back to where we began this story: Why is it that one Chicago-area district has $9,794 to spend on each of its students, while another, nearby district has three times that?

Two words: property tax.

These days, when we ask "the inhabitants in general" to help pay for their schools, we usually start with local property taxes. That's nothing new. The property tax is an old idea, older than America itself.

The problem with a school-funding system that relies so heavily on local property taxes is straightforward: Property values vary a lot from neighborhood to neighborhood, district to district. And with them, tax revenues.

To help poorer schools compensate for that local imbalance, some states have stepped in. In 2013, North Carolina provided two-thirds of its schools' funding.

"If we didn't have that, we'd be in pretty dire straits right now," says Rodney Shotwell, superintendent of Rockingham County Schools, a low-income, rural district along the state's northern border with Virginia.

This year, Rockingham got more than $5 million in extra state funding for its disadvantaged students. Shotwell says that money helped pay for teachers, instructional supplies, even custodians.

But North Carolina is the exception, not the rule.

Most of the nation's superintendents and principals will tell you that whether they can afford a year-round art teacher or new textbooks depends at least in part on the property wealth around them. Just ask Tramene Maye.

. . .

Maye is the principal of Livingston Junior High School in rural western Alabama. Most of his students come from low-income families. Sumter County is farm country, and what isn't farmland is timberland. In Alabama, both are lightly taxed. Maye gives us a guided tour of the results:

"In the girls restroom, they may have four or five stalls, but only one works," he says.

One room, no longer a classroom, leaks when it rains. Garbage cans catch some of the water, but the buckled floor and smell of mold suggest they miss plenty. Around the school, there are broken windows, peeling paint and cracked floors.

Again, some states send extra dollars to districts like Sumter that serve lots of low-income students, to help level the playing field, but Alabama isn't one of them.

Jewel Townsend is a star student at Sumter Central High, which is in better shape than the junior high. Still, she says it's hard when she travels and sees the buildings and sports facilities that other schools have.

"I see that Sumter County doesn't have that," Jewel says, her voice catching. "It's like, 'Wow, really? Why can't we have that?'"

In 2011, plaintiffs from Sumter tried to prove that the state's school funding system wasn't just unfair but was also racially discriminatory. In addition to being mainly low-income, all of Sumter's students are African-American.

A federal judge excoriated Alabama's funding system in an 800-page opinion. Still, he found the plaintiffs were not entitled to relief from the court.[5]

. . .

Of the many funding lawsuits that have played out in the nation's courts, one stands out: *San Antonio Independent School District v. Rodriguez.*

The suit, which made it to the U.S. Supreme Court, struck at the heart of the nation's school-funding system.

It was filed by Demetrio Rodriguez and other parents in Edgewood, a largely poor, Latino school district in San Antonio.[6] Edgewood is across town from a largely white district that, back then, had some of the best-funded schools in Texas.

Rodriguez's sons attended an elementary school where the third floor had been condemned. It lacked books, and many teachers weren't certified.

The plaintiffs argued that any school-funding system that depends on local property tax revenue is fundamentally unfair to poorer districts.

Specifically, the suit claimed, the way we pay for our schools violates the U.S. Constitution's equal protection clause, which says that no state shall "deny to any person within its jurisdiction the equal protection of the laws."

This was 1973, nearly 20 years after the Supreme Court used the equal protection clause to justify an end to racial segregation in America's schools.

In his decision in the landmark *Brown v. Board of Education* case,* Chief Justice Earl Warren wrote:

> "It is doubtful that any child may reasonably be expected to succeed in life if he is denied the opportunity of an education. Such an opportunity, where the state has undertaken to provide it, is a right which must be made available to all on equal terms."

The *Rodriguez* plaintiffs considered their lawsuit a natural extension of *Brown*: that disparities in school funding prevent America's students from getting that opportunity of an education on "equal terms."

The nation's schools had become more racially integrated, certainly, but were still profoundly segregated: Poor kids, black and white alike, found themselves clustered in largely poor schools.

In a split 5-4 decision, the Supreme Court ruled against Rodriguez, saying there is no right to equal funding in education under the U.S. Constitution. Not that the system is fair or balanced — just that the federal government has no obligation to make it so.

In his forceful dissent, Justice Thurgood Marshall wrote, "I cannot accept such an emasculation of the Equal Protection Clause in the context of this case."[7]

It was a turning point in the school funding debate.

"As a result of Rodriguez, the federal courts essentially washed their hands of the problem. And they turned it over to the states," says Michael Rebell, executive director of the Campaign for Educational Equity at Teachers College, Columbia University.

. . .

Across the country, schools in low-wealth districts face tough choices. Not only do they struggle to raise money locally, but many saw drastic cuts in state funding during and after the Great Recession.

According to [a] study from the Center on Budget and Policy Priorities, at least 31 states spent less money per student in 2014 than they did in 2008.[8] During that time, the study found, local funding also dropped in 18 states.

To make ends meet, schools are cutting back everywhere they can. And some are hitting bone.

The rural Coolidge Unified School District, southeast of Phoenix, had already cut its arts and music classes as well as its librarians. But that wasn't enough. The district still struggled to attract and keep good teachers — because it couldn't pay them well.

---

*Excerpts from the ruling in *Brown v. Board of Education* appear in Part VII of this volume.

So, Coolidge shaved a day off its school week. On Fridays, the district's teachers and students stay home. Because the schools are locked tight.

"To achieve savings," says Superintendent Charie Wallace, "we couldn't have people flipping on lights or turning on a computer."

The promise of a regular three-day weekend and a modest salary hike cut the district's teacher turnover rate in half this year.

"Anything I can do to pay teachers," Wallace says, "because they are the key to student achievement. They are the ones that deliver the goods."

That may explain why nearly 1 in 5 Arizona districts now uses the four-day school week.

. . .

And then there's Tiffany Anderson, the superintendent of Jennings School District just outside St. Louis, not far from Ferguson, Mo. She says many of her students come from poverty, and she's got to stretch the money she gets to help them.

"Every principal has to meet with me every month, and they have to justify how they spent every dollar," Anderson says.

She walks the walk, too. The crosswalk.

Every morning, she plays the role of crossing guard, walking kids across the street in front of one of the district's nine schools.

"The members of my staff, including myself, we have maybe 10 different roles that we juggle," Anderson says. "It's a way to really maximize that budget so we can divert dollars into the classroom."

Anderson isn't just about cutting costs, either; she's creative about finding new money. She put donated washers and dryers in some of her schools. Parents can use them in exchange for volunteering an hour in the classroom.

She has even forged some powerful outside partnerships to help pay for a district homeless shelter, health clinic and food pantry.

It's a double whammy for educators like Anderson who serve kids living in poverty: They often have less local money to work with but higher costs than other, more affluent districts. Kids can't check their poverty at the classroom door.

. . .

We began with the question: "How do we pay for our schools?"

We've traveled now from that old deluder, Satan, to segregation. From a leaky ceiling in rural Alabama to a four-day school week in Arizona. From $9,794 to $28,639.

What does it all add up to?

To be sure, many parents who live in districts that can and do spend lavishly to educate their children argue that the system works just fine. And they're not wrong. It's working *there*. But it's not working everywhere.

NOTES

1. "School Finance." *Education Week Research Center, 2016.* https://www.edweek.org/media/school-finance-education-week-quality-counts-2016.pdf.
2. *School Funding Fairness*, Rutgers University and Education Law Center, 2018, www.schoolfundingfairness.org/.

3. Reardon, Sean F. "The Widening Academic Achievement Gap between the Rich and the Poor." *Community Investments*, vol. 24, no. 2, 2012. pp. 19-39.

4. US Census Bureau. "2016 Public Elementary-Secondary Education Finance Data." *2016 Public Elementary-Secondary Education Finance*, 17 May 2018, www.census.gov/data/tables/2016/econ/school-finances/secondary-education-finance.html.

5. *Lynch et al. v. State of Alabama*, Case 5:08-cv-00450-CLS, Document 296, United States District Court Northern District of Alabama. Entered . 7 Nov. 2011. Available at: www.govinfo.gov/content/pkg/USCOURTS-alnd-5_08-cv-00450/pdf/USCOURTS-alnd-5_08-cv-00450-3.pdf.

6. Ayala, Elaine. "Rodriguez, Who Fought for Equality, Dies at 87." *San Antonio Express-News*, 23 Apr. 2013. http://www.mysanantonio.com/news/local_news/article/Rodriguez-who-fought-for-equality-dies-at-87-4456618.php.

7. San Antonio Independent School District v. Rodriguez, 411 U.S. 1 (1973) Thurgood Marshall. Dissenting opinion. Available at: documents.routledge-interactive.s3.amazonaws.com/9780415506434/document10.pdf.

8. Leachman, Michael, et al. "Most States Have Cut School Funding, and Some Continue Cutting." *Center on Budget and Policy Priorities*, www.cbpp.org/research/state-budget-and-tax/most-states-have-cut-school-funding-and-some-continue-cutting.

10   The New Face of Hunger
Tracie McMillan

On a gold-gray morning in Mitchell County, Iowa, Christina Dreier sends her son, Keagan, to school without breakfast. He is three years old, barrel-chested, and stubborn, and usually refuses to eat the free meal he qualifies for at preschool. Faced with a dwindling pantry, Dreier has decided to try some tough love: If she sends Keagan to school hungry, maybe he'll eat the free breakfast, which will leave more food at home for lunch.

Dreier knows her gambit might backfire, and it does. Keagan ignores the school breakfast on offer and is so hungry by lunchtime that Dreier picks through the dregs of her freezer in hopes of filling him and his little sister up. She shakes the last seven chicken nuggets onto a battered baking sheet, adds the remnants of a bag of Tater Tots and a couple of hot dogs from the fridge, and slides it all into the oven. She's gone through most of the food she got last week from a local food pantry; her own lunch will be the bits of potato left on the kids' plates. "I eat lunch if there's enough," she says. "But the kids are the most important. They have to eat first."

The fear of being unable to feed her children hangs over Dreier's days. She and her husband, Jim, pit one bill against the next—the phone against the rent against the heat against the gas—trying always to set aside money to make up for what they can't get from the food pantry or with their food stamps, issued by the Supplemental Nutrition Assistance Program (SNAP). Congressional cuts to SNAP last fall of $5 billion pared her benefits from $205 to $172 a month.

On this particular afternoon Dreier is worried about the family van, which is on the brink of repossession. She and Jim need to open a new bank account so they can make automatic payments instead of scrambling to pay in cash. But that will happen only if Jim finishes work early. It's peak harvest time, and he often works until eight at night, applying pesticides on commercial farms for $14 an hour. Running the errand would mean forgoing overtime pay that could go for groceries.

It's the same every month, Dreier says. Bills go unpaid because, when push comes to shove, food wins out. "We have to eat, you know," she says, only the slightest hint of resignation in her voice. "We can't starve."

• • •

Tracie McMillan is an investigative reporter who covers America's multiracial working class. Since her 2012 *New York Times* bestseller *The American Way of Eating: Undercover at Walmart, Applebee's, Farm Fields and the Dinner Table*, she has written extensively on food as a social issue.

Originally appeared in *National Geographic Magazine*. Reprinted with permission from Tracie McMillan/ National Geographic Creative.

Chances are good that if you picture what hunger looks like, you don't summon an image of someone like Christina Dreier: white, married, clothed, and housed, even a bit overweight. The image of hunger in America today differs markedly from Depression-era images of the gaunt-faced unemployed scavenging for food on urban streets. "This is not your grandmother's hunger," says Janet Poppendieck, a sociologist at the City University of New York. "Today more working people and their families are hungry because wages have declined."

In the United States more than half of hungry households are white, and two-thirds of those with children have at least one working adult—typically in a full-time job. With this new image comes a new lexicon: In 2006 the U.S. government replaced "hunger" with the term "food insecure" to describe any household where, sometime during the previous year, people didn't have enough food to eat. By whatever name, the number of people going hungry has grown dramatically in the U.S., increasing to 48 million by 2012—a five-fold jump since the late 1960s, including an increase of 57 percent since the late 1990s. Privately run programs like food pantries and soup kitchens have mushroomed too. In 1980 there were a few hundred emergency food programs across the country; today there are 50,000. Finding food has become a central worry for millions of Americans. One in six reports running out of food at least once a year. In many European countries, by contrast, the number is closer to one in 20.

To witness hunger in America today is to enter a twilight zone where refrigerators are so frequently bare of all but mustard and ketchup that it provokes no remark, inspires no embarrassment. Here dinners are cooked using macaroni-and-cheese mixes and other processed ingredients from food pantries, and fresh fruits and vegetables are eaten only in the first days after the SNAP payment arrives. Here you'll meet hungry farmhands and retired schoolteachers, hungry families who are in the U.S. without papers and hungry families whose histories stretch back to the *Mayflower*. Here pocketing food from work and skipping meals to make food stretch are so common that such practices barely register as a way of coping with hunger and are simply a way of life.

It can be tempting to ask families receiving food assistance, If you're really hungry, then how can you be—as many of them are—overweight? The answer is "this paradox that hunger and obesity are two sides of the same coin," says Melissa Boteach, vice president of the Poverty and Prosperity Program of the Center for American Progress, "people making trade-offs between food that's filling but not nutritious and may actually contribute to obesity." For many of the hungry in America, the extra pounds that result from a poor diet are collateral damage—an unintended side effect of hunger itself.

• • •

As the face of hunger has changed, so has its address. The town of Spring, Texas, is where ranchland meets Houston's sprawl, a suburb of curving streets and shade trees and privacy fences. The suburbs are the home of the American dream, but they are also a place where poverty is on the rise. As urban housing has gotten more expensive, the working poor have been pushed out. Today hunger in the suburbs is growing faster than in cities, having more than doubled since 2007.

Yet in the suburbs America's hungry don't look the part either. They drive cars, which are a necessity, not a luxury, here. Cheap clothes and toys can be found at yard sales and thrift shops, making a middle-class appearance affordable. Consumer electronics can be bought on installment plans, so the hungry rarely lack phones or televisions. Of all the suburbs in the country, northwest Houston is one of the best places to see how people live on what might be called a minimum-wage diet: It has one of the highest percentages of households receiving SNAP assistance where at least one family member holds down a job. The Jefferson sisters, Meme and Kai, live here in a four-bedroom, two-car-garage, two-bath home with Kai's boyfriend, Frank, and an extended family that includes their invalid mother, their five sons, a daughter-in-law, and five grandchildren. The house has a rickety desktop computer in the living room and a television in most rooms, but only two actual beds; nearly everyone sleeps on mattresses or piles of blankets spread out on the floor.

Though all three adults work full-time, their income is not enough to keep the family consistently fed without assistance. The root problem is the lack of jobs that pay wages a family can live on, so food assistance has become the government's—and society's—way to supplement low wages. The Jeffersons receive $125 in food stamps each month, and a charity brings in meals for their bedridden matriarch.

Like most of the new American hungry, the Jeffersons face not a total absence of food but the gnawing fear that the next meal can't be counted on. When Meme shows me the family's food supply, the refrigerator holds takeout boxes and beverages but little fresh food. Two cupboards are stocked with a smattering of canned beans and sauces. A pair of freezers in the garage each contain a single layer of food, enough to fill bellies for just a few days. Meme says she took the children aside a few months earlier to tell them they were eating too much and wasting food besides. "I told them if they keep wasting, we have to go live on the corner, beg for money, or something."

Jacqueline Christian is another Houston mother who has a full-time job, drives a comfortable sedan, and wears flattering clothes. Her older son, 15-year-old Ja'Zarrian, sports bright orange Air Jordans. There's little clue to the family's hardship until you learn that their clothes come mostly from discount stores, that Ja'Zarrian mowed lawns for a summer to get the sneakers, that they're living in a homeless shelter, and that despite receiving $325 in monthly food stamps, Christian worries about not having enough food "about half of the year."

Christian works as a home health aide, earning $7.75 an hour at a job that requires her to crisscross Houston's sprawl to see her clients. Her schedule, as much as her wages, influences what she eats. To save time she often relies on premade food from grocery stores. "You can't go all the way home and cook," she says.

On a day that includes running a dozen errands and charming her payday loan officer into giving her an extra day, Christian picks up Ja'Zarrian and her seven-year-old, Jerimiah, after school. As the sun drops in the sky, Jerimiah begins complaining that he's hungry. The neon glow of a Hartz Chicken Buffet appears up the road, and he starts in: Can't we just get some gizzards, please?

Christian pulls into the drive-through and orders a combo of fried gizzards and okra for $8.11. It takes three declined credit cards and an emergency loan from her mother, who lives nearby, before she can pay for it. When the food finally arrives, filling the car with the smell of hot grease, there's a collective sense of relief. On the drive back to the shelter the boys eat until the gizzards are gone, and then drift off to sleep.

Christian says she knows she can't afford to eat out and that fast food isn't a healthy meal. But she'd felt too stressed—by time, by Jerimiah's insistence, by how little money she has—not to give in. "Maybe I can't justify that to someone who wasn't here to see, you know?" she says. "But I couldn't let them down and not get the food."

• • •

Of course it is possible to eat well cheaply in America, but it takes resources and know-how that many low-income Americans don't have. Kyera Reams of Osage, Iowa, puts an incredible amount of energy into feeding her family of six a healthy diet, with the help of staples from food banks and $650 in monthly SNAP benefits. A stay-at-home mom with a high school education, Reams has taught herself how to can fresh produce and forage for wild ginger and cranberries. When she learned that SNAP benefits could be used to buy vegetable plants, she dug two gardens in her yard. She has learned about wild mushrooms so she can safely pick ones that aren't poisonous and has lobbied the local library to stock field guides to edible wild plants.

"We wouldn't eat healthy at all if we lived off the food-bank food," Reams says. Many foods commonly donated to—or bought by—food pantries are high in salt, sugar, and fat. She estimates her family could live for three months on the nutritious foods she's saved up. The Reamses have food security, in other words, because Kyera makes procuring food her full-time job, along with caring for her husband, whose disability payments provide their only income.

But most of the working poor don't have the time or know-how required to eat well on little. Often working multiple jobs and night shifts, they tend to eat on the run. Healthful food can be hard to find in so-called food deserts—communities with few or no full-service groceries. Jackie Christian didn't resort to feeding her sons fried gizzards because it was affordable but because it was easy. Given the dramatic increase in cheap fast foods and processed foods, when the hungry have money to eat, they often go for what's convenient, just as better-off families do.

• • •

It's a cruel irony that people in rural Iowa can be malnourished amid forests of corn-stalks running to the horizon. Iowa dirt is some of the richest in the nation, even bringing out the poet in agronomists, who describe it as "black gold." In 2007 Iowa's fields produced roughly one-sixth of all corn and soybeans grown in the U.S., churning out billions of bushels.

These are the very crops that end up on Christina Dreier's kitchen table in the form of hot dogs made of corn-raised beef, Mountain Dew sweetened with corn syrup, and chicken nuggets fried in soybean oil. They're also the foods that the U.S. government supports the most. In 2012 it spent roughly $11 billion to subsidize and insure commodity crops like corn and soy, with Iowa among the states receiving the highest subsidies. The government spends much less to bolster the production of the fruits and vegetables its own nutrition guidelines say should make up half the food on our plates. In 2011 it spent only $1.6 billion to subsidize and insure "specialty crops"—the bureaucratic term for fruits and vegetables.

Those priorities are reflected at the grocery store, where the price of fresh food has risen steadily while the cost of sugary treats like soda has dropped. Since the early 1980s the real cost of fruits and vegetables has increased by 24 percent. Meanwhile the cost of nonalcoholic beverages—primarily sodas, most sweetened with corn syrup—has dropped by 27 percent.

"We've created a system that's geared toward keeping overall food prices low but does little to support healthy, high-quality food," says global food expert Raj Patel. "The problem can't be fixed by merely telling people to eat their fruits and vegetables, because at heart this is a problem about wages, about poverty."

When Christina Dreier's cupboards start to get bare, she tries to persuade her kids to skip snack time. "But sometimes they eat saltine crackers, because we get that from the food bank," she said, sighing. "It ain't healthy for them, but I'm not going to tell them they can't eat if they're hungry."

The Dreiers have not given up on trying to eat well. Like the Reamses, they've sown patches of vegetables and a stretch of sweet corn in the large green yard carved out of the cornfields behind their house. But when the garden is done for the year, Christina fights a battle every time she goes to the supermarket or the food bank. In both places healthy foods are nearly out of reach. When the food stamps come in, she splurges on her monthly supply of produce, including a bag of organic grapes and a bag of apples. "They love fruit," she says with obvious pride. But most of her food dollars go to the meat, eggs, and milk that the food bank doesn't provide; with noodles and sauce from the food pantry, a spaghetti dinner costs her only the $3.88 required to buy hamburger for the sauce.

What she has, Christina says, is a kitchen with nearly enough food most of the time. It's just those dicey moments, after a new bill arrives or she needs gas to drive the kids to town, that make it hard. "We're not starved around here," she says one morning as she mixes up powdered milk for her daughter. "But some days, we do go a little hungry."

11 "I am Alena": Life as a Trans Woman Where Survival Means Living as Christopher

Ed Pilkington

At 8pm on Sunday, Alena Bradford will settle down like millions of other Americans in front of her TV set for the start of *I Am Cait*, the reality show following the gender transition[1] of Olympic gold medalist Caitlyn Jenner. The eight-part series on the E! channel will tell a story, as Jenner puts it, "about getting to be who you really are."

It promises to be a gripping viewing experience, given the controversial and deeply personal nature of its subject matter. But there will be few people across the country who will be watching quite as intensely as Alena.

If Jenner has become today's figurehead for an elite gender transition, in her case from sporting male hero to female pin-up on the cover of *Vanity Fair*,[2] Alena represents those who have been left behind. To her family and associates in her south Georgia town she is Christopher, an African American man with a round face, pronounced cheekbones and short black hair.

But that isn't who she is at all.

"I am Alena," she says in an unconscious echo of the title of Jenner's TV series. "I may not be externally, but I am Alena. Unfortunately, I live as Christopher."

Alena is one of tens of thousands of trans people across the United States still forced to live in the gender they were assigned at birth, stuck in a half-life in mid-transition. It's a lonely and dangerous place to be, as Caitlyn Jenner pointed out[3] in her ESPY awards speech[4] last week. "They're getting bullied, they're getting beaten up, they're getting murdered and they're committing suicide. The numbers are staggering, but they are the reality of what it's like to be trans today."

Alena's reality is that through a combination of her mother's disapproval, the threat of violence in her deep south community, joblessness and an almost complete lack of medical care, she finds herself at the age of 21 still living in a male body that she considers nothing but a "shell."

"Nothing in me feels like Christopher," she says. Yet she dresses as a man, answers to the name of Christopher and plays a role that feels—day by day, hour by hour—to be existentially wrong. "It's hard trying to be something you're not in order to please people around you. I'm trapped," she says.

Ed Pilkington is chief reporter for *Guardian US*. He is the author of *Beyond the Mother Country*.

She lives in Albany, Georgia,[5] a town of about 70,000 in the far south of the state where every street corner appears to boast an evangelical church, with prevailing social attitudes to match. "This is a Bible belt city," Alena says. "People are supposed to live by the Bible here, so it's different."

Until six months ago, Alena lived in Atlanta, Georgia's capital. She moved there when she was 18 after her mother kicked her out of the house having discovered that Alena—Christopher to her—was transgender. She came across a vial of hormone pills that Alena was taking at the start of transition, and the realization dawned on her.

Alena had known she was sexually attracted to men from a young age, about six years old she thinks. But it wasn't until high school where she made friends with a trans girl named Coco that she made the connection.

"I'm curious, so I asked Coco what being transgender was and she explained, and that was the moment I realized I wasn't a gay male, I was trans. I finally had a word for it. I knew what I'd always been feeling."

After her mother cast her out, Alena made a journey familiar to many trans people in the deep south—to the north. Eighteen months in the big city put Alena well on the road to achieving Caitlyn Jenner's challenge: getting to be who she really is. In Atlanta's more permissive environment she began to build a life as a woman. She had a job working in a call center, rented her own small apartment, and acquired a small circle of trans friends who encouraged her to present herself outwardly as Alena.

They did her makeup, told her to be strong, to be true to herself. She was amazed by her own transformation in Atlanta. "I didn't realize how whole living as a woman made me feel, dressing up and going out that way. I may not have been the cutest thing, but I felt at peace. I felt this is me."

Then last year she lost her job as a result of company cutbacks, and the whole edifice instantly crumbled. No job meant no apartment. Desperate to cling to her new life, she began sleeping in her car, but there was only so long she could go without a regular meal or shower. A month into her nomadic lifestyle, she realized she had to decide: continue living in a car as Alena, or go home to Albany as Christopher.

"I was saying I would never go back home, never, but God has a funny way of making you eat your words and swallow your pride. Here I am back at my mom's—one of the conditions of staying here is that she will not allow me to live as Alena. I want somewhere to stay? Then I live as Christopher."

And that's how it is. When we meet she is dressed in a pair of army-style camouflage pants and a tank top, a black headscarf covering up her hair that she finds distressingly male.

"It has broken my heart," she says about her return to Albany. "I feel defeated."

Two Names, Two Lives

In the small apartment she shares with her mother and younger brother, Alena keeps only male clothes. When she first started buying women's clothes her mother got mad and threw them in the trash can. Alena bought replacements, only to have her mother throw those away too. "We went back and forth for a bit until I got sick of arguing about it," she says.

The irony is that Alena sees her mother as her role model, as the woman she wants to become. "Though we have a very up and down relationship, she's my biggest inspiration, she is the person I aspire to be. My mother raised two boys on her own without ever complaining. I want to be strong like her."

Alena has told this to her mother. "She's flattered, and she isn't. She's flattered that I want to be like her, but isn't that I want to be her."

Alena's mother declined to be interviewed [for this article].

Alena has no illusions now: she won't persuade her mother to change. So to avoid another fight she keeps her women's clothes at the house of the person she calls her "gay mom," a drag queen called Nakia who acts as her mentor and guide. She has a couple of dresses and wigs and some high-heeled shoes stashed away in Nakia's cupboard.

Most of the time, Alena has to make do with knowing who she is inside while everyone else around her thinks she is the opposite. She runs two separate Facebook pages, one sanitized version as Christopher for her non-accepting family, the second as Alena where she posts her more personal thoughts.

Even when she's with Nakia she won't go out in public dressed as a woman. She knows that having only partially completed hormone treatment, she still looks like a man, or as she puts it: "My shoulders are too broad, my breasts aren't big enough for the size I am. The way I am now, I look like a football player walking down the road in a dress, and that's not a great idea in Albany."

Her mother's disapproval—in part inspired by her religious upbringing—is not unusual in these parts. It's the norm, Alena suggests. "It's how pretty much everybody thinks in south Georgia. If you're born a man you should stay a man, if you're a woman you should stay a woman."

The few times she did venture out onto the street as a woman it ended badly. "I got cat-called. They hollered as I walked down the street: 'Faggot! You're a faggot! [If] I had my gun I would shoot you.' It made me not want to come out dressed like that anymore."

Living as Themselves, and Living in Fear

The name-calling Alena can cope with. But it's more than that. It's life-threatening.

At least 10 trans women,[6] most of them black,[7] have been murdered this year and transgender rights groups describe the epidemic of violence and sexual assault as a national crisis.* Caitlyn Jenner raised the issue at the ESPYs, talking about Mercedes William, a 17-year-old trans girl whose body was found riddled with stab marks in a field in Mississippi

---

*This article appeared July 2015. By the end of that year, advocates had tracked 21 reported transgender homicide victims, nearly all trans women of color, the highest annual number since such statistics had been kept, according to the Human Rights Campaign. These numbers have continued to increase, with 29 recorded homicides in 2017, another peak year. (See https://www.hrc.org/resources/violence-against-the-transgender-community-in-2018.)

last month. This week, India Clarke, a trans woman in Tampa, Florida, was found dead with signs of blunt force trauma[8] on her torso; police have launched a murder investigation.

Dee Dee Chamblee, a member of the Transgender Law Center's Positively Trans project who lives in Atlanta, said: "In the country towns of south Georgia there are a lot of trans women whose lives are in danger every day. They are having to hide their identity, knowing that if their community finds out they become the target."

Alena herself knows from experience how dangerous it is in Albany to be visibly transgender. She is scared that if she gets discovered when she is out in the street she will find herself in a near-death or fatal situation. A few years ago she made a rare foray out into the town as Alena and was set upon by a group of men.

"I put on a dress and wig and some heels and accessories, and went out. A guy tried to talk to me in a bar. As soon as he started hitting on me I told him, I'm not what you're looking for. But he got mad, and he and his friends jumped on me."

She says the experience has left her wary of appearing in public. "You don't know how far these people are going to go. At that moment I truly understood why trans women are so scared—I didn't trick him and he jumped on me because he hated the fact that he was attracted to me. That's terrifying."

The attack has also made her determined to become "passable"—that is, to come across so convincingly as a woman that no stranger would be able to tell she is transgender. That's the only way she will ever be able to live as Alena, she believes, without forever looking over her shoulder.

But to be able to pass, she requires a steady, affordable supply of prescription hormones—something impossible to come by in Albany.

Alena finds herself in a double-bind that makes securing affordable prescription hormones for transition virtually impossible. She is one of 600,000 Georgians who have been left uninsured for healthcare[9] as a result of the Republican state's refusal to expand Medicaid under Barack Obama's Affordable Care Act[10]—a hardship that she shares with low-income citizens in 19 other states mainly across the deep south.

Even if she were entitled to Medicaid, Georgia—along with 15 other states—specifically excludes health coverage for transition-related treatment, so she wouldn't get anything anyway. A further 26 states have no policies at all regarding transgender health, rendering the system a minefield to negotiate, while only eight states plus Washington DC have reformed the rules to ensure that services are provided.

The state of play is little better with private insurance schemes—10 states plus DC require private policies to cover treatment for transition, the remaining 40 are mute on the subject.

Kellan Baker, a senior fellow at the Center for American Progress, pointed out that "many states exempt Medicaid from treatment for gender dysphoria, ignoring the overwhelming evidence of the medical needs and the psychological impact. That sets up an insurmountable barrier for low-income trans people—and trans people have a very low average income, with surveys showing[11] they suffer twice the unemployment rate of the general population with one in six living on an annual income of $10,000 or less—to finding help from the medical system."

"There's nothing here for me in Albany. Nothing"

Alena is theoretically able to obtain prescription hormones on her mother's insurance. But having scoured Albany and surrounding towns over many months, she has been unable to find a doctor willing to take her on as a patient. She does have a physician in Atlanta, but without Medicaid to pay for the bus, and having traded in her car, she can't afford the 200-mile journey.

"This is a messed-up situation," Alena says with understatement. "I know that resources are out there, that people are willing to help me, but I just can't get to them. There's nothing here for me in Albany. Nothing."

And so, like many transgender individuals, Alena gets her hormones rough-and-ready through the internet. She buys bottles of estradiol, a female sex hormone, for $30 once a month, supplemented when she has the money with Perlutal, a female contraceptive in liquid form that she injects into her muscles.

Sometimes when she needs the drugs quickly she will buy them from other trans women prepared to sell them on the buzzing black market for hormones. No figures exist to indicate the scale of black market hormones in the US, but to those like Dee Dee Chamblee who are active in the community, evidence of the trade is not hard to find.

"It's rampant. Trans women are taking half their hormones and selling the rest on. They are getting all kinds of stuff, taking just about anything to transition their bodies to match up with their minds."

Alena is aware how perilous such do-it-yourself treatment can be, administered entirely in the absence of medical supervision, with scant knowledge of the origins and strengths of the drugs, and with at best intermittent supply.

"I know I don't take hormones like I should. I take a shot when I can get it, and when I have it I take it in double doses, and when I run out I stop taking it. I know that's unhealthy."

Recently, she was present when a trans friend fell sick having injected herself with oestrogen from Mexico. "I was with her when she took the shot. The next day she was in the hospital. I knew then I wasn't taking any more of those shots. How do we know those are human hormones? We don't."

The dangers of bad drugs or medicating yourself at the wrong doses are self-evident. But forgoing the drugs can also carry mortal risks. In addition to the threat of being assaulted on the street because you are not "passable," there is also the danger of self-harm.

A study last year[12] by the National Transgender Discrimination Survey found that the stress and depression associated with failure to transition fully has a terrible cost—the prevalence of suicide attempts is 41% within the trans community, vastly more than the 4.6% of the US population as a whole.

One of the 41% is Alena, who tried to kill herself when she was 15. "It was around the time that I realized I was trans. I felt that my parents would never accept me, that I would never get to live like a woman, and at that point I would rather end my life than have to live like this."

Shedding Her Skin

Today, Alena is arguably no further towards her goal of transition than she was six years ago. What has changed, though, is the clarity of her thinking and her iron-clad determination to transition. She sees it as just a question of time.

On the second day we spend with her, we take Alena clothes shopping so that she can be fully herself just for an hour or two. She buys a $20 red-and-white chiffon dress and a $30 black wig, courtesy of *The Guardian*.

Back at the hotel she puts on her new wardrobe, adding a little lip gloss and mascara. Alena-as-Christopher transforms in front of our eyes into Alena-as-Alena.

"I haven't felt like this in a long time," she says standing in front of the mirror, stroking her long black hair like an adored cat. "I really feel like Alena now. I really do."

She pauses, and then says: "I feel beautiful."

Before she climbs back into her Christopher uniform and we drop her back at her mother's, we ask Alena if she'd be OK taking a walk in her new female clothes, to give us a more intimate sense of the challenges she faces in public.

No, she says gently. She couldn't do that. "I'm not brave enough to endure what would be thrown at me. Not now."

Alena is not there yet. She hasn't got to be who she really is.

But she will. She will get there, she's certain of that. She has it all planned out. First she'll get a job. Then she'll start saving for a security deposit on a home of her own. Finally, when she's ready, she'll leave her mother and shed her male skin.

"As soon as I have the money, I'm gone," she says. "And the minute I'm gone, Christopher is gone."

NOTES

1. Holpuch, A. (2015, June 3). "I Am Cait: Caitlyn Jenner's reality series set to premiere in July." *The Guardian*.
2. Bissinger, B. (2015, July 1). "Caitlyn Jenner: The Full Story." *Vanity Fair*.
3. Gambino, L. (2015, July 16). "Caitlyn Jenner: transgender people 'shouldn't have to take' bullying." *The Guardian*.
4. Daily News Staff. (2015, July 16). "Transcript: Caitlyn Jenner's ESPYs acceptance speech." *Daily News*.
5. The Associated Press, Gainesville, GA. (2015, September 5). "Black couple turns to fair housing law to sue neighbor and city over racial slurs." *The Guardian*.
6. Pilkington, E. (2015, July 4). "LGBT activists call for new focus on violence against transgender community." *The Guardian*.
7. Pilkington, E. (2014, August 1). "Fear and violence in transgender Baltimore: 'It's scary trusting anyone.'" *The Guardian*.
8. Stafford, Z. (2015, July 22). "Florida transgender woman beaten to death is 10th US trans murder in 2015." *The Guardian*.
9. Families U.S.A. (2015, July). "A 50-State Look at Medicaid Expansion." Available at: familiesusa.org/product/50-state-look-medicaid-expansion.

10. Siddiqui, S. (2015, July 1). "Barack Obama to Republican states: 'open your hearts' and expand Medicaid." *The Guardian.*
11. The National Center for Transgender Equality and the National Gay and Lesbian Task Force. (2009, November). "National Transgender Discrimination Survey." Available at: https://transequality.org/sites/default/files/docs/usts/USTS-Full-Report-Dec17.pdf or https://transequality.org/issues/national-transgender-discrimination-survey.
12. Haas, A. P., Rodgers, P. L., and Herman, J. L. (2014, January). "Suicide Attempts among Transgender and Gender Non-Conforming Adults." The Williams Institute. Available at: williamsinstitute.law.ucla.edu/wp-content/uploads/AFSP-Williams-Suicide-Report-Final.pdf.

12 Cause of Death: Inequality
Alejandro Reuss

Inequality Kills

You won't see inequality on a medical chart or a coroner's report under "cause of death." You won't see it listed among the top killers in the United States each year. All too often, however, it is social inequality that lurks behind a more immediate cause of death, be it heart disease or diabetes, accidental injury or homicide. Few of the top causes of death are "equal opportunity killers." Instead, they tend to strike poor people more than rich people, the less educated more than the highly educated, people lower on the occupational ladder more than those higher up, or people of color more than white people.

Statistics on mortality and life expectancy do not provide a perfect map of social inequality. For example, in 2002, the life expectancy for women in the United States was about five years longer than the life expectancy for men, despite the many ways in which women are subordinated to men. Take most indicators of socioeconomic status, however, and most causes of death, and it's a strong bet that you'll find illness and injury (or "morbidity") and mortality increasing as status decreases.

Among people between the ages of 25 and 64, those with less than a high school diploma (or equivalent) had an age-adjusted mortality rate more than three times that of people with at least some college, as of 2003. Those without a high school diploma had more than triple the death rate from chronic noncommunicable diseases (e.g., heart disease), more than 3½ times the death rate from injury, and nearly six times the death rate from HIV/AIDS, compared to those with at least some college. People with incomes below the poverty line were nearly twice as likely to have had an asthma attack in the previous year (among those previously diagnosed with asthma) as people with incomes at least twice the poverty line. Poor people were over 2½ times as likely to suffer from a chronic condition that limited their activity and over three times as likely to characterize their own health as "fair" or "poor" (rather than "good" or "very good"), compared to those with incomes over double the poverty line. African Americans have higher death rates than whites from cancer (¼ higher), heart disease (⅓ higher), stroke (½ higher), diabetes (twice as high), homicide (more than 5 times as high), and AIDS (more than 8 times as

Alejandro Reuss is an historian and economist. He has been a member of the Dollars & Sense collective for nearly 15 years, has served on the editorial committee of NACLA Report on the Americas, and has been a staff member and board member of Bikes Not Bombs (Boston). He teaches at the Labor Relations and Research Center at the University of Massachusetts–Amherst.

high). The infant mortality rate for African Americans was, in 2002–2003, over twice as high as for whites. In all, the lower you are in a social hierarchy, the worse your health and the shorter your life are likely to be.

The Worse Off in the United States Are Not Well Off by World Standards

You often hear it said that even poor people in rich countries like the United States are rich compared to ordinary people in poor countries. While that may be true when it comes to consumer goods like televisions or telephones, which are widely available even to poor people in the United States, it's completely wrong when it comes to health.

In a 1996 study published in the *New England Journal of Medicine*, University of Michigan researchers found that African-American females living to age 15 in Harlem had a 65% chance of surviving to age 65. That is less than the probability at birth of surviving to age 65 for women in India, according to 2000–2005 data. Meanwhile, Harlem's African-American males reaching age 15 had only a 37% chance of surviving to age 65. That is less than the probability at birth of surviving to age 65 for men in Haiti. Among both African-American men and women, diseases of the circulatory system and cancers were the leading causes of death.

It takes more income to achieve a given life expectancy in a rich country like the United States than it does to achieve the same life expectancy in a less affluent country. So the higher money income of a low-income person in the United States, compared to a middle-income person in a poor country, does not necessarily translate into a longer life span. The average income per person in African-American households ($15,200), for example, is about three times the per capita income of Peru. As of 2002, however, the life expectancy for African-American men in the United States was about 69 years, less than the average life expectancy in Peru. The infant mortality rate for African Americans, 13.5 per 1000 live births, is between that of Uruguay and Bulgaria, both of which have per capita incomes around $8,000.

Health Inequalities in the United States Are Not Just About Access to Health Care

Nearly one sixth of the U.S. population below age 65 lacks health insurance of any kind, private or Medicaid. Among those with incomes below 1½ times the poverty line, over 30% lack health coverage of any kind, compared to 10% for those with incomes more than twice the poverty line. African Americans under age 65 were about 1½ times as likely as whites to lack health insurance; Latinos, nearly three times as likely. Among those aged 55 to 64, uninsured people were about ⅔ as likely as insured people to have seen a primary-care doctor in the last year, and less than half as likely to have seen a specialist, as of 2002–2003. Among women over 40, about 55% of those with incomes below the poverty line had gotten a mammogram in the last two years, compared to 75% of those with incomes over twice the poverty line, as of 2003. Obviously, disparities in access to health care are a major health problem.

But so are environmental hazards; communicable diseases; homicide and accidental death; and smoking, lack of exercise, and other risk factors. These dangers all tend to affect lower-income people more than higher-income, less-educated people more than more-educated, and people of color more than whites. African-American children between the ages of 3 and 10 were nearly twice as likely to have had an asthma attack in the last year as white children, among those previously diagnosed with asthma. The frequency of attacks is linked to air pollution. Among people between ages 25 and 64, those without a high school diploma had over five times the death rate from communicable diseases, compared to those with at least some college. African-American men were, as of 2003, more than seven times as likely to fall victim to homicide as white men; African-American women, more than four times as likely as white women. People without a high school diploma (or equivalent) were nearly three times as likely to smoke as those with at least a bachelor's degree, as of 2003. People with incomes below the poverty line were nearly twice as likely to get no exercise as people with incomes over double the poverty line.

Michael Marmot, a pioneer in the study of social inequality and health, notes that so-called diseases of affluence—disorders, like heart disease or diabetes, associated with high-calorie and high-fat diets, lack of physical activity, etc., increasingly typical in rich societies—are most prevalent among the *least* affluent people in these societies. While recognizing the role of such "behavioral" risk factors as smoking in producing poor health, he argues, "It is not sufficient . . . to ask what contribution smoking makes to generating the social gradient in ill health, but we must ask, why is there a social gradient in smoking?" What appear to be individual "lifestyle" decisions often reflect a broader social epidemiology.

Greater Income Inequality Goes Hand in Hand with Poorer Health

Numerous studies suggest that the more unequal the income distribution in a country, state, or city, the lower the life expectancies for people at all income levels. A 1996 study published in the *American Journal of Public Health*, for example, shows that U.S. metropolitan areas with low per capita incomes and low levels of income inequality have lower mortality rates than areas with high median incomes and high levels of income inequality. Meanwhile, for a given per capita income range, mortality rates always decline as inequality declines.

R.G. Wilkinson, perhaps the researcher most responsible for relating health outcomes to overall levels of inequality (rather than individual income levels), argues that greater income inequality causes worse health outcomes independent of its effects on poverty. Wilkinson and his associates suggest several explanations for this relationship. First, the bigger the income gap between rich and poor, the less inclined the well-off are to pay taxes for public services they either do not use or use in low proportion to the taxes they pay. Lower spending on public hospitals, schools, and other basic services does not affect wealthy people's life expectancies very much, but it affects poor people's life expectancies a great deal. Second, the bigger the income gap between rich and poor, the lower the overall level of social cohesion. High levels of social cohesion are associated with good health outcomes for several reasons. For example, people in highly cohesive societies are more likely to be active in their communities, reducing social isolation, a known health risk factor.

Numerous researchers have criticized Wilkinson's conclusions, arguing that the real reason income inequality tends to be associated with worse health outcomes is that it is associated with higher rates of poverty. But even if they are right and income inequality causes worse health simply by bringing about greater poverty, that hardly makes for a defense of inequality. Poverty and inequality are like partners in crime. "Whether public policy focuses primarily on the elimination of poverty or on reduction in income disparity," argue Wilkinson critics Kevin Fiscella and Peter Franks, "neither goal is likely to be achieved in the absence of the other."

Differences in Status May Be Just as Important as Income Levels

Even after accounting for differences in income, education, and other factors, the life expectancy for African Americans is less than that for whites. U.S. researchers are beginning to explore the relationship between high blood pressure among African Americans and the racism of the surrounding society. African Americans tend to suffer from high blood pressure, a risk factor for circulatory disease, more often than whites. Moreover, studies have found that, when confronted with racism, African Americans suffer larger and longer-lasting increases in blood pressure than when faced with other stressful situations. Broader surveys relating blood pressure in African Americans to perceived instances of racial discrimination have yielded complex results, depending on social class, gender, and other factors.

Stresses cascade down social hierarchies and accumulate among the least empowered. Even researchers focusing on social inequality and health, however, have been surprised by the large effects on mortality. Over 30 years ago, Michael Marmot and his associates undertook a landmark study, known as Whitehall I, of health among British civil servants. Since the civil servants shared many characteristics regardless of job classification—an office work environment, a high degree of job security, etc.—the researchers expected to find only modest health differences among them. To their surprise, the study revealed a sharp increase in mortality with each step down the job hierarchy—even from the highest grade to the second highest. Over ten years, employees in the lowest grade were three times as likely to die as those in the highest grade. One factor was that people in lower grades showed a higher incidence of many "lifestyle" risk factors, like smoking, poor diet, and lack of exercise. Even when the researchers controlled for such factors, however, more than half the mortality gap remained.

Marmot noted that people in the lower job grades were less likely to describe themselves as having "control over their working lives" or being "satisfied with their work situation," compared to those higher up. While people in higher job grades were more likely to report "having to work at a fast pace," lower-level civil servants were more likely to report feelings of hostility, the main stress-related risk factor for heart disease. Marmot concluded that "psycho-social" factors—the psychological costs of being lower in the hierarchy—played an important role in the unexplained mortality gap. Many of us have probably said to ourselves, after a trying day on the job, "They're killing me." Turns out it's not just a figure of speech. Inequality kills—and it starts at the bottom.

RESOURCES

Health, United States, 2005, with Chartbook on Trends in the Health of Americans, National Center for Health Statistics, www.cdc.gov/nchs.

Health, United States, 1998, with Socioeconomic Status and Health Chartbook, National Center for Health Statistics, www.cdc.gov/nchs.

Human Development Report 2005, UN Development Programme, hdr.undp.org.

Human Development Report 2000, UN Development Programme, hdr.undp.org.

World Development Indicators 2000, World Bank.

Lisa Berkman, "Social Inequalities and Health: Five Key Points for Policy-Makers to Know," February 5, 2001, Kennedy School of Government, Harvard University.

Ichiro Kawachi, Bruce P. Kennedy, and Richard G. Wilkinson, eds., *The Society and Population Health Reader, Volume I: Income Inequality and Health.* New York: The New Press, 1999.

Michael Marmot, "Social Differences in Mortality: The Whitehall Studies," in Alan D. Lopez, Graziella Caselli, and Tapani Valkonen, eds., *Adult Mortality in Developed Countries: From Description to Explanation.* New York: Oxford University Press, 1995.

Michael Marmot, "The Social Pattern of Health and Disease," in David Blane, Eric Brunner, and Richard Wilkinson, eds., *Health and Social Organization: Towards a Health Policy for the Twenty-First Century.* New York: Routledge, 1996.

Arlne T. Gronimus et al., "Excess Mortality Among Blacks and Whites in the United States," *The New England Journal of Medicine,* 335(21), November 21, 1996.

Nancy Krieger, Ph.D., and Stephen Sidney, M.D., "Racial Discrimination and Blood Pressure: The CARDIA Study of Young Black and White Adults," *American Journal of Public Health,* 86(10), October 1996.

Kevin Fiscella and Peter Franks, "Poverty or Income Inequality as Predictor of Mortality: Longitudinal Cohort Study," *British Medical Journal,* 314(7096): 1724–1727, June 14, 1997.

PART V   SUGGESTIONS FOR FURTHER READING

Albelda, Randy, et al. *Unlevel Playing Fields: Understanding Wage Inequality and Discrimination*, 2nd ed. Economic Affairs Bureau, 2004.

Amott, Theresa L., and Julie Atthaei. *Race, Gender, and Work: A Multi-Cultural History of Women in the United States*, rev. ed. South End Press, 1999.

Aronowitz, Stanley. *How Class Works*. Yale University Press, 2004.

Bergmann, Barbara R. *The Economic Emergence of Women*, 2nd ed. Palgrave Macmillan, 2005.

Brown, Wendy. *Undoing the Demos: Neoliberalism's Stealth Revolution*. Zone Books, 2015.

Cashin, Sheryll. *The Failures of Integration: How Race and Class Are Undermining the American Dream*. PublicAffairs, 2005.

Chang, Grace. *Disposable Domestics: Immigrant Women Workers in the Global Economy*, 2nd ed. Haymarket Books, 2016.

Children's Defense Fund. *The State of America's Children*. Children's Defense Fund. Published annually.

Cooper, Melinda. *Family Values: Between Neoliberalism and the New Social Conservatism*. Zone Books, 2017.

Desmond, Matthew. *Evicted: Poverty and Profit in the American City*. Crown Publishers, 2016.

Domhoff, G. William. *Who Rules America: Power, Politics, and Social Change*. McGraw-Hill, 2006.

Duggan, Lisa. *The Twilight of Equality? Neoliberalism, Cultural Politics, and the Attack on Democracy*. Penguin, 2012.

Edin, Kathryn, and H. Luke Shaefer. *$2.00 a Day: Living on Almost Nothing in America*. Houghton Mifflin Harcourt, 2015.

Ehrenreich, Barbara. *Bait and Switch: The (Futile) Pursuit of the American Dream*. Metropolitan Books, 2005.
_____. *Nickel and Dimed*, 10th anniversary ed. Picador Books, 2011.

Gans, Herbert J. *The War Against the Poor*. Basic Books, 1995.

Glenn, Evelyn Nakano. *Forced to Care: Coercion and Caregiving in America*. Harvard University Press, 2012.

Goldin, Claudia, and Leonard Katz. *The Race Between Education and Technology*. Belknap Press, 2008.

Hacker, Andrew. *Two Nations: Black and White, Separate, Hostile, Unequal*. Scribner, 2003.

Hays, Sharon. *Flat Broke with Children: Women in the Age of Welfare Reform*. Oxford University Press, 2004.

Kessler Harris, Alice. *In Pursuit of Equity: Women, Men, and the Quest for Economic Citizenship in Twentieth-Century America*. Oxford University Press, 2001.

Klein, Naomi. *The Shock Doctrine: The Rise of Disaster Capitalism*. Picador, 2008.

Kozol, Jonathan. *Savage Inequalities: Children in America's Schools*. Crown, 1991.

Krugman, Paul. *End This Depression Now!* Norton, 2012.

MacLean, Nancy. *Freedom Is Not Enough*. Harvard University Press, 2008.

Melamed, Jodi. *Represent and Destroy: Rationalizing Violence in the New Racial Capitalism*. University of Minnesota Press, 2011.

Mishel, Lawrence, et al. *The State of Working America*, 12th ed. ILR Press, 2012.

Newman, Katherine S. *No Shame in My Game: The Working Poor in the Inner City*. Vintage Books, 2000.

New York Times. Class Matters. Times Books, 2005.

Phillips, Kevin. *Wealth in America: A Political History of the American Rich*. Broadway Books, 2002.

Poo, Ai-jen. *The Age of Dignity: Preparing for the Elder Boom in a Changing America.* The New Press, 2015.

Rank, Mark Robert. *One Nation Underprivileged: Why American Poverty Affects Us All.* Oxford University Press, 2005.

Sernau, Scott. *Social Inequality in a Global Age,* 5th ed. Sage Publications, 2017.

Shapiro, Thomas M. *The Hidden Costs of Being African American: How Wealth Perpetuates Inequality.* Oxford University Press, 2003.

Shipler, David K. *The Working Poor: Invisible in America.* Vintage Books, 2005.

Sidel, Ruth. *Unsung Heroines: Single Mothers and the American Dream.* University of California Press, 2006.

Stiglitz, Joseph E. *The Price of Inequality: How Today's Divided Society Endangers Our Future.* Norton, 2012.

Wacquant, Loïc. *Punishing the Poor: The Neoliberal Government of Social Insecurity.* Duke University Press, 2009.

Wolff, Edward N. *A Century of Wealth in America.* Harvard University Press, 2017.

In addition to these books, the websites of the following organizations are good sources for current statistics analyzed in terms of race, class, gender, and sexuality:

Asian Nation: Asian American History, Demographics and Issues: asian-nation.org/index.shtml.

Association on American Indian Affairs: www.indian-affairs.org/.

Children's Defense Fund: www.childrensdefense.org.

Economic Policy Institute: epi.org/.

Institute for Women's Policy Research: www.iwpr.org.

National Committee on Pay Equity: www.pay-equity.org.

National Urban League: www.nul.org.

Pew Research Center: https://www.pewresearch.org/.

United for a Fair Economy: www.faireconomy.org.

U.S. Bureau of Labor Statistics: www.bls.gov.

Williams Institute (independent research on sexual orientation and gender identity law and public policy): williamsinstitute.law.ucla.edu.

PART VI

Living Knowledge and Testimony

A theory in the flesh means one where the physical realities of our lives—our skin color, the land or concrete we grew up on, our sexual longings—all fuse to create a politic born of necessity. Here, we attempt to bridge the contradictions in our experience.

We are the colored in a white feminist movement.

We are the feminists among the people of our culture.

We are often the lesbians among the straight.

We do this bridging by naming our selves and by telling our stories in our own words.

—Cherríe L. Moraga

In the groundbreaking anthology *This Bridge Called My Back: Writings by Radical Women of Color*, Chicana poet and playwright Cherríe Moraga articulated the notion of "theory in the flesh"—theory that emanates from and is applicable to lived experience. Moraga argues that testimony about "flesh and blood experiences," particularly from marginalized voices, contains knowledge and articulates theory that can respond to trauma, facilitate collective healing, and grapple with complexities of identity, oppression, and resistance.[1]

Many of the readings in this volume offer statistics, historical information, and social science analysis, all of which is vital for analyzing race, class, gender, and sexuality in the United States. While statistics can tell us a great deal about life in any given society, they paint only part of the picture. They can tell us that more than 110,000 Japanese Americans were incarcerated in concentration camps during World War II, but they tell us nothing of the lives lived in those camps or of the repercussions years later of that experience. They can tell us the rates of sexualized violence on college campuses, but they cannot convey what it means to survive a sexual assault. Statistics tell a story with numbers, but to translate those numbers into experience, we must turn to living knowledge and testimony.

441

In Selection 1, Cherríe Moraga delves into her own complex identity as a light-skinned ("güera") Chicana lesbian with a Chicana mother and an Anglo father. Her experiences illustrate key critical concepts such as intersectionality, privilege, internalized oppression, and coalition building. She insists that we must face complexity, within ourselves and within our movements: "I think: *what is my responsibility to my roots: both white and brown, Spanish-speaking and English?* I am a woman with a foot in both worlds. I refuse the split. I feel the necessity for dialogue. Sometimes I feel it urgently." Moraga argues that unless "feminists confront their fear of and resistance to each other, . . . we will not survive."

In Selection 2, "Civilize Them with a Stick," Lakota writer Mary Brave Bird describes being torn from her family and community and sent to live at an Indian boarding school that she compares to a penal institution. Her experience combined religious indoctrination and corporal punishment: "All I got out of school was being taught how to pray. I learned quickly that I would be beaten if I failed in my devotions or, God forbid, prayed the wrong way, especially prayed in Indian to Wakan Tanka, the Indian Creator." In Selection 3, Deborah Miranda (an enrolled member of the Ohlone-Costanoan Esselen Nation of California) deconstructs the mythology currently being fed to schoolchildren about the California missions, juxtaposing the "imperialism, racism, and Manifest Destiny" of California's real history with the glorified and glossed-over version offered by the curriculum. "It's time," she argues, "for the Mission Fantasy Fairy Tale to end."

In Selection 4, Yuri Kochiyama tells of her experiences growing up "red, white, and blue" on the West Coast during World War II and then being incarcerated in a concentration camp in Jerome, Arkansas. She details the impact of the FBI arresting her father on the day Pearl Harbor was bombed, of President Roosevelt signing an Executive Order authorizing the removal of Japanese Americans from the West Coast, of families being divided, and of living behind barbed wire. "I was so red, white, and blue, I couldn't believe this was happening to us. America would never do a thing like this to us." The personal and collective experience "showed us that even though there is a Constitution, . . . constitutional rights could be taken away very easily."

In Selection 5, Dhaha Nur, a refugee from Somalia, tells a different story about family separation and uncertainty in the wake of a different Executive Order by a different president. Nur fled civil war at the age of five and became a U.S. citizen two decades later, eager to bring his mother to join him at last in the country he had made his home in her absence. "And 22 years later, it's not a war or even an ocean that forces our separation. It's our nation's president, whose Muslim ban . . . gave the green light to tear families like mine apart." Like Kochiyama, he struggles with the contradictions between "the values the United States aspires to" and policies that seem to run counter to those lofty ideals.

Unlike Nur, Oscar Casares and his family have been in this country for generations. In Selection 6, he describes both pride in his Mexican identity and frustrations with the regular microaggressions he encounters (from being asked "What are you?" to people calling the police on "Mexicans" in suburbia). He writes, "Like many Americans whose families came to this country from somewhere else, many children of Mexican immigrants struggle with their identity, as our push to fully assimilate is met with an even greater pull to remain anchored to our family's country of origin." The personal testimony offered by Casares is a valuable companion piece to Mireya Navarro's essay "For Many Latinos, Racial Identity Is More Culture Than Color" (Selection 8 in Part III of this volume).

In Selection 7, poet Claudia Rankine scrutinizes white people's assumptions about race and grapples with the visceral experiences of those on the receiving end of those assumptions. She uses the second person ("you") to confront readers with the intensity of the frustration experienced in each of these moments: "And yes, you want it to stop, you want the black child pushed to the ground to be seen, to be helped to his feet and be brushed off, not brushed off by the person that did not see him, has never seen him, has perhaps never seen anyone who is not a reflection of himself." The racial microaggressions detailed in these vignettes reveal both the pain felt by the targets of these recurrent aggressions and the obliviousness displayed by the perpetrators who "brush off" the incidents. By telling these stories she refuses invisibility and silencing.

Michael Scarce in Selection 8 recounts a violent sexual assault he experienced in his dorm room as a college student. While he holds the rapist fully accountable for this act of violence, Scarce also identifies the unrelenting homophobia of his fellow students as a contributing factor: "I now blame those 30 floormates for my rape as much as I blame the man who assaulted me. They created and shaped a space, both actively and through negligence, in which I was gagged, effectively silenced and unable to resist." Scarce comes to resist this silencing and becomes an antirape activist, researcher, and organizer. "The atrocities I have experienced provide a lens through which I am better able to see the complexity of injustices around me," he writes, "and I have learned to harness the resulting anger in positive and productive ways that fuel my drive for social change."

In Selection 9, Tommi Avicolli Mecca also delves into the impact of homophobic harassment, beginning with a childhood in Catholic school, and he also comes to resist the silencing imposed upon him as a child. He moves between memoir and poetry to analyze the deployment of labels like "sissy" and "faggot" as tools of control: "If you did something that didn't conform to what was the acceptable behavior of the group, then you risked being called a faggot. . . . It was the most commonly used put-down. It kept guys in line." By the end of the piece he claims pride in defying those forces that tried to keep him in line.

Eric Rodriguez (in Selection 10), Kiese Laymon (in Selection 11), and Chase Strangio (in Selection 12) offer reflective narratives that show us how the intersections of race, class, gender, and sexuality are not static and can produce contradictions when oppression and privilege are simultaneously called into play. Rodriguez analyzes the harm of gentrification in Los Angeles's Echo Park community, while also exploring his own contradictory relationship to the dynamic: "Since moving back here in July 2014, I've had one foot in my former community and the other in this new place I call 'home'—while slowly robbing my uncle of his own." College professor Laymon juxtaposes the privileges afforded by his Vassar faculty ID with the daily micro- and macroaggressions experienced by faculty and students of color: "I'm wondering what price we pay for these kinds of IDs, and what that price has to do with the extrajudicial disciplining and killing of young cis and trans black human beings." ACLU transgender rights attorney Strangio articulates the many contradictions of his own life, experiencing both invisbility and hypervisibility, both oppression and privilege. He emphasizes the complex matrix of intersectional identities: "If I can be erased and attacked, what about my friends and colleagues who are exposed to relentless surveillance, erasure and violence without such protection? What about the trans women of color for whom visibility does not lead to discomfort but to arrest or death?" Strangio also emphasizes the spaces for resistance: "Amidst the scrutiny, the savage violence, the systemic discrimination, there are communities of resistance and resilience that hold each other up."

In Selection 13, Edwidge Danticat concludes Part VI by making profound connnections between the Great Migration of African Americans fleeing the South in the early twentieth century, the 2015 racist massacre of churchgoers in Charleston, South Carolina, and the expulsion of Haitians from the Dominican Republic. Danticat writes, "we are witnessing, once again, a sea of black bodies in motion, in transit, and in danger. . . . And we will keep asking ourselves, When will this end? When will it stop?"

The selections in this part contribute testimony, analysis, and living knowledge from a diverse range of experiences, illustrating in concrete detail some of the consequences of the inequalities documented in earlier parts of this book. These selections also illustrate the need to speak our truths, hear each other's stories, and make connections across differences. As Cherríe Moraga writes, "Without an emotional, heartfelt grappling with the source of our own oppression, without naming the enemy within ourselves and outside of us, no authentic, nonhierarchical connection among oppressed groups can take place."

NOTE

1. "Entering the Lives of Others: Theory in the Flesh," in *This Bridge Called My Back: Writings by Radical Women of Color,* edited by Cherríe Moraga and Gloria Anzaldúa, 4th ed. SUNY Press, 2015, p. 19.

GUIDING QUESTIONS FOR PART VI

1. How do the personal stories in Part VI reflect specific U.S. institutions, policies, and social structures?

2. In the essay about her complex identity, Cherríe Moraga declares, "I refuse the split." What are some of the splits that she refuses? How does the idea of split identities or split allegiances operate in some of the other essays in this part? Does the idea of "refusing the split" apply to your own life? If so, how?

3. Can you identify moments when the authors of readings in this part grapple with the tensions of experiencing oppression and privilege at the same time? How does that dynamic complicate simplistic notions of identity?

4. In "Civilize Them with a Stick," Mary Brave Bird describes the often violent efforts to strip Indigenous identities from children sent to boarding schools. How was such violence justified? How were these efforts resisted?

5. What are some other examples in Part VI of societal forces and mechanisms that seek to suppress the identities of marginalized groups? Based on those examples, can you describe how that suppression is resisted?

6. Deborah Miranda writes, "Human beings have no other way of knowing that we exist, or what we have survived, except through the vehicle of story." What is her critique of the stories told by the California history curriculum about the California missions? Are there stories you recall from your elementary school curriculum that you now question?

7. Several of the writers in this part tell stories about family members. How do the family relationships described in this part convey important insights about race, class, gender, sexuality, and nationality?

8. "Like nearly every black person I know from the deep South who has one of these faculty IDs, I anticipated reckoning daily with white racial supremacy at my job," writes Kiese Laymon. He offers dual lists of "white racial supremacy": both the things he anticipated and the things he did not anticipate. What stories from his essay—and from the other readings in Part VI—fit your expectations or resonated with your own experiences? What stories most surprised you?

9. Michael Scarce's essay ends with a list of concrete strategies for change. What are the strengths and challenges of his recommendations? Can you see these recommendations being implemented at your school? Why or why not?

10. The readings in Part VI offer many examples of conflict and division. Can you identify moments of coalition or collaboration? Can you generate your own suggestions for how to create coalitions across differences? Under what circumstances would such coalitions be effective?

1 La Güera

Cherríe Moraga

It requires something more than personal experience to gain a philosophy or point of view from any specific event. It is the quality of our response to the event and our capacity to enter into the lives of others that help us to make their lives and experiences our own.

—Emma Goldman[1]

I am the very well-educated daughter of a woman who, by the standards in this country, would be considered largely illiterate. My mother was born in Santa Paula, Southern California, at a time when much of the coast and neighboring central valley was still farmland. Nearly thirty-five years later, in 1948, she was the only daughter of six to marry an anglo, my father.

I remember all of my mother's stories, probably much better than she realizes. She is a fine storyteller, recalling every event of her life with the vividness of the present, noting each detail right down to the cut and color of her dress. I remember stories of her being pulled out of school at the ages of five, seven, nine and eleven to work in the fields, along with her brothers and sisters; stories of her father drinking away whatever small profit she was able to make for the family; of her going the long way home to avoid meeting him on the street, staggering toward the same destination. I remember stories of my mother lying about her age in order to get a job as a hat-check girl at Agua Caliente Racetrack in Tijuana. At fourteen, she was the main support of the family. I can still see her walking home alone at 3 a.m., only to turn all of her salary and tips over to her mother, who was pregnant again.

The stories continue through the war years and on: walnut-cracking factories, the Voit Rubber factory, and then the electronics boom. I remember my mother doing piecework for the plant in our neighborhood. In the late evening, she would sit in front of the TV set, wrapping copper wires into the backs of circuit boards, talking about "keeping up with the younger girls." By that time she was already in her mid-fifties.

Cherríe Moraga is an award-winning poet, playwright, and essayist. A leading Chicana feminist theorist, she also helped found the advocacy network La Red Xicana Indígena and coedited *This Bridge Called My Back: Writings by Radical Women of Color.* She was an artist in residence for over 20 years at Stanford University's Department of Theater and Performance Studies and is now a professor at the University of California, Santa Barbara.

Meanwhile, I was college-prep in school. After classes, I would go with my mother to fill out job applications for her, or write checks for her at the supermarket. We would have the scenario all worked out ahead of time. My mother would sign the check before we'd get to the store. Then, as we'd approach the checkstand, she would say—within earshot of the cashier—"oh honey, you go 'head and make out the check," as if she couldn't be bothered with such an insignificant detail. No one asked any questions.

I was educated, and wore it with a keen sense of pride and satisfaction, my head propped up with the knowledge, from my mother, that my life would be easier than hers. I was educated; but more than this, I was "la güera"—fair-skinned. Born with the features of my Chicana mother, but the skin of my anglo father, I had it made.

No one ever quite told me this (that light was right), but I knew that being light was something valued in my family, who were all Chicano, with the exception of my father. In fact, everything about my upbringing, at least what occurred on a conscious level, attempted to bleach me of what color I did have. Although my mother was fluent in Spanish, I was never taught much of it at home. I picked up what I did learn from school and from overheard snatches of conversation among my relatives and mother. She often called other lower-income Mexicans "braceros," or "wet-backs," referring to herself and her family as "a different class of people." And yet, the real story was that my family, too, had been poor (some still are) and farmworkers. My mother can remember this in her blood as if it were yesterday. But this is something she would like to forget (and rightfully), for to her, on a basic economic level, being Chicana meant being "less." It was through my mother's desire to protect her children from poverty and illiteracy that we became "anglocized"; the more effectively we could pass in the white world, the better guaranteed our future.

From all of this, I experience, daily, a huge disparity between what I was born into and what I was to grow up to become. Because, as Goldman suggests, these stories my mother told me crept under my "güera" skin. I had no choice but to enter into the life of my mother. I had no choice. I took her life into my heart, but managed to keep a lid on it as long as I feigned being the happy, upwardly mobile heterosexual.

When I finally lifted the lid to my lesbianism, a profound connection with my mother reawakened in me. It wasn't until I acknowledged and confronted my own lesbianism in the flesh that my heartfelt identification with and empathy for my mother's oppression—due to being poor, uneducated and Chicana—was realized. My lesbianism is the avenue through which I have learned the most about silence and oppression, and it continues to be the most tactile reminder to me that we are not free human beings.

You see, one follows the other. I had known for years that I was a lesbian, had felt It in my bones, had ached with the knowledge, gone crazed with the knowledge, wallowed in the silence of it. Silence is like starvation. Don't be fooled. It's nothing short of that, and felt most sharply when one has had a full belly most of her life. When we are not physically starving, we have the luxury to realize psychic and emotional starvation. It is from this starvation that other starvations can be recognized—if one is willing to take the risk of making the connection—if one is willing to be responsible to the result of the connection. For me, the connection is an inevitable one.

What I am saying is that the joys of looking like a white girl ain't so great since I realized I could be beaten on the street for being a dyke. If my sister's being beaten because she's Black, it's pretty much the same principle. We're both getting beaten any way you look at it. The connection is blatant; and in the case of my own family, the difference in the privileges attached to looking white instead of brown are merely a generation apart.

In this country, lesbianism is a poverty—as is being brown, as is being a woman, as is being just plain poor. The danger lies in ranking the oppressions. *The danger lies in failing to acknowledge the specificity of the oppression.* The danger lies in attempting to deal with oppression purely from a theoretical base. Without an emotional, heartfelt grappling with the source of our own oppression, without naming the enemy within ourselves and outside of us, no authentic, nonhierarchical connection among oppressed groups can take place. When the going gets rough, will we abandon our so-called comrades in a flurry of racist/heterosexist/what-have-you panic? To whose camp, then, should the lesbian of color retreat? Her very presence violates the ranking and abstraction of oppression. Do we merely live hand to mouth? Do we merely struggle with the "ism" that's sitting on top of our heads? The answer is: yes, I think first we do; and we must do so thoroughly and deeply. But to fail to move out from there will only isolate us in our own oppression—will only insulate, rather than radicalize us.

To illustrate: a gay white male friend of mine once confided to me that he continued to feel that, on some level, I didn't trust him because he was male; that he felt, really, if it ever came down to a "battle of the sexes," I might kill him. I admitted that I might very well. He wanted to understand the source of my distrust. I responded, "You're not a woman. Be a woman for a day. Imagine being a woman." He confessed that the thought terrified him because, to him, being a woman meant being raped by men. He *had* felt raped by men; he wanted to forget what that meant. What grew from that discussion was the realization that in order for him to create an authentic alliance with me, he must deal with the primary source of his own sense of oppression. He must, first, emotionally come to terms with what it feels like to be a victim. If he—or anyone—were to truly do this, it would be impossible to discount the oppression of others, except by again forgetting how we have been hurt.

And yet, oppressed groups are forgetting all the time. There are instances of this in the rising Black middle class, and certainly an obvious trend of such "capitalist-unconsciousness" among white gay men. Because to remember may mean giving up whatever privileges we have managed to squeeze out of this society by virtue of our gender, race, class, or sexuality.

Within the women's movement, the connections among women of different backgrounds and sexual orientations have been fragile, at best. I think this phenomenon is indicative of our failure to seriously address some very frightening questions: How have I internalized my own oppression? How have I oppressed? Instead, we have let rhetoric do the job of poetry. Even the word "oppression" has lost its power. We need a new language, better words that can more closely describe women's fear of, and resistance to, one another, words that will not always come out sounding like dogma.

What prompted me in the first place to work on an anthology by radical women of color[2] was a deep sense that I had a valuable insight to contribute, by virtue of my birthright and my background. And yet, I don't really understand first-hand what it feels like being shitted on for being brown. I understand much more about the joys of it. Being

Chicana and having family are synonymous for me. What I know about loving, singing, crying, telling stories, speaking with my heart and hands, even having a sense of my own soul comes from the love of my mother, aunts, cousins . . .

But at the age of twenty-seven, it is frightening to acknowledge that I have internalized a racism and classism, where the object of oppression is not only someone *outside* my skin, but the someone *inside* my skin. In fact, to a large degree, the real battle with such oppression, for all of us, begins under the skin. I have had to confront the fact that much of what I value about being Chicana, about my family, has been subverted by anglo culture and my own cooperation with it. This realization did not occur to me overnight. For example, it wasn't until long after my graduation from the private college I'd attended in Los Angeles that I realized the major reason for my total alienation from, and fear of, my classmates was rooted in class and culture.

Three years after graduation, in an apple orchard in Sonoma, a friend of mine (who comes from an Italian Irish working-class family) says to me, "Cherríe, no wonder you felt like such a nut in school. Most of the people there were white and rich." It was true. All along I had felt the difference, but not until I had put the words "class" and "race" to the experience did my feelings make any sense. For years, I had berated myself for not being as "free" as my classmates. I completely bought that they simply had more guts than I did to rebel against their parents and run around the country hitchhiking, reading books and studying "art." They had enough privilege to be atheists, for chrissake. There was no one around filling in the disparity for me between their parents, who were Hollywood filmmakers, and my parents, who wouldn't know the name of a filmmaker if their lives depended on it; and precisely because their lives didn't depend on it, they couldn't be bothered. But I knew nothing about "privilege" then. White was right. Period. I could pass. If I got educated enough, there would never be no telling.

Three years after that, I had a similar revelation. In a letter to Black feminist, Barbara Smith (whom I had not yet met), I wrote:

> I went to a concert where Ntozake Shange was reading. There, everything exploded for me. She was speaking in a language that I knew, in the deepest parts of me, existed, and that I ignored in my own feminist studies and even in my own writing. What Ntozake caught in me is the realization that in my development as a poet, I have, in many ways, denied the voice of my own brown mother, the brown in me. I have acclimated to the sound of a white language which, as my father represents it, does not speak to the emotions in my poems, emotions which stem from the love of my mother.
>
> The reading was agitating. Made me uncomfortable. Threw me into a week-long terror of how deeply I was affected. I felt that I had to start all over again, that I turned only to the perceptions of white middle-class women to speak for me and all women. I am shocked by my own ignorance.

Sitting in that Oakland auditorium chair was the first time I had realized to the core of me that for years I had disowned the language I knew best. I had ignored the words and rhythms that were the closest to me: the sounds of my mother and aunts gossiping—half in English, half in Spanish—while drinking cerveza in the kitchen. And the hands—I had cut off the hands in my poems. But not in conversation; still the hands could not be kept down. Still they insisted on moving.

The reading had forced me to remember that I knew things from my roots. But to remember puts me up against what I don't know. Shange's reading agitated me because she spoke with power about a world that is both alien and common to me: "the capacity to enter into the lives of others." But you can't just take the goods and run. I knew that then, sitting in the Oakland auditorium (as I know in my poetry), that the only thing worth writing about is what seems to be unknown and, therefore, fearful.

The "unknown" is often depicted in racist literature as the "darkness" within a person. Similarly, sexist writers will refer to fear in the form of the vagina, calling it "the orifice of death." In contrast, it is a pleasure to read works such as Maxine Hong Kingston's *Woman Warrior*, where fear and alienation are depicted as "the white ghosts." And yet, the bulk of literature in this country reinforces the myth that what is dark and female is evil. Consequently, each of us—whether dark, female, or both—has in some way *internalized* this oppressive imagery. What the oppressor often succeeds in doing is simply *externalizing* his fears, projecting them into the bodies of women, Asians, gays, disabled folks, whoever seems most "other."

> call me
> roach and presumptuous
> nightmare on your white pillow
> your itch to destroy
> the indestructible
> part of yourself
>
> —*Audre Lorde*[3]

But it is not really difference the oppressor fears so much as similarity. He fears he will discover in himself the same aches, the same longings as those of the people he has shit on. He fears the immobilization threatened by his own incipient guilt. He fears he will have to change his life once he has seen himself in the bodies of the people he has called different. He fears the hatred, anger and vengeance of those he has hurt.

This is the oppressor's nightmare, but it is not exclusive to him. We women have a similar nightmare, for each of us in some way has been both the oppressed and the oppressor. We are afraid to look at how we have failed each other. We are afraid to see how we have taken the values of our oppressor into our hearts and turned them against ourselves and one another. We are afraid to admit how deeply *the man's* words have been ingrained in us.

To assess the damage is a dangerous act. I think of how, even as a feminist lesbian, I have so wanted to ignore my own homophobia, my own hatred of myself for being queer. I have not wanted to admit that my deepest personal sense of myself has not quite "caught up" with my "woman-identified" politics. I have been afraid to criticize lesbian writers who choose to "skip over" these issues in the name of feminism. In 1979, we talk of "old gay" and "butch and femme" roles as if they were ancient history. We toss them aside as merely patriarchal notions. And yet, the truth of the matter is that I have sometimes taken society's fear and hatred of lesbians to bed with me. I have sometimes hated my lover for loving me. I have sometimes felt "not woman enough" for her. I have sometimes felt "not man enough." For a lesbian trying to survive in a heterosexist society, there is no easy way around these emotions. Similarly, in a white-dominated world, there is little getting around racism and our own internalization of it. It's always there, embodied in someone we least expect to rub up against. When we do rub up against this person, *there* then is the challenge. *There* then is the opportunity to look at the nightmare within us. But we usually shrink from such a challenge.

Time and time again, I have observed that the usual response among white women's groups when the "racism issue" comes up is to deny the difference. I have heard comments like, "Well, we're open to *all* women; why don't they (women of color) come? You can only do so much . . . " But there is seldom any analysis of how the very nature and structure of the group itself may be founded on racist or classist assumptions. More important, so often the women seem to feel no loss, no lack, no absence when women of color are not involved; therefore, there is little desire to change the situation. This has hurt me deeply. I have come to believe that the only reason women of a privileged class will dare to look at *how* it is that *they* oppress, is when they've come to know the meaning of their own oppression. And understand that the oppression of others hurts them personally.

The other side of the story is that women of color and white working-class women often shrink from challenging white middle-class women. It is much easier to rank oppressions and set up a hierarchy than to take responsibility for changing our own lives. We have failed to demand that white women, particularly those who claim to be speaking for all women, be accountable for their racism.

The dialogue has simply not gone deep enough.

In conclusion, I have had to look critically at my claim to color, at a time when, among white feminist ranks, it is a "politically correct" (and sometimes peripherally advantageous) assertion to make. I must acknowledge the fact that, physically, I have had a *choice* about making that claim, in contrast to women who have not had such a choice and have been abused for their color. I must reckon with the fact that for most of my life, by virtue of the very fact that I am white-looking, I identified with and aspired toward white values, and that I rode the wave of that Southern California privilege as far as conscience would let me.

Well, now I feel both bleached and beached. I feel angry about this—about the years when I refused to recognize privilege, both when it worked against me and when I worked it, ignorantly, at the expense of others. These are not settled issues. This is why this work feels so risky to me. It continues to be discovery. It has brought me into contact with women who invariably know a hell of a lot more than I do about racism, as experienced in the flesh, as revealed in the flesh of their writing.

I think: *what is my responsibility to my roots: both white and brown, Spanish-speaking and English?* I am a woman with a foot in both worlds. I refuse the split. I feel the necessity for dialogue. Sometimes I feel it urgently.

But one voice is not enough, nor are two, although this is where dialogue begins. It is essential that feminists confront their fear of and resistance to each other, because without this, there *will* be no bread on the table. Simply, we will not survive. If we could make this connection in our heart of hearts, that if we are serious about a revolution—better, if we seriously believe there should be joy in our lives (real joy, not just "good times")—then we need one another. We women need each other. Because my/your solitary, self-asserting "go-for-the-throat-of-fear" power is not enough. The real power, as you and I well know, is collective. I can't afford to be afraid of you, nor you of me. If it takes head-on collisions, let's do it. This polite timidity is killing us.

As Lorde suggests in the passage I cited earlier, it is in looking to the nightmare that the dream is found. There, the survivor emerges to insist on a future, a vision, yes, born out of what is dark and female. The feminist movement must be a movement of such survivors, a movement with a future.

NOTES

1. Alix Kates Shulman, "Was My Life Worth Living?" *Red Emma Speaks.* New York: Random House, 1972, p. 388.
2. Moraga, Cherríe, and Gloria Anzaldúa. *This Bridge Called My Back: Writings by Radical Women of Color.* Watertown, Mass.: Persephone Press, 1981.
3. From "The Brown Menace or Poem to the Survival of Roaches," *The New York Head Shop and Museum.* Detroit, Mich.: Broadside, 1974, p. 48.

2

Civilize Them with a Stick

Mary Brave Bird (Crow Dog) with Richard Erdoes

Gathered from the cabin, the wickiup, and the tepee,
partly by cajolery and partly by threats,
partly by bribery and partly by force,
they are induced to leave their kindred
to enter these schools and take upon themselves
the outward appearance of civilized life.

—ANNUAL REPORT OF THE DEPARTMENT OF INTERIOR, 1901

It is almost impossible to explain to a sympathetic white person what a typical old Indian boarding school was like; how it affected the Indian child suddenly dumped into it like a small creature from another world, helpless, defenseless, bewildered, trying desperately and instinctively to survive and sometimes not surviving at all. I think such children were like the victims of Nazi concentration camps trying to tell average, middle-class Americans what their experience had been like. Even now, when these schools are much improved, when the buildings are new, all gleaming steel and glass, the food tolerable, the teachers well trained and well-intentioned, even trained in child psychology—unfortunately the psychology of white children, which is different from ours—the shock to the child upon arrival is still tremendous. Some just seem to shrivel up, don't speak for days on end, and have an empty look in their eyes. I know of an eleven-year-old on another reservation who hanged herself, and in our school, while I was there, a girl jumped out of the window, trying to kill herself to escape an unbearable situation. That first shock is always there.

Although the old tiyospaye has been destroyed, in the traditional Sioux families, especially in those where there is no drinking, the child is never left alone. It is always surrounded by relatives, carried around, enveloped in warmth. It is treated with the respect due to any human being, even a small one. It is seldom forced to do anything against its

---

Mary Brave Bird (Crow Dog) (1954–2013) was a Sicangu Lakota writer and activist involved in the American Indian Movement. Her childhood experiences of poverty, brutality, and cultural suppression led her to participate in protests against police violence and to activism promoting a deeper understanding and acceptance of Native American traditions. She wrote extensively about her experiences as a Sioux woman caught between cultures.

Richard Erdoes (1912–2008) was a photographer, artist, writer, and university lecturer who was active in the Native American civil rights movements through the twentieth century. As a writer, he collaborated with many different people to publish and illustrate Native American stories.

will, seldom screamed at, and never beaten. That much, at least, is left of the old family group among full-bloods. And then suddenly a bus or car arrives, full of strangers, usually white strangers, who yank the child out of the arms of those who love it, taking it screaming to the boarding school. The only word I can think of for what is done to these children is kidnapping.

Even now, in a good school, there is impersonality instead of close human contact; a sterile, cold atmosphere, an unfamiliar routine, language problems, and above all the mazaskan-skin, that damn clock—white man's time as opposed to Indian time, which is natural time. Like eating when you are hungry and sleeping when you are tired, not when that damn clock says you must. But I was not taken to one of the better, modern schools. I was taken to the old-fashioned mission school at St. Francis, run by the nuns and Catholic fathers, built sometime around the turn of the century and not improved a bit when I arrived, not improved as far as the buildings, the food, the teachers, or their methods were concerned.

In the old days, nature was our people's only school and they needed no other. Girls had their toy tipis and dolls, boys their toy bows and arrows. Both rode and swam and played the rough Indian games together. Kids watched their peers and elders and naturally grew from children into adults. Life in the tipi circle was harmonious—until the whiskey peddlers arrived with their wagons and barrels of "Injun whiskey." I often wished I could have grown up in the old, before-whiskey days.

Oddly enough, we owed our unspeakable boarding schools to the do-gooders, the white Indian-lovers. The schools were intended as an alternative to the outright extermination seriously advocated by Generals Sherman and Sheridan, as well as by most settlers and prospectors overrunning our land. "You don't have to kill those poor benighted heathen," the do-gooders said, "in order to solve the Indian Problem. Just give us a chance to turn them into useful farmhands, laborers, and chambermaids who will break their backs for you at low wages." In that way the boarding schools were born. The kids were taken away from their villages and pueblos, in their blankets and moccasins, kept completely isolated from their families—sometimes for as long as ten years—suddenly coming back, their short hair slick with pomade, their necks raw from stiff, high collars, their thick jackets always short in the sleeves and pinching under the arms, their tight patent leather shoes giving them corns, the girls in starched white blouses and clumsy, high-buttoned boots—caricatures of white people. When they found out—and they found out quickly—that they were neither wanted by whites nor by Indians, they got good and drunk, many of them staying drunk for the rest of their lives. I still have a poster I found among my grandfather's stuff, given to him by the missionaries to tack up on his wall. It reads:

1. Let Jesus save you.
2. Come out of your blanket, cut your hair, and dress like a white man.
3. Have a Christian family with one wife for life only.
4. Live in a house like your white brother. Work hard and wash often.
5. Learn the value of a hard-earned dollar. Do not waste your money on giveaways. Be punctual.
6. Believe that property and wealth are signs of divine approval.

7. Keep away from saloons and strong spirits.
8. Speak the language of your white brother. Send your children to school to do likewise.
9. Go to church often and regularly.
10. Do not go to Indian dances or to the medicine man.

The people who were stuck upon "solving the Indian Problem" by making us into whites retreated from this position only step by step in the wake of Indian protests.

The mission school at St. Francis was a curse for our family for generations. My grandmother went there, then my mother, then my sisters and I. At one time or other every one of us tried to run away. Grandma told me once about the bad times she had experienced at St. Francis. In those days they let students go home only for one week every year. Two days were used up for transportation, which meant spending just five days out of three hundred and sixty-five with her family. And that was an improvement. Before grandma's time, on many reservations they did not let the students go home at all until they had finished school. Anybody who disobeyed the nuns was severely punished. The building in which my grandmother stayed had three floors, for girls only. Way up in the attic were little cells, about five by five by ten feet. One time she was in church and instead of praying she was playing jacks. As punishment they took her to one of those little cubicles where she stayed in darkness because the windows had been boarded up. They left her there for a whole week with only bread and water for nourishment. After she came out she promptly ran away, together with three other girls. They were found and brought back. The nuns stripped them naked and whipped them. They used a horse buggy whip on my grandmother. Then she was put back into the attic — for two weeks.

My mother had much the same experiences but never wanted to talk about them, and then there I was, in the same place. The school is now run by the BIA — the Bureau of Indian Affairs — but only since about fifteen years ago. When I was there, during the 1960s, it was still run by the Church. The Jesuit fathers ran the boys' wing and the Sisters of the Sacred Heart ran us — with the help of the strap. Nothing had changed since my grandmother's days. I have been told recently that even in the '70s they were still beating children at that school. All I got out of school was being taught how to pray. I learned quickly that I would be beaten if I failed in my devotions or, God forbid, prayed the wrong way, especially prayed in Indian to Wakan Tanka, the Indian Creator.

The girls' wing was built like an F and was run like a penal institution. Every morning at five o'clock the sisters would come into our large dormitory to wake us up, and immediately we had to kneel down at the sides of our beds and recite the prayers. At six o'clock we were herded into the church for more of the same. I did not take kindly to the discipline and to marching by the clock, left-right, left-right. I was never one to like being forced to do something. I do something because I feel like doing it. I felt this way always, as far as I can remember, and my sister Barbara felt the same way. An old medicine man once told me: "Us Lakotas are not like dogs who can be trained, who can be beaten and keep on wagging their tails, licking the hand that whipped them. We are like cats, little cats, big cats, wildcats, bobcats, mountain lions. It doesn't matter what kind, but cats who can't be tamed, who scratch if you step on their tails." But I was only a kitten and my claws were still small.

Barbara was still in the school when I arrived and during my first year or two she could still protect me a little bit. When Barb was a seventh-grader she ran away together with five other girls, early in the morning before sunrise. They brought them back in the evening. The girls had to wait for two hours in front of the mother superior's office. They were hungry and cold, frozen through. It was wintertime and they had been running the whole day without food, trying to make good their escape. The mother superior asked each girl, "Would you do this again?" She told them that as punishment they would not be allowed to visit home for a month and that she'd keep them busy on work details until the skin on their knees and elbows had worn off. At the end of her speech she told each girl, "Get up from this chair and lean over it." She then lifted the girls' skirts and pulled down their underpants. Not little girls either, but teenagers. She had a leather strap about a foot long and four inches wide fastened to a stick, and beat the girls, one after another, until they cried. Barb did not give her that satisfaction but just clenched her teeth. There was one girl, Barb told me, the nun kept on beating and beating until her arm got tired.

I did not escape my share of the strap. Once, when I was thirteen years old, I refused to go to Mass. I did not want to go to church because I did not feel well. A nun grabbed me by the hair, dragged me upstairs, made me stoop over, pulled my dress up (we were not allowed at the time to wear jeans), pulled my panties down, and gave me what they called "swats"—twenty-five swats with a board around which Scotch tape had been wound. She hurt me badly.

My classroom was right next to the principal's office and almost every day I could hear him swatting the boys. Beating was the common punishment for not doing one's home-work, or for being late to school. It had such a bad effect upon me that I hated and mistrusted every white person on sight, because I met only one kind. It was not until much later that I met sincere white people I could relate to and be friends with. Racism breeds racism in reverse.

3 Lying to Children about the California Missions and the Indians

Deborah A. Miranda

California is a story. California is many stories. Human beings have no other way of knowing that we exist, or what we have survived, except through the vehicle of story.

In 1769, after missionizing much of Mexico, the Spaniards began to move up the west coast of North America in order to establish claims to rich resources and before other European nations could get a foothold. Together, the Franciscan priests and Spanish soldiers "built" a series of 21 missions along what is now coastal California. (California's Indigenous peoples, numbering more than 1 million at the time, did most of the actual labor.) These missions, some rehabilitated from melting adobe, others in near-original state, are now one of the state's biggest tourist attractions; in the little town of Carmel, Mission San Carlos Borromeo de Carmelo is the biggest attraction. Elsewhere, so-called Mission décor drenches Southern California, from restaurants to homes, apartment buildings, animal shelters, grocery stores, and post offices. In many neighborhoods, a bastardized Mission style is actually required by cities or neighborhood associations. Along with this visual mythology of adobe and red clay roof tiles comes the cultural storytelling that drains the missions of their brutal and bloody pasts for popular consumption.

In California schools, students come up against the "Mission Unit" in 4th grade, reinforcing the same lies those children have been breathing in most of their lives. Part of California's history curriculum, the unit is entrenched in the educational system and impossible to avoid, a powerfully authoritative indoctrination in Mission Mythology to which 4th graders have little if any resistance. Intense pressure is put upon students (and their parents) to create a "Mission Project" that glorifies the era and glosses over both Spanish and Mexican exploitation of Indians, as well as enslavement of those same Indians during U.S. rule. In other words, the Mission Unit is all too often a lesson in imperialism, racism, and Manifest Destiny rather than actually educational or a jumping-off point for critical thinking or accurate history.

In Harcourt School Publisher's *California: A Changing State*, the sacrifice for gold, riches, settlements, and violence by Spanish, English, and Russian explorers is well

Deborah A. Miranda is the author of *Bad Indians: A Tribal Memoir*, as well as the poetry collections *The Zen of La Llorona* and *Indian Cartography*, and she co-edited *Sovereign Erotics: An Anthology of Two-Spirit Literature*. A professor of English at Washington and Lee University, Miranda teaches American literature "off the canonical map." She is an enrolled member of the Ohlone/Costanoan-Esselen Nation of California and is also of Chumash and Jewish ancestry.

enunciated throughout Unit 2 and dressed in exciting language such as on page 113: "In one raid, Drake's crew took 80 pounds of gold!"

In four opening pages to Chapter 3 devoted to Father Junípero Serra, the textbook urges students to sympathize with the Spanish colonial mission:

> Mile after mile, day after day, week after week, the group traveled across the rugged terrain. As their food ran low, many of the men grew tired and sick. Father Serra himself suffered from a sore on one leg that grew worse each day. And yet he never gave up, calling on his faith in God to keep himself going.

The language jumps between an acknowledgment of the subjugation of Indigenous peoples and of mutually beneficial exchanges. In Lesson 3, "The Mission System" opens: "Indians were forced to build a chain of missions." Subsequent language emphasizes the alleged benefits to the Indians:

> At the missions, the priests worked to create loyal Spanish subjects. . . . They would *move* the California Indians into the missions, *teach them* to be Christians, and *show them* European ways. [Emphasis added.]

Visiting the mission as an adult, proud, mixed-blood California Indian woman, I found myself unprepared for gift shops well stocked with CDs of pre-researched Mission Projects; photocopied pamphlets of mission terms, facts, and history (one for each mission); coloring books; packaged models of missions ("easy assembly in 10 minutes!"); and other project paraphernalia for the discerning 4th grader and his or her worried parents.

The Carmel Mission website maintains a "4th Grade Corner" where daily life for padres and their "Indian friends" who "shared what little food and supplies they had" is blissfully described. Other websites offer "easy," "quick," and "guaranteed A+!!!" Mission Projects, targeting those anxious parents, for a price.

Generations of Californians have grown up steeped in a culture and education system that trains them to think of Indians as passive, dumb, and disappeared. In other words, the project is so well established, in such a predictable and well-loved rut, that veering outside of the worn but comfortable mythology is all but impossible.

On my visit to Mission Dolores, I found that out in a particularly visceral way.

It was over winter break, 2008. I was in San Francisco for a conference, and my friend Kimberly and I had hopped on a streetcar to visit Mission Dolores. As we emerged from the mission church via a side door into a small courtyard (featuring one of those giant dioramas behind glass), we inadvertently walked into video range of a mother filming her daughter's 4th-grade project.

Excusing ourselves, we studiously examined the diorama while the little girl flubbed her lines a few times. She was reading directly from the flyer given tourists in the gift shop and could say "basilica" but not "archdiocese," but she maintained her poise through several takes until she nailed it.

Both mothers ourselves, Kimberly and I paused to exchange a few words of solidarity about school projects with the mother, which gave Mom the chance to brag about how she and Virginia were trying to "do something a little different" by using video instead of making a model.

"That's great!" I said, giving them both a polite smile. "I'll bet your teacher will be glad to have something out of the ordinary."

"Well, it is different actually being right here," Mom said excitedly. "To think about all those Indians and how they lived all that time ago, that's kind of impressive."

I could not resist: "And better yet," I beamed, "still live! Guess what? I'm a member of the Ohlone/Costanoan-Esselen Nation myself! Some of my ancestors lived in this mission. I've found their names in the Book of Baptism." (I didn't mention that they are also listed in the Book of Deaths soon afterward.)

The mother was beside herself with pleasure, posed me with her daughter for a still photo, and wrote down my name so she could Google my work. Little Virginia, however, was shocked into silence. Her face drained, her body went stiff, and she stared at me as if I had risen, an Indigenous skeleton clad in decrepit rags, from beneath the clay bricks of the courtyard. Even though her mother and I talked a few more minutes, Virginia the 4th grader—previously a calm, articulate news anchor in training—remained a shy shadow, shooting side glances at me out of the corner of her eyes.

As Kimberly and I walked away, I thought, "That poor kid has never seen a live Indian, much less a 'Mission Indian'—she thought we were all dead!" Having me suddenly appear in the middle of her video project must have been a lot like turning the corner to find the (dead) person you were talking about suddenly in your face, talking back.

Kimberly, echoing my thoughts, chortled quietly, "Yes, Virginia, there really are live Mission Indians."

The problem is, thanks to Mission Mythology, most 4th graders will never know that and the textbooks don't help to give visibility to modern California Indians.

Throughout the rest of *California: A Changing History*, mentions of California Indians are brief and as victims fading into history. On page 242, under the heading of "A Changing Population," Harcourt states simply, "California Indians were hurt by the gold rush. . . . Many were forced off their lands when the miners found gold there."

Many pages later, California Indians are mentioned again when the textbook devotes five paragraphs to Indian Governments. Although 109 tribes are recognized in California, in the text, they are faceless and noted only by red square dots on a map.

It's time for the Mission Fantasy Fairy Tale to end. This story has done more damage to California Indians than any conquistador, any priest, and *soldado de cuera* (leather-jacket soldier), any smallpox, measles, or influenza virus. This story has not just killed us, it has also taught us to kill ourselves and kill each other with alcohol, domestic violence, horizontal racism, internalized hatred. We have to put an end to it now.

4 Then Came the War
Yuri Kochiyama

I was red, white, and blue when I was growing up. I taught Sunday school, and was very, very American. But I was also very provincial. We were just kids rooting for our high school.

My father owned a fish market. Terminal Island was nearby, and that was where many Japanese families lived. It was a fishing town. My family lived in the city proper. San Pedro was very mixed, predominantly white, but there were blacks also.

I was nineteen at the time of the evacuation. I had just finished junior college. I was looking for a job, and didn't realize how different the school world was from the work world. In the school world, I never felt racism. But when you got into the work world, it was very difficult. This was 1941, just before the war. I finally did get a job at a department store. But for us back then, it was a big thing, because I don't think they had ever hired an Asian in a department store before. I tried, because I saw a Mexican friend who got a job there. Even then they didn't hire me on a regular basis, just on Saturdays, summer vacation, Easter vacation, and Christmas vacation. Other than that, I was working like the others—at a vegetable stand, or doing part-time domestic work. Back then, I only knew of two Japanese American girl friends who got jobs as secretaries—but these were in Japanese companies. But generally you almost never saw a Japanese American working in a white place. It was hard for Asians. Even for Japanese, the best jobs they felt they could get were in Chinatowns, such as in Los Angeles. Most Japanese were either in some aspect of fishing, such as in the canneries, or went right from school to work on the farms. That was what it was like in the town of San Pedro. I loved working in the department store, because it was a small town, and you got to know and see everyone. The town itself was wonderful. People were very friendly. I didn't see my job as work—it was like a community job.

Everything changed for me on the day Pearl Harbor was bombed. On that very day—December 7—the FBI came and they took my father. He had just come home from the hospital the day before. For several days we didn't know where they had taken him. Then we found out that he was taken to the federal prison at Terminal Island. Overnight, things

---

Yuri Kochiyama (1921–2014) was a civil rights activist whose experiences as a Japanese American forced into an internment camp during World War II and then as a resident of racially diverse housing projects in New York City led her to take part in the civil rights movement. Her lifelong work for racial justice contributed to the enactment of the Civil Liberties Act in 1988.

changed for us. They took all men who lived near the Pacific waters, and had nothing to do with fishing. A month later, they took every fisherman from Terminal Island, sixteen and over, to places—not the regular concentration camps—but to detention centers in places like South Dakota, Montana, and New Mexico. They said that all Japanese who had given money to any kind of Japanese organization would have to be taken away. At that time, many people were giving to the Japanese Red Cross. The first group was thirteen hundred Isseis—my parents' generation. They took those who were leaders of the community, or Japanese school teachers, or were teaching martial arts, or who were Buddhist priests. Those categories which would make them very "Japanesey," were picked up. This really made a tremendous impact on our lives. My twin brother was going to the University at Berkeley. He came rushing back. All of our classmates were joining up, so he volunteered to go into the service. And it seemed strange that here they had my father in prison, and there the draft board okayed my brother. He went right into the army. My other brother, who was two years older, was trying to run my father's fish market. But business was already going down, so he had to close it. He had finished college at the University of California a couple of years before.

They took my father on December 7th. The day before, he had just come home from the hospital. He had surgery for an ulcer. We only saw him once, on December 13. On December 20th they said he could come home. By the time they brought him back, he couldn't talk. He made guttural sounds and we didn't know if he could hear. He was home for twelve hours. He was dying. The next morning, when we got up, they told us that he was gone. He was very sick. And I think the interrogation was very rough. My mother kept begging the authorities to let him go to the hospital until he was well, then put him back in the prison. They did finally put him there, a week or so later. But they put him in a hospital where they were bringing back all these American Merchant Marines who were hit on Wake Island. So he was the only Japanese in that hospital, so they hung a sheet around him that said, Prisoner of War. The feeling where he was was very bad.

You could see the hysteria of war. There was a sense that war could actually come to American shores. Everybody was yelling to get the "Japs" out of California. In Congress, people were speaking out. Organizations such as the Sons and Daughters of the Golden West were screaming "Get the 'Japs' out." So were the real estate people, who wanted to get the land from the Japanese farmers. The war had whipped up such a hysteria that if there was anyone for the Japanese, you didn't hear about it. I'm sure they were afraid to speak out, because they would be considered not only just "Jap" lovers, but unpatriotic.

Just the fact that my father was taken made us suspect to people. But on the whole, the neighbors were quite nice, especially the ones adjacent to us. There was already a six AM to six PM curfew and a five mile limit on where we could go from our homes. So they offered to do our shopping for us, if we needed.

Most Japanese Americans had to give up their jobs, whatever they did, and were told they had to leave. The edict [Executive Order No.] 9066—President Roosevelt's edict[*] for evacuation—was in February 1942. We were moved to a detention center that April.

---

[*]Executive Order No. 9066 does not mention detention of Japanese specifically, but was used exclusively against the Japanese. Over 120,000 Japanese were evacuated from the West Coast.

By then the Japanese on Terminal Island were just helter skelter, looking for anywhere they could go. They opened up the Japanese school and Buddhist churches, and families just crowded in. Even farmers brought along their chickens and chicken coops. They just opened up the places for people to stay until they could figure out what to do. Some people left for Colorado and Utah. Those who had relatives could do so. The idea was to evacuate all the Japanese from the coast. But all the money was frozen, so even if you knew where you wanted to go, it wasn't that simple. By then, people knew they would be going into camps, so they were selling what they could, even though they got next to nothing for it.

We were fortunate, in that our neighbors, who were white, were kind enough to look after our house, and they said they would find people to rent it, and look after it till we got back. But these neighbors were very, very unusual.

We were sent to an assembly center in Arcadia, California, in April. It was the largest assembly center on the West Coast, having nearly twenty thousand people. There were some smaller centers with about six hundred people. All along the West Coast—Washington, Oregon, California—there were many, many assembly centers, but ours was the largest. Most of the assembly centers were either fairgrounds, or race tracks. So many of us lived in stables, and they said you could take what you could carry. We were there until October.

Even though we stayed in a horse stable, everything was well organized. Every unit would hold four to six people. So in some cases, families had to split up, or join others. We slept on army cots, and for mattresses they gave us muslin bags, and told us to fill them with straw. And for chairs, everybody scrounged around for carton boxes, because they could serve as chairs. You could put two together and it could be a little table. So it was just makeshift. But I was amazed how, in a few months, some of those units really looked nice. Japanese women fixed them up. Some people had the foresight to bring material and needles and thread. But they didn't let us bring anything that could be used as weapons. They let us have spoons, but no knives. For those who had small children or babies, it was rough. They said you could take what you could carry. Well, they could only take their babies in their arms, and maybe the little children could carry something, but it was pretty limited.

I was so red, white, and blue, I couldn't believe this was happening to us. America would never do a thing like this to us. This is the greatest country in the world. So I thought this is only going to be for a short while, maybe a few weeks or something, and they will let us go back. At the beginning no one realized how long this would go on. I didn't feel the anger that much because I thought maybe this was the way we could show our love for our country, and we should not make too much fuss or noise, we should abide by what they asked of us. I'm a totally different person now than I was back then. I was naïve about so many things. The more I think about it, the more I realize how little you learn about American history. It's just what they want you to know.

At the beginning, we didn't have any idea how temporary or permanent the situation was. We thought we would be able to leave shortly. But after several months they told us this was just temporary quarters, and they were building more permanent quarters elsewhere in the United States. All this was so unbelievable. A year before we would never have thought anything like this could have happened to us—not in this country. As time went by, the sense of frustration grew. Many families were already divided. The fathers, the heads of the households, were taken to other camps. In the beginning, there was no way for the sons to get in touch with their families. Before our group left for the detention camp, we were saying goodbye almost every day to other groups who were going to places like Arizona and Utah. Here we finally had made so many new friends—people who we met, lived with, shared the time, and got to know. So it was even sad on that note and the goodbyes were difficult. Here we had gotten close to these people, and now we had to separate again. I don't think we even thought about where they were going to take us, or how long we would have to stay there. When we got on the trains to leave for the camps, we didn't know where we were going. None of the groups knew. It was later on that we learned so and so ended up in Arizona, or Colorado, or some other place. We were all at these assembly centers for about seven months. Once they started pushing people out, it was done very quickly. By October, our group headed out for Jerome, Arkansas, which is on the Texarkana corner.

We were on the train for five days. The blinds were down, so we couldn't look out, and other people couldn't look in to see who was in the train. We stopped in Nebraska, and everybody pulled the blinds to see what Nebraska looked like. The interesting thing was, there was a troop train stopped at the station too. These American soldiers looked out, and saw all these Asians, and they wondered what we were doing on the train. So the Japanese raised the windows, and so did the soldiers. It wasn't a bad feeling at all. There was none of that "you Japs" kind of thing. The women were about the same age as the soldiers— eighteen to twenty-five, and we had the same thing on our minds. In camps, there wasn't much to do, so the fun thing was to receive letters, so on our train, all the girls who were my age, were yelling to the guys, "Hey, give us your address where you're going, we'll write you." And they said, "Are you sure you're going to write?" We exchanged addresses and for a long time I wrote to some of those soldiers. On the other side of the train, I'll never forget there was this old guy, about sixty, who came to our window and said, "We have some Japanese living here. This is Omaha, Nebraska." This guy was very nice, and didn't seem to have any ill feelings for Japanese. He had calling cards, and he said "Will any of you people write to me?" We said, "Sure," so he threw in a bunch of calling cards, and I got one, and I wrote to him for years. I wrote to him about what camp was like, because he said, "Let me know what it's like wherever you end up." And he wrote back, and told me what was happening in Omaha, Nebraska. There were many, many interesting experiences too. Our mail was generally not censored, but all the mail from the soldiers was. Letters meant everything.

When we got to Jerome, Arkansas, we were shocked because we had never seen an area like it. There was forest all around us. And they told us to wait till the rains hit. This would not only turn into mud, but Arkansas swamp lands. That's where they put us—in swamp lands, surrounded by forests. It was nothing like California.

I'm speaking as a person of twenty who had good health. Up until then, I had lived a fairly comfortable life. But there were many others who didn't see the whole experience the same way. Especially those who were older and in poor health and had experienced racism. One more thing like this could break them. I was at an age where transitions were not hard—the point where anything new could even be considered exciting. But for people in poor health, it was hell.

There were army-type barracks, with two hundred to two hundred and five people to each block and every block had its own mess hall, facility for washing clothes, showering. It was all surrounded by barbed wire, and armed soldiers. I think they said only seven people were killed in total, though thirty were shot, because they went too close to the fence. Where we were, nobody thought of escaping because you'd be more scared of the swamps—the poisonous snakes, the bayous. Climatic conditions were very harsh. Although Arkansas is in the South, the winters were very, very cold. We had a pot bellied stove in every room and we burned wood. Everything was very organized. We got there in October, and were warned to prepare ourselves. So on our block, for instance, males eighteen and over could go out in the forest to chop down trees for wood for the winter. The men would bring back the trees, and the women sawed the trees. Everybody worked. The children would pile up the wood for each unit.

They told us when it rained, it would be very wet, so we would have to build our own drainage system. One of the barracks was to hold meetings, so block heads would call meetings. There was a block council to represent the people from different areas.

When we first arrived, there were some things that weren't completely fixed. For instance, the roofers would come by, and everyone would hunger for information from the outside world. We wanted to know what was happening with the war. We weren't allowed to bring radios; that was contraband. And there were no televisions then. So we would ask the workers to bring us back some papers, and they would give us papers from Texas or Arkansas, so for the first time we would find out about news from the outside.

Just before we went in to the camps, we saw that being a Japanese wasn't such a good thing, because everybody was turning against the Japanese, thinking we were saboteurs, or linking us with Pearl Harbor. But when I saw the kind of work they did at camp, I felt so proud of the Japanese, and proud to be Japanese, and wondered why I was so white, white when I was outside, because I was always with white folks. Many people had brothers or sons who were in the military and Japanese American servicemen would come into the camp to visit the families, and we felt so proud of them when they came in their uniforms. We knew that it would only be a matter of time before they would be shipped overseas. Also what made us feel proud was the forming of the 442 unit.[*]

I was one of these real American patriots then. I've changed now. But back then, I was all American. Growing up, my mother would say we're Japanese. But I'd say, "No, I'm American." I think a lot of Japanese grew up that way. People would say to them, "You're Japanese," and they would say, "No, we're Americans." I don't even think they used the hyphenated term "Japanese-American" back then. At the time, I was ashamed of being Japanese. I think many Japanese Americans felt the same way. Pearl Harbor was a shameful act, and being Japanese Americans, even though we had nothing to do with it, we still

---

[*]American soldiers of Japanese ancestry were assembled in two units: the 442 Regimental Combat Team and the 100th Infantry Battalion. The two groups were sent to battle in Europe. The 100th Battalion had over 900 casualties and was known as the Purple Heart Battalion. Combined, the units received 9,486 Purple Hearts and 18,143 individual decorations.

somehow felt we were blamed for it. I hated Japan at that point. So I saw myself at that part of my history as an American, and not as a Japanese or Japanese American. That sort of changed while I was in the camp.

I hated the war, because it wasn't just between the governments. It went down to the people, and it nurtured hate. What was happening during the war were many things I didn't like. I hoped that one day when the war was over there could be a way that people could come together in their relationships.

Now I can relate to Japan in a more mature way, where I see its faults and its very, very negative history. But I also see its potential. Scientifically and technologically it has really gone far. But I'm disappointed that when it comes to human rights she hasn't grown. The Japan of today—I feel there are still things lacking. For instance, I don't think the students have the opportunity to have more leeway in developing their lives.

We always called the camps "relocation centers" while we were there. Now we feel it is apropos to call them concentration camps. It is not the same as the concentration camps of Europe; those we feel were death camps. Concentration camps were a concentration of people placed in an area, and disempowered and disenfranchised. So it is apropos to call what I was in a concentration camp. After two years in the camp, I was released.

Going home wasn't much of a problem for us because our neighbors had looked after our place. But for most of our Japanese friends, starting over again was very difficult after the war.

I returned in October of 1945. It was very hard to find work, at least for me. I wasn't expecting to find anything good, just something to tide me over until my boyfriend came back from New York. The only thing I was looking for was to work in a restaurant as a waitress. But I couldn't find anything. I would walk from one end of the town to the other, and down every main avenue. But as soon as they found out I was Japanese, they would say no. Or they would ask me if I was in the union, and of course I couldn't be in the union because I had just gotten there. Anyway, no Japanese could be in the union, so if the answer was no I'm not in the union, they would say no. So finally what I did was go into the rough area of San Pedro—there's a strip near the wharf—and I went down there. I was determined to keep the jobs as long as I could. But for a while, I could last maybe two hours, and somebody would say "Is that a 'Jap'?" And as soon as someone would ask that, the boss would say, "Sorry, you gotta go. We don't want trouble here." The strip wasn't that big, so after I'd go the whole length of it, I'd have to keep coming back to the same restaurants, and say, "Gee, will you give me another chance?" I figure, all these servicemen were coming back and the restaurants didn't have enough waitresses to come in and take these jobs. And so, they'd say "Okay. But soon as somebody asks who you are, or if you're a 'Jap,' or any problem about being a 'Jap,' you go." So I said, "Okay, sure. How about keeping me until that happens?" So sometimes I'd last a night, sometimes a couple of nights that no one would say anything. Sometimes people threw cups at me or hot coffee. At first they didn't know what I was. They thought I was Chinese. Then someone would say, "I bet she's a 'Jap'." And I wasn't going to say I wasn't. So as soon as I said "Yeah," then it was like an uproar. Rather than have them say, "Get out," I just walked out. I mean, there was no point in fighting it. If you just walked out, there was less chance of getting hurt. But one place I lasted two weeks. These owners didn't want to have to let me go. But they didn't want to have problems with the people.

And so I did this until I left for New York, which was about three months later. I would work the dinner shift, from six at night to three in the morning. When you are young you tend not to take things as strongly. Everything is like an adventure. Looking back, I felt the people who were the kindest to me were those who went out and fought, those who just got back from Japan or the Far East. I think the worst ones were the ones who stayed here and worked in defense plants, who felt they had to be so patriotic. On the West Coast, there wasn't hysteria anymore, but there were hostile feelings towards the Japanese, because they were coming back. It took a while, but my mother said that things were getting back to normal, and that the Japanese were slowly being accepted again. At the time, I didn't go through the bitterness that many others went through, because it's not just what they went through, but it is also what they experienced before that. I mean, I happened to have a much more comfortable life before, so you sort of see things in a different light. You see that there are all kinds of Americans, and that they're not all people who hate Japs. You know too that it was hysteria that had a lot to do with it.

All Japanese, before they left camp, were told not to congregate among Japanese, and not to speak Japanese. They were told by the authorities. There was even a piece of paper that gave you instructions. But then people went on to places like Chicago where there were churches, so they did congregate in churches. But they did ask people not to. I think psychologically the Japanese, having gone through a period where they were so hated by everyone, didn't even want to admit they were Japanese, or accept the fact that they were Japanese. Of course, they would say they were Japanese Americans. But I think the psychological damage of the wartime period, and of racism itself, has left its mark. There is a stigma to being Japanese. I think that is why such a large number of Japanese, in particular Japanese American women, have married out of the race. On the West Coast I've heard people say that sixty to seventy percent of the Japanese women have married, I guess, mostly whites. Japanese men are doing it too, but not to that degree. I guess Japanese Americans just didn't want to have that Japanese identity, or that Japanese part. There is definitely some self-hate, and part of that has to do with the racism that's so deeply a part of this society.

Historically, Americans have always been putting people behind walls. First there were the American Indians who were put on reservations, Africans in slavery, their lives on the plantations, Chicanos doing migratory work, and the kinds of camps they lived in, and even, too, the Chinese when they worked on the railroad camps where they were almost isolated, dispossessed people—disempowered. And I feel those are the things we should fight against so they won't happen again. It wasn't so long ago—in 1979—that the feeling against the Iranians was so strong because of the takeover of the U.S. embassy in Iran, where they wanted to deport Iranian students. And that is when a group called Concerned Japanese Americans organized, and that was the first issue we took up, and then we connected it with what the Japanese had gone through. This whole period of what the Japanese went through is important. If we can see the connections of how often this happens in history, we can stem the tide of these things happening again by speaking out against them.

Most Japanese Americans who worked years and years for redress never thought it would happen the way it did. The papers have been signed, we will be given reparation, and there was an apology from the government. I think the redress movement itself was very good because it was a learning experience for the Japanese people; we could get out into our communities and speak about what happened to us and link it with experiences of other people. In that sense, though, it wasn't done as much as it should have been. Some Japanese Americans didn't even learn that part. They just started the movement as a reaction to the bad experience they had. They don't even see other ethnic groups who have gone through it. It showed us, too, how vulnerable everybody is. It showed us that even though there is a Constitution, that constitutional rights could be taken away very easily.

5 | San Diegan Hopes to Reunite with Mother Despite "Muslim Ban"

Dhaha Nur

President Abraham Lincoln once said, "It's not the years in your life that count. It's the life in your years." It's been over two decades since I have seen my mother—since July 1996—and I can't help but look back over those past 22 years and wonder what my life would've been like growing up with her.

My mother and I are not separated by choice. We fled Somalia when I was 5, running for our lives in the midst of a civil war. I came to the U.S. without my mother. I was young, but old enough to feel the impact of her absence. And 22 years later, it's not a war or even an ocean that forces our separation. It's our nation's president, whose Muslim ban*— introduced two years ago this week—gave the green light to tear families like mine apart.

Before the Muslim ban, I never doubted that my mother would soon be rejoined with me: her eldest son, her pride and joy. After the summer of 2014, the same summer I received my citizenship, I made it my mission to bring my mother here to the United States. Without hesitation I applied for her visa, so we could regain the years we lost to time.

Two years ago this week, when Trump first introduced the Muslim ban, we were horrified. We had already jumped through all the bureaucratic hoops, from the original visa application to supplying my mother's DNA evidence. But we continued to push for my mother's dream of seeing her son. Last August, my mother successfully completed all the requirements for her visa. We were elated, knowing we were just moments away from our dream.

And then on Oct. 11, 2018, I received the news: "Denial under Presidential Proclamation 9645."

I was devastated, and worst of all, I had no way to explain this to my mother. How could I tell her she was indefinitely banned from being with me based on nothing more than her nationality? Or that we had no appeal to a process we had trusted, and invested so much heart into? Heartbreak and hopelessness are feelings I have had to navigate before, as a former refugee.

*See "America's Love–Hate Relationship with Immigrants," by Angelica Quintero (in Part III of this volume), for details about President Donald Trump's series of executive orders seeking to ban travel from several Muslim-majority countries. See also the ACLU's "Timeline of the Muslim Ban" (https://www.aclu-wa.org/pages/timeline-muslim-ban).

Dhaha Nur is a Somali American poet and the civic engagement manager at the Partnership for the Advancement of New Americans (PANA). He is also a fellow at the Bread and Roses Center for Feminist Research and Activism.

But it hit hard, knowing that this moment was shrewdly orchestrated by an administration bent on banning others because of their faith and their homeland.

Our story is not unique; there are countless people whose lives the Muslim ban has impacted in ways that should shock the American consciousness. Marwa, a 16-year-old Syrian girl disfigured by a bomb blast, was recently informed that the United States has banned her from seeking the medical treatment she desperately needs. And in the 2 percent of cases that someone is granted a Muslim ban waiver, like the Yemeni mother who was recently granted entry to visit her 2-year-old son on life support, the right to see one's family requires a coordinated online and legal campaign.

I've long been hoping to bring my mother to the U.S., especially now that I have built a life she would be proud of. I've been very fortunate: I had the opportunity to graduate from San Diego State University, I am happily married, and I have a lovely 9-month-old daughter who my mother desperately wants to meet. But the Muslim ban sends a clear message to all the communities it impacts: the Trump administration does not believe we have the same rights and privileges as other Americans.

Trump's Muslim ban runs counter to the values the United States aspires to: religious freedom, and our commitment to affording every human being the respect and dignity they deserve. These are the values I sought when I came here. And they are the ones I ask you to affirm today, two years after the ban was introduced and so many of us flooded airports to refute it.

As a first-generation refugee, I have so much hope for my life here. I have hope for my family, for my siblings, my daughter, and, someday, for a reunification with my beloved mother. I still believe we can do better.

So on this anniversary of the Muslim ban executive order, picture my mother, far from her family and banned from seeing her son and grandchild.

I want her to be part of "the life in my years," and it will take each and every one of us standing together against the Muslim ban to make that happen.

6 Crossing the Border without Losing Your Past

Oscar Casares

Along with it being diez y seis de septiembre, Mexican Independence Day, today is my father's 89th birthday. Everardo Issasi Casares was born in 1914, a little more than a hundred years after Miguel Hidalgo y Costilla rang the church bells of Dolores, summoning his parishioners to rise up against the Spaniards.

This connection has always been important in my family. Though my father was born in the United States, he considers himself a Mexicano. To him, ancestry is what determines your identity. If you have Mexican blood, you are Mexican, whether you were born in Mexico City or New York City. This is not to say he denies his American citizenship— he votes, pays taxes and served in the Army. But his identity is tied to the past. His family came from Mexico, so like them he is Mexicano, punto, end of discussion.

In my hometown, Brownsville, Tex., almost everyone I know is Mexicano: neighbors, teachers, principals, dropouts, doctors, lawyers, drug dealers, priests. Rich and poor, short and tall, fat and skinny, dark- and light-skinned. Every year our Mexican heritage is celebrated in a four-day festival called Charro Days. Men grow beards; mothers draw moustaches on their little boys and dress their little girls like Mexican peasants; the brave compete in a jalapeño-eating contest. But the celebration also commemorates the connection between two neighboring countries, opening with an exchange of gritos (traditional cowboy calls you might hear in a Mexican movie) between a representative from Matamoros, Mexico, standing on one side of the International Bridge and a Brownsville representative standing on the other.

Like many Americans whose families came to this country from somewhere else, many children of Mexican immigrants struggle with their identity, as our push to fully assimilate is met with an even greater pull to remain anchored to our family's country of origin. This is especially true when that country is less than a quarter of a mile away—the width of the Rio Grande—from the new one. We learn both cultures as effortlessly as we do two languages. We learn quickly that we can exist simultaneously in both worlds, and that our home exists neither here nor there but in the migration between these two forces.

But for Mexican-Americans and other immigrants from Spanish-speaking countries who have been lumped into categories like Latino or Hispanic, this struggle has become even more pronounced over the last few years as we have grown into the largest minority

Oscar Casares is a writer and the director of the creative writing program at the University of Texas at Austin. His books, which focus on border-town lives and cross-cultural challenges, include the novel *Amigoland* and the short story collection *Brownsville*.

Oscar Casares "Crossing the Border without Losing your Past" originally appeared in The New York Times, September 6, 2003. Copyright © 2003 by Oscar Casares. Used with permission.

group in the United States. Our culture has been both embraced and exploited by advertisers, politicians and the media. And as we move, individually, from our small communities, where our identity is clear, we enter a world that wants to assign us a label of its choosing.

When I left Brownsville in 1985 to start at the University of Texas at Austin one of the first things I was asked was, "What are you?" "I'm Mexican," I told the guy, who was thrown off by my height and light skin. "Really, what part of Mexico are you from?" he asked, which led me to explain I was really from Brownsville, but my parents were Mexican. "Really, what part of Mexico?" Here again I had to admit they weren't really born in Mexico and neither were my grandparents or great-grandparents. "Oh," he said, "you're Mexican-American, is what you are."

Mexican-American. I imagined a 300-mile-long hyphen that connected Brownsville to Austin, a bridge between my old and new world. Not that I hadn't seen this word combination, Mexican-American, on school applications, but I couldn't remember the words being spoken to me directly. In Brownsville, I always thought of myself as being equally Mexican and American.

When I graduated that label was again redefined. One of my first job interviews was at an advertising agency, where I was taken on a tour: the media department, the creative department, the account-service department, the Hispanic department. This last department specialized in marketing products to Spanish-speaking consumers. In the group were men and women from Mexico, Puerto Rico and California, but together they were Hispanic. I was hired to work in another department, but suddenly, everyone was referring to me as Hispanic.

Hispanic? Where was the Mexican in me? Where was the hyphen? I didn't want to be Hispanic. The word reminded me of those Mexican-Americans who preferred to say their families came from Spain, which they felt somehow increased their social status. Just hearing the word Hispanic reminded me, too, of people who used the word Spanish to refer to Mexicans. "The Spanish like to get wild at their fiestas," they would say, or "You Spanish people sure do have a lot of babies."

In this same way, the word Hispanic seemed to want to be more user friendly, especially when someone didn't want to say the M word: Mexican. Except it did slip out occasionally. I remember standing in my supervisor's office as he described calling the police after he saw a car full of "Mexicans" drive through his suburban neighborhood.

Away from the border, the word Mexican had come to mean dirty, shiftless, drunken, lustful, criminal. I still cringe whenever I think someone might say the word. But usually it happens unexpectedly, as though the person has pulled a knife on me. I feel the sharp words up against my gut. Because of my appearance, people often say things in front of me they wouldn't say if they knew my real ethnicity—not Hispanic, Latino or even Mexican-American. I am, like my father, Mexican, and on this day of independence, I say this with particular pride.

7 "You Are in the Dark, in the Car . . ."
Claudia Rankine

/

You are in the dark, in the car, watching the black-tarred street being swallowed by speed; he tells you his dean is making him hire a person of color when there are so many great writers out there.

You think maybe this is an experiment and you are being tested or retroactively insulted or you have done something that communicates this is an okay conversation to be having.

Why do you feel okay saying this to me? You wish the light would turn red or a police siren would go off so you could slam on the brakes, slam into the car ahead of you, be propelled forward so quickly both your faces would suddenly be exposed to the wind.

As usual you drive straight through the moment with the expected backing off of what was previously said. It is not only that confrontation is headache producing; it is also that you have a destination that doesn't include acting like this moment isn't inhabitable, hasn't happened before, and the before isn't part of the now as the night darkens and the time shortens between where we are and where we are going.

/

When you arrive in your driveway and turn off the car, you remain behind the wheel another ten minutes. You fear the night is being locked in and coded on a cellular level and want time to function as a power wash. Sitting there staring at the closed garage door you are reminded that a friend once told you there exists a medical term—John Henryism—for people exposed to stresses stemming from racism. They achieve themselves to death trying to dodge the build-up of erasure. Sherman James, the researcher who came up with the term, claimed the physiological costs were high. You hope by sitting in silence you are bucking the trend.

Claudia Rankine is an award-winning poet and playwright whose work focuses on American cultural and emotional experience in the twenty-first century and contributes to conversations on racial violence and identity. She teaches poetry at Yale University.

/

When the stranger asks, Why do you care? you just stand there staring at him. He has just referred to the boisterous teenagers in Starbucks as niggers. Hey, I am standing right here, you responded, not necessarily expecting him to turn to you.

He is holding the lidded paper cup in one hand and a small paper bag in the other. They are just being kids. Come on, no need to get all KKK on them, you say.

Now there you go, he responds.

The people around you have turned away from their screens. The teenagers are on pause. There I go? you ask, feeling irritation begin to rain down. Yes, and something about hearing yourself repeating this stranger's accusation in a voice usually reserved for your partner makes you smile.

/

A man knocked over her son in the subway. You feel your own body wince. He's okay, but the son of a bitch kept walking. She says she grabbed the stranger's arm and told him to apologize: I told him to look at the boy and apologize. And yes, you want it to stop, you want the black child pushed to the ground to be seen, to be helped to his feet and be brushed off, not brushed off by the person that did not see him, has never seen him, has perhaps never seen anyone who is not a reflection of himself.

The beautiful thing is that a group of men began to stand behind me like a fleet of body-guards, she says, like newly found uncles and brothers.

/

The new therapist specializes in trauma counseling. You have only ever spoken on the phone. Her house has a side gate that leads to a back entrance she uses for patients. You walk down a path bordered on both sides with deer grass and rosemary to the gate, which turns out to be locked.

At the front door the bell is a small round disc that you press firmly. When the door finally opens, the woman standing there yells, at the top of her lungs, Get away from my house. What are you doing in my yard?

It's as if a wounded Doberman pinscher or a German shepherd has gained the power of speech. And though you back up a few steps, you manage to tell her you have an appointment. You have an appointment? she spits back. Then she pauses. Everything pauses. Oh, she says, followed by, oh, yes, that's right. I am sorry.

I am so sorry, so, so sorry.

/

Male-on-Male Rape
Michael Scarce

This article contains descriptions of a violent sexual assault.—Editor

In the autumn of 1989 my friend Tom and I returned from summer break to begin our sophomore year at Ohio State University. We unpacked our belongings and settled into room 332 on the third floor of Bradley Hall, an undergraduate residence hall in the south area of campus. . . .

The return of students to campus ushered in a flurry of activity as Welcome Week programs and parties abounded around us. Tom and I had been elected president and vice president, respectively, of the Gay and Lesbian Alliance, our campus gay and lesbian organization. We held weekly meetings and organized events while striving to increase membership and politicize the organization's activities. As GALA became more visible throughout autumn quarter, the organization and its officers frequently appeared in the local media, promoting GALA and challenging homophobia on campus, As our visibility increased, so did our Bradley Hall floormates' recognition that their two neighbors in room 332 were gay.

The stares and sneers from our thirty floormates began early in the academic year and slowly escalated to verbal abuse, menacing, and death threats. Messages were left on our answering machine, death threat notes were mailed to us, signs saying "Die Faggots" were posted on our door, and as the intensity of the intimidation increased, so did the frequency. Eventually the third-floor men's wing became so dangerous for Tom and me that the university was forced to evacuate everyone, relocating the male students and splitting them up across campus before someone was bashed or killed.

Tom and I were moved to a nearby Ramada Hotel, where we lived in adjoining rooms for the last few weeks of spring quarter. Both of us were escorted around campus by an armed security guard hired by the university to protect us in the midst of hostility. A protest of more than three hundred students erupted on campus soon thereafter. Some students applauded the university's relocation decision while others criticized campus officials for "pandering" to gay activists. Still others blamed the university administration for allowing the situation to escalate to a level that necessitated such drastic action. The third-floor men's wing of

Michael Scarce is a writer, researcher, activist, and health advocate who focuses on vulnerable populations. He is the author of *Smearing the Queer: Medical Bias in the Health Care of Gay Men* and *Male on Male Rape: The Hidden Toll of Stigma* and *Shame*.

The first part of this selection originally appeared in *Male on Male Rape: The Hidden Toll of Stigma and Shame*, by Michael Scarce. Published by Perseus Books. Copyright © 1997 by Michael Scarce. The sections "Defining the Term," "Denial," and "Recommendations" originally appeared in "Same-Sex Rape of Male College Students," *Journal of American College Health*, 45:4, 171–173. Reprinted by permission of the publisher (Taylor & Francis Ltd., http://www.tandfonline.com).

Bradley Hall remained vacant, sealed, and empty for the remainder of the academic year. A media frenzy ensued, with coverage from CNN to the *New York Times*. This year was devastating for me as I struggled to survive in such an environment of hostility, humiliation, and degradation. I lived in constant fear and frustration while the weight of the events took its toll on my academic performance, my relationships with family and friends, and my health.

However, the pain and violation I experienced during those months before the relocation exceeded the incidents of homophobic harassment. During winter quarter of that academic year, Tom went home for a weekend visit and I was left alone. I was nervous about what could happen to me, what those men could do to hurt and punish me. It was a weekend in February and I decided to go dancing at a gay bar downtown to get out from under the suffocating weight of it all. I went alone, expecting to meet up with friends. The music was great, the bar was hopping, and I was having a wonderful time. As I danced, I noticed a handsome man standing at the edge of the dance floor. He watched me for the duration of several songs and smiled when I returned his stares. Later we talked and I learned he was from out of town, visiting Columbus on business. After an hour of conversation and heavy flirting, I invited him to return with me to my residence hall to escape the loud music, crowd, and cigarette smoke.

On returning to my room and continuing our conversation, we grew more physically intimate with each other. We were on my bed and began to kiss. Slowly he attempted to unzip my pants, and when I resisted, he became surprisingly rough. The more I pushed his hands away, the more aggressive he became until finally he used force. I asked him to stop but was too embarrassed to raise my voice for fear that others next door or outside in the hallway would hear what was happening. I was afraid the men who hated me for being gay would use this situation as one more excuse to bash me. . . .

The walls in Bradley Hall were very thin. The air vents in the doors were so large you could hear practically everything through those wide cracks, and many of my neighbors were home that night. One yell, one shout would have attracted the attention I needed to stop what was happening, but I could not bring myself to cry out. What would my floormates think? They already hated me for being queer, so how might they react if they responded to my cries for help and burst in on that lovely scene—a man on top of me, penetrating me? There was nothing I could do except lie there and go numb.

After he left, I took a long shower, standing under the water and crying. The smell of him was on my body, his semen was between my legs, and I washed with soap over and over—lathering and rinsing continuously. I endured some minor rectal bleeding for the next day, and remained sore for many more. I did not contact the police or visit the hospital emergency room. I did not seek counseling or formal support, nor did I confide in any of my friends for several years. I was ashamed and embarrassed by what had happened, identifying the experience as a form of bad, regretted sex.

It was not until a year later that I began to make more sense of my experience. Through my academic course work in OSU's Department of Women's Studies, I took an internship with the university's Rape Education and Prevention Program, where I conducted library research on rape and sexual violence. Gradually I came to terms with the fact that I had physically and mentally resisted that night a year ago in Bradley Hall and that I had been, in fact, raped. I now blame those thirty floormates for my rape as much as I blame the man who assaulted me. They created and shaped a space, both actively and through negligence, in which I was gagged, effectively silenced, and unable to resist. Their intimidation weakened my spirit, lowered my self-worth, and forced me to appropriate a victim mentality that impeded me from regaining control of my life.

So very little has been published on the rape of adult males. As I began to search for documentation that resonated with my own assault, I was dismayed at being unable to locate many scholarly articles or even popular, first-person accounts of this form of sexual violence. Slowly, over the last few years, I have collected what scarce writing and research have been published about men raping men. Although I was raped by a gay male acquaintance, I discovered multiple other forms of same-sex rape between men—rape in prison institutions, assault by strangers, gang rape, and more.

As my knowledge and understanding of the subject has grown, so has my interest in speaking and educating others about this form of sexual violence. When I speak publicly and conduct sensitivity trainings on male rape, I relate to others the story of my own assault, for it serves as a highly useful illumination of the ways in which homophobia and other forms of oppression create climates that foster and perpetuate rape behavior. My rape in Bradley Hall was simply a microcosm of the broader rape culture we all live in, a culture that encourages and condones sexual violence wielded as a tool for the subordination and control of those with less power in our society. Scores of male survivors have approached me after speaking engagements or contacted me later to share their own rape stories with me.

As I gradually became more involved in antirape work on campus, I began facilitating sexual assault workshops for the Rape Education and Prevention Program in classrooms, residence halls, student organizations, fraternities, and sororities. My involvement continued through graduate school, and after receiving my master's degree I was hired as the full-time coordinator of the program. My transformation from helpless victim to empowered survivor has refashioned my sense of self and purpose in life. The atrocities I have experienced provide a lens through which I am better able to see the complexity of injustices around me, and I have learned to harness the resulting anger in positive and productive ways that fuel my drive for social change. I wonder if the man who raped me realizes what he has created.

Defining the Term

The term "male rape" is frequently used in reference to the same-sex rape of men. Unless carefully defined, the term may be semantically confusing because many people remain unsure whether the "male" in "male rape" is an indicator of the rapist, the victim, or both. The use of "homosexual rape" to connote men raping men is also problematic. The (homo)-sexual terminology perpetuates the stereotypical notions that all gay men are sexual predators or that gay men rape other men. On the contrary, the majority of men who rape other men are identified as heterosexual.[1]

Emphasis on the root word "sex" in "homosexual rape" also conflates consensual sex with rape behavior. Fortunately, feminist social movements since the 1970s have laid much of the groundwork for an understanding of rape as an act of power rather than of sex. Until now most research on male rape has concluded, as has research on opposite-sex rape, that the rape of men is not sexually motivated.[2] Instead, it is a form of violent power and control exercised over others. Although opposite-sex rape can be seen as a violent expression of power related to gender inequality, same-sex rape can involve other power dynamics related to physical strength, weapon use, influence of alcohol and other drugs, political strength, economic power, social power, and more.

One attempt to delineate the different kinds of male rape involves an examination of the sexual identity of both the rapist and the survivor. Viewing same-sex rape as an act of power through this lens is especially poignant, considering the controversy surrounding the dichotomization of rape and sex employed by feminist movements of the last twenty-five years. For example, the rape of gay men (or men perceived to be gay) by heterosexual men is often accompanied by misogynist verbal epithets in which the rapist degrades his victim with such language as "bitch," "girl," and so on.[3]

When same-sex rape is employed as a hate crime against gay men, usually as part of gay bashing, social inequality between heterosexual and gay men is clear evidence of a propensity to commit acts of violence. Rigidly traditional forms of hegemonic masculinity portray gay men as weak, feminine, and fit only for punishment and humiliation in the most dehumanizing way possible. "The victim may symbolize what they (the rapists) want to control, punish, and/or destroy, something they want to conquer and defeat. The assault is an act of retaliation, an expression of power, and an assertion of their strength and manhood"[4] Sexual violence within gay male relationships or between gay male acquaintances is also a serious problem, just as it is for heterosexual people and lesbian women.[5]

Same-sex rape of heterosexual men carries the stigma and shame associated with homosexuality in our culture; if the general population equates sex and rape to some degree, a man who has been raped by another man is, by implication, a homosexual. These categories could be further differentiated on the basis of whether the assault was stranger or acquaintance rape, interracial or intraracial, familial or nonfamilial, involved individual or multiple assailants, and so on. All of these factors can influence the rape experience, the dynamics of power involved, and the devastating aftermath faced by the male survivor.

Denial of the Significance of Male Rape

Discussions of adult male rape are frequently absent in campus rape education and prevention programs because the general public and popular culture have traditionally viewed rape in a context of violence against women. Although women statistically constitute the majority of rape victims, assessments in medicine, law, and education continue to deny dismiss, or diminish the significant number of men who are sexually assaulted. Male survivors of sexual assault may be less likely to report or seek treatment for their assault, in part because these men view rape crisis centers and hotlines as having been established to serve only women.[6]

• • •

How can we change existing systems to confront and deal with the phenomenon of male rape without compromising or damaging the successful sexual assault education and prevention services we have fought so hard to develop? Even an acknowledgment that men can be victims (or perpetrators) of same-sex rape may introduce a gender contradiction into the women-centered missions, objectives, and goals of some sexual assault prevention programs, disrupting the fundamental structure and philosophy upon which they may have been built.

Recommendations

Concrete suggestions for the infusion of male-rape programmatic content and services into general prevention education and crisis services are numerous. Here are six areas that campus health professionals should consider in evaluating how prepared they are to meet the needs of male rape survivors.

Prepare Resources and Referrals for Male Survivors

Are campus sexual assault centers prepared for male survivors' needs? Adequate referrals for support groups, counselors, hotlines, medical attention, financial assistance, and academic support should be at hand. Male-specific or gender-neutral literature and a short reading list should be available to the survivor. These resources should be compiled before a survivor contacts the office, not as the result of a last-minute search on behalf of a survivor in need of immediate crisis assistance.

Provide Training to Campus Health Clinic and Emergency Room Staff

Are campus health clinics and local hospital emergency rooms trained in the care of adult male survivors of rape? Many rape advocates and medical professionals never receive any such formal training. Not all hospital and statewide protocols for the forensic collection of evidence in rape cases include male-specific content. Adequate training for the examination of men's bodies is crucial, as are procedures for the identification and interpretation of physical findings.

Determine and Address the Legal Implications of Same-Sex Rape

Do law enforcement officials receive sexual assault sensitivity training? If so, is the occurrence of male rape addressed? State and local legal statutes may strongly influence the campus climate for male rape survivors. How is male-on-male rape defined by state and local laws? In many states, rape laws are gender specific, rendering the rape of men a legal impossibility.

Ensure That Campus Policies Apply to Same-Sex Sexual Violence

Do campus policies relating to rape and sexual harassment, codes of student conduct, and nondiscrimination policies allow for the possibility of same-sex sexual violence?

Conduct Prevention and Education Work in Addition to Treatment

Is any form of proactive education and prevention work being done on campus? Reacting to the rape of men is essential, but it is not enough. Absence of attention to male rape denies the reality of same-sex rape and subsequently renders male survivors invisible. Infusion of male rape content into general rape education programming can be effective, not only for the provision of information but also for signifying that the organization or office is receptive and prepared to work with male survivors. Even a basic informational handout can be effective in heightening awareness that rape of men happens in campus communities, not solely in prison populations.

Provide Culturally Competent Programs

Has population-specific awareness and programming been considered? When the entire college rape prevention programming is based on heterosexual models, the sexual assault of gay men, as part of gay bashing or acquaintance rape, is overlooked. Race, class, and other socioeconomic factors could influence the assault characteristics and impact. Single-sex campus environments, such as athletic teams, ROTC, all-male residence halls, and fraternities may also be at a higher risk for male rapes, given the hierarchical structure such environments tend to rely on and the internal power struggles that often manifest as physical violence.[7] Outreach to these communities is essential.

These suggestions are not all inclusive. The diversity of higher-education institutions will dictate the development of additional programs and differing approaches to meet the particular needs of students. More extensive research on the same-sex rape of men is needed to draw further conclusions and closer estimations of this form of violence. As the knowledge and visibility of male rape increase nationally, so will the call for expertise in prevention, education, and treatment related to same-sex rape in campus communities.

NOTES

1. Groth and Burgess, "Male Rape," 806–10; R. Hillman, "Adult Male Victims of Sexual Assault: An Underdiagnosed Condition," *International Journal of STDS and AIDS* 2(1991): 22–24; R. McMullen, *Male Rape: Breaking the Silence on the Last Taboo* (London: Gay Men's Press, 1990); P. L. Huckle, "Male Rape Victims Referred to a Forensic Psychiatric Service," *Medicine, Science, and the Law* 35 (1995): 187–19.

2. Groth and Burgess, "Male Rape"; Mezey and King, "Effects of Sexual Assault"; Hillman, "Adult Male Victims"; McMullen, *Male Rape*; Huckle, "Male Rape Victims."

3. Groth and Burgess, "Male Rape"; McMullen, *Male Rape*; and R. E. Funk, *Stopping Rape* (Philadelphia: New Society, 1993).

4. Groth and Burgess, "Male Rape," 809.

5. D. F. Duncan, "Prevalence of Sexual Assault Victimization among Heterosexual and Gay/Lesbian University Students," *Psychological Reports* 166 (1990); 65–66, D. Island and P. Letellier, *Men Who Beat the Men Who Love Them: Battered Gay Men and Domestic Violence* (New York: Harrington Park Press, 1991); C. K. Waterman, L. Dawson, and M. J. Bologna, "Sexual Coercion in Gay Male and Lesbian Relationships: Predictors and Implications for Support Services," *Journal of Sex Research* 26 (1989): 118–24.

6. Frazier, "Comparative Study"; Mezey and King, "Effects of Sexual Assault."

7. McMullen, *Male Rape*; Huckle, "Male Rape Victims"; Funk, *Stopping Rape*.

9 He Defies You Still: The Memoirs of a Sissy

Tommi Avicolli Mecca

You're just a faggot
No history faces you this morning
A faggot's dreams are scarlet
Bad blood bled from words that scarred[1]

Scene One

A homeroom in a Catholic high school in South Philadelphia. The boy sits quietly in the first aisle, third desk, reading a book. He does not look up, not even for a moment. He is hoping no one will remember he is sitting there. He wishes he were invisible. The teacher is not yet in the classroom so the other boys are talking and laughing loudly.

Suddenly, a voice from beside him:

"Hey, you're a faggot, ain't you?"

The boy does not answer. He goes on reading his book, or rather pretending he is reading his book. It is impossible to actually read the book now.

"Hey, I'm talking to you!"

The boy still does not look up. He is so scared his heart is thumping madly; it feels like it is leaping out of his chest and into his throat. But he can't look up.

"Faggot, I'm talking to you!"

To look up is to meet the eyes of the tormentor.

Suddenly, a sharpened pencil point is thrust into the boy's arm. He jolts, shaking off the pencil, aware that there is blood seeping from the wound.

"What did you do that for?" he asks timidly.

"Cause I hate faggots," the other boy says, laughing. Some other boys begin to laugh, too. A symphony of laughter. The boy feels as if he's going to cry. But he must not cry. Must not cry. So he holds back the tears and tries to read the book again. He must read the book. Read the book.

When the teacher arrives a few minutes later, the class quiets down. The boy does not tell the teacher what has happened. He spits on the wound to clean it, dabbing it with a

---

Tommi Avicolli Mecca is a radical queer activist, writer, and performer. He is the editor of *Smash the Church, Smash the State: The Early Years of Gay Liberation* and coeditor of *Avanti Popolo: Italian Writers Sail Beyond Columbus* and *Hey Paesan: Writing by Lesbians and Gay Men of Italian Descent.*

tissue until the bleeding stops. For weeks he fears some dreadful infection from the lead in the pencil point.

Scene Two

The boy is walking home from school. A group of boys (two, maybe three, he is not certain) grab him from behind, drag him into an alley and beat him up. When he gets home, he races up to his room, refusing dinner ("I don't feel well," he tells his mother through the locked door) and spends the night alone in the dark wishing he would die. . . .

These are not fictitious accounts—I *was* that boy. Having been branded a sissy by neighborhood children because I preferred jump rope to baseball and dolls to playing soldiers, I was often taunted with "hey sissy" or "hey faggot" or "yoo hoo honey" (in a mocking voice) when I left the house.

To avoid harassment, I spent many summers alone in my room. I went out on rainy days when the street was empty.

I came to like being alone. I didn't need anyone, I told myself over and over again. I was an island. Contact with others meant pain. Alone, I was protected. I began writing poems, then short stories. There was no reason to go outside anymore. I had a world of my own.

> *In the schoolyard today*
> *they'll single you out*
> *Their laughter will leave your ears ringing*
> *like the church bells*
> *which once awed you.*[2] . . .

School was one of the more painful experiences of my youth. The neighborhood bullies could be avoided. The taunts of the children living in those endless repetitive row houses could be evaded by staying in my room. But school was something I had to face day after day for some two hundred mornings a year.

I had few friends in school. I was a pariah. Some kids would talk to me, but few wanted to be known as my close friend. Afraid of labels. If I was a sissy, then he had to be a sissy, too. I was condemned to loneliness.

Fortunately, a new boy moved into our neighborhood and befriended me; he wasn't afraid of the labels. He protected me when the other guys threatened to beat me up. He walked me home from school; he broke through the terrible loneliness. We were in third or fourth grade at the time.

We spent a summer or two together. Then his parents sent him to camp and I was once again confined to my room.

Scene Three

High school lunchroom. The boy sits at a table near the back of the room. Without warning, his lunch bag is grabbed and tossed to another table. Someone opens it and confiscates a package of Tastykakes; another boy takes the sandwich. The empty bag is tossed back to the boy who stares at it, dumbfounded. He should be used to this; it has happened before.

Someone screams, "faggot," laughing. There is always laughter. It does not annoy him anymore.

There is no teacher nearby. There is never a teacher around. And what would he say if there were? Could he report the crime? He would be jumped after school if he did. Besides, it would be his word against theirs. Teachers never noticed anything. They never heard the taunts. Never heard the word, "faggot." They were the great deaf mutes, pillars of indifference; a sissy's pain was not relevant to history and geography and god made me to love honor and obey him, amen.

Scene Four

High school Religion class. Someone has a copy of *Playboy*. Father N. is not in the room yet; he's late, as usual. Someone taps the boy roughly on the shoulder. He turns. A finger points to the centerfold model, pink fleshy body, thin and sleek. Almost painted. Not real. The other asks, mocking voice, "Hey, does she turn you on? Look at those tits!"

The boy smiles, nodding meekly; turns away.

The other jabs him harder on the shoulder, "Hey, whatsamatter, don't you like girls?"

Laughter. Thousands of mouths; unbearable din of laughter. In the Arena: thumbs down. Don't spare the queer.

"Wanna suck my dick? Huh? That turn you on, faggot!"

The laughter seems to go on forever. . . .

> *Behind you, the sound of their laughter*
> *echoes a million times*
> *in a soundless place*
> *They watch how you walk/sit/stand/breathe.*[3] . . .

What did being a sissy really mean? It was a way of walking (from the hips rather than the shoulders); it was a way of talking (often with a lisp or in a high-pitched voice); it was a way of relating to others (gently, not wanting to fight, or hurt anyone's feelings). It was being intelligent ("an egghead" they called it sometimes); getting good grades. It meant not being interested in sports, not playing football in the street after school; not discussing teams and scores and playoffs. And it involved not showing fervent interest in girls, not talking about scoring with tits or *Playboy* centerfolds. Not concealing naked women in your history book; or porno books in your locker.

On the other hand, anyone could be a "faggot." It was a catch-all. If you did something that didn't conform to what was the acceptable behavior of the group, then you risked being called a faggot. If you didn't get along with the "in" crowd, you were a faggot. It was the most commonly used put-down. It kept guys in line. They became angry when somebody called them a faggot. More fights started over someone calling someone else a faggot than anything else. The word had power. It toppled the male ego, shattered his delicate facade, violated the image he projected. He was tough. Without feeling. Faggot cut through all this. It made him vulnerable. Feminine. And feminine was the worst thing he could possibly be. Girls were fine for fucking, but no boy in his right mind wanted to be like them. A boy was the opposite of girl. He was not feminine. He was not feeling. He was not weak.

Just look at the gym teacher who growled like a dog; or the priest with the black belt who threw kids against the wall in rage when they didn't know their Latin. They were men, they got respect.

But not the physics teacher who preached pacifism during lectures on the nature of atoms. Everybody knew what he was—and why he believed in the anti-war movement.

My parents only knew that the neighborhood kids called me names. They begged me to act more like the other boys. My brothers were ashamed of me. They never said it, but I knew. Just as I knew that my parents were embarrassed by my behavior.

At times, they tried to get me to act differently. Once my father lectured me on how to walk right. I'm still not clear on what that means. Not from the hips, I guess, don't "swish" like faggots do.

A nun in elementary school told my mother at Open House that there was "something wrong with me." I had draped my sweater over my shoulders like a girl, she said. I was a smart kid, but I should know better than to wear my sweater like a girl!

My mother stood there, mute. I wanted her to say something, to chastise the nun; to defend me. But how could she? This was a nun talking—representative of Jesus, protector of all that was good and decent.

An uncle once told me I should start "acting like a boy" instead of like a girl. Everybody seemed ashamed of me. And I guess I was ashamed of myself, too. It was hard not to be.

Scene Five

Priest: Do you like girls, Mark?

Mark: Uh-huh.

Priest: I mean *really* like them?

Mark: Yeah—they're okay.

Priest: There's a role they play in your salvation. Do you understand it, Mark?

Mark: Yeah.

Priest: You've got to like girls. Even if you should decide to enter the seminary, it's important to keep in mind God's plan for a man and a woman.[4] . . .

Catholicism of course condemned homosexuality. Effeminacy was tolerated as long as the effeminate person did not admit to being gay. Thus, priests could be effeminate because they weren't gay.

As a sissy, I could count on no support from the church. A male's sole purpose in life was to father children—souls for the church to save. The only hope a homosexual had of attaining salvation was by remaining totally celibate. Don't even think of touching another boy. To think of a sin was a sin. And to sin was to put a mark upon the soul. Sin—if it was a serious offense against god—led to hell. There was no way around it. If you sinned, you were doomed.

Realizing I was gay was not an easy task. Although I knew I was attracted to boys by the time I was about eleven, I didn't connect this attraction to homosexuality. I was not queer. Not I. I was merely appreciating a boy's good looks, his fine features, his proportions. It didn't seem to matter that I didn't appreciate a girl's looks in the same way. There was no twitching in my thighs when I gazed upon a beautiful girl. But I wasn't queer.

I resisted that label—queer—for the longest time. Even when everything pointed to it, I refused to see it. I was certainly not queer. Not I.

We sat through endless English classes, and History courses about the wars between men who were not allowed to love each other. No gay history was ever taught. No history faces you this morning. You're just a faggot. Homosexuals had never contributed to the human race. God destroyed the queers in Sodom and Gomorrah.

We learned about Michelangelo, Oscar Wilde, Gertrude Stein—but never that they were queer. They were not queer. Walt Whitman, the "father of American poetry," was not queer. No one was queer. I was alone, totally unique. One of a kind. Were there others like me somewhere? Another planet, perhaps?

In school, they never talked of the queers. They did not exist. The only hint we got of this other species was in Religion class. And even then it was clouded in mystery—never spelled out. It was sin. Like masturbation. Like looking at *Playboy* and getting a hard-on. A sin.

Once a progressive priest in senior year Religion class actually mentioned homosexuals—he said the word—but was into Erich Fromm, into homosexuals as pathetic and sick. Fixated at some early stage; penis, anal, whatever. Only heterosexuals passed on to the nirvana of sexual development.

No other images from the halls of the Catholic high school except those the other boys knew: swishy faggot sucking cock in an alley somewhere, grabbing asses in the bathroom. Never mentioning how much straight boys craved blowjobs, it was part of the secret.

It was all a secret. You were not supposed to talk about the queers. Whisper maybe. Laugh about them, yes. But don't be open, honest; don't try to understand. Don't cite their accomplishments. No history faces you this morning. You're just a faggot faggot no history just a faggot

Epilogue

The boy marching down the Parkway. Hundreds of queers. Signs proclaiming gay pride. Speakers. Tables with literature from gay groups. A miracle, he is thinking. Tears are coming loose now. Someone hugs him.

> *You could not control*
> *the sissy in me*
> *nor could you exorcise him*
> *nor electrocute him*
> *You declared him illegal illegitimate*
> *insane and immature*
> *But he defies you still.*[5]

NOTES

1. From the poem "Faggot," by Tommi Avicolli Mecca, published in *GPU News*, September 1979.

2. *Ibid.*

3. *Ibid.*

4. From the play *Judgment of the Roaches*, by Tommi Avicolli Mecca, produced in Philadelphia at the Gay Community Center, the Painted Bride Arts Center and the University of Pennsylvania; aired over WXPN-FM, in four parts; and presented at the Lesbian/Gay Conference in Norfolk, VA, July 1980.

5. From the poem "Sissy Poem," published in *Magic Doesn't Live Here Anymore* (Philadelphia: Spruce Street Press, 1976).

10 | Gentrification Will Drive My Uncle out of His Neighborhood, and I Will Have Helped

Eric Rodriguez

My *tío* Pedro lives behind a trendy bar on Sunset Boulevard in Los Angeles's Echo Park. The apartment owners told him the other day that the price of rent would be going up—again. He is one of many who will be pushed out by rising prices, and I am one of the very people pushing him out.

Since moving back here in July 2014, I've had one foot in my former community and the other in this new place I call "home"—while slowly robbing my uncle of his own. I don't know what the right thing to do is. I did what he and moms told me to do to avoid the gangs and violence: I got an education, and I earn more money than the rest of my family. I made it out of the neighborhood. Now, moving back feels wrong.

When I was a kid you could buy tacos at the park for a dollar. The vendors upped their prices the moment different people came into the neighborhood and were willing to pay more. Now many of the *mamis* with their thin eyebrows and big hooped earrings can't afford living here, nor can many of the shaved headed homies in white t-shirts and tattoos. They're disappearing. As are those random *tiendas* at the center of commerce on Sunset Boulevard which close every other week, only to be replaced by a new coffee shop.

My *tío* works in construction so money is not, well, flowing. Not in the way it does to the developers who buy up charming bungalows in the neighborhood and then demolish them to build mid-rise monstrosities. It's "modern" and makes money, the developers say. You don't get it, they tell me, despite having lived in one in New York City and being an alumnus of a Wall Street investment bank. I get it, I just don't agree with it. *Tío* Pedro could not afford to live in one; he actually thinks they're hideous too. And so he laments the former neighborhood, its charm and character and affordability, minus the gangs and violence, of course.

Violence was common back in the 1990s around here. The park was off-limits at night because of the drug dealing and gang fights. It's different now; the park is safer than ever. I took a girl there for a walk around the lake in the evening the other day and saw the bust of José Martí, the Cuban revolutionary whose writings and philosophy led to Cuba's independence from Spain, and smiled at the thought of how Echo Park itself had wrestled its independence from the crime and violence it was once chained to.

Eric Rodriguez is a writer, a trustee emeritus of Brown University, and a term member at the Council on Foreign Relations.

Originally appeared in *The Guardian*, August 23, 2015. Copyright © 2019 by Guardian News & Media Ltd.

But there are bizarre things happening now.

The other day a few friends and I smoked a joint near the boathouse and no one—not even the cops—cared much to stop and check things out. Back in the day it didn't go down like that at all. Don't take my word for it either; look at Frank Romero's "Arrest of the Paleteros."* Even selling ice cream those days was a crime for people of color.

One day my cousin, Echo Park Pete, was walking with me around the lake and he said, referring to the drug use: "Man, I went to jail for this shit and now people do it all the time and the cops don't give a shit." I thought about offering a plausible explanation, you know, invoking my Ivy League education, but it felt forced. It is what it is: discrimination. I kept my stupid mouth shut.

This is the *new* neighborhood. A place where coffee shops and trendy bars are popping up, and drug use at the park goes unchecked because the new people using look different than the ones previously using. One group of people is moving in and another is being moved out. Call it gentrification; call it what you want, but it's happening. I see it happening—because I'm part of it.

---

*This 1996 painting by acclaimed Chicano artist Frank Romero depicts the violent arrest of Echo Park paleteros (ice cream vendors) for not having permits.

11 My Vassar College Faculty ID Makes Everything OK

Kiese Laymon

The fourth time a Poughkeepsie police officer told me that my Vassar College Faculty ID could make everything OK was three years ago. I was driving down Wilbur Avenue. When the white police officer, whose head was way too small for his neck, asked if my truck was stolen, I laughed, said no, and shamefully showed him my license and my ID, just like Lanre Akinsiku.[1] The ID, which ensures that I can spend the rest of my life in a lush state park with fat fearless squirrels, surrounded by enlightened white folks who love talking about Jon Stewart, Obama, and civility,[2] has been washed so many times it doesn't lie flat.

After taking my license and ID back to his car, the police officer came to me with a ticket and two lessons. "Looks like you got a good thing going on over there at Vassar College," he said. "You don't wanna it ruin it by rolling through stop signs, do you?"

I sucked my teeth, shook my head, kept my right hand visibly on my right thigh, rolled my window up, and headed back to campus.

One more ticket.

Two more condescending lessons from a lame armed with white racial supremacy, anti-blackness, a gun, and a badge. But at least I didn't get arrested.

Or shot eight times.

My Vassar College Faculty ID made everything okay. A little over two hours later, I sat in a closed room on Vassar's campus in a place called Main Building.

In the center of my ID, standing dusty orange and partially hidden by shadows of massive trees, is a picture of Vassar College's Main Building. Black women students took the building over in 1969 to demand, among other things, that the administration affirmatively reckon with its investment in anti-blackness and white racial supremacy. A multiracial group of students led by Cleon Edwards occupied Main again in 1990, after Daniel Patrick Moynihan reportedly told a Jamaican Dutchess County official, "If you don't like it in this country, why don't you pack your bags and go back where you came from?"

I sat in a room in Main that day with a senior professor and two high-ranking administrators. We were having one of those meetings you're not supposed to talk about. Near the end of the meeting, this senior professor affirmed his/her commitment to "African Americans" and said I was a "fraud."

Kiese Laymon is a writer and a professor of English and creative writing at the University of Mississippi. His novels, memoirs, and short stories explore racism, family, mental health, and identity.

Originally appeared on Gawker, November 19, 2014. Reprinted with permission from the author.

I tucked both hands underneath my buttocks, rested my left knuckle beneath my ID as tears pooled in the gutters of both eyes. I'd been hungry before. I'd been beaten. I'd had guns pulled on me. I never felt as pathetic, angry, and terrified as I felt in that room.

I came into that meeting knowing that the illest part of racial terror in this nation is that it's sanctioned by sorry overpaid white bodies that will never be racially terrorized and maintained by a few desperate underpaid black and brown bodies that will. I left that meeting knowing that there are few things more shameful than being treated like a nigger by—and under the gaze of—intellectually and imaginatively average white Americans who are not, and will never have to be, half as good at their jobs as you are at yours.

I sat in that meeting thinking about the first day I got my ID. It was nine years earlier and I remember walking to the gym, maybe 100 yards behind Main Building and being asked by a white boy in yellow flip-flops if I could sell him some weed.

I just looked at his flip-flops.

And he just looked at my black neck. And when I told him that I taught English, he contorted his bushy brow, said "Word," and trotted off.

Later that year, maybe 30 yards to the left of Main Building, security routinely entered my office asking for my ID despite my name on the door and pictures of me, my Mama, and them all over my desk. In that same building, one floor lower, after I got my first book deal, I was told by another senior white member of my department that it was "all right" if I spoke to him "in ebonics." Later that year, a white senior professor walked in at the end of one of my classes and told me, in front of my students, "Don't talk back to me."

I wanted to put my palm through this man's esophagus and burn that building down, but I thought about prison and my Grandmama's health care. So I cussed his ass out and went about the business of eating too much fried cheese and biscuits at a local buffet.

A few summers later, right in front of Main Building, two security guards stopped me for walking past the President's house without identification. They threatened to call the Poughkeepsie police on me. I told the officers, "Fuck you" and "Show me your ID" for a number of reasons, but mostly because I'd sold one of them a car a few years ago, and Vassar's security officers don't carry guns.

Like nearly every black person I know from the deep South who has one of these faculty IDs, I anticipated reckoning daily with white racial supremacy at my job.

But.

I didn't expect to smell the crumbling of a real human heart when I went to the police station to get my student, Mat, who had been missing for days. Mat was a beautiful Southern black boy suffering from bipolar disorder.

I didn't anticipate hearing the hollowed terror and shame in my student Rachel's voice at 2 in the morning after she was arrested by Poughkeepsie police for jaywalking while her white friends just watched. Rachel went to jail that night.

I didn't expect to feel the cold cracked hands of administrators when we pushed the college to allow Jade, a black Phi Beta Kappa student from DC, back into school after they suspended her for a full year for verbally intimidating her roommate.

I didn't expect to taste my own tears when watching three black women seniors tell two heads of security and the Dean of the College that they, and another Asian American woman, deserve to not have security called on them for being black women simply doing their laundry and reading books on a Sunday afternoon. I didn't expect the Dean of the College and the heads of security to do absolutely nothing after this meeting.

I didn't expect to have to wrap my arms around Leo, a Chicano student who stood shivering and sobbing in front of Poughkeepsie police after getting jumped on Raymond Ave. by kids he called "my own people." Didn't expect to take him to the police station and have the questioning officer ask Leo, "Why do you use the term 'Latino'? Can you tell me what country the boys who jumped you were from?" The officer told Leo that his partner was Colombian and could tell where a person was from just by looking at them. Leo told me that he felt "most Chicano, most Latino, and most like a Vassar student" that night.

I didn't expect that.

I didn't expect to see my student Orion, a black boy from Boston, sitting palms down on the sidewalk in front of a police car a few Thursdays ago on my way from the gym. I got in the face of the two interrogating officers telling them, "He didn't do nothing" and "Leave my student the fuck alone," when I found out he was being accused of trying to steal a security golf cart.

I didn't expect the same two security guards who'd stopped me for walking in front of the President's house to tell the officers interrogating Orion that the golf cart was theirs and Orion was "a good kid, a Vassar student" who was just going to get a slice of pizza.

By the time one of the heads of Vassar security, in the presence of the current Dean of the College, told one of my colleagues and me that there was "no racial profiling on campus" and that we were making the black and brown students say there was, I expected almost everything.

I expected that four teenage black boys from Poughkeepsie would have security called on them for making too much noise in the library one Sunday afternoon. I expected security to call Poughkeepsie police on these 15- and 16-year-olds when a few of them couldn't produce an ID. I expected police to drive on the lawn in front of the library, making a spectacle of these black boys' perceived guilt.

A few days after Vassar called police on those children, a police officer visited one of the boys while he was in class and questioned him about some stolen cell phones and iPods at Vassar. When the kid said he didn't know anything about any stolen cell phones, the officer told the 15-year-old black child, who might have applied to Vassar in three years, to never go back to Vassar College again.

I didn't expect that.

Vassar College, the place that issues my faculty ID, a place so committed to access and what they call economic diversity,[3] did its part to ensure that a black Poughkeepsie child, charged with nothing, would forever be a part of the justice system for walking through a library without an ID.

There is no way on earth that a 15-year-old child visited by police officers at his school for walking through a local college library while black is going to be OK.

And neither are we.

But.

My Vassar College Faculty ID affords me free smoothies, free printing paper, paid leave, and access to one of the most beautiful libraries on Earth. It guarantees that I have really good health care and more disposable income than anyone in my Mississippi family. But way more than I want to admit, I'm wondering what price we pay for these kinds of IDs, and what that price has to do with the extrajudicial disciplining and killing of young cis and trans black human beings.

You have a Michigan State Faculty ID, and seven-year old Aiyana Stanley-Jones was killed in a police raid. You have a Wilberforce University Faculty ID and 12-year-old Tamir Rice was shot dead by police for holding a BB gun. I have a Vassar College Faculty ID and NYPD suffocated Shereese Francis while she lay face-down on a mattress. You have a University of Missouri Student ID and Mike Brown's unarmed 18-year-old black body lay dead in the street for four and a half hours.

But.

"We are winning," my mentor, Adisa Ajamu, often tells me. "Improvisation, transcendence, and resilience—the DNA of the Black experience—are just synonyms for fighting preparedness for the long winter of war."

Adisa is right. But to keep winning, to keep our soul and sanity in this terror-filled coliseum, at some point we have to say fuck it. We have to say fuck them. And most importantly, we must say to people and communities that love us, "I love you. Will you please love me? I'm listening."

We say that most profoundly with our work. We say that most profoundly with our lives. The question is, can we mean what we must say with our work and our lives and continue working at institutions like Vassar College.

Listening to our people and producing rigorous, soulful work are not antithetical. My teachers: Noel Didla, Paula Madison, Brittney Cooper, Rosa Clemente, Osagyefo Sekou, Eve Dunbar, Imani Perry, Darnell Moore, Josie Duffy, Kimberlé Crenshaw, Mark Anthony Neal, Mychal Denzel Smith, dream hampton, Regina Bradley, Marlon Peterson, Jamilah LeMieux, Luke Harris, Chanda Hsu Prescod-Weinstein, and Carlos Alamo show me this every day.

They also show me that though there's an immense price to pay in and out of so-called elite American educational institutions, the depth of this price differs based on sexuality, gender, race, access to wealth, and the status of one's dependents.

I paid the price of having sorry gatekeepers at Vassar question the validity of my book contracts, question my graduation from undergrad, question my graduation from grad school, question whether or not I was given tenure as opposed to earning it. And like you, when questioned so much, of course I outworked them, but scars accumulated in battles won sometimes hurt more than battles lost.

I gained 129 pounds. I got sick. I kept hurting someone who would have never hurt me. I rarely slept.

I kept fighting. And praying. And I got my work out. And I worked on healing. And I taught my kids. And I served my community. And I got hit again. And I swung at folks who weren't even swinging at me. And my best friend, who was also reckoning with the "Vassar" part of her Vassar Faculty ID, and I took turns lying to each other, sealing off our hearts in favor of arguments and unpaid labor. And when I earned leaves that I should have spent at home in Forest, Mississippi, with the 85-year-old woman who gave me the skills of improvisation, transcendence, and resilience, I stayed at Vassar College and guided tons of independent studies, directed flailing programs, helped incompetent administrators do their jobs, and chaired hollow committees.

My family needed me home. My soul needed to be there. But I was afraid to be somewhere where my Vassar College Faculty ID didn't matter worth a damn. I was afraid to let the Mississippi black folks who really got me oversee all my new stretch marks, afraid they'd hear the isolation and anxiety in my voice, afraid they'd find the crumpled bank receipts from money taken out at casinos. I was afraid to show my Mama, Auntie, and Grandma that I felt alone and so much sadder than the 27-year-old black boy they remember being issued a Vassar College Faculty ID 12 years ago.

OK.

A half an inch below my name on my bent ID is a nine digit identification number, and in the top left corner, hanging in the blue sky, is a 27-year-old black boy wearing an emerald green hoodie. An army green sweater-hat cocked slightly to the left is pulled over my eyes. A black book bag is slung across my right shoulder.

When I took the picture of that ID, I felt so healthy. I felt so worthy of good love. I didn't feel delivered but I felt proud that I could take care of my Mississippi family. I felt that every beating I'd gotten with shoes, extension cords, switches, belts, belt buckles, fists, and the guns of police officers was worth it. I knew that our mamas and grandmamas and aunties beat us to remind us that there was a massive price to pay for being black, free, and imperfect. I knew they beat us partially so that we would one day have a chance to wield IDs like mine as a weapon and a shield.

Twelve years after getting my Vassar College faculty ID, I sit here and know that the nation can't structurally and emotionally assault black children and think they're going to turn out OK.

Vassar College can't structurally assault and neglect black children and think they're going to turn out OK.

I can't personally assault and neglect black children and think they're going to turn out OK.

I think about time travel and regret a lot. If I could go back and tell my Mama anything, I would tell her that I love her, and I thank her, and I see her and I know that white racial supremacy, poverty, heteropatriarchy, and a lifetime as a young black woman academic with a hardheaded son are whupping her ass, but black parents can't physically and emotionally assault their black children—even in an attempt to protect them from the worst of white folks—and think they are going to turn out OK.

We are not OK. We are not OK. We have to get better at organizing, strategizing, and patiently loving us because the people who issued my Vassar College ID, like the people who issued Darren Wilson and Robert McCulloch their badges, will never ever give a fuck about the inside of our lives.

I have a Vassar College Faculty ID. I write books that some people care about. I teach my students. I take care of my Grandma. I have more access to healthy choice than most of my cousins. And I, like a lot of you, am not OK. I am not subhuman. I am not superhuman. I am not a demon. I cannot walk through bullets. I am not a special nigger. I am not a fraud. I am not OK.

But.

Unlike Mike Brown and Aiyana Stanley-Jones and Tamir Rice, I am alive. We are alive. And.

We are so much better than the sick part of our nation that murders an unarmed black boy like a rabid dog, before prosecuting him for being a nigger. We are so much better than powerful academic institutions, slick prosecutors, and the *innocent* practitioners of white racial supremacy in this nation who really believe that a handful of niggers with some special IDs, and a scar(r)ed black President on the wrong side of history, are proof of their—and really, our own—terrifying deliverance from American evil.

NOTES

1. Akinsiku, L. (2014, August 17.). *Gawker.com*. The Price of Blackness.
2. Hsu, H. (2014, December 1). *Newyorker.com*. The Civility Wars.
3. Hoffman, E. (2014, September 17). *miscellanynews.org*. VC Tops List of Economically Diverse Elite Colleges.

12

The Unbearable (In)visibility of Being Trans

Chase Strangio

During an internship in my second year of law school, I quickly realized that my transness made me both hyper-visible and completely invisible.

I am noticed.

Innocuously, that visibility is a second glance when I use the bathroom, when I am walking down the street with my toddler, when I speak and my voice does not quite match up with people's expectations. But more insidiously that visibility is the older gentleman coming up behind me while I wait for a train at Penn Station, grabbing my crotch and asking, "how much?"; it is the receptionist at the gynecologist's office telling me I don't belong there, delaying my needed medical care for dangerous lengths of time; it is the unconsented-to questions and declarations about my body.

At that internship in law school, where I first really felt this paradox of hyper-visibility and invisibility, there was something about the liminal gender space I occupied that invited attention. I didn't look quite right but no one could figure out what was "wrong." Everyone in the office knew my name and had their own way of asking (without asking)—"what are you?" Frequently this was in the form of unwanted and sexualized attention. I spent much of the internship managing questions about my body, how I had sex and from one staff member in the office, relentless requests to satisfy his own curiosity about both things.

At the same time, I walked into court every day—with relative ease because of my suit, my masculinity, my whiteness—through the separate security entrance for attorneys and law students. But once inside the courthouse, there was the constant suggestion that I was a young child accompanying my father to work every day. I would be yelled at if I didn't wear a tie—"young man, don't you understand professionalism"—but mocked if I did—"ties are not appropriate for women." One judge joked flippantly that I was "Doogie Howser" and laughed in front of a courtroom full of people. This certainly didn't help me develop confidence in myself as a person and a lawyer but it paled in comparison to the humiliation and erasure levied upon those mostly black and brown bodies who sat in court awaiting sentencing or trial or more and endless court dates.

Chase Strangio is a staff attorney with the ACLU's LGBT & HIV Project. His work focuses on advocacy and lawsuits promoting societal change on behalf of LGBT people and people with HIV, with a special focus on transgender people held in police custody, jailed, or otherwise detained. He founded the Lorena Borjas Community Fund to help LGBT immigrants with direct bail in criminal and immigration cases.

Originally appeared in *The Huffington Post*, February 2, 2016. Courtesy of Chase Strangio.

Make no mistake; none of these experiences are unique to trans-ness. Tragically few people go through the world without being surveilled and erased by the powerful and their power systems. And those who do—those who feel empowered and safe in powerful spaces—are disproportionately (if not exclusively) white, cis-, able-bodied, citizens with access to significant financial and social capital. They are the judges making jokes from the bench as they send young black men to prison for life.

Nor are the costs and consequences of this visibility evenly distributed and felt. Imagine what the cost is to those trans people who don't carry the powerful shield from systemic violence that comes with whiteness, masculinity, a legal education, a job doing LGBT work, at an organization with resources and cultural respect and recognition. If I can be erased and attacked, what about my friends and colleagues who are exposed to relentless surveillance, erasure and violence without such protection? What about the trans women of color for whom visibility does not lead to discomfort but to arrest or death?

There is unbearableness to being trans; so much visibility and so much invisibility.

I think of Ashley Arnold,[1] a 32-year-old white trans woman in federal prison in Virginia. She was hyper-visible to the officers who allegedly tormented[2] and harassed her daily. But she was invisible to the prison system and to the courts that systemically withheld her medical care. On February 25, Ashley died by suicide in her cell. When her trans sisters at FCI Petersburg tried to tell her story, make her visible on her own terms, they were punished by the prison. Disciplined for "acting as journalists."

I think of Islan Nettles,[3] a black trans woman, just 21 years old, who was brutally murdered for daring to exist in the world. When Islan walked down the street with her friends, the fact that she was trans evoked so much rage that a group of people beat her to death.

I think of CeCe McDonald,[4] a black trans woman, just 21 years old, when she almost suffered the same fate as Islan. Walking down the street in Minneapolis, her blackness and transness, prompted a group of white people to attack her and beat her. She fought back and survived. And what did she get for surviving against all odds—a manslaughter conviction and years in prison.

There is unbearableness but that unbearableness also binds us together. Amidst the scrutiny, the savage violence, the systemic discrimination, there are communities of resistance and resilience that hold each other up, that send letters and love to people in prison like Ashley's friends who are mourning her death, that organized for CeCe's release from prison, that tell stories of trans histories and leadership.

I am always struck by how many amazing trans people there are—mostly trans women of color—who don't work at big name organizations or appear in magazines or on television, but who make sure that other trans people are housed, fed, supported, and surviving.

Lorena Borjas,[5] Bamby Salcedo, Ruby Corado, Miss Major, Reina Gossett, and so many more. They are the connective tissue, the supportive framework, the breath that gives so many life and that makes trans survival beautiful and possible. Read about them, support them, donate to them.

NOTES

1. Lydon, J. (2015, March 25). *Blackandpink.org*. Prison Censorship in America: The Ashley Jean Arnold Case.
2. Zoukis, C. (2015, March 3). *Prisonlegalnews.org*. Transgender Prisoner Denied Adequate Treatment Hangs Herself.
3. Kellaway, M. (2015, March 4). *Advocate.com*. Suspect Indicted in Beating Death of N.Y. Trans Woman Islan Nettles.
4. Erdely, S. (2014, July 30). *Rollingstone.com*. The Transgender Crucible. [See Erdely's essay in Part IV of this volume.]
5. Cortes, Z. (2012, May 22). *Voicesofny.org*. Fund Seeks to Address Police Profiling of Transgender Women.

13 Black Bodies in Motion and in Pain

Edwidge Danticat

This past weekend, between not sleeping and constantly checking the news, I walked the long rectangular room at New York's Museum of Modern Art, where Jacob Lawrence's "Migration Series" is currently on display. I had seen many of the paintings before, in books and magazines, but never "in person." I'd somehow expected them to be as colossal as their subject, the fifty-five-year-plus mass migration of more than six million African-Americans from the rural south to urban centers in the northern United States. The sixty spare and, at times, appropriately stark tempera paintings in the series each measure twelve-by-eighteen inches and are underscored by descriptive captions written by the artist, whose parents moved from Virginia and South Carolina to New Jersey, where he was born. The size of the paintings quickly became inconsequential as I moved from panel to panel, the first one showing a crowd of people crammed into a train station and filing toward ticket windows marked Chicago, New York, Saint Louis, and the last panel returning us to yet another railroad station, showing that in spite of dangerous and unhealthy working conditions and race riots in the North, the migrants "kept coming."

At the end of a week when nine men and women were brutally assassinated by a racist young man in Charleston, South Carolina, and the possibility of two hundred thousand Haitians and Dominicans of Haitian descent being expelled from the Dominican Republic suddenly became very real,[1] I longed to be in the presence of Lawrence's migrants and survivors. I was yearning for their witness and fellowship, to borrow language from some of the churches that ended up being lifelines for the Great Migration's new arrivals. But what kept me glued to these dark silhouettes is how beautifully and heartbreakingly Lawrence captured black bodies in motion, in transit, in danger, and in pain. The bowed heads of the hungry and the curved backs of mourners helped the Great Migration to gain and keep its momentum, along with the promise of less abject poverty in the North, better educational opportunities, and the right to vote.

Human beings have been migrating since the beginning of time. We have always travelled from place to place looking for better opportunities, where they exist. We are not always welcomed, especially if we are viewed as different and dangerous, or if we end up,

---

Edwidge Danticat is a Haitian-American writer whose novels, short stories, and memoirs focus on women and their relationships and on issues related to power dynamics, social injustice, and poverty, as well as her own experiences as an immigrant. Her awards include a Pushcart Short Story Prize.

Originally Appeared in *The New Yorker*, June 22, 2015. Reprinted with permission from: Edwidge Danticat, *The New Yorker* © Condé Nast.

as the novelist Toni Morrison described in her Nobel lecture, on the edges of towns that cannot bear our company. Will we ever have a home in this place, or will we always be set adrift from the home we knew? Or the home we have never known.

The nine men and women who were senselessly murdered at Emanuel African Methodist Episcopal Church last Wednesday were home. They were in their own country, among family and friends, and they believed themselves to be in the presence of God. And yet before they were massacred they were subjected to a variation of the same detestable vitriol that unwanted immigrants everywhere face: "You're taking over our country, and you have to go."

In the hateful manifesto posted on his Web site, the killer, Dylann Roof, also writes, "As an American we are taught to accept living in the melting pot, and black and other minorities have just as much right to be here as we do, since we are all immigrants. But Europe is the homeland of White people, and in many ways the situation is even worse there." I wonder if he had in mind Europe's most recent migrants, especially those who have been drowning by the hundreds in the waters of the Mediterranean Sea, brown and black bodies fleeing oppression and wars in sub-Saharan and northern Africa and the Middle East. Or maybe he was thinking of all those non-white people who are European citizens, though not by his standards. This bigoted young man charged himself with deciding who can stay and who can go, and the only uncontestable way he knew to carry out his venomous decree was to kill.

In "The Warmth of Other Suns," the Pulitzer Prize–winning journalist Isabel Wilkerson writes that, during the Great Migration, "The people did not cross the turnstiles of customs at Ellis Island. They were already citizens. But where they came from, they were not treated as such." Nearly every migrant Wilkerson interviewed justifiably resisted being called an immigrant. "The idea conjured up the deepest pains of centuries of rejection by their own country," she writes.

Tragically, we do not always get the final say on how our black bodies are labelled. Those fleeing the South during the Great Migration were sometimes referred to not only as immigrants but as refugees, just as the U.S. citizens who were internally displaced by Hurricane Katrina were given that label ten years ago.

Dominicans of Haitian descent also thought themselves to be at home in the Dominican Republic. The Dominican constitution, dating back to 1929, grants citizenship to all those who are born in the country, unless they are the children of people "in transit." Dominicans of Haitian descent who were born during the past eighty-six years are still considered to be in transit. Black bodies, living with "certain uncertainty," to use Frantz Fanon's words, can be in transit, it seems, for several generations.

White supremacists such as Dylann Roof like to speak of black bodies as though they are dangerous weapons. Xenophobes often speak of migrants and immigrants as though they are an invasion force or something akin to biological warfare. In an essay called "The Fear of Black Bodies in Motion," Wallace Best, a religion and Great Migration scholar, writes that "a black body in motion is never without consequence. It is always a signifier of something, scripted and coded. And for the most part, throughout our history black bodies in motion have been deemed a threat."[2]

These days, it seems that black bodies are more threatened than they have ever been so far in this century. Or maybe we just have more ways to document the beatings, shootings, and other abuses that have been suffered in the recent past. As means of transportation have become more accessible, it also seems that we have more migration than ever. Even children are migrating by the thousands in our hemisphere, crossing several borders to flee gang violence in Central America, while hoping to be reunited with their U.S.-based parents. Still, we live in a world where, as the late Uruguayan writer Eduardo Galeano said, money can move freely, but people cannot.

Black bodies are increasingly becoming battlefields upon which horrors are routinely executed, each one so close to the last that we barely have the time to fully grieve and mourn. The massacre at Emanuel African Methodist Episcopal Church and the racist rant that preceded it highlight the hyper-vigilance required to live and love, work and play, travel and pray in a black body. These killings, and the potential mass expulsions from the Dominican Republic, remind us, as Baby Suggs reminds her out-of-doors congregation in Toni Morrison's "Beloved," that, both yonder and here, some do not love our flesh and are unwilling to acknowledge our humanity, much less our nationality or citizenship.

As many Haitian migrants and immigrants and Dominicans of Haitian descent now either go into hiding or leave the Dominican Republic out of fear, we are witnessing, once again, a sea of black bodies in motion, in transit, and in danger. And as Emanuel African Methodist Episcopal Church and the larger community of Charleston, South Carolina, prepare to bury their dead, we will once again be seeing black bodies in pain. And we will be expected to be exceptionally graceful mourners. We will be expected to stifle our rage. And we will keep asking ourselves, When will this end? When will it stop?

NOTES

1. Danticat, E. (2015, June 17). "Fear of Deportation in the Dominican Republic." *The New Yorker.*
2. Best, W. (2014, December 4). "The Fear of Black Bodies in Motion." *The Huffington Post.*

Adichie, Chimamanda Ngozi. *We Should All Be Feminists*. Anchor Books, 2015.

Allison, Dorothy. *Skin: Talking about Sex, Class and Literature*, 2nd ed. Open Road Media, 2013.

Anzaldúa, Gloria, ed. *Making Face, Making Soul/Haciendo Caras: Creative and Critical Perspectives by Women of Color*. Aunt Lute Books, 1990.

Azoulay, Katya Gibel. *Black, Jewish, and Interracial*. Duke University Press, 1997.

Baca, Jimmy Santiago. *A Place to Stand*. Grove, 2002.

Bahadur, Gaiutra. *Coolie Woman: The Odyssey of Indenture*. University of Chicago Press, 2014.

Bartlett, Jennifer, Sheila Black, and Michael Northen, eds. *Beauty Is a Verb: The New Poetry of Disability*. Cinco Puntos Press, 2011.

Baumgardner, Jennifer. *Look Both Ways: Bisexual Politics*. Farrar, Straus and Giroux, 2008.

Bayoumi, Moustafa. *This Muslim American Life: Dispatches from the War on Terror*. New York University Press, 2015.

Bean, Joseph. *In the Life: A Black Gay Anthology*. Alyson Publications, 1986.

Brown, Rita Mae. *Rubyfruit Jungle*. Bantam, 1977.

Chen, Chen. *When I Grow Up I Want to Be a List of Further Possibilities*. BOA Editions Ltd, 2017.

Clausen, Jan. *Apples and Oranges: My Journey to Sexual Identity*. Houghton Mifflin, 1999.

Coates, Ta-Nehisi. *Between the World and Me*. Spiegel & Grau, 2015.

Cofer, Judith Ortiz. *The Latin Deli*. University of Georgia Press, 1993.

Coltelli, Laura. *Winged Words: American Indian Writers Speak*. University of Nebraska Press, 1990.

Crozier Hogle, Lois, et al. *Surviving in Two Worlds: Contemporary Native American Voices*. University of Texas Press, 1997.

Danticat, Edwidge. *Breath, Eyes, Memory*. Vintage Books, 1994.

Davis, Lennard. *The Disability Studies Reader*, 5th ed. Routledge, 2016.

Delgado, Richard, and Jean Stefancic. *The Latino/a Condition: A Critical Reader*, 2nd ed. New York University Press, 2010.

Dougherty, Cyra Perry, ed. *The Anatomy of Silence: Twenty-Six Stories about All the Shit That Gets in the Way of Speaking about Sexual Violence*. Red Press, 2019.

Findlen, Barbara. *Listen Up: Voices from the Next Feminist Generation*, 2nd ed. Seal Press, 2001.

Fong, Timothy, and Larry Shinagawa. *Asian Americans: Experiences and Perspectives*. Prentice Hall, 2000.

Gay, Roxane. *Bad Feminist*. Harper Perennial, 2014.

———, ed. *Not That Bad: Dispatches from Rape Culture*. Harper Perennial, 2018.

Halberstam, Judith. *In a Queer Place and Time: Transgender Bodies, Subcultural Lives*. New York University Press, 2005.

Haley, Alex. *The Autobiography of Malcolm X*. Grove Press, 1964.

Jackson, Naomi. *The Starside of Bird Hill: A Novel*. Penguin Press, 2015.

James, Marlon. *A Brief History of Seven Killings*. Riverhead Books, 2015.

Jen, Gish. *Typical American*. Penguin, 1992.

Kim, Elaine H., Lilia V. Villanueva, and Asian Women United of California, eds. *Making More Waves: New Writings by Asian American Women*. Beacon Press, 1997.

Kimmel, Michael S., and Michael A. Messner, eds. *Men's Lives*, 9th ed. Prentice Hall, 2012.

Kingston, Maxine Hong. *The Woman Warrior*. Vintage Books, 1981.

Lahiri, Jhumpa. *The Namesake*. Mariner Books, 2003.

Linton, Simi. *My Body Politic*. University of Michigan Press, 2005.

Miranda, Deborah. *Bad Indians: A Tribal Memoir*. Heyday, 2013.

Moody, Anne. *Coming of Age in Mississippi*. Dell, 1968.

Moss, Janet. *Redefining Realness: My Path to Womanhood, Identity, Love & So Much More*. Simon & Schuster, 2014.

Moraga, Cherríe L. *A Xicana Codex of Changing Consciousness: Writings, 2000–2010*. Duke University Press, 2011.

Moraga, Cherríe, and Gloria Anzaldúa, eds. *This Bridge Called My Back*. Kitchen Table: Women of Color Press, 1983.

Nam, Vickie. *Yell-Oh Girls!* HarperCollins, 2001.

Obama, Barack. *Dreams of My Father*. Three Rivers Press, 2004.

Phi, Bao. *Thousand Star Hotel*. Coffee House Press, 2017.

Piepzna-Samarasinha, Leah Lakshmi. *Dirty River: A Queer Femme of Color Dreaming Her Way Home*. Arsenal Pulp Press, 2015.

Portes, Alejandro, and Rubén G. Rumbaut. *Legacies: The Story of the Immigrant Second Generation*. University of California Press, 2001.

Rankine, Claudia. *Citizen*. Graywolf Press, 2014.

Rebolledo, Tey Diana, and Eliana S. Rivero, eds. *Infinite Divisions: An Anthology of Chicana Literature*. University of Arizona Press, 1993.

Rehman, Bushra. *Corona*. Sibling Rivalry Press, 2013.

Rivera, Edward. *Family Installments: Memories of Growing Up Hispanic*. Penguin, 1983.

Rubin, Lillian B. *Worlds of Pain: Life in the Working-Class Family*. Basic Books, 1976.

Santiago, Esmeralda. *When I Was Puerto Rican: A Memoir*. Vintage Books, 1993.

Savage, Dan. *The Commitment: Love, Sex, Marriage, and My Family*. Plume, 2006.

Scarce, Michael. *Male on Male Rape: The Hidden Toll of Stigma and Shame*. Basic Books, 2001.

Shulman, Alix Kates. *Memoirs of an Ex-Prom Queen*. Knopf, 1972.

Silko, Leslie Marmon. *Ceremony*. New American Library, 1972.

Smith, Barbara, ed. *Home Girls: A Black Feminist Anthology*. Kitchen Table: Women of Color Press, 1983.

Stevenson, Bryan. *Just Mercy: A Story of Justice and Redemption*. Spiegel & Grau, 2014.

Terkel, Studs. *Working*. Avon Books, 1972.

Tobias, Andrew (writing as John Reid). *The Best Little Boy in the World*. Ballantine Books, 1993.

Warshaw, Robin. *I Never Called It Rape*. Harper & Row, 1988.

Wu, Frank H. *Yellow: Race in America Beyond Black and White*. Basic Books, 2003.

Zahava, Irene, ed. *Speaking for Ourselves: Short Stories by Jewish Lesbians*. Crossing Press, 1990.

Zhou, Min, and James V. Gatewood, eds. *Contemporary Asian Americans: A Multidisciplinary Reader* New York University Press, 2000.

Zia, Helen. *Asian American Dreams: The Emergence of an American People*. Farrar, Straus and Giroux, 2000.

PART VII

How It Happens: Legal Constructions of Power and Privilege

Legality is a matter of power, not a matter of justice.

—JOSEPH M. MARSHALL III

I regarded such laws as the regulations of robbers, who had no rights that I was bound to respect.

—HARRIET JACOBS

How has a nation founded upon revolutionary articulations of equality justified profound inequalities throughout its history? The previous six parts of this volume have addressed social constructions of race, class, gender, sexuality, and citizenship, through personal testimony, statistics, and analysis by contemporary scholars and activists. Part VII turns to legal documents—primarily the U.S. Constitution, federal and state laws, and court rulings—to examine the legal constructions of difference that have been deployed throughout our history to justify and reinforce oppression and privilege. Lawmakers have relied upon complex rhetorical and ideological maneuvers to rationalize genocide, slavery, mass incarceration, and discrimination, while also claiming "equality," "justice," and "freedom" as fundamental tenets. These documents are not easy to read, not only because of the content but also because of the archaic language and the legal terminology.[1] Law is often presented as a rational, objective, and neutral discourse. Reading the actual words of lawmakers and judges as they attempt to justify inequities in a democracy exposes the lie of neutrality and teaches us a great deal about the workings of our nation.

Part VII does not attempt to provide a comprehensive history of U.S. law—many key moments and issues are not represented, and legal documents cannot tell the entire story.

Laws foreground the dominant voices in society, leaving out the voices of resistance that also have shaped our nation. Some counternarratives do appear in this part (such as the Civil War amendments, the 19th Amendment, *Brown v. Board of Education*, and *Obergefell v. Hodges*), but they do not detail the political and social movements that forced changes in the legal realm; nor do they acknowledge the efforts of activists who continue to fight for justice beyond these legal victories. The readings listed at the end of Part VII include some rich accounts of social history that can supplement the study of these documents.

In the Declaration of Independence, the founders of our republic proclaimed that "all men are created equal, that they are endowed by their Creator with certain unalienable Rights, that among these are Life, Liberty and the pursuit of Happiness." When these words were written, "all men" excluded not only all women, but also Indigenous peoples, enslaved Africans and their descendants, indentured servants, and unpropertied white men. The readings in Part VII show that from the country's inception, including in the colonial era, American laws and institutions have been designed to create and maintain the privileges of wealthy white males. The discrimination documented in the early parts of this book has a long and deliberate history. Understanding this history is essential if we are to create a more just and truly democratic society.

When the early European colonizers came to this continent, there were over seven million[2] Indigenous people living on Turtle Island, an aboriginal name for North America. These peoples were divided among numerous autonomous nations, each with its own highly developed culture and rich history. The white colonizers quickly lumped these diverse peoples into a single category of supposedly inferior "Indians" and set about destroying their cultures and seizing the lands on which they lived.

The colonial governments formulated *legal* means and justifications for taking Indigenous people's land. American lawmakers and judges invoked the language and ideology of European countries (including England, Portugal, Spain, and France) that had long claimed a right of domination over non-Christian peoples and their lands. Dating back to the fifteenth century, papal bulls (edicts from the pope) laid out a "doctrine of discovery" to provide legal, political, and spiritual justification for the theft of land from Indigenous and other non-Christian peoples. For example, a 1452 papal bull directed King Alfonso V of Portugal to "invade, capture, vanquish, and subdue, all Saracens, pagans, and other enemies of Christ, to reduce their persons to perpetual slavery, and to take away all their possessions and property."[3] In the U.S. Supreme Court case *Johnson v. M'Intosh* (1823), Chief Justice John Marshall builds upon this papal authority, as well as upon British charters, to justify the seizure of Indigenous land. Marshall writes: "The right of discovery . . . is confined to countries 'then unknown to all Christian people;' . . . . Thus asserting a right to take possession, notwithstanding the occupancy of the natives, who were heathens . . . ."[4] Marshall distinguishes between what he refers to as the right of *occupancy* of the Indigenous people versus the right to *property* held by Christian nations, upholding Christian nations' "ultimate dominion" over Indigenous people and lands. "However extravagant the pretension of converting the discovery of an inhabited country into conquest may appear," Marshall argues: "if the principle has been asserted in the first instance, and afterwards sustained; if a country has been acquired and held under it; if the property of the great mass of the community originates in it, it becomes the law of the land, and cannot be questioned."[5] These legal constructions, embedded in U.S. law through this early case about property rights, have resulted in a legacy of dehumanization of and domination over Indigenous peoples.

Part VII begins with an excerpt from a 1981 report by the U.S. Commission on Human Rights tracing the relationship between tribal nations and the U.S. government. The report examines the intertwining roles of colonizaton, racism, and religion in federal Indian law and policies relating to land, education, and language. This history, with its continuing effects into the present, is informed by Justice Marshall's adoption and promulgation of the doctrine of discovery and its construction of Indigenous peoples and lands as "heathen."

The Indian Removal Act of 1830 was fairly typical of the kinds of laws that were passed to carry out the appropriation of Indigenous lands in the nineteenth century. Constructing "Indians" as inherently inferior to whites, the U.S. government did not hesitate to legislate the violent removal of Indigenous peoples from their ancestral lands (lands of great value to white settlers) to ever more remote and barren reservations. The dissolution of the Indigenous tribal system was further advanced by the Dawes General Allotment Act of 1887, which divided tribal landholdings among Indigenous individuals—thereby undermining the tribal system and the culture of which it was a part—and invented "surplus" land, resulting in the transfer of 90 million acres of Indigenous land into white ownership.[6]

In addition to stripping land and rights away from Indigenous peoples, European colonizers also kidnapped and enslaved millions of Africans, forcibly transporting them to the Americas. As early as 1526, a Spanish expedition to what is now South Carolina included enslaved Africans (who rebelled against the Spaniards some months after the expedition landed).[7] In 1619 (a year before the Pilgrims landed at Plymouth Rock), more than 20 men and women kidnapped from Angola arrived in Jamestown, having been sold to British colonists in exchange for food. Thomas Jefferson included a condemnation of King George's role in the international slave trade in his draft of the Declaration of Independence: "He has waged cruel war against human nature itself, violating its most sacred rights of life and liberty in the persons of a distant people who never offended him, captivating & carrying them into slavery in another hemisphere or to incur miserable death in their transportation thither. This piratical warfare, the opprobrium of infidel powers, is the warfare of the Christian King of Great Britain."[8]

The delegates rejected Jefferson's language and ignored the contradictions involved in breaking away from a monarchy, ushering in a democracy, and simultaneuously practicing human enslavement. A decade later, delegates to the Constitutional Convention did address the presence of slavery, but without once using the word in the Constitution. The slavery-related provisions in the originally adopted Constitution, reproduced here as Selection 4, included protection of the international slave trade, a fugitive slave law, and the "three-fifths" compromise, which counted each enslaved American as three-fifths of a person for purposes of calculating both congressional representation and taxes.

Numerous legal documents regulated the lives of enslaved people, including South Carolina's colonial law "for the Better Ordering and Governing of Negroes and Slaves" (Selection 2) and North Carolina's 1830 "Act to Prevent All Persons from Teaching Slaves to Read or Write" (Selection 5). Slave laws reveal dehumanizing constructions of race as well as the anxieties and insecurities of slaveholders—if, for example, they had believed their own fictions about black inferiority, they would not have felt the need to pass laws banning black literacy. "The Petition of the Africans, Living in Boston" (Selection 3) is a 1773 public protest against slavery and an important reminder that enslaved persons have always resisted slavery through a range of methods, including writing.

The rich body of autobiographical writings by formerly enslaved Americans also offers a dramatic counternarrative to the legal fictions of slavery. Harriet Jacobs escaped from North Carolina slavery (by hiding in her grandmother's attic crawl space for seven years before fleeing to the North) and published *Incidents in the Life of a Slave Girl, Written by Herself*, on the eve of the Civil War. Jacobs not only displays her literary genius in this work but also writes an extended critique of proslavery legal discourse. In one key line, she condemns the 1850 Fugitive Slave Act by rewriting the most famous line of the most famous Supreme Court ruling on the subject of slavery, *Dred Scott v. Sandford* (Selection 8). In that 1857 case, the Supreme Court ruled that Dred Scott had no right to be free, despite having been taken into the free state of Illinois for a period of time, and did not even have the right to bring a lawsuit, because African Americans had always been regarded as "so far inferior, that they had no rights which the white man was bound to respect." As Harriet Jacobs faces the pursuit of her family, even after she had secured their freedom in the nominally free North, she writes, "I knew the law would decide that I was his property, and would probably still give his daughter a claim to my children; but I regarded such laws as the regulations of robbers, who had no rights that I was bound to respect." She turns the lawmakers into the criminals and puts herself in the position of a judge deciding whether to respect the rights of slaveholders and slavecatchers.

Jacobs and other abolitionist activists formed a movement that helped push the question of slavery in a democracy to the forefront of national debates. During the period in which *Dred Scott* and other court cases were brought, the United States moved toward and ultimately fought a bloody civil war, a war that reflected a struggle between the Southern aristocracy and the Northern capitalists. The wealth of the Southern aristocracy was based on their ownership of land and of the black people whom they pressed into labor to work that land, and their power rested on a kind of feudal economic and political order. The Northern capitalists and their wealth, in contrast, were a product of the Industrial Revolution, and their power was directed at restructuring the nation's economic and political institutions to better serve the needs of the new industrial order. President Abraham Lincoln, who opposed slavery's expansion but did not support emancipation, eventually did sign the Emancipation Proclamation (Selection 9) as part of his efforts to bring the Civil War to an end. The proclamation declared freedom only for enslaved persons in states or parts of states in rebellion against the federal government (precisely the places not under Union control). Only in December 1865, after the war ended, were all people held as slaves officially freed by the Thirteenth Amendment (Selection 10, which also includes the Fourteenth and Fifteenth Amendments, discussed below).

While many white Americans, including the journalist and social reformer William Lloyd Garrison and other abolitionists, thought that the Thirteenth Amendment signaled the end of the need for an abolitionist movement, black abolitionist leader Frederick Douglass knew that the fight against slavery and racism was not over. In 1865, Douglass gave a speech opposing Garrison's call to disband the American Anti-Slavery Society, concluding with these words about slavery: "It has been called by a great many names, and it will call itself by yet another name; and you and I and all of us had better wait and see what new form this old monster will assume, in what new skin this old snake will come forth." As he predicted, Southern whites did not yield their privileges easily. Immediately after the ratification of the Thirteenth Amendment, the Southern states began to pass laws known as "Black Codes," which sought to reestablish the conditions of slavery. The South Carolina Black Codes (excerpted in Selection 11) led the way, denying free blacks legal rights and criminalizing them through vagrancy laws and other measures that did not apply to white people.

In 1867, feminist and abolitionist orator Sojourner Truth gave a speech to the American Equal Rights Association, asserting, "so much good luck to have slavery partly destroyed; not entirely. I want it root and branch destroyed." In 1868, Congress passed the Fourteenth Amendment (in Selection 10), which addresses some of the roots and branches of slavery. This amendment, which plays a major role in contemporary legal battles over discrimination, explicitly extended citizenship to all those "born or naturalized in the United States" and guaranteed all citizens "due process" and "equal protection" of the law. Southern resistance to extending the rights and privileges of citizenship to *all* citizens persisted, and the Southern states used all their powers, including unbridled terror and violence, to subvert the intent of the Thirteenth and Fourteenth Amendments. The Fifteenth Amendment (also in Selection 10), which explicitly granted the vote to black men, was passed in 1870 but was undermined by extralegal methods (including voter intimidation and outright terrorism) and through discriminatory legal practices, including poll taxes, literacy tests, white primaries, and restrictive registration practices.

The denial of citizenship and voting rights has also been a key element in the construction of Indigenous peoples as subordinate. Even though the Fourteenth Amendment declared the principle of birthright citizenship and the Fifteenth Amendment asserted the right of citizens to vote, a subsequent decision by the U.S. Supreme Court denied these rights to Indigenous people. In 1884, John Elk, a Winnebago man who gave up his tribal affiliation, argued that he was a citizen by virtue of the Fourteenth Amendment and should not be denied the right to vote by the state of Nebraska. In *Elk v. Wilkins* (Selection 14), the Supreme Court ruled that neither the Fourteenth nor Fifteenth Amendment applied to Elk. Indigenous peoples officially gained U.S. citizenship with the Indian Citizenship Act of 1924, although many states continued to deny their voting rights for four more decades.[9]

A racial restriction on the right of immigrants to seek naturalized citizenship was first articulated by the U.S. Congress in 1790, limiting this right to persons who were "free and white"; Congress did not remove this restriction until 1952 (see "Racial Restrictions in the Law of Citizenship," Selection 1 in Part III, for more details about such laws). People of Asian origin were particularly targeted by this restriction, with a range of consequences. Prohibition from seeking citizenship reinforced the already prevalent construction of Asians as un-American and undeserving of rights. In *People v. Hall* (1854, excerpted in Selection 7), the California Supreme Court decided that a California statute barring any "Black, or Mulatto person, or Indian" from testifying in court cases involving whites also applied to Chinese Americans. The judges asserted that the Chinese were "a race of people whom nature has marked as inferior, and who are incapable of progress or intellectual development beyond a certain point" and that they could not be allowed to "swear away the life of a citizen." Anti-Chinese hostility in parts of the United States was supported and institutionalized through the Chinese Exclusion Act (Selection 13), which remained U.S. policy from 1882 to 1943. Numerous court cases in this period addressed the question of *which* immigrants were eligible for citizenship, revealing the contradictory legal constructions of race. These cases were often based either on "scientific" evidence that assigned the plaintiff a racial category or on what the courts understood to be "common sense." The case of *U.S. v. Bhagat Singh Thind* (Selection 18) is significant in that the court conceded that Thind, an Indian Sikh immigrant, could be racially "Caucasian," but held that this designation was not equivalent to a commonsense understanding of "whiteness." Here, the ostensibly commonsense understanding—how "the common man" (meaning, clearly, the common *white* man) would interpret Thind's race—was the more powerful determinant of his racial assignment than any appeal to science, ancestry, or history.

Citizenship, while significant, has never by itself guaranteed equal rights. Jim Crow—the laws and practices of antiblack discrimination and segregation—was another strategy that the Southern states used to negate the rights of black citizens. In an act of deliberate civil disobedience, an African American man, Homer Plessy, violated Louisiana's Separate Car Act and took his case to the U.S. Supreme Court, arguing that the racial segregation of public facilities violated the Thirteenth and Fourteenth Amendments. In *Plessy v. Ferguson* (1896, Selection 15), the Supreme Court ruled that restricting black people to the use of "separate but equal" public accommodations did not deny them equal protection of the law. This decision remained in effect for six decades, until the Supreme Court's 1954 ruling in *Brown v. Board of Education of Topeka* (Selection 19). In this historic decision, the Court ruled that "[s]eparate educational facilities are inherently unequal." Nonetheless, abolishing segregation on paper was one thing; actually bringing about the integration of schools and other public facilities was another. The long and often bloody struggle to integrate public schools, housing, and employment in both the North and the South continues to this day.

Men and women of color and Indigenous peoples have long been denied basic civil rights, even when counted as citizens. For most of our history, white women considered U.S. citizens were not granted common rights of citizenship, such as the right to own property, serve on juries, and vote. Even white women with significant class privilege found themselves prevented from studying at universities, entering the professions, or controlling their own bodies. In 1848, participants in the Seneca Falls Women's Rights Convention issued "The Declaration of Sentiments" (Selection 6), a list of demands that included the right to speak in public, to enter the professions, and, most controversially, to vote. This document—modeled on the Declaration of Independence—asserted that "all men and women are created equal" and cataloged not the crimes of King George against the colonists but the "history of repeated injuries and usurpations on the part of man toward woman, having in direct object the establishment of an absolute tyranny over her." The U.S. Supreme Court's ruling in *Bradwell v. Illinois* (Selection 12), offers a concrete example of women's agency and the law's tyranny through the story of Myra Bradwell, who passed the bar exam in 1869 but was denied admission to the bar by the Illinois supreme court. Bradwell appealed the case to the U.S. Supreme Court, which invoked "divine ordinance" and "the nature of things" to uphold the Illinois court's decision. Bradwell nonetheless continued her legal activism until her death.

In 1920, the Nineteenth Amendment to the Constitution (Selection 16) was ratified, disallowing voting discrimination "on account of sex." In practice, however, women's right to vote continued to be abrogated for Indigenous women and women of color, as a result of other continuing legal barriers and socially sanctioned racist tactics, such as poll taxes and literacy tests.[10] Three years after the Nineteenth Amendment became law, the National Women's Party proposed a federal Equal Rights Amendment (Selection 17) that would outlaw sex discrimination in areas beyond the right to vote. Feminist activists lobbied for decades in support of the ERA, and it finally passed Congress in 1972, but it was never ratified. Saddled with a deadline that was not part of the original proposal, it fell three states short of ratification when time ran out in 1982. Proponents today argue that the amendment is still viable—and still necessary—and some state legislatures have revisited ratification.

Feminist activists have also lobbied for many decades for reproductive rights, including the right to determine when and whether to have a child. In *Griswold v. Connecticut* in 1965, the Supreme Court held that, based on a constitutional right to privacy, states could not bar married couples from using contraception. In the landmark *Roe v. Wade* ruling in 1973 (Selection 20), the Supreme Court struck down state laws criminalizing abortion. The *Roe* decision is based on the right to privacy, and not based on a woman's right to control her body. In fact, the medical language of the ruling in some ways emphasizes doctors' rights more than women's rights: "The decision vindicates the right of the physician to administer medical treatment according to his professional judgment." This left the way open for the impact of *Roe* to be significantly blunted by subsequent legislation and Supreme Court rulings, including *Harris v. McRae* in 1980, holding that the right to privacy did not require public funding of medically necessary abortions for women who could not afford them. In practice, this meant that middle class and wealthy women could exercise their right to abortion but that many poor women (both white women and women of color) could not. In 1994, a gathering of black women activists in Chicago coined the term "reproductive justice" to acknowledge the intersectional issues inherent in the fight by women of color to secure reproductive rights, including but also going beyond access to abortion (for example, the issue embodied in the battle to end forced sterilization). (See "Reproductive Justice in the Twenty-First Century," Selection 8 in Part IX, for a discussion of the many issues involved in the right to parent or not to parent.)

Activists also have fought for decades for LGBTQ liberation, including legal rights such as the ability to pursue certain careers (e.g., in teaching or the military), an end to antisodomy laws (which were finally struck down in 2003 by the Supreme Court's decision in *Lawrence v. Texas*), and the right to marry. In 2015, in *Obergefell* v. *Hodges* (Selection 23), the Supreme Court legalized same-sex marriage in all states. Hundreds of rights, privileges, and responsibilities flow from the right to marry (relating to immigration, adoption, taxes, inheritance, health insurance, medical decision-making, etc.), so there are significant legal consequences from this ruling. At the same time, the right to marriage alone does not guarantee LGBTQ liberation in all realms. Many activists have insisted on more transformative approaches to questions of health care, violence, discrimination, gender policing, criminalization, and other struggles facing LGBTQ people (see "Building an Abolitionist Trans and Queer Movement with Everything We've Got," Selection 10 in Part IX, for concrete examples of such movement building).

Several of the readings in this part offer hope for future activism and legal advances, but our history has shown that retrenchments are also part of the story. Hard-won rights like equal protection, due process, and voting rights are springboards for future change, but are also under threat. In 1987, in *McCleskey v. Kemp* (Selection 21), the Supreme Court handed down a ruling that severely narrowed the ability of plaintiffs to make equal protection claims under the Fourteenth Amendment. The Court ruled that claims of racial bias could only be supported by explicit evidence of discriminatory intent. Michelle Alexander (author of Selection 3 in Part IV of this volume), argues that this ruling has effectively "closed the courthouse doors" to meaningful equal protection claims and signals that "racial bias would be tolerated—virtually to any degree—so long as no one admitted it."[11]

In his dissent to *McCleskey*, Justice William Brennan argued, "we remain imprisoned by the past as long as we deny its influence in the present." This insight could also be applied to the Court's 2013 ruling in *Shelby County v. Holder* (Selection 22), widely seen as gutting the Voting Rights Act of 1965. This ruling will have a particularly lasting impact, since one of the most important tools for political change in a democracy is, of course, the right to vote.

While it is vital to note the changes made possible by social movements, the readings in this section also make it clear that American history offers no simple narrative of progress that occurs naturally with the passage of time. Martin Luther King, Jr., in his "Letter from Birmingham Jail," wrote that "time itself is neutral; it can be used either destructively or constructively." He argued that "[h]uman progress never rolls in on wheels of inevitability," but requires tireless effort. Without the hard work of individual activism and collective movement building, "time itself becomes an ally of the forces of social stagnation. We must use time creatively, in the knowledge that the time is always ripe to do right. Now is the time to make real the promise of democracy . . . ."

NOTES

1. Addressing the challenge of reading slave laws, legal scholar and judge A. Leon Higginbotham argues that "however tightly woven into the history of their country is the legalization of black suppression, many Americans still find it too traumatic to study the true story of racism as it has existed under their 'rule of law.'. . . Since the language of law shields one's consciousness from direct involvement with the stark plight of its victims, the human tragedy of the slavery system does not surface from the mere reading of cases, statutes, and constitutional provisions. Rather it takes a skeptical reading of most of the early cases and statutes to avoid having one's surprise and anger dulled by the casualness with which the legal process dealt with human beings who happened to be slaves." (*In the Matter of Color: Race and the American Legal Process: The Colonial Period*, 4th ed. Oxford University Press, 1980, p. 11.)

2. Russell Thornton, *American Indian Holocaust and Survival: A Population History Since 1492* (University of Oklahoma Press, 1990), p. 32.

3. Steven Newcomb, *Pagans in the Promised Land: Decoding the Doctrine of Christian Discovery* (Fulcrum Publishing, 2008), p. 84.

4. *Ibid.* Newcomb argues: "By categorizing indigenous peoples as heathens, Chief Justice Marshall was conceptualizing them in terms of what they were *not*: . . . *not* Christian, *not* positive, *not* good, *not* fully human, *not* civilized" (p. 103).

5. *Johnson and Graham's Lessee v. McIntosh* 21 U.S. 543 (1823). This case is the first of three rulings (known as the "Marshall trilogy") establishing U.S. federal supremacy over Indigenous peoples. The other two cases in the trilogy are *Cherokee Nation v. Georgia*, 30 U.S. 1 (1831) and *Worcester v. Georgia*, 31 U.S. 515 (1832). See also Roxanne Dunbar-Ortiz, "The Doctrine of Discovery," in *An Indigenous Peoples' History of the United States* (Beacon Press, 2014).

6. "Under that allotment legislation, for which there was no legitimate constitutional basis, Indian land holdings dropped from 138 million acres down to 48 million acres, for a loss to Indian nations of some 90 million acres of land." (Steven Newcomb, "The 1887 Dawes Act: The U.S. Theft of 90 Million Acres of Indian Land," *Indian Country Today*, Feb. 8, 2012. https:// newsmaven.io/indiancountrytoday/archive/the-1887-dawes-act-the-u-s-theft-of-90-million -acres-of-indian-land.)

7. Michael Guasco, "The Misguided Focus on 1619 as the Beginning of Slavery in the U.S. Damages Our Understanding of American History," *Smithsonian*, Sept. 13, 2017. https://www.smithsonianmag.com/history/misguided-focus-1619-beginning-slavery-us-damages-our-understanding-american-history.

8. Embodying the contradictions of our nation's founding, slaveholder Jefferson also penned other powerful lines condemning slavery (and fearing a just god in this regard). Sally Hemings had six children fathered—and enslaved—by Jefferson. "Hemings' story is an extraordinary one—since it chronicles not only a 16-year-old enslaved girl who had the life experience and presence of mind to negotiate for her unborn children's future freedom, but a founding father whose complex moral code moved him to honor his agreement with a woman he enslaved for decades." (Daina Ramey Berry, "How Sally Hemings and Other Enslaved People Secured Precious Pockets of Freedom," *History Reads*, July 9, 2018.)

9. In 1962, Utah became the last state to remove formal barriers against Indigenous voters. "But pernicious roadblocks remain to this day. Restrictive voting laws throughout the United States often carry a discriminatory effect, either by intent or consequence, for Native communities." (Peter Dunphy, "The State of Native American Voting Rights," Brennan Center for Justice, March 13, 2019. https://www.brennancenter.org/blog/state-native-american-voting-rights.)

10. See "The forgotten history of how Latinos earned the right to vote" (https://splinternews. com/the-forgotten-history-of-how-latinos-earned-the-right-t) and "Who got the right to vote when?" (https://interactive.aljazeera.com/aje/2016/us-elections-2016-who-can-vote/index.html).

11. Michelle Alexander, *The New Jim Crow* (The New Press, 2010), pp. 108–109.

GUIDING QUESTIONS FOR PART VII

1. As you read the documents in Part VII, pay attention to the *legal* constructions of race and gender. What are some of the stories that lawmakers tell about racialized and gendered differences? How do they deploy legal language to justify racial and gendered hierarchies? How do these patterns relate to the readings in Part I that analyzed *social* constructions of difference?

2. How do the constitutional provisions, statutes, and court rulings addressing slavery reveal lawmakers' fears and anxieties?

3. Can you identify self-fulfilling prophecies in these readings? Where do lawmakers invoke their own legal fictions to justify circumstances they present as natural or god-given?

4. "This is the law of the Creator," writes the judge in *Bradwell v. Illinois* (Selection 12). How does religious language function in these legal documents?

5. What do we learn about resistance from the 1773 Petition of the Africans (Selection 3) and the 1848 Declaration of Sentiments (Selection 6)? How do these writers craft their calls for social change, given the moments in which they are writing? Why is it important to study these counternarratives alongside legal documents justifying oppression?

6. The judges in *People v. Hall* (Selection 7) released a convicted murderer rather than admit the testimony of Chinese witnesses. What "logic" do they use to justify this ruling?

7. How do the South Carolina Black Codes (Selection 11) reinstitute the hierarchies of slavery? How do these codes criminalize black people? What are some present-day legacies of these laws?

8. What notions of citizenship emerge in these readings? Who counts as an American? Who is excluded, and on what basis?

9. *McCleskey v. Kemp* (Selection 21) requires explicit evidence of "discriminatory purpose" in equal protection cases. What forms of discrimination are rendered invisible by such a legal standard? You might want to look back at some of the selections in Part II (including the essays by Tatum, Haney López, and Bonilla-Silva) as you consider this question.

10. While most of the legal documents in this section enact discrimination, several (such as the Emancipation Proclamation, the Thirteenth Amendment, and the rulings in *Brown v. Board of Education*, *Roe v. Wade*, and *Obergefell v. Hodges*) offer an expansion of rights. Can you identify limitations or loopholes in some of these documents that make them less liberatory than they might seem on the surface?

11. The Equal Rights Amendment (Selection 17) was first proposed a century ago, and activists are still fighting for its adoption into the U.S. Constitution. How do readings elsewhere in this volume affect your thinking about the continuing relevance of the ERA?

1

Indian Tribes: A Continuing Quest for Survival

U.S. Commission on Civil Rights

Editor's Note: This excerpt from a government report offers historical context for the relationship between the U.S. government and Indigenous nations. Based on a series of public hearings held by the U.S. Commission on Civil Rights, the report traces the role of legal, political, and religious discourses and policies in denying rights to Indigenous peoples in the United States. First published in 1981, the report relies upon some outdated terminology. The word "Indian" has a complicated and fraught history, from its inaccurate use by Columbus to its being both reclaimed and attacked by activists and scholars (see, for example, the essay by Michael Yellow Bird in Part VIII of this volume). "Indian" is also used in this report and in the body of federal Indian law because it is codified in federal court cases, Congressional acts, executive orders, and federal regulations that refer to Indigenous nations and individuals. Terms in current usage include Indigenous peoples, First Nations, Native Americans, and American Indians. Indigenous scholars and journalists advise that, when possible, it is preferable to use the names of specific tribal nations.* Readers may view some of the other language in the report—such as "benevolent" and "civilize"— with a critical eye, while still noting the report's critique of U.S. policies and ideologies. Recent scholarly works provide a more extensive and nuanced analysis of the history of Indigenous peoples in this country, including *Pagans in the Promised Land: Decoding the Doctrine of Christian Discovery*, by Shawnee-Lenape legal scholar Steven Newcomb, and *An Indigenous People's History of the United States,* by Roxanne Dunbar-Ortiz (these two works, along with others addressing this history, are in the list of suggested readings at the end of Part VII).

Traditional Civil Rights Problems

Traditional civil rights, as the phrase is used here, include those rights that are secured to individuals and are basic to the United States system of government. They include the right to vote and the right to equal treatment without discrimination on the basis of race, religion, or national origin, among others, in such areas as education, housing, employment, public accommodations, and the administration of justice.

---

* See, for example, the Native American Journalists Association's guide "Reporting and Indigenous Terminology" (https://najanewsroom.com/reporting-guides/), which includes this statement: "Reporters should identify Indigenous people by their specific tribes, nations or communities. Headlines and text should also refer to tribes by their proper names, not a catch-all phrase . . . . Failing to use the actual name of the tribe you are reporting on is neither accurate, fair or thorough and undermines diversity by erasing the tribe's identity."

U.S. Commission on Civil Rights, *Indian Tribes: A Continuing Quest for Survival*, a report of the United States Commission on Civil Rights, June 1981, pp. 32–35.

In order to understand where American Indians stand today with respect to these rights, it is important to look at historical developments of the concept of Indian rights along with the civil rights movement in this country. The consideration given to these factors here will not be exhaustive, but rather a brief look at some of the events that are most necessary to a background understanding of this area.[1]

A basic and essential factor concerning American Indians is that the development of civil rights issues for them is in reverse order from other minorities in this country. Politically, other minorities started with nothing and attempted to obtain a voice in the existing economic and political structure. Indians started with everything and have gradually lost much of what they had to an advancing alien civilization. Other minorities have had no separate governmental institutions. Their goal primarily has been and continues to be to make the existing system involve them and work for them. Indian tribes have always been separate political entities interested in maintaining their own institutions and beliefs. Their goal has been to prevent the dismantling of their own systems. So while other minorities have sought integration into the larger society, much of Indian society is motivated to retain its political and cultural separateness.

Although at the beginning of the colonization process Indian nations were more numerous and better adapted to survival on this continent than the European settlers, these advantages were quickly lost. The colonization period saw the rapid expansion of non-Indian communities in numbers and territory covered and a shift in the balance of strength from Indian to non-Indian communities and governments. The extent to which Indians intermingled with non-Indian society varied by time period, geographical location, and the ability of natives and newcomers to get along with one another. As a general matter, however, Indians were viewed and treated as members of political entities that were not part of the United States. The Constitution acknowledges this by its separate provision regarding trade with the Indian tribes.[2] Indian tribes today that have not been forcibly assimilated, extinguished, or legally terminated still consider themselves to be, and are viewed in American law, as separate political units.

The Racial Factor

An important element in the development of civil rights for American Indians today goes beyond their legal and political status to include the way they have been viewed racially. Since colonial times Indians have been viewed as an "inferior race"; sometimes this view is condescendingly positive—the romanticized noble savage—at other times this view is hostile—the vicious savage—at all times the view is racist. All things Indian are viewed as inherently inferior to their counterparts in the white European tradition. Strong racist statements have appeared in congressional debates, Presidential policy announcements, court decisions, and other authoritative public utterances. This racism has served to justify a view now repudiated, but which still lingers in the public mind, that Indians are not entitled to the same legal rights as others in this country. In some cases, racism has been coupled with apparently benevolent motives, to "civilize" the "savages," to teach them Christian principles. In other cases, the racism has been coupled with greed; Indians were "removed" to distant locations to prevent them from standing in the way of the development of the new Western civilization. At one extreme the concept of inferior status of Indians was used to justify genocide; at the other, apparently benevolent side, the attempt was to assimilate them into the dominant society. Whatever the rationale or motive, whether rooted in voluntary efforts or coercion, the common denominator has been the belief that Indian society is an inferior lifestyle.

> It sprang from a conviction that native people were a lower grade of humanity for whom the accepted canons of respect need not apply; one did not debase oneself by ruining a native person. At times, this conviction was stated explicitly by men in public office, but whether expressed or not, it generated decision and action.[3]

Early assimilationists like Thomas Jefferson proceeded from this assumption with benevolent designs.*

> Thus, even as they acknowledged a degree of political autonomy in the tribes, their conviction of the natives' cultural inferiority led them to interfere in their social, religious, and economic practices. Federal agents to the tribes not only negotiated treaties and tendered payments; they pressured husbands to take up the plow and wives to learn to spin. The more conscientious agents offered gratuitous lectures on the virtues of monogamy, industry, and temperance.[4]

The same underlying assumption provided the basis for Andrew Jackson's attitude. "I have long viewed treaties with the Indians an absurdity not to be reconciled to the principles of our government," he said.[5] As President he refused to enforce the decisions of the U.S. Supreme Court upholding Cherokee tribal autonomy, and he had a prominent role in the forced removal of the Cherokees from Georgia and the appropriation of their land by white settlers.[6] Other eastern tribes met a similar fate under the Indian Removal Act of 1830.[7]

Another Federal Indian land policy, enacted at the end of the 19th century and followed until 1934, that shows the virulent effect of racist assumptions was the allotment of land parcels to individual Indians as a replacement for tribal ownership. Many proponents of the policy were considered "friends of the Indians," and they argued that the attributes of individual land ownership would have a great civilizing and assimilating effect on American Indians.[8] This action, undertaken for the benefit of the Indians, was accomplished without consulting them. Had Congress heeded the views of the purported beneficiaries of this policy, allotment might not have been adopted. Representatives of 19 tribes met in Oklahoma and unanimously opposed the legislation, recognizing the destructive effect it would have upon Indian culture[9] and the land base itself, which was reduced by 90 million acres in 45 years.[10]

An important principle established by the allotment policy was that the Indian form of land ownership was not "civilized," and so it was the right of the Government to invalidate

---

* For an analysis of the construction of benevolence, see "Myth 9: 'US Presidents Were Benevolent or at Least Fair-Minded Toward Indians,'" in *"All the Real Indians Died Off"* and 20 Other Myths about Native Americans, by Roxanne Dunbar-Ortiz and Dina Gilio-Whitaker, listed among the suggested readings at the end of Part VII.

that form. It is curious that the principle of the right to own property in conglomerate form for the benefit of those with a shareholder's undivided interest in the whole was a basis of the American corporate system, then developing in strength. Yet a similar form of ownership when practiced by Indians was viewed as a hallmark of savagery. Whatever the explanation for this double standard, the allotment policy reinforced the notion that Indians were somehow inferior, that non-Indians in power knew what was best for them, and that these suppositions justified the assertion that non-Indians had the power and authority to interfere with the basic right to own property.

Religion is another area in which non-Indians have felt justified in interfering with Indian beliefs. The intent to civilize the natives of this continent included a determined effort to Christianize them. Despite the constitutional prohibition, Congress, beginning in 1819, regularly appropriated funds for Christian missionary efforts.[11] Christian goals were visibly aligned with Federal Indian policy in 1869 when a Board of Indian Commissioners was established by Congress under President Grant's administration. Representative of the spectrum of Christian denominations, the independently wealthy members of the Board were charged by the Commissioner of Indian Affairs to work for the "humanization, civilization and Christianization of the Indians."[12] Officials of the Federal Indian Service were supposed to cooperate with this Board.

The benevolent support of Christian missionary efforts stood in stark contrast to the Federal policy of suppressing tribal religions. Indian ceremonial behavior was misunderstood and suppressed by Indian agents. In 1892 the Commissioner of Indian Affairs established a regulation making it a criminal offense to engage in such ceremonies as the sun dance.[13] The spread of the Ghost Dance religion, which promised salvation from the white man, was so frightening to the Federal Government that troops were called in to prevent it, even though the practice posed no threat to white settlers.[14]

The judiciary of the United States, though it has in many instances forthrightly interpreted the law to support Indian legal claims in the face of strong, sometimes violent opposition, has also lent support to the myth of Indian inferiority. For example, the United States Supreme Court in 1883, in recognizing the right of tribes to govern themselves, held that they had the exclusive authority to try Indians for criminal offenses committed against Indians. In describing its reasons for refusing to find jurisdiction in a non-Indian court in such cases, the Supreme Court said:

> It [the non-Indian court] tries them, not by their peers, nor by the customs of their people, nor the law of their land, but by *superiors* of a different race, according to the law of a social state of which they have an imperfect conception, and which is opposed to the traditions of their history, to the habits of their lives, to the strongest prejudices of their *savage nature*; one which measures the red man's revenge by the maxims of the white man's morality.[15]

In recognizing the power of the United States Government to determine the right of Indians to occupy their lands, the Supreme Court expressed the good faith of the country in such matters with these words: "the United States will be governed by such considerations of justice as will control a Christian people in their treatment of an ignorant and dependent race."[16]

Another example of racist stereotyping to be found in the courts is this example from the Supreme Court of Washington State:

> The Indian was a child, and a dangerous child, of nature, to be both protected and restrained. . . . True, arrangements took the form of treaty and of terms like "cede," "relinquish," "reserve." But never were these agreements between equals . . . [but rather] that "between a superior and an inferior."[17]

This reasoning, based on racism, has supported the view that Indians are wards of the Government who need the protection and assistance of Federal agencies and it is the Government's obligation to recreate their governments, conforming them to a non-Indian model, to establish their priorities, and to make or approve their decisions for them.

Indian education policies have often been examples of the Federal Government having determined what is "best" for Indians. Having judged that assimilation could be promoted through the indoctrination process of white schools, the Federal Government began investing in Indian education. Following the model established by army officer Richard Pratt in 1879, boarding schools were established where Indian children were separated from the influences of tribal and home life.[18,*] The boarding schools tried to teach Indians skills and trades that would be useful in white society, utilizing stern disciplinary measures to force assimilation.[19] The tactics used are within memory of today's generation of tribal leaders who recall the policy of deterring communication in native languages. "I remember being punished many times for . . . singing one Navajo song, or a Navajo word slipping out of my tongue just in an unplanned way, but I was punished for it."[20]

Federal education was made compulsory, and the policy was applied to tribes that had sophisticated school systems of their own as well as to tribes that really needed assistance to establish educational systems.[21] The ability of the tribal school to educate was not relevant, given that the overriding goal was assimilation rather than education.

Racism in Indian affairs has not been sanctioned recently by political or religious leaders or other leaders in American society. In fact, public pronouncements over the last several decades have lamented past evils and poor treatment of Indians.[22] The virulent public expressions of other eras characterizing Indians as "children" or "savages" are not now acceptable modes of public expression. Public policy today is a commitment to Indian self-determination. Numerous actions of Congress and the executive branch give evidence of a more positive era for Indian policy.[23] Beneath the surface, however, the effects of centuries of racism still persist. The attitudes of the public, of State and local officials, and of Federal policymakers do not always live up to the positive pronouncements of official policy. Some decisions today are perceived as being made on the basis of precedents mired in the racism and greed of another era.[24] Perhaps more important, the legacy of racism permeates behavior and that behavior creates classic civil rights violations. . . .

---

* For more on the topic of these boarding schools, see "Civilize Them with a Stick," by Mary Brave Bird (Selection 2 in Part VI of this volume).

NOTES

1. This section does not cover rights of Indians with respect to tribal governments.
2. U.S. Const. Art. 1, §8.
3. D'Arcy McNickel, *Native American Tribalism* (New York: Oxford University Press, 1973), p. 56.
4. U.S. Congress, American Indian Policy Review Commission, *Final Report Submitted to Congress*, Volume 1, 1977, pp. 52–53.
5. McNickel, *Native American Tribalism*, p. 56.
6. *Final Report*, p. 54.
7. Act of May 28, 1830, ch. 148, 4 Stat. 411.
8. McNickel, *Native American Tribalism*, pp. 80–81.
9. Ibid., p. 85.
10. Ibid., p. 83.
11. *Final Report*, p. 53.
12. Francis P. Prucha, *American Indian Policy* (Norman, Oklahoma: University of Oklahoma Press, 1964), pp. 33–38.
13. Federal Agencies Task Force, *American Indian Religious Freedom Act Report* (Department of the Interior, 1979), pp. 5–6.
14. *Final Report*, pp. 67–68.
15. *Ex Parte Crow Dog*, 109 U.S. 556, 571 (1883).
16. *Missouri, Kansas, and Texas Railway Co. v. Roberts*, 152 U.S. 114, 117 (1894).
17. *State v. Towessnute*, 154 P. 805, 807 (Wash. Sup. Ct. 1916), quoting *Choctaw Nation v. United States*, 119 U.S. 1, 27 (1886).
18. *Final Report*, pp. 63–64.
19. Ibid.
20. Peter Macdonald, chairman, Navajo Tribe, testimony, *Hearing Before the U.S. Commission on Civil Rights*, Window Rock, Arizona, Oct. 22–24, 1973, vol. I, p. 18.
21. *Final Report*, p. 64.
22. See, e.g., President Nixon's July 8, 1970, Message to the Congress, Recommendations for Indian Policy, H. Doc. No. 91–363, 91st Cong., 2d sess.
23. Ibid.; Indian Self-Determination and Education Assistance Act, Pub. L. No. 93–638, 88 Stat. 2203 (1975); Indian Child Welfare Act of 1978, Pub. L. No. 95–608, 92 Stat. 3096; U.S. Department of the Interior, *Report on the Implementation of the Helsinki Final Act* (1979).
24. Robert T. Coulter, testimony, *Hearing Before the U.S. Commission on Civil Rights*, Washington, D.C., Mar. 19–20, 1979, vol. I, pp. 205–07.

2 An Act for the Better Ordering and Governing of Negroes and Slaves (South Carolina, 1712)

Editor's Note: Colonial America relied upon a racialized system of human enslavement, undergirded by ideological constructions of racial inferiority and highly developed codes governing the enslaved. Slave laws reveal both the profound violence of slavery and the anxiety of white slaveholders who feared black people's communication, rebellion, and escape. In 1712, South Carolina passed "An Act for the better ordering and governing of Negroes and Slaves." This comprehensive measure served as a model for slave codes in the South during the colonial and national periods. Eight of its thirty-five sections are reproduced below. The Act argues that the colony cannot operate without enslaved labor, defines such labor in racialized terms, and empowers white colonists to "beat, maim or . . . kill" those who resist their enslavement. The Act also authorizes penalties (fines rather than violence) for free persons who refuse to punish the enslaved.

Whereas, the plantations and estates of this province cannot be well and sufficiently managed and brought into use, without the labor and service of negroes and other slaves; and forasmuch as the said negroes and other slaves brought unto the people of this Province for that purpose, are of barbarous, wild, savage natures, and such as renders them wholly unqualified to be governed by the laws, customs, and practices of this Province; but that it is absolutely necessary, that such other constitutions, laws and orders, should in this Province be made and enacted, for the good regulating and ordering of them, as may restrain the disorders, rapines and inhumanity, to which they are naturally prone and inclined, and may also tend to the safety and security of the people of this Province and their estates; to which purpose,

I. *Be it therefore enacted,* by his Excellency William, Lord Craven, Palatine, and the rest of the true and absolute Lords and Proprietors of this Province, by and with the advice and consent of the rest of the members of the General Assembly, now met at Charlestown, for the South-west part of this Province, and by the authority of the same, That all negroes, mulatoes, mustizoes or Indians, which at any time heretofore have been sold, or now are held or taken to be, or hereafter shall be bought and sold for slaves, are hereby declared slaves; and they, and their children, are hereby made and declared slaves, to all intents and purposes; excepting all such negroes, mulatoes, mustizoes or Indians, which heretofore have been, or hereafter shall be, for some particular merit, made and declared free, either by the Governor and council of this Province, pursuant to any Act or law of this Province, or by their respective owners or masters; and also, excepting all such negroes, mulatoes,

From Thomas Cooper and David J. McCord, eds., Statutes at Large of South Carolina (10 vols., Columbia, 1836–1841), VII, 352–357.

mustizoes or Indians, as can prove they ought not to be sold for slaves. And in case any negro, mulatoe, mustizoe or Indian, doth lay claim to his or her freedom, upon all or any of the said accounts, the same shall be finally heard and determined by the Governor and council of this Province.

II. And for the better ordering and governing of negroes and all other slaves in this Province, *Be it enacted* by the authority aforesaid, That no master, mistress, overseer, or other person whatsoever, that hath the care and charge of any negro or slave, shall give their negroes and other slaves leave, on Sundays, hollidays, or any other time, to go out of their plantations, except such negro or other slave as usually wait upon them at home or abroad, or wearing a livery; and every other negro or slave that shall be taken hereafter out of his master's plantation, without a ticket, or leave in writing, from his master or mistress, or some other person by his or her appointment, or some white person in the company of such slave, to give an account of his business, shall be whipped; and every person who shall not (when in his power) apprehend every negro or other slave which he shall see out of his master's plantation, without leave as aforesaid, and after apprehended, shall neglect to punish him by moderate whipping, shall forfeit twenty shillings, the one half to the poor, to be paid to the church wardens of the Parish where such forfeiture shall become due, and the other half to him that will inform for the same, within one week after such neglect; and that no slave may make further or other use of any one ticket than was intended by him that granted the same, every ticket shall particularly mention the name of every slave employed in the particular business, and to what place they are sent, and what time they return; and if any person shall presume to give any negro or slave a ticket in the name of his master or mistress, without his or her consent, such person so doing shall forfeit the sum of twenty shillings; one half to the poor, to be disposed of as aforesaid, the other half to the person injured, that will complain against the person offending, within one week after the offence committed. And for the better security of all such persons that shall endeavor to take any runaway, or shall examine any slave for his ticket, passing to and from his master's plantation, it is hereby declared lawful for any white person to beat, maim or assault, and if such negro or slave cannot otherwise be taken, to kill him, who shall refuse to shew his ticket, or, by running away or resistance, shall endeavor to avoid being apprehended or taken.

III. *And be it further enacted* by the authority aforesaid, That every master, mistress or overseer of a family in this Province, shall cause all his negro houses to be searched diligently and effectually, once every fourteen days, for fugitive and runaway slaves, guns, swords, clubs, and any other mischievous weapons, and finding any, to take them away, and cause them to be secured; as also, for clothes, goods, and any other things and commodities that are not given them by their master, mistress, commander or overseer, and honestly come by; and in whose custody they find any thing of that kind, and suspect or know to be stolen goods, the same they shall seize and take into their custody, and a full and ample description of the particulars thereof, in writing, within ten days after the discovery thereof, either to the provost marshall, or to the clerk of the parish for the time being, who is hereby required to receive the same, and to enter upon it the day of its receipt, and the particulars to file and keep to himself; and the clerk shall set upon the posts of the church door, and the provost marshall upon the usual public places, or places of notice, a short brief, that such lost goods are found; whereby, any person that hath lost his goods may the better come to the knowledge where they are; and the owner going to the marshall or clerk, and proving, by marks or otherwise, that the goods lost belong to him, and paying twelve pence for the entry and declaration of the same, if the marshall or clerk be convinced that any part of the goods certified by him to be found, appertains to the party inquiring, he is to direct the said party inquiring to the place and party where the goods be, who is hereby required to make restitution of what is in being to the true owner; and every master, mistress or overseer, as also the provost marshall or clerk, neglecting his duty in any the particulars aforesaid, for every neglect shall forfeit twenty shillings.

IV. And for the more effectual detecting and punishing such persons that trade with any slave for stolen goods, *Be it further enacted* by the authority aforesaid, That where any person shall be suspected to trade as aforesaid, any justice of the peace shall have power to take from him suspected, sufficient recognizance, not to trade with any slave contrary to the laws of this Province; and if it shall afterwards appear to any of the justices of the peace, that such person hath, or hath had, or shipped off, any goods, suspected to be unlawfully come by, it shall be lawful for such justice of the peace to oblige the person to appear at the next general sessions, who shall there be obliged to make reasonable proof, of whom he bought, or how he came by, the said goods, and unless he do it, his recognizance shall be forfeited. . . .

VII. And *whereas*, great numbers of slaves which do not dwell in Charlestown, on Sundays and holidays resort thither, to drink, quarrel, fight, curse and swear, and profane the Sabbath, and using and carrying of clubs and other mischievous weapons, resorting in great companies together, which may give them an opportunity of executing any wicked designs and purposes, to the damage and prejudice of the inhabitants of this Province; for the prevention whereof, *Be it enacted* by the authority aforesaid, That all and every the constables of Charlestown, separately on every Sunday, and the holidays at Christmas, Easter and Whitsonside [*sic*], together with so many men as each constable shall think necessary to accompany him, which he is hereby empowered for that end to press, under the penalty of twenty shillings to the person that shall disobey him, shall, together with such persons, go through all or any the streets, and also, round about Charlestown, and as much further on the neck as they shall be informed or have reason to suspect any meeting or concourse of any such negroes or slaves to be at that time, and to enter into any house, at Charlestown, or elsewhere, to search for such slaves, and as many of them as they can apprehend, shall cause to be publicly whipped in Charlestown, and then to be delivered to the marshall, who for every slave so whipped and delivered to him by the constable, shall pay the constable five shillings, which five shillings shall be repaid the said marshall by the owner or head of that family to which the said negro or slave, doth belong, together with such other charges as shall become due to him for keeping runaway slaves; and the marshall shall in all respects keep and dispose of such slave as if the same was delivered to him as a runaway, under the same penalties and forfeiture as hereafter in that case is provided; and every constable of Charlestown which shall neglect or refuse to make search as aforesaid, for every such neglect shall forfeit the sum of twenty shillings. . . .

IX. *And be it further enacted* by the authority aforesaid, That upon complaint made to any justice of the peace, of any heinous or grievous crime, committed by any slave or slaves, as murder, burglary, robbery, burning of houses, or any lesser crimes, as killing or stealing any meat or other cattle, maiming one the other, stealing of fowls, provisions, or such like trespasses or injuries, the said justice shall issue out his warrant for apprehending the offender or offenders, and for all persons to come before him that can give evidence; and if upon examination, it probably appeareth, that the apprehended person is guilty, he shall commit him or them to prison, or immediately proceed to tryal of the said slave or slaves, according to the form hereafter specified, or take security for his or their forthcoming, as the case shall require, and also to certify to the justice next to him, the said cause, and to require him, by virtue of this Act, to associate himself to him, which said justice is hereby required to do, and they so associated, are to issue their summons to three sufficient freeholders, acquainting them with the matter, and appointing them a day, hour and place, when and where the same shall be heard and determined, at which day, hour and place, the said justices and freeholders shall cause the offenders and evidences to come before them, and if they, on hearing the matter, the said freeholders being by the said justices first sworn to judge uprightly and according to evidence, and diligently weighing and examining all evidences, proofs and testimonies (and in case of murder only, if on violent presumption and circumstances), they shall find such negro or other slave or slaves guilty thereof, they shall give sentence of death, if the crime by law deserve the same, and forthwith by their warrant cause immediate execution to be done, by the common or any other executioner, in such manner as they shall think fit, the kind of death to be inflicted to be left to their judgment and discretion; and if the crime committed shall not deserve death, they shall then condemn and adjudge the criminal or criminals to any other punishment, but not extending to limb or disabling him, without a particular law directing such punishment, and shall forthwith order execution to be done accordingly.

X. And in regard great mischiefs daily happen by petty larcenies committed by negroes and slaves of this Province, *Be it further enacted* by the authority aforesaid, That if any negro or other slave shall hereafter steal or destroy any goods, chattels, or provisions whatsoever, of any other person than his master or mistress, being under the value of twelve pence, every negro or other slave so offending, and being brought before some justice of the peace of this Province, upon complaint of the party injured, and shall be adjudged guilty by confession, proof, or probable circumstances, such negro or slave so offending, excepting children, whose punishment is left wholly to the discretion of the said justice, shall be adjudged by such justice to be publicly and severely whipped, not exceeding forty lashes; and if such negro or other slave punished as aforesaid, be afterwards, by two justices of the peace, found guilty of the like crimes, he or they, for such his or their second offence, shall either have one of his ears cut off, or be branded in the forehead with a hot iron, that the mark thereof may remain; and if after such punishment, such negro or slave for his third offence, shall have his nose slit; and if such negro or other slave, after the third time as aforesaid, be accused of petty larceny, or of any of the offences before mentioned, such negro or other slave shall be tried in such manner as those accused of murder, burglary, *etc.* are before by this Act provided for to be tried, and in case they shall be found guilty a fourth time, of any of the offences before mentioned, then such negro or other slave shall be adjudged to suffer death, or other punishment, as the said justices shall think fitting; and any judgment given for the first offence, shall be a sufficient conviction for the first offence; and any after judgment after the first judgment, shall be a sufficient conviction to bring the offender within the penalty of the second offence, and so for inflicting the rest of the punishments; and in case the said justices and freeholders, and any or either of them, shall neglect or refuse to perform the duties by this Act required of them, they shall severally, for such their defaults, forfeit the sum of twenty-five pounds. . . .

XII. *And it is further enacted* by the authority aforesaid, That if any negroes or other slaves shall make mutiny or insurrection, or rise in rebellion against the authority and government of this Province, or shall make preparation of arms, powder, bullets or offensive weapons, in order to carry on such mutiny or insurrection, or shall hold any counsel or conspiracy for raising such mutiny, insurrection or rebellion, the offenders shall be tried by two justices of the peace and three freeholders, associated together as before expressed in case of murder, burglary, *etc.*, who are hereby empowered and required to try the said slaves so offending, and inflict death, or any other punishment, upon the offenders, and forthwith by their warrant cause execution to be done, by the common or any other executioner, in such manner as they shall think fitting; and if any person shall make away or conceal any negro or negroes, or other slave or slaves, suspected to be guilty of the beforementioned crimes, and not upon demand bring forth the suspected offender or offenders, such person shall forfeit for every negro or slave so concealed or made away, the sum of fifty pounds; *Provided, nevertheless,* that when and as often as any of the beforementioned crimes shall be committed by more than one negro, that shall deserve death, that then and in all such cases, if the Governor and council of this Province shall think fitting, and accordingly shall order, that only one or more of the said criminals should suffer death as exemplary, and the rest to be returned to the owners, that then, the owners of the negroes so offending, shall bear proportionably the loss of the said negro or negroes so put to death, as shall be allotted them by the said justices and freeholders; and if any person shall refuse his part so allotted him, that then, and in all such cases, the said justices and freeholders are hereby required to issue out their warrant of distress upon the goods and chattels of the person so refusing, and shall cause the same to be sold by public outcry, to satisfy the said money so allotted him to pay, and to return the overplus, if any be, to the owner; *Provided, nevertheless,* that the part allotted for any person to pay for his part or proportion of the negro or negroes so put to death, shall not exceed one sixth part of his negro or negroes so excused and pardoned; and in case that shall not be sufficient to satisfy for the negro or negroes that shall be put to death, that the remaining sum shall be paid out of the public treasury of this Province.

3 The Petition of the Africans, Living in Boston (1773)

Editor's Note: Enslaved persons have always resisted enslavement, in a variety of ways. In the 1770s, Africans in America strategically invoked the liberatory discourses of both the Old Testament and the American revolutionaries in their calls for justice. These early petitions and letters, reaching a wide audience by way of newspapers and pamphlets, planted the seeds for the abolition of slavery in Massachusetts a decade later.* Black poet Phillis Wheatley, for example, published a 1774 letter she wrote to Mohegan minister Samson Occom, highlighting the hypocrisy of American revolutionaries who sought to shake off British chains while enslaving their fellow humans. Kidnapped from Senegal/Gambia and sold to a Boston family at age eight, Wheatley wrote, "[I]n every human Breast, God has implanted a Principle, which we call Love of Freedom . . . and by the Leave of our Modern Egyptians I will assert, that the same Principle lives in us. . . . How well the Cry for Liberty, and the reverse Disposition for the Exercise of oppressive Power over others agree,—I humbly think it does not require the Penetration of a Philosopher to determine." The 1773 "humble petition" reproduced here—the first black-authored public protest submitted to a New England legislature—uses a deferential tone but at the same time boldly invokes the Christian deity as "no respecter of Persons" and as the inspiration for antislavery discourse on both sides of the Atlantic. The author, Felix, alludes to Britain's 1772 *Somerset* ruling, which deemed slavery "odious" and which freed a Boston slave brought to England, but did not end slavery in the British colonies. Opponents of slavery quickly published Felix's petition as a pamphlet titled "Some observations on the expediency of the petition of the Africans, living in Boston," expanding the domain of this legislative appeal into public discourse.

To His Excellency Thomas Hutchinson, Esq; Governor; To The Honorable His Majesty's Council, and To the Honorable House of Representatives in General Court assembled at Boston, the 6th Day of *January*, 1773. The humble petition of many Slaves, living in the Town of Boston, and other Towns in the Province is this, namely, That your Excellency

---

* According to Chernoh Sesay, Jr., "With the petitions by Felix and others, black agitation expanded into the realms of print culture and public debate." Massachusetts ends slavery implicitly in its state Constitution in 1780, and explicitly in a state Supreme Court ruling three years later. ("The Revolutionary Black Roots of Slavery's Abolition in Massachusetts," *The New England Quarterly*, Vol. 87, No. 1 [March 2014], pp. 111, 130.)

Excerpted from: The appendix: or, Some observations on the expediency of the petition of the Africans, living in Boston, &c. lately presented to the General Assembly of this province. To which is annexed, the petition referred to. Likewise, Thoughts on slavery. With a useful extract from the Massachusetts Spy, of January 28, 1773, by way of an address to the members of the Assembly. By a Lover of Constitutional Liberty. Boston, E. Russell. Pages 9–10.

and Honors, and the Honorable the Representatives would be pleased to take their unhappy State and Condition under your wise and just Consideration.

We desire to bless God, who loves Mankind, who sent his Son to die for their Salvation, and who is no Respecter of Persons; that he hath lately put it into the Hearts of Multitudes on both Sides of the Water, to bear our Burthens, some of whom are Men of great Note and Influence; who have pleaded our Cause with Arguments which we hope will have their weight with this Honorable Court.

We presume not to dictate to your Excellency and Honors, being willing to rest our Cause on your Humanity and Justice; yet would beg Leave to say a Word or two on the Subject.

Although some of the Negroes are vicious, (who doubtless may be punished and restrained by the same Laws which are in Force against other of the King's Subjects) there are many others of a quite different Character, and who, if made free, would soon be able as well as willing to bear a Part in the Public Charges; many of them of good natural Parts, are discreet, sober, honest, and industrious; and may it not be said of many, that they are virtuous and religious, although their Condition is in itself so unfriendly to Religion, and every moral Virtue except *Patience*. How many of that Number have there been, and now are in this Province, who have had every Day of their Lives embittered with this most intolerable Reflection, That, let their Behaviour be what it will, neither they, nor their Children to all Generations, shall ever be able to do, or to possess and enjoy any Thing, no, not even *Life itself*, but in a Manner as the *Beasts that perish*.

We have no Property! We have no Wives! No Children! We have no City! No Country! But we have a Father in Heaven, and we are determined, as far as his Grace shall enable us, and as far as our degraded contemptuous Life will admit, to keep all his Commandments: Especially will we be obedient to our Masters, so long as God in his sovereign Providence shall *suffer* us to be holden in Bondage.

It would be impudent, if not presumptuous in us, to suggest to your Excellency and Honors any Law or Laws proper to be made, in relation to our unhappy State, which, although our greatest Unhappiness, is not our *Fault*; and this gives us great Encouragement to pray and hope for such Relief as is consistent with your Wisdom, Justice, and Goodness.

We think ourselves very happy, that we may thus address the Great and General Court of this Province, which great and good Court is to us, the best Judge, under God, of what is wise, just and good.

We humbly beg Leave to add but this one Thing more: We pray for such Relief only, which by no Possibility can ever be productive of the least Wrong or Injury to our Masters; but to us will be as Life from the dead.

Signed,
FELIX

4 United States Constitution: Slavery Provisions (1787)

Editor's Note: While the word "slavery" does not appear in the U.S. Constitution, this founding document protected the institution of slavery in several of its provisions. One of the major debates at the 1787 Constitutional Convention hinged on whether or not to include the enslaved population in calculating taxes and Congressional representation. Southern delegates wanted to count enslaved persons in determining representation in the House but exclude their numbers in determining a state's share of the direct tax burden. The northern delegates' point of view was exactly the opposite. The "three fifths" compromise (Article I, Section 2, whereby three-fifths of the enslaved were to be counted for both representation and taxes) was a victory for southern slaveholders, as were the provision to protect the international slave trade for two decades (Article I, Section 9) and the fugitive slave clause (Article IV, Section 2). In describing the debate, Maryland delegate Luther Martin declared that giving national sanction to the slave trade "ought to be considered as *justly exposing* us to the *displeasure* and *vengeance* of *Him*, who is equal Lord of all, and who views with equal eye the poor *African slave* and his *American master!*"

Article I, Section 2. Representatives and direct Taxes shall be apportioned among the several States which may be included within this Union, according to their respective Numbers, which shall be determined by adding to the whole Number of free Persons, including those bound to Service for a Term of Years, and excluding Indians not taxed, three fifths of all other Persons. . . .

Article I, Section 9. The Migration or Importation of such Persons as any of the States now existing shall think proper to admit, shall not be prohibited by the Congress prior to the Year one thousand eight hundred and eight, but a Tax or duty may be imposed on such Importation, not exceeding ten dollars for each Person. . . .

Article IV, Section 2. No Person held to Service or Labour in one State, under the Laws thereof, escaping into another, shall, in Consequence of any Law or Regulation therein, be discharged from such Service or Labour, but shall be delivered up on Claim of the Party to whom such Service or Labour may be due.

5 | An Act to Prevent All Persons from Teaching Slaves to Read or Write, the Use of Figures Excepted (North Carolina, 1830)

Editor's Note: Justifications of slavery constructed people of color as inherently servile, ignorant, and intellectually inferior to whites, but widespread antiliteracy laws revealed white fears that enslaved persons and free blacks could, in fact, wield the written word as a potent weapon. Literate people could read abolitionist newspapers, forge passes, and communicate with each other. In 1829, free black Bostonian David Walker, originally from North Carolina, published his fiery *Appeal to the Coloured Citizens of the World*. Copies of this bold call for revolt were smuggled into North Carolina and elsewhere, intensifying fears of insurrection and anxiety about literacy. In 1830, North Carolina passed a law prohibiting anyone from teaching enslaved people to read or write. The Act spells out different penalties based on the offender's identity: "a white man or woman" can be fined or imprisoned but not whipped; an enslaved teacher is punished with a specified number of lashes on "his or her bare back"; and a free person of color can face the worst penalties of a white or enslaved lawbreaker. The diversity of potential offenders considered in the Act also reveals the range of Americans challenging racist presumptions of black ignorance and inferiority.

Whereas the teaching of slaves to read and write, has a tendency to excite dissatisfaction in their minds, and to produce insurrection and rebellion, to the manifest injury of the citizens of this State:

Therefore,

Be it enacted by the General Assembly of the State of North Carolina, and it is hereby enacted by the authority of the same, That any free person, who shall hereafter teach, or attempt to teach, any slave within the State to read or write, the use of figures excepted, or shall give or sell to such slave or slaves any books or pamphlets, shall be liable to indictment in any court of record in this State having jurisdiction thereof, and upon conviction, shall, at the discretion of the court, if a white man or woman, be fined not less than one hundred dollars, nor more than two hundred dollars, or imprisoned; and if a free person of color, shall be fined, imprisoned, or whipped, at the discretion of the court, not exceeding thirty-nine lashes, nor less than twenty lashes.

II. *Be it further enacted,* That if any slave shall hereafter teach, or attempt to teach, any other slave to read or write, the use of figures excepted, he or she may be carried before any justice of the peace, and on conviction thereof, shall be sentenced to receive thirty-nine lashes on his or her bare back.

III. *Be it further enacted,* That the judges of the Superior Courts and the justices of the County Courts shall give this act in charge to the grand juries of their respective counties.

From Acts Passed by the General Assembly of the State of North Carolina at the Session of 1830–1831. (Raleigh, 1831), 11.

6 Declaration of Sentiments and Resolutions, Seneca Falls Convention (1848)

Editor's Note: The Declaration of Sentiments, adopted in July 1848 at Seneca Falls, New York, at the first woman's rights convention, is the most famous document in the early history of U.S. feminism. Like the Declaration of Independence, it contains a bill of particulars, but the Declaration of Sentiments itemizes not King George's offenses against the colonists but "usurpations on the part of man toward woman." Elizabeth Cady Stanton wrote the bulk of the document, with Lucretia Mott proposing the final resolution. Stanton and Mott began planning the Convention after attending the 1840 World's Anti-Slavery Convention in London and finding themselves and other women segregated behind a screen. In protest, the acclaimed abolitionist Frederick Douglass sat behind the screen with them. Douglass attended the 1848 Seneca Falls Convention, and he spoke passionately in favor of the most controversial resolution—the one calling for women's right to vote. It narrowly passed (the only resolution not receiving unanimous support) and helped inaugurate the woman's suffrage movement in the United States.

Declaration of Sentiments

When, in the course of human events, it becomes necessary for one portion of the family of man to assume among the people of the earth a position different from that which they have hitherto occupied, but one to which the laws of nature and of nature's God entitle them, a decent respect to the opinions of mankind requires that they should declare the causes that impel them to such a course.

We hold these truths to be self-evident: that all men and women are created equal; that they are endowed by their Creator with certain inalienable rights; that among these are life, liberty, and the pursuit of happiness; that to secure these rights governments are instituted, deriving their just powers from the consent of the governed. Whenever any form of government becomes destructive of these ends, it is the right of those who suffer from it to refuse allegiance to it, and to insist upon the institution of a new government, laying its foundation on such principles, and organizing its powers in such form, as to them shall seem most likely to effect their safety and happiness. Prudence, indeed, will dictate that governments long established should not be changed for light and transient causes; and accordingly all experience hath shown that mankind are more disposed to suffer, while evils are sufferable, than to right themselves by abolishing the forms to which they were accustomed. But when a long train of abuses and usurpations, pursuing invariably the same object, evinces a design to reduce them under absolute despotism, it is their duty to throw off such government, and to provide new guards for their future security. Such has been the patient sufferance of the women under this government, and such is now the necessity which constrains them to demand the equal station to which they are entitled.

The history of mankind is a history of repeated injuries and usurpations on the part of man toward woman, having in direct object the establishment of an absolute tyranny over her. To prove this, let facts be submitted to a candid world.

He has never permitted her to exercise her inalienable right to the elective franchise.

He has compelled her to submit to laws, in the formation of which she had no voice.

He has withheld from her rights which are given to the most ignorant and degraded men—both natives and foreigners.

Having deprived her of this first right of a citizen, the elective franchise, thereby leaving her without representation in the halls of legislation, he has oppressed her on all sides.

He has made her, if married, in the eye of the law, civilly dead.

He has taken from her all right in property, even to the wages she earns.

He has made her, morally, an irresponsible being, as she can commit many crimes with impunity, provided they be done in the presence of her husband. In the covenant of marriage, she is compelled to promise obedience to her husband, he becoming, to all intents and purposes, her master—the law giving him power to deprive her of her liberty, and to administer chastisement.

He has so framed the laws of divorce, as to what shall be the proper causes, and in case of separation, to whom the guardianship of the children shall be given, as to be wholly regardless of the happiness of women—the law, in all cases, going upon the false supposition of the supremacy of man, and giving all power into his hands.

After depriving her of all rights as a married woman, if single, and the owner of property, he has taxed her to support a government which recognizes her only when her property can be made profitable to it.

He has monopolized nearly all the profitable employments, and from those she is permitted to follow, she receives but a scanty remuneration. He closes against her all the avenues to wealth and distinction which he considers most honorable to himself. As a teacher of theology, medicine, or law, she is not known.

He has denied her the facilities for obtaining a thorough education, all colleges being closed against her.

He allows her in Church, as well as State, but a subordinate position, claiming Apostolic authority for her exclusion from the ministry, and, with some exceptions, from any public participation in the affairs of the Church.

He has created a false public sentiment by giving to the world a different code of morals for men and women, by which moral delinquencies which exclude women from society, are not only tolerated, but deemed of little account in man.

He has usurped the prerogative of Jehovah himself, claiming it as his right to assign for her a sphere of action, when that belongs to her conscience and to her God.

He has endeavored, in every way that he could, to destroy her confidence in her own powers, to lessen her self-respect, and to make her willing to lead a dependent and abject life.

Now, in view of this entire disfranchisement of one-half the people of this country, their social and religious degradation—in view of the unjust laws above mentioned, and because women do feel themselves aggrieved, oppressed, and fraudulently deprived of their most sacred rights, we insist that they have immediate admission to all the rights and privileges which belong to them as citizens of the United States.

In entering upon the great work before us, we anticipate no small amount of misconception, misrepresentation, and ridicule; but we shall use every instrumentality within our power to effect our object. We shall employ agents, circulate tracts, petition the State and National legislatures, and endeavor to enlist the pulpit and the press in our behalf. We hope this Convention will be followed by a series of Conventions embracing every part of the country.

Resolutions

WHEREAS, The great precept of nature is conceded to be, that "man shall pursue his own true and substantial happiness." Blackstone in his Commentaries remarks, that this law of Nature being coeval with mankind, and dictated by God himself, is of course superior in obligation to any other. It is binding over all the globe, in all countries and at all times; no human laws are of any validity if contrary to this, and such of them as are valid, derive all their force, and all their validity, and all their authority, mediately and immediately, from this original; therefore,

Resolved, That such laws as conflict, in any way, with the true and substantial happiness of woman, are contrary to the great precept of nature and of no validity, for this is "superior in obligation to any other."

Resolved, That all laws which prevent woman from occupying such a station in society as her conscience shall dictate, or which place her in a position inferior to that of man, are contrary to the great precept of nature, and therefore of no force or authority.

Resolved, That woman is man's equal — was intended to be so by the Creator, and the highest good of the race demands that she should be recognized as such.

Resolved, That the women of this country ought to be enlightened in regard to the laws under which they live, that they may no longer publish their degradation by declaring themselves satisfied with their present position, nor their ignorance, by asserting that they have all the rights they want.

Resolved, That inasmuch as man, while claiming for himself intellectual superiority, does accord to woman moral superiority, it is pre-eminently his duty to encourage her to speak and teach, as she has an opportunity, in all religious assemblies.

Resolved, That the same amount of virtue, delicacy, and refinement of behavior that is required of woman in the social state, should also be required of man, and the same transgressions should be visited with equal severity on both man and woman.

Resolved, That the objection of indelicacy and impropriety, which is so often brought against woman when she addresses a public audience, comes with a very ill-grace from those who encourage, by their attendance, her appearance on the stage, in the concert, or in feats of the circus.

Resolved, That woman has too long rested satisfied in the circumscribed limits which corrupt customs and a perverted application of the Scriptures have marked out for her, and that it is time she should move in the enlarged sphere which her great Creator has assigned her.

Resolved, That it is the duty of the women of this country to secure to themselves their sacred right to the elective franchise.

Resolved, That the equality of human rights results necessarily from the fact of the identity of the race in capabilities and responsibilities.

Resolved, therefore, That, being invested by the Creator with the same capabilities, and the same consciousness of responsibility for their exercise, it is demonstrably the right and duty of woman, equally with man, to promote every righteous cause by every righteous means; and especially in regard to the great subjects of morals and religion, it is self-evidently her right to participate with her brother in teaching them, both in private and in public, by writing and by speaking, by any instrumentalities proper to be used, and in any assemblies proper to be held; and this being a self-evident truth growing out of the divinely implanted principles of human nature, any custom or authority adverse to it, whether modern or wearing the hoary sanction of antiquity, is to be regarded as a self-evident falsehood, and at war with mankind.

At the last session Lucretia Mott offered and spoke to the following resolution:

Resolved, That the speedy success of our cause depends upon the zealous and untiring efforts of both men and women, for the overthrow of the monopoly of the pulpit, and for the securing to woman an equal participation with men in the various trades, professions, and commerce.

7 | *People v. Hall* (1854)

Editor's Note: Bias against the Chinese and other people of color was endemic in nineteenth-century California, but perhaps no single document so well demonstrates that bias as this majority opinion handed down by the chief justice of the California supreme court. The ruling struggles to interpret the word "Indian" to include the Chinese for the purpose of enforcing California's antitestimony laws, and it resulted in the release of George Hall, a white man who had been convicted of murdering a Chinese man.

The appellant, a free white citizen of this State, was convicted of murder upon the testimony of Chinese witnesses.

The point involved in this case, is the admissibility of such evidence.

The 394th section of the Act Concerning Civil Cases, provides that no Indian or Negro shall be allowed to testify as a witness in any action or proceeding in which a White person is a party.

The 14th section of the Act of April 16th, 1850, regulating Criminal Proceedings, provides that "No Black, or Mulatto person, or Indian, shall be allowed to give evidence in favor of, or against a white man."

The true point at which we are anxious to arrive, is the legal signification of the words, "Black, Mulatto, Indian and White person," and whether the Legislature adopted them as generic terms, or intended to limit their application to specific types of the human species.

Before considering this question, it is proper to remark the difference between the two sections of our Statute, already quoted, the latter being more broad and comprehensive in its exclusion, by use of the word "Black," instead of Negro.

Conceding, however, for the present, that the word "Black," as used in the 14th section, and "Negro," in 394th, are convertible terms, and that the former was intended to include the latter, let us proceed to inquire who are excluded from testifying as witnesses under the term "Indian."

When Columbus first landed upon the shores of this continent, in his attempt to discover a western passage to the Indies, he imagined that he had accomplished the object of his expedition, and that the Island of San Salvador was one of those Islands of the Chinese sea, lying near the extremity of India, which had been described by navigators.

Acting upon this hypothesis, and also perhaps from the similarity of features and physical conformation, he gave to the Islanders the name of Indians, which appellation was universally adopted, and extended to the aboriginals of the New World, as well as of Asia.

The People of the State of California v. George W. Hall, 4 Cal. 399 (1854).

From that time, down to a very recent period, the American Indians and the Mongolian, or Asiatic, were regarded as the same type of human species. . . .

. . . That this was the common opinion in the early history of American legislation, cannot be disputed, and, therefore, all legislation upon the subject must have borne relation to that opinion. . . .

. . . In using the words, "No Black, or Mulatto person, or Indian shall be allowed to give evidence for or against a White person," the Legislature, if any intention can be ascribed to it, adopted the most comprehensive terms to embrace every known class or shade of color, as the apparent design was to protect the White person from the influence of all testimony other than that of persons of the same caste. The use of these terms must, by every sound rule of construction, exclude every one who is not of white blood. . . .

. . . We have carefully considered all the consequences resulting from a different rule of construction, and are satisfied that even in a doubtful case we would be impelled to this decision on grounds of public policy.

The same rule which would admit them to testify, would admit them to all the equal rights of citizenship, and we might soon see them at the polls, in the jury box, upon the bench, and in our legislative halls.

This is not a speculation which exists in the excited and overheated imagination of the patriot and statesman, but it is an actual and present danger.

The anomalous spectacle of a distinct people, living in our community, recognizing no laws of this State except through necessity, bringing with them their prejudices and national feuds, in which they indulge in open violation of law; whose mendacity is proverbial; a race of people whom nature has marked as inferior, and who are incapable of progress or intellectual development beyond a certain point, as their history has shown; differing in language, opinions, color, and physical conformation; between whom and ourselves nature has placed an impassable difference, is now presented, and for them is claimed, not only the right to swear away the life of a citizen, but the further privilege of participating with us in administering the affairs of our Government. . . .

. . . For these reasons, we are of opinion that the testimony was inadmissible. . . .

8 *Dred Scott v. Sandford* (1857)

The question is simply this: Can a negro, whose ancestors were imported into this country, and sold as slaves, become a member of the political community formed and brought into existence by the Constitution of the United States, and as such become entitled to all the rights, and privileges, and immunities, guarantied by that instrument to the citizen? One of which rights is the privilege of suing in a court of the United States in the cases specified in the Constitution.

It will be observed, that the plea applies to that class of persons only whose ancestors were negroes of the African race, and imported into this country, and sold and held as slaves. The only matter in issue before this court, therefore, is whether the descendants of such slaves, when they shall be emancipated, or who are born of parents who had become free before their birth, are citizens of a State, in the sense in which the word citizen is used in the Constitution of the United States. And this being the only matter in dispute on the pleadings, the court must be understood as speaking in his opinion of that class only, that is, of those persons who are the descendants of Africans who were imported into this country, and sold as slaves.

. . .

It becomes necessary, therefore, to determine who were citizens of the several States when the Constitution was adopted. And in order to do this, we must recur to the Governments and institutions of the thirteen colonies, when they separated from Great Britain and formed new sovereignties, and took their places in the family of independent nations. We must inquire who, at that time, were recognised as the people or citizens of a State, whose rights and liberties had been outraged by the English Government; and who declared their independence, and assumed the powers of Government to defend their rights by force of arms.

In the opinion of the court, the legislation and histories of the times, and the language used in the Declaration of Independence, show, that neither the class of persons who had been imported as slaves, nor their descendants, whether they had become free or not, were then acknowledged as a part of the people, nor intended to be included in the general words used in that memorable instrument.

It is difficult at this day to realize the state of public opinion in relation to that unfortunate race, which prevailed in the civilized and enlightened portions of the world at the time of the Declaration of Independence, and when the Constitution of the United States was formed and adopted. But the public history of every European nation displays it in a manner too plain to be mistaken.

From Benjamin C. Howard, Report of the Decision of the Supreme Court of the United States in the Case Dred Scott . . . (Washington, 1857), 9, 13–14, 15–17, 60.

They had for more than a century before been regarded as beings of an inferior order, and altogether unfit to associate with the white race, either in social or political relations; and so far inferior, that they had no rights which the white man was bound to respect; and that the negro might justly and lawfully be reduced to slavery for his benefit. He was bought and sold, and treated as an ordinary article of merchandise and traffic, whenever a profit could be made by it. This opinion was at that time fixed and universal in the civilized portion of the white race. It was regarded as an axiom in morals as well as in politics, which no one thought of disputing, or supposed to be open to dispute; and men in every grade and position in society daily and habitually acted upon it in their private pursuits, as well as in matters of public concern, without doubting for a moment the correctness of this opinion.

And in no nation was this opinion more firmly fixed or more uniformly acted upon than by the English Government and English people. They not only seized them on the coast of Africa, and sold them or held them in slavery for their own use, but they took them as ordinary articles of merchandise to every country where they could make a profit on them, and were far more extensively engaged in this commerce than any other nation in the world.

The opinion thus entertained and acted upon in England was naturally impressed upon the colonies they founded on this side of the Atlantic. And, accordingly, a negro of the African race was regarded by them as an article of property, and held, and bought and sold as such, in every one of the thirteen colonies which united in the Declaration of Independence, and afterwards formed the Constitution of the United States. The slaves were more or less numerous in the different colonies, as slave labor was found more or less profitable. But no one seems to have doubted the correctness of the prevailing opinion of the time.

The legislation of the different colonies furnishes positive and indisputable proof of this fact.

. . .

The language of the Declaration of Independence is equally conclusive:

It begins by declaring that, "when in the course of human events it becomes necessary for one people to dissolve the political bands which have connected them with another, and to assume among the powers of the earth the separate and equal station to which the laws of nature and nature's God entitle them, a decent respect for the opinions of mankind requires that they should declare the causes which impel them to the separation."

It then proceeds to say: "We hold these truths to be self-evident: that all men are created equal; that they are endowed by their Creator with certain unalienable rights; that among them is life, liberty, and the pursuit of happiness; that to secure these rights, Governments are instituted, deriving their just powers from the consent of the governed."

The general words above quoted would seem to embrace the whole human family, and if they were used in a similar instrument at this day would be so understood. But it is too clear for dispute, that the enslaved African race were not intended to be included, and formed no part of the people who framed and adopted this declaration; for if the language, as understood in that day, would embrace them, the conduct of the distinguished men who framed the Declaration of Independence would have been utterly and flagrantly inconsistent with the principles they asserted; and instead of the sympathy of mankind, to which they so confidently appealed, they would have deserved and received universal rebuke and reprobation.

Yet the men who framed this declaration were great men—high in literary acquirements—high in their sense of honor, and incapable of asserting principles inconsistent with those on which they were acting. They perfectly understood the meaning of the language they used, and how it would be understood by others; and they knew that it would not in any part of the civilized world be supposed to embrace the negro race, which, by common consent, had been excluded from civilized Governments and the family of nations, and doomed to slavery. They spoke and acted according to the then established doctrines and principles, and in the ordinary language of the day, and no one misunderstood them. The unhappy black race were separated from the white by indelible marks, and laws long before established, and were never thought of or spoken of except as property, and when the claims of the owner or the profit of the trader were supposed to need protection.

The state of public opinion had undergone no change when the Constitution was adopted, as is equally evident from its provisions and language.

The brief preamble sets forth by whom it was formed, for what purposes, and for whose benefit and protection. It declares that it is formed by the *people* of the United States—that is to say, by those who were members of the different political communities in the several States—and its great object is declared to be to secure the blessings of liberty to themselves and their posterity. It speaks in general terms of the *people* of the United States, and of *citizens* of the several States, when it is providing for the exercise of the powers granted or the privileges secured to the citizen. It does not define what description of persons are intended to be included under these terms, or who shall be regarded as a citizen and one of the people. It uses them as terms so well understood, that no further description or definition was necessary.

But there are two clauses in the Constitution which point directly and specifically to the negro race as a separate class of persons, and show clearly that they were not regarded as a portion of the people or citizens of the Government then formed.

One of these clauses reserves to each of the thirteen States the right to import slaves until the year 1808, if it thinks proper. And the importation which it thus sanctions was unquestionably of persons of the race of which we are speaking, as the traffic in slaves in the United States had always been confined to them. And by the other provision the States pledge themselves to each other to maintain the right of property of the master, by delivering up to him any slave who may have escaped from his service, and be found within their respective territories. By the first above-mentioned clause, therefore, the right to purchase and hold this property is directly sanctioned and authorized for twenty years by the people who framed the Constitution. And by the second, they pledge themselves to maintain and uphold the right of the master in the manner specified, as long as the Government they then formed should endure. And these two provisions show, conclusively, that neither the description of persons therein referred to, nor their descendants, were embraced in any of the other provisions of the Constitution, for certainly these two clauses were not intended to confer on them or their posterity the blessings of liberty, or any of the personal rights so carefully provided for the citizen.

. . .

Upon the whole, therefore, it is the judgment of this court, that it appears by the record before us that the plaintiff in error is not a citizen of Missouri, in the sense in which that word is used in the Constitution; and that the Circuit Court of the United States, for that reason, had no jurisdiction in the case, and could give no judgment in it. Its judgment for the defendant must, consequently, be reversed, and a mandate issued, directing the suit to be dismissed for want of jurisdiction.

9 The Emancipation Proclamation
Abraham Lincoln

January 1, 1863

Whereas, on the twenty-second day of September, in the year of our Lord one thousand eight hundred and sixty two, a proclamation was issued by the President of the United States, containing, among other things, the following, to wit:

"That on the first day of January, in the year of our Lord one thousand eight hundred and sixty-three, all persons held as slaves within any State or designated part of a State, the people whereof shall then be in rebellion against the United States, shall be then, thenceforward, and forever free; and the Executive Government of the United States, including the military and naval authority thereof, will recognize and maintain the freedom of such persons, and will do no act or acts to repress such persons, or any of them, in any efforts they may make for their actual freedom.

"That the Executive will, on the first day of January aforesaid, by proclamation, designate the States and parts of States, if any, in which the people thereof, respectively, shall then be in rebellion against the United States; and the fact that any State, or the people thereof, shall on that day be, in good faith, represented in the Congress of the United States by members chosen thereto at elections wherein a majority of the qualified voters of such State shall have participated, shall, in the absence of strong countervailing testimony, be deemed conclusive evidence that such State, and the people thereof, are not then in rebellion against the United States."

Now, therefore I, Abraham Lincoln, President of the United States, by virtue of the power in me vested as Commander-in-Chief, of the Army and Navy of the United States in time of actual armed rebellion against authority and government of the United States, and as a fit and necessary war measure for suppressing said rebellion, do, on this first day of January, in the year of our Lord one thousand eight hundred and sixty-three, and in accordance with my purpose so to do publicly proclaimed for the full period of one hundred days, from the day first above mentioned, order and designate as the States and parts of States wherein the people thereof respectively, are this day in rebellion against the United States, the following, to wit:

Arkansas, Texas, Louisiana (except the Parishes of St. Bernard, Plaquemines, Jefferson, St. Johns, St. Charles, St. James[,] Ascension, Assumption, Terrebonne, Lafourche, St. Mary, St. Martin, and Orleans, including the City of New-Orleans), Mississippi, Alabama, Florida, Georgia, South-Carolina, North-Carolina, and Virginia (except the forty-eight counties designated as West Virginia, and also the counties of Berkley, Accomac, Northampton, Elizabeth-City, York, Princess Ann, and Norfolk, including the cities of Norfolk & Portsmouth[)]; and which excepted parts are, for the present, left precisely as if this proclamation were not issued.

And by virtue of the power, and for the purpose aforesaid, I do order and declare that all persons held as slaves within said designated States, and parts of States, are, and henceforward shall be free; and that the Executive Government of the United States, including the military and naval authorities thereof, will recognize and maintain the freedom of said persons.

And I hereby enjoin upon the people so declared to be free to abstain from all violence, unless in necessary self-defence; and I recommend to them that, in all cases when allowed, they labor faithfully for reasonable wages.

And I further declare and make known, that such persons of suitable condition, will be received into the armed service of the United States to garrison forts, positions, stations, and other places, and to man vessels of all sorts in said service.

And upon this act, sincerely believed to be an act of justice, warranted by the Constitution, upon military necessity, I invoke the considerate judgment of mankind, and the gracious favor of Almighty God.

In witness whereof, I have hereunto set my hand and caused the seal of the United States to be affixed.

Done at the City of Washington, this first day of January, in the year of our Lord one thousand eight hundred and sixty-three, and of the Independence of the United States of America the eighty-seventh.

By the President:
Abraham Lincoln

William H. Seward,
Secretary of State

10 United States Constitution: Thirteenth (1865), Fourteenth (1868), and Fifteenth (1870) Amendments

Editor's Note: In the aftermath of the Civil War, these three amendments sought to protect the rights of previously enslaved Americans. A century and a half later, all three amendments continue to play a key role in contemporary civil rights debates. The Thirteenth Amendment bans involuntary servitude, with the significant exception of "punishment for crime." The Fourteenth Amendment articulates the principle of birthright citizenship and guarantees "equal protection" and "due process" under law. The Fifteenth Amendment protects the right to vote from being abridged based on "race, color, or previous condition of servitude."

Amendment XIII [Ratified December 6, 1865]

Section 1. Neither slavery nor involuntary servitude, except as a punishment for crime whereof the party shall have been duly convicted, shall exist within the United States, or any place subject to their jurisdiction.

    Section 2. Congress shall have power to enforce this article by appropriate legislation.

Amendment XIV [Ratified July 9, 1868]

Section 1. All persons born or naturalized in the United States, and subject to the jurisdiction thereof, are citizens of the United States and of the state wherein they reside. No State shall make or enforce any law which shall abridge the privileges or immunities of citizens of the United States; nor shall any State deprive any person of life, liberty, or property, without due process of law; nor deny to any person within its jurisdiction the equal protection of the laws.

    Section 2. Representatives shall be apportioned among the several states according to their respective numbers, counting the whole number of persons in each state, excluding Indians not taxed. But when the right to vote at any election for the choice of Electors for President and Vice-President of the United States, Representatives in Congress, the executive and judicial officers of a State, or the members of the Legislature thereof, is denied to any of the male inhabitants of such State, being twenty-one years of age, and, citizens of the United States, or in any way abridged, except for participation in rebellion, or other crime, the basis of representation therein shall be reduced in the proportion which the number of such male citizens shall bear to the whole number of male citizens twenty-one years of age in such State.

Section 3. No person shall be a Senator or Representative in Congress, or elector of President and Vice-President, or hold any office, civil or military, under the United States, or under any State, who, having previously taken an oath, as a member of Congress, or as an officer of the United States, or as an executive or judicial officer of any State, to support the Constitution of the United States, shall have engaged in insurrection or rebellion against the same, or given aid or comfort to the enemies thereof. But Congress may by a vote of two-thirds of each House, remove such disability.

Section 4. The validity of the public debt of the United States, authorized by law, including debts incurred for payment of pensions and bounties for services in suppressing insurrection or rebellion, shall not be questioned. But neither the United States nor any State shall assume or pay any debt or obligation incurred in aid of insurrection or rebellion against the United States, or any claim for the loss or emancipation of any slave; but all such debts, obligations, and claims, shall be held illegal and void.

Section 5. The Congress shall have power to enforce, by appropriate legislation, the provisions of this article.

Amendment XV [Ratified February 3, 1870]

Section 1. The right of citizens of the United States to vote shall not be denied or abridged by the United States or by any State on account of race, color, or previous condition of servitude.

Section 2. The Congress shall have power to enforce this article by appropriate legislation.

11 South Carolina Black Codes (1865)

Editor's Note: Within days of the Thirteenth Amendment's becoming part of the U.S. Constitution, the South Carolina legislature passed an extensive set of laws known as "Black Codes," essentially reestablishing the terms of slavery, and other states quickly followed suit. W. E. B. Du Bois described the black codes that swept the South as "an astonishing affront to emancipation" and an "indisputable attempt on the part of the Southern states to make Negroes slaves in everything but name." Renamed "servants" or "apprentices," blacks in South Carolina were limited in their movements, and "masters" were authorized to recapture, "correct," and "chastise" those in their service. In addition to questions of labor, the codes regulated matters of marriage, barring interracial relationships and mandating the "consent of the master" before a black apprentice could marry. Persons of color were barred from numerous trades and were required to obtain licenses for certain kinds of work, and then were punished for the "crimes" of "vagrancy and idleness." Those convicted could be sentenced to hard labor and "hired" out to landowners, exploiting the loophole in the Thirteenth Amendment that allowed involuntary servitude for those convicted of a crime.

An Act to Establish and Regulate the Domestic Relations of Persons of Color, and to Amend the Law in Relation to Paupers and Vagrancy

HUSBAND AND WIFE

I. The relation of husband and wife amongst persons of color is established.

II. Those who now live as such, are declared to be husband and wife. . . .

VIII. One who is a pauper, or a charge to the public, shall not be competent to contract marriage. Marriage between a white person and a person of color, shall be illegal and void.

IX. The marriage of an apprentice shall not, without the consent of the master, be lawful. . . .

MASTER AND APPRENTICE

XV. A child over the age of two years, born of a colored parent, may be bound by the father, if he be living in the District, or in case of his death or absence from the District,

The Statutes at Large of South Carolina Vol. XII containing the Acts from December 1861 to December 1866. An Act to Establish and Regulate the Domestic Relations of Persons of Color and to Amend the Law in Relation to Paupers and Vagrancy, Act No. 4733. General Assembly, 19 December 1865 (Columbia, SC: Republican Printing Corp., 1875): 269–285. South Carolina Department of Archives and History, Columbia, South Carolina.

by the mother, as an apprentice, to any respectable white or colored person, who is competent to make a contract—a male until he shall attain the age of twenty-one years and a female until she shall attain the age of eighteen years.

XVI. Illegitimate children, within the ages above specified, may be bound by the mother.

XVII. Colored children, between the ages mentioned, who have neither father nor mother living in the District in which they are found, or whose parents are paupers, or unable to afford to them maintenance, or whose parents are not teaching them habits of industry and honesty, or are persons of notoriously bad character, or are vagrants, or have been, either of them convicted of an infamous offense, may be bound as apprentices by the District Judge, or one of the Magistrates for the aforesaid term.

XVIII. Males of the age of twelve years, and females, of the age of ten years, shall sign the indenture of apprenticeship and be bound thereby.

XIX. When the apprentice is under these ages, and in all cases of compulsory apprenticeship, where the infant refuses assent, his signature shall not be necessary to the validity of the apprenticeship. . . .

XXII. The master or mistress shall teach the apprentice the business of husbandry, or some other useful trade or business, which shall be specified in the instrument of apprenticeship; shall furnish him wholesome food and suitable clothing; teach him habits of industry, honesty and morality; govern and treat him with humanity; and if there be a school within a convenient distance, in which colored children are taught, shall send him to school at least six weeks in every year of his apprenticeship, after he shall be of the age of ten years: *Provided,* That the teacher of such school shall have the license of the District Judge to establish the same.

XXIII. The master shall have authority to inflict moderate chastisement and impose reasonable restraint upon his apprentice, and to recapture him if he depart from his service.

XXIV. The master shall receive to his own use the profits of the labor of his apprentice. . . .

CONTRACTS FOR SERVICE

XXXV. All persons of color who make contracts for service or labor, shall be known as servants, and those with whom they contract shall be known as masters.

XXXVI. Contracts between masters and servants, for one month or more, shall be in writing, be attested by one white witness, and be approved by the Judge of the District Court, or by a Magistrate. . . .

XLIII. For any neglect of the duty to make a contract as herein directed, or the evasion of that duty by the repeated employment of the same persons for periods less than one month, the party offending shall be guilty of a misdemeanor, and be liable on conviction to pay a sum not exceeding fifty dollars, and not less than five dollars, for each person so employed. No written contract shall be required, when the servant voluntarily receives no remuneration, except food and clothing. . . .

REGULATIONS OF LABOR ON FARMS

XLV. On farms or in out-door service, the hours of labor, except on Sunday, shall be from sun-rise to sun-set, with a reasonable interval for breakfast and dinner. Servants shall rise at the dawn in the morning, feed, water and care for the animals on the farm, do the usual and needful work about the premises, prepare their meals for the day, if required by the master, and begin the farm work or other work by sun-rise. The servant shall be careful of all the animals and property of his master, and especially of the animals and instruments used by him, shall protect the same from injury by other persons, and shall be answerable for all property lost, destroyed or injured by his negligence, dishonesty or bad faith.

XLVI. All lost time, not caused by the act of the master, and all losses occasioned by neglect of the duties hereinbefore prescribed, may be deducted from the wages of the servant; and food, nursing and other necessaries for the servant, while he is absent from work on account of sickness or other cause, may also be deducted from his wages. Servants shall be quiet and orderly in their quarters, at their work and on the premises; shall extinguish their lights and fires, and retire to rest at seasonable hours. Work at night, and out-door work in inclement weather, shall not be exacted unless in case of necessity. Servants shall not be kept at home on Sunday, unless to take care of the premises, or animals thereupon, or for work of daily necessity, or on unusual occasions; and in such cases only so many shall be kept at home as are necessary for these purposes. Sunday work shall be done by the servants in turn, except in cases of sickness or other disability, when it may be assigned to them out of their regular term. Absentees on Sunday shall return to their homes by sun-set. . . .

XLVIII. Visitors or other persons shall not be invited, or allowed by the servant, to come or remain upon the premises of the master, without his express permission.

XLIX. Servants shall not be absent from the premises without the permission of the master.

RIGHTS OF MASTER AS BETWEEN HIMSELF AND HIS SERVANT

L. When the servant shall depart from the service of the master without good cause, he shall forfeit the wages due to him. The servant shall obey all lawful orders of the master or his agent, and shall be honest, truthful, sober, civil, and diligent in his business. The master may moderately correct servants who have made contracts, and are under eighteen years of age. He shall not be liable to pay for any additional or extraordinary services or labor of his servant, the same being necessary, unless by his express agreement. . . .

PAUPERS

LXXXI. When a person of color shall be unable to earn his support, and is likely to become a charge to the public, the father and grand-fathers, mother and grand-mothers, child and grand-child, brother and sister of such person, shall, each according to his ability, contribute monthly, for the support of such poor relative, such sum as the

District Judge, or one of the Magistrates, upon complaint to him, shall deem necessary and proper; and on failure to pay such sum, the same shall be collected by summary order or process.

MECHANICS, ARTISANS AND SHOP-KEEPERS

LXXII. No person of color shall pursue or practice the art, trade or business of an artisan, mechanic or shop-keeper, or any other trade, employment or business (besides that of husbandry, or that of a servant under a contract for services or labor) on his own account and for his own benefit, or in partnership with a white person, or as agent or servant of any person, until he shall have obtained a license therefor from the Judge of the District Court, which license shall be good for one year only. This license the judge may grant upon petition of the applicant, and upon being satisfied of his skill and fitness, and of his good moral character . . . : *Provided, however,* That upon complaint being made and proved to the District Judge of an abuse of such license, he shall revoke the same, and: *Provided, also,* That no person of color shall practice any mechanical art or trade, unless he shows that he has served an apprenticeship in such trade or art, or is now practicing such trade or art. . . .

VAGRANCY AND IDLENESS

XCV. These are public grievances, and must be punished as crimes.

XCVI. All persons who have not some fixed and known place of abode, and some lawful and reputable employment; those who have not some visible and known means of a fair, honest and reputable livelihood; all common prostitutes; those who are found wandering from place to place, vending, bartering, or peddling-any articles or commodities, without a license from the District Judge, or other proper authorities; all common gamblers; persons who lead idle or disorderly lives, or keep or frequent disorderly or disreputable houses or places; those who, not having sufficient means of support, are able to work and do not work; those who, (whether or not they own lands, or are lessees or mechanics,) do not provide a reasonable and proper maintenance for themselves, and families; those who are engaged in representing publicly or privately, for fee or reward, without license, any tragedy, interlude, comedy, farce, play, or other similar entertainment, exhibition of the circus, sleight of hand, wax work or the like; those who for private gain, without license, give any concert or musical entertainment of any description; fortune tellers; sturdy beggars; common drunkards; those who hunt game of any description, or fish on the land of others, or frequent the premises, contrary to the will of the occupants; shall be deemed vagrants, and be liable to the punishment hereinafter provided.

XCVII. Upon information, or oath, of another, or upon his own knowledge, the District Judge or a Magistrate shall issue a warrant for the arrest of any person of color known or believed to be a vagrant, within the meaning of this Act. The Magistrate may proceed to try, with the assistance of five freeholders, or call into his aid another

Magistrate, and the two may proceed to try, with the assistance of three freeholders, as provided by the Act of 1787, concerning vagrants; or the Magistrate may commit the accused to be tried before the District Court. On conviction, the defendant shall be liable to imprisonment, and to hard labor, one or both, as shall be fixed by the verdict, not exceeding twelve months.

XCVIII. The defendant, if sentenced to hard labor after conviction, may, by order of the District Judge, or Magistrate, before whom he was convicted, be hired for such wages as can be obtained for his services, to any owner or lessee of a farm, for the term of labor to which he was sentenced, or be hired for the same labor on the streets, public roads, or public buildings. The person receiving such vagrant shall have all the rights and remedies for enforcing good conduct and diligence at labor that are herein provided in the case of master and servant.

12 *Bradwell v. Illinois* (1873)

Editor's Note: Myra Bradwell passed the Illinois bar exam in 1869, but the Illinois Supreme Court denied her admission to the bar. She filed multiple briefs, invoking the Fourteenth Amendment and countering the argument that her status as a married woman rendered her unfit to practice law. Bradwell appealed the case to the U.S. Supreme Court, which ruled against her and upheld a state's right to deny women the right to practice law, invoking "divine ordinance" and the "natural and proper timidity and delicacy which belongs to the female sex." Despite being denied the right to practice law, Bradwell drafted legislation to protect the rights of married women and widows, worked for women's suffrage, and helped other women gain the right to practice law and enter other professions. Myra Bradwell was finally admitted to the bar in 1890.

. . . The claim of the plaintiff, who is a married woman, to be admitted to practice as an attorney and counsellor-at-law, is based upon the supposed right of every person, man or woman, to engage in any lawful employment for a livelihood. The Supreme Court of Illinois denied the application on the ground that, by the common law, which is the basis of the laws of Illinois, only men were admitted to the bar, and the legislature had not made any change in this respect, but had simply provided that no person should be admitted to practice as attorney or counsellor without having previously obtained a license for that purpose from two justices of the Supreme Court, and that no person should receive a license without first obtaining a certificate from the court of some county of his good moral character. In other respects it was left to the discretion of the court to establish the rules by which admission to the profession should be determined. The court, however, regarded itself as bound by at least two limitations. One was that it should establish such terms of admission as would promote the proper administration of justice, and the other that it should not admit any persons, or class of persons, not intended by the legislature to be admitted, even though not expressly excluded by statute. In view of this latter limitation the court felt compelled to deny the application of females to be admitted as members of the bar. Being contrary to the rules of the common law and the usages of Westminster Hall from time immemorial, it could not be supposed that the legislature had intended to adopt any different rule.

The claim that, under the fourteenth amendment of the Constitution, which declares that no State shall make or enforce any law which shall abridge the privileges and immunities of citizens of the United States, the statute law of Illinois, or the common law prevailing in that State, can no longer be set up as a barrier against the right of

Bradwell v. State of Illinois, 83 U.S. (16 Wall.) 130 (1873).

females to pursue any lawful employment for a livelihood (the practice of law included), assumes that it is one of the privileges and immunities of women as citizens to engage in any and every profession, occupation, or employment in civil life. . . . It certainly cannot be affirmed, as an historical fact, that this has ever been established as one of the fundamental privileges and immunities of the sex. On the contrary, the civil law, as well as nature herself, has always recognized a wide difference in the respective spheres and destinies of man and woman. Man is, or should be, woman's protector and defender. The natural and proper timidity and delicacy which belongs to the female sex evidently unfits it for many of the occupations of civil life. The constitution of the family organization, which is founded in the divine ordinance, as well as in the nature of things, indicates the domestic sphere as that which properly belongs to the domain and functions of womanhood. The harmony, not to say identity, of interest and views which belong, or should belong, to the family institution is repugnant to the idea of a woman adopting a distinct and independent career from that of her husband. So firmly fixed was this sentiment in the founders of the common law that it became a maxim of that system of jurisprudence that a woman had no legal existence separate from her husband, who was regarded as her head and representative in the social state; and, notwithstanding some recent modifications of this civil status, many of the special rules of law flowing from and dependent upon this cardinal principle still exist in full force in most States. One of these is, that a married woman is incapable, without her husband's consent, of making contracts which shall be binding on her or him. This very incapacity was one circumstance which the Supreme Court of Illinois deemed important in rendering a married woman incompetent fully to perform the duties and trusts that belong to the office of an attorney and counsellor.

It is true that many women are unmarried and not affected by any of the duties, complications, and incapacities arising out of the married state, but these are exceptions to the general rule. The paramount destiny and mission of woman are to fulfil the noble and benign offices of wife and mother. This is the law of the Creator. And the rules of civil society . . . must be adapted to the general constitution of things, and cannot be based upon exceptional cases.

The humane movements of modern society, which have for their object the multiplication of avenues for woman's advancement, and of occupations adapted to her condition and sex, have my heartiest concurrence. But I am not prepared to say that it is one of her fundamental rights and privileges to be admitted into every office and position, including those which require highly special qualifications and demanding special responsibilities. In the nature of things it is not every citizen of every age, sex, and condition that is qualified for every calling and position. It is the prerogative of the legislator to prescribe regulations founded on nature, reason, and experience for the due admission of qualified persons to professions and callings demanding special skill and confidence. This fairly belongs to the police power of the State; and, in my opinion, in view of the peculiar characteristics, destiny, and mission of woman, it is within the province of the legislature to ordain what offices, positions, and callings shall be filled and discharged by men, and shall receive the benefit of those energies and responsibilities, and that decision and firmness which are presumed to predominate in the sterner sex.

For these reasons I think that the laws of Illinois now complained of are not obnoxious to the charge of abridging any of the privileges and immunities of citizens of the United States.

Mr. Justice SWAYNE and Mr. Justice FIELD concurred in the foregoing opinion of Mr. Justice BRADLEY. The CHIEF JUSTICE dissented from the judgment of the court, and from all the opinions.

13 The Chinese Exclusion Act (1882)

An Act to Execute Certain Treaty Stipulations Relating to Chinese

PREAMBLE: Whereas, in the opinion of the Government of the United States the coming of Chinese laborers to this country endangers the good order of certain localities within the territory thereof: Therefore,

Be it enacted by the Senate and House of Representatives of the United States of America in Congress assembled, That from and after the expiration of ninety days next after the passage of this act, and until the expiration of ten years next after the passage of this act, the coming of Chinese laborers to the United States be, and the same is hereby, suspended; and during such suspension it shall not be lawful for any Chinese laborer to come, or having so come after the expiration of said ninety days, to remain within the United States.

SEC. 2. That the master of any vessel who shall knowingly bring within the United States on such vessel, and land or permit to be landed, any Chinese laborer, from any foreign port or place, shall be deemed guilty of a misdemeanor, and on conviction thereof shall be punished by a fine of not more than $500 for each and every such Chinese laborer so brought, and may be also imprisoned for a term not exceeding one year.

SEC. 3. That the two foregoing sections shall not apply to Chinese laborers who were in the United States on the 17th day of November, 1880, or who shall have come into the same before the expiration of ninety days next after the passage of this act . . .

SEC. 4. That for the purpose of properly identifying Chinese laborers who were in the United States on the 17th day of November, 1880, or who shall have come into the same before the expiration of ninety days next after the passage of this act, and in order to furnish them with the proper evidence of their right to go from and come to the United States of their free will and accord, as provided by the treaty between the United States and China dated November 17, 1880, the collector of customs of the district from which any such Chinese laborer shall depart from the United States shall, in person or by deputy, go on board each vessel having on board any such Chinese laborer and cleared or about to sail from his district for a foreign port, and on such vessel make a list of all such Chinese laborers, which shall be entered in registry-books to be kept for that purpose, in which shall be stated the name, age, occupation, last place of residence, physical marks or peculiarities, and all facts necessary for the identification of each of such Chinese laborers, which books shall be safely kept in the custom-house; and every such Chinese laborer so departing from the United States shall be entitled to, and shall receive, free of any charge or cost upon application therefor, from the collector or his deputy, at the time such list is taken, a certificate, signed by the collector or his deputy and attested by his seal of office, in such form as the Secretary of the Treasury shall prescribe, which certificate shall contain a statement of the name, age, occupation, last place of residence, personal description, and facts of identification of the Chinese laborer to whom the certificate is issued, corresponding with the said list and registry in all particulars. . . .

SEC. 5. That any Chinese laborer mentioned in section four of this act being in the United States, and desiring to depart from the United States by land, shall have the right to demand and receive, free of charge or cost, a certificate of identification similar to that provided for in section four of this act to be issued to such Chinese laborers as may desire to leave the United States by water; and it is hereby made the duty of the collector of customs of the district next adjoining the foreign country to which said Chinese laborer desires to go to issue such certificate, free of charge or cost, upon application by such Chinese laborer, and to enter the same upon registry-books to be kept by him for the purpose, as provided for in section four of this act.

SEC. 6. That in order to the faithful execution of articles one and two of the treaty in this act before mentioned, every Chinese person other than a laborer who may be entitled by said treaty and this act to come within the United States, and who shall be about to come to the United States, shall be identified as so entitled by the Chinese Government in each case, such identity to be evidenced by a certificate issued under the authority of said government, which certificate shall be in the English language or (if not in the English language) accompanied by a translation into English, stating such right to come, and which certificate shall state the name, title, or official rank, if any, the age, height, and all physical peculiarities, former and present occupation or profession, and place of residence in China of the person to whom the certificate is issued and that such person is entitled conformably to the treaty in this act mentioned to come within the United States. . . .

SEC. 7. That any person who shall knowingly and falsely alter or substitute any name for the name written in such certificate or forge any such certificate, or knowingly utter any forged or fraudulent certificate, or falsely personate any person named in any such certificate, shall be deemed guilty of a misdemeanor; and upon conviction thereof shall be fined in a sum not exceeding $1,000, and imprisoned in a penitentiary for a term of not more than five years.

SEC. 8. That the master of any vessel arriving in the United States from any foreign port or place shall, at the same time he delivers a manifest of the cargo, and if there be no cargo, then at the time of making a report, of the entry of the vessel pursuant to law, in addition to the other matter required to be reported, and before landing, or permitting to land, any Chinese passengers, deliver and report to the collector of customs of the district in which such vessels shall have arrived a separate list of all Chinese passengers taken on board his vessel at any foreign port or place, and all such passengers on board the vessel at that time. . . .

SEC. 9. That before any Chinese passengers are landed from any such vessel, the collector, or his deputy, shall proceed to examine such passengers, comparing the certificates with the list and with the passengers; and no passenger shall be allowed to land in the United States from such vessel in violation of law. . . .

SEC. 11. That any person who shall knowingly bring into or cause to be brought into the United States by land, or who shall knowingly aid or abet the same, or aid or abet the landing in the United States from any vessel of any Chinese person not lawfully entitled to enter the United States, shall be deemed guilty of a misdemeanor, and shall, on conviction thereof, be fined in a sum not exceeding $1,000, and imprisoned for a term not exceeding one year.

Sec. 12. That no Chinese person shall be permitted to enter the United States by land without producing to the proper officer of customs the certificate in this act required of Chinese persons seeking to land from a vessel. . . .

Sec. 13. That this act shall not apply to diplomatic and other officers of the Chinese Government traveling upon the business of that government, whose credentials shall be taken as equivalent to the certificate in this act mentioned, and shall exempt them and their body and household servants from the provisions of this act as to other Chinese persons.

Sec. 14. That hereafter no State court or court of the United States shall admit Chinese to citizenship; and all laws in conflict with this act are hereby repealed.

Sec. 15. That the words "Chinese laborers," wherever used in this act, shall be construed to mean both skilled and unskilled laborers and Chinese employed in mining.

Approved, May 6, 1882.

14   *Elk* v. *Wilkins*, 1884

Editor's Note: This case has implications for questions of voting rights, birthright citizenship, and tribal sovereignty. John Elk, a Winnebago man born on a reservation in Iowa and later moving to Nebraska and giving up his tribal affiliation, was denied the right to vote on the grounds that he was not a U.S. citizen. The Fourteenth Amendment articulated the principle of birthright citizenship in its provision that "All persons born or naturalized in the United States, and subject to the jurisdiction thereof, are citizens of the United States and of the State wherein they reside." The Supreme Court considered the question of whether Elk had been made a citizen by the Fourteenth Amendment and decided against him. Congress ended the exclusion of Native Americans from citizenship through passage of the Indian Citizenship Act of 1924, but many states continued to deny voting rights to Native Americans for decades. In 1962, New Mexico became the last state to officially enfranchise Native Americans.

MR. JUSTICE GRAY delivered the opinion of the Court.

. . . The plaintiff, in support of his action, relies on the first clause of the first section of the Fourteenth Article of Amendment of the Constitution of the United States, by which "all persons born or naturalized in the United States, and subject to the jurisdiction thereof, are citizens of the United States and of the State wherein they reside"; and on the Fifteenth Article of Amendment, which provides that "the right of citizens of the United States to vote shall not be denied or abridged by the United States or by any State on account of race, color, or previous condition of servitude." . . .

The petition, while it does not show of what Indian tribe the plaintiff was a member, yet, by the allegations that he "is an Indian, and was born within the United States," and that "he had severed his tribal relation to the Indian tribes," clearly implies that he was born a member of one of the Indian tribes within the limits of the United States, which still exists and is recognized as a tribe by the government of the United States. Though the plaintiff alleges that he "had fully and completely surrendered himself to the jurisdiction of the United States," he does not allege that the United States accepted his surrender, or that he has ever been naturalized, or taxed, or in any way recognized or treated as a citizen, by the State or by the United States. Nor is it contended by his counsel that there is any statute or treaty that makes him a citizen.

The question then is, whether an Indian, born a member of one of the Indian tribes within the United States, is, merely by reason of his birth within the United States, and

From Elk v. Wilkins, 112 United States Reports: Cases Adjudged in the Supreme Court (New York: Banks & Brothers).

of his afterwards voluntarily separating himself from his tribe and taking up his residence among white citizens, a citizen of the United States, within the meaning of the first section of the Fourteenth Amendment of the Constitution. . . .

Indians born within the territorial limits of the United States, members of, and owing immediate allegiance to, one of the Indian tribes (an alien, though dependent, power), although in a geographical sense born in the United States, are no more "born in the United States and subject to the jurisdiction thereof," within the meaning of the first section of the Fourteenth Amendment, than the children of subjects of any foreign government born within the domain of that government, or the children born within the United States, of ambassadors or other public ministers of foreign nations.

This view is confirmed by the second section of the Fourteenth Amendment, which provides that "representatives shall be apportioned among the several States according to their respective numbers, counting the whole number of persons in each State, excluding Indians not taxed." Slavery having been abolished, and the persons formerly held as slaves made citizens, this clause fixing the apportionment of representatives has abrogated so much of the corresponding clause of the original Constitution as counted only three-fifths of such persons. But Indians not taxed are still excluded from the count, for the reason that they are not citizens. Their absolute exclusion from the basis of representation, in which all other persons are now included, is wholly inconsistent with their being considered citizens. . . .

The plaintiff, not being a citizen of the United States under the Fourteenth Amendment of the Constitution, has been deprived of no right secured by the Fifteenth Amendment, and cannot maintain this action.

MR. JUSTICE HARLAN, with whom concurred MR. JUSTICE WOODS, dissenting.

. . . It seems to us that the Fourteenth Amendment, insofar as it was intended to confer national citizenship upon persons of the Indian race, is robbed of its vital force by a construction which excludes from such citizenship those who, although born in tribal relations, are within the complete jurisdiction of the United States. . .

Born . . . in the territory, under the dominion and within the jurisdictional limits of the United States, plaintiff has acquired, as was his undoubted right, a residence in one of the states, with her consent, and is subject to taxation and to all other burdens imposed by her upon residents of every race. If he did not acquire national citizenship on abandoning his tribe and becoming, by residence in one of the states, subject to the complete jurisdiction of the United States, then the Fourteenth Amendment has wholly failed to accomplish, in respect of the Indian race, what, we think, was intended by it, and there is still in this country a despised and rejected class of persons with no nationality whatever, who, born in our territory, owing no allegiance to any foreign power, and subject, as residents of the states, to all the burdens of government, are yet not members of any political community, nor entitled to any of the rights, privileges, or immunities of citizens of the United States.

15 | *Plessy* v. *Ferguson* (1896)

Editor's Note: In 1883 the U.S. Supreme Court opened the floodgates for states to pass Jim Crow segregation laws when it struck down the Civil Rights Act of 1875, which had banned discrimination in public accommodations. The Louisiana legislature passed the Separate Car Act in 1890 providing that "all railway companies carrying passengers . . . in this State shall provide separate but equal accommodations for the white and colored races."

Thirty-year-old shoemaker and activist Homer Plessy deliberately challenged the constitutionality of this law when he bought a first-class ticket on the East Louisiana Railway on June 7, 1892, and took a seat in the coach reserved for whites. This act of civil disobedience was strategized by Plessy and the New Orleans civil rights organization Comité des Citoyens, and he had every intention of being arrested. Upon conviction of a violation of the 1890 statute, Plessy appealed to the supreme court of Louisiana, which upheld his conviction, and finally to the U.S. Supreme Court, which pronounced the Louisiana law constitutional, on May 18, 1896. The 7–1 majority opinion of the Court was delivered by Justice Henry B. Brown. In his dissent, John Marshall Harlan offered the prophecy that "the judgment rendered this day will, in time, prove to be quite as pernicious as the decision made by this tribunal in the Dred Scott case."

The "separate but equal" justification for racial discrimination remained the law of the land for nearly six decades, until the Court reversed the ruling in 1954, in *Brown v. Board of Education* (see excerpts from the *Brown* ruling later in Part VII of this volume).

. . . The constitutionality of this act is attacked upon the ground that it conflicts both with the Thirteenth Amendment of the Constitution, abolishing slavery, and the Fourteenth Amendment, which prohibits certain restrictive legislation on the part of the States.

1. That it does not conflict with the Thirteenth Amendment, which abolished slavery and involuntary servitude, except as a punishment for crime, is too clear for argument. Slavery implies involuntary servitude—a state of bondage: the ownership of mankind as a chattel, or at least the control of the labor and services of one man for the benefit of another, and the absence of a legal right to the disposal of his own person, property and services. . . .

   A statute which implies merely a legal distinction between the white and colored races—a distinction which is founded in the color of the two races, and which must always exist so long as white men are distinguished from the other race by color—has no tendency to destroy the legal equality of the two races, or reestablish

From Plessy v. Ferguson, 163 U.S. 537 United States Reports: Cases Adjudged in the Supreme Court (New York, Banks & Brothers, 1896).

a state of involuntary servitude. Indeed, we do not understand that the Thirteenth Amendment is strenuously relied upon by the plaintiff in error in this connection.

2. By the Fourteenth Amendment, all persons born or naturalized in the United States, and subject to the jurisdiction thereof, are made citizens of the United States and of the State wherein they reside; and the States are forbidden from making or enforcing any law which shall abridge the privileges or immunities of citizens of the United States, or shall deprive any person of life, liberty or property without due process of law, or deny to any person within their jurisdiction the equal protection of the laws. . . .

The object of the amendment was undoubtedly to enforce the absolute equality of the two races before the law, but in the nature of things it could not have been intended to abolish distinctions based upon color, or to enforce social, as distinguished from political equality, or a commingling of the two races upon terms unsatisfactory to either. Laws permitting, and even requiring, their separation in places where they are liable to be brought into contact do not necessarily imply the inferiority of either race to the other, and have been generally, if not universally, recognized as within the competency of the state legislatures in the exercise of their police power. The most common instance of this is connected with the establishment of separate schools for white and colored children, which has been held to be a valid exercise of the legislative power even by courts of States where the political rights of the colored race have been longest and most earnestly enforced. . . .

While we think the enforced separation of the races, as applied to the internal commerce of the State, neither abridges the privileges or immunities of the colored man, deprives him of his property without due process of law, nor denies him the equal protection of the laws, within the meaning of the Fourteenth Amendment, we are not prepared to say that the conductor, in assigning passengers to the coaches according to their race, does not act at his peril, or that the provision of the second section of the act, that denies to the passenger compensation in damages for a refusal to receive him into the coach in which he properly belongs, is a valid exercise of the legislative power. Indeed, we understand it to be conceded by the State's attorney, that such part of the act as exempts from liability the railway company and its officers is unconstitutional. The power to assign to a particular coach obviously implies the power to determine to which race the passenger belongs, as well as the power to determine who, under the laws of the particular State, is to be deemed a white, and who a colored person. . . .

It is claimed by the plaintiff in error that, in any mixed community, the reputation of belonging to the dominant race, in this instance the white race, is *property*, in the same sense that a right of action, or of inheritance, is property. Conceding this to be so, for the purposes of this case, we are unable to see how this statute deprives him of, or in any way affects his right to, such property. If he be a white man and assigned to a colored coach, he may have his action for damages against the company for being deprived of his so called property. Upon the other hand, if he be a colored man and be so assigned, he has been deprived of no property, since he is not lawfully entitled to the reputation of being a white man.

In this connection, it is also suggested by the learned counsel for the plaintiff in error that the same argument that will justify the state legislature in requiring railways to provide separate accommodations for the two races will also authorize them to require separate cars to be provided for the people whose hair is of a certain color, or who are aliens, or who belong to certain nationalities, or to enact laws requiring colored people to walk upon one side of the street, and white people upon the other, or requiring white men's houses to be painted white, and colored men's black, or their vehicles or business signs to be of different colors, upon the theory that one side of the street is as good as the other, or that a house or vehicle of one color is as good as one of another color. The reply to all this is that every exercise of the police power must be reasonable, and extend only to such laws as are enacted in good faith for the promotion of the public good, and not for the annoyance or oppression of a particular class. . . .

We consider the underlying fallacy of the plaintiff's argument to consist in the assumption that the enforced separation of the two races stamps the colored race with a badge of inferiority. If this be so, it is not by reason of anything found in the act, but solely because the colored race chooses to put that construction upon it. The argument necessarily assumes that if, as has been more than once the case, and is not unlikely to be so again, the colored race should become the dominant power in the state legislature, and should enact a law in precisely similar terms, it would thereby relegate the white race to an inferior position. We imagine that the white race, at least, would not acquiesce in this assumption. The argument also assumes that social prejudices may be overcome by legislation, and that equal rights cannot be secured to the negro except by an enforced commingling of the two races. We cannot accept this proposition. If the two races are to meet upon terms of social equality, it must be the result of natural affinities, a mutual appreciation of each other's merits and a voluntary consent of individuals.

16 United States Constitution: Nineteenth Amendment (1920)

Amendment XIX [Ratified August 18, 1920]

Section 1. The right of citizens of the United States to vote shall not be denied or abridged by the United States or by any State on account of sex.

   Section 2. Congress shall have power to enforce this Article by appropriate legislation.

17 Equal Rights Amendment (Proposed 1923)

Editor's Note: In 1972, fifty years after its 1923 introduction, the Equal Rights Amendment (ERA) won Congressional approval, but it is still not law. Proposed Constitutional amendments need the ratification of three-fourths of the state legislatures, and the ERA fell three states short by its 1982 deadline. More than three decades later, revived interest in the amendment has led state legislatures to revisit ratification, with Nevada ratifying in 2017 and Illinois in 2018. Proponents argue that since the congressionally imposed deadline is not part of the text of the amendment itself, the measure is still viable. If adopted, the ERA would require a higher standard to evaluate sex-based distinctions in the law. Sex discrimination in federal and state laws would have to be viewed by courts as "inherently suspect" and subject to "strict scrutiny." When justices use the strict scrutiny test (the highest standard of judicial review), the differential treatment must serve a "compelling state interest" (and not merely have a "rational basis").

Section 1. Equality of rights under the law shall not be denied or abridged by the United States or any state on account of sex.

 Section 2. The Congress shall have the power to enforce, by appropriate legislation, the provisions of this article.

 Section 3. This amendment shall take effect two years after the date of ratification.

18 *U.S. v. Bhagat Singh Thind* (1923)

Editor's Note: The Naturalization Act of 1790 limited access to naturalized citizenship to "free white persons," and the courts handed down inconsistent rulings about who qualified as "white." In 1922, the Supreme Court held that Japanese immigrant Takao Ozawa could not become a citizen because he was "clearly . . . not Caucasian." A year later, Indian immigrant and U.S. Army veteran Bhagat Singh Thind argued that as a member of the Aryan race and a Caucasian, he should be allowed to apply for citizenship. The Supreme Court changed their standard from just a year before and ruled that not science but a "common understanding, by unscientific men" of what white means would determine who was white. Not only was Thind denied the opportunity to become a citizen by this ruling, but Indian immigrants who had already been naturalized had their citizenship rescinded. The racial restriction on naturalization remained in place until the McCarran Walter Act in 1952.

Mr. Justice SUTHERLAND delivered the opinion of the Court.

This cause is here upon a certificate from the Circuit Court of appeals requesting the instruction of this Court in respect of the following questions:

"1. Is a high caste Hindu, of full Indian blood, born at Amrit Sar, Punjab, India, a white person within the meaning of section 2169, Revised Statutes?

"2. Does the Act of February 5, 1917 (39 Stat. L. 875, section 3), disqualify from naturalization as citizens those Hindus, now barred by that act, who had lawfully entered the United States prior to the passage of said act?"

. . .

Section 2169, Revised Statutes, provides that the provisions of the Naturalization Act "shall apply to aliens, being free white persons, and to aliens of African nativity and to persons of African descent."

If the applicant is a white person within the meaning of this section he is entitled to naturalization; otherwise not. In *Ozawa v. United States*, 260 U. S. 178, we had occasion to consider the application of these words to the case of a cultivated Japanese and were constrained to hold that he was not within their meaning. As there pointed out, the provision is not that any particular class of persons shall be excluded, but it is, in effect, that only white persons shall be included within the privilege of the statute. "The intention was to confer the privilege of citizenship upon that class of persons whom the fathers knew as white, and to deny it to all who could not be so classified. It is not enough to say that the framers did not have in mind the brown or yellow races of Asia. It is necessary to go farther

United States v. Bhagat Singh Thind, 261 U.S. 204 (1923).

and be able to say that had these particular races been suggested the language of the act would have been so varied as to include them within its privileges," . . . . Following a long line of decisions of the lower federal courts, we held that the words imported a racial and not an individual test and were meant to indicate only persons of what is *popularly* known as the Caucasian race. But, as there pointed out, the conclusion that the phrase "white persons" and the word "Caucasian" are synonymous does not end the matter. It enabled us to dispose of the problem as it was there presented, since the applicant for citizenship clearly fell outside the zone of debatable ground on the negative side; but the decision still left the question to be dealt with, in doubtful and different cases, by the "process of judicial inclusion and exclusion." Mere ability on the part of an applicant for naturalization to establish a line of descent from a Caucasian ancestor will not *ipso facto* and necessarily conclude the inquiry. "Caucasian" is a conventional word of much flexibility, as a study of the literature dealing with racial questions will disclose, and while it and the words "white persons" are treated as synonymous for the purposes of that case, they are not of identical meaning—*idem per idem*.

In the endeavor to ascertain the meaning of the statute we must not fail to keep in mind that it does not employ the word "Caucasian" but the words "white persons," and these are words of common speech and not of scientific origin. The word "Caucasian" not only was not employed in the law but was probably wholly unfamiliar to the original framers of the statute in 1790. When we employ it, we do so as an aid to the ascertainment of the legislative intent and not as an invariable substitute for the statutory words. Indeed, as used in the science of ethnology, the connotation of the word is by no means clear and the use of it in its scientific sense as an equivalent for the words of the statute, other considerations aside, would simply mean the substitution of one perplexity for another. But in this country, during the last half century especially, the word by common usage has acquired a popular meaning, not clearly defined to be sure, but sufficiently so to enable us to say that its popular as distinguished from its scientific application is of appreciably narrower scope. It is in the popular sense of the word, therefore, that we employ it as an aid to the construction of the statute, for it would be obviously illogical to convert words of common speech used in a statute into words of scientific terminology when neither the latter nor the science for whose purposes they were coined was within the contemplation of the framers of the statute or of the people for whom it was framed. The words of the statute are to be interpreted in accordance with the understanding of the common man from whose vocabulary they were taken. See *Maillard v. Lawrence*, 16 How. 251, 261.

They imply, as we have said, a racial test; but the term "race" is one which, for the practical purposes of the statute, must be applied to a group of living persons *now* possessing in common the requisite characteristics, not to groups of persons who are supposed to be or really are descended from some remote, common ancestor, but who, whether they both resemble him to a greater or less extent, have, at any rate, ceased altogether to resemble one another. It may be true that the blond Scandinavian and the brown Hindu have a common ancestor in the dim reaches of antiquity, but the average man knows perfectly well that there are unmistakable and profound differences between them today; and it is not impossible, if that common ancestor could be materialized in the flesh, we should discover that he was himself sufficiently differentiated from both of his descendants to preclude his racial classification with either. The question for determination is not, therefore, whether by the speculative processes of ethnological reasoning we may present a probability to the scientific mind that they have the same origin, but whether we can satisfy the common understanding that they are now the same or sufficiently the same to justify the interpreters of a statute—written in the words of common speech, for common understanding, by unscientific men—in classifying them together in the statutory category as white persons. . . .

. . . We are unable to agree with the District Court, or with other lower federal courts, in the conclusion that a native Hindu is eligible for naturalization under § 2169. The words of familiar speech, which were used by the original framers of the law, were intended to include only the type of man whom they knew as white. The immigration of that day was almost exclusively from the British Isles and Northwestern Europe, whence they and their forbears had come. When they extended the privilege of American citizenship to "any alien, being a free white person," it was these immigrants—bone of their bone and flesh of their flesh—and their kind whom they must have had affirmatively in mind. The succeeding years brought immigrants from Eastern, Southern and Middle Europe, among them the Slavs and the dark-eyed, swarthy people of Alpine and Mediterranean stock, and these were received as unquestionably akin to those already here and readily amalgamated with them. It was the descendants of these, and other immigrants of like origin, who constituted the white population of the country when § 2169, reënacting the naturalization test of 1790, was adopted, and there is no reason to doubt, with like intent and meaning.

. . .

What we now hold is that the words "free white persons" are words of common speech, to be interpreted in accordance with the understanding of the common man, synonymous with the word "Caucasian" only as that word is popularly understood. As so understood and used, whatever may be the speculations of the ethnologist, it does not include the body of people to whom the appellee belongs. It is a matter of familiar observation and knowledge that the physical group characteristics of the Hindus render them readily distinguishable from the various groups of persons in this country commonly recognized as white. The children of English, French, German, Italian, Scandinavian, and other European parentage quickly merge into the mass of our population and lose the distinctive hallmarks of their European origin. On the other hand, it cannot be doubted that the children born in this country of Hindu parents would retain indefinitely the clear evidence of their ancestry. It is very far from our thought to suggest the slightest question of racial superiority or inferiority. What we suggest is merely racial difference, and it is of such character and extent that the great body of our people instinctively recognize it and reject the thought of assimilation.

It is not without significance in this connection that Congress, by the Act of February 5, 1917, c. 29, § 3, 39 Stat. 874, has now excluded from admission into this country all natives of Asia within designated limits of latitude and longitude, including the whole of India. This not only constitutes conclusive evidence of the congressional attitude of opposition to Asiatic immigration generally, but is persuasive of a similar attitude toward Asiatic naturalization as well, since it is not likely that Congress would be willing to accept as citizens a class of persons whom it rejects as immigrants.

It follows that a negative answer must be given to the first question, which disposes of the case and renders an answer to the second question unnecessary, and it will be so certified.

Answer to question No. 1, No.

19 | *Brown v. Board of Education of Topeka* (1954)

Mr. Chief Justice Warren delivered the opinion of the Court.

These cases come to us from the States of Kansas, South Carolina, Virginia, and Delaware. They are premised on different facts and different local conditions, but a common legal question justifies their consideration together in this consolidated opinion.[1]

In each of the cases, minors of the Negro race, through their legal representatives, seek the aid of the courts in obtaining admission to the public schools of their community on a nonsegregated basis. In each instance, they had been denied admission to schools attended by white children under laws requiring or permitting segregation according to race. This segregation was alleged to deprive the plaintiffs of the equal protection of the laws under the Fourteenth Amendment. In each of the cases other than the Delaware case, a three-judge federal district court denied relief to the plaintiffs on the so-called "separate but equal" doctrine announced by this Court in *Plessy* v. *Ferguson*, 163 U.S. 537. Under that doctrine, equality of treatment is accorded when the races are provided substantially equal facilities, even though these facilities be separate. In the Delaware case, the Supreme Court of Delaware adhered to that doctrine, but ordered that the plaintiffs be admitted to the white schools because of their superiority to the Negro schools.

The plaintiffs contend that segregated public schools are not "equal" and cannot be made "equal," and that hence they are deprived of the equal protection of the laws. Because of the obvious importance of the question presented, the Court took jurisdiction.[2] Argument was heard in the 1952 Term, and reargument was heard this Term on certain questions propounded by the Court.[3] . . .

In approaching this problem, we cannot turn the clock back to 1868 when the Amendment was adopted, or even to 1896 when *Plessy* v. *Ferguson* was written. We must consider public education in the light of its full development and its present place in American life throughout the Nation. Only in this way can it be determined if segregation in public schools deprives these plaintiffs of the equal protection of the laws.

Today, education is perhaps the most important function of state and local governments. Compulsory school attendance laws and the great expenditures for education both demonstrate our recognition of the importance of education to our democratic society. It is required in the performance of our most basic public responsibilities, even service in the armed forces. It is the very foundation of good citizenship. Today it is a principal instrument in awakening the child to cultural values, in preparing him for later professional training, and in helping him to adjust normally to his environment. In these days, it is doubtful that any child may reasonably be expected to succeed in life if he is denied the opportunity of an education. Such an opportunity, where the state has undertaken to provide it, is a right which must be made available to all on equal terms.

Brown v. Board of Education of Topeka, 347 U.S. 483 (1954).

We come then to the question presented: Does segregation of children in public schools solely on the basis of race, even though the physical facilities and other "tangible" factors may be equal, deprive the children of the minority group of equal educational opportunities? We believe that it does.

In *Sweatt v. Painter*, in finding that a segregated law school for Negroes could not provide them equal educational opportunities, this Court relied in large part on "those qualities which are incapable of objective measurement but which make for greatness in a law school." In *McLaurin v. Oklahoma State Regents*, the Court, in requiring that a Negro admitted to a white graduate school be treated like all other students, again resorted to intangible considerations: ". . . his ability to study, to engage in discussions and exchange views with other students, and in general, to learn his profession." Such considerations apply with added force to children in grade and high schools. To separate them from others of similar age and qualifications solely because of their race generates a feeling of inferiority as to their status in the community that may affect their hearts and minds in a way unlikely ever to be undone. The effect of this separation on their educational opportunities was stated by a finding in the Kansas case by a court which nevertheless felt compelled to rule against the Negro plaintiffs:

> "Segregation of white and colored children in public schools has a detrimental effect upon the colored children. The impact is greater when it has the sanction of the law; for the policy of separating the races is usually interpreted as denoting the inferiority of the negro group. A sense of inferiority affects the motivation of a child to learn. Segregation with the sanction of law, therefore, has a tendency to [retard] the educational and mental development of negro children and to deprive them of some of the benefits they receive in a racial[ly] integrated school system."[4]

Whatever may have been the extent of psychological knowledge at the time of *Plessy v. Ferguson*, this finding is amply supported by modern authority.[5] Any language in *Plessy v. Ferguson* contrary to this finding is rejected.

We conclude that in the field of public education the doctrine of "separate but equal" has no place. Separate educational facilities are inherently unequal. Therefore, we hold that the plaintiffs and others similarly situated for whom the actions have been brought are, by reason of the segregation complained of, deprived of the equal protection of the laws guaranteed by the Fourteenth Amendment. This disposition makes unnecessary any discussion whether such segregation also violates the Due Process Clause of the Fourteenth Amendment.[6]

Because these are class actions, because of the wide applicability of this decision, and because of the great variety of local conditions, the formulation of decrees in these cases presents problems of considerable complexity. On reargument, the consideration of appropriate relief was necessarily subordinated to the primary question—the constitutionality of segregation in public education. We have now announced that such segregation is a denial of the equal protection of the laws. In order that we may have the full assistance of the parties in formulating decrees, the cases will be restored to the docket, and the parties are requested to present further argument on Questions 4 and 5 previously propounded by the Court for the reargument this Term.[7] The Attorney General of the United States is again invited to participate. The Attorneys General of the states requiring or permitting segregation in public education will also be permitted to appear as amici curiae upon request to do so by September 15, 1954, and submission of the briefs by October 1, 1954.

It is so ordered.

NOTES

1. In the Kansas case, *Brown v. Board of Education*, the plaintiffs are Negro children of elementary school age residing in Topeka. They brought this action in the United States District Court for the District of Kansas to enjoin enforcement of a Kansas statute which permits, but does not require, cities of more than 15,000 population to maintain separate school facilities for Negro and white students. Kan. Gen. Stat. § 72–1724 (1949). Pursuant to that authority, the Topeka Board of Education elected to establish segregated elementary schools. Other public schools in the community, however, are operated on a nonsegregated basis. The three-judge District Court, convened under 28 U.S.C. §§ 2281 and 2284, found that segregation in public education has a detrimental effect upon Negro children, but denied relief on the ground that the Negro and white schools were substantially equal with respect to buildings, transportation, curricula, and educational qualifications of teachers. 98 F. Supp. 797. The case is here on direct appeal under 28 U.S.C. § 1253.

   In the South Carolina case, *Briggs v. Elliot*, the plaintiffs are Negro children of both elementary and high school age residing in Clarendon County. They brought this action in the United States District Court for the Eastern District of South Carolina to enjoin enforcement of provisions in the state constitution and statutory code which require the segregation of Negroes and whites in public schools. S.C. Const., Art. XI, § 7; S.C. Code § 5377 (1942). The three-judge District Court, convened under 28 U.S.C. §§ 2281 and 2284, denied the requested relief. The court found that the Negro schools were inferior to the white schools and ordered the defendants to begin immediately to equalize the facilities. But the court sustained the validity of the contested provisions and denied the plaintiffs admission to the white schools during the equalization program. 98 F. Supp. 529. This Court vacated the District Court's judgment and remanded the case for the purpose of obtaining the court's views on a report filed by the defendants concerning the progress made in the equalization program. 342 U.S. 350. On remand, the District Court found that substantial equality had been achieved except for buildings and that the defendants were proceeding to rectify this inequality as well. 103 F. Supp. 920. The case is again here on direct appeal under 28 U.S.C. § 1253.

   In the Virginia case, *Davis v. County School Board*, the plaintiffs are Negro children of high school age residing in Prince Edward County. They brought this action in the United States District Court for the Eastern District of Virginia to enjoin enforcement of provisions in the state constitution and statutory code which require the segregation of Negroes and whites in public schools. Va. Const., § 140; Va. Code § 22–221 (1950). The three-judge District Court, convened under 28 U.S.C. §§ 2281 and 2284, denied the requested relief. The court found the Negro school inferior in physical plant, curricula, and transportation, and ordered the defendants forthwith to provide substantially equal curricula and transportation and to "proceed with all reasonable diligence and dispatch to remove" the inequality in physical plant. But, as in the South Carolina case, the court sustained the validity of the contested provisions and denied the plaintiffs admission to the white schools during the equalization program. 103 F. Supp. 337. The case is here on direct appeal under 28 U.S.C. § 1253.

   In the Delaware case, *Gebhart v. Belton*, the plaintiffs are Negro children of both elementary and high school age residing in New Castle County. They brought this action in the Delaware

Court of Chancery to enjoin enforcement of provisions in the state constitution and statutory code which require the segregation of Negroes and whites in public schools. Del. Const., Art. X, § 2; Del. Rev. Code § 2631 (1935). The Chancellor gave judgment for the plaintiffs and ordered their immediate admission to schools previously attended only by white children, on the ground that the Negro schools were inferior with respect to teacher training, pupil-teacher ratio, extracurricular activities, physical plant, and time and distance involved in travel. 87 A.2d 862. The Chancellor also found that segregation itself results in an inferior education for Negro children (see note 4, *infra*), but did not rest his decision on that ground. Id., at 865. The Chancellor's decree was affirmed by the Supreme Court of Delaware, which intimated, however, that the defendants might be able to obtain a modification of the decree after equalization of the Negro and white schools had been accomplished. 91 A.2d 137, 152. The defendants, contending only that the Delaware courts had erred in ordering the immediate admission of the Negro plaintiffs to the white schools, applied to this Court for certiorari. The writ was granted, 344 U.S. 891. The plaintiffs, who were successful below, did not submit a cross-petition.

2. 344 U.S. 1, 141, 891.

3. 345 U.S. 972. The Attorney General of the United States participated both Terms as amicus curiae.

4. A similar finding was made in the Delaware case: "I conclude from the testimony that in our Delaware Society, State-imposed segregation in education itself results in the Negro children, as a class, receiving educational opportunities which are substantially inferior to those available to white children otherwise similarly situated." 87 A.2d 862, 865.

5. K. B. Clark, Effect of Prejudice and Discrimination on Personality Development (Midcentury White House Conference on Children and Youth, 1950); Witmer and Kotinsky, Personality in the Making (1952), c. VI; Deutscher and Chein, The Psychological Effects of Enforced Segregation: A Survey of Social Science Opinion, 26 J. Psychol. 259 (1948); Chein, What Are the Psychological Effects of Segregation Under Conditions of Equal Facilities?, 3 Int. J. Opinion and Attitude Res. 229 (1949); Brameld, Educational Costs, in Discrimination and National Welfare (MacIver, ed., 1949), 44–48; Frazier, The Negro in the United States (1949), 674–681. And see generally Myrdal, An American Dilemma (1944).

6. See *Boling v. Sharpe*, post, p. 497, concerning the Due Process Clause of the Fifth Amendment.

7. "4. Assuming it is decided that segregation in public schools violates the Fourteenth Amendment

   "(a) would a decree necessarily follow providing that, within the limits set by normal geographic school districting, Negro children should forthwith be admitted to schools of their choice, or

   "(b) may this Court, in the exercise of its equity powers, permit an effective gradual adjustment to be brought about from existing segregated systems to a system not based on color distinctions?

"5. On the assumption on which questions 4(a) and (b) are based, and assuming further that this Court will exercise its equity powers to the end described in question 4(b),

   "(a) should this Court formulate detailed decrees in these cases;

   "(b) if so, what specific issues should the decrees reach;

   "(c) should this Court appoint a special master to hear evidence with a view to recommending specific terms for such decrees;

   "(d) should this Court remand to the courts of first instance with directions to frame decrees in these cases, and if so what general directions should the decrees of this Court include and what procedures should the courts of first instance follow in arriving at the specific terms of more detailed decrees?"

20 *Roe* v. *Wade* (1973)

Editor's Note: This historic decision affirmed a woman's right to terminate her pregnancy by abortion. The ruling was based upon the right of privacy founded on both the Fourteenth and Ninth Amendments to the Constitution. The Court ruled that this right of privacy protected the individual from interference by the state in the decision to terminate a pregnancy during the early portion of the pregnancy. At the same time, it recognized the interest of the state in regulating decisions concerning the pregnancy during the later period.

JUSTICE BLACKMUN delivered the opinion of the Court.

X

. . . [W]e do not agree that, by adopting one theory of life, Texas may override the rights of the pregnant woman that are at stake. We repeat, however, that the State does have an important and legitimate interest in preserving and protecting the health of the pregnant woman, whether she be a resident of the State or a nonresident who seeks medical consultation and treatment there, and that it has still another important and legitimate interest in protecting the potentiality of human life. These interests are separate and distinct. Each grows in substantiality as the woman approaches [410 U.S. 113, 163] term and, at a point during pregnancy, each becomes "compelling."

With respect to the State's important and legitimate interest in the health of the mother, the "compelling" point, in the light of present medical knowledge, is at approximately the end of the first trimester. This is so because of the now-established medical fact . . . that until the end of the first trimester mortality in abortion may be less than mortality in normal childbirth. It follows that, from and after this point, a State may regulate the abortion procedure to the extent that the regulation reasonably relates to the preservation and protection of maternal health. Examples of permissible state regulation in this area are requirements as to the qualifications of the person who is to perform the abortion; as to the licensure of that person; as to the facility in which the procedure is to be performed, that is, whether it must be a hospital or may be a clinic or some other place of less-than-hospital status; as to the licensing of the facility; and the like.

This means, on the other hand, that, for the period of pregnancy prior to this "compelling" point, the attending physician, in consultation with his patient, is free to determine, without regulation by the State, that, in his medical judgment, the patient's pregnancy should be terminated. If that decision is reached, the judgment may be effectuated by an abortion free of interference by the State.

With respect to the State's important and legitimate interest in potential life, the "compelling" point is at viability. This is so because the fetus then presumably has the capability of meaningful life outside the mother's womb. State regulation protective of fetal life after viability thus has both logical and biological justifications. If the State is interested in protecting fetal life after viability, it may go so far as to proscribe abortion [410 U.S. 113, 164] during that period, except when it is necessary to preserve the life or health of the mother.

Measured against these standards, Art. 1196 of the Texas Penal Code, in restricting legal abortions to those "procured or attempted by medical advice for the purpose of saving the life of the mother," sweeps too broadly. The statute makes no distinction between abortions performed early in pregnancy and those performed later, and it limits to a single reason, "saving" the mother's life, the legal justification for the procedure. The statute, therefore, cannot survive the constitutional attack made upon it here.

This conclusion makes it unnecessary for us to consider the additional challenge to the Texas statute asserted on grounds of vagueness. See United States v. Vuitch, 402 U.S., at 67–72.

XI

To summarize and to repeat:

1. A state criminal abortion statute of the current Texas type, that excepts from criminality only a life-saving procedure on behalf of the mother, without regard to pregnancy stage and without recognition of the other interests involved, is violative of the Due Process Clause of the Fourteenth Amendment.

   a. For the stage prior to approximately the end of the first trimester, the abortion decision and its effectuation must be left to the medical judgment of the pregnant woman's attending physician.

   b. For the stage subsequent to approximately the end of the first trimester, the State, in promoting its interest in the health of the mother, may, if it chooses, regulate the abortion procedure in ways that are reasonably related to maternal health.

   c. For the stage subsequent to viability, the State in promoting its interest in the potentiality of human life [410 U.S. 113, 165] may, if it chooses, regulate, and even proscribe, abortion except where it is necessary, in appropriate medical judgment, for the preservation of the life or health of the mother.

2. The State may define the term "physician," as it has been employed in the preceding paragraphs of this Part XI of this opinion, to mean only a physician currently licensed by the State, and may proscribe any abortion by a person who is not a physician as so defined. . . .

This holding, we feel, is consistent with the relative weights of the respective interests involved, with the lessons and examples of medical and legal history, with the lenity of the common law, and with the demands of the profound problems of the present day. The decision leaves the State free to place increasing restrictions on abortion as the period of pregnancy lengthens, so long as those restrictions are tailored to the recognized state interests. The decision vindicates the right of the physician to administer medical treatment according to his professional judgment up to the points where important [410 U.S. 113,

166] state interests provide compelling justifications for intervention. Up to those points, the abortion decision in all its aspects is inherently, and primarily, a medical decision, and basic responsibility for it must rest with the physician. If an individual practitioner abuses the privilege of exercising proper medical judgment, the usual remedies, judicial and intra-professional, are available.

XII

Our conclusion that Art. 1196 is unconstitutional means, of course, that the Texas abortion statutes, as a unit, must fall. The exception of Art. 1196 cannot be struck down separately, for then the State would be left with a statute proscribing all abortion procedures no matter how medically urgent the case. . . .

21 | *McCleskey v. Kemp* (1987)

Editor's Note: According to the NAACP Legal Defense Fund, "Few cases involving the inter-section of race, criminal law, and procedure have had the reach and impact of *McCleskey v. Kemp*. . . . Ultimately, the *McCleskey* decision set the stage for more than 20 years of dra-matically increasing racial disparities within the criminal justice system."[1] Warren McCleskey was sentenced to death in 1978. He challenged his sentence, offering an extensive statistical analysis of more than 2,000 murder cases in the state, showing that racial bias permeated Georgia's application of capital punishment. Justice Powell—who later told his biographer that he regretted his vote in this 5-4 ruling—dismissed the statistical evidence of pervasive racial bias, stating that sentencing disparities are "inevitable." The U.S. Supreme Court not only rejected McCleskey's appeal (allowing him to be executed), but also ruled that *racial bias could not be challenged under the Fourteenth Amendment in the absence of positive proof of discriminatory intent.* This narrow and very difficult to apply criterion for find-ing bias has implications in areas beyond capital punishment. This ruling effectively "closed the courthouse doors" to any meaningful challenges to bias in the criminal justice system, including racial disparities in stop-and-frisk practices, arrest patterns, plea bargains, con-viction rates, and criminal penalties.[2] Several readings elsewhere in this volume[3] make the point that contemporary racism is often subtle, systemic, institutionalized, masked, and ostensibly "color blind" (not necessarily overt, explicit, individual, and intentional), yet the Court here insists upon explicit declarations of individual discriminatory intent. This means that, absent a smoking gun, victims of discrimination cannot even be heard in court.[4] Legal scholar Anthony Amsterdam called this case "the *Dred Scott* decision of our time."[5]

---

[1] https://www.naacpldf.org/case-issue/landmark-mccleskey-v-kemp/.

[2] Michelle Alexander, *The New Jim Crow: Mass Incarceration in the Age of Colorblindness* (listed among the suggested readings at the end of Part VII), p. 139. An excerpt from Alexander's book is in Part IV of this volume.

[3] See selections by Michelle Alexander, Beverly Tatum, Ian Haney López, Eduardo Bonilla-Silva, and Angela Davis, among others.

[4] Michelle Alexander calls the holding in *McClesky* the "damning step" in how "a formally colorblind criminal justice system [can] achieve such racially discriminatory results." She writes, "Close the courthouse doors to all claims by defendants and private litigants that the criminal justice system operates in racially discriminatory fashion. Demand that anyone who wants to challenge racial bias in the system offer, in advance, clear proof that the racial disparities are the product of intentional racial discrimination—i.e., the work of a bigot. This evidence will almost never be available in the era of colorblindness . . . ." (p. 103).

[5] Adam Liptak, "New Look at Death Sentences and Race," *The New York Times*, April 29, 2008.

McCleskey v. Kemp, 481 U.S. 279 (1987).

JUSTICE POWELL delivered the opinion of the Court.

This case presents the question whether a complex statistical study that indicates a risk that racial considerations enter into capital sentencing determinations proves that petitioner McCleskey's capital sentence is unconstitutional under the Eighth or Fourteenth Amendment. . . .

His petition raised 18 claims, one of which was that the Georgia capital sentencing process is administered in a racially discriminatory manner in violation of the Eighth and Fourteenth Amendments to the United States Constitution. In support of his claim, McCleskey proffered a statistical study performed by Professors David C. Baldus, Charles Pulaski, and George Woodworth (the Baldus study) that purports to show a disparity in the imposition of the death sentence in Georgia based on the race of the murder victim and, to a lesser extent, the race of the defendant. . . .

Even assuming the study's validity, the Court of Appeals found the statistics "insufficient to demonstrate discriminatory intent or unconstitutional discrimination in the Fourteenth Amendment context, [and] insufficient to show irrationality, arbitrariness and capriciousness under any kind of Eighth Amendment analysis." . . .

As a black defendant who killed a white victim, McCleskey claims that the Baldus study demonstrates that he was discriminated against because of his race and because of the race of his victim. In its broadest form, McCleskey's claim of discrimination extends to every actor in the Georgia capital sentencing process, from the prosecutor who sought the death penalty and the jury that imposed the sentence to the State itself that enacted the capital punishment statute and allows it to remain in effect despite its allegedly discriminatory application. We agree with the Court of Appeals, and every other court that has considered such a challenge, that this claim must fail.

Our analysis begins with the basic principle that a defendant who alleges an equal protection violation has the burden of proving "the existence of purposeful discrimination." [*Whitus v. Georgia*, 1967] A corollary to this principle is that a criminal defendant must prove that the purposeful discrimination "had a discriminatory effect" on him. [*Wayte v. United States*, 985] Thus, to prevail under the Equal Protection Clause, McCleskey must prove that the decisionmakers in *his* case acted with discriminatory purpose. . . .

. . . Because discretion is essential to the criminal justice process, we would demand exceptionally clear proof before we would infer that the discretion has been abused. The unique nature of the decisions at issue in this case also counsels against adopting such an inference from the disparities indicated by the Baldus study. Accordingly, we hold that the Baldus study is clearly insufficient to support an inference that any of the decisionmakers in McCleskey's case acted with discriminatory purpose. . . .

To evaluate McCleskey's challenge, we must examine exactly what the Baldus study may show. . . . There is, of course, some risk of racial prejudice influencing a jury's decision in a criminal case. There are similar risks that other kinds of prejudice will influence other criminal trials. . . . The question "is at what point that risk becomes constitutionally unacceptable, ..." [*Turner v. Murray*, 1986] McCleskey asks us to accept the likelihood allegedly shown by the Baldus study as the constitutional measure of an unacceptable risk of racial prejudice influencing capital sentencing decisions. This we decline to do.

At most, the Baldus study indicates a discrepancy that appears to correlate with race. Apparent disparities in sentencing are an inevitable part of our criminal justice system. . . .

McCleskey's claim, taken to its logical conclusion, throws into serious question the principles that underlie our entire criminal justice system. The Eighth Amendment is not limited in application to capital punishment, but applies to all penalties. . . . Thus, if we accepted McCleskey's claim that racial bias has impermissibly tainted the capital sentencing decision, we could soon be faced with similar claims as to other types of penalty. . . .

The Constitution does not require that a State eliminate any demonstrable disparity that correlates with a potentially irrelevant factor in order to operate a criminal justice system that includes capital punishment. . . .

JUSTICE BRENNAN, dissenting.

. . . The Court assumes the statistical validity of the Baldus study, and acknowledges that McCleskey has demonstrated a risk that racial prejudice plays a role in capital sentencing in Georgia . . . . Nonetheless, it finds the probability of prejudice insufficient to create constitutional concern. . . . Close analysis of the Baldus study, however, in light of both statistical principles and human experience, reveals that the risk that race influenced McCleskey's sentence is intolerable by any imaginable standard. . . .

The statistical evidence in this case . . . relentlessly documents the risk that McCleskey's sentence was influenced by racial considerations. . . .

Evaluation of McCleskey's evidence cannot rest solely on the numbers themselves. We must also ask whether the conclusion suggested by those numbers is consonant with our understanding of history and human experience. Georgia's legacy of a race-conscious criminal justice system, as well as this Court's own recognition of the persistent danger that racial attitudes may affect criminal proceedings, indicates that McCleskey's claim is not a fanciful product of mere statistical artifice.

For many years, Georgia operated openly and formally precisely the type of dual system the evidence shows is still effectively in place. The criminal law expressly differentiated between crimes committed by and against blacks and whites, distinctions whose lineage traced back to the time of slavery. . . .

History and its continuing legacy . . . buttress the probative force of McCleskey's statistics. Formal dual criminal laws may no longer be in effect, and intentional discrimination may no longer be prominent. Nonetheless, as we acknowledged in Turner, "subtle, less consciously held racial attitudes" continue to be of concern, . . . and the Georgia system gives such attitudes considerable room to operate. The conclusions drawn from McCleskey's statistical evidence are therefore consistent with the lessons of social experience. . . .

The Court . . . states that its unwillingness to regard petitioner's evidence as sufficient is based in part on the fear that recognition of McCleskey's claim would open the door to widespread challenges to all aspects of criminal sentencing. . . . Taken on its face, such a statement seems to suggest a fear of too much justice. Yet surely the majority would acknowledge that if striking evidence indicated that other minority groups, or women, or even persons with blond hair, were disproportionately sentenced to death, such a state of affairs would be repugnant to deeply rooted conceptions of fairness. The prospect that there may be more widespread abuse than McCleskey documents may be dismaying, but it does not justify complete abdication of our judicial role. . . .

Warren McCleskey's evidence confronts us with the subtle and persistent influence of the past. His message is a disturbing one to a society that has formally repudiated racism, and a frustrating one to a Nation accustomed to regarding its destiny as the product of its own will. Nonetheless, we ignore him at our peril, for we remain imprisoned by the past as long as we deny its influence in the present. . . .

22 | *Shelby County v. Holder* (2013)

Editor's Note: "Today, the Supreme Court stuck a dagger into the heart of the Voting Rights Act of 1965, one of the most effective pieces of legislation Congress has passed in the last 50 years," said Representative John Lewis of *Shelby County v. Holder*, which overturned a key provision of that landmark civil rights law. Section 5 of the 1965 law required jurisdictions with a history of voting discrimination to seek federal approval before enacting new voting regulations. They could obtain this "preclearance" only after proving the new regulations would not result in "denying or abridging the right to vote on account of race or color." In *Shelby County v. Holder*, the Court struck down Section 4, which provided a formula for determining the jurisdictions required to seek preclearance. "Our country has changed," wrote Chief Justice John Roberts, arguing that some of the act's "extraordinary measures" are no longer justified. In her dissent, Justice Ruth Bader Ginsburg, noting that voting discrimination has evolved into more subtle barriers, argued that dispensing with the preclearance requirement for jurisdictions with a history of discrimination is like "throwing away your umbrella in a rainstorm because you are not getting wet." In the years following the ruling, states have enacted voter ID laws, voter purges, and other measures that might have been disallowed under preclearance rules.*

Chief Justice Roberts delivered the opinion of the Court.

The Voting Rights Act of 1965 employed extraordinary measures to address an extraordinary problem. Section 5 of the Act required States to obtain federal permission before enacting any law related to voting—a drastic departure from basic principles of federalism. And Section 4 of the Act applied that requirement only to some States—an equally dramatic departure from the principle that all States enjoy equal sovereignty. This was strong medicine, but Congress determined it was needed to address entrenched racial discrimination in voting, "an insidious and pervasive evil which had been perpetuated in certain parts of our country through unremitting and ingenious defiance of the Constitution." . . .

---

* Fifteen states were subject to preclearance by the formula in the 1965 act: nine states as a whole (Alabama, Alaska, Arizona, Georgia, Louisiana, Mississippi, South Carolina, Texas, and Virginia) and specific counties or townships in six other states (California, Florida, Michigan, New York, North Carolina, and South Dakota). Eight of those fifteen states are among the many jurisdictions that have enacted restrictive voting measures since *Shelby County v. Holder*. The Brennan Center for Justice (https://www.brennancenter.org/issues/voting-rights-elections) provides updated and more detailed information on this topic. Also see "The Georgia Governor's Race Has Brought Voter Suppression into Full View," by Vann R. Newkirk II (Selection 2 in Part IV of this volume), for a detailed discussion of the "labyrinth" of contemporary voter disenfranchisement.

Shelby County v. Holder, 570 U.S. 529 (2013).

Nearly 50 years later, [these measures] are still in effect; indeed, they have been made more stringent, and are now scheduled to last until 2031. There is no denying, however, that the conditions that originally justified these measures no longer characterize voting in the covered jurisdictions. . . . Since that time, Census Bureau data indicate that African-American voter turnout has come to exceed white voter turnout in five of the six States originally covered by Section 5, with a gap in the sixth State of less than one half of one percent. . . .

At the same time, voting discrimination still exists; no one doubts that. The question is whether the Act's extraordinary measures, including its disparate treatment of the States, continue to satisfy constitutional requirements. . . .

The Fifteenth Amendment was ratified in 1870, in the wake of the Civil War. It provides that "[t]he right of citizens of the United States to vote shall not be denied or abridged by the United States or by any State on account of race, color, or previous condition of servitude," and it gives Congress the "power to enforce this article by appropriate legislation."

"The first century of congressional enforcement of the Amendment, however, can only be regarded as a failure." . . . In the 1890s, Alabama, Georgia, Louisiana, Mississippi, North Carolina, South Carolina, and Virginia began to enact literacy tests for voter registration and to employ other methods designed to prevent African-Americans from voting. . . . Congress passed statutes outlawing some of these practices and facilitating litigation against them, but litigation remained slow and expensive, and the States came up with new ways to discriminate as soon as existing ones were struck down. Voter registration of African-Americans barely improved. . . .

Inspired to action by the civil rights movement, Congress responded in 1965 with the Voting Rights Act. Section 2 was enacted to forbid, in all 50 States, any "standard, practice, or procedure . . . imposed or applied . . . to deny or abridge the right of any citizen of the United States to vote on account of race or color.". . . Section 2 is permanent, applies nationwide, and is not at issue in this case.

Other sections targeted only some parts of the country. At the time of the Act's passage, these "covered" jurisdictions were those States or political subdivisions that had maintained a test or device as a prerequisite to voting as of November 1, 1964, and had less than 50 percent voter registration or turnout in the 1964 Presidential election. . . . Such tests or devices included literacy and knowledge tests, good moral character requirements, the need for vouchers from registered voters, and the like. . . .

. . . Section 5 provided that no change in voting procedures could take effect until it was approved by federal authorities in Washington, D. C.—either the Attorney General or a court of three judges. . . . A jurisdiction could obtain such "preclearance" only by proving that the change had neither "the purpose [nor] the effect of denying or abridging the right to vote on account of race or color." . . .

Sections 4 and 5 were intended to be temporary; they were set to expire after five years. . . .

In 2006, Congress . . . reauthorized the Voting Rights Act for 25 years, . . . without change to its coverage formula. . . . Section 5 now forbids voting changes with "any discriminatory purpose" as well as voting changes that diminish the ability of citizens, on account of race, color, or language minority status, "to elect their preferred candidates of choice." . . .

The Constitution and laws of the United States are "the supreme Law of the Land." . . . State legislation may not contravene federal law. The Federal Government does not, however, have a general right to review and veto state enactments before they go into effect. . . .

Outside the strictures of the Supremacy Clause, States retain broad autonomy in structuring their governments and pursuing legislative objectives. Indeed, the Constitution provides that all powers not specifically granted to the Federal Government are reserved to the States or citizens. Amdt. 10. . . .

The Voting Rights Act sharply departs from these basic principles. It suspends "all changes to state election law—however innocuous—until they have been precleared by federal authorities in Washington, D. C." . . . States must beseech the Federal Government for permission to implement laws that they would otherwise have the right to enact and execute on their own, subject of course to any injunction in a Section 2 action. . . .

And despite the tradition of equal sovereignty, the Act applies to only nine States (and several additional counties). . . .

Nearly 50 years later, things have changed dramatically. . . .

There is no doubt that these improvements are in large part because of the Voting Rights Act. The Act has proved immensely successful at redressing racial discrimination and integrating the voting process. . . . During the "Freedom Summer" of 1964, in Philadelphia, Mississippi, three men were murdered while working in the area to register African-American voters. . . . On "Bloody Sunday" in 1965, in Selma, Alabama, police beat and used tear gas against hundreds marching in support of African-American enfranchisement. . . . Today both of those towns are governed by African-American mayors. Problems remain in these States and others, but there is no denying that, due to the Voting Rights Act, our Nation has made great strides.

Yet the Act has not eased the restrictions in Section 5 or narrowed the scope of the coverage formula in Section 4(b) along the way. Those extraordinary and unprecedented features were reauthorized—as if nothing had changed. In fact, the Act's unusual remedies have grown even stronger. . . .

The Government falls back to the argument that because the formula was relevant in 1965, its continued use is permissible so long as any discrimination remains in the States Congress identified back then—regardless of how that discrimination compares to discrimination in States unburdened by coverage. . . .

There is no valid reason to insulate the coverage formula from review merely because it was previously enacted 40 years ago. If Congress had started from scratch in 2006, it plainly could not have enacted the present coverage formula. It would have been irrational for Congress to distinguish between States in such a fundamental way based on 40-year-old data, when today's statistics tell an entirely different story. And it would have been irrational to base coverage on the use of voting tests 40 years ago, when such tests have been illegal since that time. But that is exactly what Congress has done. . . .

Our decision in no way affects the permanent, nationwide ban on racial discrimination in voting found in Section 2. We issue no holding on Section 5 itself, only on the coverage formula. Congress may draft another formula based on current conditions. Such a formula is an initial prerequisite to a determination that exceptional conditions still exist justifying such an "extraordinary departure from the traditional course of relations between the States and the Federal Government." . . . Our country has changed, and while any racial discrimination in voting is too much, Congress must ensure that the legislation it passes to remedy that problem speaks to current conditions.

Justice Ginsburg, with whom Justice Breyer, Justice Sotomayor, and Justice Kagan join, dissenting.

In the Court's view, the very success of Section 5 of the Voting Rights Act demands its dormancy. Congress was of another mind. Recognizing that large progress has been made, Congress determined, based on a voluminous record, that the scourge of discrimination was not yet extirpated. The question this case presents is who decides whether, as currently operative, Section 5 remains justifiable, this Court, or a Congress charged with the obligation to enforce the post–Civil War Amendments "by appropriate legislation." With overwhelming support in both Houses, Congress concluded that, for two prime reasons, Section 5 should continue in force, unabated. First, continuance would facilitate completion of the impressive gains thus far made; and second, continuance would guard against backsliding. Those assessments were well within Congress' province to make and should elicit this Court's unstinting approbation.

"[V]oting discrimination still exists; no one doubts that." . . . But the Court today terminates the remedy that proved to be best suited to block that discrimination. The Voting Rights Act of 1965 (VRA) has worked to combat voting discrimination where other remedies had been tried and failed. Particularly effective is the VRA's requirement of federal preclearance for all changes to voting laws in the regions of the country with the most aggravated records of rank discrimination against minority voting rights. . . .

. . . Early attempts to cope with this vile infection resembled battling the Hydra. Whenever one form of voting discrimination was identified and prohibited, others sprang up in its place. This Court repeatedly encountered the remarkable "variety and persistence" of laws disenfranchising minority citizens. . . .

Patently, a new approach was needed.

Answering that need, the Voting Rights Act became one of the most consequential, efficacious, and amply justified exercises of federal legislative power in our Nation's history. Requiring federal preclearance of changes in voting laws in the covered jurisdictions—those States and localities where opposition to the Constitution's commands were most virulent—the VRA provided a fit solution for minority voters as well as for States. . . .

Although the VRA wrought dramatic changes in the realization of minority voting rights, the Act, to date, surely has not eliminated all vestiges of discrimination against the exercise of the franchise by minority citizens. Jurisdictions covered by the preclearance requirement continued to submit, in large numbers, proposed changes to voting laws that the Attorney General declined to approve, auguring that barriers to minority voting would quickly resurface were the preclearance remedy eliminated. . . . Efforts to reduce the impact of minority votes, in contrast to direct attempts to block access to the ballot, are aptly described as "second-generation barriers" to minority voting.

Second-generation barriers come in various forms. One of the blockages is racial gerry-mandering, the redrawing of legislative districts in an "effort to segregate the races for purposes of voting." . . . Whatever the device employed, this Court has long recognized that vote dilution, when adopted with a discriminatory purpose, cuts down the right to vote as certainly as denial of access to the ballot. . . .

True, conditions in the South have impressively improved since passage of the Voting Rights Act. Congress noted this improvement and found that the VRA was the driving force behind it. . . . But Congress also found that voting discrimination had evolved into subtler second-generation barriers, and that eliminating preclearance would risk loss of the gains that had been made. . . .

The Court stops any application of Section 5 by holding that Section 4(b)'s coverage formula is unconstitutional. It pins this result, in large measure, to "the fundamental principle of equal sovereignty." . . . In *Katzenbach*, however, the Court held, in no uncertain terms, that the principle "applies only to the terms upon which States are admitted to the Union, and not to the remedies for local evils which have subsequently appeared." . . .

[T]he Court strikes Section 4(b)'s coverage provision because, in its view, the provision is not based on "current conditions." . . . It discounts, however, that one such condition was the preclearance remedy in place in the covered jurisdictions, a remedy Congress designed both to catch discrimination before it causes harm, and to guard against return to old ways. . . . Volumes of evidence supported Congress' determination that the prospect of retrogression was real. Throwing out preclearance when it has worked and is continuing to work to stop discriminatory changes is like throwing away your umbrella in a rainstorm because you are not getting wet.

But, the Court insists, the coverage formula is no good; it is based on "decades-old data and eradicated practices." . . . Even if the legislative record shows, as engaging with it would reveal, that the formula accurately identifies the jurisdictions with the worst conditions of voting discrimination, that is of no moment, as the Court sees it. Congress, the Court decrees, must "star[t] from scratch." . . . I do not see why that should be so. . . .

The sad irony of today's decision lies in its utter failure to grasp why the VRA has proven effective. The Court appears to believe that the VRA's success in eliminating the specific devices extant in 1965 means that preclearance is no longer needed. . . . With that belief, and the argument derived from it, history repeats itself. . . . In truth, the evolution of voting discrimination into more subtle second-generation barriers is powerful evidence that a remedy as effective as preclearance remains vital to protect minority voting rights and prevent backsliding.

Beyond question, the VRA is no ordinary legislation. It is extraordinary because Congress embarked on a mission long delayed and of extraordinary importance: to realize the purpose and promise of the Fifteenth Amendment. For a half century, a concerted effort has been made to end racial discrimination in voting. Thanks to the Voting Rights Act, progress once the subject of a dream has been achieved and continues to be made.

The record supporting the 2006 reauthorization of the VRA is also extraordinary. . . . After exhaustive evidence-gathering and deliberative process, Congress reauthorized the

VRA, including the coverage provision, with overwhelming bipartisan support. It was the judgment of Congress that "40 years has not been a sufficient amount of time to eliminate the vestiges of discrimination following nearly 100 years of disregard for the dictates of the 15th amendment and to ensure that the right of all citizens to vote is protected as guaranteed by the Constitution." . . . That determination of the body empowered to enforce the Civil War Amendments "by appropriate legislation" merits this Court's utmost respect. In my judgment, the Court errs egregiously by overriding Congress' decision.

23 Obergefell v. Hodges (2015)

Justice Kennedy delivered the opinion of the Court.

The Constitution promises liberty to all within its reach, a liberty that includes certain specific rights that allow persons, within a lawful realm, to define and express their identity. The petitioners in these cases seek to find that liberty by marrying someone of the same sex and having their marriages deemed lawful on the same terms and conditions as marriages between persons of the opposite sex.

I

These cases come from Michigan, Kentucky, Ohio, and Tennessee, States that define marriage as a union between one man and one woman. . . . The petitioners are 14 same-sex couples and two men whose same-sex partners are deceased. The respondents are state officials responsible for enforcing the laws in question. The petitioners claim the respondents violate the Fourteenth Amendment by denying them the right to marry or to have their marriages, lawfully performed in another State, given full recognition.

. . .

II

Before addressing the principles and precedents that govern these cases, it is appropriate to note the history of the subject now before the Court.

A

From their beginning to their most recent page, the annals of human history reveal the transcendent importance of marriage. The lifelong union of a man and a woman always has promised nobility and dignity to all persons, without regard to their station in life. Marriage is sacred to those who live by their religions and offers unique fulfillment to those who find meaning in the secular realm. Its dynamic allows two people to find a life that could not be found alone, for a marriage becomes greater than just the two persons. Rising from the most basic human needs, marriage is essential to our most profound hopes and aspirations.

. . .

Obergefell v. Hodges, 576 U.S. _____ (2015).

. . . Far from seeking to devalue marriage, the petitioners seek it for themselves because of their respect and need for its privileges and responsibilities. And their immutable nature dictates that same-sex marriage is their only real path to this profound commitment.

Recounting the circumstances of three of these cases illustrates the urgency of the petitioners' cause from their perspective. Petitioner James Obergefell, a plaintiff in the Ohio case, met John Arthur over two decades ago. They fell in love and started a life together, establishing a lasting, committed relation. In 2011, however, Arthur was diagnosed with amyotrophic lateral sclerosis, or ALS. This debilitating disease is progressive, with no known cure. Two years ago, Obergefell and Arthur decided to commit to one another, resolving to marry before Arthur died. To fulfill their mutual promise, they traveled from Ohio to Maryland, where same-sex marriage was legal. It was difficult for Arthur to move, and so the couple were wed inside a medical transport plane as it remained on the tarmac in Baltimore. Three months later, Arthur died. Ohio law does not permit Obergefell to be listed as the surviving spouse on Arthur's death certificate. By statute, they must remain strangers even in death, a state-imposed separation Obergefell deems "hurtful for the rest of time." . . .

April DeBoer and Jayne Rowse are co-plaintiffs in the case from Michigan. They celebrated a commitment ceremony to honor their permanent relation in 2007. They both work as nurses, DeBoer in a neonatal unit and Rowse in an emergency unit. In 2009, DeBoer and Rowse fostered and then adopted a baby boy. Later that same year, they welcomed another son into their family. The new baby, born prematurely and abandoned by his biological mother, required around-the-clock care. The next year, a baby girl with special needs joined their family. Michigan, however, permits only opposite-sex married couples or single individuals to adopt, so each child can have only one woman as his or her legal parent. If an emergency were to arise, schools and hospitals may treat the three children as if they had only one parent. And, were tragedy to befall either DeBoer or Rowse, the other would have no legal rights over the children she had not been permitted to adopt. This couple seeks relief from the continuing uncertainty their unmarried status creates in their lives.

Army Reserve Sergeant First Class Ijpe DeKoe and his partner Thomas Kostura, co-plaintiffs in the Tennessee case, fell in love. In 2011, DeKoe received orders to deploy to Afghanistan. Before leaving, he and Kostura married in New York. A week later, DeKoe began his deployment, which lasted for almost a year. When he returned, the two settled in Tennessee, where DeKoe works full-time for the Army Reserve. Their lawful marriage is stripped from them whenever they reside in Tennessee, returning and disappearing as they travel across state lines. DeKoe, who served this Nation to preserve the freedom the Constitution protects, must endure a substantial burden.

. . .

III

. . .

The nature of injustice is that we may not always see it in our own times. The generations that wrote and ratified the Bill of Rights and the Fourteenth Amendment did not presume to know the extent of freedom in all of its dimensions, and so they entrusted to future generations a charter protecting the right of all persons to enjoy liberty as we learn its meaning. When new insight reveals discord between the Constitution's central protections and a received legal stricture, a claim to liberty must be addressed.

Applying these established tenets, the Court has long held the right to marry is protected by the Constitution. In *Loving v. Virginia*, . . . which invalidated bans on interracial unions, a unanimous Court held marriage is "one of the vital personal rights essential to the orderly pursuit of happiness by free men." The Court reaffirmed that holding in *Zablocki v. Redhail*, . . . which held the right to marry was burdened by a law prohibiting fathers who were behind on child support from marrying. The Court again applied this principle in *Turner v. Safley*, . . . which held the right to marry was abridged by regulations limiting the privilege of prison inmates to marry. . . .

. . .

. . .The four principles and traditions to be discussed demonstrate that the reasons marriage is fundamental under the Constitution apply with equal force to same-sex couples.

A first premise of the Court's relevant precedents is that the right to personal choice regarding marriage is inherent in the concept of individual autonomy. This abiding connection between marriage and liberty is why *Loving* invalidated interracial marriage bans under the Due Process Clause. . . . Like choices concerning contraception, family relationships, procreation, and childrearing, all of which are protected by the Constitution, decisions concerning marriage are among the most intimate that an individual can make. . . .

. . .

The nature of marriage is that, through its enduring bond, two persons together can find other freedoms, such as expression, intimacy, and spirituality. This is true for all persons, whatever their sexual orientation. . . .

A second principle in this Court's jurisprudence is that the right to marry is fundamental because it supports a two-person union unlike any other in its importance to the committed individuals. This point was central to *Griswold* v. *Connecticut*, which held the Constitution protects the right of married couples to use contraception. . . .

. . .

. . . Marriage responds to the universal fear that a lonely person might call out only to find no one there. It offers the hope of companionship and understanding and assurance that while both still live there will be someone to care for the other.

As this Court held in *Lawrence*, same-sex couples have the same right as opposite-sex couples to enjoy intimate association. *Lawrence* invalidated laws that made same-sex intimacy a criminal act. . . . But while *Lawrence* confirmed a dimension of freedom that allows individuals to engage in intimate association without criminal liability, it does not follow that freedom stops there. Outlaw to outcast may be a step forward, but it does not achieve the full promise of liberty.

A third basis for protecting the right to marry is that it safeguards children and families and thus draws meaning from related rights of childrearing, procreation, and education. . . . By giving recognition and legal structure to their parents' relationship, marriage allows children "to understand the integrity and closeness of their own family and its concord with other families in their community and in their daily lives." . . .

As all parties agree, many same-sex couples provide loving and nurturing homes to their children, whether biological or adopted. And hundreds of thousands of children are presently being raised by such couples. . . .

Excluding same-sex couples from marriage thus conflicts with a central premise of the right to marry. Without the recognition, stability, and predictability marriage offers, their children suffer the stigma of knowing their families are somehow lesser. They also suffer the significant material costs of being raised by unmarried parents, relegated through no fault of their own to a more difficult and uncertain family life. The marriage laws at issue here thus harm and humiliate the children of same-sex couples. . . .

That is not to say the right to marry is less meaningful for those who do not or cannot have children. An ability, desire, or promise to procreate is not and has not been a prerequisite for a valid marriage in any State. . . .

Fourth and finally, this Court's cases and the Nation's traditions make clear that marriage is a keystone of our social order. . . . This idea has been reiterated even as the institution has evolved in substantial ways over time, superseding rules related to parental consent, gender, and race once thought by many to be essential. . . .

For that reason, just as a couple vows to support each other, so does society pledge to support the couple, offering symbolic recognition and material benefits to protect and nourish the union. . . . These aspects of marital status include: taxation; inheritance and property rights; rules of intestate succession; spousal privilege in the law of evidence; hospital access; medical decisionmaking authority; adoption rights; the rights and benefits of survivors; birth and death certificates; professional ethics rules; campaign finance restrictions; workers' compensation benefits; health insurance; and child custody, support, and visitation rules. . . .

. . .

The limitation of marriage to opposite-sex couples may long have seemed natural and just, but its inconsistency with the central meaning of the fundamental right to marry is now manifest. With that knowledge must come the recognition that laws excluding same-sex couples from the marriage right impose stigma and injury of the kind prohibited by our basic charter. . . .

. . .

The right of same-sex couples to marry that is part of the liberty promised by the Fourteenth Amendment is derived, too, from that Amendment's guarantee of the equal protection of the laws. . . .

. . .

. . . The Court now holds that same-sex couples may exercise the fundamental right to marry. No longer may this liberty be denied to them. *Baker v. Nelson* must be and now is overruled, and the State laws challenged by Petitioners in these cases are now held invalid to the extent they exclude same-sex couples from civil marriage on the same terms and conditions as opposite-sex couples.

IV

There may be an initial inclination in these cases to proceed with caution—to await further legislation, litigation, and debate. The respondents warn there has been insufficient democratic discourse before deciding an issue so basic as the definition of marriage. . . .

Yet there has been far more deliberation than this argument acknowledges. There have been referenda, legislative debates, and grassroots campaigns, as well as countless studies, papers, books, and other popular and scholarly writings. There has been extensive litigation in state and federal courts. . . .

. . .

Finally, it must be emphasized that religions, and those who adhere to religious doctrines, may continue to advocate with utmost, sincere conviction that, by divine precepts, same-sex marriage should not be condoned. The First Amendment ensures that religious organizations and persons are given proper protection as they seek to teach the principles that are so fulfilling and so central to their lives and faiths, and to their own deep aspirations to continue the family structure they have long revered. The same is true of those who oppose same-sex marriage for other reasons. In turn, those who believe allowing same-sex marriage is proper or indeed essential, whether as a matter of religious conviction or secular belief, may engage those who disagree with their view in an open and searching debate. The Constitution, however, does not permit the State to bar same-sex couples from marriage on the same terms as accorded to couples of the opposite sex.

V

These cases also present the question whether the Constitution requires States to recognize same-sex marriages validly performed out of State. As made clear by the case of Obergefell and Arthur, and by that of DeKoe and Kostura, the recognition bans inflict substantial and continuing harm on same-sex couples.

. . . Leaving the current state of affairs in place would maintain and promote instability and uncertainty. For some couples, even an ordinary drive into a neighboring State to visit family or friends risks causing severe hardship in the event of a spouse's hospitalization while across state lines. In light of the fact that many States already allow same-sex marriage—and hundreds of thousands of these marriages already have occurred—the disruption caused by the recognition bans is significant and ever-growing. . . .

. . .

* * *

No union is more profound than marriage, for it embodies the highest ideals of love, fidelity, devotion, sacrifice, and family. In forming a marital union, two people become something greater than once they were. As some of the petitioners in these cases demonstrate, marriage embodies a love that may endure even past death. It would misunderstand these men and women to say they disrespect the idea of marriage. Their plea is that they do respect it, respect it so deeply that they seek to find its fulfillment for themselves. Their hope is not to be condemned to live in loneliness, excluded from one of civilization's oldest institutions. They ask for equal dignity in the eyes of the law. The Constitution grants them that right.

The judgment of the Court of Appeals for the Sixth Circuit is reversed.

It is so ordered.

Accomando, Christina. *"The Regulations of Robbers": Legal Fictions of Slavery and Resistance.* Ohio University Press, 2001.

Acuña, Rudolpho. *Occupied America: A History of Chicanos,* 7th ed. Prentice Hall, 2010.

Alexander, Michelle. *The New Jim Crow.* The New Press, 2012.

Anderson, Karen. *Changing Women: A History of Racial Ethnic Women in Modern America.* Oxford University Press, 1997.

Baxandall, Rosalyn F., Linda Gordon, and Susan Reverby, eds. *America's Working Women: A Documentary History—1600 to the Present,* rev. ed. Norton, 1995.

Bell, Derrick. *Silent Covenants: Brown v. Board of Education and the Unfulfilled Hopes for Racial Reform.* Oxford University Press, 2005.

———. *Race, Racism, and American Law,* 6th ed. Aspen Publishers, 2008.

Berry, Mary Frances. *Justice for All: The United States Commission on Civil Rights and the Continuing Struggle for Freedom in America.* Knopf, 2009.

Cacho, Lisa Marie. *Social Death: Racialized Rightlessness and the Criminalization of the Unprotected.* New York University Press, 2012.

Cluster, Dick, ed. *They Should Have Served That Cup of Coffee.* South End Press, 1999.

Cott, Nancy F. *Root of Bitterness: Documents of the Social History of American Women,* 2nd ed. Northeastern Press, 1996.

Crenshaw, Kimberlé, et al. *Critical Race Theory: The Key Writings That Formed the Movement.* The New Press, 1996.

Davis, Mike. *Prisoners of the American Dream: Politics and Economics in the History of the U.S. Working Class.* Verso, 2000.

D'Emilio, John, and Estelle B. Freedman. *Intimate Matters: A History of Sexuality in America,* 3rd ed. University of Chicago Press, 2012.

Dray, Philip. *There Is Power in the Union: The Epic Story of Labor in America.* Anchor, 2012.

Duberman, Martin Baum, Martha Vicinus, and George Chauncey, Jr., eds. *Hidden from History: Reclaiming the Gay and Lesbian Past.* New American Library, 1989.

Dunbar-Ortiz, Roxanne. *An Indigenous Peoples' History of the United States.* Beacon Press, 2015.

———, and Dina Gilio-Whitaker. *"All the Real Indians Died Off": And 20 Other Myths about Native Americans.* Beacon Press, 2016.

Elinson, Elaine, and Stan Yogi. *Wherever There's a Fight: How Runaway Slaves, Suffragists, Immigrants, Strikers, and Poets Shaped Civil Liberties in California.* Heyday Books, 2010.

Fleischer, Doris Zames, and Frieda Zames. *The Disability Rights Movement from Charity to Confrontation.* Temple University Press, 2001.

Flexner, Eleanor, and Ellen Fitzpatrick. *Century of Struggle: The Woman's Rights Movement in the United States,* 3rd ed. Harvard University Press, 1996.

Freedman, Estelle B. *No Turning Back: The History of Feminism and the Future of Women.* Ballantine, 2003.

Giddings, Paula. *When and Where I Enter: The Impact of Black Women on Race and Sex in America.* William Morrow, 1996.

Gilmore, Ruth Wilson. *Golden Gulag: Prisons, Surplus, Crisis, and Opposition in Globalizing California.* University of California Press, 2007.

Higginbotham, A. Leon. *In the Matter of Color: Race and the American Legal Process: The Colonial Period,* 4th ed. Oxford University Press, 1980.

Jacobs, Harriet. *Incidents in the Life of a Slave Girl, Written by Herself.* 1861. Penguin, 2000.

Katz, Jonathan. *Gay American History: Lesbians and Gay Men in the U.S.: A Documentary History,* rev. ed. Plume, 1992.

Kessler-Harris, Alice. *In Pursuit of Equity: Women, Men, and the Quest for Economic Citizenship in 20th-Century America,* rev. ed. Oxford University Press, 2003.

Meyer, Doug. *Violence against Queer People: Race, Class, Gender, and the Persistence of Anti-LGBT Discrimination.* Rutgers University Press, 2015.

Mogul, Joey L., Andrea J. Ritchie, and Kay Whitlock. *Queer (In)Justice: The Criminalization of LGBT People in the United States.* Beacon Press, 2012.

Murolo, Priscilla, A. B. Chitty, and Joe Sacco. *From the Folks Who Brought You the Weekend: A Short, Illustrated History of Labor in the United States.* The New Press, 2003.

Newcomb, Steven. *Pagans in the Promised Land: Decoding the Doctrine of Christian Discovery.* Fulcrum Publishing, 2008.

Ortiz, Paul. *An African American and Latinx History of the United States.* Beacon Press, 2018.

Pérez, Emma. *The Decolonial Imaginary: Writing Chicanas into History.* Indiana University Press, 1999.

Richie, Beth E. *Arrested Justice: Black Women, Violence, and America's Prison Nation.* New York University Press, 2012.

Rios, Victor. *Punished: Policing the Lives of Black and Latino Boys.* New York University Press 2011.

Roberts, Dorothy. *Killing the Black Body: Race, Reproduction, and the Meaning of Liberty,* 2nd ed. Vintage, 2017.

Robson, Ruthann. *Lesbian (Out)Law: Survival under the Rule of Law.* Firebrand Books, 1992.

Ross, Loretta, and Rickie Solinger. *Reproductive Justice: An Introduction.* University of California Press, 2017.

Ruiz, Vicki L., and Ellen Carol DuBois, eds. *Unequal Sisters: An Inclusive Reader in U.S. Women's History,* 4th ed. Routledge and Kegan Paul, 2007.

Silliman, Jael, and Anannya Bhattacharjee. *Policing the National Body: Race, Gender, and Criminalization.* South End Press, 2002.

Spade, Dean. *Normal Life: Administrative Violence, Critical Trans Politics and the Limits of Law.* South End Press, 2011.

Stanley, Eric, and Nat Smith. *Captive Genders: Trans Embodiment and the Prison Industrial Complex,* 2nd ed. AK Press, 2015.

Stevenson, Bryan. *Just Mercy: A Story of Justice and Redemption.* Spiegel & Grau, 2015.

Stryker, Susan. *Transgender History: The Roots of Today's Revolution,* 2nd ed. Seal Press, 2017.

Takaki, Ronald. *A Different Mirror: Multicultural American History.* Little, Brown, 1993.

———. *From Different Shores: Perspectives on Race and Culture in America,* 2nd ed. Oxford University Press, 1994.

Tang, Eric. *Unsettled: Cambodian Refugees in the New York City Hyperghetto.* Temple University Press, 2015.

Wagenheim, Kal, and Olga Jiménez de Wagenheim, eds. *The Puerto Ricans: A Documentary History,* rev. ed. Markus Wiener, 2013.

Zinn, Howard. *A People's History of the United States.* Harper Perennial Modern Classics, 2010.

PART VIII

Maintaining Race, Class, and Gender Hierarchies

[S]tereotypes have a life beyond facts. Their origin lies in a culture's ideology—the general system of beliefs by which it lives—and they are sustained across generations by diverse cultural transmissions . . . . Stereotypes, then, are not the products of bad science, but are social constructions that perform central functions in maintaining society's conception of itself.

—RICHARD MOHR

Ideological orthodoxy so permeates the plutocratic culture that it is often not felt as indoctrination. The most effective forms of tyranny are those so deeply ingrained, so thoroughly controlling, as not even to be consciously experienced as constraints.

—MICHAEL PARENTI

As colonized people many of us have internalized and adapted to the colonizer's dominant ideology, which has perpetuated our subjugation and repression. . . . However, this can change if Indigenous and non-Indigenous Peoples intelligently resist American colonialism and begin the process of decolonizing . . .

—MICHAEL YELLOW BIRD

The most effective forms of social control are often invisible. Tanks in the streets and armed militia are obvious reminders that people are not free, and they provide a focus for anger and an impetus for rebellion. More effective, in many cases, are the beliefs and attitudes a society fosters to rationalize and reinforce prevailing distributions of power and opportunity. It is here that stereotypes and ideology have an important role to play. Philosopher Richard D. Mohr argues that stereotypes emerge from a culture's dominant ideology and that they function to maintain existing power relations. They shape how we see ourselves and others, and they determine whom we hold responsible for society's ills. Stereotypes help to persuade people that differences in wealth, power, and opportunity are reflections of natural differences among people, not the results of the economic and political organization of society. These distortions of reality go beyond rationalizing inequality to rendering it invisible. Once again we find that the social constructions of gender, race, and class are at the heart of a belief system that makes the prevailing distribution of wealth and opportunity appear natural and inevitable rather than deliberate and alterable.

The selections in Part VIII examine some of the ways in which we are socialized to buy into belief systems that reinforce existing social roles and class positions and blunt social criticism. Stereotypes and dominant ideology are perpetuated by the institutions in which we live and grow: Education, religion, and our families, along with the media, encourage us to adopt a particular view of the world and our place in it. These institutions shape our perceptions of others and give us a sense of our own future. By making inequities and suffering appear to be the result of personal or group deficiency rather than the consequences of injustice, dominant representations of race, class, and gender tend to reconcile people to the status quo and distract them from the need to seek change. Violence and the threat of violence reinforce ideology and offer the prospect of pain or death to those who challenge the prevailing system or its conventions and prescriptions.

In the first selection in Part VIII, Mark Snyder draws on psychological research to show how important people's expectations are not only in shaping their perceptions of others but also in influencing the behavior of the people they stereotype. In particular, this research raises serious questions about the "objectivity" of interviewers' evaluations of job candidates and college applicants. The studies cited suggest that how interviewers see others often says more about their own unconscious stereotyping and expectations than about the individuals themselves. As Snyder points out, some of the most interesting studies in education show that teachers' expectations are at least as important as children's innate ability in determining how well children do in school. People's unconscious beliefs can have powerful consequences for the life chances and well-being of others.

In Selection 2, Sharlene Hesse-Biber explores some of the consequences of dominant ideologies of gender, including gendered constructions of worth and beauty. Patriarchy, heterosexism, and economics are bound together if, in her words, "[a] woman's sense of worth in our culture is still greatly determined by her ability to attract a man." By examining cultural messages from the media and from the numerous industries that profit from women's insecurities, Hesse-Biber exposes the ways in which women have been encouraged to internalize an artificial and generally unattainable standard of beauty. While she begins with one young woman's individual story, Hesse-Biber emphasizes that the root causes of eating disorders and struggles with body image lie in patriarchy and capitalism.

In Selection 3, Michael Parenti offers an account of our society as a plutocracy, a system of rule by and for the rich, rather than a democracy, a system of rule by and for all the people. Parenti discusses the ways in which our social institutions are organized to perpetuate rule by the rich and the ways in which we are socialized to embrace a system of beliefs that reinforces the existing social hierarchy. He suggests that all of us are receiving a clear message that material success is the measure of a person's worth, along with the dangerously false assumption that, by implication, the poor aren't worth very much and so we should not waste society's resources on them.

Constructing a particular group as worthless creates a profoundly dangerous dynamic. In Selection 4, Jason Stanley addresses the dangers of fascist politics, including tools of dehumanization and "unreality." His own family fled Nazi Germany, and his analysis is informed by this history, but the real purpose of his work is to empower us to see the patterns of fascism in present-day politics. "The dangers of fascist politics come from the particular way in which it dehumanizes segments of the population," he writes. "By excluding these groups, it limits the capacity for empathy among other citizens, leading to the justification of inhumane treatment, from repression of freedom, mass imprisonment, and expulsion to, in extreme cases, mass extermination." Addressing the deployment of conspiracy theories and attacks on journalism, Stanley warns, "A fascist leader can replace truth with power, ultimately lying without consequence,"

Dehumanization and lies have been central to antisemitism, which is often a key feature of fascist politics. Selection 5, a 2017 report issued by Jews for Racial & Economic Justice (JFREJ), analyzes the historical and present-day workings of antisemitism. "Like all oppressions," they argue, antisemitism "has deep historical roots and uses exploitation, marginalization, discrimination, and violence as its tools. Like all oppressions, the ideology contains elements of dehumanization and degradation via lies and stereotypes about Jews, as well as a mythology. The myth changes and adapts to different times and places, but fundamentally it says that Jews are to blame for society's problems." The report reveals the "conjuring trick" embedded in antisemitism, the "misdirection" that covers up the actual sources of inequality in society: "when people's rage is misdirected toward Jews, larger systems of economic injustice are shielded from scrutiny or even enhanced."

In Selection 6, Michael Yellow Bird dissects the everyday ways in which colonial ideology permeates our contemporary cultural artifacts, including team logos, cowboy hats, children's toys, and the money in our wallets. He defines colonialism as not only the "invasion, subjugation, and occupation of one people by another" in the past, but also the ongoing practices of "exploitation and control of Indigenous Peoples in the United States." Yellow Bird interweaves stark details from U.S. history with personal stories to illuminate both "the colonial master narrative" and the impact of internalized oppression. Ultimately he calls for all of us to decolonize not just the icons of colonialism but also, and more importantly, our thought patterns. The "antidotes to colonialism" that he encourages Indigenous Peoples to employ include: "courage, intelligent resistance, development of a counterconsciousness and discourse, and a fierce, ongoing critical interrogation of American colonial ideology."

Several of Yellow Bird's examples of colonialism include references to education. In both the content of curriculum and the inequities of school funding, education plays an immense role in reproducing the social hierarchy. In Selection 7, Jonathan Kozol, who has written numerous books about the "savage inequalities" of the U.S. educational system, describes what he calls "the governmentally administered diminishment in the value of children of the poor." Kozol's thesis is that education in the United States continues to be separate and unequal to such an extent that it both constitutes and perpetuates a system of apartheid.

Angela Davis argues in Selection 8 that "[t]he deterioration of public education, including prioritizing discipline and security over learning in public schools located in poor communities," is related to our nation's economic and ideological investments in prisons. She contends that the prison industrial complex in the United States performs a sleight of hand by making social problems seemingly disappear. "But prisons do not disappear problems," she writes, "they disappear human beings. And the practice of disappearing vast numbers of people from poor, immigrant, and racially marginalized communities has literally become big business." Davis examines racialized criminalization, gendered patterns of imprisonment, private prisons, the exploitation of prison labor, and unequal surveillance. She offers an intersectional analysis that makes visible the intertwining roles of race, class, and gender in perpetuating these problems. "Once the aura of magic is stripped away from the imprisonment solution, what is revealed is racism, class bias, and the parasitic seduction of capitalist profit."

Gregory Mantsios also addresses the "magic" of disappearing the realities of inequality. In Selection 9, he argues that in addition to fostering racial, ethnic, gender, and class stereotypes, the media's programming and perspectives affect our ability to "see" class at all. "By ignoring the poor and blurring the lines between working people and the upper class," he writes, "the news media creates a universal middle class." By adopting the perspective of those who are most privileged, the media distorts the realities of daily life and encourages most of us to identify with the needs and interests of a privileged few.

The next selection examines the influence of Hollywood on the (mis)representation of Muslims. Jon Ronson writes in Selection 10 about typecasting and the role of the entertainment industry in fueling the conflation of Islam and terrorism. He speaks with Muslim actors about how they negotiate the ethical concerns of playing one-dimensional, stereotyped roles and the pragmatic concerns of finding work and paying the bills. Ronson notes that those of us who consume the television shows and movies that perpetuate these stereotypes are complicit in this misrepresentation.

In Selection 11, Richard Kim details heartbreaking stories of teenagers and even younger children who have committed suicide after being subjected to antigay bullying. He reflects, "when faced with something so painful and complicated as gay teen suicide, it's easier to go down the familiar path, to invoke the wrath of law and order, to create scapegoats out of child bullies who ape the denials and anxieties of adults, to blame it on technology or to pare down homophobia into a social menace called 'anti-gay bullying' and then confine it to the borders of the schoolyard." Kim shifts the responsibility for this dynamic from the shoulders of young bullies to adult family members, lawmakers, and media-makers. Rather than calling for punishment of bullies, he calls on us to make a better world: "It's tougher, more uncertain work creating a world that loves queer kids, that wants them to live and thrive. But try—try as if someone's life depended on it."

The final selection turns to the deadly consequences of stereotyping in relation to law enforcement and 911 calls. Tressie McMillan Cottom examines the tragic case of a young black man who survived a car crash only to be shot to death by police as he sought help. Cottom interrogates the idea that black people should be responsible for keeping themselves safe by signaling—through whistling classical music, for example—that they are not threatening. There are daily costs to "the constant background processing that stereotyped people engage," she writes. "It's like running too many programs in the background of your computer as you try to play a YouTube video." Cottom also identifies the valuable "social-psychological privilege" experienced by people in the dominant group who aren't forced to adapt their behavior to manage the effects of assumptions and stereotypes. She sees social-psychological and structural factors intertwining when stereotypes "can be aided and abetted by organizational processes like the characterization of a police call to 911 and structural legitimacy like the authority of the police to shoot first and ask questions later."

GUIDING QUESTIONS FOR PART VIII

1. Several readings in this volume have asked us to consider not only *individuals* but also *institutions* and *structures* as we work to understand unequal power and privilege. Identify specific examples from Part VIII where the author uses a personal story to illustrate how social, political, and economic institutions are inextricably interwoven with individual experiences.

2. Understanding the role of institutions affects where we look for solutions and for strategies for change. Sharlene Hesse-Biber argues, "An addiction model of behavior assumes that the cause and the cure of the problem lies within the individual." What does she see as the root causes of eating and body image struggles, causes that lie outside the individual? How does this analysis of *causes* change how we might imagine *solutions*?

3. Several readings in Part VIII examine history—histories of fascism, antisemitism, colonialism, and other systems of hierarchy. Why is it so important to examine history to understand our present moment?

4. How do the readings in Part VIII argue that media representations both reflect and help shape dominant ideology? Can the media also be a force for challenging dominant representations? Can you give some examples of such challenges in the media?

5. Michael Yellow Bird identifies several everyday cultural artifacts, from toys to money, that carry ideological messages. How does he try to "decolonize" those objects? What ideological meanings and histories of colonialism are contained in some of the objects in your daily life? Can you think of ways to "begin the process of decolonizing"?

6. People often defend stereotypes by arguing that they contain a kernel of truth. The readings in Part VIII reject that notion and demonstrate that stereotypes exist to reinforce dominant ideology and unequal power relations. Identify some examples from the readings that reveal the origin and function of specific stereotypes.

7. Jason Stanley notes that "fascist ideology seeks to naturalize group difference." Why is that such a key step in generating a politics of "us" and "them"? Do you see this dynamic operating in other readings in Part VIII? Can you identify examples of the strategic deployment of the "us" and "them" framework in political rhetoric today?

8. Angela Davis argues, "Racism has undermined our ability to create a popular critical discourse to contest the ideological trickery that posits imprisonment as key to public safety." What does she mean by "ideological trickery"? What is covered up by this trickery? Do you see "ideological trickery" analyzed in other essays in Part VIII?

9. Davis asks us to imagine alternatives to building more prisons. Richard Kim asks us to imagine "a world that loves queer kids." As you read the social critiques in each of the articles in Part VIII, consider the type of world you would like to live in. What steps can you take to help bring that world into existence?

1 Self-Fulfilling Stereotypes

Mark Snyder

Gordon Allport, the Harvard psychologist who wrote a classic work on the nature of prejudice, told a story about a child who had come to believe that people who lived in Minneapolis were called monopolists. From his father, moreover, he had learned that monopolists were evil folk. It wasn't until many years later, when he discovered his confusion, that his dislike of residents of Minneapolis vanished.

Allport knew, of course, that it was not so easy to wipe out prejudice and erroneous stereotypes. Real prejudice, psychologists like Allport argued, was buried deep in human character, and only a restructuring of education could begin to root it out. Yet many people whom I meet while lecturing seem to believe that stereotypes are simply beliefs or attitudes that change easily with experience. Why do some people express the view that Italians are passionate, blacks are lazy, Jews materialistic, and lesbians mannish in their demeanor? In the popular view, it is because they have not learned enough about the diversity among these groups and have not had enough contact with members of the groups for their stereotypes to be challenged by reality. With more experience, it is presumed, most people of good will are likely to revise their stereotypes.

My research over the past decade convinces me that there is little justification for such optimism—and not only for the reasons given by Allport. While it is true that deep prejudice is often based on the needs of pathological character structure, stereotypes are obviously quite common even among fairly normal individuals. When people first meet others, they cannot help noticing certain highly visible and distinctive characteristics: sex, race, physical appearance, and the like. Despite people's best intentions, their initial impressions of others are shaped by their assumptions about such characteristics.

What is critical, however, is that these assumptions are not merely beliefs or attitudes that exist in a vacuum; they are reinforced by the behavior of both prejudiced people and the targets of their prejudice. In recent years, psychologists have collected considerable laboratory evidence about the processes that strengthen stereotypes and put them beyond the reach of reason and good will.

My own studies initially focused on first encounters between strangers. It did not take long to discover, for example, that people have very different ways of treating those whom they regard as physically attractive and those whom they consider physically unattractive, and that these differences tend to bring out precisely those kinds of behavior that fit with stereotypes about attractiveness.

Mark Snyder is a social psychologist and a professor at the University of Minnesota.

From *Psychology Today*, January 1982. Copyright © 1982 by Psychology Today. www.Psychologytoday.com.

In an experiment that I conducted with my colleagues Elizabeth Decker Tanke and Ellen Berscheid, pairs of college-age men and women met and became acquainted in telephone conversations. Before the conversations began, each man received a Polaroid snapshot, presumably taken just months before, of the woman he would soon meet. The photograph, which had actually been prepared before the experiment began, showed either a physically attractive woman or a physically unattractive one. By randomly choosing which picture to use for each conversation, we insured that there was no consistent relationship between the attractiveness of the woman in the picture and the attractiveness of the woman in the conversation.

By questioning the men, we learned that even before the conversations began, stereotypes about physical attractiveness came into play. Men who looked forward to talking with physically attractive women said that they expected to meet decidedly sociable, poised, humorous, and socially adept people, while men who thought that they were about to get acquainted with unattractive women fashioned images of rather unsociable, awkward, serious, and socially inept creatures. Moreover, the men proved to have very different styles of getting acquainted with women whom they thought to be attractive and those whom they believed to be unattractive. Shown a photograph of an attractive woman, they behaved with warmth, friendliness, humor, and animation. However, when the woman in the picture was unattractive, the men were cold, uninteresting, and reserved.

These differences in the men's behavior elicited behavior in the women that was consistent with the men's stereotyped assumptions. Women who were believed (unbeknown to them) to be physically attractive behaved in a friendly, likeable, and sociable manner. In sharp contrast, women who were perceived as physically unattractive adopted a cool, aloof, and distant manner. So striking were the differences in the women's behavior that they could be discerned simply by listening to tape recordings of the woman's side of the conversations. Clearly, by acting upon their stereotyped beliefs about the women whom they would be meeting, the men had initiated a chain of events that produced *behavioral confirmation* for their beliefs.

Similarly, Susan Anderson and Sandra Bem have shown in an experiment at Stanford University that when the tables are turned—when it is women who have pictures of men they are to meet on the telephone—many women treat the men according to their presumed physical attractiveness, and by so doing encourage the men to confirm their stereotypes. Little wonder, then, that so many people remain convinced that good looks and appealing personalities go hand in hand.

Sex and Race

It is experiments such as these that point to a frequently unnoticed power of stereotypes: the power to influence social relationships in ways that create the illusion of reality. In one study, Berna Skrypnek and I arranged for pairs of previously unacquainted students to interact in a situation that permitted us to control the information that each one received about the apparent sex of the other. The two people were seated in separate rooms so that they could neither see nor hear each other. Using a system of signal lights that they operated with switches, they negotiated a division of labor, deciding which member of the pair would perform each of several tasks that differed in sex-role connotations. The tasks varied along the dimensions of masculinity and femininity: sharpen a hunting knife (masculine), polish a pair of shoes (neutral), iron a shirt (feminine).

One member of the team was led to believe that the other was, in one condition of the experiment, male; in the other, female. As we had predicted, the first member's belief about the sex of the partner influenced the outcome of the pair's negotiations. Women whose partners believed them to be men generally chose stereotypically masculine tasks; in contrast, women whose partners believed that they were women usually chose stereotypically feminine tasks. The experiment thus suggests that much sex-role behavior may be the product of other people's stereotyped and often erroneous beliefs.

In a related study at the University of Waterloo, Carl von Baeyer, Debbie Sherk, and Mark Zanna have shown how stereotypes about sex roles operate in job interviews. The researchers arranged to have men conduct simulated job interviews with women seeking positions as research assistants. The investigators informed half of the women that the men who would interview them held traditional views about the ideal woman, believing her to be very emotional, deferential to her husband, home-oriented, and passive. The rest of the women were told that their interviewer saw the ideal woman as independent, competitive, ambitious, and dominant. When the women arrived for their interviews, the researchers noticed that most of them had dressed to meet the stereotyped expectations of their prospective interviewers. Women who expected to see a traditional interviewer had chosen very feminine-looking makeup, clothes, and accessories. During the interviews (videotaped through a one-way mirror) these women behaved in traditionally feminine ways and gave traditionally feminine answers to questions such as "Do you have plans to include children and marriage with your career plans?"

Once more, then, we see the self-fulfilling nature of stereotypes. Many sex differences, it appears, may result from the images that people create in their attempts to act out accepted sex roles. The implication is that if stereotyped expectations about sex roles shift, behavior may change, too. In fact, statements by people who have undergone sex-change operations have highlighted the power of such expectations in easing adjustment to a new life. As the writer Jan Morris said in recounting the story of her transition from James to Jan: "The more I was treated as a woman, the more woman I became."

The power of stereotypes to cause people to confirm stereotyped expectations can also be seen in interracial relationships. In the first of two investigations done at Princeton University by Carl Word, Mark Zanna, and Joel Cooper, white undergraduates interviewed both white and black job applicants. The applicants were actually confederates of the experimenters, trained to behave consistently from interview to interview, no matter how the interviewers acted toward them.

To find out whether or not the white interviewers would behave differently toward white and black job applicants, the researchers secretly videotaped each interview and then studied the tapes. From these, it was apparent that there were substantial differences in the treatment accorded blacks and whites. For one thing, the interviewers' speech deteriorated when they talked to blacks, displaying more errors in grammar and pronunciation. For another, the interviewers spent less time with blacks than with whites and showed less "immediacy," as the researchers called it, in their manner. That is, they were less friendly, less outgoing, and more reserved with blacks.

In the second investigation, white confederates were trained to approximate the immediate or the nonimmediate interview styles that had been observed in the first investigation as they interviewed white job applicants. A panel of judges who evaluated the tapes agreed that applicants subjected to the nonimmediate styles performed less adequately and were more nervous than job applicants treated in the immediate style. Apparently, then, the blacks in the first study did not have a chance to display their qualifications to the best advantage. Considered together, the two investigations suggest that in interracial encounters, racial stereotypes may constrain behavior in ways to cause both blacks and whites to behave in accordance with those stereotypes.

Rewriting Biography

Having adopted stereotyped ways of thinking about another person, people tend to notice and remember the ways in which that person seems to fit the stereotype, while resisting evidence that contradicts the stereotype. In one investigation that I conducted with Seymour Uranowitz, student subjects read a biography of a fictitious woman named Betty K. We constructed the story of her life so that it would fit the stereotyped images of both lesbians and heterosexuals. Betty, we wrote, never had a steady boyfriend in high school, but did go out on dates. And although we gave her a steady boyfriend in college, we specified that he was more of a close friend than anything else. A week after we had distributed this biography, we gave our subjects some new information about Betty. We told some students that she was now living with another woman in a lesbian relationship; we told others that she was living with her husband.

To see what impact stereotypes about sexuality would have on how people remembered the facts of Betty's life, we asked each student to answer a series of questions about her life history. When we examined their answers, we found that the students had reconstructed the events of Betty's past in ways that supported their own stereotyped beliefs about her sexual orientation. Those who believed that Betty was a lesbian remembered that Betty had never had a steady boyfriend in high school, but tended to neglect the fact that she had gone out on many dates in college. Those who believed that Betty was now a heterosexual tended to remember that she had formed a steady relationship with a man in college, but tended to ignore the fact that this relationship was more of a friendship than a romance.

The students showed not only selective memories but also a striking facility for interpreting what they remembered in ways that added fresh support for their stereotypes. One student who accurately remembered that a supposedly lesbian Betty never had a steady boyfriend in high school confidently pointed to the fact as an early sign of her lack of romantic or sexual interest in men. A student who correctly remembered that a purportedly lesbian Betty often went out on dates in college was sure that these dates were signs of Betty's early attempts to mask her lesbian interests.

Clearly, the students had allowed their preconceptions about lesbians and heterosexuals to dictate the way in which they interpreted and reinterpreted the facts of Betty's life. As long as stereotypes make it easy to bring to mind evidence that supports them and difficult to bring to mind evidence that undermines them, people will cling to erroneous beliefs.

Stereotypes in the Classroom and Work Place

The power of one person's beliefs to make other people conform to them has been well demonstrated in real life. Back in the 1960s, as most people well remember, Harvard psychologist Robert Rosenthal and his colleague Lenore Jacobson entered elementary-school classrooms and identified one out of every five pupils in each room as a child who could be expected to show dramatic improvement in intellectual achievement during the school year. What the teachers did not know was that the children had been chosen on a random basis. Nevertheless, something happened in the relationships between teachers and their supposedly gifted pupils that led the children to make clear gains in test performance.

It can also do so on the job. Albert King, now a professor of management at Northern Illinois University, told a welding instructor in a vocational training center that five men in his training program had unusually high aptitude. Although these five had been chosen at random and knew nothing of their designation as high-aptitude workers, they showed substantial changes in performance. They were absent less often than were other workers, learned the basics of the welder's trade in about half the usual time, and scored a full 10 points higher than other trainees on a welding test. Their gains were noticed not only by the researcher and by the welding instructor, but also by other trainees, who singled out the five as their preferred coworkers.

Might not other expectations influence the relationships between supervisors and workers? For example, supervisors who believe that men are better suited to some jobs and women to others may treat their workers (wittingly or unwittingly) in ways that encourage them to perform their jobs in accordance with stereotypes about differences between men and women. These same stereotypes may determine who gets which job in the first place. Perhaps some personnel managers allow stereotypes to influence, subtly or not so subtly, the way in which they interview job candidates, making it likely that candidates who fit the stereotypes show up better than job seekers who do not fit them.

Unfortunately, problems of this kind are compounded by the fact that members of stigmatized groups often subscribe to stereotypes about themselves. That is what Amerigo Farina and his colleagues at the University of Connecticut found when they measured the impact upon mental patients of believing that others knew their psychiatric history. In Farina's study, each mental patient cooperated with another person in a game requiring teamwork. Half of the patients believed that their partners knew they were patients, the other half believed that their partners thought they were nonpatients. In reality, the nonpatients never knew a thing about anyone's psychiatric history. Nevertheless, simply believing that others were aware of their history led the patients to feel less appreciated, to find the task more difficult, and to perform poorly. In addition, objective observers saw them as more tense, more anxious, and more poorly adjusted than patients who believed that their status was not known. Seemingly, the belief that others perceived them as stigmatized caused them to play the role of stigmatized patients.

Consequences for Society

Apparently, good will and education are not sufficient to subvert the power of stereotypes. If people treat others in such a way as to bring out behavior that supports stereotypes, they may never have an opportunity to discover which of their stereotypes are wrong.

I suspect that even if people were to develop doubts about the accuracy of their stereotypes, chances are they would proceed to test them by gathering precisely the evidence that would appear to confirm them.

The experiments I have described help to explain the persistence of stereotypes. But, as is so often the case, solving one puzzle only creates another. If by acting as if false stereotypes were true, people lead others, too, to act as if they were true, why do the stereotypes not come to *be* true? Why, for example, have researchers found so little evidence that attractive people are generally friendly, sociable, and outgoing and that unattractive people are generally shy and aloof?

I think that the explanation goes something like this: Very few among us have the kind of looks that virtually everyone considers either very attractive or very unattractive. Our looks make us rather attractive to some people but somewhat less attractive to other people. When we spend time with those who find us attractive, they will tend to bring out our more sociable sides, but when we are with those who find us less attractive, they will bring out our less sociable sides. Although our actual physical appearance does not change, we present ourselves quite differently to our admirers and to our detractors. For our admirers we become attractive people, and for our detractors we become unattractive. This mixed pattern of behavior will prevent the development of any consistent relationship between physical attractiveness and personality.

Now that I understand some of the powerful forces that work to perpetuate social stereotypes, I can see a new mission for my research. I hope, on the one hand, to find out how to help people see the flaws in their stereotypes. On the other hand, I would like to help the victims of false stereotypes find ways of liberating themselves from the constraints imposed on them by other members of society.

2 | Am I Thin Enough Yet?

Sharlene Hesse-Biber

Ever since I was ten years old, I was just a very vain person. I always wanted to be the thinnest, the prettiest. 'Cause I thought, if I look like this, then I'm going to have so many boyfriends, and guys are going to be so in love with me, and I'll be taken care of for the rest of my life. I'll never have to work, you know?

—Delia, College Senior

What's Wrong with This Picture?

Pretty, vivacious, and petite, Delia was a picture of fashionable perfection when she first walked into my office. Her tight blue jeans and fringed Western shirt showed off her thin, 5-ft frame; her black cowboy boots and silver earrings completed a presentation that said, "Look at me!"

The perfect picture had a serious price. Delia had come to talk about her "problem." She is bulimic. In secret, she regularly binges on large amounts of food, then forces herself to vomit. It has become a powerful habit, one that she is afraid to break because it so efficiently maintains her thin body. For Delia, as for so many others, being thin is everything.

"I mean, how many bumper stickers have you seen that say 'No Fat Chicks,' you know? Guys don't like fat girls. Guys like little girls. I guess because it makes them feel bigger and, you know, they want somebody who looks pretty. Pretty to me is you have to be thin and you have to have like good facial features. It's both. My final affirmation of myself is how many guys look at me when I go into a bar. How many guys pick up on me. What my boyfriend thinks about me."

Delia's Story

Delia is the eldest child, and only girl, in a wealthy Southern family. Her father is a successful dentist and her mother has never worked outside the home. They fought a lot when she was young—her father was an alcoholic—and they eventually divorced. According to Delia, both parents doted on her.

Sharlene Hesse-Biber is a professor of sociology and director of the women's studies program at Boston College. She has published widely, focusing on women and body issues, mixed research methods, and feminist pedagogy. Her books include *The Cult of Thinness*.

"I've never been deprived of anything in my entire life. I was spoiled, I guess, because I've never felt any pressure from my parents to do anything. My Dad would say, 'Whatever you want to do, if you want to go to Europe, if you want to go to law school, if you don't want to do anything . . . whatever you want to do, just be happy.' No pressure."

He was unconcerned about her weight, she said, but emphasized how important it was to be pretty. Delia quickly noticed this message everywhere, especially in the media.

"I am so affected by *Glamour* magazine and *Vogue* and all that, because that's a line of work I want to get into. I'm looking at all these beautiful women. They're thin. I want to be just as beautiful. I want to be just as thin. Because that is what guys like."

When I asked what her mother wanted for her, she recited, "To be nice and pretty and sweet and thin and popular and smart and successful and have everything that I could ever want and just to be happy." "Sweet and pretty and thin" meant that from the age of ten she was enrolled in a health club, and learned to count calories. Her mom, who at 45 is "beautiful, gorgeous, thin," gave her instructions on how to eat.

"'Only eat small amounts. Eat a thousand calories a day; don't overeat.' My mom was never critical like, 'You're fat.' But one time, I went on a camping trip and I gained four pounds and she said, 'You've got to lose weight.' I mean, she watched what I ate. Like if I was going to get a piece of cake she would be, 'Don't eat that.'"

At age 13 she started her secret bingeing and vomiting. "When I first threw up I thought, well, it's so easy," she told me. "I can eat and not get the calories and not gain weight. And I was modeling at the time, and I wanted to look like the girls in the magazines."

Delia's preoccupation with thinness intensified when she entered high school. She wanted to be a cheerleader, and she was tiny enough to make it. "When I was sixteen I just got into this image thing, like tiny, thin . . . I started working out more. I was Joe Healthy Thin Exercise Queen and I'd just fight eating because I was working out all the time, you know? And so I'm going to aerobics two or three times a day sometimes, eating only salad and a bagel, and like, no fat. I just got caught up in this circle."

College in New England brought a new set of social pressures. She couldn't go running every day because of the cold. She hated the school gym, stopped working out, and gained four pounds her freshman year. Her greatest stress at college had nothing to do with academics. "The most stressful thing for me is whether I'm going to eat that day, and what am I going to eat," she told me, "more than getting good grades."

After freshman year Delia became a cheerleader again. "Going in, I know I weighed like 93 or 94 pounds, which to me was this enormous hang-up, because I'd never weighed more than 90 pounds in my entire life. And I was really freaked out. I knew people were going to be looking at me in the crowd and I'm like, I've got to lose this weight. So I would just not eat, work out all the time. I loved being on the squad, but my partner was a real jerk. He would never work out, and when we would do lifts he'd always be, 'Delia, go run. Go run, you're too heavy.' I hadn't been eating that day. I had already run seven or eight miles and he told me to run again. And I was surrounded by girls who were all so concerned about their weight, and it was just really this horrible situation."

College life also confirmed another issue for Delia, a cultural message from her earliest childhood. She did *not* want to be a breadwinner. She put it this way, "When I was eight I wanted to be President of the United States. As I grew older and got to college I was like, wow, it's hard for women. I mean, I don't care what people say. If they say the society's liberated, they're wrong. It's still really hard for women. It's like they look through a glass window [*sic*]. They're vice presidents, but they aren't the president. And I just figured, God, how much easier would it be for me to get married to somebody I know is going to make a lot of money and just be taken care of . . . I want somebody else to be the millionaire." . . .

Economic and career achievement is a primary definition of success for men. (Of course, men can also exhibit some self-destructive behaviors in pursuit of this success, such as workaholism or substance abuse.) Delia's upbringing and environment defined success for her in a different way. She was not interested in having a job that earned $150,000 a year, but in marrying the guy who did. She learned to use any tool she could to stay thin, to look good, and to have a shot at her goal.

No wonder she was reluctant to give up her behavior. She was terrified of losing the important benefits of her membership in the Cult of Thinness. She knew she was hurting psychologically and physically, but, in the final analysis, being counted among "the chosen" justified the pain.

"God forbid anybody else gets stuck in this trap. But I'm already there, and I don't really see myself getting out, because I'm just so obsessed with how I look. I get personal satisfaction from looking thin, and receiving attention from guys."

I told Delia about women who have suggested other ways of coping with weight issues. There are even those who advocate fat liberation, or who suggest that fat is beautiful. She was emphatic about these solutions.

"Bullshit. They live in la-la land . . . I can hold onto my boyfriend because he doesn't need to look anywhere else. The bottom line is that appearance counts. And you can sit here and go, 'I feel good about myself twenty pounds heavier,' but who is the guy going to date?"

A Woman's Sense of Worth

Delia's devotion to the rituals of beauty work involved a great deal of time and energy. She weighed herself three times a day. She paid attention to what she put in her mouth; when she had too much, she knew she must get rid of it. She had to act and look a certain way, buy the right clothes, the right makeup. She also watched out for other women who might jeopardize her chances as they vied for the rewards of the system.

A woman's sense of worth in our culture is still greatly determined by her ability to attract a man. Social status is largely a function of income and occupation. Women's access to these resources is generally indirect, through marriage.[1] Even a woman with a successful and lucrative career may fear that her success comes at the expense of her femininity. . . .

Cultural messages on the rewards of thinness and the punishments of obesity are everywhere. Most women accept society's standards of beauty as "the way things are," even though these standards may undermine self-image, self-esteem, or physical well-being. Weight concerns or even obsessions are so common among women and girls that they escape notice. Dieting is not considered abnormal behavior, even among women who are not overweight. But only a thin line separates "normal" dieting from an eating disorder.[2] . . .

Profiting from Women's Bodies

Because women feel their bodies fail the beauty test, American industry benefits enormously, continually nurturing feminine insecurities. Ruling patriarchal interests, like corporate culture, the traditional family, the government, and the media, also benefit. If women are so busy trying to control their bodies through dieting, excessive exercise, and self-improvement activities, they lose control over other important aspects of selfhood that might challenge the status quo.[3] In the words of one critic, "A secretary who bench-presses 150 pounds is still stuck in a dead-end job; a housewife who runs the marathon is still financially dependent on her husband."[4]

In creating women's concept of the ideal body image, the cultural mirror is more influential than the mirror reflecting peer group attitudes. Research has shown that women overestimate how thin a body their male and female peers desire. In a recent study using body silhouettes, college students of both sexes were asked to indicate an ideal female figure, the one that they believed most attractive to the same-sex peer and other-sex peer. Not only did the women select a thinner silhouette than the men,[5] but when asked to choose a *personal* ideal, rather than a peer ideal, the women selected an even skinnier model.

Advertisements and Beauty Advice: Buy, Try, Comply

Capitalism and patriarchy most often use the media to project the culturally desirable body to women. These images are everywhere—on TV, in the movies, on billboards, in print. Women's magazines, with their glossy pages of advertising, advertorials, and beauty advice, hold up an especially devious mirror. They offer "help" to women, while presenting a standard nearly impossible to attain. As one college student named Nancy noted in our interviews,

> The advertisement showed me exactly what I should be, not what I was. I wasn't tall, I wasn't blonde, I wasn't skinny. I didn't have thin thighs, I didn't have a flat stomach. I am short, have brown curly hair, short legs. They did offer me solutions like dyeing my hair or a workout or the use of this cream to take away cellulite. . . .

Not everyone is taken in, of course. One student I interviewed dismissed the images she saw in the advertising pages of magazines as "constructed people."

> I just stopped buying women's magazines. They are all telling you how to dress, how to look, what to wear, the type of clothes. And I think they are just ridiculous. . . . You can take the most gorgeous model and make her look terrible. Just like you can take a person who is not that way and make them look beautiful. You can use airbrushing and many other techniques. These are not really people. They are constructed people.

Computer-enhanced photography has advanced far beyond the techniques that merely airbrushed blemishes, added highlights to hair, and lengthened the legs with a camera angle. The September 1994 issue of *Mirabella* featured as a cover model "an extraordinary image of great American beauty." According to the magazine, the photographer "hints that she's something of a split personality . . . it wasn't easy getting her together. Maybe her identity has something to do with the microchip floating through space, next to that gorgeous face . . . true American beauty is a combination of elements from all over the world." In other words, the photo is a computerized composite. It is interesting that *Mirabella's* "melting pot" American beauty has white skin and predominantly Caucasian features, with just a hint of other ethnicities.

There are a number of industries that help to promote image, weight, and body obsession, especially among women. If we examine the American food and weight loss industries, we'll understand how their corporate practices and advertising campaigns perpetuate the American woman's dissatisfaction with her looks.

The American Food Industry: Fatten Up and Slim Down

. . . It is not uncommon for the average American to have a diet cola in one hand and high-fat fries and a burger in the other. Food and weight loss are inescapably a key part of the culture of the 1990s. The media bombard us with images of every imaginable type of food—snack foods, fast foods, gourmet foods, health foods, and junk foods. Most of these messages target children, who are very impressionable, and women, who make the purchasing decisions for themselves and their families. At the same time women are subjected to an onslaught of articles, books, videos, tapes, and TV talk shows devoted to dieting and the maintenance of sleek and supple figures. The conflicting images of pleasurable consumption and an ever leaner body type give us a food consciousness loaded with tension and ambivalence.

Social psychologist Brett Silverstein explains that the food industry, like all industries under capitalism, is always striving to maximize profit, growth, concentration, and control. It does so at the expense of the food consumer. "[It] promotes snacking so that consumers will have more than three opportunities a day to consume food, replaces free water with purchased soft drinks, presents desserts as the ultimate reward, and bombards women and children with artificially glamorized images of highly processed foods."[6]

Diet foods are an especially profitable segment of the business. . . .

In 1983, the food industry came up with a brilliant marketing concept, and introduced 91 new "lite" fat-reduced or calorie-reduced foods.[7] The success of lite products has been phenomenal. The consumer equated "lightness" with health. The food industry seemed to equate it with their own expenses—lite foods have lower production costs than "regular" lines, but they are often priced higher. . . .

The Diet and Weight-Loss Industry: We'll Show You the Way

. . . Increasingly, American women are told that they can have the right body if only they consume more and more products. They can change the color of their eyes with tinted contacts, they can have a tanned skin by using self-tanning lotion. They can buy cellulite control cream, spot firming cream, even contouring shower and bath firming gel to get rid of the "dimpled" look. One diet capsule on the market is supposed to be the "fat cure." It is called Anorex-eck, evoking the sometimes fatal eating disorder known as anorexia. It promises to "eliminate the cause of fat formation . . . so quickly and so effectively you will know from the very start why it has taken more than 15 years of research . . . to finally bring you . . . an ultimate cure for fat!"[8] . . .

There are currently more than 17,000 different diet plans, products, and programs from which to choose.[9] Typically, these plans are geared to the female market. They are loaded with promises of quick weight loss and delicious low-calorie meals. . . .

Many of these programs produce food products that they encourage the dieter to buy. The Jenny Craig member receives a set of pre-packaged meals that cost about $10 per day. (It allows for some outside food as well.) Some diet companies are concerned with the problem of gaining weight back and have developed "maintenance" products. Maintenance programs are often expensive and their long-term outcomes are unproven. What *can* be proven are bigger profits and longer dependence on their programs.

The Dis-eased Body: Medicalizing Women's Body Issues

The therapeutic and medical communities tend to categorize women's eating and weight problems as a disease.[10] In this view, behavior like self-starvation or compulsive eating is often called an addiction. An addiction model of behavior assumes that the cause and the cure of the problem lies within the individual. Such an emphasis fails to examine the larger mirrors that society holds up to the individual.[11]

. . . While a disease model lessens the burden of guilt and shame and may free people to work on change, it also has political significance. According to feminist theorist Bette S. Tallen, "The reality of oppression is replaced with the metaphor of addiction." It places the problem's cause within a biological realm, away from outside social forces.[12] Issues such as poverty, lack of education and opportunity, racial and gender inequality remain unexamined. More important, a disease-oriented model of addiction, involving treatment by the health care system, results in profits for the medical-industrial complex. Addiction, Tallen notes, suggests a solution that is personal—"Get treatment!"—rather than political—"Smash patriarchy!" It replaces the feminist view, that the personal is political, with the attitude of "therapism," that the "political is personal."[13] One of Bette Tallen's students told her that she had learned a lot from reading *Women Who Love Too Much* after her divorce from a man who had beaten her. Tallen suggested that "perhaps the best book to read would not be about women who love too much but about men who hit too much."[14]

The idea that overweight is a disease, and overeating represents an addiction, reinforces the dis-ease that American women feel about their bodies. The capitalist and patriarchal mirror held before them supports and maintains their obsession and insecurity. . . .

Women continue to follow the standards of the ideal thin body because of how they are rewarded by being in the right body. Thinness gives women access to a number of important resources: feelings of power, self-confidence, even femininity; male attention or protection; and the social and economic benefits that can follow. . . .

NOTES

1. Pauline B. Bart, "Emotional and Social Status of the Older Woman," in *No Longer Young: The Older Woman in America. Proceedings of the 26th Annual Conference on Aging*, ed. Pauline Bart et al. (Ann Arbor: University of Michigan Institute of Gerontology, 1975), pp. 3–21; Daniel Bar-Tal and Leonard Saxe, "Physical Attractiveness and Its Relationship to Sex-Role Stereotyping," *Sex Roles* 2 (1976): 123–133; Peter Blumstein and Pepper W. Schwartz, *American Couples: Money, Work and Sex* (New York: William Morrow, 1983); Glen H. Elder, "Appearance and Education in Marriage Mobility," *American Sociological Review* 34 (1969): 519–533; Susan Sontag, "The Double Standard of Aging," *Saturday Review* (September, 1972), pp. 29–38.

2. J. Polivy and C. P. Herman, "Dieting and Binging: A Causal Analysis," *American Psychologist* 40 (1985):193–201.

3. Ilana Attie and J. Brooks-Gunn, "Weight Concerns as Chronic Stressors in Women," in *Gender and Stress*, eds. Rosalind K. Barnett, Lois Biener, and Grace Baruch (New York: Free Press, 1987), pp. 218–252.

4. Katha Pollitt, "The Politically Correct Body," *Mother Jones* (May 1982): 67. I don't want to disparage the positive benefits of exercising and the positive self-image that can come from feeling good about one's body. This positive image can spill over into other areas of one's life, enhancing, for example, one's self-esteem, or job prospects.

5. See Lawrence D. Cohn and Nancy E. Adler, "Female and Male Perceptions of Ideal Body Shapes: Distorted Views Among Caucasian College Students," *Psychology of Women Quarterly* 16 (1992): 69–79; A. Fallon and P. Rozin, "Sex Differences in Perceptions of Desirable Body Shape," *Journal of Abnormal Psychology* 94 (1985): 102–105.

6. Brett Silverstein, *Fed Up!* (Boston: South End Press, 1984), pp. 4, 47, 110. Individuals may be affected in many different ways, from paying too much (in 1978, concentration within the industry led to the overcharging of consumers by $12 to $14 billion [p. 47]) to the ingestion of unhealthy substances.

7. Warren J. Belasco, "'Lite' Economics: Less Food, More Profit," *Radical History Review* 28–30 (1984): 254–278; Hillel Schwartz, *Never Satisfied* (New York: Free Press, 1986), p. 241.

8. Advertised in *Parade* magazine (December 30, 1984).

9. Deralee Scanlon, *Diets That Work* (Chicago: Contemporary Books, 1991), p. 1.

10. See Stanton Peele, *Diseasing of America: Addiction Treatment Out of Control* (Lexington, MA: D.C. Heath and Co., 1989).

11. There are a few recovery books that point to the larger issues of the addiction model. Anne Wilson Schaef's book, *When Society Becomes an Addict*, looks at the wider institutions of society that perpetuate addiction. She notes that society operates on a scarcity model. This is the "Addictive System." This model assumes that there is never enough of anything to go around and we need to get what we can. Schaef sees society as made up of three systems: A White Male System (the Addictive System), A Reactive Female System (one where women respond passively to men by being subject to their will), and the Emerging Female System (a system where women lead with caring and sensitivity). Society needs to move in the direction of the Emerging Female System in order to end addiction. Another important book is Stanton Peele's *Love and Addiction*. Another book by Stanton Peele, *The Diseasing of America: How the Addiction Industry Captured Our Soul* (Lexington, MA: Lexington Books, 1989), stresses the importance of social change in societal institutions and advocates

changing the given distribution of resources and power within the society as a way to overcome the problem of addiction. See Anne Wilson Schaef, *When Society Becomes an Addict* (New York: Harper & Row, 1987), and Stanton Peele, *Love and Addiction* (New York: New American Library, 1975).

12. Bette S. Tallen, "Twelve Step Programs: A Lesbian Feminist Critique," NWSA *Journal* 2 (1990): 396.
13. Tallen, "Twelve Step Programs: A Lesbian Feminist Critique," 404–405.
14. Tallen, "Twelve Step Programs: A Lesbian Feminist Critique," 405.

3 | Institutions and Ideologies
Michael Parenti

Corporate Plutocracy

American capitalism represents more than just an economic system; it is a *plutocracy*, that is, a social order ruled mostly for and by the rich. Along with business enterprises and banks, the nation's *cultural institutions*—that is, its universities, publishing houses, mass-circulation magazines, newspapers, television and radio stations, professional sports teams, foundations, hospitals, churches, private museums, and charities—are mostly chartered as corporations, ruled by boards of directors (or "trustees" or "regents" as they might be called) composed overwhelmingly of affluent business people who exercise final judgment over institutional matters.

Consider the university. Private and public institutions of higher education are run by boards of trustees with authority over all matters of capital funding and budget; curriculum and tuition; degree awards; and hiring, firing, and promotion of faculty and staff. Daily decision-making power is delegated to administrators but can be easily recalled by the trustees when they choose. Most trustees are successful business people who have no administrative or scholarly experience in higher education. As trustees, they take no financial risks because their decisions are covered by insurance paid out of the university budget. Their main function seems to be to exercise oligarchic control over the institution.

Almost all of "our" cultural institutions are ruled by nonelected self-perpetuating boards of affluent corporate representatives who are answerable to no one but themselves. We the people have no vote, no portion of the ownership, and no legal decision-making power within these institutions.

We are taught to think that capitalism breeds democracy and prosperity. The private-enterprise system, it is said, creates equality of opportunity, rewards those who show ability, relegates the slothful to the lower rungs, creates national prosperity, and bolsters democracy. Little is said about how capitalism has supported and flourished under some of the most repressive regimes and impoverished Third World nations.

The corporate enterprise system places a great deal of emphasis on commercial worth: how to compete and get ahead. As Ralph Nader notes, the free market "only stimulates one value in society—the acquisitive, materialistic, profit value." What about the values relating to justice, health, occupational and consumer safety, regard for future generations, and equitable social relations?[1]

Michael Parenti is a political scientist, author, cultural critic, and speaker. His books include *Profit Pathology and Other Indecencies* and *Waiting for Yesterday: Pages from a Street Kid's Life*.

Among the key purveyors of plutocratic culture is our educational system. From grade school onward, students are given a positive picture of America's history, institutions, and leaders. Teachers tend to concentrate on the formal aspects of government and accord scant attention to the influence that wealthy, powerful groups exercise over political life. Instructors who wish to introduce a more revealing view invite critical attention from their superiors. High school students who attempt to explore controversial issues in student newspapers have frequently been overruled by administrators and threatened with disciplinary action.

School texts seldom give more than passing mention to the courageous history of labor struggle or the corporate exploitation of working people at home and abroad. Almost nothing is said of the struggles of indigenous Americans (or Native American "Indians"), indentured servants, small farmers, and Latino, Asian, Middle Eastern, and European immigrants. The history of resistance to slavery, racism, and U.S. expansionist wars goes largely untaught in our classrooms.[2]

Schools and media are inundated with informational materials provided free by the Pentagon and large corporations to promote a highly favorable view of the military and to boost privatization, deregulation of industry, and other blessings of the free market.[3] Numerous conservative think tanks and academic centers have emerged, along with conservative journals, conferences, and endowed chairs, all funded by right-wing foundations, big corporations, and superrich individuals.

Many universities and colleges have direct investments in corporate America, holding stock portfolios worth billions of dollars. Such bountiful endowments are to be found especially in elite Ivy League schools like Yale, Harvard, Brown, Columbia, and others. More and more college presidents and other top administrators are drawn directly from corporate America with no experience in teaching, research, or university administration. Their salaries are skyrocketing and their fringe benefits are increasingly lavish, including such things as year-long paid leaves at full salary. Some administrators and faculty earn handsome sums as business consultants. Corporate logos are appearing in classrooms and student union buildings. Academic-based scientific research is being increasingly funded and defined by corporations that have a vested interest in the results of the research. With its financing of chairs and study programs, private industry is influencing who is hired and what is taught.[4]

Meanwhile library budgets, scholarships, course offerings, teaching staff, and student services are being cut back. At most universities and colleges, tuition has climbed more than 30 percent in the last decade. Tenured and other full-time faculty positions are being replaced with underpaid part-time adjuncts. Some 40 percent of all college teachers are adjuncts, working for no benefits, and carrying heavy teaching loads for paltry pay.[5]

Ideological Orthodoxy

In academia, politically radical faculty, and even students, have suffered politically motivated negative evaluations and loss of stipends, grants, and jobs. Professors, journalists, managers, bureaucrats, and most other professionals who wish to advance their careers learn to go along with things as they are and avoid espousing radical views that conflict with the dominant economic interests of capitalist society.[6] . . .

Although we are often admonished to think for ourselves, we might ask if our socialization process puts limits on doing so. Ideological orthodoxy so permeates the plutocratic culture that it is often not felt as indoctrination. The most effective forms of tyranny are those so deeply ingrained, so thoroughly controlling, as not even to be consciously experienced as constraints.

In a capitalist society, mass advertising sells not only particular products but a way of life, a glorification of consumer acquisitiveness. Born of a market economy, the capitalist culture downplays cooperative efforts and human interdependence. People are expected to operate individually but toward rather similar goals. Everyone competes against everyone else, but for the same things. "Individualism" in this corporate-dominated culture refers to acquisitiveness and careerism. We are expected to get what we can for ourselves and not be too troubled by the problems faced by others. This attitude, considered inhuman in some societies, is labeled approvingly as "ambition" in our own and is treated as a quality of great social value.

Whether or not this "individualism" allows one to have much control over one's own life is another story. The decisions about the quality of the food we eat, the goods we buy, the air we breathe, the prices we pay, the wages we earn, the way work tasks are divided, the modes of transportation available to us, and the images we are fed by the media are usually made by people other than ourselves.

People who occupy privileged positions within the social hierarchy become committed to the hierarchy's preservation and hostile toward demands for a more equitable social order. Economically deprived groups are seen as a threat because they want more, and more for the have-nots might mean less for the haves. Class bigotry is one of the widely held forms of prejudice in American society and the least examined.

The plutocratic culture teaches that material success is a measure of one's worth, and because the poor are not worth much, then society's resources should not be squandered on them. In capitalist society, the poor are generally seen as personally deficient, the authors of their own straitened circumstances. Rarely are they considered to be the victims of poverty-creating economic forces: high rents, underemployment, low wages, unattended illnesses, disabilities, and other such features of the free market. As the American humorist Will Rogers once said, "It's no crime to be poor, but it might as well be."

In a society where money is the overriding determinant of one's life chances, the drive for material gain is not merely a symptom of a greed-driven culture but a factor in one's very survival. As corporate power tightens its grip over the political economy, many people have to work still harder to keep their heads above water. Rather than grasping for fanciful luxuries, they struggle to provide basic necessities. If they need more money than was essential in earlier days, it is partly because essentials cost so much more.

Because human services are based on ability to pay, money becomes a matter of life and death. To have a low or modest income is to run a higher risk of insufficient medical care, homelessness, and job insecurity, and to have less opportunity for education, recreation, travel, and comfort. Thus, the desire to "make it," even at the expense of others, is not merely a wrong-headed attitude but a reflection of the material conditions of capitalist society wherein no one is ever really economically secure except the superrich, and even they forever seek to secure and advance their fortunes through further capital accumulation.

For those who enjoy the best of everything, the existing politico-economic system is a smashing success. For those who are its hapless victims, or who are concerned about the well-being of all and not just themselves, the system leaves a great deal to be desired. . . .

Public Opinion: Which Direction?

The opinions most Americans have about socioeconomic issues are decidedly more progressive than what is usually enunciated by political leaders and right-wing media pundits. Surveys show substantial majorities strongly favoring public funding for Social Security, nursing home care, and lower-priced prescription drugs. Substantial majorities support unemployment insurance, disability assistance, job retraining, child care, price supports for family farms, and food stamps for the needy, while opposing tax cuts for the very rich and privatization of social services. Large majorities want improvements in managed health care and favor a universal health insurance program run by the government and funded by taxpayers. The public generally supports a stronger, not a weaker, social safety net. By nearly three to one, the public rejects cutbacks in Medicare and Social Security.[7]

Large majorities feel that the gap between rich and poor is growing, and that government has a responsibility to try to do away with poverty and hunger, that abortion should be a decision made by a woman and her doctor, and that racial minorities should be given fair treatment in employment—but not special preferences in hiring and promotion. After many years of strong support for organized labor, Americans became much less positive toward unions during the grim days of the 2009 recession.[8]

Sixty percent agree that large corporations wield too much power. A majority believes that corporate executives care very little about the environment, are given to falsifying company accounts, and are lining their own pockets. Large majorities say that corporations have too much influence over government. Most Americans are concerned about the environment. A majority also favors the death penalty and being "tough" on crime. Yet 60 percent agree that the president has no right to suspend the Bill of Rights in time of war or national emergency. By a five-to-three majority, Americans support the idea of a public health plan to compete with private insurance. Only 25 percent of Americans say banks are honest and trustworthy.[9]

In sum, on many important issues, a majority seems to hold positions at variance with those maintained by ideological conservatives and reactionaries and closer to the ones enunciated by liberals and progressives.

Opinion polls are only part of the picture. There is the whole history of democratic struggle that continues to this day and remains largely untaught in the schools and unreported in the media. It is expressed in mass demonstrations, strikes, boycotts, and civil disobedience—targeting such things as poverty, unemployment, unsafe nuclear reactors, nuclear missile sites, and U.S. wars abroad. There have been mass mobilizations in support of legalized abortion, women's rights, gay and lesbian rights, and environmental protections. There have been organized housing takeovers for the homeless, protests against police brutality, and noncompliance with draft registration. The Selective Service System admitted that over the years some 800,000 young men have refused to register (the actual number is probably higher).[10] At the same time, major strikes have occurred in a wide range of industries, showing that labor militancy is not a thing of the past.

This is not to deny that there remain millions of Americans, including many of relatively modest means, who succumb to the culture of fear propagated by right-wing reactionaries. They fear and resent gays, ethnic minorities, feminists, immigrants, intellectuals, liberals, peace activists, environmentalists, evolutionary scientists, communists, socialists, labor unions, Muslims, and atheists. They swallow the reactionary line that government is the enemy (not the powerful interests it serves), and they are readily whipped into jingoistic fervor when their leaders go to war against vastly weaker nations.

Yet this society does not produce large numbers of conservative activists. There are no mass demonstrations demanding tax cuts for the rich, more environmental devastation, more wars, . . . or more corporate accumulation of wealth.

Despite the mind-numbing distractions of a mass culture and the propaganda and indoctrination by plutocratic institutions, Americans still have concerns about important issues. Political socialization often produces contradictory and unexpected spin-offs. When opinion makers indoctrinate us with the notion that we are a free and prosperous people, we, in fact, begin to demand the right to be free and prosperous. The old trick of using democratic rhetoric to cloak an undemocratic class order can backfire when people begin to take the rhetoric seriously and translate it into democratic demands.

There are those who love justice more than they love money, those who do not long for more acquisitions but for a better quality of life for all.

Democracy: Form and Content

Americans of all political persuasions profess a dedication to democracy, but they tend to mean different things by the term. . . . *Democracy* refers to a system of governance that represents in both *form* and *content* the interests of the broad populace. Decision makers are to govern for the benefit of the many, not for the advantages of the privileged few. The people hold their representatives accountable by subjecting them to open criticism, the periodic check of elections, and, if necessary, recall and removal from office. Democratic government is limited government, the antithesis of despotic absolutism. . . .

We are taught that capitalism and democracy go together. The free market supposedly creates a pluralistic society of manifold groups, a "civic society" that acts independently of the state and provides the basis for political freedom and prosperity. In fact, many capitalist societies—from Nazi Germany to today's Third World dictatorships—have private-enterprise systems but no political freedom, and plenty of mass destitution. And the more open to free-market capitalism they become, the poorer they seem to get. In such systems, economic freedom means the freedom to exploit the labor of the poor and get endlessly rich. Transnational corporate capitalism is no guarantee of a meaningful political democracy, neither in Third World countries nor in the United States itself.

When it works with any efficacy, democracy is dedicated to protecting the well-being of the many and rolling back the economic oppressions and privileges that serve the few. Democracy seeks to ensure that even those who are not advantaged by wealth or extraordinary talent can earn a decent livelihood. The contradictory nature of "capitalist democracy" is that it professes egalitarian political principles while generating enormous disparities in material well-being and actual political influence.

Some people think that if you are free to say what you like, you are living in a democracy. But freedom of speech is not the sum total of democracy, only one of its necessary conditions. Too often we are free to say what we want, while those of wealth and power are free to do what they want to us regardless of what we say. Democracy is not a seminar but a system of power, like any other form of governance. Freedom of speech, like freedom of assembly and freedom of political organization, is meaningful only if it is heard and if it keeps those in power responsive to those over whom power is exercised.

Nor are elections a sure test of democracy. Some electoral systems are so thoroughly controlled by well-financed like-minded elites or rigged by dishonest officials that they discourage meaningful dialogue and broad participation. Whether a political system is democratic or not depends not only on its procedures but on the actual material benefits and the social justice or injustice it propagates. A government that pursues policies that by design or neglect are so steeply inequitable as to damage the life chances of large sectors of the population is not democratic no matter how many elections it holds.

It should be repeated that when we criticize the lack of democratic substance in the United States, we are not attacking or being disloyal to our nation itself. Quite the contrary. A democratic citizenry should not succumb to state idolatry but should remain critical of the powers that work against the democratic interests of our nation and its people.

NOTES

1. Nader quotes in *Home and Gardens*, August 1991.
2. On the biases of textbooks, see Michael Parenti, *History as Mystery* (City Lights, 1999), 11–21.
3. Mark Maier, "High-School Economics: Corporate Sponsorship and Pro-Market Bias," *Dollars and Sense*, May/June 2002.
4. Jennifer Washburn, *University Inc.: The Corporate Corruption of Higher Education* (Basic Books, 2005); also report in *Chronicle of Higher Education*, 17 November 2008.
5. *San Francisco Chronicle*, 13 November 2005.
6. Stephen Best, Anthony J. Nocella II, and Peter McLaren (eds.), *Academic Repression: Reflections from the Academic Industrial Complex* (AK Press, 2009).
7. Economic Policy Institute, www.epinet.org/pulse; *New York Times*, 24 May 2005; Public Citizen's Health Research Group, *Health Letter*, June 2004.
8. Gallup Polls, http://www.gallup.com/.
9. http://harrisinteractive.com/harris_poll/HarrisPoll.
10. Stephen Kohn, *The History of American Draft Law Violations 1658–1985* (Greenwood Press, 1986).

4 | How Fascism Works
Jason Stanley

Introduction

… Before World War II, Charles Lindbergh typified American heroism with his daring flights, including the first solo transatlantic flight, and his celebration of new technology. He parlayed his fame and heroic stature into a leading role in the America First movement, which opposed America's entrance into the war against Nazi Germany. In 1939, in an essay entitled "Aviation, Geography, and Race," published in that most American of journals, *Reader's Digest*, Lindbergh embraced something close to Nazism for America:

> It is time to turn from our quarrels and to build our White ramparts again. This alliance with foreign races means nothing but death to us. It is our turn to guard our heritage from Mongol and Persian and Moor, before we become engulfed in a limitless foreign sea.[1]

The year 1939 was also when my father, Manfred, then six years old, escaped Nazi Germany, leaving Tempelhof Airport in Berlin in July with his mother, Ilse, after spending months in hiding. He arrived in New York City on August 3, 1939, his ship sailing past the Statue of Liberty on its way to dock. We have a family album from the 1920s and '30s. The last page has six different pictures of the Statue of Liberty gradually coming into view.

The America First movement was the public face of pro-fascist sentiment in the United States at that time.[2] In the twenties and thirties, many Americans shared Lindbergh's views against immigration, especially by non-Europeans. The Immigration Act of 1924 strictly limited immigration into the country, and it was specifically intended to restrict the immigration of both nonwhites and Jews. In 1939, the United States allowed so few refugees through its borders that it is a miracle that my father happened to be among them.

In 2016, Donald Trump revived "America First" as one of his slogans, and from his first week in office, his administration has ceaselessly pursued travel bans on immigration, including refugees, specifically singling out Arab countries. Trump also promised to deport the millions of nonwhite Central and South American undocumented workers in the United States and to end legislation protecting the children they brought with them from deportation. In September 2017, the Trump administration set a cap of forty-five

---

Jason Stanley is a professor of philosophy at Yale University whose books include *How Fascism Works: The Politics of Us and Them*, *How Propaganda Works*, and *Hustle: The Politics of Language* (forthcoming). He also serves on the board of the Prison Policy Initiative, which researches the harm of mass criminalization.

thousand on the number of refugees that will be allowed into the United States in 2018, the lowest number since presidents began placing such limits.

If Trump recalled Lindbergh specifically with "America First," the rest of his campaign also longed for some vague point in history—to "Make America Great Again." But when, exactly, was America great, in the eyes of the Trump campaign? During the nineteenth century, when the United States enslaved its black population? During Jim Crow, when black Americans in the South were prevented from voting? A hint about the decade that was most salient to the Trump campaign emerges from a November 18, 2016, *Hollywood Reporter* interview with Steve Bannon, the then president-elect's chief strategist, in which he remarks about the era to come that "it will be as exciting as the 1930s." In short, the era when the United States had its most sympathy for fascism.

In recent years, multiple countries across the world have been overtaken by a certain kind of far-right nationalism; the list includes Russia, Hungary, Poland, India, Turkey, and the United States. The task of generalizing about such phenomena is always vexing, as the context of each country is always unique. But such generalization is necessary in the current moment. I have chosen the label "fascism" for ultranationalism of some variety (ethnic, religious, cultural), with the nation represented in the person of an authoritarian leader who speaks on its behalf....

My interest in this [work] is in fascist *politics*. Specifically, my interest is in fascist tactics as a mechanism to achieve power. Once those who employ such tactics come to power, the regimes they enact are in large part determined by particular historical conditions. What occurred in Germany was different from what occurred in Italy. Fascist politics does not necessarily lead to an explicitly fascist state, but it is dangerous nonetheless.

Fascist politics includes many distinct strategies: the mythic past, propaganda, anti-intellectualism, unreality, hierarchy, victimhood, law and order, sexual anxiety, appeals to the heartland, and a dismantling of public welfare and unity....

The dangers of fascist politics come from the particular way in which it dehumanizes segments of the population. By excluding these groups, it limits the capacity for empathy among other citizens, leading to the justification of inhumane treatment, from repression of freedom, mass imprisonment, and expulsion to, in extreme cases, mass extermination....

The most telling symptom of fascist politics is division. It aims to separate a population into an "us" and a "them" ... Giving a description of fascist politics involves describing the very specific way that fascist politics distinguishes "us" from "them," appealing to ethnic, religious, or racial distinctions, and using this division to shape ideology and, ultimately, policy. Every mechanism of fascist politics works to create or solidify this distinction.

Fascist politicians justify their ideas by breaking down a common sense of history in creating a mythic past to support their vision for the present. They rewrite the population's shared understanding of reality by twisting the language of ideals through propaganda and promoting anti-intellectualism, attacking universities and educational systems that might challenge their ideas. Eventually, with these techniques, fascist politics creates a state of unreality, in which conspiracy theories and fake news replace reasoned debate.

As the common understanding of reality crumbles, fascist politics makes room for dangerous and false beliefs to take root. First, fascist ideology seeks to naturalize group difference, thereby giving the appearance of natural, scientific support for a hierarchy of human worth. When social rankings and divisions solidify, fear fills in for understanding between groups. Any progress for a minority group stokes feelings of victimhood among the dominant population. Law and order politics has mass appeal, casting "us" as lawful citizens and "them," by contrast, as lawless criminals whose behavior poses an existential threat to the manhood of the nation. Sexual anxiety is also typical of fascist politics as the patriarchal hierarchy is threatened by growing gender equity.

As the fear of "them" grows, "we" come to represent everything virtuous. . . . "We" are hardworking, and have earned our pride of place by struggle and merit. "They" are lazy, surviving off the goods we produce by exploiting the generosity of our welfare systems, or employing corrupt institutions, such as labor unions, meant to separate honest, hardworking citizens from their pay. "We" are makers; "they" are takers.

Many people are not familiar with the ideological structure of fascism, that each mechanism of fascist politics tends to build on others. . . . I have written this [work] in the hope of providing citizens with the critical tools to recognize the difference between legitimate tactics in liberal democratic politics on the one hand, and invidious tactics in fascist politics on the other. . . .

Unreality

When propaganda succeeds at twisting ideals against themselves and universities are undermined and condemned as sources of bias, reality itself is cast into doubt. We can't agree on truth. Fascist politics replaces reasoned debate with fear and anger. When it is successful, its audience is left with a destabilized sense of loss, and a well of mistrust and anger against those who it has been told are responsible for this loss.

Fascist politics exchanges reality for the pronouncements of a single individual, or perhaps a political party. Regular and repeated obvious lying is part of the process by which fascist politics destroys the information space. A fascist leader can replace truth with power, ultimately lying without consequence. By replacing the world with a person, fascist politics makes us unable to assess arguments by a common standard. The fascist politician possesses specific techniques to destroy information spaces and break down reality.

Anyone looking at current U.S. politics, or current Russian politics, or current Polish politics, would immediately note the presence and political potency of *conspiracy theories*.

The task of defining conspiracy theories presents difficult issues. The philosopher Giulia Napolitano has suggested that we should think of conspiracy theories as "aimed" at some out-group, and in the service of some in-group. Conspiracy theories function to denigrate and delegitimize their targets, by connecting them, mainly symbolically, to problematic acts. Conspiracy theories do not function like ordinary information; they are, after all, often so outlandish that they can hardly be expected to be literally believed. Their function is rather to raise general suspicion about the credibility and the decency of their targets. . . .

The 2016 U.S. presidential election was marred by a series of conspiracy theories. These were aimed against several targets, including Hillary Clinton, the Democratic candidate, as well as Muslims and refugees. Perhaps the most bizarre such theory was "Pizzagate." According to those who spread it, leaked emails from John Podesta, Clinton's campaign manager, were said to spell out secret coded messages about the trafficking of young children for sex to Democratic congressmen, conducted from a pizzeria in Washington, DC. The theories were circulated on social media and, given their bizarre nature, achieved surprisingly wide currency. Though it was just one among several bizarre conspiracy theories about Clinton and the Democrats, it received outsized national attention, not just for its extreme oddity but because Edgar Maddison Welch, a man from North Carolina, actually showed up, gun in hand, at the pizzeria to confront its owners and free the supposed sexual slaves. The goal of this conspiracy was to connect its targets, Democrats, to acts of extreme depravity.

The University of Connecticut philosopher Michael Lynch has used the example of "Pizzagate" as evidence for the thesis that conspiracy theories are not intended to be treated as ordinary information. Lynch points out that if one were actually supposed to believe that there was a pizzeria in Washington, D.C., that was trafficking in child sex slaves for Democratic congressmen, it would be entirely rational to act as Edgar Maddison Welch acted. And yet, Welch was roundly *condemned* by those who promulgated the "Pizzagate" conspiracy for his actions. Lynch's point is that the "Pizzagate" conspiracy was not intended to be treated as ordinary information. The function of conspiracy theories is to impugn and malign their targets, but not necessarily by convincing their audience that they are true. In the case of "Pizzagate," the conspiracy theory was intended to remain at the level of innuendo and slander.

Donald Trump came to mainstream political attention by attacking the press for their supposed censorship of the conspiracy theory called "birtherism," the belief that President Obama was born in Kenya and therefore not eligible to be president of the United States. In an interview with CNN on May 29, 2012, Trump railed at Wolf Blitzer and CNN for not covering the topic, because, according to Trump, they were working for Obama. Fox News, in contrast, provided Trump a ready platform to promote his conspiracy theories. President Trump is not an outlier here; conspiracy theories are the calling cards of fascist politics. Conspiracy theories are tools to attack those who would ignore their existence; by not covering them, the media is made to appear biased and ultimately part of the very conspiracy they refuse to cover. ...

Fascist politicians discredit the "liberal media" for censoring discussion of outlandish right-wing conspiracy theories, which suggests mendacious behavior covered up by the veneer of liberal democratic institutions. Conspiracy theories play to the most paranoid elements of society—in the case of the United States, fear of foreign elements and Islam (as in the "birther" theory that President Barack Obama was born a Muslim in Kenya).... The goal of the conspiracies is to cause widespread mistrust and paranoia, justifying drastic measures, such as censoring or shutting down the "liberal" media and imprisoning "enemies of the state." ...

Hannah Arendt, perhaps the twentieth century's greatest theorist of totalitarianism, gave clear warning of the importance of conspiracy theories in antidemocratic politics. In *The Origins of Totalitarianism,* she writes:

> Mysteriousness as such became the first criterion for the choice of topics. . . . The effectiveness of this kind of propaganda demonstrates one of the chief characteristics of modern masses. They do not believe in anything visible, in the reality of their own experience; they do not trust their eyes and ears but only their imaginations, which may be caught by anything that is at once universal and consistent in itself. What convinces masses are not facts, and not even invented facts, but only the consistency of the system of which they are presumably part. Repetition ... is only important because it convinces them of consistency in time.[3]

Because the audience for conspiracy theories readily discount their own experience, it is often unimportant that the conspiracy theories are demonstrably false. Texas House Bill 45, the "American Laws for American Courts" bill signed into law by Texas governor Greg Abbott in June 2017, is intended to block Muslims from bringing Sharia law into the state. That Muslims are trying to sneakily transform Texas into an Islamic republic is deeply improbable—as is the hypothesis that President Obama is a secret Muslim pretending to be a Christian in order to overthrow the U.S. government. These conspiracy theories are effective nevertheless because they provide simple explanations for otherwise irrational emotions, such as resentment or xenophobic fear in the face of perceived threats. The idea that President Obama is secretly a Muslim pretending to be a Christian in order to overthrow the U.S. government makes rational sense of the irrational feeling of threat many white people had upon his ascension to the presidency. That Muslims are trying to sneak Sharia law into Texas makes rational sense of the feeling of fear caused by a combination of religious nationalists spreading anti-Muslim xenophobia, and ISIS propaganda videos of terrorist acts committed on far-off shores. Once a public accepts the comfort of conspiracy thinking as an explanation for irrational fears and resentments, its members will cease to be guided by reason in political deliberation.

Spreading wild conspiracy theories benefits fascist movements. And yet how can this be, if reason always wins out in the public square of liberal democracy? Shouldn't liberal democracy promote a full airing of all possibilities, even false and bizarre ones, because the truth will eventually prevail in the marketplace of ideas? ...

... But the notion of a "marketplace of ideas," like that of a free market generally, is predicated on a Utopian conception of consumers. In the case of the metaphor of the marketplace of ideas, the Utopian assumption is that conversation works by exchange of reasons, with one party offering its reasons, which are then countered by the reasons of an opponent, until the truth ultimately emerges. But conversation is not just used to communicate information. Conversation is also used to shut out perspectives, raise fears, and heighten prejudice. The philosopher Ernst Cassirer writes in 1946, remarking on the changes wrought by fascist politics on the German language:

> If we study our modern political myths and the use that has been made of them we find in them, to our great surprise, not only a transvaluation of all our ethical values but also a transformation of human speech. . . . New words have been coined, and even the old ones are used in a new sense; they have undergone a deep change of meaning. This change of meaning

depends upon the fact that these words which formerly were used in a descriptive, logical, or semantic sense are now used as magic words that are destined to produce certain effects and to stir up certain emotions. Our ordinary words are charged with meanings; but these new-fangled words are charged with feelings and violent passions.[4]

The argument for the "marketplace of ideas" presupposes that words are used only in their "descriptive, logical, or semantic sense." But in politics, and most vividly in fascist politics, language is not used simply, or even chiefly, to convey information but to elicit emotion.

The argument from the "marketplace of ideas" model for free speech works only if the underlying disposition of the society is to accept the force of reason over the power of irrational resentments and prejudice. If the society is divided, however, then a demagogic politician can exploit the division by using language to sow fear, accentuate prejudice, and call for revenge against members of hated groups. Attempting to counter such rhetoric with reason is akin to using a pamphlet against a pistol....

...The effect of ... myriad conspiracy-theory-producing websites across the world, including in the United States, has been to destabilize the kind of shared reality that is in fact required for democratic contestation....

Disagreement requires a shared set of presuppositions about the world. Even dueling, requires agreement about the rules. You and I might disagree about whether President Obama's healthcare plan was good policy. But if you suspect that President Obama was an undercover Muslim spy seeking to destroy the United States, and I do not, our discussion will not be productive. We will not be talking about the costs and benefits of Obama's health policy, but rather about whether any of his policies mask a devious antidemocratic agenda.

... Allowing every opinion into the public sphere and giving it serious time for consideration, far from resulting in a process that is conducive to knowledge formation via deliberation, destroys its very possibility. Responsible media in a liberal democracy must, in the face of this threat, try to report the truth, and resist the temptation to report on every possible theory, no matter how fantastical, as long as someone advances it.

What happens when conspiracy theories become the coin of politics, and mainstream media and educational institutions are discredited, is that citizens no longer have a common reality that can serve as background for democratic deliberation. In such a situation, citizens have no choice but to look for markers to follow other than truth or reliability. What happens in such cases, as we see across the world, is that citizens look to politics for tribal identifications, for addressing personal grievances, and for entertainment. When news becomes sports, the strongman achieves a certain measure of popularity. Fascist politics transforms the news from a conduit of information and reasoned debate into a spectacle with the strongman as the star.

Fascist politics, as we have seen, seeks to undermine trust in the press and universities. But the information sphere of a healthy democratic society does not include just democratic institutions. Spreading general suspicion and doubt undermines the bonds of mutual respect between fellow citizens, leaving them with deep wells of mistrust not just toward institutions but also toward one another. Fascist politics seeks to destroy the relations of mutual respect between citizens that are the foundation of a healthy liberal democracy, replacing them ultimately with trust in one figure alone the leader. When fascist politics is at its most successful, the leader is regarded by the followers as singularly trustworthy.

In the 2016 U.S. presidential election, Donald Trump repeatedly and openly lied, and openly flouted long-sacrosanct liberal norms. The U.S. mainstream media dutifully reported his many lies. His opponent, Hillary Clinton, followed liberal norms of equal respect; her one violation of these norms, which occurred when she called some of the supporters of her opponent "deplorables," was endlessly thrown back in her face. And yet again and again, Americans found Trump to be the more authentic candidate. By giving voice to shocking sentiments that were presumed to be unsuitable for public discourse, Trump was taken to be *speaking his mind*. This is how, by exhibiting classic demagogic behavior, a politician can come to be seen as the more authentic candidate, even when he is manifestly dishonest.

The possibility of this kind of politics arises under certain conditions in a democracy.[5] In another kind of propagandists twisted meaning, politicians can convey the message that they are the representative of the common good by explicitly attacking the common good. To see how this perplexing situation is possible, one can look at how in the U.S. political system these conditions have arisen in the recent past.

In Federalist Paper No. 10, James Madison argued that the United States had to take the form of a representative democracy and seek to elect leaders who best represented the values of democracy. An election campaign is supposed to present candidates seeking to show that they have the common interests of all citizens at heart. Two factors have eroded the protections that representative democracy is supposed to provide. First, candidates must raise huge sums to run for office (ever more so since the 2010 Citizens United decision by the U.S. Supreme Court). As a result, they represent the interests of their large donors. However, because it is a democracy, they must also try to make the case that they represent the common interest. They must pretend that the best interests of the multinational corporations that fund their campaigns are also the common interest.

Second, some voters do not share democratic values, and politicians must appeal to them as well. When large inequalities exist, the problem is aggravated. Some voters are simply more attracted to a system that favors their own particular religion, race, gender, or birth position. The resentment that flows from unmet expectations can be redirected against minority groups seen as not sharing dominant traditions; goods that go to them are represented by demagogic politicians, in a zero-sum way, as taking goods away from majority groups. Some voters see such groups, rather than the behavior of economic elites, as responsible for their unmet expectations. Candidates must attract these voters while appearing not to flout democratic values. As a result, many politicians use coded language to exploit resentment, as in the Republican Party's "Southern strategy," in order to avoid the charge of excluding the perspectives of opposing groups. As the infamous Republican political strategist Lee Atwater … explained that racist intent had to be made less overt over time … :

> By 1968 you can't say "nigger"—that hurts you, backfires. So you say stuff like, uh, forced busing, states' rights, and all that stuff, and you're getting so abstract. Now, you're talking

about cutting taxes, and all these things you're talking about are totally economic things and a byproduct of them is, blacks get hurt worse than whites. . . .[6]

. . .

Ever since Plato and Aristotle wrote on the topic, political theorists have known that democracy cannot flourish on soil poisoned by inequality. It is not merely that the resentments bred by such divisions are tempting targets for a demagogue. The more important point is that dramatic inequality poses a mortal danger to the shared reality required for a healthy liberal democracy. Those who benefit from inequalities are often burdened by certain illusions that prevent them from recognizing the contingency of their privilege. When inequalities grow particularly stark, these illusions tend to metastasize. What dictator, king, or emperor has not suspected that he was chosen by the gods for his role? What colonial power has not entertained delusions of its ethnic superiority, or the superiority of its religion, culture, and way of life, superiority that supposedly justifies its imperial expansions and conquests? In the antebellum American South, whites believed that slavery was a great gift to those who were enslaved. The harshness of Southern planters to enslaved persons who sought to flee or rebel was in no small part due to their conviction that such behavior revealed lack of gratitude.

Extreme economic inequality is toxic to liberal democracy because it breeds delusions that mask reality, undermining the possibility of joint deliberation to solve society's divisions. Those who benefit from large inequalities are inclined to believe that they have earned their privilege, a delusion that prevents them from seeing reality as it is. Even those who demonstrably do not benefit from hierarchies can be made to believe that they do; hence the use of racism to ensnare poor white citizens in the United States into supporting tax cuts for extravagantly wealthy whites who happen to share their skin color.

Liberal equality means that those with different levels of power and wealth nevertheless are regarded as having equal worth. Liberal equality is, by definition, meant to be compatible with economic inequality. And yet, when economic inequality is sufficiently extreme, the myths that are required to sustain it are bound to threaten liberal equality as well.

The myths that arise under conditions of dramatic material inequality legitimize ignoring the proper common referee for public discourse, which is the world. To completely destroy reality, fascist politics replaces the liberal ideal of equality with its opposite: hierarchy.

NOTES

1. Charles Lindbergh, "Aviation, Geography and Race," *Reader's Digest*, Nov. 1939, 64–67.
2. See Richard Steigmann-Gall, "Star-spangled Fascism: American Interwar Political Extremism in Comparative Perspective," *Social History*, 42:1 (2017): 87–104.
3. Hannah Arendt, *The Origins of Totalitarianism* (New York: Harcourt, Brace, 1973). 351.
4. Ernst Cassirer, "The Technique of the Modern Political Myths," chapter 18 of *The Myth of the State* (New Haven: Yale University Press, 1946).
5. See Oliver Hahl, Minjae Kim, and Ezra Zuckerman, "The Authentic Appeal of the Lying Demagogue," *American Sociological Review*, February 2018.
6. https://www.thenation.com/article/exclusive-lee-atwaters-infamous-1981-interview-southern-strategy/.

5 Understanding Antisemitism

Jews For Racial & Economic Justice

Originating in European Christianity, antisemitism is the form of ideological oppression that targets Jews. In Europe and the United States, it has functioned to protect the prevailing economic system and the almost exclusively Christian ruling class by diverting blame for hardship onto Jews. Like all oppressions, it has deep historical roots and uses exploitation, marginalization, discrimination and violence as its tools. Like all oppressions, the ideology contains elements of dehumanization and degradation via lies and stereotypes about Jews, as well as a mythology. The myth changes and adapts to different times and places, but fundamentally it says that Jews are to blame for society's problems.

. . .

Engaging in a pattern of behavior that should feel familiar to anyone listening to today's right-wing rhetoric about immigration and refugees, Christian nobility from antiquity on through the Renaissance curried favor with their populations by placing restrictions on economic opportunities for Jews, and sometimes isolating them physically by confining them to what came to be called ghettos.[1,2] Prohibited from owning land or joining tradesmen's guilds, Jews were restricted to jobs that Christians found distasteful or were prohibited by the Church, such as money-lending and tax collecting.[3] (There is recent scholarship that contradicts this sequence of events, and suggests that Jews arrived in the cities of early Europe armed with very high literacy rates for the era, seeking better jobs, which means that antisemitic restrictions on Jews were a form of backlash and protectionism.[4]) Regardless of the chicken-and-egg nature of this debate, this era saw the genesis of many anti-Jewish myths.[5] Laws that funneled Jews into certain professions such as money lending could only serve to reinforce these stereotypes. . . . After centuries of church indoctrination claiming that Jews rejected Jesus, had killed the son of God, and were agents of the devil, it was easy for European Christians to believe that Jews were the cause of their problems. Whether it was spreading the Black Plague or hoarding a community's wealth, they were an ideal group to scapegoat. This meant that attention and anger was diverted away from the people who levied the taxes and toward the "strange," "greedy" Jews tasked with collecting them.

Once this mythology was established, it followed Jews throughout Europe, and was exported to the Middle East, North Africa, and the Americas through colonialism and imperial conquest.

Jews For Racial & Economic Justice (JFREJ) pursues racial and economic justice in New York City. JFREJ advocates for a sustainable world with an equitable distribution of economic and cultural resources and political power.

Before European colonialism, Jews in the Middle East and North Africa (MENA), Central Asia, and the Balkans, lived as one religious minority among many, sometimes socially restricted or targeted for violence as non-Muslims, but most of the time not singled out for persecution or racialized in the way European Jews were. . . . Over centuries of coexistence in many Islamic territories, there were indeed sporadic attacks, forced conversions and mass killings of Jews. But the same was true for Christians and other non-Muslim minorities. The key distinction is that there was no specifically anti-Jewish ideology that bore any resemblance to European antisemitism, and for long stretches of time, Jews lived safely alongside their Muslim neighbors. This history disproves narratives that assert universal persecution as the permanent condition of Jews in the world, rather than describing antisemitism as a historically specific product of European society that can also be interrupted. That's why the histories of Mizrahi and Sephardi Jews throw a beautiful wrench into attempts (by the right and sometimes the left) to manipulate Jewish fear by universalizing Ashkenazi historical trauma.[*] This erasure of Mizrahi and Sephardi history fuels Islamophobia by spreading an inaccurate story about Jewish experiences outside of Europe. . . .

In What Ways Is Antisemitism Different Than Other Oppressions Such As Anti-Black Racism?

Many oppressions, such as anti-Black racism in the United States, could be said to require a fixed hierarchy or binary values system. Whites are supreme; Blacks are on the bottom. Men are born to rule; women are meant to be obedient. There are variations and nuances—putting women on pedestals of virtue, etc.—but we understand these to be ultimately in service of the original proposition.

By contrast, antisemitism is often described as "cyclical." The Jewish experience in Europe has been characterized as cycling between periods of Jewish stability and even success, only to be followed by periods of intense anti-Jewish sentiment and violence. This is directly related to the stereotypes and myths about Jews, which push the idea that Jews are secretly very powerful—that they control the economy of a town, a country or even the world and thus that they are ruining the "true" character of these places. . . . But if Jews were truly as collectively powerful as the antisemitic myths say—if they actually controlled the societies in which they lived throughout European history—they would have been able to protect themselves from anti-Jewish violence and bigotry. The truth is that they have historically been small minorities in almost every country they have migrated to, without the ability to control their own destinies, let alone those of the entire nation. When the workers in these countries got angry about their exploitation, the most accessible targets were often Jews, rather than the elite political and economic actors who actually had power over the system and who were almost exclusively Christian. Antisemitism—ever

---

[*]Mizrahim are Jews of the Middle East and North Africa and their descendants; Sephardim are Jews of Spain and Portugal and their descendants; Ashkenazim are Jews of Germany, France, and Eastern Europe and their descendants.

present in European culture—rises and becomes institutionalized; then violence; purges and forced migration; resettlement. Repeat.

. . .

At different times and places in history, the amount of success that Jews were allowed has varied, and at any given time many Jews remained poor or working-class. But the result of anti-Jewish oppression has remained consistent: when people's rage is misdirected toward Jews, larger systems of economic injustice are shielded from scrutiny or even enhanced. European capitalism developed hand-in-hand with antisemitism, and as such the oppression of Jews has been a systemic feature in the functioning of capitalism for centuries.

Throughout Europe and in the U.S., when times are good, antisemitism may seem like nothing more than a set of stereotypes and attitudes about Jews—a nuisance. . . . But when times got tough and non-Jewish poor and working-class people got angry about their own oppression, visible, prospering Jews have often been lifted up as the cause of societal problems, and all Jews (wealthy or not) have been blamed. During such times, Jews are attacked in gossip and graffiti, vilified in the media, physically assaulted, collectively punished, pushed out of communities or whole countries, and sometimes killed. Antisemitism that had been simmering below the surface has erupted into institutional exclusion and systemic violence.

Nazi Germany is a clear example of this dynamic, as well as the most extreme act of antisemitic violence in world history. Prior to Hitler's rise to power, Jews were, on the whole, an assimilated and comfortable minority in Germany.[6] . . . However, after World War I, most Germans experienced deep economic hardship from the war and the economic reparations demanded by the victors. As the German economy worsened and sections of the country and its colonies were redistributed to other countries, Germans became outraged at what they saw as injustice against them. Meanwhile, Germany was also experiencing a large wave of Jewish immigration as refugees fled Eastern Europe. Many of these Jews were not only new immigrants, but were associated with (or accused of being associated with) communist movements in their home countries.[7] After the worldwide depression began in 1929, this outrage needed an outlet, and Adolf Hitler was able to rise to power, stoking a tide of hatred toward Jews, Romani, queer people and others—those already considered "outsiders" or "pollutants" in popular imagination.[8] Much as Donald Trump weds his appeals to racism and xenophobia with a pro-white working-class, nationalist narrative, Hitler combined his bigotry with populist, pro-working-class policies and intensely pro-German nationalist sentiment. . . . In his rise to power, Hitler was able to stoke Germany's collective hatred of Jews and place the blame for Germany's failings on them, which expanded public support for discriminatory policies and practices, and ultimately led to widespread violence, systematic expunging and murders, and the attempted genocide of the Jewish people. The Nazis exterminated 6 million Jews in death camps and mass murders, about ⅔ of the European Jewish population. The global Jewish population is only just now, in 2017, approaching its pre-Holocaust numbers. There were also many non-Jewish victims of Nazism including about 1.8 million Polish people, 250,000–270,000 people with disabilities, 90,000–220,000 Romani, and 5,000–15,000 queer people.[9] As the famous Martin Niemöller poem* makes clear, the scapegoating of one group lays the groundwork for the targeting of the next and the next. The acceptability of antisemitism ultimately leaves every marginalized group vulnerable.

In the words of Aurora Levins Morales:

> ". . . The oppression of Jews is a conjuring trick, a pressure valve, a shunt that redirects the rage of working people away from the 1%, a hidden mechanism, a set up that works through misdirection, that uses privilege to hide the gears. . . ."

. . .

Examples of These False Narratives Today

The false association of Jews with money does not preclude a legitimate critique of capital or capitalists—banks, the real estate industry, or other financial actors. But all too often, people fail to separate the two. We see this expressed subtly when people in labor and housing justice coalitions say "my Jewish landlord" (especially if the landlords are visibly observant Jews) or "my Jewish employer." They may not be explicitly anti-Jewish, but the fact that they mentioned "Jewishness" at all is a sign of how anti-Jewish sentiment is insidiously connected to wealth, greed, and control in the American consciousness. (How many times have you heard someone complain about a Presbyterian landlord or a Lutheran employer?) Jews who are slumlords, bad bosses, and racist bureaucrats aren't that way because they're Jewish. Like people from every ethnic group, they are participating in a system of racialized capitalist exploitation. In order for our movements to build effective anti-racist, working-class-based coalitions and actions, Jews who oppress must be challenged because of their roles in that system, not because of their Jewishness.

The slippage from economic misery to blaming the Jews is an easy one to make, given that these ideas about Jews (dirty, greedy, conspiratorial) pervade Western culture. . . .

*First they came for the Communists
And I did not speak out
Because I was not a Communist

Then they came for the Socialists
And I did not speak out
Because I was not a Socialist

Then they came for the trade unionists
And I did not speak out
Because I was not a trade unionist

Then they came for the Jews
And I did not speak out
Because I was not a Jew

Then they came for me
And there was no one left
To speak out for me

[A]ntisemitism frames the function[ing] of capitalism as a problem of human or communal mischief rather than as intrinsic to capitalism itself. Capitalism isn't oppressive because Jews are ruining it; capitalism is oppressive because capitalism is oppressive. . . .

On the campaign trail, Donald Trump occasionally offered legitimate criticisms of the role of offshoring and Wall Street speculation. But his final campaign ad, which featured Jewish financiers (George Soros, Lloyd Blankfein) and Federal Reserve Chairperson Janet Yellen (also Jewish), suggests . . . antisemitic conspiracy [theory] instead of actual economic critique. This is nefarious not only because it leads to violence, such as recent threats against Jewish community centers and other Jewish institutions, but because it provides simplistic and facile answers (Jewish control! Jewish greed!) to a complicated, structural set of problems that are not the fault of any one religious group.

. . .

Is Criticism of Israel Antisemitic?

Criticisms of Israel and Zionism are not inherently or inevitably anti-Jewish. All states, movements and ideologies should be scrutinized, and all forms of injustice denounced. It is not anti-Jewish to denounce oppressive acts committed by Jews. . . .

Leaders of the Jewish state and the Jewish leaders and institutions that support them worldwide must be held accountable for their oppression of Palestinians and the continued occupation of Palestinian land. However, we must not become confused about the nature, cause, or, sadly, the sheer ordinariness of Israeli state violence and the pain visited upon Palestinians. It does not in any way minimize the suffering of Palestinians to say that their oppression is comparable to many other terrible human rights disasters being committed worldwide by non-Jews. There is nothing about the Jewishness of Israeli leaders that makes their rockets more deadly or their walls more brutal—it is simply militaristic nationalism. . . . We must criticize Jews who support the oppression of Palestinians on the same terms and by the same standards that we hold for all oppressors the world over—we are enraged because of what they do, not by who they are.

It is also important to understand that for many Jews past and present, Zionism has not been seen as a colonialist project but as the right for Jews to have a physical place of self-determined safety. For many Jews, the State of Israel has felt like the only thing standing between them and another Holocaust. This fear, rooted in very recent historical trauma, is why grounded and valid protests against Israeli government policy or Zionism are sometimes heard by Jews as threats to the safety of the Jewish people as a whole. Actual violence against Jews or other antisemitic acts in the U.S., Europe, the Middle East, and around the globe only compound these fears and further a tragic dynamic.

The political right in the United States and Israel often trades on this fear and uses false or inflated charges of antisemitism to delegitimize pro-Palestinian activism and undermine attempts to hold Israel accountable for its actions. . . . And while critiquing Israel and Zionism is not inherently or inevitably anti-Jewish, it *is* possible for Jews and non-Jews alike to attack Zionism or Israel with language that echoes anti-Jewish tropes or exceptionalizes Israeli actions in a way that furthers antisemitism. For example, Jew-hater,

Holocaust-denier and Ku Klux Klan leader David Duke has been trying to popularize the term "Zio" (short for Zionist) as a stand-in for Jew—a transparently disingenuous way to attack Jews without being accused of antisemitism.

Anti-Jewish and Anti-Muslim Oppression Are Closely Related

Antisemitism and Islamophobia are not only entangled, but deeply rooted in the same systems of white supremacy and Christian hegemony that have also driven ongoing genocide against indigenous people, and bigotry toward non-Christians from other parts of the world.

The history of Spain during the 14th and 15th centuries is one of the most clear examples of this shared past. Before there were modern-day conceptions of race, there were theories about racial inferiority based on religion—the concept of *limpieza de sangre*—specifically based on who was not Christian. Both Jews and Muslims were racialized in strikingly similar ways under this framework: as separate races than Christians, as biological pollutants, as perpetually suspect religious infidels, even after conversion. The last Moorish stronghold in Granada fell to the Catholic monarchs in 1492, consolidating what would become Spain under one Christian faith. . . .

It is significant that the Spanish Inquisition was launched by the same Christian rulers, in the same place and the same year that Columbus set sail with the blessings of the Spanish crown to discover "India." When he and his *conquistadores* "discovered" the "New World," they referred to indigenous sites of worship as "mosques" and "synagogues," and ultimately used the same tactics for conversion, torture, and genocide on native peoples that they practiced on Muslims and Jews in Catholic Spain. . . .

What Is the Relationship Between Antisemitism and White Supremacy Today?

We must be careful to draw a distinction between white supremacists—including neo-Nazis and white nationalists—and the system of white supremacy (especially as it developed in the United States). Both draw on the same ideological roots, but the former describes—in broad terms—a group of people who are preoccupied with particular aspects of that ideology, and with either maintaining it through violence and the threat of violence, or overthrowing the current multicultural order in favor of a white ethnostate. The latter is the air we breathe, the water we swim in—the prerequisite soil for American capitalism to flower.

The assimilation of different groups of European immigrants (such as the Irish and Italians) into whiteness has been a core component of maintaining and extending white supremacy in this country since its founding.[10,11] In the U.S., Jews long had privilege in the racial hierarchy over Black people and Native peoples. For example, in the 1705 Virginia Slave Codes, Jews and Muslims, though prohibited from having Christian servants, could own Native and African descendent slaves.[12] But they were still in a fluid, shifting, non-white category at many times and places during the first 150 years of American history. This clearly changed in the second half of the 20th century as light-skinned Jews got the all-access pass to whiteness, and American institutions relaxed rules and behaviors that excluded Jews.* Jews with white skin privilege took advantage of their new freedoms and access, and in the process, accepted and participated in the white supremacy–based racial hierarchy of U.S. society and culture.

Jews of color have not, of course, had access to the same white privilege. . . .

. . .

Though they may currently be thoroughly engaged with white supremacy culture, white Jews are not immune from the antisemitic agendas of white supremacists. In the U.S. today, antisemitism is central to the ideology of the neo-Nazi and white nationalist movements. As Eric K. Ward documents in his powerful essay, "Skin in the Game: How Antisemitism Animates White Nationalism," "At the bedrock of the [white nationalist] movement is an explicit claim that Jews are a race of their own, and that their ostensible position as White folks in the U.S. represents the greatest trick the devil ever played."[13] As such, antisemitism also interacts with racism in complex ways.

. . .

. . . As long as white Jews remain tacitly invested in white supremacy—though it may benefit them in the short term—they leave in place the ideological roots necessary for the re-emergence of violent antisemitism in the future. And if white Jews remain complicit in white supremacy then like all white people they will be forever compelled to seek safety through separateness and self-interest—poisonous ideas which must be perpetually defended by walls, guns and badges both at home and abroad.

It is critical to make clear that as long as Jews have been in this country many have struggled against white supremacy and for collective liberation. Jewish anti-racist activists have backed movements, organized and campaigned, and risked and given their lives fighting racism. . . . For Jews and non-Jews engaged in this work today, the resurgence of white supremacist groups is a powerful opportunity to find new ways forward and forge new relationships born out of mutual interest and deeply shared values. . . .

NOTES

1. Cahnman, Werner J. "Socio-Economic Causes of Antisemitism." *Social Problems*, vol. 5, no. 1, 1957, pp. 21–29. JSTOR, www.jstor.org/stable/798945.
2. https://www.myjewishlearning.com/article/jewish-ghettos-of-europe/.
3. United States Holocaust Memorial Museum. "Antisemitism in History: The Early Modern Era, 1300–1800." *Holocaust Encyclopedia*. https://www.ushmm.org/wlc/en/article. php?ModuleId=10007172. Accessed on 10/30/2017.
4. Botticini, Maristella, and Zvi Eckstein, *The Chosen Few: How Education Shaped Jewish History, 70–1492*. Princeton University Press, 2012. JSTOR, www.jstor.org/stable/j.ctt7rv92.

*For a discussion of this change in attitudes, see "How Jews Became White Folks, and What That Says About Race in America," by Karen Brodkin (Selection 4 in Part I of this volume).

5. https://academic.oup.com/ahr/article/119/1/229/20497/Maristella-Botticini-and-Zvi-Eckstein-The-Chosen.
6. Hertz, Deborah, *How Jews Became Germans: The History of Conversion and Assimilation in Berlin*. New Haven, London, Yale University Press, 2007. JSTOR, www.jstor.org/stable/j.ctt5vktjn.
7. http://ieg-ego.eu/en/threads/europe-on-the-road/jewish-migration#19141948ExpulsionShoahandthefoundationofIsrael.
8. https://www.ushmm.org/wlc/en/article.php?ModuleId=10008222.
9. https://www.ushmm.org/wlc/en/article.php?ModuleId=10008193.
10. Ignatiev, Noel, *How the Irish Became White*, Routledge Classics, 2008.
11. Guglielmo, Thomas, "No Color Barrier: Italians, Race, and Power in the United States," in *Are Italians White? How Race Is Made in America*, edited by Jennifer Guglielmo and Salvatore Salerno, Routledge 2003.
12. https://www.encyclopediavirginia.org/_An_act_concerning_Servants_and_Slaves_1705.
13. Ward, Eric K., "Skin in the Game: How Antisemitism Animates White Nationalism," *The Public Eye*, June 29, 2017, retrieved from http://www.politicalresearch.org/2017/06/29/skin-in-the-game-how-antisemitism-animates-white-nationalism/#sthash.QspASGyl.bUQpZ9Sy.dpbs.

6 | Cowboys and Indians: Toys of Genocide, Icons of American Colonialism

Michael Yellow Bird

Colonialism is the invasion, subjugation, and occupation of one people by another. In *Postcolonialism: An Historical Introduction* (2001), Robert J. C. Young concludes that the United States of America, the world's last remaining significant colonial power, continues to dominate external territories without the consent of the indigenous inhabitants.[1] However, one does not have to go abroad to analyze the practice of American colonialism since the exploitation and control of Indigenous Peoples[2] in the United States continues unabated. This essay examines cowboys and Indians as part of the colonial canon asserting white supremacy and Indigenous inferiority. I begin by telling how my encounter with a bag of toy cowboys and Indians reminded me that Indigenous Peoples face the humiliation of American colonialism on a daily basis. I next recount how a master cowboys and Indians narrative was used to support and maintain the oppression of people in the tribal community where I was raised. I end with a discussion concerning the importance of decolonizing cowboys and Indians.

Toys of Genocide

It seems I am constantly offended by the colonial representations and words used to describe (or more accurately subjugate) Indigenous Peoples in the United States. Images such as big-nosed Indian sports team mascots and words like "redskins" and "squaw" quickly come to mind. Cowboys and Indians have, for me, come to symbolize America's past and present infatuation with colonization and genocide.

For the past year, I have been accepting invitations from an Indigenous colleague and her family to come to their place to visit and have dinner, go hiking, watch cult videos, celebrate birthdays and holidays, and meet relatives from out of town. . . . Sometimes we discuss global or tribal politics or the environmental degradation of Mother Earth. Other times we talk about our responsibility as First Nations intellectuals and the microassaults we experience from everyday colonial society or about our teaching and research in the academy and the effects that resistant students and colleagues have on our

Michael Yellow Bird is a citizen of the Three Affiliated Tribes (Mandan, Hidatsa, and Arikara). He is a professor and the director of the Tribal Indigenous Studies program at North Dakota State University.

Originally published in *Wicazo Sa Review*, 19, no. 2, 2004. Copyright © 2004 by University of Minnesota Press. Used with permission.

attempts to decolonize their thinking and our academic disciplines. Inevitably, our conversation always turns to how American colonialism has damaged our reservation communities: alcoholism, poverty, poor health, internalized hatred, social factionalism, and the brain drain (the exodus of our most talented tribal members from our communities due to the lack of opportunity or challenge, being from the wrong family, or jealousy). . . .

A couple of weeks ago, on my way over for my ritual dinner and visit, I stopped to get the ice cream. Remembering the children's delight when they received their toys at Christmas, I first went in search of a present for each. I walked down the toy aisle until I found the Matchbox car section where I picked out one for each of the two boys, and then carefully sidestepped my way farther down the aisle looking for an appropriate gift for the daughter. I stopped at the bubbles section and picked out the largest bottle, which was on the highest shelf. Pleased with my selections, I turned toward the freezers of ice cream and came face-to-face with several near-identical plastic bags full of little red toy Indians and blue cowboys. I was momentarily stunned as I gazed at this nauseating display of Americana. However, a panoply of interactions between the receptors and neuropeptides in my gut and brain caused me to smile with delight because I had been talking about these little genocidal toys just a few weeks earlier with students in my Diversity and Oppression class. After explaining to them my most "neutral" scholarly disdain for these toys, I attempted to put these seemingly benign little figures into a larger cultural context that I thought might help students see more precisely what I was attempting to convey. You might call it a teaching moment. Often, I find it is effective to help students understand the oppression of Indigenous Peoples by paralleling our situation with that of other more well-known groups of color.

I said, "Imagine if children could also buy bags of little toy African-American slaves and their white slave masters, or Jewish holocaust prisoners and their SS Nazi guards, or undocumented Mexicans and their INS border patrol guards." I paused a moment for greater effect. "Imagine if the African-American set included little whips and ropes so the white slave masters could flog the slaves that were lazy and lynch those who defied them. Imagine if the border guards in the Mexican toy set came with little nightsticks to beat the illegal aliens, infrared scopes on their rifles to shoot them at night, and trucks to load up those they caught." I continued, "Imagine if the Jewish and Nazi toys included little barbed-wire prison camps and toy trains to load up and take the prisoners to the toy gas chambers or incinerators, batteries not included." When I finished I asked for feedback on what I thought was a most brilliant exemplar and repartee to American colonialism. To my dismay no one answered or showed any emotion. Students seemed paralyzed. I waited as they remained fixed and dilated giving me "the thousand-yard stare." Their lack of response caused me to wonder if it were possible to create permanent disconnect between receptors and neuropeptides in people by sharing such toxic images and words.

I set down the toy cars and bubbles and grabbed one of the bags of cowboys and Indians and carefully tilted it toward me to read the front of the package. As I read, I pulled the bag from the small metal display rod so I could see what the little figures were wearing and the weapons they were brandishing: cowboy hats and fully feathered war bonnets; six-guns and rifles, bows and arrows. These guys were ready for battle. I turned over the bag, interested to read who manufactured them (Magic) and where they were made (China), since half the toys sold in the United States (about $20 billion worth in 2001) *are* made in China under brutal sweatshop conditions made possible by the avarice or, in economic terms, the "bottom line" of several different prominent American toy companies. As I gazed at the figures, I thought about all those young Chinese women forced to work in these American toy factories for seventeen cents an hour, sixteen hours a day, seven days a week, for months at a time; workers who spend all day in 104-degree room temperatures around machines that cause hearing loss and chemicals that make them sick and faint on the job; workers who agonizingly perform the same job operation three thousand times a day and work an overtime schedule that leaves them with as little as two or three hours of sleep per night. Workers who are worn out and used up by the time they reach age thirty to thirty-five and are quickly removed and replaced by a constant stream of younger workers.[3] I wondered how many young Chinese women have died or been poisoned by breathing in the toxic chemicals in molten plastic while they poured the red liquid to make the Indians and the blue to make the cowboys; all this so American kids can practice killing Indians.

I decided to buy the cowboys and Indians and take them to my class for a show-and-tell session, thinking I would let my students play with them and then discuss what malevolent tendencies came alive in their play. I also thought that discussing the connection between these little genocidal toys and the exploitation of Chinese women by American multinational toy companies would be interesting, especially if I were able to input my theory that a reason these figures are tolerated is due to the subconscious demands of white American supremacy over Indigenous Peoples. I walked confidently to the checkout stand, but as I got closer I began to psychologically deflate, remembering that I am closely related to those little red guys in the bag while the white cashiers, despite their lack of cowboy hats, dirty faces, boots, and six-guns, are relatives of those little blue guys: the ones who killed my kind. I placed the ice cream down first and threw all the toys together hoping that the cowboys and Indians wouldn't draw too much attention from the cashier. Everything totaled twelve dollars. Twelve dollars! I uttered an inaudible ouch as the cashier cowboy quickly colonized the portion of my economic livelihood I earned through my decolonization work with non-Indigenous university students.

I mistakenly pulled out a one-dollar bill from my wallet, thinking it was a twenty. The cashier stared at me as I put it back, but not before I looked at the picture of George Washington, remembering that cowboys call this guy one of the founding fathers of the United States while the Seneca called him "Caunotaucarius" (the town destroyer). I recalled a conversation with a Seneca brother who informed me that the father of this country sent American troops through his people's territory burning down villages, destroying all crops and stored foodstuffs, killing many, and leaving the rest to starve through the bitter winter.

I pulled out a five and searched for another and a couple of ones with no luck. Ah yes, Abraham Lincoln, the great emancipator pictured on the five-dollar bill, "freed" black slaves and gave orders to hang thirty-eight Dakotas following the so-called Dakota Uprising in Minnesota. This hanging was called the "greatest mass execution in U.S. history," and, according to the *Guinness Book of Records*, lynching these Dakotas made "Old Honest Abe" the record holder for the largest hanging of people from one gallows.[4] During Lincoln's presidency, the Dakota were mistreated, cheated, and abused by white settlers, Indian agents, and traders who had pushed them off their lands, leaving them only one-tenth of their original territory. They were starving because the wild game was gone from their hunting grounds, which were claimed by white settlers. They were also deceived in the treaties that they made with the United States and did not get annuities and food promised to them. When Dakota chief Little Crow requested food from Indian agent Thomas Calbraith for his starving people, he was condescendingly told by trader Andrew Myrick that they should "eat grass or their own dung."[5]

I put back the five and finally pulled out a twenty and gave it to the cashier who put it in the register while she counted my change. As I waited, I remembered that Andrew Jackson, the brave Indian fighter on the twenty-dollar bill, was called the "devil" by the Creek Nation because of his wanton slaughter of unarmed Creeks. "At the Battle of Horse Shoe Bend, Jackson and his troops surrounded eight hundred Creeks and killed almost all of them, including women and children. Afterward his soldiers made bridle reins of skins taken from the corpses; they also cut off the tip of each dead Indian's nose for a body count."[6] Jackson was also responsible for illegally driving the Cherokees off their homelands in Georgia and force-marching them to Oklahoma, but not before five to eight thousand (mostly elders, children, and women) died on the "trail of tears." As I collect my change, it occurs to me that I got rid of the Cherokee/Creek killer, but now have three more town destroyers and one more Dakota executioner.

I finally arrived at the home of my friends and received the customary affectionate hugs and greetings from all. I handed over the ice cream to the parents to be refrigerated and dug the toys out of the bag to hand out to the kids. Forgetting the cowboys and Indians were in the bag, I took them out at the same time as the other toys. The youngest, responding like other young feral boys his age, immediately yelled "these are mine," snatched them out of my hand before his brother and sister could react, and dove toward a corner protecting his cache while we all looked on. I quickly responded, saying, "Oh, those little toys are for my students; I have another really nice toy for you." However, when he saw that the car I was holding was much smaller, he hunkered down on his prize and cried "no, no, no" as his mother attempted to extricate the bag from his little, powerful, white-knuckled clutch. As he and his mother wrestled for supremacy over the toys, I quickly intervened saying, "It's OK, you can have them ... he can have them," which brought some relief for all. . . .

Later in the evening, when visiting between us adults waned, the two boys brought me their large sky blue Tupperware container of toys and asked me to play with them. I agreed, and we sat at the dining table looking at all the different little cars, trucks, and animal figures. I cringed as I observed that they had already added the cowboys and Indians to their collection. I began to pray silently that we wouldn't play with these guys because I knew I would want the Indians to kill all the cowboys, and it wouldn't be pretty. As the boys looked over the toys, I sent them powerful silent thoughts intended to discourage them from wanting to play with these little figures. My telekinetic abilities failed, and the boys took them out and separated them into what seemed like positions of battle. I watched without protest even though my fierce anticolonial perspicacity told me that these are the toys of genocide, icons of colonialism, and little boys should not be allowed to play with them because it will create a subconscious desire to kill real Indians. As I pondered these thoughts, I suddenly realized that I could experiment with how the boys play with these toys. When all the figures are on the table, I ask, "What shall we do with these guys?" Neither answers. Realizing I need to coach them a bit, I ask, "Who are the bad guys and who are the good guys . . . which guys are supposed to get killed?" My research questions are suddenly contaminated when the boys quickly reach into the Tupperware container and pull out a brontosaurus and a T. rex and began knocking down everybody, saying, "We have to kill them all." Unable to restrain my latent tendencies of revenge, I grabbed a pterodactyl and started making what I think are pretty good pterodactyl sounds while I used my guy to peck out the eyes of the cowboy who most looked like John Wayne.

Cowboys and Indians: the Master Narrative

> The colonizer's falsified stories have become universal truths to mainstream society, and have reduced Aboriginal culture to a caricature. This distorted reality is one of the most powerful shackles subjugating Aboriginal people. It distorts all Indigenous experiences, past and present, and blocks the road to self determination.[7]

Years ago, when I was a child, my play with toy cowboys and Indians would have ended much differently than my above story. Having been inculcated with the master narrative, or what Howard Adams calls "the colonizer's falsified stories," my cowboys would have heroically killed the dinosaurs and then the Indians. Like many children on the North Dakota reservation where I grew up, my young mind had been intellectually conscripted by the local Bureau of Indian Affairs school to battle the delusion that we Indians were equal in standing to whites. Like most reservation schools during this era, not only was our education inferior and biased, it was also well versed in the oppression, control, and intellectual and cultural domination of us little brown prisoners. We quickly discovered that what we believed was not important unless it was about the great deeds of George Washington (the town destroyer) or Abraham Lincoln (the Dakota executioner) or other significant dead white guys. We learned that we did not know anything of value, nor did we have anything important to contribute from our culture unless it supported the myths of white supremacy. In junior high school we continued to learn we were primitive, superstitious people who should be thankful that God was on the side of the white people who came to the "new world" to settle and help us have a better life.

In high school, lectures or readings rarely mentioned Indigenous Peoples except at Thanksgiving when we were told that this day was special because (white) Pilgrims came here to escape religious persecution and then had a fine dinner with the Indians. Of course, we were never told just how expensive that fine dinner was. Years later, after reading the works of historian Alfred W. Crosby and demographer Henry F. Dobyns, I learned that all along the Eastern seaboard, during the time of the Pilgrims, the infectious diseases of whites wiped out between 60 to 90 percent of the Indigenous populations while colonists simultaneously murdered and terrorized children, women, and other unarmed Native civilians. For instance, in 1623 Captain William Tucker brought his soldiers to a Powhatan village to negotiate a peace treaty. After the treaty was concluded, he convinced the Indians to drink a toast and served them poisoned wine. About two hundred died instantly. Tucker's men then killed another fifty and brought home a number of the heads of their victims.[8]

The master narrative confirmed Indians were inferior to whites by way of a seemingly inexhaustible supply of western movies and TV programs that showed huge numbers of Indians could be easily defeated by a few cowboys with large, shiny, phallic-shaped pistols and an endless reserve of bullets. As a child I observed that whenever the TV Indians battled with the TV cowboys, not only did we spectacularly lose, but to add insult to this injury we were also presented as screaming, grunting, unreasonable savages who unjustly assaulted and/or killed what seemed like the most helpless, likeable, and innocent white people in the world. The TV Indians were the poorest of war tacticians, buffoons really, who would unfailingly ride directly into a great volley of bullets only to be killed over and over again in movie after movie. . . .

Perhaps what gave the master narrative the greatest credibility was that most of the men in my small reservation community made an everyday affair of wearing some vestige of cowboy apparel: hats, boots, shirts with mother-of-pearl buttons, silver belt buckles with golden inlaid bucking bulls or horses, and hand-tooled leather belts with an individual's first or last name engraved in western-style letters. Wanting so much to emulate the dress of our male role models, whom we noticed often occupied the alpha position in our community because of how they behaved, talked, and dressed, we young boys took to nagging our parents about getting us cowboy boots and clothes. . . .

The everyday discourse of people in my community was also highly supportive of the master narrative. Many of the men called each other "cowboy," and some would self-identify as an Indian cowboy. Often when male children cooperated or did some good deed they would be praised by being called cowboys. One of the groups that policed our appearance were the older men in my community who would often say that we (young boys) didn't look like cowboys at all but instead "looked like girls" whenever our hair got even the slightest bit long. My grandfather, a product of Indian boarding schools who sported a crew-cut hairstyle, never failed to rescue us from this name calling. I remember many hot summer days when he would round up us boys (his grandsons) and take us to my mother's house and give us "marine-style" haircuts (which we called skinners) while my mother and our older female relatives looked on and praised our cooperation saying, "Gee, you look good now, you look just like a cowboy." However, getting our heads shaved was never a pleasant experience since it felt like being emotionally robbed of our spirit and our ability to say no. With tears running down our little brown, dirt-stained faces, we would walk out of the house, eyes cast down, feeling humiliated and violated, looking like small brown skinheads. I don't ever recall any adults saying to us, "Gee, you look good now, you look like an Indian."

I also recall that many times when a small boy was crying his heart out due to bonking his head against a chair or the floor, mothers or fathers, grandparents, or other older relatives would often try to get him to calm down by saying, "Oh, cowboys don't cry. Look at the cowboy, look at the cowboy." The cowboy discourse followed me into young adulthood, and I recall as a teen that whenever I stayed with a particular uncle to help him with his ranch chores, he often communicated to me in no uncertain terms that, when I worked for him, I had to act like a cowboy. This often meant I didn't eat or rest much, and if I got hurt I had to "tough it out." . . . Despite this uncle's loyalty to this image and lifestyle, he experienced a lot of racism and taunting from some of the white cowboys he interacted with because, to them, he was just an Indian posing as a cowboy. And because only whites can be "true" cowboys, he settled for being an "Indian cowboy" whenever he felt the sting of racism.

Fortunately, my desire to be a cowboy or to have any association with this image quickly faded during my teen years following my reading of Vine Deloria Jr.'s *Custer Died for Your Sins.*[9] During this same time I was fortunate enough to be exposed to different Indigenous spokespersons and groups, such as the American Indian Movement (AIM), who were advancing powerful political ideas that supported and extended Deloria's critique of American colonial society. Deloria's book was important to me since I found it to be a brilliant, honest, and courageous work that exposed, fiercely critiqued, and neutralized the myths and lies of the master narrative that, for the first fifteen years of my life, had made me into a compliant little Indian, inculcated with the belief that I was an inferior member of society because of my race. The words and ideas of other Indigenous leaders and groups gave me the permission that I needed to begin letting go of the shame that was imposed on me by the colonizer for being an Indian. In the end, both enabled me to begin searching for similar thinking that would prepare me to become intelligently outraged at the lies, distortions, and omissions that Americans had carefully and resolutely forced on our peoples.

Decolonizing Cowboys and Indians

Because decolonization requires a telling of the truth and completely calling into question the colonial structure,[10] it took some years before I stopped wearing cowboy apparel, believing the colonial master narrative, and referring to myself or other Indigenous Peoples as "Indians," "American Indians," "Native Americans," "cowboys," or "Indian cowboys." It also took some years for me to understand that colonialism is a sickness, an addiction to greed, supremacy, power, and exploitation and that cowboys and Indians are one of the colonizer's drugs of choice. Cowboys and Indians are this nation's most passionate, embedded form of hate talk.

Colonialism has taught many Indigenous Peoples to be silent, passive, compliant victims who participate in, excuse, enable, or ignore the colonizer's addictive behaviors. Left unchecked, colonialism has continued to flourish, devastate, and suppress Indigenous Peoples, keeping them in the perpetual role of "the Indian," causing many to say, do, and think things they never would if their minds and hearts were free from American colonial rule. There are, however, antidotes to colonialism that Indigenous Peoples can and must employ: courage, intelligent resistance, development of a counterconsciousness and discourse, and a fierce ongoing critical interrogation of American colonial ideology.

No matter how they have been portrayed in the past or present, cowboys and Indians are the consummate example of American colonialism. They represent the overt and hidden hatred and fear that many Americans harbor toward Indigenous, dark-skinned peoples. They are symbolic of the white colonizer's claim of superiority and Indigenous Peoples' inferiority. Cowboys have remained, in the hearts of most Americans, an evocative representation of American values: love of freedom, fairness, individualism, toughness, enterprise, forward-looking attitude, and whiteness. Indians, on the other hand, have remained the savage, primitive, losing, dark-skinned, evil, antagonistic enemy. . . .

I would guess there are few American boys who grew up before the 1970s who did not play cowboys and Indians: U.S. presidents, vice presidents, Supreme Court justices, congressmen, police chiefs, religious clergy, and schoolteachers—the folks that now run this country. It is not unreasonable to expect that this "star-studded" group killed a lot of Indians during their boyhood war games believing it was the right thing to do. In fact, the cowboys and Indians phenomenon has been directly implicated as contributing to the killing of other dark-skinned people in other parts of the world who have been regarded as impediments to American colonial progress. During the Vietnam War the United States often thought of Vietnam in images of the American West and cast the Vietnamese in the role of Indians.[11] It was common for American soldiers to refer to enemy territory (free-fire zones) as "Indian Country" and for American soldiers to brutally massacre Vietnamese while fantasizing they were killing Indians. One of the most infamous massacres embodying the cowboys and Indians theme was My Lai, where American soldiers murdered as many as five hundred unarmed civilians—old men, women, and children. A unit of Charlie Company, First Battalion, Twentieth Infantry, the soldiers responsible for this slaughter, said that My Lai was inevitable because the Viet Cong were regarded as Indians.[12] In *Facing West: The Metaphysics of Indian Hating and Empire Building*, Richard Drinnon says that one way the Indian-hating fantasies among American soldiers in Vietnam was fulfilled was by cutting off the ears of an enemy, which was equated to the scalping of an Indian.[13] . . .

Calling the enemies of the United States "Indians" and their lands "Indian Country" did not end with Vietnam. I remember the cowboys and Indians theme came up during C-Span television coverage of the American invasion of Iraq in early 1991. On the afternoon of February 19, 1 was at home listening to several military officers briefing reporters in Riyadh, Saudi Arabia, regarding the upcoming strategies of Operation Desert Storm. At one point during the presentation, Brigadier General Richard Neal said that the U.S. military wanted to be confident of a speedy victory once they committed land forces to "Indian Country." What he said had no visible effect on the audience: cameras kept snapping pictures and reporters kept on taking notes. However, I was shocked and outraged and became even more so as I thought about how this country had manipulated young Indigenous men and women and their tribal communities to take part in this hysterical American invasion of Iraq even though their own tribal lives, lands, sovereignty, and resources were, and still are, controlled and threatened by the colonial policies and arrogance of the United States of America.

. . .

America has carefully made sure that Indigenous Peoples continue to fulfill the role of a racial and cultural scapegoat in the game of cowboys and Indians. However, it is hardly an amusing situation since Indigenous Peoples experience numerous humiliating assaults from colonial society, for instance, control and manipulation of their tribal governments by the U.S. federal government, land and resource theft and destruction by U.S. multinational corporations, control and exploitation of tribal gaming and economic revenue by state governments, poorly funded on-reservation substandard schools that continue teaching the prevaricated history of the colonizer, and the continued use of racist images and words to describe Indians.

As colonized peoples, many of us have internalized and adapted to the colonizer's dominant ideology, which has perpetuated our subjugation and repression. As a result we have developed a certain sense of internalized denigration and personal contempt within our consciousness resulting in self-effacing and destructive behaviors. However, this can change if Indigenous and non-Indigenous Peoples intelligently resist American colonialism and begin the process of decolonizing cowboys and Indians, beginning by telling the truth about the racist intent of the cowboys and Indians phenomenon. We must also intelligently interrogate and reform the colonial structure of this nation and challenge the written false histories of the American colonizer. Indigenous Peoples must consciously refuse to be little red plastic toy Indians participating in the racist American myths and policies of white colonial supremacy. Whites must refuse to be little blue plastic toy cowboys blindly accepting their position of privilege in society and, instead, truthfully amend this nation's history and practice of colonialism while seeking justice on behalf of those they have colonized here and abroad. Until this is done, cowboys and Indians will continue to be toys of genocide, icons of colonialism.

. . .

NOTES

1. Robert J. C. Young, *Postcolonialism: An Historical Introduction* (Oxford: Blackwell Publishers, 2001).

2. I do not use the terms "Indian," "American Indian," or "Native American" when I write or speak of the Indigenous Peoples who reside in what is now referred to as the United States of America. I consider these names to be counterfeit, colonized identities imposed by European Americans who attempt to keep Aboriginal Peoples in a perpetual state of colonization through the use of such racist labels. Instead I use the terms "First Nations" or "Indigenous Peoples." In this essay I use "Indian" as a term of subjugation.

3. For a detailed report of the American toy industry in China, see *Toys of Misery: A Report of the Toy Industry in China*, authored by the National Labor Committee, New York, January 2002 (http://www.nlcnet.org).

4. *The Guinness Book of Records* (New York: Bantam Books, 1993). Also see Dee Brown, *Bury My Heart at Wounded Knee: An Indian History of the American West* (New York: Henry Holt, 1991).

5. Brown, *Bury My Heart at Wounded Knee*, 40.

6. Ronald Takaki, *A Different Mirror: A History of Multicultural America* (Boston: Little, Brown, 1993), 85.

7. Howard Adams, *A Tortured People: The Politics of Colonization* (Penticton, BC: Theytus Books, 1995), I.

8. Takaki, A *Different Mirror.*

9. Vine Deloria Jr., *Custer Died for Your Sins: An Indian Manifesto* (New York: Macmillian, 1969).

10. Frantz Fanon, *The Wretched of the Earth* (New York: Grove Press, 1968).

11. David Espy, "America and Vietnam: The Indian Subtext," in *The Journal of American Culture and Literature Uprising: The Protests and the Arts,* ed. David Landrey and Blige Mutluay (Buffalo: Poetry/Rare Books Collection, State University of New York, 1994).

12. Statement of Robert B. Johnson, Captain, U.S. Army, West Point Class of 1965, "Free Fire Zones? We Called It Indian Country: America's Vietnamese Killing Fields," U.S. House of Representatives, War Crimes Hearings, April 29, 1971, http://www.iwchildren.org/veterans/goodcadindian.htm.

13. Richard Drinnon, *Facing West: The Metaphysics of Indian Hating and Empire Building* (New York: Schocken Books, 1990).

7

Still Separate, Still Unequal: America's Educational Apartheid

Jonathan Kozol

Many Americans who live far from our major cities and who have no firsthand knowledge of the realities to be found in urban public schools seem to have the rather vague and general impression that the great extremes of racial isolation that were matters of grave national significance some thirty-five or forty years ago have gradually but steadily diminished in more recent years. The truth, unhappily, is that the trend, for well over a decade now, has been precisely the reverse. Schools that were already deeply segregated twenty-five or thirty years ago are no less segregated now, while thousands of other schools around the country that had been integrated either voluntarily or by the force of law have since been rapidly resegregating. . . .

"There are expensive children and there are cheap children," writes Marina Warner, an essayist and novelist who has written many books for children, "just as there are expensive women and cheap women." The governmentally administered diminishment in value of the children of the poor begins even before the age of five or six, when they begin their years of formal education in the public schools. It starts during their infant and toddler years, when hundreds of thousands of children of the very poor in much of the United States are locked out of the opportunity for preschool education for no reason but the accident of birth and budgetary choices of the government, while children of the privileged are often given veritable feasts of rich developmental early education.

In New York City, for example, affluent parents pay surprisingly large sums of money to enroll their youngsters, beginning at the age of two or three, in extraordinary early-education programs that give them social competence and rudimentary pedagogic skills unknown to children of the same age in the city's poorer neighborhoods. The most exclusive of the private preschools in New York, which are known to those who can afford them as "Baby Ivies," cost as much as $24,000 for a full-day program. Competition for admission to these pre-K schools is so extreme that private counselors are frequently retained, at fees as high as $300 an hour, to guide the parents through the application process.

At the opposite extreme along the economic spectrum in New York are thousands of children who receive no preschool opportunity at all. Exactly how many thousands are denied this opportunity in New York City and in other major cities is almost impossible to know. Numbers that originate in governmental agencies in many states are incomplete and imprecise and do not always differentiate with clarity between authentic pre-K

Jonathan Kozol has written extensively on the state of education in the United States since the 1960s. His books include *Death at an Early Age* and *Savage Inequalities: Children in America's Schools*.

Adapted from *The Shame of the Nation* (Crown Publishers, 2005). Reprinted by permission of the author.

programs that have educative and developmental substance and those less expensive child-care arrangements that do not. But even where states do compile numbers that refer specifically to educative preschool programs, it is difficult to know how many of the children who are served are of low income, since admissions to some of the state-supported programs aren't determined by low income or they are determined by a complicated set of factors of which poverty is only one.

There are remarkable exceptions to this pattern in some sections of the nation. In Milwaukee, for example, virtually every four-year-old is now enrolled in a preliminary kindergarten program, which amounts to a full year of preschool education, prior to a second kindergarten year for five-year-olds. More commonly in urban neighborhoods, large numbers of low-income children are denied these opportunities and come into their kindergarten year without the minimal social skills that children need in order to participate in class activities and without even such very modest early-learning skills as knowing how to hold a crayon or a pencil, identify perhaps a couple of shapes and colors, or recognize that printed pages go from left to right.

Three years later, in third grade, these children are introduced to what are known as "high-stakes tests," which in many urban systems now determine whether students can or cannot be promoted. Children who have been in programs like those offered by the "Baby Ivies" since the age of two have, by now, received the benefits of six or seven years of education, nearly twice as many as the children who have been denied these opportunities; yet all are required to take, and will be measured by, the same examinations. Which of these children will receive the highest scores? The ones who spent the years from two to four in lovely little Montessori programs and in other pastel-painted settings in which tender and attentive and well-trained instructors read to them from beautiful storybooks and introduced them very gently for the first time to the world of numbers and the shapes of letters, and the sizes and varieties of solid objects, and perhaps taught them to sort things into groups or to arrange them in a sequence, or to do those many other interesting things that early childhood specialists refer to as prenumeracy skills? Or the ones who spent those years at home in front of a TV or sitting by the window of a slum apartment gazing down into the street? There is something deeply hypocritical about a society that holds an eight-year-old inner-city child "accountable" for her performance on a high-stakes standardized exam but does not hold the high officials of our government accountable for robbing her of what they gave their own kids six or seven years earlier.

Perhaps in order to deflect these recognitions, or to soften them somewhat, many people, even while they do not doubt the benefit of making very large investments in the education of their own children, somehow—paradoxical as it may seem—appear to be attracted to the argument that money may not really matter that much at all. No matter with what regularity such doubts about the worth of spending money on a child's education are advanced, it is obvious that those who have the money, and who spend it lavishly to benefit their own kids, do not do it for no reason. Yet shockingly large numbers of well-educated and sophisticated people whom I talk with nowadays dismiss such challenges with a surprising ease. "Is the answer really to throw money into these dysfunctional and failing schools?" I'm often asked. "Don't we have some better ways to make them 'work'?" The question is posed in a variety of forms. "Yes, of course, it's not a perfectly fair system as it stands. But money alone is surely not the sole response. The values of the parents and the kids themselves must have a role in this as well you know, housing, health conditions, social factors." "Other factors"—a term of overall reprieve one often hears—"have got to be considered, too." These latter points are obviously true but always seem to have the odd effect of substituting things we know we cannot change in the short run for obvious solutions like cutting class size and constructing new school buildings or providing universal preschool that we actually could put in place right now if we were so inclined.

Frequently these arguments are posed as questions that do not invite an answer because the answer seems to be decided in advance. "Can you really buy your way to better education for these children?" "Do we know enough to be quite sure that we will see an actual return on the investment that we make?" "Is it even clear that this is the right starting point to get to where we'd like to go? It doesn't always seem to work, as I am sure that you already know," or similar questions that somehow assume I will agree with those who ask them.

Some people who ask these questions, although they live in wealthy districts where the schools are funded at high levels, don't even send their children to these public schools but choose instead to send them to expensive private day schools. At some of the well-known private prep schools in the New York City area, tuition and associated costs are typically more than $20,000 a year. During their children's teenage years, they sometimes send them off to very fine New England schools like Andover or Exeter or Groton, where tuition, boarding, and additional expenses rise to more than $30,000. Often a family has two teenage children in these schools at the same time, so they may be spending more than $60,000 on their children's education every year. Yet here I am one night, a guest within their home, and dinner has been served and we are having coffee now; and this entirely likeable, and generally sensible, and beautifully refined and thoughtful person looks me in the eyes and asks me whether you can really buy your way to better education for the children of the poor.

As racial isolation deepens and the inequalities of education finance remain unabated and take on new and more innovative forms, the principals of many inner-city schools are making choices that few principals in public schools that serve white children in the mainstream of the nation ever need to contemplate. Many have been dedicating vast amounts of time and effort to create an architecture of adaptive strategies that promise incremental gains within the limits inequality allows.

New vocabularies of stentorian determination, new systems of incentive, and new modes of castigation, which are termed "rewards and sanctions," have emerged. Curriculum materials that are alleged to be aligned with governmentally established goals and standards and particularly suited to what are regarded as "the special needs and learning styles" of low-income urban children have been introduced. Relentless emphasis on raising test scores, rigid policies of nonpromotion and nongraduation, a new empiricism and the imposition of unusually detailed lists of named and numbered "outcomes" for each isolated parcel of instruction, an oftentimes fanatical insistence upon uniformity of teachers in their management of time, an openly conceded emulation of the rigorous approaches of the military and a frequent use of terminology that comes out of the world of industry and commerce—these are just a few of the familiar aspects of these new adaptive strategies.

Although generically described as "school reform," most of these practices and policies are targeted primarily at poor children of color; and although most educators speak of these agendas in broad language that sounds applicable to all, it is understood that they are valued chiefly as responses to perceived catastrophe in deeply segregated and unequal schools.

"If you do what I tell you to do, how I tell you to do it, when I tell you to do it, you'll get it right," said a determined South Bronx principal observed by a reporter for the *New York Times*. She was laying out a memorizing rule for math to an assembly of her students. "If you don't, you'll get it wrong." This is the voice, this is the tone, this is the rhythm and didactic certitude one hears today in inner-city schools that have embraced a pedagogy of direct command and absolute control. "Taking their inspiration from the ideas of B. F. Skinner . . . ," says the *Times*, proponents of scripted rote-and-drill curricula articulate their aim as the establishment of "faultless communication" between "the teacher, who is the stimulus," and "the students, who respond."

The introduction of Skinnerian approaches (which are commonly employed in penal institutions and drug-rehabilitation programs), as a way of altering the attitudes and learning styles of black and Hispanic children, is provocative, and it has stirred some outcries from respected scholars. To actually go into a school where you know some of the children very, very well and see the way that these approaches can affect their daily lives and thinking processes is even more provocative.

On a chilly November day four years ago in the South Bronx, I entered P.S. 65, a school I had been visiting since 1993. There had been major changes since I'd been there last. Silent lunches had been instituted in the cafeteria, and on days when children misbehaved, silent recess had been introduced as well. On those days the students were obliged to sit in rows and maintain perfect silence on the floor of a small indoor room instead of going out to play. The words SUCCESS FOR ALL, the brand name of a scripted curriculum—better known by its acronym, SFA—were prominently posted at the top of the main stairway and, as I would later find, in almost every room. Also frequently displayed within the halls and classrooms were a number of administrative memos that were worded with unusual didactic absoluteness. "Authentic Writing," read a document called "Principles of Learning" that was posted in the corridor close to the principal's office, "is driven by curriculum and instruction." I didn't know what this expression meant. Like many other undefined and arbitrary phrases posted in the school, it seemed to be a dictum that invited no interrogation.

I entered the fourth grade of a teacher I will call Mr. Endicott, a man in his mid-thirties who had arrived here without training as a teacher, one of about a dozen teachers in the building who were sent into this school after a single summer of short-order preparation. Now in his second year, he had developed a considerable sense of confidence and held the class under a tight control.

As I found a place to sit in a far corner of the room, the teacher and his young assistant, who was in her first year as a teacher, were beginning a math lesson about building airport runways, a lesson that provided children with an opportunity for measuring perimeters.

On the wall behind the teacher, in large letters, was written: "Portfolio Protocols: 1. You are responsible for the selection of [your] work that enters your portfolio. 2. As your skills become more sophisticated this year, you will want to revise, amend, supplement, and possibly replace items in your portfolio to reflect your intellectual growth." On the left side of the room: "Performance Standards Mathematics Curriculum: M-5 Problem Solving and Reasoning. M-6 Mathematical Skills and Tools . . ."

My attention was distracted by some whispering among the children sitting to the right of me. The teacher's response to this distraction was immediate: his arm shot out and up in a diagonal in front of him, his hand straight up, his fingers flat. The young co-teacher did this, too. When they saw their teachers do this, all the children in the classroom did it, too.

"Zero noise," the teacher said, but this instruction proved to be unneeded. The strange salute the class and teachers gave each other, which turned out to be one of a number of such silent signals teachers in the school were trained to use, and children to obey, had done the job of silencing the class.

"Active listening!" said Mr. Endicott. "Heads up! Tractor beams!" which meant, "Every eye on me."

On the front wall of the classroom, in handwritten words that must have taken Mr. Endicott long hours to transcribe, was a list of terms that could be used to praise or criticize a student's work in mathematics. At Level Four, the highest of four levels of success, a child's "problem-solving strategies" could be described, according to this list, as "systematic, complete, efficient, and possibly elegant," while the student's capability to draw conclusions from the work she had completed could be termed "insightful" or "comprehensive." At Level Two, the child's capability to draw conclusions was to be described as "logically unsound"; at Level One, "not present." Approximately 50 separate categories of proficiency, or lack of such, were detailed in this wall-sized tabulation.

A well-educated man, Mr. Endicott later spoke to me about the form of classroom management that he was using as an adaptation from a model of industrial efficiency. "It's a kind of 'Taylorism' in the classroom," he explained, referring to a set of theories about the management of factory employees introduced by Frederick Taylor in the early 1900s. "Primitive utilitarianism" is another term he used when we met some months later to discuss these management techniques with other teachers from the school. His reservations were, however, not apparent in the classroom. Within the terms of what he had been asked to do, he had, indeed, become a master of control. It is one of the few classrooms I had visited up to that time in which almost nothing even hinting at spontaneous emotion in the children or the teacher surfaced while I was there.

The teacher gave the "zero noise" salute again when someone whispered to another child at his table. "In two minutes you will have a chance to talk and share this with your partner." Communication between children in the class was not prohibited but was afforded time slots and, remarkably enough, was formalized in an expression that I found included in a memo that was posted on the wall beside the door: "An opportunity . . . to engage in Accountable Talk."

Even the teacher's words of praise were framed in terms consistent with the lists that had been posted on the wall. "That's a Level Four suggestion," said the teacher when a child made an observation other teachers might have praised as simply "pretty good" or "interesting" or "mature." There was, it seemed, a formal name for every cognitive event within this school: "Authentic Writing," "Active Listening," "Accountable Talk." The ardor to assign all items of instruction or behavior a specific name was unsettling me. The adjectives had the odd effect of hyping every item of endeavor. "Authentic Writing" was, it seemed, a more important act than what the children in a writing class in any ordinary school might try to do. "Accountable Talk" was some thing more self-conscious and significant than merely useful conversation.

Since that day at P.S. 65, I have visited nine other schools in six different cities where the same Skinnerian curriculum is used. The signs on the walls, the silent signals, the curious salute, the same insistent naming of all cognitive particulars, became familiar as I went from one school to the next.

"Meaningful Sentences," began one of the many listings of proficiencies expected of the children in the fourth grade of an inner-city elementary school in Hartford (90 percent black, 10 percent Hispanic) that I visited a short time later. "Noteworthy Questions," "Active Listening," and other designations like these had been posted elsewhere in the room. Here, too, the teacher gave the kids her outstretched arm, with hand held up, to reestablish order when they grew a little noisy, but I noticed that she tried to soften the effect of this by opening her fingers and bending her elbow slightly so it did not look quite as forbidding as the gesture Mr. Endicott had used. A warm and interesting woman, she later told me she disliked the regimen intensely.

Over her desk, I read a "Mission Statement," which established the priorities and values for the school. Among the missions of the school, according to the printed statement, which was posted also in some other classrooms of the school, was "to develop productive citizens" who have the skills that will be needed "for successful global competition," a message that was reinforced by other posters in the room. Over the heads of a group of children at their desks, a sign anointed them BEST WORKERS OF 2002.

Another signal now was given by the teacher, this one not for silence but in order to achieve some other form of class behavior, which I could not quite identify. The students gave exactly the same signal in response. Whatever the function of this signal, it was done as I had seen it done in the South Bronx and would see it done in other schools in months to come. Suddenly, with a seeming surge of restlessness and irritation—with herself, as it appeared, and with her own effective use of all the tricks that she had learned—she turned to me and said, "I can do this with my dog."

"There's something crystal clear about a number," says a top adviser to the U.S. Senate committee that has jurisdiction over public education, a point of view that is reinforced repeatedly in statements coming from the office of the U.S. education secretary and the White House. "I want to change the face of reading instruction across the United States from an art to a science," said an assistant to Rod Paige, the former education secretary, in the winter of 2002. This is a popular position among advocates for rigidly sequential systems of instruction, but the longing to turn art into science doesn't stop with reading methodologies alone. In many schools it now extends to almost every aspect of the operation of the school and of the lives that children lead within it. In some schools even such ordinary acts as children filing to lunch or recess in the hallways or the stairwells are subjected to the same determined emphasis upon empirical precision.

"Rubric For Filing" is the printed heading of a lengthy list of numbered categories by which teachers are supposed to grade their students on the way they march along the corridors in another inner-city district I have visited. Someone, in this instance, did a lot of work to fit the filing proficiencies of children into no more and no less than thirty-two specific slots:

"Line leader confidently leads the class. . . . Line is straight. . . . Spacing is right. . . . The class is stepping together. . . . Everyone shows pride, their shoulders high . . . no slumping," according to the strict criteria for filing at Level Four.

"Line is straight, but one or two people [are] not quite in line," according to the box for Level Three. "Line leader leads the class," and "almost everyone shows pride."

"Several are slumping. . . . Little pride is showing," says the box for Level Two. "Spacing is uneven. . . . Some are talking and whispering."

"Line leader is paying no attention," says the box for Level One. "Heads are turning every way. . . . Hands are touching. . . . The line is not straight. . . . There is no pride."

The teacher who handed me this document believed at first that it was written as a joke by someone who had simply come to be fed up with all the numbers and accounting rituals that clutter up the day in many overregulated schools. Alas, it turned out that it was no joke but had been printed in a handbook of instructions for the teachers in the city where she taught.

In some inner-city districts, even the most pleasant and old-fashioned class activities of elementary schools have now been overtaken by these ordering requirements. A student teacher in California, for example, wanted to bring a pumpkin to her class on Halloween but knew it had no ascertainable connection to the California standards. She therefore had developed what she called "The Multi-Modal Pumpkin Unit" to teach science (seeds), arithmetic (the size and shape of pumpkins, I believe—this detail wasn't clear), and certain items she adapted out of language arts, in order to position "pumpkins" in a frame of state proficiencies. Even with her multi-modal pumpkin, as her faculty adviser told me, she was still afraid she would be criticized because she knew the pumpkin would not really help her children to achieve expected goals on state exams.

Why, I asked a group of educators at a seminar in Sacramento, was a teacher being placed in a position where she'd need to do preposterous curricular gymnastics to enjoy a bit of seasonal amusement with her kids on Halloween? How much injury to state-determined "purpose" would it do to let the children of poor people have a pumpkin party once a year for no other reason than because it's something fun that other children get to do on autumn days in public schools across most of America?

"Forcing an absurdity on teachers does teach something," said an African-American professor. "It teaches acquiescence. It breaks down the will to thumb your nose at pointless protocols to call absurdity 'absurd.'" Writing out the standards with the proper numbers on the chalkboard has a similar effect, he said; and doing this is "terribly important" to the principals in many of these schools. "You *have* to post the standards, and the way you know the children know the standards is by asking them to *state* the standards. And they do it—and you want to be quite certain that they do it if you want to keep on working at that school."

In speaking of the drill-based program in effect at P.S. 65, Mr. Endicott told me he tended to be sympathetic to the school administrators, more so at least than the other teachers I had talked with seemed to be. He said he believed his principal had little choice about the implementation of this program, which had been mandated for all elementary schools in New York City that had had rock-bottom academic records over a long period of time. "This puts me into a dilemma," he went on, "because I love the kids at P.S. 65." And even while, he said, "I know that my teaching SFA is a charade . . . if I don't do it I won't be permitted to teach these children."

Mr. Endicott, like all but two of the new recruits at P.S. 65—there were about fifteen in all—was a white person, as were the principal and most of the administrators at the school. As a result, most of these neophyte instructors had had little or no prior contact with the children of an inner-city neighborhood; but, like the others I met, and despite the distancing between the children and their teachers that resulted from the scripted method of instruction, he had developed close attachments to his students and did not want to abandon them. At the same time, the class- and race-specific implementation of this program obviously troubled him. "There's an expression now," he said. "The rich get richer, and the poor get SFA." He said he was still trying to figure out his "professional ethics" on the problem that this posed for him.

White children made up "only about one percent" of students in the New York City schools in which this scripted teaching system was imposed,[1] according to the *New York Times,* which also said that "the prepackaged lessons" were intended "to ensure that all teachers—even novices or the most inept"—would be able to teach reading. As seemingly pragmatic and hardheaded as such arguments may be, they are desperation strategies that come out of the acceptance of inequity. If we did not have a deeply segregated system in which more experienced instructors teach the children of the privileged and the least experienced are sent to teach the children of minorities, these practices would not be needed and could not be so convincingly defended. They are confections of apartheid, and no matter by what arguments of urgency or practicality they have been justified, they cannot fail to further deepen the divisions of society.

There is no misery index for the children of apartheid education. There ought to be; we measure almost everything else that happens to them in their schools. Do kids who go to schools like these enjoy the days they spend in them? Is school, for most of them, a happy place to be? You do not find the answers to these questions in reports about achievement levels, scientific methods of accountability, or structural revisions in the modes of governance. Documents like these don't speak of happiness. You have to go back to the schools themselves to find an answer to these questions. You have to sit down in the little chairs in first and second grade, or on the reading rug with kindergarten kids, and listen to the things they actually say to one another and the dialogue between them and their teachers. You have to go down to the basement with the children when it's time for lunch and to the playground with them, if they have a playground, when it's time for recess, if they still have recess at their school. You have to walk into the children's bathrooms in these buildings. You have to do what children do and breathe the air the children breathe. I don't think that there is any other way to find out what the lives that children lead in school are really like.

High school students, when I first meet them, are often more reluctant than the younger children to open up and express their personal concerns; but hesitation on the part of students did not prove to be a problem when I visited a tenth-grade class at Fremont High School in Los Angeles. The students were told that I was a writer, and they took no time in getting down to matters that were on their minds.

"Can we talk about the bathrooms?" asked a soft-spoken student named Mireya.

In almost any classroom there are certain students who, by the force of their directness or the unusual sophistication of their way of speaking, tend to capture your attention from the start. Mireya later spoke insightfully about some of the serious academic problems that were common in the school, but her observations on the physical and personal embarrassments she and her schoolmates had to undergo cut to the heart of questions of essential dignity that kids in squalid schools like this one have to deal with all over the nation.

Fremont High School, as court papers filed in a lawsuit against the state of California document, has fifteen fewer bathrooms than the law requires. Of the limited number of bathrooms that are working in the school, "only one or two . . . are open and unlocked for girls to use." Long lines of girls are "waiting to use the bathrooms," which are generally "unclean" and "lack basic supplies," including toilet paper. Some of the classrooms, as court papers also document, "do not have air conditioning," so that students, who attend school on a three-track schedule that runs year-round, "become red-faced and unable to concentrate" during "the extreme heat of summer." The school's maintenance records report that rats were found in eleven classrooms. Rat droppings were found "in the bins and drawers" of the high school's kitchen, and school records note that "hamburger buns" were being "eaten off [the] bread-delivery rack."

No matter how many tawdry details like these I've read in legal briefs or depositions through the years, I'm always shocked again to learn how often these unsanitary physical conditions are permitted to continue in the schools that serve our poorest students—even after they have been vividly described in the media. But hearing of these conditions in Mireya's words was even more unsettling, in part because this student seemed so fragile and because the need even to speak of these indignities in front of me and all the other students was an additional indignity.

"The problem is this," she carefully explained. "You're not allowed to use the bathroom during lunch, which is a thirty-minute period. The only time that you're allowed to use it is between your classes." But "this is a huge building," she went on. "It has long corridors. If you have one class at one end of the building and your next class happens to be way down at the other end, you don't have time to use the bathroom and still get to class before it starts. So you go to your class and then you ask permission from your teacher to go to the bathroom and the teacher tells you, 'No. You had your chance between the periods . . .'

"I feel embarrassed when I have to stand there and explain it to a teacher."

"This is the question," said a wiry-looking boy named Edward, leaning forward in his chair. "Students are not animals, but even animals need to relieve themselves sometimes. We're here for eight hours. What do they think we're supposed to do?"

"It humiliates you," said Mireya, who went on to make the interesting statement that "the school provides solutions that don't actually work," and this idea was taken up by several other students in describing course requirements within the school. A tall black student, for example, told me that she hoped to be a social worker or a doctor but was programmed into "Sewing Class" this year. She also had to take another course, called "Life

Skills," which she told me was a very basic course—"a retarded class," to use her words—that "teaches things like the six continents," which she said she'd learned in elementary school.

When I asked her why she had to take these courses, she replied that she'd been told they were required, which as I later learned was not exactly so. What was required was that high school students take two courses in an area of study called "The Technical Arts," and which the Los Angeles Board of Education terms "Applied Technology." At schools that served the middle class or upper-middle class, this requirement was likely to be met by courses that had academic substance and, perhaps, some relevance to college preparation. At Beverly Hills High School, for example, the technical-arts requirement could be fulfilled by taking subjects like residential architecture, the designing of commercial structures, broadcast journalism, advanced computer graphics, a sophisticated course in furniture design, carving and sculpture, or an honors course in engineering research and design. At Fremont High, in contrast, this requirement was far more often met by courses that were basically vocational and also obviously keyed to low-paying levels of employment.

Mireya, for example, who had plans to go to college, told me that she had to take a sewing class last year and now was told she'd been assigned to take a class in hairdressing as well. When I asked her teacher why Mireya could not skip these subjects and enroll in classes that would help her to pursue her college aspirations, she replied, "It isn't a question of what students want. It's what the school may have available. If all the other elective classes that a student wants to take are full, she has to take one of these classes if she wants to graduate."

A very small girl named Obie, who had big blue-tinted glasses tilted up across her hair, interrupted then to tell me with a kind of wild gusto that she'd taken hairdressing twice! When I expressed surprised that this was possible, she said there were two levels of hairdressing offered here at Fremont High. "One is in hairstyling," she said. "The other is in braiding."

Mireya stared hard at this student for a moment and then suddenly began to cry. "I don't want to take hairdressing. I did not need sewing either. I knew how to sew. My mother is a seamstress in a factory. I'm trying to go to college. I don't need to sew to go to college. My mother sews. I hoped for something else."

"What would you rather take?" I asked.

"I wanted to take an AP class," she answered.

Mireya's sudden tears elicited a strong reaction from one of the boys who had been silent up till now: a thin, dark-eyed student named Fortino, who had long hair down to his shoulders. He suddenly turned directly to Mireya and spoke into the silence that followed her last words.

"Listen to me," he said. "The owners of the sewing factories need laborers. Correct?"

"I guess they do," Mireya said.

"It's not going to be their own kids. Right?" "Why not?" another student said.

"So they can grow beyond themselves," Mireya answered quietly. "But we remain the same."

"You're ghetto," said Fortino, "so we send you to the factory." He sat low in his desk chair, leaning on one elbow, his voice and dark eyes loaded with a cynical intelligence. "You're ghetto—so you sew!"

"There are higher positions than these," said a student named Samantha.

"You're ghetto," said Fortino unrelentingly. "So sew!"

Admittedly, the economic needs of a society are bound to be reflected to some rational degree within the policies and purposes of public schools. But, even so, there must be *something* more to life as it is lived by six-year-olds or by teenagers, for that matter, than concerns about "successful global competition." Childhood is not merely basic training for utilitarian adulthood. It should have some claims upon our mercy, not for its future value to the economic interests of competitive societies but for its present value as a perishable piece of life itself.

Very few people who are not involved with inner-city schools have any real idea of the extremes to which the mercantile distortion of the purposes and character of education have been taken or how unabashedly proponents of these practices are willing to defend them. The head of a Chicago school, for instance, who was criticized by some for emphasizing rote instruction that, his critics said, was turning children into "robots," found no reason to dispute the charge. "Did you ever stop to think that these robots will never burglarize your home?" he asked, and "will never snatch your pocketbooks. . . . These robots are going to be producing taxes."

Corporate leaders, when they speak of education, sometimes pay lip-service to the notion of "good critical and analytic skills," but it is reasonable to ask whether they have in mind the critical analysis of *their* priorities. In principle, perhaps some do; but, if so, this is not a principle that seems to have been honored widely in the schools I have been visiting. In all the various business-driven inner-city classrooms that I have observed in the past five years, plastered as they are with corporation brand names and managerial vocabularies, I have yet to see the two words "labor unions." Is this an oversight? How is that possible? Teachers and principals themselves, who are almost always members of a union, seem to be so beaten down that they rarely even question this omission.

It is not at all unusual these days to come into an urban school in which the principal prefers to call himself or herself "building CEO" or "building manager." In some of the same schools teachers are described as "classroom managers."[2] I have never been in a suburban district in which principals were asked to view themselves or teachers in this way. These terminologies remind us of how wide the distance has become between two very separate worlds of education.

It has been more than a decade now since drill-based literacy methods like Success For All began to proliferate in our urban schools. It has been three and a half years since the systems of assessment that determine the effectiveness of these and similar practices were codified in the federal legislation, No Child Left Behind, that President Bush signed into law in 2002. Since the enactment of this bill, the number of standardized exams children must take has more than doubled. It will probably increase again after the year 2006, when standardized tests, which are now required in grades three through eight, may be required in Head Start programs and, as President Bush has now proposed, in ninth, tenth, and eleventh grades as well.

The elements of strict accountability, in short, are solidly in place; and in many states where the present federal policies are simply reinforcements of accountability requirements that were established long before the passage of the federal law, the same regimen has been in place since 1995 or even earlier. The "tests-and-standards" partisans have had things very much their way for an extended period of time, and those who were convinced that they had ascertained "what works" in schools that serve minorities and children of the poor have had ample opportunity to prove that they were right.

What, then, it is reasonable to ask, are the results?

The achievement gap between black and white children, which narrowed for three decades up until the late years of the 1980s—the period in which school segregation steadily decreased—started to widen once more in the early 1990s when the federal courts began the process of resegregation by dismantling the mandates of the *Brown* decision[*]. From that point on, the gap continued to widen or remained essentially unchanged; and while recently there has been a modest narrowing of the gap in reading scores for fourth-grade children, the gap in secondary school remains as wide as ever.

The media inevitably celebrate the periodic upticks that a set of scores may seem to indicate in one year or another in achievement levels of black and Hispanic children in their elementary schools. But if these upticks were not merely temporary "testing gains" achieved by test-prep regimens and were instead authentic education gains, they would carry over into middle school and high school. Children who know how to read—and read with comprehension—do not suddenly become nonreaders and hopelessly disabled writers when they enter secondary school. False gains evaporate; real gains endure. Yet hundreds of thousands of the inner-city children who have made what many districts claim to be dramatic gains in elementary school, and whose principals and teachers have adjusted almost every aspect of their school days and school calendars, forfeiting recess, canceling or cutting back on all the so-called frills (art, music, even social sciences) in order to comply with state demands, those students, now in secondary school, are sitting in subject-matter classes where they cannot comprehend the texts and cannot set down their ideas in the kind of sentences expected of most fourth- and fifth-grade students in the suburbs. Students in this painful situation, not surprisingly, tend to be most likely to drop out of school.

In 48 percent of high schools in the nation's 100 largest districts, which are those in which the highest concentrations of black and Hispanic students tend to be enrolled, less than half the entering ninth-graders graduate in four years. Nationwide, from 1993 to 2002, the number of high schools graduating less than half their ninth-grade class in four years has increased by 75 percent. In the 94 percent of districts in New York State where white children make up the majority, nearly 80 percent of students graduate from high school in four years. In the 6 percent of districts where black and Hispanic students make up the majority, only 40 percent do so. There are 120 high schools in New York, enrolling nearly 200,000 minority students, where less than 60 percent of entering ninth-graders even make it to twelfth grade.

The promulgation of new and expanded inventories of "what works," no matter the enthusiasm with which they're elaborated, is not going to change this. The use of horta-tory slogans chanted by the students in our segregated schools is not going to change this.

---

[*]See the excerpt from the ruling in *Brown v. Board of Education* in Part VII of this volume.

Desperate historical revisionism that romanticizes the segregation of an older order (this is a common theme of many separatists today) is not going to change this. Skinnerian instructional approaches, which decapitate a child's capability for critical reflection, are not going to change this. Posters about "global competition" will certainly not change this. Turning six-year-olds into examination soldiers and denying eight-year-olds their time for play at recess will not change this.

"I went to Washington to challenge the soft bigotry of low expectations," said President Bush in his campaign for reelection in September 2004. "It's working. It's making a difference." Here we have one of those deadly lies that by sheer repetition is at length accepted by surprisingly large numbers of Americans. But it is not the truth; and it is not an innocent misstatement of the facts. It is a devious appeasement of the heartache of the parents of the black and brown and poor, and if it is not forcefully resisted it will lead us further in a very dangerous direction.

Whether the issue is inequity alone or deepening resegregation or the labyrinthine intertwining of the two, it is well past the time for us to start the work that it will take to change this. If it takes people marching in the streets and other forms of adamant disruption of the governing civilities, if it takes more than litigation, more than legislation, and much more than resolutions introduced by members of Congress, these are prices we should be prepared to pay. "We do not have the things you have," Alliyah told me when she wrote to ask if I would come and visit her school in the South Bronx. "Can you help us?" America owes that little girl and millions like her a more honorable answer than they have received.

NOTES

1. SFA has since been discontinued in the New York City public schools, though it is still being used in 1,300 U.S. schools, serving as many as 650,000 children. Similar scripted systems are used in schools (overwhelmingly minority in population) serving several million children.

2. A school I visited three years ago in Columbus, Ohio, was littered with "Help Wanted" signs. Starting in kindergarten, children in the school were being asked to think about the jobs that they might choose when they grew up. In one classroom there was a poster that displayed the names of several retail stores: J. C. Penney, Wal-Mart, Kmart, Sears, and a few others. "It's like working in a store," a classroom aide explained. "The children are learning to pretend they're cashiers." At another school in the same district, children were encouraged to apply for jobs in their classrooms. Among the job positions open to the children in this school, there was an "Absence Manager" and a "Behavior Chart Manager," a "Form Collector Manager," a "Paper Passer Outer Manager," a "Paper Collecting Manager," a "Paper Returning Manager," an "Exit Ticket Manager," even a "Learning Manager," a "Reading Corner Manager," and a "Score Keeper Manager." I asked the principal if there was a special reason why those two words "management" and "manager" kept popping up throughout the school. "We want every child to be working as a manager while he or she is in this school," the principal explained. "We want to make them understand that, in this country, companies will give you opportunities to work, to prove yourself, no matter what you've done." I wasn't sure what she meant by "no matter what you've done," and asked her if she could explain it. "Even if you have a felony arrest," she said, "we want you to understand that you can be a manager someday."

8 Masked Racism: Reflections on the Prison Industrial Complex

Angela Davis

Imprisonment has become the response of first resort to far too many of the social problems that burden people who are ensconced in poverty. These problems often are veiled by being conveniently grouped together under the category "crime" and by the automatic attribution of criminal behavior to people of color. Homelessness, unemployment, drug addiction, mental illness, and illiteracy are only a few of the problems that disappear from public view when the human beings contending with them are relegated to cages.

Prisons thus perform a feat of magic. Or rather the people who continually vote in new prison bonds and tacitly assent to a proliferating network of prisons and jails have been tricked into believing in the magic of imprisonment. But prisons do not disappear problems, they disappear human beings. And the practice of disappearing vast numbers of people from poor, immigrant, and racially marginalized communities has literally become big business.

The seeming effortlessness of magic always conceals an enormous amount of behind-the-scenes work. When prisons disappear human beings in order to convey the illusion of solving social problems, penal infrastructures must be created to accommodate a rapidly swelling population of caged people. Goods and services must be provided to keep imprisoned populations alive. Sometimes these populations must be kept busy and at other times—particularly in repressive super-maximum prisons and in INS detention centers—they must be deprived of virtually all meaningful activity. Vast numbers of handcuffed and shackled people are moved across state borders as they are transferred from one state or federal prison to another.

All this work, which used to be the primary province of government, is now also performed by private corporations, whose links to government in the field of what is euphemistically called "corrections" resonate dangerously with the military industrial complex. The dividends that accrue from investment in the punishment industry, like those that accrue from investment in weapons production, only amount to social destruction. Taking into account the structural similarities and profitability of business–government linkages in the realms of military production and public punishment, the expanding penal system can now be characterized as a "prison industrial complex."

Angela Davis is a scholar, teacher, and activist who has been involved in social justice advocacy for most of her life. She has published more than ten books, including *Women, Race, and Class*; *Are Prisons Obsolete?*; and *Abolition Democracy: Beyond Prisons, Torture, and Empire*.

This article was first published in *ColorLines Magazine* (now Colorlines.com), Fall 1998. Reprinted by permission of the author.

The Color of Imprisonment

Almost two million people are currently locked up in the immense network of U.S. prisons and jails. More than 70 percent of the imprisoned population are people of color. It is rarely acknowledged that the fastest growing group of prisoners are black women and that Native American prisoners are the largest group per capita. Approximately five million people—including those on probation and parole—are directly under the surveillance of the criminal justice system.[1]

Three decades ago, the imprisoned population was approximately one-eighth its current size. While women still constitute a relatively small percentage of people behind bars, today the number of incarcerated women in California alone is almost twice what the nationwide women's prison population was in 1970. According to Elliott Currie, "[t]he prison has become a looming presence in our society to an extent unparalleled in our history—or that of any other industrial democracy. Short of major wars, mass incarceration has been the most thoroughly implemented government social program of our time."

To deliver up bodies destined for profitable punishment, the political economy of prisons relies on racialized assumptions of criminality—such as images of black welfare mothers reproducing criminal children—and on racist practices in arrest, conviction, and sentencing patterns. Colored bodies constitute the main human raw material in this vast experiment to disappear the major social problems of our time. Once the aura of magic is stripped away from the imprisonment solution, what is revealed is racism, class bias, and the parasitic seduction of capitalist profit. The prison industrial system materially and morally impoverishes its inhabitants and devours the social wealth needed to address the very problems that have led to spiraling numbers of prisoners.

As prisons take up more and more space on the social landscape, other government programs that have previously sought to respond to social needs—such as Temporary Assistance to Needy Families—are being squeezed out of existence. The deterioration of public education, including prioritizing discipline and security over learning in public schools located in poor communities, is directly related to the prison "solution."

Profiting from Prisoners

As prisons proliferate in U.S. society, private capital has become enmeshed in the punishment industry. And precisely because of their profit potential, prisons are becoming increasingly important to the U.S. economy. If the notion of punishment as a source of potentially stupendous profits is disturbing by itself, then the strategic dependence on racist structures and ideologies to render mass punishment palatable and profitable is even more troubling.

Prison privatization is the most obvious instance of capital's current movement toward the prison industry. While government-run prisons are often in gross violation of international human rights standards, private prisons are even less accountable. In March [1998], the Corrections Corporation of America (CCA),[2] the largest U.S. private prison company, claimed 54,944 beds in 68 facilities under contract or development in the U.S., Puerto Rico, the United Kingdom, and Australia. Following the global trend of subjecting more women to public punishment, CCA recently opened a women's prison outside Melbourne. The company recently identified California as its "new frontier."

Wackenhut Corrections Corporation (WCC), the second largest U.S. prison company, claimed contracts and awards to manage 46 facilities in North America, the United Kingdom, and Australia. It boasts a total of 30,424 beds as well as contracts for prisoner health care services, transportation, and security.

Currently, the stocks of both CCA and WCC are doing extremely well. Between 1996 and 1997, CCA's revenues increased by 58 percent, from $293 million to $462 million. Its net profit grew from $30.9 million to $53.9 million. WCC raised its revenues from $138 million in 1996 to $210 million in 1997. Unlike public correctional facilities, the vast profits of these private facilities rely on the employment of non-union labor.

The Prison Industrial Complex

But private prison companies are only the most visible component of the increasing corporatization of punishment. Government contracts to build prisons have bolstered the construction industry. The architectural community has identified prison design as a major new niche. Technology developed for the military by companies like Westinghouse [is] being marketed for use in law enforcement and punishment.

Moreover, corporations that appear to be far removed from the business of punishment are intimately involved in the expansion of the prison industrial complex. Prison construction bonds are one of the many sources of profitable investment for leading financiers such as Merrill Lynch. MCI[3] charges prisoners and their families outrageous prices for the precious telephone calls which are often the only contact prisoners have with the free world.

Many corporations whose products we consume on a daily basis have learned that prison labor power can be as profitable as third world labor power exploited by U.S.-based global corporations. Both relegate formerly unionized workers to joblessness and many even wind up in prison. Some of the companies that use prison labor are IBM, Motorola, Compaq, Texas Instruments, Honeywell, Microsoft, and Boeing. But it is not only the hi-tech industries that reap the profits of prison labor. Nordstrom department stores sell jeans that are marketed as "Prison Blues," as well as t-shirts and jackets made in Oregon prisons. The advertising slogan for these clothes is "made on the inside to be worn on the outside." Maryland prisoners inspect glass bottles and jars used by Revlon and Pierre Cardin, and schools throughout the world buy graduation caps and gowns made by South Carolina prisoners.

"For private business," write Eve Goldberg and Linda Evans (a political prisoner inside the Federal Correctional Institution at Dublin, California) "prison labor is like a pot of gold. No strikes. No union organizing. No health benefits, unemployment insurance, or workers' compensation to pay. No language barriers, as in foreign countries. New leviathan prisons are being built on thousands of eerie acres of factories inside the walls. Prisoners do data entry for Chevron, make telephone reservations for TWA, raise hogs, shovel manure, make circuit boards, limousines, waterbeds, and lingerie for Victoria's Secret—all at a fraction of the cost of 'free labor.'"

Devouring the Social Wealth

Although prison labor—which ultimately is compensated at a rate far below the minimum wage—is hugely profitable for the private companies that use it, the penal system as a whole does not produce wealth. It devours the social wealth that could be used to subsidize housing for the homeless, to ameliorate public education for poor and racially marginalized communities, to open free drug rehabilitation programs for people who wish to kick their habits, to create a national health care system, to expand programs to combat HIV, to eradicate domestic abuse—and, in the process, to create well-paying jobs for the unemployed.

Since 1984 more than twenty new prisons have opened in California, while only one new campus was added to the California State University system and none to the University of California system. In 1996–97, higher education received only 8.7 percent of the State's General Fund while corrections received 9.6 percent. Now that affirmative action has been declared illegal in California, it is obvious that education is increasingly reserved for certain people, while prisons are reserved for others. Five times as many black men are presently in prison as in four year colleges and universities. This new segregation has dangerous implications for the entire country.

By segregating people labeled as criminals, prison simultaneously fortifies and conceals the structural racism of the U.S. economy. Claims of low unemployment rates—even in black communities—make sense only if one assumes that the vast numbers of people in prison have really disappeared and thus have no legitimate claims to jobs. The numbers of black and Latino men currently incarcerated amount to two percent of the male labor force. According to criminologist David Downes, "[t]reating incarceration as a type of hidden unemployment may raise the jobless rate for men by about one-third, to 8 percent. The effect on the black labor force is greater still, raising the [black] male unemployment rate from 11 percent to 19 percent."

Hidden Agenda

Mass incarceration is not a solution to unemployment, nor is it a solution to the vast array of social problems that are hidden away in a rapidly growing network of prisons and jails. However, the great majority of people have been tricked into believing in the efficacy of imprisonment, even though the historical record clearly demonstrates that prisons do not work. Racism has undermined our ability to create a popular critical discourse to contest the ideological trickery that posits imprisonment as key to public safety. The focus of state policy is rapidly shifting from social welfare to social control.

Black, Latino, Native American, and many Asian youth are portrayed as the purveyors of violence, traffickers of drugs, and as envious of commodities that they have no right to possess. Young black and Latina women are represented as sexually promiscuous and as indiscriminately propagating babies and poverty. Criminality and deviance are racialized. Surveillance is thus focused on communities of color, immigrants, the unemployed, the undereducated, the homeless, and in general on those who have a diminishing claim to social resources. Their claim to social resources continues to diminish in large part because law enforcement and penal measures increasingly devour these resources. The prison industrial complex has thus created a vicious cycle of punishment which only further impoverishes those whose impoverishment is supposedly "solved" by imprisonment.

Therefore, as the emphasis of government policy shifts from social welfare to crime control, racism sinks more deeply into the economic and ideological structures of U.S. society. Meanwhile, conservative crusaders against affirmative action and bilingual education proclaim the end of racism, while their opponents suggest that racism's remnants can be dispelled through dialogue and conversation. But conversations about "race relations" will hardly dismantle a prison industrial complex that thrives on and nourishes the racism hidden within the deep structures of our society.

The emergence of a U.S. prison industrial complex within a context of cascading conservatism marks a new historical moment, whose dangers are unprecedented. But so are its opportunities. Considering the impressive number of grassroots projects that continue to resist the expansion of the punishment industry, it ought to be possible to bring these efforts together to create radical and nationally visible movements that can legitimize anti-capitalist critiques of the prison industrial complex. It ought to be possible to build movements in defense of prisoners' human rights and movements that persuasively argue that what we need is not new prisons, but new health care, housing, drug programs, jobs, and education. To safeguard a democratic future, it is possible and necessary to weave together the many and increasing strands of resistance to the prison industrial complex into a powerful movement for social transformation.

EDITOR'S NOTES

1. Updated statistics as of 2019: Approximately 2.3 million people are incarcerated in U.S. prisons and jails, and almost 7 million people are under the direct surveillance of the criminal justice system.
2. In 2016, CCA rebranded itself as "CoreCivic."
3. Formerly a major U.S. telecommunications company, MCI became part of Verizon in 2006.

9 Media Magic: Making Class Invisible

Gregory Mantsios

Of the various social and cultural forces in our society, the mass media is arguably the most influential in molding public consciousness. Americans spend an average twenty-eight hours per week watching television. They also spend an undetermined number of hours reading periodicals, listening to the radio, and going to the movies. Unlike other cultural and socializing institutions, ownership and control of the mass media is highly concentrated. Twenty-three corporations own more than one-half of all the daily newspapers, magazines, movie studios, and radio and television outlets in the United States.[1] The number of media companies is shrinking and their control of the industry is expanding. And a relatively small number of media outlets is producing and packaging the majority of news and entertainment programs. For the most part, our media is national in nature and single-minded (profit-oriented) in purpose. This media plays a key role in defining our cultural tastes, helping us locate ourselves in history, establishing our national identity, and ascertaining the range of national and social possibilities. In this essay, we will examine the way the mass media shapes how people think about each other and about the nature of our society.

The United States is the most highly stratified society in the industrialized world. Class distinctions operate in virtually every aspect of our lives, determining the nature of our work, the quality of our schooling, and the health and safety of our loved ones. Yet remarkably, we, as a nation, retain illusions about living in an egalitarian society. We maintain these illusions, in large part, because the media hides gross inequities from public view. In those instances when inequities are revealed, we are provided with messages that obscure the nature of class realities and blame the victims of class-dominated society for their own plight. Let's briefly examine what the news media, in particular, tells us about class.

About the Poor

The news media provides meager coverage of poor people and poverty. The coverage it does provide is often distorted and misleading.

Gregory Mantsios is founder and director of the Murphy Institute for Worker Education and Labor Studies, an organization established by New York City labor unions and the City University of New York to offer educational opportunities to union members and serve as an academic resource for the labor movement.

The Poor Do Not Exist

For the most part, the news media ignores the poor. Unnoticed are forty million poor people in the nation—a number that equals the entire population of Maine, Vermont, New Hampshire, Connecticut, Rhode Island, New Jersey, and New York combined. Perhaps even more alarming is that the rate of poverty is increasing twice as fast as the population growth in the United States. Ordinarily, even a calamity of much smaller proportion (e.g., flooding in the Midwest) would garner a great deal of coverage and hype from a media usually eager to declare a crisis, yet less than one in five hundred articles in the *New York Times* and one in one thousand articles listed in the *Readers' Guide to Periodic Literature* are on poverty. With remarkably little attention to them, the poor and their problems are hidden from most Americans.

When the media does turn its attention to the poor, it offers a series of contradictory messages and portrayals.

The Poor Are Faceless

Each year the Census Bureau releases a new report on poverty in our society and its results are duly reported in the media. At best, however, this coverage emphasizes annual fluctuations (showing how the numbers differ from previous years) and ongoing debates over the validity of the numbers (some argue the number should be lower, most that the number should be higher). Coverage like this desensitizes us to the poor by reducing poverty to a number. It ignores the human tragedy of poverty—the suffering, indignities, and misery endured by millions of children and adults. Instead, the poor become statistics rather than people.

The Poor Are Undeserving

When the media does put a face on the poor, it is not likely to be a pretty one. The media will provide us with sensational stories about welfare cheats, drug addicts, and greedy panhandlers (almost always urban and Black). Compare these images and the emotions evoked by them with the media's treatment of middle-class (usually white) "tax evaders," celebrities who have a "chemical dependency," or wealthy businesspeople who use unscrupulous means to "make a profit." While the behavior of the more affluent offenders is considered an "impropriety" and a deviation from the norm, the behavior of the poor is considered repugnant, indicative of the poor in general, and worthy of our indignation and resentment.

The Poor Are an Eyesore

When the media does cover the poor, they are often presented through the eyes of the middle class. For example, sometimes the media includes a story about community resistance to a homeless shelter or storekeeper annoyance with panhandlers. Rather than focusing on the plight of the poor, these stories are about middle-class opposition to the poor. Such stories tell us that the poor are an inconvenience and an irritation.

The Poor Have Only Themselves to Blame

In another example of media coverage, we are told that the poor live in a personal and cultural cycle of poverty that hopelessly imprisons them. They routinely center on the Black urban population and focus on perceived personality or cultural traits that doom the poor. While the women in these stories typically exhibit an "attitude" that leads to trouble or a promiscuity that leads to single motherhood, the men possess a need for immediate gratification that leads to drug abuse or an unquenchable greed that leads to the pursuit of fast money. The images that are seared into our mind are sexist, racist, and classist. Census figures reveal that most of the poor are white, not Black or Hispanic, that they live in rural or suburban areas, not urban centers, and hold jobs at least part of the year.[2] Yet, in a fashion that is often framed in an understanding and sympathetic tone, we are told that the poor have inflicted poverty on themselves.

The Poor Are Down on Their Luck

During the Christmas season, the news media sometimes provides us with accounts of poor individuals or families (usually white) who are down on their luck. These stories are often linked to stories about soup kitchens or other charitable activities and sometimes call for charitable contributions. These "Yule time" stories are as much about the affluent as they are about the poor: they tell us that the affluent in our society are a kind, understanding, giving people—which we are not.[*] The series of unfortunate circumstances that have led to impoverishment are presumed to be a temporary condition that will improve with time and a change in luck.

• • •

Despite appearances, the messages provided by the media are not entirely disparate. With each variation, the media informs us what poverty is not (i.e., systemic and indicative of American society) by informing us what it is. The media tells us that poverty is either an aberration of the American way of life (it doesn't exist, it's just another number, it's unfortunate but temporary) or an end product of the poor themselves (they are a nuisance, do not deserve better, and have brought their predicament upon themselves).

By suggesting that the poor have brought poverty upon themselves, the media is engaging in what William Ryan has called "blaming the victim."[3] The media identifies in what ways the poor are different as a consequence of deprivation, then defines those differences as the cause of poverty itself. Whether blatantly hostile or cloaked in sympathy,

---

[*]American households with incomes of less than $10,000 give an average of 5.5 percent of their earning to charity or to a religious organization, while those making more than $100,000 a year give only 2.9 percent. After changes in the 1986 tax code reduced the benefits of charitable giving, taxpayers earning $500,000 or more slashed their average donation by nearly one-third. Furthermore, many of these acts of benevolence do not help the needy. Rather than provide funding to social service agencies that aid the poor, the voluntary contributions of the wealthy go to places and institutions that entertain, inspire, cure, or educate wealthy Americans—art museums, opera houses, theaters, orchestras, ballet companies, private hospitals, and elite universities. (Robert Reich, "Secession of the Successful," *New York Times Magazine*, February 17, 1991, p. 43.)

the message is that there is something fundamentally wrong with the victims—their hormones, psychological makeup, family environment, community, race, or some combination of these—that accounts for their plight and their failure to lift themselves out of poverty.

But poverty in the United States is systemic. It is a direct result of economic and political policies that deprive people of jobs, adequate wages, or legitimate support. It is neither natural nor inevitable: there is enough wealth in our nation to eliminate poverty if we chose to redistribute existing wealth or income. The plight of the poor is reason enough to make the elimination of poverty the nation's first priority. But poverty also impacts dramatically on the nonpoor. It has a dampening effect on wages in general (by maintaining a reserve army of unemployed and underemployed anxious for any job at any wage) and breeds crime and violence (by maintaining conditions that invite private gain by illegal means and rebellion-like behavior, not entirely unlike the urban riots of the 1960s). Given the extent of poverty in the nation and the impact it has on us all, the media must spin considerable magic to keep the poor and the issue of poverty and its root causes out of the public consciousness.

About Everyone Else

Both the broadcast and the print news media strive to develop a strong sense of "we-ness" in their audience. They seek to speak to and for an audience that is both affluent and like-minded. The media's solidarity with affluence, that is, with the middle and upper class, varies little from one medium to another. Benjamin DeMott points out, for example, that the *New York Times* understands affluence to be intelligence, taste, public spirit, responsibility, and a readiness to rule and "conceives itself as spokesperson for a readership awash in these qualities."[4] Of course, the flip side to creating a sense of "we," or "us," is establishing a perception of the "other." The other relates back to the faceless, amoral, undeserving, and inferior "underclass." Thus, the world according to the news media is divided between the "underclass" and everyone else. Again the messages are often contradictory.

The Wealthy Are Us

Much of the information provided to us by the news media focuses attention on the concerns of a very wealthy and privileged class of people. Although the concerns of a small fraction of the populace, they are presented as though they were the concerns of everyone. For example, while relatively few people actually own stock, the news media devotes an inordinate amount of broadcast time and print space to business news and stock market quotations. Not only do business reports cater to a particular narrow clientele, so do the fashion pages (with $2,000 dresses), wedding announcements, and the obituaries. Even weather and sports news often have a class bias. An all-news radio station in New York City, for example, provides regular national ski reports. International news, trade agreements, and domestic policy issues are also reported in terms of their impact on business climate and the business community. Besides being of practical value to the wealthy, such coverage has considerable ideological value. Its message: the concerns of the wealthy are the concerns of us all.

The Wealthy (as a Class) Do Not Exist

While preoccupied with the concerns of the wealthy, the media fails to notice the way in which the rich as a class of people create and shape domestic and foreign policy. Presented as an aggregate of individuals, the wealthy appear without special interests, interconnections, or unity in purpose. Out of public view are the class interests of the wealthy, the interlocking business links, the concerted actions to preserve their class privileges and business interests (by running for public office, supporting political candidates, lobbying, etc.). Corporate lobbying is ignored, taken for granted, or assumed to be in the public interest. (Compare this with the media's portrayal of the "strong arm of labor" in attempting to defeat trade legislation that is harmful to the interests of working people.) It is estimated that two-thirds of the U.S. Senate is composed of millionaires.[5] Having such a preponderance of millionaires in the Senate, however, is perceived to be neither unusual nor antidemocratic; these millionaire senators are assumed to be serving "our" collective interests in governing.

The Wealthy Are Fascinating and Benevolent

The broadcast and print media regularly provide hype for individuals who have achieved "super" success. These stories are usually about celebrities and superstars from the sports and entertainment world. Society pages and gossip columns serve to keep the social elite informed of each others' doings, allow the rest of us to gawk at their excesses, and help to keep the American dream alive. The print media is also fond of feature stories on corporate empire builders. These stories provide an occasional "insider's" view of the private and corporate life of industrialists by suggesting a rags to riches account of corporate success. These stories tell us that corporate success is a series of smart moves, shrewd acquisitions, timely mergers, and well thought out executive suite shuffles. By painting the upper class in a positive light, innocent of any wrongdoing (labor leaders and union organizations usually get the opposite treatment), the media assures us that wealth and power are benevolent. One person's capital accumulation is presumed to be good for all. The elite, then, are portrayed as investment wizards, people of special talent and skill, whom even their victims (workers and consumers) can admire.

The Wealthy Include a Few Bad Apples

On rare occasions, the media will mock selected individuals for their personality flaws. Real estate investor Donald Trump and New York Yankees owner George Steinbrenner, for example, are admonished by the media for deliberately seeking publicity (a very un-upper class thing to do); hotel owner Leona Helmsley was caricatured for her personal cruelties; and junk bond broker Michael Milkin was condemned because he had the audacity to rob the rich. Michael Parenti points out that by treating business wrongdoings as isolated deviations from the socially beneficial system of "responsible capitalism," the media overlooks the features of the system that produce such abuses and the regularity with which they occur. Rather than portraying them as predictable and frequent outcomes of corporate power and the business system, the media treats abuses as if they were isolated and atypical. Presented as an occasional aberration, these incidents serve not to challenge, but to legitimate, the system.[6]

The Middle Class Is Us

By ignoring the poor and blurring the lines between the working people and the upper class, the news media creates a universal middle class. From this perspective, the size of one's income becomes largely irrelevant: what matters is that most of "us" share an intellectual and moral superiority over the disadvantaged. As *Time* magazine once concluded, "Middle America is a state of mind."[7] "We are all middle class," we are told, "and we all share the same concerns": job security, inflation, tax burdens, world peace, the cost of food and housing, health care, clean air and water, and the safety of our streets. While the concerns of the wealthy are quite distinct from those of the middle class (e.g., the wealthy worry about investments, not jobs), the media convinces us that "we [the affluent] are all in this together."

The Middle Class Is a Victim

For the media, "we" the affluent not only stand apart from the "other"—the poor, the working class, the minorities, and their problems—"we" are also victimized by the poor (who drive up the costs of maintaining the welfare rolls), minorities (who commit crimes against us), and workers (who are greedy and drive companies out and prices up). Ignored are the subsidies to the rich, the crimes of corporate America, and the policies that wreak havoc on the economic well-being of middle America. Media magic convinces us to fear, more than anything else, being victimized by those less affluent than ourselves.

The Middle Class Is Not a Working Class

The news media clearly distinguishes the middle class (employees) from the working class (i.e., blue collar workers) who are portrayed, at best, as irrelevant, outmoded, and a dying breed. Furthermore, the media will tell us that the hardships faced by blue collar workers are inevitable (due to progress), a result of bad luck (chance circumstances in a particular industry), or a product of their own doing (they priced themselves out of a job). Given the media's presentation of reality, it is hard to believe that manual, supervised, unskilled, and semiskilled workers actually represent more than 50 percent of the adult working population.[8] The working class, instead, is relegated by the media to "the other."

• • •

In short, the news media either lionizes the wealthy or treats their interests and those of the middle class as one in the same. But the upper class and the middle class do not share the same interests or worries. Members of the upper class worry about stock dividends (not employment), they profit from inflation and global militarism, their children attend exclusive private schools, they eat and live in a royal fashion, they call on (or are called upon by) personal physicians, they have few consumer problems, they can escape whenever they want from environmental pollution, and they live on streets and travel to other areas under the protection of private police forces.[*9]

The wealthy are not only a class with distinct life-styles and interests, they are a ruling class. They receive a disproportionate share of the country's yearly income, own a disproportionate amount of the country's wealth, and contribute a disproportionate number of their members to governmental bodies and decision-making groups—all traits that William Domhoff, in his classic work *Who Rules America*, defined as characteristic of a governing class.[10]

This governing class maintains and manages our political and economic structures in such a way that these structures continue to yield an amazing proportion of our wealth to a minuscule upper class. While the media is not above referring to ruling classes in other countries (we hear, for example, references to Japan's ruling elite),[11] its treatment of the news proceeds as though there were no such ruling class in the United States.

Furthermore, the news media inverts reality so that those who are working class and middle class learn to fear, resent, and blame those below, rather than those above, them in the class structure. We learn to resent welfare, which accounts for only two cents out of every dollar in the federal budget (approximately $10 billion) and provides financial relief for the needy,[**] but learn little about the $11 billion the federal government spends on individuals with incomes in excess of $100,000 (not needy),[12] or the $17 billion in farm subsidies, or the $214 billion (twenty times the cost of welfare) in interest payments to financial institutions.

Middle-class whites learn to fear African Americans and Latinos, but most violent crime occurs within poor and minority communities and is neither interracial[***] nor interclass. As horrid as such crime is, it should not mask the destruction and violence perpetrated by corporate America. In spite of the fact that 14,000 innocent people are killed on the job each year, 100,000 die prematurely, 400,000 become seriously ill, and 6 million are injured from work-related accidents and diseases, most Americans fear government regulation more than they do unsafe working conditions.

---

*The number of private security guards in the United States now exceeds the number of public police officers. (Robert Reich, "Secession of the Successful," *New York Times Magazine*, February 17, 1991, p. 42.)

**A total of $20 billion is spent on welfare when you include all state funding. But the average state funding also comes to only two cents per state dollar.

***In 92 percent of the murders nationwide the assailant and the victim are of the same race (46 percent are white/white, 46 percent are black/black, 5.6 percent are black on white, and 2.4 percent are white on black). (FBI and Bureau of Justice Statistics, 1985–1986, quoted in Raymond S. Franklin, *Shadows of Race and Class*, University of Minnesota Press, Minneapolis, 1991, p. 108.)

Through the media, middle-class—and even working-class—Americans learn to blame blue collar workers and their unions for declining purchasing power and economic security. But while workers who managed to keep their jobs and their unions struggled to keep up with inflation, the top 1 percent of American families saw their average incomes soar 80 percent in the last decade.[13] Much of the wealth at the top was accumulated as stockholders and corporate executives moved their companies abroad to employ cheaper labor (56 cents per hour in El Salvador) and avoid paying taxes in the United States. Corporate America is a world made up of ruthless bosses, massive layoffs, favoritism and nepotism, health and safety violations, pension plan losses, union busting, tax evasions, unfair competition, and price gouging, as well as fast buck deals, financial speculation, and corporate wheeling and dealing that serve the interests of the corporate elite, but are generally wasteful and destructive to workers and the economy in general.

It is no wonder Americans cannot think straight about class. The mass media is neither objective, balanced, independent, nor neutral. Those who own and direct the mass media are themselves part of the upper class, and neither they nor the ruling class in general have to conspire to manipulate public opinion. Their interest is in preserving the status quo, and their view of society as fair and equitable comes naturally to them. But their ideology dominates our society and justifies what is in reality a perverse social order—one that perpetuates unprecedented elite privilege and power on the one hand and widespread deprivation on the other. A mass media that did not have its own class interests in preserving the status quo would acknowledge that inordinate wealth and power undermines democracy and that a "free market" economy can ravage a people and their communities.

NOTES

1. Martin Lee and Norman Solomon, *Unreliable Sources*, Lyle Stuart (New York, 1990), p. 71. See also Ben Bagdikian, *The Media Monopoly*, Beacon Press (Boston, 1990).
2. Department of Commerce, Bureau of the Census, "Poverty in the United States: 1992," *Current Population Reports, Consumer Income*, Series P60–185, pp. xi, xv, 1.
3. William Ryan, *Blaming the Victim*, Vintage (New York, 1971).
4. Benjamin Demott, *The Imperial Middle*, William Morrow (New York, 1990), p. 123.
5. Fred Barnes, "The Zillionaires Club," *The New Republic*, January 29, 1990, p. 24.
6. Michael Parenti, *Inventing Reality*, St. Martin's Press (New York, 1986), p. 109.
7. *Time*, January 5, 1979, p. 10.
8. Vincent Navarro, "The Middle Class—A Useful Myth," *The Nation*, March 23, 1992, p. 1.
9. Charles Anderson, *The Political Economy of Social Class*, Prentice Hall (Englewood Cliffs, N.J., 1974), p. 137.
10. William Domhoff, *Who Rules America*, Prentice Hall (Englewood Cliffs, N.J., 1967), p. 5.
11. Lee and Solomon, *Unreliable Sources*, p. 179.
12. *Newsweek*, August 10, 1992, p. 57.
13. *Business Week*, June 8, 1992, p. 86.

10 | You May Know Me from Such Roles as Terrorist #4

Jon Ronson

The right-wing action hero gave Maz Jobrani hope. This was 2001. Maz had been trying to make it as an actor in Hollywood for three years, but things were going badly for him. He was earning peanuts as an assistant at an advertising agency. But then his agent telephoned: Did Maz want to play a terrorist in a Chuck Norris movie? So Maz read the screenplay for *The President's Man: A Line in the Sand,* and he found within it a moment of promising subtlety.

"Chuck Norris plays a professor of Middle Eastern studies," Maz tells me. We're sitting in a coffee shop in Westwood, Los Angeles. Maz is a goateed man in his early forties who was born in Tehran but moved with his family to the San Francisco Bay Area when he was 6. "There's a scene where he's talking to his students about Afghanistan. One of the students raises his hand and says something like, 'Uh, professor, they're all fanatics, so why don't we just kill them all?' And the Chuck Norris character goes, 'Now, now. They're not all bad.' And I thought, 'Wow! A nuance!'"

The nuance gave Maz hope. Did this mean they'd allow him to make his character nuanced? Maz was aware that fixating on this one line might have been self-deluding, like a drowning man clutching driftwood in a hurricane. But he agreed to take the part. Then, at the wardrobe fitting, they handed him his turban.

"I said, 'Whoa, whoa! No! Afghans in America don't wear turbans. Plus, this guy's a terrorist. He's not going to draw attention to himself. You tell the producers I want to bring authenticity to this character.' The wardrobe supervisor replied, 'All right, all right, I'll talk to them.'"

The message came back from Chuck Norris's people that the turban was mandatory.

And then came Maz's death. It was the one thing he'd been excited about, because the script alluded to a short fight immediately preceding it. Hand-to-hand combat with Chuck Norris!

"But on the day of the scene," Maz says, "Chuck Norris told his son, who was the director, 'Oh, I'll just take a gun and I'll shoot him.' Oh, great! I don't even get a fight!"

"So how exactly did you get shot?" I ask Maz.

"Okay, so I'm about to set off a bomb at a refinery," he replies. "Chuck Norris runs in. I run away, because I'm scared. He gets behind the computer and starts dismantling the bomb, because he's a genius. I come running back in carrying an Uzi. And I try to shoot

---

Jon Ronson is an award-winning author, screenwriter, investigative journalist, musician, and filmmaker.

Originally published in *GQ*, July 2015. Copyright © Condé Nast. Used with permission.

him. But he takes out his gun and shoots me." Maz shrugs. "I start to yell, '*Allah*—' Bang! I'm down. I don't even get 'Allahu Akbar!' out. It was horrible, man."

Maz shakes his head at the memory. It was humiliating. Actually, it was worse than humiliating—it was a harbinger. Maz understood, as he lay dead in that refinery, that Hollywood didn't want him to be an actor. Hollywood wanted him to be a caricature. "I started acting in junior high," he says. "I was in *Guys and Dolls*. I was Stanley Kowalski. In my head, before coming to Hollywood, I thought, 'I can play anything.'" But instead he'd become the latest iteration in Hollywood's long history of racist casting, reducing his religion and culture to a bunch of villainous, cartoonish psychopaths. He knew he had to get out.

I glance at my phone. It's 1 P.M. We're running late to meet three of Maz's friends at a nearby Lebanese restaurant. We jump into Maz's car.

Maz refuses to take terrorist parts nowadays. He's primarily a stand-up comedian instead, a very funny and successful one. In fact, he's just published a memoir, *I'm Not a Terrorist, But I've Played One on TV*. But Maz's friends at the restaurant haven't been so lucky. They still make their livings as actors, which means they still play terrorists all the time.

Maz and I hurry into the restaurant, apologizing for being late. We order a *mezze* plate for five. These men have been killed while committing acts of terrorism on *Homeland* and *24*, in *The Kingdom* and *Three Kings* and *True Lies*, and in too many other films and shows to list. We've barely sat down when Waleed Zuaiter, a Palestinian-American actor in his early forties, recounts for me his death scene on *Law & Order: Criminal Intent*. This was about a year after September 11. "I play a guy from a sleeper cell," Waleed says. "I'm checking my e-mails. I hear the cops come in, and the first thing I go for is my box cutter. There's literally a box cutter in the scene."

"Was this in an office?" I ask Waleed.

"It was in my home!" he replies. "I just *happened* to have a box cutter lying around." Waleed shakes his head, bemused. "The cops burst in, and next thing you know I've got the box cutter to some guy's neck. And then one of the cops shoots me."

"I die in *Iron Man*," says Sayed Badreya, an Egyptian man with a salt-and-pepper beard. "I die in *Executive Decision*. I get shot at by—what's his name?—Kurt Russell. I get shot by everyone. George Clooney kills me in *Three Kings*. Arnold blows me up in *True Lies* . . ."

As Sayed and Waleed and the others describe their various demises, it strikes me that the key to making a living in Hollywood if you're Muslim is to be good at dying. If you're a Middle Eastern actor and you can die with charisma, there is no shortage of work for you.

Here's another irony in the lives of these men: While they profoundly wish they didn't have to play terrorists, much of our lunch is taken up with them swapping tips on clever ways to stand out at terrorist auditions.

"If I'm going in for the role of a nice father, I'll talk to everybody," Sayed tells the table. "But if you're going for a terrorist role, don't fucking smile at all those white people sitting there. Treat them like shit. The minute you say hello, you break character."

"But it's smart at the end of the audition to break it," adds Hrach Titizian, who at 36 is the youngest actor here. "'Oh, thanks, guys.' So they know it's okay to have you on set for a couple of weeks."

Then Waleed says something you don't often hear actors say, because most actors regard their competition with dread: "Whenever it's that kind of role and we see each other at the auditions, it's so comforting. We're not in this alone. We're in this together."

We're in this together. By this Waleed is referring to a uniquely demeaning set of circumstances. I'm sure practically *all* actors, Muslim or otherwise, feel degraded. Most have no power over their careers—what roles they can play, how their performances are edited. But Muslim actors are powerless in unusually hideous ways. The last time one became a big star in America was back in 1962—Omar Sharif in *Lawrence of Arabia.* These days they get offered terrorist roles and little else. And we—the paying public—barely even notice, much less worry about it. Where's the outrage? There is none, except from the actors themselves. These roles are ethically nightmarish for them, and the stress can wreak havoc on their lives. Waleed's father, for instance, threatened never to talk to him again if he ever played a terrorist. I thought that was bad enough. But then I meet another actor who had it much worse.

• • •

Ahmed Ahmed was raised a strict Muslim in Riverside, California, by his Egyptian-immigrant parents—a mother who learned English from watching soap operas, and a gas-station-attendant father who ended up buying an automotive shop. The day Ahmed told them he was quitting college to try his luck in Hollywood, his father asked if he was gay and didn't speak to him for seven years.

When I meet Ahmed at the French Roast Café in downtown New York City, he echoes Waleed's thoughts about the camaraderie among these actors. "It's always the same guys at every audition. Waleed, Sayed Badreya . . . You're all sitting in a row in the waiting room. Oftentimes the casting offce is right next to you. The door's shut, but you can hear what's going on."

"What do you hear?" I ask him.

"Oh, you know," he says. "'ALLAHU AKBAR!' And then . . ." Ahmed switches to the voice of a bubbly casting director. "'Thank you! That was *great!*' And the guy walks out, sweating. And you walk in and they're, 'Hey! Thanks for coming in! Whenever you're ready!' And you're thinking, 'How do I do it differently from the guy before me? Do I go louder?'"

When he auditioned for *Executive Decision,* he went louder. *Executive Decision* is, I realize as I talk to people from this world, considered the ground zero (as it were) of ludicrous portrayals of Islamic terrorists. This was 1996, and Ahmed was in his mid-twenties. "My agent had called me. 'There's this film. It's a $55 million action suspense thriller starring Kurt Russell, Halle Berry, and Steven Seagal. They want to bring you in to read for one of the parts.' I said, 'What's the part?' She said, 'Terrorist Number Four.' I said, 'I don't want to do it.' She said, 'It's three weeks of work. It pays $30,000.'"

And so Ahmed read for the part. "My lines were 'Sit down and obey or I will kill you in the name of Allah.' And the director goes, 'Brilliant! Do it again. But this time, can you give me more of that Middle Eastern, you know . . .' I go, 'Anger?' He goes, 'Yes! Yes! Angry!'"

Feeling a flash of actual anger, Ahmed decided to ridicule the process by going stupidly over-the-top.

"And the next day," he says, "my agent calls me up: 'You booked it.'"

By the time *Executive Decision* came out later that year, Ahmed says, his life had "become dark. Boozing on the Sunset Strip. After-hours parties. I'd wake up at 2 P.M. and do it all over again. It's the same people in the clubs every night. Everyone's trying to fill a void."

"Were you doing all that boozing because you felt guilty for playing terrorists?" I ask him.

"There was an element of that," he replies. "There was an element of not working between those parts. And then I had an epiphany. I called my agent: 'Hey! Don't send me out on these terrorist parts anymore. I'll be open for anything else, but not the terrorist stuff.'" Ahmed pauses. "After that, she never called."

"How often did she call before then?" I ask him.

"Oh, three or four times a week."

And so Ahmed made a decision: "Get the fuck out of Hollywood." He went to Mecca. And what he saw there were "four and a half million people dressed in white — rich, poor, walking side by side, asking for blessings from God."

For ten solid years after his trip to Mecca, Ahmed quit acting and became a stand-up comedian. He still performs regularly, but he says he'll take a terrorist role from time to time if a good one comes along. After all, he notes, nobody accuses Robert De Niro of betraying other Italian-Americans when he plays a mobster.

• • •

The evening after our lunch in Westwood, I visit Sayed Badreya, the older Egyptian actor, at his Santa Monica apartment. When I arrive, he's online, looking at photographs of Arabian horses.

"I'm involved in breeding them," he says, "because I don't know if I can keep playing these same parts." He says his daughter was once asked at school what her father did for a living and she replied, "He hijacks airplanes."

Sayed takes his work seriously and has always gone to great lengths to research his roles. In 1991, he started attending a mosque in Culver City, one that was known to attract some militant worshippers, so he could study Islamic radicalism up close. A few years later, some of the mosque's worshippers went to a movie and recognized Sayed. Back at the mosque after Friday prayers, they surrounded him. "They were yelling, right in my face: 'You're helping the Zionist Jews of Hollywood in their agenda to make Islam look bad. For money, you're giving up your heritage.'"

"How were you responding?" I ask.

"I felt guilty," he says. "I knew they were sort of right. But I yelled back at them, 'We have to take their money to make our own movie and tell our own story!' We were yelling so hard we were showering each other with spit."

"What was the movie of yours they saw?" I ask him.

"*Executive* fucking *Decision*," he says.

Sayed says he does all he can to intersperse his terrorist roles with more helpful portrayals of Muslims. He wrote and starred in a well-regarded film, *AmericanEast*, charting the struggles of Muslims in America post-9/11. But he has to play terrorists to pay the bills, so he at least tries to be a realistic one. He does side work as a technical consultant, advising directors on the accuracy of their films. He worked in this capacity on *Executive Decision*. "We had a really beautiful moment in an Arabic wedding scene," Sayed says. "And the producer, Joel Silver, saw it and said, 'No, no. This is nice. I want a fucking bad Arab. We don't want a good Arab.'"

Almost all of the wedding scene was cut from the film, Sayed says. But here's a scene that wasn't cut: One of the terrorists takes a quick break from killing people to read the Koran. "If I'm playing a guy chosen to hijack a plane, that means I'm one of the top soldiers. I'm going on a mission. I'm not going to Mecca. He might recite something in his head if he's religious, but he's not going to open the Bible. But producers get really sensitive if you say, 'No, that's not accurate.'"

In an e-mailed statement, Joel Silver denied the "bad Arab" incident, adding, "Any editorial decisions, made twenty years ago, were strictly creative, and not to perpetuate any stereotypes." I didn't hear back from any of the other producers or directors I approached. Not Peter Berg (*The Kingdom*, another film that has a bad reputation with Muslim actors for its portrayal of the Islamic world), nor Stephen McEveety (Mel Gibson's collaborator on *The Passion of the Christ* and the producer of the *The Stoning of Soraya M.*, in which an Iranian husband has his wife stoned to death), nor Joel Surnow, the co-creator of *24*. Maz told me that his most offensive acting offer ever was for a Joel Surnow production—Fox's short-lived comedy *The 1/2 Hour News Hour*. Maz says he was asked to audition for a sketch about a Middle Eastern architect pitching to rebuild the Twin Towers. The joke was that his design included a bull's-eye right on the building. Howard Gordon, the man behind *Homeland* and *24*, is the only producer I persuade to talk to me. He calls me from his car.

"I came to this issue when I was accused of having Islamophobia in *24*," he says. "We had a family, essentially, of terrorists on the show. The Muslim Public Affairs Council provided an education for me on the power of images."

"What did they say?"

"They asked me to imagine what it might be like to be a Muslim, to have people fear my faith," he replies. "I felt very sympathetic. I didn't want to be a midwife to xenophobia."

Since then, he says, he has done his best. And people have noticed. When I was having lunch with Maz and the other actors at the Lebanese restaurant in Westwood, Howard was one of the only mainstream producers they praised. (*Three Kings'* David O. Russell was another.)

"Anyone with a conscience has to take this seriously," Howard tells me. "I'd often hidden behind the defense that *24* was a counterterrorism show. We rationalized to ourselves that our primary task was to tell a compelling story." But the truth, he knew, was darker than that: "We all have our personal biases and fears—I suspect we're wired to feel threatened by the 'other.' And I include myself in that category."

● ● ●

In the lobby of a chichi old hotel in Midtown Manhattan, Anthony Azizi warns me that this interview might get heated. And indeed it does. If you want to know the impact that a lifetime of doing these movies can have on a man, spend some time with Anthony Azizi.

Anthony is a veteran of various *CSIs* and *NCISs* and *24*. His death scene in *24*, he says, made it onto a Yahoo list of best deaths ever. (His throat gets slit with a credit card.) He's a big, handsome, intense man who is not, by the way, a Muslim. He's a member of the Iranian spiritualist faith the Bahá'í.

"Hollywood has the power to snap its fingers and make whoever it wants a star," he begins. "It specifically and purposefully doesn't want to see an Arab or a Middle Eastern star. There's too much prejudice and racism—and the people running it, I don't need to go into the specifics of their backgrounds. . . ."

I think I know what he's getting at. But all sorts of producers—not just Jews—are behind insensitive movie portrayals of Muslims. There's Chuck Norris. There's John Musker, director of 1992's *Aladdin*, in which all the "good Arabs" have American accents and all the "bad Arabs" have pseudo-Middle Eastern accents. Stephen McEveety (*The Stoning of Soraya M.*) is Catholic.

Anthony carries on, turning his anger toward Jon Stewart's *Rosewater*, in which the Mexican actor Gael García Bernal plays the Iranian-Canadian reporter Maziar Bahari. "Man, if I saw Jon Stewart, you'd have to hold me back. How dare you hire a Mexican-American to play an Iranian-American, with all these amazing Iranian-American artists. I can't stand it. I'm sick of it. I speak Spanish fluently. . . ."

He effortlessly slides into perfect Spanish for a few seconds, then returns to being Anthony. "Why am I not being hired for Mexican or Latino roles?" he says. "You play my roles, but I can't play yours, and I speak Spanish just as well? Go fuck yourself." Anthony picks up my recorder. "Go fuck yourself, Jon Stewart!" he yells. "Have me on your show if you have the balls! You don't have the balls!"

He's really shouting now. The hotel receptionists keep glancing nervously over at us, wondering whether to intervene. "Hollywood people are pussies!" he rants. "They're racist! They don't want to say, 'I just built a Middle Eastern star!' Here's how I see it—and this is probably the most controversial thing I'll ever say: The only Middle Eastern star was Omar Sharif. The minute he had a relationship with a Jewish-American woman named Barbra Streisand was the death knell for any other Arab-American actor's career. Hear it again! The minute he had a sexual relationship with a Jewish . . ."

"I don't underst—" I start to say.

"How dare you make that an incident where no Arab-American actor can ever get a career again!"

Finally I get my question out, or at least some of it: "But what's the connection between Omar Sharif purportedly having an affair with Barbra Streisand and—"

"I think there's a certain type of producer that doesn't want to see that happen," he says. "They don't want their gem—Barbra Streisand was the gem of the Jewish community—sleeping with the Arab heathen! It caused huge riots in Egypt, too. I'd say the same thing to the Egyptian community. . . ."

Sure, Anthony's Barbra Streisand outburst is crazy. If there *is* a racist conspiracy in Hollywood to rob Middle Eastern actors of roles, it's not a great idea to rail against it with a racist-conspiracy theory of one's own. But think about what Anthony has been subjected to in his career. He and the other men in this story are going through something that future generations will regard as outrageous. They're the bloodthirsty Red Indians surrounding the settlers' wagons in *Stagecoach*. They're the black savages in *The Birth of a Nation* (who were played by white actors in blackface). They are the people Hollywood will be apologizing to tomorrow.

"Don't question my talent," Anthony says. "I should be a star by now. But I'm not. So you explain why."

Perhaps the closest this community has to a star is Navid Negahban. He played, most famously, Abu Nazir in *Homeland* and also the Iraqi in *American Sniper* who helps the U.S. military locate "the butcher." He was Ali, the stoner in *The Stoning of Soraya M.*

"Everyone I've met seems really talented," I tell Anthony. "So why do you think Navid, of all of you . . .?"

"He's hot right now, playing bad guys," Anthony replies. "He loves to play those roles. I love Navid. He's my brother. But there's no longevity in those roles. You always get whacked. Everybody who's still alive in *Homeland* is white! Where is Abu Nazir? He got whacked, 'cause he's brown."

• • •

Getting to meet Navid isn't easy. One minute he's filming in upstate New York, the next he's doing motion capture as a video-game character in Los Angeles before flying off to shoot a movie in Morocco. But I manage to catch him for an hour at a coffee shop near Columbus Circle in New York City. He's already there, chatting with another on-screen terrorist, Herzl Tobey *(The Shield, 24, Homeland)*. They've been working on a movie together upstate, so Navid has brought him along to meet me. Navid is very dashing, with an old-fashioned matinee-idol air to him.

"I'm sure you've had a few of the others say, 'I won't do terrorists anymore,'" he says as I sit down.

"Yes," I say.

"I've told them that's the biggest mistake," says Navid. "If we don't play those roles, the character becomes a caricature. [The producers] might get some actor from a different background who looks Middle Eastern." Herzl nods, adding, "The writer is sitting here in America, writing about a world he's completely unfamiliar with. So of course he won't be able to write it with the full depth and sensuality that comes with that world. It's up to us to bring that depth."

I tell Navid that I've noticed that the more prominent the Middle Eastern actor, the more awesome the death. Back when Maz was just starting out, he barely got 'Allah' out before Chuck Norris shot him. But Navid is at the top of the pecking order, the closest thing we have to the late Omar Sharif. I ask him to remind me how Abu Nazir died on *Homeland*.

"Oh, he was graceful," Navid replies. "It was so . . ." He smacks his lips. "He's sitting very gracefully on the floor. On his knees. He's ready. The soldiers run in. Everybody's yelling. But he's calm. He's just looking at all of them very, very calmly. And then he reaches into his pocket and they shoot him. And there's a Koran in his pocket." Navid smiles wistfully. "That was beautiful," he says. "I die well."

11

Against "Bullying" or On Loving Queer Kids

Richard Kim

When I read that 18-year-old Rutgers freshman Tyler Clementi had committed suicide by jumping off the George Washington Bridge after two other students posted a video of him having sex with another man online, my heart dropped. Tyler grew up in New Jersey and played the violin, and I did too. I don't know what life was like for Tyler before he chose to end it, but my early high school years were spent improvising survival strategies. I mentally plotted the corridors where the jocks hung out and avoided them. I desperately tried to never go to the bathroom during the school day. I was Asian and gay, stood 5'2", weighed 95 pounds and when I got excited about something—which was often—my voice cracked into a register normally only heard among Hannah Montana fans. If it weren't for the fact that I ran really fast and talked even faster and enjoyed the protection of a few popular kids and a couple of kind-hearted teachers—well, it's not hard to imagine a similar fate.

I say all this not to elicit pity—I'm a bigger boy now, and I bash back—but to make it clear that I'm conditioned to abhor people who bully queer kids. There's nothing—nothing—that raises my hackles more than seeing an effeminate boy being teased. But I also find myself reluctant to join the chorus of voices calling for the law to come down hard on Dharun Ravi and Molly Wei, the Rutgers students who posted the video and who are now facing "invasion of privacy" charges. If convicted they could face up to 5 years in prison; some gay rights groups like Garden State Equality are calling for the two to be prosecuted under New Jersey's hate crimes law, which could double the sentence.

What Ravi and Wei did was immature, prurient, and thoughtless; it undoubtedly played some role in what became an awful, awful tragedy. That they acted with homophobic malice, that they understood what the consequences of their actions might be, or that their prank alone, or even chiefly, triggered Clementi's suicide is far less clear. There's no record of Ravi and Wei discriminating against gays in the past, and there's nothing exceptionally homophobic about the tweet Ravi sent—"I saw him making out with a dude. Yay." One could easily insert "fat chick" or "masturbating to porn" into the scenario, which wouldn't have made it any more acceptable—or legal—for Ravi and Wei to surreptitiously broadcast the incident, but might have provided just as much titillation and inducement anyway. More importantly, we know virtually nothing about Clementi's life prior to his

---

Richard Kim is on the editorial board of *The Nation* and is coeditor with Betsy Reed of the anthology *Going Rouge: Sarah Palin, An American Nightmare*. He has taught at New York University and Skidmore College.

last days, including how he felt about his sexuality or whether or not he found affirmation of it at home, among his friends or on the campus at large.

But for some gays and liberals shaken by Clementi's suicide, the complexities and unknowns don't seem to matter. It's convenient to make Ravi and Wei into little monsters singularly responsible for his death. In the words of Malcolm Lazin—the director of Equality Forum, a gay rights group that's calling for "murder by manslaughter" charges, a demand echoed on sympathetic blogs and Facebook pages—the duo's conduct was "willful and premeditated," an act so "shocking, malicious and heinous" that Ravi and Wei "had to know" it would be "emotionally explosive." Each and every one of these accusations is entirely speculative at this point, a fact that you'd think Lazin, a former US assistant district attorney, would bear in mind before rounding up the firing squad.

Clementi's is the latest in a rash of suicides by gay teenagers, most of them boys. In September alone the body count includes Billy Lucas, a 15-year-old from Indiana who hanged himself after repeatedly being called a "fag" by his classmates; Asher Brown, a 13-year-old Texan who shot himself after his fellow students performed "mock gay acts" on him during gym class; and 13-year-old Seth Walsh from California who hanged himself from a tree in his backyard after being teased for years for being gay. In each of these cases, news reports focused almost exclusively on the bullies—other kids who were 12, 13, 14, 15 years old—as the perpetrators in what's been dubbed "an epidemic of anti-gay bullying." In each of these cases, liberals and gays expressed dismay that the bullies weren't being charged with crimes. Few of the articles asked what home life was like for these gay teens or looked into what role teachers, schools and the broader community played in creating an environment where the only escape from such routine torment seemed death. And too few (with the exception of Ellen DeGeneres and Sarah Silverman) drew the line to the messages mainstream adult America, including its politicians and preachers, sends every day.

It's not hard to do. Senator Jim DeMint of South Carolina is in the news of late for doubling down on his 2004 statement that out gay people (and unwed mothers) should be banned from teaching in public schools. Both New Hampshire Senate candidate Kelly Ayotte and Nevada Senate candidate Sharron Angle support making gay adoption illegal, as did Florida's Charlie Crist until he flipped his position and tacked to the center in his race against Tea Partier Marco Rubio, who still supports the ban. These right-wing policies would discriminate against gay adults, but what fuels them is the anxiety that having openly gay men and women teaching and raising kids would make it known to children that being gay is a survivable, even joyous, condition. As such the real targets are queer kids, and the message is quite simple: Please, don't exist.

At least the right is relatively honest in its brutality. Oregon has no ban on gay teachers, but that didn't stop the Beaverton school district, which is located just outside lefty Portland and has an anti-discrimination policy that includes sexual orientation, from removing Seth Stambaugh from his fourth grade classroom. A 23-year-old teaching intern, Stambaugh responded to a student's question about why he wasn't married by saying that gay marriage is illegal in Oregon. A spokeswoman for the school board claimed that the action wasn't discriminatory, but rather based on concerns about Stambaugh's "professional judgment and age appropriateness."

And there you have a pithy example of the limits of liberal tolerance; even in communities that would denounce the DeMints of the world, a palpable phobia remains when it comes to *the children*. Gay teachers should teach, until they teach about the plain realities of being gay. (It's this vacuum of education that's inspired Dan Savage's direct-to-teen YouTube campaign *It Gets Better*). Let's just have the kids figure it out themselves and come out when they're all grown up, rather than ask pesky questions we'd rather not try to answer: What does the "closet" mean for a kid who announces she's gay when she's 11, or 5, or wants to marry someone like Mommy and not Daddy? What to make of the fact that your little boy begs to dress exclusively like Taylor Swift? Is he gay or trans or just going through a phase—and oh God, isn't not knowing the worst of it?

Even for liberals who like to think of themselves as pro-gay, this is uncharted territory, little discussed except perhaps in the deepest corners of Park Slope. So when faced with something so painful and complicated as gay teen suicide, it's easier to go down the familiar path, to invoke the wrath of law and order, to create scapegoats out of child bullies who ape the denials and anxieties of adults, to blame it on technology or to pare down homophobia into a social menace called "anti-gay bullying" and then confine it to the borders of the schoolyard.

It's tougher, more uncertain work creating a world that loves queer kids, that wants them to live and thrive. But try—try as if someone's life depended on it. Imagine saying I really wish my son turns out to be gay. Imagine hoping that your 2-year-old daughter grows up to be transgendered. Imagine not assuming the gender of your child's future prom date or spouse; imagine keeping that space blank or occupied by boys and girls of all types. Imagine petitioning your local board of education to hire *more* gay elementary school teachers.

Now imagine a world in which Tyler Clementi climbed up a ledge on the George Washington Bridge—and chose to climb back down instead. It's harder to do than you might think.

12 When You Forget to Whistle Vivaldi

Tressie McMillan Cottom

Last week Jonathan Ferrell had a horrible car crash. He broke out the back window to escape and walked, injured, to the nearest home hoping for help. Ferrell may have been too hurt, too in shock to remember to whistle Vivaldi. Ferrell is dead.[1]

Social psychologist Claude Steele revolutionized our understanding of the daily context and cognitive effects of stereotypes and bias. The title of his book alludes to a story his friend, *New York Times* writer Brent Staples, once shared.[2] An African American man, Staples, recounts how his physical presence terrified whites as he moved about Chicago as a free citizen and graduate student. To counter the negative effects of white fear he took to whistling a classical music piece by Italian composer Vivaldi. It was a signal to the victimless victims of his blackness that he was safe. Dangerous black men do not listen to classical music, or so the hope goes. The incongruence between Staples' musical choices and the stereotype of him as a predator was meant to disrupt the implicit, unexamined racist assumptions of him. It seems trite perhaps, an attempt to make whites feel at ease unless we recall the potential consequences of white dis-ease for black lives.

I do not know many black people who do not have a similar coping mechanism. I have been known to wear university branded clothing when I am shopping for real estate. A friend straightens her hair when she is job seeking. Another friend, a Hispanic male, told me that he shaves all his facial hair when entertaining white clients to signal that he is respectable. While stereotype threat can occur to any member of any group, it occurs most frequently and with more dangerous consequences for groups for whom there are more and stronger negative beliefs.

Of course, the oft-quoted idiom that respectability politics will not save you is true. Just as wearing long johns is not a preventative measure against rape for women, affecting middle class white behaviors is not a protective measure but a talisman. In exerting any measure of control over signaling that we are not dangerous or violent or criminal we are mostly assuaging the cognitive stress that constant management of social situations causes.

That stress has real consequences. Steele inspired an entire body of research on those effects. When the object of a stereotype is aware of the negative perception of her, that

---

Tressie McMillan Cottom is a sociologist, an author, and a professor at Virginia Commonwealth University. She writes widely on issues of inequality, work, higher education, and technology. She is the author of *Lower Ed: The Troubling Rise of For-Profit Colleges in the New Economy* and coeditor of *Digital Sociologies.*

Originally published September 18, 2013. Republished with permission from Tressie McMillan Cottom.

awareness constrains all manner of ability and performance. From testing scores of women who know the others in the room believe women cannot do math to missing a sports play when one is reminded that Asians don't have hops, the effects of stereotype threat are real.

Perhaps more interesting to me is what Steele described as the constant background processing that stereotyped people engage. It's like running too many programs in the background of your computer as you try to play a YouTube video. Just as the extra processing, invisible to the naked eye, impacts the video experience, the cognitive version compromises the functioning of our most sophisticated machines: human bodies.

I mentioned just today to a colleague that for all we social scientists like to talk about structural privilege it might be this social-psychological privilege that is the most valuable. Imagine the productivity of your laptop when all background programs are closed. Now imagine your life when those background processes are rarely, if ever, activated because of the social position your genetic characteristics afford you.

Of course, privilege is sometimes structural. But the murder of Jonathan Ferrell reminds us that activation of stereotype threat in daily interactions can be aided and abetted by organizational processes like the characterization of a police call to 911 and structural legitimacy like the authority of the police to shoot first and ask questions later. I am choosing to ignore how that process was set in motion. Perhaps better feminist scholars than myself can explore the historical, cultural gendered fear that legitimizes the unconscious bias of black men as sexual and criminal predators. I find I do not have the stomach for it today.

I just read an article that quotes Ferrell's family at length. His family's attorney did not just want us to know that Ferrell was a friend and son but that: "He's engaged to be married, he has a dog and a cat, he was driving a Toyota Camry, he survived an accident, had 3.7 GPA, a chemistry major. This is not someone who posed a threat to the officers or anyone else, this is an everyday American."

A 3.7 GPA.

They want us to know that their murdered friend, son, brother and cousin had a 3.7 GPA.

Ferrell may have been too injured, too shocked to whistle Vivaldi to all he encountered the night he was shot. It may not have helped if he had through slammed doors, over police sirens, and gunfire. But even in death his family cannot help but signal to us all that he was a student and, by extension, a human being whose death should matter.

Whistling Vivaldi in tribute, a talisman and hope that justice will hear what its executioners did not.

NOTES

1. Lee, T. (2013, September 25). "The 911 call that led to Jonathan Ferrell's death." http://www.msnbc.com/msnbc/the-911-call-led-jonathan-ferrells

2. Pronin, E. (2010, May 1). "Not Just Whistling Vivaldi." https://thesituationist.wordpress.com/2010/05/01/emily-pronin-reviews-whistling-vivaldi/

Chomsky, Noam. *On Power and Ideology*. Haymarket Press, 2015.

Cole, David. *No Equal Justice: Race and Class in the American Criminal Justice System*. The New Press, 2000.

Fenelon, James V. *Redskins? Sport Mascots, Indian Nations and White Racism*. Routledge, 2016.

Fraser, Steve, and Gary Gerstle. *Ruling America: A History of Wealth and Power in a Democracy*. Harvard University Press, 2005.

Giroux, Henry. *American Nightmare: Facing the Challenge of Fascism*. City Lights Publishers, 2018.

Goings, Kenneth W. *Mammy and Uncle Mose: Black Collectibles and American Stereotyping*. Indiana University Press, 1994.

Hall, Stuart, Jessica Evans, and Sean Nixon, eds. *Representation*, 2nd ed. Sage, 2013.

Harding, Sandra, and Merrill B. Hintikka. *Discovering Reality: Feminist Perspectives on Epistemology, Metaphysics, Methodology, and Philosophy of Science*, 2nd ed. Springer, 2007.

Harvey, David. *Spaces of Global Capitalism: A Theory of Uneven Geographical Development*. Verso, 2006.

Holtzman, Linda. *Media Messages: What Film, Television, and Popular Music Teach Us About Race, Class, Gender, and Sexual Orientation*. M. E. Sharp, 2000.

hooks, bell. *Black Looks: Race and Representation*, 2nd ed. Routledge, 2014.

Jhally, Sut. *The Spectacle of Accumulation: Essays in Culture, Media and Politics*. Peter Lang International Academic Publishers, 2011.

Kimmel, Michael. *Guyland: The Perilous World Where Boys Become Men*. Harper, 2009.

Klein, Naomi. *No Logo: 10th Anniversary Edition*. Picador, 2009.

Lewis, Amanda E. *Race in the Schoolyard*. Rutgers University Press, 2003.

Loewen, James. *Lies My Teacher Told Me: Everything Your American History Textbook Got Wrong*, rev. ed. New Press, 2008.

Madrick, Jeff. *The Case for Big Government*. Princeton University Press, 2008.

Mazzocco, Dennis W. *Networks of Power: Corporate TV's Threat to Democracy*. South End Press, 1999.

Morrison, Toni. *The Origin of Others*. Harvard University Press, 2017.

Orenstein, Peggy. *Cinderella Ate My Daughter: Dispatches from the Frontlines of the New Girlie-Girl Culture*. Harper, 2012.

Parenti, Michael. *Inventing Reality: The Politics of New Media*, 2nd ed. St. Martin's Press, 1992.

Sadker, David, Myra Sadker, and Karen Zittleman. *Still Failing at Fairness: How Gender Bias Cheats Boys and Girls in School and What We Can Do About It*. Scribner, 2009.

Schor, Juliet B. *Born to Buy: The Commercialized Child and the New Consumer Culture*. Scribner, 2004.

Snyder, Timothy. *On Tyranny: Twenty Lessons from the Twentieth Century*. Tim Duggan Books, 2017.

Stanley, Jason. *How Fascism Works: The Politics of Us and Them*. Random House, 2018.

Steele, Claude. *Whistling Vivaldi: How Stereotypes Affect Us and What We Can Do*. Norton, 2011.

Thompson, Becky W. *A Hunger So Wide and So Deep*, 2nd ed. University of Minnesota Press, 1996.

Valenti, Jessica. *The Purity Myth: How America's Obsession with Virginity Is Hurting Young Women*. Seal Press, 2009.

Yates, Michael D., ed. *More Unequal: Aspects of Class in the United States*. Monthly Review Press, 2007.

PART
IX

Social Change: Revisioning the Future and Making a Difference

For we have, built into all of us, old blueprints of expectation and response, old structures of oppression, and these must be altered at the same time as we alter the living conditions which are a result of those structures. For the master's tools will never dismantle the master's house.
—AUDRE LORDE

Abolition is not just about closing the doors to violent institutions, but also about building up and recovering institutions and practices and relationships that nurture wholeness, self-determination, and transformation. . . . Abolition is about breaking down things that oppress and building up things that nourish. Abolition is the practice of transformation in the here and now and the ever after.
—MORGAN BASSICHIS, ALEXANDER LEE, AND DEAN SPADE

An intersectional understanding of the nature and causes of systems of advantage and oppression based on race, class, and gender is a critical step toward dismantling these systems. How we define a problem affects how we imagine solutions and how we try to implement them. That is why so much of this book is devoted to defining and analyzing the nature of these systems. Only when we appreciate the subtle and complex factors that combine to create a society in which wealth, privilege, and opportunity are unequally apportioned will we be able to formulate viable proposals for bringing about social justice.

What, then, have the selections in this book told us about racism, sexism, heterosexism, and class exploitation? First, the complex ways in which these systems intersect and overlap mean that there is no single cause for any of them. Eliminating these systems of advantage and oppression will involve changes at every level—personal, social, political, and economic. It will require us to think differently about ourselves and others and to see the world

679

through new lenses. We will have to learn to pay close attention to our own attitudes and behaviors. We will have to reevaluate every institution in society and critically appraise the ways in which each privileges some people and disadvantages others. As we identify the ways in which our society reproduces the forms of inequality and privilege that we have been studying, we will have to act to change them. In short, we must scrutinize every aspect of our personal, economic, political, and social life with a view to asking whose interests are served and whose rights are denied when the world is so organized.

In Selection 1, poet and essayist Audre Lorde asserts that we will need to begin by redefining the meaning of difference. "The old definitions," she states, "have not served us, nor the earth that supports us." Our profit-driven economy, she argues, trains us to respond to differences with "fear and loathing" toward those defined as "other" and toward othered identities within ourselves. Lorde refuses this dynamic: "My fullest concentration of energy is available to me only when I integrate all the parts of who I am, openly, allowing power from particular sources of my living to flow back and forth freely through all my different selves, without the restrictions of externally imposed definition." Identifying herself as a "Black lesbian feminist socialist mother of two," Lorde asserts that real differences among people do exist. She argues, however, that it is *not* these differences that separate us but rather "our refusal to recognize those differences" and the role they play in shaping our relationships and social institutions. Denying or distorting those differences keeps us apart; embracing them "as a springboard for creative change" can provide a new starting point from which to work together to reconstruct our world.

In Selection 2, cultural critic bell hooks joins Audre Lorde in urging us to rethink difference in "a world governed by politics of domination." Both hooks and Lorde are central figures in laying the groundwork for contemporary intersectional feminism, a feminist movement revisioned to acknowledge the ways in which "sexism, racism, and class exploitation constitute interlocking systems of domination." hooks argues, "Feminist struggle to end patriarchal domination should be of primary importance to women and men globally not because it is the foundation of all other oppressive structures but because it is that form of domination we are most likely to encounter in an ongoing way in everyday life," particularly in the sphere of the family. She sees love as a vital mediating element in feminist revolution: "Working together to identify and face our differences—to face the ways we dominate and are dominated—to change our actions, we need a mediating force that can sustain us so that we are not broken in this process, so that we do not despair."

In Selection 3, Amit Taneja's journey to feminist consciousness hinges on his willingness to face the ways in which he is both oppressed and privileged. He traces his movement "from oppressor to activist" through a series of "snapshots"—moments in his life when he came to realize that, even as a "poor, immigrant, big-boned, non-Christian, gay person of color," he still received male privilege and had a duty to challenge patriarchal oppression. Taneja uses this personal transformation as a point of departure to call upon all of us to commit to social justice activism at the structural level, "not just on paper but also in practice."

Confronted by the enormous scale of the work to be done, many of us feel overwhelmed and disheartened. In Selection 4, educator and pastor Andrea Ayvazian suggests that one way to overcome a sense of immobilization and despair is to recognize our multiple social identities and engage in allied behavior. According to Ayvazian, "Allied behavior is intentional, overt, consistent activity that challenges prevailing patterns of oppression, makes privileges that are so often invisible visible, and facilitates the empowerment of persons targeted by oppression." When they consciously and deliberately work to dismantle forms of oppression from which they benefit, allies can be powerful agents of change.

Whereas Ayvazian's essay focuses on members of the dominant group, in Selection 5, Kristin Anderson and Christina Hsu Accomando expand the focus from allied behavior to coalition work, which involves working collectively for social change across precisely the sorts of differences identified by Lorde. They identify several pitfalls of superficial allied behavior—when "ally" operates merely as an identity, performance, or simplistic binary. In contrast, "coalition work is inherently intersectional," collaborative, and action based. Several of the readings that follow provide concrete examples of contemporary coalition work.

In Selection 6, Black Lives Matter cofounder Alicia Garza describes the genesis of the movement and the intersectional identities at its heart: "Black Lives Matter affirms the lives of Black queer and trans folks, disabled folks, Black-undocumented folks, folks with records, women, and all Black lives along the gender spectrum. It centers those that have been marginalized within Black liberation movements. It is a tactic to (re)build the Black liberation movement." She critiques those who fail to understand the complexity of the movement, who appropriate the movement's work without acknowledging the source, and who "drop 'Black' from the equation of whose lives matter." Garza supports "active solidarities" across differences but cautions against the construction of false unities. She writes: "Progressive movements in the United States have made some unfortunate errors when they push for unity at the expense of really understanding the concrete differences in context, experience, and oppression." Like Lorde and hooks, Garza encourages activists to redefine—but not erase—differences.

Civil rights activist Tarana Burke, in Selection 7, also tells the story of a movement's origin and calls on activists, the media, and the public to honor and build upon the original goals. In 2006, Burke launched Me Too as a grassroots movement to support survivors of sexualized violence, particularly young women of color in underserved communities. A decade later, #MeToo rose to international prominence as women in the Hollywood entertainment industry spoke out against sexual harassment. Burke critiques the mischaracterization of the movement as being focused on "taking down" powerful men. Rather, the focus of the movement she founded has always been on the healing of survivors. She writes: "Everyday people—queer, trans, disabled, men, and women—are living in the aftermath of a trauma that tried, at the very worst, to take away their humanity. This movement at its core is about the restoration of that humanity." While the mainstream media have focused on individual white women's stories (as also pointed out in Selections 11 and 12 in Part IV of this volume), Burke emphasizes the diversity of survivors and the need to address systemic causes: "The work of #MeToo builds on the existing efforts to dismantle systems of oppression that allow sexual violence, patriarchy, racism, and sexism to persist."

In Selection 8, human rights activist Loretta Ross and historian Rickie Solinger describe reproductive justice as a transformative framework and a twenty-first-century movement. They define reproductive justice as a human rights approach that places women of color at the center and fights equally for "(1) the right *not* to have a child; (2) the right to *have* a child; and (3) the right to parent children in safe and healthy environments." Such a framework necessitates intersectional analysis, coalitions across differences, and creative movement-building. In addition, "Storytelling is a core aspect of reproductive justice practice because attending to someone else's story invites us to shift the lens—that is, to imagine the life of another person and to reexamine our own realities and reimagine our own possibilities."

Activist, scholar, and prison abolitionist Angela Davis asks us to radically reimagine our reliance on prisons. In Selection 9, she asks this fundamental question: "If jails and prisons are to be abolished, then what will replace them?" To begin exploring that question, Davis must first challenge our current way of thinking about prisons. The prison industrial complex (also explored in her essay "Masked Racism"—Selection 8 in Part VIII) is more than jails and prisons: "It is a set of symbiotic relationships among correctional communities, transnational corporations, media conglomerates, guards' unions, and legislative and court agendas." Thus, imagining alternatives involves a "constellation" of approaches, including "demilitarization of schools, revitalization of education at all levels, a health system that provides free mental and physical care to all, and a justice system based on reparation and reconciliation rather than retribution and vengeance."

The abolitionist authors of Selection 10 also call for transformative strategies that radically reimagine justice, specifically using trans and queer lenses. Dean Spade (a law professor and founder of the Sylvia Rivera Law Project), legal advocate Alexander Lee, and performer Morgan Bassichis critique not only interlocking systems of domination, but also the ways in which mainstream gay rights movements have reinforced the police state. They identify a range of social problems and juxtapose "official" and transformative solutions. Calling for creative coalitions and "trickle up" change, they highlight diverse examples of visionary activism. The abolitionist trans and queer movement they advocate envisions abolition as not just "closing the doors to violent institutions," but also building up institutions and practices that "nurture wholeness, self-determination, and transformation." Ultimately, they argue for "the practice of transformation in the here and now."

In Selection 11, immigrant rights activist Gaby Pacheco offers advice and strategies from one youth-led movement to another. In 2010, Pacheco led a 1500-mile immigrant rights march from Florida to Washington, D.C. On the eve of the 2018 "March for Our Lives" to end gun violence, led by survivors of a mass shooting at a high school in Parkland, Florida, Pacheco shares her experiences as a source of both inspiration and caution. Now in her 30s, she highlights the courage and energy that young people bring to organizing, while also encouraging this new generation of leaders to learn from those who came before. "The young activists of today are more adept with social media than we were," she points out. "But I would encourage them to get out into the streets to talk to people. Our march took four months, and we spent time in the communities we visited." She also emphasizes the importance of foregrounding multiple voices, recognizing the complexity of identity, and building coalitions across differences.

In the final selection of Part IX, Chief Arvol Looking Horse, spiritual leader of the Lakota, Dakota, and Nakota Nations, articulates both disappointment and hope a year after the closing of the camp at Standing Rock Reservation and the movement forward of the Dakota Access Pipeline. Nevertheless, "Standing Rock has marked the beginning of an international movement that will continue to work peacefully, purposefully, and tirelessly for the protection of water along all areas of poisonous oil pipelines and across all of Mother Earth." There are many reasons to work in coalition, and in this case, the stakes are extremely high. Looking Horse writes, "Water is a source of life, not a resource. . . . We must continue to work together for the health and well-being of our water and our Earth."

GUIDING QUESTIONS FOR PART IX

1. How do the authors in Part IX use intersectional analysis? Why is it important to look at everything—including strategies for resistance—through an intersectional lens? Which movements discussed in Part IX are reimagined through intersectional lenses?

2. "[T]he master's tools will never dismantle the master's house," writes Audre Lorde. How can we forge new tools to transform our society? What are some examples of new tools in the readings in Part IX?

3. bell hooks argues that "[s]mall groups remain an important place for education for critical consciousness." What do you think she means by "critical consciousness"? According to hooks, what are some advantages of small-group conversations over classrooms and other more official spaces for education? In the twenty-first century, how might social media play a role in creating small-group conversations?

4. "As we work to be loving, to create a culture that celebrates life, that makes love possible, we move against dehumanization, against domination," argues bell hooks. How does she imagine love playing a role in feminist politics? How do you think love can counter dehumanization and domination?

5. Amit Taneja writes, "Feminist ideology recognizes the complexities of how oppression affects us and involves a much larger lens than only women's rights." How do the readings in Part IX reveal what this larger lens involves?

6. "Many of us are in positions of oppressor and oppressed at the same time," Taneja points out. "This knowledge must fuel our passion for ending oppression by abdicating and resisting norms that give us privilege over others." What are some concrete examples of how people can resist their own privileges? Can you identify life-altering moments (Taneja calls them "snapshots") in your own experience when you resisted privilege, challenged oppression, or bridged differences?

7. What are the pitfalls of ally behavior and identity, according to Anderson and Accomando? How does coalition politics offer an alternative set of practices for working across differences?

8. Alicia Garza describes creating #BlackLivesMatter as a response to the murder of Trayvon Martin; she also states that "Black Lives Matter is a unique contribution that goes beyond extrajudicial killings of Black people by police and vigilantes." How does she describe the larger goals of the movement she cofounded?

9. According to Tarana Burke, what were the intended purposes of the Me Too movement? How have the media misrepresented the aims of the movement? How does Burke

counter those misrepresentations? What does she see as the rigorous work that still lies ahead?

10. Why does Angela Davis close her chapter with the story of Amy Biehl? What lessons might we draw from this story that offer hope for "reconciliation and restorative justice" rather than retribution?

11. Morgan Bassichis, Alexander Lee, and Dean Spade identify several "big problems" facing queer and trans people in U.S. society. How do the transformative approaches they discuss differ from the "official" solutions offered by mainstream organizations?

12. How are environmental issues tied to systems of domination? According to Chief Arvol Looking Horse, why is protecting water such an important cause for an international movement? What does he mean when he writes, "Standing Rock is everywhere"? What does he mean when he writes, "we are at the crossroads"?

1

Age, Race, Class, and Sex: Women Redefining Difference

Audre Lorde

Much of Western European history conditions us to see human differences in simplistic opposition to each other: dominant/subordinate, good/bad, up/down, superior/inferior. In a society where the good is defined in terms of profit rather than in terms of human need, there must always be some group of people who, through systematized oppression, can be made to feel surplus, to occupy the place of the dehumanized inferior. Within this society, that group is made up of Black and Third World people, working-class people, older people, and women.

As a forty-nine-year-old Black lesbian feminist socialist mother of two, including one boy, and a member of an interracial couple, I usually find myself a part of some group defined as other, deviant, inferior, or just plain wrong. Traditionally, in american society, it is the members of oppressed, objectified groups who are expected to stretch out and bridge the gap between the actualities of our lives and the consciousness of our oppressor. For in order to survive, those of us for whom oppression is as american as apple pie have always had to be watchers, to become familiar with the language and manners of the oppressor, even sometimes adopting them for some illusion of protection. Whenever the need for some pretense of communication arises, those who profit from our oppression call upon us to share our knowledge with them. In other words, it is the responsibility of the oppressed to teach the oppressors their mistakes. I am responsible for educating teachers who dismiss my children's culture in school. Black and Third World people are expected to educate white people as to our humanity. Women are expected to educate men. Lesbians and gay men are expected to educate the heterosexual world. The oppressors maintain their position and evade responsibility for their own actions. There is a constant drain of energy which might be better used in redefining ourselves and devising realistic scenarios for altering the present and constructing the future.

Institutionalized rejection of difference is an absolute necessity in a profit economy which needs outsiders as surplus people. As members of such an economy, we have *all* been programmed to respond to the human differences between us with fear and loathing and to handle that difference in one of three ways: ignore it, and if that is not possible, copy it if we think it is dominant, or destroy it if we think it is subordinate. But we have no

Audre Lorde (1934–1992) was a poet, essayist, and prominent black feminist theorist. In the 1980s she cofounded Kitchen Table: Women of Color Press, and she later taught at John Jay College of Criminal Justice and Hunter College and served as the poet laureate of New York. Her many books include *Zami: A New Spelling of My Name, Sister Outsider,* and *The Cancer Journals.*

patterns for relating across our human differences as equals. As a result, those differences have been misnamed and misused in the service of separation and confusion.

Certainly there are very real differences between us of race, age, and sex. But it is not those differences between us that are separating us. It is rather our refusal to recognize those differences, and to examine the distortions which result from our misnaming them and their effects upon human behavior and expectation.

Racism, the belief in the inherent superiority of one race over all others and thereby the right to dominance. Sexism, the belief in the inherent superiority of one sex over the other and thereby the right to dominance. Ageism. Heterosexism. Elitism, Classism.

It is a lifetime pursuit for each one of us to extract these distortions from our living at the same time as we recognize, reclaim, and define those differences upon which they are imposed. For we have all been raised in a society where those distortions were endemic within our living. Too often, we pour the energy needed for recognizing and exploring difference into pretending those differences are insurmountable barriers, or that they do not exist at all. This results in a voluntary isolation, or false and treacherous connections. Either way, we do not develop tools for using human difference as a springboard for creative change within our lives. We speak not of human difference, but of human deviance.

Somewhere, on the edge of consciousness, there is what I call a *mythical norm*, which each one of us within our hearts knows "that is not me." In america, this norm is usually defined as white, thin, male, young, heterosexual, christian, and financially secure. It is with this mythical norm that the trappings of power reside within society. Those of us who stand outside that power often identify one way in which we are different, and we assume that to be the primary cause of all oppression, forgetting other distortions around difference, some of which we ourselves may be practicing. By and large within the women's movement today, white women focus upon their oppression as women and ignore differences of race, sexual preference, class, and age. There is a pretense to a homogeneity of experience covered by the word *sisterhood* that does not in fact exist.

Unacknowledged class differences rob women of each others' energy and creative insight. Recently a women's magazine collective made the decision for one issue to print only prose, saying poetry was a less "rigorous" or "serious" art form. Yet even the form our creativity takes is often a class issue. Of all the art forms, poetry is the most economical. It is the one which is the most secret, which requires the least physical labor, the least material, and the one which can be done between shifts, in the hospital pantry, on the subway, and on scraps of surplus paper. Over the last few years, writing a novel on tight finances, I came to appreciate the enormous differences in the material demands between poetry and prose. As we reclaim our literature, poetry has been the major voice of poor, working class, and Colored women. A room of one's own may be a necessity for writing prose, but so are reams of paper, a typewriter, and plenty of time. The actual requirements to produce the visual arts also help determine, along class lines, whose art is whose. In this day of inflated prices for material, who are our sculptors, our painters, our photographers? When we speak of broadly based women's culture, we need to be aware of the effect of class and economic differences on the supplies available for producing art.

As we move toward creating a society within which we can each flourish, ageism is another distortion of relationship which interferes with our vision. By ignoring the past, we are encouraged to repeat its mistakes. The "generation gap" is an important social tool for any repressive society. If the younger members of a community view the older members as contemptible or suspect or excess, they will never be able to join hands and examine the living memories of the community, nor ask the all important question, "Why?" This gives rise to a historical amnesia that keeps us working to invent the wheel every time we have to go to the store for bread.

We find ourselves having to repeat and relearn the same old lessons over and over that our mothers did because we do not pass on what we have learned, or because we are unable to listen. For instance, how many times has this all been said before? For another, who would have believed that once again our daughters are allowing their bodies to be hampered and purgatoried by girdles and high heels and hobble skirts?

Ignoring the differences of race between women and the implications of those differences presents the most serious threat to the mobilization of women's joint power.

As white women ignore their built-in privilege of whiteness and define woman in terms of their own experience alone, then women of Color become "other," the outsider whose experience and tradition is too "alien" to comprehend. An example of this is the signal absence of the experience of women of Color as a resource for women's studies courses. The literature of women of Color is seldom included in women's literature courses and almost never in other literature courses, nor in women's studies as a whole. All too often, the excuse given is that the literatures of women of Color can only be taught by Colored women, or that they are too difficult to understand, or that classes cannot "get into" them because they come out of experiences that are "too different." I have heard this argument presented by white women of otherwise quite clear intelligence, women who seem to have no trouble at all teaching and reviewing work that comes out of the vastly different experiences of Shakespeare, Molière, Dostoyefsky, and Aristophanes. Surely there must be some other explanation.

This is a very complex question, but I believe one of the reasons white women have such difficulty reading Black women's work is because of their reluctance to see Black women as women and different from themselves. To examine Black women's literature effectively requires that we be seen as whole people in our actual complexities—as individuals, as women, as human—rather than as one of those problematic but familiar stereotypes provided in this society in place of genuine images of Black women. And I believe this holds true for the literatures of other women of Color who are not Black.

The literatures of all women of Color recreate the textures of our lives, and many white women are heavily invested in ignoring the real differences. For as long as any difference between us means one of us must be inferior, then the recognition of any difference must be fraught with guilt. To allow women of Color to step out of stereotypes is too guilt provoking, for it threatens the complacency of those women who view oppression only in terms of sex.

Refusing to recognize difference makes it impossible to see the different problems and pitfalls facing us as women.

Thus, in a patriarchal power system where whiteskin privilege is a major prop, the entrapments used to neutralize Black women and white women are not the same. For example, it is easy for Black women to be used by the power structure against Black men, not because they are men, but because they are Black. Therefore, for Black women, it is necessary at all times to separate the needs of the oppressor from our own legitimate conflicts within our communities. This same problem does not exist for white women. Black women and men have shared racist oppression and still share it, although in different ways. Out of that shared oppression we have developed joint defenses and joint vulnerabilities to each other that are not duplicated in the white community, with the exception of the relationship between Jewish women and Jewish men.

On the other hand, white women face the pitfall of being seduced into joining the oppressor under the pretense of sharing power. This possibility does not exist in the same way for women of Color. The tokenism that is sometimes extended to us is not an invitation to join power; our racial "otherness" is a visible reality that makes that quite clear. For white women there is a wider range of pretended choices and rewards for identifying with patriarchal power and its tools.

Today, with the defeat of ERA,* the tightening economy, and increased conservatism, it is easier once again for white women to believe the dangerous fantasy that if you are good enough, pretty enough, sweet enough, quiet enough, teach the children to behave, hate the right people, and marry the right men, then you will be allowed to co-exist with patriarchy in relative peace, at least until a man needs your job or the neighborhood rapist happens along. And true, unless one lives and loves in the trenches it is difficult to remember that the war against dehumanization is ceaseless.

But Black women and our children know the fabric of our lives is stitched with violence and with hatred, that there is no rest. We do not deal with it only on the picket lines, or in dark midnight alleys, or in the places where we dare to verbalize our resistance. For us, increasingly, violence weaves through the daily tissues of our living—in the supermarket, in the classroom, in the elevator, in the clinic and the schoolyard, from the plumber, the baker, the saleswoman, the bus driver, the bank teller, the waitress who does not serve us.

Some problems we share as women, some we do not. You fear your children will grow up to join the patriarchy and testify against you, we fear our children will be dragged from a car and shot down in the street, and you will turn your backs upon the reasons they are dying.

The threat of difference has been no less blinding to people of Color. Those of us who are Black must see that the reality of our lives and our struggle does not make us immune to the errors of ignoring and misnaming difference. Within Black communities where racism is a living reality, differences among us often seem dangerous and suspect. The need for unity is often misnamed as a need for homogeneity, and a Black feminist vision mistaken for betrayal of our common interests as a people. Because of the continuous battle against racial erasure that Black women and Black men share, some Black women still refuse to recognize that we are also oppressed as women, and that sexual hostility against Black women is practiced not only by the white racist society, but implemented within our Black communities as well. It is a disease striking the heart of Black nationhood, and silence will not make it disappear. Exacerbated by racism and the pressures of powerlessness, violence against Black women and children often becomes a standard within our communities, one by which manliness can be measured. But these woman-hating acts are rarely discussed as crimes against Black women.

*See the full text of the Equal Rights Amendment (ERA) in Part VII of this volume.

As a group, women of Color are the lowest paid wage earners in america. We are the primary targets of abortion and sterilization abuse, here and abroad. In certain parts of Africa, small girls are still being sewed shut between their legs to keep them docile and for men's pleasure. This is known as female circumcision, and it is not a cultural affair as the late Jomo Kenyatta insisted, it is a crime against Black women.

Black women's literature is full of the pain of frequent assault, not only by a racist patriarchy, but also by Black men. Yet the necessity for and history of shared battle have made us, Black women, particularly vulnerable to the false accusation that anti-sexist is anti-Black. Meanwhile, womanhating as a recourse of the powerless is sapping strength from Black communities, and our very lives. Rape is on the increase, reported and unreported, and rape is not aggressive sexuality, it is sexualized aggression. As Kalamu ya Salaam, a Black male writer, points out, "As long as male domination exists, rape will exist. Only women revolting and men made conscious of their responsibility to fight sexism can collectively stop rape."[1]

Differences between ourselves as Black women are also being misnamed and used to separate us from one another. As a Black lesbian feminist comfortable with the many different ingredients of my identity, and a woman committed to racial and sexual freedom from oppression, I find I am constantly being encouraged to pluck out some one aspect of myself and present this as the meaningful whole, eclipsing or denying the other parts of self. But this is a destructive and fragmenting way to live. My fullest concentration of energy is available to me only when I integrate all the parts of who I am, openly, allowing power from particular sources of my living to flow back and forth freely through all my different selves, without the restrictions of externally imposed definition. Only then can I bring myself and my energies as a whole to the service of those struggles which I embrace as part of my living.

A fear of lesbians, or of being accused of being a lesbian, has led many Black women into testifying against themselves. It has led some of us into destructive alliances, and others into despair and isolation. In the white women's communities, heterosexism is sometimes a result of identifying with the white patriarchy, a rejection of that interdependence between women-identified women which allows the self to be, rather than to be used in the service of men. Sometimes it reflects a diehard belief in the protective coloration of heterosexual relationships, sometimes a self-hate which all women have to fight against, taught us from birth.

Although elements of these attitudes exist for all women, there are particular resonances of heterosexism and homophobia among Black women. Despite the fact that woman-bonding has a long and honorable history in the African and African-american communities, and despite the knowledge and accomplishments of many strong and creative women-identified Black women in the political, social and cultural fields, heterosexual Black women often tend to ignore or discount the existence and work of Black lesbians. Part of this attitude has come from an understandable terror of Black male attack within the close confines of Black society, where the punishment for any female self-assertion is still to be accused of being a lesbian and therefore unworthy of the attention or support of the scarce Black male. But part of this need to misname and ignore Black lesbians comes from a very real fear that openly women-identified Black women who are no longer dependent upon men for their self-definition may well reorder our whole concept of social relationships.

Black women who once insisted that lesbianism was a white woman's problem now insist that Black lesbians are a threat to Black nationhood, are consorting with the enemy, are basically un-Black. These accusations, coming from the very women to whom we look for deep and real understanding, have served to keep many Black lesbians in hiding, caught between the racism of white women and the homophobia of their sisters. Often, their work has been ignored, trivialized, or misnamed, as with the work of Angelina Grimke, Alice Dunbar-Nelson, Lorraine Hansberry. Yet women-bonded women have always been some part of the power of Black communities, from our unmarried aunts to the amazons of Dahomey.

And it is certainly not Black lesbians who are assaulting women and raping children and grandmothers on the streets of our communities.

Across this country, as in Boston during the spring of 1979 following the unsolved murders of twelve Black women, Black lesbians are spearheading movements against violence against Black women.

What are the particular details within each of our lives that can be scrutinized and altered to help bring about change? How do we redefine difference for all women? It is not our differences which separate women, but our reluctance to recognize those differences and to deal effectively with the distortions which have resulted from the ignoring and misnaming of those differences.

As a tool of social control, women have been encouraged to recognize only one area of human difference as legitimate, those differences which exist between women and men. And we have learned to deal across those differences with the urgency of all oppressed subordinates. All of us have had to learn to live or work or coexist with men, from our fathers on. We have recognized and negotiated these differences, even when this recognition only continued the old dominant/subordinate mode of human relationship, where the oppressed must recognize the masters' difference in order to survive.

But our future survival is predicated upon our ability to relate within equality. As women, we must root our internalized patterns of oppression within ourselves if we are to move beyond the most superficial aspects of social change. Now we must recognize differences among women who are our equals, neither inferior nor superior, and devise ways to use each others' difference to enrich our visions and our joint struggles.

The future of our earth may depend upon the ability of all women to identify and develop new definitions of power and new patterns of relating across difference. The old definitions have not served us, nor the earth that supports us. The old patterns, no matter how cleverly rearranged to imitate progress, still condemn us to cosmetically altered repetitions of the same old exchanges, the same old guilt, hatred, recrimination, lamentation, and suspicion.

For we have, built into all of us, old blueprints of expectation and response, old structures of oppression, and these must be altered at the same time as we alter the living conditions which are a result of those structures. For the master's tools will never dismantle the master's house.

As Paulo Freire shows so well in *The Pedagogy of the Oppressed,*[2] the true focus of revolutionary change is never merely the oppressive situations which we seek to escape, but that piece of the oppressor which is planted deep within each of us, and which knows only the oppressor's tactics, the oppressors' relationships.

Change means growth, and growth can be painful. But we sharpen self-definition by exposing the self in work and struggle together with those whom we define as different from ourselves, although sharing the same goals. For Black and white, old and young, lesbian and heterosexual women alike, this can mean new paths to our survival.

> *We have chosen each other*
> *and the edge of each other's battles*
> *the war is the same*
> *if we lose*
> *someday women's blood will congeal*
> *upon a dead planet*
> *if we win*
> *there is no telling*
> *we seek beyond history*
> *for a new and more possible meaning.*[3]

NOTES

1. From "Rape: A Radical Analysis, An African-American Perspective" by Kalamu ya Salaam in *Black Books Bulletin*, vol. 6, no. 4 (1980).
2. Seabury Press, New York, 1970.
3. From "Outlines," unpublished poem.

2 Feminism: A Transformational Politic

bell hooks

We live in a world in crisis—a world governed by politics of domination, one in which the belief in a notion of superior and inferior, and its concomitant ideology—that the superior should rule over the inferior—affects the lives of all people everywhere, whether poor or privileged, literate or illiterate. Systematic dehumanization, worldwide famine, ecological devastation, industrial contamination, and the possibility of nuclear destruction are realities which remind us daily that we are in crisis. Contemporary feminist thinkers often cite sexual politics as the origin of this crisis. They point to the insistence on difference as that factor which becomes the occasion for separation and domination and suggest that differentiation of status between females and males globally is an indication that patriarchal domination of the planet is the root of the problem. Such an assumption has fostered the notion that elimination of sexist oppression would necessarily lead to the eradication of all forms of domination. It is an argument that has led influential Western white women to feel that feminist movement should be *the* central political agenda for females globally. Ideologically, thinking in this direction enables Western women, especially privileged white women, to suggest that racism and class exploitation are merely the offspring of the parent system: patriarchy. Within feminist movement in the West, this has led to the assumption that resisting patriarchal domination is a more legitimate feminist action than resisting racism and other forms of domination. Such thinking prevails despite radical critiques made by black women and other women of color who question this proposition. To speculate that an oppositional division between men and women existed in early human communities is to impose on the past, on these non-white groups, a world view that fits all too neatly within contemporary feminist paradigms that name man as the enemy and woman as the victim.

Clearly, differentiation between strong and weak, powerful and powerless, has been a central defining aspect of gender globally, carrying with it the assumption that men should have greater authority than women, and should rule over them. As significant and important as this fact is, it should not obscure the reality that women can and do participate in politics of domination, as perpetrators as well as victims—that we dominate, that we are dominated. If focus on patriarchal domination masks this reality or becomes the means by

bell hooks is a writer, professor, and cultural critic whose books include *Talking Back: Thinking Feminist, Thinking Black*; *Teaching to Transgress: Education as the Practice of Freedom*; and *Feminism Is for Everybody*.

which women deflect attention from the real conditions and circumstances of our lives, then women cooperate in suppressing and promoting false consciousness, inhibiting our capacity to assume responsibility for transforming ourselves and society.

Thinking speculatively about early human social arrangement, about women and men struggling to survive in small communities, it is likely that the parent–child relationship with its very real imposed survival structure of dependency, of strong and weak, of powerful and powerless, was a site for the construction of a paradigm of domination. While this circumstance of dependency is not necessarily one that leads to domination, it lends itself to the enactment of a social drama wherein domination could easily occur as a means of exercising and maintaining control. This speculation does not place women outside the practice of domination, in the exclusive role of victim. It centrally names women as agents of domination, as potential theoreticians, and creators of a paradigm for social relationships wherein those groups of individuals designated as "strong" exercise power both benevolently and coercively over those designated as "weak."

Emphasizing paradigms of domination that call attention to woman's capacity to dominate is one way to deconstruct and challenge the simplistic notion that man is the enemy, woman the victim; the notion that men have always been the oppressors. Such thinking enables us to examine our role as women in the perpetuation and maintenance of systems of domination. To understand domination, we must understand that our capacity as women and men to be either dominated or dominating is a point of connection, of commonality. Even though I speak from the particular experience of living as a black woman in the United States, a white-supremacist, capitalist, patriarchal society, where small numbers of white men (and honorary "white men") constitute ruling groups, I understand that in many places in the world oppressed and oppressor share the same color. I understand that right here in this room, oppressed and oppressor share the same gender. Right now as I speak, a man who is himself victimized, wounded, hurt by racism and class exploitation is actively dominating a woman in his life—that even as I speak, women who are ourselves exploited, victimized, are dominating children. It is necessary for us to remember, as we think critically about domination, that we all have the capacity to act in ways that oppress, dominate, wound (whether or not that power is institutionalized). It is necessary to remember that it is first the potential oppressor within that we must resist—the potential victim within that we must rescue—otherwise we cannot hope for an end to domination, for liberation.

This knowledge seems especially important at this historical moment when black women and other women of color have worked to create awareness of the ways in which racism empowers white women to act as exploiters and oppressors. Increasingly this fact is considered a reason we should not support feminist struggle even though sexism and sexist oppression is a real issue in our lives as black women (see, for example, Vivian Gordon's *Black Women, Feminism, Black Liberation: Which Way?*). It becomes necessary for us to speak continually about the convictions that inform our continued advocacy of feminist struggle. By calling attention to interlocking systems of domination—sex, race, and class—black women and many other groups of women acknowledge the diversity and complexity of female experience, of our relationship to power and domination. The intent is not to dissuade people of color from becoming engaged in feminist movement. Feminist struggle to end patriarchal domination should be of primary importance to women and men globally not because it is the foundation of all other oppressive structures but because it is that form of domination we are most likely to encounter in an ongoing way in everyday life.

Unlike other forms of domination, sexism directly shapes and determines relations of power in our private lives, in familiar social spaces, in that most intimate context—home—and in that most intimate sphere of relations—family. Usually, it is within the family that we witness coercive domination and learn to accept it, whether it be domination of parent over child, or male over female. Even though family relations may be, and most often are, informed by acceptance of a politic of domination, they are simultaneously relations of care and connection. It is this convergence of two contradictory impulses—the urge to promote growth and the urge to inhibit growth—that provides a practical setting for feminist critique, resistance, and transformation.

Growing up in a black, working-class, father-dominated household, I experienced coercive adult male authority as more immediately threatening, as more likely to cause immediate pain than racist oppression or class exploitation. It was equally clear that experiencing exploitation and oppression in the home made one feel all the more powerless when encountering dominating forces outside the home. This is true for many people. If we are unable to resist and end domination in relations where there is care, it seems totally unimaginable that we can resist and end it in other institutionalized relations of power. If we cannot convince the mothers and/or fathers who care not to humiliate and degrade us, how can we imagine convincing or resisting an employer, a lover, a stranger who systematically humiliates and degrades?

Feminist effort to end patriarchal domination should be of primary concern precisely because it insists on the eradication of exploitation and oppression in the family context and in all other intimate relationships. It is that political movement which most radically addresses the person—the personal—citing the need for transformation of self, of relationships, so that we might be better able to act in a revolutionary manner, challenging and resisting domination, transforming the world outside the self. Strategically, feminist movement should be a central component of all other liberation struggles because it challenges each of us to alter our person, our personal engagement (either as victims or perpetrators or both) in a system of domination.

Feminism, as liberation struggle, must exist apart from and as a part of the larger struggle to eradicate domination in all its forms. We must understand that patriarchal domination shares an ideological foundation with racism and other forms of group oppression, that there is no hope that it can be eradicated while these systems remain intact. This knowledge should consistently inform the direction of feminist theory and practice. Unfortunately, racism and class elitism among women has frequently led to the suppression and distortion of this connection so that it is now necessary for feminist thinkers to critique and revise much feminist theory and the direction of feminist movement. This effort at revision is perhaps most evident in the current widespread acknowledgement that sexism, racism, and class exploitation constitute interlocking systems of domination—that sex, race, and class, and not sex alone, determine the nature of any female's identity, status, and circumstance, the degree to which she will or will not be dominated, the extent to which she will have the power to dominate.

While acknowledgement of the complex nature of woman's status (which has been most impressed upon everyone's consciousness by radical women of color) is a significant corrective, it is only a starting point. It provides a frame of reference which must serve as the basis for thoroughly altering and revising feminist theory and practice. It challenges and calls us to re-think popular assumptions about the nature of feminism that have had the deepest impact on a large majority of women, on mass consciousness. It radically calls into question the notion of a fundamentally common female experience which has been seen as the prerequisite for our coming together, for political unity. Recognition of the inter-connectedness of sex, race, and class highlights the diversity of experience, compelling redefinition of the terms of unity. If women do not share "common oppression," what then can serve as a basis for our coming together?

Unlike many feminist comrades, I believe women and men must share a common understanding—a basic knowledge of what feminism is—if it is ever to be a powerful mass-based political movement. In *Feminist Theory: From Margin to Center,* I suggest that defining feminism broadly as "a movement to end sexism and sexist oppression" would enable us to have a common political goal. We would then have a basis on which to build solidarity. Multiple and contradictory definitions of feminism create confusion and undermine the effort to construct feminist movement so that it addresses everyone. Sharing a common goal does not imply that women and men will not have radically divergent perspectives on how that goal might be reached. Because each individual starts the process of engagement in feminist struggle at a unique level of awareness, very real differences in experience, perspective, and knowledge make developing varied strategies for participation and transformation a necessary agenda.

Feminist thinkers engaged in radically revisioning central tenets of feminist thought must continually emphasize the importance of sex, race, and class as factors which *together* determine the social construction of femaleness, as it has been so deeply ingrained in the consciousness of many women active in feminist movement that gender is the sole factor determining destiny. However, the work of education for critical consciousness (usually called consciousness-raising) cannot end there. Much feminist consciousness-raising has in the past focused on identifying the particular ways men oppress and exploit women. Using the paradigm of sex, race, and class means that the focus does not begin with men and what they do to women, but rather with women working to identify both individually and collectively the specific character of our social identity.

Imagine a group of women from diverse backgrounds coming together to talk about feminism. First they concentrate on working out their status in terms of sex, race, and class using this as the standpoint from which they begin discussing patriarchy or their particular relations with individual men. Within the old frame of reference, a discussion might consist solely of talk about their experiences as victims in relationship to male oppressors. Two women—one poor, the other quite wealthy—might describe the process by which they have suffered physical abuse by male partners and find certain commonalities which might serve as a basis for bonding. Yet if these same two women engaged in a discussion of class, not only would the social construction and expression of femaleness differ, so too would their ideas about how to confront and change their circumstances. Broadening the discussion to include an analysis of race and class would expose many additional differences even as commonalities emerged.

Clearly the process of bonding would be more complex, yet this broader discussion might enable the sharing of perspectives and strategies for change that would enrich rather than diminish our understanding of gender. While feminists have increasingly given "lip service" to the idea of diversity, we have not developed strategies of communication and inclusion that allow for the successful enactment of this feminist vision.

Small groups are no longer the central place for feminist consciousness-raising. Much feminist education for critical consciousness takes place in Women's Studies classes or at conferences which focus on gender. Books are a primary source of education, which means that already masses of people who do not read have no access. The separation of grassroots ways of sharing feminist thinking across kitchen tables from the spheres where much of that thinking is generated, the academy, undermines feminist movement. It would further feminist movement if new feminist thinking could be once again shared in small group contexts, integrating critical analysis with discussion of personal experience. It would be useful to promote anew the small group setting as an arena for education for critical consciousness, so that women and men might come together in neighborhoods and communities to discuss feminist concerns.

Small groups remain an important place for education for critical consciousness for several reasons. An especially important aspect of the small group setting is the empha-sis on communicating feminist thinking, feminist theory, in a manner that can be easily understood. In small groups, individuals do not need to be equally literate or literate at all because the information is primarily shared through conversation, in dialogue which is necessarily a liberatory expression. (Literacy should be a goal for feminists even as we ensure that it not become a requirement for participation in feminist education.) Reform-ing small groups would subvert the appropriation of feminist thinking by a select group of academic women and men, usually white, usually from privileged class backgrounds.

Small groups of people coming together to engage in feminist discussion, in dialectical struggle make a space where the "personal is political" as a starting point for education for critical consciousness can be extended to include politicization of the self that focusses on creating understanding of the ways sex, race, and class together determine our individual lot and our collective experience. It would further feminist movement if many well known feminist thinkers would participate in small groups, critically re-examining ways their works might be changed by incorporating broader perspectives. All efforts at self-transfor-mation challenge us to engage in ongoing, critical self-examination and reflection about feminist practice, about how we live in the world. This individual commitment, when coupled with engagement in collective discussion, provides a space for critical feedback which strengthens our efforts to change and make ourselves new. It is in this commitment to feminist principles in our words and deeds that the hope of feminist revolution lies.

Working collectively to confront difference, to expand our awareness of sex, race, and class as interlocking systems of domination, of the ways we reinforce and perpetuate these structures, is the context in which we learn the true meaning of solidarity. It is this work that must be the foundation of feminist movement. Without it, we cannot effectively resist patriarchal domination; without it, we remain estranged and alienated from one another. Fear of painful confrontation often leads women and men active in feminist movement to avoid rigorous critical encounter, yet if we cannot engage dialectically in a committed, rigorous, humanizing manner, we cannot hope to change the world. True politicization—coming to critical consciousness—is a difficult, "trying" process, one that demands that we give up set ways of thinking and being, that we shift our paradigms, that we open ourselves to the unknown, the unfamiliar. Undergoing this process, we learn what it means to struggle and in this effort we experience the dignity and integrity of being that comes with revolutionary change. If we do not change our consciousness, we cannot change our actions or demand change from others.

Our renewed commitment to a rigorous process of education for critical consciousness will determine the shape and direction of future feminist movement. Until new perspectives are created, we cannot be living symbols of the power of feminist thinking. Given the privileged lot of many leading feminist thinkers, both in terms of status, class, and race, it is harder these days to convince women of the primacy of this process of politicization. More and more, we seem to form select interest groups composed of individuals who share similar perspectives. This limits our capacity to engage in critical discussion. It is difficult to involve women in new processes of feminist politicization because so many of us think that identifying men as the enemy, resisting male domination, gaining equal access to power and privilege is the end of feminist movement. Not only is it not the end, it is not even the place we want revitalized feminist movement to begin. We want to begin as women seriously addressing ourselves, not solely in relation to men, but in relation to an entire structure of domination of which patriarchy is one part. While the struggle to eradicate sexism and sexist oppression is and should be the primary thrust of feminist movement, to prepare ourselves politically for this effort we must first learn how to be in solidarity, how to struggle with one another.

Only when we confront the realities of sex, race, and class, the ways they divide us, make us different, stand us in opposition, and work to reconcile and resolve these issues will we be able to participate in the making of feminist revolution, in the transformation of the world. Feminism, as Charlotte Bunch emphasizes again and again in *Passionate Politics*, is a transformational politics, a struggle against domination wherein the effort is to change ourselves as well as structures. Speaking about the struggle to confront difference, Bunch asserts:

> A crucial point of the process is understanding that reality does not look the same from different people's perspective. It is not surprising that one way feminists have come to understand about differences has been through the love of a person from another culture or race. It takes persistence and motivation—which love often engenders—to get beyond one's ethnocentric assumptions and really learn about other perspectives. In this process and while seeking to eliminate oppression, we also discover new possibilities and insights that come from the experience and survival of other peoples.

Embedded in the commitment to feminist revolution is the challenge to love. Love can be and is an important source of empowerment when we struggle to confront issues of sex, race, and class. Working together to identify and face our differences—to face the ways we dominate and are dominated—to change our actions, we need a mediating force that can sustain us so that we are not broken in this process, so that we do not despair.

Not enough feminist work has focussed on documenting and sharing ways individuals confront differences constructively and successfully. Women and men need to know what is on the other side of the pain experienced in politicization. We need detailed accounts of the ways our lives are fuller and richer as we change and grow politically, as we learn to live each moment as committed feminists, as comrades working to end domination. In reconceptualizing and reformulating strategies for future feminist movement, we need to concentrate on the politicization of love, not just in the context of talking about victimization in intimate relationships, but in a critical discussion where love can be understood as a powerful force that challenges and resists domination. As we work to be loving, to create a culture that celebrates life, that makes love possible, we move against dehumanization, against domination. In *Pedagogy of the Oppressed*, Paulo Freire evokes this power of love, declaring:

> I am more and more convinced that true revolutionaries must perceive the revolution, because of its creative and liberating nature, as an act of love. For me, the revolution, which is not possible without a theory of revolution—and therefore science—is not irreconcilable with love . . . The distortion imposed on the word "love" by the capitalist world cannot prevent the revolution from being essentially loving in character, nor can it prevent the revolutionaries from affirming their love of life.

That aspect of feminist revolution that calls women to love womanness, that calls men to resist dehumanizing concepts of masculinity, is an essential part of our struggle. It is the process by which we move from seeing ourselves as objects to acting as subjects. When women and men understand that working to eradicate patriarchal domination is a struggle rooted in the longing to make a world where everyone can live fully and freely, then we know our work to be a gesture of love. Let us draw upon that love to heighten our awareness, deepen our compassion, intensify our courage, and strengthen our commitment.

3

From Oppressor to Activist: Reflections of a Feminist Journey

Amit Taneja

My gay friends say I'm part of the "family," but sometimes strangers call me "fag."
I was born in India, but I have been called a "sand n****r."
I became a Canadian citizen recently, but I am still called an "Indo-Canadian."
I am working on my doctorate, but I anticipate being in large debt for my education through my late forties.
I am Hindu, but I am often asked if I have found Jesus.
I am fluent in English, but it is my fourth language.
I am big boned, but I am often mistaken as fat and unhealthy.
I work legally in the U.S., but my official status according to the government is "Alien Employee."

Introduction

As a poor, immigrant, big-boned, non-Christian, gay person of color who happens to be working in a country where Others are feared, some people would say that I have a lot going against me. And they would be right. However, despite all that works against me, I still feel that I have power. Correction: A lot of power. You see, I was born with a penis and I was taught early on that this simple fact meant I was inherently superior to about half of the human population. The mere sighting of my anatomy at birth outlined my destiny in this life as being smarter, taller, faster, stronger, funnier, and in general just "better" than women. That is what I was taught.

Despite all the messages that were bored into my brain about my supposed male superiority, I have come to a place of questioning, resisting, and actively changing the tape that plays as the background music in my head. I have come to fight the sexist messages that I was raised with and, more importantly, to duck and cover from, deflect, and strike back against the thousands of similar messages that come my way on a daily basis.

I write this essay as snapshots of a life-changing journey. It is not a complete story, or even chronological for that matter. But it is a story of important markers on my path of becoming a feminist. This journey brought me from a place of unquestioned male power

---

Amit Taneja is the dean for diversity, equity, and inclusion at College of the Holy Cross. His research focuses on the intersections of race, class, gender, and sexual orientation for LGBT students of color on historically white college campuses.

and privilege to experiencing oppression myself. The journey ends at my resting place as a life-long, hardcore, die-hard, to-my-last-breath, capital "F" Feminist.

Snapshot #1: Get Your Brother Some Water

Summers in India were hot, and while little girls helped their mommies cook and clean at home after school, little boys could run around being rascals, playing cricket, and flying kites. I remember coming home one afternoon after a long day of playing marbles with the other boys. No sooner had I entered the room, my mom asked my younger sister to get me a tall glass of water with ice. My sister resisted and complained, "Why do I have to get him water? He never gets me water when I come home!" My grandmother immediately chastised her, saying that such talk would keep her single all her life, and that she would never land a husband. (My grandmother was more right than she could have known. My sister is a lesbian and now walks around proudly wearing her "Well-Behaved Women Hardly Ever Make History" T-shirt.)

I remember this story about the water so vividly. I might have made a face at my sister while agreeing with my grandmother. Whatever my grandma said made a lot of sense to me at the time. I was brought up to believe that the man is the breadwinner, the decision maker, the provider, and the protector for his family. Women exist to serve the men and children in their lives. These notions made it seem reasonable that it was my sister's job . . . no, change that to duty . . . to bring me water.

I remember this story because of the way my sister looked at me. There was part contempt, part anger, some pain, and perhaps resignation to her fate as a woman. I don't know precisely what she was thinking, but I remember feeling guilty when she came back with a glass of water. I only took a sip (even though I was parched). Somehow I felt that I didn't deserve that glass of water just because I was a boy and she was a girl. But I knew that to question the system would be wrong. I put that event deep in my memory scrapbook, but the seeds of questioning my male privilege were planted for years to come.

Snapshot #2: Isn't 99 Percent Good Enough?

Sonali Mehta* and I were good friends in high school in India. We had a fierce, but friendly, competition over who would get the top rank in math each semester. Sometimes I came out ahead, and sometimes she did. Many a teacher commented that Sonali was very gifted in math and sciences, *especially for being a girl*. We both tied with 96 percent on our preliminary practice tests before our provincial board exams at the end of twelfth grade. We both studied hard for our exams and the pressure was on for the final showdown. We took the exam and immediately compared notes. It seemed that Sonali and I both had the same answers to most of the questions.

Fast-forward. Two months later. We nervously opened our grade envelopes. I peeked with one eye open and saw my score was 97 percent in math. Another friend saw my grades and yelled over my shoulder, "Sonali, Amit got 97 percent. How did you do?"

*Pseudonyms used.

All heads turned in our direction, and I saw Sonali sitting quietly with a tear running down her cheek. Oh no! This was supposed to be a friendly competition. She couldn't have done that bad to be crying! I went over to comfort her and saw her grades lying on her desk. Her crying became louder and more noticeable. The paper read, "Math 99 percent." I was really confused at this point. She got the highest marks, but yet she was sad. I asked why she was crying, and Sonali said that she was upset because she did not get a perfect score of 100 percent. I responded by saying, "You still have the highest grade in our class! " She quietly replied, "I am a girl. I am told over and over again that I am exceptionally good at math as far as girls go. I didn't want to be just exceptionally good. I wanted to be perfect; to prove them all wrong! You wouldn't understand." Suddenly it all made sense. And from that day on, I have cringed (and always confront people) when I hear the words "especially gifted for a girl."

Snapshot #3: The Oppressor Becomes Oppressed

It was the beginning of my freshman year in college, and my family and I had immigrated to Canada nine months earlier. I had a Presidential Full Tuition Scholarship in Engineering and I was determined to do well in school. I wanted to build bridges because they fascinated and scared me at the same time. While I was preparing for the adjustment to living on my own, I also became fascinated and scared by feelings of attraction toward men. I was actively exploring the idea of accepting my same-sex feelings and eventually "coming out" but, at the time, I felt very unsure.

I was sitting in the dorm lounge watching television during the first week of classes when a gay character came on the sitcom. One of my floormates said how much he hated fags, and another agreed by saying that he would "beat the crap out of any fag" he met. Uh oh! Cancel the coming out. I did not need to be hated on, much less beaten for being gay. The obvious path to avoid this was to deny all feelings for men and be as straight-acting and macho as I could.

I started out small by trying to be a heterosexual man (or what I thought it meant to be a heterosexual man). At first that meant making small comments about women, their bodies, their breasts. But that didn't seem enough. I kept thinking that "real men" would be able to see through my façade, so I had to step it up and be more macho than most men to prevent my dirty secret from emerging. I had to turn into Captain Hyper-Hetero, the imaginary superhero who safeguarded masculinity by being the manliest man possible.

I started talking more loudly in the presence of other men (while avoiding all contact with women). I kept telling others that I was looking for sexual adventures with women (okay it was a lot more graphic than that, but I choose not to repeat or remember the details). Soon word got around about my comments, and the women in my building were avoiding me because I was an all-around sexist jerk.

The plan was working. Men thought I was a player and women didn't want to have anything to do with me. Until one day a female neighbor reached out to me, and pointed out that my comments were hurtful, demeaning, and revolting. I was treating women like "meat," and that was not going to get me anywhere. I realized that I was causing harm and fear amongst the women who lived close to me. This was not really me. I was ashamed of what I had done. I just blurted out, "I am gay, and I am trying to hide behind this mask of being super straight." I knew at that moment that I had a critical choice to make and I could not lead a life of lies. More importantly, I could now relate to what it felt like to be oppressed. It was a life-altering moment, and I found love and forgiveness from the women around me when they heard my story. We stayed up late at night, eating ice cream and sharing stories of oppression and fear, while building dreams of a future filled with confidence and hope. And we also created a list of the most eligible bachelors in our dorm, but that is another story for another time.

Snapshot #4: Fitting the Gender Box

After the demise of Captain Hyper-Hetero I decided to come out more publicly. Life was good and I was trying to fit in with the straight world while finding my place within the gay community. The more out I became on campus, the more I was targeted by messages of homophobia from the straight community and racism and classism from the queer community. Straight men questioned my masculinity and often made assumptions that being gay meant that I had to be effeminate. It seemed like I didn't fit in completely in either the straight world or the gay world. I was too femme for the straight boys, and not femme enough for the pretty, out, campy, white, gay crowd. Drag queens in the gay bars were relentless in making fun of my outfit, my accent, and my looks. I dressed too breeder for their liking and I was told that I needed to "gay it up a little." I was told, "Go get some Abercrombie, honey!"

I went looking for Abercrombie clothing, but I could neither fit in it nor afford it. At the same time, the straight men (and sometimes straight women) would belittle the "queeny fags" and the "butch dykes." It seemed to me that if drag queens and butch dykes did not exist, then straight people would only see the "normal gays (and lesbians)" like me, and there would be little reason for them to hate us. I was being taught the message that those who transgress gender boundaries are bad and should be looked down upon. And I bought that message for a while (until I took women's studies courses, and things changed).

I realized through these experiences that the roots of homophobia lie in sexism. People are taught to be afraid of those who defy gender norms because doing so topples the power granted to men over women. Homophobia is an offshoot of sexist ideology, and even gay and lesbian people are not immune from homophobic thinking because sexism is active and alive in our society.

Snapshot #5: Boys Go to College

In 2001, I moved from Canada to the United States to pursue graduate studies. I recently shared with an American buddy of mine that being born in India (which is a very gender segregated society) I was exposed to numerous messages about male superiority from an early age. He thought that such thinking was "barbaric and idiotic," and he felt good knowing that we lived in a country where young children are not taught such gibberish.

"Whoa, hold on a second. Is that really true?" I replied. "Are young children in the United States not taught notions of male superiority? I don't think it is a lot different here," I said. The messages about gender inequality are a lot more covert in U.S. culture, but they have the same effect.

My friend was not quite convinced so I shared with him the story of a recent visit to my partner's family in Ohio. My partner's brother has two children: a five-year-old boy named Colin and a four-year-old girl named Grace, who was asked by her parents to recite the new poem she'd been taught. In a shy tone she recited the following to us:

> Boys go to college to get smarter
> Girls go to Jupiter to get stupider

Grace's poem was met with a loud round of laughter from an assortment of adults including grandparents, uncles, aunts, and cousins. Everyone laughed except me. The smiling, laughter, and clapping following the performance signified to Grace that her poem was met with approval. In fact, later that night Grace offered to recite the poem again when new company arrived. It was heart-breaking and eye-opening to see that the adults in the room did not understand the significance of the message that was being taught to Grace and reinforced for everyone else.

From the time they are born, little boys and girls are taught gender "appropriate" behaviors, dress, and hobbies. But they are also taught to dream and aspire in gendered ways. It is no coincidence that little boys want to grow up to be firefighters, police, and pilots, while girls want to be princesses who live in Barbie's Dream House. I wonder what would happen to men and women's self-esteem and career aspirations if children were taught that they could be whatever they wanted to be. I think we should all dream of the day when good-minded men, women, and those in-between make a commitment to egalitarian parenting and continually striving to create social change.

Snapshot #6: The Glass Cubicle: Complicating Gender

During college, I worked at a fast food restaurant for three summers. Make that three l-o-n-g summers. Nicole,* a co-worker who had worked at the chain for five years, said that she was thinking of leaving. I asked her why, and she responded that she did not see herself getting promoted anytime soon. She explained that except for one woman who worked the weekend graveyard shift, all the managers were men. Nicole said that the vast majority of the male supervisors and managers had worked at the establishment for a lot less time than her, and that she was never promoted.

Frustrated from being passed over for a promotion several times, Nicole approached the owner with her concerns. He denied there was any sexism at play, and mentioned that the men who had been promoted were "just better workers." To prove his point he called a staff meeting and asked if anyone was unhappy with promotions or had any concerns. The owner was known to be moody and petty. Although several women had privately shared their frustrations with me, no one spoke up out of fear. The owner said that since no one had anything to say, there must not be a problem. All too often, silence is taken as a form of agreement when in reality the silence is saying a lot more. Nicole was shortly moved to the evening shifts which conflicted with her family commitments, and she quit within a month.

I share this snapshot because it had profound meaning for me. I always envisioned the glass ceiling as something that affected professional women like lawyers and MBAs. The truth is, though, that working-class women are even more prone to its effects. To this day, women still make around seventy-seven cents on the male dollar. This wage difference is exacerbated by race. And when we consider class, (dis)abilities, nationality, immigration status, and race, it becomes clear that some women don't just experience the vertical push of the glass ceiling. They're getting pressed from all sides. The glass ceiling doesn't tell the whole story: Some women's lives are confined within a small glass cubicle. Feminist ideology recognizes the complexities of how oppression affects us and involves a much larger lens than only women's rights.

Snapshot #7: Sexism within the Queer Community

I was hanging out with some gay male friends, when one of them stubbed his toe and let out a cry of pain. One of the other men in the group yelled "Stop being a pussy and take it like a man!" Later that evening, another queer man claimed that he was "allergic to vagina in every way possible." When I pointed out the sexist and misogynistic undertones of their comments, these men became very defensive and claimed that they had little to nothing in common with women, and they couldn't care less about women's issues. Another one responded that he could "barely tolerate the dykes at the pride marches."

Unfortunately, these comments are part of many gay men's repertoires. Some gay men deal with gender and sexuality by either acting macho, or by being a "mean girl" and hating on other "bitches." While my friends claimed their comments were made in jest and with no ill intent, these words actually have a damaging effect on their individual psyches and on the soul of the queer rights and women's rights movements.

I've struggled to explain gay men's sexist behavior. Queer people are oppressed in many ways by heteronormative society. Maybe some gay men deal with this particular powerlessness by hanging onto their male privilege. Perhaps this is also why some white queers are unwilling to acknowledge their skin privilege and the racism within the gay community.

I think it is important for social justice activists to confront sexism within the queer community and challenge misogynistic thinking. There is a grave problem within our community when some gay men claim that they can "barely tolerate" lesbian women. Only certain people with social position have the power to "tolerate" another human being. Of all people, gay men should know what it feels like to be "tolerated." Those of us who don't have social power are often taught to hope for tolerance at best. For many of us, full inclusion and acceptance are not even on the menu of options. The gender split within the queer community needs to be addressed because our internal and external struggles are connected by sexist and misogynistic ideologies. I have hope that activism from the transgender, intersexed, and genderqueer community will help educate others in meaningful ways.

Acknowledging and Resisting Privilege

The preceding seven snapshots portray my understanding of oppression and provide the foundation of my feminism. I want to bring this essay to a close by considering the biggest challenge in my journey to being a feminist: acknowledging and resisting privilege.

I experience oppression in a number of ways because of the intersection of my sexual orientation, race, ethnicity, national origin, class, language, and religion. As I said, I am a poor, big-boned, immigrant, gay man of color. Some days I feel the weight of the world on my shoulders. *I can't imagine what a day without oppression feels like.* Yet, still, I know that I have male privilege. The issues for me are multiple: How do I acknowledge and resist my male privilege? And why should I refuse one form of advantage when I am disenfranchised in so many others?

I've toyed with these ideas for a long time and here's what I've come up with: A common thread links all forms of oppression. It is not possible to fight just one form of oppression while neglecting others. And often we ignore how privilege and oppression are heavily mediated by class; that is, by the power and money that provide access to refuge and support, and open doors for people who are subjugated in other ways. This insight helps me reconcile my struggle between being multiply oppressed while also wanting to keep my male privilege.

I have learned that our personal decisions must reflect and support our political ideologies. We are not relieved from responsibility for politically conscientious action by claiming that our personal and political lives do not mix. Those of us who are oppressed don't have a choice. Our personal decisions are seen and treated as political, whether we want them to be or not! I cannot enter a same-sex marriage and expect that decision to be seen as politically neutral. Neither can I hold hands with my partner in public, nor try to be a foster parent without my actions having political meaning assigned to them.

The Advocate, America's largest gay and lesbian publication, recently posed the following question: "Is the gay community welcoming to people of color?" While I understand the intent of the question, I also see the implicit assumption that the gay community is white, and that white people have the power to accept (or tolerate) queer people of color. We need to problematize these assumptions and how we compartmentalize our identities. While some of our struggles may appear different on the surface, we are all connected through our intersecting identities and through the common experience of oppression.

We need to understand that there is no such thing as completely disconnected identities. Race, class, gender, sexual orientation, age—and all other signifiers of identity—intersect in meaningful and powerful ways to shape our individual and collective experiences. We must always talk about women's rights and gay and lesbian rights while also thinking about xenophobia, classism, racism, transphobia, etc. Doing so allows us to acknowledge the existence of those of us who carry multiple burdens, but also strengthens all our movements under one collective stance. We should not worry about which oppression is worse than the other, but about the fact that all oppression is worth speaking out against. Many of us are in positions of oppressor and oppressed at the same time. This knowledge must fuel our passion for ending oppression by abdicating and resisting norms that give us privilege over others. Women's rights are the same as civil rights, which are the same as gay rights, which are the same as immigrant rights. We are all connected and only together will we be able to create lasting change.

Lastly, I want to encourage readers to make a personal and political commitment to social justice activism. I am suggesting something well beyond the realm of participating in diversity training or signing an online petition. Some people believe that acts like these absolve them of their moral responsibility to participate in social justice activism. The typical corporate diversity training does little to make us examine our assumptions and merely gives us license to continue to exercise our power while maintaining a superficial front of understanding and tolerance. True social justice work starts with grassroots activism and extends in scope from local to national to global. We need to keep moving forward. We need to work for social justice until we reach a place where equal opportunity exists for everyone not just on paper, but also in practice.

4 Interrupting the Cycle of Oppression: The Role of Allies as Agents of Change

Andrea Ayvazian

Many of us feel overwhelmed when we consider the many forms of systemic oppression that are so pervasive in American society today. We become immobilized, uncertain about what actions we can take to interrupt the cycles of oppression and violence that intrude on our everyday lives. One way to overcome this sense of immobilization is to assume the role of an ally. Learning about this role—one that each and every one of us is capable of assuming—can offer us new ways of behaving and a new source of hope.

Through the years, experience has taught us that isolated and episodic actions—even dramatic, media-grabbing events—rarely produce more than a temporary blip on the screen. What does seem to create real and lasting change is highly motivated individuals—usually only a handful at first—who are so clear and consistent on an issue that they serve as a heartbeat in a community, steadily sending out waves that touch and change those in their path. These change agents or allies have such a powerful impact because their actions embody the values they profess: their behavior and beliefs are congruent.

What Is an Ally?

An ally is a member of a dominant group in our society who works to dismantle any form of oppression from which she or he receives the benefit. Allied behavior means taking personal responsibility for the changes we know are needed in our society, and so often ignore or leave to others to deal with. Allied behavior is intentional, overt, consistent activity that challenges prevailing patterns of oppression, makes privileges that are so often invisible visible, and facilitates the empowerment of persons targeted by oppression.

I use the term "oppression" to describe the combination of prejudice plus access to social, political, and economic power on the part of a dominant group. Racism, a core component of oppression, has been defined by David Wellman as a system of advantage based on race. Wellman's definition can be altered slightly to describe every other form of oppression. Hence we can say that sexism is a system of advantage based on gender, that heterosexism is a system of advantage based on sexual orientation, and so on. In each form of oppression there is a dominant group—the one that receives the unearned advantage, benefit, or privilege—and a targeted group—the one that is denied that advantage, benefit, or privilege. We

Andrea Ayvazian is the director of the Sojourner Truth School for Social Change Leadership. She holds degrees from Oberlin College, the University of North Carolina–Chapel Hill, Duke University, the Graduate School of the Union Institute, and Yale Divinity School.

From *Fellowship* (January/February 1995). Reprinted by permission of Rev. Dr. Andrea Ayvazian, pastor of the Haydenville Congregational Church.

know the litany of dominants: white people, males, Christians, heterosexuals, able-bodied people, those in their middle years, and those who are middle or upper class.

We also know that everyone has multiple social identities. We are all dominant and targeted simultaneously. I, for instance, am simultaneously dominant as a white person and targeted as a woman. A white able-bodied man may be dominant in those categories, but targeted as a Jew or Muslim or as a gay person. Some people are, at some point in their lives, entirely dominant; but if they are, they won't be forever. Even a white, able-bodied, heterosexual, Christian male will literally grow out of his total dominance if he reaches old age.

When we consider the different manifestations of systematic oppression and find ourselves in any of the categories where we are dominant—and therefore receive the unearned advantages that accrue to that position of advantage—we have the potential to be remarkably powerful agents of change as allies. Allies are whites who identify as anti-racists, men who work to dismantle sexism, able-bodied people who are active in the disability rights movement, Christians who combat anti-Semitism and other forms of religious prejudice. Allied behavior usually involves talking to other dominants about their behavior: whites confronting other whites on issues of racism, men organizing with other men to combat sexism, and so on. Allied behavior is clear action aimed at dismantling the oppression of others in areas where you yourself benefit—it is proactive, intentional, and often involves taking a risk.

To tether these principles to everyday reality, just think of the group Parents, Families and Friends of Lesbians and Gays (PFLAG) as the perfect example of allied behavior. PFLAG is an organization of (mainly) heterosexuals who organize support groups and engage in advocacy and education among other heterosexuals around issues of gay and lesbian liberation. PFLAG speakers can be heard in houses of worship, schools, and civic organizations discussing their own commitment to securing gay and lesbian civil rights. Because they are heterosexuals speaking (usually) to other heterosexuals, they often have a significant impact.

The anti-racism trainer Kenneth Jones, an African American, refers to allied behavior as "being at my back." He has said to me, "Andrea, I know you are at my back on the issue of race equity—you're talking to white people who cannot hear me on this topic, you're out there raising these issues repeatedly, you're organizing with other whites to stand up to racism. And I'm at your back. I'm raising issues of gender equity with men, I am talking to men who cannot hear you, I've made a commitment to combat sexism."

Available to each one of us in the categories where we are dominant is the proud and honorable role of ally: the opportunity to raise hell with others like us and to interrupt the cycle of oppression. Because of our very privilege, we have the potential to stir up good trouble, to challenge the status quo, and to inspire real and lasting change. William Strickland, an aide to Jesse Jackson, once said: "When a critical mass of white people join together, rise up, and shout a thunderous 'No' to racism, we will actually alter the course of history."

Reducing Violence

When I ponder the tremendous change a national network of allies can make in this country, I think not only of issues of equity and empowerment, but also of how our work could lead to diminishing levels of violence in our society. Let us consider for a moment the critical connection between oppression and violence on one hand, and the potential role of allied behavior in combating violence on the other.

A major source of violence in our society is the persistent inequity between dominant and targeted groups. Recall that oppression is kept in place by two factors:

1. Ideology, or the propagation of doctrines that purport to legitimize inequality; and
2. Violence (or the threat of violence) by the dominant group against the targeted group.

The violence associated with each form of systemic oppression noticeably decreases when allies (or dominants) rise up and shout a thunderous "No" to the perpetuation of these inequities. Because members of the dominant group are conferred with considerable social power and privilege, they carry significant authority when confronting perpetrators of violence in their own group—when whites deter other whites from using violence against people of color, when heterosexuals act to prevent gay bashing, and so on.

. . .

In our society, oppression and violence are woven together: one leads to the other, one justifies the other. Furthermore, members of the dominant group who are not perpetrators of violence often collude, through their silence and inactivity, with those who are. Allied behavior is an effective way of interrupting the cycle of violence by breaking the silence that reinforces the cycle, and by promoting a new set of behavior through modeling and mentoring.

Providing Positive Role Models

Not only does allied behavior contribute to an increase in equity and a decrease in violence, but allies provide positive role models that are sorely needed by today's young people. The role of ally offers young people who are white, male, and in other dominant categories a positive, proactive, and proud identity. Rather than feeling guilty, shameful, and immobilized as the "oppressor," whites and other dominants can assume the important and useful role of social change agent. There have been proud allies and change agents throughout the history of this nation, and there are many alive today who can inspire us with their important work.

I often speak in high school classes and assemblies, and in recent years I have taken to doing a little informal survey from the podium. I ask the students if they can name a famous living white racist. Can they? Yes. They often name David Duke—he ran for President in their lifetime—or they sometimes name Senator Jesse Helms; and when I was in the midwest, they named Marge Schott, the owner of the Cincinnati Reds.* It does not take long before a hand shoots up, or someone just calls out one of those names.

---

*White supremacist David Duke, a former grand wizard of the Ku Klux Klan, ran for president in 1988 and 1992 and served in the Louisiana state legislature. Jesse Helms, a five-term senator from North Carolina, was known for his opposition to civil rights legislation and his racially charged campaign tactics. Marge Schott, who was twice banned from baseball because of her offensive statements, used anti-black and anti-Asian slurs and made statements supportive of Adolf Hitler.

Following that little exercise, I ask the students, "Can you name a famous living white anti-racist (or civil rights worker, or someone who fights racism)?" Can they? Not very often. Sometimes there is a whisper or two, but generally the room is very quiet. So, recently, I have been saying: forget the famous part. Just name for me any white person you know in your community, or someone you have heard of, who has taken a stand against racism. Can they? Sometimes. Occasionally someone says "my mom," or "my dad." I have also heard "my rabbi, my teacher, my minister." But not often enough.

I believe that it is difficult for young people to grow up and become something they have never heard of. It is hard for a girl to grow up and become a commercial airline pilot if it has never occurred to her that women can and do fly jet planes. Similarly, it is hard for young people to grow up and fight racism if they have never met anyone who does.

And there *are* many remarkable role models whom we can claim with pride, and model ourselves after. People like Laura Haviland, who was a conductor on the Underground Railroad and performed unbelievably brave acts while the slave-catchers were right on her trail; Virginia Foster Durr, a southern belle raised with great wealth and privilege who, as an adult, tirelessly drove black workers to and from their jobs during the Montgomery bus boycott; the Rev. James Reeb, who went south during the Mississippi Freedom Summer of 1964 to organize and march; Hodding Carter, Jr., editor and publisher of a newspaper in the Mississippi Delta who used his paper to battle for racial equity and who took considerable heat for his actions. And more: the Grimke sisters, Lucretia Mott, William Lloyd Garrison, John Brown, Viola Liuzzo.

There are also many contemporary anti-racists like Morris Dees, who gave up a lucrative law practice to start the Southern Poverty Law Center and Klanwatch in Alabama and bring white supremacists to trial; Anne Braden, active for decades in the civil rights struggle in Kentucky; Rev. Joseph Barndt, working within the religious community to make individual churches and entire denominations proclaim themselves as anti-racist institutions. And Peggy McIntosh, Judith Katz, and Myles Horton. And so many others. Why don't our young people know these names? If young people knew more about these dedicated allies, perhaps they would be inspired to engage in more anti-racist activities themselves.

Choosing Our Own Roles

We also need to consider our role as allies. In our own communities, would young people, if asked the same questions, call out our names as anti-racists? In areas where we are dominant, is our struggle for equity and justice evident? When we think about our potential role as allies, we need to recall a Quaker expression: "Let your life be your teaching." The Quakers understand that our words carry only so much weight, that it is our actions, our daily behaviors, that tell the true story.

In my own life I struggle with what actions to take, how to make my beliefs and my behaviors congruent. One small step that has had interesting repercussions over the last decade is the fact that my partner (who is male) and I have chosen not to be legally married until gay and lesbian couples can be married and receive the same benefits and legal protection that married heterosexual couples enjoy. A small step, but it has allowed us to talk with folks at the YMCA about their definition of "family" when deciding who qualifies for their "family plan"; to challenge people at Amtrak about why some "family units" receive discounts when traveling together and others do not; and to raise questions in the religious community about who can receive formal sanction for their loving unions and who cannot. These are not earth-shattering steps in the larger picture, but we believe that small steps taken by thousands of people will eventually change the character of our communities.

When we stop colluding and speak out about the unearned privileges we enjoy as members of a dominant group — privileges we have been taught for so long to deny or ignore — we have the potential to undergo and inspire stunning transformation. Consider the words of Gandhi: "As human beings, our greatness lies not so much in being able to remake the world, as in being able to remake ourselves."

In my own community, I have been impressed by the efforts of three middle-aged males who have remade themselves into staunch allies for women. Steven Botkin established the Men's Resource Center in Amherst, Massachusetts twelve years ago and put a commitment to eliminating sexism in its very first mission statement. Another Amherst resident, Michael Burkart, travels nationwide and works with top executives in Fortune 500 companies on the issue of gender equity in their corporations. And Geoff Lobenstine, a social worker who identifies as an anti-sexist male, brings these issues to his work in Holyoke, Massachusetts.

Charlie Parker once said this about music: "Music is your own experience, your thoughts, your wisdom. If you don't live it, it won't come out of your horn." I think the same is true about us in our role as allies — it is our own experience, our thoughts, our wisdom. If we don't live it, it won't come out of our horn.

Preparing for the Long Haul

Now I would be the first to admit that personally and professionally the role of ally is often exhausting. I know that it involves challenges — being an ally is difficult work, and it can often be lonely. We must remember to take care of ourselves along this journey, to sustain our energy and our zest for those ongoing challenges.

We must also remember that it is hard to go it alone: allies need allies. As with any other struggle in our lives, we need supportive people around us to help us to persevere. Other allies will help us take the small, daily steps that will, in time, alter the character of our communities. We know that allied behavior usually consists of small steps and unglamorous work. As Mother Teresa once said: "I don't do any great things. I do small things with great love."

Finally two additional points about us in our role as allies: First, we don't always see the results of our efforts. Sometimes we do, but often we touch and even change lives without ever knowing it. Consequently, we cannot measure our success in quantitative terms. Like waves upon the shore, we are altering the landscape — but exactly how, may be hard to discern.

Doubts inevitably creep up about our effectiveness, about our approach, about the positions we assume or the actions we take. But we move forward, along with the doubts, the uncertainty, and often the lack of visible results. In our office, we have a famous William James quote on the wall to sustain us: "I will act as though what I do makes a difference." And, speaking personally, although my faith gets rattled, I try to act as though what I do does make a difference.

Second, there is no such thing as a perfect ally. Perfection is not our goal. When I asked my colleague Kenneth Jones what stood out for him as the most important characteristic of a strong ally, he said simply: "being consistently conscious." He didn't say "never stumbling," or "never making mistakes." He said: "being consistently conscious." And so we do our best: taking risks, being smart, making errors, feeling foolish, doing what we believe is right, based on our best judgment at the time. We are imperfect, but we are steady. We are courageous but not faultless. As Lani Guinier said: "It is better to be vaguely right than precisely wrong." If we obsess about looking good instead of doing good, we will get caught in a spiral of ineffective action. Let's not get side-tracked or defeated because we are trying to be perfect.

And so we move ahead, pushing ourselves forward on our growing edge. We know that although none of us are beginners in dealing with issues of oppression and empowerment, none of us are experts either. These issues are too complex, too painful, and too pervasive for us to achieve a state of clarity and closure once and for all. The best we can hope for is to strive each day to be our strongest and clearest selves, transforming the world one individual at a time, one family at a time, one community at a time.

. . .

Within each individual is the potential to effect enormous change. May we move forward, claiming with pride our identities as allies, interrupting the cycle of oppression, and modeling a new way of behaving and believing.

5 | The Pitfalls of Ally Performance: Why Coalition Work Is More Effective Than Ally Theater

Kristin J. Anderson and Christina Hsu Accomando

Ally activism can be an important and inspiring starting point in the early stages of social justice work for activists first grappling with their privileges. An *ally* is often defined as someone from a dominant group who is working on efforts to dismantle the form of privilege their group receives.[1] Examples include white people supporting Black Lives Matter, straight and cis folk supporting LGBTQ rights, men condemning rape culture. Obviously, allies are better than oppressors, and ally hearts generally are in the right place. However, a problematic type of ally *performance* has insinuated itself into present-day activist discourse, especially on social media. Claiming "ally" *as an identity* can limit and stifle the potential for lasting change because it centers the privileged individual, renders identity unidimensional, and shifts attention from a sustained political movement to the individual activist's identity. In contrast, actively participating in a movement in which groups work in *coalition across differences* can be a powerful means of changing society over the long term. In what follows, we identify four pitfalls of ally activism and conclude with an overview of the theory and practice of coalition work as an alternative model.

First, if "ally" is merely an identity marker, it becomes a description of who you *are*, rather than what you *do*. That's a problem because when it comes to social change, the work you do with others as part of a movement is more important than who you think you are. If your social justice profile crumbles when you cannot use the term "ally," then you might be stuck in the ally *identity*, and that identity by itself has no substance. If you cannot work without that label, then maybe you are not really doing any useful work.

Second, wearing "ally" as an identity can easily slip into a performance. Princess Harmony Rodriguez refers to this dynamic as "Ally Theater,"[2] part of what Indigenous Action Media calls the "Ally Industrial Complex."[3] The concern here is about activists who focus on performing an identity for an audience of disadvantaged folk rather than doing the hard and often unseen work of social change. To get out of the surface-level ally theater

Kristin J. Anderson is a psychology professor at the Center for Critical Race Studies at the University of Houston–Downtown. She is the author of *Modern Misogyny: Anti-Feminism in a Post-Feminist Era* and *Benign Bigotry: The Psychology of Subtle Prejudice*.

Christina Hsu Accomando is a professor of English and of critical race, gender, and sexuality studies at Humboldt State University. Her publications include *"The Regulations of Robbers": Legal Fictions of Slavery and Resistance*.

Revised February 2019 specifically for *Race, Class, and Gender in the United States: An Integrated Study*, 11th edition. Used with permission from the authors.

loop, white people need to challenge other whites about racism—even when no one else is watching. Straight and cis people need to confront other straight and cis people on their assumptions about gender and sexuality—even when no one else is watching. Challenging people in your own identity group is one of the most important and difficult tasks of allies. You must be willing to do the work even when the work is invisible.

A third problem with "ally" arises when activists get divided into dominant-group do-gooders and subordinate-group people-who-need-help. This framework reduces complicated relationships and social positions to a simplistic and static binary. In fact, we all carry multiple identities as we navigate the world and our activism. Most of us are simultaneously in some privileged and some targeted positions—you might be a cis woman of color or a white man with a physical disability. The binary construction of *ally* and *other* can slide into the implication that the work of well-meaning people in the dominant group is uniquely valuable to the helpless activists in the targeted group. As Benjamin Dixon says, allies aren't heroes, they're sidekicks.[4]

Finally, the use of the term "ally" has shifted over time from a descriptor other activists might use about you to something more self-serving and narcissistic, something you call yourself: "As an ally, I . . . ." Declaring yourself an ally distinguishes you from other people in your own group ("I'm white, but I'm one of the good ones") and also sets you apart from the activists you are attempting to work with. Declaring yourself an ally centers your dominant and privileged status and, unintentionally, can become an *othering* gesture. For instance, some straight people exhibit their support for the queer community with "Straight but not narrow" t-shirts and buttons. On the one hand, we can appreciate the sentiment of support offered by such a gesture, especially when straight support of queer people involves risk. On the other hand, the straight-but-not-narrow frame also declares, *I'm* not one of *them*, but I support them. Such self-labeling allows you to showcase your support of a group targeted for violence while simultaneously keeping yourself separate and away from peril.

We propose an alternative framing of social justice work that de-centers "ally" and instead brings into focus more complexity, more action, and less posing. Instead of ally-as-identity or ally-as-performance, we would like to shift the focus to a more productive way of understanding the role of activists who work across differences: *coalition work*.

Coalition work focuses less on individual identity and more on the work that different groups engage in to struggle collectively for social change. Whereas you can call yourself an ally alone in a room (or retweeting yourself on Twitter), you do coalition work only by engaging with people different from yourself. And such work is inherently challenging and risky. As Bernice Johnson Reagon says, "Most of the time you feel threatened to the core and if you don't, you're not really doing no coalescing."[5]

Rather than simplistically binary, coalition work is inherently intersectional. Unlike *ally*, *coalition* makes visible complex (and fraught) organizing and movement building among activists in different social positions. The 1% at the top of the power structure does well when the bottom 99% fractures and fails to form progressive alliances. We can chart different historical moments when coalition work among marginalized groups panicked the ruling elite, who then furiously deployed divisive tactics to keep those groups fragmented along various lines (particularly racial). For instance, Blacks and landless whites came together in Bacon's Rebellion in 1676, an early coalition that so alarmed the governing elite that they responded with everything from state violence to new laws to keep Blacks and poor whites in separate subordinate places.[6] And we can chart moments when marginalized groups forged ways to create coalitions instead of falling into the horizontal hostility[7] that serves the elite, as when Filipino and Mexican farmworkers built alliances in the historic Delano grape strike (1965–1970) that led to the formation of the United Farm Workers.[8]

Today, activists have the opportunity to form productive and dynamic coalitions around issues such as better schools, a living wage, immigration rights, ending racialized violence, and ending sexualized violence. Here are some examples of coalition work on such issues:

- In 2012, the Chicago Teachers Union went on strike for better wages and benefits, while also protesting against racist policies in the school district. The union is largely white and the students are largely African American and Latinx but commentators noted that "[b]y highlighting the fact that its members' fight for 'good teaching conditions' was intertwined with the fight against segregated schooling, racist probationary policies, poverty and the criminalization of students, the union showed in practice how the politics of solidarity and the recognition of shared interests can contribute to a powerful struggle."[9] Parents of color overwhelmingly supported the teachers.

- In 2017, the Movement for Black Lives (a coalition of groups fighting to end violence against Black communities) and Fight for $15 (a movement to raise the federal minimum wage to $15 per hour) initiated their first joint national action and organized protests for racial and economic justice in two dozen cities.[10]

- While labor unions have often been pitted against immigrants (in another example of horizontal hostility that serves the ruling elite), key unions representing four million workers have joined together as Working Families United to support permanent protections for recipients of Deferred Action for Childhood Arrivals (DACA) and the Temporary Protected Status (TPS) program.[11] The TPS program (rescinded by the Trump administration) offered thousands of immigrants from El Salvador, Haiti, Nicaragua, Sudan, and Honduras authorization to work and protection from deportation.

- Recent attention to the ongoing movement to end sexualized violence also has revealed dynamic coalitions. Civil rights activist Tarana Burke launched Me Too in 2006 as a grassroots movement to support survivors of sexualized violence, particularly young women of color. A decade later, #MeToo rose to international prominence as women in Hollywood protested sexual harassment. In 2017, Alianza Nacional de Campesinas (representing 700,000 Latina farmworkers) issued an open statement of solidarity with the Hollywood women, prompting the formation of "Time's Up" as a movement and legal defense fund to support workers across the labor spectrum as they fight harassment. In 2018, farmworker activists Lupe Gonzalo, Nely Rodriguez, Silvia Perez, and Julia de la Cruz (all from the Coalition of Immokalee Workers) published an open letter to Time's Up, calling for specific acts of solidarity toward concrete solutions, including the expansion of the Fair Food Program, a worker-driven monitoring program that seeks to eliminate human rights violations "from rape to modern-day slavery."[12]

Coalition work demands more from an activist than does being an ally (see the table below). The hope of being called an ally is not why you do the work. You engage in activism because, independent of your label, it's important work. Coalition work is an active process, not a passive identity, nor a feel-good performance for status points. Whereas ally theater is often both a starting point and an end point, coalition work is continuous, and it is hard work. "Some people will come to a coalition and they rate the success of the coalition on whether or not they feel good when they get there," says Bernice Johnson Reagon. "They're not looking for a coalition; they're looking for a home! They're looking for a bottle with some milk in it and a nipple, which does not happen in a coalition."[13]

Coalition work recognizes that fighting oppression binds us together and that it's the ruling elite who benefit when we fail to forge alliances for social change. Coalition work is also risky. We'll make mistakes. But working for liberation requires courage.

Ally Theater	Coalition Work
Ally as Identity: Ally is something I *am*. I wear "Ally" as a label.	*Coalition Work Is Action*: It is something we *do*.
Ally as Performance: Focus is on audience appreciation, and, frequently, the performance is foisted upon people in the targeted group the ally claims to be supporting.	*Coalitions Require Work*: Focus is on engaging with other activists across differences, doing the difficult work of social transformation.
Ally as Simplistic Binary: I in the dominant group will help out *you* in the oppressed group.	*Coalition Work Is Intersectional*: Everyone comes to the table with multiple identities. Most of us are in some dominant groups and some targeted groups. Effective coalition work helps undermine the insidious divide-and-conquer strategy that the elite has counted on for centuries.
Ally as Self-Serving: I call myself an ally, whether others do or not. My privilege and dominant status set me apart from others in my group. At the same time, proclaiming "ally" asserts my difference from the targeted group: "I'm straight but not narrow" advertises both my tolerance *and* my privilege. My identity as an ally feels good.	*Coalition Work Acknowledges Privilege*: Coalition work is about dismantling systems of oppression and acknowledging one's location in the matrix of domination and privilege. Coalition work is uncomfortable. Everyone is implicated, no one is off the hook.

NOTES

1. See Andrea Ayvazian, "Interrupting the Cycle of Oppression," also in Part IX of this volume.

2. http://www.bgdblog.org/2015/06/caitlyn-jenner-social-media-and-violent-solidarity-calling-out-abusive-material-sharing-it/

3. www.indigenousaction.org/accomplices-not-allies-abolishing-the-ally-industrial-complex/

4. https://www.bestoftheleft.com/6_rules_of_being_a_good_ally_benjamin_dixon_show_thebpdshow

5. Bernice Johnson Reagon, "Coalition politics: turning the century." In Barbara Smith (ed.), *Home Girls: A Black Feminist Anthology* (Kitchen Table Press, 1983), p. 356.

6. See Pem Davidson Buck, "Derailing Rebellion: Inventing White Privilege," in Part I of this volume, and Michelle Alexander, *The New Jim Crow: Mass Incarceration in the Age of Colorblindess* (The New Press, 2012), pp. 22–26.

7. Audre Lorde refers to the "tactic of encouraging horizontal hostility to becloud more pressing issues of oppression." She decries moments when "energy is being wasted on fighting each other over the pitifully few crumbs allowed us," rather than fighting a "vertical battle" against the actual structural systems of oppression, a fight that "could result in real power and change." She points out that "[i]t is the structure at the top which desires changelessness and which profits from these apparently endless kitchen wars" (see Lorde, "Scratching the Surface," in *Sister Outsider* [Crossing Press, 1984], p. 48).

8. http://ufw.org/research/history/mexicans-filipinos-joined-together/

9. Khury Petersen-Smith and Brian Bean argue for a politics of solidarity over a rhetoric of ally-ship: "We believe that ally-ship is a step in the right direction—but we need to go well beyond it if our objective is overcoming racism and winning Black liberation. Our case is that the politics of solidarity—encapsulated in the old labor movement slogan 'An injury to one is an injury to all' and given concrete expression in strikes and struggles like the CTU's—can take us forward." https://socialistworker.org/2015/05/14/fighting-racism-and-the-limits-of-allyship.

10. Maha Ahmed quotes Chicago Black Lives Matter organizer Kofi Ademola: "Poverty is violence, and over 300,000 people in Chicago are living in deep poverty. The struggles against white supremacy and capitalism have always been intertwined." http://inthesetimes.com/working/entry/20019/fight_for_15_and_the_movement_for_black_lives_join_forces.

11. https://www.workingfamiliesunited.org/union-members-to-congress-permanent-protections-for-tps-is-a-labor-issue/

12. https://ciw-online.org/blog/2018/02/an-open-letter/

13. Reagon, p. 359.

6 A Herstory of the #BlackLivesMatter Movement

Alicia Garza

I created #BlackLivesMatter with Patrisse Cullors and Opal Tometi . . . as a call to action for Black people after 17-year-old Trayvon Martin was posthumously placed on trial for his own murder [on February 26, 2012] and the killer, George Zimmerman, was not held accountable for the crime he committed. It was a response to the anti-Black racism that permeates our society and also, unfortunately, our movements.

Black Lives Matter is an ideological and political intervention in a world where Black lives are systematically and intentionally targeted for demise. It is an affirmation of Black folks' contributions to this society, our humanity, and our resilience in the face of deadly oppression.

We were humbled when cultural workers, artists, designers and techies offered their labor and love to expand #BlackLivesMatter beyond a social media hashtag. Opal, Patrisse, and I created the infrastructure for this movement project—moving the hashtag from social media to the streets. Our team grew through a very successful Black Lives Matter ride,[1] led and designed by Patrisse Cullors and Darnell L. Moore, organized to support the movement that is growing in St. Louis, MO, after 18-year old Mike Brown was killed at the hands of Ferguson Police Officer Darren Wilson [on August 9, 2014]. We've hosted national conference calls focused on issues of critical importance to Black people working hard for the liberation of our people. We've connected people across the country working to end the various forms of injustice impacting our people. We've created space for the celebration and humanization of Black lives.

The Theft of Black Queer Women's Work

As people took the #BlackLivesMatter demand into the streets, mainstream media and corporations also took up the call; #BlackLivesMatter appeared in an episode of *Law & Order: SVU* in a mash up containing the Paula Deen racism scandal and the tragedy of the murder of Trayvon Martin.

Suddenly, we began to come across varied adaptations of our work—all lives matter, brown lives matter, migrant lives matter, women's lives matter, and on and on. While imitation is said to be the highest form of flattery, I was surprised when an organization called

---

Alicia Garza is an Oakland-based organizer and writer and the special projects director for the National Domestic Workers Alliance. She cofounded Black Lives Matter in 2013.

to ask if they could use "Black Lives Matter" in one of their campaigns. We agreed to it, with the caveat that (a) as a team, we preferred that we not use the meme to celebrate the imprisonment of any individual and (b) that it was important to us they acknowledged the genesis of #BlackLivesMatter. I was surprised when they did exactly the opposite and then justified their actions by saying they hadn't used the "exact" slogan and, therefore, they deemed it okay to take our work, use it as their own, fail to credit where it came from, and then use it to applaud incarceration.

I was surprised when a community institution wrote asking us to provide materials and action steps for an art show they were curating, entitled "Our Lives Matter." When questioned about who was involved and why they felt the need to change the very specific call and demand around Black lives to "our lives," I was told the artists decided it needed to be more inclusive of all people of color. I was even more surprised when, in the promotion of their event, one of the artists conducted an interview that completely erased the origins of their work—rooted in the labor and love of queer Black women.

Pause.

When you design an event / campaign / et cetera based on the work of queer Black women, don't invite them to participate in shaping it, but ask them to provide materials and ideas for next steps for said event, that is racism in practice. It's also hetero-patriarchal. Straight men, unintentionally or intentionally, have taken the work of queer Black women and erased our contributions. Perhaps if we were the charismatic Black men many are rallying around these days, it would have been a different story, but being Black queer women in this society (and apparently within these movements) tends to equal invisibility and non-relevancy.

We completely expect those who benefit directly and improperly from White supremacy to try and erase our existence. We fight that every day. But when it happens amongst our allies, we are baffled, we are saddened, and we are enraged. And it's time to have the political conversation about why that's not okay.

We are grateful to our allies[2] who have stepped up to the call that Black lives matter, and taken it as an opportunity to not just stand in solidarity[3] with us, but to investigate the ways in which anti-Black racism is perpetuated in their own communities. We are also grateful to those allies who were willing to engage in critical dialogue with us about this unfortunate and problematic dynamic. And for those who we have not yet had the opportunity to engage with around the adaptations of the Black Lives Matter call, please consider the following points.

Broadening the Conversation to Include Black Life

Black Lives Matter is a unique contribution that goes beyond extrajudicial killings of Black people by police and vigilantes. It goes beyond the narrow nationalism that can be prevalent within some Black communities, which merely call on Black people to love Black, live Black and buy Black, keeping straight cis Black men in the front of the movement while our sisters, queer and trans and disabled folk take up roles in the background or not at all. Black Lives Matter affirms the lives of Black queer and trans folks, disabled folks, Black-undocumented folks, folks with records, women and all Black lives along the gender spectrum. It centers those that have been marginalized within Black liberation movements. It is a tactic to (re)build the Black liberation movement.

When we say Black Lives Matter, we are talking about the ways in which Black people are deprived of our basic human rights and dignity. It is an acknowledgment [that] Black poverty and genocide is state violence. It is an acknowledgment that 1 million Black people . . . locked in cages in this country—one half of all people in prisons or jails—is an act of state violence. It is an acknowledgment that Black women continue to bear the burden of a relentless assault on our children and our families and that [that] assault is an act of state violence. Black queer and trans folks bearing a unique burden in a hetero-patriarchal society that disposes of us like garbage and simultaneously fetishizes us and profits off of us is state violence; the fact that 500,000 Black people in the US are undocumented immigrants and relegated to the shadows is state violence; the fact that Black girls are used as negotiating chips during times of conflict and war is state violence; [the fact that] Black folks living with disabilities and different abilities bear the burden of state-sponsored Darwinian experiments that attempt to squeeze us into boxes of normality defined by White supremacy is state violence. And the fact that the lives of Black people—not ALL people—exist within these conditions is [a] consequence of state violence.

When Black people get free, everybody gets free.

#BlackLivesMatter doesn't mean your life isn't important—it means that Black lives, which are seen as without value within White supremacy, are important to your liberation. Given the disproportionate impact state violence has on Black lives, we understand that when Black people in this country get free, the benefits will be wide reaching and transformative for society as a whole. When we are able to end hyper-criminalization and sexualization of Black people and end the poverty, control, and surveillance of Black people, every single person in this world has a better shot at getting and staying free. When Black people get free, everybody gets free. This is why we call on Black people and our allies to take up the call that Black lives matter. We're not saying Black lives are more important than other lives, or that other lives are not criminalized and oppressed in various ways. We remain in active solidarity with all oppressed people who are fighting for their liberation and we know that our destinies are intertwined.

And, to keep it real—it is appropriate and necessary to have strategy and action centered around Blackness without other non-Black communities of color, or White folks for that matter, needing to find a place and a way to center themselves within it. It is appropriate and necessary for us to acknowledge the critical role that Black lives and struggles for Black liberation have played in inspiring and anchoring, through practice and theory, social movements for the liberation of all people. The women's movement, the Chicano liberation movement, queer movements, and many more have adopted the strategies, tactics and theory of the Black liberation movement. And if we are committed to a world where all lives matter, we are called to support the very movement that inspired and activated so many more. That means supporting and acknowledging Black lives.

Progressive movements in the United States have made some unfortunate errors when they push for unity at the expense of really understanding the concrete differences in context, experience and oppression. In other words, some want unity without struggle. As people who have our minds stayed on freedom, we can learn to fight anti-Black racism by examining the ways in which we participate in it, even unintentionally, instead of the worn out and sloppy practice of drawing lazy parallels of unity between peoples with vastly different experiences and histories.

When we deploy "All Lives Matter" as to correct an intervention specifically created to address anti-blackness, we lose the ways in which the state apparatus has built a program of genocide and repression mostly on the backs of Black people—beginning with the theft of millions of people for free labor—and then adapted it to control, murder, and profit off of other communities of color and immigrant communities. We perpetuate a level of White supremacist domination by reproducing a tired trope that we are all the same, rather than acknowledging that non-Black oppressed people in this country are both impacted by racism and domination, and simultaneously, BENEFIT from anti-black racism.

When you drop "Black" from the equation of whose lives matter, and then fail to acknowledge it came from somewhere, you further a legacy of erasing Black lives and Black contributions from our movement legacy. And consider whether or not when dropping the Black you are, intentionally or unintentionally, erasing Black folks from the conversation or homogenizing very different experiences. The legacy and prevalence of anti-Black racism and hetero-patriarchy is a lynch pin holding together this unsustainable economy. And that's not an accidental analogy.

In 2014, hetero-patriarchy and anti-Black racism within our movement is real and felt. It's killing us and it's killing our potential to build power for transformative social change. When you adopt the work of queer women of color, don't name or recognize it, and promote it as if it has no history of its own such actions are problematic. When I use Assata's powerful demand[4] in my organizing work, I always begin by sharing where it comes from, sharing about Assata's significance to the Black Liberation Movement, what its political purpose and message is, and why it's important in our context.

When you adopt Black Lives Matter and transform it into something else (if you feel you really need to do that—see above for the arguments not to), it's appropriate politically to credit the lineage from which your adapted work derived. It's important that we work together to build and acknowledge the legacy of Black contributions to the struggle for human rights. If you adapt Black Lives Matter, use the opportunity to talk about its inception and political framing. Lift up Black lives as an opportunity to connect struggles across race, class, gender, nationality, sexuality and disability.

And, perhaps more importantly, when Black people cry out in defense of our lives, which are uniquely, systematically, and savagely targeted by the state, we are asking you, our family, to stand with us in affirming Black lives. Not just all lives. Black lives. Please do not change the conversation by talking about how your life matters, too. It does, but we need less watered down unity and more active solidarities with us, Black people, unwaveringly, in defense of our humanity. Our collective futures depend on it.

NOTES

1. Akiba Solomon, "Get on the Bus: Inside the Black Life Matters 'Freedom Ride' to Ferguson," Colorlines, Sept. 5, 2014.

2. "Asian Grassroots Statement for Justice for Trayvon Martin." Asian Pacific Environmental Network. July 23, 2013.

3. Marisa Franco, "If Michael Brown was the Last, Not the Latest." NotOneMoreDeportation. com, August 18, 2014.

4. "It is our duty to fight for our freedom. It is our duty to win. We must love each other and support each other. We have nothing to lose but our chains." Assata Shakur, "To My People." TheTalkingDrum.com.

7 | The Me Too Movement: The Rigorous Work That Still Lies Ahead

Tarana Burke

Twelve years ago, I could never have predicted all that has happened in the past 12 months. Historically, in this country, there has been very little space to talk about sexual violence in ways that focus on survivors and solutions, especially in the media. Cases that should have signaled a serious, persistent problem were reduced to salacious gossip and tawdry headlines; the last year hasn't done much to change that.

Some might see the cases of Harvey Weinstein and Les Moonves as bookends to this year. But look closer and you'll find at both the beginning and the end are survivors and allies refusing to stay silent while people in power inflict harm without recourse. And we've just scratched the surface. To many in the public, that seems to translate to the belief that the outing of perpetrators is the main goal of the #MeToo movement when that is the furthest from the truth. Calling out individual bad actors doesn't get us to the root of the problem.

It's no secret that Hollywood runs off power, privilege and access, and because of that it is important in this moment to also examine the ways that unchecked privilege and power accumulate and are wielded against the most vulnerable. We know this doesn't just happen in Hollywood, so we have to do the same kind of rigorous investigation and analysis of the culture within all our major corporations and communities that consistently allows sexual violence to occur again and again.

What the world recognizes as the #MeToo movement was built on the labor of everyday people who survived sexual violence in a number of forms. Some were harassed, some survived child sexual abuse or other kinds of sexual assault, but all of them endeavored to stand in their truth. All at once starting last October, millions of people raised their hands and voices to be counted among the number of people who had experienced sexual harassment, assault and abuse. More than 12 million in 24 hours on Facebook. Half a million in 12 hours on Twitter. And the numbers kept growing. But as soon as the mainstream media got over the shock of the sheer volume of those who counted themselves in, it immediately pivoted back to what was happening in Hollywood. While that was driven by the dynamic investigative journalism of people like Ronan Farrow of *The New Yorker*, what was happening around the world was driven by the courage of people from all walks of life. If we don't shift our focus and actually look at the people saying, "Me too," then

---

Tarana Burke founded the Me Too movement in 2006. She is a civil rights activist, the senior director of Girls for Gender Equity, and the founder of the nonprofit Just Be Inc., which promotes the health and well-being of young women of color.

Originally appeared in *Variety* in fall of 2018. Used with permission.

we are going to waste a really valuable opportunity to change the nature of how we think about sexual violence in this country.

If we could pull back from focusing on the accused and zero in on the ones speaking out, we would see common denominators that bridge the divide between celebrity and everyday citizens: the diminishing of dignity and the destruction of humanity. Everyday people—queer, trans, disabled, men and women—are living in the aftermath of a trauma that tried, at the very worst, to take away their humanity. This movement at its core is about the restoration of that humanity.

This is one reason that the weaponization of #MeToo has been so shocking. Several men and some women, many of whom are rich and powerful, have mischaracterized this movement out of their own fears and inability to hold a nuanced perspective. These same folks are quick to assign blame to the victims of violence based on the media's obsession with who will be "found out" next. So, instead of homing in on the pervasiveness of sexual violence, the focus is on the accused and what's at stake for them: What's going to happen to their careers? What are the consequences for the companies that employed them? What are the consequences for the industry they're in? But how many articles were written about the consequences for the women still working at places like NBC and CBS? The details of those experiences are going to mirror those of so many people. Knowing those stories gives voice to those who survived sexual violence as opposed to the people who perpetrate the violence.

All of the shouting and headlines about who #MeToo is going to take down next creates a kind of careless perception that invalidates the experiences of survivors who risk everything coming forward, whether it's telling their stories, sharing a hashtag or being transparent and vulnerable about some of the worst things that have happened in their lives.

The din of naysayers has, in many regards, severely overshadowed the beauty of what has happened this year. It has been a year of great liberation and empowerment. Every day I meet people who have moved from victim to survivor by simply adding their own "Me too" to the chorus of voices. They have freed themselves from the burden that holding on to these traumas often creates and stepped into the power of release, the power of empathy and the power of truth. They have looked their demons in the face and lived to see another day, and they have become the empirical proof that we can win the fight to end sexual violence.

Moving into 2019, some concrete things must happen in order to build on the momentum we have gained in the last year, starting with changing how we talk about the #MeToo movement. This is a survivors' movement created for and by those of us who have endured sexual violence. The goal is to provide a mechanism to support survivors and move people to action. Any other characterization severely handicaps our ability to move the work forward.

We also need to have a more intentional public dialogue about accountability, and not just the kind that focuses on crime and punishment, but on harm and harm reduction. Narrowing our focus to investigations, firings and prison can hinder the conversation and the reality that accountability and justice look different for different people. We need to refine our approaches for seeking justice to reflect that diversity. Sexual violence happens on a spectrum, so accountability has to happen on a spectrum. And that means various ways of being accountable are necessary. Survivors have to be central to that accountability, and they must be the ones leading and dictating what that accountability looks like. Without that, there's no clear path for people, especially public figures, to regain the trust of those they've harmed and let down. This is playing out publicly as many of the celebrities and entertainers whose behavior was exposed are now attempting comebacks without having made amends to those they harmed, publicly apologizing, or acknowledging how they're going to change their behavior, industries, or communities to help end sexual violence.

Apologies, in and of themselves, are not work. They precede work. The men who are trying to come back have not done any work. Not that I have seen. Oftentimes it's about intent versus impact. So even if you think you're innocent of the actions you're being accused of, human decency dictates that you say, "OK. I want to hear what your experience in that moment was." Terry Crews is a perfect example. He said, "My experience with this thing was that you made me feel that I was humiliated. I was overpowered. You took away my dignity." There is not a plot to excommunicate people for life, but the accused should have the respect, at least, to show that they're committed to change. Show your work.

It is also necessary for us to expand the scope of the movement in the mainstream. In 2006, I launched the #MeToo movement because I wanted to find ways to bring healing into the lives of black women and girls. But those same women and girls, along with other people of color, queer people and disabled people, have not felt seen this year. Whether it was the near abandonment of Lupita Nyong'o when she revealed her experience with Weinstein, or Lena Dunham's support of the man Aurora Perrineau accused of rape, there was a sharp difference in the response to black women coming forward. Russell Simmons has 18 accusations of rape, sexual assault and sexual misconduct against him, largely by black women, and yet there is no media frenzy around him or his accusers. The depth and breadth of sexual violence in this country can't be quantified, but it definitely doesn't discriminate, and we won't begin to really understand its impact unless we look at the whole story.

I can't stress how critical our next steps are. It's been almost 30 years since Anita Hill testified in front of the Senate Judiciary Committee about the sexual harassment she endured at the hands of now Justice Clarence Thomas. It is so disheartening that we're here again, but it's just another reminder about where we are as a country and how this movement still has to be powered by everyday people who vote, who are vocal, who are active, who are tuned in and aware of how it's bigger than Hollywood, and bigger than politics.

For our part we are building out our work both online with the October launch of our new comprehensive website [metoomvmt.org] and on the ground through programming and partnerships. We have also partnered with the New York Women's Foundation to create a #MeToo movement fund that will raise $25 million to put toward working to end sexual violence over the next five years. Our goal is to keep expanding the work and building the movement.

For too long women and others living on the margins have managed to survive without our full dignity intact. It can't continue to be our reality. The work of #MeToo builds on the existing efforts to dismantle systems of oppression that allow sexual violence, patriarchy, racism and sexism to persist. We know that this approach will make our society better for everyone, not just survivors, because creating pathways to healing and restoration moves us all closer to a world where everyone knows the peace of living without fear and the joy of living in your full dignity. I intend to keep doing this work, from within this amazing movement, until we get there.

8 Reproductive Justice in the Twenty-First Century

Loretta J. Ross and Rickie Solinger

Why Does Reproductive Justice Matter?

We begin with one woman's story, to illustrate how reproductive justice can change what we know about the past, how we interpret the present, and how we envision the future. We also begin with a story because we want to show how storytelling is an act of subversion and resistance. Stories help us understand how others think and make decisions. They help us understand how our human rights—and the human rights of others—are protected or violated. Storytelling is a core aspect of reproductive justice practice because attending to someone else's story invites us to shift the lens—that is, to imagine the life of another person and to reexamine our own realities and reimagine our own possibilities.

. . .

At this historical moment, narratives have become a key strategy for making social justice claims to change the world. Social justice groups all over the world are using stories to explain—and claim—their power to "build a bridge across our fears of what has never been before," in the words of Black feminist Audre Lorde.[1] . . . Reproductive justice helps break our silences to ask many questions about knowledge and beliefs, about the nature of society, about who benefits and who is harmed. We break our silences to ask why lethal inequalities persist. We trust in the power of personal and cultural biographies.

The Political Is Personal: A Reproductive Justice Story
Imagine you're a young woman in college on a scholarship in [your] first semester, because great grades helped you graduate at sixteen. You're majoring in chemistry, eventually headed to medical school. You've met someone who might be your future husband, a first-year law student who teaches you how to drive, and helps you improve your already good study habits. He patiently explains how to conquer both precalculus and pinochle. A thousand miles from home, you're enjoying both your first "adult" relationship and the freedom and responsibility of going to college.

Loretta J. Ross is a feminist academic and activist who cofounded the SisterSong Women of Color Reproductive Justice Collective in 1997. Her books include the coedited collection *Radical Reproductive Justice: Foundation, Theory, Practice, Critique.*

Rickie Solinger is an historian, a curator, and an award-winning author. She focuses on the politics of welfare, reproductive rights, and incarceration.

By the second semester, you've had sex with him three times. Of course you're a little worried, because you didn't use condoms each time. You're not old enough to get other birth control without your conservative parents' permission.

And then it happens. Your period is two weeks late. Your mind seizes on a frenzied set of oh-my-god questions: "OMG! What will my family say? OMG! Can I stay in school? OMG! Can I tell my boyfriend and will he freak out? OMG! I only work part-time; will I lose my job? OMG! I believe in abortion, but what if he doesn't? OMG! What will I do?"

This young woman does not even know for sure that she is pregnant, but she will soon realize that the answers to her OMG questions determine whether or not she's ready to become a mother. If she has the economic, emotional, and moral support of her family and partner, maybe she will continue the pregnancy. If she doesn't, maybe she will seek an abortion for what might have been a wanted pregnancy under other circumstances.

Nearly every woman who has unprotected sex with a man and is scared by a late period has faced these OMG panics. Many women confront these difficult situations that pro-choice/pro-life abortion debates rarely mention. Not every unplanned pregnancy is unwanted, and not every wanted pregnancy leads to a birth. The OMG questions involving education, financial security, family relationships, and the partner's reaction are far upstream from the "to be or not to be" question of motherhood. The pro-choice side is primarily concerned about legality, safety, and access. The pro-life side emphasizes morality, religion, and the potential life of the unborn child. . . . Both sides fail to understand that the answers to the OMG questions are the actual logic chain that a woman goes through when she is deciding to continue or end a pregnancy.

Of course, not every pregnant woman is in total control of her decisions. She may be mentally disabled. She may be physically disabled, unable to marshal the necessary resources to have a real choice. He may be a transman rejected by a health care provider. Or she may live on a Native American reservation with access only to health care provided by the Indian Health Service, which prohibits abortions. Or, in the eyes of the law, she may simply be too young to have an abortion, even though she is not too young to become a mother. To understand and respond to stories like these, we needed reproductive justice.

Birthing and Defining Reproductive Justice

. . .

I—Loretta—had experiences that were like the ones that this first-year college student had. They were part of my Black feminist journey. I was that young woman with the OMG panic in 1970. Twenty-four years later, I helped create the reproductive justice framework with eleven other Black women meeting in Chicago in 1994 at a larger pro-choice conference advocating for health care reform.[2] . . . At the time, the Clinton administration's plan for health care reform avoided the issue of reproductive health care, especially abortion, an attempt to placate Republican opponents.

. . .

We . . . objected to the ways that [the Clinton administration's] proposals isolated reproductive rights issues from other social justice issues (the OMG questions) for vulnerable people. The proposals on the table did not make connections between the decision to become a mother—or not—and extremely relevant issues such as economics, immigration, and incarceration. [T]he twelve Black women at the pro-choice conference in 1994 collectively questioned the primacy of abortion, but not its necessity. We placed *ourselves* in the center of our analysis and made the case that while abortion was a crucial resource for us, we also needed health care, education, jobs, day care, and the right to motherhood. Taking this position was a powerful example of *centering*, placing oneself in the center of the lens in order to discover new ways of describing reality from a particular standpoint. These fresh perspectives—so different from the endless and debilitating debates that focused exclusively on abortion—radically shifted our thinking and launched the concept of reproductive justice by splicing together the equation of *reproductive rights + social justice = reproductive justice.*

Reproductive justice is not difficult to define or remember. It has three primary values: (1) the right *not* to have a child; (2) the right to *have* a child; and (3) the right to *parent* children in safe and healthy environments. In addition, reproductive justice demands sexual autonomy and gender freedom for every human being. The problem is not defining reproductive justice but achieving it.

Our group of twelve, an informal alliance we called Women of African Descent for Reproductive Justice, decided to launch an ad campaign to challenge the Clinton administration's strategy and to get the attention of Washington policy makers. We crafted a national statement for Black women regarding our demands for health care reform. Six weeks after the Chicago meeting, we raised the funds to place a full-page signature ad in both the *Washington Post* and *Roll Call* (a publication that serves all the people who work in Congress and on Capitol Hill) on August 16, 1994, under the more media-friendly name Black Women on Health Care Reform. Almost 850 African American women joined, including professor Angela Davis, novelist Alice Walker, and supermodel Veronica Webb.[3]

Our group created the concept of reproductive justice and a nascent movement out of our need to develop a response to a public policy proposal for health care reform that, as it stood, failed to meet the needs of women. As Black women, we shared a unique standpoint that expressed how the reproductive privileges of some women depended on the reproductive disciplining of other women in ways that did not challenge racism or other vehicles of inequality. This new reproductive justice perspective began to explain how all people experience their reproductive capacity according to multiple intersecting factors including their class, race, gender, sexuality, status of their health, and access to health care.

In 1994 we had no idea we were literally at the forefront of a new movement that would revolutionize reproductive political activism in the United States. Yet at the end of the twentieth century, reproductive justice offered new visions of self-determination, collective unity, and liberatory practices. Reproductive justice was a breathtaking and innovative theoretical breakthrough that changed the way that mainstream and grassroots groups in the United States and abroad thought about reproductive politics.

. . .

In 2003, the SisterSong Women of Color Reproductive Health Collective organized its first national conference and featured a plenary and workshop on reproductive justice.[4]

SisterSong challenged the speakers to address these questions: What is reproductive justice? Could it serve as a new way for women of color to address reproductive injustices? Could it be used to build a movement by and for women of color to address reproductive politics in the United States? The six hundred participants at SisterSong's conference enthusiastically supported this revolutionary concept. Reproductive justice began to march from the margins to the center of reproductive activism to protect the human rights of all women.

At the 2003 conference, the Feminist Majority Foundation, NARAL Pro-Choice America, the National Organization for Women (NOW), and the Planned Parenthood Federation of America asked SisterSong to help organize a national march for women's rights to take place in Washington, DC, in 2004. After some negotiation, members of SisterSong and other women of color, particularly members of the National Latina Institute for Reproductive Health, the Black Women's Health Imperative, and the National Asian Pacific American Women's Forum, agreed to help organize the April 25, 2004, March for Women's Lives, which reportedly became the largest protest in U.S. history with 1.15 million participants. NARAL and Planned Parenthood originally wanted to call the event the March for Freedom of Choice, focusing exclusively on abortion and birth control. But women of color insisted that the name be changed to the March for Women's Lives, a more inclusive name,[5] and demanded that the organizers move beyond a singular focus on abortion to include other reproductive justice and human rights issues.[6] The impact of the march helped to advance the concept of reproductive justice, and in the minds of many analysts, its new reproductive justice focus helped the march achieve its unprecedented size. The National Organization for Women became the first mainstream women's organization to use the phrase "reproductive justice" when it promoted the March in a 2003 newsletter.[7]

The first book focusing on reproductive justice, *Undivided Rights: Women of Color Organize for Reproductive Justice,* was published in 2004. This book introduced the concept to an even broader activist and academic public, particularly students and young people. The book detailed the histories of Native American, Asian Pacific Islander, Latina, and African American activists working in local and national community-based organizations devoted to reproductive health, sexual autonomy, and human rights.[8]

The book told a vibrant history that was largely unknown to the general public, but after these events in 2003 and 2004, the recognition of women of color as a growing power base within U.S. reproductive politics accelerated. This was an important shift because up until that time, women of color were largely seen as objects of reproductive control by family planners, elected officials, demographers, and eugenicists. The development of the reproductive justice framework forcefully demonstrated the agency of women of color and the power of our movement to produce new theories, new knowledge, and new forms of activism that could alter the American political and economic landscape.

. . .

. . .Today, many women of color and their allies are producing a prodigious body of work on reproductive justice in the United States and internationally. For example, in 2014 the social development minister of South Africa, Bathabile Dlamini, announced that reproductive justice was the conceptual framework she used to determine health policies for her nation.[9] The New York City Department of Health and Mental Hygiene has adopted the reproductive justice perspective to inform and guide all of its work in its Bureau of Maternal, Infant, and Reproductive Health, which will surely be a model for other municipal health departments around the country. This global explosion of reproductive justice activism and its fertile scholarship have sparked a radical provocation and an interruption of narrow, repetitive, and unproductive debates on abortion.

We think of reproductive justice as an open source code that people have used to pursue fresh critical thinking regarding power and powerlessness. The results of this analysis are only beginning to emerge. As musician, activist, and scholar Bernice Johnson Reagon said, "Most of the things that you do, if you do them right, are for people who live long after you are long forgotten. That will only happen if you give it away."[10] Women of color offered reproductive justice to the feminist world as an important contribution to political and social analysis of reproductive politics. In the process, they successfully transformed reproductive activism at the beginning of the twenty-first century.

One key to the success of reproductive justice is that this framework infers a universality that has previously eluded the women's movement, while avoiding essentialism. That is, reproductive justice does not insist that one set of meanings or experiences describes the experiences of all people. On the contrary, reproductive justice insists that no particular reproductive experience is superior to or more authentic than other experiences. Reproductive justice is universally applicable because every human being has the same human rights, a foundational reproductive justice principle. While reproductive justice was created by women of color, its precepts apply not only to women of color. But only women of color created a theoretical breakthrough in this arena that is universally relevant.

The reproductive justice framework begins with the proposition that while every human being has the same human rights, not everyone is oppressed the same way, or at the same time, or by the same forces. Nevertheless, the experiences of oppression and struggling against oppression are constants in human experience. Most of us have had or will have the experience of being unjustly degraded and rendered powerless by another individual or by an institution, often because of our personal characteristics such as gender, race, class, religion, or sexual orientation.

Reproductive justice incorporates "standpoint theory" and its concept of shifting lenses to understand these matters. This concept helps us interrogate a host of injustices that may seem tangential to reproductive health, rights, and justice—for example, gentrification, environmental degradation, incarceration migration, and militarization. Reproductive justice looks at how these issues intersect with each other and how, at various points of intersection, they affect the reproductive bodies of women and individuals.

Intersectionality: Do Differences Divide?

. . . In 1989 critical legal theorist Kimberlé Williams Crenshaw named the concept "intersectionality" to illustrate how racial and gender oppression interact in the lives of Black women. She used a traffic metaphor: Black women stand at the intersection of Race and Gender Streets, vulnerable to injury from cars traveling along either axis. Crenshaw explained that neither race nor gender by itself could capture the particular experiences of Black women.[11] Only when we imagine the intersection of race and gender can we imagine the needs and perspectives of African American women. . . .

. . .

. . . The deeply influential 1977 Combahee River Collective's statement by Black feminists including Barbara Smith, Demita Frazier, and Beverly Smith, introduced the term "identity politics" and argued that racial and sexual discrimination, homophobia, and classism were "multifaceted and interconnected."[12] In *This Bridge Called My Back*, Chicana activists, theorists, and writers Cherríe Moraga and Gloria Anzaldúa wrote about the linkages of class, race, sexuality, and feminism in a way that explored the concept of intersectionality nearly a decade before Crenshaw named it. This family lineage provided a strong platform for launching a new theoretical framework offering all human beings a chance to explore their own intersecting identities and to resist being forced into a one-dimensional box.

. . .

The concept of intersectionality has evolved to describe a system of advantages and disadvantages dependent on markers of difference. The result is not an account of identity but an explanation of power disparities. Sometimes *identity politics*—making claims for recognition and resources based on, for example, race or sexual orientation—can overwhelm efforts to build a human rights movement. Indeed, differences can be a platform for positive creative change, or they can build barriers that separate people into bitter, competitive groups.

When activists assume that only those with whom they share particular identities are acceptable, safe, or credible, they are promoting a mechanical "angel/devil" practice of radical struggle, creating a false binary. This kind of "purity politics" foments criticism, shaming, and silencing—and turns naturally occurring political disagreements into excuses for dismissing the voices of others. Purity politics harms the chance, as Toni Cade Bambara put it, to "make revolution irresistible."[13] In the reproductive justice movement, we always need to emphasize that using difference as a weapon is contrary to our framework. Using difference as a weapon thwarts the transformative and radical solidarity of reproductive justice as people become "identity bullies." No one wins in the Oppression Olympics. In order to achieve reproductive justice, we need a united human rights movement that includes all persons and their voices.[14]

On the other hand, identity politics can be a positive force. As people explore their multidimensional identities, they sometimes seek a "safe space" with others like them, a space in which to explore the meanings and power of these joyfully ambiguous realizations. They want and deserve a nurturing space in which to decide who they are and how they want the world to recognize who they are. This is the essence of identity politics, to help create that womb-like safe space where one is fed, nurtured, and encouraged to grow.

But when people mistake the collective movement for a womb—that is, a very safe place—they sometimes become fierce language disciplinarians or boundary-watchers who experience their lack of safety outside the womb as a form of violence. When this happens, a human rights movement—in this case, the movement for reproductive justice—is harmed.

It may be a hard lesson, but the road to human rights is not necessarily a protected space. Over and over we've seen that antioppression work does not necessarily guarantee or provide a safe space free from painful triggers. If being oppressed is dangerous, why would anyone assume that fighting oppression—the toxic forces of capitalism, homophobia, racism, sexism, ableism, transphobia, nativism—can take place in a safe space? Did the sit-in activists in the civil rights movement experience safety? Do the antiviolence feminists who confront rapists and batterers expect safety? Do the Dreamers who are fighting for respect and legal rights as immigrants live in safe spaces? Are fast-food workers fighting for the $15-an-hour minimum wage too afraid of being fired to protest? In short, coalition work is often scary and challenging. Indeed, Bernice Johnson Reagon warned that coalition work "is the most dangerous work you can do. . . . Some people will come to a coalition and they rate the success of the coalition on whether they feel good when they get there. They are not looking for a coalition; they are looking for a home!"[15] The reproductive justice framework is defined by coalition politics and cannot achieve its human rights goals without building coalitions.

. . .

Movement Building Through Reproductive Justice

. . . As individuals, we cannot change the systemic reproductive injustices we face. We must work together in solid alliances that put our own lives in the center of the lens through which we theorize, strategize, and organize.

As an action strategy for movement building, reproductive justice requires working across social justice issues, bringing diverse issues and people together and revealing differences and commonalities using the human rights framework. Reproductive justice offers the human rights movement an opportunity to build a movement of solidarity in which differences are strengths, not liabilities.

. . .

In the process of making the reproductive justice framework effective in the world, we have shifted from individual resistance to proactive organizing with a new vision for political engagement. This shift transcends siloed single-issue identity politics. Rather, it connects multi-issue, multiracial, and poly-vocal movements across borders, incorporates multiple and variable identities, and interrogates the structures below the surfaces of our sufferings. The shared values we can unearth, name, and celebrate have the potential to create solutions. We especially aim to create a culture of caring that can transform U.S. society through social justice activism.

> In our world, divide and conquer must become define and empower.
>
> —Audre Lorde[16]

The reproductive justice movement has connected many activists across progressive movements, including many new activists, through shared core values. It has changed the public discourse on reproductive health and rights issues in the United States by connecting to broader progressive movements. Collectively, we are pressing our ideas into public policies that address the structural and systemic issues that contribute to reproductive oppression. We seek to achieve institutional and public accountability for the conditions in our communities that compromise our ability to possess our human rights. Women-of-color organizations that work on a variety of issues, such as HIV/AIDS, midwifery, abortion rights, health disparities, abstinence, teen pregnancy, breast cancer, environmental justice, police brutality, and immigrants' rights, among others, are working together in the spaces created by reproductive justice. . . .

. . .

To some degree each of these new movements is shifting its analysis toward the global human rights framework. Will this shift finally facilitate common human rights grounding for all justice movements and offer a shared vision and set of practices? While this process is barely under way and cannot as yet be measured, those committed to bringing human rights home to the United States are excited about the prospect for movement building that this development seems to promise. The reproductive justice movement, with its distinct commitment to personal storytelling, can help create a culture of collaboration among human rights activists, enabling us to organize with people who think differently about issues or who focus on different issues but who agree to work together to achieve human rights goals. As a transformative framework, reproductive justice can revolutionize our approach to reproductive politics.

NOTES

1. Audre Lorde, *Sister Outsider: Essays and Speeches* (Trumansburg, NY: Crossing Press, 1984), 37.
2. These were the twelve founding mothers of the concept of reproductive justice and their affiliations at the time:

   Toni M. Bond, Chicago Abortion Fund
   Reverend Alma Crawford, Religious Coalition for Reproductive Choice
   Evelyn S. Field, National Council of Negro Women
   Terri James, American Civil Liberties Union of Illinois
   Bisola Maringay, National Black Women's Health Project, Chicago Chapter
   Cassandra McConnell, Planned Parenthood of Greater Cleveland
   Cynthia Newbille, National Black Women's Health Project (now Black Women's Health Imperative)
   Loretta J. Ross, Center for Democratic Renewal
   Elizabeth Terry, National Abortion Rights Action League of Pennsylvania
   "Able" Mabel Thomas, Pro-Choice Resource Center, Inc.
   Winnette P. Willis, Chicago Abortion Fund
   Kim Youngblood, National Black Women's Health Project

3. Black Women on Health Care Reform held a press conference the next day to underscore the purpose of the ad. The press conference featured African American Congresswomen Eleanor Holmes Norton, Maxine Waters, Carrie Meek, Cynthia McKinney, and Eva Clayton.

4. The women in the 2003 SisterSong plenary and workshop on reproductive justice included the following:

   Byllye Avery, National Black Women's Health Project Founder
   Adriane Fugh Berman, National Women's Health Network
   Jatrice Gaithers, Planned Parenthood of Metropolitan Washington
   Rosalina Palacios, National Latina Health Organization
   Dorothy Roberts, Northwestern University School of Law
   Malika Saada Saar, Rebecca Project for Human Rights founder
   Eveline Shen, Asian Pacific Islanders for Reproductive Health
   Jael Silliman, Ford Foundation (affiliation listed for identification only)
   Barbara Smith, Combahee River Collective cofounder

5. The name March for Women's Human Rights was originally suggested at the SisterSong conference, but was likely little understood by some of the mainstream groups, so a name used for previous marches was recycled.
6. These included environmental justice issues, the war against Iraq, and the international debt crisis of the Global South.
7. Zakiya Luna, "Marching toward Reproductive Justice: Coalitional (Re) Framing of the March for Women's Lives," *Sociological Inquiry* 80, no. 4 (November 2010): 554–78.
8. Jael Silliman, Marlene Gerber Fried, Loretta Ross, and Elena Gutiérrez, *Undivided Rights: Women of Color Organize for Reproductive Justice* (Boston: South End Press, 2004).
9. Rebecca Davis, "Minister Bathabile Dlamini: Reproductive Justice's Newly Vocal Champion," *Daily Maverick*, June 11, 2014, http://www.dailymaverick.co.za/article/2014–06–11-minister-bathabile-dlamini-reproductive-justices-newly-vocal-champion/.
10. Bernice Johnson Reagon, "Coalition Politics: Turning the Century," in *Home Girls: A Black Feminist Anthology*, ed. Barbara Smith (New York: Kitchen Table Press, 1983), 365.
11. Kimberlé Crenshaw, "Intersectionality and Identity Politics: Learning from Violence against Women of Color" in *Feminist Theory: A Reader,* 2nd ed., ed. Wendy Kolmar and Frances Bartkowski (New York: McGraw-Hill, 2005), 50.
12. The Combahee River Collective's name commemorated a river in South Carolina where 750 slaves were freed on June 2, 1863, in a raid planned and led by ex-slave Harriet Tubman, the only military campaign in American history planned and led by a woman. Combahee River Collective, "Black Feminist Statement," in *All the Women Are White, All the Blacks Are Men, But Some of Us Are Brave: Black Women's Studies*, ed. Gloria T. Hull, Patricia Bell Scott, and Barbara Smith (Westbury, NY: Feminist Press, 1982).
13. Gloria Anzaldúa and Cherríe Moraga, *This Bridge Called My Back,* 2nd ed. (New York: Kitchen Table Press, 1983), 263. Also available in *Savoring the Salt: The Legacy of Toni Cade Bambara*, ed. Linda Janet Holmes and Cheryl A. Wall (Philadelphia: Temple University Press, 2007); Thabiti Lewis, *Conversations with Toni Cade Bambara* (Jackson; University of Mississippi Press, 2012).
14. Bernice Johnson Reagon wrote, "The 'our' must include everybody you have to include in order for you to survive." "Coalition Politics: Turning the Century," in *Homegirls: A Black Feminist Anthology*, ed. Barbara Smith (New York: Kitchen Table Press, 1983), 365.
15. Reagon,"Coalition Politics," 359.
16. Audre Lorde, "The Master's Tools Will Never Dismantle the Master's House," *Sister Outsider: Essays and Speeches* (Trumansburg, NY: Crossing Press, 1984), 112.

9 Are Prisons Obsolete? Abolitionist Alternatives

Angela Davis

Forget about reform; it's time to talk about abolishing jails and prisons in American society . . . Still—abolition? Where do you put the prisoners? The 'criminals'? What's the alternative? First, having no alternative at all would create less crime than the present criminal training centers do. Second, the only full alternative is building the kind of society that does not need prisons: A decent redistribution of power and income so as to put out the hidden fire of burning envy that now flames up in crimes of property—both burglary by the poor and embezzlement by the affluent. And a decent sense of community that can support, reintegrate and truly reha- bilitate those who suddenly become filled with fury or despair, and that can face them not as objects—'criminals'—but as people who have committed illegal acts, as have almost all of us.
—Arthur Waskow, Institute for Policy Studies[1]

If jails and prisons are to be abolished, then what will replace them? This is the puzzling question that often interrupts further consideration of the prospects for abolition. Why should it be so difficult to imagine alternatives to our current system of incarceration? There are a number of reasons why we tend to balk at the idea that it may be possible to eventually create an entirely different—and perhaps more egalitarian—system of justice. First of all, we think of the current system, with its exaggerated dependence on imprison- ment, as an unconditional standard and thus have great difficulty envisioning any other way of dealing with the more than two million people who are currently being held in the country's jails, prisons, youth facilities, and immigration detention centers. Ironically, even the anti-death penalty campaign tends to rely on the assumption that life imprison- ment is the most rational alternative to capital punishment. As important as it may be to abolish the death penalty, we should be conscious of the way the contemporary cam- paign against capital punishment has a propensity to recapitulate the very historical pat- terns that led to the emergence of the prison as the dominant form of punishment. The death penalty has coexisted with the prison, though imprisonment was supposed to serve as an alternative to corporal and capital punishment. This is a major dichotomy A critical engagement with this dichotomy would involve taking seriously the possibility of linking the goal of death penalty abolitionism with strategies for prison abolition.

It is true that if we focus myopically on the existing system—and perhaps this is the prob- lem that leads to the assumption that imprisonment is the only alternative to death—it is

Angela Davis is a scholar, teacher, and activist who has been involved in social justice advocacy for most of her life. She has published more than ten books, including *Women, Race, and Class*; *Are Prisons Obsolete?*; and *Abolition Democracy: Beyond Prisons, Torture, and Empire*.

very hard to imagine a structurally similar system capable of handling such a vast population of lawbreakers. If, however, we shift our attention from the prison, perceived as an isolated institution, to the set of relationships that comprise the prison industrial complex, it may be easier to think about alternatives. In other words, a more complicated framework may yield more options than if we simply attempt to discover a single substitute for the prison system. The first step, then, would be to let go of the desire to discover one single alternative system of punishment that would occupy the same footprint as the prison system.

Since the 1980s, the prison system has become increasingly ensconced in the economic, political and ideological life of the United States and the transnational trafficking in U.S. commodities, culture, and ideas. Thus, the prison industrial complex is much more than the sum of all the jails and prisons in this country. It is a set of symbiotic relationships among correctional communities, transnational corporations, media conglomerates, guards' unions, and legislative and court agendas. If it is true that the contemporary meaning of punishment is fashioned through these relationships, then the most effective abolitionist strategies will contest these relationships and propose alternatives that pull them apart. What, then, would it mean to imagine a system in which punishment is not allowed to become the source of corporate profit? How can we imagine a society in which race and class are not primary determinants of punishment? Or one in which punishment itself is no longer the central concern in the making of justice?

An abolitionist approach that seeks to answer questions such as these would require us to imagine a constellation of alternative strategies and institutions, with the ultimate aim of removing the prison from the social and ideological landscapes of our society. In other words, we would not be looking for prisonlike substitutes for the prison, such as house arrest safeguarded by electronic surveillance bracelets. Rather, positing decarceration as our overarching strategy, we would try to envision a continuum of alternatives to imprisonment—demilitarization of schools, revitalization of education at all levels, a health system that provides free physical and mental care to all, and a justice system based on reparation and reconciliation rather than retribution and vengeance.

The creation of new institutions that lay claim to the space now occupied by the prison can eventually start to crowd out the prison so that it would inhabit increasingly smaller areas of our social and psychic landscape. Schools can therefore be seen as the most powerful alternative to jails and prisons. Unless the current structures of violence are eliminated from schools in impoverished communities of color—including the presence of armed security guards and police—and unless schools become places that encourage the joy of learning, these schools will remain the major conduits to prisons. The alternative would be to transform schools into vehicles for decarceration. Within the health care system, it is important to emphasize the current scarcity of institutions available to poor people who suffer severe mental and emotional illnesses. There are currently more people with mental and emotional disorders in jails and prisons than in mental institutions. This call for new facilities designed to assist poor people should not be taken as an appeal to reinstitute the old system of mental institutions, which were—and in many cases still are—as repressive as the prisons. It is simply to suggest that the racial and class disparities in care available to the affluent and the deprived need to be eradicated, thus creating another vehicle for decarceration.

To reiterate, rather than try to imagine one single alternative to the existing system of incarceration, we might envision an array of alternatives that will require radical transformations of many aspects of our society. Alternatives that fail to address racism, male dominance, homophobia, class bias, and other structures of domination will not, in the final analysis, lead to decarceration and will not advance the goal of abolition.

It is within this context that it makes sense to consider the decriminalization of drug use as a significant component of a larger strategy to simultaneously oppose structures of racism within the criminal justice system and further the abolitionist agenda of decarceration. Thus, with respect to the project of challenging the role played by the so-called War on Drugs in bringing huge numbers of people of color into the prison system, proposals to decriminalize drug use should be linked to the development of a constellation of free, community-based programs accessible to all people who wish to tackle their drug problems. This is not to suggest that all people who use drugs—or that only people who use illicit drugs—need such help. However, anyone, regardless of economic status, who wishes to conquer drug addiction should be able to enter treatment programs.

Such institutions are, indeed, available to affluent communities. The most well known program is the Betty Ford Center, which, according to its Web site, "accepts patients dependent on alcohol and other mood altering chemicals. Treatment services are open to all men and women eighteen years of age and older regardless of race, creed, sex, national origin, religion or sources of payment for care."[2] However, the cost for the first six days is $1,175 per day, and after that $525 per day.[3] If a person requires thirty days of treatment, the cost would amount to $19,000, almost twice the annual salary of a person working a minimum-wage job.

Poor people deserve to have access to effective, voluntary drug treatment programs. Like the Betty Ford program, their operation should not be under the auspices of the criminal justice system. As at the Ford Center, family members also should be permitted to participate. But unlike the Betty Ford program, they should be free of charge. For such programs to count as "abolitionist alternatives," they would not be linked—unlike existing programs, to which individuals are "sentenced"—to imprisonment as a last resort.

The campaign to decriminalize drug use—from marijuana to heroin—is international in scope and has led countries such as the Netherlands to revise their laws, legalizing personal use of such drugs as marijuana and hashish. The Netherlands also has a history of legalized sex work, another area in which there has been extensive campaigning for decriminalization. In the cases of drugs and sex work, decriminalization would simply require repeal of all those laws that penalize individuals who use drugs and who work in the sex industry. The decriminalization of alcohol use serves as a historical example. In both these cases, decriminalization would advance the abolitionist strategy of decarceration—that is, the consistent reduction in the numbers of people who are sent to prison—with the ultimate aim of dismantling the prison system as the dominant mode of punishment. A further challenge for abolitionists is to identify other behaviors that might be appropriately decriminalized as preliminary steps toward abolition.

One obvious and very urgent aspect of the work of decriminalization is associated with the defense of immigrants' rights. The growing numbers of immigrants—especially since the attacks on September 11, 2001—who are incarcerated in immigrant detention centers, as well as in jails and prisons, can be halted by dismantling the processes that punish people for their failure to enter this country [with the required] documents. Current campaigns that call for the decriminalization of undocumented immigrants are making important contributions to the overall struggle against the prison industrial complex and are challenging the expansive reach of racism and male dominance. When women from countries in the southern region are imprisoned because they have entered this country to escape sexual violence, instead of being granted refugee status, this reinforces the generalized tendency to punish people who are persecuted in their intimate lives as a direct consequence of pandemics of violence that continue to be legitimized by ideological and legal structures.

Within the United States, the "battered women's syndrome" legal defense reflects an attempt to argue that a woman who kills an abusive spouse should not be convicted of murder. This defense has been abundantly criticized, both by detractors and proponents of feminism; the former do not want to recognize the pervasiveness and dangers of intimate violence against women and the latter challenge the idea that the legitimacy of this defense resides in the assertion that those who kill their batterers are not responsible for their actions. The point feminist movements attempt to make—regardless of their specific positions on battered women's syndrome—is that violence against women is a pervasive and complicated social problem that cannot be solved by imprisoning women who fight back against their abusers. Thus, a vast range of alternative strategies of minimizing violence against women—within intimate relationships and within relationships to the state—should be the focus of our concern.

The alternatives toward which I have gestured thus far—and this is only a small selection of examples, which can also include job and living wage programs, alternatives to the disestablished welfare program, community-based recreation, and many more—are associated both directly and indirectly with the existing system of criminal justice. But, however mediated their relation might be to the current system of jails and prisons, these alternatives are attempting to reverse the impact of the prison industrial complex on our world. As they contest racism and other networks of social domination, their implementation will certainly advance the abolitionist agenda of decarceration.

Creating agendas of decarceration and broadly casting the net of alternatives helps us to do the ideological work of pulling apart the conceptual link between crime and punishment. This more nuanced understanding of the social role of the punishment system requires us to give up our usual way of thinking about punishment as an inevitable consequence of crime. We would recognize that "punishment" does not follow from "crime" in the neat and logical sequence offered by discourses that insist on the justice of imprisonment, but rather punishment—primarily through imprisonment (and sometimes death)—is linked to the agendas of politicians, the profit drive of corporations, and media representations of crime. Imprisonment is associated with the racialization of those most likely to be punished. It is associated with their class and, as we have seen, gender structures the punishment system as well. If we insist that abolitionist alternatives trouble these relationships, that they strive to disarticulate crime and punishment, race and punishment, class and punishment, and gender and punishment, then our focus must not rest only on the prison system as an isolated institution but must also be directed at all the social relations that support the permanence of the prison.

An attempt to create a new conceptual terrain for imagining alternatives to imprisonment involves the ideological work of questioning why "criminals" have been constituted as a class and, indeed, a class of human beings undeserving of the civil and human rights accorded to others. Radical criminologists have long pointed out that the category "lawbreakers" is far greater than the category of individuals who are deemed criminals since, many point out, almost all of us have broken the law at one time or another. Even President Bill Clinton admitted that he had smoked marijuana at one time, insisting, though, that he did not inhale. However, acknowledged disparities in the intensity of police surveillance—as indicated by the present-day currency of the term "racial profiling" which ought to cover far more territory than "driving while black or brown"—account in part for racial and class-based disparities in arrest and imprisonment rates. Thus, if we are willing to take seriously the consequences of a racist and class-biased justice system, we will reach the conclusion that enormous numbers of people are in prison simply because they are, for example, black, Chicano, Vietnamese, Native American or poor, regardless of their ethnic background. They are sent to prison, not so much because of the crimes they may have indeed committed, but largely because their communities have been criminalized. Thus, programs for decriminalization will not only have to address specific activities that have been criminalized—such as drug use and sex work—but also criminalized populations and communities.

It is against the backdrop of these more broadly conceived abolitionist alternatives that it makes sense to take up the question of radical transformations within the existing justice system. Thus, aside from minimizing, through various strategies, the kinds of behaviors that will bring people into contact with the police and justice systems, there is the question of how to treat those who assault the rights and bodies of others. Many organizations and individuals both in the United States and other countries offer alternative modes of making justice. In limited instances, some governments have attempted to implement alternatives that range from conflict resolution to restorative or reparative justice. Such scholars as Herman Bianchi have suggested that crime needs to be defined in terms of tort and, instead of criminal law, should be reparative law. In his words, "[The lawbreaker] is thus no longer an evil-minded man or woman, but simply a debtor, a liable person whose human duty is to take responsibility for his or her acts, and to assume the duty of repair." [4]

There is a growing body of literature on reshaping systems of justice around strategies of reparation, rather than retribution, as well as a growing body of experiential evidence of the advantages of these approaches to justice and of the democratic possibilities they promise. Instead of rehearsing the numerous debates that have emerged over the last decades—including the most persistent question, "What will happen to the murderers and rapists?"—I will conclude with a story of one of the most dramatic successes of these experiments in reconciliation. I refer to the case of Amy Biehl, the white Fulbright scholar from Newport Beach, California, who was killed by young South African men in Guguletu, a black township in Capetown, South Africa.

In 1993, when South Africa was on the cusp of its transition, Amy Biehl was devoting a significant amount of her time as a foreign student to the work of rebuilding South Africa. Nelson Mandela had been freed in 1990, but had not yet been elected president. On August 25, Biehl was driving several black friends to their home in Guguletu when a crowd shouting antiwhite slogans confronted her, and some of them stoned and stabbed her to death. Four of the men participating in the attack were convicted of her murder and sentenced to eighteen years in prison. In 1997, Linda and Peter Biehl—Amy's mother and father—decided to support the amnesty petition the men presented to the Truth and Reconciliation Commission. The four apologized to the Biehls and were released in July 1998. Two of them—Easy Nofemela and Ntobeko Peni—later met with the Biehls, who, despite much pressure to the contrary, agreed to see them.[5] According to Nofemela, he wanted to say more about his own sorrow for killing their daughter than what had been possible during Truth and Reconciliation hearings. "I know you lost a person you love," he says he told them during that meeting. "I want you to forgive me and take me as your child."[6]

The Biehls, who had established the Amy Biehl Foundation in the aftermath of their daughter's death, asked Nofemela and Peni to work at the Guguletu branch of the foundation. Nofemela became an instructor in an after-school sports program and Peni an administrator. In June 2002, they accompanied Linda Biehl to New York, where they all spoke before the American Family Therapy Academy on reconciliation and restorative justice. In a *Boston Globe* interview, Linda Biehl, when asked how she now feels about the men who killed her daughter, said, "I have a lot of love for them." After Peter Biehl died in 2002, she bought two plots of land for them in memory of her husband so that Nofemela and Peni can build their own homes.[7] A few days after the September 11 attacks, the Biehls had been asked to speak at a synagogue in their community. According to Peter Biehl, "We tried to explain that sometimes it pays to shut up and listen to what other people have to say, to ask: 'Why do these terrible things happen?' instead of simply reacting."[8]

NOTES

1. Arthur Waskow, resident, Institute for Policy Studies, *Saturday Review*, 8 January 1972, quoted in Fay Honey Knopp, et al., *Instead of Prisons: A Handbook for Abolitionists* (Syracuse, N.Y.: Prison Research Education Action Project, 1976), 15–16.
2. www.bettyfordcenter.org/programs/programs/index.html
3. www.bettyfordcenter.org/programs/programs/prices.html
4. Herman Bianchi, "Abolition: Assensus and Sanctuary," in *Abolitionism: Toward a Non-Repressive Approach to Crime*, eds. Herman Bianchi and René Swaaningen (Amsterdam: Free University Press, 1986), 117.
5. Anthropologist Nancy Schepper-Hughes described this astonishing turn of events in a talk she delivered at UC Berkeley on September 24, 2001, entitled "Un-Doing; The Politics of the Impossible in the New South Africa."
6. Bella English, "Why Do They Forgive Us," *Boston Globe*, 23 April 2003.
7. Ibid.
8. Gavin Du Venage, "Our Daughter's Killers Are Now Our Friends," *The Straits Times* (Singapore), 2 December 2 2001.

10 Building an Abolitionist Trans and Queer Movement with Everything We've Got

Morgan Bassichis, Alexander Lee, and Dean Spade

Editor's Note: When this essay was first published in 2011, most states and the federal government did not recognize same-sex marriage. The authors critique mainstream LGBT organizations for their narrow focus on legalizing same-sex marriage as the primary solution to injustice. On June 26, 2015, the U.S. Supreme Court in *Obergefell* v. *Hodges* struck down marriage bans and legalized same-sex marriage nationwide (see an excerpt from the *Obergefell* ruling in Part VII of this volume). While that landmark ruling had a significant impact on public policy and the lives of many LGBT people, these authors argue for more transformative approaches to collective liberation. Their vision of an abolitionist trans and queer movement aims to radically challenge dominant institutions such as marriage, prisons, and the military.

As we write this, queer and trans people across the United States and in many parts of the world have just celebrated the fortieth anniversary of the Stonewall Rebellion. On that fateful night back in June 1969, sexual and gender outsiders rose up against ongoing brutal police violence in an inspiring act of defiance. These early freedom fighters knew all too well that the NYPD—"New York's finest"—were the frontline threat to queer and trans survival. Stonewall was the culmination of years of domination, resentment, and upheaval in many marginalized communities coming to a new consciousness of the depth of violence committed by the government against poor people, people of color, women, and queer people both within US borders and around the world. The Stonewall Rebellion, the mass demonstrations against the war in Vietnam, and the campaign to free imprisoned Black-liberation activist Assata Shakur were all

---

Morgan Bassichis is a performer and writer whose essays have been published in the *Radical History Review, Captive Genders*, and other anthologies.

Alexander Lee is a screenwriter, director, and transgender rights attorney. He founded the Transgender, Gender Variant and Intersex Justice Project.

Dean Spade is a writer, lawyer, law professor, and founder of the Sylvia Rivera Law Project. His publications include *Normal Life: Administrative Violence, Critical Trans Politics and the Limits of Law.*

---

powerful examples of a groundswell of energy demanding an end to the "business as usual" of US terror during this time.

Could these groundbreaking and often unsung activists have imagined that only forty years later the "official" gay rights agenda would be largely pro-police, pro-prisons, and pro-war—exactly the forces they worked so hard to resist? Just a few decades later, the most visible and well-funded arms of the "LGBT movement" look much more like a corporate strategizing session than a grassroots social justice movement. There are countless examples of this dramatic shift in priorities. What emerged as a fight against racist, anti-poor, and anti-queer police violence now works hand in hand with local and federal law enforcement agencies—district attorneys are asked to speak at trans rallies, cops march in Gay Pride parades. The agendas of prosecutors—those who lock up our family, friends, and lovers—and many queer and trans organizations are becoming increasingly similar, with sentence- and police-enhancing legislation at the top of the priority list. Hate crimes legislation is tacked on to multi-billion dollar "defense" bills to support US military domination in Palestine, Iraq, Afghanistan, and elsewhere. Despite the rhetoric of an "LGBT community," transgender and gender-non-conforming people are repeatedly abandoned and marginalized in the agendas and priorities of our "lead" organizations—most recently in the 2007 gutting of the Employment Non-Discrimination Act of gender identity protections. And as the rate of people (particularly poor queer and trans people of color) without steady jobs, housing, or health-care continues to rise, and health and social services continue to be cut, those dubbed the leaders of the "LGBT movement" insist that marriage rights are the way to redress the inequalities in our communities.

For more and more queer and trans people, regardless of marital status, there is no inheritance, no health benefits from employers, no legal immigration status, and no state protection of our relationship to our children. Four decades after queer and trans people took to the streets throwing heels, bottles, bricks, and anything else we had to ward off police, the official word is that, except for being able to get married and fight in the military,[1] we are pretty much free, safe, and equal. . . .

Fortunately, radical queer and trans organizing for deep transformation has also grown alongside this "trickle-down"[2] brand of "equality" politics mentioned above. Although there is no neat line between official gay "equality" politics on the one hand, and radical "justice" politics on the other, it is important to draw out some of the key distinctions in how different parts of our movements today are responding to the main problems that queer and trans people face. This is less about creating false dichotomies between "good" and "bad" approaches, and more about clarifying the actual impact that various strategies have, and recognizing that alternative approaches to the "official" solutions are alive, are politically viable, and are being pursued by activists and organizations around the United States and beyond. In the first column, we identify some of these main challenges; in the second, we summarize what solutions are being offered by the well-resourced[3] segments of our movement; and in the third, we outline some approaches being used by more radical and progressive queer and trans organizing to expand possibilities for broad-based, social-justice solutions to these same problems.

The Current Landscape		
Big Problems	**"Official" Solutions**	**Transformative Approaches**
Queer and trans people, poor people, people of color, and immigrants have minimal access to quality healthcare	Legalize same-sex marriage to allow people with health benefits from their jobs to share with same-sex partners	Strengthen Medicaid and Medicare; win universal healthcare; fight for transgender health benefits; end deadly medical neglect of people in state custody
Queer and trans people experience regular and often fatal violence from partners, family members, community members, employers, law enforcement, and institutional officials	Pass hate crimes legislation to increase prison sentences and strengthen local and federal law enforcement; collect statistics on rates of violence; collaborate with local and federal law enforcement to prosecute hate violence and domestic violence	Build community relationships and infrastructure to support the healing and transformation of people who have been impacted by interpersonal and inter-generational violence; join with movements addressing root causes of queer and trans premature death, including police violence, imprisonment, poverty, immigration policies, and lack of healthcare and housing
Queer and trans members of the military experience violence and discrimination	Eliminate bans on participation of gays and lesbians in US military	Join with war resisters, radical veterans, and young people to oppose military intervention, occupation, and war abroad and at home, and demand the reduction/elimination of "defense" budgets
Queer and trans people are targeted by an unfair and punitive immigration system	Legalize same-sex marriage to allow same-sex international couples to apply for legal residency for the non-US citizen spouse	End the use of immigration policy to criminalize people of color, exploit workers, and maintain the deadly wealth gap between the United States and the Global South; support current detainees and end ICE raids, deportations, and police collaboration

Big Problems	"Official" Solutions	Transformative Approaches
Queer and trans families are vulnerable to legal intervention and separation from the state, institutions, and/or nonqueer people	Legalize same sex marriage to provide a route to "legalize" families with two parents of the same sex; pass laws banning adoption discrimination on the basis of sexual orientation	Join with struggles of queer/trans and non-queer/trans families of color, imprisoned parents and youth, native families, poor families, military families, and people with disabilities to win community and family self-determination and the right to keep kids, parents, and other family members in their families and communities
Institutions fail to recognize family connections outside of heterosexual marriage in contexts like hospital visitation and inheritance	Legalize same-sex marriage to formally recognize same-sex partners in the eyes of the law	Change policies like hospital visitation to recognize a variety of family structures, not just opposite-sex and same-sex couples; abolish inheritance and demand radical redistribution of wealth and an end to poverty
Queer and trans people are disproportionately policed, arrested, and imprisoned, and face high rates of violence in state custody from officials as well as other imprisoned or detained people	Advocate for "cultural competency" training for law enforcement and the construction of queer- and trans-specific and "gender responsive" facilities; create written policies that say that queer and trans people are equal to other people in state custody; stay largely silent on the high rates of imprisonment in queer and trans communities, communities of color, and poor communities	Build ongoing, accountable relationships with and advocate for queer and trans people who are locked up to support their daily well-being, healing, leadership, and survival; build community networks of care to support people coming out of prison and jail; collaborate with other movements to address root causes of queer and trans imprisonment; work to abolish prisons, establish community support for people with disabilities and eliminate medical and psychiatric institutionalization, and provide permanent housing rather than shelter beds for all people without homes

. . .

Reclaiming a Radical Legacy

Despite the powerful and destructive impacts that the renewed forces of neoliberal global-ization and the "New World Order" have had on our communities and our social move-ments, there are and always have been radical politics and movements to challenge the exploitation that the United States is founded upon. These politics have been developed in communities of color and in poor and working-class, immigrant, queer, disability, and feminist communities in both "colonized" and "colonizing" nations, from the Black Pan-ther Party in Oakland to the Zapatistas in Chiapas to the Audre Lorde Project in New York. As the story of Stonewall teaches us, our movements didn't start out in the court-room; they started out in the streets! Informing both the strategies of our movements as well as our everyday decisions about how we live our lives and form our relationships, these radical politics offer queer communities and movements a way out of the murderous politics that are masked as invitations to "inclusion" and "equality" within fundamentally exclusive, unequal systems. Sometimes these spaces for transformation are easier to spot than others—but you can find them everywhere, from church halls to lecture halls, from the lessons of our grandmothers to the lessons we learn surviving in the world, from the post-revolutionary Cuba to post-Katrina New Orleans.

These radical lineages have nurtured and guided transformative branches of queer and trans organizing working at the intersections of identities and struggles for collective lib-eration. . . . In the chart below, we draw out a few specific strands of these diverse radical lineages that have paved the way for this work. In the first column, we highlight a value that has emerged from these radical lineages. In the second column, we lift up specific organizations striving to embody these values today.[4]

Deepening the Path of Those Who Came Before	
Radical Lineage	**Contemporary Descendant**
Liberation is a collective process! The con-ventional nonprofit hierarchical structure is actually a very recent phenomenon, and one that is modeled off corporations. Radi-cal organizations, particularly feminist and women of color–led organizations, have often prioritized working collectively—where group awareness, consensus, and wholeness is valued over majority rule and individual leadership. Collectivism at its best takes up the concerns of the few as the concerns of the whole. For example, when one member of a group or community cannot attend an event or meeting because the building is not wheelchair accessible, it becomes a moment for all to examine and challenge ableism in our culture—instead of just dismissing it as a "problem" that affects only people who use wheelchairs.	The **Sylvia Rivera Law Project**[5] (SRLP), among many other organizations, has shown just how powerful working collectively can be—with their staff and volunteers, majority people of color, majority trans and gender-non-conforming governing collective, SRLP is showing the world that how we do our work is a vital part of the work, and that doing things collectively helps us to create the world we want to see as we're building it.

Radical Lineage	Contemporary Descendant
"Trickle up" change! We know that when those in power say they will "come back" for those at the bottom of the social and economic hierarchy, it will never happen. . . . The changes required to improve the daily material and spiritual lives of low-income queer and transgender people of color would by default include large-scale transformation of our entire economic, education, healthcare, and legal systems. When you put those with the fewest resources and those facing multiple systems of oppression at the center of analysis and organizing, everybody benefits.	**Queers for Economic Justice**[6] in New York City and the **Transgender, Gender Variant, and Intersex Justice Project**[7] in San Francisco are two great examples of "trickle up" change—by focusing on queers on welfare, in the shelter system, and in prison systems, these groups demand social and economic justice for those with the fewest resources and the smallest investment in maintaining the system as it is.
Be careful of all those welcome mats! Learning from history and other social-justice movements is a key principle. Other movements and other moments have been drained of their original power and purpose and appropriated for purposes opposing their principles, either by governments working to dilute and derail transformation or by corporations looking to turn civil unrest into a fashion statement (or both). Looking back critically at where other movements have done right and gone wrong helps us stay creative and accountable to our communities and our politics.	**Critical Resistance**[8] is a great example of this commitment. In the group's focus on prison abolition (instead of reform), its members examine their strategies and potential proposals through the question "Will we regret this in ten years?" This question is about taking a long-term view and assessing a potential opportunity (such as any given proposal to "improve" or "reform" prisons or sentencing laws) against their commitment to abolishing—not expanding or even maintaining—the prison industrial complex. The message here is that even though it might feel nice to get an invitation to the party, we would be wise to ask about the occasion.
For us, by us! The leadership, wisdom, and labor of those most affected by an issue should be centralized from the start. This allows those with the most to gain from social justice to direct what that justice will look like and gives allies the chance to directly support their leadership.	. . . At **FIERCE!**[9], it is the young people directly facing the intersections of ageism, racism, xenophobia, homophobia, and transphobia who identify what the problems, priorities, and strategies should be rather than people whose expertise on these issues derives from advanced degrees or other criteria. The role of people not directly affected by the issues is to support the youth in manifesting their visions, not to control the political possibilities that they are inventing.

Radical Lineage	Contemporary Descendant
Let's practice what we preach! Also known as "praxis," this ideal strives for the alignment of what we do, why we're doing it, and how we do it—not just in our formal work, but also in our daily lives. . . . If we believe that people of color have the most to gain from the end of racism, then we should support and encourage people of color's leadership in fights to end white supremacy, and for a fair economy and an end to the wealth gap. People in our organizations should get paid equally regardless of advanced degrees, and our working conditions and benefits should be generous. If we support a world in which we have time and resources to take care of ourselves, as well as our friends, families, and neighbors, we might not want to work sixty hours a week.	An inspiring example of praxis can be found in the work of **Southerners on New Ground**[10] (SONG), based in Atlanta, Ga. SONG strives to integrate healing, spirit, and creativity in their work organizing across race, class, gender, and sexuality to embody new (and old!) forms of community, reflective of our commitments to liberation. SONG and other groups show that oppression is traumatic, and trauma needs to be addressed, acknowledged, and held both by individuals and groups of people. If trauma is ignored or swept under the rug, it just comes back as resentment, chaos, and divisiveness. We are all whole, complex human beings that have survived a great deal of violence to get where we are today. Our work must support our full humanity and reflect the world we want to live in.
Real safety means collective transformation! Oppressed communities have always had ways to deal with violence and harm without relying on police, prisons, immigration, or kicking someone out—knowing that relying on those forces would put them in greater danger. Oppressed people have often known that these forces were the main sources of violence that they faced—the central agent of rape, abuse, murder, and exploitation. The criminal punishment system has tried to convince us that we do not know how to solve our own problems and that locking people up and putting more cops on our streets are the only ways we can stay safe or heal from trauma. Unfortunately we often lack other options. Many organizations and groups of people have been working to interrupt the intergenerational practices of intimate violence, sexual violence, hate violence, and police violence without relying on the institutions that target, warehouse, kill, and shame us.	Groups like **Creative Interventions** and **generationFIVE** in Oakland, Calif., **Communities Against Rape and Abuse** in Seattle, Wash., and the Audre Lorde Project's **Safe OUTside the System (SOS) Collective**[11], have been creating exciting ways to support the healing and transformation of people who have survived and caused harm, as well as the conditions that pass violence down from one generation to another. Because violence touches every queer and trans person directly or indirectly, creating ways to respond to violence that are transformative and healing (instead of oppressive, shaming, or traumatizing) is a tremendous opportunity to reclaim our radical legacy. We can no longer allow for our deaths to be the justification for so many other people's deaths through policing, imprisonment, and detention. Locking people up, having more cops in the streets, or throwing more people out will never heal the wounds of abuse or trauma.

. . .

So You Think We're Impossible?

This stuff is heavy, we realize. Our communities and our movements are up against tremendous odds and have inherited a great deal of trauma that we are still struggling to deal with. A common and reasonable response to these conditions is getting overwhelmed, feeling defeated, losing hope. In this kind of emotional and political climate, when activists call for deep change like prison abolition (or, gasp, an LGBT agenda *centered around* prison abolition), our demands get called "impossible" or "idealistic" or even "divisive." As trans people, we've been hearing this for ages. After all, according to our legal system, the media, science, and many of our families and religions, we shouldn't exist! Our ways of living and expressing ourselves break such fundamental rules that systems crash at our feet, close their doors to us, and attempt to wipe us out. And yet we exist, continuing to build and sustain new ways of looking at gender, bodies, family, desire, resistance, and happiness that nourish us and challenge expectations.

. . .

What would it mean to *embrace*, rather than *shy away from*, the impossibility of our ways of living as well as our political visions? . . . We see the abolition of policing, prisons, jails, and detention not strictly as a narrow answer to "imprisonment" and the abuses that occur within prisons, but also as a challenge to the rule of poverty, violence, racism, alienation, and disconnection that we face every day. Abolition is not just about closing the doors to violent institutions, but also about building up and recovering institutions and practices and relationships that nurture wholeness, self-determination, and transformation. Abolition is not some distant future but something we create in every moment when we say no to the traps of empire and yes to the nourishing possibilities dreamed of and practiced by our ancestors and friends. Every time we insist on accessible and affirming healthcare, safe and quality education, meaningful and secure employment, loving and healing relationships, and being our full and whole selves, we are doing abolition. Abolition is about breaking down things that oppress and building up things that nourish. Abolition is the practice of transformation in the here and now and the ever after.

NOTES

1. In the wake of the 2011 repeal of Don't Ask Don't Tell, queer and trans people who oppose the horrible violence committed by the US military all over the world have been disappointed not only by pro-military rhetoric of the campaign to allow gays and lesbians to serve, but also by the new debates that have emerged since then about ROTC on college campuses. Many universities that have excluded the military from campuses are now considering bringing it back to campus, and some activists are arguing that the military should be kept off campus because trans people are still excluded from service. The terms of this debate painfully embraces US militarism, and forgets that long-term campaigns to exclude the US military from college campuses and to disrupt military recruitment campaigns and strategies are based in not only the horrible violence of the military toward service members but also the motivating colonial and imperial purposes of US militarism.

2. This is a reference to the "trickle-down" economic policies associated with the Reagan Administration, which promoted tax cuts for the rich under the guise of creating jobs for middle-class and working-class people. The left has rightfully argued that justice, wealth, and safety do not "trickle down," but need to be redistributed first to the people at the bottom of the economic and political ladder. Trickle down policies primarily operate as another opportunity to distribute wealth and security upward.

3. By this we mean the advocacy work and agenda-setting done by wealthy (budgets over $1 million) LGBT-rights organizations such as the Human Rights Campaign and the National Lesbian and Gay Task Force.

4. We recognize that we mention only relatively well-funded organizations and mostly organizations in the San Francisco Bay Area and New York City, two strongholds of radical organizing and also places where a significant amount of resources are concentrated. There are hundreds of other organizations around the country and the world that we do not mention and do not know about. *What organizations or spaces do you see embodying radical values?*

5. The Sylvia Rivera Law Project at http://www.srlp.org.

6. Queers for Economic Justice at http://www.q4ej.org.

7. Transgender, Gender Variant, and Intersex Justice Project at http://www.tgijp.org.

8. Critical Resistance at http://www.criticalresistance.org.

9. FIERCE! at http://www.fiercenyc.org.

10. Southerners on New Ground at http://www.southernersonnewground.org .

11. See Creative Interventions at http://www.creative-interventions.org, generationFIVE at http://www.generationfive.org, and Communities Against Rape and Abuse at http://www.cara-seattle.org. For examples of LGBTQ-specific organizations creating community-based responses to violence, see the Audre Lorde Project's Safe Outside the System Collective in Brooklyn (www.alp.org), the Northwest Network of BTLG Survivors of Abuse in Seattle, and Community United Against Violence (CUAV) in San Francisco (www.cuav.org).

11 What the Dreamers Can Teach the Parkland Kids

Gaby Pacheco

Editor's Note: The Dreamers are immigrant youth activists—many of them undocumented students—named for the Development, Relief and Education for Alien Minors (DREAM) Act, a federal bill repeatedly introduced since 2001 but not signed into law. The DREAM Act would have provided a multiphase process for granting legal status to certain undocumented immigrants who were brought to the United States as children. The "Parkland kids" are a group of students who became activists after surviving the mass shooting at Marjory Stoneman Douglas High school in Parkland, Florida, where a 19-year-old former student killed 17 people on February 14, 2018. Survivors Emma González, David Hogg, Jaclyn Corin, and Matt Deitsch, among others, organized a national "March for Our Lives" to end gun violence.

It was Jan. 1, 2010, the beginning of a new decade. Instead of sleeping in after what should have been a fun night bringing in the new year, my friends and I were up early putting on matching Nike sneakers to start walking the 1,500 miles from Miami to Washington.

This is what set off the "Dreamer" movement, which fights for the rights of immigrant youth and their families. What began with me and my friends Carlos, Juan and Felipe walking turned into a national campaign joined by tens of thousands of young people.

I've been thinking of those early days a lot, ever since the teenage survivors of last month's deadly school shooting started demanding stricter gun controls and rallying other young people to their cause. That shooting happened in Parkland, Fla., just an hour from where our Dreamer march began. And next weekend, those teenagers will be joined by tens of thousands of others as they, too, march on Washington.

Young people have an incredible ability to drive change. But it's not easy. I offer my own experience in case it provides any comfort or guidance.

My activism was born out of necessity and rage. I learned I was undocumented when I was in the eighth grade. My senior year, my college counselor told me that I could not go to college. She advised hiding my immigration status and staying quiet. I quickly realized that adults live a more cautious, fearful life than young people, and their conservative views on how to tackle issues couldn't help me. It was up to me to find a way for myself and others like me to go to college.

Gaby Pacheco is the program director for TheDream.US, a college access program for undocumented immigrant youth. She served as political director of United We Dream and helped lead the 2010 Trail of Dreams. Pacheco, who was eight when she and her family migrated from Ecuador, was the first undocumented Latina to testify before Congress.

One of the first things I learned, when my friends and I started to get some attention, is how quickly politicians try to co-opt youth movements for their own agendas. Both Republicans and Democrats claimed to care about immigrants, but both parties continued to deport people and failed to pass immigration reform. The same thing is already happening to the Parkland kids. I saw politicians turn a recent town hall for the parents, teachers and students into a platform to debate not a solution to gun violence, but which party was better.

Young activists must learn to trust their instincts and not let these debates distract them from their goals. At the same time, they have to trust the wisdom and experience of those who preceded them.

Before embarking on our march, I had the opportunity to meet with the Rev. James Lawson, who helped coordinate the 1963 March on Washington. He served as one of the advisers for our walk. The struggle of black people in America, not just during the civil rights movement but today, is one we knew we had to understand and emulate. We called our walk the Trail of Dreams as a tribute to the Rev. Dr. Martin Luther King Jr., as well as a memorial to the Native Americans who died in the Trail of Tears.[1] We wanted to remind people how many atrocities have been carried out in this county in the name of "law and order."

The young activists of today are more adept with social media than we were. But I would encourage them to get out into the streets to talk to people. Our march took four months, and we spent time in the communities we visited. We rested on Mondays because weekends were when people were most likely to be free to walk with us.

One challenge in every social justice movement is making sure it's not dominated by a single voice. At the beginning, I was surprised to be criticized by fellow activists because I was not a Mexican immigrant. I did not have to walk across the border; my family came to this country from Ecuador on an airplane, with a tourist visa. My parents bought an apartment before we arrived. Because I was more privileged than many others, I tried to put them front and center when reporters came to talk to us. Learning to give up your seat so others can have a voice helps legitimize and strengthen your movement.

This is very important for the Parkland teenagers, many of whom are white and well off—the kind of kids the news media typically pays the most attention to. They have met with students from Chicago, where young people have long been speaking out about gun violence without much national attention.[2] But they can and ought to do more.

At the same time, as a woman, I also knew I had to speak out, because my voice was often ignored. One day, two male reporters asked me, "Where are the students who are walking?"

I smiled and said, "I am one of them, how can I help you?"

They looked at me and said, "No, the people who are walking, where are the boys?"

This kept on happening. Maybe they didn't think a woman could walk 18 miles a day, or maybe they thought that because I was overweight, I couldn't possibly do this. After a CNN interview during which I had to force myself into the conversation, I shared what I had been experiencing with my fellow walkers. They decided that from then on, I would be the first person to speak at events.

Perhaps the hardest thing about being part of a youth movement is transitioning out of it. I am now 33. It's been 17 years since the introduction of the Dream Act, and still it has not passed. Part of me feels like I have failed.

I am still involved, but not at the forefront of the fight. I realized I could no longer go days without sleep, working on strategy and giving interviews. I needed a succession plan. And I wanted to help mentor other smart and motivated young people. Perhaps the Parkland students will be luckier than we were, and will see stricter gun control enacted before they hit their 30s. But if not, they will have to pass on the baton. This is important not just for the continuity of a movement but also for the sanity of the individuals within it.

Finally, people are going to attack any activist in the spotlight. Being vocal in the age of social media is hard. My advice to the youth activists of today is: Don't read the comments. And if you do, don't take what they say personally. While it is worth your time to listen respectfully to those who think differently from you, when someone is insulting you, it's best to ignore them.

I will always be an advocate, but it will take people who are brave, energetic—and young—to keep the fire burning. Thankfully, the resilience and strength of the Parkland students and the next generation of Dreamers fill me with hope.

NOTES

1. History.com Editors. "Trail of Tears." History, A&E Television Networks, 5 Mar. 2019, www.history.com/topics/native-american-history/trail-of-tears.

2. Mary Schmich. "In a Florida Poolside Visit, Chicago Teens Glimpse Parkland Students' Lives, and Find Gun Violence in Common." *Chicago Tribune*, 8 Mar. 2018, www.chicagotribune.com/news/columnists/schmich/ct-met-parkland-shooting-chicago-students-mary-schmich-20180308-story.html.

12 Standing Rock Is Everywhere: One Year Later

Chief Arvol Looking Horse

One year after the closing of the camp at the Standing Rock Reservation, Standing Rock is everywhere. Our collective water has been assaulted for many generations to the possible point of no return.

Our Elders foretold of a Black Snake and how the Water of Life—"Mni Woc'oni," which is our first medicine—would be affected if we did not stop this oncoming disaster. Mni Woc'oni is part of our creation story, and the same story that exists in many creation stories around Mother Earth.

When we say "Mni Woc'oni"—Water of Life—people all over the world are now beginning to understand that it is a living spirit: it can heal when you pray with it and die if you do not respect it. We wanted the world to know there have been warnings in our prophecies and, as we see it, those warnings are now taking place. It was said water would be like gold. It was said that our spirit of water would begin to leave us.

We are at the crossroads.

In April 2016, after receiving concerns about the construction of an oil pipeline, I was invited to Sacred Stone Camp at the northeastern border of the Standing Rock Reservation in North Dakota to assist with a water ceremony. At that time, not many were there, but it was enough to create a prayer to wake up the people. I told the young people that Standing Rock is everywhere.

Later that month, our indigenous youth set out on foot to run from the Standing Rock Reservation to Washington D.C. in an attempt to bring attention to the poisonous bitumen oil pipeline coming through our treaty territory. For our young people, it was important to explain to U.S. government leaders that this was unacceptable.

As I look back at my experiences at Standing Rock, I think about the circle we created through prayer on December 4, 2016. Our traditional Elders asked all nations to join us and stand in prayer. Thousands, including many religious representatives, joined in prayer on that very cold day. An invitation video was made and sent all over the world.

After the prayers were offered to the fire, I asked the people to surround the camp and ride horseback around the whole perimeter. On this day, President Obama and

Chief Arvol Looking Horse is the author of *White Buffalo Teachings* and a columnist for *Indian Country Today*. At the age of 12, he was given the responsibility of becoming the 19th Generation Keeper of the Sacred White Buffalo Calf Pipe. He is recognized as a chief and the spiritual leader of the Lakota, Dakota, and Nakota Nations.

his administration halted the Dakota Access Pipeline by denying the U.S. Army Corps of Engineers an easement that would have allowed the pipeline to cross beneath Lake Oahe.

The closing of the camp at Standing Rock a year ago and the continued construction of the Dakota Access Pipeline has been a great disappointment. So, too, was the November 2017 spill of 210,000 gallons of oil from the Keystone Pipeline, west of the Sisseton Wahpeton Reservation, despite the tribe's fight against it since 2003. So, too, was the April 2011 spill of 1.2 million gallons of oil onto Lubicon Cree territory, northeast of Peace River.

What happened at Standing Rock has awakened many of my own people, and people across the world.

It was at Standing Rock that so many came together to share their stories and knowledge of what was happening in their territory, sharing ideas on how to move toward sustainable living in our relationship to land, water, and food.

Standing Rock has marked the beginning of an international movement that will continue to work peacefully, purposefully, and tirelessly for the protection of water along all areas of poisonous oil pipelines and across all of Mother Earth.

In the protection of Mni Woc'oni, it is more than oil pipelines threatening the well-being and future of our water. Near the native territory of the Sisseton Wahpeton Oyate, concentrated animal feeding operations or "CAFOs" are draining and degrading the land and water. As a result, the air is toxic, swamps have dried up, and aquifers, to which the people are supposed to have water rights, are being drained. Residents have mortgaged their homes to fight these threats in court and lost. In other places—in mining spills across South America and Africa and at Fukushima—man has gone too far.

Water is a source of life, not a resource.

My life's work has been to bring attention to water and to unite all nations, all faiths in one prayer. As Keeper to the White Buffalo Calf Woman Bundle, I have also brought attention to the white animals being born, signaling us of changes globally.

As an indigenous leader, I have supported the establishment of a World Peace and Prayer Day, the UN Declaration on the Rights of Indigenous Peoples and, most recently, the Nayzul Declaration.*

In our tradition, we pray for everything we eat and drink so our minds can be good. When the environment that we live in is sick and suffering, so too are the minds and decisions of our leaders.

We must continue to work together for the health and well-being of our water and our Earth.

In a Sacred Hoop of Life, there is no ending and no beginning.

Hec'ed Onipikte (that we shall live).

---

*Issued on February 22, 2018, the Nayzul (meaning "in our spirit") Declaration was an outcome of the 2017 Nobel Peace Prize Forum in Oslo. "We recognize it is in the direct interest of Indigenous peoples that all nations shift to energy technologies that do not create dangerous climate disruption. We must work together to ensure all mineral extractive processes genuinely provide for free, prior and informed consent of Indigenous stakeholders." https://www.nobelpeaceprize.org/Nobel-Peace-Prize-Forum/2017-Across-Dividing-Lines/Press-release-The-Nayzul-Declaration-and-the-Nobel-Peace-Prize-Forum-Oslo.

PART IX

SUGGESTIONS FOR FURTHER READING

Barber, William J., II. *Revive Us Again: Vision and Action in Moral Organizing*. Beacon Press, 2018.

Boggs, Grace Lee, and Scott Kurashige. *The Next American Revolution: Sustainable Activism for the 21st Century*. University of California Press, 2012.

Carruthers, Charlene A. *Unapologetic: A Black, Queer, and Feminist Mandate for Radical Movements*. Beacon Press, 2018.

Chen, Ching-In, Jai Dulani, and Leah Lakshmi Piepzna-Samarasinha, eds. *The Revolution Starts at Home: Confronting Intimate Violence within Activist Communities*. AK Press, 2016.

Chenoweth, Erica, and Maria Stephan. *Why Civil Resistance Works: The Strategic Logic of Nonviolent Conflict*. Columbia University Press, 2011.

De Robertis, Carolina. *Radical Hope: Letters of Love and Dissent in Dangerous Times*. Vintage, 2017.

Engler, Mark, and Paul Engler. *This Is an Uprising: How Nonviolent Revolt Is Shaping the Twenty-First Century*. Bold Type Books, 2016.

Featherstone, Liza. *Selling Women Short: The Landmark Battle for Workers' Rights at Wal-Mart*. Basic Books, 2004.

Fletcher, Bill, Jr. *"They're Bankrupting Us!" And 20 Other Myths about Unions*. Beacon Press, 2012.

Fujiwara, Lynn, and Shireen Roshanravan, eds. *Asian American Feminisms and Women of Color Politics*. University of Washington Press, 2018.

Gilio-Whitaker, Gina. *As Long as Grass Grows: The Indigenous Fight for Environmental Justice from Colonization to Standing Rock*. Beacon Press, 2019.

Imarisha, Walidah. *Octavia's Brood: Science Fiction Stories from Social Justice Movements*. AK Press, 2015.

INCITE! *Color of Violence: The INCITE! Anthology*. Duke University Press, 2016.

Iyer, Deepa. *We Too Sing America: South Asian, Arab, Muslim and Sikh Immigrants Shape Our Multiracial Future*. The New Press, 2015.

Kivel, Paul. *Uprooting Racism: How White People Can Work for Racial Justice*, 4th ed. New Society Publishers, 2017.

Love, Bettina. *We Want to Do More Than Survive: Abolitionist Teaching and the Pursuit of Educational Freedom*. Beacon Press, 2019.

Marable, Manning. *The Great Wells of Democracy: The Meaning of Race in American Life*. Basic Books, 2003.

McCarthy, Timothy Patrick, ed. *The Radical Reader: A Documentary History of the American Radical Tradition*. The New Press, 2003.

Nadasen, Premilla. *Household Workers Unite: The Untold Story of African American Women Who Built a Movement*. Beacon Press, 2015.

Piepzna-Samarasinha, Leah Lakshmi. *Care Work: Dreaming Disability Justice*. Arsenal Pulp Press, 2018.

Reddy, Maureen T., ed. *Everyday Acts against Racism: Raising Children in a Multiracial World*. Seal Press, 1996.

Reich, Robert B. *Beyond Outrage: What Has Gone Wrong with Our Economy and Our Democracy, and How to Fix It*. Vintage, 2012.

Ritchie, Andrea J. *Invisible No More: Police Violence against Black Women and Women of Color.* Beacon Press, 2017.

Ross, Loretta, Lynn Roberts, Erika Derkas, Whitney Peoples, and Pamela Bridgewater Toure, eds. *Radical Reproductive Justice: Foundation, Theory, Practice, Critique.* Feminist Press, 2017.

Savage, Dan, and Terry Miller, eds. *It Gets Better: Coming Out, Overcoming Bullying, and Creating a Life Worth Living.* Plume, 2012.

Snyder, Timothy. *On Tyranny: Twenty Lessons from the Twentieth Century.* Tim Duggan Books, 2017.

Solnit, Rebecca. *Hope in the Dark: Untold Histories, Wild Possibilities.* 2nd ed. Haymarket Books, 2016.

Soskin, Betty Reid. *Sign My Name to Freedom: A Memoir of a Pioneering Life.* Hay House, 2018.

Spring, Joel. *Deculturalization and the Struggle for Equality: A Brief History of the Education of Dominated Cultures in the United States,* 7th ed. McGraw-Hill, 2012.

Stoltenberg, John. *The End of Manhood: Parables on Sex and Selfhood.* 2nd ed. Routledge, 1999.

Sudbury, Julia, and Margo Okazawa-Rey, eds. *Activist Scholarship: Antiracism, Feminism, and Social Change.* Paradigm Publishers, 2009.

Thompson, Becky. *A Promise and a Way of Life: White Antiracist Activism.* University of Minnesota Press, 2001.

Zepeda-Millán, Chris. *Latino Mass Mobilization: Immigration, Racialization, and Activism.* Cambridge University Press, 2017.

INDEX